1812
NAPOLEON'S
INVASION OF

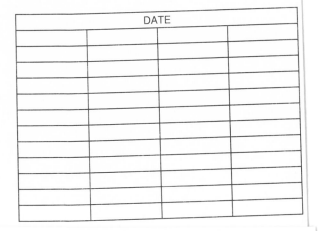

DATE		

This edition of *1812: Napoleon's Invasion of Russia*
first published 2000 by
Greenhill Books, Lionel Leventhal Limited, Park House,
1 Russell Gardens, London NW11 9NN
and
Stackpole Books, 5067 Ritter Road,
Mechanicsburg, PA 17055, USA.

British Library Cataloguing in Publication Data
Britten Austin, Paul
1812, Napoleon's invasion of Russia
1. Napoleon, I, Emperor of the French, 1769–1821 – military
leadership
2. Napoleonic Wars, 1800–1815 – Campaigns – Russia
I. Title   II, 1812, march on Moscow
III. 1812, Napoleon in Moscow   IV. 1812, the great retreat
V. 1812, Napoleon's invasion of Russia
940.2'7

ISBN 1-85367-415-X

Library of Congress Cataloging-in-Publication Data
Austin, Paul Britten
1812 – Napoleon's invasion of Russia/Paul Britten Austin
p.   cm.
Trilogy in one volume of the following previously published works:
1812: The march on Moscow; 1812: Napoleon in Moscow; and 1812:
The great retreat.
Includes bibliographical references and index.
ISBN 1-85367-415-X
1. Napoleonic Wars, 1800–1815 – Campaigns – Russia.
2. Russia – History, Military – 1801–1917.
3. Napoleon, I, Emperor of the French, 1769–1821 – military leadership.
I. Title: Napoleon's invasion of Russia.   II. Title.
DC235 A855 2000
940.2'74–dc21
00-038075
CIP

Publishing History
1812: Napoleon's Invasion of Russia consists of *1812: The March on
Moscow, 1812: Napoleon in Moscow* and *1812: The Great Retreat* bound in
one paperback volume. These three books are reproduced exactly as
the original editions, with a small number of factual amendments.

Printed and bound in Great Britain by
Creative Print and Design (Wales), Ebbw Vale

1812
THE MARCH ON MOSCOW

'It's for posterity to judge whether I made a mistake in going to Moscow.'

Napoleon, at St Helena

'When I read history, which is a subject for everyone, I've made a habit of taking into account who the writer is. When they are soldiers, one looks to matters concerning their profession and, more especially, to descriptions of actions in which they have themselves taken part.'

Montaigne: *Essaies*

'Reading modern history is generally the most tormenting employment a man can have: one is plagued with the actions of a detestable set of men called conquerors, heroes, and great generals, and we wade through pages loaded with military detail...'

Arthur Young (1741-1820)

'I always prefer an eye-witness to a line of reasoning.'

Baron Fain: *Mémoires*

1812
THE MARCH ON MOSCOW

PAUL BRITTEN AUSTIN
Foreword by David G. Chandler

GREENHILL BOOKS, LONDON
STACKPOLE BOOKS, PENNSYLVANIA

To my son THOM
and my grandson BENNY
without whose patient encouragement
and computer expertise this work
would never have been possible.

This edition of *1812: The March on Moscow*
first published 1993 by
Greenhill Books, Lionel Leventhal Limited, Park House,
1 Russell Gardens, London NW11 9NN
and
Stackpole Books, 5067 Ritter Road,
Mechanicsburg, PA 17055, USA.

British Library Cataloguing in Publication Data
Austin, Paul Britten
1812: March on Moscow
I. Title
940.27
ISBN 1-85367-154-1

Designed and edited by DAG Publications Ltd.
Designed by David Gibbons; edited by Michael Boxall.
Printed and bound in Great Britain by
Creative Print and Design (Wales) Ebbw Vale

Note:
First references to the eyewitnesses
whose accounts make up this 'documentary'
of Napoleon's invasion of Russia appear in
italic.

CONTENTS

FOREWORD
BY DAVID G. CHANDLER,
M.A. (OXON.), D.LITT., F.R.HIST.S., F.R.G.S
HEAD, DEPARTMENT OF WAR STUDIES, R.M.A. SANDHURST

Of all the many campaigns of war throughout History from the onset of the age of gunpowder down to the opening of the 20th century, Napoleon's invasion of Tsarist Russia in 1812 is probably the best known throughout the world – and for good reason. In terms of scale, both of man-power engaged and of geographical extent, the only applicable word is epic. Well over half a million of Napoleon's soldiers were involved, and eventually almost as many warriors of Alexander I. From Berlin to Moscow is one thousand miles, and for the French and their allies seven hundred of these, once the River Niemen had been crossed, were through hostile and mainly barren expanses of forest and plains. For Napoleon the Niemen was to prove his Rubicon: fateful and irreversible results were to follow – leading to his twin downfalls – first in April 1814, then (after the episode of exile in Elba) the ultimate cataclysm of Waterloo in 1815. The scale of operations in 1812 almost beggar belief, and the casualties – military and civilian, French invaders and Russian defenders – cause a shudder even today, despite the horrendously greater losses of two successive World Wars in the 20th century. But it must be remembered that populations were far smaller in 1812 than in either 1914 or 1939 – so proportionately there is less differentiation than at first appears to be the case.

The famous Prussian soldier-philosopher-historian, Carl von Clausewitz, once called warfare 'a passionate drama'. So it is to be sure – and one major attribute of this new treatment of an old subject by Paul Britten Austin is his use of the words, recollections and, occasionally incorrect, memories – for the passage of time can play the strangest tricks with human memory, as every historian who has ever attempted to debrief or question old soldiers will be only too well aware – of one hundred and more survivors who participated in the dramatic events of one hundred and eighty-one years ago in eastern Europe. The bare historical events have been recounted time and again – there have been four notable treatments in the last five years alone – but there has never been one quite like this before or on such a scale.

For it is the story of 1812 as seen by eye-witnesses – French, Russian, Ukrainian, Germans of many kinds and Italians prominent amongst them – of many ranks and military as well as civilian avocations – that forms the main focus of this new treatment; in other words, the human angle. War, when all is said and done, is about human beings under the combined stresses in multi-variant proportions of discomfort, hunger, homesickness, boredom and danger, with occasional brief minutes of sheer elation or absolute terror thrown in to add a little 'spice' as it were.

To borrow a proposition from Euclid, the Ancient Alexandrian geometrician, 'a whole is the sum of all of its parts'. On both sides, over a million armed men – including some women fighting in Davydov's irregular partisan bands – and perhaps three more million civilians, became directly involved in one way or another in Napoleon's invasion of Russia and the subsequent cataclysm that overwhelmed his army. Over 650,000 Frenchmen and their allies entered Russia (to include reserves); only an estimated 110,000 lived to pass back over the River Niemen (to include the forces on the flanks and retiring ahead of the main army group) – and probably as many as 75% of the survivors were suffering from starvation, frost-bite, wounds and illnesses from which they soon died or remained crippled by for the rest of their lives. The armies and inhabitants of Holy Russia certainly fared even worse, although they had the solace of ultimate victory over a foreign enemy led by one of the two greatest military geniuses of all History. More we shall never know.

Of the active and literate participants, Paul Britten Austin has woven together the stories of 100 human beings – or one ten thousandth part of the men who shared in this campaign, a mere 0.1%, a tenth of a tenth of a tenth part. He has needed all of 400 pages to bring us from the unopposed crossing of the River Niemen on 21 June with barely a foe in sight to the French occupation of a deserted Moscow just 85 days later. Martial events both great and small crowd his canvas – ranging from huge set-piece battles such as Borodino or Smolensk to tiny skirmishes and outpost actions that never received a name. But what lay beyond Moscow? We know the bare historical facts, to be sure: Napoleon's lingering for a month in Moscow hoping for peace-overtures from Tsar Alexander which never came: the start of the long retreat in fine autumnal weather; the unnecessary check at Malojaroslavetz; the fatally redesignated line of retreat past Borodino to Smolensk as the weather changed for the worst; battles of all shapes and sizes with the harrying and pursuing Russians under command of Kutusov at such places as Krasnoe and Orsha; the huge drama of the crossing of the River Beresina under close enemy fire; the fate of the straggling thousands; the breakdown of formation cohesion and individual discipline as the survivors – deserted by their Emperor from 5 December as he headed back for Paris to quell rumours of his supposed death, to crush conspiracies, and above all to start building a new army ready to meet the advancing Allied hordes of the Sixth Coalition – limped back through rapidly deteriorating weather conditions, the temperature plummeting to minus 30 degrees on some occasions and the casualty figures from exposure to the elements rather than the foe soaring; and then, the very last man of all to leave the soil of Holy Mother Russia – the totally unrecognizable Marshal Ney, already dubbed the 'bravest of the brave' by his master – on his rag-wrapped feet, unshaven and unwashed after ten days of desperate actions in command of the rearguard, a private-soldier's musket carried in the crook of his left arm: all this has still to come in an eagerly-awaited second volume.

Here is all the drama of Ancient Greek tragedy within the bounds of a single campaign. Great aspirations, fatal miscalculations, heroic and intrepid contenders, immense but ultimately flawed achievements, and, towards the end, the 'twilight of the gods' leading inexorably on to the nemesis of cataclysmic failure: and, last but not least, the founding of a new legend to beguile, fascinate and horrify successive generations of mankind. It all represents a new Heroic Age with a vengeance.

Little wonder that the great novelist Tolstoi made this story the second half of the greatest historical novel of all time – *War and Peace*. Nor that this great book has fascinated successive generations of film-makers. Many will remember Aubrey Hepburn and Henry Fonda starring in the American *Paramount Films* version (1966), with Herbert Lom as Napoleon, to be followed – and indeed surpassed – by Sergei Bondarchuk's definitive seven-and-a-half hour masterpiece, *Voina I Mir*, made between 1963 and 1967, employing over 20,000 Soviet soldiers as battle-extras. Then there came BBC Television's first great colour multipart epic in 20 episodes (1972) by David Conroy and John Davis working to Jack Pulman's scripts (which used a cast of famous British actors headed by Morag Hood, Tony (now Sir Anthony) Hopkins and Alan Dobie in the key roles, not to forget the services of 2,500 Yugoslav territorial soldiers for the great battle-scene shot in two main locations near the Danube and the city of Novi Sad (the ancient Peterwardein). And now, most recently of all, Cromwell Production's one hour home-video, *The Road to Moscow* (1992), in the *Campaigns in History* series. The writer of this introduction has had the great good fortune to be actively involved as a military adviser for both the last two projects.

So much for the media treatments; far more significantly, many notable military historians have produced some memorable works of scholarship on the 1812 Campaign. One thinks of General Jackson's *Seven Roads to Moscow* (1958), Antony Brett-James's anthology, *1812: Eyewitness Accounts of Napoleon's Defeat in Russia* (1966), Alan Palmer's *With Napoleon in Russia* (1967), C. Vossler's *With Napoleon in Russia* (1969), Christopher Duffy's *Borodino: Napoleon against Russia* (1972), Curtis Cate's *The War of the Two Emperors* (1985), John Nicholson's *Napoleon, 1812* (1986), George Nafziger's *Napoleon's Invasion of Russia* (1988), and Richard Riehn's *1812: Napoleon's Russian Campaign* (1990) – and even my own small in-house offering for British Army officers studying for the Junior Command and Staff Course (Part Four, Correspondence Course), *Napoleon's Campaign in Russia 1812* (1986) (which unexpectedly led directly to the inauguration of the *Osprey Campaign Series*) – is to mention but nine since 1958. Thus there has been no lack of recent treatments of this theme.

One day in 1973 a concept took root in the publisher Lionel Leventhal's office to create a wholly different on-the-ground account of 1812. Then, in 1979, (the original) Arms and Armour Press republished the *Memoirs of Sergeant Bougogne*, mainly covering the terrible retreat. The present volume has taken almost 20 years to reach fruition, and a second is already on the way, a project which has taken up perhaps a quarter of its author's productive life. In style it comes nearest to Antony Brett-James's

10

1966 offering. But whereas Brett-James was a professional linguist and military historian of the 'Sandhurst school', Paul Britten Austin is first and foremost a writer on cultural subjects and a professional translator, whose hitherto most celebrated work is his study of the extraordinary 18th-century Swedish poet *Carl Michael Bellman*, and his congenial translations, so much admired by W. H. Auden, of Bellman's immortal songs. Among other books he has also written *The Organ-Maker's Wife*, a dramatic novel of Reformation days, it too a unique verbal – albeit fictional – reconstruction of a past age. The author calls the present work 'a word-film shot by over 100 of the survivors'. Very few indeed have been translated into English before, and he interweaves their accounts to constitute an unforgettable historical tapestry. Incidentally, always abstaining from comment or innuendo, it is also a probing study of the perils of omnipotence, or anyway of Napoleon's near absolute power. There are indeed many levels in this remarkable *jeu d'esprit*, which is also a *tour de force*.

Not that Paul Britten Austin is a stranger to military history. He is the son of F. Britten Austin, the celebrated historical short-story writer of the 1930s, who also wrote those two fascinating historical novels that Wavell recommended as essential reading for all aspiring military men: *The Road to Glory* (1936), treating of the young Bonaparte's First Italian Campaign, and *Forty Centuries Look Down*, which deals with Napoleon in Egypt. They were to have been the first two volumes in a series devoted to Napoleon's complete career; but alas death intervened and only two were ever written. Indeed even they might never have seen the light of day but for Paul, aged 10. One day, walking with his father to visit the Invalides ("as a boy I was dotty about Napoleon") he piped up and asked the great man why he didn't write Napoleon's life as a novel. We can be grateful for those two remarkable books in the 1930s, but also for this new and very different project seeing the light of day over 60 years later.

It is indeed a vast project – but one which has been brilliantly brought off. As the historian Hudson wrote of Napoleon himself: 'This is his distinction, and if necessary, his excuse. When an achievement lasts so long and bears such fruit, it produces its own justification.'

1812: The March on Moscow, provides brilliant insight into men at war. The book is almost as epic as the campaign.

David G. Chandler
Hindford and RMA Sandhurst

PREFACE

Of the third of a million men with whom Napoleon, on Midsummer Day 1812, invaded Russia, few ever got back. The ghastly story of the retreat has been often told; the story of the advance less frequently. Yet it's no less dramatic – in some ways more so.

This book is a word-film, shot by more than 100 of the survivors. My 'cameramen' came from almost every country in Europe – Frenchmen, Dutchmen, Germans, Swiss, Italians... Most reliable of course are the diaries. Lejeune says that his was

'smaller than my hand, and I carried it against my heart. It's all torn, all soaked by storms and sweat caused by Russia's extreme heats...'

The always critical Labaume – whose account was the first to appear in print only two years later, while Napoleon was temporarily away on Elba[1] – says that his, too, was based on just such a diary:

'Reduced, like all my companions in arms, to struggling for the ultimate needs, pierced with cold, tormented by hunger, prey to all kinds of sufferings, unsure at each rising of the sun whether I'd see its last rays that evening, doubting in the evening whether I'd see a new day, all my feelings focused in this one desire: to live to preserve the memory of what I was seeing. Every night, seated in front of a wretched campfire in a temperature of 20-25 degrees below freezing,[2] surrounded by dead and dying, I'd retrace the day's events. The same knife I used for cutting up horsemeat was used for sharpening crows' feathers. A pinch of gunpowder diluted in the hollow of my hand with melted snow served me for ink, and a cannon for a writing desk! It was by the light of Moscow in flames I've described the sack of that city. It was on the banks of the Berezina I've traced my account of that fatal crossing...'

Glory-seeking Césare de Laugier, too, scribbled his down 'with a piece of charcoal by the light of some house or village in flames, on certain days below 28 degrees of frost'. Even Sergeant Bourgogne's immortal classic, written to exorcize terrible memories, may have been based on a diary. So certainly are the memoirs of Caulaincourt, Napoleon's loyal but always critical Boswell:

'My notes were made everywhere, at my desk and in camp every day and at all times of day; they are the work of every moment, I have touched up nothing, because although there were moments when the man showed himself, it was the demigod one mostly recognized. More than once the thought occurred to me that this journal, written under the Emperor's very eyes, might fall into his hands; but that reflection didn't check my pen. No doubt truth chilled his goodwill, but his strong and lofty character raised him above all criticism made in good faith.'

How many hundreds, perhaps thousands, of other diaries perished with their writers? For a generation afterwards Europe echoed with the reminiscences of old soldiers recounting their tales in every language. Little Coignet, the smallest grenadier in the Imperial Guard, wrote his down at the age of 70 in intervals of playing endless games of manille and piquet in a cafe at Auxerre; and when he died left 600 francs for his surviving comrades to drink his health after his funeral and sing a song that went to the tune of Béranger's *Le Vieux Sergeant*. Amazingly, we've a *photograph* of him, taken in old age. So it didn't happen all that long ago!

Always it's the details that fascinate! To edit even a small part of these thousands of kilometres of 'film' into a comprehensible dramatic pattern has been no small labour.

For reasons of space I have *not*:

(a) tried to see events from the Russian side. War, unless one is taken prisoner, is always a one-sided experience;

(b) entered into tactical intricacies – the war-gamer is referred to George F. Nafziger's *Napoleon in Russia* (Presidio Press, Novato CA, 1988), which also contains an admirable précis of Franco-Russian relations 1806-12, as well as a great deal of statistical information. For an overall view of the 1812 drama Curtis Cate's *The War of the Two Emperors* (Random House, NY, 1985) cannot be bettered; nor for information on Napoleon's armies in general, can John R. Elting's *Swords Around a Throne* (The Free Press, New York, 1988). For a strategic overview I've followed David Chandler's classic *Campaigns of Napoleon* (Macmillan, New York, 1966);

(c) for reasons of space been able to follow other corps than those making up the 'Moscow army'. Even II and VI Corps' operations have had to be skimped;

(d) ascribed to my protagonists thoughts or feelings they have not themselves put on record;

(e) tried to evaluate, except occasionally in the notes, the accuracy of my eye-witnesses' memories, or how much is hindsight. On the whole, anyone ploughing through all these memoirs will gain the impression that the writers are mostly telling very exactly what they experienced, whether in the present (diaries) or past (memoirs). Sometimes, but rarely, they catch one another out telling fibs or exaggerating their own exploits. Ségur's masterpiece is particularly inaccurate, as Gourgaud long ago pointed out, and I've only drawn on it very little.

A word about my translation method. However vivid in themselves, my eye-witnesses' nineteenth-century prose is slower, more fraught with subordinate clauses and therefore heavier than ours; and to have rendered their sentences in all their syntactical intricacy would often have been to lose much of their contemporary speed and impact. I have therefore taken certain liberties with punctuation, syntax and even tense. Even the exact order of phrases, sentences and paragraphs may not tally. But the sense does, always. When omitting and abbreviating I have also skipped the customary '...'. Most of the originals can in any case be consulted in the Bibliothèque National, Paris, or elsewhere. In a word, I've tried to render my authors' prose as if they'd used typewriters or word-processors, not goose quills. Or, in Labaume's case, crows' feathers.

Paul Britten Austin
Dawlish, Devon

ACKNOWLEDGEMENTS

My grateful thoughts go to the late Antony Brett-James who, having travelled this ground before me, generously lent me many a rare volume (now in the Staff College Library). Also to David Chandler, for his unfailing encouragement and suggestions, and giving me the benefit of his unparalleled expertise. I am also especially grateful to my sister-in-law, Else Fisher-Bergman, for indefatigably writing into my computer hundreds of semi-illegible fragments of text, scribbled down in various libraries. And lastly to Mr Peter Harrington, Librarian of the Anne S. K. Military Collection, Brown University, Providence, Rhode Island, USA, for generously waiving copyright fees on many of the illustrations; likewise to the Royal Library, Stockholm, for free access to its wonderfully sharp edition of Faber du Faur's engravings. Last but not least, my wife, the Swedish novelist Margareta Bergman, deserves a special accolade for allowing endless breakfast-table monologues about the doings of these long-dead heroes to disturb her own much more profound reflections.

CHAPTER 1

OVERTURE TO 1812

'Half-way between Bedlam and the Pantheon!' – a new war with Russia? – Colonel Ponthon goes down on his knees – Napoleon's nightmare – economics – the Master of the Horse is naïve – Polish quagmires – 'without transport all is useless' – Sergeant Coignet fills cartridges – Lieutenant Bourgoing shuffles his recruits – seven armies march north – 'he arrived like the Prince of Darkness' – fireworks at Dresden – Narbonne's fruitless errand – Turkey and Russia make peace – 'Alexander the Great marched on India'

One early March night in 1812, young Villemain, secretary to General Count Louis de Narbonne,[1] aide-de-camp to the Emperor Napoleon, was sitting in his master's carriage in the courtyard of the palace at St-Cloud, reading Chateaubriand's newly published *Journey to Jerusalem*, when
'suddenly there was a noise, as of servants. The horses, more bored than I, pricked up their ears. The carriage moved forward several paces; and the general, flinging himself briskly into it, ordered the coachman to drive to Foreign Minister Maret's house, in Paris.'
Reputedly an illegitimate son of the dissolute and effete Louis XV, the 57-year-old but already white-haired Narbonne 'admired Napoleon personally, but didn't like his absolute and military empire, and thought it doomed to perish if it didn't mend its ways'. But according to what he'd tell his temperamental First Ordnance Officer *Gaspard Gourgaud* on St Helena, Napoleon didn't give a damn for what others thought or felt; only for what they said and did. And he enjoyed Narbonne's intelligent and cultivated conversation and was glad to have this scion of the *ancien régime* about his own imperial but thoroughly bourgeois person. As his coach rolled swiftly out of the courtyards – Villemain goes on – Narbonne
'put his hand to his bald forehead, as if passing in review all he'd just heard. And said in a low voice: "What a man! What stupendous ideas! What dreams! Where find a fireguard against such a genius? It staggers belief! We're half-way between Bedlam and the Pantheon. Each time I see him I'm worried sick. His specious reasonings, his optimistic sophisms, his gigantic illusions, are all engraved in his mind, and in a tête-à-tête come out as ineffaceable axioms."'
What the two men have been discussing is a new war with Russia. In 1807 Tsar Alexander had bound his defeated country, under the Treaty of Tilsit, to exclude British goods from her ports. The Continental System was the one great stranglehold Napoleon had on his arch-enemy. Only Russia's total defeat could have led to such a result, for she needed British industrial products and colonial goods as much as the British market needed bar iron from Russia's rapidly expanding iron industry. But soon economics had spoken louder than politics. By 1811 the rouble, which in

1807 had stood at 2.90 francs, had fallen as low as 1.50 francs. In vain Napoleon had first remonstrated, then fulminated against the import licences Alexander – imitating his own example – had begun to grant for goods delivered in neutral, namely American, vessels. And by 1810 both empires had begun to prepare for a new war.

It was a prospect which filled at least one of Napoleon's officers with dread. Engineer-Colonel Ponthon had been attached as an observer to the Russian Army after Tilsit; and his reports had been so detailed and well-written that Napoleon had afterwards brought him into his war cabinet. But Ponthon, it seems, was also a man of moral courage. One day he'd literally gone down on his knees and begged Napoleon 'in the name of France's happiness and your own glory' to abstain from invading Russia:

"The peoples under your yoke, Sire, will never be true allies. Your army will find neither food nor forage. The first rains will make the terrain impassable. And if the campaign drags on into winter, how will the troops stand up to temperatures of minus 20 to 30 degrees?"
Staring sternly at Ponthon, Napoleon had let him have his say. It seems his words had even had some effect. For several days afterwards the Grand Equerry General *Armand de Caulaincourt* noticed Napoleon had looked troubled – but then overcome his doubts by telling everyone 'this is going to be a short war, over in two months'. Even, if all went well, within a fortnight.

But the man who is trying hardest of all to avert this new war is Caulaincourt himself. Having been the French Ambassador at Petersburg during four years of mounting tension, he too realizes what an invasion of Russia must entail. Indeed in early 1811 he'd found his mission impossible and asked to be recalled, on grounds that the climate was 'ruining his health'.[3] Caulaincourt had been replaced by General Lauriston, a soldier of tougher fibre.

Before he'd left, the Tsar had given him a singular token of his friendship. It's the secret grief of Caulaincourt's life that in 1800 Napoleon, then First Consul of the French Republic, had implicated him in the arrest – if not the actual execution – of the young Duke of Enghien. In the eyes of all supporters of the *ancien régime* this judicial murder of a member of the Bourbon family, by which the First Consul had once and for all alienated the reaction, was an unforgivable crime. But as it happened Tsar Alexander, too, was under suspicion of having connived at another assassination: that of his own father Tsar Paul. And before parting with Caulaincourt he'd given him a certificate to the effect that he'd never believed him guilty of Enghien's death, and added to it the prestigious Order of St Andrew and his own miniature, signed on the back 'a present from a friend'. Although Napoleon liked to see familiar faces around him, such amiable sentiments on the eve of a new and, as he hoped, decisive war didn't please him. And for a while the Master of the Horse had been under a cloud. The government-controlled theatres had been allowed to lampoon him as a sentimental dove, forever extolling the virtues of eternal peace. And at court, where he'd resumed his normal duties, Napoleon had kept twitting him with his having let himself be 'seduced' by the Tsar's 'wily and Asiatic' character. Not perhaps that he really has anything against their friendship. This 'purely political' war once over and the Tsar of all the Russias again brought to heel, it can come in handy when it's a question of signing a new peace. And by and by Caulaincourt had been taken back into favour.

During their several long conversations in that spring of 1812 he claims he never minced his words. One day the talk turned to Poland, partitioned between Austria, Prussia and Russia in 1794 and in 1807 erected by Napoleon into a Grand Duchy, its territory aggrandized with parts of East Prussia. Although the thousands of patriotic Poles serving with the French armies are longing to see their ancient kingdom restored *in toto*, Napoleon says he has no intention of doing any such thing. In that case, Caulaincourt ripostes, he doesn't understand why he has sacrificed his alliance with Russia.

'Napoleon smiled and pinched my ear: "Are you really so fond of Alexander?" – "No Sire, but I'm fond of peace."'

There lay the difference. In vain Caulaincourt stresses the dangers of another war in the far north, with 220,000 soldiers already tied up in Spain fighting Wellington and the guerrillas. Napoleon simply turns a deaf ear. And when Caulaincourt tries to disabuse him of his notion that Russian aristocrats are no different from their western European counterparts and after 'a good battle... fearing for their palaces' will force the Tsar to make peace, Napoleon simply won't believe him:

"I don't want war, and I don't want Poland."

The Poles, he'd told Narbonne, with whom he'd also discussed the matter, were 'a trivial nation'. Why were they always divided among themselves?

'I love the Poles on the field of battle. They're a valiant race. As for their free veto, their diets-on-horseback with drawn sabres, I want none of all that! I've thought the matter over very carefully. In Poland I want a camp, not a forum. The war I'm going to wage on Alexander will be a courteous one, with 2,000 pieces of artillery and 500,000 soldiers, but without any insurrection. It's not for me to reestablish a breeding-ground of republicanism in the heart of Europe. No, my dear Narbonne, all I want out of Poland is a disciplined force, to furnish a battlefield. That's the whole question: how excite the spirit of national liberation in Poland, without re-exciting the fibre of liberalism? And where would I find a king for Poland? I haven't got one in my own family, and it'd be dangerous to take one from somewhere else.'

The difficulty with this new war, he'd gone on, was wholly of a moral order:

'Whilst using the material force accrued from the Revolution, it's necessary to unleash no passions, to raise Poland without emancipating it, and assure the independence of western Europe without reanimating any republican ferment. There you've the whole problem in a nutshell.'

It was the Russian government which, by systematically evading the terms of the Tilsit treaty, was forcing on a new war. And when Caulaincourt contradicts him and says 'it's not the Russian government, Sire, which wants a war, but your own, which is losing no opportunity of hastening it on,' Napoleon merely smiles the seductive smile which – all eye-witnesses agree – neither friend nor foe could resist,[4] pinches Caulaincourt's ear and tells him he's naïve and 'doesn't understand politics'. Whereupon the Master of the Horse takes out his notebook, in which, before leaving Petersburg, he has taken the precaution of jotting down the Tsar's exact words: 'If the Emperor Napoleon makes war on me,' Alexander had said,

'it's possible, even probable, we'll be defeated – that is, assuming we fight. The Spaniards have often been defeated, yet they aren't beaten. And they're not so far from Paris! We shall take no risks. We've plenty of elbow room. I shan't be the first to draw the sword; but I'll be the last to sheath it. If the fighting goes against me I'll retire to Kamtcharka [in Siberia]. Our climate, our winter, will fight on our side.'

Napoleon, who has listened with closest attention, 'even with some astonishment', remains silent awhile:

'The harder he found it to persuade me, the more art and persistence he deployed to reach his ends. From his calculated wiles and the language he employed anyone would have thought I was one of the great powers he was so concerned to win over. That was how he acted toward anyone he wished to persuade – and he was always trying to persuade someone. "When I need anyone," he said, "I don't put too fine a point upon it. I'll kiss his arse."'

Narbonne's assessment of Napoleon's character as he rides into Paris, talking to his young secretary, coincides exactly with Narbonne's:

'He's naturally fond of truth. His pride is immense. Yet he's patient, attentive. Though he's an excellent conversationalist, one must be able to stand firm when contradicting him. And that's hard, faced with so much power and genius! One ends up by letting oneself be convinced. You put your hands over your eyes, doubt, and ask yourself whether even so such a man's logic isn't the truth, and his ambition a presentiment of the future?'

If Napoleon possessed the art of fascinating everyone, Caulaincourt goes on,

'it was because he'd already fascinated himself. He spared no pains, no trouble to gain his ends, in small matters as in great. One could say he gave himself wholly over to his ends. Always he developed all possible means, all his faculties, and all his attention, and directed them to whatever matter was just then in hand. Never was there a man more fascinating when he chose to be! Woe to him who admitted a single modification... it led from concession to concession, to the end *he* had in view! You had to stick to the question as it appeared to you, and above all not follow the Emperor in his digressions; for as soon as he ran into opposition he unfailingly shifted the centre of argument.'

As for Alexander's repeated assurances that he'll fight to the death, he dismisses them as verbiage. So the two men wrangle on hour after hour, Napoleon always manoeuvring for position. When Caulaincourt says his mobilization against Russia is

'"either for a political end or to gratify his fondest passion". Napoleon asks laughing: "What passion is that?" "War, Sire." Protesting weakly it wasn't so, he tweaked my ear and said jokingly; "You certainly don't mince your words. It's time to go to dinner."'

Not all critics, however, are being fobbed off with such amiable banter. For many years the French consul-general in Petersburg, de Lesseps, a man 'deeply familiar with Russian life and affairs', has been

'looking after the interests of French shipping better than his own. This honest man was in as bad odour as myself, for not providing trumped up evidence conducive to a new war. Beyond all suspicion of bribery, his thirty years of service, his probity, his well-known trustworthiness, all went for nothing. With his own hand Napoleon had cancelled his annual expense account, and he was faced with being deprived of all means of earning a living.'

As yet, however, few Western Europeans know much about Russian life. And those who do are too valuable to be spared. Before the year is out de Lesseps, much to his own reluctance, will find himself civil governor of a Moscow in ashes.

'The detractors of this great epoch,' Caulaincourt assures us, 'may say what they like; never was a sovereign surrounded by more capable men. Honest, full of zeal and devotion, we remained moderate, and above all good Frenchmen. Never was the truth so dinned into a sovereign's ears, but alas to no effect.'

As early as at his last frustrating meeting with Alexander, at Erfurt four years earlier, Napoleon's more intuitive self had been warned of the true state of their apparently cordial relationship. On a raft moored in the middle of the Niemen at Tilsit, each had tried to out-charm the other – and Napoleon, undoubtedly, had come off best. But by 1810, privily encouraged by Talleyrand's murmurs that 'the giant has feet of clay', it had been the Tsar who'd begun to call the tune. And one night Napoleon's First Valet *Constant Wairy*,[5] asleep as usual in the next room, had been awakened by 'dull and plaintive cries, as of someone being strangled'. Jumping out of bed, 'with such precautions as my alarm permitted' he'd opened the door:

'Going over to the bed, I saw His Majesty lying across it in a convulsive posture, his sheets and bedcover thrown off and all his person in a terrible state of nervous constriction. Inarticulate sounds were coming from his open mouth, his chest seemed deeply oppressed, and he was pressing one fist against the hollow of his stomach. Terrified to see him like this, I speak to him. When he doesn't reply, I shake him lightly. At this the Emperor wakes up with a loud cry and says: "What is it? What is it?" [And then, interrupting Constant's apologies] "You've done quite right, my dear Constant. Ah! my friend, what a horrible nightmare! A bear was ripping open my chest and tearing my heart out." Whereupon the Emperor got up and walked to and fro in the room while I was rearranging his bedclothes. He was obliged to change his shirt, the one he had on being drenched in sweat. The memory of this dream followed him a very long while. He often spoke of it, each time trying to extract different deductions from it and relate it to circumstances.'

That Napoleon has forseen the coming campaign's exceptional difficulties, at least in part, there is no question. None of his others have called for such meticulous planning. Or for so huge a mobilization of men and resources. 'Without transport,' he'd written in 1811 to his stepson Eugène de Beauharnais, Viceroy of Italy, 'all is useless'. And as early as June that year his 'geometrical mind' had begun wrestling with the problem.

Unprecedented mobility had always been a condition of Napoleonic blitzkrieg. And therefore the French armies had always lived off the rich lands they had conquered. But the far north was a different matter, as Sergeant *Jean-Roch Coignet*, the 2nd Guard Grenadiers' little drill instructor, all too vividly remembers. In Poland's sandy quagmires in 1806

'we'd had to tie on our shoes with string under the insteps. Sometimes, when the bits of string broke and our shoes got left behind in the mud, we had to take hold of our hind leg and pull it out like a carrot, lift it forward, and then go back and look for the other one. The same manoeuvre over and over, for two days on end.'

Neither were Lithuanian roads – insofar as they existed – like western European ones. 'In this part of the world,' the Prussian lieutenant *H.A. Vossler* of Prince Louis' Hussars will soon be discovering, 'all heavy transportation normally goes by sledge in winter. Roads aren't as important as in more southerly climes.'

Although the French army has a Supply Train, it consists of only 3,500 men and 891 vehicles, certainly not enough to maintain an invasion force of at least a third of a million men. For that's what's in question. One day, taking aside his War Minister Clarke on the terraces of St-Cloud, Napoleon had confided to him: 'I'm planning a great expedition. The men I shall get easily enough. The difficulty is to prepare transport.'

Huge quantities of rice, flour and biscuit will have to be assembled and paid for. Well there's gold and enough for that! The gold millions extorted from Prussia as reparations for her attack on him in 1806 and, in 1805 and 1810, from Austria, are lying in the Tuileries cellars, to which only Napoleon himself and his infinitely hard-working, enormously capable Intendant-General *Pierre Daru*[6] have keys. By March 1812 he's hoping to have 270,000 quintals of wheat, 12,000 of rice, 2,000,000 bushels of oats, equivalent to 20 million rations of bread and rice – enough for 400,000 men and 50,000 horses for 50 days. Since armies are also apt to be thirsty and brandy is also needed for amputations, on 29 December he has already ordered the Minister of Administration of the Army to buy at Bordeaux '28 million bottles of wine, 2 million bottles of brandy', i.e., 200 days' rations of wine and 130 of brandy for 300,000 men.

But the transport question remains. On such terrain will the existing 1,500 large-wheeled battalion wagons, each drawn by eight horses and capable of carrying 10,000 rations, suffice to feed the army for 25 days, the time needed for his swift campaign? Although really too heavy, h'd at first assumed that they would. But next day he had thought the matter over. If such a wagon is

'"loaded with biscuit, it has to be in barrels, otherwise the biscuit crumbles, and the men complain. Nor is it suitable for grain, flour, oats, bales of hay, or barrels of wine or brandy. So each battalion must keep its wagon for its normal needs. All others must be replaced by good carriers' wagons with big wheels, each drawn by eight horses and driven by four men, or, if need be, by three,"

all of them, preferably, foreigners. On 4 July 1811, writing to the head of his supply corps, he'd come to the conclusion that a wholly new, much lighter kind of cart must also be invented, "normally designed to carry 4,000 rations, or if necessary 6,000, and driven by two men and four horses'. Since even these can't be counted on to cope with the terrain at its worst, an even lighter type of cart must be designed, drawn by a single horse, used to walking nose to tail, "so that only one man will be needed for several carts". Oxen, too, will be useful. Even when prodded on by conscripts not used to wielding a goad, they can at least eat grass by the wayside before themselves being eaten.

How long will the biggest army in the history of European warfare be able to sustain itself amid Lithuania's conifer forests? Long enough, at least, Napoleon has calculated, to roll up and annihilate its enemy.

To defend their vast country the Russians, he knows, have two armies, plus a third, currently engaged fighting the Turks in Moldavia. The First West Army is commanded by Barclay de Tolly, a Lithuanian of Scottish descent who, remarkably, had once served in the ranks and who since the Friedland disaster, as Minister for War, has modernized the Russian army on French lines. It's being concentrated around Vilna (Vilnius). The Second West Army, commanded by the fiery and temperamental Georgian Prince Bagration, is cantoned further south around Grodno, 75 miles further up the Niemen. By driving a wedge between Barclay and

Bagration in a surprise attack of the kind he has so often launched before, Napoleon, with the reputation of his own invincibility and no fewer than ten army corps and three 'reserve' cavalry corps at his disposal, is planning to defeat them in detail. And if all goes well the campaign will indeed be over within a couple of weeks.

But how, on a given day in the summer of 1812, concentrate the Grand Army, with its 150,000 horses and 1,000 guns, on the banks of the Niemen – frontier between Poland and Russian Lithuania? That's the immense logistic problem he has set himself. And on which day? Neither too early – summer comes late to the North and the corn must be ripe for fodder. Nor too late; with autumn coming on in mid-August that would be to risk the very winter campaign so feared by Colonel Ponthon. Midsummer Day should be about right.

All over Europe units are being reinforced. Regiments normally four battalions strong are being increased to five. In its Courbevoie barracks outside Paris the infantry regiments of the Imperial Guard – an entire crack army corps 50,000 strong – are being brought up to scratch. Two whole companies of oldsters, 'only too happy to be assigned such pleasant duties', are being weeded out from the 2nd Grenadiers and replaced by 'superb men who keep arriving daily' from the Line, for which Guard NCOs are in turn being trained to take commissions. While teaching a squad of officer cadets their new command duties Sergeant Coignet is having them teach *him* his ABC, while the adjutants-major train them in theory. Such is the system, and

'Napoleon himself checked up on the results. For fifteen days a hundred men, presided over by the adjutants-major, were making up cartridges. To avoid any danger of an explosion they had to wear shoes without hobnails, taken off and inspected every two hours. We made up 100,000 packets. The moment this harvest was in – major manoeuvres in the plain of St-Denis, and reviews at the Tuileries, together with sizeable artillery parks, wagons and ambulances! The Emperor had them opened and himself climbed up on a wheel to make sure they were full.'

The regiments of the Young Guard, too, are hurriedly being brought up to strength. Its officers, taken from the Old Guard, will still draw their higher pay; but otherwise its regiments are really no different from those of the Line. Now it's to consist of thirteen regiments of tirailleurs, thirteen of voltigeurs, one of fusilier-grenadiers, one of fusilier-chasseurs, one of flankers, one of éclaireurs, and one of national guards – 'ten distinct denominations for infantry units armed in exactly the same way and all carrying the same model of standard-issue musket'. Paul de Bourgoing, a well-educated young lieutenant of the 5th Tirailleurs just back from fighting in Spain, is present as the new recruits come in,

'fifteen hundred young men in blouses, waistcoats, village costumes, or citizens of various provinces of the vast French Empire, traipsing over the vast barrack square to the rattle of sixteen drums. The drummers had almost all been taken from the Pupils of the Guard [a regiment consisting wholly of soldiers' sons]. Almost all were Dutchmen. Some, from Amsterdam and Frisia, were only fifteen. Great care had been taken not to let any one company contain too many nationals of any one country: "That won't be good either for discipline or for warfare," my major told me. "Shuffle them together like a pack of cards! Choose the twelve men who seem to have the thickest beards, or are likely to grow them. Above all, don't take any blondes or redheads; only men with black beards, whom you'll place out in front.'"

Carrying axes and wearing tall bearskins and white leather aprons, these are to be sappers and march at the head of the regimental column:

'So I passed these 1,500 two-year-old chins in review as swiftly as possible. Most were still beardless. Scarcely 25 or 30 of them were destined ever to see their maternal hearths again.'

On the Elbe, meanwhile, an Army of Observation, soon to become I Corps, is being drilled to a degree of efficiency 'almost equalling the Imperial Guard' under its fearsomely disciplinarian commander, Marshal Davout, Prince of Eckmühl. One of its strongest infantry regiments, the 85th Line, has spent the winter in the strongly fortified town of Glogau, 'as in a besieged city'. Its 1st battalion's portly 2nd major *C.F.M. Le Roy*[6] is a staunch democrat who regards all blue-blooded persons with contempt, Napoleon as 'an enterprising genius' and the Russians as barbarians. After 'deciding to be born in the midst of a nation execrated by all others', he'd begun his military career 'by chance' as a conscript in 1795 but 'continued it by taste'. During that winter of 1811/12 he has been amused to see how at the Grand Casino the wives of the local nobility, 'without fear of besmirching their sixteen quarterings of nobility' have been happy to gamble and dance with the young officers; and, not least, how 'more than one felt an impulse to fall into [the] Line – and enjoyed doing so'.

In Southern Germany, too, the various principalities of the French-dominated Confederation of the Rhine are reluctantly supplying fresh contingents to General Vandamme's VIII Corps. Meanwhile Jerome Bonaparte, King of Westphalia, Napoleon's troublesome youngest brother, though destitute of military experience, is no less reluctantly preparing himself to assume overall command both of it, as well as Prince Poniatowski's V (Polish) Corps and General Reynier's Saxons (VII). None of these sacrifices, though unwelcome, are novel. In 1806 the little duchy of Saxe-Coburg had been overrun by the bluecoats; and only ten months have gone by since the kind-hearted Duchess Augusta[7] was pained to see

'the fragments of our poor little contingent return from Spain – eighteen men out of 250! Most of the losses haven't been due to actual fighting, but mainly to disease, scarcity and neglect, added to the hardships caused by the Spanish climate. Half the town turned out to meet the survivors,' she'd noted in her diary. Now she's depressed to see a fresh contingent march out,[8] this time northwards.[9]

What is their destination? Coignet, in Paris, may not know; but all these tens of thousands of conscripted Germans certainly do. Writing home to his family for some pocket money for this new campaign, one of Davout's corporals hears it's going to be India, a country evidently populated by monkeys ['*aux Singes*' = *aux Indes*]. Which way? Via Russia, of course, whose emperor is, for the third time, to be 'taught a lesson'.

This new Grand Army is certainly not only made up of willing soldiers. Far from it. All over Europe – even from faraway Naples where Napoleon's glamorous brother-in-law *Joachim Murat* is putting his *lazzaroni* and released convicts into exceptionally colourful uniforms – all unmarried 18-year-olds who haven't been able to afford to pay for a substitute to go and get killed for them[10] and who've drawn the recruiting sergeant's shortest straw – all, that is, who haven't fled to the hills and become 'bandits' – are being accompanied to the outskirts of their towns or villages by weeping relatives who never expect to see them again. As usual, desertion en route for the depots is wholesale. Most of the reluctant peasants whom Lieutenant *Heinrich von Brandt*[11] is seeing co-opted into the 2nd Vistula Regiment at Posen have never in their lives worn boots or slept in a bed and 'only knew of white bread and coffee by hearsay' and are having to be kept to the colours by a combination of good food and lodgings and, for deserters ('almost all were caught') 50 to 60 strokes of the cane on their backsides. After fetching a whole route-regiment of deserters from the Ile de Ré to Lübeck *Joseph Guitard*[12] a tall chestnut-haired captain in Coignet's regiment, is having to go back into Prussia and fetch another. The equivalent of a whole division of the Grand Army consists of such would-be deserters.

Napoleon, of course, knows perfectly well what he's about, and whose interests he's serving. The French nation's of course. But who are the 'nation'? The middle classes, of course, as opposed to *le peuple*, whom he one day boasts to Narbonne that he has "pacified by arming it". Adding as a corollary: "In my hands war has become the antidote to anarchy." As for the old aristocracy, those of them who've rallied to the cause of an upstart throne "borne up", as Napoleon himself realized, "on the bayonets of the Imperial Guard, all sons of self-owning peasants", some are really devoted to his cause, if not always, like Caulaincourt and Narbonne, to his policies. Others, perhaps most, are decidedly ambivalent: "A blue is always a blue, a white always a white," he'll ruefully tell his First Ordnance Officer Gaspard Gourgaud one day on St Helena.

Among aristocratic officers wholeheartedly devoted to his cause is General Count *Philippe de Ségur.* One day during the Consulate this son of a distinguished father, both bitter enemies of the Revolution, had been loitering outside the Tuileries gates in a state of such deep depression that he was contemplating suicide, when a troop of Chasseurs of the Consular Guard had come trotting out. On this scion of France's ancient military

caste the sight of their brilliant green and red uniforms and other accoutrements had had an effect only comparable to that of St Paul's vision en
route for Damascus. Throwing in his lot with the new Caesar, the young
Philippe de Ségur had gone and joined up; and like his fellow aristocrat
Montesquiou Fézensac had of course been swiftly promoted. After various
exploits he is now an officer at Imperial Headquarters, where his special
task as Assistant Prefect of the Palace is to supervise the pack mules which,
on campaign, transport the imperial gold dinner service and other
domestic chattels. If half of de Ségur's mind is deep in military matters,
the other is no less deep in classical literature; and it's by no means impossible that he's already contemplating a great historical work – not that
either he or anyone else, in this spring of 1812, can envisage what it will
be. Filled with what will turn out to be a passionate, if, in the event – in
Gourgaud's eyes – altogether too ambivalent admiration for his idol, he is
already well aware that of all the allies being pressed into service in this
gigantic expedition 'only the Italians and Poles were really enthusiastic for
our cause'.

Of none of the Grand Army's officers is this truer than of a certain
Elban officer, by name *Césare de Laugier* (or Loggia). Setting out from
Milan in February with the rest of Prince Eugène's IV Corps, the
adjutant-major of the Guards of Honour of the Kingdom of Italy, each
company of which comes from a different North Italian city and has a dif-
ferent-hued facing to its green-and-white uniform, has crossed the Alps
and gone into cantonments in Southern Germany, where he's sure the
inhabitants 'love' them. Inside its new-fangled Grecian-style helmet, whose
huge plumed and combed crest culminates in an agressively beaked, rapa-
cious and gilded eagle's head, Césare de Laugier's head is full of notions
of antique military exploits. Not a little naïve himself, he paints a touching picture of his compatriots' mentality:

'They know no other divinity than their sovereign. No other reason
but force. No other passion but glory. All is levelled out in discipline
and passive obedience, the soldier's prime virtue. Ignorant of what's
in store for them, they're so convinced of the justice of their cause
that they never try to find out which country it is they're being sent
to. Having heard it said at each war's commencement that they're
destined to deal the final blow to the Englishmen's tottering power,
they end up by confusing all existing powers with England. They
assess the distance separating them from it by the number of
marches they, for several years now, have been making from one side
of Europe to the other, without ever reaching that country which,
goal of all their efforts, vanishes before their eyes.'

Reviewed on 14 May on the esplanade at Glogau outside that town's fortifications, the adjutant-major will write in his diary:

'The whole of IV Corps is under arms. The Viceroy got here yesterday. The Royal Guard, occupying as of right the right of the front
line, which is very long, finds itself situated in the town cemetery.

Only the graves interrupt our regular alignment. Some superstitious minds are trying to extract a sinister presage from this circumstance, and are complaining of our being put here. The Roman legions would certainly have sacrificed to their gods to exorcize such sinister auguries.'

But evidently Prince Eugène, a somewhat stolid but very capable soldier, is above such fears; and, in an order of the day expressess his satisfaction with IV Corps' turnout. Nothing could make the Guardia d'Onore's adjutant-major feel more ecstatic.

As ever, there are political complications. Some, unlike the domestic ones,[13] can't be ironed out by imperial edict. For some time now the French and British embassies in Constantinople have been outvying each other in the art of bribing Turkish officials. The French to keep Turkey at war with Russia; the British to get them to make peace. And since the Turks have recently been getting the worst of it there's a distinct danger of British gold weighing heavier than French, thus freeing General Tormassov's Army of Moldavia to march northwards and threaten the Grand Army's southern flank. An eventuality Napoleon hopes he has guarded himself against by forcing his new-found father-in-law, the Emperor Francis, to provide him with 30,000 Austrians under Prince Schwarzenberg. Well, not exactly forcing, because there has been a price for it: that he guarantee his fellow-emperor the quiet possession of his ill-gotten Polish dominions in Galicia, wrested from the Poles in 1794. Here's an insoluble clash of claims: the Poles' that he shall reintegrate Galicia in their dreamed of kingdom. The Austrians' that he shan't.

Sweden, resoundingly defeated by Russia in 1809, is another problem. At that all-time ebb in her affairs, with Finland and even the Åland islands lost, her parliament, its elbow jogged by an independently minded young subaltern who'd happened to be in Paris at the time, had elected Napoleon's one-time rival Marshal Bernadotte to be that country's Crown Prince. One of the first things he'd found out on arriving in Stockholm was that his adoptive country's all-important iron industry was no less dependent than Russia's on the British market. And Franco-Swedish relations had rapidly gone from bad to worse. Finally Berndotte had declared himself neutral in the great power struggle; and in May 1810 Count Lagerbielke, the Swedish Ambassador in Paris, had been received in audience at the Tuileries:

'I'd never seen the Emperor so utterly furious, it exceeded anything one can imagine. He declared angrily that he hadn't slept one hour all night because of his Swedish business. "You could let me get some rest, I need it! British prisoners of war have been returned without compensation, isn't that so, Monsieur de Cadore?" (The Minister, all a-tremble, didn't fail to answer this question, like all others, in the affirmative.)'

For an hour and a quarter Napoleon had talked and shouted, so often repeating himself and interrupting his own line of thought that Lagerbielke would afterwards have some difficulty in clearly recalling all he'd said. He'd spared Sweden at the end of the 1807 war, he'd shouted, but had been 'deceived' by Lagerbielke:

'Neutrality no longer exists. Britain doesn't recognize it, neither can I. You're suffering? Don't you think I suffer, that France, Bordeaux, Holland and Germany are suffering? That's why there must be an end to it. Peace on the seas must be sought, no matter what the cost.' (Here the Emperor became terrifyingly angry.) 'Well, Sweden alone is responsible for the crisis I find myself in! Sweden has done me more harm than all five Coalitions put together. Open war, or else reliable friendship. Choose now. There's my last word. Farewell. May I see you again under happier circumstances.'[14]

With these words the Corsican Tyrant had walked out of the room,[15] leaving the Swede amazed to find the antechamber deserted 'even by the duty officer... whether in obedience to orders or out of voluntary politeness, the Emperor on several occasions having raised his voice to such a degree of loudness it was impossible not to hear him in the next room.' And early in 1812, while Narbonne and Napoleon were having their fascinating conversations at St-Cloud, Davout had been ordered to occupy Swedish Pomerania by a *ruse de guerre*, seize all Swedish shipping in its ports and have the Swedish garrisons sent back to France as prisoners of war.

This, for the Swedes, had been the last straw. Bernadotte had declared Sweden neutral, made peace with Britain, and opened secret negotiations with the Tsar.

Prussia is yet another problem, albeit apparently not too serious a one. Stripped of almost half her land area, and still seething with resentment after the stupendous war indemnities still being paid since 1806, she, as an 'ally' of France, has been ordered to provide the Grand Army with a 30,000-man contingent to protect its left wing, in the same way as the Austrians are to protect its right. This has caused the Berlin court to put out secret feelers to Vienna – feelers which, after three no less ruinous defeats, have fallen on deaf ears. Even so, just to make sure there are no misunderstandings, Marshal Oudinot is ordered to occupy Berlin with his 30,000-strong II Corps, while Narbonne at the same time is sent there to exercise his old-style diplomacy on a traumatized Prussian court.

All through the spring and early summer of 1812 Europe's roads resound to the tramp of marching boots as no fewer than seven armies march northwards. Each division sets out after the one ahead of it at two-day intervals. With a distance of 100 paces (70m) between battalions, its regiments march 'in two files sharing the road whose crown they leave free'. Halting for 'five minutes in every hour and at three-quarters of the day's march for half an hour' and with a day's rest every fifth, they tramp on northwards at an average speed of 25 miles a day. Every second day they pick up rations, provided along the route by Count Daru's[16] administration. 'The step of the NCO who marches at the head of the regiment,' explains that amusing raconteur Captain *Elzéar Blaze* (who is himself lucky enough not to be sent to Russia),

'must be short and regular; for if the right advances at a regular pace, the left will have to gallop. The least obstacle on the road, even if it's only a runnel to cross, and if the first man to encounter the obstacle pauses for even half a second, the men in the last battalion will have to run for a quarter of an hour to catch up. All this an experienced officer sees at a glance; orders a brief halt; and everything resumes its wonted course. After we've marched an hour there's a five-minute halt, to light our pipes. This is known as *la halte des pipes*. The soldier must never be deprived of any of his pleasures. Everyone dines on what he has in his pack, and then off we go again, breaking each league with five-minute halts.'

Looking out of his window in Dresden, capital of the kingdom of Saxony, a nine-year-old boy, *Wilhelm von Kügelgen*, watches them go by:

'The long dark columns of the Old Guard with their proud eagles, tall bearskins, and martial faces hovering like gloomy dream-pictures. The warlike sound of drums and pipes; then the ghostly figures of the pioneers with glinting axes and long black beards, and behind them the endless transport columns. Day after day they passed under our window, man by man, brigade after brigade. I saw almost all the arms of the Grand Army: the tall carabiniers with plumed helmets and gilded cuirasses; the light chasseurs, hussars, voltigeurs; all types of infantry and artillery with good horse-drawn vehicles. And, lastly, long columns of pontoon-bridging and other military equipment.'

It's at Dresden, namely, that the new Charlemagne has ordered the kings and princes of a conquered Europe to come and do him homage. Since few if any – the King of Saxony apart – are sincerely attached to his cause, perhaps a festive display of political and military might will impress on everyone the futility of stirring up trouble behind his back? His father-in-law the Emperor of Austria is to be guest of honour and his young daughter, Marie-Louise, Empress of the French, leading lady – Prussia's king and queen have to beg to be allowed in and even then are only grudgingly admitted.

What, one wonders, are the 47-year-old upstart emperor's thoughts as, with his young blonde empress seated at his side, the imperial cortège leaves Paris at 5.30 a.m. on 9 May, for 'the supreme effort, the most difficult task of all?' – namely, by crushing Russia to crush Britain and secure for himself and for France the domination of the world? Is he perhaps even hoping the Dresden event may, in itself, suffice to bring the Tsar to heel? Otherwise what was the meaning of his rueful aside to his police prefect, just before leaving:

'Well, one must finish what one has started!'

No previous campaign, as far as we know, had been preluded by such a remark.

Von Kügelgen goes on:

'One stormy night when the torches would hardly burn he arrived like the Prince of Darkness. Flashes of lightning lit the sky, and peals of thunder mingled with the populace's half-hearted cheers and the ghostly ringing of churchbells. There was a good deal to be seen in Dresden at this time. The presence of so many armies filled the town with martial pomp. Bells pealed and cannons boomed to welcome the princes. Grand parades and manoeuvres entertained them. At night the town shone under the magical glare of a thousand lamps. A broad rainbow of gay paper lanterns arched the sky high above the Elbe, which reflected every colour of the spectrum, the prettiest light-effect one could possibly imagine. Fireworks crackled in the air. Every house was filled to the brim with soldiers who talked, laughed and swore in almost every European language.'

The romantic poet Heinrich Heine, too, sees him

'high on horseback, the eternal eyes set in the marble of that imperial visage, looking on, calm as destiny, at his guards as they march past. He was sending them to Russia, and the old grenadiers glanced up at him with so anxious a devotion, such sympathy, such earnestness and lethal pride: *Ave Caesar, morituri te salutant!*

Among the princelings who are anxiously waiting here to placate him, two of Duchess Augusta's sons have every reason to be worried. For a third brother has been so imprudent as to take a commission in the Russian army, causing Napoleon, like an angry landlord, to threaten to 'chase' their father out of his duchy. But at the festivities what impresses them most is

'the contrast between the very human Emperor Franz, with his friendly courteous bearing,[17] and Napoleon, decidedly curt and rude, though possibly not intentionally so, merely over-elated by his extraordinary luck and cleverness. The adulation and sickening flattery with which he's everywhere received further increase the contemptuous, harsh attitude peculiar to him.'

An assessment certainly not shared by Napoleon's First Secretary. Baron *Claude-François Méneval*[18] has

'many opportunities to observe these august assemblies. In the vast apartments of the Dresden palace I contemplated the procession headed by Napoleon. The Empress of Austria's health being too feeble for her to stand the fatigue of walking through all these apartments, the Emperor walked ahead of her, hat in one hand, the other resting on the door of her sedan chair, as he talked gaily to her. All who witnessed these social events agreed that by his affability, intellect and seductive manners he exerted an irresistible ascendancy over his noble guests. He was the most amiable and charming man in the world when he wanted to be.'

Napoleon may be invincible, the Duchess concedes in her diary: but at what cost in human blood and suffering?

The Tsar meanwhile has left Petersburg for Vilna, in a last-minute attempt to enlist the support of his more influential Lithuanian subjects. And when Lauriston follows and applies for an audience, refuses to receive him. So Narbonne, at Berlin, gets new instructions. He too is to go to Vilna, ostensibly to try and save the peace, actually to sniff out all he can about Russo-Swedish and Russo-Turkish relations and, in the event of the Russian army crossing the Niemen, try to negotiate a truce "to give His Majesty time to reach the front".

Narbonne is more welcome than Lauriston. Invited to dinner, he delivers Napoleon's personal message:

"In the last analysis, there's only one, but very important, issue between us and Russia: of neutral nations and of English trade. Compared with this, Poland doesn't matter. His Majesty has only French interests at heart."

To this Alexander, who also has the knack of being all things to all men, replies that he'll neither be the aggressor, nor will he

"sign a peace dictated on Russian territory. The Russian nation doesn't recoil in the face of danger. All Europe's bayonets on my frontier won't make me alter my language."

Deeply impressed by so firm and dignified a stance, no sooner is Narbonne back at his lodgings than three high Russian officials come knocking at his door. His carriage, they tell him, is already harnessed up and ready to leave. The Tsar has even been so considerate as to have it provisioned out of his own kitchen with food for the journey. Reaching Dresden on 24 May at the height of the festivities, Narbonne brings his master four items of information. One is correct. The others not. The Russians won't break the peace, he tells him, nor will they cross the Niemen. But if he, Napoleon, does so, then he "has the impression they'll immediately give battle. And Russia will at once ally herself with Britain." As for the Swedes, though it's true their Crown Prince seems to be siding with Alexander, there's still no pact between them. Neither is there any prospect of a Russo-Turkish peace.

(Actually, unknown both to Napoleon and his envoy but loyal to the interests of his adoptive country, Bernadotte has already assured the Tsar that Sweden will remain neutral until the moment comes for her to show her hand. At the same time he has urged Alexander to stand fast. As for Turkey, only two days earlier, on 22 May, a certain one-eyed General Kutusov, who had come off very much second best at Austerlitz in 1804, has met the Grand Vizir at Budapest and signed a peace treaty between

Russia and Turkey. Two events in the light of which Napoleon will say on St Helena that his invasion of Russia was a mistake.)

Paying scant heed to his envoy's report, Napoleon launches out into another rhetorical flight of the kind that had so worried Narbonne at St-Cloud:

"Very well, then! Let destiny be accomplished, and Russia be crushed under my hatred of England! At the head of four hundred thousand men, paid and equipped on a hitherto unexampled scale, with reserves on our flanks, with a Lithuanian corps of the same blood as some of the populations we'll be passing through, I don't fear this long road fringed with deserts. After all, my dear fellow,' he went on as if in an exalted dream, 'this long road is the road to India. Alexander the Great set out to reach the Ganges from a distance no less great than from Moscow. Imagine Moscow taken – Russia crushed – the Tsar reconciled or dead in some palace conspiracy – a new and dependent throne, perhaps. And tell me whether we a great army of Frenchmen and auxiliaries from Tiflis would have to do more than touch the Ganges with a French sword for the whole scaffolding of Britain's mercantile greatness to collapse. It'd be a gigantic expedition, I admit; but possible in the nineteenth century. At a blow, France will have conquered the independence of the West and the freedom of the seas."

Five days later he'll leave for the army.

In one of Davout's baggage wagons is a map of India. Just in case.[19]

CHAPTER 2

THE RAPE OF POLAND

A Dutch diplomat turns soldier – a heavily laden army – pillage and violence –
'Napoleono magni Caesari' – miserable villages, splendid châteaux – Brandt visits
his parents – a campaign for men only – cantinières – 'this child should be with his
mother' – Napoleon dictates in a terrible voice – a priest with his wits about him –
'terror and desolation are let loose in Poland'

On 11 June, writes *Dedem van der Gelder*, the army was set in motion. A dap-
per little man, more suited for the profession his father had put him into
than for the military life he'd always hankered after, Dedem had been a
Dutch diplomat. But after the incorporation of his country into France in
1810 he'd gone to Fontainebleau and offered his services. Napoleon had
wanted to give him a military governorship in the Netherlands. But 'not
wanting to begin by shooting my compatriots' Dedem had asked for a post
on active service; whereupon Napoleon, who was increasingly short of
educated officers, had promoted him *général de brigade* and sent him to
Davout at Hamburg, where the Iron Marshal – surprisingly in view of
Dedem's lack of military experience – had entrusted him with the command of 2nd Infantry Brigade, under his brother-in-law Friant. And it had
been in that capacity Dedem had taken part in the treacherous occupation of Swedish Pomerania, an operation he, having been Dutch
Ambassador in Stockholm and still having many friends there, found
utterly distasteful.[1]

The whole army is maximally burdened. Each infantryman, at least in I
Corps, is carrying on his back bread and flour for 20 days – Dedem says a
bag containing ten pounds of flour and another with ten pounds of rice.
It's just as well. For three days on end little *Jean-Marc Bussy*, a voltigeur of
the 3rd Swiss Regiment, sees 'not a village, not a house'. Besides his musket (ten pounds), he's carrying *inside* his pack:
  2 shirts,
  1 pair of thick linen trousers,
  1 pair of thick black linen half-gaiters,
  1 brush-bag,
  1 bandage and lint, and
  2, or perhaps 3, pairs of shoes [right and left foot identical], together
  with spare hobnails and soles.
On either side of his pack:
  4 'biscuits' (large slices of twice-baked bread, each weighing sixteen
  ounces).
Under his pack is slung a canvas bag containing five pounds of flour.
Thereto in a canvas bandoleer, two loaves of bread, each weighing three
pounds, i.e., bread for four days, biscuit for four more, and flour for
seven, the whole weighing 58 pounds (25.5kg), enough for him to live on

for fifteen days. Passing through Warsaw with VIII Corps, another voltigeur, lance-corporal *William Heinemann* of the Brunswick Chasseurs – though an old campaigner[2] he'd made made an abortive attempt to escape in Germany – swaps his extra pairs of shoes for 'forty eggs and some bunches of radishes'. Such initiatives might perhaps pass muster in Vandamme's corps: not under Davout's fiercely disciplined regiments. Upon some young soldiers of Dedem's brigade throwing away their sacks of flour, the colonel of the 127th, reviewing them, had ordered the empty sacks to be filled with sand. The guilty men were to carry them until further notice. This, says Caulaincourt, did the trick, 'the more so as the time for filling them with flour never came'.

Nor is it only the infantry which is so heavily burdened. The 2nd ('Red') Lancers of the Guard are a new élite regiment. Although their uniform emulates that of the famous 1st (Polish) Guard Lancers, albeit with reversed colours – scarlet with dark-blue facings and yellow trimmings – the unit consists mostly of Dutchmen. Originally Napoleon had intended it to be a cuirassier regiment for the Guard; but in the end, for lack of sufficiently powerful horses, has equipped it with lances. And a great deal else besides. At Koenigsberg its farriers – one per company – have been issued with a big axe 'for felling forests or butchery', and each troop's brigadier with eight little hatchets, for sharpening stakes to tether their horses and build shacks and bivouacs. Finally, besides lance, carbine, ammunition, and other regulation equipment, each trooper has to find room for a sickle, fastened on his horse's rump on top of his cylindrical portmanteau, for cutting standing crops and grass. All these extras, on top of the lancers' heavy harness, are already proving too much for their mounts:

'In the long run all the regiment's companies had some horses hurt. Since most of these sores appeared on the right side, it was their withers which were wrung, and we assumed this was due to the combined weight of lance and carbine. We tried to remedy this in every thinkable way: by shifting the lance from right to left, and then by having the carbine carried on the hook of the bandoleer. But we soon saw that this latter measure had the drawback of more or less causing the trooper to lean forward under its weight and thus cause fresh sores.'

If this is the state of affairs in a 'light' cavalry regiment, what, one wonders, can it be like for massively weighted cuirassiers and carabiniers, wearing their plumed and maned brass helmets and 16lb steel cuirasses?

But though the rank and file are burdened to the last ounce, some of the supply wagons obviously aren't. Arriving at Gumbinnen on the Polish-Prussian border on 21 June, Napoleon dictates an angry letter to Berthier:

'The wagons of the select headquarters have left here only half-loaded. Send an express courier forthwith, with an order to assemble the whole load on 20 wagons, and for the 20 empty ones to be sent

to Insterburg to reload. Tell the supply officer I'm displeased with him for going forward in this way with his wagons empty. I've sometimes seen nonchalant administrators, but never any more stupid.' Each officer and soldier, Dedem goes on, has been
  'summarily ordered to relieve his Prussian hosts of ten days' rations. The countryside was stripped of horses and vehicles to carry forage, and even of straw. Altogther 90,000 horses were officially requisitioned from the Prussians, who [although nominally allies] were treated at very least as a conquered people. In other words, the order about 10 days' rations had been nothing but an authorization of pillage and violence.'

Pillage and violence, indeed, are the real order of the day. On Napoleon's arrival at Gumbinnen the civil authorities complain to him that a local landowner, whose château has been taken over by the Guard, has been found at the bottom of a well, whether having committed suicide or been thrown down no one knows. But though Napoleon orders an immediate 'very serious' joint investigation by themselves and the Guard's commanders, nothing is done about it.

Official manifestations staged by a cowed administration are not the less spectacular for all these distresses. At Posen on 29 May, Lieutenant *Heinrich von Brandt* of the Vistula Legion[3] has seen the Emperor
  'eloquently received under a triumphal arch bearing the words "Heroi invincibli". The town hall's five big windows were decoated with a transparency of the civic arms, alternating with the initials of Napoleon, the Empress Marie Louise,[4] the French eagle and the escutcheon of the Grand Duchy. On the church tower, which the Emperor could see from his windows, the illuminations showed a gigantic crown of laurels surmounting this motto: "Napoleoni magno Caesari et victori". A vast crowd from the surrounding countryside was bivouacked in all the squares, notably in the one called Place Napoleon, and which, before the year was out, would resume the name of Frederick William! Only the old 'grumblers' (for we Poles had some among us) remained rather aloof amid the general hubbub. They maintained that the enthusiasm was partly artificial and stimulated by the authorities, who wanted to throw dust in the Emperor's eyes.'

But though the Poles, according both to Ségur and Brandt, really are enthusiastic for the French cause, they're finding themselves no less roughly handled than the unwilling and resentful Prussians. The troops, for their part, are appalled by the extreme and appalling poverty of their villages. 'What a contrast', exclaims Le Roy, 'between the beautiful German villages, which had yielded us all we needed, and these little Polish towns where we only found miserable Israelites, rife with vermine and the scab.' Colonel *Lubin Griois* of the Guard Horse Artillery – a great lover of Italian opera and, not least, Italian women (though he doesn't despise the Germans, despite their resistance to being seduced and their eventual capitulation) – agrees wholeheartedly:

'Thinly populated, the villages lie far apart, and the towns are almost wholly occupied by Jews. They are as wretched as their inhabitants. All peasants are the property of their lords, whose magnificent châteaux contrast sharply with the poverty of the shacks, and whose superb gardens and numerous servants offer a luxury and splendour unknown in France. That part of the countryside which wasn't forest was covered as far as the eye could see with fields of rye, promising the richest of harvests. But soon these fields were devastated in order to nourish our horses, for which we had the greatest difficulty in finding any dry forage.'

Colonel *St-Chamans*, riding along at the head of his 7th Chasseurs, is finding it repugnant to obey orders

'to take away all the grain, brandy and cattle we could find between the Vistula and the Niemen. I must admit it was very cruel of us, after spending a few days in the home of the lord of some village or of some farmer who'd received us well, and often better, than we were in France, to thank them on leaving by carrying off their carriages, grain and cattle. These unhappy people begged us with groans to modify the rigour of an order which, from their having been well off, plunged them into poverty. I fancy all the officers tried to soften their fate. But even with such concessions we still did them a lot of harm.'

Even crueller, it is, if one is oneself Polish. Passing through Strzelnow, between Posen and Thorn, Brandt pays a brief visit to his parents:

'It was this part of old Poland which had suffered worst. The evils of the 1807 war had been followed without pause by the miseries of the Continental Blockade, by epidemics among humans and animals, and now by the continual troop movements. My parents, once well-off proprietors, had had the costly honour of first putting up Marshal Ney, then the Prince of Württemberg. All their forage had been taken away by the artillery trains, and the daily and nightly requisitions had taken their horses. In a word, everything was happening exactly as in an enemy country, apart from the government vouchers, repayable only after a long period. For me the forty-eight hours I spent in my father's house were as many hours of torture.'

No woman, whatever her social rank, is to be allowed to cross the Niemen. So among all these thousands of marching men there can be only very few, apart from the formidable breed of Mutter Courages, the sutleresses, or *cantinières*. 'It was a fine profession, the cantinière's,' writes Elzéar Blaze:

'These ladies had usually begun by following a soldier who'd inspired them with tender sentiments. At first one saw them making their way on foot with a barrel of brandy slung over one shoulder. Eight days later they were comfortably seated on a horse they'd found. To right, to left, in front, behind, barrels and saveloy sausages, cleverly disposed, balanced each other. The month was never out without a two-horse wagon, filled with provisions of all kinds, being there as evidence of the growing prosperity of their trade. An officer knew no greater pleasure than to lend them money. They were much less afraid of the Cossacks and the bands of stragglers who would sometimes strip them of their crowns than that some of their insolvent debtors might get killed. In camp the cantinière's tent is the company's sitting room, bar, café.'

Many of course have children, usually by a succession of fathers, many of whom have slain their predecessor in a duel. Some of the boys are destined to become drummer-boys. But one of General Friant's surgeons, by name Déchy, who left Paris 'by the light of the immense tail of that year's comet' has brought his 13-year-old son. At Mecklenburg they find the 2nd Division 'encamped around the town, within sight of the British cruisers we could see from the coast'. From there they go on via Thorn to Insterberg, where an immense artillery park has been set up:

'At 9 a.m., June 22, a great rumour arose in the town. Soldiers with a martial air the like of which had never been seen and covered in dust, were drawing up in battle array on the public square. It was the Foot Grenadiers of the Guard. The whole population stood around,' young Déchy among them. Once again it's Napoleon who's approaching. Since he's rumoured to be less than two hours away, the boy runs to tell his father, who promptly dons his sombre uniform – blue with yellow trimmings – and his fore-and-aft hat, and goes out beyond the suburbs to meet the Emperor. At a crossroads, one kilometre outside town,

'we saw in the plain a whirl of dust. It was the Emperor's carriage. Drawn by six little local horses driven by three peasants, with a mameluke on the box and only escorted by a few horse-gunners, it was making slow progress along the sandy road. To the Emperor's left we saw a sleeping man, whose head, knocking against the panel, fell back on His Majesty's shoulder.'

Déchy's father immediately recognizes the sleeper as Marshal Berthier, Prince of Neuchâtel, Napoleon's chief-of-staff and the army's major-general:

'As the carriage turned a corner its wheels sank deep into the sand and brought it to a standstill. By a natural movement the Emperor stuck his head out of the window, looked at us, and signed to my father to come closer.'

Seeing he's the doctor in charge of the Isterberg hospital, Napoleon wants to know whether its patients' health is satisfactory. The last artilleryman, Dr Déchy replies proudly, has just been given a clean bill of health. 'The Emperor took this news with pleasure. Then he asked my father who this child was he was holding by the hand.' On being told it was his son,

'the Emperor's face took on a stern impression. And he said: "Monsieur, this child ought to be at school or with his mother, not here. When orders are given for no women to follow the army, such orders should a fortiori be extended to include children." To excuse himself my father risked this answer: That when he'd taken me with him he hadn't expected to find himself so far from France. "Monsieur, anyone who belongs to the army in any capacity whatsoever must be prepared for anything."

A brief encounter which will be decisive for the boy's whole life.

And now it's sunset, 22 June. And this time it's the turn of the inhabitants of the little town of Wilkowiszki, about a day's march from the Niemen, to see

'a cloud of dust approaching along the road and hear trumpets heralding the Emperor's approach. A few moments later he appeared, seated alone in his carriage. Five trumpeters rode ahead, and he had an escort of officers and NCOs. He made straight for the castle, where a lodging had been prepared for him.'

His study, the local priest Butkevicius goes on, had been installed in

'a rustic pavilion surrounded by poplars. Numerous maps were spread out on his desk. Although the weather was very hot, Napoleon kept his dark greatcoat on and his little hat which he wore while talking to his generals and marshals, who all stood uncovered to listen. Through its coating of dust the Emperor's features showed signs of fatigue, annoyance and displeasure caused by the news he'd received on the way. His ill humour turned to anger when he was told that not only the army, but even the Guard, was short of provisions. Throughout his stay he was certainly in a very bad mood, because he dictated letters in a terrible voice. He didn't sleep that night, and everywhere people were organizing ovens to bake bread.'

Doubtless it's in the same 'terrible voice' he now dictates his declaration of war. Dated Wilkowiszki 22 June 1812, it's in the form of a proclamation to the army:

"Soldiers! The second Polish war has begun. The first ended at Friedland and Tilsit. At Tilsit Russia swore to be an eternal ally of France and to make war on Britain. Today she is violating these oaths. She refuses any explanation of her strange behaviour, so that the French eagles have been unable to recross the Rhine, which would be to leave our allies at her mercy. Russia is being swept away by her fate, her destinies must be accomplished. Does she think we are degenerates? Aren't we still the soldiers of Austerlitz? She makes us choose between dishonour and war. The choice cannot be in doubt. So let us march on, across the Niemen, and carry the war on to her territory. The second Polish war will be as glorious as the first, but the peace we shall conclude will carry its own guarantee. It will put an end to the baneful influence Russia for fifty years has been exercising on the affairs of Europe. – Napoleon."

The Reverend Butkevicius, at least, has his wits about him. Next day he invites Brandt to dinner, shows him a bed Napoleon has allegedly just done him the honour of sleeping in, likewise the table on which he'd signed his declaration of war. And in return for being allowed to keep 'at least one bull' offers Brandt 'two bottles of the imperial liqueurs and a glass of schnapps for each officer'. The bottles are afterwards found to contain... water, and cause Brandt to reflect that good nature is seldom rewarded, least of all in wartime. Before leaving Wilkowiski he has to requisition

'a whole herd of 50 cows, watched over by a very pretty girl. In despair at seeing us grab her herd, this Amaryllis weeps, wrings her hands, and finally throws herself at my feet, begging me to leave her at least two cows for her parents. Which I did without exacting any kind of ransom, though she seemed resigned to make great sacrifices to soften my heart.'

Catching up next day, a subaltern, left behind to escort the regimental baggage, tells Brandt of the

'disorders being committed and the confusion and indiscipline already prevailing in this immense army. "Everyone", he said, "is doing whatever he likes, taking from wherever he can. Frenchmen, Italians, Württembergers, Badeners, Bavarians, even Poles, are sacking the country just as they like. If this goes on much longer we'll be eating each other, like starving rats. The Emperor must be blind to such excesses."

In fact he isn't. Only, as usual, overestimating the power and range of his authority. From Thorn he'd written to Berthier to tell Davout that

'when you gave him orders to procure food for twenty days you assumed this would be done under regular forms and without stripping the countryside; that terror and desolation are let loose in Poland; and that he shall take the promptest measures to prevent the country from being devastated, otherwise we'll find ourselves in the same situation as we were in Portugal.'

By and by they will, and worse. Even so, riding on at a brisk 15 miles per hour through the immense forest of Pilkowiski, '25-miles broad by 37-mile long', Caulaincourt sees his master has no reason to be dissatisfied with the results of Davout's efforts:

'The troops marching along the road were superb, and received the Emperor with real enthusiasm. The men of I Corps were noticeable for their fine uniforms and general smartness. They could rival the Guard. All this mass of youth was full of ardour and good health.'

With certain exceptions. In the forest another eye-witness overtakes 'a fat major on a horse driving on stragglers with a long cane, who were answering him with loud shouts of abuse'.

CHAPTER 3

MIDSUMMER AT THE NIEMEN

'At present we must give back what doesn't belong to us' – 'his air was gay, even mischievous' – Major Le Roy's cookpot goes missing – Dumonceau stumbles on I Corps – a sunshade of pine branches – a staggering spectacle – birds of paradise – effectives – the Imperial Guard – the cavalry – the veterans – three classes of officers – recruits at Posen – too young an army – an immense baggage train – 'what a crowd of protégés!' – Napoleon falls off his horse – 'a military promenade to Petersburg and Moscow'

On Midsummer's Eve, 1812, the patriotic Polish count *Roman Soltyk* is resting in his bivouac not far from the Niemen's 'sluggish yellow waves' and probably swatting the mosquitoes which are so numerous in those latitudes at that time of year, when

'a travelling coach drawn by six swift coursers arrived at a brisk trot by the Königsberg road and stopped abruptly in the middle of our camp. It was only escorted by a few Chasseurs of the Guard, whose horses were exhausted and out of breath.'

Soltyk is an artillery officer. His friend *Josef Grabowski* calls him 'a handsome man but a bit of a boaster, who always made a good impression on the French by speaking their language with all its refinements. Above all he was remarkable for his knowledge of the theory and practice of gunnery'. Judge Soltyk's excitement when

'the carriage door opened, and we saw Napoleon get vivaciously out. He was wearing his uniform of a chasseur of the Guard and was accompanied by Berthier. None of his aides-de-camp put in an appearance. Shortly afterwards General Bruyères arrived, alone, at a gallop. The Emperor, apparently much wearied by his journey, wore a preoccupied air.'

Soltyk and some other officers run over:

'Taking several quick steps toward our major, Napoleon asked where the regiment's commanding officer was. Untroubled by the colonel's absence – he was still resting – Major Suchorzewski replies that he's standing in for him, and was at his orders. Whereupon the Emperor asked which road led to the Niemen, where our outposts were, and various other questions as to the Russians' whereabouts. While interrogating us in this way he said he wanted to change his coat, asking for a Polish uniform.¹ It had been agreed, or rather ordered, that no French soldier should be visible to the Muscovites. So he took off his coat, and the Prince of Neuchâtel, Suchorzewski, myself and Colonel Pagowski, who'd just come running up, likewise. Also General Bruyères.'

So now there they are

'five or six of us, standing around the Emperor in our shirtsleeves, in the middle of our bivouac, holding our uniforms in our hands. A singular sight! Of all our uniforms Colonel Pagowski's greatcoat and forage cap fitted the Emperor best. At first we'd offered him a lancer officer's chapka [flared helmet], but he declined, saying it was too heavy. All this took only a few minutes. Berthier, too, donned a Polish uniform. The colonel's two horses were quickly brought up. Napoleon mounted one, and Berthier the other. Since Lieutenant Zrelski's company was doing outpost duty that day, he was detailed off to accompany the Emperor as guide.'

The party proceed to the hamlet of Alexota, three miles downstream, 'opposite and only a cannonshot distant from the little walled town of Kovno'. Three days earlier Soltyk had, from this point, drawn a map of the Niemen's eastern shore. Here

'the Emperor dismounted in the courtyard of a doctor's house whose windows overlooked the Niemen and gave him a good view of the surroundings. Without showing himself, and with his horses carefully hidden in the courtyard, he reconnoitred the country perfectly. Back at our bivouac he wants to have details of the enemy's positions. More particularly he asks me where the main Muscovite bodies were, whether on Vilia's left or right bank? Doubtless he wanted to know whether the route to Vilna was open.'

A glance at the map shows the sense of Napoleon's question. It's at Kaunas – known in those days as Kovno – that the Vilia, after winding westwards from Vilna, flows into the Niemen. As usual he has taken his enemy on the hop.[2] Barclay de Tolly's First West Army is 75 miles away, concentrated around Vilna. Bagration's Second West Army is 75 miles further up the Niemen, at Grodno. Will his enemies never learn? His plan is to defeat them in detail, just as he'd done during his very first campaign back in 1796. And this time he has overwhelming numbers to do it with.

Flanked along the Vilia's north-western bank by Oudinot's II Corps and headed by Murat's immense command (I, II, III and IV 'reserve' Cavalry Corps), a main striking force, Davout's mostly French I Corps and Ney's Württembergers (III Corps), backed up by the Imperial Guard, will make a beeline for Vilna. While Oudinot fends off Wittgenstein's Finnish corps northwards towards Petersburg, farther down the Niemen at Tilsit Macdonald's (mostly Prussian) X Corps will drive northwards and besiege Riga, on the Baltic. Meanwhile farther upstream, at Grodno, three more army corps – Poniatowski's Poles (V), Reynier's (Saxons) (VII) and Vandamme's Westphalians (VIII) – advancing from Warsaw, will strike at Bagration, who at the same time will be prevented from liaising with Barclay by being stricken in flank by Eugène's (mostly Italian) IV Corps, supported by Saint-Cyr's Bavarians (VI), who are to cross the Niemen midway between Kovno and Grodno, at Piloni, and thus safeguard the main force's right flank as it advances swiftly on Vilna. First Barclay, then

Bagration, will be caught between overwhelming forces; and the war will be over in its allotted two or three weeks. Such is Napoleon's perfectly designed plan, and there's no reason in the world why it shouldn't succeed.

All possible contingencies having been taken care of, the Poles return to their bivouac. And as they do so Soltyk notices

'a visible change in the Emperor's face. His air was gay, even mischievous. No doubt he relished the idea of the surprise he was preparing for the Muscovites for the morrow, and whose results he'd calculated in advance. We brought him some refreshments, which he ate on the main road in our midst. He seemed to take pleasure in his change of costume and twice asked us whether the Polish uniform didn't suit him. Having breakfasted, he said laughingly: "At present we must give back what doesn't belong to us." Taking off his borrowed garments, he resumed his uniform of a Chasseur of the Guard, climbed back into his carriage and, accompanied by Berthier, left abruptly.'

Not far away from Soltyk's bivouac but evidently out of sight of it, 'in a vast plain of standing corn', there's another, whose men, though they're wearing Polish-style uniforms, aren't Poles but Dutchmen. It's the 2nd ('Red') Lancers of the Imperial Guard. The Belgian Captain *François Dumonceau* is in command of its 2nd squadron's 6th troop. In the oppressive heat – the temperature is up in the 30s – he has just had all the trouble in the world to clear a way through the immense masses of men on the only highroad through the Pilkowisky forest. Now his regiment is on a war footing, with loaded carbines. And though no one is allowed to unsaddle, their sickles have come into use and are harvesting the half-ripe corn. Fortunately their bivouac is close to a small stream. As for victuals,

'a wise providence had just brought three oxen on to the scene to supplement what was left of our provisions issued to us the day before yesterday. Unfortunately we lacked firewood for our camp fires, and were having to go a long way to get some. At about 7 p.m., just as we were settling in, a violent storm passed over us and for more than half an hour drenched us in torrents of rain.'

As yet the 85th Line's five battalions are still trudging on through the forest; and when a tremendous thunderstorm breaks out and the rain comes lashing down, Major Le Roy, his friend Lieutenant Jacquet and his ever resourceful 'philistine' (servant) Guillaume are instantly soaked through. All around them the storm is bringing pines and spruces crashing down and great lightning flashes, striking the tallest pines, have started a forest fire which Dumonceau, looking back over his shoulder, assumes is a smokescreen 'lit deliberately to conceal the army's concentration'.

Of none of the thousands of officers approaching the Niemen that day could it be more truly said that armies march on their stomachs than of Le Roy. A good portly man i'sooth, his diary is nothing so much as a record of how he gets his dinner each day and what it consists of. Alas, no sooner has his battalion emerged at long last from the endless forest and begun to bivouac in another soaking cornfield, than Guillaume is horrified to find that the major's iron cookpot, his most treasured possession, has gone missing – and with it their rice rations! 'But only since we've left the forest,' says the ever-optimistic Guillaume. 'Quite right,' rejoins Le Roy. 'And since you're wet through anyway you can take the same road back again. You'll be sure to find it. Run along now and fetch us back our wet-nurse.'

Said and done. The cookpot is found by the roadside, as well as – amazingly – the rice stowed inside it. Not far away is another of I Corps' regiments, the 57th Line. And one of its lieutenants, the 21-year-old *Aubin Dutheillet*, is watching his men

'slaughter such cows or other animals following in the wake of each unit as we had need of, making broth of our flour and cooking pancakes amid the embers of our campfires.'

Not all units are as well supplied. And despite all the elaborate arrangements – the company of bricklayers and bakers Davout has sent on ahead to build ovens at the river bank, the 'enormous flocks and herds and immense parks of wagons laden with food each regiment was dragging behind it to the Niemen', etc., – other units, belonging to less strictly disciplined corps, are already beginning to feel hungry.

An unusually observant man, all the 22-year-old Dumonceau can see from his 'solitary spot' is

'a few stragglers or isolated wagons searching about for their units in this vast plain. Only to our left, in the neighbourhood of Nougardisky, could we make out a little group of white tents, which we took to be the Emperor's. Seized by a desire to witness the passage of the Niemen, which we assumed was just then going on,'

he requests permission to go and take a look. Gets it. Mounts. And rides off. The horse he's riding is 'an excellent Polish cross-bred mare, a dark 5-year-old bay, well built and full of vigour and liveliness' called Liesje. When he'd bought her in East Prussia her tangled mane had hung down to her knees and her previous owner had begged him 'with tears in his eyes not to disentangle it, as the animal's life depended on it'. But Liesje has had to submit to comb, shears and bit, and of Dumonceau's three horses she's already his favourite:[3]

'Penetrating the curtain of woods bounding our horizon, I reach the end of the plateau. There, through the gaps in the dense foliage, I discover the river. Its yellowish waters, flowing along a river bed about 50 metres wide, washed the foot of our high ground, circumventing a kind of promontory on the opposite bank, and presenting a low unbroken plain, sandy and deserted, about three miles long and perhaps three-quarters wide. The only object to be seen anywhere was a little shack, flanked by two arid pines like parasols.'

But no sign of an enemy, or even inhabitants:

'No bridge had yet been established, nor was there any sign of any preparations to construct one. Everywhere reigned only a profound silence. But furthest away to my left, opposite the promontory, I thought I could make out some troops. Going in that direction, I encounter an artillery column, coming down by a very narrow hollow road. Following in its tracks, I reach a kind of hollow, three-quarters of a mile wide, surrounded by high ground, opposite the elbow formed by the river bank. At the centre of this basin a little hillock, shaped like a truncated cone, rose abruptly to a height of six or seven metres. Since it was sloped at its rear, two guns had been hauled up. Screened by bushes, I saw they were trained on the opposite bank. At the base of the mound was a big farm.'

And in the same instant, behind the farm, Dumonceau sees

'an imposing mass of infantry drawn up in close order, on several very extensive lines. Several similar lines of artillery and cavalry stood behind them, and out in front a mass of pontoons, loaded on their drays. It was Marshal Davout's army corps, resting silently under arms! I tried to bypass them and get closer to the river bank. But a sentry placed at its approaches stopped me, saying it was forbidden to reveal oneself. They were waiting for nightfall and definitive orders to start the crossing.'

Napoleon's reconnaissance in Polish uniform, Caulaincourt notes in his diary, had been made during the morning:

'Arrived at Naugaraidski at 1 a.m. Mounted Gonzalon. Wore a Polish cloak, black silk cap, with General Haxo, the Prince of Neuchâtel and the Master of the Horse to reconnoitre the Niemen. Followed the river bank along the left bank from below Kovno to a league and half above it. Returned to Naugaraidski at 3 p.m. Went into his tent.'

On another hillock, some 300 paces from the river bank and a few yards from his blue-and-white striped tents, Guard sappers have improvised a sunshade of pine branches. And he evidently spends some part of the sultry afternoon under it, watching the divisions debouch from the Pilkowski forest and drawing up on the sloping plain. Marshal Oudinot's remarkable factotum 'Grenadier' *François Pils*[4] finds a moment to open his watercolour box and sketch the scene. Besides Napoleon himself, only his Armenian bodyguard *Roustam Raza*[5] can be made out with any certainty as he stands there holding one of the Emperor's six Arab greys.

When, at about midday, Berthier's ADCs turn up, one of them, the future painter of ballet-like battle scenes, Baron *Louis-François Lejeune*[6] finds the scene from the imperial hillock

'the most extraordinary, the most pompous, the most inspiring spectacle imaginable – of all sights the one which, by exaggerating the extent of his power, both material and moral, is most capable of inebriating a conqueror. Under our gaze, around the culminating point we occupied, were seven reigning princes, King Murat prancing about in his theatrical costume at the head of the cavalry, all

Europe's most handsome men in parade uniforms, and all its finest horses. In the distance the massed battalions covered the plain with their sparkling bayonets and emulated the blazing sun, whose flashing mirage was reflected in the river waters and in lakes ruffled by a light breeze. The salutes of thousands of trumpets and drums – the enthusiastic shouts acclaiming the Emperor whenever he appeared – so much devotion and discipline, shortly to set in motion this multitude whose immensity lost itself on the horizon where its weapons still twinkled like so many stars – all this exalted everyone's confidence in the chief who was leading us.'

All day division after division debouches from the forest; until by the time the 2nd Cuirassiers, in Nansouty's I Cavalry Corps, emerges on to the plateau, Sergeant-major *Auguste Thirion*[7] finds

'the ground so thick with men and horses we could hardly find a spot to bivouac on. No anthill is more agitated. And the variety of uniforms, moving in all directions, the noise arising from this multitude, and the incessant uproar of drums, trumpets and bands – all made the moment solemn and the scene a curious one.'

Another of the shadowy figures up there on the imperial hillock may well be *Planat de la Faye*[8]. A lieutenant in the Artillery Train, to his own great surprise, he has been appointed ADC to General Lariboisière, once Lieutenant Napoleone Buonaparte's messmate, but now commanding all the Grand Army's artillery. Unexampled though it is for a mere lieutenant of the Train to be offered such a position, Planat, faced with the choice between 1,800 and 2,500 francs a year and the prospect of further brilliant advancement on Lariboisière's staff, has naturally jumped at this chance, which among other things will enable him to send home more pay to his two impecunious brothers, especially as 'on campaign one spends almost nothing, and the habitual distractions of military men weren't to my taste'. Planat is a close friend of Lariboisière's son Honoré who is his fellow-ADC:

'Nothing was commoner than to see generals' sons situated like this. It was supposed to vaccinate them with the germs of the most brilliant military qualities. But the sternest general is almost always the feeblest and most indulgent father.'

Though enhanced with silver aiguillettes – the emblem of a staff officer – Planat's iron-grey uniform is admittedly nothing like as spectacular as the one Lejeune has designed for himself and his aristocratic colleagues on Berthier's staff:

'Scarlet tight-fitting trousers, with two gold stripes down the sides, a sky-blue pélisse trimmed with white fox-fur and, across the chest, gold brandenburger lacings, crossed transversely by a broad scarlet shoulder-strap. The tall new-style black-peaked hussar helmet, likewise scarlet, sported an inverted gold chevron on either side and around the top a gold lace band. The dangling scarlet schabraque, too, was fringed with gold lace and had a gold eagle in the centre,'

44

a painting to which Secretary Fain adds some finishing touches. The shako, he says, was

'ornamented with a white aigrette of heron's plumes and the uniform's effect still further heightened by gilt cordings and a mass of gold tassles and buttons. A superb silk and gold sash, a little cartridge case, a sabretache and a damascened sword completed their outfit. Their parade horses were Arab greys with long fluttering silky manes and hussar-style bits with braidings and gold tufts.'

So magnificent a horseman in the full pride and vigour of his youth can of course sit on nothing less than 'a gold and scarlet festooned panther skin', likewise edged with gold and sporting scarlet tassles. One of Lejeune's colleagues has even gone so far as to fit his pélisse with *diamond* buttons.[9]

How many men are assembled that day at the Niemen? How many horses? How many guns? The most authentic – if not necessarily the most accurate – assessment is on a slip of paper afterwards preserved by Napoleon's ambitious, jealous and fiery-tempered First Ordnance Officer, the 28-year-old Gaspard Gourgaud.[10] 'Scribbled all over in the Emperor's handwriting' it gives a total of 350,000 combatants, whereof 155,000 Frenchmen (but that would include Dutchmen), 162,000 allies, and 984 guns.

Crème de la crème is of course the Imperial Guard. An army corps in itself, with its own infantry, engineer, cavalry and artillery regiments, officers and rankers alike have been skimmed off from Line. At the Courbevoie barracks Coignet had seen them come in. Each had served for five years, done at least two campaigns, and would now draw pay a rank above what they'd have got in the Line. The Guard Artillery was superb. Major *Jean-François Boulart*, a man who in odd moments likes to play the flute, has brought one of the Guard's three artillery columns all the way from its depot at La Fère, outside Paris. In their tall plaqueless bearskins and dark-blue red-trimmed uniforms, he says, his gunners were

'a magnificent object of general admiration. On 5 June the Emperor had come and reviewed my artillery. He wasn't a man to make compliments, but he found it handsome. He had the goodness to spend a lot of time in my company.'

The Guard is a law unto itself. Outside its own hierarchy it is absolutely no respecter of persons. Sarcastically known as 'The Immortals' because its infantry units, at least, practically never fight, its function is to give the knockout blow in battle and in the unimaginable eventuality of a retreat ('a word unknown in the French army') provide a kind of marching bastion. It also gets all the pickings. If not the largest of all the corps (Davout's numbered 70,000), the Guard, 43,000 strong plus the 8,300 Poles of Claparède's Vistula Legion and the Hessian Royal Guard, is certainly the most formidable.

Many of the other cavalry regiments are especially magnificent. Major *Marcelline Marbot's*[11] 23rd Chasseurs, serving with Oudinot's II Corps and numbering – quite exceptionally – 2,000 mounted men, was as fine a regiment as that beau sabreur says he'd ever seen, or ever would:

'Not that it comprised out-of-the-way individuals of transcendent merit; but there was no one who wasn't up to his duties. Everyone marched in step, both in point of bravery and zeal. All the officers, intelligent and sufficiently educated, lived as true brothers-in-arms. So also with the NCOs. And since the troopers followed this good example, they lived in perfect harmony. Almost all being old veterans of Austerlitz, Iéna, Friedland and Wagram, most sported the triple or double stripe. General Bourcier, whose task it had been to find mounts for these vast masses of cavalry, had given the 23rd Chasseurs the tallest and finest horses he could find. So this regiment was known as the carabiniers of the light cavalry.'

Jean-Michel Chevalier, a long-serving lieutenant of the Chasseurs of the Imperial Guard, its senior cavalry regiment, may think the Saxon Guard Cuirassiers 'not very elegant, with cast iron cuirasses weighing 30 pounds and more, and a Roman-style helmet'; but some of the Italian Guard regiments, it's generally agreed, are superb. For Murat's Neapolitan Guard, resplendent in sky-blue or yellow uniforms, 'the Marquis of Livorno had formed one of the most beautiful regiments you could hope to see. He'd summoned old French and German military men and himself set them an example of enterprise and strict discipline.' The Guardia d'Onore of the Kingdom of Italy – of which Césare de Laugier is adjutant, too, is

'composed of young men of the best Italian families, each being supported by his family with 1,200 frs a year [a Line lieutenant's pay]. It drew attention to itself by its handsome turnout and good discipline.'

Cuirassier Sergeant-major Thirion is rhapsodic:

'Never had more beautiful cavalry been seen! Never had the regiments reached such high effectives. And never had cavalry been so well mounted. Our regiments were so numerous that three had been adjudged enough for a division.'

At the same time he's critical of the way it's organized and commanded:

'Each regiment formed a brigade in itself, with a brigadier-general commanding it: a vicious organization, however, because a regiment isn't a proper command for a general, and it tended to annihilate its colonel's authority.'

All the Line infantry regiments, too, have a backbone of veterans – men like Captain *Charles François* of the 36th Line, nicknamed 'the Dromedary of Egypt' because he'd fought at the Pyramids and once been a Turkish slave. Ségur says such old-timers could easily be recognized

'by their martial air. Nothing could shake them. They had no other memories, no other future, except warfare. They never spoke of anything else. Their officers were either worthy of them or became it.

For to exert one's rank over such men one had to be able to show them one's wounds and cite oneself as an example.'

De Laugier – still trudging across Poland in the heats toward Poloni – is noticing how his Italian veterans, men who'd fought in Spain at the sieges of Saragossa and Gerona,

'are stimulating the new arrivals with their warlike tales, so that the conscripts brighten up. The continual marching is giving them a military bearing. By so often exaggerating their own feats of arms, the veterans oblige themselves to authenticate by their conduct what they've led others to believe of them.'

If many of these 'old' campaigners, men of thirty or forty, have never been promoted, it's usually because they can't read or write. Another of Berthier's brilliant aides, Major *Montesquiou de Fézensac*, a scion of one of France's most ancient military families, who'd joined up as a ranker at the time of the Boulogne Camp, divides the army's officers at this time into three categories:

'The first class, made up of graduates recently out of military school, zealous, trained, but inexperienced and little developed physically, were from the outset unable to stand up to the campaign's excessive fatigues. The second class, quite the contrary, consisted of ex-NCOs whose total lack of education should have blocked their further promotion, but who'd been commissioned so as to keep up the spirit of emulation and replace the enormous losses caused by such murderous campaigns; excellent soldiers, for the rest, hardened to fatigues and from long habit knowing everything war can teach in the lower ranks. The third class, halfway between, was made up of educated officers in the prime of life, formed by experience, and all inspired with a noble ambition to distinguish themselves and carve out a career. Unfortunately these were the least numerous.'

Into which class would he have put sergeant – soon to become sous-lieutenant – Jean-Roch Coignet? Certainly the second. A guardsmen had to be at last 5 feet 7 inches tall. And the 2nd Grenadiers' little drill sergeant had only been smuggled in by padding out the soles of his boots with a pack of cards. As we've seen, he'd only recently learnt his alphabet, certainly with an eye to the infinitely desirable commission which 'on campaign could make all the difference between life and death' especially if one had the misfortune – as both Le Roy and Fézensac had in 1807 – to be taken prisoner. Yet that hot day at the Niemen, Coignet is responsible for part of the Imperial Treasure.[12]

If the regiments drawn up on the river bank that blazing afternoon have a fault it is that they contain altogether too many young soldiers. No regiment in I Corps is stronger than the 85th Line. Yet when Le Roy had joined it in East Prussia he'd found his battalion 'consisted entirely of young soldiers needing a lot of care; not,' he adds, 'that this would save them from being subjected to the same demands as our veterans, or from having the same marches exacted of them'. And already, after the three-day march across Poland, only four-fifths have even reached the Niemen. The average age of Bourgoing's fellow-subalterns in the 5th Tirailleurs is hardly over twenty.

Although troopers take much longer to train, the cavalry, too, is full of striplings. General Count Dejean, who'd raised 40,000 new troopers in Alsace, had confessed to Napoleon at the Tuileries that 'half of them hadn't the necessary vigour to wield a sabre. "If it hadn't been for Your Majesty's express orders I'd have sent them back to the depots." – "You'd have done very ill if you had," Napoleon had replied tartly. And explained that sheer numbers "combined with the supposed quality of my regiments of already known worth," exaggerated in the newspapers and passing from mouth to mouth, had the result that "on the day I open a campaign I'm preceded by a moral power that makes up for the real effectives I haven't been able to obtain." Which no doubt is why, though at Hanover they'd been given 'very beautiful horses,' Colonel *St-Chamans'* young recruits for the 7th Chasseurs

'who'd left the depots in France without even having learnt to sit a horse or any of a trooper's duties on the march or on campaign, if the truth be told didn't know how to use them, and wouldn't be able to turn them against the old and tried cavalry to be opposed to us.'

Results which had shocked Napoleon himself. Appearing suddenly on horseback at the 2nd Vistula Regiment's march-past at Insterberg, he'd said 'in the curt strident voice he used on his bad days "I find these young men too young. What I need is people who can stand fatigues. Men who're too young only fill the hospitals."'

But what is striking everybody most of all as the army debouches on the wooded slopes on that blazing afternoon is the immense, the unprecedented numbers of vehicles. Never has Captain *Girod de l'Ain*, ADC to General Dessaix, commanding a division of I Corps, or anyone else

'seen such immense preparations. The Emperor had assembled all the forces of Europe for this expedition; and each one of us had followed his example and brought with him everything he possessed. Each officer had at least one carriage, and the generals several. The number of horses and servants was prodigious.'

An officer's 'philistine' cooks, launders and, on occasion, marauds for him. Even subalterns such as Paul de Bourgoing have brought one: a plucky little 13-year-old Parisian street urchin, by name Victor, who'd done his damnedest to join the 5th Tirailleurs as a drummer-boy, but been turned down because of his tender age and puny physique, and whom Bourgoing has taken on out of sheer compassion.

The host of domestics is partly explained by the strict rule which forbids any officer to employ a ranker as batman. In the Imperial Guard it is 'forbidden, under pain of dismissal, for a chasseur or a grenadier to tend an officer's horse, or even hold it by the bridle. So we took old fife-players who had served out their time, soldiers' children or retired veterans.'

Gone too are the republican days when any officer under the rank of major had had to hoof it with his men. For the top brass alone the famous Parisian coachbuilder Gros-Jean has built no fewer than 300 carriages, specially for the campaign.[13] Colonel Count *François Roguet* of the 1st Grenadiers, who has just covered 1,200 miles in sixteen weeks in his own travelling carriage to take command of the Guard's 2nd Division, has brought with him six servants, twelve horses and two wagons filled with his personal effects, among them books and a great many maps. Girod de l'Ain goes on:

'Much of the baggage train, it's true, was made up of vehicles stocked up with provisions while crossing Prussia and Poland. But add the trains of the big artillery parks, the pontoon bridges, the ambulances, etc., and you can judge what such an army looked like.'

Least competent – and certainly least popular – of all branches of the service is the Administration. By no means all the war commissaries and intendants responsible for all these thousands of transports can be prevailed upon to emulate their chief, the indefatigable Daru, an administrator of utmost probity and energy. 'What a mob of fellows wearing collars of every hue!' exclaims Artillery Inspector *Paixhans*:

'What a brilliant crowd of youthful protégés! Their holy persons filled with self-importance but oblivious of their functions, not even knowing what their duties consisted in, with an arrogance only equalled by their ineptitude, they regarded themselves as our superiors. In their wake, what a dirty sombre swarm of subordinate agents, a cloaque of ineptitude, baseness and rapacity!'

Colonel St-Chamans, too, is discovering to his dismay that compared with the Army of Andalusia, which he has just left, the Grand Army's administration is

'full of types who'd never seen war, and who were saying out loud they'd only come on this campaign to make their fortunes'.

A certain pudgy and no little conceited captain of dragoons, by name *Henri Beyle*,[14] one day to become one of France's greatest novelists, is in it mostly for the experience. A younger cousin of Daru's, he has secured himself a job as a war commissary by paying court to Daru's wife.

As for the horses, their numbers, either at the Niemen or still in the rear, are almost beyond belief. Over and above the cavalry's 80,000 mounts there are 50,000 draft horses and more than 10,000 officers' mounts – in all 140,000.

And now it's afternoon. Friant's crack infantry division, which is to spearhead the advance, has turned up late. And to get his orders Dedem, too, has to mount the imperial hillock. Meanwhile the rest of the division stands waiting in column at its base. The scene may be spectacular; but Dedem finds the mood up there strangely sombre:

'I went up to the group of generals in Napoleon's entourage. A grim silence, almost a feeling of consternation, reigned among them. Upon my allowing myself a little gaiety, General Auguste de Caulaincourt (the Governor of the Pages and brother to the Master of the Horse) signed to me, and said in a low voice: "No one here is laughing. It's a historic occasion [*une journée*]." He gestured toward the other bank, as if to add: "There's our tomb!"

Hindsight? Or foresight? Caulaincourt says his brother was always in pain from his old wounds and 'often longed for death'. Has he a premonition of his own death in battle six weeks later? Or has he perhaps been influenced by his elder brother's outspoken antipathy to this new war? Or is it the complete lack of news. Where, exactly, are the Russians? Quartermaster-General *Anatole de Montesquiou* is noticing how 'Davout, the staff, everyone,' is complaining that

'none of their spies are coming back. The only sign of life on the opposite shore was an occasional patrol of Cossacks. The corps on our right knew no more about the enemy's movements than we did. A major got the idea of crossing the river, alone, to find out what was happening on the opposite bank. Not a sentry, not a soldier did he find. Proceeding further, he interrogated some inhabitants, who told him the enemy had retired, and he came back to inform the Emperor. This was certainly to render an important service; yet being improvised and outside the hierarchy it lacked legality. And the Emperor's righteous anger was extreme.'

At 6 p.m., Caulaincourt goes on, Napoleon

'mounted Friedland, inspected the pontoon train on the Kovno road, reconnoitred towards Marienpol. Returned at 8 p.m. At 9 p.m. mounted the same horse and rode over the high ground and the river banks from the point opposite Kovno to where the pontoons had been thrown across. After spending two hours dictating orders he decided to make a moonlight reconnaissance, closer to the river, to decide exactly where to cross. To avoid attracting attention from any Russian outposts he left everybody, without exception, at a distance. Accompanied only by General Haxo of the Engineers, he rode to and fro along the bank, before rejoining his staff.'

It is now that an incident occurs that in any other circumstance would go unheeded, but which strikes both Berthier and Caulaincourt as ominous. By no means a good horseman, only an indefatigable one,[15] Napoleon rode, says Odenleben,

'like a butcher. Without moving his legs, holding the reins loosely in his right hand, the left hanging down, he looked as if he'd been hung up in his saddle. At a gallop his torso swayed forwards and sideways with the horse's movements.'

And this summer he has also put on a lot of weight. 'His Majesty,' Captain Count *Boniface de Castellane*, an orderly officer who's seeing him daily at close quarters at IHQ, writes in his diary, 'has put on a good deal of weight, and rides with more difficulty than before. The Grand Equerry has to give him a hand up when he mounts.' That evening, Napoleon is riding through a wheatfield in the moonlight, followed by Caulaincourt and Berthier, when

'a hare, starting up between his horse's legs, caused it to swerve slightly.[16] The Emperor, who hadn't a good seat, rolled to the ground; but got up again so quickly that he was on his feet again before I could reach him to lend him a hand. He mounted again without saying a word. The ground was very soft, and he suffered only a slight bruise on his hip.'

In spite of themselves, says Caulaincourt, men are superstitious on the eve of great events: 'Instantly the reflection occurred to me that it was a bad augury. Nor was I the only one to think so, for the Prince of Neuchâtel seized my hand and said: "We'd better not cross the Niemen. This is a bad omen!"'

At first Napoleon says nothing; but

'by and by he began to joke with Berthier and me about his fall. Yet his bad temper and forebodings were obvious, no matter how he tried to conceal them. In other circumstances he'd have blamed the charger which had caused this silly accident, and wouldn't have spared the Master of the Horse. As it was, he affected the utmost serenity, and did all he could to banish the gloomy doubts no one could help feeling.'

Gossip is general:

'Some of the headquarters staff observed that the Romans wouldn't have crossed the Niemen. All that day the Emperor, usually so cheerful and active when his troops were carrying out extensive operations, was very serious and preoccupied.'

At dinner that evening he asks Caulaincourt whether his fall has given rise to much talk? What are Russian peasants like? Are they likely to form guerrilla bands, as the Spaniards have done? Barclay, he suspects, is concentrating his forces around the little town of Novo-Troki, a dozen or so miles on this side of Vilna. Surely his ex-ambassador to Petersburg doesn't think his 'brother Alexander' will give up the Lithuanian capital without a fight?

Between hasty mouthfuls – dinner never takes more than fifteen minutes – Caulaincourt opines with his usual candour[17] that, in a campaign where the theatre of war is so vast, he 'doesn't much believe in pitched battles'. Hasn't the Tsar himself told him that if the fighting should go against him he'll retire to Siberia? Barclay can afford to yield a lot of ground, 'if only to lead you a long way from your base and oblige you to divide your forces'.

'"Then I've got Poland!" retorts Napoleon briskly. "And in the eyes of the Poles Alexander will have earned everlasting shame by giving it up without a fight. To give me Vilna is to lose Poland."'

But didn't he tell Caulaincourt at the Tuileries that he doesn't want Poland anyway?

The Grand Army's self-confidence, General Count *Philippe de Ségur* assures us, was boundless:[18]

'It was going to be a military promenade to Petersburg and Moscow. One last effort, and maybe everything would be achieved. This being the last opportunity that would present itself, we were loth to let it slip out of our hands. We should have been embarrassed by the glorious stories others would have to tell of it.'

Of course there are sceptics. And one or another of our writers even claims to have foreseen the disaster. One of Boulart's immediate subordinates is a certain Captain *Pion des Loches*. A more than unusually inveterate grumbler, he claims that he

'foresaw clearly that this campaign would bring about the Emperor's ruin; and though I loved neither his person nor his government, the prospect of his fall terrified me, on account of the consequences it would have'.

But such seers must have been few.[19] And certainly no one, that Midsummer's Eve, could have forseen that of this vast and glittering host at most some 20,000 ragged, stunned, starving, stinking, frostbitten men, a handful of women and almost none of its 140,000 horses would recross the frozen river six months later. Young Déchy was among the most impressed: 'What men! What an epoch!' he'd exclaim, long afterwards. 'Alas,' sighs that man of steel, cuirassier Sergeant-major Thirion,

'how many of the personages in this picture are still alive to tell the tale today! What became of these conquerors of Europe? With few exceptions all died – some the beautiful death of a soldier on the field of battle; others of misery and hunger.'

CHAPTER 4

'GET INTO VILNA!'

A tremendous thunderstorm – 'A desert' – a lethal diet for horses – an abandoned countryside – pillage – quagmires – Captain Fivaz writes his will – Lyautey listens to the band – a military promenade – Napoleon leaves Kovno – desperate looters – a carriageful of commanders – Murat – Davout – Berthier – strategic considerations – 'I sow dissension among my generals' – a serious mistake – where's Barclay? – Dumonceau flanks the army – Montbrun loses his temper – a skirmish – into Vilna – Ségur's brother taken prisoner

Three bridges are to be thrown, at 100-metre intervals. And at 10 p.m. Eblé's engineers begin launching the pontoons from their 12-horse drays. To cover the operation, three companies of the 13th Light cross silently in skiffs, land on the opposite bank and lie down in the sand, 'hiding behind the little escarpment formed by the river bank'. By now the night sky is full of glimmering stars.[1]

Soltyk, whose fluent French has meanwhile attached him to Imperial Headquarters' topographical department, is perhaps the very first staff officer to cross, with orders to bring Napoleon some villagers:[2]

'It was so dark we didn't know whether we had any enemy in front of us or not. As far as we could see, no patrol, no scout appeared at any point. Only after about 100 men had established themselves on the right bank did we hear a distant sound of galloping horses, and a strong troop of Muscovite hussars halted at about a hundred paces from our weak advance guard. Dark though it was, we recognized them by their white plumes.[3] Coming toward us, the officer in command shouts out in French: "*Qui vive?*" "France!" our men reply quietly. "What are you doing here? F... off!" "You'll soon see!" our skirmishers reply resolutely. Whereon the officer goes back to his men and orders them to fire their carbines. None of ours reply. And the enemy hussars disappear at a gallop.'

Ségur, with his literary turn of mind, thinks he hears *three* shots – like *les trois coups* in a French theatre – 'and this irritated Napoleon'. Even though the Russian army is 75 miles away.

At 3 a.m. Dumonceau is roused by his regiment's silver trumpets 'joyously sounding the reveille and, immediately afterwards, the saddle-up'. The Red Lancers not being scheduled to move down to the river until well into the forenoon, General Count Colbert, its commanding officer, 'formed us up in square. After a flourish of trumpets had prepared us for it, Adjutant Fallot, in a resounding voice, read out the Emperor's proclamation.' So also in all the other regiments. To Captain *Pierre Auvray* of the 23rd Dragoons it seems that the army reacts with 'unparalleled enthusiasm. Its sentiments were shared by everyone around Napoleon, whether Frenchmen or foreigners.' So also Ségur:

'The word Niemen inflamed our imagination. Everybody was on fire to get across it – a desire the more natural as the miserable conditions in Poland had been daily augmenting our privations. To put an end to our complaints we were made to see the enemy's country as a promised land.'

At 4 a.m. the sun rises over the plains of Lithuania beyond the bridges; and Planat de la Faye, watching from the top of the imperial hillock, sees how

'the army, in parade uniforms, begins defiling in good order on to the three bridges. At its head each regiment had its band playing fanfares, mingled with the shouts of "Vive l'Empereur!". It all seemed like one vast military parade.'

Major Boulart of the Guard Artillery, too, is impressed:

'Unit after unit came and took up its position on the heights, ready when its turn came to cross the bridges. Arriving from all sides, they seemed to be springing up out of the ground. These 200,000 men, assembled in a small space, pressing incessantly on to the bridges then rallying on the vast plain on the right bank and going off in various directions, were a magnificent spectacle, perhaps unique in history.'

His colleague Colonel *Lubin Griois* – that great lover of the good things of life, and more particularly of Italian music and women – will always remember how the sun 'flashed on the arms and cuirasses of the innumerable troops of all nations as they poured uninterruptedly over the three bridges. All these troops rivalled each other in ardour and covered both banks to a great distance.' And to Lieutenant Chevalier of the Guard Chasseurs – who sincerely believes Napoleon has 'done everything in his power to avoid this war' – it all seems positively supernatural, 'as if the earth were producing armed men instead of harvests'.

By now, after exhausting forced marches of 35 miles a day, Ney's III Corps too has turned up; and as it emerges from the Pilkowiski forest one of its Württemberg artillery officers, Major *Faber du Faur*, sketches the scene, showing some Württemberg grenadiers in the foreground and, in the distance, a glimpse of columns crossing the three pontoon bridges. 'As soon as the first division was established on the far bank,' Ségur goes on,

'the Emperor, seized with sudden impatience, galloped cross-country as fast as his horse could go to the forest bordering the river. In his haste he seemed to be wanting to reach the enemy all on his own.'

Pure literary imagination, explodes Gourgaud. 'Has the Assistant Prefect of the Palace taken his characters from the madhouse?' On this occasion, however, Ségur seems to be right, even if his manner of expressing himself is melodramatic. To Caulaincourt, riding a few paces behind him with a map of the district dangling on a leather thong from his left buttonhole, Napoleon seems to be 'amazed to learn that the Russian army had retreated. Several reports had to be given him and various people brought before him before he'd believe the news. He followed the advance guard's movements for more than five miles, pressing the whole army forward and questioning all the country folk he could find, yet without obtaining any positive news. Poles were sent out in all directions to collect information.'

No enemy being in sight – or 'only an occasional Cossack lance flashing on the horizon' – Napoleon returns to his headquarters on the left bank. And at about 1 p.m. makes a second, more ceremonious entry into Lithuania, this time at the head of the Imperial Guard, which 'crossed the river to the sound of its bands'.[5]

The crossing is proceeding so smoothly and swiftly that as the Red Lancers ride down to join the rest of the Guard cavalry Dumonceau is wondering where all the scores of regiments have gone to. Already Davout's I Corps, making a bee-line for Vilna, has completely 'disappeared into the vast plains beyond'. Debouching from the bridges together with the Guard's four other cavalry regiments (Chasseurs, Grenadiers, Dragoons, and 1st (Polish) Lancers) the Red Lancers turn left and 'at a steady trot' follow 'a broad sandy road' downstream.

By and by Kovno comes into sight. 'A well-built little town set in an amphitheatre of pinewoods', it puts Lieutenant Vossler of Prince Louis' Hussars in mind of an Italian city. No enemy is defending its walls. And to Colonel St-Chamans, riding quickly through the streets at the head of his 7th Chasseurs, most of the inhabitants still seem to be there. 'They received us in a friendly fashion and no one did them any harm.'

Dumonceau's Dutchmen are still pushing their way along the sandy road 'amid a crush of all kinds of vehicles in the stifling almost insupportable heat', when

'the sky became charged with electricity which rumbled horribly in clouds that came rolling up at a speed we'd never seen the like of. At about 3 p.m. the lightning struck, close at hand. It killed two men and three horses.'

Back at the bridges the storm breaks so suddenly that the 2nd Cuirassiers, leading unit of Montbrun's II Cavalry Corps, hardly have time to unbuckle their white capes and

'the 6th Troop was still on the bridge, when a clap of thunder burst with such violence that all our heads, as if in a drill movement, jerked down on to our horses' necks. I've seen many storms in my life, but never any to approach that thunderclap on the Niemen! The cloudburst had flung its thunderbolt at the pontoon bridge which 6th Company were just then crossing. It fell in little stones, some of which struck against our cuirasses. One of them hit M. Henri Vandendrier on the cheek. Either the thunderclap or the rattling of the hailstones so terrified the colour-sergeant's horse that it leapt into the river and reached the shore swimming. All we saw above the water during his voyage was the poor bather's head and the pole of the standard attached to his saddle! Never have I received such a waterspout on my body!'

There the storm is violent but brief – by the time Thirion's men have drawn up to the right of the bridges in line with the 1st Lancers it has already gone over. But at Kovno, only a couple of miles away, where the 'burning torrential rain' drenches Dumonceau for two hours, it has also flooded the Vilia, whose only bridge has been burnt by the Russian rearguard. And the swollen waters are holding up the French pursuit. By and by Napoleon himself turns up on the scene and orders young Colonel Géheneuc[5] of the 6th Light Infantry to take some Polish lancers and find a ford. Said and done. Accompanied by two other resolute swimmers, Géheneuc swims his horse over to the far bank. But returning to his regiment, sees a Polish lancer being swept away by the current, and leaps

'fully clothed into the river to save him. This action, praiseworthy enough in itself, the Emperor considered unbecoming in a colonel at the head of his regiment in the presence of the enemy and told him so.'[9]

Heroics are all very well. What's wanted is some pontoons. And Napoleon orders Lariboisière to lend Haxo the battalion of military labourers of the so-called Navy of the Danube. To Lejeune's painterly eye the scene as they get down to work is positively Raphaelesque:

'The Emperor, though drenched through like the rest of us, was present at the rebuilding of the bridge. He impressed an extraordinary activity on all who were working at it, including two hundred of General Haxo's engineers [sic], stripped naked.'

The Russians have also destroyed the permanent timber bridge over the Niemen. But it's soon restored, and other units are streaming across. Ordering Haxo to throw a fourth pontoon bridge, plus two more on piles, Napoleon leaves the scene at about 8 p.m. and makes for his new headquarters in a convent, about half a mile outside the town.

Normally it should be the duty of the Prefect of the Palace, *Louis-François Joseph de Bausset* – a man so corpulent that Spanish chairs have a way of collapsing under his bulk – to select a building for IHQ. But Bausset is still in Paris, and according to Gourgaud the task is falling on Ségur, his first assistant. Which among other things means it's unlikely he witnessed the scene at the Vilia. Yet evidently it's in some such semi-mythical version as he'll afterwards give that the incident, passing through the army and being steadily improved as it goes, reaches Dumonceau. Just as he's settling into his wet bivouac outside the town walls he hears from some comrades 'who'd gone into town to do some shopping' an even more melodramatic version. It had been the Emperor himself, they tell him, who, 'supported by two troopers', had risked his life trying to cross the swollen stream!

'Seeing us arrive in the dishevelled state inflicted by the storm on our faces and clothes,' Lejeune goes on, 'the little town's inhabitants and its many monasteries' religious brought us abundant refreshments. It was their habitual luxury to drink iced honey-water and a beer of their own admirable brew. But this sudden transition to iced liquors, avidly gulped down by men drenched in rain and sweat, instantly made many of us ill.'

Dedem's infantry brigade has been one of the first to cross the Niemen, and by now must be miles down the Vilna road; so he too can only be reporting by hearsay when he says that the first units to enter Kovno had harmed neither the town nor its inhabitants:

'We found any amount of supplies; but soon an order comes to place sentries at the doors and allow neither soldiers, officers nor generals to enter. Everything is reserved for the Imperial Guard. It alone is allowed into town. The other corps, including the advance guard, marched round outside its walls. The inhabitants fled, spreading consternation far and wide.'

And by the time Lieutenant *Carl von Martens* of III Cavalry Corps passes through, everything in Kovno has been smashed up:

'Camp fires were still smoking in the market place, the furniture had been taken out of the houses and the windows shattered. At most a Jew was to be seen here and there. One glance was enough. Kovno was a totally plundered town.'

The 'liberation' of Lithuania has begun.

For Dumonceau's Dutchmen, grilling their meat rations at a stick's end outside Kovno town walls, their first brief summer night on Lithuanian soil is dank and chill. Sergeant-major Thirion, too, is shivering and so are all the other steel-clad men whom I Cavalry Corps' kindly and philosophical senior veterinary surgeon Dr *Raymond Faure* sees

'wrapped in their big white mantles, seeming as much by their heroic bearing as by their nigh colossal forms to be the very embodiments of a force everything must yield to'.

Thirion's horse, a magnificent Hanoverian, can hardly lift its hoofs and 'tottered like a drunken man. I walked him up and down in front of my company to warm him and get the blood circulating.' Such a damp chilly night is unexpectedly disastrous. When dawn breaks over the wet trampled rye fields, Thirion realizes

'this night had cost us as dearly as a battle. Everyone has told of the numbers of horses lost that night. No one how many men! But what was the loss of mere men? Horses cost money; the army's ranks repopulated themselves by decree, one more felling in the human forest.'

Fortunately, Dr Faure goes on,

'a gentle dawn refreshed the air and seemed just what was needed to reanimate the forces of vegetation, always busily reproducing while men seemed only to meditate destruction'.

The French high command has assumed that Lithuania's wide fields, stretching away to the sombre spruce forests, will be ripe for harvesting and yield plenty of fodder. They aren't. The northern summer has come two weeks late and green crops of rye and barley are a lethal diet for the horses. Dumonceau and his colleagues have to be

'exceedingly careful not to feed them the barley until after the green corn; and even then only very little at a time. But above all not to let them drink for a long while afterwards. Otherwise the barley, suddenly swelling inside the stomach, caused violent cholics, such as almost invariably led to sudden death.'

Already he has blotted his copybook by emulating his general's habit, famous throughout the army, of smoking a meerschaum on the march. Now something more serious happens. One of his troopers ignores the order and his horse drops dead. And Dumonceau gets a swingeing reprimand. 'Two other captains were in like case as myself.'

The Red Lancers and the rest of the Guard cavalry spend that day in what seems a senseless exercise of the kind endemic in military life:

'In the morning, unexpectedly, the trumpets on all sides sound "To horse!", as if we've been surprised by the enemy. In a jiffy the various regiments assemble. Coming and placing himself at our head and preceded by an advance guard, the Duke of Istria [Marshal Bessières, commanding the Guard Cavalry] leads us by column of troops along the same road we'd taken yesterday to get here. Then he turns off to the left, into the road being followed by the King of Naples' and Marshal Davout's columns.'

Since the Imperial Guard always has absolute right of way, its cavalry's irruption into the chaos prevailing around the bridgeheads – the crossing will go on for three days – can hardly have diminished it, or helped Generals Guilleminot and *Jomini* in their vain efforts to control it. No matter. The six proud cavalry regiments continue their promenade. For that's what it turns out to be. Towards evening

'with the left, i.e., the Horse Grenadiers, at our head, we finally retrace our steps along a fine paved highway through an immense sombre forest, out of which, to our vast amazement, we emerge in front of our bivouac of that same morning, which we immediately re-occupy.'

Davout's infantry divisions had cheered as they passed under Napoleon's all-seeing eye: if many commanding officers have so far managed to maintain strict discipline it's been by telling the ranker 'once we're on Russian territory we'll take anything we like'. But no sooner have Dedem's men debouched on to the Niemen's right bank than he's horrified to hear them

'burst out into joyful shouts, horrible to hear, as if to say: "At last, we're on enemy territory! Now our officers won't punish us when we make the bourgeois[6] wait on us!'

Otherwise the whole army is a bit frightened at the sight of so sparsely populated and poverty-stricken a countryside. Dedem finds himself in 'a desert'. What kind of a land is this they've come to 'liberate'? 'Not a soul in sight, not an inhabitant in the villages we were passing through.' Even men who've served in Spain – and there are many – soon begin to feel depressed by its sombre aspect. Captain *Karl von Suckow* of the Württemberg Cavalry and his men are 'all struck by the absence of any birds flying up at our approach'. And in Dr Faure the 'countryside's repulsive appearance' is 'giving rise to serious reflections'.

Certainly the Lithuanian peasants aren't welcoming their liberators. After two failed harvests the abandoned barns have been stripped to the last grain of corn, and the patriotic Soltyk is grieved to see how

'the terrified people who cultivated this land, all but for a few poor people who came to our bivouacs to beg for bread, were fleeing to the woods, uttering dolorous cries and invoking the divine pity'.

Grenadier-Captain *Guillaume Bonnet* of the 18th Line, Ney's III Corps, following the Vilia's serpentine left bank, is shocked to see how the peasants' clothing consists of only

'a shirt, a pair of coarse cloth trousers, a hooded cloak of sheepskin and some kind of a fur cap. The women's dress is virtually the same. The head is wrapped in bad linen, the face pale, and the skin blackened by smoke.'

As for their villages, they're even more squalid than the Polish ones. Spending his first night in Lithuania in a hamlet whose name he hasn't been able to identify, the commander of the (Polish) Vistula Legion, the newly married General Claparède, writes home[7] to his young bride:

'The inhabitants and their houses are very ugly and extremely dirty, and the latter only differ from the peasants' log cabins in possessing a chimney or two. When the weather is fine, I sleep under a shelter of branches and manage very well; or else, when it's bad, in my carriage.'

The serfs' dwellings, writes Captain *Abraham Rosselet* of the 1st Swiss,

'are built of pieces of timber laid on top of each other without any framework. The chinks are blocked up with moss. To let in some daylight people cut out a sort of porthole, opened and closed by means of slots or grooves. One finds no furniture and seldom a bed, however wretched. There's only one room, a sort of stable, big enough to accommodate the family and animals. A quarter of it is taken up by a big stove which also serves as a bed. Here mother, father, daughter and son-in-law sleep together on straw and everything goes on much as in a rabbit warren.'

Although General Compans, commanding Davout's crack 5th Division, is finding the countryside 'quite attractive', he refuses even to set foot inside such hovels. And though all are deserted, many aren't available for a second occupation, since the first-comers have a way of lighting so rousing a fire in the primitive stove that first the chimney, then the cottage itself goes up in flames and not infrequently cremates its exhausted occupants.

Although the harvest isn't ripe, Major Faber du Faur advancing with Ney's heavy artillery, sees

'the fields being devastated by foragers. As sole traces of our brief visit we left behind us empty huts, fields stripped and forests thinned out.' – 'Crops trampled down, ancient trees felled, hamlets, entire timber villages of thatched houses devastated, thrown down and almost vanished – thatch, doors, shutters, furniture – all was being carried off to the bivouacs, the terrible and inevitable effect of warfare, above all when waged with such huge masses of men.'

All this is only justifiable, the patriotic Soltyk consoles himself, as being incidental to a war of national liberation.

The Supply Train takes no priority over anyone, and in no time the marching columns have pushed its 'heavy wagons and smaller carts' off the roads. Every battalion has such a wagon; but even these either turn up late at the bivouacs, where they find the exhausted men fast asleep, or else after they've already left again; or perhaps not at all. German officers such as Lieutenant Vossler are infuriated that their

'laboriously and often humiliatingly acquired provisions fall a prey to the French commissariat. Many of the regiments had no more than three days' supply of rations. Because of the countryside's total devastation, we had to subsist on the flesh of exhausted starving cattle, of which each regiment dragged at least one herd with it.'

Some of these herds, lackadaisically goaded onwards by their 'fearsomely unqualified drivers', have come from as far afield as Hungary or Italy. And they too soon fall behind:

'From the very first day the ranker found himself very badly fed. For lack of bread, and often of vegetables, he ate too much meat, which was plentiful. This rapid movement without supplies exhausted and destroyed all the resources and houses along the way. The advance guard,'

complains Dedem, whose brigade is marching in its wake, 'lived quite well, but the rest of the army was dying of hunger.'

The 18-year-olds, particularly, are finding it impossible to keep up. Marching ever onwards in the steadily falling rain, Claparède's veterans from Spain see 'the Young Guard, marching immediately ahead of us, sowing stragglers behind it. Each instant we came upon them, stretched out beside the roadside and sometimes across it, pell-mell with dead horses.' Von Suckow, too, is distressed to see how

'these exceptional marches were thinning our ranks to an exceptional degree. Within no time thousands of men had disappeared.'

'Our drink', Dedem goes on,

'consisted of a brackish liquid scooped from stinking wells and putrid ponds. Under these circumstances it isn't surprising if, within two or three days of crossing the Niemen, the army, and in particular the infantry, was being ravaged by diseases, particularly dysentery,[8] ague and typhus.'

Sous-lieutenant Dutheillet of the 57th Line is seeing how at the hourly *halte des pipes* the generals are having 'to station sentries, so that the men shan't pull down their trousers almost in the column's very ranks'. Then the drums beat again. The cornets shrill, ordering the light infantrymen back into the ranks. The trumpets blare 'To horse!'. And the troops stagger on, some marchers actually asleep as they march, 'only kept on their feet by two limp arms flung round the necks of two sturdier comrades'. Staff officers are distinguishable by a red armband tied in a bow. And now and then one, carrying an order, comes cantering along the edge of the road.

Napoleon, says Caulaincourt, 'would gladly have given wings to the army'. But the Lithuanian roads are militating against it. Lieutenant Vossler sees that

'most of the road from the Niemen to Vilna is either so sandy or so marshy that even in the most favourable weather conditions it presents great problems to the passage of heavy wagons and matériel. These difficulties were multiplied almost beyond endurance on the short but correspondingly steep slopes of the many ravines which intersect the road at right angles.'

Certain stretches are paved with transversely laid pine trunks. But since they're often decayed, there are gaps as lethal to a horse's legs as the green rye is to its belly. Elsewhere are quagmires. 'The roads were bottomless, unviable,' writes General *Jean Rapp*, Napoleon's favourite ADC:

'We drowned in mud or collapsed from weakness or hunger. Ten thousand horses had died within a distance we travelled in two days.'

Really that many? Murat's chief-of-staff, General *Augustin-Daniel Belliard*, puts the figure at 8,000. Some think only 5,000. And Captain *Franz Roeder*,[9] following on a few days later with the Hessian Footguards, will count '3,000 horses lying dead by the roadside, together with other rotting corpses which at this season of the year made a hideous stench'. He'll also see 'hundreds of dismounted cavalry trekking away westwards in the hope of finding remounts'. A general, says the Flemish war-commissary *Bellot de Kergorre*, had already been detailed off to get all these stinking cadavers buried. The weather, too,

'seemed to be doing its best to contribute to our discomforture. Before crossing the Niemen we'd been thoroughly parched by the persistent oppressive heats. Thereafter we endured three days of continuous and torrential rain, followed by alternating periods of unbearable heat and downpours whose like I've never known. Under skies now unbearably hot, now pouring forth freezing rain, we were either smothered in sand or knee-deep in mud.'

Despite his privileged position at imperial headquarters Ségur is finding midday 'the moment of greatest discouragement. Then the heat became intolerable. Then the sky, heavy with thick clouds, seemed almost to press on the ground, oppressing us with all their weight.'

Taking blocks of ice from the peasants' outdoor ice cellars, the 3rd Württemberg Chasseurs pass them 'from hand to hand until they were either consumed or melted away'.

From the very first days there are suicides:

'Hundreds of men, feeling they could no longer endure such hardships, killed themselves. Every day we heard isolated shots ring out in the woods near the road. Patrols, sent to investigate, always came back to report: "It's a cuirassier, a hussar, an infantryman, a Frenchman or an ally, who's just taken his own life..."'

In these sombre circumstances even a hardened veteran such as the Swiss Captain *François Fivaz*,[10] who has fought in all the wars of the Consulate and Empire, even though as yet he is 'hardly embarked upon this accursed war which can lead to no good', feels he's had enough. Staggering into his bivouac in the evening of 26 June, he sits down to write his will:

'In the name of God, amen! – Having given mature reflection to the inconveniences of the military estate and its few advantages, I feel it is my fatherly duty to forbid any of my sons to embrace this profession. I recommend my wife and my children to God and to our relatives, who are to be consulted on everything, and that she shall have exclusive charge of our children's education. She is full of good sense. Had I consulted her I should never have left my own country.'

What has happened to the romance of war? *Hubert de Lyautey*, a young lieutenant in the Guard artillery, may be 'enchanted by the bivouacs besides the shores of lakes, where in the warm evenings the bands play one after another in the dusk, and by the spectacle of these long lines of campfires on which the moon sometimes came and shed its light'. Few can be sharing his lyrical feelings.

Most of Napoleon's campaigns had started in similar fashion. None quite like this.

'When the army was carrying out major manoeuvres at great distances,' writes Gourgaud,

'he remained at his headquarters, attending to the interior administration of France and replying to the reports sent him daily by his ministers in Paris, until the marching corps were almost in the positions he had indicated. To economize with his time, he calculated his moment of departure so as to be at the head of his corps in the same moment as his presence there became necessary. Then he travelled swiftly by carriage. Yet even during such a transit he wasn't idle. He busied himself reading despatches and immediately sent off replies. Sometimes the mail brought by the Paris courier arrived at the same time.'

Not until dawn on 26 June does he leave the Kovno monastery. And once again it's presumably Ségur's task to go on ahead and make arrangements for the next headquarters. In this case they're to be in a handsome white-pillared manor-house near the village of Jejwe (or Ewë), half-way to Vilna.[11] It seems Napoleon has set out on horseback; for he's riding along, followed by his glittering staff, when he's stopped

'by the supplications and cries of a venerable old man, M. Prozov, an ex-soldier and a good patriot. Surrounded by his family he was flee-ing from his home, only a musket shot's distance from the main road. Stragglers had invaded it and were devastating it from top to bottom. He begged Napoleon's justice and protection. Moved by the poor old man's straits and indignant at the soldiers' behaviour, the Emperor grants him a safeguard, and orders me to take some men of the escort, surround Prozov's house and seize those responsible. I'm to take them to the provost-marshal and tell him to have them shot.'

Shocked by the pillage, but even more appalled at the rigour of his orders, Soltyk has

'Prozov's house surrounded by some lancers. Many of the marauders were making off in all directions. Thirteen were seized and brought before me. Finding myself their judge and master, with power of life and death, I at least wanted to know what their crime was. So I inter-rogated each in turn and had my lancers search them. They replied that they had had no food and had vainly asked their commander for some. Unable to distribute any rations, he'd authorized them to get whatever they could, wherever they could. And indeed nothing was found on them except the food they'd taken – admittedly by force – in M. Prozov's house.'

Letting them off with a reprimand which he knows can only be futile, Soltyk catches up with IHQ, wondering anxiously what to say. But no ques-tions are asked. The whole incident has already been forgotten. Soon the Emperor exchanges his horse for a 'light travelling carriage or droshki'. As Dedem's brigade slogs on through a pine forest it comes bouncing by, and he catches a glimpse of its occupants. Besides Napoleon himself they are: the army's major-general and Napoleon's chief-of-staff, Alexandre Berthier; the commander of its four 'reserve' cavalry corps, Joachim Murat, King of Naples; and Davout, Prince of Eckmühl.

No three commanders could be more different, or more mutually antipathetic.

Well over six feet tall, immensely handsome and vain, Murat speaks in a husky voice with a strong Gascon accent and has what in a woman would be called bedroom eyes. One of his many baggage wagons is filled with perfumes, and each morning he appears in a new and highly theatrical get-up of his own devising. Not a little peeved to have been the only reign-ing prince excluded from the Dresden *son et lumière*, he has nothing to gain from this new campaign which is taking him away from his Neapolitan kingdom and his adored children. On morosely reporting for duty at Danzig, he'd been promptly bawled out for his wife's intrigues with the Austrian government and told he looked 'sickly'. Whereafter his imperial brother-in-law, after cowing him with talk of 'pitiless punishments', had softened his tone and appealed to him, as an old comrade-in-arms. 'I took turn and turn about with anger and sentimentality,' he'd told Duroc, Berthier, Caulaincourt and Bessières cynically at dinner that evening,

> 'because that's all that's needed with this Italian pantalone. At bottom he has a good heart. He loves me even more than he does his lazzaroni. He only has to set eyes on me to be my man. But far away from me, anyone can flatter and approach him, like all people without character.'

And Murat of course had come to heel, protesting his sincere devotion. 'There were not, I believe,' Napoleon will say at St. Helena,

> 'two such officers in the world as Murat for the cavalry, and Drouot for the artillery. Murat was a most singular character. Twenty-four years earlier, when he was only a captain, I'd made him my aide-de-camp, and thereafter raised him to be what he became. He loved, I may rather say, adored me. In my presence he was as it were awe-stricken, ready to fall at my feet. With me, he was my right arm. Order Murat to attack and destroy four or five thousand men in such or such a direction, it was done in a flash. But left to himself he was an imbecile, without judgement. It's more than I can understand how so brave a man could be so cowardly.'

The carriage's second occupant is a man of totally different stamp. Bald and bespectacled, with a head bearing a striking resemblance to Seneca's, Davout, Prince of Eckmühl, is in all points Murat's exact opposite. An extreme disciplinarian, at Mecklenburg he'd placed General Dalton, one of Dedem's fellow-brigadiers, under arrest and cited him in the order of the day for spending more than regulations permitted on his table. But Davout is a brilliant administrator and a first-class corps commander. If Murat has little tactical and less strategic sense, Davout has both in eminent degree, treating his staff as he does everyone else, with icy detachment and no consideration whatever for their creature comforts. Biot describes him as 'the most slovenly of men' and 'incontrovertibly the least polite of our marshals'. He's utterly unpopular with everyone. General *François Roguet*, commanding the 2nd Guard Grenadiers, complains of his always 'interfering in everything, trying to do everything himself, and forever scolding and fulminating'. Only Dedem has a good word to put in for him:

> 'If ever I have to make war again, it's under Marshal Davout I'd wish to do so. The Prince of Eckmühl is the man who best knows how to obey, and thereby has learnt to command. There was never a chief more severe in point of discipline, juster, or who occupied himself more with the welfare of the ranker, his instruction and his needs; and no sovereign ever had a more faithful or devoted servant.'

While conceding that Davout had 'twice laid a heavy iron hand on Prussia and each time showed a hardness outrageous to humanity', Dedem acquits him of all self-seeking:

'His hands were as pure as gold. He never took anything for himself. He was always the father of his army. He liked people to think he was more ill-natured than he really was. Those he ordered to be shot[12] had fully merited it under the military laws of all countries, and the number was small compared with that of the guilty.'

If Napoleon is just now treating Davout with a certain coolness, it's perhaps because he, like the whole army, is well aware that his dour but efficient marshal is aspiring to the throne of Poland. And anyway Davout's loyalty, unlike Murat's, is unshakeable.

Such are the two commanders whose corps are spearheading the main striking force. Their mutual detestation is only equalled by the 'terrible hatred' prevailing between Davout and the carriage's fourth occupant: Napoleon's all-seeing, all-fixing, all-remembering – yet little understanding chief-of-staff, Marshal Alexandre Berthier, Prince of Neuchâtel:

'No one ever saw greater exactitude, a more entire submission, a more absolute devotion. Busy all day, it was by writing at night he rested from the day's fatigues. Often he'd be summoned in the middle of his sleep to change all his work of yesterday, and sometimes his only reward was unjust or, at very least, severe reprimands. Yet nothing slowed down his zeal.'

Berthier and Davout haven't seen each other for several years, but on their having recently done so at Hamburg the occasion had been marked by a blazing row. Having no talent whatever for independent command, Berthier has never forgiven Davout for rescuing an army he'd put gravely at risk. Berthier too is a slovenly man. He speaks in a nasal voice and usually keeps his hands in his pockets – that is, when he hasn't got one finger in his nose. His badly cut clothes hang on him like a sack:

'Short, ill-grown without actually being deformed, he had a head slightly too large for his body, hair rather tousled than curly, neither dark nor fair; hands, ugly by nature, made still uglier by forever biting his nails, so that his fingers were almost always bleeding. Add to this a rather severe stammer and the grimaces he made – well, if not exactly grimaces, then odd jerky movements – to anyone who wasn't directly impressed by his elevated status he seemed to cut a very comical figure.'

Unlike Davout, he's extremely decent to his staff, treating them with

'that blend of kindness and brusqerie which made up his character. Often he seemed to pay no heed to us. But we were sure on occasion to gain his whole attention, and during his long military career he never failed to advance any of the officers employed under his orders.'

Though exercising none of the functions of a modern chief-of-staff, Berthier's grasp of each unit's strength, its whereabouts and march route have for many years always been immaculate. 'I count for nothing in the Army,' he once wrote to Marshal Soult. 'I receive the marshals' orders on His Majesty's behalf, and I sign his orders for him. But personally I am nothing.' And again: 'The Emperor needs neither advice nor to have his plans drawn up for him. No one knows his thoughts, and it's our duty simply to obey.' When taking Napoleon's orders, which he writes down in a green notebook, Berthier like everyone else always stands hat in hand – a hat of the same Swiss civilian cut as his master's and which it is his unique privilege to wear.[13]

Nor is Berthier, in this summer of 1815, quite the man he has been, as those in daily contact with him will shortly be noticing. 'Unfortunately,' Dedem sees, Berthier is ' already beginning to be the old man. All that shop was badly run. Few talents and much presumption.' And Ségur agrees:

'Berthier's mental forces were declining. Since 1805 he'd hated every war. His talent resided above all in his meticulousness and memory. At any hour of the day or night whatsoever he was able to go through the most numerous news and orders.'

Even First Secretary Méneval, though deeply respecting Berthier's 'loyalty of character and sense of responsibility', feels forced to admit that

'I shouldn't be telling the truth if I didn't also say that in proportion to the honours and wealth which had come Berthier's way, his serious and real qualities had declined. Several times during the 1812 campaign the Emperor reproached him in my presence for his carelessness. "Berthier," he told him, "I'd give my right arm for you to be back at Grosbois. Not merely are you no use to me at all, you're harming me." After these altercations Berthier sulked and wouldn't come to dinner. Then the Emperor would send for him, and himself wouldn't sit down to table before he was there. Putting his arm round his neck, he'd tell him they were inseparable, etc., tease him about Mme. Visconti,[14] and finally sit down at table facing him.'

Of his doggily faithful, endlessly painstaking chief-of-staff Napoleon once said candidly:

'Truly, I can't understand how a relationship which looks like friendship can have arisen between Berthier and myself. Useless sentiments don't amuse me, and Berthier is so mediocre. Yet at bottom, when nothing turns me against him, I do believe I'm not without a certain penchant for him.'

And again: 'Out of this goose I've made an eagle.'

One would think a command structure compounded at top level of such mutual antipathies and jealousies can hardly be making for good collaboration. Yet far from discouraging them, Napoleon confessedly fosters them. 'You see,' he'd told the Tsar in the days of their friendship (words the Tsar will soon be repeating to Napoleon's arch-enemy Madame Germaine de Staël, she too just then on her way to Moscow)'

'I always try to sow dissension among my generals so that each shall discover the others' shortcomings. By my way of treating people around me I keep all their jealousies alive. One day one of them imagines himself preferred; the next, another. So no one can be sure of being in my good books.'
In this summer of 1812 Napoleon is nearly 43, Davout 42, Murat 45, and Berthier 59. Like Murat, Berthier only has three more years to live.

Seeing the open carriage go bouncing along the sandy road it seems to Dedem that its four occupants looked 'astonished, maybe terrified' to see neither inhabitants nor foe. Terrified is hardly a word to use of four such war-hardened commanders. Worried they certainly are. Although three days have gone by, the first of all strategic desiderata – knowledge of the enemy's whereabouts and movements – still hasn't been met.

And what is Jerome doing?

The danger with outflanking movements is that they can themselves be outflanked; and Eugène's march across Poland, which is to guard against the eventuality of Bagration taking the main striking force in flank, has been seriously delayed. And Napoleon, by crossing the Niemen on 24 June rather than next day as originally planned, has left his right flank in the air. Here's a delaying factor which, unlike the weather, the appalling roads or lack of food, can't be ignored. Already Napoleon has had to curb Murat's headlong gallopings in pursuit of the foe: "There can be no question of your actually marching into Vilna," he writes to Davout some time after leaving the droshky, to warn him of the danger of Wittgenstein, eluding both Oudinot, on the Vilia's right bank, and Ney on its left, taking him in flank.

But most important of all, will Barclay stand and fight? And if so, where? Surely Davout's I Corps, with its 60 cannon, should long ago have made contact with the enemy somewhere near the little town of Novo-Troki? 'To prevent any minor Russian success at the campaign's outset,' says Dedem,

'Napoleon had ordered even the least reconnaissance to be made at brigade strength. The result was to exhaust the horses and men by useless gallopings after foes who refused to cross sabres with them.'

At most some Poles, 'sent up to some high ground, reported seeing an enemy rearguard afar off retiring toward Vilna. And only a few very keen-sighted officers claimed to have spotted Cossacks in the distance.'

That night the heavens open again. And all along the Vilna road the rain comes pelting down, forcing Major Boulart to spend the night in one of his artillery wagons. In a freezing wet dawn, somewhere beyond Ewë, he climbs out to see in front of him 'a quarter of my horses lying on the ground, some dead or almost, the others shivering'. Harnessing up the survivors, he orders men and horses to march – not so much because there's any great hurry, 'but to restore their circulation'. The 2nd

Company of the 9th Artillery Regiment, too, is losing its Frisians at an alarming rate. 'Exposed to this rain as long as it lasted, and after living for several days off barley and other standing crops,' Lieutenant *N. J. Sauvage* sees in the morning

'two or three of these beasts in their death-throes or laid out lifeless in front of each ammunition wagon. At their side we saw our gunners and soldiers of the Train standing in a gloomy silence, tears in their eyes, trying to avert their gaze from this afflicting scene. Troops of horned cattle, driven by detachments from the various units, were wandering about as their drivers tried to get out of the terrible weather.'

Away to the left Captain *Pierre Pelleport* is following the twists and turns of the Vilia, a river, he notices, which 'flows slowly and isn't very deep. Its course is embarrassed by rocks and it never stops winding'. In the hot weather his men have been 'throwing away their waistcoats'. But now, his fellow-captain Bonnet writes in his diary on 27 June,

'we've ceased hugging the riverline to continue our way over the hills which follow its left bank at a distance. A violent storm has frozen and drenched us, penetrating us to our very bones. At 1 a.m. we arrived in much diminished numbers at... From Kalwary to here we've made a wide circuit, doubtless a manoeuvre. The countryside is densely covered with vegetation. The few cultivated fields are sown with extraordinarily tall rye, the forests extremely thick.'

All Colbert's lancers, seconded to Murat's advance guard, and detailed off to cover its sensitive right flank, scour a 'beautiful undulating countryside' but meet no living soul. Dumonceau notices how his regiment's thousand Dutchmen, as if troubled by finding themselves alone amidst so much emptiness,[16] keep inclining insensibly to their left, in towards Novo-Troki. By and by their three Polish lancer interpreters elicit scraps of information from some peasants. The Russian army is 'retiring towards the interior under General Toutchkoff'.

By now the great masses of Nansouty's and Grouchy's cavalry corps are only some fifteen miles from Vilna. And still there's no sign of a general engagement! Next day (27 June) the 30th Line are tramping onwards through the steadily falling rain when Voltigeur-captain François sees

'the Emperor sitting on the steps of an inn. He watched us go by in the very best order. After our division had marched past he left like lightning on horseback for the outposts.'

At long last some Russians have been intercepted; and they have told Napoleon that the Tsar is still at Vilna, where Bagration has been ordered to join him. The Lithuanian capital lies in a crescent of hills, with its back to the Vilia, and any attempt by the Russians to defend it with less than equal forces will only be to invite another disaster of the kind they'd suffered at Friedland in 1807. Hearing that the information he'd received is false, and afraid that Barclay will give him the slip, Napoleon now sends orders to General Montbrun, commander of II Cavalry Corps, to get into

Vilna with all speed. Above all he must save the immense grain stores assembled there by the Russian commissariat.

After Murat, the 42-year-old Montbrun is the most prestigious and popular of all the Grand Army's cavalry commanders, and is certainly not a man to sleep on the job. Dedem calls him 'a fine warrior, brilliant with glory, an officer of talent, but too ardent'. On the other hand, if what Staff-captain *Hubert Biot* says is true, he's ill-served by his four ADCs:

'Squadron-leader Martin, in charge of his carriages, who never appeared under fire; Squadron-leader Hubert, who had altogether too high an opinion of himself and only deigned to budge on grand occasions; and Captain Caillot, colder than cold, a mere nothing. Remained only young Linz, an officer full of goodwill, bravery and dash.'

Vossler, the only officer in Prince Louis' hussars who can speak even halting French, has much the same opinion. He has spent the last few days of

'very cold drizzling rain, either in Montbrun's retinue or else riding both myself and my horses to a standstill delivering messages and orders. The first night had found me in pouring rain by a dying campfire, without food or drink, silently cursing my French comrades, who had plenty of both but were in no mood to share it. The second had passed in delivering a message to the King of Naples, at whose headquarters I was at least served a decent meal.'

Ill-served or not, Montbrun now becomes the victim of a muddle. Seize Vilna? That's an exploit Murat wants to reserve for himself! Finding Montbrun's corps mounted at an earlier hour than he'd ordered, he asks him why. In obedience to the Emperor's direct orders, Montbrun replies.

'What order?'

'To get into Vilna before the Russians can leave it.'

'No need. I'll deal with that myself!'

'But I've the Emperor's personal orders!'

'What the hell does that matter, providing the thing's done?' says Murat in his husky Gascon voice, and orders Montbrun to follow on behind Nansouty's I Cavalry Corps. Whereupon the whole cumbersome cavalry mass, with Bruyère's light brigade scouting ahead, moves on – evidently at no great speed – towards Vilna.

At that moment Napoleon himself, who only a few moments ago has left Captain François (Morand's division) trudging on through the drizzle, appears on the scene. Seeing Montbrun riding at the head of his corps but in the tail of the operation, he gallops furiously up to him and, livid with rage, threatens to exile him to the rear for such incompetence. Montbrun tries to excuse himself.

'Shut up!' shouts Napoleon.

'But, Sire.'

'Will you be quiet?'

Napoleon's threats and reprimands become more and more angry. Montbrun appeals with a glance to Murat. But seeing him tongue-tied, loses his temper. Draws his sword and – grasping it by its point – flings it over his shoulder. With a shout of "Go to hell, the whole lot of you!" he puts spurs to his horse, leaving the weapon quivering in the soggy ground more than forty paces away. Napoleon, pale with fury and surprise, stands stock-still. Then he too, without another word, plies spurs to his horse, leaving the spectators dumbfounded.

Surely Montbrun will be court-martialled, sent to a fortress, or at very least dismissed the army?

Nothing of the sort. That evening Murat receives a cold inquiry: "His Majesty wishes to know why General Montbrun didn't reach Novo-Troki until midday?" No doubt Murat plucks up enough courage to explain. For nothing more is heard of that matter, either. On the other hand no small conciliatory gesture follows, of the kind Napoleon is in the habit of making towards objects of his wrath, deserved or undeserved. Montbrun is left in command of his divisions. But will remain under a cloud.[17]

'Nothing resembles the view as one surveys Vilna from the hills all around,' Oudinot's courageous young duchess will think, reaching the brow of Ponari Hill when she gets there, four months later, to nurse her wounded husband. 'Although the Vilia vainly wends its way through a countryside it seems unable to fertilize, a multitude of domes and church towers rise brilliantly above the thirty-six convents.' But now, from this vantage point, Dumonceau at about 2 or 3. p.m. on 18 June sees 'that vast city swathed in thick smoke, whose cause we didn't know'.

It's coming from the burning grain stores.

To save the honour of Russian arms and give the fires time to do their work the Russian rearguard are making a token stand on the southern heights. Ordered to take the town by assault, General Wathier de St-Alphonse, however, only sends 'a strong detachment of élite companies, under the llth Chasseurs' colonel'. Captain *Tomas-Joseph Aubry* is ordered to support it with 100 men of the 12th Chasseurs:

'I'd hardly got to the point indicated, loaded my men's firearms and drawn them up in line of battle, than what do I suddenly hear but a troop coming at the gallop down this main road I'm guarding. It's its colonel, returning flat out with his troopers, a very superior force he's bumped into at his heels. Never did I see a man more relieved than when he saw my squadron coming to his aid! He'd been utterly routed. My chasseurs caught a number of the riderless horses that came after him. At the sight of my squadron drawn up in line, the enemy ceased his pursuit. I didn't have to fire so much as a pistol shot.'

Is it signs of this affray that Dumonceau, approaching the town with the rest of the Guard cavalry, sees 'at the entrance to a defile, where the ground was violently churned up on all sides by numerous cavalry, which seemed to bear witness to a sharp engagement'? There he sees his first enemy corpse. Stretched out at the corner of a hedge, the dead man is 'clad in a bizarre greyish-brown costume, which only seemed military because of its regularity, and which we supposed to belong to a Russian militiaman'.

Soltyk claims that it's the 6th Polish Lancers, led by Major Suchorzewski, who are the first unit to enter Vilna, at 8 a.m. on 28 June; but their exploit 'not being authorized from above, gained no official mention, was even regarded as reprehensible'. What they do get is a delirious welcome:
> 'Our entry was a triumph. Streets and public places were full of people. All the windows were adorned with wildly enthusiastic ladies. Valuable carpets hung on the façades of several houses. Every hand seemed to be waving a handkerchief, and shouts of joy kept ringing out.'

One patriotic Lithuanian lady – like everyone else she's wearing the national colours, white and crimson – sees the Poles come 'galloping in, full-tilt, sabres drawn yet laughing, waving their pennons, also in the national colours'. Captain *Victor Dupuy's* 7th Hussars, too, are welcomed 'with the most joyous acclamations. The ladies in their party dresses were throwing down flowers and biscuits to us from the windows – a kindly forethought useless to us as we were unable to dismount and pick them up.'

Everywhere in the streets Ségur sees people
> 'embracing and congratulating each other. Old men appeared again in their former costume, with its memories of honour and independence. They wept with joy at the sight of the national banners being followed by innumerable crowds.'

Galloping straight through the town and across the half-burned Vilia bridge, the Polish lancers fling themselves at the Russian rearguard, capturing 'five hundred prisoners and a good deal of baggage'. So far so good. But nine miles beyond the town Soltyk sees the red-and-green uniformed 8th Hussars run into serious resistance. Although the Cossack irregulars scatter at their approach, the scarlet-clad Cossacks of the Russian Imperial Guard stand all too firm:
> 'Only a few hundred yards from us Captain Ségur fell in the midst of a party of the enemy who took him prisoner. He was the brother of the one who has written the history of this unhappy campaign.' – At 'the same moment I arrived at Vilna, Duroc, the Grand Marshal of the Palace, called me over, squeezed my hand, and told me that two leagues beyond the city my brother, flung imprudently into a wood by his general, had just run into three regiments of the Russian Guard while mounting a hillside. His company had been crushed; and he himself had disappeared! At this news, I hurried to my brother's hussars. Those that were left were still drawn up in line of battle in front of the scene of their defeat.'

They tell Ségur[18] how his brother had

'several times tried to cut his way out, but been felled by a lance-thrust, and then, while struggling to get up from the ground, by several more. Some Russian officers had dragged him away into the forest. One of the hussars gestured toward a conifer forest and the sandy slope of the broad highway which went into it. Bloodstained shreds of uniforms lay scattered in the middle of the road. In each I trembled to recognize my brother, particularly when the faces were hidden in the sand and their hair was black and their stature great. What anguish when the hussar who accompanied me, seizing these heads by their hair and brusquely turning them round, showed me their features!'

But none is his brother. So Ségur, 'defying the order forbidding all communications with the enemy', quickly gets hold of a trumpeter and scribbles some hasty words to his brother. Then, equipping his servant with a purse of money, accompanies him and the trumpeter into the wood. 'Only after I'd left it again did I catch sight of the first Russian scouts. Soon the servant and the trumpeter were among them. An hour of anxiety followed, the cruellest in my whole life.'

Dusk falls. What's become of his emissaries? The Russians know he's a high-ranking officer at IHQ. Will they try to capture him too? No. Here, at last, comes the trumpeter – dead drunk:

'The Russians had received him so cordially he was unable to speak. But he brought me some lines written by a generous hand. My brother's wounds, though serious, weren't mortal. His name and courage assured him a gentle and honourable captivity. I breathed again.'

In Paris Napoleon had told Caulaincourt he'd wage a 'polite war' against Alexander; and that, for officers of Ségur's status, is what it still is. Hardly for others. Riding sadly back into Vilna, he hears a shot ring out, 'followed by an unusual murmur'. A French infantryman who's just blown his brains out is lying in the middle of the road. His comrades are staring down at him in consternation when a second shot is heard. Everyone runs over. Another suicide. The spectators, Ségur says, 'exclaimed with their usual exaggeration that if this went on, the whole army would go the same way'.

According to another of Pajol's ADCs, Captain *Jean-Pierre Dellard*, the 8th Hussars' setback 'wouldn't have happened if General Wathier de St-Alphonse, who was to have debouched on the enemy's left by the Wacha and Novo-Troki roads, hadn't turned up too late'. And in fact he's relieved of his commmand. It's taken over by General Sébastiani – who won't do much better. But Captain Aubry and his chasseurs are deeply affected by their ex-commander's disgrace. None of them will be either decorated or promoted.

By now Murat has ridden in at the head of Bruyère's division, and Vilna's narrow streets are packed with men and horses. Even before entering the city, Napoleon's photographic memory has recalled – no doubt in connection with a large donation he'd made to its university in 1810 – the name of a certain Professor Sniadecky, its aged rector. Sent off to fetch him, Soltyk finds the old man

'wearing the Academy uniform. He wanted to put on silk stockings instead of his boots. I told him my mission admitted of no delay. When he insisted, I said: "Rector, it's of no consequence. The Emperor attaches no importance to externals which only impress the vulgar. Science is the garb of the wise. Let's be off." And he acquiesced with good grace.'

Next day old Sniadecky will find himself co-opted willy-nilly into a provisional government, together with six other notables who haven't left with the Russians.

But what has happened to the first-comers' delirious welcome? Either it must have subsided remarkably quickly, or else Caulaincourt is projecting his own pessimistic frame of mind on to the situation:

'The Emperor passed through Vilna without making himself known. The town seemed deserted. Not a face showed at a single window, not a sign of enthusiasm or even curiosity. Everything was gloomy. Passing straight through the town, he inspected the burnt Vilia bridge, the terrain beyond the city, and the magazines the enemy had set fire to and which were still burning. Hastening on the repairs to the bridges, he gave orders for defensive outworks, and then returned and went to the palace.'

In this case 'the palace', as IHQ is always called on campaign, is in the palace of the Archbishop of Vilna, vacated only two days ago by the Tsar. 'Although his return was made public,' Caulaincourt goes on,

'and the Household, the Headquarters, the Guard and all the paraphernalia indicating his presence had been established there, the population didn't show the slightest interest. The Emperor was struck by this. Entering his study, he remarked: "The Poles hereabouts aren't like the ones at Warsaw. They're cooler than Poles and much more reticent."'

He's right. They're Lithuanians. Since 1807 the Tsar has made great efforts to win over the wealthier segment of the population, and now it's divided between pro-French and pro-Russian factions. And in fact many of the town's leading families have left with the Russian army. Near the town gate Dumonceau, riding in earlier that morning, has noticed

'a kind of cloister with a chapel. Its bell tower was a parti-coloured striped ball, the first bizarre Russian bell tower we'd seen. Its walls were placarded all over with lengthy proclamations in Russian we'd have liked to decipher.'

Not all, however, are in Russian, for Labaume says 'everyone could read them'. It's Alexander's dignified if wordy reply to Napoleon's declaration of war:

"We have long noticed on the part of the Emperor of the French proceedings hostile to Russia, but have always hoped to avert them by conciliatory and pacific means. Finally, seeing the continual renewal of obvious offences and despite our desire to preserve the peace, we have been constrained to complete and assemble our armies. However, we still flatter ourselves we shall reach a reconciliation by remaining on the frontiers of our empire... ready only to defend ourselves..."

By 'suddenly attacking our army at Kovno' Napoleon has become the aggressor:

"Seeing, therefore, that nothing can make him accessible to our desire to keep the peace, it only remains for us, while invoking the Almighty, witness and defender of the truth, to succour us, to oppose our forces to the enemy's. We do not need to remind corps and unit commanders and the soldiers of their duty and their courage. The blood of the valorous Slavs runs in their veins. Warriors! You are defending religion, the country and freedom! I am with you. God is against the aggressor. – Alexander"

Looking up at the ancient ruined citadel, Dumonceau has also seen flying on its summit an 'immense white and sky-blue flag, said to be the colours of the Jagallons, ancient sovereigns of Lithuania'.[19] As his lancers walk their horses through the streets past 'the wreckage of military stores that were smoking and even still in flames' they see here and there 'soldiers rifling them to extract a few remains of victuals'. So he leaves behind some of his men, duly provided with sacks, to 'gather up some oats, of which we saw some half-burnt morsels'. Oats are all that have been saved, but so smoked the horses won't eat them. All the corn has been consumed by the flames.

Just as Planat de la Faye and the artillery staff are installing themselves in town, the weather suddenly changes. 'A gale, followed by a cold rain, lasted for almost two days.' Out on the Kovno road the long continuous cloudburst overtakes Sergeant Coignet that evening just as his little convoy of two treasury wagons is reaching a village near Vilna, causing him hurriedly to take shelter inside one them. But Dumonceau's men find themselves locked up inside a walled monastery garden, where they have no shelter at all and where they're having to make do with the most meagre of rations, sent them by a municipality which is already at its wits' end in suddenly having to feed all these thousands of men and horses.

'The rain was coming down in bucketsful, accompanied by a glacial cold which we felt the more keenly for its following immediately on the overwhelming heats. Soon the soil of the garden, churned up and drowning in water, was nothing but a vast swamp of mud. We stood knee-deep in it, having neither straw to lie down on nor any shelter, and without wood to light a fire. And then, to cap it all, came a terrible hurricane. Finding it equally hard to stand up or lie down, we squatted dozing on our mantles in the mud; and awoke only to find the rain still pouring down and the hurricane growing steadily more furious. Chimneys and tiles were coming down all around us. Equally tormented whether lying down or standing up, all we could do was crouch there under our capes. Arms and equipment were lying in the mud. Our dismal fires had gone out. Our horses were shivering at least as violently as ourselves. Several succumbed during the night or else died next day, destroyed by cold and misery.'

All this the new Guard regiment resents so much the more because 'rightly or wrongly we supposed the other Guard cavalry regiments were lodged with the inhabitants and that this was a mere caprice of General Colbert, and that we were being treated as illegitimates, pariahs. We observed between ourselves that not one of our superior officers, nice and snug in the neighbouring houses, put his nose out into the wind to enquire after our sufferings.'

Not until the evening of the following day (29 June) will adjutants arrive, order the trumpeters to sound the fall-in, and distribute billets. Next morning, when Coignet peers out of his treasury wagon, it's to find 'the ground in the nearby cavalry bivouac covered with horses, dead from cold. Climbing out, I saw three of mine had perished. I imme-diately distributed the survivors among my four wagons. The poor beasts were trembling so violently that no sooner were they har-nessed up than they smashed everything, throwing themselves about wildly in their halters. They were mad, prancing about with rage. On reaching the road we found some dead soldiers who hadn't been able to stand up to this appalling storm, and this demoralized a great many of our men.'

Far away to the south-west, too, a Lieutenant *Sauvage*, struggling on east-wards through the same rainstorm with one of Jerome's artillery parks, sees his young drivers shedding tears over their dead teams.

It's 'heartbreaking' for Napoleon, Caulaincourt sees, to have been cheated of his 'good battle'. But supposing there'd been one? In Lieutenant Brandt's view 'it could only have been indecisive; the ground was so thoroughly soggy, neither artillery, cavalry, nor even infantry could have budged except with extreme difficulty'.

As for the Russians' withdrawal, it strikes the French as extremely well-planned and orderly. And will continue to do so.

CHAPTER 5

BAGRATION GIVES DAVOUT THE SLIP

A disappointing conquest – a letter from the Tsar – Sergeant Bertrand gatecrashes a supper party – sudden departures – the trap is sprung – a heart-rending spectacle – the Tsar's emissary – where's Jerome? – Caulaincourt is upset – the Italian army crosses the Niemen – frustrations at Novo-Troki – impossibilities at Grodno – 'tell him it's impossible to manoeuvre in worse fashion' – Dumonceau meets the Iron Marshal – forced marches – a disgraceful scene

Vilna may not be the 'fine city of 40,000 souls' Napoleon writes of in his letter to Marie Louise – actually it has only half as many – nor is it politically any great capture. Few people in western Europe can even have heard of it. Yet it forms a forward base from which the main army, like a two-headed snake, can strike either at Barclay, retreating north-eastwards towards the River Dwina and the Drissa Camp, or at Bagration, coming up from Grodno; or, should they make junction, at both. Hardly less important, the vast stocks of food and other supplies assembled at Danzig and Königsberg can be brought up by barge along the Vilia; the thousands of stragglers and would-be deserters can be netted in; and a Lithuanian army raised for the 'national' cause. But is there one? Ségur says Napoleon has been

'counting on four million Lithuanians. Only a few thousand supported him. The inhabitants seemed little disposed to respond to appeals made to their patriotism. Moreover the Russians weren't far away, and no decisive action had yet been fought.'

And that's the crux of the matter.

On the morning of 29 July he's dealing with these and a myriad other urgent matters when a despatch arrives from Davout. A certain Count Balashoff, the Tsar's police minister, has presented himself at the outposts with a personal letter from Alexander, asking to be taken to Murat. Receiving him politely, Murat has told him that he, for his part, 'most earnestly hopes our two emperors will come to an understanding, and that this war, begun against all my inclinations, will be over as soon as possible.' Which is true. All he wants is to get back to Naples.

Relieving Balashoff of the Tsar's letter, Davout, not so politely, has sent it on to Napoleon, with a request for further orders. Opening the letter in the presence of Duroc, Berthier, Bessières and Caulaincourt, Napoleon finds that it is in fact in the Tsar's handwriting and asks why 'in times of deepest peace and without any preliminary declaration of war' the Emperor of the French has invaded Russian territory. The letter proposes that he withdraw behind the Niemen, pending negotiations.

This is too much:

'Alexander's laughing at me!' Napoleon exclaims. 'Does he imagine I've come to Vilna to negotiate trade treaties? I've come to finish off the barbarian colossus of the North, once and for all. They must be thrust back into their snow and ice, so that for a quarter of a century at least they won't be able to interfere with civilized Europe. The sword is drawn. The Tsar sees his army has been cut in two. He wants to come to terms. The acquisition of Finland has turned his head. If he must have victims, let him defeat the Persians; but don't let him meddle in Europe's affairs. My manoeuvres have disconcerted the Russians. Before a month has passed they'll be on their knees to me.' Not, he adds hastily, that he has any personal grievance against Alexander. He'll treat his emissary well. But since a police minister presumably has his eyes and ears about him, Balashoff is to be brought to Vilna by 'another route' so as not to have a chance to see the frightful wreckage of men, horses and *matériel* lining the Kovno road. Anyway the whole thing's just a gambit to gain time...

By no means everyone has had a roof over his head this drenching night. The 85th Line have bivouacked outside the town under pine trees. And together with the rest of Gudin's 3rd division of I Corps, the 7th Light, 'up to its ankles in water and mud took up its position in a hollow, en masse and by divisions.[1] But just as Carabinier-sergeant *Bertrand* is expecting, as so often before, to pass the night standing 'with musket grounded in this morass', he has a stroke of luck. The adjutant comes and tells him he's been selected for orderly duty at Davout's headquarters, which he finds is in a house between The Palace and Murat's, in the next best house in town. There NCO orderlies 'from all arms' are crammed together in a single room. All have but one longing – to go off and find something to eat; but are only being allowed to do so one by one. Looking about him for somewhere to lie down, Bertrand opens some double doors and is surprised to see in the next room

'two townsmen and two other persons in turbans seated around a well-lit table, on which was a good dinner. Valets dressed in the Emperor's livery were waiting on them. Stupefied, I didn't know whether to advance or retreat. But not yet knowing how to beat a retreat, I go in, raising my hand to my shako. "What do you want?" says one of my two turbans. "A corner where I can get some rest. But I see this isn't the place, please excuse me." – "If there's only you," replies the turban whom I'd recognized as Roustam, the Emperor's mameluke, "come in. Your division has been in the advance guard all day. You must be dead beat." Amazed at my lucky windfall, I valiantly plant my fork in a chicken wing, followed by an iced ham, the whole washed down with the finest vintages. The second turban, Murat's mameluke,[2] orders up a square-shaped bottle wrapped in straw, and we drink the healths of the Emperor, of his worthy spouse, of the Prince Imperial, of King Murat.'

Since his hosts' generosity is at the expense of *their* hosts it knows no bounds. But just as they're stuffing his pack with provisions Bertrand hears someone shouting for 'the sentry from the 7th Light'. Profusely thanking the two mamelukes, he hurries off – with urgent orders to General Gudin. What orders? We'll see in a moment.

And indeed Sergeant Bertrand is by no means alone in having to go out again into the wind and pelting rain. At the 2nd Lancers' monastery Dumonceau and his fellow-captain Post are just turning in for what they hope is going to be the campaign's first comfortable night when 'to our annoyance, the sound of the trumpets was heard under our windows'. Resisting the temptation to pretend they're deaf, they get back into their saturated uniforms and go downstairs. And there, in the terrible wind and rain, they stand holding their horses' reins:

'Our trumpeters kept reiterating their calls, but the regiment responded only very slowly. And when, toward midnight, the time came to leave, it still lacked over a hundred men and two officers.'[3]

Yet another officer who's had to spend a most uncomfortable night encamped in the mud outside the town is Grouchy's artillery commander, Colonel Griois. As morning comes he's just limbering up his batteries and wondering how he'll ever get them some food and forage, when counter-orders arrive – to unlimber again and wait until all the teams and guns he's had to leave behind on the Kovno road have caught up. Never in all his military career has his colleague Major Boulart known the Guard artillery to suffer such losses – most, he's sure, avoidable if only he'd been given the oats ration Napoleon had promised him during their pleasant chat together at Thorn. How can he report them to 'Old Thunderer', General Sorbier, the Guard artillery's commander? Only yesterday he'd been complimented by him on the excellent state of

'the teams of 20 vehicles, 90 train horses and 70 peasant ponies. I expected Sorbier to be stupefied. But he'd already been informed of the other divisions' losses, and listened without apparent emotion to mine.'

Now Boulart is to stay outside Vilna until they've been made good. But his colleague Griois is to leave,

'bringing with me such guns and ammunition wagons as I could harness up to healthy horses, and leave the rest of our artillery at Vilna, together with the lame horses and useless men'.

So saying, Grouchy had ridden off, 'indicating roughly which direction I should follow to rejoin him'. Even so, not until 4 p.m. (29 June) is Griois able to get going, 'with about two-thirds of what I'd brought this far, escorted by 50 dragoons from the dragoon division Grouchy had left behind.'

There's a reason for these hasty departures.

Early in the course of that drenching night of 28/9 June Napoleon has at last got what he takes to be reliable news of Bagration, said to be marching toward Svetsianya, due east of Vilna. And has instantly sent off orders to Murat, Ney and Oudinot not to press Barclay too hard, but, on the contrary, let him get as far as possible from what is now to be the real scene of action. And at 2 a.m. another staff officer had galloped off with equally urgent orders to Davout, who's already gone on ahead in the direction of Ochmiana. To his extreme chagrin his corps has already been lopped of three of its finest infantry divisions.[4] Instead of marching under his command, Friant, Gudin and Morand are to provide a powerful striking force to support Murat's cavalry, while the rest of I Corps, plus Nansouty's (I) and Grouchy's (II) Cavalry Corps, marching in three columns, is to interpose itself between the two Russian armies. Nansouty, to the left, is to circumvent Bagration's advance guard. Davout will attack his centre. And the right-hand column (Grouchy's corps, with its cuirassier division, headed by Griois' horse artillery) is to pin down his rearguard – all on the assumption that Bagration is by now being hard-pressed by Jerome's 55,000 infantry and cavalry, coming up from Grodno. That is to say, four whole army corps, to be backed up – as soon as they've crossed the Niemen – by Eugène (IV) and Saint-Cyr (VI), are to envelop Bagration from all sides – 110,000 men against a mere 45,000, and annihilate him. After which it will be Barclay's turn.

Riding out of the town gate at midnight, the Red Lancers take the Smorgoni road 'in the direction of Miednicky' to protect Nansouty, on Davout's left flank, against any attempt by Barclay to intervene in the great enveloping movement. Dumonceau is happy to see that the Lithuanian peasants, 'in return for promises to respect their homes', are hastily consenting to supply his men with food and forage. At Smorgoni, which turns out to be a small town almost wholly made up of wooden houses,[6] his men can at last snatch 'two hours' happy sleep in its town square and cemetery'. Then the trumpets sound again. The lancers fall-in. And after five or six more hours' march they catch up with the rest of I Corps at the small town of Ochmiana. From time to time Dumonceau hears shots still being fired, Barclay's rearguard having only been dislodged that afternoon. But fails to catch even a glimpse of what's going on. The long summer day drawing to a close and 'the smoke from the campfires beginning to mingle with everything', he bivouacks and waters his horses.

The situation being what it is – or at any rate what on 30 June it seems to be – it's with a certain glee that Napoleon prepares to receive the Tsar's emissary. Duly brought to Vilna by the 'roundabout route', Balashoff has slept the night at Berthier's headquarters. And after breakfast is fetched by the one-eyed chamberlain Count Turenne. Conducted upstairs to 'the selfsame room from which, five days ago, Alexander had despatched me on my errand', he finds himself in the presence of Napoleon. The interview's twists and turns, its seemingly erratic leaps and angry outbursts, its cat-and-mouse tirades interspersed with sudden bouts of *faux bonhomie*, all bear the authentic Napoleonic hallmark. After some preliminary remarks ('I've seized one of his fairest provinces without firing a shot, and here we are, neither he nor I knowing what we're fighting for...') Napoleon declares Alexander has insulted him by demanding he withdraw behind the Niemen:

'At this moment, the gale blew a window open. Napoleon went over to it (we were both pacing the room) and quickly shut it. And upon its again blowing open – by now he was no little agitated – he didn't bother to shut it again, but tore it from its frame and flung it out into the street.'

So little has it been his intention to attack Russia, Napoleon goes on, he has even sent his personal carriages to Spain, where he'd really wanted to go. 'I know a war between France and Russia is no trifling matter, either for Russia or France. I've made extensive preparations, and my forces are three times as big as yours. I know the size of your armies as well as you do, perhaps better.' (Which he does. Upon the editor of *The Lithuanian Courier* setting the Russian effectives at 300,000, Napoleon had sardonically shown him a torn and crumpled despatch, intercepted from Barclay's chief-of-staff, which showed they at most added up to 185,000.)

Accusing Alexander of having connived at the assassination of his father, Tsar Paul, in 1802, he goes on to inveigh against Alexander's foreign associates, whose relatives, he says, he'll 'chase out of Europe'. Nor does he conceal his annoyance at Barclay's having refused battle in front of Vilna. 'I don't know Barclay de Tolly, but to judge from his first moves he hasn't much military talent.' A lecture follows on the folly of assembling stores, only to burn them: 'Did you think I'd just have a look at the Niemen and not cross it? Aren't you ashamed? With all Europe behind me, how can you resist me?'

'We shall do our best, Sire.'

Immediately Napoleon (who a moment before has been boasting of the Poles' unshakeable loyalty to himself) begins blandly talking about a settlement under which Alexander should 'in due course get the Duchy of Warsaw'.

And invites Balashoff to dinner.[6]

Even worse nourished and over-marched than the main body, Jerome's leading divisionss have only been making eighteen miles a day across Poland in the blazing heat. Only that morning have they, after immense efforts and sufferings,[7] entered an abandoned Grodno. A 24-year-old Westphalian lieutenant *Friedrich Giesse*, who'd not had a bite to eat for five successive nights, has seen his men die of thirst after drinking muddy river water. Another subaltern, *Eduard Ruppel*, seeing his 2nd Westphalian Hussars sprinkle their horsemeat with gunpowder for lack of salt, had trembled to think that this, so far from being the last stages of a campaign, was only its outset. Then the rains had come down; and the

Westphalians' and Saxons' horses, too, had begun to die. Now, struggling into Grodno without even having made contact with the enemy, Jerome receives a peremptory order from Vilna. He's to

"unleash the Poles, put the advance guard under Poniatowski's orders. Give him all your light troops and yourself be always ready to support him. Don't be afraid to put your troops at risk. Bagration has plenty else to think about besides turning back to fight and manoeuvre. All he's trying to do is to get clear away out into the countryside. So harass the Russians. Delay their march if they advance. Bar their way if they retire."

All of which is good tactics, but, in the circumstances, very much easier said than done. Everyone in Jerome's three corps, from general to drummer boy, is dead beat. Even Vandamme, one of Napoleon's very toughest generals, and Maison, Jerome's no less capable chief-of-staff, realize the troops must rest up. And when Jerome tries to enforce the imperial order to march, Vandamme protests. Whereupon a piqued Jerome, playing the emperor,[8] promptly dismisses him.

This is bad enough. But to make matters worse Jerome finds the worst possible replacement to command VIII Corps. Namely the youthful Bonaparte's one-time comrade-in-arms General Junot. A choice which will turn out to be perhaps the campaign's single most damaging act.[9] Foreseeing disaster, Vandamme appeals to Napoleon. Receives no reply. And goes home.

That same morning too Eugène's Italians and Saint-Cyr's Bavarians have at last arrived at the Niemen. Crossing Poland, the Elban officer Cesare de Laugier has written in his diary:

'Our very swift march and the sandy terrain are putting more and more distance between us and the wagons carrying the food that's been assembled. But it would be unjust to accuse the head of the army of improvidence. For the time being we must subsist as best we can, aim at the main goal, i.e., make contact with the enemy; fall on him with a colossal mass of men; win a decisive victory; and conclude a glorious peace!'

Now, after literally stumbling on the Niemen at Piloni, the Italian Royal Guard 'find the Viceroy, the Duke of Abrantès (Junot) and the staff surveying the construction of a bridge'. One of the regiments which cross it as soon as it's ready – the (mostly Swiss) 35th Line – has in its ranks a Genevan shepherd, *Pierre-Louis Mayer*. Although his professional knowhow has come in handy when driving flocks of requisitioned sheep across Poland, he's finding it a 'sad forboding of having to steal to live'. And now, at the pontoon bridge, he sees

'incomparable torments and weeping. A commandant of engineers, supervising four sentries, was only allowing one cantinière per battalion to cross. All unauthorized persons, and those unhappy women who'd followed their lovers in the capacity of vivandières and laundresses, were being stopped.'

Most of these women, he fancies (rightly, as it will turn out) will nevertheless rejoin by and by. But the 36 horses he also sees lying there dead from hunger are gone for good. In the afternoon, Cesare de Laugier again scribbles in his diary:

'the first divisions have crossed over in the greatest order and silence. Since the Viceroy believes the enemy to be nearby, he has forbidden us to light fires.'

At Vilna, meanwhile, Napoleon is dining with his Russian guest. That afternoon in his office his second secretary, Baron *A-J-F. Fain*,[10] has heard him,

'while walking rapidly to and fro, mutter to himself: "Return behind the Niemen...?" Containing himself, he meditates his reply. Soon, ignoring this condition [that he should return behind the Niemen], so hurtful to his feelings, he returns to the main point at issue. "Those fellows only want a few days' respite. They're laughing at all that's most sacred and all they're thinking of is how to save Bagration. Very well then, let's busy ourselves solely with what's been begun so well."'

Also present at that dinner are Marshals Duroc, Berthier and Bessières, and Caulaincourt. In the last four years Jomini's *Treatise on Great Operations in Warfare* have had almost as great an influence on Russian military thinking as Barclay's army reforms. And Napoleon's opening shot is an allusion to the Tsar's underhand efforts to recruit the services of this Swiss writer, whose highest ambition – year after year frustrated by Berthier – is to become his chief-of-staff:

'"Your generals imagine they can resist me because they've read Jomini. But knowing the principles isn't everything."

BALASHOFF (according to himself): "The Russians, like the French, say all roads lead to Rome. The road to Moscow is a matter of choice. Charles XII went via Poltava."

NAPOLEON: "I've no intention of making the same blunder." And then, by way of a joke: "My brother Alexander has turned Caulaincourt into a proper Russian."

CAULAINCOURT: "Sire, I'm a very good Frenchman. The marks of kindness the Tsar Alexander has so often honoured me with were in reality addressed to Your Majesty. As your faithful servant, Sire, I'll never forget them."'

But Napoleon, who's having a good time, takes Caulaincourt's irritation in good part: 'I hear the Emperor Alexander wants to take command himself. Why? It'd be to assume responsibility for a defeat. War is my profession. I'm used to it. But he isn't. He's an emperor by birth. He should rule, and appoint a general to command the army. If the general does his job well, he can reward him. If not, he can punish and discharge him.'[11]

And so the conversation goes on. By now they must have come to the coffee, for Napoleon, pacing the room, goes up to Caulaincourt and taps him lightly on the neck: "Well, you old St Petersburg courtier, why don't you say something? Are the general's horses ready for him? Give him some of mine. He's got a long journey ahead of him."

Seeing Balashoff off, Caulaincourt asks to be kindly remembered to the Tsar. Then, returning to the dining room, tells Napoleon 'in a trembling voice' (Ségur) he's 'a better Frenchman than those who've cried up this war'. And asks to resign – or be given a commission in Spain, with permission to set out tomorrow.

'NAPOLEON: "I was only joking. You know perfectly well I esteem you. Just now you're talking foolishly and I shan't reply to what you're saying."'

'Bessières tugged at one of my coattails, and Berthier at the other. Between them they drew me aside and begged me to cease my retorts. Seeing I was beyond listening to reason, Napoleon, who, I'm bound to admit, kept his patience and spoke with the same kindness, retired to his study. I'd lost my head completely.'

Next morning, when Caulaincourt doesn't appear at the levée,

'first Berthier then Duroc came and remonstrated with me. Seeing I didn't appear, the Emperor, having taken some turns about the town and after halting by the bridge, gave orders for me to be sought for and fetched. Unable to refuse obedience, I joined him while he was inspecting the outworks in front of Vilna.'

Napoleon pinches his ear: '"Are you mad, wanting to leave me?" With these words he galloped off, reined in his horse; and soon afterwards began talking of other matters.'

And that was that.

After the pontoon bridge at Piloni has been crossed by the Italian Royal Guard 'under the Viceroy's eyes' they're followed by the 35,000 men of Pino's division who, says Cesare de Laugier,

'broke out into spontaneous acclamations. The movement has been carried out with the same order, the same discipline, the same turnout and the same brio as if it had been a parade movement on some festive occasion in front of the prince's palace in Milan.'

But no sooner are they on the right bank than, out of a clear sky, comes an ominous rumble. Cannon fire? Every one strains his ears. General Roguet is sure they're about to be attacked; and Eugène, despite his instructions to advance with all speed to plug the gap between the main force and Jerome at Grodno, sends off a Colonel Battaglia to Vilna for orders. After which the Italians pile arms. Their first bivouac on Lithuanian soil, like the main army's before them, looks like being cold, dank and misty. But then, suddenly,

'a furious gust of wind upsets our stacked muskets and flings disorder into the camp. The horizon is covered with black clouds. Soon we're enveloped in a cloud of dust, drenched by torrents of rain which have now been falling with unheard of violence for thirty-six hours. Roads and fields are swamped; the heat we've been enduring for several days has changed into a very keen cold. The horses are dying like flies. Many of them have perished during the night and we must expect many more to do so.'

In a pallid dawn, after a night when no campfire would stay alight, 'pierced through to the bone with cold, half-asleep and at our wits' end, we look like phantoms or shipwrecked men saved from the waters. A lack of food is aggravating our situation.'

Quitting their 'accursed bivouac', the Italians find the little town of Kronie deserted down to its last inhabitant. All it can offer is some very welcome brandy. While they're gulping it down, here comes Colonel Battaglia, back from Vilna with a flea in his ear. The two corps' halt at Piloni, the irate Emperor has written scathingly to his stepson, is 'ridiculous. General Roguet has no common sense. These delays are turning all IV Corps' fatigues into pure losses. His Majesty wants to hear undelayedly from that officer the reasons for such an idiotic supposition.'

So that day (2 July) the Army of Italy, bedraggled and hungry and with its horses too 'falling by the hundreds', makes tracks for Vilna. 'All along the road we met with nothing but dead horses, overturned vehicles and scattered baggage. And here we are, exposed to cold, rain and famine – in July!' Next day the Viceroy instals his headquarters in 'a château near the miserable village of Rouicontouï, very near the fork in the road leading to Novo-Troki'. Novo-Troki itself, despite 'an impressive abbey and a picturesque castle on an islet', turns out to be only

'a little town of about 300 houses, every single one of which has been stripped bare by its owner. Entering the town, the Viceroy has found himself surrounded by a swarm of Jews, each dirtier than the others, followed by a long line of women, old men and children, who prostrate themselves before him, howling and weeping and begging him to protect them against the men's rapacity. They're scattering through the town and pillaging everything. Nowhere have we found any straw to lie on, and to get forage for the horses we've had to go nearly seven miles.'

Though hardened to warfare in Catalonia, the Guardia d'Onore's adjutant-major is horrified by the pillage. But can do nothing to prevent it. 'Discipline, temperance, military honour, the superior officers' wise foresight, all are collapsing,' his diary laments. In vain Eugène sends urgent messages to Vilna, begging for food. 'The help we've been given from there is so meagre it hardly suffices for one day.' All IV Corps finds at Novo-Troki to fill its 30,000 empty stomachs are great quantities of linden honey. Gobbling it down, many men instantly fall victim to 'dysentery'.

By now the Italians are longing for only one thing – to get to Vilna. Judge their disappointment next day when orders arrive to stay where they are:

'Everyone cried out with vexation, saying our corps is doomed. They've tried to console us by saying we'll be going to Witebsk and

Smolensk, and that those two towns will make us forget all about Vilna.'
- obviously they've no idea of how many versts[12] they'll have to march to get there. Newspapers arriving from Vilna tell how Napoleon has 'set up some kind of provisional government of Lithuania, whose first concern has been to create five regiments of infantry and five of cavalry'. The flower of the young Vilna nobility, Laugier notes with something of his earlier enthusiasm, is forming a guard of honour under the command of Prince Oginski:

'Many young men of good family and 300 students from the university have enrolled, and are providing themselves with uniforms at their own expense. What a contrast to the abandonment of these houses and the flight of the population!'

Less encouragingly, the Vilna hospitals are reported as being choked with the sick.

That day the former Swiss shepherd Mayer confesses to a small but horrible murder:

'I saw a calf grazing peacefully in a garden around a hut. I go up to him and the poor beast lets me take him. I attack him, throw him down, and half cut his throat with my knife. As long as I live I'll recall the effect produced on me by this kind of murder. I said to myself: "What kind of a soul can assassins have who commit such a crime on their own kind?" But we've got to eat.'

Next day he makes up for it by saving a Russian landlord's daughter from being raped by a Pole.

So three days pass. Then IV Corps sets off for fresh fields and new tribulations.

Jerome's reply to his order to 'unleash the Poles' has thrown Napoleon into a rage less certainly feigned than his diplomatic ones. None of his cavalry probes in the direction of Ochmiana, his brother has written, have found Bagration's army. The fateful import is obvious. Somehow or other Bagration is managing to slip away, probably in the direction of Minsk. And the danger of this happening and the entire grand strategy being set at nought mmake him send a furious answer galloping off to Grodno:

"To the Prince of Neuchâtel, Major-general: *Mon Cousin.* Tell him [Jerome] it would be impossible to manoeuvre in worse fashion. I am severely displeased at his failure to place all the light troops at Poniatowski's disposal and so harass Bagration. Tell him he has robbed me of the fruit of my manoeuvres and of the best opportunity ever offered in war – all because of his extraordinary failure to grasp the first principles of warfare."

Nor is Napoleon's mood improved by a letter from Poniatowski to Berthier. Although his officers have accepted a 33 per cent cut in salary, Poniatowski has written, they've actually received no pay at all and can't even buy food. One of the secretaries[13] scribbles a letter to Berthier. He's to tell Poniatowski that

'His Majesty is most displeased that you should speak to him of pay and bread when it's a question of pursuing the enemy. The Emperor could not but be pained to see that Poles are such bad soldiers. His Majesty hopes to hear no more such talk.'

Stung by this reprimand, the Poles make a new and convulsive effort. And on 5 July, near the little town of Mir, their advance guard at last makes contact with Platov's retiring rearguard. Without waiting to be supported by artillery or infantry which are anyway a whole day's march to their rear, they fling themselves at the Cossacks – and get a bloody nose. Next day an entire cavalry division – 3,000 lancers, this time reinforced by infantry – is flung in. And is no less badly mauled.

Meanwhile the 85th Line, Le Roy's regiment, is spearheading Davout's corps as it probes for signs of Bagration's army. On 1 July the regiment had turned off 'sharply to the right, parallel with the Grodno road near Surviliski, to link up with the Westphalian army, which was to our right but in arrears'. And indeed is still at Grodno. Next day, failing of course to make any such junction, the 85th had taken 'the Minsk road, via Volokzin and Rahow'. Bumping into what he takes for Bagration's advance guard, Captain Biot, riding on south-eastwards with Pajol's cavalry, finds it's only a convoy Bagration has sent to Barclay.

Who will get to Minsk first – Davout or Bagration?

On 3 July the sun comes out again and is greeted with cheers by the men of the Vistula Legion; sent off from Vilna as an afterthought and to make up for Davout's loss of Friant's, Gudin's and Morand's divisions, they're marching down the Minsk road to catch up with I Corps and bring its nominal strength up to 50,000 men.

Next day at dawn Dumonceau, provided with a Polish interpreter, is ordered to probe the countryside toward Zabrès, on the Berezina, 'a name which as yet meant nothing to us'. Although his two troops of lancers run into Barclay's rearguard, they find the bridge over the Vilia's upper reaches still intact. Rejoining his fellow-officers at dinner, Dumonceau overeats, and is smitten with a cruel fit of indigestion; but next day in the afternoon (5 July) he's sent out again, this time under the regiment's veteran commandant Coti, to save the bridge by a night attack. Although the cool night air dissipates his dyspepsia, by the time the detachment gets there

'the bridge had just been burnt. Only a few half-consumed piles remained, still more or less in flames above the water. A cavalry trooper posted on the far side fired a shot at us and then cleared off.'

Nine miles further on, after finding a 'a deep and uncertain ford', they reach Zabrès at daybreak, to find it's just been evacuated by the Russian cavalry. Although the Dutchmen's sudden appearance at their town gate throws the locals into confusion, they're generous with useful information. I Corps, they say, is only five or six miles away to the right. So Coti sends off Dumonceau, 'accompanied by six of our best lancers and a mounted guide', to tell Davout he's at Zabrès. It's a dangerous mission. His guide is

'a kind of country gentleman of ferocious appearance, bearded, a black bearskin on his head, dressed in a Polish tunic, armed with a sabre and two pistols at his waist – in a word, got up like a comic-opera brigand and evidently very much exalted'.

But since Dumonceau knows no Polish and the Pole no French, the latter's patriotic eloquence is as lost on everyone as it is on the unending pine trees. Just as all this incomprehensible talk is showing signs of ebbing away, the party, deep in the forest solitudes, catch sight of some villagers who are furiously driving away 'some horsemen armed with long perches in guise of lances'. "Cossacks! Cossacks!," shouts the bellicose guide, eager to join in the fray. But that's none of Dumonceau's business and, to his guide's disgust, he refuses.

Reaching the town of Volagin, he finds I Corps bivouacked. Asks for Davout's headquarters and finds him at dinner in the local château, 'a great seigneurial building, with vast dependencies'. Dry and severe, and wearing his bifocal spectacles, Davout notes what Dumonceau has to say; bids him curtly sit down beside him at table with the rest of his staff. Pays him no more attention. As it happens, Dumonceau has met the Prince of Eckmühl before he had been made a prince, on the eve of Austerlitz. Shall he remind him of it? Dumonceau finds he lacks the courage. The meal over, Davout gets up from table and, saying he'll have some orders for him to take back to Colbert, leaves the room:

'Everyone made haste to follow him, except one little elderly senior officer, seated at the table's end, who muttered something about there surely not being all that hurry. The marshal heard and snapped back a few words as he left the room. Then I saw him address the lady of the manor with infinite courtesy, hoping he was disturbing her as little as possible. After which he went out and, with some of his aides packed around him, took his place on the lengthwise seat of a char-à-banc that stood waiting at the base of the peristyle.'

After a well-deserved nap Dumonceau tries to obtain his orders; but gets no help from Davout's disgruntled staff, who keep bitching about their chief's 'brusqueries, his haughty character and excessive severity'. Hadn't he only yesterday 'pitilessly had an unfortunate grenadier shot for pillaging?'[14] By and by Davout 'collarless, in his shirtsleeves on account of the heat, emerges from his office, severely reprimanding a grey-headed senior officer who's coming out backwards, resolutely but deferentially excusing himself'. Seeing Dumonceau standing there, the Iron Marshal calms down and calls him into the office, the whole of the middle of which is taken up by a huge table covered with maps and papers. At a card table by the window an officer whose acquaintance Dumonceau has made in Holland is sitting writing. And it's to him Davout dictates Colbert's orders. That very evening he's to force the inhabitants of Zabrès, 'on pain of military execution', to start rebuilding the burnt bridge. More importantly, Dumonceau is to tell him – verbally, if his despatches should be at risk – that I Corps' destination is Minsk. Colbert himself is to make for Veleika, to protect its rear.

'"You remember those place names, I suppose? Minsk and Veleika?"

"Yes yes, M. le Maréchal. But I'll jot them down in my notebook anyway."

"Quite right, get going." And with a slight inclination of his head the marshal dismissed me.'

And it's at Veleika, on 7 July, the Red Lancers have their first real clash with the enemy:

'We carried the bridge over the Vilia by a brisk attack before they could burn it. We seized a considerable convoy of camp equipment, a military pay chest and various baggage, among them a sutler's store of rice, oatmeal, salt, coffee, tea, sugar and such haberdasheries as thread, cordage, ribbons, buttons, clasps, etc., of which my servant took in an ample stock. The convoy's escort managed to make off into the woods after firing a few shots at us.'

The weather is again blazing. Even in this new crack lancer regiment men and horses are falling sick; and before leaving the captured stores (for the Italians to lay famished hands on) Colbert has to evacuate a second big batch of sick Dutchmen back to Vilna.

For three days 'at an even more rapid pace than before', through 'an agreeable countryside, covered with rich cornfields and fine forests where there are plenty of bees' I Corps makes forced marches for Minsk. Once again it's leaving in its wake hundreds, if not thousands of 'starving stragglers, marauders, and sick and exhausted men'. Until, on 8 July, Biot, General Pajol's ADC, with 200 men of the 6th Hussars and 200 of the 2nd Chasseurs, enters the capital of White Russia:

'I was ignorant of the marshal's order forbidding anyone to enter the town. When I got near it, I ordered my troop to a canter, passed through Minsk, and went and took up a position on the far side. We'd arrived in the nick of time. A Russian colonel, ADC to Bagration, was already in the town hall, busy collecting victuals for his army corps. He'd had to jump on his horse and make off as fast as he could go.'

Proud of his achievement, Biot reports back to Pajol; who sends him to Davout. Who, to Biot's dismay, flies into a rage: '"What! You've flouted my express orders, and entered Minsk? I'll have you shot!" Fortunately, I didn't lose my head; and replied bravely: "I didn't go *into* Minsk, M. le Maréchal. I went round it." – "In that case how do you know about that

Russian staff colonel?'" From an aged Russian official, Biot says. Dressed in full uniform, with stars and decorations and attended by footmen and lackeys, fulsomely declaring himself an old friend of France, he'd come in an open carriage drawn by four magnificent greys to present his compliments to the head of the French army. Davout doesn't believe a word of it: 'Odd, that bit about the old fellow being smothered in Russian decorations!'

Compared to Vilna, Minsk, with its mere 3,000 inhabitants, and though 'fortified, with its two citadels', turns out to be only a small town. 'This little town's streets', Lieutenant *Jacquemot*[21] of the 5th Artillery Regiment will write when he reaches it three months later, 'are dark and dirty. Though there are any number of churches and convents, the Jews are in a majority, disgusting, doing all the business and above all the money-lending.' But its great military stores – 3,600 quintals of flour, 22,000 bushels of oats, 6,000 quintals of hay, and 200 firkins of brandy – are intact, and their preservation is 'the greatest service its inhabitants could render the French army. Though united to Russia', Brandt notes proudly, 'they were still Polish at heart.'

Le Roy, of course, is particularly happy to be able to replenish his larder. Seeking out a Polish count whose guest he'd been as a prisoner of war in 1807, the Lucullan major finds his benefactor is ill and

'his house full of administrative officers of the kind who, for a few services they do us, without in any way participating in its victories, often disturb an army's march and are the only ones to profit by them'.

But Davout lets him station two NCOs to protect his friend's property against these parasites.

Pierre Auvray, arriving at Minsk four days later with the 21st Dragoons on 12 July just as the 85th are leaving, will be less lucky. His unit is sent straight through the town to the outposts beyond:

'No rations were distributed. Severe orders were at once issued against marauding, though we'd lived on nothing else since we'd entered Lithuania. In this unhappy situation we were glad the town's Jews brought us food for our money. Brandy and beer were cheap.'

'We'd stayed there for three days,' Le Roy goes on, 'during which we'd been given every sort of victuals and were made to erect great huts, as if we were going to establish ourselves there for a long time to come.'

All Davout's marching has been in vain. Bagration has eluded him. Making tracks by forced marches for the lower reaches of the Berezina, he's aiming to join up with Barclay in the interior.[15]

The realization that this is so throws Davout into an icy rage. And a scapegoat is needed. All the regiments have left innumerable stragglers. The 57th Line has left 1,400 men behind, and the 25th almost 1,700. Each company of Brandt's 2nd Vistula Regiment, for instance, is lacking 'on an average 15 to 20 men', 800 out of its nominal strength of 2,400 having been left 'lying on the roads, in the fields and marshes, some dead, others lacking strength to keep up with us. Other regiments, with nominal strengths of 4,000, have suffered proportionately'. But the 33rd Line, it too consisting largely of Dutchmen, is in specially sorry case.[16]

The 11th of July being a Sunday, a grand parade is ordered in the town square. Follows a scene the like of which no one has ever witnessed before. 'When the Prince of Eckmühl lost his temper he was like Vesuvius in eruption,' writes Sergeant *Henri-Pierre Everts*:

'Having attended Mass,[17] His Excellency, surrounded by several generals and a numerous staff, appears at the parade. Hardly is he there than he comes galloping toward our élite companies, yelling at us in a voice of thunder and losing his temper in an utterly brutal manner. Reaching our fusilier companies, he again begins cursing us in a monstrous manner on account of our stragglers, threatening to have every tenth man present shot. Our divisional and brigade generals, like our colonel, also get a terrible bawling out.'

By and by Davout calms down:

'Our unit isn't to have the honour of marching past him with the others, but shall instantly return to its bivouac.'

Turning to one of his ADCs, Davout asks him what punishment is suitable. The ADC suggests the regiment shall be made to march past with reversed arms, 'musket butts in the air'. Said and done. The band of 57th Line, says Lieutenant Dutheillet,

'was ordered to play during this shameful execution. General Barbangère and many of his officers refused to be associated with the disgraceful event, and quit the ranks under the eyes of the Marshal, who couldn't force them to stay there. But the mass of the regiment marched past under the officers still on parade; and I was there.'[18]

Everyone is utterly indignant. But although General Dessaix immediately goes out into the plain to the 33rd's bivouac and orders the men to fall in just as they are, without greatcoats or muskets, and explains that it isn't they, who've stayed with the colours, but the stragglers His Most Serene Highness the Prince of Eckmühl is so angry with, it does nothing to dispel the baneful impression. 'I'd never heard of such a thing,' Everts concludes indignantly. Nor has anyone else.

More horrible, if less 'disgraceful' scenes are to follow. When Le Roy and the 85th and the rest of I Corps march out of Minsk on 12 July to make for the Berezina in further pursuit of Bagration, the 33rd, except for its 3rd Battalion, is left behind. It is occupy Minsk, which 'certainly couldn't be left without troops, since the Russians were still occupying the fortified town of Bobruisk, on our right and another force of 15,000 men, under General Ertel, was at Moziev, in our rear. Furthermore, Napoleon is intending to turn Minsk into a base and a great storehouse for the army.

First and foremost Davout's thousands of stragglers are to be rounded up and brought back to their duties. Everts goes on:

'The governor of Minsk, a Polish general who had a name very hard to pronounce, which I've forgotten, and whose signature I could never read, staked everything on preventing the countryside from being devastated in this way.'

Flying columns are being sent out daily, and

'each day numbers of these disbanded men were brought back into town; many of them were condemned by court-martial and immediately shot. But this did not suffice, for the governor kept receiving complaints from landlords of the intolerable way in which they were being maltreated, they and their peasants.'

One day when Everts is at table with His Excellency just such a complaint comes in:

'He ordered me to go out with a column of infantry and cavalry (Polish lancers), about 1,000 men strong, and punish on the spot all who didn't submit or follow me. I asked for one of his ADCs who also spoke French, and was willingly granted one.'

On the second day out of Minsk he sends back some 500 stragglers and marauders 'whom I'd disarmed. To prevent more trouble I had all their muskets, whose barrels I'd removed, placed on carts.' His prisoners are twice as many as their escort, and 'to my great regret I was obliged and materially constrained to have two men from an Illyrian regiment shot who with blows of their muskets had struck and killed a sergeant-major of my cavalry, whom I had at my side.' Thanks to the governor's Polish ADC he can explain to all his men and their prisoners, drawn up in line, the reasons for this sentence.

'I ordered a corporal and four men to step out of the ranks and shoot these rebels. I was the more obliged to take such rigorous measures as a violent and mutinous spirit was very openly manifesting itself among those who had belonged to these bands of furious men. I consecrated eight days to this disagreeable and wearisome mission, daily arresting some hundreds of stragglers and sending them into town. But the rumour of my presence seemed to have spread terror, and at Minsk a military commission was in permanent session. One needs oneself to have witnessed all the numbers of pillaged and devastated houses I saw, and their unfortunate inhabitants, fully to grasp the barbarity and the horror of the spectacle.'

Yet Everts is well aware that it's the excessive speed of Davout's advance that has caused them:

'It was without precedent and exceeded human strength. Often after a march of almost 40 leagues (160 versts) [120 miles], the troops were hardly allowed to rest for a mere couple of hours. So they weren't able to use the few victuals they still had on them. The horses of superior officers, though only walking, came to a halt between their riders' legs and collapsed on the ground. No one bothered. In this campaign neither men nor beasts had a right to rest or nourishment if they were to keep up with the rapidity of our operations.'

CHAPTER 6

PROBLEMS AT VILNA

'The Emperor's incredible activity' – 'I could wish that carriage to the devil' – Planat learns the hard way – why no prisoners? – General Tayrayre is worried – how get on without maps? – 'we had to hunt for life's barest necessities' – the pillage of Lithuania – 'under the Law of 21 Brumaire' – IHQ on parade – Coignet gets his epaulette – Fézensac has a nice time – the diplomatic corps – the Polish question – 'how many leagues is it to Moscow?' – 'our fatuous and unlimited confidence in Napoleon's genius' – Sébastiani surprised – two incompatible governors

Jomini would afterwards call Napoleon's two weeks at Vilna 'a fatal mistake'. But where else could he have been? So long as the outcome of the enveloping movement is uncertain he can pursue neither Bagration nor Barclay.

Certainly he's not idle. 'During his stay at Vilna', Caulaincourt assures us, 'the Emperor showed incredible activity. ADCs, orderlies and staff officers were forever on the roads. He waited with insatiable impatience for reports from the corps on the march.'

Baron Pierre-Paul Denniée, an inspector of reviews in Berthier's cabinet, sees how 'the Emperor alone set everything in motion. He alone gave directions inside all departments of the General Staff.' His quarters in the archbishop's palace consists as always of three rooms *en suite*. The innermost, his bedroom, contains one of his three folding iron green-curtained campaign beds. The middlemost, his office, has a big map table in the centre of it and in each corner a chair and a small table, for the four secretaries. The outermost room, lastly, is for the duty adjutants. Although Berthier has his own headquarters in the third best building available in town, there's also a room for him, and it is there that he spends most of his days and nights.

The pace is hectic. To his secretaries' ever-scratching quills – and sometimes to all four at once, or if no secretary is available, then to anyone who is – the Emperor dictates, always at breakneck speed, an endless stream of detailed orders. No one is exempt. Everyone, says First Secretary Méneval, has to sit down and do their stint:

'So fast did the Emperor dictate, no one but the person who'd written it down could have transcribed a clean copy. As soon as his idea has matured he begins walking slowly to and fro in the room. Then, in a serious, sharply emphatic tone of voice and with never a pause, he begins dictating. As inspiration comes to him, it finds expression in a livelier tone of voice and a kind of jerky movements of his right arm, whose sleeve he begins plucking at. He has no difficulty in formulating his thoughts. Sometimes the form is incorrect. Yet this very lack of correctness sets its lively stamp on his language, always admirably depicting what he wants to say.'

Everything proceeds swiftly and methodically. "Tomorrow! Night brings good advice," Méneval hears him say sometimes. At other moments, often, he'll joke and laugh with his secretaries, and at such times his usually mild thoughtful air breaks into a 'gentle caressing smile'. His terrifying rages pass over quickly, and his threats, though drastic, are almost never implemented.

All orders are addressed to Berthier, who passes them on to Colonel Salomon, his chief assistant, to copy into the order book before despatch. This is always done in duplicate, sent by two separate adjutants, and Napoleon is notified of the times of their departures. Nor does he ever send a new order to the same recipient without first consulting the order book. Secrecy is absolute, confined to himself, to his chief topographer, little Colonel *Bacler d'Albe*,[2] and 'perhaps to Berthier'.

'A little dark fellow, handsome, amiable, highly educated, talented and a clever draughtsman', Bacler d'Albe is Napoleon's most intimate collaborator. As chief cartographer it's his business to see to it that the maps are 'corrected and the various units' marches and lines of operation worked out'. Also to summarize, immediately on receipt, any important despatch. For seventeen years d'Albe has hardly had a moment to himself. One of the orderly officers, Captain Castellane, who doesn't like him, calls him scathingly 'the topographer par excellence, the great topographer, who has no excess of intelligence'. But Napoleon thinks otherwise[2] – always his first words on returning to his maps are "Fetch d'Albe!" And there are moments when Méneval sees the two of them lying flat on the big map table and hears them 'let out loud cries as their heads bumped together'.

No one ever knows from moment to moment what Napoleon's next move will be. After dictating his last word he exclaims: "To horse! My carriage!" And everyone has to scramble for it:

'This he called "keeping my people in good breath". As soon as he has formed a plan, he rings. Abruptly, the office door opens. An usher of the household comes forward and shouts in a loud voice: "The Emperor!" ' – a shout repeated by the grenadiers on sentry duty at the various doors, who present arms. At the same moment a carriage or a saddle-horse is brought round to the exit,'

and Caulaincourt emerges, carrying the imperial riding-whip, followed by Napoleon himself, 'walking quickly. He mounted. And left like a flash of lighting'. Well, not quite. On 7 July Captain Castellane confides to his diary:

'When I'm on duty I follow the Emperor when he rides out. We go the whole way at a walk. When the Emperor travels, he does most of the journey by carriage. This is very tiring for the officers who have to follow, because His Majesty, having rested up when the time comes for him to mount, assumes that the rest of us, who've covered the distance on horseback, are also. And behaves accordingly. Sometimes I could wish this confounded carriage to the devil. When His

Majesty's on the move there's not a moment of rest to be expected the clock round.'

Not a few of the innumerable orders pouring out from Napoleon's office are being passed on by Salomon to Lariboisière, head of the artillery. Which in effect means to Lieutenant Planat de la Faye, who forwards them to his assistants. These assistants, who are his seniors in rank, are six arrogant but badly educated artillery captains:

'I give them my minutes to copy, and sometimes, when their copies aren't sufficiently legible, make them begin all over again. The Emperor wants to be informed of the state of affairs, both matériel and personnel, at all his reserve depots, from Metz to Vilna. He's writing letter after letter to hasten on the arrival of everything in the rear; and each letter from him means I'm having to write at least twenty.'[3]

All this pen-pushing on a starved stomach – for there's a terrible shortage of food – is causing the six artillery captains to dub him sarcastically their 'man of letters'. Poor Planat! He's learning the hard way that

'in war one shouldn't make oneself too indispensable. Almost always one ends up by becoming the dupe or victim of such devotedness, in which vanity plays so large a part. It's precisely those officers who spare themselves most and sin least by excess of zeal who get on best. A little worldly-wise charlatanism and boasting goes much further.'

A lesson also being learnt by Sergeant-major Thirion. After taking him into his confidence, the commander of his cuirassier brigade, 'General Bruno, of Metz, an excellent man who liked to tell tall stories, and whom I really ought to be annoyed with, overwhelmed me with missions and rides, while my companions took it easy.'

After only two days at Vilna even the artillery staff, 'exhausted by marching and working', have no bread, indeed nothing to eat apart from what they've been able to steal from the villages en route. And after four even Caulaincourt is finding it has 'become necessary to search for life's barest necessities'. Many of the inhabitants are already reduced to 'living on berries'.

Small wonder then if, as at Minsk, thousands of starving deserters are pillaging the countryside. Marshal Mortier, the Young Guard's jovial giant of a commander, is setting their number at 30,000, equivalent of a whole army corps. The Lithuanian gentry are appalled at this side-effect of their supererogatory liberation. Heinrich von Brandt talks to 'a Lithuanian gentleman, an old soldier, who'd come to offer his services to the French Army, but found he must leave again in all haste to defend his property against the pillagers'. And when another, Eismont by name, makes so bold as to remind some French officers how Pharaoh's host, though innumerable, had all been drowned in the Red Sea, his frankness almost costs him his life:

'One of these madcaps drew a 3-foot dagger and ran at me, shout-ing: "Die, thou unbeliever in the earthly god and his inscrutable order of things!" After that, I've learnt to hold my tongue. A third Lithuanian landowner arrived on the steps of the Palace in rags, after soldiers had killed his serfs and driven his wife and daughter mad.'

Nor are the Lithuanians the only sufferers. Back at Novo-Troki, Césare de Laugier sees the newly appointed French sub-prefect turn up on foot, after being pillaged by stragglers. Whereupon his escort had eaten his provisions and made off with his horses; so that he when he'd got to Novo-Troki, Fézensac says, he was 'almost naked. Everyone took this man, who was to be our chief administrator, for a spy.'

Normally, says Ségur, Napoleon winked at pillage. But obviously things are going too far; and already on 2 July he has signed an order that all marauders 'if found guilty' are to be court-martialled and shot. And two days later he signs another, for the "despatch of cavalry detachments under staff officers to catch the stragglers, of whom many are committing crimes and end up by falling into the hands of the Cossacks". Immediately three flying columns, each consisting of 100 men and subdivided into ten patrols of ten men apiece (30 gendarmes, 30 Dragoons of the Guard, 30 lancers and ten local mounted guards) under a superior officer, have set out from Vilna with orders to go wherever 'they might be invited by the inhabitants'. Marauders convicted of crimes by the provost-court are to be 'executed within 24 hours, conformably with the Law of 21 Brumaire, Year V'. But though Coignet soon sees 'gendarmes everywhere, picking up stragglers', what can 300 men do against 30,000? Although 'military commissions and the making of several examples frightened a number of stragglers into returning to their duty, order was only indifferently restored,' says Caulaincourt.

Where, in this vast shortage of everything, are the immense supplies of foodstuffs, assembled at Danzig? Despite the heavy rains the Vilia, a shal-low river at the best of times, has in places almost dried out. And it isn't until 9 July that Napoleon personally supervises the arrival of the first barges.[3]

Every day new units are arriving and wanting rations. All are reviewed by Napoleon with his usual close attention to detail. On Monday, 8 July it's the turn of the Old and Young Guard. On the Tuesday, of the ambu-lances, 'lightly equipped to follow the army on the battlefields'. And on 10 July Fézensac has 'an opportunity of observing in every detail the way the General Staff is made up:

'The Administration, directed by the Intendant-General Count Dumas, was subdivided into an administrative service proper; ordon-nateurs, inspectors of reviews and war commissaries; the health ser-vice; doctors, surgeons and pharmacists; the victualling service in its various branches, and all kinds of employees.'

Berthier's aristocratic ADC doesn't know whether to be more impressed or dismayed by the

'great number of officers of all grades, commanded by General Mouthon. At a distance one would have thought they were troops drawn up in battle order. Just imagine the entire headquarters staff assembled at one spot. Imagine the prodigious numbers of domestics, of lead-horses, of baggage of all kinds which it had to drag along in its wake, and you'll have some notion of the spectacle offered by the headquarters.'

Since Vilna's market place isn't big enough to contain it, the extraordinary parade takes place in a plain beyond the town, where Dr *Réné Bourgeois* is also among the witnesses. Unfortunately, he sees, looking up at the sky, a storm was brewing.

'Thunder was heard grumbling in the distance. The sky got darker and darker. Finally, at the very moment when Napoleon emerged from the town, thick blue-black clouds let fly a deluge of rain. The Emperor refused to be deterred. But soon lightning flashes, cracks of thunder and an impetuous wind, raising whirlwinds, forced him to dismount, so as not to be carried away. In all haste he took refuge behind an ammunition wagon. Whereon everyone dispersed in the darkness to find shelter. The review couldn't take place and Napoleon went back into the town drenched to the skin. Likewise his suite.'

But why are there no prisoners? All officers arriving at IHQ from the various corps are immediately asked how many have been taken. 'The Emperor was anxious to get some trophies, so as to encourage the Poles. But no one gave him any.' This doesn't prevent him from making provision for them:

'As soon as there are 1,200 of them, they are to be divided up into twelve companies of 100 men apiece and marched in four days to Kovno, under a strong detachment commanded by a major and escorted by a Baden company of 100 men, 40 mounted Prussians, and a squad of five gendarmes.'

The returning Niemen barges, he thinks, will serve admirably to transport the prisoners – after they've taken a day's rest locked up in a church at Kovno – downstream to Tilsit, 'if it presents no difficulties, at the bottom of the holds and strictly supervised'. Should navigation prove difficult, or water transport take longer than land transport, then, issued with four days' bread rations, they're to be marched along the Niemen's left bank to Königsberg and thence to Pilau 'where they're to be shut up in a prison'. From there the officers and NCOs are to be sent on to Danzig, where 'vast localities are to be prepared to hold 10,000 prisoners'.

All this is very well, or would be if there were any. But Captain Franz Roeder, arriving at Kovno on 15 July to join the Hessian Footguards, only sees 850, 'mostly hospital orderlies, stragglers or officials'. His friend

General Tayrayre, the town's military governor ('one of the most modest Frenchmen I've ever met, as well as being a sympathetic and extremely honest man') has 'counted on finding all needful equipment, but been horrified to find neither tents, bandages nor blankets, and no prospects of getting any'. Inviting Roeder to dinner, he asks him to become his ADC, – a post the fiery-tempered captain would gladly accept 'if I could have gone with him to headquarters, but it's precisely there he won't be needing an adjutant of my stamp, and a German to boot'. High administrative officials, Tayrayre tells him, are obviously in no hurry to reach Lithuania and take up their duties: 'God knows what'll happen when the Grand Army is extended over such immeasurable distances and advancing at speed.'

Hasn't everything been thought of?

Everything, it seems, except maps.

Even while still en route for Vilna, General Compans had realized the sketchy nature of the campaign map. 'Everyday', he'd written home to his young bride,

'I'm becoming aware of the inadequacy of the maps we have; so I've bought a compass to guide me. Although I'm not used to this instrument I'm not unhopeful that it'll enable me to find St Petersburg or Moscow.'

Poring over the campaign map, specially engraved and printed on an enormous and unwieldy roll of paper, even the usually admiring Soltyk is beginning to realize that

'the geographical notions of the Muscovite empire entertained in Napoleon's office were about as imperfect as could be, and likewise of its topography. At all hours Napoleon kept interrogating the Polish General Soholnicki about such matters. On my offering to rectify the place names' orthography, I was ordered to write them in on the map, so that Napoleon could have a better idea of his whereabouts.'

As for the outlandish place names, the locals have never so much as heard of them. And since all the verst-posts have been removed by the Russians it's hardly surprising if smaller fry, who've no maps at all, are going astray; or if a half-witted psychopath like Roeder's irascible Colonel Follenius (Roeder himself, oddly enough, seems to have had some kind of a map) manages to lose his way and yet stumble on his destination a day too early! Even Davout has only been issued with *six* copies of the campaign map – one for himself, and one for each of his divisional commanders,

'but none for the generals commanding the artillery or engineers, for the generals commanding the light cavalry, nor for any of the army's generals of brigade. I therefore implore Your Highness to send me a dozen copies, which I shall distribute to the army corps, and which will be most usefully employed,

he'd written to Berthier before leaving Vilna on 30 June.

All of which points to a gross over-centralization of command. In

Napoleon's office little Baron Fain, who's sure everything's going well, notes in his journal that his master

'is only telling each of the participants about the bit that concerns him. The whole remains in his thoughts. Like writings in invisible ink which only fire can bring out, his military combinations will remain unperceived until revealed on the field of battle.'

And Tayrayre, at Kovno, is perfectly right in his apprehensions. Already the theatre of war is fanning out dangerously. For several days Oudinot has marched in pursuit of Wittgenstein without so much as catching up with his rearguard. Then, on 28 June, while he and his staff were taking breakfast in a farmhouse, a Polish lancer of his escort had found a Russian straggler asleep under a bush; and Marbot's light cavalry advance guard ('any army's eyes and ears') had seen Wittgenstein's corps drawn up in front of the little market town of Weselowo. Oudinot, says Marbot who affects to despise his talents as a corps commander, had amiably refused to believe his reports – until, proceeding to the edge of the forest, he and his staff had had to jump ditches to elude bouncing Russian roundshot. A small but full-scale battle had followed. The Russians had been driven out of Weselowo. And Oudinot had sent off a report of his victory to Vilna. But the distance between him and IHQ was now so great that it had taken three days before he received an acknowledgement.

Neither to Fain nor to Napoleon does it seem to occur that a system that leaves little or nothing to the corps commanders' initiative, when applied over such great and ever-growing distances, must in the end come unstuck.

Although victuals are so hard to come by, Fézensac's fortnight at Vilna, at least, is passing pleasantly enough. Nor is it the first time he's been here. As a pampered prisoner of war in 1807, captured while carrying Ney's despatches, this scion of the old French aristocracy had made many acquaintances in the town. This time too

'there was nothing burdensome about our duties. Assemblies, balls, concerts succeeded one another uninterruptedly. We found it hard to recognize the capital of a country ravaged by two hostile armies, and whose inhabitants were being reduced to indigence and despair.'

In Berthier's *salon de service*, where they aren't 'even allowed to read or write', the 'heart-breakers' preserve 'a profound silence' as they take turn and turn about, two at a time, one to receive, the other to despatch messages. But since these are normally carried by

'other staff officers, our turn only came every fourth or fifth day, when none of us was out on mission, something that happened only rarely. As Berthier himself always lodged physically close to the Emperor, his own lodgings belonged to his aides. It was most agreeable, in the midst of war and without having to take the least trouble, to find oneself better lodged and fed than anyone else in the army. At times it was as if we were in Paris.'

It's also at Vilna that the ambassadors of Austria, Prussia and the – still neutral – United States of America have foregathered, nothing doubting the outcome. Their opposite number is the former journalist, now Napoleon's minister of foreign affairs, *Hugues Bernard Maret*, Duke of Bassano.[5] A rare survivor of the pre-revolutionary diplomatic service, though certainly not the peer of his formidable but devious forerunner Talleyrand,

'M. Maret distinguished himself by the elegance of his manners, as much as by the solidity and pleasantness of his mind. His devotion to Napoleon arose from the conviction he'd gained from day to day of this great man's superiority.'

Secretary Fain notes his singular gift of wholeheartedly supporting policies of which he personally disapproved. His ducal title, he says, had been 'acquired by the most legitimate means, for it was the price of hard work and the most honourable services'. Maret is in effect Napoleon's prime minister 'and under any other man would have been so by right'. But just now Napoleon is not particularly pleased with the efforts of his diplomatic service. Relationships with Turkey, Sweden and the USA are all extremely sensitive. One day Fain sees Napoleon

'vivaciously drop his reading of the English newspaper to open despatches announced from the USA. They're of greater interest. The Americans are at war with the British. He exclaimed: "If this rupture had occurred earlier it might perhaps have contributed to keep Alexander inside the Continental System!"'

And in fact an American army will shortly – if not very successfully – be invading Canada. News from Spain, on the other hand, isn't so good. After starving out Masséna's army, Wellington has left his impregnable position among the hills round Torres Vedras and is steadily driving it back into Spain. As for the Turks, Napoleon still doesn't know a peace has been signed between them and the Russians. Nor is Sweden's neutrality to be taken for granted.

Lastly, and most urgently, there's the Polish question.

Ambivalent attitudes yield ambiguous choices. Abbé *Pradt*,[6] Bishop of Malines, the man Napoleon has chosen as his ambassador-extraordinary to the Grand Duchy of Warsaw, has immediately shown himself unequal to his task. Two days before the Niemen crossings the Warsaw Diet had assembled and in a fever of excitement declared the Kingdom of Poland re-established. And all that's needed now to trigger off a national uprising which can provide the Grand Army with thousands of 'Polish Cossacks' is a word from Napoleon, confirming the decision.

A word he's determined not to utter. After all, there's his father-in-law the Emperor Francis to consider, and his guaranteed claim on Polish Galicia; as a quid pro quo for Schwarzenberg's 30,000 Austrians, fending off a potential threat to the Grand Army's southernmost flank from the Russian Army of Moldavia.

On 5 July Napoleon hears that Pradt, after three days of high-flown rhetoric in the Diet, instead of skilfully directing its patriotic fervour, has quite simply dissolved it. For a moment, utterly furious, he thinks of replacing Pradt with the strongly pro-Polish Narbonne. But reflecting no doubt that this could be equally disastrous in the opposite direction, refrains from doing so. Finally, on 11 July, an eight-man delegation gets to Vilna – but only after being seriously molested en route by marauders. Roman Soltyk's father is one of the delegates. At a solemn Te Deum in the cathedral Captain *Fantin des Odoards* of the 2nd Guard Grenadiers (Coignet's regiment) watches them renew their oath of fidelity to a united Poland in front of the high altar:

'The tremendous enthusiasm of all present was particularly noticeable among the women. All wore on their bosoms a large rosette in the Lithuanian colours, crimson and blue.'

Afterwards, in the archbishop's palace, Maret solemnly receives the delegates' petition and presents it, no less ceremoniously, to his all-puissant master who, Fézensac sees, receives it 'with benevolence'. Whereupon the delegation's francophile spokesman, the aged Wybicki, steps forward and appeals pathetically: 'Sire, say but the word, say Poland exists. For the world your decree will be the equivalent of reality!'

Will it? Solemn oaths and ceremonies are one thing. Power politics quite another. Napoleon's reply is at once candid and evasive:

'I love your nation. For sixteen years now I've seen your soldiers beside me on the battlefields of Italy and Spain. I applaud all you've done. But in lands so distant and far-flung you must above all place your hopes in the efforts of the local population. Let me add that having guaranteed the Emperor of Austria the integrity of his domains I cannot sanction any moves or manoeuvres that might trouble his peaceful possession of his remaining Polish provinces.'

Hasn't he already hinted to Balashoff that he's reserving 'Polish' Lithuania as an important pawn in his future peace negotiations with Alexander?

Faces fall. There'll be no Polish uprising. But at the ball that follows, Fantin des Odoards has

'a better opportunity of judging the fair sex of Vilna, of whose charms I'd formed a favourable opinion at the religious service. This time I was filled with quite another sort of admiration when I saw them animated by dancing, pleasure and patriotism and noticed how white and rounded were the objects rising and falling under the national colours during the gentle embraces of the waltz.'

Dedem, the ex-diplomat, says he'd often seen his colleagues neglect to take Napoleon at his word when he'd told them the plain truth about his intentions. So now. After dinner that evening he takes one of the delegates aside and tells him confidentially: "I see you aren't well off. I advise you not to compromise yourself vis-à-vis the Emperor of Russia. I may make peace with him at any moment."

On one of those days in Vilna Berthier presents the Line regiments' needs for new subalterns. As usual they're to be picked from among Guard NCOs. And little Coignet, much to his dismay, finds he's among the candidates:

'Since the Foot Chasseurs had left, all these promotions fell on us. We had to be in our places at two o'clock to be presented to the Emperor. At midday I was in the public square with my packet of letters under my arm, to distribute them. Taking me by the arm, Major Belcourt squeezed it hard and said: "Mon brave! Today you're going to be promoted lieutenant in the Line!" – "Thank you, but I don't want to go back to the Line." – "And I tell you today you'll be wearing a lieutenant's epaulette. If the Emperor sends you to the Line, I give you my word I'll bring you back into the Guard. So, don't answer back! Two o'clock, on the square, without fail!"'

And at two o'clock sharp they're there, all twenty-two of them

'all in one row. The Emperor arrives to review us. Beginning at the right, looking these handsome NCOs up and down from head to foot, he says: "These'll make fine regimental officers!" Coming to me, he sees I'm the smallest. The major says to him: "He's our instructor, and doesn't want to be sent to the Line." – "What's that? You don't want to go to the Line?" – "No, Sire. I want to stay in your Guard." -"Very well, then, I appoint you to my select staff." – How happy I was to be able to stay close to the Emperor!'

sighs Coignet. But adds: 'I didn't guess I was leaving paradise to fall into hell. That same evening my comrades shot my pack.' And next day, presenting himself for his new duties, he's

'graciously received by the general, whose face showed he loved old soldiers. "Well, so you'll be on duty close to the Emperor. If you don't mind, you'll do me the kindness of cutting off your long moustaches. The Emperor doesn't like moustaches at his headquarters. So you'll have to sacrifice them."'

For a few hours Coignet, stripped of his sergeant's stripes and his moustache, feels 'like a demoted NCO' – a loss made up for that evening by a large sabre, an officer's fore-and-aft hat and a gold epaulette from the quartermaster's store. All these new accoutrements have been paid for personally by General Monthyon, who even offers him a horse from his own stable. As it happens some soldiers of the Train – remarkably in view of the present acute dearth of horsepower – have already made him a present of 'a fine horse, together with its saddle and portmanteau'. Thus equipped, he presents himself for his first task as a commissioned officer. It will be extremely exacting.

Even as late as 14 July IHQ is still in the dark as to Barclay's plans. The Russian commander has four options. Either (a) to withdraw northwards and defend Petersburg; in which case Napoleon will attack him with an overpowering concentration, consisting of Murat's cavalry, Oudinot's II, Ney's III, Eugène's IV, St-Cyr's VI Corps and the Imperial Guard. Or (b) he can shut himself up in the Drissa Camp – in which case the invaders' vastly superior forces will quite simply outflank it and take him from the rear. Or again (c) he can stand and fight on the River Dwina near the little town of Kamen. Or lastly, (d) he can try to make junction with Bagration by retiring on to the important city of Witebsk.

Whichever of these courses Barclay opts for, Glubokoïe, a small town 90 miles east of Vilna on the Witebsk road, 24 miles due south of the Drissa Camp, commands a central position. And already on 7 July the Guard has been ordered to leave for there. For its three-day march it's to carry on its backs 90,000 bread rations, sufficient for ten days.

'The bridging equipment, the engineer units, the artillery, and everyone who leaves must take with them half-rations for six days, and three-quarters of a pound or a pound of meat per man.'

Four more days' bread rations,

'loaded on the headquarters auxiliary vehicles, must be assured by two convoys leaving on 11 and 12 July and on those vehicles replacing the 2nd, 9th, 10th and 11th Battalions and on such others as may yet arrive, so that during 10 and 11 July 11,000 quintals of flour shall have followed the Guard, which makes 360,000 bread rations or ten days of victuals assured for the Guard and headquarters; which, added to the ten days' rations the Guard will carry, will make bread for ten days.'

Whoever else is going to go hungry, the Guard isn't:

'If the army doesn't march, other convoys will arrive. If it does, it'll find resources in the towns. But I cannot be tranquil until the Guard and headquarters have 20 days' rations assured, since the Guard, marching last, should set an example of discipline. In this account the biscuits and brandy, etc., contained in the headquarters' 40 wagons should not be included, these being a last resource.'

(How the Guard, marching last, can set an example isn't clear.)

All these preparations have been made and all these orders given when, on 14 July, some mortifying news comes in. An entire cavalry brigade of General Sébastiani's advance guard, commanded by General St-Gèniez, has been surprised, driven into a swamp and forced to surrender. This is distressing enough. But does it portend a Russian counter-offensive? Immediately Napoleon decides to advance his headquarters to Glubokoïe.

Before he can leave Vilna, however, two appointments must be made. Lithuania must have a governor; and so must Vilna. To the first post he has already appointed a Dutch general *Dirk van Hogendorp*. A stiff and stuffy but in his own eyes irreproachable officer whom Napoleon had honoured by making him his ADC but 'laughed at because I hadn't even asked for the Cross of the Legion of Honour,' but whom he esteemed, Hogendorp claims, because he'd flouted his orders to burn down a Prussian town, is already on his way to take up his duties. For the second post, as military governor of Vilna, Napoleon selects a man of completely different, not to say incompatible, character.

If Napoleon had needed a chief-of-staff with ideas of his own, the Swiss General Jomini, author of *The Grand Operations of Warfare*, the greatest military work of the age, would have been his man. But he has no such need.[8] And in the end an exasperated Jomini, aware of his own status as the recognized theorist *par excellence* of modern warfare, had begun to listen to siren tones from Petersburg, steadily upping his price until the secret negotiations, which Napoleon of course had known about all along, had fallen through; or rather, at the critical moment, had been scotched, on the one hand by threats against which Jomini's status as a Swiss citizen availed nothing, on the other by giving him a post at IHQ – as official historian of the forthcoming campaign. So far, however, his only task has been to police the Niemen bridges.

But now, on the eve of the Emperor's departure, he's invited to dinner. Also present are two members of the Polish delegation:

"How many leagues is it from Vilna to Moscow, M. Vibicki?" Napoleon asks, by way of making table talk. And before the other can answer: "Two hundred and fifty, I believe? Hardly forty days' march of six leagues apiece!"

"Oh certainly, Your Majesty can easily be in Moscow in forty days!"

"You see how easy it is to skip distances by movements on maps! I prefer to take two years. If the Russian gentlemen fancy I'm going to run after them they're mistaken. We'll go as far as to Smolensk, and enter into cantonments on the Dwina. I'll resume my headquarters here, send for the Théâtre Français, and finish the job off next spring. Isn't that wise, *Monsieur le tacticien?*"

"Very wise," Jomini (says he) replied. "But even wiser to make peace without going any further."

"Ah, that's quite another matter!"

Dinner over, Napoleon takes him aside and says: "Any amount of guns and wagons are being left here. I'm expecting convoys of oxen from Hungary and Galicia. You'll manufacture as many yokes as are needed. From Danzig and Kovno you'll bring up convoys of flour, which can only get here by the Vilia. You'll construct the necessary barges. The town must be defended against any surprise assault, so you'll dig such trenches around it as are requisite.'

Jomini is also to rope in all the stragglers, victual the reserve corps, organize hospitals, bury several thousand dead horses, and, in general, teach the Lithuanians their new duties. It'll be for Hogendorp and his colleague General *Roch Godart* to raise a Lithuanian army. Nor is this all.

Next day Jomini is dismayed to receive a 16-page memorandum, listing a host of other tasks.

Napoleon, true to his divide-and-rule tactics, couldn't have chosen two more mutually antipathetic fellow-governors.

How had that ignominious surrender of an entire cavalry brigade come about? Captain Zalusky of the Polish Guard Lancers – he who'd so narrowly escaped drowning at Kovno – has virtually foreseen it.

It is Napoleon's habit on the eve of an important departure to send out his light travelling carriages

'in various directions, partly because he didn't really know where he'd make contact with the Russians, and partly to deceive his enemies as to his real intentions'.

And it's with one of these *calèches* Zalusky, with his 1st Squadron of the Polish Guard Lancers, has been sent ahead to Murat's headquarters at a place called Belmont. During their three-day march they talk en route to an intelligent Russian prisoner,

'an elderly NCO from Docturov's corps. When we asked him why they were abandoning so many towns and terrain without standing and fighting, he, neither frightened nor boastful, replied that their plan was to draw us as far as they could into the interior, where we'd gradually grow weaker: and then surround us and stifle us.[9] However, our fatuity and limitless confidence in Napoleon's genius made light of these auguries. We could have been asked to conquer the moon, and we'd have responded with "Forward, march!"'

And just now Zalusky is anyway less interested in the campaign's outcome than in what may be happening – with the Russians only a couple of miles away – on one of his mother's estates at Druï, on the Dwina. Belmont turns out to be a palatial residence owned by an Italian, who's much more concerned for his herd of prize cattle than for the Polish pennons surrounding his house. Zalusky seeks permission to visit Montbrun and Sébastiani near Druï; and gets it, on condition that he bring back some provisions for his squadron 'and notably for its officer corps', who are 'suffering from a complete dearth of everything'. Reaching Druï with a corporal and four lancers, he's just in time to participate in a scuffle with some Cossacks, in which 'Sébastiani, with the impetuosity typical of the French generals, personally fought among the Uminski Hussars'. Then the Cossacks withdraw to the other side of the river. Behind the Dominican monastery 'which had done so much good in the town,' Zalusky goes on,

'there was an island in the Dvina which could facilitate any attack from that quarter. It was a spot which called for great vigilance. I was afraid the French cavalry's advance guard, made up of two chasseur regiments under General St-Gèniez – who also commanded the Uminski Regiment – might be attacked on this side. Next day I left, feeling dissatisfied – a feeling which grew considerably when, arriving at Sébastiani's headquarters, I found him clad only in his shirt, resting on a camp-bed in the middle of a room in an inn, under a tent of green cloth, rubbing his shins! Stupefied at this sight, I began to fear seriously for his advance guards, and for him personally.'

Despite his military dash, Sébastiani, a relative of the Bonapartes, is more diplomat than soldier. Dedem describes him as

'intelligent, of a rare impudence and immorality. Though short of stature, he had a pleasant appearance and knew how to insinuate himself and captivate others.'

After General Wathier de St-Alphonse's dismissal for his inertia outside Vilna, command of his advance guard has fallen on General St-Gèniez. When Sébastiani asks Zalusky what he's seen, he replies:

'"a corps of 40,000 men with numerous artillery whose guns one could count gleaming in the sunshine, all commanded by Wittgenstein!" At this name he exclaimed: "Wittgenstein's a bungler who doesn't know his job!" More and more I began to fear such vain self-assurance would be punished."[10]

At lunch Zalusky is no less dazzled by his host's table silver than by his knowledge of Polish affairs. Sent back to Murat with an account of the state of affairs at Druï, he's received by the King of Naples, who in a long tête-à-tête, extols the Polish ladies' charms, saying he's bored with the throne of Naples and would much prefer to command 100,000 Polish cavalrymen. Finally Zalusky, 'enchanted to have discovered a candidate for the Polish crown, but absolutely sceptical about the pretender's political worth', withdraws. And next day, sure enough, comes

'the nastiest news – viz. that the Russian general Kulmiew had crossed the Dwina with 5,000 cavalry and infantry, and having thrown a bridge over the island without being seen, had fallen on Colonel Uminski's advance guard, crushed it, rounded on St-Gèniez' brigade and taken it prisoner – a defeat the more painful for its being our first, and for a French general being captured in it.'

But Barclay has served notice that his withdrawal won't lack teeth.

CHAPTER 7

WITH THE ADVANCING COLUMNS

Barclay's options – a swift leap – how to make 700 deserters march – 'God, what a scene!' – Jerome quits – 'we felt our hearts beating faster' – Major Rossetti seizes his chance – a tragic execution – the long road to Glubokoïë – a solitary adjutant-major – Italians in distress – marauding and pillaging – an intellectual commander – 'Tell General Jomini' – 'He gave himself over to the greatest gaiety'

At 11 p.m. on 18 July the imperial cortège, preceded at a regulation 50 paces by twelve light cavalry troopers and followed by the four escort squadrons,[1] rolls out of the town gate and at a brisk eighteen miles per hour sets off down the Sventsiany road. Napoleon's own carriage is

'a very simple yellow coupé, in which he could shut himself up as in a berline. There was a mattress to sleep on, paper, pens, ink, a little travelling library and a nécessaire; numerous drawers offered all the resources of a house on wheels.'

Flanked by ADCs and ordnance officers riding at its doors, it's preceded by Caulaincourt's carriage and followed by two more, for Berthier and the interpreter Hyde d'Ideville, and a servant, with a spyglass on a thong and a leather case holding writing materials and a pair of compasses. After these four vehicles comes a lighter 'calèche which served to transport the Emperor from one army corps to another, or to cover in a few hours a road for which the troops needed a whole day'. A 'brigade' of thirteen saddle-horses brings up the rear. Relays of the same strength have been placed out by Caulaincourt's office at 10 to 15-mile intervals. Since all the rest of headquarters staff have either, like Fézensac, gone on ahead or will follow after, 'the Emperor made this leap very quickly. He took with him only a very small number of officers.'

At about midnight, travelling on through the light summer night, the party comes on a bivouac at a crossroads. In command and all alone except for a single drummer-boy *Sous-lieutenant* Coignet is already regretting his sergeant's stripes. His column, which all day has been marching to tap of drum, consists of 700 Spanish deserters from Dedem's brigade.[2] After they'd been inspected by Napoleon in a compound at Vilna, they'd trekked out eastwards:

'Soon we found ourselves engulfed by forests. Leaving my place at the head of the battalion I'd placed my little musician on the right, to mark step, and gone to the rear to make all the stragglers follow on. At nightfall I'd seen my deserters slipping away into the forest, and could do nothing to bring them back. It's too dark. It's enough to make one chew one's horse's reins with mortification! What to do with such soldiers? I tell myself: "The whole lot are going to desert!"'

But now, after only two hours, the head of his reluctant column has halted at this crossroads, in open country:

'By the time the rear turned up, the camp fires had already been lit. Judge my surprise. "What are you fellows doing here? Why aren't you marching?" – "We've marched far enough, we need to rest and eat." The fires were made up, and the pots had been put on. At midnight, here's the Emperor passing, with his escort. Seeing my bivouac all lit up, he orders a halt and calls me over to the door of his carriage. "What are you doing here?" – "But, Majesty, it's not I who am giving the orders, it's them. I've been bringing up the rear, and found the head of the battalion encamped with their fires alight. Lots of my deserters have already gone back to Vilna. What can I do, alone, with seven hundred stragglers?" – "Do what you can, I'll give orders to have them arrested."'

The escort drives on, leaving Coignet in ever-deepening trouble. At dawn he has

'the fall-in beaten; and at daybreak away we go. I tell them the Emperor's going to have all deserters arrested. I march until midday. Emerging from the forest, I see a herd of cows grazing in a meadow. And there are my soldiers going off with their panikins to milk the cows! What can I do but wait? Again and again they find some cows, and we have to stop. That evening they again camp before nightfall. Not much fun for me! At last I reach some woods, very remote from any towns. Away to my right I see a forest fire is spreading, and I catch sight of my troops making off into the burnt woods. I gallop off to compel them to come back to the road. Judge my surprise when I see these soldiers about-face and firing at me! I'm forced to let go my grip. These soldiers of Joseph Napoleon were in a plot. There were 133 of them. Not one Frenchman had mingled with these brigands. Back at my detachment, I form them up in a circle around me, and tell them: "I shall be obliged to make my report. Be Frenchmen, and follow me! I've had enough of bringing up the rear. That's your business. By the right, march!"'

Apparently many of them obey; because by evening Coignet reaches a village where some cavalry are guarding a fork in the road, to direct passing troops. And he makes his report to its colonel, who orders the battalion to camp:

'On the basis of the directions I give him he summons his Jews and an interpreter. Guessing my deserters' whereabouts, he sends off 50 mounted chasseurs, with Jews to guide them. Half-way there, they meet with some oppressed peasants seeking help. Getting there at midnight, they surround the village and surprise the Spaniards in their sleep. Seize them. Disarm them. Throw their muskets into a cart. The men, too, are put into little carts, with a strong escort. At 8 a.m. the 133 Spaniards arrive and have their hobbles removed. Lining them up in a single rank, the colonel tells them: "You've behaved badly, I'm going to form you up in squads. Are there any sergeants or corporals among you, to form your units?" And here are two sergeants, showing their stripes, hidden under their greatcoats. "Stand over there. Any corporals?" – Three corporals make themselves known. "Stand over there! No more? Good! Now, you others draw lots." Anyone who drew a white ticket was put on one side, and anyone who drew a black one on the other. When they'd all done it, he tells them: "You've stolen. You've set fire to property. You've fired on your officers. The law condemns you to death. You shall suffer your sentence... I could have you all shot; I spare half of you. Let it be a lesson to the others. Commander, load your battalion's firearms! My adjutant will give the order to fire." We shot sixty-five of them. God, what a scene! Distraught at heart, I set off at once. But the Jews were content.'

Before leaving Vilna Napoleon has written to Bessières that if the supposed Russian counter-offensive should develop, his intention is
'to move against the enemy from all sides. If, on my arrival at Sventsiany tomorrow, I discover it's been a false alarm, I shall resume the move to Glubokoië.'
Evidently it is. For after reaching Sventsiany at 10 a.m. on 19 July and spending the day there, he reaches his destination at 1 or 2 p.m. next day. Dominated by a huge Carthusian monastery where general headquarters has already installed itself, Glubokoië turns out to be quite an exceptionally big town, whose 'closely huddled timber houses, twelve to fifteen feet high but looking like primitive huts', spread out for half a mile in all directions. Opinions about the surroundings differ – in Caulaincourt's eyes it's 'a stretch of very beautiful countryside', which Fezensac, for his part finds to be 'of sad and savage appearance'. While Dr Réné Bourgeois feels he's 'in Lapland'.

Entering the Carthusian monastery – or possibly he's already heard about it en route – Napoleon gets a second piece of news, even more mortifying than the loss of St-Géniez's brigade. While still hoping to trap Bagration he has secretly instructed Davout, on making junction with Jerome, to take over his three corps, thus uniting the army's right wing. But Davout isn't the most tactful of men at the best of times, and hasn't waited so long. When Jerome had appeared on the scene he'd informed him by despatch from Minsk that he was now his superior. For Jerome, who hadn't wanted any part in this war anyway, this had been the last straw.[1] After being reprimanded for not achieving the impossible he, the King of Westphalia, is to subordinate himself to a mere prince! Without even confiding his orders to his chief-of-staff, General Maison, he has quite simply gone off home to Cassel, taking his white-uniformed Royal Westphalian Guard with him.

Napoleon, all eye-witnesses agree, has a singular faculty of being able to control himself in difficult situations. And all he says is: 'What a silly prank!' After which, Fain notices, 'the Emperor shut up this grievance in his heart and said no more about it'. Even so he can't wholly contain his annoyance. And Davout is sharply reprimanded for disclosing his secret orders 'before the two armies were on the field of battle and would have needed a single commander'.

Or perhaps it's a bit of good news from another quarter that has soothed his irritation? For the last two years several thousand Russians have been busy throwing up an immense system of earthworks on the Dwina, the so-called Drissa Camp. Consisting of three concentric galleries, defended by a 36-foot deep trench, its 600 guns ensconced behind a 360-foot glacis were to command a murderous field of fire whose sandy terrain had been cleared of every tree, shrub and bush for 3,000 yards in all directions. It's in this formidable earthwork fortress that, if the Tsar's Prussian adviser's plan is followed, Barclay's retiring First West Army is to shut itself up and be besieged by Napoleon, who will, if all goes well, passively sit down and let himself be assailed in the rear by Bagration – and annihilated.

On the eve of Napoleon's departure from Vilna (17 July) the van of Montbrun's cavalry corps had approached the Drissa Camp's fortifications in the most gingerly fashion. Dr von Roos and many of his comrades in the the 3rd Württemberg Chasseurs had

'felt our hearts beating quicker as we came nearer. The great redoubt, which was of an unusual height, was provided with numerous gunports. The closer we came, the deeper became the silence. Not the least clink of arms was heard. The men didn't cough. The horses didn't neigh. Expecting at each instant to be received by cannonfire, we continued our soundless approach.'

But then, suddenly, the silence is broken by

'formidable bursts of laughter. In the gigantic redoubt there was neither a man nor a gun left! Its sole occupant was a little peasant, whom we'd first taken for a sentry. He'd been taking a stroll along the top.'

There must have been some poor communications between Murat's headquarters and Montbrun's; for on the previous day one of Murat's Neapolitan staff officers had already discovered that the camp had been abandoned. Sent there under a white flag of truce, 'ostensibly with 200 louis for General St-Gèniez, captured on the 15th', Major *Marie-Joseph Rossetti*'s

'true instructions had been to observe what enemy forces were entrenched in the Drissa Camp. General Sébastiani had given me a select escort of twelve hussars and ordered St-Gèniez's brother, who was also his ADC, to accompany me with the general's carriage and servants. One hour before midnight I'd come within musket shot of the entrance to the camp, preceded by a trumpeter who every three minutes sounded calls announcing a bearer of a flag of truce. But what was my surprise to find the camp abandoned and all the fortifications stripped of their guns!'

Rossetti had entered one of the redoubts, notified Sébastiani, and drawn up a plan 'of these works which had cost such enormous sums and two years' labour'. Although his immediate trumpetings had gone unanswered, next day, farther along the river, he's courteously received by the Russian General Bagawout who invites him to lunch and gives his hussars any amount of victuals – no doubt to impress on them how well supplied the Russian army is compared with the French. St-Gèniez's carriage is shipped to him across the river. And now Murat has sent Rossetti to take the news to Napoleon, who at first

'seemed not to believe me. But having read the King of Naples' despatches and found in them the sketches I'd made of this camp, he couldn't contain himself for joy. Pacing quickly to and fro, he said to the Prince of Neuchâtel: "You see! The Russians don't know how to make either war or peace! They give up their 'palladium' without firing a shot! Come along! One more real effort on our part and my brother will repent of having taken my enemies' advice. – Well, Monsieur le Napolitain, come back in two hours and I'll have despatches for you to take to your King."'

But Rossetti, who isn't a Neapolitan for nothing, replies:

'"Sire, ever since I've been in the service I've always fought in the French ranks and for France, and I'll never exchange my title of Frenchman for that of Neapolitan or of any other nation." The Emperor replied: "That's good, and that's how I see the matter." And turning to the Prince of Neuchâtel: "Appoint him colonel. Make a note of it."'[4]

Not everyone is so fortunate. For at least one good-natured man the Drissa Camp has been the ignominious end of life's long road. If the fortifications had been abandoned, the more remote approaches had been hotly contested. For the 7th Light the affair had been a

'general, hot and protracted affair. In front of the scene of the fighting was a rich chapel, attached to a big abbey two leagues further on. On the hillock crowned by this chapel the Russians had placed a battery, which was captured after a fierce resistance. In the course of this action the chapel was sacked. As soon as we were masters of the position, companies were placed to safeguard it, in conformity with the Emperor's severe orders on the point.'

No doubt impressed by his unfortunate experiences in Spain, Ney carries out his orders to the letter. 'To rid themselves of the stolen objects,' Carabinier-sergeant Bertrand goes on,

'those who'd committed this impious sacrilege had turned to a chasseur in my regiment. Known as the rag-and-bone man, he made a habit of buying and selling. All regiments had such men, so-called Jews. This chasseur had been my bedmate. He was good-natured, willing, loved and esteemed by us all. But the poor fellow had been weak enough to buy two sacred vessels off these looters. The marshal having received some complaints, he orders our regiment's packs to be searched. The four battalions are at once formed up in open ranks, arms and packs lying open on the ground. In each company one of its three officers inspects one rank. My poor comrade is revealed as at very least a receiver of stolen goods. We're ordered to take up our packs, pick up our arms, and close ranks. The battalions form square. The unfortunate chasseur is brought out, judged, condemned to death, and shot by the men of his own company. The whole affair didn't last an hour.'

Before setting out again, Bertrand and his heart-broken comrades hardly have time

'to dig a ditch at the foot of a big oak, where the old soldier from Iéna, Eylau, Friedland and Wagram, who'd only a moment ago still been fighting bravely, slept his last sleep. A victim of military duty, his cries of despair went on ringing a long time in my ears. We left this place of sorrow and mourning and marched for Witebsk.'

IHQ's saddle-horses may have made the 90 miles from Svenziany to Glubokoië 'in eighteen hours without one of them falling sick'. The Old Guard, carrying on its backs 90,000 bread rations and 'three-quarters of a pound or a pound of meat per man' and followed by 11,000 quintals of flour, have taken three; and the Young Guard – those who've got so far – five. Many don't reach Glubokoië at all. Overtaking it en route, Fézensac had been particularly grieved to see the dust-caked green-uniformed corpses of the Regiment of Flankers, 'made up of very young men', littering the roadside:

'Since leaving St-Denis this regiment had only enjoyed one day's rest at Mayence, and one at Marienwerder on the Vistula. Even on those days when they marched, they were still being drilled when they got to their destination, the Emperor having found them insufficiently trained. Thus this regiment was the first to be destroyed.'

Although no less young, the 5th Tirailleurs of the Young Guard seem to be doing somewhat better, perhaps because of the stern care being taken of them by their colonel. As they march day after day across 'the feeble undulations of Russia's verdant terrain, the long avenues of immense silver birches, that graceful tree of the North with its lightsome foliage' Lieutenant Paul de Bourgoing hears his mostly beardless conscripts

'going through the whole repertoire of songs which the soldiers and officers could remember. Each nation made its contribution. A song only had to be sung once or twice for it to soon be known by the whole group. Usually one or two verses were sung solo and then repeated in unison by the rest of the column. In our unit songs from Languedoc, Provence, or Picardy alternated with those from Paris, Piedmont or other parts of the Empire. In our ranks we had Frenchmen from Genoa, Amsterdam, Mainz and Erfurt; so we sang in every language and dialect. Here's one specially composed for our unit. I give only the chorus:

Les tirailleurs sans souci,
Où sont-ils...? Les voici.
Où sont-ils...? Les voici.

Repeated in unison after being sung by the best tenor in the leading company, this question, posed in a strong voice by the best singer and answered twice far down the battalion's long column, had a gaiety all its own.'

Yet even in the Tirailleurs the mood is far from 'carefree':

'In our young soldiers the solitudes of Russia, their monotony, produced a deep sadness, having all the qualities of homesickness; and several cases of suicide occurred in our new regiments. Yet the weather was fine, we were at the height of summer. In these latitudes and at this season the days last until half-past eleven in the evening or until midnight, and it's impossible to say whether one owes this veiled but persistant light, reigning over the countryside, to dawn or sunset.'

Unfortunately, since Paul de Bourgoing speaks German and a smattering of Polish, Colonel Hennequin, 'a man of iron authority who only laughed when he was burning himself up, otherwise irreproachable and of uncontested merit, but also of an inflexibility recalling the heads of Ancient Rome's legions', has appointed him regimental adjutant-major – 'an officer attached to no company, and who has neither captain nor soldier under him'. As such, Bourgoing is finding he's keenly missing

'the mutual assistance, the solidarity of the bivouac, the daily convivialities of simple wartime meals, where each man contributes his ration of victuals and in nearby copses helps cut the silver birch or pine branches which, put together to form a shelter, cover the earth we're to rest on'.

Although each evening as the Young Guard halts 'the roofs of interlaced branches' are forming 'a straight line as far as the eye could see and enlivening the scene when the fires were lit', Bourgoing can only turn sadly to his colonel. But Colonel Baron Hennequin is,

'giving much more thought to what orders he should give me than to my 20-year-old appetite. Returning from missions made on foot so as to save my horse a double day's work, I often found the fire out and the supper eaten.'

Not that his little Parisian street urchin Victor isn't doing his utmost to feed his lieutenant:

'One evening, a few days' march from Vilna, all he can find upon my return from my round of the outposts at 11 p.m. is two fistfuls of dried peas, gathered with great difficulty. He'd had to climb up one of those big wooden walls or latticeworks, 30 foot high, which the Polish and Lithuanian peasants erect behind their barns to dry their winter vegetables on. I recommend to no one my supper menu of July 16, 1812.'

But officer and servant share the peas.

IV Corps' wretched Italians are in even worse case. Smarting no doubt from his rebuke for the day 'ridiculously' lost at the Niemen, the normally stolid Eugène is forcing the pace as he moves up from Novo-Troki to plug the gap left by Davout's march on Minsk. Having divided IV corps into two columns, he himself is leading the first towards Ochmiana at so fast a trot that 'the horses of the Queen's Dragoons escorting him kept falling one by one'. The other, consisting of Pino's 15th Division which at Glogau, in May, had consisted of 'more than 13,000 men, so accustomed to warfare that General Pino, though captain-in-chief of the Royal Guard, thought it an honour to command them' – is

'having to protect its artillery on a very bad road rendered impracticable by the passage of cavalry. Overtaken by darkness and the least movement being extremely dangerous, it's had to remain all night in this bog. Add to all this a horrible gale and rain coming down in bucketsful,'

and at dawn Pino has to turn back, his guide having utterly lost his way. All day, in broiling heat, Pino's division 'wanders about for ages'. And when, after 'crossing immense forests without finding food or water, and making interminable detours', it at last, after forty-eight hours, rejoins the other column, Césare de Laugier shudders to think what's to become of

'its sick, the soldiers exhausted by dysentery and those who've strayed from their units and who, despite all Pino's, his generals' and his subalterns' precautions, it's had to leave behind'.

In these dire predicaments *Albrecht Adam*, a painter of battle scenes who started out in life as a cakemaker and has accompanied Eugène's staff to Russia in search of them, is beginning to lose heart. Even so, riding through 'a long dense wood' he can't help smiling to see how

'out of sheer exhaustion many riders fell asleep on horseback and kept banging their heads against trees, so that helmets fell off, or were only held on lopsidedly by the chinstraps. A few troopers slithered to the ground,'

a ridiculous contretemps that Césare de Laugier is too proud of his regiment's superb Grecian-style helmets even to mention. But, the ex-cake-maker goes on remorselessly,

'the Italian Guardia d'Onore, with their exceptionally tall helmets, fared particularly ill. The weary horses often stumbled and fell. Whole columns of hundreds of these poor beasts were in the most pitiful state; with sores on their withers or backs, stopped up with tow and discharging a stream of pus, they had to be led by the bridle. Having lost weight until their ribs stood out, they looked a very picture of abject misery.' 'Two whole months on the march,' he'll write to his wife three days later, 'and to what purpose? It distresses me to have to waste God-given time so wretchedly. War – a terrible word. It means no regard for the well-being or destruction of whole nations, and woe betide anyone who makes this termagent's acquaintance and has a heart that still beats for humanity!'

In all the advancing columns of men, horses, wagons, carriages, artillery parks and guns, relations between the French and their so-called allies have already become unendurably strained. None of the dangers and hardships is so irksome to an anonymous artillery lieutenant in III Corps as the serious daily quarrels that keep breaking out:

> 'If anything broke on a wagon or a gun, or if an exhausted horse had to be unharnessed, the vehicle, cut off by the troops coming on behind, very likely couldn't rejoin its battery until evening. The French infantry were so unpleasant and brutal that more often than not their officers, to prevent some unfortunate godforsaken gun from even travelling near – let alone ahead of – them would order bayonets to be levelled at its lead-horses, and strike the men of the Train – behaviour that aroused our intense hatred and bitterest resentment. Again and again our battery, after spending half a day with utmost difficulty following the brigade along appalling tracks, had to turn back and search for the road being followed by the infantry. Yet when we got to it no one would let us into the column, and we had to try and secure ourselves a tiny place on the road either by dint of asking pleasantly, but sometimes with oaths and insults, and often at sword-point. As I was the only French-speaking officer it always fell to me to conduct these wrangles.'

Few of the villages along the way can boast even twenty cottages, and only rarely do these even stand beside the main roads. On the other hand there's usually an inn -

> 'but what an inn! All it offers is small beer, bad brandy, and a kind of dough they call bread. These houses resemble their occupants – distressingly dirty! They're run exclusively by Jews, who do everything – are innkeepers, merchants, tailors, cobblers, almost every profession.'

A despised blessing, for the Lithuanian Jews are the only people in this godforsaken country the troops, or at any rate their officers, can converse with, either in Low German or a smattering of Latin. Almost always they've got something to sell to a famished soldier. Particularly in demand are the little rough-haired Polish ponies known as *konyas*, which are even being used to help pull the artillery. Paixhans sees how impossible a task it is for them alone: 'Twelve such little horses produce no more effect when harnessed up to the shaft of a heavy wagon than two teams of six on a light vehicle. Yet we'd still enough big horses to harness them up last.' Heinrich von Brandt is shocked to see

> 'these unfortunate little animals being wasted in their thousands. Knowing what a hard life they were used to, we exacted a lot of work from them, yet took no care of them at all. They perished in masses and were then replaced. Some drew the artillery, foodstuffs, baggage, etc. All the stragglers rode on them and dragged them along with them. Without them it's certain we could never have marched at all.'

When the poor little beasts are exhausted, his men just unharness them and leave them

'standing or lying there. Then the cannon and wagons rolled over them and their steaming guts got entangled in the wheels. No one cared – what with human beings hardly being treated any better.'

But by no means everything is being paid for or obtained under official forms. On the contrary, everyone is grabbing anything he can lay his hands on, not only from the peasants and the manor-houses along the way, but also from other units. One day Pion des Loches' company of Guard artillery finds its few remaining provisions have been stolen out of its wagon by some Bavarians – and next day itself promptly pillages a manor-house. Vital to each unit's survival is the

'mounted rabble or – to give it its proper name – robber band which was swarming around it, to left and right, in front and in the rear, using as its base the regiment as it marched in good order along the highroad. All carried large and small haversacks and bottles to hide their plunder in, and were armed with swords, pistols, even carbines. Roaming far and boldly on the flank, if ever they got back again they brought supplies for the troops. The work was dangerous, and many lost their lives – in agony, if they fell into the clutches of the infuriated peasants.'

On the other hand, they are providing the advancing columns with a kind of flank patrol, 'because if ever they bumped into enemy detachments they came flying back in a hurry, uttering loud cries'.

Obviously absurd though it is to forbid starving men to pillage, many are being shot for doing so. Three or four days out of Vilna, Dr von Roos sees

'a division of cuirassiers formed up in square. In the middle four soldiers were digging up the earth. We were told a court-martial had condemned them to death for flouting orders. They were going to be shot; but first had to dig their own graves. Had these four unfortunates known what they were missing out on',

he'll reflect afterwards, 'they might have counted themselves lucky.'

Between individual pillage and organized marauding there lies, namely, a fine but crucial distinction. All units except the Imperial Guard trudging along under its supplies of flour and biscuit, are sending out detachments to relieve the locals of their 'superfluous' grain, horses and cattle. Always commanded by an officer – 'the most intelligent ones', Roeder adds – their prime objectives are the manor-houses, where

'you find more or less everything needed for man as a social being, even a library and politeness. It's the nobleman who in his house has everything needed for keeping body and soul together.'

Many of these lie at a considerable distance from the five or six-mile front spanned by each corps as it advances. Usually their proprietors have fled, leaving them under the authority of a steward who may speak French, or again, may not. After being relieved of its 'superfluous' assets, each such estate is provided with a 'safeguard', a signed document exempting it from further contributions, and a picket to enforce it. One day Lance-corporal *Wilhelm Heinemann*[5] is being wined and dined by a Russian landlord and his party of Brunswick Chasseurs are busy rummaging about upstairs when suddenly a footman enters:

'Pale as a corpse, he said some words in Russian to his master, words I didn't understand. The count, too, blenched. Jumping up, he begged me in French to be a good fellow and stop my comrades doing whatever it was they were up to. Though of no use to them, it would be a catastrophe for himself.'

Coming across a lead-lined trunk in the count's bedroom, the voltigeurs have opened it with an axe.

'Inside, it was divided up into numerous compartments, in each of which were little bits of shiny paper oddly printed in all colours, red, white, blue, yellow, green. So elegant and neat were their colours they seemed to be a lot of playthings.'

It's the count's entire cash fortune the Brunswickers have taken for playing cards and are helping themselves to the prettiest, offering Heinemann several fistfuls. His host assures him they're coupons he has to issue against deliveries of goods within his administrative district – 'worthless to the soldiers but vital to himself'. But Heinemann has already seen paper currency in Austria,[6] and smiles at this fib, replying in French – which his men don't understand – 'Least of all these 500-rouble notes!' Upon his convincing them that the 'toys' really are worthless, of one them flings a bundle of white banknotes 'worth at least 50,000 roubles' back into the chest. And the count, overjoyed, is only too happy to accept his apologies for all the cartloads of farm produce he's being obliged to requisition; entertains him to the best his house can produce; and they part as friends for life. 'Where life has so little value, money has even less; and I didn't have the heart to take my part of this rich booty.'

One day *Thomas Legler*, too, an officer in the 1st Swiss Regiment, marching eastwards with II Corps after Wittgenstein, is ordered, like two other lieutenants, to go out marauding. Each is allocated a sergeant, a corporal, and twelve grenadiers. But... how proceed in such totally unknown countryside? Perhaps it's best to follow in the tracks of the French? On the other hand they'll have no use for estates which have already been given safeguards. After much discussion the three Swiss lieutenants decide to go off in different directions. And soon Legler's party sight a manor-house:

'The baron who owned it was in the drawing-room, surrounded by his servants. Addressing him in French, I gave him to understand I needed food. He replied, also in French, assuring me that the French had already taken all he owned.'

Really? Legler, sceptical, orders his men to ransack the house. 'This threat led to us being given a little bread and boiled meat with schnapps. Meanwhile my grenadiers had found twelve sacks of grain in the barn.' Even this won't go very far for the hungry 1st Swiss. Seizing the manor's cook as a guide, Legler forces the baron to tell him the whereabouts of the nearest manor. Tying the cook's hands with a rope's end, Legler tells his men, in loud clear French, that if he isn't back by 6 p.m., they're to put a bullet through the baron. 'These words, uttered in a tone of command, brought out beads of sweat on the baron's forehead. Running over to his cook, he spoke to him at length – probably begging him to make sure we got back safely!' At first the cook had tried to run away. But now he calms down,

> 'assuring the baron he hoped we'd be back, fully pleased and contented. This order of mine may strike the reader as inhuman. But he should consider my situation. I didn't know where the enemy was, or whether I'd even be able to find my way back to our camp. But I secretly told the sergeant to let the baron go free as soon as we were out of sight.'

After an hour and a quarter of 'following side roads and long stretches of forest where we didn't meet a soul', the guide brings them to the next manor. 'In several spots we saw horses and horned cattle and on our way the grenadiers captured a well-grown horse.' Approaching this second manor with all due caution, Legler enters and interrogates its proprietor as to the Russian army's whereabouts. This second 'baron' is so 'very amiable and accommodating' as to station four lookouts, throw open all his doors, give the Swiss some bread, brandy and dinner, and

> 'made his servants help us pack and load: with the result that by about 3 o'clock I'd already 20 one-horse carts fully laden with foodstuffs. On my showing him my horse lacked a saddle, he immediately provided it with an English saddle and harness.'

Even dinner is served. Legler advises his host to hide his valuables in a place of safety,

> 'for soon the French would be there, and they wouldn't be content merely with food. Handing him back his silver spoons and forks, I advised him to hide them away as quickly as possible. We Swiss desired nothing but food. At first the good baron wants to make me a present of his table silver; but when he sees I set no value on it he pats my shoulder and says: "honest fellow!"'

Just as Legler is about to leave, one of his grenadiers comes running, shouting: 'The French are coming!' Quite right. Here's a chasseur officer, with four troopers:

> 'Seeing my neatly laden carts, he gives a start. And more particularly takes a fancy to my saddled horse. "That belongs to us, and so do all those oats you've got there!" says one of his chasseurs, trying to grab the horse. But the grenadier holding it threatens to shoot him down.'

On the French officer threatening to report him, Legler tells him to go to the devil – or if he doesn't like it, he can get down off his horse and they'll settle the matter between them. 'But it went no further than French sabre-rattling. And suddenly the Frenchman and his four chasseurs dashed off, followed by Swiss curses.'[7]

Alas, this has only been the beginning of the poor landowner's misfortunes:

'Hardly has the last cart gone forty paces from the manor-house than we catch sight of a strong detachment of French light infantry approaching it. A quarter of an hour later, thick smoke billows up behind us, out of which we soon see flames rising. It seemed very likely the French, embittered at finding nothing to seize, had set fire to it – a revenge often taken by troops reaching a farm that had already been plundered.'

On their way back Legler's party come across other units, driving a lot of cattle before them. 'In the woods, chance brought into my hands first a few, then more, then finally 60 head of cattle; and I didn't hesitate to drive them in front of us.' At dusk Legler is back at camp. But what about the other two detachments? All – except one grenadier – have been captured by the Russians. 'I thanked God for my good luck in escaping.' Bread, butter, cheese, ham, brandy, honey and salt Legler has aplenty – 'brandy and flour for several days for the rank and file, and corn and oats for the regiment's horses. This,' he concludes, 'was the first and last time I went out on a marauding expedition.'

Disputes over such booty can be furious. Upon Pino's division turning up at Veleika at the same time as a French one, and finding the biscuit stores which had been captured by the Red Lancers,

'the French, being the first comers, have possessed themselves of them. We Italians, arriving at their heels, lay claim to our share. We've shared the sufferings, are dying of hunger, and have equal rights. The general makes representations to that effect to Prince Eugène.'

But the Viceroy just shrugs his shoulders and says it's a case of first-come-first-served. Isn't possession nine points of the law? Pino, who has several officers with him, waxes eloquent about his division's urgent needs. But all Eugène says is:

"Well, gentlemen, you can f—— off! You're asking for something impossible. And if you don't like it you can go back to Italy. I don't give a damn for you. Let me tell you I'm no more afraid of your swords than I am of your stilettos!"

Hitherto, Laugier goes on indignantly,

'the Italians' affection for the Viceroy had never been in question. His youth, the care he was taking of the rank and file, his status as the Emperor's adoptive son, all had contributed to making him loved. But this injurious phrase, escaping him in a moment of anger, keenly wounded our Italian hearts.'[8]

The delegation is just leaving the château when they see thick smoke coming from it. It's on fire, and already partly in ashes. The Royal Guard comes running and at the orders of the very officers who'd just been told to f— off make every effort to demolish everything adjacent to the Viceroy's quarters. But this only leads to another altercation between the Viceroy and General Pino, who says 'with utmost firmness: "Very well, since Your Highness won't render the Italians the justice they deserve, I'll get it from the Emperor." And lays his sword on Eugène's table. Which forces him to try to calm him. 'Today,' the Guardia d'Onore's adjutant-major notes, 'for the first time, Italy has been reminded that Prince Eugène isn't an Italian.' And by now even he's beginning to feel despondent:

'All these factors are contributing to deprive a unit of the brio of its first days. From day to day it becomes steadily more exhausted, dwindles away. The state of weakness it finds itself reduced to inevitably diminishes the numbers of the detachments sent out to look for victuals. And so there we are! Out of the need to survive, out of humanity, out of compassion, out of sheer necessity, we have to tolerate these regrettable pillagings we'd so like to prevent. And off the men go. Sometimes they come back. At others, not. When they do, it's little they bring back with them. The bivouacs, the fastings, the forced marches are thinning our files. Numerous soldiers who possess a deep and inflexible sense of honour prefer to die of inanition rather than support a life which has become horrible to them. Though up to now they've carried their packs and their arms with an imperturbable fortitude and truly heroic firmness, they fall exhausted, measure their length on the ground. Alas! few dare linger behind to succour them. Nor have they the means to do so, and the fear of getting lost in these immense solitudes, coupled with our fear of vengeful peasants, prevails over the compassion we feel for them.'[9]

When the Bavarian infantry of General *Gouvion St-Cyr*'s VI Corps had arrived at Vilna it had been in such splendid trim, and his cavalry so impressive that, despite his protests, Napoleon had hived off the cavalry to strengthen IV Corps. As for the infantry, it had been given only twelve rations of bad bread per man for eight days' marching; and now, as it turns up at Glubokoïe it's in such an appalling state that Napoleon refuses even to review it. 'I was reprimanded', writes St-Cyr,

'for not making my troops march fast enough. In Napoleon's eyes fatigue, sicknesses and lack of victuals weren't legitimate excuses for a delay of a few hours, even though when VI Corps had left each bivouac the manor-houses had immediately been turned into hospitals and each day it had left behind the equivalent of a battalion.'[10]

St-Cyr is an intellectual and a convinced republican who has never fallen under the imperial spell. And Napoleon, who has a genius for coping with anyone who can be cajoled, flattered, intimidated, fooled or bribed, is apt to be suspicious, not to say caustic, towards men of independent judgement and principles. Which is why this is St-Cyr's first high command. But whether Napoleon now feels he has gone too far, or because he wishes to to exert his charms and genius upon him, the imperial reprimand is followed by the usual gesture of conciliation. At their interview he

'wore an air of putting on a great deal of spontaneity, and passed in review most of the various French generals, living or dead, who'd gained reputations in the revolutionary wars'.

And not only them, 'but also his marshals' – i.e., St-Cyr's superiors,

'distributing praise or blame. The art of war, he said, was of all arts the hardest. A general needed intelligence; but what was rarer, great character. He'd sent Marmont into Spain. "He has plenty of intelligence, I still can't gauge his draught, but I'll soon be able to judge, for today he's on his own.""[11]

If Napoleon possessed the art of fascinating everyone, says Caulaincourt,

'it was because he'd already fascinated himself. In small matters as well as great, he spared no pains to gain his ends. One could say he gave himself wholly over to them. Always he developed all possible means, all his faculties, and all his attention, and directed them to whatever matter was just then in hand. Never was there a man more fascinating when he chose to be!'

In his youth, St-Cyr had been an actor, and if there's one thing he detests and can see through it's theatricality. This makes him perhaps of all the Grand Army's corps commanders the one who's just now best able to weigh up its commander-in-chief:

'He disclosed his plan of campaign, and gave all his excellent reasons for it. It was dictated by foresight and genius. By following it, all past errors could still easily be corrected.'[12]

After his reprimand St-Cyr has been feeling gloomy. But now, either flattered or genuinely impressed – or both – he feels his hopes rising again.[12] And indeed, whether it's because he's beginning to feel he hasn't quite got the situation under control or for some other reason, the Emperor is dealing out reprimands left and right. Even Lariboisière, his old mess-mate from college days, gets his share:

"His Majesty is being told there are 600 wagons at Vilna, 40,000 artillery rounds, and a great quantity of infantry cartridges, so there is no need to transport ammunition to Vilna. We are going to have a battle which will consume an enormous quantity of ammunition. The Emperor asks what is to be done to replace them. Should empty artillery wagons be sent back to Vilna? In that case, at least a month or six weeks will be needed for them to rejoin. All possible means must be used to bring the biggest quantity of infantry and artillery ammunition wagons up to the army."

In the same way, Grouchy, instead of being congratulated when his cavalry corps, in the van of Davout's army, manages to grab huge stores of flour at the important town of Orsha, is curtly asked why he hasn't sent the flour to Glubokoïe "where the centre is assembling and where we're in direst need?"

Nor is it the moment for Jomini's lucid expositions – which are reaching Napoleon almost daily – of why he can't do all the things he's been told to. And on the eve of leaving Berthier is ordered:

"Inform Geneneral Jomini it's absurd his saying there's no bread when he receives 500 quintals of flour every day; that instead of complaining, he should get up at four every morning and go in person to the mill and commissariat and see to it that 30,000 bread rations are prepared; and that he'll achieve nothing by merely sleeping and moaning. Tell him the Emperor himself, busy though he is, visits the commissariat every day; that I don't see why he criticizes the Lithuanian government for having put all the prisoners into a single regiment; that this kind of thing indicates a critical spirit which can only harm the development of events, whereas he should be encouraging the government and helping it. Write to General Jomini to have all the muskets in the hospitals collected, and that in this way he'll find some that can be used."

Even on 22 July Napoleon is still uncertain of Barclay's movements. Is he withdrawing toward Polotsk or Witebsk? But that day he and St-Cyr are at supper when some crucial information comes in. Gleaned from a Polish deserter, it shows clearly that it's Witebsk – on the Moscow road.

'Having calculated he'd be able to catch up with Barclay, he gave himself over to the greatest gaiety. Even though the French army no longer enjoyed the numerical superiority it had enjoyed at the Niemen, he believed he could bring him to a battle, which, if it occurred, would be greatly to our advantage.'

One of Oudinot's ADCs happening just then to be at Glubokoïë, Berthier is told to send him back with orders for II Corps to move toward Sebeje, thus forcing Wittgenstein to cover the Petersburg road and place still greater distance between himself and Barclay:

"Since Wittgenstein hasn't even 10,000 infantry, the Duke of Reggio can march straight at him. We're marching on Witebsk. Tell him to sweep the right bank of the Dwina and push back Wittgenstein at the sword's point. Even so, he should leave a small garrison at Polotsk in case he [Wittgenstein] throws himself to the left. When I get to Witebsk I'll direct a corps to the Newel, which will communicate with him."

Having dictated these orders, Napoleon climbs into his carriage and – at long last – sets out for the front.

CHAPTER 8

FIRST CLASHES

Polotsk – how Murat wasted the cavalry – putrid hay bundles – the most dangerous moment – an extraordinary costume – 'they never say anything to me!' – Napoleon wounds Italian sensibilities – psychological warfare – d'Hautpoul's orders – two ladies get wet – chaos at Beschenkowiczi – von Muraldt reconnoitres in only one boot

Sick at heart at the thought of the moment, if it ever comes, when he'll get back to Toulouse and have to tell the rag-and-bone man's parents of their son's ignominious end, Sergeant Bertrand has marched with III Corps, not for Witebsk, but for Polotsk. 'At least Polotsk looks like a city,' he sighs into his diary on 24 July, seeing its green onion spires slowly come up the horizon. 'It boasts seven or eight church towers and two big monasteries.'[1] Chasseur Lieutenant *Maurice Tascher*,[2] a nephew of ex-empress Josephine, serving in Montbrun's corps, calls it less enthusiastically 'a town sprung up in the heart of a village'. Lying astride the Petersburg and Riga roads, Polotsk is destined to become the pivot of II Corps' operations.

Murat's cavalry, leading this advance, is wasting away at an alarming rate. Already only three-quarters of the troopers who'd crossed the Niemen are still with the colours. Of the light cavalry, only half. And everyone is agreeing that this is due, not to enemy action as such, but to its disgraceful mismanagement. 'The King of Naples', a nameless officer of the 16th Chasseurs writes home,

'is personally very brave, but has few military talents. He knows very well how to use cavalry in front of the enemy, but is ignorant of the art of preserving it. At high noon the horses are dropping from weariness and want.'

The chief cause of the cavalry's destruction,' Victor Dupuy agrees, is

'the scant care taken of it. Having fought all day, we were made to bivouack in windmills, on high arid ground, bare of all resources. Only with the greatest difficulty did we manage to obtain some bad forage.' – 'We marched all day. We made hourly – often two-hourly – halts, during which we could have refreshed some of the horses. But no. Strict orders not to unbridle. Death struck. We had to bivouack in the middle of forests, without making sure whether there was any forage or water nearby. Next day we had to march and fight as if we'd lacked for nothing.'

For all the light cavalry regiments the first glimmer of dawn is the most dangerous moment:

'In the French army the outposts were habitually under arms one hour before sunrise. This was called 'doing the dawn'.[3] Usually we assembled without any signal. It all took place in a deathly silence.

Then the infantry rested under arms and the cavalry remained dismounted, holding our horses by their bridles. In this fashion we waited, sometimes for three or four hours on end, for any detachments sent out on patrol or reconnaissance to come in. If we weren't to leave we went back to our bivouac, feeling safe. One of the squadrons unsaddled to rub down its horses. Each of the others followed suit, turn and turn about. Thus the horses were perpetually saddled up and laden day and night, the men always dressed and armed, ready to fight at any instant.'

All, no doubt, a model of military efficiency and in the ordinary way of things Dumonceau would have approved. But persisted in day after day, week after week, it's proving disastrous. Each morning it's the light cavalry, joined by Murat in person, that opens the march, the hussar and chasseur regiments being followed by the dragoons and lancers, escorting the cuirassiers.

Day after day the Russian rearguard carries out the same manoeuvre. By pretending to make a stand, it lures Murat into mounting a full-scale attack – and then melts away into the forests. Towards midday the heat becomes intolerable; and the chasseurs and hussars,

'seeing the Russians dismount, unbridle their horses and give them something to eat. Yet General St- Germain kept us standing in battle array, bridle on arm, at our horses' heads.'

Old St-Germain, commanding 11th Heavy Cavalry Division, is

'a swordsman who owed his promotion to his bravery and dash. On entering Russia, he'd ordered that each trooper should make up an 8 to 12-lb truss of hay, well twisted and uniformly rolled, and set it on top of his mantle strapped to his portmanteau, with the wallet of food and oats, thus raising the load behind our backs to shoulder level. Constantly exposed to rain, sun and dust, the hay ended up by being not merely inedible, but got heavier and heavier and more and more unhealthy.'

Finally Thirion's colonel lets him go and speak to the other two colonels. Wouldn't they, too, like to get rid of their rotten trusses?

'Being ADC to the Emperor, Colonel Doudenarde of the 3rd Cuirassiers, a man of most imperious character, didn't give a damn for General St-Germain, and hastened to accept. As for Colonel Murra of the 9th, he'd never have taken such an initiative himself. But backed up by his two colleagues, he too consents. Returning to my regiment, I give the order to chuck away the bales. A hurrah of joy goes up from all down the line. In a jiffy the bundles are untwisted, scattered to the wind. When the division mounts, the general flies into a terrible rage. But what's done is done! And the crude words that made up General St-Germain's vocabulary went the same way as the putrid hay.'

Each night, Thirion goes on,

'the light cavalry ahead of us bivouacked on a line parallel to ours, with 50 men on outpost duty. We, behind them, had 150. And yet our scouts were placed, pistol in hand, only 100 metres from the first line! Protected as we were by the eight light cavalry regiments ahead of us, we'd no need to fear a surprise attack. A simple colour-guard to the regiment's right, near the colonel's bivouac, would have sufficed. Those 150 horses had carried their riders on their backs all day and on the morrow would have to set out on another 12-hour march.'

Without a drop of water to drink and only an occasional nibble of wayside grasses, they arrive at the next bivouac utterly spent, collapse, and have to be shot by their riders, who, adding horsemeat to a soup of uncut rye, promptly go down with diarrhoea, an affliction not conducive to brilliant exploits on horseback. The 22-year-old Prussian Lieutenant *Count von Wedel* is seeing how 'a hundred Cossacks who knew the district and its least track could, without danger to themselves, put the wind up an entire army corps'. Certainly they know how exploit Murat's mania for chasing them. 'I can still see that marvellous officer's outlandish costume,' Karl von Suckow of the Württembergers will write long afterwards:

'On his long black curly hair he wore a Renaissance-style hat, adorned with large white plumes waving in the wind and held in place by a diamond clasp. Around his bare neck an antique Spanish-style ruff over a sort of light-blue velvet tunic, all bedecked with gold embroidery and held in tight at the waist by a silk sash of the same colour as the tunic and tipped at both ends with gold fringes. White worsted breeches in huge deerskin boots of the kind fashionable during the Thirty Years War, with massive gold spurs.'

On one memorable occasion Dr von Roos, too, sees him wearing 'a red Spanish cloak. On others a green one, with boots à la hongroise, sometimes red, sometimes green, sometimes yellow'. But everyone, not least the retreating enemy, admires him:

'Herculean in strength, excessively gallant, admirably cool in the midst of danger, his daring, his elegant costume inspired an extraordinary veneration among the Cossacks.'

One day Victor Dupuy witnesses

'their almost magical respect for him. There was a swamp we had to cross, and my general had ordered me to go and reconnoitre a path through it. I was riding ahead with three troopers when I saw the King of Naples at the far end of a little wood, looking out over a narrow stretch of flat ground in front of the swamp. He was all alone. In front of him, on the other side of the flat ground, some 40 mounted Cossacks were gazing at him, leaning on their lances. Seeing us emerge from the wood, they make a move. Taking it for an attack, I shout to my men: "Hussars! Cover the King!" No sooner have we taken up our positions in front of him than the Cossacks fire several shots, one of which strikes my horse's leg. Noticing this, the King says to me, laughing: "Serves you right! What have you come here for? They never say anything to me!'"

Nor is it only the cavalry that's suffering from Murat's precipitate leadership.'If Murat didn't spare the cavalry, he spared the infantry even less.' Dedem's infantry brigade is one of those that have been detached from I Corps to support Murat, and thirty days of a campaign conducted in this headlong fashion, he realizes, have already 'cost the French and Allied cavalry more horses than ten pitched battles'. With the result that Friant's crack division, too, has dwindled to a mere two-thirds of its original strength and the commander of its 1st Infantry Brigade is bitterly regretting being separated from Davout'.

On 23 July the Italians, farther to the south, reach the village of Botscheikovo on the Oula, 'a river joined to the Berezina by the Lepel Canal and linking the Dnieper with the Dwina, the Baltic with the Mediterranean.' They are resting up 'in an immense field of rye' and the Viceroy is deep in a long discussion with his chief-of-staff General Dessoles when suddenly Napoleon's imminent arrival is announced. Instantly the order is given to don parade uniforms. And the word goes round: 'The Emperor's coming!' It's the first time IV Corps has seen him. At once everyone is all agog, and Césare de Laugier, no less excited, snatches a moment to jot down in his diary:

'The Emperor's going to reconnoitre the army's advanced positions, here, at exactly this spot where we're its advance guard! At this news, here's the entire camp in a turmoil! Officers and men, we hurriedly strip ourselves of our marching clothes, to don our finest uniforms. Everyone wallops, brushes, launders, polishes. Valises and trunks are brought into the middle of our camp. Linen and clothes are hung up to air. The comings and goings of those who're loading and unloading the vehicles, the songs, the laughter, the jokes flying to and fro – all throw our camp into a gay mood, an explosion of the gaiety natural to us Italians which lends the countryside a festive air it's never worn before and very likely never will again. In the twinkling of an eye our dusty route-coats have been replaced by clean uniforms, opulently smothered in gold and silk.'

And now here he is:

'The Emperor arrives. The troops, ranked in battle order, present to the eye a scene of utmost brilliance. But what does he do? Cross the post-road in his carriage; get out of it near the bridge, where he listens to some reports; goes and visits some positions; gives some orders; and then leaves again, to rejoin the Imperial Guard at Kamen! What a disappointment! In a vile humour we strip ourselves of our beautiful uniforms; and slowly, without a word, put on our tattered marching clothes again.'

'This man, for whom we've come so far,' the adjutant-major goes on bitterly, 'for whom we have been willing to shed our blood, and on whose account we've already put up with such fatigues, didn't even deign to throw us a glance. Curiosity at least, we tell ourselves, should have impelled him to glance at his subjects, his faithful allies, and speak to them. What has he to reproach us with? A glance, a word, a smile of complaisance costs so little! Men are so easily contented. The masses so effortlessly enchained! Instead – *"Niente, niente, niente!"* – that's what I'm hearing said all around me as, feeling melancholy, I've come back to my bivouac.'

The incident is perhaps too painful for Albrecht Adam's artistic soul. For he skips it. Altogether the ex-cakemaker is becoming disenchanted with 'this senseless war' which so far hasn't even yielded him any battle-scenes.

As for the Russians, they're literally leaving neither horse nor straggler behind them. But one day, they leave something else instead. Leaflets. Picking one up, Césare de Laugier reads:

'Italian soldiers! You're being forced to march to a new war. They're trying to convince you it's because the Russians don't set a proper value on your valour. No, comrades, we appreciate it, as you'll soon see on a day of battle. But reflect! One army will succeed to another. You're 1,200 miles from your reinforcements. Don't let yourselves be deceived by our first movements! You know us Russians too well to believe we're running away. We'll accept battle; and your retreat will be difficult. We say to you, as between comrades: "go home en masse" . Place no faith in perfidious words that you're fighting for peace. No, you're fighting for the insatiable ambition of a sovereign who simply doesn't want peace, and who makes a sport of spilling his brave men's blood. Go home to your own country; or while waiting to do so accept if you prefer it asylum in Russia, where you'll forget the very words "conscription", "levée", "the *ban*" and "the *arrière ban*"[6] and the whole of this military tyranny which never for a moment lets you evade its yoke.'

'This document', comments Eugène's always critical staff captain Labaume, 'contained such great truths that everyone was amazed it was allowed to spread.' The Guardia d'Onore, at least, is unable to grasp them. And gets busy penning ripostes,[7] which 'the least corporal is furnishing himself with before setting out for an outpost or reconnaissance, so as to pass it over to the Russian outposts'. Napoleon, too, feels such a riposte is in order. When one such leaflet is brought to him he comments: 'My brother Alexander stops at nothing!' And under the pseudonymn 'A Letter from a Grenadier' dictates a reply, to be printed in the Paris newspapers.

Instead of standing and fighting near the little town of Kamen, on the Dwina, as Napoleon has been expecting him to, Barclay is now seen to be retiring along the river's southern bank. So orders are given for the army to cross it at the small town of Beschenkowiczi.[8] And next day, after a five-hour march, the Army of Italy, still in the van, gets there to find Bruyère's and St-Germain's cavalry divisions already on the river bank. They're having trouble with some Russian sharpshooters, ensconced on the far bank, beyond the burnt bridge, while in the plain beyond some Russian cavalry are manoeuvring.

This is the first time the Italians have seen the enemy. And to protect the sappers who are to throw new bridges two guns are immediately brought to bear. 'Some sailors of the Royal Guard swim across to fetch the ferry and drive the Russians out of houses on the opposite shore.' This forces the Russians to evacuate Beschenkowiczi and 'leave us in peace to work on the bridges'.

Meanwhile, 200 yards further downstream, General Preyssing's Bavarian light cavalry (seconded to IV Corps at Vilna) have found a ford. Labaume thinks the Bavarians' 'way of marching, the precision of their drill and the sagacity of their scouting' exemplary. Troop after troop is taking the plunge, swimming the river and scrambling up the steep sandy bank opposite, Eugène sits his horse and directs the operation – all as in Adam's print. In the distance we see the Bavarians making for Beschenkowiczi's little timber houses, on the skyline. All doubtless as it was in reality. Or was it? In fact the

'tumult and confusion can hardly be conceived. Imagine, after a month of separation, all the various army corps arriving on the same day and at virtually the same hour! The infantry are levelling their bayonets at the guns, shouting and threatening to cut the artillery and cavalry wagons' traces. Drivers and troopers are cramming themselves together, refusing to let anyone through. The officers are finding it hard to prevent the men from coming to blows. The men, at their wits' end, are complaining of the staff's lack of foresight, which they see as the cause of all this indescribable muddle.'

The Italian sappers have just constructed their first bridge between 'the Dwina's high and steep banks' when, at 2 p.m., Napoleon turns up – and 'in a very dry tone of voice' criticizes its construction, 'which in truth was very defective'. As for the Emperor's and 'his staff's great activity' Albrecht Adam keeps finding his eye returns to

'a striking individual wearing a light-blue coat trimmed all over with gold braid, red trousers edged with gold, a strange hat lavishly decked with plumes. I couldn't make him out. What struck me most was that he'd so much business near the Emperor, who, like the whole of his suite, was on foot. In the end I asked an officer who was standing beside me: "Maybe you can solve an enigma. How come the Emperor has so much to do with that drum major?" Surprised, the officer looked at me and said: "What do you mean?" I explained. "My God!" he exclaimed, "but that's Murat, the King of Naples!"'

Labaume sees Napoleon, 'determined to cross over to the other side', traverse the rickety bridge on foot, mount his horse, and join the Bavarians who've halted there in the plain. Or is it an optical illusion? With the rest of IV Corps' four Bavarian chasseur regiments Lieutenant *Albrecht von Muraldt* has had to 'swim the river to cover him on this reconnaissance', and he sees Napoleon, Berthier and Murat cross in a little boat,

'to be sure of the enemy's strength there. At a loss of two men carried away by the current and drowned, we reached the other shore. After we'd drawn up in line of battle, the Emperor himself put himself at our head and personally led the reconnaissance.'

Alas, von Muraldt hasn't reckoned with the imperial tempo. Having pulled off a boot to void it of the Dwina's water, he's only wearing the other:

'The signal "Mount!" was sounded, and despite my most desperate efforts it had been more than I could do to pull my wet boot on again. So I'd had to get into the saddle with a boot on one foot but none on the other. Everyone laughed at me, which didn't improve matters. At a quick trot or canter the Emperor rode with us for two hours, but without coming upon the enemy. After which we returned to Beschenkowiczi. I was ordered to stay at the outposts, and because of the enemy's supposed proximity not dismount all night, nor light any fire. You can imagine what a long night that was for me!'

Not until he gets back to his regiment next morning will he get his 'damned boot' on again. But some Bavarian troopers, wounded by enemy fire when crossing the river, have fared much worse. IHQ having installed itself in the town's little houses, General Preyssing sends von Muraldt to its military governor to request billets for them. The governor, a French general of brigade, receives him politely in a ground-floor room where a 'tall man in a buttoned-up blue greatcoat was sitting writing' in one corner. At that moment a French general appears on horseback in the open doorway, accompanied by his two ADCs and an orderly officer. Not even bothering to dismount, he begins cursing and swearing and complaining that his lodgings aren't worthy of a 'lieutenant-general attached to General Headquarters. I demand you instantly find me something else!' Polite as ever, the commandant points out that, what with lodgings being needed for the Emperor and all the headquarters staff, there's very little choice.

'The man doesn't accept this sensible reply, but starts insulting the governor, who's standing there in the doorway. Suddenly the tall man gets up from his writing-table, pushes the governor aside, and in a voice of thunder roars up at the raging general: "If you aren't satisfied, you can f— off! D'you think we've nothing better to do than listen to your f—ing complaints?" The man on horseback only had to set eyes on the tall man to whip off his hat, bend his back in an equestrian bow, and stammer out an apology. But the tall man just tells him to go to the devil and returns to his writing-table.'

Muraldt, who has 'watched this scene open-mouthed', asks another officer who the tall man is. It's Caulaincourt. 'So I was no longer surprised at the raging general's suddenly obsequious behaviour.' But quarters are found for the Bavarian wounded; and by and by Captain Roeder and his Hessian Guards will turn up to look after them.

Nansouty's I Cavalry Corps have already crossed the Dwina farther downstream two days before, near Drissa, where the river is 'between 80 and 90 yards wide, its waters rushing between great boulders. Several attempts to bridge it were frustrated by its swift current and rocky bed.' Prince Henry of Württemberg's Hussars 'swam across in columns, but lost a fair number of riders and many more horses'. And when the turn had come for the 3rd Württemberg Chasseurs to cross, Dr von Roos had

'followed the procedure I'd recently grown used to. Accompanying the first squadron as it moved down to the river bank, I ordered two well-mounted NCOs to take me between them. They did so willingly; and into the water we went... and across. Swimming swiftly and easily, we soon reached the further bank. But from our heels up to our thighs, yes, even up to our ribs, we were as soaked as our horses. None of our men were drowned; but the next regiment didn't get over without loss.'

Safely on the other side, the Württembergers had lit their pipes, shared any brandy they'd left in their flasks, and lit their campfires:

'But the persistent rain didn't give us a chance to dry our clothes. Sorriest of all, we were, for two of the regiment's wives – the highly esteemed Frau Worth, who could always fend for herself, and the careful Frau Weiler. Sergeant-majors' wives both, they were riding little horses, so their clothes and baggage had sunk deeper than ours, and they'd no greater prospects of getting dry.'

CHAPTER 9

BATTLE AT OSTROWNO

Systematized flight of the population – IHQ hears gunfire – Murat doesn't wait for the infantry – 'we're wondering how it'll end' – an artist gets his battle – 'Murat, his wildness inflamed' – Thirion sits it out – the mortification of being overlooked -after the battle – a fatality of strategies

A splendid highway, flanked by double avenues of silver birches, leads from Beschenkowiczi to Witebsk across 'an immense plateau, full of swamps and quagmires. One only had to make a hole with one's foot or a spade to get water. The entire army was suffering severely from heat, lack of food, and bad water.'

Now the march order is Murat, Eugène, Ney, Davout's three detached infantry divisions under Lobau, and the Imperial Guard. Only at Beschenkowiczi does Napoleon tumble to a sinister fact which Caulaincourt and everyone else has 'noticed two days ago', namely that the population's wholesale flight is being organized by the Russian authorities. 'All the upper classes had fled, except the Jesuits.'

He has just finished dictating orders for Oudinot and St-Cyr[1] when there comes a rumble of distant gunfire:

'At this sound everything becomes animated. It's the first time since the campaign opened that IHQ finds itself in the vicinity of a combat. So the Russians have made up their minds to dispute Witebsk with us! We make haste to leave.' – 'All reports gave us to believe the enemy would stand and give a major battle in front of Witebsk. The regiments' ardour was extreme, and we all shared it.'

Like everyone else Fézensac is 'suffering severely from heat, lack of food and bad water'. Eugène's staff are just about to leave when an ADC arrives flat out from General Delzons, commander of 13th Division. With his usual impetuousness Murat, without waiting for Delzons' infantry to come up, has flung his light cavalry into some woods packed with Russian sharpshooters.

'The sound of the guns redoubling, His Highness at once ordered his headquarters baggage to halt, and, followed only by his principal officers, hastened on towards Ostrowno.'

Once again it's been the 8th Hussars who, together with the 9th Polish Lancers, have been suffering. Marching along the Witebsk road in column, they'd been approaching a rise in the ground which prevented them from seeing far ahead; and when they eventually saw the Russians massed in line 'with never a skirmisher out in front'[2] they'd taken them for friendly units. Sending an officer to liaise, they'd been shaken to see him cut down and taken prisoner. Whereupon the regiment, supposing itself to be supported on each side by other columns, which had in fact halted, has furiously charged the Russians ahead of them, and then to left and right, and finally returned with some prisoners, but also losses. All this Ségur hears about – since his brother's capture outside Vilna, he has doubtless been keeping in personal touch with his regiment. Surgeon Réné Bourgeois, arriving on the scene, sees

'a hussar of the 8th lying face down on the road, his cranium taken off by a roundshot. The general in command had come and said that if the enemy went on firing, they must charge the guns. The shots beginning again, his soldiers had left like lightning, and soon after had come back with eight guns and prisoners. By the time we were told of this, both sides of the road were already littered with wounded, either prisoners or French. We saw hussars, holding their horses' bridle in one hand and a pistol in the other, bringing back prisoners, making them run in front of them on foot. I dressed the more urgent cases.'

Lieutenant *von Kalckreuth* of the 2nd Prussian Hussars, too, has been in the thick of it:

'We were very close to the enemy and lost many men and horses from his artillery, which our regiment, too, had to attack. We managed to pass between the Russian guns, but a violent infantry fire from the nearby forest forced us to retire.'

Although in a second charge they'd 'sabred many of the gunners and tried to carry off the guns', the Prussians, not getting the support they'd counted on from the 7th French Hussars, had again had to retire with heavy losses to a position where they're being continuously fired on with grapeshot 'that thinned our ranks considerably'.

Meanwhile the heavy cavalry has drawn up in line behind the artillery, and in no time the fighting has developed into a full-scale engagement. Sergeant-major Thirion and his 2nd Cuirassiers find themselves in front of a Russian line

'bristling with guns. On our side we'd only two divisions of cavalry, led by King Murat. The road forms an elbow; and a few paces in front of it Bruyères' division deployed in line to the right of the road, with our division to its left and the road between us. The two were standing in line on a single front, parallel to the Russian one. Because of a wood the Russian army didn't stretch as far to the left as we did. So all the burden of the day fell on General Bruyères' light division and on ours, and above all on my regiment, whose right touched the road. The enemy had placed his batteries astride it, exactly facing us.'

When two French regiments are routed, together with the artillery supporting them, Piré's light cavalry division is flung in, and in its turn routs three similar Russian regiments. But by now Eugène's infantry divisions are arriving on the scene. Laugier sees his men are all on fire to

'measure ourselves against this hitherto invisible enemy. We can read contentment on all faces. And then – it's in our hearts to avenge the insult' when Eugène had spurned their stilettos. And in fact Delzons' leading division drives the Russians right back into the forest. Such is the beginning of a full-scale battle that will last two days. Only at nightfall do the heavily outnumbered Russians fall back on to their second position.

Next morning, advancing across the battlefield before entering the forests, von Kalckreuth's hussars use their sabres hastily to cover 'at least with a little earth' as many as possible of their comrades who'd fallen in yesterday's charges. In a clearing in the woods six more of them are killed and five wounded by grapeshot from Russian guns they can't even see. Although the Italians are in motion at 4 a.m., 'the sun already lighting up the field of yesterday's carnage', they've no time to bury '400 corpses, almost all Russian. Weapons, broken wheels, shattered ammunition wagons, helmets and haversacks litter the ground.' Their divisions follow on at one-hour intervals, and at 6 a.m. Eugène can inspect his light infantry battalions' outposts and study the Russians' new and 'formidable position' among trees and boulders, barring the road to Witebsk – where, it's being said, the Russians have assembled huge stores.

This second position, too, is covered by a ravine or hollow way. Its right rests on the Dwina's swampy shore and its left on dense forest. For a field of battle, it has a most peculiar feature. Down its middle runs a long strip of forest, thickly garrisoned with Russian sharpshooters. Behind this island of conifers, are more dense woods, out of whose depths the Russians can see without being seen.

Again IV Corps deploys. And Laugier jots down the Italians' battle array in his diary:

'The 8th Light in line facing the enemy, thus covering the formation of the Croat Regiment to the left of the road, behind which is the 84th in column of divisions. The battalions of the 92nd Regiment, preceded by the 3rd Italian Light Infantry, are in line by échelons on the other side of the road. The 106th forms the reserve, and the cavalry is disposed to support the movement. A light brigade crosses the Dwina to cover the left of our line. The artillery and cavalry are distributed along our front.'

Now his watch shows it's 10 o'clock:

'Here and there sharpshooters are opening fire. The Russian guns have been crossing our column as we've been forming up in our assigned places. The Royal Guard's artillery is ordered forward and begins firing at the Russian batteries; by drawing their fire makes it less dangerous for us to cross the open terrain to take up our battle positions.'

Whereafter the Italians launch a general attack; but are

'resisted with the greatest intrepidity. Wishing to envelop our left, the enemy general brings a strong body of cavalry out of the wood touching the Dwina. The King of Naples has it charged by a regiment of hussars, but these are beaten and thrown back. Whereon the viceroy orders General Huard, commanding the left of Delzons' division, composed of the Croat Regiment and the 84th, to advance. The first shock is to his advantage. He crosses the ravine and everything yields to his troops' impetuosity. On the right the battalions of the 3rd Light and the 92nd, who're to penetrate the forest, form up under the Russian fire.'

But the Russians bring up their reserves and Huard's brigade is routed by sheer weight of numbers:

'Almost immediately an extraordinary disturbance, an undulation in the masses, terrible shouts, attract all our eyes to our left. A division of cuirassiers, too exposed to fire, is retiring at a trot to give place to Broussier's division, which is going to Delzons' assistance. The earth trembles under the horses' weight.'

Though Césare de Laugier can no longer see exactly what's going on, he's alarmed to realize that the two wings seem out of touch! To steady his Guards at such a frightening moment, Eugène rides across their front, says he's relying on them today. Muskets and swords are waved. Shouts of 'Avanti la Guardia!' But still the Russians are coming on, and as they emerge from the forest to annihilate Delzons' division and seize its guns their shouts, too, can be heard. At this moment too the 'hitherto invisible' Russian sharpshooters emerge from their hiding-places. Everyone in the Guardia d'Onore 'is asking himself how this is going to end'. Impossible to bring the guns to bear without firing on Huard's routed brigade! The first line is falling back on the second, 'at grave risk of causing extreme confusion, an irreparable disorder, and of rendering resistance impossible. This state of affairs cannot last long.'

At such a moment Murat is supreme. 'Only a cavalry attack could be of any use.' Riding out in front of a line of red and white pennons which stretches from the Dwina's swamp on the right to the island of forest in the centre, he intends to harangue the Polish lancer division – but finds himself in a most awkward, not to say comical position. The Poles need no exhortation. With tremendous élan, like several thousand pig-stickers, they charge, driving the King of Naples like a wild boar before them. And Murat, unable to see or command, has no option but to 'lead' them:

'The brave Poles threw themselves on the Russian battalions. Not a man escaped. Not a prisoner was taken. Everything was killed, everything perished. Not even the forest could provide protection against the slashing sabres,'

he'll write that evening. Only thanks to his Herculean physique and the prowess of his gilded scimitar does he survive in the ensuing scrum. 'At the same moment', he goes on,

'the squares began moving up with seven-league boots. General Girard, who was leading the left-hand battalions, made a swing to the right, hastening down the highroad to fall on the enemy's rear. The troops to the right made the same movement. General Piré supported them, attacking the enemy at the head of the 8th Hussars.

This regiment was overthrown and only had the forest and hollow roads to thank for its salvation. The whole division followed the movement. The infantry advanced along the highroad. The cavalry rushed down from the higher ground. And I ordered the artillery to fire at the five or six regiments that were resisting us.'

Is it just then, or at some other moment, that Albrecht Adam sees

'the King of Naples at close quarters, his wildness inflamed by the fighting and opposition. He roared hither and thither, cursing and scolding, urging on his troops. Dashing to and fro, he seemed to fly, and his noble steed was all lathered. The noble Prince Eugène, displaying calm and prudence, presented a very strange contrast. Always he preserved his solemn, noble bearing.'

So, for that matter, does the intrepid war artist:

'My long-cherished desire to see a battle at close quarters and find myself involved in it was now at last being fulfilled. On this occasion I really heard the musketballs whine. Yet didn't let it distract me from drawing. During those two days I saw enough to provide me with material for a lifetime of painting battles! Although the Prince's officers and ADCs treated me amiably enough, before the action had commenced they hadn't been able to refrain from teasing me: "Just now our Adam is always hanging around. But once the bullets start flying we'll have to search for him!" When the first cannon-balls landed near us, an ADC, who looked rather pale, remarked: "Well, Monsieur Adam, how do you find this?" I replied rather tartly: "I find we're in a battle." Several hours later, when I was in a very tight spot, another well-intentioned officer came up and said this was no place for me, and I could go to the rear. I replied that I didn't value my own life more highly than the Prince's, and that if one wanted to paint battles one must have witnessed them.'

Such was the ex-cakemaker's baptism of fire which, true to his calling, he has been able to contemplate with true aesthetic detachment.

Sergeant-major Thirion, sitting his Turkish horse hour after hour in the scorching sun, has no such option. Roasted in his 16-pound steel cuirass (able to stop a musket ball at 45 paces but not a cannon-ball), tormented like everyone else by a burning thirst, he simply has to stay put while the Russian guns slowly decimate his regiment.

'We cuirassiers were an easy target. A few paces in front of me Commandant Dubois sat a white horse, and his position had caused him to be recognized as a superior officer.'

At one moment Murat makes the Prussian Black Lancers charge down the main road at two battalions of Russian artillery and infantry, in squares on either side of it; and from his high ground Thirion sees how

'this charge, made calmly at a trot, not proving successful, this cavalry retired as calmly as it had advanced. It was the first time I'd seen cavalry charge at that pace and come back from it without any shouting, any disorder. "By and by, cuirassiers!" shouted Murat, passing across our front, "Your turn will soon come!"

But it never does. For six solid hours the 2nd Cuirassiers, their lungs filled with the acrid smoke of battle, sit there in the blazing heat while the roundshot rips through and over them, a gleaming steely target for the Russian guns. Fortunately the Russian gunners tend to misjudge their trajectories and aim too high, so that – when it's all over – Thirion and his comrades are amazed to find only 187 of them have been killed. But of the 27 men in his own troop, only eleven have survived – and are counting themselves lucky to have done so.

Some units, perhaps many, are mortified to find their exploits have escaped official notice. To his left Thirion had seen the 7th Hussars make a brilliant charge against Russian infantry and cavalry, and only lose a few men in so doing.

'A short way away to our left', writes Dupuy, 'the 9th Polish Lancers pierced a square of Muscovite chasseurs and wiped it out.' To Thirion it had seemed

'these men had become fighting mad. How many didn't I see who, with arm or leg bandaged, returned to the scrum at a flat-out gallop, forcefully eluding those of their comrades who tried to hold them back.'

At the height of the action General Jacquinot had sent Dupuy to inform Bruyères of the 7th Hussars' exhilarating success. And on his way he'd paused a moment to tell General Bessières, once his colonel and now commanding the cuirassier brigade, all about it. Yet no one – absolutely no one – afterwards commends the 7th Hussars' brilliant charge! It's been omitted from all mention in favour of Piré's brigade, and General Jacquinot afterwards goes and complains bitterly to Murat. But all he gets for an answer is: 'My dear general, what do you expect? I don't know who's written this bulletin, nor how. But in truth I don't recognize myself in it.' Which is odd, seeing that it's based on his own report. 'This victory,' Surgeon Faure is thinking sadly,

'if that's what our success in so obstinate a fight can be called, was brilliant. But the surroundings offered no means of gathering its fruits. Ostrowno was a village of a few poor smoky houses. There was no one to pay these soldiers' courage the tribute of admiration they'd so well merited. Not even the smallest table could be laid where we could recount the day's exploits. After such actions one wants to absorb oneself wholly in one's experiences, and it's hard to think about anything less serious.'

Only next morning do he and his surgeons of I Cavalry Corps began their ministrations:

'There were still some dead on the road, but the greater number of those who'd been there had been flung into the ditches. Some trees had been damaged or cut down by roundshot. Off the road, where there'd been several cavalry charges, the greensward was churned up, and men were lying in every posture and mutilated in a variety of ways. Some had been burnt quite black by the explosion of an ammunition wagon. Others, who seemed dead, were still breathing. As we approached we heard them complaining. They lay on their back, their head sometimes resting on some comrade already dead for several hours, in a state of apathy, in a kind of sleep of pain they were loth to come out of, heeding no one around them. They asked for nothing, doubtless because they knew there was nothing to hope for; nor did they beg for the help already so many times refused. The Prussian lancers were walking about the places where they'd made charges, gloomily contemplating the remains of some hardly recognizable friends. In such a situation one accuses fate. The soldier is generous. He bears no grudge against whomever it is makes him fight, nor those he's fighting against. Here and there lay horses, broken harness, exploded ammunition wagons, twisted sabres, pistols, broken muskets. The ground was covered with débris. The brave hussars of the 8th lay in great numbers among the dead, having mingled their blood with the enemy's. A little further on we recognized the place where the Russians had attended to their wounded.'

Towards 3 p.m. Faure had seen 'the Emperor come and cast his master's eye on the scene. No emotion appeared on his face. His sensitivity had passed so many tests!' And in fact he'd played almost no part in the battle. No more, therefore, has Captain Zalusky, whose 1st Polish Lancer Squadron is one of the four (one from each Guard cavalry regiment) on escort duty,

'even though I was close to the Emperor, who examined the enemy's movements from a hillock. When the Russian cavalry appeared, we made a movement to protect the monarch if need should arise.'

In the upshot the Russians have left behind eight guns, several hundred prisoners and some 2,000 dead and wounded. Planat de la Faye, reaching the battlefield later next day, will study it for several hours, and be

'deeply pained to see some poor wounded Russians, exposed for the last three or four days to the sun's heat and the chill of the nights without help. Their misery and complaints made so much the greater impression on me as I'd learnt enough Russian in 1801 [his father had had business in Moscow] to know what they were begging for, but which I couldn't give them.'

Faure too is deeply worried. He and his fellow-surgeons are sending the wounded back to Beschenkowiczi. But what will become of them, with 'even the able-bodied hardly able to manage?' The Russians seemed to have suffered four times as much as the French. If so, Thirion thinks it's because, though the enemy had more guns, the French horse-gunners' fire had been more rapid and accurate. That morning, where his regiment had yesterday stood its ground so staunchly,

'two rows of dead horses marked the place it had occupied. As for our comrades who'd been killed, we buried them in the evening, each unit making it its duty to give burial to those of its men who had perished.'

And as the army marches on toward Witebsk surgeon Réné Faure sees 'the road covered with crests of enemy helmets'.

As soon as it was all over Albrecht Adam had got Eugène to sign some of his sketches – to prove he'd really been there.

CHAPTER 10

WHAT FEZENSAC HEARD ON MISSION

'We had to get hold of information as best we could' – a fatal game of billiards – a nervous Colbert smokes his meerschaum – 'Render unto Caesar...' – a most uncomfortable night – Le Roy commands Davout's advance guard – battle at Novo-Saltka – 'the Russians were walls which had to be demolished' – Davout steadies a regiment – forty ducats for a miniature – Girod de l'Ain is again passed over

What neither Barclay nor Napoleon know is that on 23 July Davout, at Novo-Salta, near Molihew, about 100 miles away to the south, has barred Bagration's attempt to break through northwards to effect liaison at Witebsk and that Bagration is now marching instead for Smolensk, 80 miles further east. Because of the very speed with which Napoleon has been driving a wedge between the two Russian armies, what had at best been a rhetorical idea – endless withdrawal and a war of attrition – is fast becoming a disastrous reality. Although Napoleon's communications with Davout are more direct than Barclay's with Bagration, his need for news of what is happening to I Corps is almost as urgent as Barclay's for news of the Second West Army. Who will make junction first?

At Beschenkowiczi Fézensac had shared the excitement at the sound of the guns. But he's not been at Ostrowno. He's on mission:

'On the morning of the 25th the Prince of Neuchâtel ordered me to follow the army's route as far as Molihew, where I should find the Prince of Ekhmühl. My instructions were to send back ordnance officers to inform the Emperor immediately of anything fresh I might learn. He was particularly concerned to know how the Prince of Ekhmühl was situated vis-à-vis Prince Bagration, and whether V and VIII corps were able to support him. At the first cannon shots announcing the King of Naples' attack I left. A Polish officer went with me to question the locals.'

En route Fézensac and his Pole stop off at Polish manor-houses,

'whose lords supplied us with horses. The country was quiet and no one had any news. That night we reached Kochanov, where General Grouchy was commanding a cavalry corps, whose advance guard was established at Orsha, under the orders of General Colbert.'

This is of course the Red Lancers. On 21 July two of their squadrons had been part of the pincer movement which had snatched the Russians' great flour stores at Orsha. 'Lying on the banks of the Dnieper – the Boristhenes of antiquity' – Orsha, the last major town in Lithuania, had reminded Dumonceau of Vilna and Kovno:

'It contained several big monasteries, was crossed by several broad streets, and in the centre, together with several others, was a vast market place, surrounded by a wooden balustrade painted in the Russian national colours, black, yellow and white. Here the Dnieper flows peacefully through a gorge at the end of the plateau. There was no bridge, only a ford, whence a sloping causeway on piers led straight up to the town, situated on the slopes of some high ground.' But now Colbert, having pushed on from Orsha, is feeling nervous. Already a reconnaissance party of another of Grouchy's light cavalry regiments, the 21st Chasseurs, has been 'rudely attacked by thousands of Cossacks and driven back with lances at their backs, with a loss of 200 men'. And he realizes his own regiment is out on a limb. If he should be attacked in force, Grouchy's cavalry corps is too far to his rear to come to his aid. As for his Dutchmen, they're altogether too phlegmatic, too little on the *qui vive.*

Quite right. That day Dumounceau, who is duty captain, he has posted out one of his two lieutenants, Baron van Zuylen van Nijevekt, in the direction of Babinowiczi, 'which lies on the edge of a lake, on the far side of a stream, in a plain fringed by the vast forest of the same name'. He has taken care to place Van Zuylen's outposts in an 'advantageous position amid bushes, where he could scan the plain, the woods, and the highroad leading eastwards in the direction of Witebsk'. And all would perhaps have been well if Dumonceau, in this jittery situation, had stayed with his lieutenant. But 'after the return of his dawn patrols' van Zuylen, to get food and forage from the inhabitants and 'lulled by the assurances they lavished upon us' retires with some of his men to an inn at Babinowisky, for a game of billiards with his fellow-lieutenant Wichel. 'His troop under arms, horses still saddled up and bridled,' and ready to rush out at the least alert, he has just laid aside his sabre, when a lancer, 'flat out and his horse white with foam', comes dashing back along the road. A brigade of Uhlans of the Russian Imperial Guard, 'probably forewarned by the locals as to our detachment's habits and dispositions', has captured all but four of his men! In the same instant the Uhlans come galloping into town and surround the inn.

Grabbing up their carbines, Van Nijevekt and his men defend themselves by firing down from the inn's dormer windows. Had any help been near to hand, this should have sufficed to keep the Uhlans at bay. But there isn't. And his whole troop has to surrender.[1]

After this nasty incident Colbert has promptly withdrawn his regiment to a safer position west of Orsha – with orders that the duty squadron be changed every two hours during the night:

'At about midnight I, in my turn, was on my way to relieve the squadron posted out on the plateau, and passed the general's and his staff's bivouac – a long shelter, open in front, lit up by a big fire some distance from its centre. There I saw all our numerous staff lying stretched out on straw, deeply asleep, while the general alone kept watch, sitting in his stable-litter, peaceably smoking his meerschaum, and giving an example of vigilance.'

Next morning Fézensac turns up. And no doubt Colbert tells him about the contretemps, if only because he has since learnt that the Uhlans had been commanded by no lesser a personage than the Tsar's brother, Grand Duke Constantine.[2] It had been while probing for Bagration along the Smolensk-Orsha road that they'd bumped into Dumonceau's outposts.

What conclusion does Fézensac draw from this? Certainly that on 24 July Barclay had still been in the dark as to Bagration's whereabouts; was perhaps unaware that he'd been fended off by Davout at Novo-Salta[3] and is therefore unable to come to Barclay's assistance in front of Witebsk.

By and by Grouchy comes up to Colbert's support. His 'three divisions, seven to eight thousand men', are followed next day by VIII Corps, 'all Westphalians, arriving from Borissow'. By evening Colbert feels secure enough to receive the 6th Hussars' officers, 'whom he seemed to know of old, and offered them a glass of punch at his bivouac. But to everyone's astonishment none of our regimental officers is invited,' no doubt as a tacit reprimand for van Zuylen's ineptitude. Most of Babinowiczi's inhabitants have fled,

'fearing such reprisals by us as the event of the 24th might warrant. Those who'd stayed behind were interrogated as to the fate of our detachment. They told us some of the details I've mentioned above. Resistance at the inn had lasted half an hour.'

And indeed by the time Lieutenant Auvray of the 23rd Dragoons gets there the town is being given over to pillage. But the Red Lancers have to move on. Towards midnight

'two squadrons, one from our regiment and one from the 6th Hussars, had to get on their horses and leave to reconnoitre. I was with the party. The night was dark, the road very broad and irregular. Having hardly had as much sleep as I needed, I dozed off again on my horse. Riding on at random, I overtook our advance guard, and would have got lost if an old hussar, scouting ahead, hadn't woken me up.'

Shortly afterwards Dumonceau sights some Cossacks: 'Peasants, brought from a nearby village, told us everyone was saying the whole Russian army was concentrated around Witebsk.'

But Fézensac is on his way again:

'On the 26th at daybreak we reached Chlow, a very commercial little Jewish town; and, during the forenoon, at Molihew, where I Corps was. I had occasion to note the order and discipline which still distinguished the Prince of Eckmühl's troops.'

Davout tells him about the battle at Salta-Novka which has headed off Bagration and forced him, 'despairing of making junction with Barclay', to cross the Dnieper. Now he's retiring toward Smolensk. He himself is going to follow the Dnieper upstream as far as Orsha, 'to close the distance between himself and the rest of the army'.

It's a Sunday. And once again Davout, that convinced atheist, attends divine service. Coming out, he receives the Archimandrite and recommends to him 'that he recognize the Emperor Napoleon as his sovereign and to substitute his name in public prayers for that of the Emperor Alexander. He reminded him of the words of the Gospel: to render unto Caesar that which is Caesar's, adding that by Caesar is meant the stronger. The Archimandrite promised to conform with this instruction, but in a tone of voice which showed how little he approved of it.'

Should Fézensac that morning bump into Le Roy – which is by no means impossible, for his exploits at Salta-Novka have attached him to Davout's headquarters – there's a lot he can hear from him. One imagines Le Roy telling him how I Corps 'without even noticing it' had crossed the Berezina, 'at this time of year fordable at all points, with water only half-way up our legs' at Borissow, on the heels of Grouchy's cavalry corps. As he'd ridden over the 300m-long timber bridge Captain Auvray had noticed how

'between the fortifications and the town lies a marsh, intersected by the river bank, making the passage almost impossible without a bridge. Our arrival had prevented the Russians from burning the one that existed. They also had sixteen heavy calibre guns, meant for the fortifications. If the enemy had been able to finish his works there, Borissow would have been a fortified town.'[4]

Four more days on the march and I Corps had reached Molihew.

'The enemy had reached the Dnieper at the same moment as ourselves, but a little farther downstream. We detached a few companies of our first battalion; encountering no resistance, they took possession of the town.'

All of which Le Roy might well have followed up with his personal and, as usual, no little culinary account of the preliminaries of the fierce battle that had followed:

'At about 9 a.m. [20 July] the 3rd Chasseur Regiment, which made up the advance guard, was taken by surprise and thrown back at a run on to the infantry line, which just had time to fly to arms and face the Russian cavalry. More than 150 chasseurs and the regiment's colonel were captured or killed. Not having left my battalion, I soon had it assembled under arms. At the sound of the first shots, the Prince, seeing a battalion under arms, comes hastening up, speaks to me, and orders me to leave at once and follow the river. The army would be following my movement. My men eat their soup as they march. I realize they need to; and make for the Dnieper, to my left, by which I can gauge my position. Entangled in the plenteous ravines along the riverbank'

Le Roy realizes to his dismay that his battalion has become isolated. Worse, just as he reaches a little manor-house overlooking the river he hears a couple of shots ring out; and prepares for a desperate fight. But it's only two Cossacks. His men have killed one and taken both their horses. Beyond he sees a small town. Its 'filthy ragged Jews told me the

Russian cavalry had just pillaged it and taken away all the food'. Bad news for Le Roy. After barricading the bridge over a little muddy stream at the town entrance and posting sentries, he goes up to some high ground, to survey the town below him. Beyond the stream he sees several enemy regiments lined up in echelon between two forests on both its banks. Concluding that he has nothing to fear for the moment, he gives the order: 'Make the soup!' Then, summoning 'an elderly lieutenant I knew to be a good marauder', he sends him to visit the little manor-house in the battalion's rear. 'If inhabited, he was to ask for food; if deserted, as I presumed it was, to rifle it without breaking anything or letting his detachment take the least thing.' And come back as soon as possible.

All Le Roy can see from his observation post, to his right, is a single squadron of red-clad Cossacks. From which he infers that his own main body can't be far off:

'I went back into town. Having made sure the Russians hadn't pillaged or even exacted anything from the inhabitants, I had some bread and beer brought. As I was distributing these victuals to my men, I saw my marauder arriving with a cart filled with delicacies. There were biscuits, almonds, biscuits of all kinds, there were big fat sausages, some rice, some vermicelli, some figs, some dried dates, some raisins; in a word, we'd a complete dessert. A little barrel of spirits, which I ordered to be reduced to a temperature of seventeen degrees, sufficed for a ration to each man. For the officers the marauder had set aside a score of bottles of Bordeaux and four round loaves of rather fine bread. Hardly had the distribution been made than I heard, behind me: "Qui vive!" And "To arms!".

The battalion springs to arms. But it's only the 85th's adjutant-major, accompanied by several staff officers; and, at their heels, Davout himself, 'who told me how surprised he was to find me two whole leagues ahead of the army'. Well, Le Roy's luck has held. He's been facing the entire Russian Second West Army! 'But tomorrow', says Davout, 'I hope to have my revenge', i.e., for the damage done to the 3rd Chasseurs. That evening the Iron Marshal approves Le Roy's dispositions: and indeed is quite unusually friendly, perhaps because he knows he's heavily outnumbered:

'Unlike his usual self, he says some nice polite things to me. At that moment General Friedrichs arrives, and in a brusque military manner demands to know who'd ordered me to advance so boldly and expose myself and my battalion to being carried off. "I did," replied the Marshal. "This officer has been following my orders; and without this action, which to you seems so foolhardy, I'd have been groping about until evening. Whereas, as it is, I know for certain where the enemy is, and tomorrow I intend to have a go at him."'

Golden words Le Roy hastens to share with his men. At dawn the regiment's other battalions turn up and relieve him of his anxieties, which have been considerable, especially as he has 'no great confidence in my recruits, who as yet hadn't received their baptism of fire'.

If staff-captain *Girod de l'Ain* had also been among Fézensac's informants two days later, he too could have told him a thing or two; notably about Davout's singular way of treating his divisional generals. On the eve of the battle even the elderly cuirassier general Valence had had to spend the night, soupless and strawless, on the bare floor of Davout's antechamber 'like so many orderlies'. Chairs being too few to go round, the generals and their aides had ignored them as invidious, but 'very fed up, as you'll believe. The Marshal didn't so much as offer us a glass of water.'

After his uncomfortable night Girod de l'Ain had suggested to Dessaix that he go off on his own and reconnoitre the Dnieper's swampy banks. Finding no Russians, he'd returned to find Dessaix' and Compans' divisions drawn up in line in some narrow, wooded, swampy terrain. The main road plunged into a ravine, where a wooden bridge crossed a steep-banked muddy stream. Dessaix' division was to the right of the bridge, Compans' to its left. To their right was some open ground. 'Four or five houses had been loop-holed.'

Nothing had happened until about 10 a.m. Then, out of the dense forest ahead, great masses of Russians had emerged in attack columns, only to be stopped dead in their tracks by

'lively artillery fire and musketry. For several minutes they let themselves be shot down without budging. We had a new chance to recognize that the Russians, as we said, were "walls which had to be demolished".'[5]

Le Roy takes up the tale:

'Our artillery and the enemy's pounded each other from one plateau to the other at caseshot range. The stream's two banks were lined with both nations' sharpshooters, who only had some willows for cover. Each shot took its effect in the enemy masses, who were trying to force a way through and throw us back into Molihew.'

Davout himself had not turned up until about midday. And instead of going up to Dessaix, commanding his right centre, had approached one of his brigadiers. Finding himself so coldly treated, Dessaix had

'dismounted and gone off, saying he'd no more orders to give, and nothing remained for him but to hand over his command to someone else. At that moment the enemy seemed to make a new and serious effort to cross the ravine. After a long and lively fusillade, a battalion of the 108th (Colonel Achard), which was in the front line, makes to retire, a movement noticed by the Marshal. And instantly we see the latter go to the head of this battalion, halt it on the spot, make it face about toward the enemy, and give it drill orders as if on parade.'

Ignoring Achard's protests that he'd only been retiring because all his ammunition is spent, Davout, his back to the Russians, goes on giving parade orders, 'as if'd been a hundred leagues from the enemy'. In the end Achard has physically to turn the short-sighted marshal around, to convince him of their extreme proximity. Whereupon, Le Roy goes on,

'the Marshal threw forward a regiment along the road. It attacked
the enemy and forced him to retreat. And as it was late we remained
masters of the ground. We saw the enemy, who'd built three bridges
during the fighting, placing himself between us and the river. He'd
sacrificed a corps of 3,000 élite soldiers to save the rest of his army.
Never in my life did I see so much damage caused by our artillery!
Guns, horses, men, roadside trees, all piled on top of one another,
beyond recognition. To our left we saw whole ranks of Russian cavalry carried off by the grapeshot or killed by the fusillades.'

According to Le Roy the French hadn't taken a single prisoner – which
can only be a lapse of memory. For, on 7 August, Davout will write in his
report to Berthier: 'The enemy left on the field upwards of 1,200 dead
and more than 4,000 wounded, of whom seven or eight hundred are in
our hands, as well as 152 prisoners.' But next day they'd collected six broken Russian guns, four thousand muskets and rendered a great deal of
matériel unserviceable:

> 'That day a spokesman presented himself under a flag of truce to ask
> for the body of an artillery captain who'd been engaged to the gen-
> eral's daughter, and for this young lady's portrait, which the officer
> had been wearing round his neck. It had come into the hands of one
> of our voltigeurs. He got forty ducats for it. As for the body, it was
> buried with ours – friends and enemies, all were flung into a big hole
> on the bank of the stream.'

Having been lopped of Lobau's three divisions, I Corps had been too
weak to pursue the Russians and spent two whole days burying the dead.
Girod de l'Ain thinks the outcome would have been more decisive if it
hadn't been for dissension between Davout and his divisional commanders.

Dissatisfaction is rife over rewards. All the divisional staffs have been
overlooked; thus also for 'the seventh or eighth time' Girod de l'Ain, even
though Davout now for the second time requests the Cross for him. All
regimental claims, on the other hand, are being granted – no doubt
Fézensac carries them back with him to Berthier in his scarlet and gold
sabretache. For his mission is accomplished:

> 'That evening I left by the same road as I'd come by. The next day,
> approaching the [main] army, I learnt that the three days I'd been
> away had been filled with brilliant combats, in which the Russian
> army had been pushed back from one position to another, as far as
> the walls of Witebsk. I crossed the battlefields still covered with the
> debris of these three combats, and on the evening of the 26th [*sic*,
> he must mean 27 July] reached headquarters, where I gave an
> account of my mission to the Emperor and the Prince of Neuchâtel.
> The army was encamped in battle order opposite the Russian army.
> Only the Luchiesa stream separated them. The Emperor's tents had
> been erected on an eminence in the centre.[6] Everyone was expecting
> a general engagement next day.'

CHAPTER 11

AN ARMY VANISHES

The Russian army at last! – Homeric stand of some Parisian tirailleurs – a bewildering delay – 'is everyone here asleep?' – an army vanishes – the Grand Army enters Witebsk – golden dishes for a council-of-war

The invaders' joy was immense. There, at last, in full view on the far side of an undulating plain, 'deployed near the town on a big plateau dominating all the roads it can be reached by' lay the Russian army. At last the moment has come for the blow that will decide the campaign?

'Only the Luchiesa stream and our outposts at the foot of the plateau lay between us. After the 13th Division had moved up, it bore off to the right. The Viceroy, riding at the head of the 14th, which followed, passed over the low hills dominating the plateau where the enemy were encamped.'

Albrecht Adam reins in his horse and sketches the scene: in the distance the line of tirailleurs and voltigeurs – nearer, long massed lines of men – artillery teams moving up – cocked-hatted ADCs, galloping hither and thither, heeded by no one. A dead man, arms outstretched, lies in the foreground. Eugène's horse rears. An adjutant gallops up, pointing. The green-coated Italian Guard grenadiers stand packed in reserve, wearing their bearskins. Shortly afterwards, Lieutenant Kalckreuth, moving up into the first line, sees Napoleon ride up to the outposts and dismount:

'Immediately four Guard chasseurs got off their horses and, carbine in hand, formed a square around the Emperor which no one might enter without his express order. He observed the enemy for a quarter of an hour, and then left us.'

First across the Luchiesa bridge – apparently intact – are two voltigeur companies of the 9th Line, followed by 'the 16th Chasseurs à Cheval, led by General Piré'. These are followed at a gallop by Murat himself. And after him the leading battalion of the 53rd Line (Broussier's division). But then Césare de Laugier is alarmed to see

'a hidden battery of twelve guns suddenly unmasking against them! In a twinkling of an eye they find themselves surrounded by Cossacks and hussars. Seeing this, the chasseurs halt, firmly awaiting the shock; and when the Russians are only 30 paces away, fire their carbines. But the discharge doesn't suffice to check the Russian cavalry's impetus. Some of the chasseurs' files fall into disarray, and they're flung back en masse on to the French infantry.'

A very brisk fire from the 53rd, 'formed up in square and presenting an unbreakable front', receives the Russian cavalry, 'exhausting all attempts to drive it in. To get clear, the Russian cavalry swerves to its right and falls on the voltigeur companies which, with their backs to the Dwina, are facing them.'

Follows a combat of truly Homeric proportions. Caulaincourt is among the fascinated spectators, 'all the rest of the army, encamped on a low hill in the form of an amphitheatre and encouraging them with its reiterated applause'. 'These brave fellows' (Césare de Laugier seems to be noting it all down in his diary as soon ever he can),

'placed out along the stream amidst some bushes and houses on the ravine's far side, were surrounded by a cloud of cavalry, against which they kept up a steady fire in support of our feeble squadrons, emptying many saddles and doing such damage that by degrees they force the enemy off our squadrons' flank. Several times we see five or six of these light infantrymen stand back to back, some fifty paces from the enemy squadrons sweeping down on them, and hold their fire until at point-blank range, surrounded on all sides, we give them up for lost. But these brave men, by forming a compact mass and using every advantage offered by the terrain, put up such an energetic resistance that they enable the troopers of the 16th Chasseurs to rally and be reinforced by fresh cavalry, which hastens to deliver them.'

The 16th Chasseurs' repulse has caused 'a certain confusion in our ranks. But Napoleon was there, and it couldn't last'. From a slight eminence crowned by a burnt windmill, to the left of the main road, he'd been 'watching all the manoeuvres and ordered a regiment of cavalry retire, to leave the bridge free for the 13th Division. This retrograde movement spread terror in our rear, composed as it was of a mass of employees, army suppliers or sutlers, folk who easily take fright and, always afraid for their loot, do armies more harm than good.'

Following up their success, the Russian Guard Lancers even reach the hillock's foot, so that the service squadrons – which today consist of Chasseurs à Cheval and Polish Lancers – hardly have time to form square around its foot. Whereupon Murat, whose impetuosity in sending forward the 16th Chasseurs without adequate infantry support has caused the setback, beside himself with fury and supported only by his staff and personal escort, flings himself at the intruders. Astounded at this extraordinary apparition, the Russian Lancers, though 'thirty times more numerous' than his handful of 60 troopers, turn tail and flee. As for the gallant light infantrymen, Laugier goes on,

'the Emperor said to several of them who'd brought him prisoners and asked for the Cross: "You're all brave lads, and you all deserve it." They were the object of the whole army's admiration. Some were killed, many wounded; but even these, unless completely disabled, were loth to abandon their comrades. I can't say how deeply I regret having lost the names of the officers and NCOs, and even the number of this gallant regiment.'

But Labaume and many others[1] make a note of it. It's the 9th Line, 'Captains Guyard (or Guillard) and Savary. All were Parisians.'

After this contretemps the moment has come for a general deployment.

'Everyone is forming a thousand conjectures, each in his own way, most favourable to our leader. At 2 p.m. we at last see new ADCs detaching themselves from the group always surrounding the Emperor, to go to the various corps. The soldiers give vent to their joy. The drums beat. Everyone's under arms. Now the silence is only broken by the redoubled firing of the Russian guns. Enthusiastically the troops are getting under way,'

when something bewildering happens. Napoleon calls off his attack.

'All of a sudden we hear it's not a question of attacking, but of camping. The light infantry receive an order to cease firing and retire from the positions they've occupied. To the military operation succeeds the less heroic repose of the camp. We look at each other, stupefied, vexed. What! Now, when enfeebled by sufferings and hunger, after endless marches to reach this enemy, we at last see him, can almost touch him, and all the circumstances are favourable, an untimely decision, a quite pointless deferment, has snatched victory from our hands! Surprise stands written on all our faces. Silently we interrogate the faces of our superiors to divine in them the cause of this inexplicable holdup.'

What can be causing this wholly untypical delay, just now, at the campaign's critical moment? And at exactly what time has Fézensac returned with the crucial news that Bagration can't possibly turn up and reinforce Barclay's mere 75,000 men? Was it the previous evening? Or is it now, on the 27th? True, III Corps and the Imperial Guard, too, are 'only joining gradually' along the great silver-birch lined highway from Beschenkowiczi:

'Everyone's astounded at this suspension of hostilities at the very moment when the armies are standing face to face. Everyone's asking where the Emperor is and what his plans can be. Some think he's only waiting for all his forces to join before launching a serious attack. Others are sure Ney and Montbrun's cavalry, advancing along the Dwina's other bank, are going to turn the Witebsk position and thus cut off the Russians' retreat.'[1]

But in such a situation assurance has to be doubly sure – so far from home and especially when faced by the staunch Russian 'walls' which had almost spelt defeat at Eylau in 1807. Is it this that gives him pause?[2] Certainly it's neither doubt nor lethargy. Caulaincourt sees how cheerful he is

'and already beaming with pride, confident of measuring his strength with the enemy and obtaining a result that should give some colour to his already over-extended expedition. He spent the day in the saddle, reconnoitering the terrain in every direction, even to a considerable distance.'

But the battle has been deferred. And it isn't until after sunset, when 'the rays of the setting sun had been reflected in Witebsk's golden cupolas' and darkness is already falling that III Corps passes through the Italians' lines, through Friant's, Morand's and Gudin's divisions (the ones Davout could so well have done with at Novo-Saltka) and through the Imperial

148

Guard, and takes up its assigned position. 'It's we who are to lead the attack!' Captain Bonnet notes excitedly in his diary, no doubt by the fluttering light of a campfire. 'Up here this high ground we've occupied appears as one vast mass of light.'

For his part Fezensac is spending the evening with Berthier's other ADCs, 'talking about my mission and listening to the tale of the combats that had just taken place'; everyone else, Césare de Laugier writes in his diary, is thinking only of the morrow, which is to

'decide Russia's fate, once and for all. Everyone is determined to put an end to these endless marches and privations by a crushing victory. Hasn't he ended all his wars in this way, forced his enemies to submit to his law?'

That evening the adjutant-major of the Guardia d'Onore has seen 'various ADCs sent out of our line to the right' and even the Viceroy sent off in person in the same direction:

'Some time afterwards he has come back, all out of breath and in a sweat. The Emperor says to him, brusquely: "You were more diligent when you were only colonel of my guard!" This unexpected reprimand, made in a loud voice, is immediately being repeated.'

What's it due to? No one knows – perhaps a lingering resentment at Eugène's timidity on the banks of the Niemen which, together with Jerome's alleged irresolution in the campaign's early stages, had cost him its immediate success? At midnight, again, the vélites of the Italian Guard are bivouacked around Eugène's tent, 'not far from the banks of the Luchiesa' and their adjutant is getting some much-needed sleep, when there's

'a sound of approaching footsteps and our camp's sentinels' challenges awaken us. It's the Emperor, followed by a few officers who've come to visit the Viceroy. As he approaches the royal tent we all recognize his imperious exclamation, of a kind only he can permit himself: "Is everyone here asleep?"'

Eugène goes off with his stepfather to the front line to look at the enemy and 'from officers who've accompanied him on this tour of inspection I know he's given orders for the battle he's flattering himself he'll be able to deliver today. Then each of us has gone back to his tent.' Only very late does Napoleon, accompanied as usual by Caulaincourt, return to his, 'after himself seeing to and checking up on everything'. But already at 1.30 a.m. he's on horseback again. And still the dying glow of innumerable Russian campfires covers the plain to the east...

Even amidst all the shocks still in store for them in this bewildering campaign – in which, as one chief-of-staff puts it, 'nothing was destined to happen as it did in others' – the invaders will remember the one they get at 4 a.m. on 28 July, as Witebsk's cupolas begin to stand out against the first glimmer of dawn, as among the worst. A shaken de Laugier scribbles in his diary:

'July 28. Hardly has the very faintest appearance of dawn allowed us to scrutinize the horizon than, without uttering a word, we're all staring out across this immense plain that stretches away in front of us. Yesterday it was covered with the enemies we're so impatient to attack. Today it spreads out before our eyes, deserted, abandoned!' Employing a device as old as war itself, and leaving its campfires burning, 'not merely has the enemy vanished. He has left no trace to show which way he's gone.' Not a man, not a wagon, not a horse, not a single piece of equipment – not even a footprint in the wind-blown sands[3] – have Barclay's men left behind them. Dedem and Laugier are by no means the only ones to be staggered at this vanishing act of an entire army 'as if by magic – and not merely the army, but even its very traces!'

For Napoleon the shock is of course immense. As the sun, rising over Witebsk, blazes from the east into all those thousands of staring eyes, can it be the Tsar's words Caulaincourt had read out to him verbatim from his notebook in Paris flit through his mind? "If the Emperor Napoleon makes war on me, it's possible, even probable, we'll be defeated – that is, assuming we fight." Ahead lie the immense expanses of a Russia whose real frontier the Grand Army still hasn't even reached...

A second disappointment follows, in its way hardly less keen or to the point. After 'examining, very closely and more than once, every part of the enemy's positions, especially their bivouacs, to estimate their exact strengths', Napoleon and his entourage ride up to the town gate. There, writes Soltyk,

'he'd expected to be met by locals, imploring his clemency. But the Russians had taken with them many eminent people as hostages, and we found few notables in Witebsk to form the deputation he demanded. When it appeared before the Emperor he was walking up and down on the greensward near the main road, his arms crossed on his chest and deep in thought. At first the Polish gentlemen, awe-stricken and unprepared to find themselves face to face with the great man and all out of breath after having done a couple of miles on foot, didn't know what to say. In vain I prompt them to open the conversation. They seem to be waiting for the Emperor to question them; and this evidently annoys him. After two or three questions about the enemy army, he tells them in a curt tone of voice that his army needs food and forage, and above all bread. Then, abruptly breaking off the conversation, ends it by saying: "I see there are no more Poles here. This isn't Polish country any more!"'[4]

And indeed when, at 11 a.m., he enters the town it's to find it empty. Virtually the entire population – 20,000 souls – have fled. 'Passing rapidly through the streets', the Master of the Horse is with him as

'he rejoins his Guard, which, like the other troops, is already marching along the Smolensk road. Flattering himself we'll catch up with the enemy rearguard, he hastens forward the movement of the van, asking the King of Naples at all costs to get hold of some prisoners and send them to him. But not even a peasant can we find, to show us which way the enemy has gone! No inhabitants are to be seen, no prisoners to be taken, not a single straggler to be picked up, nor any spies. For some hours we have to play at being huntsmen and follow the enemy's tracks in every direction. But to what purpose? What's the use? What route have his masses of men and artillery followed? No one knows, and for some hours no one will; for in every direction there are signs of them. We're in the heart of populated Russia, yet, if I may be permitted the simile, are like a vessel without a compass in the midst of a vast ocean, knowing nothing of what's happening around us.'

Following on the heels of Murat's cavalry, the Italians, too, are 'straying hither and thither in every direction in an immense plain without being able to find any trace of his retreat: not an abandoned vehicle, not a single dead horse, not even a single straggler'. Labaume and his colleagues on Eugène's staff are 'in this state of uncertainty, perhaps unique of its kind, when Colonel Kliski, searching the countryside for a peasant, at last found a Russian soldier asleep under a bush'.

And it's not until Murat's leading hussars, floundering at times up to their horses' knees in the soft sandy soil, are eighteen miles beyond Witebsk that they at last catch up with the Russian rearguard. 'Suddenly it halts, about-faces, and waits for the hussars to attack. But they're unable to spur their horses, too dead-beat to charge.' Worse, at the little town of Lochesna, junction of the Sarowiczi and Surash roads, they fall into an ambush. And whole troops are decimated. Those who survive and make for the rear have to lead their mounts which are no longer able to carry them.

It's there, as evening falls, that Napoleon finally halts, intending to spend the night in a 'poor little cottage'; but on second thoughts orders his tents to be raised. Around them the Italian Royal Guard forms a hollow square – 'it's the first time since the campaign opened that circumstances accord us this distinction, to which we, in the absence of the Imperial Guard, are anyway entitled'. Albrecht Adam's quick pencil sketches the scene. And Césare de Laugier notices 'several of our most prominent generals entering the Emperor's tent. We conclude that they're going to decide what to do.'

And in fact, uniquely, Napoleon has summoned a council-of-war. Present are only Eugène, Murat and his chief-of-staff General Belliard, and the light cavalry General Lefèbvre-Desnouëttes.[5] Murat isn't even asked for his opinions. But Belliard, 'a bluff frank soldier, who could be counted on to relate the plain facts,' replies: "Sire, if we go on marching six more days like this we'll have no cavalry left." From Berthier, too, Napoleon hears – incredulously – how the advance guard's horses are so worn out they've not even been able to charge. After alluding to the ancient "Scythians and their scorched earth policy", he agrees to call a halt.

The council-of-war is followed however by a magnificent meal, served up as usual on a gold dinner service, on tables outside the imperial tents – with scant respect for the Italians' feelings. All they have for dinner after a six-hour march in glaring sunshine through a dense dust cloud, stumbling over the soft sandy soil, and with the thermometer at 29 degrees Réaumur, is

'a little muddy and unhealthy water. The men cannot but observe with surprise and indignation the abundance both in the dishes and the exquisite wines on the imperial household's table, whilst they are themselves in the most extreme penury. They find the contrast disgusting and humiliating.'

Laugier hopes the 'army's chiefs may find it a profitable lesson. Cato of old, and Bonaparte himself in Egypt and crossing the Alps,' he adds in a footnote,

'had marched on foot, bareheaded under the sun's rays and shared their hard bread with their men, knowing what influence such conduct had on their armies. On this occasion he, perhaps over-preoccupied, hasn't reflected what a bad impression it must be making on us to see so splendid a banquet, at which the least of his servants has a place, whilst his soldiers, who're sacrificing their lives for him, lack even bread and water.'

Yet even this doesn't lessen the Napoleonic charisma. And when, at 6 p.m., the Emperor comes out of his tent,

'the Royal Guard salute him with the usual acclamations. Napoleon is hatless, has his sword at his side. A folding chair is brought him. Sitting down on it, he puts some questions to two vélites on sentry duty at the entrance of his tent. His expressive features bear the imprint of health and vitality. Turning to an officer of the same vélites, the one closest to him, he asks him what the effectives of his regiment are, how many men have been lost on the march; whether there are many sick. The officer replies: "Sire, we have some companies which still haven't lost one man from Italy to here." Without showing any surprise, the Emperor replies: "What! They're still as strong as when they left Milan?" "Yes, Your Majesty." Then, after a brief pause: "Your regiment still hasn't measured itself against the Russians?" "No, Sire, but it's eagerly looking forward to doing so."'

Glancing at the 'old "moustaches" of Austerlitz', Napoleon reminds them that the blood of the Romans runs in their veins, and that they must never forget it. As de Laugier's comrades are listening spellbound to his every word, a senior Austrian officer, 'his simple white uniform contrasting singularly with the rich coats of the officers around the Emperor', is announced. He has brought a despatch from Schwarzenberg. So many years the whitecoats have been the Italians' enemy! 'He hands the Emperor an envelope, then follows him into his tent.' The Italians tell one another that he's come to report Schwarzenberg's junction with Reynier's Saxons and his imminent arrival on the scene.[6]

But next morning, says Caulaincourt, Napoleon returned to Witebsk 'in a deep gloom'.

As well he might.

CHAPTER 12

WORRIES AT WITEBSK

Its superb churches – a dingy headquarters – Napoleon's tetchiness – 'the army is lost' – 'why wait here for eight months?' – 'the Emperor is being deceived' – 'the heat's worse than in Paris' – Dr Mestivier is called in – 'the insolent arrogant Goliath' – Dumonceau fights off ants – a very pretty Spaniard – an Italian victory – Lejeune visits II Corps – a messenger from Schwarzenberg

Witebsk lies on the left bank of the Dwina at a point where it 'flows along a deep broad bed, two-thirds dry in summer, leaving on each side a broad sandy beach that reaches up to the foot of high vertical cliffs'. Seen from afar Witebsk pleases Captain *Berthezène* by its 'smiling appearance'. And to Captain Bonnet of the 18th Line 'its many churches and immense monasteries' had announced 'a great city with some impressive buildings, in the same style as Polotsk'. Franz Roeder, turning up a fortnight later with the Hessians, will admire

'the dusky golden darkness of the ancient church of Ivan Boheslav and the fine icons on its screen, separating nave from sanctuary, the altar, the towers, and the bells hung on both sides of the street. Also the great and very beautiful church of St Zapor, whose high altar is concealed by a screen covered in gold and wonderful paintings, and whose bells are hung deep in one of the two front towers which, being roofed with copper and golden balls, shine magnificently from a distance.'

While thinking the Jesuits' church – 'overlaid with an enormous amount of gold and ornamentation, where the simple Poles must feel themselves to be in the antechamber of the Lord God Himself' – a bit tasteless, he'll none the less be impressed by it, too. And find 'the charming new post office and the hexagonal street lamps flanking the main street' wholly to his taste; likewise the 'Vauxhall' [pleasure park] on Castle Hill, 'among avenues of silver birches, with a little wooden temple, a swing and a dance-hall'.

Otherwise Witebsk isn't much of a place. Entering it, the invaders are 'very disagreeably surprised' to find it criss-crossed by ravines. 'From the outside the houses, all higgledy-piggledy, small, low and built of wood, have the most wretched appearance' and their interiors offer Berthezène, at least, no comfort. Even the governor's palace, on the main square, is of timber. Fain, settling in, is disgusted to find that

'apart from several large rooms suited to a headquarters, hardly a few sticks of furniture are to be found in it. But we've soon made up the Emperor's lodging (a carpet of green cloth, the maps laid out, the book box, the big portfolio, the nécessaire and the little iron bed, these everywhere suffice for him). The rest of its layout offers only garrets.'

Outside its windows the main square is encumbered by 'a lot of miserable huts', and since this won't do for a parade ground they are to be imperiously demolished. But the heat is so extreme that the party of Guard sappers put on this fatigue take five days over it. An antique chapel also has to go. Constant, the First Valet, sees the inhabitants assemble

'in great numbers, loudly expressing their displeasure. But the Emperor has permitted them to take away the sacred objects and they've calmed down. We saw them with great pomp carry away some very tall wooden saints, which they deposited in other churches.'

As usual, only the Guard is being given billets. Riding through on 31 July, Dumonceau[1] sees the houses 'for as far as three miles around full of soldiers of the Young Guard. We saw them at all the open casement windows, busy sprucing themselves up and repairing their clothing, etc.' And he hopes similar lodgings have been reserved for himself. 'Witebsk has lost its inhabitants,' notes Réné Bourgeois. 'Never again will its population offer so numerous an affluence, or so brilliant!'

Brilliant perhaps. But though one of Napoleon's first measures on returning to the town has been to order the construction of 36 bakers' ovens, the food shortage is no less keen and frustrating than at Vilna. A day or two later Captain Faré of the 2nd Guard Grenadiers writes home that,

'prices are higher here than in Paris. Everything is madly expensive. The people at Imperial Headquarters are rich and pay for everything with its weight in gold. And we're obliged to pay at the same rate. A pound of butter sells at forty sous, a white loaf at thirty, and vegetables in proportion. So far we've been given no allowance, and there's no sign of us getting any.'

Fain sees his master 'with Count Mathieu Dumas calculating that each oven can yield 30,000 bread rations'. 'No one,' says Fézensac,

'concerned himself more with the army's supplies and hospitals than Napoleon did. But giving orders wasn't enough. They also had to be capable of being carried out.'

The bread rations may be sufficing for the Guard, or anyway part of it. But even Boulart's gunners, bivouacked for eight days on end in the blazing heat on the debris of the Russian army's camp and without even a tree to shade them, are getting neither bread nor meat, and he is having

'to send out marauding parties to get us cattle, sheep, wheat, oats or flour. After which we had to do our own slaughtering, grinding and cooking.'

If this is the state of affairs in the Guard artillery it is *a fortiori* worse in the Line. After a couple of days Dedem, too, is having to send out whole battalions 'to distances of 20 to 25 miles, so as not to die of starvation'. Apparently there's plenty to be obtained from such maraudings, even if few perhaps are faring as well as Captain François' company of the 30th Line, who never 'lack for anything. My men used the rights given to them, and I often had five to nine carts full of victuals following me on the way back.'

The Russians' vanishing act has clearly given Napoleon a shock. Rarely if ever has anyone seen him in such a tetchy mood. Each morning he reviews one Guard brigade on the enlarged main square. 'The Emperor insisted on everyone turning out. In the presence of the general staff and the assembled Guard he went into the smallest details of the army's administration.' The detested commissaries and the medical officers are 'summoned and obliged to declare the state of their supplies'. How are the sick being treated in the hospitals? How many dressings have been got together for the wounded? "You don't realize how sacred your task is!" he barks at them. "All you want to do is to sleep between white sheets! It's in the open air, it's in the mud one must sleep! Glory doesn't lie in soft ways, it's only found in privations!"'

This tirade makes 'a very bad impression' on at least one veteran. General Delaborde, commanding a division of the Young Guard,[2] is a man who 'walked with a limp, liked to crack solemn-faced jokes and was endowed with an intrepid heart that drew all with it', tells Paul de Bourgoing, whom he has taken over from the 5th Tirailleurs as his interpreter:

'I don't take the Emperor's bad temper this morning as a good omen. He fulminated against his commissaries to console the fighting men who were present. But our grenadiers have feelings no less sensitive than ours. They looked sarcastic, and soon they'll be demanding bread of him, not words.'

But the reprimands continue. The bridge over the Dwina not being built quickly enough, old General Chasseloup of the Engineers, too, is told crudely: 'You engineer officers, you're never ready. When we need you, that's fine. But when we don't need you any longer, we don't give a damn for you.' Witnessing the scene from only a few paces away, even the usually uncritical Soltyk finds himself reflecting that

'what rendered General Chasseloup's position sadder was that a fine but abundant rain was falling, and this old and respectable warrior, whose head was bald, was standing there in front of the Emperor hat in hand, without the latter telling him to put it on again.'

But what shocks everyone most of all is the Emperor's treatment of the army's universally loved and admired chief surgeon, Baron *Dominique Larrey*. Although the army's medical service has been grievously neglected and Larrey's reiterated requests for adequate supplies have been largely ignored,[3] its indefatigable chief has seen to it that

'all the 2,300 men wounded in the fighting of 25-7 July had received first aid on the field of battle. I myself had carried out 56 of the 100 amputations, and only eight of my patients had died,'

- a miracle of improvisation, seeing that the ambulances still haven't caught up. 'We had to use the soldiers' linen to give first aid, and even use our own shirts.' And now sick and wounded are lying all jumbled up on the floors of Witebsk's magnificent churches. Although they, fortunately, at least have wooden floorboards, Caulaincourt, ordered to visit these hotbeds of infection, is deeply shocked. Whereon Napoleon visits them himself – and bombards Larrey with reproaches. 'Not one of the *commis-saires-ordonnateurs*, solely concerned with formalities of administration and the triplication of requisition forms, opened his mouth to defend me.' Suffocating with indignation, Larrey tries to defend himself. But already Napoleon has turned on his heel and walked out. Everyone is shaken. It's the first time he's ever had a hard word for 'the most honourable man I've ever known'.

But facts speak louder than words. Returning to his own headquarters, Larrey immediately sends in a detailed report, attaching copies of all his fruitless requests for medical supplies. And at his levée next morning Napoleon ostentatiously pushes the other generals aside, comes up to him, and takes him by both hands: 'Now I know what's been going on! I want you to know that I regard you as one of the State's best servants and as my friend.' Larrey's report is forwarded to the no less hard-working and devoted Intendant-General Mathieu Dumas, 'to know why linen has been lacking on the field of battle'.

The explanation is simple. Most of the ambulances' horses have died en route.

Mounting indiscipline is another worrying factor, particularly in the Guard. And Caulaincourt's younger brother Auguste, he who'd looked so sombre on that hillock by the Niemen, is detailed to set things to rights. Likewise two other high-ranking officers, one to discipline the cavalry, the other the infantry.

Since entering Poland the army has marched nearly 900 miles. By now only two-thirds of the effectives that 'with joyous acclamations' had crossed the Niemen are still with the eagles. Vilna, its most advanced base, lies 200 miles to its rear. At least a third of the horses have died. And even to Colonel Boulart and his Guard gunners, who have 'done 650 leagues since La Fère, this distance seemed immense; and we liked to think we could go no further'. Everywhere in the rear thousands of 'stragglers are destroying everything'. Yet even marauding, writes the *Marquis de Chambray*[4], has been

'unable to provide bread, flour, enough brandy. There'd been no time to turn the grain into flour. Such mills as stood by the roads, not having been protected by safeguards, were being burnt and sacked. The food convoys had lagged behind and were no longer rejoining. Great numbers of hospitals had had to be set up, but were always insufficient and badly organized, and their sick could hardly be given the basic necessities, provisions not having been calculated for so great a number of sick men and been no less delayed than anything else that depended on transport.'

In these unprecedented circumstances all too many experienced men are beginning to feel that words and facts, intentions and realities, have parted company. Fézensac sees how 'men of sagacity and experience' are 'becoming more than a little worried. They asked themselves not merely what would become of this army if it were beaten, but how it could even support further losses from more marches and more serious combats.'

Paul de Bourgoing, who's busy cutting up General Delaborde's copy of the unwieldy campaign map and glueing it on to two dozen of his chief's red-and-white check handkerchiefs, is noticing that it's 'more especially the old thinkers, those we called the 'brain-diggers' [*les songe-creux*] if they were officers, and 'the old grumblers' [*les vieux grognards*] if they were rankers, who were murmuring'. Dedem has a subordinate who falls exactly into this category. One of his three colonels, 'a distinguished and very intelligent officer, albeit of a sardonic disposition', Colonel Pouchelon, commanding the 33rd Line, had fought at Eylau. He is married to a wealthy Polish girl, and has local acquaintances. One day he takes Dedem aside and tells him frankly: 'I'm sending all my effects to the rear. The army is lost.'

As for the ex-diplomat Dedem himself, General Friant is finding him altogether too much the sea-lawyer; and says so to Napoleon. When the Dutchman dares admire the Russian retreat, he's 'told coldly that there was no such word as retreat in the French army's dictionary. Nevertheless I hoped ours would by and by be as elegant.'[5]

What to do? Advance still further? Retreat? Stay put? Witebsk hasn't even a town wall, only the endless palings we see in Chagall's paintings. Least of all will it be defensible in winter, when the Dwina will freeze and lose its strategic significance. Yet retreat is unthinkable. The political effect incalculable. So what to do? There are times when Napoleon, who in odd moments is reading the history of Charles XII,[6] seems to be seriously considering digging in at Witebsk.

'We shan't commit the same folly,' he tells Narbonne airily. 'We must stay here this year and finish the war off next spring.' In vain Caulaincourt tries to disabuse him of an idea he is venting ever more often: that 'the winter here is no worse than in Paris, only longer'. And when Caulaincourt, who has shivered through four severe winters at Petersburg, assures him it's indeed not merely much longer but very much worse, he just makes fun of him.

But the Master of the Horse sees that all talk of wintering at Witebsk is in fact only talk: 'He saw clearly that the French liked active, not defensive warfare. "Not merely does winter threaten us with its frosts. It also menaces us with diplomatic intrigues,"' Napoleon explains to his ex-ambassador. And Secretary Fain, observing him at even closer quarters, sees how two words are now obsessing him: 'Peace', and 'Moscow':

'Why wait here for eight months when twenty days' march are enough for us to reach our goal?' he asks him rhetorically in his office. 'We must be in Moscow within the month, under pain of never entering it! In war, luck is half of everything. If one always waited for a coincidence of completely favourable conditions one would never finish anything off.' A successful battle, he assures his Second Secretary, will enable him to threaten either of Russia's two capitals:

'Peace and Moscow will accomplish and terminate my warlike expeditions. The European System will have been founded, and it'll simply be a question of organizing it. The cause of the century will have won out, and the Revolution be accomplished. No longer will it be a question of accommodating it with the one it hasn't destroyed. This enterprise is mine. I've given it long-term preparation, perhaps at the expense of my popularity. No matter. My glory will be in the success and in my equity. Back in France, in the bosom of the fatherland, great, strong and magnificent, tranquil and glorious, I shall associate my son with me as Emperor. My dictatorship will be over.'

All this is very well, but belongs to a highly speculative future. And Ségur – just at how close quarters the assistant prefect of the palace is observing him is hard to say – sees Napoleon at Witebsk as a man in the throes of an impossible choice,

'straying about his apartments, as if pursued by this dangerous temptation [to march on Moscow]. He takes up his work, drops it, and takes it up again. He walks aimlessly about, asks what time it is and, utterly preoccupied, comes to a halt. Then he begins to hum, and walks on again. In his perplexity he addresses these words to anyone he meets: "Well, what shall we do then? Shall we stay here? Shall we advance further? How halt on so glorious a course?" Not waiting for an answer, he goes on wandering about. He seems to be looking for something or someone to make up his mind for him. Finally, altogether overwhelmed by the weight of so considerable a thought, and as if overcome by such immense uncertainty, he throws himself down on one of the rest couches he's had laid out on the floors of his rooms.'

History? Or literature? Sheer romantic novel-writing, declares Gourgaud scornfully. Yet that Napoleon is an insomniac is no secret to his First Valet:

'More in this campaign than in any other the Emperor often got up at nights, put on his dressing-gown and worked in his office. Very often he suffered from bouts of insomnia he couldn't overcome. Then, his bed seeming insupportable to him, he'd suddenly get out of it, went over and picked out a book and while walking to and fro began to read. Feeling his head a bit refreshed, he went back to bed. It was rare for him to sleep straight through two nights in succession.'

And Ségur goes on drawing his pen-portrait:

'Impatience seizes on him. We see how restless he is, either weighed down by inaction or preferring danger to the boredom of waiting, or agitated by hope. The image of Moscow obsesses his mind. Already we're beginning to foresee that so ardent a genius, restless, accustomed to taking short cuts, won't wait eight months, now he feels his goal is within reach. At first he seems not to dare to admit to so great a temerity, even to himself; but little by little he's getting used to it. Then he deliberates; and this great irresolution, tormenting his spirit, takes possession of his whole person.'

At times he agrees with Caulaincourt that he's gone far enough. But then 'the thousand and one things that ought to have opened his eyes vanish before the slightest incident that can revive his hopes – a captured Russian officer who promises battle in front of Smolensk, for instance. He believes there'll be a battle because he wants one. And believes he'll win it because it's essential he shall. No amount of reasoning can enlighten him. The spectacle of his soldiers, their enthusiasm at the sight of him, the reviews and parades, and above all the King of Naples' and certain other generals' frequently coloured reports have gone to his head.'

And all the time the atmosphere in the rickety old timber palace overlooking the town square is becoming more and more tense. Even Lieutenant Bourgoing, tagging along in Delaborde's suite, notices how 'unusually careless the Emperor is in his expressions when speaking to his officers'. Poniatowski's V Corps not having caught up on time, one of the prince's ADCs is told rudely: 'Your prince is just a cunt.'

Never, says Caulaincourt, have his colleagues 'seen the Emperor in such a touchy state of mind'. He has taken a dislike to Berthier's staff, and in particular to Count Monthyon, 'its moving spirit'. Likewise to Dumas, the zealous head of the administration. Also to Paymaster-General Joinville. Poor nail-biting Berthier is being 'snapped at all day long':

'Duroc, without yielding, wrapped himself in a cloak of impassivity. Lobau became rude. As for Caulaincourt and Daru, the one turned pale and the other flushed with anger. The former impetuous and dogged, the latter dry and cold, they vehemently contradicted the Emperor's denials of the facts.'

Daru, in particular, isn't mincing his words. 'War's a game you're good at,' he tells Napoleon bluntly. 'But here we aren't fighting men, we're fighting nature.' But few make so bold or speak so to the point. If the always critical Dedem van der Gelder can 'find one excuse for Napoleon, it's the cruel way in which he was being deceived by the reports made to him'. For instance by Friant,

'a man of handsome physique, a martial air, and brave, not malicious, but whose manners when he let himself go a bit reminded one of his origins as a simple grenadier in the Royal Guard. He was a real master of manoeuvre. Otherwise "only intelligent on the field of battle", as his brother- in-law Davout agreed.'

When news comes in that the admired Dorsenne, commander of the two Guard grenadier regiments, has died in Paris, it's Friant who's publicly given the accolade and promoted to succeed him – but asked, even so, to remain with his division for the campaign:

'You'll be more useful there than at the head of these veterans who march of their own accord. Besides, I'm always close to them, and you're one of those rare men I'd like to see everywhere I'm not,' Napoleon tells him. Yet Friant isn't hesitating to flatter Napoleon's wishes by making nonsense of d'Ideville's patient statistical work. His division, Dumas tells Napoleon, has food for ten days,

'whereas we were already at our wits' end to get any at all. As usual, I spoke my mind plainly about our position, and had a violent altercation with Friant. He wanted me to produce a report on the 33rd Line and say it amounted to 3,200 men, whilst I knew that in reality no more than 2,500 men, at most, were left. Friant, who was under Murat's orders, said Napoleon would be angry with his chief. He preferred to introduce an error. And Colonel Pouchelon provided the mendacious report required.'

Later Dedem hears from Lobau that the army's effectives have been inflated by 35,000 men.

Likewise the food supplies – something even such veterans as Captain François instinctively understand:

'Despite all the care the Emperor took to get us food, his orders were only being carried out on paper. He was being fooled by the administrators' returns. These brigands led him to believe the army had been given victuals and was provisioned for a fortnight.'

Worst of all is the heat. It's terrific. Over and over again in his almost daily letters to Marie-Louise[7] Napoleon keeps mentioning 'the unbearable heat, 27 degrees [Réaumur]. It's as hot as in the South' (2 August): and on 7 August: 'The heat here is worse than in Paris, we're suffocating.'

Never before has Constant seen his master so bothered by the weight of his own clothes. Vain though he is about his hands' whiteness, the Emperor is breaking his invariable habit of wearing gloves when he goes out and is allowing his hands to get sunburnt. Nor is he sleeping well. 'The Emperor has slept two hours,' Narbonne scribbles in his diary:

'He has been physically very poorly [*très souffrant*]. He has taken some opium, prepared by Dr Méthivier:[8] "Duroc, we must march or die. An Emperor dies on his legs; and then he doesn't die at all. You're afraid of the Prussians, between Moscow and France. Remember Iéna, and rely even more on their fear than their hatred. But for that we must march, we must act."'

And again, almost illegibly: 'The Emperor has been ill again. "We must put an end to this fever of doubt".' One morning he shows Narbonne the dawn,

'already brightening on the horizon. "We've still almost three months of fine weather ahead of us," he told me. "I needed less than that for Austerlitz and Tilsit."'

But ill or well, nothing abates his activity. 'During night's silent hours' Fain sees him

'studying his regiments' and the various army corps' returns. He compares them with those of a fortnight ago, to know his losses in detail and how they've been compensated for. With equal attentiveness he consults the bulletin of troops on the march. In it he follows from day to day the arrival of his reinforcements, never letting a moment go by when he can give them fresh orders. In this way he contrives to know the enemy army just about as well as he knows his own.[9] Perhaps even better.'

From now on Lelorgne d'Ideville 'who understands and speaks Russian' is always to ride behind him. And the daily routine of top-speed dictations goes on unimpeded. Caulaincourt's courier service, too, is functioning impeccably. Each day the locked leather despatch cases brought by relays of couriers are arriving and leaving. 'Each day the Paris courier is being opened, read and replied to. The private correspondence with the Duke of Bassano at Vilna is no less regular.'

Newspapers, too, are arriving. Not always with good news. Here's a worrying item. The Turks have made peace with Russia "precisely at the moment when they should have made war on their traditional enemies. It's such a gross mistake I could never have foreseen it!" declares Napoleon; and fires off a reprimand to Maret at Vilna for not having out-lavished the British gold at Constantinople. Another almost equally unpleasant item throws doubt on Sweden's neutrality:

"Bernadotte is quite capable of forgetting he's a Frenchman by birth. But the Swedes are too energetic and enlightened not to revenge themselves for all the injuries done them since the days of Peter the Great,"

is Napoleon's comment. That the Tsar is in Moscow, arousing popular patriotic feeling, he knows already; also that the city's governor, a certain Count Rostopchin, is assembling men and money for its defence. But what's this? Far from thinking of calling it a day and making peace, here's his 'brother' Alexander, declaring a 'national' – not merely a 'political' – war against him; and what that can mean the French already know from Spain. And what's this? The Moscow Archimandrite, head of the Russian Orthodox Church, is calling him

'a Moloch, the insolent, arrogant Goliath from the frontiers of France, a tyrant who wants to destroy the whole earth. The religion of peace, that sling of David, shall soon bring him down and cut off the head of his bloodthirsty arrogance.'

'These expressions of hatred he had repeated to him several times,' Fain goes on:

'They astonished and disquieted him. Who had been instrumental in bringing about such a change in the Tsar's mind? His own moderation concerning the fate of Poland, which had upset and cooled the

Poles, had been partly due to his wish for a political settlement with Russia; which was now declaring him an outlaw.'

One day a rumour passes through the army that Alexander, like Tsar Paul before him, has been assassinated, on suspicion of suing for peace. And next morning at his levée Napoleon, 'with a joyous and satisfied air' announces it for a fact, only for it to turn out shortly afterwards to have been unfounded.[10]

Altogether his political position is hardly less problematic than the military one. It's no revolutionary army that is bivouacked around Witebsk, but an imperial one. And when the local gentry complain that the 'peasants in the surroundings, hearing people talk of liberty and independence, have thought themselves authorized to rise against their lords, and are indulging in the most abandoned licence,' the usual flying columns are immediately sent out to crush them. 'It was a question of stopping a movement that could degenerate into a civil war. Some examples are made. And order is soon re-established' – obviously to Fezensac's aristocratic satisfaction. Remarkably, the local landlords are even 'authorized to have the peasants arrest marauders, disarm them and bring them in'. And Chambray is astounded to see an

'altogether extraordinary spectacle: in the midst of our successes to see Lithuanian serfs marching our disarmed soldiers. Any who had been pillaging were condemned to death. Had this order been rigorously carried out, thousands of soldiers would have had to be shot, since marauding was the sole means of survival, no distributions having been made. Those on whom pillaged objects were found were brought before military courts. As many as 80 were judged at a time and condemned to death. But only two or three of the guiltiest were executed.'

Perhaps this is why Boulart's gunners are suddenly ordered to a village five miles away, where there's a fine Polish château 'which really merited the name'. Its mistress, however, is in town and has only left her furniture there. 'As for food, it was I who offered her some. This lady', says the flute-playing major, 'had a real Polish head, remarkably exalted, and held the Russians in horror.' If Napoleon will only re-establish the Kingdom of Poland, she tells him, the whole country will rise *en masse* to support him. But that's exactly what he has decided not to do.

And here's some bad news for Colonel Tschüdi of the Joseph Napoleon Regiment. Quite unexpectedly here's little Coignet turning up with his surviving Spanish deserters, like 350 bad halfpennies. Who 'immediately they take to their heels to rejoin their regiment'. Tschüdi is 'so furious with them he wants to have them all shot, too'. Only when Coignet points out that they've had their pardon and 'only the Emperor himself can reverse it' does their Swiss colonel drop the idea.

And here's another, less questionable reinforcement. Disappointed in their hopes of comfortable billets in town and bivouacked on the sandy

plain beyond the town where they're doing outpost duty 'to protect imperial headquarters on that side', the Red Lancers suddenly receive an
afflux of 200 fresh men from their Versailles depot, 'mainly former hussars of our 3rd Dutch Regiment, back from Spain. This brings the regiment's effectives, already reduced to 600 of the horses it had counted
when leaving Versailles,' up to 800, i.e., to four-fifths of its original
strength. Dumonceau, whose company now numbers 102 troopers, is
   'making the best of a certain abundance of straw to build myself a
   good hut with two compartments, provided with a table and a bench,
   where I was perfectly at my ease from the hot sunshine and the rain.
   I busied myself with my correspondence, interrupted since Königsberg. Now bread was arriving regularly from the town, which further
   provided us with all sorts of stores,'
including sugar. But though Dumonceau puts his little larder under his
pillow, 'safe from gourmands', it's only to have it gobbled up by... ants.
   Vélite-Sergeant *François Bourgogne* of the Young Guard's Fusiliers-
Grenadiers was very likely one of the lucky ones whom Dumonceau had
seen polishing their arms in comfortable billets when he'd first ridden
into the town. No sooner had Bourgogne settled in than he'd been visited
by 'twelve young men from my own part of the country [Condé]; ten were
drummers, one a drum-major, and the twelfth a corporal of voltigeurs.
They all wore side-arms.' Alas, he has nothing to offer them; but the
drum-major insists on his going back with them to share some 'wine, gin,
and other things that'll do you good' and which his unit has
   'taken from the Russian general, together with a little cart holding
   his kitchen. "We've put it all into the canteen cart with our cantinière. Florencia's a pretty Spaniard. She might be taken for my wife:
   I protect her – honourably, I can tell you!" As he said this he struck
   the hilt of his long rapier. "She's a good woman: ask the others – no
   one dares say anything else. She took a fancy to a sergeant, who was
   to have married her: but he was murdered by a Spaniard from
   Bilbao, and until she's chosen someone else she must be taken care
   of."
'We sat down near the cantinière's cart,' Sergeant Bourgogne goes on.
'She really was a very pretty Spaniard, and she was overjoyed to see us, as
we'd just come from her own country, and could speak her language
pretty well – the dragoon Flament best of all. So we spent the night in
drinking the Russian general's wine and talking of our own country.'
   But not everything is pretty, and some things are hideous. One such
warm evening as Dedem is taking a stroll behind his brigade's line of huts
he's horrified to hear a grenadier boasting to a comrade: 'D'you remember the damned face that little bugger made when I had him on my bayonet and was putting him closer and closer to the fire, and how his mother
screamed?' Dedem says his recruits 'were tender-hearted enough, but
many old soldiers had lost all sensibility'. As for the Spaniards, they'd long

remained well-disciplined, 'but once let loose they surpassed the French in horrors and abominations'.

Lieutenant Paul de Bourgoing, for his part, is finding life much more agreeable than in the arduous days when he'd been Colonel Hennequin's factotum. Delaborde's staff consists of 'two ADCs, a surgeon and a major-domo with the irreproachable turn-out of a maître d'hôtel of one of today's fine houses'. There too are a Polish lancer called Gorski and a Prussian gunner. All are enjoying a superior standard of living. 'From that moment my depression passed over. I was surrounded by people I liked, and that's the first condition of contentment' – especially as Bourgoing's admiration for his 48-year-old general knows no bounds. One day some straw catches fire close to some ammunition wagons. Their crews and everyone else run for their lives. But Delaborde just limps over and calmly quenches the flames.

The delicate Planat de la Faye, by contrast, isn't feeling at all well. Ever since the shock of the Russians' rope-trick he's been

'so ill and so weakened by continual dysentery that I was tempted to quit the army. But the point of honour kept me there, and it's true to say that in the army, by a sort of state of grace and without ceasing to do one's job, one puts up with illnesses which in any other place would lay you out on your pallet. What's more, you recover without being missed or having a doctor.'

Some of the stores being gratefully consumed by Dumonceau may well have come from a small but welcome victory won by the Italians. 'Immediately on halting at Witebsk,' Fain had written in his private journal, 'the Emperor ordered the Viceroy to push outposts towards Nevel, by the Surash–Veleija road', chiefly to get news of II Corps' operations against Wittgenstein. On 1 August, at the junction of the rivers Carplia and Dwina and of the Moscow and Petersburg roads, General Villata's Italian brigade and a battalion of Croats had just been about to enter the Jewish town of Surash, 'the most advanced point yet reached by the French armies', and were finding it full of stores, when some men of the 2nd Italian Chasseurs reported that a weakly escorted enemy convoy was trying to cross the river to get to Veleija-Luki. Immediately Eugène had ordered his Russian-speaking ADC Colonel Bianco to take 200 picked men and grab it. After a 27-mile march they'd sighted the convoy – escorted, Césare de Laugier hears afterwards, by four infantry battalions and 300 cavalry. The cavalry tries to cover the infantry just as it's about to cross the bridge over the Dwina:

'Realizing they can't escape us, the Russian force forms square on the far side of the Dwina and entrenches itself behind its carts and vehicles. Though outnumbered, Colonel Bianco orders the charge to be sounded; the Russian cavalry are put to flight, and his own men are received with a shower of musketballs. A deep ditch protects the Russian kraal; but the remains of a causeway enable two Italians to cross it at a time. Bianco is wondering what to do. His chasseurs' shouts, demanding to be allowed to charge, tell him. Headed by Quartermaster-sergeant Grassini, five frontal charges are made, to no avail. Finally they manage to penetrate a weak spot in the improvised wheeled fortress and take 500 prisoners and 150 vehicles filled with food and ammunition. We lost some 40 men, killed or wounded, among them six officers.'

Would the Italians be allowed to keep their spoils? Certainly part of them. On the other hand Eugène must have known that Grouchy had been reprimanded for not sending the fruits of his Orsha coup to Glubokoïe; and at Surash his Italians are

'living in a state of penury which is, in fact, a trifle too great. Encamped far from river banks, we're suffering horribly from thirst. To get at water, the men are digging down into the soil with their bayonets, and even if they're so happy as to find some, it's so terribly muddy it can't even be drunk until it's been filtered through their handkerchiefs.'

'Faithful to their system,' Ceesare de Laugier goes on,

'the Russians (wherever we've left them time to) have been burning almost all the stores, scattering the harvests, and destroying everything they haven't been able to carry off. This has thrown the various corps back on to living off their own resources and making troublesome excursions whose only result is to destroy the bases of discipline, impoverish the population and exasperate it against us.'

But necessity knows no law. The Bavarian chasseurs have just rejoined IV Corps; and one day Lieutenant *Albrecht von Muraldt* is doing a little marauding on his own account when he bumps into no less a personage than General Montbrun, 'who bawled me out, even saying something about having me shot and so forth'. But taking Montbrun's 'hellfire sermon' for the empty threat it certainly is, he gets safely back to his bivouac 'with some brandy and bread'.

Away to the north, near Polotsk, a kind of stalemate has arisen between Oudinot and Wittgenstein, who instead of letting himself be pushed back on Petersburg is 'manoeuvring with considerable ability between II and X Corps'. On 1 August Oudinot had lured General Koulnieff across the Dwina, where he'd run headlong into a masked battery of 40 French guns. Koulnieff's force had been annihilated and he himself had been killed. Oudinot had captured fourteen guns, thirteen ammunition wagons and more than 2,000 prisoners. But the success (for which Marbot in his boastful way claims exclusive credit) hadn't been followed up, and Verdier's division had been driven back on to the French camp. 'I've seen few battlefields which offered such a picture of carnage,' Oudinot had written home. 'The ground for two miles is covered with their dead.' Thereafter both sides had retired – Oudinot into Polotsk. And on 5 August an irritated Napoleon sends off d'Hautpoul to Polotsk, with orders not to return 'until he can give an account of the Russians' defeat'. That same evening (whether conformably to the usual duplication of despatches or for some other reason Fain doesn't say) Lejeune, too, is sent off. After finding a shortcut by fording the Dwina and 'having with difficulty covered a distance of 105 miles', he reaches Polotsk after 24 hours, and is received in style by Oudinot in the Jesuits' great building, where the marshal explains to him how 'the Russians, by letting themselves be driven back, are trying to draw the French into a desert, where they'll be destroyed by hunger'. This is the sole reason – Lejeune can tell His Majesty – why, after several reverses but also such a signal success, he, Oudinot, has withdrawn to Polotsk, there 'undelayedly to issue his men with rations and put them into a state to begin anew'.

All this may be true. But Lejeune finds II Corps shockingly depleted, hardly 20,000 men. Dysentery, typhus, desertion and exhaustion have already reduced it to half-strength. 'Of the 2,000 men of the 1st Swiss who'd left Paris,' Captain *Louis Begos*[11] of the 2nd Swiss assures us, 'hardly 1,200 were in a state to fight.'

Fain explains that Napoleon's planning always allowed for reverses; and his response to Oudinot's request for reinforcements had been to send him St-Cyr's Bavarians. This should have been an adequate blood transfusion. But the Germans – all witnesses agree – didn't have the French flair for marauding and 'wanted to cook everything properly and get a full night's sleep'. Already starved of rations, VI Corps' wretched Bavarians are now suffering worse than anyone. On 6 August, after retracing many endless miles, they're seen by Franz Roeder just as he and his faithful sergeant-major Vogel are comfortably installing themselves in Beschenkowiczi castle. 'Surprised to see them so mightily cast down, and the soldiers dragging themselves so wearily along,' Roeder wonders whether there can even be two-thirds of the number that had crossed the Niemen; and concludes that it's their officers' fault for not taking better care of them. Many more will die en route, some only a mile and a half from Polotsk, where Colonel St-Chamans will see

'such a terrible epidemic raging among the Bavarians that they almost all fell sick, and died in their thousands. Men who were well yesterday, fell ill in the morning and were dead by evening. When they left the camp only 3,000 remained.'

For four days Lejeune follows Oudinot's movements as his corps again drives back the Russians, 'without anything of note happening, except the difficulty of feeding the army in this land of sands, forests and lakes. On 11 August, after working with the Duke and General Gouvion de St-Cyr, I left again for Witebsk.' But when he gets there he finds Napoleon in no mood to reckon with troublesome realities beyond his reach. In Oudinot's explanations of his inactivity he sees only excuses. By advancing on Opotscka and Novorjev he was convinced the marshal would have found the means to feed his army. So back to Polotsk goes Lejeune, this time to order Oudinot to 'keep abreast of the main army' in its advance on

Smolensk – for that, in spite of everything, is what Napoleon has in mind. Meanwhile all important communications with the Austrians are being carried by another of Berthier's ADCs. On 2 August Colonel Flahaut, the 'best dancer and biggest ladykiller in France'[12] had left for Schwarzenberg's headquarters, followed next day, Fain says, by 'a trusty Polish officer with a duplicate of the same order'. According to Captain *Joseph Grüber*,[13] a Bavarian in the Austrian service, Schwarzenberg 'didn't dare do anything without orders from Napoleon'. And this is why he has sent Grüber with a despatch of his own, requesting instructions:

'I travelled as fast as I could by mail coach. Reaching the spot where the great Emperor, on horseback and surrounded by his marshals, was waiting for some troops to march past, I jump out, apply to an officer of his entourage, and am immediately taken to Marshal Duroc, to whom I hand my despatch. Duroc rides over to Napoleon, ordering me to follow. Napoleon takes a pinch of snuff from his waistcoat pocket – always, as I've learnt afterwards, full of tobacco – throws me a sombre glance, reads the despatch and says to me: "Do you speak French?" "Fluently, Your Majesty." "Good," the Emperor says, taking another pinch of snuff from his waistcoat pocket. And asks one of his generals, whom I was afterwards told was Berthier, for the map of Volhynia. At the same time he orders Duroc to inhibit the troops' march-past, and together with myself begins examining the map. Questioning me on the operations of Schwarzenberg's corps, he follows with the forefinger of his right hand each point I indicate to him on the map as having been the theatre of our struggles. And finally says to me: "My friend, you're well informed!" Then, turning to Berthier, he tells him that Schwartzenberg's report agrees perfectly with my exposé. Whereupon he most amiably orders me to accompany Duroc and get all necessary instructions for Schwarzenberg from the bureau of operations. "Tell your Field Marshal", the Emperor concluded, "to hurry up and turn back on his tracks and disengage General Reynier at Kowel; and get back as quickly as ever you can. It's urgent."'

After 'a plenteous *déjeuner à la fourchette* washed down with a bottle of champagne' while waiting for his instructions, Grüber leaves again by coach. And next day reports to Schwartzenberg. His mission, he claims, would prove crucial to the Austrians' and Saxons' fate. 'Had they advanced into Old Russia they too must infallibly have perished.'

CHAPTER 13

THE GREAT MANOEUVRE

A strategic masterstroke – Sébastiani routed a second time – the Grand Army concentrates at the 'Borysthenes' – Neverovski's fighting rearguard – Napoleon's 42nd birthday – Poniatowski doesn't understand politics – Coignet sent on mission – alarms and excursions at Witebsk – each army has its smell

Only one thing is more dangerous in warfare than to change one's lines of communication in the presence of the enemy, and that's to expose one's flank to him while doing so. Yet this is what Napoleon, behind all the grandiloquent talk, is now planning to do.

Between him and the two Russian armies, astride the Smolensk road, lies Murat's cavalry screen. And between all three and the Dnieper, to his right, lies a vast belt of primitive forests.[1] Each army corps being in principle able to move at any moment in any direction, Napoleon has been secretly planning to take advaantage of this forest, move I, III, IV, V, VIII Corps and the Guard crabwise, cross the Dnieper, and march swiftly on Smolensk, grab it, and – before Barclay and Bagration realize what's happening – attack them in the rear. Flung helter-skelter back on to Oudinot and St-Cyr – who it is to be hoped are advancing from Polotsk – both Russian armies will be caught in a gigantic trap and annihilated.

Orders have already been sent to the various corps to march for the river, and some have already broken camp, when on 8 August some unexpected news comes in. In pouring rain – the weather has suddenly broken – 10,000 (some say 12,000) Russian cavalry and Cossacks, supported by twelve guns, have flung themselves on Sébastiani's advance guard at Inkovo, and – for the second time in the campaign – routed it.

Vossler, Tascher, Roos and Aubry have all been in it. At first the Prussian and Polish cavalry stand firm. But then they're forced back through their own tents 'many of which were still standing, so that the guy-ropes kept tripping us up'. Lieutenant Tascher's horse is killed under him by the Russian guns and he owes his life to his sergeant-major who dismounts and gives him his own, only to be himself overwhelmed by Cossacks and taken prisoner.[2] Dr Roos too is entangled in the affray, but manages somehow or other to save all his wounded from capture. In the end the 24th Light, Sébastiani's forward infantry regiment, after putting up a staunch resistance, is forced to abandon its 'fine voltigeur battalion in a wood it couldn't get out of'. For a moment there's even a danger of a complete rout. But by and by Montbrun – some think much too tardily – comes up from Rudnia with the rest of II Cavalry Corps and its horse artillery, and saves the situation. After it's all over Vossler proudly notes in his diary that

'such a withdrawal as we carried out on this occasion can almost be regarded as a victory. Despite his immense superiority, the enemy

didn't at any time succeed in breaking our ranks.'
Which is to put a good face on it. Sébastiani has lost ten officers and 300 men; and a violent altercation breaks out between him and Montbrun who, Aubry explains, 'weren't on the best of terms, the inferior officer being in command of his superior'. Both are being widely blamed for the loss of a lot of cavalry and the voltigeur battalion.

Is this the beginning, at last, of a Russian counter-offensive? Napoleon immediately cancels his grand enveloping movement – a hesitation as to the enemy's movements reflected in those of the Red Lancers. They've just passed through Witebsk and in the afternoon of 9 August are already well on their way to the Rudnia road, and are getting ready to leave before daybreak next morning 'when urgent orders come to turn back at once towards Witebsk'. After retracing their steps for four or five hours they meet a convoy of wounded, who tell them all about the Inkowo affair and how the Cossacks' pursuit had only been halted by 'a regiment of Württemberg Chasseurs of their division, who'd formed square, thus giving I and II Cavalry Corps time to arrive and stem it'.

What's going to happen now? From what these casualties have to say it seems a new and more grave engagement is certainly imminent, though they're sure Ney's corps will be able to contain it.

Colbert thinks the matter over. Concludes that his regiment's support is no longer urgently needed. And bivouacs on a hilltop between Witbesk and Rudnia. Although the rain is still falling steadily, Dumonceau is enjoying a splendid view of the landscape, when he sees a horseman galloping towards him. It's one of Murat's ADCs 'on his way to IHQ, who tells us the enemy is definitely retreating'. Withdrawing his lancers a mile or two, Colbert grudgingly allows his captains to decide for themselves – on their own responsibility – whether to disperse their companies among nearby farms or to bivouac in the rain. Seizing this unexpected chance of a dry night, Dumonceau installs his company in

'a spacious farm with barns, less than half a mile from the one where regimental headquarters were. It was surrounded by high wooden walls, with only one exit, surmounted by a tall dovecote, whence we had a wide view out over the surroundings. I shut myself up in it, with all my unit sheltered in the barns. The entrance door was barricaded, and a sentry placed in the dovecote. It was like being in a fortress.'

But the Russians don't follow up their success.[3] And next day the grand operation across the Dnieper is resumed.

Everywhere the downpour is soaking the terrain. Liozna, on 11 August, is just a 'big village full of mud', where the artillery finds the going heavy, as do the Italians trudging through it all the long way to Liouvavitschi. There they see

'all the King of Naples' cavalry coming back from the environs of Rudnia and Inkowo – but instead of taking the Rudnia road it turned left, as before, to cross the Dnieper at a point much less far upstream than the place where we were to cross. The assembly of the entire army on the banks of this river proclaimed our overt intention of crossing it and attacking Smolensk by the left bank, to seize the town.'

And still the rain drenches down. Muddy marches and counter-marches are being made to find viable roads through a countryside almost void of inhabitants. Some have to be repaired by the sappers, who, 'better still, make a new one out of fascines, branches and earth'. Some of the corps are coming up via Orsha, others via Babinowiczi:

'This immense gathering of men at one point increased our misery and redoubled the confusion and disorder prevailing on the main roads. Lost soldiers were vainly looking for their regiments. Others carrying urgent orders could only execute them by encumbering the roads. The upshot was a frightful confusion on bridges and at defiles.'

At last, on 12 August, the rain gives over. And at dawn next day Dumonceau's men continue their march in brighter weather. The knowledge that they're approaching the 'Borysthenes' – limit of the ancient world – is setting all educated minds aquiver.[4] Aren't they the worthy descendants of ancient Greece and Rome? Who are going still farther? Césare de Laugier's glamorous reflections, however, evaporate

'when all we see is an ordinary little river flowing between narrow banks. Its waters are so steeply embanked you can hardly see the river until you actually come upon it.'

The road through the forests being blocked by Davout's corps, the Red Lancers don't reach the Dnieper until about midday. Across to Rossasna, 'a miserable-looking little town', three trestle bridges have just been thrown; and already the columns are pouring over. In the distance on the opposite bank Dumonceau sees

'III Cavalry Corps, recognizable by the 6th Hussars' red dolmans and the resplendent helmets of its dragoon division, deployed in the plain and moving towards the left in a long column. It was becoming obvious that the whole army was on the move and converging towards this point for some grand operation we'd been summoned to take part in',

and the panorama of which delights them. Dr Roos, too, sees 'crowds of infantry and huge artillery trains'. Obliged to wait until next day to cross, Dumonceau's regiment goes

'to bivouac on the left of the town in a hemp field, whose strong stalks, over six feet high, served for us to build excellent shelters. After that the entire Imperial Guard turned up successively. Ranging itself near us, it soon covered the surroundings for a distance of three miles, naturally causing a lively animation. Close by us they were raising the Emperor's tents. He was expected at any moment. This stimulated us to take particular care to make sure our camp was regularly laid out, thinking he might come and visit, or at least glance at it.'

Dumonceau is staggered by this

'mass of 170,000 men, assembled as if by magic at a given spot on the enemy's left, and dragging in its train a confused multitude of folk and carts and carriages, whose disordered mob seemed rather a migration of nomads, above all in view of a herd of cattle and sheep we saw moving to one side across the fields, escorted by a detachment of I Corps, which it belonged to.'

Although the ripe standing crops give the Guard cavalry plenty of forage for its horses, the fortnight's rations, issued at Witebsk, are already running out; and the supply wagons, as usual, haven't caught up:

'A few feeble distributions didn't at all meet our needs. The entire army marching en masse devoured the countryside's resources like a cloud of grasshoppers, without satisfying anyone's needs. Each of us had to live on any flour or grain he had with him. There was hardly any more question of bread or meat. We made soup of flour in water or biscuits baked in the ashes which now had to suffice to keep us alive.'

At about 6 or 7 p.m. on 14 August

'reiterated shouts of acclamation on all sides told us the Emperor had arrived. He didn't come to his tents at all, just went straight to join the advance guard, which we made haste to follow.'

That day Grouchy's van is riding through Liady – the easternmost town in Lithuania and 'the last where we saw any Jews' – and out along the great tree-lined highroad toward Krasnoië – the first in Russia – and the rest of Murat's cavalry and Davout's corps are coming on behind, when the whole mass suddenly and unexpectedly runs into resistance. Dumonceau's men, in their wake, are riding through Liady's

'single muddy street paved with logs, broken at various points, and going down a steep slope towards a stream whose half-broken bridge had been supplemented by two others hastily thrown on either side, and mounting the opposite bank to another similar plateau, when we hear the distant rumble of the guns, to which is added, more and more distinctly as we advance, the crackle of musketry'.

What opposition can this be? Certainly it's extremely dogged. By and by it becomes clear that Bagration has intentionally left behind a division at Krasnoië, 'at the intersection of the Constantinople-Petersburg road', precisely to guard against the eventuality of Napoleon trying to seize Smolensk by a *coup de main*. And now Neverovski's sixteen infantry battalions, four squadrons of dragoons and four of Cossacks and eight guns are stubbornly defending the threshold of Old Russia. First dividing his little army into two close columns, then forming a huge single compact 'filled' square, Neverovski, who has altogether too many raw recruits, is retreating slowly across the open plain, along the long straight Smolensk road with its double avenues of silver birches; and he's contesting every inch of the ground. Although Murat flings in wave after wave of cavalry, first Nansouty's cavalry corps, then Montbrun's cuirassiers, neither can make the least impression on this vast mass of Russian bayonets.

What's needed is grapeshot and canister.

Unfortunately, just behind Krasnoïë, Griois' guns have got bogged down in a steep and narrow defile.[5] And Murat, as usual, is altogether too impatient:

'Scarcely has the 2nd Württemberg Artillery got within the most efficient range for grapeshot, hardly has it opened fire to make a breach in this mass of men and blast open a passage for the cavalry, than Murat's boiling valour pushes regiment after regiment in front of our battery and against this compact mass, several times charging it himself, sabre in hand, without being able to break in. The gaps are always closed up, leaving no traces.'

Even when breaches are made (Fain will note in his diary that evening) the

'very inexperience of the Russian peasants making up this force gave them an inertia which took the place of resistance. This manoeuvre repeated itself from each position to the next, until at last Neverovski finds himself near a forest defile by which he escapes, having lost 2,000 men.'

Again the weather is blazing; and that evening the broad road, its silver birches hanging their silent boughs in the stupendous heat, is littered with dead and wounded. 'Such', says Dedem caustically, 'was the bloody affair of Krasnoïë, which Napoleon called a battle because he was present at it.' Although evidently he'd done his best to be. Advancing cross-country toward the sound of the guns, the Red Lancers had been overtaken by him at a gallop, 'followed by his numerous staff':

'Later we found him halted, on foot, standing by the roadside, holding a riding-whip, his left arm behind his back, in front of a fire which had gone out and whose ashes he was absent-mindedly lashing at, apparently heedless of the cries of Vive l'Empereur! the men were incessantly saluting him with as they went by, more than ever because of its being "Napoleon Day". He was alone, except for Prince Poniatowski, who in a most animated fashion seemed to be telling him something. The staff were assembled at a certain distance.'

What were they talking about?

Ever since his V Corps, despite its immense efforts, had failed to grab Bagration by the tail, Napoleon's wrath with Jerome 'had fallen instead on Poniatowski, who had really made forced marches'. Poniatowski being liable to fits of melancholia and depression, this hadn't mended matters:

'I don't know whether it was on this solemn day his ADC Antoine Potocki arrived at Napoleon's headquarters. But it seemed to me it was only then we, the Polish officers of the Guard, heard how the Polish army corps had dwindled. There were really no more than 11.000 under arms. Although we knew Dombrowski's division with a brigade of cavalry had been detached from the main body,[6] we were overcome with sadness at the thought of Poland's military power being so feeble, above all just now, when the first real battle should shortly be taking place.'

Poniatowski has had to appeal to Davout to put in a word on his behalf. And now, standing there by the roadside as Colbert's lancers again file by, he's urging Napoleon to mobilize Poland and thus consolidate the army's rear, instead of marching on Moscow. But the Polish prince, who'd turned down the Tsar's handsome offers of advancement if he'd side with him, gets nowhere. Napoleon simply tells him he doesn't understand matters of high policy.

That evening the Italians, too, hear cannonfire; and hasten their footsteps. But the booming of the guns turns out to be only a salute, fired at Murat's orders to mark the Emperor's birthday. 'The army's commanders have gone to compliment him on the occasion,' notes Césare de Laugier, normally so concerned to put the best construction on things; but adds: 'the troops are definitely not thinking of celebrating this day as they usually do'. At the reception Fain hears Napoleon tell Murat, Ney and Eugène – what by now must be obvious – that he's going to seize Smolensk and take Barclay in the rear.[7] His commanders, by way of making up for the failure to crush Neverovski, have made him a birthday present of his eight guns, fourteen artillery wagons and 1,500 prisoners. 'While they were entertaining themselves with these hopes,' writes Major Boulart, whose gunners have had to drag away the captured Russian pieces and whose own cannon are among those firing the salute,

'the bands of the regiments were heard, and a 100-gun salute all down the line. Napoleon observed that they couldn't afford to waste gunpowder; but smiled when Murat replied that it had been captured from the Russians.'

Gourgaud says he told the Viceroy: 'Everything is preparing for a big battle. I shall win it and we'll see Moscow.' Ségur notices that Eugène makes no reply to this, but hears him observe to Mortier as he leaves the meeting: 'Moscow is going to be our downfall.' 'Duroc, the most reserved of all, was saying he couldn't foresee when we'd get home again.'

Such were Napoleon's forty-third birthday celebrations.

That day, too, Rapp has arrived from Danzig, where he has been governor, via Vilna. Planat notices that 'despite his elevated status' Rapp still has 'the lively gait of a hussar officer'. At Vilna Napoleon's favourite ADC has found both Hogendorp and Jomini a good deal more optimistic about the campaign's outcome than he himself is beginning to be: "You've come from Vilna?" Napoleon asks him. "What's Hogendorp doing? Nothing, I suppose. Has he got any woman with him?" And when Rapp says he doesn't know: "If he's got his wife with him she must go back to France or he must send her back to Germany. Berthier must write to him about it."[8] And when Rapp describes the 'sad picture' of the immense numbers of stragglers, etc., he's seen in the rear: "That's the usual result of long marches. I'll strike a lightning blow and everything will come together again."

That auspicious day it's Sous-lieutenant Coignet's turn to be on orderly duty at IHQ. Suddenly he's called for. One positively feels how the little fellow trembles with emotion as he stands there at attention in front of his idol, his new officer's hat under his arm, his single gold epaulette glittering in the sunshine on his left shoulder and his dangling gold sword-knot quivering:

'"*You*," says Napoleon – no longer using the familiar *tu* to an NCO, but the polite *vous*, to an officer, "you are to go immediately to Witebsk with these orders. They impose on everyone, of any arm whatever, to help you unsaddle your horses. If need be, all horses at relay posts are at your disposal – except those of the artillery! Do you possess one yourself?" "Two, Sire!" "Take them. When you've ridden one to death, take the other. I expect you back already tomorrow. It's three o'clock. Get going!"

'I mount my horse. Count Monthyon says to me: "Get moving, my dear chap. Take your other horse by its bridle and lead it behind you on the way. But saddle them both. Leave your best saddle here with my domestics; you've not got a moment to lose!" Away I go like lightning, leading my second horse by the hand. As soon as the first's legs give way under it I dismount, unsaddle and saddle up again, all in one movement, and leave my poor beast standing where he is. Ride on. Deep inside a wood, I come across some cantinières on their way to rejoin their corps. "Halt there! A horse, at once! I'll leave you mine here, together with its harness. I'm in a hurry! Unharness my horse!" "We've four fine Polish horses here," says the cantinière. Which d'you want?" "This one. Harness it up, quick! Not a minute to lose!" Alas, that excellent horse, he carried me far. In the forest I come across a relay post, guarding the main road. Ride up to its commander, shout: "See here my orders! Quick, a horse! You can keep mine!"'

Not an hour is lost en route for Witebsk. Clattering down the main street between its two rows of octagonal lampposts, Coignet finds General Charpentier, the military governor, installed – not in the 'wretched timber palace' overlooking the main square – but in a stone building, which according to Roeder, was down by the Dnieper bridge:

'I hand over my despatches. He reads through them; says: "Give this officer his dinner, lay him down on a mattress for an hour's rest; get a good horse ready for him and a chasseur as escort. Near the forest he'll find a regiment camped. He can change horses at the relay posts in the forest."'

Witebsk being essentially indefensible, its garrison, only a few thousand infantry and fewer cavalry, is forever having the jitters. Roeder – who'll get there next day – will find all its churches and hospitals packed with sick and wounded; and the 'French and Italians prodigiously slack in the execution of their duty. The guard and piquets sleep. The sentries are allowing anyone to enter who wants to, or at least anyone who can speak loud enough in French.' There are constant alarms and excusions about Cossacks in the neighbourhood. The newly arrived Hessians are just about to parade in full uniform on the main square to celebrate *their* young prince's name-day, when

'everything is suddenly thrown into a ridiculous uproar because a few Cossacks have been sighted, who're said to have carried off a forager. The entire garrison spring to arms, and when they've ridden out it's discovered that we're really only surrounded by a few dozen Cossacks dodging about hither and thither. In this way they'll be able to bring the whole garrison to hospital in about fourteen days without losing a single man.'

Scare over. Although still in full uniform and suffering from 'dysentery', Roeder has to do picket duty for twenty-four hours. To keep himself awake and set his sleepy men an example, he orders them to place a small writing-desk out in the middle of the street, down there by the bridge. Standing at it, he writes a long letter home to his new bride Sofie, friend of his tragically deceased Mina, whom he'd married before again going off to war (an attraction he can never resist) to provide a mother for their children. When he's finished, he takes out his diary and writes in it what amounts to another epistle – to the soul of his dead but much more passionately loved Mina. He doesn't give a fig for the immortality of the soul, he writes, unless it means he'll be reunited with her. As for the Grand Army, he has taken in its plight at a glance:

'On the march to Witebsk yesterday we met several cavalry depots of men who'd been sent back from regiments where either the riders had no horses or the horses no riders. They came, for example, from the fine 2nd Carabiniers, two regiments of cuirassiers and one of hussars, who every day are falling sick from the everlasting marching and bivouacking under the open sky. If the Russians want to send half our army to the dogs by the winter, all they have to do is to make us march hither and thither, with the individual units kept continually under arms. Then if they give us a few battles we'll be in a tough spot, so long as they have plenty of light troops.'

But all this will be next day; and just now Coignet, the true believer, is sleeping the sleep of the diligent on his straw mattress...

To the advancing army it seems as if the Cossacks are burning the entire country. An illusion of course. The swath of devastation the Cossacks and the Grand Army are together cutting in the immensities of the Russian countryside is at most some thirty miles wide. When von Roos' troopers are

'separated from the army for a few days and wandering around the countryside, we met neither friend nor foe, only occasional peasants busy with the harvest. The further away from our route they were working, the less they bothered about us and the harder they went on with their labours. We crossed the Dnieper several times, likewise several smaller streams, and also main roads, from which we could see whether Russians or our own troops had passed, because we recognized the horses' hoofmarks from the way they were shod and from the wheel tracks. Troops always leave behind something by which one can ascertain their nationality. As soon as a column has passed, one notices a smell that's peculiar to each army, and which the veterans instantly recognize.'

One evening Dumonceau's Dutchmen pass through just such an abandoned Russian encampment:

'Behind it was a hollow where the men had gone to meet calls of nature. I noticed a considerable volume of heaps of excrement covering the ground and from it concluded that the enemy army must have any amount of food to eat.'

Dr Roos is drawing similar conclusions:

'Normally it's rather hard to identify the ownership of camp sites, but even here this campaign had the special feature that the excrement left by men and animals behind the Russian front indicated a good state of health, whereas behind ours we found the most obvious possible signs that the entire army, men and horses alike, must be suffering from diarrhoea.'

Every time he reaches a new bivouac Dr Roos brews peppermint or camomile tea for his troopers

'in one or two kettles hung over the fire, serving it to all who needed it. If these items weren't available, then our people drank tea made of balm-mint and elder-blossom. To any who were particularly ill I allowed tincture of opium and Hoffmann's drops [a mixture of alcohol and ether] with these drinks. In this way we managed tolerably well, as long as my supplies lasted.'

At the large village of Katyn, on the Dnieper, the Red Lancers come across another abandoned camp, this time of Cossacks:

'Our generals, not feeling they should content themselves with appearances, had the opposite bank explored by some dismounted cavalrymen, who swam the river with their sabres between their teeth. From the height of the dominating bank, occupied by ourselves, we anxiously watched the outcome of this reconnaissance, made by completely naked men. They found nothing. Only some cables and other bridging materials seemed to indicate that the Russians had planned to take the French in flank.'

After Liady the sombre Lithuanian forests come at long last to an end. Everywhere the rich harvest, which has begun to be reaped but then abandoned, is putting new flesh on the cavalry's scraggy nags. Three miles further on, at the village of Sinacki, the Italians bivouack in really idyllic scenery, and Césare de Laugier sits scribbling in his diary as he watches

the other corps go by, leaving IV Corps in reserve:
'The columns of infantry, cavalry and artillery are marching at an urgent pace and in line, at short intervals so as to be able to deploy at the first obstacle. But this military arrangement has the grave defect of trampling the corn underfoot over a distance of 300 paces on either side of the road.'

The troops may be hurrying on towards what is hopefully an undefended Smolensk; but Napoleon himself, it seems, is in no great hurry. All day he lingers at Liady until he's 'sure the bridge over the Dnieper had been destroyed' so he can't himself be suddenly taken in flank or rear.

CHAPTER 14

THE WALLS OF SMOLENSK

A four-mile wall – 'the bravest feat I've seen' – Bagration's dark masses – a chivalrous challenge – what was Murat wearing? – Barclay relieved of the supreme command – 'the Emperor's staking out a battlefield' – effectives on 16 August – 'At last I've got them!' – a useful ford – fraternizing in the heat – Le Roy brings a herd of cows – an Italian idyll – a professor of swimming – Coignet returns from Witebsk – a painful episode

Smolensk, Russia's third most important city, lies on a steep reverse slope and is intersected by the Dnieper. Its older part, on the south bank, is surrounded by four miles of walls, 'very high, built of deep red bricks blackened by time, and flanked by 32 large towers[1] – some polygonal, others square, others again capped with dovecot-shaped roofs'.

Emerging on to the slopes facing the Krasnoië suburb at about 10 a.m. (16 August) III Corps sees to its left a great earthwork. Assuming he has only Neverovski's 4,000 survivors to deal with, Ney tries a *coup de main* by sending forward a single battalion of the 44th Line. Preceded by skirmishers, it drives the Russians out of the dry moat that everywhere covers the approaches, and is even within an ace of taking the earthwork. 'That's the bravest feat of arms I've seen since I've been making war!' Ney exclaims. And is promptly hit in the neck by a spent musketball. Only his tall collar, embroidered with gold acanthus leaves, saves him.

It also shows him that he's mistaken. Already 20,000 infantry and 72 guns of Raevsky's division, supported by 'a fair amount of cavalry', are holding the city. Arriving with Murat's advance guard, Colonel Griois' horse gunners have

'found the high ground all round Smolensk occupied by units of enemy cavalry. Our own charged them vigorously, pursuing them as far as the town walls, until held up by gunfire and musketry. Immediately I advanced my guns. Forming battery at two points, they opened a lively cannonade on the town, which kept continuously firing back at us.'

Griois' guns are busy banging away when he realizes that, at his side, someone is sitting a fabulously caparisoned horse:

'His beautiful brown hair fell down in tresses on to his shoulders. His harness, too, was bizarre but magnificent, and its beauty enhanced by the grace and deftness with which he handled his horse.'

It"s Murat, of course, who has spent the night at Ney's headquarters. Griois is too busy to note exactly what costume he's wearing.[2] Only that it's

'utterly theatrical. On anyone else it would have been ridiculous; but it seemed cut to his stature, the perfect accompaniment to an altogether brilliant valour, all his own.'

Enchanted with the vivacity and accuracy of the horse gunners' shooting, Murat keeps exclaiming in his husky voice: 'Bravo, boys! Knock that scum over. You shoot like angels!' And here come several squadrons of Russian dragoons; but the 7th French Dragoons, supported by the 23rd Line, move forward to drive them off: 'The two bodies approached each other at a gallop and the affray was intense and murderous. I've seen few cavalry charges driven home more thoroughly.' But in the end the Russians 'retire in disorder beneath the walls. And my artillery bombarded them so effectively at half-range that all our roundshot and shells fell in their midst and increased their disarray.'

But who are those 'dark masses' a keen-eyed Württemberg artillery officer has spotted in the distance, advancing at such a rate that they 'seemed to be running'[3]

'At first we took them for Junot's (VIII) corps, which we knew had gone astray. But then we saw it was the entire Russian army. Hearing of Neverovski's defeat [sic], it had woken up out of its trance and was making tracks for Smolensk, so as not to be cut off from the Moscow road.'

Since Ney's own supports are only coming up slowly, and 'upon the fortress suddenly belching troops and the fire of sixty guns', the Marshal calls off the badly mauled 44th, and waits for the situation to stabilize. Above all the Russian army mustn't be panicked into staging a further retreat.

'Taking out spyglasses at a great distance,' Captain Zalusky and his fellow-officers in the Polish Guard Lancers study 'with a certain emotion its walls, ancient witnesses to the siege they'd withstood in the days of Sigismund III'. 'Too frail to support the weight of heavy-calibre guns', Fézensac notices, they bristle with lighter pieces. He also sees that, 'though far from being built on the modern system, their great extent and height (8 metres) together with the broad ditch and covered way defending its approaches' will make the city hard to storm.

There'd been a chevalieresque prelude to all this. Approaching the 1st Guard Lancers on a grey horse, a Cossack officer

'at a distance of one hundred paces, or even less, challenged us in Polish to fight him. But Colonel Kozictulski wouldn't let anyone budge. Whereupon the Cossack shouted out: "Now you can capture me!" Got off his horse, and even started to unsaddle it. Finally, seeing he couldn't lure us out of our ranks, he remounted and went back to his own men. Their cannon fired a hundred rounds at us, without hurting anyone.'

But Griois' cannon go on firing until evening: 'Soon it had become general on all fronts as the corps batteries turned up one by one, and added their fire to ours. I had two guns dismounted and several men and horses killed.'

It had not been until late the previous evening that Napoleon had realized that the Russian high command had tumbled to his manoeuvre.

Leaving his bivouac at Koroutnia at 8 a.m., he'd crossed the intervening 20 miles at a gallop and at 1 p.m. reined in his horse above the heights above the city. 'We've just got here,' Fain jots down in his journal:
'The Emperor is staking out a field of battle between our line and the ramparts. Everything is being foreseen against the eventuality of the enemy emerging through the gates; or, if the Russian general should hesitate, of carrying the place by assault. But how believe Barclay de Tolly will hesitate? This time he's united with Bagration, and it's a question of Russia's third most important city!'
While waiting for the Russians to come out and fight, Fain hears 'a fusillading being kept up all along the line'. And Dumonceau, not far away, is noting how between himself and these massive walls, which 'put him in mind of what medieval cities must have looked like', there lies a ravine,
'on whose far side the enemy had had time to occupy some half-demolished houses. And about a mile away, where the Dnieper's further bank was covered with bushes, a suburb had been entrenched and its timber houses loopholed. Beyond, on the heights dominating the city, the Russian army was in position, ready to support the divisions which are going to defend Smolensk.'
As for the dry moat, or covered way, it
'supported a spacious glacis and everywhere separated it from the suburbs. There were only two gates. Access to one was covered by an arrow-shaped redoubt; to the other, by a modern terraced construction. The only other issue on the river side was by a simple passage down to the bridges.'

Again the time has come for the Grand Army to count its effectives. Fortunately for us, Fain jots down the returns:

	At the Niemen	At Smolensk
Imperial Guard	43,000	24,000
I Corps (Davout)	79,000	60,000
III Corps (Ney)	44,000	22,000
V Corps (Poniatowski)	39,000	22,000
Murat's cavalry	42,000	18,000
TOTALS	247,000	146,000
and in the rear		
IV Corps (Eugène)	52,000	30,000
VIII Corps (Junot)	18,700	14,000
GRAND TOTALS	318,000	190,800

Despite the units it has had to leave behind to garrison Minsk and Molihew (Sergeant Everts' 33rd Light, for instance), only Davout's corps is relatively intact. And the army's artillery, despite its shortage of horse-power, remarkably so. Gourgaud, whose business as First Ordnance Officer it is to get in its returns from Lariboisière – effectively, from Planat de la Faye, gives a detailed rundown:

'57×12-pounders, 267×8-pounders, 32×4-pounders, 2×3-pounders, 10×6.4 howitzers, 122×5.6 howitzers: altogether 490 pieces and 2,477 ammunition wagons, 'which makes up a total of 2,967 vehicles, the bridging equipment, forges, spare parts, wagons, etc., not included'.

The dwindling of the Guard has been due, of course, to the huge numbers of Young Guard conscripts lost en route. Many cavalry units have sunk pathetically. In III Corps, now at half-strength, von Suckow's company, 150 troopers strong when it set out from Württemberg, now has only 38.

Against Barclay's and Bagration's 115,000 behind those massive if antiquated walls, Napoleon still has – at least nominally – 190,000. Training his spyglass on Raevsky's troops as they come pouring into the city over the Dnieper bridge, he exclaims: 'At last – I've got them!' At long last the moment has arrived for the grand Austerlitz-style battle he has envisaged from the outset. Most of the long hot day, Caulaincourt says, was devoted to getting as close to the fortifications as possible and straightening out the battle line. Meanwhile, on either side of a little stream which separates the two armies the skirmishers are dodging about among bushes, taking potshots at one another. Gradually it becomes evident to officers on both sides that nothing much is going to be expected of them today. And with 'both sides feeling the need to water our horses', Lieutenant Lyautey's battery of the Guard Artillery unharnesses half its guns:

'Going down into the ravine I accompanied the horses with a few gunners, leaving behind enough to service the guns, if need arose. The Russians drank on one bank. We on the other. Not understanding each other very well, we conversed with gestures. We offered liquor and tobacco; and in this we were the more generous. Soon afterwards these good friends of ours fired a few shots. I found an officer who spoke good French, and we exchanged a few words.'

The 9th Lancers are among the light infantry on the left wing, with Bruyères' division drawn up in three lines behind them. At midday Lieutenant Wedel witnesses even more extensive fraternization. Swarms of Russian dragoons and Cossacks have been attacking the French skirmishers then falling back 'to lure us into the bushes where some infantry were concealed and which opened fire, forcing us to beat a hasty retreat. This mutual playfulness lasted quite a while.' But now the Russian fire ceases:

'Placing out some of their light infantrymen at intervals of some 15 to 20 paces, they sheath their swords as a sign they don't want to go on fighting. We follow their example, disposing our skirmishers in similar fashion at 100 metres or so from each other, with orders not to shoot. Now a Russian dragoon officer comes forward a few paces and salutes us, making signs with a bottle. I follow suit, and place myself in front of our line of skirmishers. In this way we come to within 30 metres of one another; whereupon the Russian calls out in French:

'Mon camarade! There's no sense in tiring our horses and killing each others' men to no purpose. Let's take a drink together instead. By and by we'll have all the time in the world to fight.'

We come closer and enjoy a friendly drink together, while further away other troops are still fighting. Soon several other Russian officers come forward. Upon my making to retire, my dragoon officer says:

'I promise you on my word of honour they won't do you any harm.'

So I stay put, and we have a friendly chat. His rum tasted good in my mouth. Unfortunately, I couldn't offer him any in return.'

Gradually more and more officers from both sides are joining in. Likewise 'our Frau Ehmke, a pretty woman who always rode about among the light infantry with two little kegs of brandy on her horse. She poured the Russians a free drink, but made us pay dearly for ours. A young lieutenant of our regiment, Piessac by name, had a girlishly pretty face, and got a kiss from an elderly bearded Russian.'

The 9th Lancers, though nominally Polish, are a ragbag of all nationalities; and there are Poles in the Russian army too:

'Because of our Polish uniforms a Polish-born Uhlan officer took us for Poles, and wanted to make enquiries about his compatriots. Hearing that a Polish lancer regiment was standing behind us in the second line, he rode fearlessly over to it, as fast as his horse could carry him. We thought he meant to desert. But that wasn't at all his intention! He just wanted to meet his compatriots and air his embittered views about Barclay de Tolly's way of waging war. When he heard we wished for nothing better than a pitched battle that would decide the war's outcome, and how tired we were of wandering about in a country that could offer us so few resources, he replied that, if we were hoping for such a battle in front of Smolensk, we'd be disappointed. He'd bet anything we'd enter Smolensk tomorrow; and that the Russians would slip away without fighting.'

But now General Bruyère notices what's going on, and sends an ADC to put a stop to it – and capture the Uhlan. 'But he rode so slowly – doubtless on purpose – that the Pole was warned in time by another officer, and hurried off.'

Le Roy, too, is taking it easy. Arriving from Molihew with 'bread, brandy and flour, likewise a large herd of cows which I placed at the regiment's disposal', he's amazed to hear he's been promoted *chef de bataillon* – Davout hasn't forgotten his resourceful behaviour at Salta Nowka. Not that there's any battalion of the 85th for him to command – as yet. But the portly major is reckoning with getting one after tomorrow's slaughter.

As for the Italians, they're positively enjoying themselves. A couple of miles to the rear they've bivouacked beside an idyllic lake fringed by a silver birch wood, whose 'pellucid waters invite us to bathe'. Albrecht Adam's lithograph shows the scene exactly; and Césare de Laugier fills in other details -

'the Viceroy's carriages and wagons... the generals and other officers scattered throughout the wood... groups of officers and men resting with their backs against tree trunks or stretched out at full length on the ground... other groups busy making their soup. Further away a circle has been formed and a peaceful discussion is going on. Still others either going off foraging or else returning. Along the shores of the lake many of us are busy doing our washing, whilst others, out of necessity or for pleasure' (as Labaume, also struck by the scene, puts it) 'are waging war on the little flock of geese and ducks that have escaped the Cossacks'.

Carabinier-sergeant Bertrand of the 7th Light is also in for a dip, but of another kind. He's just looking forward to a quiet night, even if it's to be his last, when his battalion is ordered to reconnoitre the river bank downstream from the city:

'We were commanded by a staff colonel, and had two guns with us. After three hours' marching our little advance guard is attacked by cavalry. The two companies of voltigeurs and granadiers are thrown forward. First in square then in open order, they push the enemy cavalry in front of them. We clear the rough ground at the double, so fast our cannon can't keep up with us. Arrived at the limit of a big ravine – no more cavalry! And in front of us the Dnieper!'

The Russians having crossed it in little skiffs, the staff-colonel says they must go and fetch them from the far bank:

'Since I'm the regiment's professor of swimming, I collect my 20 pupils, plus 30 volunteers. Our weapons and effects we leave in the battalion's care. Our guns are in battery. At a given signal we throw ourselves into the water. The enemy sends us a few musketballs; but a whiff of grapeshot puts him to flight, and we're able to bring back the fifteen boats. One swimmer has been killed and disappeared under the waves. Two have been lightly wounded on the head and neck. Just as the voltigeurs are embarking, a staff officer brings an order: we're to go back to our corps. We don't have to be asked twice. Already the daylight was fading, and night operations are always troublesome.'

Coignet, too, on his way back from Witebsk, is experiencing some tense moments. His hour's rest at an end, General Charpentier had come into the room:

'"Your packet's waiting for you, my friend, get going! Unless something should hold you up en route you'll get there within twenty-four hours, including the time you'll need for unsaddling and saddling up." I leave with a good mount and my escort. In the forest I find a regiment encamped. Show its colonel my orders. Hardly giving himself time to read them, he says: "Adjutant-major, give him a horse. It's the Emperor's orders!"

'I'd counted on finding cavalry posts in the forest. No sign of any! All had fled or been taken prisoner. Now I'm on my own, without any escort. Seeing some dismounted cavalrymen in the offing, I thoughtfully slow my horse to a walk. So they shan't catch sight of me, I take a roundabout way. Cossacks, certainly, standing there, waiting. Suddenly, just as I'm slipping along the forest fringe, a peasant comes out of it. Says to me: "Cossacks!" Well, I'd already seen them. Without an instant's hesitation I dismount and grab my peasant; show him some gold in one hand and my pistol in the other. Comprehending me, he says: "Toc, toc!" Which means "that's good!" I stuff the gold back into my waistcoat pocket, and while holding the horse's reins under one arm and my cocked pistol in my left hand, I take my Russian under my right arm. When he's led me to the main road, he says: "Nien, nien cossacks!"

Recognizing the highroad from its avenue of silver birches, he's beside himself with joy:

'I give my peasant three napoleons, promptly mount my horse. How I spurred that poor beast's flanks! The road vanishes behind me and even before my galloping horse has time to stumble I'm lucky enough to find a farm. Rush into the farmyard. There I see three young surgeons. I dismount, make a dash for the stable: "That horse, at once! I'll leave you mine. Read these orders!" Once again I mounted a good horse, who certainly knew how to get a move on. Yet to reach my goal I'd need yet another one. Night was falling, and I could no longer make out the road. Luckily I came across four well-mounted officers. Same ceremony begins all over again: "Try and read the Emperor's orders that you're to replace my horse." A fat gentleman whom I take to be a general says to the others: "Unsaddle your horse and give it to this officer. His orders are urgent. Help him!" I'm saved. Reaching the battlefield, here I am now, searching about for the Emperor. Everywhere the same reply: "I don't know."'

Darkness has fallen, so it must be at about 10 p.m. as not only Coignet but also Captain Biot are groping around amid the camp fires, searching for imperial headquarters. Though it wasn't his turn, Biot has been sent by Pajol with despatches for Montbrun and Napoleon. Coignet, for his part, almost wanders into the Russian lines:

'I push on. Catching sight of some camp fires to my left I leave the road. I'm just passing close by a battery when someone shouts out: "Qui vive?" "Orderly officer!" "Halt! You're going towards the enemy!" "Where's the Emperor?" "Follow me, I'll take you to my CO." We find him. He says: "Take him to the Emperor's tent." "Thanks." Reaching the tent, I have myself announced. General

Monthyon comes out, says: "Oh, so it's you, is it, *mon brave!* I'll present you at once to the Emperor." He thought I'd been taken prisoner. Whereon my general says to the Emperor: "Here's Your Majesty's officer, back from Witebsk." I hand him my despatches. The Emperor notices what a state I'm in: "How did you manage to get through the forest? Weren't there any Cossacks there?" "With gold, Sire! A peasant saved me by showing me a way round." "How much did you give him?" "Three napoleons." "And your horses?" "I've none left." "Monthyon, make good his travel expenses, his two horses and those sixty francs that peasant so well deserved. Give my old grumbler here time to get his breath back. For his two horses, six hundred francs and the post charges! I'm pleased with you!'"

What can it have been that was so urgent in those despatches? Perhaps Coignet's mission had partly been to test the state of communications to the rear? If so, Napoleon would also have been informed by Biot – it must have been one of Pajol's light cavalry regiments, guarding them, that Coignet had seen bivouacked in the forest– and there's certainly reason for anxiety. A couple of days later chasseur Lieutenant Maurice Tascher, will write in his diary: 'The Cossacks are on both flanks of the French army and in its rear. They're taking lots of prisoners and have cut the Liouvavitski road.'

But Sergeant Bertrand, still marching through the night, is 'only encountering a few poor isolated houses. Not until the moment when the regiment is about to leave do we rejoin it. It's been able to get some rest and have something to eat. But we ... we've sixteen hours of marching in our legs.'

While Coignet had been away there's been a painful incident in front of Napoleon's tent. Some staff officers looking through their spyglasses have thought that they could see Russian troops moving in *both* directions across the Dnieper bridge which links the city's two halves. Does this mean another midnight flit?[4] A fresh retreat? Murat (says Ségur) gloomily declares there'll be no battle, but is promptly contradicted by Davout. 'As for the Emperor, he believed what he wanted to.' This is too much for Murat. Who explodes: 'Since they won't stand and fight, to run after them is to go too far. It's time to call a halt!'

Napoleon tells him sharply not to meddle in matters he doesn't understand; and goes into his tent, followed by Murat. No one hears what follows. But when Murat comes out again he looks deeply depressed, angry and agitated:

'The word "Moscow" several times escaped his lips. Afterwards the King of Naples was heard to say he'd gone down on his knees to his brother-in-law, begged him to call a halt; but that all Napoleon could see in front of him was Moscow, declaring that honour, glory, repose

– all, for him, lay there. It was this "Moscow" that had been our undoing.'

Fact or fiction? Gourgaud says it's just another of Ségur's fables. Having 'spent part of the night in the Emperor's tent, we can assure the reader these allegations are false'. Well, perhaps: or partly. Maybe Murat didn't actually go down on his knees. But the morrow will confirm his despair. Evidently Napoleon feels challenged, for he tries to get Caulaincourt to agree with him. But Caulaincourt replies drily that, in his view, since the Russians can no longer take the offensive, they'll again retreat.

'"In that case," Napoleon burst out in the tones of a man who'd suddenly made up his mind, "by abandoning Smolensk, one of Russia's holy cities, the Russian army will have dishonoured itself in the eyes of its own nation and put me in a strong position. We'll drive them back a bit further, so they can't disturb us. I'll fortify my positions, give the troops a rest, and organize the country from our base at Witebsk – and see how Alexander likes that! I'll raise Poland in arms and later on, if necessary, decide between Moscow and Petersburg."'

In that moment Caulaincourt sees him as 'sublime, great, far-seeing, as on the day of his most brilliant victory'. And reiterates his long-standing view that it's the Russian plan to 'lure him further and further from his base, and shut him up among snow and ice. It was imperative we didn't go along with their little game. His Majesty seemed to approve of my reflections.' But when Caulaincourt hastens to report their conversation to Berthier and asks him 'to do everything in his power to support this wise decision, he seemed to doubt whether it would outlive the taking of Smolensk'.

CHAPTER 15

SMOLENSK – THE FIRST SHOCK

How thick are those walls? – Murat tries to get himself killed – seen in cinemascope – 'his face was a sickly hue and his look sombre' – Junot arrives – François is in the thick of it – a Russian hero – 'I'd gladly have hidden in a mousehole' – an immense furnace – Caulaincourt is worried – the Russians evacuate their holy city – Napoleon visits the battlefield – 'in six weeks we'll have peace' – Smolensk a charnel – 'a human face lay in the mud like a glove' – 'I felt I'd left hell behind me' – 'the gay strains of our bands' – 'they implored God's succour against us' – Le Roy revisits a distraught friend – Larrey does wonders – a ghastly wound

Again the sun rises in a cloudless sky; and the topographer-in-chief jots down in his journal:

'8 a.m. The Russians are beginning to pour out of the town. Our outposts are retiring, and the fighting which is now beginning is only for the houses in the outermost suburbs. Nor are they the same troops as yesterday. At dawn Raevski's men have left the city to liaise with Bagration. Today it's General Docturov, reinforced by Konownitzin's division, who's to defend Smolensk.'

As early as 3 a.m. Captain François has seen his division's light infantry regiment open a skirmishing fire, and I Corps begin to manoeuvre. And at 9 a.m. Sergeant Bertrand, suffering from lack of sleep after his night march, finds the 7th Light caught up in

'masses of troops of all kinds, debouching in every direction. Each takes up his proper place in the firing line. The Emperor appears. Like the generals in his suite he's covered in dust from head to foot. He rides up to the right of our division to give his orders. Near my company Marshal Ney dismounts, takes me by the arm, and leads me up to the top of a small hillock. Placing his telescope on my shoulder, he peers steadily through it for a full five minutes. After which he goes off and gives the Emperor an account of what he has seen.'

For a moment there's been another scare when 'some strong columns are seen moving off along the Moscow road'. Surely it's not going to be the same story as at Witebsk? 'No. Barclay's lines are standing motionless on the hills of the Petersburg suburb. Only Bagration is leaving.' Immediately Napoleon orders the bridge linking the old city with the new to be shelled by 30 heavy guns:

'The battery so harasses the enemy that his columns are crossing the bridge at the double. Obviously they're in full retreat. The Emperor wants to unleash an assault, and some officers decide to reconnoitre the wall, but haven't a scaling ladder.'

Nor are there any siege guns – the siege train is several hundred miles away with Macdonald's X Corps, investing Riga. But how will those red brick walls stand up to 12-pounders? How thick are they, really? The artillery staff are just passing in front of one of the town gates when a blast of grapeshot is fired at them at short range. It's Planat's baptism of fire. By a miracle no one's hurt. And Lariboisière tells his 'man of letters' to go and tell General Sorbier, commanding the Guard Artillery, to bring up a battery of 12-pounders as close as possible and try to batter a breach. Returning, Planat is 'present at the first attempt. Though a score of rounds were fired at point-blank range, they hardly managed to flake off a few fragments of bricks from the walls.' Davout, too, has brought up several such batteries. Roman Soltyk, that expert on ballistics, turns up 'at the very moment when Marshal Davout ordered his battery of 12-pounders to open fire'. It doesn't take him long to see they're just wasting ammunition, the more so as

'we were concentrating our fire on the wall, instead of on its flanking towers, whose lesser thickness would have enabled our artillery to bring them down. I was just returning from carrying a report to the Emperor. Halting there momentarily, I had occasion to admire our gunners' ability and Davout's courage, exposed as he was to the most murderous fire.'

Indeed all hell is let loose. The French position is completely dominated by some high ground on the other side of the Dnieper, and 40 Russian guns are replying. Amid bursting shells and rip-roaring roundshot Davout receives another visitor: Fézensac, sent by Berthier, quickly reaches the same conclusion. The walls are quite simply too thick.

But Napoleon, the gunner-emperor, feels he must see for himself. Mounting his horse he orders Captain *Chlapowsky* of the Polish Guard Lancers, whose turn it is to command the escort squadron, 'to chase away the Cossacks from the far side of the ravine'. A Russian shell bursts right in the midst of his lancers; and a moment later they're attacked by Cossacks. One of them lunges his lance at Chlapowsky, who parries the thrust with his sabre. But his horse suffers a nasty wound, from the tip of its ear to its nostril.

Nor is Davout alone in exposing himself. Nor – quite needlessly – is Murat. Leading his horse by the reins a few paces behind the King, his Neapolitan ADC sees

'the gunners, crushed by the battery dominating us, falling beside their guns. The gun carriages were being smashed, the guns overthrown. Ignited by the enemy shells, ammunition wagons keep exploding with a terrific crash. It was at that moment one such wagon blew up, only ten paces away from us, throwing me to the ground – fortunately without worse harm to myself than to stun me, leaving me stone deaf for two days to come. But horse and harness were torn to shreds.'

A most puzzling scene ensues. Half-grilled alive in their steel cuirasses, their maned helmets gleaming in the sun as it rises ever higher in the sky, the 2nd Cuirassiers have been standing 'more or less out of range of the roundshot, some of which got as far as to our horses' hoofs'; and since 'another opportunity mightn't present itself' Thirion is curious to see such an artillery battle at close quarters. Accompanied by a comrade, Baffcop by name, 'whose adventurous character I knew', he walks forward until he's in the very midst of one of Sorbier's batteries:

'Reaching this point, I find myself amidst a rain of cannon-balls. Never was I better able to appreciate the dangers run by the artillery, how much valour and what cool heads are needed for this branch of the service! Not only are the Guard batteries, in whose midst I stood, being rapidly bombarded by the artillery in the fortress, they're also being taken in flank by other Russian batteries, set up on an eminence on the other side of the river. How a man or a horse could have escaped from this mass of roundshot coming from two sides and crossing each other in the middle of these batteries, each gun with its six horses and an ammunition wagon, is more than I can conceive.'

And yet here's Murat – strolling to and fro 'with the calm which distinguished him when under fire, smiling at everyone, encouraging the gunners and promising them his wonted success'. This time we know what he was wearing, for he's been seen a few moments earlier by I Corps' paymaster *Duverger* sporting 'a gold-braided pelisse, a pair of flesh-coloured pantaloons that showed off his figure, and a toque on his head, adorned by a tuft of luxurious feathers'. Surprised to see two cuirassier officers standing there, Murat comes up and asks: 'What the devil are you doing here, gentlemen?' Their presence, they explain, is due to a passionate interest in siegecraft. Murat smiles and walks away, leaving Thirion puzzled. Why was the King of Naples, normally surrounded by a numerous staff, alone? 'No ADCs. No escort. What had become of this obligatory accompaniment of a high commander? Had they dispersed, carrying orders?' Or had they all been killed by 'the roundshot which was raining down at this point?'

Evidently he hasn't noticed Belliard, who explains the mystery.

Murat, depressed after the previous evening's conversation, is quite simply trying to get himself killed. When Rossetti had been stunned by the exploding ammunition wagon, Belliard had protested: 'Sire, you'll only get yourself killed – without glory, and to no purpose.' But Murat, mumbling repeatedly 'Moscow, Moscow', tells him irritably to go away. And when Belliard points out that all he'll succeed in doing will be to get his staff killed, bursts out furiously: 'Very well, then, retire! And leave me here alone! Surely you can see your group is giving the enemy a target for his fire?' The officers had scattered – which is why Thirion doesn't see them. But Belliard persists: 'Sire, Your Majesty has decided to get himself killed today. Permit me to do the same at your side.' At this, he says, Murat 'with a gesture of fury and despair, walked quickly away from the spot'.

'Soon we had to admit the operation was impossible. The walls resisted our roundshot. So the breaching project was abandoned, and the Emperor gave orders for them to be mined. But neither could this method, though surer, be implemented, the circumstances being so urgent. So our artillery was employed to enfilade the wall and dismount the enemy guns by firing ricochets. In this way,'

concludes Soltyk, that expert on gunnery and ballistics, 'it sent a great number of shells into the town, causing several fires to break out'.

Meanwhile the infantry assault columns have been massing on the slopes. In the centre, says Captain François of the 36th Line, 'I Corps manoeuvred en masse under the enemy's fire'. But to Dumonceau the forenoon seems to be passing quietly enough. Only when the sun is blazing down from its zenith are the 2nd Guard Lancers ordered to stand to arms. And an ADC leads them forward to the rim of the ravine:

'From there we had a view over the entire enemy army on the plateau opposite us, likewise of the assault columns massing on the slopes opposite the town gates. A crowd of curious persons from the artillery parks and baggage train who'd nothing to do and no need to bestir themselves came running up and lined the valley's rim to watch, as if from the top of an amphitheatre.'

But so far not a single enemy soldier has shown himself in front of the suburbs. And by and by Morand's division forms up

'in a compact column[1] and descends from where we are by the broad Micislaw road. Provisionally leaving one of its brigades in reserve near a bridge at the bottom, it throws out a screen of skirmishers. They're just reaching the crest, when two enemy squadrons, coming up from behind the suburb, draw up on the plain opposite, ready to charge as soon as the line shall appear on the plateau. These skirmishers, still sheltered by the crest of the hill, have no inkling of the danger they are in, though we, from our dominant position, can see it perfectly. Alarmed for the outcome, the crowd of spectators all around us try to ward off Fate by shouts and gesticulations, as if these could be understood at such a distance! But here too our battery comes to the rescue. We can see the cannon-balls ricocheting in front of the enemy squadrons, reaching them and carrying confusion among their ranks, and, after a few instants' hesitation, forcing them to retire. Each of these successes fills our crowd of onlookers with enthusiasm. They applaud noisily, clapping their hands and shouting "Bravo! Bravo!" as if at the theatre. On the skirmishers reaching the crest of the plateau we see them carry out a sudden flank movement at the double, in the direction of a large enclosed area visible at some distance to their right, and which seems to be a cemetery. One by one they get inside it and vanish. To make this movement they've had to pass in front of two long loopholed buildings, or timber outhouses, from which comes a lively fusillade... but so swiftly have they passed in front of it, it only causes them the loss of one man, who's left lying on the ground before our eyes.'

Meanwhile Morand's assault column has been mounting the slope without meeting any resistance. But now

'two enemy guns emerge from the suburb, appear at the head of the incline, and open fire. Whereupon a French battery, sited close beside us on the plateau's edge, crushes them by its superior weight of fire, forcing them to withdraw. Meanwhile the column, moving off the road to the left so as to get more room to manoeuvre, imperturbably goes on climbing the hill. Reaching its brow, it drives before it a confused mass of enemy skirmishers who've been sent out to meet it.'

Now it's within sight of the suburb's first houses,

'which receive it with a sudden rolling fusillade. Marching quickly on these buildings, they turn their extreme right, take them from behind, and thus displace the scene of the fighting to their rear, where it disappears from view. Attacking these houses at the *pas de charge*, the column flows around them and penetrates them at all points, amidst whirling smoke which thereafter hides this engagement going on inside the suburb from our view.'

And now the Red Lancers are themselves being called for. This time it's Friant's division which, together with III Cavalry Corps, is to attack the Roslawl suburb, and they're to support the movement. This assault, too, is followed by some fascinated spectators on a hillock. To the right they see

'Poniatowski's V Polish Corps, deployed in line, marching as if on parade across an open plain, rising imperceptibly toward the Nikolskoïe and Rasaska suburb. A Russian battery, placed out slightly ahead on the slope, unceasingly vomits whirlwinds of smoke and fire, to which the artillery advancing ahead of the Polish line replies. Still further to the right, at the far end of the line, the King of Naples' cavalry seems to be strongly engaged with a cloud of Cossacks.'

Now Dumonceau himself gets some orders. He's to take two troops of lancers and observe the flank of the suburb opposite them, thus guaranteeing the regiment from any surprises on that side. 'Even so, I find I'm being fired on by the skirmishers embuscaded behind garden hedges. In no time two of my men are lightly wounded and a musket-ball rips my mantle, which I'm wearing bandoleer-style, as is the usage when on outpost duty.' Colbert, informed, feels he shouldn't leave the two troops exposed; and orders them to retire.

Only after reiterated efforts – in which Dedem van der Gelder, riding at the head of his infantry brigade, is hit in the chest by a spent musket-ball and has a horse killed under him – does Friant's division penetrate its target. But all Dumonceau can see now is 'a lot of movement, and numerous wounded streaming back out of all the exits. Finally a decisive movement seems to be happening. We see III Cavalry Corps suddenly fling itself in columns of troops into the suburb's broad main street and disappear there, enveloped in a cloud of dust and smoke.' Whereupon Davout flings the entire weight of I Corps at the Malakhofskaia Gate and the strongly pallisaded redoubt covering it. But the Red Lancers have 'no part to play in such engagements. As soon as the suburbs had been captured we returned to our bivouac. None of the Imperial Guard's other units had budged.'

And here – at last – after wandering aimlessly about the countryside is Junot's VIII Corps.

His troops too, are utterly discouraged. 'Depression and weariness with life had spread through the Westphalian army,' says that proud veteran from Wagram, Lance-corporal Wilhelm Heinemann. That morning the Brunswick Chasseurs had just put their cooking pots on to make their soup, and had even sent out marauders to find some bread and flour, when the order had come to get moving again.

'The half-boiled broth had to be thrown away. The meat is tied to our straps – a cruel fate for hungry soldiers! To run for two hours, embarrassed with musket and pack, after already suffering so much from famine, shortages and wearisome marches, is no light matter. Several gave up the ghost and fell exhausted. Others shot themselves in despair. The thunder of the guns is coming closer and closer. We're made to march past Napoleon at the double. How different everthing is from what it had once been at Lobau! Then the French army had been all enthusiasm – one thunderous shout of "Vive l'Empereur!"; and he himself lively as a bird on his dazzling white horse, surrounded by a general staff whose splendour and brilliance seemed better suited to a parade than to serious fighting. Now the Emperor and his entourage were so covered in dust we could hardly make out the colours of their uniforms. Pale and lethargic, his face a sickly hue and his glance sombre, he sat immobile, a bad portrait of himself. Horse and rider were both visibly exhausted.'

As the Westphalians, silent and panting in the dust clouds, double past, a singular detail catches Heinemann's eye: 'On one side the Emperor's underclothes were torn open from knee to hip, baring his leg.' Heinemann thinks it 'shows he isn't sparing himself'.

'On our way', Dumonceau goes on,

'we passed across the front of a handsome regiment of lancers of the Royal Westphalian Guard, formed up in reserve. It was wearing black helmets with a lot of copper ornament, which attracted our attention. We observed one another with curiosity. As they pointed us out we could hear them saying among themselves in German: "Holländer, Holländer". Among them our comrade Captain Bellefroid saw one of his brothers.'

But of Junot himself, the blonde handsome friend of Napoleon's youth, 'whose face, bearing and turnout eight or nine years before had surpassed all the army's officers at the Boulogne Camp,' nothing is left. Secretary Fain is shocked to see him

Armand de Caulaincourt, Master of the Horse and Napoleon's left-hand man. 'Five foot eight inches tall, with a frank and honest appearance... liked and respected by all... an admirable officer, a military man through and through...', he was candidly against the war. Responsible for headquarters transports and the courier service, on campaign he rode immediately to the left of the Emperor's carriage and, upon his exchanging it for one of his Arab greys, held his stirrup as he mounted. By the summer of 1812 this had become more than a ritual gesture.

Above: Three penal regiments – 38,000 deserters – had supplied the Grand Army with the equivalent of a whole infantry division. A political dinner plate, probably from 1814, reminds the diner of a sight all too common during the Empire.

Below: The crossing of the Niemen, 24 June 1812 – engraving by Christian Wilhelm von Faber du Faur, a Württemberg artillery major in Ney's III Corps. 'Full of ardour, lulled by the most beautiful hopes, everyone hastened to reach Russian soil.' The columns crossing the three pontoon bridges are glimpsed in the distance.

Above: Grenadier Pils' watercolour sketch of the sunshade of pine branches erected by Guard sappers for Napoleon on a hillock about 100 yards from the Niemen. The man he's talking to is Marshal Oudinot – "a good fellow, but not much brains" – commander of II Corps.

Below: Philippe de Ségur's *[left]* enthralling history of the disastrous campaign is so full of errors and strokes of the imagination that they were scathingly criticized by his former colleague First Ordnance Officer Gaspard Gourgaud *[right]*. They fought a duel over it. In Russia, Ségur, as Assistant Prefect of the Palace, was in charge of the headquarters mules, which among other things carried Napoleon's gold dinner service.

Below right: The ex-Armenian slave Roustam Raza, Napoleon's bodyguard, slept with drawn scimitar across the door to his bedroom and accompanied him wherever he went, dressed in 'mameluke' costume. – *Portrait attributed to Gros.*

Above:'The stoutness he acquired during his reign's last years had developed his torso more than the lower part of his body, yielding an impression of a majestic and imposing bust which lacked a base in due proportion,' – Méneval. Girodet de Roucy Triason's portrait sketch of early 1812, too, confirms Castellane's statement that Napoleon had put on a lot of weight.

Below: Marshal Davout, Prince of Eckmühl, commander of I Corps. A fierce disciplinarian, he had no consideration whatever for his staff. Murat mocked him to his face for wearing spectacles.

Above: Marshal Berthier, Prince of Neuchâtel, the army's major-general and head of the General Staff. In 1812 his powers were declining. In reality he was less than handsome, and no little slovenly. Always biting his bleeding fingernails, he would burst into tears when reprimanded by his exacting taskmaster.

Below: Joachim Murat, King of Naples. An incomparable cavalry commander in battle, on the march he took no care whatever of his four huge 'reserve' cavalry corps. He had no taste for the Russian. He wore fantasical uniforms of his own invention.

Above: Faber du Faur's 12-pounders get stuck in a muddy hollow beyond Vilna and have to turn back, temporarily depriving Ney of his reserve artillery as he chases Barclay de Tolly's 1st West Army eastwards. 'Several hundred horses perished there.'

Below: The Italian Guardia d'Onore on the march. The artist, ex- cakemaker Albrecht Adam, had attached to Prince Eugène's staff in search of battle scenes. Long forced marches in burning heat were less to his taste.

Above: The route-march made through impossible terrain by Pino's division of IV Corps to catch up with the advancing columns was not actually witnessed by Albrecht Adam. His touching picture is thus mostly an 'artist's impression'.

Below: Surgeon Heinrich von Roos 'saw enormous cuirassiers riding little Polish horses so small their riders' legs dragged along the ground'. Faber du Faur thought it 'a spectacle at once sad and funny to see carabiniers and cuirassiers, colossi with gigantic limbs, pass our camp at Rudnia on these scraggy horses'. – *Faber du Faur*.

Above: The Napoleonic soldier, in Russia as elsewhere, didn't steal – he 'found'. But the dividing line between authorized marauding and individual pillage could suddenly shift, exposing looters to the firing squad. Grenadiers from III Corps. – *Faber du Faur.*

Below: Only the well-educated Hessian captain Franz Roeder, a stickler for justice, has a good word to say for the Lithuanian Jews. Colonel Bacler d'Albe, Napoleon's topographer-in-chief and closest collaborator, too, found time to draw 'Polish Jews presenting soldiers of the Grand Army with their merchandise'.

Above: Prince Eugène directing the Italian troops' crossing of the Dwina at Beschenkowiczi, 24 July. – *Albrecht Adam.*

Below: 'At least Polotsk looks like a city,' thought Sergeant Bertrand of the 7th Light, reaching it on 24 July. 'It boasts seven or eight church towers and two big monasteries' – one was the seat of the Jesuit order. Polotsk would be the scene of two major battles. – *Faber du Faur*

Above: Napoleon arrives on the scene at the end of the battle of Ostrowno, 26 July. When it was over, Albrecht Adam asked Eugène to sign his sketches, to prove he'd really been in the thick of it. Actually the two-day battle was only a rearguard action, to give Bagration a chance to liaise with Barclay in front of Witebsk. *Albrecht Adam.*

Below: In front of Witebsk, midday 27 July. Surely the decisive battle is at hand? 'The Army of Italy and Murat's cavalry attack the highway supporting the Russian army's left wing.' But Napoleon unexpectedly called off his attack – and next day the Russians had literally vanished. – *Albrecht Adam.*

Above: The Dnieper (the Borysthenes of antiquity) turned out to be "an ordinary little river, so steeply embanked you can hardly see it before you stumble on it". The gigantic concentration described by Dumonceau, and necessary for the flank march on Smolensk. Ney's III Corps crossing at Rossasna, under Napoleon's supervision. – *Faber du Faur.*

Below: Beyond Krasnoi. Murat's fruitless cavalry attacks on the massed square of Neverovski's division as it carries out its fighting withdrawal on to Smolensk get in the way of Ney's guns. – *Faber du Faur.*

Above: The bombardment of Smolensk, 8 August. The ancient town wall proved impermeable to the invaders' roundshot. – *Albrecht Adam.*

Below: Smolensk in flames. Around 'the cathedral cupolas rising above the plain that hid it from our sight, by 10 p.m. we saw rising from the town centre columns of fire, which seemed like a mountain peak. Growing steadily, they formed a jet of fire that turned night into day and lit up the smiling Smolensk countryside.' – *Faber du Faur.*

Above: The heroic Russian NCO who'd died among the shattered willow trees while obstinately sniping at the Württemberg artillery. 'Next day, Aug 9, visiting the spot out of pure curiosity, we found our enemy's body lying face downward among the broken and splintered trees. He'd been killed by one of our roundshot.' – *Faber du Faur.*

Below: Württemberg gunners firing from the walls of Smolensk at the New Town beyond the Dnieper, where the Russian rearguard is still hanging on. 9 Aug. – *Faber du Faur*

Above: Troops moving up to the firing line at Valutina-Gora, 10 August, where the campaign might have been decided if it hadn't been for Junot's ineptitude. The engaving gives a vivid idea of the early autumn landscape. – *Faber du Faur*

Below: The roads in the army's wake were littered with stragglers, wounded, dead and dying men. "Even if I hadn't been able to see the Moscow road, I'd only have had to follow its smell." – *Faber du Faur.*

Above: This early 19th century print gives an authentic idea of the great masses of men crammed together on a Napoleonic battlefield, particularly on 7 September 1812, at Borodino. Also of the rather gloomy weather conditions.

Below: Murat about to take refuge in a square of the 25th Division, having mistaken Russian for Saxon cuirassiers on account of their white jackets. The artist has omitted his heroic Negro servant Narcisse, who risked his own life to alert the square. – *Faber du Faur.*

Above: The 5th Cuirassiers storm the Raevsky Redoubt. 'Overthrowing everything in front of them, they turn the redoubt, entering it by the throat.' But Auguste Caulaincourt, who has guided the movement, lies dead, shot through the heart. His ADC, Lieutenant Wolbert, kneels by his side. – *Early 19th-c. engraving.*

Below: "The whole ploughed up plain, strewn with wreckage and débris and hemmed in by gloomy dark trees, conspired to give the field [of Borodino] a dreadful aspect. Everywhere soldiers were wandering about among the corpses, rifling their dead comrades' packs for food." – *Faber du Faur.*

Above: The wooden noticeboard erected by Marshal Lefebvre on the spot where the popular Montbrun – who in a moment of irritation had told Napoleon to go to the devil – was killed by a howitzer shell. The board was still standing in 1813. In the *background* Borodino church. *Left mid-distance* part of Semenovskaya and one of the flêches. – Lithographic colour-print in J.T. James: *Views of Russia, Sweden and Poland*, London, 1826.

Below: The Grand Army outside Moscow, 14 September. – *Gudin,* one of his idealized engravings *Entrances of the French into Foreign Capitals.*

'come and present himself in a leisurely way at the imperial tent. But Napoleon had gone down into the plain. The general sits down like a man utterly exhausted. He complains of having gone astray on the march. Is afraid he has sunstroke. Asks for something to drink. Wine won't quench his thirst. Offered a carafe of water, he drains it off at a gulp. By and by he becomes more animated. But it's all up with him. His eye no longer lights up at the sight of a battlefield.'[2]

Although his outflanking manoeuvre has failed, there's still a chance of cutting the Moscow road and thus cutting the Russian army off from its line of retreat. But to do this a whole corps will have to cross the Dnieper upstream. And the only one available is Junot's. According to Ségur there was 'a broad and commodious passage only three miles upstream from the town' to the east. So far, for lack of VIII Corps, attempts to find the ford seem to have been half-hearted. But now Belliard, Murat's resourceful chief-of-staff

'orders a few troopers to follow him, and pushing a band of Cossacks into the river upstream of the town, sees on the opposite bank the Smolensk–Moscow road all covered with artillery and marching troops. But the troopers sent to find a ford rode for six miles without finding one and drowned several of their horses.'

Ségur even says Napoleon 'pushed his own horse in that direction, rode several versts, wearied and came back again'. But is the lethargic Junot really capable of crossing the Dnieper and 'with a river at his back, a fortified town, and an enemy army' pinning down so fierce a bulldog as Bagration? Evidently Napoleon is hoping so. For that's what he orders him to do.

In the centre I Corps is fiercely engaged. After 'manoeuvring en masse under the enemy's fire' its other divisions have 'captured the plateau of Mulchowa'. During this operation the 30th Line is ordered by Davout to advance to the attack and 'we lose a lot of men when drawing up under the Russian guns'. To the left the 7th Light certainly aren't being spared:

'In front of us the Russians were waiting for us in a deep ravine covered with shrubs and bushes. We're thrown in by battalions, by companies. The ground is extremely rough, and breaks up our formations; few or none of our officers manage to keep their men with them – except our captain. His name was Moncey,[5] and he'd been one of the Emperor's pages. He's followed by a half-section – I being its fourth man – who are to distribute his orders. At one particular moment I find I've ten Russians in front of me. Having burnt off a cartridge, we're obliged to play with our bayonets, which hardly troubles us. Soon the Russian guns fell silent – in all that scrum and confusion they'd harm their own men as much as us. We're slowly advancing amid this hand-to-hand fighting, when the cry *"En avant!"* is heard. The drums beat the attack. And everyone dashes forward at the double, upwards and out of the ravine, driving everything before him. To our right the bombardment redoubles – and we who by now, without excessive losses, have reached the foot of the walls, have to suffer the fire from the guns up there in the towers and bastions.'

The 'Dromedary of Egypt', too, is in the thick of it. The cemetery's loop-holed walls have been forced, but now graves and mausoleums are providing almost equally good cover for both sides. Captain François' men have broken in only to find themselves exposed to threefold fire: from Russian sharpshooters dodging about among the graves, from enfilading cannon, and from others which are 'vigorously belabouring us from a tower'. Soon Colonel Bouquet has to withdraw François' men

'behind the counterscarp of the ditch surrounding the cemetery. From his higher level the enemy go on throwing roundshot and some kind of triple-vented shells at us. At 2 p.m. one of these falls in front of my company, spewing out flame from its three vents. I run over, pick it up, and drop it into a well a few yards behind me. I burn my hands a little; also the front of my coat. But the superior officers and the whole battalion shout *"Bravo! Vive le Capitaine François!"* If that shell had exploded, it'd have blown up two ammunition wagons to the battalion's left.'

Thereafter the fighting 'became horrible'. Slowly François and his comrades drive back the Russians 'even to the cannon's mouth'. The Russians' resistance astounds everyone. Defying their officers' orders merely to stand firm, the Russian light infantry in the cemetery can only be restrained from counter-attacking by blows with the flats of their officers' swords. 'Major-general Tsilbulski, on horseback in full uniform, told me he couldn't keep his men under control. Over and over again they after exchanging a few shots with the Frenchmen in the cemetery tried to throw them out of it at bayonet point.' A 22-year-old Russian officer who has ridden out of the town to watch the fighting finds

'General Schevitch of the Lifeguard Hussars inspiring the gunners by his presence. One of the town's clergy was personally sighting several of the guns. Letting the Frenchmen get as close as possible, as soon as they were within caseshot range [about 200 yards] the artillery officer, a young man of approximately the same age as myself, flung them down on the ground in enormous heaps. I'd often seen men fall; but never so many knocked over by a single salvo! Only a second earlier the poor victims had been advancing with fixed bayonets and pale faces. Now most of them lay dead or mutilated, lying there armless and legless, drowning in their own blood. Eager to avenge its comrades with a hailstorm of musketry, another column comes on. Many of our gunners are shot down.'[4]

Farther to the left, Ney's corps is no less heavily engaged. Hour after hour Major Faber du Faur's Württemberger battery stands firing a few yards from a little stream where 'a Russian chasseur distinguished himself by his staunchness and courage. He'd taken up position in front of us behind a few willow trees, on the very banks of the stream. Neither by concentrating our fire on him, nor by using a large-calibre gun to bring down all the trees where he was dodging about[5] could we silence him. He went on shooting at us until nightfall.'

Standing 50 paces away from one of Davout's 12-pounder batteries near his bespectacled marshal – he's been attached to his staff – Le Roy too catches sight of a single detached Russian soldier

'walking to and fro, as if guarding something of great importance. Recognizing me despite his extreme near-sightedness, Davout says: "Go and see what that fellow's doing." Without for one moment taking my eyes off the man's movements, against which I've furnished myself with a good pair of pistols, I gallop over and approach him. There seems to be nothing nothing hostile about him, so I assume he must be standing guard over a superior officer, wounded or dead.

The plump major approaches to within six paces. And the Russian

'points with the tip of his bayonet towards a body, apparently seated against a garden hedge. I return at once to make my report to the Marshal, who has already forgotten all about it. Seems surprised, and he remarks: "Our men wouldn't submit to such discipline; and I think they'd be right not to."

Strange words to come from the Iron Marshal. His and the Guard's 12-pounder batteries[5] have cleared the ravine with their enfilading fire. But that's a game at which two can play. As wave after wave of the blue lines roll forward over it, von Suckow, for one, is beginning to feel angry. What's the sense of such massive attacks against troops which at any moment can withdraw behind those towering walls? He sees

'a French staff officer, without even reconnoitering the terrain, lead the Württemberg Light Infantry – in particular its superb Foot Chasseurs – straight up to the high wall, where they're simply mown down. Decimated and furious at being forced to carry out such an absurd mission, they're obliged to beat a retreat, after losing five officers within only a few minutes.'

On the hither side of the ravine the surgeons have their work cut out. Keen to see the battle at close quarters, Paymaster Duverger has made his way forward through a little copse, from whose far end he can clearly see both armies' movements. Just then

'a blast of grapeshot struck a dragoon a few paces away, and gave me notice I'd do well to moderate my curiosity. So I retired towards a dressing station. A gunner had just been brought in, supported by a young officer who was shedding big tears. His arm was shattered. The amputation took place. During it the poor fellow uttered loud cries, begging for someone to kill him. Suddenly a dull rumour announces the Emperor's arrival, and after a moment or two he appears, followed by a brilliant staff. "Sire, I'm wounded, come to me, come to me!" Napoleon hears him, and comes over: "What do you want of me?" – "Sire, three of my brothers have been killed in your service. Look, I'm no longer in a state to serve you any more. I recommend myself to your bounty."

Napoleon tells Berthier to 'make a note of the wounded man's name in his notebook,[6] and he complained no more'. At that moment Duverger also sees Murat gallop up. And after him, Ney, 'but dressed in his uniform of a marshal of France. The Emperor's two lieutenants gave their superior an account of their operations and then, after a few minutes' discussion, both left.'

Again and again observers on the ravine's edge, von Suckow among them, see how

'we gained ground and broke into the suburbs, only to be dislodged by renewed Russian efforts. But then, suddenly, everything succeeds at once, except Ney's attack, which should have been decisive but has been neglected. The enemy is thrown back brusquely behind his walls. Everything which doesn't make haste to follow suit perishes. Even so, our columns, in mounting to this assault, have left behind them a long broad trail of blood, wounded and dead. One platoon of a battalion which had presented its flank to the Russians, we'd noticed, had lost an entire rank from a single cannon-ball – 22 men falling to the same shot. In this way Ney's error of the previous day with one battalion was repeated by the entire army.'

At about nightfall the city goes up in flames. Everywhere the Russians have been driven back to its walls. Nowhere have they been penetrated. At their foot, covered in blood and dust, Captain François and his comrades don't so much see Smolensk burn as hear it. The roar of his guns having at last fallen silent, Major Faber du Faur is noticing how

'The noise and uproar of the stormy day is followed by a profound silence, only broken by the roaring and crackling of flames consuming the houses. By about 10 p.m. the whole of that part of the city which stood on the far side of the river had become a single flame, mirrored in the Dnieper's waters, in the purple glow of the walls, and in the holy city's tartar towers.'

To Dumonceau, looking on from his bivouac in the vicinity of Napoleon's tents, it seems the flames are

'leaping up from behind those sombre walls like an immense furnace and reaching a considerable height under a cloudless sky, splendid with stars. It was a spectacle of marvellous beauty, or anyway, grandeur.'

That night educated men from all over Europe can drink their fill of what they called 'the sublime' – a kind of beauty defined by Edmund Burke[7] as comprising an element of the grandiose and terrible. Another aesthete, who has probably spent the long hot day in perfect safety amid the baggage train or perhaps been one of the idle spectators on the rim of the ravine – Captain Beyle, alias Stendhal, is thinking Smolensk in flames 'an entrancing sight... such a singular spectacle'.[8] The silhouette of its crenellated towers and walls is putting Paul de Bourgoing and his comrades at General Delaborde's headquarters in mind of Homer's description of Troy in flames. While to Major Boulart 'the Russian sharpshooters, posted on the ramparts, like devils in hell or figures in a Chinese shadow play, offered a picturesque spectacle of an entirely novel kind'. In their bivouacs farther away men can only see

'the cathedral cupolas rising above the plain that hid it from our sight. By 10 p.m. we saw rising from the town centre columns of fire, which seemed like a mountain peak. Growing steadily, they formed a jet of fire that turned night into day and lit up the smiling Smolensk countryside.'

But to the Master of the Horse, 'wandering sleeplessly about', this is 'a terrible sight'. He's feeling deeply worried, not to say depressed:

'The conflagration only grew worse as the night wore on. I reflected dismally on what this outcome must infallibly lead to if the Emperor didn't put into effect his good intentions of the previous day. All the time my conversation with him came back to me, and consoled me a little. But the Prince of Neuchâtel's remarks on that subject made themselves felt at least as strongly, and my earlier experiences made me share his opinion and fears.'

Despite the stupendous conflagration the night is turning cold. And at about 2.a.m. Caulaincourt goes up to 'the camp fire burning in front of the Emperor's tent, on the side facing the town' and sits down beside it:

'I was beginning to feel drowsy, when His Majesty came up, with the Prince of Neuchâtel and the Duke of Istria [Bessières]. They gazed at the flaming town. It lit up the whole horizon, which was also sparkling with our camp fires:

"An eruption of Vesuvius!" cried the Emperor, clapping me on the shoulder and rousing me from my torpor. "Isn't that a fine sight, my Master of the Horse?" "Horrible, Sire!"

"Bah!" riposted the Emperor. "Remember, gentlemen, what one of the Roman emperors said: 'an enemy's corpse always smells good!'" We were all shocked by this remark. At once I recalled what the Prince of Neuchâtel had said, and the Emperor's observation long haunted my inmost thoughts.'

Caulaincourt and Berthier exchange 'meaningful glances, as men do who understand each other without need of words'. But Napoleon is sitting 'silent in front of his tent', watching the holocaust.

An hour before midnight, as the fire is beginning to die down, some marauders who've 'made their way into the town through some old breaches the enemy hadn't even bothered to repair' are the first to enter. Venturing up to the foot of the walls, an NCO of the 107th has quietly climbed it. Encouraged by the silence reigning all around him, he's gone into the town, bumped into some of Poniatowski's Poles and 'recognizing their slavonic accents took them for Russians. Fearing himself a prisoner, he fell into a panic'. But gradually others, too, come clambering in over the debris of the town's shattered gates. 'After the powder magazines had been blown up', Rossetti goes on, 'Cossacks had been sent galloping through the streets, telling everyone the Russian army was going to retreat and urging anyone who wanted to go with it to make haste, before the Dnieper bridge was demolished.' Thousands have done so.[9] At 5 a.m. Napoleon is told the place has been evacuated.

It's been the bloodiest storming attempt Surgeon-General Larrey has ever seen:

'The approaches to the gates, the breaches, and the main streets were full of dead and dying, almost all Russians. Their losses were immense. It would have been hard to count the huge number of dead we found successively in the town's ditches, the ravines, along the river bank and at the bridgehead.'

That morning the Red Lancers, most exceptionally, are allowed to unsaddle; and Dumonceau decides to go and take a closer look at the ruined suburbs in the direction of the Malakhofskaia Gate, so repeatedly but vainly assaulted by Morand's division:

'Everywhere the terrain was ground to dust, encumbered with scattered debris, with twisted or broken weapons, dead men and horses. All were monstrously swollen, something we attributed to decomposition in the extreme heat. Already putrescent, they gave off a foul stench. They'd begun to be buried. Our own wounded had already been taken to the ambulances and disappeared; but the Russians' had been left lying on the ground. We saw them sitting in the shade of houses, their backs to the walls, calm and impassive, resignedly waiting for someone to come and succour them. Some French surgeons were busy giving first aid. Further on, they were being loaded on to ambulance wagons. Elsewhere artillery wagons were busy picking up weapons scattered over the ground. The suburb's houses, too, all of which had been broken into, abandoned and overthrown, were full of corpses and debris.'

At first it had been the Russians who'd suffered worst. But the closer the assailants had come to the town gate, the more thickly the French and Polish dead littered the ground. At first only officers are allowed inside the city. Major Boulart is one of them. 'Inside the town the sights become even more horrible: houses all in flames, houses burnt down, corpses, a population in despair.' 'The enemy corpses,' Dumonceau sees to his horror,

'were literally piled up on top of each other. One could hardly take a step without trampling on them. It was the same behind the redoubt in the space separating it from the town gate, where artillery trains had passed over these heaps of human remains, crushing them in a thick sludge of flesh, broken bones and bleeding wreckage. Beside a wheel I saw the mask of a human face whose posterior had been separated from it and which was lying in the mud like a glove.'

Artillery colonel *Michel Combe* sees how the Russian wounded from earlier engagements too 'lay here in piles, charred, almost without human form, among the smouldering ruins and flaming rafters. The postures of many corpses showed what terrible torments they must have gone through before dying. I trembled with horror at the spectacle, which always haunts my memory.' All this might conceivably have made sense, Dumonceau thought, if the battle could have been called a victory. But 'though the advantage incontestibly lay with us, it didn't seem to offer any decisive result of the kind we'd been hoping for'. Leaving the town, Le Roy, 'choking from the smoke and dust, shaken by what we saw, made haste to get out of the city. I felt I'd left hell behind me.'

Dumonceau is walking down the cobbled main street ('all the rest were tortuous and narrow') when he hears the brash sound of military music. The Italians, beside their idyllic lake, have played no part in the battle.[10] But now 'proud and grim' the Italian Guard is the first unit to enter the charred city

'to the gay strains of our bands. Not once since hostilities had begun had we seen such scenes. We were deeply shaken. I saw a cart filled to the brim with torn off human limbs being carried away for burial far from the bodies they'd belonged to. On the thresholds of surviving houses groups of wounded stood imploring our help. In the streets the only living beings were French and Allied soldiers, straying about in search of something the flames hadn't devoured. The fire, which by now had been put out, had consumed both itself and half the buildings, the market, the houses and most of the dwellings. And it was in the midst of these heaps of cinders and corpses we made ready to spend the night.'

Of the 18,000 souls Smolensk had numbered before the catastrophe, all but one-sixth have left. Its 2,000 timber houses have virtually all been laid in ashes – and the few that haven't are now being 'invaded by the soldiers, leaving the homeless owner and part of his family standing outside his door, weeping over the deaths of his children and the loss of all he'd owned'. Mostly it's the stone or brick buildings that have survived. Prominent among them is the cathedral. Stepping inside, de Laugier sees

'whole families covered in tatters, distraught, shedding tears, exhausted, debilitated, famished, squatting on the paving around the altars. Their eyes, fixed on us, tell us of their agony. All seem to tremble as we approach, are near to crying out in horror at the very sight of us. Turning back to their altars they implore God's help against us. The alarm spreads; a loud outcry breaks out that the French have come to offer them violence. There's a rush towards the high altar. Thunderstruck, the very grenadiers come to a halt. Then the priest raises his voice and manages to obtain silence. Whereupon he utters a long and energetic discourse. To us, who can't understand him, he seems to be giving expression to their fears, which, allayed, give place to a sad, resigned confidence.'

Never in his life has Césare de Laugier heard such fervent prayer. Even Le Roy, convinced deist though he is, is impressed:

'Entering, I see to my amazement the whole temple lit up, as for some grand religious festival. It's full of women, old men and children who've taken refuge in it. Popes, caring little for what was going on on earth were officiating and imploring heaven's assistance. Most of these people have with them their most precious belongings and are lying on them, sure their enemies' rapacity won't go so far as to despoil them even in their very temples. And they were right about that. Just as I, moved, was studying these unfortunates, more than five hundred soldiers came into the church. Surprised and astonished at such a spectacle, they took off their hats as they did so and assumed a diffident and contemplative air, which pleased me.'

But Laugier leaves 'this abode of misery, my heart swollen, firmly resolved not to budge again from our camp'.

Not until 10 a.m. does Napoleon, accompanied by Berthier, Murat, Davout, Ney, Lobau, and of course Caulaincourt, 'mount his horse, reconnoitre the curtain wall to the east, and enter the city through an ancient breach'. Out in front, at the regulation 50-metre interval, Lieutenant *Louis-Joseph Vionnet* is riding at the head of the Horse Grenadiers' duty troop:

'The Emperor visited the battlefield, and I was part of his escort. Halting briefly in front of the great earthwork known as the Citadel, Napoleon contemplated it a moment and seemed to hesitate. Then – to the despair of all present, with the sole exception of the implacable Davout – he declared: "Before the month's out we'll be in Moscow. In six weeks we'll have peace."'

Words, comments the Master of the Horse drily, 'which by no means convinced everyone, at least so far as peace was concerned'. After touring the charred city Napoleon stations himself by the demolished Dnieper bridge to hasten on its repair. A few yards away Colonel Rossetti and the rest of Murat's suite stand respectfully looking on:

'Squatting down on his haunches in front of a hut, he closely examined the position just abandoned to him by the Russians. After a quarter of an hour, no longer able to contain his joy, he declared delightedly: "Poor wretches! Fancy giving up such a position to me! Come on, we'll have to march on Moscow." Immediately a lively discussion arose between the Emperor, the Marshals and high officers of his entourage.'

Should the army cross the Dnieper and pursue the enemy? Or wouldn't it be more prudent to stay in Smolensk?

'As if to put some distance between them and himself, the Emperor walks on ahead a few paces. The King, Berthier, Davout, Ney, Caulaincourt and Lobau go after him, and we stay behind. The discussion between the Emperor and the heads of the army lasted more than an hour. Afterwards we heard that everyone except Davout had opposed the Emperor's project. The upshot of this conference, so utterly important for the destiny of France, was the order to depart on the morrow. The Emperor mounted his horse, and we went back into Smolensk. It was midday. The heat was stunning.'

Acute disappointment always tends to make Murat ill.[11] So now:

'We had him transported to his headquarters, where he was obliged to take to his bed. At about 3 p.m. the Emperor sent for him. Murat sent him his reply: that he had nothing to add to what he'd said that morning – that the Emperor could dispose of his life, but not make him change his mind.'

A refusal which, to Napoleon, certainly means nothing. But Paris and Vilna are another matter. From the governor's palace – one of twenty or so surviving stone buildings – he, in his own hand, as usual, scribbles a letter to Marie-Louise: "*Mon amie*, I've been in Smolensk since this morning. I've taken this city from the Russians, having killed 3,000 of their men and wounded three times that number. My health is good, the heat extreme. My affairs are going well." That would do for Paris. For Maret and the foreign powers' ambassadors at Vilna something more is needed:

"The heat is extreme, there's a lot of dust, and all this is rather tiring. The entire enemy army was here; it was ordered to give battle, but didn't dare to. We've taken Smolensk by frontal assault. It's a very large city, with solid walls and fortifications. We've killed three to four thousand of the enemy's men, their wounded were three times as many. We've found many guns here. Several divisional generals are said to have been killed. The Russian army is retiring toward Moscow, disgruntled and disheartened."

Too exhausted even to sign this hotch-potch of fact and fiction, 'after dictating this letter', the secretary added, 'His Majesty promptly threw himself down on his bed'. According to Fézensac the 'many guns' only amounted to 'a few old iron cannon in bad condition' and a modicum of stores. 'We hadn't taken a single prisoner.'

That afternoon the interpreter Hyde d'Ideville presents a priest (can he have been 'the only one we found in Smolensk' as Ségur claims) to the Emperor. Supposing him to have intentionally burnt down the city, 'the venerable priest firmly reproached him for what he called his acts of sacrilege. The Emperor listened attentively to him: "But your own church," he said at last. "Is it burnt down?" – "No, Sire," replied the priest. "God will be more powerful than you. As I've opened it to all those unfortunates the fire has left without other asylum He will protect it." Moved, Napoleon replied: "You're right. Yes, God will watch over war's innocent victims. He will reward you for your courage." With these words Napoleon sent him back to his temple with an escort.'

It must have been shortly afterwards that the 28-year-old Breton war commissary *Bellot de Kergorre* sees that a posse of Guard grenadiers has been stationed in the cathedral's central aisle, 'to keep order and ensure respect for this asylum'. At first the devotees refuse all help; but after the priest's homily return to their places and accept the meagre rations the French distribute to them.

Back in 1809 Le Roy had been a prisoner of war here, and been billeted on an Italian resident, whose house was next door to the cathedral. Not being the man to let his emotions distract him from practical business, he's making for the Italian's house when he sees that another, which belongs to another person who'd befriended him, the Countess Krapowski, is on fire. But nothing can be done about it, and he assumes that she has 'anyway retired to her estates to avoid contact with the armies. So I walked down the main street and found my Italian in a terrible state of emotion.' His house has been invaded by the soldiery. 'Remembering me at once, he takes me to witness to the value of his services to French prisoners of war.' Le Roy clears the house of its unwelcome guests, and 'the good fellow tells me how during the forenoon some Frenchmen had broken in and robbed him of 40,000 roubles, fruit of twenty years' savings' – a figure which in Le Roy arouses only scepticism:

'While we're quietly chatting, my Italian catches sight of a score of fresh pillagers, who, under pretext of looking for victuals, are paying him a domiciliary visit. Abruptly breaking off our conversation, my man starts tearing his hair and, in an Italian accent that stresses the last syllable of every word, screaming at the top of his voice that they're the very ones who've just robbed him of the 20,000 roubles. My God! Never in all my life had I heard anyone yell like that! Terrified, the marauders promptly evacuate his home. Whereupon seeing them safely outside he comes back to me and calmly resumes our conversation.'

The French, says the Italian, had done wisely not to mount a night assault, because 'more than 60,000 men had been stationed about the town's streets and squares to defend it until all their artillery and baggage had reached the other river bank'. Passing his friend's house again after his visit to the cathedral, Le Roy sees it's 'full of halted soldiers resting there, calmly waiting for the bridges to be re-established. The Guard was lodged in town, and was keeping order and discipline.'

Dumonceau too wants to take a look inside the cathedral. But gets there too late. A sentry, posted outside its door, turns him away. Instead he walks down the steep main street to the Dnieper Bridge, where he gets permission from an infantry major to go up on to the ramparts; but looking out across the river to the New Town sees little sign of the Russian rearguard, which is occupying it.

Otherwise everybody is searching for something to eat. The distinction between legitimate marauding and crude looting enables War Com-missary Kergorre to find shelter with an apothecary,

'out of whose house we evicted some looters. We ourselves, by means of organized marauding, managed to get hold of some victuals: a little butter, flour, a bad cheese, wine made from plums. There was no shortage of butcher's meat. We even got hold of a cow, which we kept with us for the next fortnight.'

One thing of which there is an abundance is roast pork. The Belgian Sergeant *Scheltens*[12] of the 2nd Guard Grenadiers sees how 'the hungry pigs straying about in the ruins found this roast [namely, dead Russians] excellent. We killed these voracious animals, which didn't come amiss in our bivouacs.' But the 5th Tirailleurs aren't so lucky; and have to make do with some 'green apples, still unripened by the northern sun' they've found 'in the pockets of some dead Russian grenadiers, recognizable by the three copper grenades on their very low and concave shakos'. While searching for his dinner Dedem van der Gelder, severely bruised in the chest from that spent musket-ball, comes across the corpse of the governor of Smolensk 'killed by a roundshot'. His supper, when he gets it, consists of 'a large amount of jam, together with two superb pineapples and some peaches. I'd have preferred a nice soup.'

There's the usual incredible wastage. In the lower part of the Old City, largely spared by the flames, Heinrich von Brandt sees 'great stocks of leather and furs being spoiled and lost, something we'd regret the more cruelly later on. I even saw soldiers, not understanding their value, throwing whole armfuls of paper roubles into the fire.'

Captain François has been commended for gallantry by his colonel. But Carabinier-sergeant Bertrand is mourning a friend, shot through the head by a musket-ball. Also the loss of his red pompom another missile has snatched from his shako.

The mood is utterly sombre. On his way back to his unit Césare de Laugier falls in with one of Eugène's ADCs, a Pole. Both try to find a scapegoat for the disaster. Upon de Laugier declaring it's all the fault of the Lithuanians 'for not imitating their compatriots in the Grand Duchy' the Pole ripostes hotly that there's nothing wrong with Lithuanian patriotism – the fault is mostly the officers who, 'instead of busying themselves with food and medicines for their wretched men have filled their wagons with Bordeaux wines and champagne'.

Neither to the Elban nor the Pole does it occur that Lithuanians aren't Poles; but a people who had themselves once had an empire that stretched to the Black Sea.

CHAPTER 16

DEATH IN THE SACRED VALLEY

*Von Suckow takes a cold dip – struggle for the northern suburbs – Barclay's danger-
ous detour – Ney held up by a feint – where's Junot? – a broken bridge – Valutina –
massacre of 65 voltigeurs – Junot's inexplicable reluctance – General Gudin falls –
furious assault by the 7th Light – Murat's letter to his daughter – 'Junot's had
enough of it' – rewards among scenes of carnage – a dissenter is sent home – St-Cyr
gets his marshal's baton – 'Forward, always forward!' – Larrey's heroic feats of
surgery – a visit to Ney's headquarters – Davout takes over the van*

And still the fighting isn't over. Far from it. The Württembergers had
spent the previous evening trying to flush the Russian rearguard out of
the northern suburbs – the so-called New Town – and the much reduced
25th Division has had to wade the Dnieper, its waters up to their chests,
while being shot at not only by the Russians but also by the brown-coated
Portuguese, whose supporting fire from the city walls is falling short and
wounding some of von Suckow's troopers. Also stationed on those walls
are Faber du Faur's guns. 'Prey to a devouring thirst' his men had forced
a terrified Russian girl to bring them water, and between salvos Faber du
Faur has had time to sketch one of his guns being served by its
crested-helmeted crew – Russian girl, yoke, buckets and all.

But the suburbs prove impenetrable. And at least the rank and file have
to take a second dip as they recross the Dnieper. Meanwhile von Suckow is
finding it 'a real pleasure' to watch the French pontooneers at work
throwing a pontoon bridge:

'Although the water was very cold and they must have had empty
stomachs they did their job playfully. It was a veritable bombardment
of jokes and quips and witticisms. *Que voulez-vous?* They were true
Frenchmen. As for our officers, the pontooneers with typically
French courtesy put some boats at our disposal. No sooner are we
back in the streets again than one of Ney's orderly officers, a tall personage of astonishing thinness, arrives flat out, shouting at a great
distance from his starving nag: "Go back! Go back across the river,
it's the Marshal's orders!"'

But the Württembergers have had theirs direct from Napoleon, who has
evidently forgotten to inform Ney. Just as they're about to take a third
cold bath, von Suckow's colonel turns up and refuses to let them do any
such thing – a piece of insubordination loudly supported by the arrival of
an imperial ADC. Nevertheless, though soaked through, they're forbidden to light fires. 'Next morning we had a considerable number of officers and men sick, and to keep warm even they had to spend the chilly
night walking briskly to and fro.'

Now, as dawn breaks, Napoleon too is on those northern walls, trying
to discern through his spyglass the line of Barclay's retreat. In fact he sees

little – except the dense smoke and flames billowing up across the river. Instead of retreating eastwards toward Moscow, Barclay seems to be taking the road northwards, toward Petersburg.[1]

Meanwhile Ney's infantry regiments – Captain Bonnet's 17th Line among them – are making their way through the blazing suburbs:

'Early that morning the Russian rearguard, though few in numbers, had still been there on the other side of the river. But by 4 a.m., when our troops had mounted the high ground on the right bank, they'd disappeared. Having crossed the bridge, we turned to the right and took the new Moscow road.'

Following on with I Corps among the still burning houses, Paymaster Duverger sees how seven to eight thousand Russian wounded

'had all perished, devoured by the fire their compatriots had lit to impede our march. I moved among the debris of these men and among the houses, very much afraid of the pitfalls opened up at each step by cellars and wells, scarcely masked by cinders and charred timbers, and religiously avoiding corpses which the fire had carbonised and reduced to dimensions of infancy.'

Le Roy, too, sees how

'each house, each courtyard – even the gardens – were full of dead and wounded, abandoned without help. The greater number were nothing but semi-incinerated, mutilated and hideous corpses. In the last house I counted 27 who'd already succumbed, plus some others who'd withdrawn into the courtyard. These unfortunates watched us pass without so much as a sigh.'

Amidst all these horrors, once again, the bands are playing, cornets shrilling and drums beating as the leading units march eastward, supported by the Württemberg artillery: 'Soon we'd set up our guns where only a moment ago enemy battalions had been stationed. The debris of their weapons, littered all over the ground, showed how furiously this point had been disputed.'

But suddenly something unexpected happens. 'A cannon-ball smashed into our ranks, ploughing up the plain. Earth and stones flew around us with the rapidity of lightning. The roundshot kept ricocheting from the walls and in the rear of our position.' The roundshot are coming from Faber du Faur's left, which bewilders Ney, who's assuming it's Barclay's rearguard he has ahead of him. Failing to realize that it's only a feint designed to hold him up,[2] and instead of screening off this diversion and by-passing it, wastes a whole hour deploying unit after unit.

Meanwhile Murat, notwithstanding his (probably psychosomatic) temperature of yesterday, is already on horseback and protecting Ney's right flank as his cavalry crosses valley after valley. Still farther to the right, beyond some very rough and wooded terrain, lies the Dnieper. And everyone is taking it for granted that by now Junot must have crossed it near the village of Pruditchino, and is moving in energetically to cut off

Barclay's retreat. But where is he? What's he doing? Why is there no sign of him?

Ney's advance guard, this hot morning, is being led by two companies of the 7th Hussars. Eight miles along the road, descending into a marshy valley, they find the little bridge broken and themselves exposed to grape and roundshot being fired at them by a solitary battery on the far slope. No question, obviously, of crossing the stream! Veering off 'into a wood to our left to place ourselves out of the line of fire', word is sent back to General Jacquinot, who in turn, accompanied by Lieutenant Victor Dupuy, gallops back to inform Ney,

'who seemed annoyed by these news and repeated several times "But are you sure? Have you seen it?" – "No, M. le Maréchal," the general replied, "but I soon shall." And left at once, as fast as his horse could carry him, with me following. As we pass across their front the hussars shout out to us "The bridge is broken. Don't go there!" We halt on the bank of the stream. The enemy battery is keeping up a very lively fire. Roundshot and grape are raining down all round us. "The bridge is broken," I say to the general, "don't let's amuse ourselves counting its planks!" We turned about and left again at the same speed.'

This time Jacquinot has seen the bridge with his own eyes and can assure Ney it really is broken. '"Very well, then!", the marshal said laughing': and orders his leading units to deploy.

Such is the beginning of what will turn out to be the exceedingly bloody battle of Valutina-Gora.

Rushed to the spot by Barclay, more and more Russian infantry are deploying on the opposite slope. For the fate of Russia hangs in the balance. Captain Bonnet can

'see the Russian column very clearly. Gunfire was being exchanged. Finally the 10th Division went up in column a little to our left and briskly drove them off. The regiment then remained in observation on the main road. At 2 p.m. Marshal Ney comes in person to order us to move up. We follow the main road at the tail of the 4th Line, the idea being to surprise the Russian rearguard and tumble it head over heels. The 4th Regiment had found it encamped [*sic*]; but it had put up a vigorous resistance, and the charge had been beaten back. Our regiments veered off from the road to the right, crossing a muddly ditch full of water. We took up our position on the heights opposite the Russian line, which we couldn't see very clearly, as it was screened by big woods and bushes. The 4th battalion was detached and marched off to the right, following the line of the hills. A lancer of the 9th came toward us, saying the Russians could be seen advancing against us.'

Detached with his grenadier company, Bonnet realizes

'almost immediately that the cavalry had mistaken us and our voltigeurs, already out ahead of us, for the enemy. So instead of dispersing my grenadiers in skirmishing order, I wait. Then, noticing the Russians are increasing the numbers of their skirmishers in front of the 1st battalion which we'd left behind us as we'd extended to the right, I face left, deploy into the line of skirmishers and march on. My grenadiers' line is on the slope of the hill, opposite another occupied by the Russians, who're in much greater numbers. We repulse all their attempts to advance, restricting ourselves to this because we'd orders not to press the enemy at this point. It rained musket-balls.'

But now many more of Ney's units are having to be fed in besides the 4th and 18th Line. From a wood in the rear von Suckow and his comrades in the Württemberg cavalry are fascinatedly watching the struggle:

'The valley, called by the Russians – God knows why – the Sacred Valley,[3] offered a singular view. At our feet reigned a veritable chaos, the thunder of the guns interrupting the crackling of musketry, drumrolls, orders in French, in German, Polish, Italian and Portuguese, thousands of vociferating individuals on foot or horseback stumbling over each other, and – enveloping it all – an impenetrable dust!'

One of his officers makes to graze his grey in front of the wood – and promptly brings down a cannonade on to the inactive Württembergers, 'wounding many to no purpose, either by roundshot or branches falling from the trees. Until all the men began shouting at the officer to bring in that white horse!' Faber du Faur has time to sketch the scene as regiment after regiment moves up. Finally Ney has deployed his entire corps – without making the least headway.

'While Ney was making his frontal attack, Murat was flanking him on both sides with his cavalry, but without being able to bring it into action. Some woods to the left and swamps to the right were impeding his movements. Both were awaiting the effect of a flank march by the Westphalians, under Junot.'

But where is he? 'Murat', writes his ADC Colonel Rossetti, 'judging that he should have come up and be engaged but astonished not to hear him attacking, leaves his cavalry, and crosses the wood and the swamps with General Denon and myself'. As it happens the first unit of VIII Corps they come to is Lance-corporal Heinemann's voltigeur company of the Brunswick Chasseurs. They've been posted far out ahead when

'suddenly a little group of horsemen comes galloping toward us. It's the King of Naples and his suite – a massive figure of a man, with brown, strong features and a black beard [sic – perhaps Murat hadn't shaved that morning?]. We recognize him by his magnificent theatrical costume and a square flat cap decorated with innumerable ostrich plumes and diamond brooches. Halting in front of our captain, he shouts: "What are you doing here? Forward! Through those thickets, in line of skirmishers, against the enemy! The army'll come up behind you!"'

Leaving them with this order, Murat rides off in search of Junot's headquarters. Napoleon too is wondering what's become of him. Earlier in the day he'd ridden out along the Petersburg road to try to fathom Barclay's movements, but hearing of the action at Valutina has finally taken up his command post at a point some five miles – Gourgaud says 'a league' – along the Moscow highway. By that time it must surely be obvious to him that a full-scale battle is developing. Yet at 5 p.m., still ignorant of Junot's movements, or rather lack of them, and after ordering Davout to send in two of his divisions to turn the Russian left, he, 'regarding the day as over' (Gourgaud) goes back to Smolensk, leaving Davout ('who seemed rightly discontented to see these fine corps he'd formed and on whose behalf he'd given himself so much trouble sacrificed to the King of Naples' imprudent valour') to commit Compans' and Gudin's crack divisions to the ever more embittered struggle, while Friant's men stand with shouldered arms ready to support them.

Before going back to Smolensk, however, Napoleon has sent Gourgaud to Murat, with

'several officers (among others M. Rohan Chabot, ADC to General Count Narbonne) under his orders, charging him to co-ordinate the movements of Marshal Ney, the King of Naples and the Duke of Abrantès and to send him reports on the affair'.

To their amazement both Murat and Gourgaud find VIII Corps motionless with piled arms. Galloping up to its commander, Murat yells:

'"What are you doing there? Why aren't you advancing? You're unworthy to be the last dragoon in Napoleon's army!" "My cavalry's no use. It's no match for the Russian battalions. Besides I've no definite orders to attack." "Then I'll do it instead! I'll put some fire into these Westphalians of yours!" Galloping up to General Hammerstein's light cavalry brigade and shouting "Follow me, brave Westphalians!", the King of Naples is immediately followed by this allegedly worthless cavalry, who overthrow the screen of Russian sharpshooters and fling them back. Returning to Junot, he says: "Now you can finish it off. Your glory is there, and your marshal's baton."'

And when Junot still shows no sign of budging, Gourgaud asks him what he's to tell the Emperor.

'The Duke of Abrantès was surrounded by his staff, and seemed utterly depressed. He replied angrily: "You'll tell him, Monsieur, that I've taken up my position, because night has fallen.' In vain the ordnance officer riposted that there were almost four more hours of daylight, that Marshal Ney was suffering badly from the frontal attack he was having to make; all his representations were useless. The Duke of Abrantès wouldn't move.'

No sooner had Murat left them than Heinemann's voltigeur company (of whom 77 of its original 150 'strong young men, wrenched from their distant fatherland' have succumbed to the campaign's rigours') 'as if guessing what was to follow already' have spread out in open order and begun advancing toward the distant enemy:

'Beyond us lay an open field. We waited for our regiments to come up in support. First we caught brief glimpses of groups of Cossacks; then of Russian hussars; and, soon afterwards, whole lines of enemies, swathed in dust clouds. Several units seemed to be moving out to their flank. We look behind us, to see if any of our own are coming up. Not a chance! Not a weapon gleams behind us in the wood. We're all on our own. And at each moment our danger is growing. Innumerable swarms of Cossacks are advancing on us, darkening the air with dust clouds, their forest of lances rolling on like a fog to envelop us.'

If only their captain ('a brave Hessian named Worm') would order the cornet to sound a hasty retreat! But no. His 'inflexible military honour' forbids it. Instead,

'the cornet is calling in our skirmishers, spread out to right and left, and the Cossacks are cutting off our retreat. Realizing we must now become the victims of our own obedience, we stop thinking and obey. Our little force forms a double square, six ranks deep – an insignificant little troop amidst countless enemies! Sabre in hand, our captain steps out boldly from the square, baring his chest to the Cossack skirmishers. He'll be the first to fall, going on ahead to prepare night quarters for 65 comrades in eternity. No little scared, but all our muskets at the ready, we await the enemy. Comes the order: "By platoons, fire!" On the instant all our muskets go off. With thumping heart, swathed in a thick cloud of gunpowder smoke, each of us awaits what the next minute will bring. It must decide whether we're to live or die.'

But it's thumbs down for the brave Brunswickers.

'With a thousandfold hurrah the galloping Cossacks break into our defenceless group from all sides. After a mere couple of minutes our front ranks are lying on the ground, stabbed through by a thousand lances. Our muskets' smoke disperses to reveal a horrible bloodbath. None of us sees the least chance of escaping the slaughter now beginning. The Cossacks are making such easy work of us, our inability to resist seems to stir their blood-lust to madness. Surrender is out of the question. As if driven by some obscure instinct, anyone who's still alive throws himself down on the ground and plays dead. Comes a moment of horrible waiting. Happy he who finds himself lying under heaps of corpses! Even if the blood of those of our comrades who've been stabbed through seeps down over our bodies, if their limbs twitch and jerk on top of ours, if the dying breathe their last sighs into our ears and their corpses press upon us – at least there's still a chance of surviving underneath this terrible rampart. In such lethal need it's every man for himself!

'The lances stab furiously into heaps of dead and living. many a chest or neck is crushed under the horses' hoofs. The Russians' green hussars, avid to join in in this monstrous feast of slaughter, are only prevented from making free use of their sabres by their own densely packed masses as they advance.

'I was one of the few still alive. Blood was seeping through my uniform, soaking me to the skin and glueing my eyelids together. Though still not wounded, I could hear the clash of lances and sabres, mingled with our assassins' dull oaths, muttering between their teeth their terrible *"Pascholl! Sabacki Franzusky!"* [Die, dog of a Frenchman!] as they exerted all their strength to probe the bodies of the dead with their lances and sabres, to see whether beneath them there mightn't be something still alive. Finally my turn comes. A lance-thrust, passing through the chest and back of a comrade who was lying on top of me, strikes my skull a glancing blow and rips open the skin. Yet I feel no pain. Lying there half-conscious, all I long for is an end to the slaughter.'

But now a new danger threatens. The Cossacks have dismounted. Savagely heaving aside the dead, they're trying to find anyone who may still be alive.

'In this terrible moment I can't help opening my eyes to see what's going on. Suddenly I'm aware of a bearded face with white teeth, bending closely down over me, and hear the Cossack's savage scornful laugh as he finds another victim to slaughter. A hundred arms drag me out from amidst the mangled corpses. And above me I see innumerable lances raised, ready to stab me – when, all of a sudden, familiar sounds suddenly ring out. Orders shouted in German! The clash of weapons! Heavenly music... The blue Westphalian hussars are fighting the Cossacks and Russian green hussars hand to hand, and after them come our chasseurs. The Cossacks depart, cursing. Only a few still go on eagerly searching for plunder; then even these gallop off, and all is quiet around our square's burial place.

'Anyone who was still alive and had the strength to do so, stood up. Only the sacred number thirteen were saved, as if by a miracle. Not one unwounded had escaped the butcher's chopping block. We were so dreadfully bloodied and covered in dust no one could recognize anyone else. Not until we'd washed our faces and hands in a stream did many of us recognize some friend.'

Hammerstein's cavalry, too, is done for. Drawn by wildly fleeing Cossacks into an improvised ambush, they're systematically mown down by Russian batteries – batteries Barclay, precisely against this eventuality, has placed along the Moscow road – before they can deploy against a line of Russian élite hussars. Lieutenant Eduard Rüppell, in the thick of it, is finding the Russians' fire 'precise as on a parade ground exercise'.

And that's the end of Junot's *manoeuvre sur les derrières.*

Out on the fiercely contested slopes of the Sacred Valley the fusillade has been going on for three hours, during which time, says Bonnet, 'the Russians were regularly relieved five or six times'. Carabinier-sergeant Bertrand's shako, minus its red pompom, is destined to suffer further mutilations. At the first rumble of gunfire, the 7th Light had been

'ordered to open our cartridge pouches and adjust the shot. A second order, and we're made to advance at the double and enter a wood where Compans' division is at grips with the enemy. This division inclines to the left and mine (Gudin's) replaces it. Hardly has the head of our column debouched from the woods than we're swept by grapeshot. We find we're facing a high steeply edged plateau, at whose foot flows a stream ten to twelve metres wide. The only bridge having been destroyed by the Russians, we must cross this broad ditch under a storm of musketry and roundshot. Our superior officers set the example by jumping into the water. The drums beat the charge. And soon my regiment and the 12th Line, eight battalions in all, are on the other bank. Two battalions of my regiment are sent forward as skirmishers over the entire front of the plateau occupied by the enemy. We encounter some felled trees, which hold us up and oblige us to make a long detour. In the midst of these difficulties our brave General Gudin is just coming toward me when he falls, felled by a roundshot.'

Gudin is one of the army's most popular generals. He has just dismounted and is standing in the middle of the road, about to lead his division into battle, when a 'ricocheting roundshot' tears off one of his legs at the thigh, and the other just below the knee.

Night falls without any abatement in the fighting. And the moon comes out. From his vantage point von Suckow is watching some Illyrians as they descend into the valley,

'to an accompaniment of drums and the sharp screeching sound of fifes.[4] I saw nothing wrong with their using these alleged instruments of music. What astonished me was the tune they were playing: "Let's be happy we're alive!" I couldn't help remarking to a comrade on the bitter irony of leading men to their deaths while offering them such advice! In the moonlight we could very clearly make out the Russian sharpshooters on the crest as they fired. The scene was one of the most interesting. We could see each skirmisher as his shot went off, and clearly made out his green tunic and white trousers.'

At the second assault the Illyrians succeed, but not without heavy losses:

'We were present at a continuous march-past of wounded being carried to the rear. A great number must have succumbed to their wounds, nothing having been arranged to receive them and everything being lacking that would have been needed to organize an ambulance'

The Württember cavalry too is suffering heavily. So heavily that General Marchand 'a man of the *ancien régime*, elegant and chivalrous, the very type of the gentleman and benevolent commander standing there beside his horse toying with his gold snuffbox, had spared us further losses when the Illyrians asked for supports to be thrown in'.

Yet the fighting is only getting still more furious. And up on the far slope Sergeant Bertrand is fighting for his life:

'Either side becomes doubly determined. Feeling a supreme effort is needed, the cry of "En avant!" coming from all voices and the charge being furiously beaten, sweeps us up. Finally, after a terrible scrimmage, we carry the redoubt which is our objective, having turned the battery flanking it. The enemy withdraws by making a stand along the fringe of the wood. Night is just falling on this carnage when we hear our Colonel Rome say "Soldiers of the 7th Light! The Emperor wants to be master of this wood, he wants us to enter it." Immediately, without further orders, the drums again beat the charge. A voice says: "Colonel, we've no cartridges!" "You've got your bayonets," replies our colonel. And into the wood we go, heads down. I'm pursuing an officer when two Russians try to surprise me from behind. "Look out, Bertrand!", shouts one of my comrades, "Stand your ground! I'm coming!" We shake off our two adversaries, I jab at mine with my bayonet so that his eye comes out of its socket.'

This attack seems to have been what was needed to force the Russians to relinquish their grip. And Gourgaud confirms it:

'a considerable column of Russian grenadiers made a bayonet charge against a battalion of the 7th Light and another of the 12th Line. In this mêlée a lieutenant of voltigeurs of the 12th (M. Etienne) flung himself on the Russian general and having hit him twice on the head with his sabre, took him prisoner in the midst of his men.'

'This fighting,' Bertrand ends,

'cost us great losses. From the stream to the crest of the plateau the ground was covered with dead, dying and wounded. The Russians were even more sorely tried than we were. And they were definitely out after my head, because two musket-balls went through my shako.'

According to Bourgoing both the Spaniards, under Count de Bourmont, and the Portuguese fought valiantly: 'The Castilian loyalty and courage didn't gainsay themselves, and the same goes for the Portuguese Legion, both infantry and cavalry, which sustained considerable losses.'

Finally, at about 11 p.m. the firing dies away. And Murat returns to his bivouac, where he pens a sad little letter to his daughter Letitia in faraway Naples:

'Today is my birthday, today the whole family will be gathered and I'm sorry I'm not in your midst, dear children, to receive your best wishes and the beautiful flowers my Letitia would have brought me. I'd have given her a rose in exchange to put in her hair, not that she has any need of it to be pretty... Your letter has made me shed many tears, but my tears have done me a lot of good...'

Incredible numbers of wounded come streaming back through the night. Dr René Faure, ordered up from Smolensk with I Cavalry Corps, crosses 'the Dnieper bridge at midnight. The night was sombre and we could hardly make out the road. As day broke we saw many wounded infantrymen coming back to the town. The youngest had lost their martial air. But the officers' features wore quite a different expression. Those who couldn't walk were letting themselves be carried, but were calm. It called for an effort to vanquish the pain. One league from the town we saw a carriage coming toward us, escorted by soldiers with lighted torches. General Gudin, who'd had a thigh carried away in the combat whose firing we'd heard, was being carried to the town with every care brave soldiers could manage.'

The morning of 20 August dawns in a dense mist. After the sun has broken through, the Red Lancers, 'grilled in a furnace-like atmosphere not relieved by a breath of air', are watching a lot of riderless horses galloping about and many wounded fellow-Dutchmen from the 127th Line making for the rear:

'After them appeared a group of soldiers carrying a stretcher covered with a mantle accompanied by a staff officer and a surgeon, from whose afflicted looks we guessed it was some important officer they were carrying. And the officer told us it was the brave and regretted General Gudin who'd had his two legs carried away at the knee by a cannon-ball.'

Gourgaud claims it was he who brought the sad news of Gudin's obviously fatal wound to Napoleon. Also of Junot's ineptitude:

'"Junot's had enough of it," Napoleon said, turning to Berthier. "He didn't want to turn the Russian position. He's caused us this very bloody affair, and of our losing Gudin... I don't want him to command the Westphalians; he'll have to be replaced by Rapp, who speaks German."'

But Caulaincourt hears some of Junot's friends, Berthier among them, intervene on his behalf. So nothing is done about it.

All their lives men will remember with horror the monstrous scene of carnage at Valutina. Early that morning the Württemberg cavalry, descending into the Sacred Valley, had

'no water to give the dying nor bandages for the wounded. We had to cross the frightful scenes of slaughter. It all offered a monstrous sight to the eye, which will never efface itself from my mind,'

von Suckow will write fifty years afterwards.

'At 3 p.m. Napoleon himself appears on the scene, and exclaims: "Ah, that's how I like to see a battlefield, three enemy to each dead Frenchman!" But by then Murat (according to Dedem) has already 'had the corpses of the French dead stripped. He wanted to make His Majesty believe all those he saw were Russians. The Emperor, seemingly not too convinced, reproached his brother-in-law for having sacrificed too many men by a frontal attack on a position which could have been turned,'

- which must also have been Davout's view. 'The corpses were heaped up under the feet of the escort's horses and hindered the regiments' alignment,' Le Roy would tell his grandsons thirty years later. The men of Gudin's division,' writes Ségur – and Rossetti echoes his words,

'were drawn up on top of their companions' and Russian corpses, amidst half-broken trees, on ground ripped up by roundshot, encumbered with the debris of arms, torn clothing, military utensils, overthrown vehicles and scattered limbs. Gudin's battalions were no longer more than platoons. All around was the smell of powder. The Emperor couldn't pass along their front without having to avoid corpses, step over them or push them aside. He was lavish with rewards. The 12th, 21st and 127th Line and the 7th Light received 87 decorations and promotions.'

As for the 7th Light, 'which had suffered particularly', it receives 32 Crosses. One of them goes to Bertrand's young Captain Moncey, the former imperial page who'd performed so valiantly in front of Smolensk. The 127th, however, is a new regiment, and therefore still lacks an eagle. Now it gets one. Brandt is among the onlookers:

'In this setting the ceremony, impressive in itself, took on a truly epic character. The regiment formed square. In the ranks I could make out many a face still blackened with powder, and much equipment still stained with blood. The colonel and his officers were drawn up in a semi-circle around the Emperor. "Soldiers!" he said, "Here's your eagle! It will serve you as a rallying point in moments of danger. Swear to me never to abandon it, to stay always in the path of honour, to defend our country and never to let France, our France, be insulted!"'

What the Dutch conscripts think about being called Frenchmen, Brandt doesn't say:

'But all replied, as a man: "We swear it!" Then the Emperor took the eagle from Marshal Berthier's hands and gave it to the colonel, who in turn handed it to the colour-bearer. At the same instant the square opened, the men formed line, and the colour-bearer, preceded by drums and the band, came to take up his battle station in the centre of the élite platoon. A grenadier sergeant of the same regiment was promoted second lieutenant on the spot. "Have this gallant fellow proclaimed at once," said Napoleon. The colonel pronounced the sacramental words, but abstained from embracing his new officer. "Well, colonel? The accolade! The accolade!" the Emperor said sharply. Nor was it the moment to forget it. Decorations, promotions and monetary awards rained down like hailstones. One could perceive that Napoleon felt an imperative need, both in himself and in others, to react against gloomy thoughts. Coming to the 95th Line, he tells the colonel to give him the names of those who'd distinguished themselves yesterday. As the colonel naturally began with the officers, when he came to the sixth or seventh name, the Emperor interrupted him: "How is it, colonel? Are all your rankers chicken-hearted?" And he personally summoned those NCOs and men who were pointed out to him as worthy of promotion or a decoration to step out from the ranks. Contemplating this scene, I submitted to the irreistible fascination Napoleon exercised whenever and wherever he wanted to.'

A few yards from the Emperor staff-captain Girod de l'Ain (he who is forever being balked of his Legion of Honour) is standing chatting with another ADC when his foot strikes against a little box, tied with string. 'We were no little surprised to find inside it two Crosses of the Legion.' Having already been several times recommended, Girod and his friend pocket one apiece -against possible future use. But Colonel Rossetti, that boasted Frenchman, is in ecstasy:

'Never did a field of victory offer a more exalting spectacle! The gift of this well-merited eagle, the pomp of these promotions, the shouts of joy, the glory of these warriors, rewarded on the very spot where they'd gained it, how many good things all at once! But we were deploring the loss of 4,000 brave men.'

Even the critical Labaume concedes that 'all antiquity cannot offer anything more heroic than such a sight amid the dead and dying.'

Next day it's the Italians' turn. Reviewed 'in a vast plain a little below the heights beyond Smolensk where they'd camped' they don their parade uniforms for the second time. And Napoleon, in his most flattering mood, rewards them for their behaviour at Witebsk – and is greeted with acclamations in his native tongue. The cheering, Laugier notes, isn't being 'ordered or incited by the colonels, but comes from the hearts of all these soldiers who, greedy for glory, have grown old in the camps. The Emperor passed brilliantly along the troops' front, spoke to several officers and also to many of the men, asking them whether they were content, whether they'd suffered on the march. More than once he got the reply: "Our only grievance, Sire, is not to have seen the enemy as often as the other corps have." "You'll be seeing them," Napoleon replied. And these were no vain words of flattery. Because flattery is little known to the soldier. These are the whole army's sentiments. The ceremony ended after sunset.'

What Laugier almost certainly doesn't know is why IV Corps' chief-of-staff is suddenly allowed to go back to Paris. Nor, evidently, does Labaume, even though he must have been associating with him daily:

'General Dessoles, disgusted by his services being overlooked, only wanted to enjoy in peace the esteem his talents had brought him.

The army, remembering how he'd shared the glory and disgrace of Moreau, showed its discontent. The Emperor yielded to the requests of this clever general, and granted him an honorable retreat and a pension.'

That's the official version. Actually Dessoles' mail, like so many other people's, has been snapped up by the secret office in the Rue Coq-Héron; and the contents and tenor of his correspondence have unmasked him as an inveterate grumbler and dissident. Packed off back to France, he's replaced by General Guilleminot.

Next day, though the Vistula Legion hasn't taken any part in the fighting, it too is reviewed on the main square. The last time Lieutenant Brandt had paraded before the Emperor had been on the Place du Carousel in Paris; and on that occasion, despite all his arduous service in Spain, Napoleon hadn't regarded him as ripe for promotion. But clearly his photographic memory for faces is no myth:

'I was one of the officers designated. There were fourteen of us who, summoned by the colonel, stepped forward out of the ranks. The Emperor halts, looks at me, draws me towards him by a button of my uniform – as his habit was – and says: "This one should have been promoted captain already, in Paris. Make him captain-adjutant-major." Continuing his tour along the front of the regiment, he notices a sergeant who'd been decorated and is wearing the three stripes that signify twenty years of service. "How is it this man isn't an officer yet?" "Sire, he can't read or write". "It's all one! These poor illiterate fellows no one wants to know about often make the best officers. Make him standard-bearer and second lieutenant of grenadiers. I'm sure he wasn't behindhand at the storming of Saragossa."'

The Russian general (Toutchkoff III) whom Voltigeur-lieutennt Etienne had seized by his collar, turns out to be the brother of his own divisional commander, General Toutchkoff II. And is therefore amiably received. And when, a moment later, a flag of truce arrives to get news of him, Napoleon seizes his opportunity and says that Toutchkoff may by all means write and tell his brother he's well – a letter, however, to be accompanied by another. Dictated to Fain and signed not by Napoleon but by Berthier, it informs the recipient that 'this general has left in good health for Metz:

'On this occasion'[here the Emperor himself takes the pen, and all the rest is in his own semi-illegible handwriting between the lines of his dictated draft) – "on this occasion I renew to Your Excellency the proposal I have made for an exchange of prisoners and for regularizing communications between the two armies; likewise the manner of treating flags of truce. His Majesty is pained to see the evils the country is suffering under. He wishes the Emperor of Russia would leave behind civil governors, to take care of the common people and of property; it is a usage which has been followed in almost all wars. The Emperor, M. le Baron, whom I have informed of the contents of this letter[!], charges me to present his compliments to the Emperor Alexander if he is with the army, or otherwise in your first report to him. Tell him that neither the vicissitudes of war, nor any circumstance, can alter the esteem and friendship he feels for him."

There's nothing, Napoleon tells Toutchkoff, he wants so much "as to conclude peace. We've burnt enough powder and shed enough blood. We must end this some time. But," he adds threateningly: "for Moscow to be occupied would be the equivalent to a girl losing her honour." No more than another letter which Berthier had written from Vilna does this one, though delivered, get an answer.

On the evening of 20 August, 'at the very moment when Napoleon amid incredible scenes of carnage was distributing rewards to the combatants of the previous three days', Lejeune gets back from Polotsk. He has the most welcome news. St-Cyr, taking over from Oudinot who's been seriously wounded,[5] has won the campaign's first signal victory. Hard-pressed by Wittgenstein, on 16 August he'd feigned a withdrawal across the Dnieper, returned under cover of night and in the afternoon of 18 August, too late for any major engagement to be expected, attacked Wittgenstein and routed him.

The news comes at exactly the right moment. And Napoleon sends St-Cyr his marshal's bâton. But Gudin, who'd been generally regarded as next in line for one, has died in agony, despite all Larrey's ministrations. And the artistically minded Lejeune is ordered to arrange a Homeric funeral:

'I guided the procession to the Great Bastion, where I'd had his grave dug and which was to be this illustrious warrior's mausoleum. On the dead man's body I placed a score of muskets, broken in the fighting, arranging them star-wise, so that one day, when Time, which destroys everything, shall uncover a hero's ossuaries, this trophy of arms will draw upon them the same sentiments of attention and respect as we accord to the remains of the valiant Gauls under their antique tumuli.'

Both Bourgoing and Boulart are among the mourners. Bourgoing feels in the air

'a general anxiety. In this grim and religious silence it was easy to see how deeply worried we were for the future. Everyone had had enough of fatigues, chancy affairs and glory for one campaign. No one was keen to go any further. Everyone was frankly avowing his need and wish to halt.'

Quartermaster Anatole de Montesquiou, at headquarters, is finding that 'when we came with orders several of the very generals we'd earlier found so compliant, so confident of success, now received us gruffly with a:

"Well, so it's 'Forwards, forwards, always forwards, is it? Hasn't he had enough yet? Won't he ever?'" And Fézensac:

'The King of Naples never ceased reiterating that the troops were exhausted, that the horses, which only had thatch to eat, could no longer stand up to such fatigues, and that we were risking losing everything by advancing further. His advice didn't prevail. And the order was given to march on.'

Only young officers like Planat de la Faye are in favour: 'we were expecting a great battle which would decide the campaign'.

Never was the old phrase about 'grasping a wolf by the throat' more applicable than to Napoleon at Smolensk. He can neither go forward nor stay where he is. Nor, least of all, retreat.

As for Smolensk itself, it's 'one vast hospital'. Although Larrey and his medical staff find 'some brandy, wines and a few medicines and our reserve ambulances had at last caught up' nothing suffices. The surgeons are working day and night.[6] 'Already during the second night we already lacked anything to bandage the wounded with.' Among the fifteen surviving brick buildings he's using are the Archives:

'In lieu of linen dressings, which had been used up after the first few days, we made use of paper found there. The parchment served for splints and bandages; tow and birch cotton (setula alba) served as lint; and the papers also did good service for bedding down the sick. But what difficulties had to be surmounted! What trouble we had to go to! Even so, despite the scanty means at our disposal, all indicated operations had been carried out within the first 24 hours. Myself I amputated eleven arms at the scapulo-humeral articulation,'

i.e., through the shoulder joint.[7] Despite all Larrey's efforts Surgeon Kerkhove calls the Smolensk hospitals 'cloaques of misery and infection, where one could observe all the influence of putrid miasmas on causing hospital gangrene by the suppuration of wounds'. Stumbling on such a hospital whose 100 wounded had been completely overlooked, Rapp, says Ségur, 'didn't fail to tell the horrible details to Napoleon, who had his own wine and several pieces of gold distributed to these unfortunates, still clinging to life or sustaining it with revolting foods'.

There are also the dead. On 21 August Berthier, who's having his work cut out to get all the corpses buried, informs Napoleon by letter that though 600 men have been detailed off, 'this operation is still far from finished. To accelerate it, we shall virtually have to employ Russian prisoners. I beg you to let us use 200 of them.'

So badly has III Corps been mauled at Valutina, it can no longer form the advance guard. Granted a 3-day halt to replenish its *matériel* and calculate how much ammunition it has expended, a Württemberg artillery officer finds that 'between July 2 and Aug 2 we'd fired off 214 shells, 433 six-pounder cannon-balls, eleven howitzer shells, and 30 six-pounder caseshot. The loss of horses was very serious and the few which could be replaced by little Russian farm horses were of scant help to us. Time and again the long-indulged hope of getting some captured remounts had been disappointed.'

Paul de Bourgoing has a brother who's one of Ney's ADCs; and gets permission to go and see him. On his way he crosses the battlefield, where he sees the corpses all jumbled up 'the French and Russian infantry having fought face to face, shot at each other point-blank, to the right, to the left, ahead, to the rear, in large and small detachments.' And a mile or two further on reaches Ney's headquarters, a 12ft x 12ft hut of leafy branches. 'An excellent shelter against the sun, but detestable against rain, they in no way resembled those of the other top brass' – Murat's, for instance, comfortably installed in a timber château some five miles further on along the Moscow road. Dedem, who's finding in Ney a great source of malicious gossip about goings on in top circles, regards the redheaded marshal as

'a man of brilliant courage and energy on the field of battle. But outside the theatre of war he was feeble, couldn't make up his mind, and let himself be swayed by his advisers. Basically detesting Napoleon, at odds with the Prince of Neuchâtel, jealous of the other marshals, the only one he was on good terms with was Macdonald. Not very communicative, withdrawn, he rarely saw the generals who served under him.'

And the 28-year-old Intendant *A-D. Pastoret*, who's been left behind at Witebsk to organize that town's supplies declares: 'He wasn't a good-natured man, this Duke of Elchingen; but he was a clever man.' Even more than with his fellow-marshals, war is more than a profession for Ney. It's a religion. And the horrible action at Valutina and its subsequent heroics must have suited him down to the ground. His headquarters, Bourgoing goes on,

'hardly differed from an ordinary officer's. When I got there, Ney was alone. But a few yards away a meal, set for 20 persons, was laid out on the greensward, awaiting his numerous aides. It was served up on a superb dish. Plates, huge bowls, etc., all in silver, symmetrically laid out on the greensward, which served as an oval table around which we sat down, or rather stretched ourselves out in a recumbent position, leaning on our elbows like guests at a sumptuous feast of the great conquerors of Ancient Rome.'

Bourgoing is struck by the great variety of III Corps' uniforms and admires the various regiments' accoutrements. Particularly

'the fine Württemberg cavalry's stood out, having in many cases been arbitrarily chosen by its colonels. The crest of its helmets, instead of being a comb or floating out behind like that of our dragoons, was flung forward, half concealing these old warriors' foreheads. They were Ney's cavalry escort.'

His visit over, Bourgoing returns to the charred city, only to hear, much to his disgust, that General Delaborde is to remain behind as governor, pending Jomini's arrival from Vilna. A couple of days later, after Napoleon has left, he and the rest of Delaborde's staff will move into the vacated palace. All they find there is a few insignificant scraps of paper, among them a little list of Napoleon's laundry which Bourgoing pockets as a souvenir. Also a whole edition, 'several thousand copies' of 'the celebrated Desaugier's drinking songs'. Had they been officially ordered? Or sent from Paris by mistake? Mediocre both as literature and as poetry – 'surprisingly so, to have come from the author of *Paris à cinq heures du matin* and many other masterpieces of French *esprit* and frank gaiety' – it had been tactful, he thought, not to have distributed them to the men 'just now when everyone was being tormented by thirst'.

As for Lejeune and his colleagues on Berthier's staff, all they can 'extract from this brief stay in this deserted town was a few dips in the Dnieper. These bathes repaired our protracted fatigues and disposed us to resume our own painful work as invaders...'

CHAPTER 17

STRAGGLERS AND PRISONERS

A loaded musket goes off – hobbling to the rear – 'they weren't the same columns' – a Turk's faith – 'what's all this fuss?' – gangrene – but what a camp! – a miracle – something out of the Arabian Nights – Cossacks and peasants – Heinemann is taken prisoner – a transport – Winzingerode's humanity – 'inhuman cruelty only possible in a land of masters and slaves'

Thousands of wounded, stragglers and looters are swarming on the army's flanks and in its rear. One of them, now, is Lance-corporal Heinemann. After the massacre of their square at Valutina those Brunswick Chasseurs who'd survived – many are suffering from dysentery – feel they've done enough:

'For a moment we hoped to be allowed to return to our fatherland. But in tight spots the ranker is mere cannonfodder. And we'd hardly got our breath back before we had to rejoin our battalion and march, once again, against the enemy.'

Obliged to relieve himself under a tree, Heinemann's sergeant is just propping his loaded musket against its trunk when it goes off; and the ball passes through his foot. No transport to the rear is available. So Wilhelm is detailed off to help him back to the Smolensk hospitals. "Now, comrade," jokes the intrepid sergeant, "we'll see how two men can manage on three legs." "If it's God's will, sergeant, all will be well in the end," says Heinemann, who has his pious moments. "What can't a man do, if he must and will?"

They'll soon find out. 'Up to now we'd been marching in the van with the strongest, who'd no inkling of what a dissolving army looks like.' Hobbling back along the highway, the two men see, for the first time, what things are like in the army's rear:

'These were no longer the same columns. Already they were beaten men, looking only for a spot on this foreign soil to lie down and die. Our comrades went marching past us in open columns. First came the strongest, then the weaker, then others whose strength was almost at an end. And last of all the dying, dragging themselves along at the tail. If any sank down, the thick dust soon covered him, like a pall over a bier. Many went past us, silent and unfeeling. Others joked desperately: "Give my love to mother!" – "If thy foot offend thee, cast it away!" jokes a former candidate for the priesthood. And a junior surgeon offers to amputate it.'

Now and again the two men exchange philosophical reflections. The sergeant, who's a great curser and swearer, sits down for a moment on a dead horse, opining that even if all men are sinners, as Wilhelm has been taught, the story of God's punishment on Adam is disagreeable to a soldier. "So I don't want to hear any more of that stuff! I'm sticking to my

221

good Turk's faith: that everything's pre-ordained. Do what one will, none of us escapes his fate." Heinemann, too little the philosopher to discuss such deep matters, hastily agrees that some such belief is indispensable on campaign. As dusk falls, some vehicles come rolling by, raising the two men's hopes. But no, they belong to the Italian army, and a wounded Westphalian is no concern of theirs. Meanwhile the sergeant's foot is becoming agonizingly painful. Gangrene? Hoping against hope it isn't, the two men struggle on westwards. Realizing they've no mercy to hope for from the exasperated peasants, still less any help, they daren't even seek shelter in any cottage that still may be left standing.

The hot dusty day is followed by an icy foggy night, lethal to a seriously wounded man. Encountering a stray horse, they kill it, cut out its liver and entrails, and dine on horsemeat grilled over a fire of broken wheelspokes, salting it with gunpowder. But this only worsens the sergeant's thirst, which is already becoming terrible, and his swigs at the brandy flask only inflame it still further. To keep warm he spends the night inside the horse's cadaver.

Morning comes. And with it an insight that two men, after all, can't get very far on three legs. "Courage, comrade," Heinemann exhorts. "We've still a long way to go to get to mother's coffeepot!". A reflection at which both men burst into tears.

Now it's the evening of the second day; and by this time Heinemann is virtually carrying his companion. But what's that over there? Five French generals 'nonchalantly wrapped in their greatcoats' are sitting round a brightly burning camp fire for which a cottage's furniture is serving as firewood.

'Their fine-limbed Arab racehorses, little though they can have been used to such fare, were eating the rotted thatch. A little distance away servants in braided livery, their brown black-bearded faces emaciated from hunger and fatigues, were bending over a smaller fire, baking a kind of bread from flour and water on hot stones.'
The two stragglers beg for a share, but are brusquely refused. However, one of the generals, 'whose open greatcoat revealed golden epaulettes adorned with the French eagles', gets up and, coming over, wants to know what the fuss is about. Isn't Heinemann speaking French? Is he a Frenchman? If so, what corps does he belong to? Wasn't it the Westphalian army which had just passed this way? Heinemann salutes, explains proudly how he'd fought under the Emperor at Wagram and Aspern, been demobilized, and had rejoined under the Westphalian flag. It's not on his own behalf he's begging, he says, but for his wounded comrade. The general reprimands his lackeys and the two Westphalian stragglers get some of 'the almost inedible bread'.

But there's a limit to even the greatest courage. By next evening the sergeant knows he's done for. Sitting down beside a cannon 'whose wheels had sunk so deep into the ground that no force had been able to extricate it' and a dead horse which had given up its life while trying to, he declares: 'Here's a resting place worthy of a dying soldier.'

Heinemann protests. He'll nurse his wounded foot. 'For the last time, then,' replies the other. Quite right. Taking off the bandage, what do they see? 'There to our silent horror were the black and dark-red stripes, creeping up from his wound to his leg.' 'So that's it, then,' says the sergeant stoically. 'Even the best of us can be branded like that. It won't be long now until it stops my heartbeats.'

Seeing even less hope for his comrade than for himself, Heinemann reluctantly agrees to leave him there to die. Which he does – but not before the sergeant has told him his own tragic love story and entrusted him with his last wishes, in the unlikely event of his ever getting home to Hildesheim.[1]

And now Heinemann, utterly alone, is wandering at random in the vast stretches of Russian landscape beyond Smolensk.

'Fed up and tired of living, I strayed about on the desolate misty heathlands into the night's deep dusk. By the time I'd reached the forest stretching away toward the horizon to the right of the road it was already pitch dark.'

The forest's silver birches gleam in the murk. Underfoot are the soft mosses, 'and overhead hardly a star. I wondered whether I wasn't myself a shadow, moving in the kingdom of the dead.' Now he hears wolves howling – but in the same instant descries a glimmer of camp fires. Friendly? or Russian? He has no means of knowing. If Russian, do they belong to regular troops, or Cossacks? If the former, perhaps he can save himself by claiming to have deserted the French eagles. If the latter,

'I could be sure of being plundered, beaten with knouts and imprisoned, with a few lance-thrusts into the bargain. If they were refugees from neighbouring villages and the men were away, I could only hope for the women's compassion. The men would have made no bones about killing a *sabacky Franzusky*.'

Well, it's a camp. But what a camp! 'The language I heard being spoken wasn't Russian, but Italian. Yet I knew from of old how the Italians hated the French.' Suddenly he's witness to a drama of jealousy. A lieutenant of the Neapolitan Guard Chasseurs – 'an immense figure of a man, black-bearded and sallow' – has just been assassinated by his rival for smiling at a cantinière. While pretending to embrace the assassin in the dark his *inamorata* stabs him in the back. Deeply shaken, Heinemann joins the crowd round the camp fires.

'They were camp followers, straying about on the army's left flank, searching for food. Here I saw men and women of every race, dressed half in uniform, half in civilian clothes. Almost all the women were past their first youth.'

The only attractive one is she of the dagger – whose charms we shan't waste time describing.

'There were Croats with long moustaches in braided fur jackets, both men and women. Also gypsies, among them pretty but dark-hued beauties, dancing to tambourines, zither and violin. Also a group of Bavarian sutlers... in a word, a real cross-section of those people who made up the baggage train of all the many nations Napoleon's iron will had driven into the icy North.'

With them they have a great variety of wagons, oxen, ponies, mules and donkeys. But also bread. So Wilhelm tenders 'a 5-franc piece as my letter of credence. "*Chè volete, can francese?*" [What do you want, you dog of a Frenchman?] shouts a man with a bloody knife between his teeth, who's busy skinning a hare. "*Matalete il can francese!*" [Kill that French dog!] shouted another.'

The 'French dog', though he hasn't eaten for four days, thinks it the better part of prudence to turn instead to some Bavarians who are roasting potatoes in the ashes. 'If we have any over, *kamerad*,' says a tall sly type, half soldier, half hobo, 'we'll be taking it to the army, where we'll get a hundred francs for a meal, instead of your wretched five!'

So Lance-corporal Heinemann has to grope about in the dark for his dinner among the gardens of a nearby deserted village. He finds a well but lacks any vessel or rope to draw up its sweet-smelling water. And for a moment contemplates throwing himself into it. Finally he drops off to sleep in a barn – with a corpse for bedfellow. In the morning the camp-followers have vanished, leaving only the ashes of their fires.

Once again he's utterly alone – terrified of being found by vengeful peasants and beaten to death, expecting every moment to see a roving Cossack patrol come galloping toward him. Climbing over the fence of the village church, he lies down among the graves under a horse-chestnut tree. Longs only to put an end to himself – but in the same instant realizes that the tree harbours a bees' nest. Thousands of soldiers, he knows, have sickened and died from eating too much of that 'sweet poison'. But now, all hope of salvation gone, he decides that he may as well die of eating honey as any other way. Knocking down the bees' honeycomb, he drives them out of it with gunpowder smoke, 'and with my sabre cut myself a large slice from the comb' – and is promptly stung on the lip for his pains. 'A bee's sting had saved me from suicide.' The reflection throws him into pious thoughts. Entering the shattered church 'plundered even of its icons, filled with a lively sense of the ever-present God' he sinks down in prayer before the altar. But coming out again, sees no sign of the daily bread he has prayed for. 'More inconsolable than ever, I stood in the open place on the far side of the plundered and half-burned village and stared out across the hemp fields towards the grim forest nearby.' He has just primed his musket and is putting its muzzle to his eye – when the miracle occurs: in the shape of a fat pig, which comes galloping towards him from a field! And is shot instead.

'We'll go halves, comrade!' shouts a German voice. And from round the corner of one of the houses a Prussian hussar emerges on a limping horse. After dinner the two men, having loaded it with hams and pork cutlets, start their search for the army. But everywhere for several versts on each side of its route the countryside has been systematically laid waste. So deciding to push on northwards out of this devastated zone, they by and by come on another deserted village. The only food they can find in it is a heap of grain inside a cottage, which they roast in its stove. They also find a horse, whose owner has fled at their approach, and a cart. So they load it with the rest of the grain. And find a second horse, which makes three. Seeing another, obviously inhabited village below them in the plain, they decide to pretend to be quartermasters, with orders to find lodgings for 500 cavalry and a whole infantry regiment. A Jew who speaks a little German interprets. And in return for some victuals and a night's sleep they offer to divert the approaching regiment elsewhere. And the village elders kiss their hands.

But the peasants aren't all that easily fooled. 'In the morning, meeting only with threatening and suspicious glances', the two men make haste to leave; come off best in a rearguard skirmish with the furious peasants, and go on. By and by they come across an isolated but singularly splendid manor-house. Never in his life has Heinemann seen the likes of its interior décor: 'costliest clocks, immense mirrors reaching up to the ceiling, polished floors of inlaid woods, the finest stucco work and fresco paintings, marble, gilt, and curtains, wallcoverings and furniture all clad in thick satin'. It's like something out of the Arabian Nights. A veritable palace. It too has been abandoned by its owner; but not by some of his female servants, by his aged French-speaking superintendent, or by his poultry. Execution is promtly done among the poultry. And in this paradise the Prussian hussar – his name is Matthias Klarges – promptly strikes up a liaison with a kitchenmaid called Olga. On the other hand, his moral indignation at so much wealth knows no bounds:

'"Know what, brother? The owner of all this couldn't have spent so much on it if he hadn't squeezed it out of his peasants. And such a tyrant deserves to be punished. Don't you think we'd bring down God's blessing on us if we smashed it all up and then set fire to his nest?" And before I could prevent him, he'd drawn his sabre and shattered a mirror and a costly table-top.'

The two stragglers barricade themselves for the night at the top of the stairs with heaps of furniture, light a bonfire to illumine the environs, and lie down booted and spurred to get some sleep amid eiderdown bolsters. But the Prussian has fallen in love with his Olga, and talks the night away about how lovely it would be to become her husband, even if it means marrying her – however many blows of the knout it may entail. And besides 'they can kill us just as easily if we leave as if we stay'. Hearing whispers in the night and a shuffling of feet on the gravel, they imagine they're being attacked and discharge their firearms into the dark – and kill the wretched Olga. Tragic moment, highly theatrical. (Did it really happen? Or only nearly? Or not at all?) 'My comrade had flung himself upon her, smothered her in kisses and himself in her blood....' Next morning they find their broadside has also slain the old French superintendent, who lies there expiring in his own blood. So that's that. They leave, the Prussian hussar consoling himself with the soldierly reflection that tears can't revive the dead: 'A soldier must let himself be shot to death, if fate has cast a bullet for him. But the regulations say nothing about dying of grief.'

Next day, coming across 'a fine large village, with a golden cupola in its midst, gleaming in the sunshine like a ball of fire', the Prussian strokes his ginger moustaches and declares he's formed a taste for luxury. Why not take it by storm? Heinemann, more cautious, points out that they've already enough food to keep them alive for many days. At very least his friend, who after all forms their little convoy's cavalry arm, should reconnnoitre before they attack. Which he does. Runs into Cossacks. And, leaving his comrade in the lurch, disappears at a terrified gallop over the horizon. For the second time Heinemann knows his last hour has come:

'Horrified, I saw what the lie of the ground had hidden from my sight. To right and left across the hemp field some Cossacks were racing toward me, long lances lowered; and, straight out of the village, on his magnificent dappled horse, comes a Cossack officer. I give myself up for lost. Climbing down from the cart, I place myself out in the field, and grasping my musket prepare to sell my life dearly. I'm surrounded on all sides.'

But suddenly the Cossacks swerve from their target, and a voice summons him in French:

'*"Pardon, camerade! Abattez vos armes!"* The officer was a slim man, in the flower of his age. His black beard and healthy hue lent his big dark eye and the pure oriental profile an expression of perfect manliness. His clothes, blue and silver, opulent but tasteful, and his whole posture and the resounding tone in which he addressed me in an educated language inspired confidence in his humanity.'

Luckily, Heinemann remembers something. The Russians are said to be reserving their most virulent hatred for the French, but treating their German prisoners less harshly. So, forgetting all about Wagram, etc., he pretends not to understand, and says – in German: "I'm not French, I'm German."

"Throw down your weapons, then!" the officer replies in accented German. For a moment, even if it must mean his own instant death from the Cossacks' lance points, Heinemann feels an impulse to shoot him. But thinks better of it, throws away musket and sabre and falls on his knees.

'"Further away!" Immediately he comes galloping at me, his pistol cocked, sabre dangling from his arm. Also the other Cossacks, with felled lances. I commend my soul to God and my body to the earth, seeming in all my limbs already to feel the pain of the lances' stabs, the bullets piercing my brain. Everything goes black. I can hardly stand upright. I've a first taste of blows from the flats of their sabres, smarting on my shoulders and back.'

In his despair he yells out that a whole squadron of hussars is in the offing. But this only exhilarates the officer: 'Good, the more prisoners the better!' But of course there are no hussars. And his own has fled.

'To begin with he drove me before him at a run, his horse's hoofs at my heels. One of his men was told to keep an eye on me. So far none of the village's peasants had appeared. Soon there came several. So far I hadn't been maltreated. But we halted at a distance from the village and the Cossacks begin visiting me, plundering me in the crude open-hearted way so typical of them. I was their first prisoner. They took all my money, and the one who got it patted me amiably on my cheek, calling me Patruschka, little father. But a second Cossack let me understand that if I didn't produce some more I'd have a taste of the knout. A third greedily grabbed my tchapska, while a fourth went through my wallet, which was inside it, looking for any rouble notes. To me my wallet was endlessly valuable. It contained no money, but everything I held holy, letters from my mother and other personal papers.'

Although his captors try to protect him, the enraged villagers bombard him with stones and dirt, toss him to and fro among themselves and beat him about the head, 'and the women were worst of all. Blood was running down my face. One moment I was lying on the ground, being trampled under their feet; the next, they'd grabbed me up by my clothes and hoisted me high in the air, to rip off my shiny buttons. In this way my uniform was torn to shreds.'

Retrieved and driven away by the Cossacks, Heinemann is amazed to find himself among a lot of other Westphalian prisoners, all from his own regiment. Its voltigeur company had been reconstituted after the massacre at Valutina, but they'd been captured 'not without putting up a fierce resistance, while out on a marauding expedition, the battalion being in dire need of everything'. They're hardly in better case than himself. All have been captured after putting up a valiant resistance in a manor-house, but having to yield to numbers. At first Heinemann has taken his comrades for 'peasants armed with sabres'. Even their valiant Captain Telge, the only officer to have escaped the massacre, is among them. Stripped of his uniform, his only clothing is a Russian nobleman's scarlet nightgown.

Afraid that they are in fact going to be attacked by Prussian cavalry, Cossacks fling their prisoners, most of whom are wounded and some very badly, on to wagons and gallop away with them, into ever more desolate tracts of countryside and swamps, where the Brunswickers, driven on at lance-point, have to jump from one tussock to the next so as not to sink up to their waists in muddy water 'covered with a sort of blueish film that in no way did anything to cheer up the dreary landscape'. Soaked through, starving, at nightfall they're packed into pigstyes where they stand and shiver, although their captors at least heave over some straw on which they can collapse. 'Cossacks and peasants kept watch all around us.'

At midnight they're peremptorily awakened by voices and a freezing north wind. A ferocious-looking long-bearded man with a lantern and a knife is searching about among the wounded. 'All I could see was that four Russians were holding down a prisoner on the ground.' Taking it for granted he's their executioner, Heinemann is 'overtaken by a trembling so violent I'd never known its like'. But no. Here's a foot flung aside, there an arm. He's 'one of those kind-hearted Samaritans who are used to cutting off arms and legs by the dozen, like calves' heads. Our wounds are bound up, the bandages a soldier has to carry on him' are put to their proper use.

And now, before dawn, the 'French dogs' are being ordered out, two by two, through the gate. And outside stand two rows of peasants, with armfuls of bread:

'A bit was flung to each of us, and we were allowed to drink out of a well used by the cattle. Such was the beginning of a chain of efforts and sufferings no pen can describe.'

One day they reach the headquarters of General Winzingerode, a German aristocrat in the Russian service,[2] who sympathizes with their plight:

'As a native of Germany he took special care of his compatriots. He had soup made for the prisoners, and bought back Captain Telge's uniform for him from a Cossack whose plunder it was. He spoke quite amiably to us and tried to revive our fallen courage, promising us we'd from now on be treated well, would be placed in a proper transport and find a good soup waiting for us at every stopping place. Orders were given that the Germans in particular should be treated kindly since everyone knew they were only serving Napoleon because they were forced to.'

But in Russia promises are one thing; realities another. Their sufferings begin again. Closely herded together like cattle, they're driven on day after day at a brisk trot along foul muddy roads or rotten causeways by peasants armed with clubs:

'Anyone who has ever marched in a column knows how wearisome it is to march close behind the man in front of you. But unable to move on without tramping on his heels, after only an hour's marching the strongest man was powerless.'

The Russian peasants' treatment of the prisoners, Heinemann says, 'bore witness to a low bestiality without a trace of humanity in it'. Anyone who collapses is first beaten half to death by the peasants, to try and make him get up; then, when they themselves have to keep up with the column, is left to receive more blows in passing by others following, until

'finally the Cossacks who closed the column reach the point where the man, beaten half to death, lies pale, motionless, covered in filth and no longer even looking like a human being. Now the last attempts are made to revive him with a score or so blows of the knout, and if even these don't have the desired effect, a couple of peasants grab hold of the poor fellow's legs and drag him aside to wait for the wagons which, according to orders, are to pick up the dead and inane. One can imagine that the unwelcome guest isn't received on it without oaths and blows – and the most inhuman cruelty, impossible in any other country than where there are only masters and slaves.'

Few such unfortunates survive. Farther and farther northwards 'towards the measureless interior of Russia our columns of exhausted captives – images of the uttermost human misery – made their way'. Until at last on the Russian Christmas Day (5 January) they reach Archangel, on the White Sea.

Thousands are sharing the same fate.[3]

CHAPTER 18

DUST, HEAT AND THIRST

An uninviting landscape – an impenetrable dust cloud – disappointments at Doroghoboui – news from Moscow – 'I'm going still further away' – Dumonceau sees the army go by – the Cossacks – their appearance – with the vanguard's guns – first signs of autumn – Murat and Davout at loggerheads – the city of fishes – an interrupted funeral – 'the Russians are preparing to give battle' – 'I've a good job, I'm emperor' – 'he made the most comical grimaces'

Now I Corps is in the van, and on the same day that Paul de Bourgoing had dined al fresco at Ney's headquarters the Red Lancers have resumed their scouting. Although all traces indicate a retreat on Moscow, not a soul is to be seen. As for the landscape, it's completely unlike what it had been before Smolensk: 'dreary and desolate, covered only by scrub and conifers'. All the villages lie in ashes. Following on with III Corps and suffering from three bruises sustained at Valutina, Captain Bonnet, 'once again crossed the Dnieper and found on this bank a poverty-stricken landscape, forests and sands, few cultivated fields'.

But gradually it improves. On 21 August Maurice Tascher is amazed to see a long-forgotten sight – 'some peasants busy harvesting their fields. Our men are wrenching the grain out of their hands to feed the horses.' At Prudiche, three days later, some houses are still left standing 'after all the troops had passed through'. The Italians, too, stare at some cattle peacefully grazing in the fields, 'as if at an extraordinary sight'. But are more considerate. Politely asking for some food and permission to rest up, they're given 'food for one day and some horned cattle'. Now Césare de Laugier is finding the landscape 'more attractive and cultivated'. Finding himself amid an abundant supply of necessities, the ranker is 'forgetting his past fatigues'. And on 25 August Tascher's hussars reach the fair-sized town of Janoviczi,

'wholly of timber. Some Jews have remained. Our soldiers are busy plundering them. A fine lake. The Cossacks have carried off a great number of our stragglers and marauders. We keep coming upon great holes, filled with linen and other chattels.'

And indeed, on each side of the great Moscow highway, a wave of organized and indiscriminate violence is rolling into Old Russia:

'In each company were certain men, excellent marchers, who were clever at going out to search for food. They went to the villages, where they plundered all they could, were guilty of all sorts of excesses, and often, after cutting the old men's throats, raping the women and setting fire to the village, returned to their company with some sacks of flour on a small cart drawn by a nanny-goat, a cow, some supplies, i.e., when these hadn't been taken from them by the Imperial Guard or other units they had to pass through. The officers congratulated these marauders and held them up as examples to be emulated by their comrades.'

Le Roy tells the same grim story:

'Each unit sent out a detachment, now on one flank, now on the other. To find inhabited villages, deserted at our approach, it had to cross the whole army, sometimes between 12 and 15 miles in extent. All was there for the taking and we carried away everything edible. Next day it all had to be done over again. The enemy frequently carried off these detachments, who were immediately put to death by peasant insurgents, excited against us by their popes.'

An 'inconvenient' thing about such ruthless marauding, in Le Roy's eyes, is that it's 'accustoming the rank and file to make a profession of it. Almost always it was the same men who asked to go off *à la picorée*, to be free and, though running the greatest dangers, avoid the shooting.'

And day after day the hot Russian sun is scorching down.

On 23 August, now 60 miles east of Smolensk, Ney's vanguard comes within sight of Doroghoboui, a largish town lying in a sloping amphitheatre, which offers 'a superb defensive position'. Le Roy jumps to the conclusion that it's here the Russians are at last going to stand and fight. So does Murat. And sends off an ADC to Smolensk. His arrival precipitates IHQ's departure after midnight on the 24th. After travelling along the Moscow highway in his closed carriage, Napoleon gets to Doroghoboui to find it's been fired by the Cossacks, and his own troops are in occupation. Makes some scathing remarks to Murat. Establishes his headquarters. And the advance goes on.

Estafettes (couriers), meanwhile, have brought worrying news. Marching northwards with the Army of Moldavia, Tormasoff has broken into the southern theatre of war, thus threatening the advancing army's right rear. Rapp and his colleagues discuss the army's remoteness from its lines of communication:

'Probably Napoleon had overheard us. Coming in to us, he talked at length about the precautions he'd taken to keep his back free, the corps forming our wings, and the chain of posts from the Niemen that linked us up to the places where we now were. "Tormassoff", he told us, "has put the wind up old and young alike in Warsaw, who've fancied him already master of Prague. But he's had to pull out quicker than he came."'

With these words Napoleon goes back into his office and 'in an indifferent tone of voice, but loud enough for each one of us to hear' begins dictating instructions to Marshal Victor to bring up X Corps to Vilna.[1] He is also given command of all the troops in Lithuania and in Witebsk and Smolensk provinces: "Dombrowski's division, seven to eight thousand strong, is manoeuvring between Molihew, Minsk and Bobruisk. Four battalions of Illyrians, the two battalions and cannon of the 129th Regiment, two battalions of the 33rd Light must go to Smolensk..." After calling in and re-organizing all these widely scattered units, Victor is to "reopen communications between Smolensk and headquarters, should they be cut, and, if need be, come to the army's rescue."'

That day (26 August) the Italians, following a separate road out to the left of the main column, are having a spot of trouble. A little river called the Wop, whose waters are 'flowing calmly and peacefully between rather steep banks' and aren't very deep, is barring their path. The artillery and carriages, Laugier writes irritably in his diary, 'have only with some difficulty got across.'² Otherwise the roads are getting better.

Not a drop of rain has fallen for a whole month. And Bonnet, when his battalion forces the pace to catch up with III Corps some fifteen miles east of Doroghoboui, finds that he's marching through a dense cloud of white dust:

'the entire army in a single mass, marching along a fine highroad in four columns, two of infantry on either side of the road, the artillery on the road itself. You can't see ten paces ahead of you.'

Oddly, on each side of the double avenues of silver birches, the infantry divisions are extended in battle order, and flanked by long lines of cavalry. Perhaps Dumonceau sees Bonnet go by. Called in from their scoutings, the Red Lancers have a long wait by the roadside. They're particularly impressed by the appearance of the 48th Line (I),

'four handsome battalions marching in closed formation, as if on parade. It enjoyed the unique privilege of wearing its number in copper figures on its pouches. Behind it came a brown-clad Portuguese regiment, wearing English-style shakos. After them³ came Ney's corps, among which we noticed a fine Württemberg regiment and a Spanish one, whose uniforms rather closely resembled that of the Portuguese. These troops were marching over the open fields in columns of platoons, on either side of the road, leaving it free for the artillery and baggage which in its enormous confusion presented the most bizarre sight – a weird muddle, made up of every thinkable kind of vehicle; teams of horses, individuals' riding horses, vivandières riding on their nags like a desert Arab on his dromedary, all amidst a mass of pack mules and infantrymen, knapsacks on their backs and muskets hanging bandoleer-fashion as they rode along on little Russian cobs whose legs were shorter than their riders. And amidst all this mass of people the funniest sights: men struggling with the most refractory animals, etc. For two hours, without for a moment feeling bored to see this motley pass along our front, we stood there resting while waiting for the Imperial Guard.'

Boulart's Guard batteries are among those taking the crown of the road. And he isn't the only man to be 'suffering worse from heat and thirst during these ten days than perhaps I've ever done in my life'. So is Girod de l'Ain:

'the heat was excessive: I'd never known it worse even in Spain. But there's a difference: in Russia it doesn't last long. The main Moscow road is sandy, and the army, marching abreast in several serried columns, raised such dust clouds we couldn't see one another two yards off. Our eyes, ears and nostrils were full of it and our faces caked with it. This heat and dust made us extremely thirsty, as can well be imagined, and water was hard to come by. Will you believe men when I say that I saw men lying on their bellies to drink horses' urine in the ditch! On this march and in a rift in the dust cloud, i.e, after a halt long enough for it to settle, I at least had the pleasure of seeing the heavy cavalry division, composed of carabiniers and cuirassiers, fourteen regiments in all. Their cuirasses and helmets, glinting in the sun, made a splendid sight.'

Riding along in their midst, Thirion can't 'make out the trooper ahead. Often we lost sight of our own horses' ears, and had to trust to instinct and these poor horses' acute vision, their eyes not being like human ones.' Caulaincourt explains the heavy cavalry regiments' advanced position as necessary to support the advance guard at a moment's notice. The steel-clad men are having to sit their saddles from 3 a.m. until late in the evening. 'Is there a soldier in the world today who could do the same?'

Von Brandt's Polish veterans, too, are making comparisons with Spain. 'The whirling gusts of wind raised such thick clouds of dust we often couldn't even see the big trees lining the road.' Many try to protect their eyes with

'little bits of windowpane. Others marched with their shakos under one arm and their head swathed in a handkerchief, only leaving in it an opening big enough to let themselves be led and to breathe through. Others made themselves leafy garlands.'

Beyond the flanking cavalry lines swarm great swarms of Cossacks. On 27 August Dumonceau, for the first but by no means last time, sees them *en masse,*

'dressed in every thinkable fashion, with every kind of head-dress. Lacking the least uniformity of appearance, dirty-looking and clad in rags, riding on nasty thin little horses with long necks, low heads, a long mane and guided only by a simple rein, and armed with a long simple whip with a kind of nail at the end, they wheeled in confused and apparently enormous disorder, and to me seemed like swarming insects.'

But Colbert, taking his meerschaum out of his mouth, tells him:

'They're admirable as light cavalry. At the outposts, for reconnaissances, they leave nothing to be desired. But they'll never really attack you as long as you stand firm and don't let yourself be distracted by their deafening shouts. The artillery only has to show up, and they'll vanish in a jiffy. Threaten them with a pistol or any kind of firearm, and they'll avoid you. They never risk a man-to-man combat unless they're several against one. Their traps and ambushes are always cleverly thought out. Nor are they cruel, though less inclined to kill you than to take you prisoner.'

And indeed only yesterday evening (26 August) the 'savages' have snapped up one of Prince Eugène's ADC. Sent across to the main column to get Murat's orders for IV Corps 'he hasn't come back,' Laugier had written in his diary, 'so we've understood what's happened to him'. But Le Roy as usual, though 'dead-beat and dusty as could be' has managed to come by his dinner. His battalion has just bivouacked

'between two woods, where there's a small lake. To freshen up, I take a dip and (remembering my youthful days) amuse myself by searching among the rushes. Am sure there must be fish there. In the end I manage to fill my handkerchief with three little fishes, which, boiled in salt water, were relished by the adjutant's mess.'

Above all it's the young Polish officers, Chlapolwsky says, who are happy to be emulating their 17th-century ancestors by advancing into Old Russia. Like the Italians to its left, Poniatowski's V Corps is flanking the main column to the right. Sent to it on some mission, Labaume is impressed by the Poles' appearance, which he unjustly ascribes to 'the Polish army having passed through a less devastated landscape than had fallen to our lot. Since it hadn't suffered at all,[4] it was still superb.' Other Polish units, in Latour Maubourg's IV Cavalry Corps, following on at a considerable distance to the rear, are reminded that day of the brevity of the northern summer. Allowed to rest up at Mscicslaw, the doyen or 'marshal' of the local nobility proposes to take General *Boris Turno*[5] and his officers on a tour of the town:

'Dusk was casting an uncertain light over our bivouacs and the lonely landscape, and the sky was covered in grey cold mists. Yet at various points on the horizon something was beginning to stir, at the same time as a kind of mute but incessant trembling sound was heard. The air seemed to be populated; far off in the mist some white objects appeared. It was swans leaving, making a clapping sound with their beaks.'

"Yes, it's the swans leaving this countryside and Russia, to seek a milder climate,' their guide tells them. 'Don't think it's an empty or unsure portent. It's terror of the ice that changes these creatures' habits. They've an intimation of what's to come." Undeterred by this portent, General Roznicki, approaching Czerepowo two days later,

'orders the Polish troops to halt, forms us up in square and reminds us that we're standing at the limit of the Jagellons' and Batory's one-time empire. After painting for us the heroic aspects of our nation's glorious past he invites all present to dismount and pick up a little dust so as to be able to remind our descendants of this glorious event which has brought us back to Poland's former limits.'

From Doroghoboui IHQ has moved on to 'a big house or manor on a hillock beside the River Ouja, at Slavkowo. 'There we found a little corn, the more valuable for the enemy having left us nothing at Smolensk.'

Here several units – Guard units, one supposes – at last get some bread. And Napoleon some news from Moscow. At Smolensk he'd heard that on 24 July the Tsar had entered his 'old' capital. Now d'Ideville reads to him news of 'how Alexander had assembled the nobility and the more prosperous class and, without hiding from them the state's situation, asked them to obtain help from all district governments'.

The evening being warm, IHQ is entertained to a concert and Faber du Faur's gunners, too, as they pass along the broad highway, hear 'music, floating out of a handsome manor-house to the left of the road'.

From Slavkowo Napoleon sends detailed instructions to his outlying corps commanders:

"I am going even further away. The day after tomorrow I shall be at Viazma, five days' march from Moscow. Probably there will be a battle which will open the city gates to me. Act above all in such a manner that any Russians confronting you shall not march against me."

St-Cyr, Napoleon thinks, has more than enough troops to inspire Wittgenstein's respect.[6] As if aware he'll shortly be needing fresh armies, he sends off a decree to Paris for the immediate implementation of the 1813 call-up. As for Smolensk, he remarks to Fain, he's "going to put in a superior commander, one who if need be can take over and act according to circumstances. The city is to be the central point in our communications." It will be Marshal Victor, coming forward with IX Corps, made up of Frenchmen, Germans and Poles.

These scorching days Lejeune is doing a lot of cantering to and fro along the dusty highway between Murat's and Berthier's headquarters; and can't help noticing how the Russians are still

'withdrawing in admirably good order and evidently wishing to defend all positions that offer any advantage. In this way our advancing cavalry had to keep forming columns of attack supported by the artillery, and which only conquered a little ground after exchanging many discharges of grape and attacks with the sabre. This meant a lot of time was being consumed in making but little progress – and still we were over 300 miles from Moscow! By day we sat our horses amid cannonfire. At nights we sat by our camp fires without the slightest scent of any roast beef hanging from pothooks to console our exhausted stomachs.'

Many days Murat, who's still forcing the pace, is covering

'thirty to thirty-six miles. The men were in the saddle from 3 a.m. to 10 p.m. By the end of the day our horses were so wearied that a mere skirmish could cost us several brave fellows, their horses not being able to keep pace.'

Of the 7th Hussars' 1,500 men and horses who'd galloped so gaily into Vilna hardly 1,000 are left; of the 11th Hussars only 300. And Victor Dupuy's existence has become utterly trying:

'Each day from 5 a.m. onwards we were skirmishing with the Cossacks, and sometimes this went on until as late as 10 or 11 p.m. They were carrying off everything they could from the villages and driving away the inhabitants, who fled into the forests. After which they set fire to the village. If we made some bold manoeuvre or brisk attack and didn't give them time to, their artillery fired incendiary shells and produced the same effect by setting alight the thatched roofs – a way of waging war we experienced as greatly to our disadvantage. After days almost totally given up to combats and physical effort we could hardly find enough to eat, and often we'd nothing to give the horses, whose numbers were daily dwindling in an alarming fashion.'

The further the army advances, Lejeune is noticing, 'the worse the devastation. Everything had been burnt and the horses didn't even find any straw on the roofs to live off. Everything lay in ashes.'

Worst off of all are the advance guard's gunners. Immense efforts are being required of Colonel *Séruzier*'s twelve companies, manhandling and serving the 72 light 6-pounders and 24lb howitzers attached to Montbrun's leading cavalry corps:

'My horse artillery and the divisions of light cavalry escorting them fought serious combats with the Russians. We were having to bombard each other for two or three hours at a time, before the enemy were so kind as to leave us a position where we could pass the night. At each withdrawal he blocked the roads and destroyed the bridges. I was every bit as busy rebuilding them. Each evening I saw my men drop from weakness and exhaustion. I went into the water up to my waist and planted the first piquet. Despite their exhaustion, my behaviour gave my men back a little energy. They got up, forced me to retire, and without saying a word got busy repairing the passage.'

Afterwards Boulart won't be able distinctly to recall all these places,

'so uniform is their appearance: largely featureless terrain, offering nothing clear-cut; rather fine harvests; plenty of forests, where the silver birch woods seemed commonest; broad unpaved roads, indicated on either side only by a row or two of magnificent trees.'

The horde of camp-followers the army is dragging along in its wake is being swelled by ever more numerous sick and stragglers. Though very young and vigorous men, lieutenants Vossler (Prince Louis' Hussars), and Dutheillet (57th Line), both suffering grievously from 'dysentery', are at each moment afraid to see their regiments fade away ahead into the advancing dustcloud. Which is exactly what happens to Dutheillet:

'I'd become so weak, and my stomach so oversensitive it couldn't even stand the weight of my swordbelt. I'd attached everything to my horse, together with my haversack and portemanteau. Obliged to dismount to obey a call of nature, I didn't even have time to tether my horse or hold him by bridle. While I'm thus occupied, a regiment of cuirassiers passes by at a trot. My horse, excited, jumps the hedge between us and runs off, carrying with him all my possessions. I try to run after him and demand him back, but haven't the strength. Unable to go a step further I come to a halt, there on the road. What upset me most, apart from the loss of my possessions, was that I could hear gunfire. Knowing my regiment was one of the leading units, I was afraid it might be engaging the enemy, and that my absence would be noticed. This idea was more than I could stand.'

But here's the 111th Line, in I Corps' 3rd brigade, passing by. Dutheillet recognizes a mounted officer, tells him of his misadventure and begs for the loan of his horse to rejoin the 57th. Gets it, and that evening sends it back by his servant. Vossler, too, who has lost all the horses he'd crossed the Niemen with and is riding a 'scruffy Cossack pony', is feeling so weak he can hardly stay on its back without help. Prince Louis' hussars are trying to catch up:

'Apart from some objects too heavy to carry away, such as great hogsheads of spirits, etc., we were finding no supplies or provisions of any kind. All along the highway from Doroghoboui we came across nothing but desolation. The towns had been taken over by the French administration, who stretched themselves out comfortably in such houses as were still standing and in the many and sometimes beautiful monasteries and churches. After Doroghoboui we'd come across many soldiers, sometimes enormously many, who out of sheer exhaustion had collapsed by the roadside, and for lack of all help were dying where they lay. The sight did much to increase our anxieties for the condition of the Grand Army's cavalry and artillery.'

Yet another officer who's feeling very ill and is straggling is Major *Friedrich Wilhelm von Lossberg,*[7] one of Junot's Westphalians. Remarkably, his wife will get his letter at Detmold:

'Feeling ill this morning I had to take medicine from the regiment's doctor, so I couldn't mount my horse until several hours after the army corps had left. This has given me a chance to observe, at close quarters, the miseries and disorder it's leaving in its wake. What masses of carriages haven't I come upon, "kikbitkas" [closed sledges on wheels], whole hordes of cattle with their drovers of all nationalities, either isolated or in big groups! Many were moribund, and most rode wretched konyas. Even if I hadn't been able to see the Moscow road, I'd only have had to follow its smell. At every hundred yards, at least, I was near to tumbling over some horse which had collapsed, or a bullock that had been slaughtered and whose guts lay across the road. In each village or isolated house I came across unburied soldiers, our own and the enemy's. To take a little rest in the shade and drink a little coffee – my servant had everything with him to prepare it – I dismounted beside a building. But it turned out to be in such bad shape, so utterly filthy, and so full of stragglers from every corps, I sat down on the grass a little way off, beside a naked corpse. So feelingless had I become, only one thought absorbed me: "What luck this fellow hasn't had time to putrefy! Otherwise I'd have had to drink my coffee out in the hot sun!'"

Von Lossberg confesses that this day's experiences have convinced him that 'Napoleon doesn't give a damn how many of his soldiers collapse by the roadside, or whether human strength suffices to pursue and if possible attack and destroy the Russian army.' During the twelve days since leaving Smolensk Lieutenant Hubert Lyautey, that lover of military music, is noticing that 'almost a tenth of the army' has melted away from dysentery and desertion'.

Worse, but hardly a matter for surprise, Caulaincourt is noticing that discipline is beginning to break down. On 28 August, as the advance guard is approaching the important town of Viazma and IHQ is following on 'a few leagues behind', Murat's ADC Colonel Rossetti realizes that 'the army, thirsty from marching, heat and dust', has no water: 'Fights were breaking out over muddy wells, which soon got stirred up and fouled. The Emperor himself had to be content with liquid mud.'

As for Davout and Murat, they're becoming more and more exasperated with each other. And at the crossing of the Osma on 27 August – another day of which we have exceptionally many and vivid glimpses – one of Davout's battery commanders refuses to obey Murat's orders to fire, Davout having forbidden it – doubtless to save ammunition.

And now the van is approaching Viazma, 'a small town, but for Russian conditions a very large one'. Or, as Larrey puts it,

'a rather considerable town, well adapted to serve as a storage point for trade between the two parts of Russia. It contained enormous stocks of oil, brandy, soap, sugar, coffee, leather and furs.'

Surrounded by the serpentine Viazma River,[8] it dominates both the plain and, on the Smolensk road, the entrance to a big defile. To eyes inflamed by white dust and the glaring sun its green onion spires hover like a veritable mirage, so that to Dedem it seems 'brand-new'; and to Maurice Tascher 'a superb town, which at a distance appears to be a forest of church towers' – Césare de Laugier, who's heard that Viazma's 1,900 houses are normally occupied by 13,000 inhabitants, thinks he can count 32 spires. No one on the Italian staff has 'seen anything so beautiful or inviting since Witebsk. But Captain Chlapowsky of the 1st Guard Lancers is a patriotic Pole and denigrates everything after Smolensk, the last place where the population had 'at least understood' Polish. To him Viazma is 'just a dozen brick houses around the main marketplace'.

As the army approaches the town 'a mass of cavalry debouches from all sides and camps in the environs'. Entering it in the van with Grouchy's corps, Pierre Aubry finds its streets 'paved with logs, its perimeter vast and its streets irregular'. Alas, its immense stocks of flour and grain are already on fire. To save what he can, Murat orders 'a regiment of carabiniers' to cross the bridge. Unfortunately Davout has already allotted the bridge to

the 57th as part of a general well-planned attack, and they've already begun crossing it. Instantly there's a blazing row:
'The Prince of Eckmühl was near the bridge. The carabiniers' colonel went up to him, saying he'd come on behalf of the King of Naples to ask to be allowed to pass. "You're not going to," the Marshal tells him. "If the King of Naples needs cavalry, I need infantry, and this bridge has been allotted me by the Emperor." Upon the colonel insisting, the Marshal orders Colonel Charrière: "Fire on that regiment if it takes another step." The carabinier colonel turns on the Marshal: "I'm retiring – at your orders, and am going to tell the King." "Go on, then, tell him it's Marshal Davout who's forbidden you to cross by this bridge." Seeing the Marshal near the bridge and the Emperor there too, the King of Naples, furious, comes up and reproaches him in the harshest terms with having held up the cavalry.'

Worse, Murat seizes his chance to reproach Davout for having made the 33rd Light, at Minsk, march past with reversed arms:
'"When one wears bifocal spectacles, M. le Maréchal, one should give up campaigning. I tell you this, not because I'm your king. Even if I were your equal I'd say the same thing." Furious, the Marshal replies that Murat isn't his king, and never will be. The Emperor put an end to this loss of tempers by ordering the Marshal to carry a battery of guns that was firing grape at us; which we did, at the double.'

Beside himself with rage, Murat sends off Belliard to tell Napoleon that under such circumstances he, the King of Naples, can no longer command the advance guard. Doubtless Napoleon, after Murat's headlong imbecilities at Krasnoië, realizes only too well that it's Davout who's in the right. But the ranks and dignities of Napoleonic society must be upheld, even in the face of commonsense. And he resolves the problem by ordering Berthier to place Compans' division temporarily under Murat's command. Whereupon an exasperated Davout tells Berthier:
'That man acts like a lunatic! He engages his cavalry without even first reconnoitring the ground, he has his men massacred in totally pointless attacks to obtain results which could equally well be obtained by means of simple demonstrations that wouldn't cost the life of a single man!'

Evidently someone passes on these words to Murat; who wants to challenge Davout to a duel. And when Belliard restrains him – bursts into tears.

All the long way since Smolensk great curtains of smoke have been lying over a horizon in flames. Yet no one at IHQ seems to have tumbled to the implications:
'Some of us had thought this way in which the cities and market towns were always going up in flames as we entered them was as much due to confusion in our vanguard as to the Cossack rearguard,

who cared very little for Russia's weal or woe. At first, I admit, I'd shared the same view, nor had I been able to understand what the Russians' intention could be in destroying all their public buildings and even their private houses – little use could they be to us.'

But now, at Viazma, it isn't only the loyal Caulaincourt or the querulous Pion des Loches who's wondering why none of its houses contain a single Russian civilian:

'As we approached the outskirts of Viazma it dawned on me that they were intentionally luring us far inland, to take us by surprise later on, or wear us down with hunger and cold. It wasn't only along the army's path fires were burning, but in other directions, far and near. At night the entire horizon was aglow.'

And now at last even Napoleon, Caulaincourt sees, is beginning to understand the implications of this scorched earth policy:

'He ordered my brother to take a strong Guard detachment next day and follow close on the enemy's heels, so as to enter the city at the same time as his rearguard, and find out for certain what was really going on, and whether the Russians were really setting fire to Viazma. The order was carried out to the letter. Though the enemy rearguard put up a defence, my brother, after a hot fight, entered Viazma at top speed, together with some skirmishers. Already the city was in flames in various places. He saw the Cossacks were setting fire to it with inflammable materials. He found some of these lying about in spots where the fire had broken out before they'd abandoned the town. From some inhabitants who'd stayed behind in their houses and, in particular, from a very intelligent baker, he heard how, long before we'd got there, a detachment of the Cossack rearguard had completed its preparations. The same moment we'd come into sight the town had been set fire to.'

Everyone at IHQ feels bewildered, 'the Emperor as much as those around him, though he pretended to poke fun at this way of waging war. In a joking tone of voice he spoke to me about "people who burn down their houses so we shouldn't be able to pass the night in them".' But the Master of the Horse is 'struck by serious reflections to which this terrible measure gave rise, and on the consequences and duration of a war where the enemy, from the very outset, had made such terrible sacrifices'.

Even while Murat's cavalry is making its attack, Le Roy, who's been fighting on some high ground fourteen kilometres away, has seen 'whirlwinds of fire and smoke devouring the town'. Now, entering it, he finds this

'superb town hadn't a single inhabitant left. To hold up our artillery's advance through the ashes the Russians had set fire to and destroyed 125 palaces [sic]. Locks, weights and other debris bore witness to the householders' former occupations. Only the cross still rose triumphant amidst so many ruins – as on Doomsday,' a strange reflection for a convinced deist. Although the Russian rear-guard, Fain says, had paid particular attention to burning down bridges and the bazaar, two battalions are ordered to fight the conflagration and manage to save two-thirds of the city, which are immediately plundered. Particularly of course by the Guard – e.g., by Boulart's gunners. He's particularly impressed to see houses 'better built than most. Since only part of the town had had time to fall a prey to the flames it could offer more resources.' These Caulaincourt appreciates the more as

'in Poland we'd lacked for everything. At Witebsk, with endless trouble, we'd been able to eat sparingly. At Smolensk, by ransacking the whole countryside, we'd found cornfields, grain, flour, cattle and even fodder, but neither brandy nor wine. After Doroghoboui everything had been in flames. But Viazma's shops and cellars were well-supplied, even opulent. Soon we found that the houses had their hiding-places, where we found an abundance of everything. The men went marauding and since no rations were distributed, nor could be, for lack of transport, no one could stop them.'

Although Lieutenant Lyautey is amazed to see 'chickens and goose feathers at each bivouac', the Master of the Horse notices

'some of the officers going without. Not having entered the houses until they'd been plundered, they couldn't share the spoils. In this way it could happen that beside the men's camp fire where chickens and sheep were being grilled and hams frizzled amidst hundreds of eggs a general or other superior officer sat eating black bread.'

Fish, too, is in plentiful supply. So much so that Sergeant Bertrand's comrades baptize Viazma 'the town of fishes'. Amidst such a cornucopea marauding, however, is a high-risk business. Looking out of a window of the house occupied by IHQ, 'a big one, on the right as you come in', Fain sees

'a sutler go by, arrested by the police while plundering a house. Taken before a court-martial, he'd been condemned to death. His legs would hardly carry him. As the picket taking him to the place of execution was passing in front of the house the Emperor asked what all the noise was about, and ordered us to tell the condemned man he'd pardoned him. The wretched sutler, already half-dead, was overwhelmed by such strong feelings that he dropped dead in terrible convulsions.'

Evidently Fain has a moment's respite from the endless dictations. For he goes on:

'Behind the house's courtyard, at the far end of a garden laid out in the English style, there's a little rotunda, an elegant copy of a Greek temple, supported by six pillars.'

A nearby building arouses his and his companions' curiosity:

'Crossing the street, we find it's a church. Its great door is closed. We walk round it. The side doors, too, are closed. We knock, knock again. No one replies. We call out several times. Finally a Russian of rather furtive aspect puts in an appearance, sees no sign of soldiers, and risks approaching us. He's the sacristan or bell-ringer. We use our few words of Russian to reassure him and, to prove we've not come to take anything away, give him something. Our religious demeanour as we follow him in under the sacred vaultings finally restores his confidence.'

But what a scene! In front of the high altar, on an open bier, lies the corpse of a venerable old man with a long white beard, a mitre on his head, his body swathed in the most superb pontificals.

'Around the catafalque, candles and all the funeral arrangements – this is what the sacristan shows us. We're dumbfounded. Our guide, no longer afraid to speak, says a lot of things we can't understand.'

Finally, they grasp what he's telling them. Just as the church's pontiff, probably the bishop of Viazma,

'had come down the altar steps he'd succumbed to terror at the tumult which had preceded our advance guard. His face at his last hour still preserved the serenity of the just.'

His clergy had just begun chanting the Office for the Dead when the Cossacks had ordered everyone to leave. 'Populace and clergy had fled, all except this unfortunate fellow who'd just opened up to us, and who'd stayed behind to keep watch over the dead man as long as possible.'

Deeply moved, Fain and his colleagues tell Napoleon. Who orders them to take a detachment and complete the old man's funeral. 'The aged pontiff is to be placed in the crypt prepared for him by the clergy.'

From the advance guard's reports as they come in it's becoming obvious, at least to Fain, that the Russians – at last – are preparing to give battle in a prepared position 'at Tsarewo-Zaimitche, near the Vlichewo post-house, between Viazma and Ghjat',[9] i.e., only a day's march ahead.

Among the many orders to Berthier Fain has had to take down in his self-invented shorthand is a letter destined for Vilna. That city's two governors (Maret has written) are hopelessly at loggerheads. Hogendorp and Jomini can't see eye to eye about the least thing. Obedient to Napoleon's orders, a 1,000-man detachment has been sent out under a Major Hell to occupy the Drissa Camp – and has been lost. The detachment had been about to set out when an entire Russian corps had been reported in the vicinity; whereupon Jomini had sensibly postponed Major Hell's departure:

'Hogendorp: "You're to obey the Emperor's orders!"

Jomini: "The Emperor certainly wouldn't have ordered a thousand men to engage a whole army corps!"

Hogendorp: "The battalion will leave."

Jomini: "Then I must have the order in writing."'

Getting it, he'd refused to endorse it; and to avert, if possible, the impending catastrophe, had given the wretched Major Hell some cavalry to reconnoitre with and advised him to exercise all possible caution and, if his task turned out impossible, not persist in it. But the inevitable happened. Overwhelmed by Russian cavalry, Hell and half his men had been killed. QED. Another major, a Pole, on the Vilna civil authorities refusing him a billet, had flown into a rage and smashed some windows. Jomini supports the major. Hogendorp orders Jomini to place him under arrest. Jomini refuses to obey. Appeals to his friend, Foreign Minister Maret, and at the ball given to celebrate the Emperor's birthday appears in his company. 'Go home!' shouts Hogendorp, 'or I'll send you to prison under an escort of grenadiers!.'

And now a perplexed Maret is asking for instructions.

Fortunately Smolensk needs a governor – Delaborde's Young Guard division is needed for the approaching battle, and it'll be some little time before Marshal Victor can get there. Napoleon cuts the Gordian knot by ordering Berthier to appoint Jomini, adding: 'Speak firmly to General Hogendorp to moderate his enthusiasm and give no further cause for complaint.' (A reprimand addressed, according to Hogendorp, to Jomini.)

One unit which partakes neither of fish nor fowl that evening in Viazma is the 16th Chasseurs. One of its officers 'commanding an advanced post of a hundred horses on the evening of the Viazma affair' becomes a victim of the cavalry's overweening command structure so deprecated by Thirion:

'I was left at my post until midday the following day without anyone relieving me, and under strict orders not to unbridle. Yet the horses had been harnessed since 6 a.m. the previous day. During the night, having nothing for my outpost, nor even any water close to hand, I sent an officer to tell the general of my plight, asking for some bread and above all some hay. He replied that his business was to make us fight, not to feed us. This meant our horses went for thirty hours without drinking. When I returned with my outpost we were just about to move on. I was given an hour to refresh my detachment, after which I had to rejoin the column at a trot, and was obliged to leave behind a dozen men whose horses could no longer walk. The King of Naples and the generals in his wake were much more occupied with their own affairs than with the troops.'

Only Lejeune's aesthetic appreciation of the bivouac scenes compensates for lack of a proper dinner:

'Life at the advance guard wasn't without its charms. I particularly noted the night of 28/9 August. A beautiful château, seen from afar, seemed to promise King Murat a thoroughly royal residence where he could spend the night. But at close quarters the traces of the fire revealed only smoking ruins, and we had to set up our bivouac at the foot of this château in the prettiest silver birch wood I've ever seen. These trees with their alabaster-white barks were mingled with pines and spruces, whose slender and hardy forms offered delightful arbours. The Polish lancers, bivouacked around us on undulating ground, had planted their lances under these birches' garlands, and the breeze agitated the thousand floating tricolour pennons which adorned their iron points. The flames of our bivouacs, the smoke of our kitchens where enormous braziers were deceptively keeping us waiting – the activity – the gaiety – even the appetite of all these young men who, greedy for glory, were laughingly tightening their belts, hole by hole, after insufficient meals – all this produced a charming effect. Nor was I the only to find it agreeable.'

Von Suckow, too, is experiencing 'superb autumn days, only saddened toward evening by the prospect of the meal awaiting us at the bivouac. Its composition was always the same: a soup of greasy water with fat, seasoned with gunpowder pretending to be salt.' Unlike the French, this is a condiment, Dr von Roos notices, that his Germans, 'absolutely had to have, with a bit of emaciated cow or horse. Apart from this detail of our fare, a very important one, it's true, we'd no reason to complain at all of our fate.' Honey, on the other hand, is to be had in abundance; but can have disastrous effects:

'Russia is a country peopled with bees. Near even the most wretched hut there were always beehives. One even found them in the woods. These industrious insects, who'd confided the delicious fruits of their labours to the hollows of old trees, hadn't at all expected the Grand Army's troopers, passing nearby, to annex their precious hoards. Our men's swollen faces when they came back from such razzias were sufficient proof of the vigour with which these little animals had defended their property.'

Nor is this the whole of the bees' vengeance. The Württembergers boil the honeycombs, and make themselves ill.

'Every morning the Emperor mounted his horse and passed rapidly from one headquarters to the next, through the midst of the masses following the main Moscow road. As he came abreast of the various units they halted and formed up in line of battle. The drums beat a salute, the eagles of the Grand Army dipped before the great man. Prolonged acclamations were heard. Joy shone on all the soldiers' faces; in his person they seemed to have concentrated all their desires, all their hopes. Only the Guard was forbidden to receive the Emperor with vivats, since they always surrounded his person. If too frequent the shout would so to speak have become banal.'

Soltyk is still seeing things through the rose-coloured spectacles of his Polish patriotism:

'One evening after we'd left Viazma behind us, IHQ was set up in a beautiful meadow. Here and there the foliage of immemorial oaks spread their exquisite shade, which was most enjoyable – it was one of those red hot days which are rather usual at that time of year. In these northern climes the nights can begin to feel rather chilly even while the sun's rays are still blazing hot at midday. Having taken his usual lunch, Napoleon was walking to and fro in the shade of these century-old trees. Not far from him were standing a number of generals and other officers of his household, among them myself. We came very close to him and could clearly hear everything he said. Sometimes he even directed his words to some of his generals. He spoke at length and in the most lively fashion, with the strong conviction which was the hallmark of his eloquence.'

Soltyk says he's sorry he can't give a verbatim transcript of Napoleon's 'impassioned improvisation'. On the other hand he's not going to commit the 'unforgivable error of putting a single thought into my hero's mouth, or even a turn of speech he didn't use'. He'll repeat only what he, immediately on his return to the topographical staff's bivouac, has jotted down:

'First he spoke of Alexander, Hannibal and Caesar, and discussed the special merits now of one, now of another, characterizing each with a few remarkable words. Then, turning his thoughts back to the present circumstances, he said: "True greatness doesn't consist in wearing a purple coat or a grey one. It consists in raising oneself above one's condition. Take me, for example. I've a good job. I'm emperor. I could live in the midst of all the delights of a great capital, let myself be swallowed up by life's pleasures and indolence. Well, I'm waging war for the glory of France, for mankind's happiness, for the future. Here I am, in your midst, at the bivouac. I can be hit by a roundshot in some battle, just like anyone else. I'm raising myself above my condition. Everyone in his own sphere should do the same. There we have real greatness."'

Unfortunately the imperial monologue is interrupted by a despatch. Few prisoners, says Caulaincourt,

'had been taken at Valutina, and in the great pursuit we'd made none at all – not so much as a cart had been seized! Like everyone else the Emperor was amazed at this retreat of an army of 100,000 men, who didn't leave a single straggler or a solitary wagon behind. Not even a horse to mount a guide was to be found within a radius of 30 miles. Often we couldn't find anyone to serve the Emperor as a guide. Often the same man led us for three or four days on end through a countryside he knew no better than we did. The vanguard was in the same plight.'

But now, about six miles from the little town of Ghjat, Murat has at last caught two prisoners. One is a Cossack, whose horse had been killed just as he was making his escape from a village he'd been plundering. The other, captured shortly afterwards, is a Negro who claims to be cook to General Platow, the Cossacks' Hetman.

Napoleon, in his peremptory manner, plies them both with questions. Their replies strike Caulaincourt as 'so odd they're worth noting'. The Negro, for his part, refuses to believe it's Napoleon he's talking to – how can he be so close to the French van? He keeps asking who it is, and 'at the same time making the most comical grimaces and contortions. When again told it really was Napoleon he was speaking to, he bowed, prostrated himself several times, and then began to dance, sing and make every imaginable contortion,'

and claims to have eavesdropped the Russian commanders' talk while waiting on Platow at table. But though he gossips about the various generals' rivalries it's clear he knows nothing about the Russian army's movements. The Cossack, brought in next, is

'a man between 30 and 35, dark, five foot tall, with an open and intelligent face, a serious air, with quick eyes, and was particularly troubled at having lost his horse, his money, and what he called his little package, i.e., the effects he'd taken or stolen, which he carried on his saddle and used for padding out his seat. The Emperor told me to give him some gold pieces, and lent him a horse from the stables.'

This loosens the prisoner's tongue.' "If Napoleon had had Cossacks in his army", he says,

"he'd have been Emperor of China long ago. If the Russian generals were in the van with the Cossacks, or even with the Russian troops, the French wouldn't now be at the gates of Ghjat, for there are many more Russians and Cossacks than there are Frenchmen, and the Cossacks aren't afraid of the French.'"

The Cossacks, he says, like Murat for the fine show he makes. He's a brave fellow, always first under fire. Word has gone round that he's not to be killed, "but they'd like to capture him". Everyone, he says, is expecting a big battle in front of Moscow:

'news which to the Emperor seemed highly probable, afforded him the greatest pleasure, and which he repeated to everyone: "This plan of theirs will give me Moscow. But a good battle would finish the war off sooner and lead us to peace. And that's where we're bound to end up."'

CHAPTER 19

THE GATHERING STORM

Retire to Smolensk? – a pretty little town – two days' rest – a glut of officers – Le Roy serves carp for dinner – Dumonceau is nearly run over – a yellow carriage gets singed – 'we could make out the Russian lines' – desperate struggle for the Schevardino redoubt – 'The Emperor's temperament was eminently nervous' – his bad cold – noises in the night

Suddenly it's autumn. For two days on end (29 and 30 August) its first cold rains come lashing down. Icy torrents are making the going impossible. Dumonceau isn't the only one who's getting

'stuck in the mud at every step. In the evening, overwhelmed by fatigue, soaked to the bone and filthy, we halted in a wretched bivouac that offered no shelter and where the suffering caused by the cold stormy night was added to those from all kinds of privations.'

Lejeune, as he rides to and fro with orders from Berthier's headquarters, is alarmed to notice how 'discouragement seemed to be overwhelming the army'. And even says that

'Berthier, though very timid about proffering his advice, made so bold as to counsel the Emperor to retreat. Napoleon took this proposal very much amiss, and told him he could clear out if he was tired, but promised to retire if the rains persisted.'

The coolness between them, Lejeune will notice, lasts 'several days, though without interrupting their continuing working relations'. "It's already autumn here, no longer summer," Napoleon writes to Marie-Louise. And indeed the first day of September brings a stupendous thunderstorm, killing with its lightning a trooper of the 2nd Carabiniers and injuring several others. As at the Niemen, the cold rain is causing 'both men and horses to sicken'. On the other hand Dumonceau is wondering whether it isn't preventing the Cossacks from setting fire to the villages, so that only the towns and manor-houses are now going up in flames. Others think it must be due to their being pressed so hard by the advance guard.

The hard-marched 85th has spent its last August night camped in gardens surrounding a manor-house with 'a superb stretch of water. The whole staff lodged in the house.' Suspecting the presence of finny friends in its pond, Le Roy had undressed, got into the water, and begun searching in the rushes:

'Quite right. Soon I feel an enormous carp who has half buried himself in the mud, and as the water is noticeably running away, we soon see his golden back. Pressing it hard, we grab him and finally, not without great efforts, manage to tumble him up on to the bank. We carry him to the château, where he gets the welcome he deserves. The kitchen is perfectly appointed – much better, in fact, than the

247

cellar, where all we find is some bad beer which, thirsty as we are, we nevertheless find delicious.'

But now, on 3 September, just as everyone's in despair, the sun comes out again; and there's no more talk of retiring on Smolensk. 'The sky turned blue,' writes Labaume, 'and I was sent to King Murat to urge him to continue his advance.' From 4 to 6 September Le Roy and the 85th march 'with great circumspection, being sure they were waiting for us at Borodino, on the Kolotchka, only five miles ahead'. Between I Corps and the Russians lies only the 'pretty little town of Ghjat,' the most important one on the Smolensk-Moscow road, bisected by the little river of the same name'.

This time, though Ghjat is 'surrounded by streams flowing through small lakes', measures are taken to enter it at a rush, before it can be put to the torch. Through heavy fire from a Russian battery, Murat and Eugène ride in slowly at a slow walk, each trying to look less concerned than the other, 'even though they calmly see several of their entourage fall under the enemy shots'. Despite the steady downpour – it's raining again – the river is so low that IV Corps, following in the wake of I Corps, can cross it on foot.

Le Roy is relieved to find that only the town's eastern side has been fired – 'unfortunately the side with the bazaar and merchants'.

Although the Red Lancers are advancing across country, Colbert seems to be urging them forward at a considerable rate, perhaps in hopes of some brilliant feat of arms 'like the one at Somosierra'.[2] But the extreme congestion at the entrance to Gjhat forces the regiment to bivouac. To get some food and forage they send out a marauding party to a 'village some soldiers said was well-provided'. But hardly has the party gone out than they have to move on again. Just then Dumonceau has no particular duties to perform and, anxious for his possessions, lingers with the regiment's baggage until the marauders shall return. But when they have, trying to catch up again, his sabre gets caught in a wheel of a wagon. This throws him from his horse and he's very nearly run over in the crush. And by the time he's mounted again – the regiment has vanished! Wandering about looking for it in fields beyond the town, he and his horse have to pass the night in a remote barn. 'Luckily it was full of hay.' To judge by her whinnyings, his Liesje seems to be as anxious as her rider. But though Dumonceau tries to stay awake and on the *qui vive*, he drops off into so deep a sleep that he doesn't wake up again until long after daybreak:

'Behind me, on the heights to the right of Ghjat, was a sizeable cavalry bivouac, dominated by lance pennons like ours, agitated by the wind, and at the bottom of the slope some red-uniformed troopers were watering their horses at a nearby lake.'

Hastening to rejoin them, he finds everyone has been so worried by his absence that Jean, his servant, who has feared him lost, greets him with tears in his eyes. Even Colbert has enquired after him several times. And now he's back 'restricted himself to reproaching me with the risks I'd exposed myself to by not sticking with the regiment. Everything was ready to receive me, and soon I was restored by a good breakfast, which I badly needed.'

Evidently the Italians have been following in the wake of Murat's cavalry; for by the time Laugier enters Ghjat's log-paved main street Napoleon, entering at 2 p.m., has already reconnoitred the great plateau dominating the town, 'the hospital, which was by the town gate and not been set fire to, and was hastening on the bridges' reconstruction and the troops crossing them'. Although even fewer inhabitants have stayed behind than at Viazma, Caulaincourt is delighted to see that all the stone houses along the main street and riverside are full of every kind of provisions -'flour, eggs and butter, everything we'd so long gone without'. Those inhabitants who've stayed behind report that the Russian army has just been reinforced by Miladorovitch's 50,000 Cossacks and a lot of artillery.[3] They also confirm that Barclay has been replaced by the one-eyed Kutusov. Since Kutusov is known to the French – quite unjustly – as 'the general who'd run away at Austerlitz', everyone is delighted. And Napoleon orders two days' rest. To Berthier, Ghjat, 2 September 1812:

"*Mon cousin*, give the King of Naples, the Prince of Eckmühl, the Viceroy, Prince Poniatowski orders to rest today, rally their troops, and at 3 p.m. to hold a roll-call and let me know definitely the number of men who will be present at the battle; to have all weapons, cartridge pouches, the artillery and the ambulances inspected; to let the men know that we are approaching the moment of a general engagement, and that they must prepare for it. Further, you must let me know the number of unshod horses which will be present and how much time would be needed to reshoe the cavalry and put it in shape for battle.'

An order which is passed on to the various corps commanders in a circular couched in the flowery language of old French chivalry. General Romeau (Davout's chief-of-staff) to Dedem:

"Sept 2. I have the honour to inform you that it is Monseigneur Marshal the Prince of Eckmühl's intention that the troops be forewarned that we are approaching the moment of a general battle, and that they should prepare for it."

'Each man in I Corps', writes Dedem, 'was issued with five packets of cartridges. Weapons were cleaned. All able-bodied men were withdrawn from the baggage train and came back into the ranks.' At 3 p.m. the review is duly held, and returns made. How grand, by now, is the Grand Army?

Evidently word soon gets round as to the figures for total effectives, for Laugier records them in his diary: 103,000 infantry, 30,000 cavalry, 587 guns. But many units have dwindled terribly. The 25th Division, originally consisting of four 4-battalion Line regiments (Württembergers, Illyrians, Poles, Portuguese) plus four more of light infantry, now has 'companies which hardly could put seven or eight muskets in a row'. Of Nansouty's light cavalry division which crossed the Niemen 7,500 horsemen strong, Victor Dupuy finds less than 1,000 are left, 'and certainly it wasn't enemy fire which had made this immense breach!' Despite the reinforcements which reached the Red Lancers at Witebsk, only 700 of the original 1,200 are still with the pennons. Above all there are altogether too many offi-cers:

> 'At least they'd been able to afford to buy a little food, even if at fan-tastically inflated prices. An officer doesn't have to carry a heavy haversack, and he rides a horse. Finally, we had the moral factor on our side.'

The result is an extraordinary imbalance between them and other ranks – hardly an officer is missing from Ney's twelve Württemberger bat-talions. Since they now number in all no more than a mere 1,450 men they're reformed as only three:

> 'The entire officer corps formed up in a single rank in a meadow a few yards from our bivouac. Accompanied by his chief surgeon, our divisional general passed along in front of it, stopping in front of each of us in turn, and asking after our state of health. In accor-dance with the doctor's assessment, he either orders us to one of the battalions, or else puts us on the non-active list; which means follow-ing in the army's tracks at a distance of one or two days' march.'

Von Suckow himself, found hale, is one of those sent to a battalion.

The story is doubtless much the same in the other corps, the Old Guard excepted.

Enjoying his two-day repose on the plateau beyond the town, Le Roy pays a courtesy visit to his old regiment, the 108th. One of its sous-lieutenants gives him a fine Polish pony, with 'a strong back, a hanging mane, a lively eye and in other respects well proportioned'. He can no longer afford to feed both it and himself.[4] Le Roy passes the pony on to his faithful servant Guillaume, to carry their larder and the precious iron cookpot which so nearly hadn't even got across the Niemen.

Just as it's about to march, IV Corps is rejoined by Preyssing's Bavarian cavalry. Laugier and Labaume, reaching first one then a second 'pretty lit-tle manor-house', find to their distress it's been thoroughly wrecked. At Pokrow,

> 'a well laid out park, beautiful long alleys, newly built pavilions evinc-ing the owner's good taste, agreeable life-style and luxurious furni-ture, precious crystals, fine porcelain vases – all is scattered or in fragments. Extremely costly books are lying on the ground.'

Labaume too notes how Pokrow's 'freshly decorated pavilion only offered an image of the most horrible devastation. Everywhere we saw only shat-tered furniture, bits of precious porcelain strewn about the garden, and expensive engravings ripped out of their frames and scattered to the winds.' No matter. The main thing is that it has plenteous stocks of corn and forage. Stolidly setting up his headquarters amidst all this cultural wreckage, Prince Eugène gives IV Corps, too, an extra day's rest 'for isolated men to catch up. The order about men serving as coachmen has been repeated, so we can be at full strength on the day of battle.'

Of all the army's units except the artillery the baggage train alone hasn't dwindled en route. And many commanders 'out of insouciance, weakness, weariness or compassion' aren't bothering to obey the order to send their carriages to the rear.

"Ghjat, Sept 2, 1812. *Mon Cousin*. The headquarters staff are of no help to me, nor is the provost-general of military police, nor yet the baggage-master; no one is doing his duty as he should. You have received my orders about the baggage; take care the first baggage I'll order to be burnt isn't that of the general staff. If you've no baggage-master, nominate one, so that all the baggage marches under one command. It's impossible to see a worse order than the one prevailing."

All these hundreds of officers' carriages, rolling placidly along behind their units, are getting badly on Napoleon's nerves:

"Ghjat, Sept 3, 1812. *Mon Cousin*, write to the corps commanders that we are losing a lot of men every day because of their disorderly way of searching for food; that it's urgent that they shall concert with the various unit commanders on measures to be taken to put an end a state of affairs which is threatening the army with destruction; that the number of prisoners taken by the enemy daily amounts to several hundreds; that the soldiers must be prevented under the severest penalties from leaving their units and be sent out to get food in the same way as forage; that a general or other superior officer shall command all maraudings."

Strange orders to be issued so late in the day and, on the eve of battle, scarcely capable of being enforced? Perhaps it's because he's angry with himself for even momentarily considering a retreat on Smolensk that Napoleon's fury now falls on Berthier. Neither that day nor for four to come will they eat at the same table. And when Napoleon, overtaking the marching columns at a gallop on 4 September, sees some carriages still intermingled with the artillery trains, it's the last straw. Among them is a fine yellow carriage. Jumping down from 'Moscow'[5] – the charger Caulaincourt has allotted him today – he orders a squad of the escort chasseurs to halt and set fire to the obnoxious carriage – which as it happens belongs to Narbonne:

'M. de Narbonne pointed out that it might mean some officer who'd lose a leg on the morrow being stranded. "It'll cost me even more tomorrow if I've no artillery!" the Emperor rejoined. And, turning to Berthier: "I only wish it had been yours. It'd make an even greater impression. I keep on coming across it all the time." "Behind Your Majesty's own carriage," Berthier replied. "It's all Caulaincourt's fault! However that may be, I've promised to burn it if I come across it. And you needn't sulk over my threat, either – I won't spare my own carriage more than anyone else's. I'm commander-in-chief and must set an example."

Girod de l'Ain, Castellane and other staff officers watch the chasseurs fetch straw and firewood and 'several flaming brands from the bivouac we'd just abandoned; and the Emperor waited until the carriage has caught alight before riding on again'. A calèche and a light trap following behind it are to suffer the same fate. 'No sooner had the fire caught', says Caulaincourt, 'than the Emperor galloped off, and the coachmen, I believe, rescued their slightly singed vehicles.' As Girod de l'Ain confirms: 'Hardly had he ridden a hundred metres than people made haste to quench the flames, after which the carriage rejoined the column as before.' Castellane says Narbonne 'gave the soldiers ten louis for putting out the fire they'd themselves lit'. And Villemain, Narbonne's secretary, adds a characteristic PS:

'Regretting his impulsiveness, but anyway wishing to make good the loss to a man he was fond of, Napoleon suggested to Duroc that he send 1,000 napoleons to M. de Narbonne, "who isn't rich". Duroc, always cultivated and meticulous, after a moment's hesitation as to the proper way of doing this, at the first halt went to the trouble of putting some gold coins in an elegant case adorned with the imperial arms, placed it underneath some exquisitely selected books, and had it all taken to the general. M. de Narbonne opened the case and studied the volumes with pleasure. As for the gold, he sent it immediately with a friendly word to the colonel of a regiment whose young soldiers he'd been tormented to see so harassed that day, and whose ranks were already anxiously thinned. He asked him to distribute the gift among the men of his unit. Next day, before setting out, when everyone was in his proper place, the Emperor said to him gently:

"Well, Narbonne, the damage to the baggage has been made good. You've been reimbursed."

"Yes, Sire, and am grateful. But in a fashion Your Majesty unquestionably would permit I've only kept the letter and of the case's contents only some books, among them, Seneca's two essays: De beneficiis, and De Patientia. They're good to have about one on campaign."'

Napoleon, says Villemain, perfectly understood both the allusion and the Latin titles, and said nothing. But the tale gets round. 'By way of making an example,' Laugier notes in his diary, 'Napoleon has had a carriage belonging to his ADC Narbonne burnt in his presence by some grenadiers of the Guard.'

During the moonlit night of 3/4 September Dumonceau is on duty, his special task being to make sure the horses are watered. So brilliant is the moonlight and so translucent the air he's able to make out objects five kilometres away. And is amazed to see 'all these thousands of men lying resting in the night's silence, like so many graves in a gigantic necropolis'.

By now everyone knows the Russians are waiting for them only a couple of hours' march further on. And that evening (4 September) Séruzier's horse artillery, arriving outside the village of Gridnowo, is more than usually severely rebuffed before it can throw out the Russian rearguard:

'Elsewhere the usual ill-prepared attacks had, as usual, been thrown back, albeit with unusual violence; and estafettes had been sent galloping back to say the entire Russian army was dug in along the slopes beyond a little stream.'

The devastation along the route, too, is becoming steadily more thorough. Everyone notices it.

'Not a blade of grass, not a tree. We never come to a village which hasn't been plundered from top to bottom. Impossible to find the least nourishment for our horses, to renew our larder, or even light a camp fire for the night.'

The Russians have 'laid waste the entire plain we were obliged to camp on. They'd mown the long grass, felled the woods, burnt down the villages. In a word, had left us nothing to eat, nothing to keep our horses alive, nothing to shelter us.'

And the weather is miserable.

The morning of 5 September dawns chill and foggy, with drizzling rain. Only when the mist lifts can Dumonceau look out over 'an open slightly undulating plain where we see our immense column stretching away as far as the eye could reach'. Between the leading units and strong Russian rearguards there are ever more embittered engagements. The 11th Hussars, in particular, catch a bad cold.

So does the Italian light cavalry, marching as usual to the left of the main column. Isn't that the sound of gunfire, away to its right?

'Over there we even see great clouds of smoke rising to the sky, and draw the conclusion that we can't be far from the Moscow post-road which the main column is marching along. [It can only be Séruzier's guns, again at grips with the enemy.] By and by we see, far away, the Russian cavalry gathering, with obvious intent to bar our way. The Viceroy orders the 3rd Italian Chasseurs to attack.'

As usual, it's a trap. Just as the chasseurs are about to reach the Russians 'a great mass of enemies come rushing out at us from a wood, with their usual hurrahs. A terrible scrum ensues.' Finally the Russians withdraw under the protection of infantry and artillery firing at the Italians out of the forest. And IV Corps again joins up with Murat's cavalry divisions.

Now it's 2 p.m. and 'only the advance guard is making some slow progress. The army has halted and formed columns of battalions at several points where there's rising ground.' Looking away across the vast plain to his right, Césare de Laugier sees an immense building, surrounded by white walls. 'The coloured tiles of its roofs gleam in the sunbeams through the dense dust being raised by our enormous masses of cavalry, and stress the savage and grim aspect of the countryside all about.' Although it has the appearance of a town, it is in fact Kolotskoïe Abbey, which 'built in the days of the Goths, has often served as a citadel during civil wars, and is still surrounded by trenches'. A mile and a half beyond it a stream winds its placid way eastwards toward the enemy positions.

The Italian light cavalry snatches the manor-house of Woroniemo before the Cossacks can set fire to it. But no sooner have Eugène's aides installed themselves in it and the Viceroy himself has just taken a couple of turns on its terrace, than Napoleon turns up. Von Muraldt, who's there with Eugène's Bavarian cavalry, sees them

'gallop flat out across our regiments' front, the imperial entourage dashing with loosened reins at a distance behind them. At this sight all IV Corps' eight cavalry regiments raise such a cheer of "*Vive l'Empereur!*" that the domestics and orderlies, who've been out watering the lead horses, take it for a Cossack "hurrah", and come rushing back in panic. You can imagine how we laughed.'

After which Napoleon goes back 'to the unit he's marching with' and Eugène sets his troops in motion again. The unit in question is the Red Lancers:

'Advancing swiftly behind the Emperor, who'd just broken into a gallop, we overtook the various army corps, and almost simultaneously with the advance guard came within view of Borodino, and toward midday halted about three-quarters of a league from that place. Beyond a last undulation of the terrain, straight in front of us, it showed a group of five globular towers at the base of a long line of sheer and wooded heights which, crossing our front, stretched out far on either hand. It was on these heights the enemy army was at long last awaiting us.'

The battlefield Kutusov (or rather one of his aides) has chosen for his great stand is a gently rising plain, flanked by sparse woods, between the old and new Moscow roads. For the great numbers of men who are going to be involved it's no little cramped. The easily fordable Kolotchka stream runs diagonally across it NE-SW. And a tributary, the Semenovskaya, fronts and – in its higher reaches, out of sight of the French – intersects the Russian position. Assuming for some reason that Napoleon will focus his onslaught on the village of Borodino, Kutusov has arranged his two armies quite eccentrically. While Barclay de Tolly's extreme right, where Borodino village, standing above the Kolotchka's west bank, forms a hardly tenable salient, is confronting almost no enemy at all, Bagration's left, facing the French centre, can fairly easily be outflanked. The Kolotchka, easily fordable at most points, separates the two armies 'by turning sharp left at the foot of the heights and some distance further on flowing into the River Moskowa. But to Dumonceau's right front, at a point before this bend, 'the escarpments of its right bank disappeared, flattening out into a low, unbroken and open plain that rose gradually, first towards the two villages of Schevardino and Borodino, ranged on a line parallel to the stream's course, then, beyond, to big woods of high brush-wood, lining the horizon a mile and a half away.'

Among the hundreds of new arrivals closely studying this frightening field of battle which is going to offer the Russian guns maximum fire power and the invaders almost no cover at all, is a Saxon dragoon officer, named *von Lessnig*.[6] As far as his inquisitive spyglass can see,

'the whole ground to the left and right and straight ahead was cov-ered with a growth of hazel bushes, juniper and other brushwood which rose to at least a man's height. To the left centre, about a thousand paces distant, stood a village and a nice Byzantine church, which rose from a gentle tree-covered slope and had a pretty tower plated in green copper. To our right was a ridge, covered along almost all its length with masses of Russian infantry and artillery. On some of the highest points, as I could see clearly through my tele-scope, the Russians had thrown up earthworks with notches cut in them that seemed to be embrasures for the artillery. Obliquely to the right of our regiment rose the towers of Mojaisk and the nearby monastery. Though they were an hour's march away, they lent a touch of beauty to the brooding gloom of this wild and barren neighbourhood.'

From IV Corps' camp von Muraldt through his spyglass can 'clearly make out the mouths of the redoubt's heavy calibre guns and in general every-thing else going on in the Russian camp'. The Mojaisk church tower, beyond the line of woods, is in fact about eight miles off. But to the right, much closer, projecting and detached from the Russian front, are two vil-lages. Between them Dumonceau sees,

'a broad, tall hillock, like a truncated cone, which we took for a redoubt. Some individuals were visible on its summit, probably put there to observe; and at its base and behind its flanks we could make out two black masses, which could only be the heads of columns intended to support it.'

Although 'prevented from seeing the enemy position clearly by the smoke from the villages he was setting fire to', Lejeune and his colleagues are able to make out that it is 'armed with 12 to 20 guns'. Clearly, before any-thing else can happen, this outspur or salient, threatening the French right, will have to be nipped off. 'The Emperor', Lejeune goes on, 'imme-diately ordered it to be attacked by Compans' division,' supported by Nansouty's and Montbrun's cavalry corps. And an order is sent off to Poniatowski, who is marching along the 'old' Moscow road, to the army's right, that his Poles are to advance through the woods and take this advanced enemy position in flank and rear. Colonel Griois, looking on with the rest of the army at Compans' division as it peels off to the right, thinks it 'wonderful to see our troops' keenness. The beauty of the scene was enhanced by the splendid sky and the setting sun, reflected on the muskets and sabres. They were proud to have been chosen as the first to get to grips with the enemy.'

The enemy, Labaume[7] sees, are

'sending considerable forces to defend the redoubt's approaches. First, General Compans bombarded it with all the artillery he had to hand, as far as possible to overthrow the entrenchment, embankment and the palisades. As soon as he thought them in a state to receive the assault, he launched Colonel Charrier at the head of the 57th.'

This is at about 5 p.m. Gourgaud, who is also certainly watching, takes up the tale:

'Between Compans' right and the wood, some of the King of Naples' cavalry advanced, but was contained by the enemy artillery and cavalry. General Compans, at the head of the 57th and the 61st, aimed toward the right of the hillock. At the same time he made General Dupelain march to its left with the 25th, on the Schevardino side. He had the 111th placed still farther to the left, in order to turn the Russians' right. While carrying out his movement Compans was attacked by masses of cavalry,'

and is personally hit in the left arm.

'But he took clever advantage of the lie of the land and of some wattle fencing that enabled him to go on, despite these cavalry masses, and even to repulse them with great loss. Soon a most murderous fusillade started up on this side, between Compans' two regiments and the Russian infantry supporting the redoubt's left flank. Only separated by a couple of dozen yards, the troops on either side of the wattle fences were protected from each other up to chest level. Thus this sanguinary fusillade lasted three-quarters of an hour; its vivacity and noise made it impossible to hear the general's order to advance with the bayonet, a manoeuvre which would have cost us a lot of men.'

Although the Russians are suffering even more heavily from this almost point-blank fusillade, Gourgaud says they can't get their men to attack either. Several voltigeur companies, ordered up by Compans on to a neighbouring mound only 120 yards away, direct a murderous fire into the redoubt. But though night is now falling neither side seems to be gaining the upper hand:

'Wanting at all costs to extricate himself from this terrible situation, Compans took a battalion of the 57th and, having opened up the fences on his right, made it advance in close column of divisions, covering four guns charged with grape that marched behind it. He led this battalion against the extreme right of the Russians flanking the redoubt. When he was 100 yards away, he unmasked his battery, whose grapeshot ravaged the enemy terribly. Profiting from the disorder he saw in their ranks, his battalion charged with its bayonets,' and the Russians give way. Compans, his wound treated, orders a second assault. This too being repulsed, 'Compans, irritated by these obstacles and impatient of success, threw in a lively attack at the redoubt's rear' – the one just described by Gourgaud – 'himself marching in at Charrier's side at the head of the 57th'. When, simultaneously, the 61st come sweeping into the redoubt, they find, Gourgaud says, 'gunners, horses, every living thing had been been destroyed by our voltigeurs' fire'.

Unfortunately this isn't the end of the matter. Recaptured by Russian grenadiers, the shattered redoubt has to be stormed a second time, this time by Morand's and Friant's crack divisions, supported by Nansouty's cavalry corps. More and more Russian troops too are being fed into this crepuscular struggle, which in the gathering dusk is developing into a wholly undesirable encounter battle. Napoleon sends off an aide to Poniatowski, urging him to make haste. 'For two hours night had been shedding its shadows on the combatants, whose determination seemed to grow with the difficulties, and we were getting worried.' But at just the right moment Poniatowski's Poles emerge from the woods. And Heinrich von Brandt, watching at a distance, realizes it's all over: 'Suddenly a huge shout reached us, brought by a violent gust of wind.'

Napoleon orders the victorious troops to remain in position, the infantry in squares. A wise precaution. For hardly has darkness fallen than Thirion sees 'a line of cavalry deploying into line of battle in front of a wood behind the captured redoubt'. Advancing rapidly and taking the 111th by suprise, it breaks into its square, kills a lot of men and seizes its guns. But the other regiments stand their ground in a darkness

'which though not so dark we couldn't make out this movement, was dark enough to prevent us from seeing which arm it was composed of. General Nansouty orders the Red Lancers of Hamburg[8] to charge the Russian cavalry and throw it back. This regiment flew to the attack, delivered its charge and fell on the enemy with felled lances, aimed at the body. The Russian cavalry received the shock without budging, and in the same moment as the French [sic] lance-heads touched the enemy's chests the regiment about-faced and came back towards us as if it in its turn had been charged. We, the 2nd and 3rd Cuirassiers, thought this a poor show, and moved briskly forward to support them and repulse the enemy cavalry.'

But at the cuirassiers' approach the Russian cavalry calmly withdraw into the woods. As for the Hamburg Lancers, nothing can induce them to launch a second attack. What their lances had struck against in the murk had been the black breastplates of the Cuirassiers of the Russian Imperial Guard, iron on iron. 'Which only goes to show', Thirion concludes, 'what an effect one arm can have on another.'

At about midnight, the entire Russian force begins to draw off, abandoning the costly and, in fact, wholly superfluous bastion. This preliminary struggle has cost Compans the lives of 500 of his crack infantrymen, and 1,000 wounded. The intrepid Colonel Charrier is promptly promoted general, but his 'handsome regiment' too has lost any amount of men. 'The 61st had lost a whole battalion there.' 'Battlefield thick with enemy dead,' Caulaincourt jots down in his notebook, late at night.

An order is issued for all wounded to be taken to the Kolotskoië Abbey. Is anyone complying? All Dr von Roos, 'while waiting to be ordered into the battle line and after passing ditches filled with arms and legs and corpses', finds when he gets to the immense abbey buildings at a late hour, are 'some persons from Napoleon's suite and the personnel of the imperial printing press'. Soltyk, ordered to interrogate Russian wounded, can't

'get any important information out of them. They all wore such an exasperated air, they wouldn't utter a single word. So these proud Moscovites, my country's oppressors, now had to feel in their turn the terrible effects of a foreign invasion!'

Oddly, von Roos' troopers have suddenly been issued with their arrears of pay. Von Roos himself would 'gladly have dispensed with the 3 thalers because of their weight, and because it was impossible to find anything to buy.' Not merely is there nothing to buy – or steal; there are no civilians about, Rapp realizes, to give any information: 'Women, children, old men, cattle, everything, had vanished.'

Meanwhile, as division after division has been turning up, 'an immense crowd had been establishing itself' in the open fields. One such regiment, hastening up from the rear 'almost always through flames from burning barns and houses', is Maurice de Tascher's chasseurs. Passing through Ghjat they'd found it a 'charming little town'; and when the 18th Line had left it on 4 September, Bonnet had written in his diary 'Ghjat was intact; only one or two houses burnt'. But then, a couple of hours later, Tascher is sent back to it and by then 'nothing remained'. A conflagration, caused, according to Faber du Faur, by 'wounded men's stupidity and inexperience in lighting fires in timber houses' and aggravated by a violent west wind, had 'laid the greater part of the town in ashes, among it the main street of stone houses'.

While the battle for the Schevardino salient had been going on 'the Palace' had been installed under canvas near Walomiewo, 'only about a mile and a quarter from the enemy's position. The Emperor's tent was placed in the midst of the Guard' – a little below and very close to the position occupied by Boulart's guns, drawn up there in battery:

'There wasn't the least dwelling or barn in the surroundings and the whole Imperial Guard, Young and Old, was concentrated there around the Emperor's tents, five army corps and cavalry crammed together to a depth of three miles and then, to the rear, the crowded assemblage of the central mass of parks and convoys. All afternoon the Emperor had stayed with us, walking to and fro on the edge of the ravine, his hands behind his back, now and then observing what was going on through his spyglass.'

As for the Russians, they are

'encamped as it were on an amphitheatre. They lit many fires, whose resplendent, almost symmetrical clarity gave this hill an enchanting appearance, in sharp contrast to our bivouacs where the soldier, lacking firewood, was reposing amid shadows, hearing all around him only the groans of the unfortunate wounded.'

Eugène, for his part, has pitched his tent amidst the Italian Guard Cavalry. But everyone else, says Labaume, who's thinking the the Russian position has been much weakened by the loss of the Schevardino redoubt,

'lay down amidst the bushes and slept profoundly, despite the vehement wind and an excessively cold rain. We were in a sandpit, with a long curtain of osiers and foliage hiding Walweiewo, where the Emperor had established his headquarters.'

Always Dumonceau has an eye to the welfare and sufferings of the horses:

'Their misery was great. Apart from a slender ration of oats brought up from Ghjat, they'd nothing to eat but a few bits of straw or grass, everywhere disputed on all sides, and to find which our men had to wander about during part of the night.'

Others are wandering about in search of other things. A Württemberg artillery officer, sent to the rear with four wagons to replenish his unit's ammunition, is having a peculiarly difficult time:

'Everywhere I met with refusal. The divisional reserve was unwilling to issue any ammunition because they said they needed it for the impending battle, and the large corps reserve was still far to the rear, some of it back in Smolensk. Eventually I came on a reserve park whose commander explained that he'd give me as much ammunition as I required provided I brought him a note from the Intendant-General of Artillery, General Lariboisière, who was usually in the Emperor's suite.'

Riding quickly off, he finds Napoleon amidst his staff in the courtyard of Kolotskoïe Abbey,

'pacing up and down and indulging in the innocent pleasure of whacking his boot with a riding-whip. Several officers from whom I inquired the whereabouts of General Lariboisière, replied curtly "I've no idea." But the Emperor, who must have noticed me stumbling about repeating my question, called out to me: "What are you looking for?" "Sire," I replied, "I'm looking for General Lariboisière, to get him to give me a voucher for some ammunition." "Which unit are you from?" "I belong to General Beurmann's light battery. Yesterday and this morning we've burnt up all our powder, and I don't think I'll get the ammunition we're short of without a written note from General Lariboisière." 'The Emperor turned to his suite and shouted "General Lariboisière!" Everybody set about finding the general, and when he turned up the Emperor said to him "Give this officer what he needs." I made the Emperor a deep and cheerful bow, and got everything I needed. At 6 p.m. that evening, with two full ammunition wagons, I rejoined the battery, which for lack of ammunition had remained close to where we'd fought in the morning.'

Labaume, for his part, is busy making a sketch map of the environs. And at about midnight IV Corps' new chief-of-staff comes and tells him the Emperor needs it. Perhaps it's from having studied it that Caulaincourt makes his night reconnaissance: 'visited bivouacs, inspected the captured redoubt and several times rode up and down the line to judge the Russian position with my own eyes'.

But Napoleon, in his tent, is feeling rotten. The Emperor's constitution', writes Yvan, his surgeon, 'was eminently nervous. He was subject to psychosomatic influences and usually the spasm would distribute itself between the stomach and the bladder.'

And now he has caught a very bad cold. 'He was tormented', Yvan goes on,

'by the equinoctial winds, by the mists, the rain and the bivouac. He was utterly susceptible to the atmosphere. If he were to maintain his equilibrium, his skin had to carry out all its functions. As soon as his tissue became constricted, whether the cause was psychological or atmospheric, the irritable apparatus [sic] had a more or less serious effect on him; and from that followed a violent cough, accompanied by ischuria. All these effects passed over as soon as the dermal functions were re-established. When the irritation went to the stomach, he would suffer from nervous coughings which exhausted his moral and physical strength to the point where his intelligence was no longer the same.'[10] Usually the bladder, too, was involved in the spasm; and then he was under the influence of an annoying and tiring situation. Horse-riding added to his sufferings. All these accidents together fell upon him at the moment of the battle.'

Summoned to his tent, Dr Mestivier is greeted with the words:

'"Well, doctor, you see I'm growing old, my legs swell, I urinate with difficulty, doubtless it's the humidity of these bivouacs, because I live only through my skin."' Mestivier notes

'a continual dry cough, breathing difficult and spasmodic, urine only coming out drop by drop and with pain... muddy [sic] and full of sediment; the lower part of the legs and feet extremely oedmatose; the pulse feverish and intermittent around the twelfth beat.[11] All these grave symptoms gave cause for justifiable fears of a chest hydropsy.'

Since his patient has 'a high temperature' Chief-pharmacist Sureau is sent for to prepare a potion. Unfortunately its ingredients are 'with the heavy baggage an hour away'. Ségur says that General Lauriston, 'who told me this himself', helped him to place cataplasms on his stomach.

CHAPTER 20

THE MOUTHS OF THE GUNS

An early reconnaissance – outflank the Russians? – effectives – 'in a lugubrious silence... the mouths of the guns' – nothing to eat – Kutusov's 'tomfoolery' – 'a masterpiece' – 'an officer of furtive appearance' – Capt. François gets a nasty leg wound – premonitions – 'like wandering shades' – muddles in the night – 'like the atmosphere before a storm' – 'parade uniforms as if for a holiday' – 'better a horrific end than a horror without end' – 'a profound silence reigned everywhere' – Napoleon's command post

Although 6 September dawns grey, cold and chilly, 'at the first glimmer of daylight [6 a.m.]' Napoleon is on horseback, 'together with Berthier, Eugène, two officers and myself', says Lejeune.

'Without any other suite, he began to traverse the enemy's front. Nowhere were our outposts more than a pistol shot from the enemy's, and neither were firing at the other. The Emperor profited from this circumstance to acquaint himself with the means of getting close to the Russians, in greater detail and closer quarters. Since he was riding on ahead, he found himself face to face with a patrol of 20 Cossacks, four paces away from us – I was a bit worried to see him thus expose himself to the risk of being carried off by a few men who might be hiding behind a bend in the ravine. But it was they who fancied themselves taken by surprise. They were just turning their horses' heads when, seeing our little group put our horses to the gallop to get away from them, they came after us for several hundred paces. Before returning from this reconnaissance, which promised him a major battle for the morrow, the Emperor ordered me to go along the line again and make him a pencil drawing of its topography and also bring him some views of the terrain.'[1]

In this, the first reconnaissance of three, he notes particularly that the Russians have thrown up three earthworks. The largest and most formidable of these, somewhat to the French left but in the centre of their lopsidedly arranged position, crowns a height. Provided with wolftraps and bristling with outward sloping stakes, its eighteen[2] heavy-calibre guns not only sweep the gentle plain sloping away NNW toward Borodino village, whose green church towers are clearly visible, but also the entire French centre. Through their glasses the French can see that this formidable obstacle, unlike the other two fieldworks – shallow, obtuse-angled redans or flèches – is also closed at the rear, but not at its 'gorges', i.e., its ends. If only Napoleon were able to get a still closer view, or the thick mist were not obscuring his field of vision, he'd be able to detect, somewhat to the left rear of the other two flèches, between them and the Grand Redoubt and somewhat retired, yet a third flèche of the same sort. But it lies just out of sight. All three of the visible fieldworks seem to stand on the same ridge. He can't see what lies beyond. Only that the Russians, on the rim of the plateau beyond the high-banked Semenovskaya stream, are busy dismantling Semenovskaya village.

Their entire position is packed with two, perhaps three, lines of densely massed troops. Obviously a frontal assault is going to be extremely costly to both sides. And the whole position is deceptively strong.

Can it be turned? Away to his right, towards the village of Utitza and the old Moscow post-road, along which Poniatowski's Poles performed so well yesterday evening, there's a prehistoric tumulus. But the whole of this part of the battlefield is screened off by woods and thickets. Probes in that direction show that resistance there is unlikely to be what it could be. Perhaps he should combine an all-out onslaught on the Russian centre with a strategic outflanking movement? Attack them also in the rear, roll up the whole Russian army and fling it into the River Moscowa – as at Friedland? But here numbers are of the essence. If his effectives were even nearly what they'd been at Witebsk, there'd be no question of the outcome. And the manoeuvre would be perfectly possible. But they aren't.

To Kutusov's 90,000 infantry, 24,000 cavalry (7,000 of them Cossacks, of little or no use in a pitched battle) and 640 guns, Napoleon has nearly 90,000 infantry, 29,500 cavalry and 587 guns. Only 130,000 against 125,000 – too slight an advantage. For an outflanking force to succeed it must consist of V Corps and at least part of I Corps. And this would gravely weaken his main striking power. Further, any such movement will depend on surprise, and have to be carried out by night. It can go adrift, turn up late, or prove impossible to co-ordinate. And though Russian armies aren't regarded as being as sensitive as others to what goes on in their rear,[3] Kutusov might only have to get the least wind of such a move to decamp again – the very last thing Napoleon or anyone else wants.

His slight superiority in numbers, furthermore, is outweighed by the fact, revealed by his spyglass, that many more of the Russian guns are real battery pieces: 'bone crushers' as the men call them. And the Russian horses are in infinitely better trim. As to the morale factor, it's about equally balanced. Although the Russian masses are totally exposed to artillery, they're notorious not only for their prowess with the bayonet but also for their extreme stolidity under fire. On the French side, on the other hand, there's not a man who isn't grimly aware of the absolute need for victory. A defeat will be a rout. Only half a cannonshot away from the Russian guns' muzzles Le Roy and his 'cold-blooded' fellow veterans of the 85th are having

'gloomy reflections on the outcome of a battle fought 2,400 miles from France, and about what would become of oneself if wounded. As for death, we didn't give it a thought. As to who'd win the battle, we were so vain as to believe it would be to our advantage.'

Seeing the Emperor pass his telescope along the Russian lines, Dedem, his brigade fronting I Corps, hears him mutter: 'a big battle ... lots of people ... many, many dead'; but then, turning to Berthier, 'the battle is ours'. Words, no doubt, he hopes will be passed on to the rest of the staff and thence to the army.

But his cold is getting worse. Several times his uraemia forces him to dismount, and Ségur sees him 'pausing a long while, his forehead pressed against the wheel of one of our guns'.

At 11 a.m. he sends Rapp out on a new reconnaissance, with orders to get as close as he can to the enemy lines. 'I removed my white plumes, put on a soldier's shako, and examined everything with greatest precision. Only a single chasseur of the Guard accompanied me. At several points I was so close I was inside their outposts.' Upon his approaching too close to Borodino village, 'separated from our outposts by a deep and narrow hollow way, they fired a few grapeshot at me and I drew back'. Reporting back to Napoleon, he finds him with Murat and Berthier. All are agreed that, if they don't attack, the Russians will. Now Berthier, too, orders up his horse and himself emulates Rapp's reconnaissance in detail. 'He was given the same reception as I'd had, canister forced him to retire.' Eugène, too, is keen to get a no less maximally detailed idea of the battle-field. And orders Labaume to correct the map he'd made yesterday

'by traversing the entire line and trying to approach the enemy as closely as possible to disclose the accidents of the ground he was encamped on, and above all make sure there weren't any masked batteries, or ravines we didn't know about'.

But neither does Labaume spot Bagration's third, northernmost flèche; nor does he realize that the Russian position is bisected by the upper reaches of the Semenovskaya. It'll be his map Eugène will use next day.[4]

All day the sun shines down out of a clear autumn sky. The compact ranks, division after division, are almost a mile deep.[5] Although the cen-tre, 85,000 men, or two-thirds of the entire army, packs a stupendous punch, yet veterans of all ranks, scanning the equally dense green-clad masses on the opposing heights, are thinking very serious thoughts. For several days now Ségur has been noticing how

'the troops had been strangely quiet, the kind of silence you associ-ate with a state of great expectation or tension, like the atmosphere before a storm, or the feeling in a crowd where people are suddenly plunged into a situation of great danger'.

'A strange thing, modern battles,' soliloquizes Thirion: 'Two armies grad-ually turn up on a piece of ground, place themselves symmetrically facing each other, their artillery 100 metres to the front. All these preliminaries are carried out with calm barrack-square precision. From one army to the other are heard the commanders' sonorous voices. In a lugubrious silence you see being turned on you the mouths of the guns which are going to send you death.'

Fézensac, at headquarters, is finding

'something sad and imposing in the appearance of these two armies preparing to cut each other's throats. All the regiments had been given orders to put on their parade uniforms, as if for a holiday. The Imperial Guard, above all, seemed rather to be disposing itself for a parade than a fight. Nothing was more striking than these old soldiers' sang-froid. On their faces one read neither disquiet nor enthusiasm. In their eyes a new battle was only one more victory, and it was enough to look at them to share this noble confidence.'

But one of them at least, Boulart, spends the day deep in serious reflections:

'What if we're beaten at 750 to 800 leagues from France, what terrible risks we'll run! Can even one of us hope to see his own country again? If we're the victors, will peace follow at once? That's hardly likely in the Russian nation's unequivocal state of exasperation!'

Yet morale is high. Letters written home that day[6] show how eager the officers, at least, are to rejoin in time for the battle. One who does so that evening is Lieutenant Vossler. Riding into camp he finds the army in

'good and sanguine spirits. We were congratulated on all sides upon our timely arrival. If one discounted our men's pale worn faces, the whole army seemed alive with a cheerful bustle. Most of the troops were busy polishing and preparing weapons for the morrow, and the order reached us to make an early night of it, so as to be ready for the morning's work. Many a soldier stretched himself out carefree and contented, little thinking that this would be his last night on earth. But the thought was common to us all: things couldn't go on much longer as they were. Though the army's numerical strength had shrunk alarmingly, the very considerable forces that remained consisted of the strongest and most experienced troops, and the bold and fiery eyes peering out from haggard faces promised certain victory.'

Girod de l'Ain, Dessaix's ADC, is one of the many who are

'able to make private observations on the points I had within view in front of me, and to judge which would be more and which less nasty to carry. For the rest, throughout the whole of the 6th, I believe, not a single musket shot was fired. All rejoiced to find themselves on the eve of this longed for battle which, we convinced ourselves, was going to decide things. For my part, after quite a long promenade reconnoitring the two armies' respective positions, I came back to our bivouac, where I whiled away my time taking my first lesson in chess from Commandant Fanfette, who was crazy about this game and always carried on him a little cardboard chessboard folding into eight pieces and most ingeniously fashioned by himself.'

Alas, almost no one has anything much to eat. Vossler dines on

'a miserable plateful of bread soup boiled with the stump of a tallow candle. But in my famished condition even this revolting dish

seemed quite appetizing. I lay down and slept as peacefully as if the coming day was to have resembled its fellow as one egg does another.'
In the Young Guard some of Sergeant Bourgogne's comrades of the Fusiliers-Grenadiers are

'cleaning muskets and other weapons; others were making bandages for the wounded, some made their wills, and others again sang or slept in perfect indifference. The whole of the Imperial Guard received orders to appear in full uniform.'

Ordered to attach all the Württemberg, Bavarian and Polish horse artillery to his own batteries, Colonel Séruzier, contemplating the packed green lines ahead of them, realizes only too well what an effort is going to be required. His 108 guns have been split into three major divisions, arranged in such a way that his French batteries have odd numbers, and the Allied equal 'so that each allied battery found itself in line between two French'. Stretched out in an undulating line they occupy nearly three miles of terrain! At 10 a.m. one of his subordinates, General Beurmann, the Saxon who'd found it so hard to replenish his ammunition, had

'summoned all the officers and made a speech in broken German, in which he informed us that the great battle would begin at 2 p.m. that very afternoon. He stressed that under no circumstances, even if enemy shells tore down whole rows of us, even if the Cossacks attacked in flank and from behind, were we to lose our presence of mind. He expressly forbade the evacuation of the wounded during the battle, it would take too many men out of the firing-line. The wounded would be taken care of after the battle. He closed by saying "I shall load you with decorations, because such brave men as you are can never be adequately rewarded."'

Is Napoleon really intending to attack that day? Evidently Beurmann has thought so. But

'at 1 p.m. he returned and told us that on account of the thick mist, which had only lifted at noon, the Emperor hadn't completed his reconnaissance, so the battle wouldn't begin until dawn next day. On receiving this news we spent the whole afternoon cooking and eating, so that whatever happened we shouldn't have to make the journey into the next world on an empty stomach.'

Shortly afterwards comes a false alarm. Murat fancies he can see the Russians retiring, and sends in a report to that effect. But Napoleon, grabbing his spyglass, is relieved to see long columns of artillery wagons still being fed into the Russian lines. And something else. At that moment the invaders are entertained to a curious spectacle:

'Knowing how pious and superstitious his men were, Kutusov didn't fail to have the image of a saintly Russian bishop [sic] pass along the front.'

Actually it's the venerated Black Virgin, rescued from the flames of Smolensk, whom Lejeune and everyone else sees being borne in procession across the Russian lines. 'It excited enthusiasm in all ranks and we could hear the joyful hurrahs of 160,000 Russians applauding as it passed them.' Rapp sees Napoleon's features light up. 'He looked with greatest pleasure on Kutusov's procession. "Good," he said to me. "They're occupying themselves with tomfoolery and won't escape us any longer."' Neither is Rapp impressed:

'St Michael's sword is undoubtedly a terrible sword; but cheerful soldiers are even better. So Kutusov wasn't stingy with the liquor, which did much to enliven the Cossacks' enthusiasm. We had neither preachers nor prophets, nor even any food to eat. But we'd a long and honourable heritage to defend. We were going to decide whether we or the Tartars were going to give laws to the world.'

Although the French haven't a single chaplain in their enlightened ranks,[7] at about midday luck has provided them, too, with a totem. Just arrived from St-Cloud the obese prefect of the palace, de Bausset, has brought with him a letter from Marie Louise and a large portrait, newly painted by Gérard, of the infant King of Rome. It shows the little boy in his cradle, playing cup-and-ball with the globe and an imperial sceptre.[8] On his return from a second reconnaissance, begun at about 2 p.m., the proud father, finding the painting already hung in his tent 'as a surprise', immediately declares it 'a masterpiece', and has it taken down and set up on an easel outside, to be admired by all. And there, at about 3 p.m., it's seen by Heinrich von Brandt who's been 'ordered to carry a message to general headquarters. The soldiers, and above all the veterans, were strongly moved. The officers became all the more concerned for the campaign's outcome.' Vernissage over, Napoleon orders the painting packed up again:

"Take him away, he's too young to see a field of battle," Gourgaud quotes him as saying.

But Brandt also hears about, and sees, another arrival, of more sinister portent. An acquaintance on the staff points out to him

'an officer of furtive appearance who seemed utterly worn out. It was Colonel Fabvier, Marmont's ADC. He'd just ridden flat out from the depths of Spain to tell the Emperor of the disaster where Wellington had decisively beaten Marmont. There under seal of secrecy I heard this bit of bad news, of which many officers, even of high rank, would know nothing until they got back from the campaign.'

Fabvier had been wounded at Salamanca, where Marmont had sacrificed his army to try and save his loot. It has taken him 32 days to cross Europe, including a brief stop in Paris. To Ségur it seems that Napoleon receives him indulgently, perhaps because of the impending crisis of his own campaign. Gourgaud gets quite the opposite impression: 'When the Emperor heard how Marmont had compromised the French army to satisfy a purely personal ambition he gave vent to the sharpest dissatisfaction.' But though the Master of the Horse sees that 'the affairs of Russia were just then too serious for the Emperor to pay much attention to the Duke of Ragusa's reverses in the Peninsula,' Fézensac, doubtless coming and going with messages from Berthier's tent, notices how all that evening Napoleon 'despite his preoccupations', keeps Fabvier with him.[9]

Just as he's surveying the scene one last time from the high ground behind Borodino, Davout comes riding up. Give him 40,000 men, his own and Poniatowski's, he offers, and he'll outflank the weak Russian left and so 'finish off the battle, the campaign, and the whole war'. Napoleon listens intently. Reflects. But declares the gambit too risky: "No! The movement would be far too great. It'd take me away from my objective and lose me too much time!" And when Davout wants to argue the toss, he's told to shut up; and rides off muttering.[10]

So the day has passed in a mood of grim expectation, but also of resolve. Evidently it's difficult to suppress all interchanges with the enemy. Although

'all engagement was carefully avoided that day, Morand's division's tirailleurs had begun to press the Russian sharpshooters and the Prince of Eckmühl ordered me to ride flat out and stop the firing all down the line.'

Evidently Dedem doesn't ride fast enough; at least not fast enough to save Captain François from a nasty leg wound:

'Having rejoined my regiment I give orders for roll-call. I've lost 23 men. Then I have myself dressed by the surgeon major of the 30th, who probes my wound, passing his probe in through the opening made by the ball. Then I hobble back to my company, and spend the rest of the night with them.'

This will be by no means the only wound that the Dromedary of Egypt will sustain. Nor has the 30th's skirmish been the only clash that evening. The 111th Line, having tangled with some Russian cavalry, Dedem orders Colonel Tschüdy to extricate it. And Tschüdy promptly arranges a kind of ambush. Forming up his remaining 400 Spaniards in square near Semenovskaya's flaming timber cottages, he sends forward his voltigeurs with orders to take pot-shots at the troopers and then, when they come to drive them off, to run back toward the square. Dazzled by the flames, their pursuers are mown down by compact fire from 400 Spanish muskets. At Lariboisière's headquarters, meanwhile, Planat de la Faye and his six staff captains are even busier than usual:

'The Emperor wanted to know exactly how many musket rounds there were, and what munitions in the reserve packs. To get all this information one had to run after units on the march, and turn to officers loth to give them, having other things to see to. However, in the name of the Emperor everything became possible. By the end of the day General Lariboisière gave him an exact report on the army's supplies of artillery rounds and infantry cartridges.'

As evening falls the sky clouds over, and a drizzling rain sweeps across the bivouacs. Under cover of it Napoleon makes a last reconnaissance. And when he gets back tells Fain how 'as he'd passed across the front of

Borodino some discharges of grapeshot had forced him to make a detour'.

Towards evening, in the same driving rain, the Guard artillery moves over and takes up position near the captured redoubt. Boulart's, attached as always, to the Chasseur brigade, is lined up between the redoubt and a little copse.

Many men are having presentiments, real or imaginary, of their fate next day. Sent by Pajol to obtain orders from II Cavalry Corps' commander, Biot finds the handsome, well-liked Montbrun

'leaning over his map, deep in thought. When I was announced, he began by asking me if I'd dined. I replied in the negative; whereupon he added "In that case you shall dine with us." Soon afterwards his manservant came in and announced that a certain Verchère, an orderly officer on the general's staff, had returned from accompanying Mme. Montbrun as far as Warsaw. "Bring him in," said the general. The officer in question handed him a letter and a packet, and as he took the latter Montbrun exclaimed, "I know what this is. You left my wife in good health, did you not? As for her letter, we'll read it after the battle."

For some obscure reason Colonel Désirad, commanding his 2nd Brigade, has no such illusions. Biot hears him remark to several of his old friends in the Dragoons of the Guard: 'I think this will be my last battle.'

Not until 8 p.m. does General Dessaix, and therefore presumably also the other divisional generals, get his orders. 'We read them by the light of the camp fire we were crouched around, half asleep. But this reading was much too interesting to us not to pay it the greatest attention.' His division's orders, Girod de l'Ain sees, are

'to get under way at daybreak and in closed columns and at short distance follow the Compans Division's march and support it in its attack on the enemy redoubts [i.e. flèches] it had to carry.'

By no means everyone dines as well as Biot that evening. Brandt's Poles of Claparède's corps are

'cruelly feeling the lack of food. We dined on grilled corn and horsemeat. The night was cold and rainy. Many officers and soldiers, drenched through and perhaps obesssed by sad presentiments, tried in vain to sleep. They got up and like wandering shades walked to and fro in front of the camp fires.'

Colonel Combe's ears are 'ceaselessly assaulted by the endless and confused noise of moving artillery and cavalry columns'. And indeed in the darkness there are all sorts of muddles. At about midnight Pion des Loches' reserve battery, ordered to leave the Young Guard's artillery and move up into the line with the Guard Foot Artillery, is just doing so when suddenly Napoleon appears:

'"What's that artillery there? What are you doing here?"'

Pion explains that an ordnance officer, i.e., one of Gourgaud's subordinates, has given him the order. '"He's a bloody fool. I've already got too much artillery here. Go back to your corps."'

'That was an order doubtless easily given. But where is this army corps [*sic*] I'd left at midnight? No point in asking. First gun left and left again, and my battery formed in column to retire. After marching for half an hour I see Marshal Mortier and gallop up to him.'

Pion des Loches explains he's been sent back by the Emperor himself. '"Who gave you the order to move?"

"An ordnance officer, speaking in the Emperor's name." "Those f— fools are always speaking in the Emperor's name. Has anyone ever heard of a corps being deprived of its reserve artillery on the eve of a battle?"'

Mortier tells him he's not to obey anyone but himself, and even if orders come from the Emperor he's not to execute them before he, Mortier, has confirmed them.

'Next I run into General Lallemand. "Haven't you seen General Desvaux's batteries?" asks Lariboisière's chief-of staff. "No." "If you see him anywhere, tell him I'm looking for him, and that he's to take two batteries to General Sorbier." "And where's General Sorbier?" But Lallemand had gone on and was no longer listening.'

Such muddles are by no means confined to the artillery. The 23rd Dragoons are one of the regiments transferred to IV Corps to strengthen the left flank. 'Marching and countermarching all night in the enemy's presence,' they're experiencing

'a terrible cold. A number of horses got stuck in the mud as we crossed several ravines where there were running streams. Our misery was at its worst since 3 September. I wasn't able to cook any meat, and during the little time when we got any rest that night we were forbidden to light a fire, leave our horses' bridles, or even speak. It was in this terrible position we waited for day to break.'

A Westphalian captain, *Linsingen*[11] by name, can't

'escape a feeling of something immense, destructive, hanging over us all. This mood led me to look at my men. There they were, sleeping all around me on the cold hard soil. I knew them all very well, and knew that many of these brave troops couldn't survive until tomorrow evening, but would be lying torn and bloody on the battlefield. For a moment it was all too easy to wish the Russians would just steal away again during the night. But then I remembered our sufferings of the past weeks. Better a horrific end than a horror without end! Our only salvation lay in a battle we must win!'

And all the time, as night deepens, Napoleon is feeling less and less well. General Lauriston, Caulaincourt's successor in the Petersburg embassy, is one of the duty ADCs, and helps place some 'emollient poultices' on his stomach. Another, Rapp, though trying to snatch some sleep 'in the room separated off by a canvas partition and reserved for the duty ADC' is all the time aware that his chief is worrying whether there's any sign of the enemy slipping away again. 'The Emperor slept very little. I woke him several times to give him reports from the outposts. All proved the Russians were expecting an attack.' At 3 a.m. he calls for a glass of hot punch and summons Rapp:

'"Well, Rapp. today we're to have to do with that Kutusov fellow, the man, you remember, who was commandant of Braunau during the Austerlitz campaign. He stayed in its fortress for three months without even budging from his room. Didn't even mount his horse to inspect the fortifications."'[12]

Ségur, who can hardly have had any business in the imperial tent that night, reports another, less probable but perhaps not quite impossible soliloquy:

'"What is war? A barbarous profession, whose whole art consists in being stronger at a given point!" He goes on to complain about the fickleness of Fortune which he says he's beginning to experience. A nervous fever, a dry cough, extreme poorliness are consuming him! During the rest of the night he tries in vain to quench a burning thirst.'

By and by he gets up and works for a while with Berthier. His proclamation to the army has already been dictated and sent to the imperial printing works in the Kolotskoïe monastery to be set, printed off, and distributed to the colonels:

'Soldiers! Here is the battle you have so ardently desired. Now victory depends on you: we need one. Victory will give us any amount of supplies, good winter quarters and a prompt return to our native land. Fight as you did at Austerlitz, Friedland, Witebsk and Smolensk, and posterity will proudly remember your conduct on this great day. May it be said of each one of us: "He fought in the great battle under the walls of Moscow!"'

At 4 a.m. he gives some last-minute instructions to the corps commanders. And at 5 a.m. one of Ney's staff officers comes to tell him the Russians are still in position: 'The army is awaiting Your Majesty's order to attack.'

Forbidden like everyone else to light fires, the Italian Royal Guard have spent the night lying on the damp ground. And just before dawn Eugène, finding his regiments unnecessarily exposed, withdraws them behind a fold in the ground. While doing so he's dismayed to find his batteries, drawn up 1,750 yards from the Russians, are 600 yards out of effective range! As they're being hauled forward Césare de Laugier is at every moment expecting the enemy

'to oppose this, but they didn't. It was a question who'd first break the terrifying silence. 5.30 a.m.: 'the sun is dissipating the mist. Immediately ADCs are being sent out in all directions by the Emperor, doubtless to make sure his orders given during the night have been carried out. A luminous burst of light, appearing on the horizon, is the signal for a solemn flourish, beaten or sounded at the same instant in the army corps.'

The proclamation has arrived from the monastery:

'The drum beats, and each colonel has it read out to his regiment, in parade uniform. We of the Italian Guard, formed up in close columns of companies without intervals between our battalions, listen to it on the reverse slope of the hill where the Italian battery is. Everyone admires the frankness, the simplicity, the imposing force of this proclamation, so well suited to our circumstances.'

To the Italians' right, next to Broussier's division, de Laugier sees in the dawn light Morand's division is massed in echelons; beyond it – both have been temporarily detached from I Corps and placed under Eugène – is Gérard's. And beyond and behind them is Grouchy's cavalry corps. 'So we were in the first line! To our left, along the Woina stream, in two lines, near Borodino, was Delzon's division, and, on the banks of the Kolotchka, the light cavalry under Ornano.' The Royal Guard itself is standing massed immediately behind Broussier's division. As for Ornano's eight light cavalry regiments, whose business it is to protect the army's left flank, they're 'so squeezed in between a little wood and some batteries' that the 1st, 2nd, 3rd and 4th Bavarian Chevauxlegers have no room to manoeuvre: 'Behind us stood two heavy cavalry regiments and, further off, the Italian Guard and an infantry brigade belonging to our corps. In front of us a Bavarian battery of horse artillery that throughout the campaign had been assigned to Preyssing's brigade was moving up.' Incomprehensibly, no one has thought of placing some light infantry in the wood to Ornano's left – an oversight they'll by and by become only too acutely conscious of. If Laugier were able to see beyond Nansouty's, Montbrun's and Latour-Maubourg's enormous cavalry masses, away to his right, and, beyond them, Ney's III and Davout's I Corps, supported in turn by Junot's VIII and the Imperial Guard, he'd see that, far out on the army's extreme right, beyond low but thick woods, Poniatowski's Poles are already moving forward to probe the weak and over-exposed Russian left.

At that moment – 5.30 a.m. – while the whole army is 'waiting for the first glimmer of dawn and Poniatowski's first musket shots' – Napoleon summons his aides, and leaves his tent, exclaiming as he does so (according to Ségur):

'"We have them at last! It's a trifle cold, but the sun's bright. It's the sun of Austerlitz! March on! We'll break open the gates of Moscow!"'

After which, as Caulaincourt holds his stirrup, he mounts his horse and followed by him and Berthier, rides slowly over towards his command post in front of the ruined Schevardino redoubt and 'to the fringe of the wood in front' – passing as they do so close to Boulart's battery, stationed between it and the redoubt. In the 'cold, misty and calm weather' the Red Lancers, too, have been

'led in silence, followed by the whole Guard, towards the Schevardino Redoubt. Beyond it we turned at a right angle to the left, and there drew up in closed column, less than a mile from an open space about 600 metres wide, between the woods on either hand and protected by two long entenchments dug the previous day by Marshal Davout's troops to secure this position. Behind the latter the Old Guard infantry came and deployed by battalions, at considerable intervals, having behind them all the reserve artillery; on their right were the three divisions of the Young Guard and, to their left, the five cavalry regiments. The first line was made up of the Chasseurs, Lancers and Dragoons, the second of the Grenadiers and the élite company [of Gendarmes]. A profound silence reigned everywhere, not a shot had been exchanged.'

Dumonceau sees the Emperor

'come and take up his position to our right, in front of the centre of his Old Guard, whence he could see all the movements as they developed in front of us. He dismounted, and someone brought him a chair, which he sat down on astraddle, his arms resting on its back, his spyglass in his hand, paying close attention to what was going on under his eyes. Berthier and Bessières stood a few paces from him and the rest of his suite a bit further behind.'

Among them, a few yards no doubt behind Berthier, Lejeune too sees him 'sit down on the steep bank of the outer slope, where he followed all the movements, spyglass in hand. The Guard was placed behind him, as in an amphitheatre. The appearance of all these crack troops, beautiful to behold in their impatience to go into action and secure a victory, made a most imposing spectacle.'

And there, all eye-witnesses agree, he'll stay until well into the afternoon.

CHAPTER 21

HOLOCAUST AT BORODINO

'Like an earthquake' – disaster for the 106th – Dutheillet storms a flèche – an unprecedented stream of wounded generals – Morand's attack – two sorts of wound – a gap in the Russian centre – 'send in the Guard!' – 'why doesn't he retire to the Tuileries?' – Ney's picnic – Ouvarov's diversion – the dying cavalry – Montbrun is killed – storming the Great Redoubt – 'take this fool away' – Thirion comforts a doomed recruit – cavalry struggles – 'won't this battle ever end?' – thousands of dead and dying men

The first shot is fired at 6 a.m. Once again Lariboisière and his staff have 'gone to the I Corps' 12-pounder battery, which was to open the firing. At this signal all the batteries along the whole line opened up; and the enemy wasn't slow to reply.[1] At that moment General Lariboisière, throwing a glance at the officers who were with him, caught sight of his son Honoré, who'd been seconded for such service. He reprimanded him severely and ordered him to withdraw, but it was easy to see he was more filled with a tender concern for him than for the rules of the service. Only half-obeying his father's orders, poor Honoré, a trifle confused, retired and stood a few paces away, behind a little silver birch wood to our right. Then we went on to III Corps' battery, where General Fouchier was.'

That first shot had been followed by a second. Then – after a horrible silence – the guns on both sides explode, in a whirlwind of shot and shell the like of which no one has ever seen. Soltyk, watching from a few paces behind Napoleon, has

'never heard anything like it. At moments the uproar was so terrible it was more like broadsides discharged from warships than a land artillery engagement.'

Others think it's 'like an earthquake'. To Dr von Roos, busy moving his dressing-station forward to 'a gully in places thick with bushes and through which flowed a small, easily jumpable stream' [the Semenovskaya] it's 'as if all Europe's voices were making themselves heard, in all its languages'.

The losses on the long march have compelled Napoleon to pack his centre, not with infantry, but with Murat's four cavalry corps. And that's where General Pajol has drawn up his light cavalry division, brigade behind brigade. At the second discharge Captain Biot, sitting his horse beside him, sees

'a horse running along our front, its rider thrown on to its cruppers. I recognized poor Colonel Désirad. A Russian roundshot had taken off his cranium. From then on we were uninterruptedly assailed by roundshot and grape. Everything that fell beyond the second line went on to strike the third; not a shot was lost.'

As usual, the Russian gunners are aiming too high. And roundshot at the very limit of their trajectory come bouncing along the grass at Napoleon's command post. Boulart, standing there with his batteries not a hundred paces away, even sees some pass over the Emperor's head: 'Captain Pantinier, commanding a battery of Friedrich's division, was killed near to and even behind us, before his division came into line.'

But already the first move is being made. Borodino village, a kind of salient on the hither side of the stream, is held by a crack division of Jägers of the Russian Imperial Guard. Only a narrow plank bridge over the Kolotchka links it with its supports.[2] And at 6.30 Delzon's division, headed by the 106th Line in column of platoons, is seen moving to the attack 'with unbelievable speed'. Already the leading Italian battalions have only 200 yards to go. Clearly the salient is completely untenable. And the Jägers are ordered to set fire to the village and evacuate it. Although 'the limit of the 106th's orders' is to capture the village, nothing can restrain it from chasing the Jägers as they, annihilated by the Italian guns, are retreating helter-skelter over the bridge. On the slope beyond, leading gently upwards to the distant Great Redoubt, three other Russian regiments are arrayed. But the 92nd Line, coming up in support and 'listening only to the voice of the guns, advances at the double, crosses the bridges and attacks the three hostile regiments.'[3] Hurrying over the bridge to recall them, General Plauzonne, their brigade commander, is killed. And in the same instant the impetuous 92nd are shattered by a massive counter-attack. After which the remains of Delzons' two regiments withdraw into the burning village, which the Russians don't bother to try and recapture.

Each side has taken a pawn.

Simultaneously with this tactical move on the left an all-out frontal assault is being delivered by I Corps on the right. Its objective is the two southern-most flèches. Lejeune, standing only a few yards to the rear of Napoleon's command post, sees how Compans, preceded by a barrage from 108 guns whose sudden torrent of shells causes

'the peaceful plain and silent slopes to erupt in swirls of fire and smoke, followed almost at once by countless explosions and the howling of cannon shot ripping through the air in every direction, has the honour of being the first to cross his infantry's fire with the Russians. Directing it at their centre to the left of the Passarevo wood, it was his task to mount the heights and carry the flèches barring his passage.'

In no time at all his heads of columns

'have disappeared into a cloud of dust infused by a reddish glow by the radiant sun. The deafening sound of our cannonade was interspersed with a sound that seemed like a distant echo, and came from the batteries on the left around Borodino [and] from beyond the woods to our right', where Poniatowski is advancing towards the village of Utitza.[4]

'The guns's roar and thunder, the crackling and crashing of musketry, the whining and soughing of roundshot large and small, the screams of the wounded and dying, oaths in every language during cavalry and bayonet attacks, the words of command, the cornet signals, the fifes and drums and thereto the masses' wave-like motion backwards and forwards in a smoke of gunpowder, shrouding friend and enemy alike in an obscurity so deep it was often only from the rows of flashing flames one could make out the enemy regiments' positions or their batteries as they came riding up – the impression of all this went through the marrow of one's bones. Anyone who claims to go into enemy fire without an oppressive feeling is a poltroon.'

This being in high degree a *journée*, Lejeune and his colleagues, too, are doubtless wearing their white fox-trimmed sky-blue pélisses, their tight-fitting double gold-striped scarlet trousers, and their gold-chevroned and white ostrich-plumed hussar helmets. From Napoleon's command post he sees the 57th enter the right-hand flèche at the *pas de charge*. And soon it seems to Sous-lieutenant Dutheillet, who's in the thick of it, that his men (6th Coy, 6th Bn) aren't merely fighting but actually winning the battle single-handed:

'The Russians had made a few abbatis which were charged and carried by our last three battalions, while the two first turned them to the right. To our left we'd a redoubt [flèche] which was firing murderously at us. Being at the regiment's left and one of the closest to the redoubt, I began shouting: "at the redoubt, let's march against the redoubt!" And together with some of our battalion's officers and two or three hundred men I flung myself at it. The Russians, seeing our resolution, retired. We entered the redoubt, pursuing them for more than 200 paces beyond our conquest. Meanwhile our colonel has been told of our success and he sends the regiment's fat major Liègre (or Liégue) to command the men who've taken the redoubt. I can say without fear of contradiction that I was one of the first, and was following the Russians, ready to receive the reinforcements behind them, when Major Liègre, a brave old soldier, seeing we weren't by any means numerous enough to repulse the enemy, massed with their cavalry in the ravines, sent us the order to come back into the redoubt to defend and keep it. For a while longer we resisted his orders, wanting to pursue the enemy, and telling the officer he'd sent to us: "Have us supported by other troops." But Major Liègre hadn't any.'

For the rest of the 57th, busy with the wood to its right, is feeling ill-supported. Dutheillet's company, attacked by artillery and fresh Russian troops, repeatedly beats them off. But Major Liègre falls dead at his feet, killed by grapeshot. 'General Teste's ADC suffered the same fate; and by this time I was so short of footwear I stripped the unfortunate ADC, still not cold, of the boots he had on his feet to put them on my own!' The Russians 'like the brave soldiers they were' renew their attacks on the flèche:

'A brave officer of that nation, seeing his men about to fall back, placed himself across the entrance to the redoubt and did everything he could to prevent them leaving it, but was shot through the body. Our men rushing forward with the bayonet, I ran towards this officer to protect him if he was still alive; but he died shortly after. I took his belt as a souvenir of his courage, and the men shared the rest of his equipment.'

The flèche so brilliantly captured by the 57th and then lost again to the Russian 7th Combined Grenadier Division is the southernmost. But soon all the terrain the 5th Division has gained is lost, as three Russian cavalry regiments sweep Compans' men on to his supports, Dessaix's 4th. As this happens Compans, already wounded in the left arm two days ago, is hit again, this time in the shoulder by a musket-ball. This second wound is serious, and Dessaix has to take over both divisions:

'To follow Compans' division's movement we'd had to descend rather a steep slope from the plateau, through dense thickets. Hardly had we emerged from the wood than General Dessaix receives orders to take command of Compans' division. Accompanied only by Captain de Bourget, Lieutenant Magnan and myself, he galloped to its head. We got there just as the first redoubts had been taken by storm. They were nothing but redans – i.e., chevron-shaped campaign works not closed at their throat, in such a way that the enemy's second line swept their interior with the sharpest musketry and grape. So it was a lot harder to gain a foothold and stay there than to have stormed them. Also, the 5th Division's troops had been massed behind these works and in folds of the ground, as far as possible to shelter from fire while waiting until fresh attacks were made. General Dessaix, whose great personal courage one had to recognize, remained a few instants totally exposed beside one of these redoubts, examining the Russian units' position and movement. And I was near him, contemplating the same view, when a mustket-ball came and smashed a bottle of brandy he'd taken care to provide himself with in one of his saddle's pistol holsters. It was more than he could do not to exclaim angrily, turning to me: "I owe that to your damned white horse!"

And indeed, Girod de l'Ain concedes, his horse was of a brilliant whiteness and a target for enemy skirmishers:

'During the few moments we'd halted there Captain du Bourget, for better shelter, had pushed his horse into the ditch of the redoubt. Having seen us dash off ahead at a gallop, he'd tried to follow us. But hardly had he emerged from the ditch than he was hit by a roundshot and fell dead.'

By now Compans' plan for a two-pronged attack seems to have been forgotten. Napoleon sends Rapp to take over his ravaged division, and Dessaix returns to his own, which by now has moved up into the first line. But almost immediately Rapp too is hit

'several times within the space of an hour; first slightly, by two musket-balls, then in the left arm by a roundshot which carried away parts of my coat and shirtsleeve, leaving my bare arm showing. At that moment I was at the head of the 61st Regiment, whose acquaintance I'd first made in Egypt. Soon I received my wound: it was a shot in my left thigh, which threw me off my horse. This was the twenty-second time I'd been wounded during my campaigns. I felt obliged to leave the field, and informed Marshal Ney to that effect, whose troops were mingled with mine. General Dessaix, the only general of this division who hadn't been wounded, took my place.'

But soon it'll be Dessaix's turn. Girod de l'Ain goes on:

'We'd advanced a certain distance and were standing in column on the edge of a wood stretching away to to our right, when we saw a charge of Russian cuirassiers coming at us like a tempest. They weren't exactly aiming at us, but at a battery of 30 of our guns which, under cover of our advance, had come and taken up position a little to our left rear. Although this charge suffered from our fire as it passed us, it didn't slow it down, no more than the discharges of grape from our battery, which it overthrew out of the cuirassiers' reach sabring those gunners who weren't able to throw themselves down between the wheels of the guns and ammunition wagons. But soon, thrown back in disorder by some French squadrons, they again passed across our column's flank and again suffered under our fire and the bayonet thrusts of a crowd of our soldiers who, leaving the ranks, ran out in front of them to cut off their retreat.'

To the French it seems there are about 1,500 cuirassiers, of whom

'scarcely 200 got back to their lines. All the rest, men and horses, remained on the ground. I don't recall our taking a single prisoner. They only wore breastplates, and these, like their helmets, were painted black. Hardly had the cuirassiers disappeared than, a little way off, we caught sight of a mass of infantry which had advanced under shelter of their charge. Left exposed and isolated after the cuirassiers' retreat, it had halted. And in the same instant we saw it as it were swirling around itself and then retiring in some disorder. As it did so, however, it, in turn, unmasked a battery, which sent us several volleys of grape, causing us considerable losses. It was also at this moment that General Dessaix had his right forearm shattered by a roundshot. Lieutenant Morgan and I took him to the rear until we were out of range of the enemy's fire.'

Le Roy, on Davout's staff, is following him about the left centre of the French front. And at 8 a.m. or thereabouts Davout's horse is killed under him, badly bruising and stunning its rider. In no time a rumour reaches headquarters that not merely his horse but the unpopular marshal himself has been killed. But Davout comes to; refuses, though badly bruised, to relinquish his command; and sends Le Roy back to IHQ to give the lie to the rumour:

'I went to tell the General Staff, which I found close to the famous redoubt we'd taken yesterday. The Emperor was seated on the reverse slope of a ditch, his left elbow resting on it. With his right hand he was observing the enemy's movements through his telescope. I heard him tell an ADC: "Hurry up and tell Ney to advance."

Le Roy is surprised to notice that a whole Guard grenadier regiment with plaqueless bearskins and red plumes is clad in white; and assumes, wrongly, they're the Westphalian Royal Guard.[5] Then he returns to the scrum. It's at the very moment he gets there that Dessaix's arm is shattered by a musket-ball. And he is immediately replaced by General Gérard, 'a man of sense and merit, who by his sang-froid and his ability consoled us for the loss we'd sustained'.

And in fact an unprecedented stream of wounded high-ups is flowing back towards Larrey's dressing-station, established in the rear of the Imperial Guard. Accompanying their wounded general, Girod de l'Ain and his other ADCs encounter

'several surgeons coming forward to attend to the wounded, among others the King of Naples' chief surgeon, who gave our general first aid. After examining his wound he strongly advised him to allow his forearm to be amputated. Larrey, who followed immediately after, was of the same opinion, insisting even more strongly that the general should resign himself to it. For the rest, it was Larrey's system on campaign – a system he applied for excellent reasons – to amputate any gravely fractured limb. So he told the general: "Doubtless we might have some chance of success if we tried to save your arm. But for that you'd need a long period of quite special care and resources you can't reasonably count on on campaign and in a country like this, a thousand leagues away from your own. Numberless fatigues and privations still await you and you're running the risk of fateful accidents, whilst within a fortnight you can be sure of your amputation wound forming a perfect scar."'

But Dessaix remains 'deaf to these exhortations and unshakeable in his determination to keep his arm.'[6] The wounded Rapp is there too:

'I had my wound bandaged by Napoleon's surgeon, and that prince [sic] himself came and visited me: "How are things going? You never get off unscathed!" "Sire, I think it'll be necessary to unleash your Guard." "I'll take care not to; I've no desire to see it destroyed. Furthermore it isn't needed. I'm sure to win the battle anyway."'[7]

That Rapp should make such a suggestion so early in the day shows how impressed he is by the Russian resistance.

Knowing that Dessaix's two brothers, one a doctor, the other a commandant, will soon be with him, Girod de l'Ain leaves him in a place of safety with the lieutenant, and returns to the firing line. There he places himself at the disposition of General Friederich, who's taken over;

'In rejoining the division I found Colonel Achard of the 108th[8] a little to the rear of the position it had occupied. With him he only had a handful of men and his eagle. "That's all that's left of my regiment," he told me sadly.'

Nor has the 4th division gained any more ground. 'Nothing important had happened in my absence.' Friant's division, too, has been standing massed in support. But now he, too, is hit; and has to hand it over to General Dufour, his senior brigadier.

Up at the front the slaughter is horrible. Voltigeur-corporal Dumont of the 61st Line is hit in the upper arm by a musket-ball. 'Soon afterwards my wound began to pain me, and I went to the ambulance to have the ball extracted.' He hasn't gone many paces before he meets the regiment's pretty Spanish cantinière Florencia:

'She was in tears. Some men had told her that nearly all the regiment's drummers were killed or wounded. She said she wanted to see them, to help them if she could. So in spite of the pain I was suffering from my wound I made up my mind to accompany her. We were walking amidst wounded men. Some moved painfully and only with difficulty, others were being carried on litters.'

Suddenly, as they pass near to one of the flèches,[9] Florencia starts to utter heart-rending cries:

'But when she caught sight of all the drums of the regiment strewn on the ground she became like a madwoman. "Here, my friend, here!" she screamed. "They're here!" And so they were, lying with broken limbs, their bodies torn by grapeshot. Mad with grief, she went from one to the other, speaking softly to them. But none of them heard. Some, however, still gave signs of life, among them the drum-major she called her father. Stopping by him and falling on her knees she raised his head and poured a few drops of brandy between his lips.'

But at that moment the Russians try to retake the flèche,

'and the firing and cannonade began again. Suddenly the Spanish woman cried out with pain. She'd been stricken by a ball in her left hand, which crushed her thumb and entered the shoulder of the dying man she was holding. She fell unconscious.'

Dumont, with his one good arm, tries to carry her to back to the baggage and ambulance; but it's more than he can do. Fortunately,

'a dismounted cuirassier came by, close to us. He didn't have to be asked. Only said: "Quick! we must hurry, this isn't a nice place to be." In fact the bullets were whistling around us. Without more ado he lifted up the young Spaniard and carried her like a child. She was still unconscious. After walking for ten minutes we got to a little wood where there was an ambulance of the Guard artillery. Here

Florencia came to her senses. M. Larrey, the Emperor's surgeon, amputated her thumb, and extracted the ball from my arm very cleverly.'

By now about two or three hours have passed. And still no significant progress is being made, either in the centre or on either wing. After the 92nd's and the 106th's destruction in front of Borodino village, Eugène, 'whose skirmishers had just dislodged the Russian chasseurs from among the bushes in front of the main battery and along the banks of the Kolotchka', had been ordered to mount a full-scale attack on the Great Redoubt. And the Italian Royal Guard is standing in reserve 'on the left of the Kalotchka, so as to be able to move to right or left in case its presence becomes necessary." Its adjutant-major can't resist the temptation to go and have a look at what's going on:

'Still too young to have been present at one of these famous battles, and hitherto only in a position to have seen combats, certainly sanguinary ones but where no such great masses had figured, only partial actions, sieges, engagements of 10,000 to 18,000 men, how often I've longed to be witness to and be an actor in so gigantic a conflict!'

So he and two other officers get Colonel Moroni's permission to mount the ridge in front of them, where the Italian guns are firing:

'Never in my life shall I forget the sublime impression yielded by the view of this long and vast carnage. No viewpoint could have been more favourable than ours. At a glance we embrace the sinuosities of the terrain, the folds of the ground, the positions of the various arms, the actions engaged on all hands. A marvellous panorama! Far off I see a very thick wood that makes me think of Tasso's and Ariosto's beautiful descriptions. Out of it spurt at each instant great jets of flame accompanied by terrible detonations. Then, under cover of these whirlwinds of fire and smoke, deep masses are deploying to advance under cover of no less terrible a fire. The sun flashes on the arms and cuirasses of infantry and cavalry marching to meet each other. At this moment the 30th Regiment, led by General Bonamy, goes to the attack.'

And of course the 'Dromedary of Egypt', despite his leg wound of the previous evening, is at his post:

'We draw up our battle line at a level ten feet below the plain, which is masked by the ravine's ridge; and General Morand orders us to march against the enemy's great battery [i.e., the Great Redoubt]. Passing along the line to encourage the men and coming in front of my company, he sees I've been seriously wounded: "Captain," he says to me, "you won't be able to keep up, retire to the colour-guard." I answer him: "General, this day holds too much attractions for me not to share the glory this regiment is going to win." "I see you for the man you are," replies the general, taking me by the hand. And passes on along the battle line amid the roundshot falling from all quarters.'

As for Laugier, who can 'see it all as a spectator at a circus might make out what's going on in the ring below him', he's seized with an 'indescribable anxiety. I can't take my eyes off this group of heroes. The men's turnout is admirable.' François' regiment

'gets the order to advance. Arrived on the ridge of the ravine, at half-range from the Russian battery, we're crushed by its grapeshot and by the fire of others taking us in flank. But nothing checks us. Like my voltigeurs and despite my wounded leg I skip and jump about to let the iron balls go their way as they come rolling into our ranks. Whole files and half-platoons are falling under the enemy's fire, leaving broad gaps.'

Now Césare de Laugier's aesthetic ecstasy

'suddenly gives place to a feeling of pity. This unhappy regiment which I've just been admiring is letting itself be massacred, and fresh Russian batteries have just been placed to reply to the Italian ones on the heights where I am.'

Captain François, skipping about among the roundshot, goes on:

'General Bonamy, who's at the head of the 30th, orders us to halt in the midst of the grapeshot. He rallies, and on we go, at the *pas de charge*. A Russian line tries to stop us. We fire a regimental volley at thirty paces and pass over it. We rush toward the redoubt and try to get in through the embrasures. I enter just as one gun has fired. The Russian gunners receive us with blows of their handspikes and ramrods. We fight them man to man and find them to be formidable adversaries. A great number of Frenchmen fall into the wolfpits pell-mell with Russians who're in them already. Once inside the redoubt I defend myself against the gunners with my sabre and slash down more than one.'

Looking on from the vantage point of the Bavarian Chasseurs, massed with the rest of Ornano's cavalry behind Borodino village, von Muraldt sees even Eugène, normally so stolid and unemotional, carried away with enthusiasm. He 'waved his hat in the air and cried "The battle's won!"'

All Colonel Griois, waiting with his guns in a dip in the ground with Grouchy's cavalry, can see is immense quantities of smoke rising over the enemy position; but he hears all the more. And he too assumes that the great fieldwork has been taken:

'A grenadier who'd been wounded in this attack came back, covered in blood and drunk on glory, to confirm for us this happy success which, by opening the enemy centre and separating his two wings, seemed to decide the victory for us.'

Such indeed is the 30th's impetuosity that François and his men have

'overrun the redoubt by more than 50 paces. But not being followed by our division's other regiments – with the exception of a battalion of the 13th Light, who're supporting us, they too are at grips with the Russians – we're forced to beat a retreat, recrossing the redoubt, the Russian line – which has sprung to its feet again – and the wolf-pits. In this way our regiment is shattered. We rally behind the redoubt, always under enemy grapeshot, and attempt a second charge. But not being supported we're too few to succeed. And with only eleven officers and 55 men we retire. All the rest have been killed or wounded. The brave General Bonamy, who'd never quit his post at the head of the regiment, has been left inside the redoubt.'

Suffering from no fewer than fifteen wounds, bleeding and helpless, Bonamy has only saved his own life by shouting out "I'm the King of Naples!" Believing him, they take him to Kutusov's headquarters, three miles behind the battleline, where the Russian commander-in-chief, completely out of touch with the stupendous conflict, is spending the day lunching and chatting with his handsome young staff officers. Kutusov calls for a surgeon, but otherwise pays him no special attention.

'I'd been through more than one campaign,' François, back on the slope in front of the Grand Redoubt, goes on,

'but never had I found myself in such a bloody mêlée or up against such tenacious soldiers as the Russians. I was in a deplorable state, my shako had been carried away by grapeshot and the tails of my coat had remained in their hands. I was bruised all over, and the wound in my left leg was hurting dreadfully. After a few minutes' rest on a plateau where we'd rallied, I fainted from loss of blood. Some voltigeurs brought me round and carried me to General Morand who'd been wounded in the chin by grapeshot. He recognized me, gave me his hand and when he'd been bandaged signed to a surgeon to attend to me.'

Realizing the triumph has been premature, it seems to Griois that the 30th have failed for lack of adequate support:

'At about the same time a mass of Russian cuirassiers charged on our right, and from where we were we could see it was causing a certain amount of disorder.'

And in fact Eugène has to send Gérard's division to support Morand's right, which is being briskly counter-attacked by two Russian dragoon regiments. As they chase the remnant of the 30th down the slope and lunge at its reserves Césare de Laugier admires the way the 7th Light (Sergeant Bertrand's regiment)

'instantly forms square, lets the dragoons advance and then opens a well-nourished fire by files, which in the twinkling of an eye covers the terrain with men and horses, dead or wounded, forming a new barrier around these brave battalions.'[10]

Griois too sees this mass of cavalry promptly driven back and overthrown, leaving

'the whole esplanade in front of the entrenchment covered by its dead. Half an hour later even sharper firing and hurrahs told us the Russians were still in the works.'

Hearing the Italian Royal Guard ordered to stand to arms, its adjutant-major, still casting lingering glances over his shoulder, goes back to his post.

In the little ravine of the Semenovka whose waters are flowing red with blood, surgeon Roos, with cannon-balls flying overhead and plunging deep into its reverse slope or else rolling towards him down the forward one, is tending his Saxon, Westphalian and Württemberger wounded, 'and even Russians'. He's noticing how deep wounds caused by flying shell fragments, even though they often tear whole chunks out of limbs, etc., bleed very little; whereas cutting wounds do so profusely:

'A cuirassier of the Saxon bodyguard, an extraordinarily big man, presented such a wound in his left buttock. The muscles, torn away, revealed the bared femur from the knee to the big trochanter. The wound wasn't bleeding. The Saxon showed himself full of energy. He said: "My wound is terrible, but I'll cure quickly because I'm healthy and have pure blood!" A very young officer of the same regiment seemed less confident. He wasn't robust, like the other. He was fine and delicate. A musket-ball had passed through the deltoid. It wasn't the pain that made him complain, but the fear of being crippled, the certainty of not being able to count on anyone helping him, and the distance he was at from his own country. I felt full of compassion for him and if we'd been in Dresden, instead of at Borodino, I'd have been only too glad to have placed him in his mother's care.'

This morning all Roos has had to eat has been a mouthful of bread, given him by another surgeon who's borrowing his instruments, washed down with a gulp of cold water from the stream:

'The numbers of wounded turning up were enormous. Other surgeons had joined us. Thanks to their collaboration we were able to give more active help. Many of these unfortunates died on the spot. Ambulances were evacuating those who'd been given first aid. The doctors hadn't been told in advance which point they should evacuate their wounded to, as in other campaigns.'

It's at just such a dressing-station that Captain François is having his wound attended to:

'The doctor comes over to me and examines my wound. Thrusting his little finger into the hole made by the musket-ball, he seizes his lancet, makes the usual cross on each hole, and puts his probe right through my leg between its two bones. "Lucky wound, this," he says, pulling out some splinters. Then he gives me first aid and tells me to go to the army's ambulance at Kolotskoïe,'

where the wounded can already be counted 'in thousands'.

In the centre, meanwhile, a third battle is raging around the flaming embers of Semenovskaya village. Against it – together with the Great Redoubt it's the key to the whole Russian position – III Corps is being thrown in, in wave after wave.[11] Evidently its attacks are overlapping those of I Corps, for Captain Bonnet, too, sees as his objective 'three redoubts' – which can only be the Bagration flèches:

'By a movement to our right we fling ourselves across some bushes and come close to the first redoubt, which is carried by our leading troops. Whereon the regiment marches on the second, its four battalions in line one behind another. Half-way between the first and the second redoubt Commandant Fournier is wounded, and I take command of the battalion – reform it in column, the right on the ditch of the redoubt we've already taken. I've got the flag. I'm awaiting the moment to act. The colonel comes up to me on foot and I ask his permission to send the flag back to that part of the corps which was close to the first redoubt and on the fringe of the copse from which we're emerging. It was done.'

But unfortunately after five minutes Russian sharpshooters

'arrive in good order a little to the left, and a dense column to our right. I deploy my battalion and, without firing, march straight at the column. It recoils. When carrying out this movement we were so exposed to grapeshot from the guns in the village that I saw my battalion falling and being breached like a crenellated wall. But still we went on.'

Reaching the edge of the ravine that separates the village from the crest of the ravine, the 18th Line runs headlong into another column

'which is marching gravely and without hurry. All that's left on its legs of the 4th Battalion makes a half turn, and we withdraw slowly, firing on this column, and re-enter the redoubt. But the place, being open on their side, isn't tenable. I'm the last to jump up on to its parapet, just as a Russian's about to grab my greatcoat. In one leap I jump the ditch. They must have fired 20 shots at me, almost point-blank, without hitting anything except my shako. We withdrew as far as to the bushes near the first redoubt.'

No sooner have the 18th taken refuge in the bushes than they're repeatedly charged by Russian cuirassiers. And it isn't until about midday that the Russians finally evacuate the ruins of what, a few hours before, was the village of Semenovskaya.

A sore throat, a bad cold, migraine and an agonizingly overfull bladder are no friends of a commander-in-chief at the crisis of his fortunes. Soltyk, only about 30 or 40 paces away from Napoleon, is observing him closely. Not paying the least attention to the Russian shells which now and then explode nearby,

'now he'd sit down on the ground; now walk to and fro quietly humming a tune, sometimes mechanically putting his hand in his waistcoat pocket to take out some pills he'd been prescribed against his cold. His face simultaneously expressed preoccupation and impassibility. He also addressed a few brief words to members of his suite, telling them to take his orders to the battlefield.'

At one moment the Polish General Kossakowski 'having picked up a Russian grape cartridge with old rusty brown iron, whose wounds are said to be the most dangerous', and holding it up

'as evidence of Muscovite foul play, went up to him and showed it to him, adding that all means were fair against such enemies. The Emperor replied vivaciously: "Oh, I don't give a damn for them!" Then added immediately: "But that stuff won't carry far."'

How much can he see of the vast conflict going on at his feet? Only Ney's corps and 'almost all the cavalry assembled under Murat', thinks Chlapowsky, who's standing not far away with his squadron of the 1st Polish Lancers. He too thinks the Emperor is ill: 'now walking up and down, now sitting on his folding chair. At no moment did he mount his horse.' Lejeune, making comparisons with Wagram, Essling, Eylau and Friedland, is astonished not to see him 'deploy the activity which produces success.' The rumour that the Emperor isn't well also reaches Dr Flize, medical officer in one of the Guard regiments:

'Not once did Napoleon mount his horse during the whole battle.[12] He walked on foot with his suite of officers, passing ceaselessly to and fro. A steady stream of adjutants took his orders and rode away.'

One of them is Lejeune:

'Returning from all my missions I always found him there sitting in the same posture, following all the movements through his pocket spyglass and giving his orders with imperturbable calm. But we weren't so happy as to see him, as formerly, going to galvanise with his presence the points where too vigorous a resistance made success doubtful. Each of us was astonished not to find the active man of Marengo, Austerlitz, etc. We didn't know Napoleon was ill and that it was this that was making it impossible for him to act in the great struggles taking place under his eyes, exclusively in the interests of his glory. We weren't very satisfied; our judgements were severe.'

Boulart, standing among his guns, horses and ammunition wagons a few yards in front of his command post, sees the Emperor himself, 'his arms crossed on his chest, walking agitatedly to and fro in a small space in the very centre of my own battery. Farther off, groups of officers and generals were standing spyglass in hand. In previous battles the Emperor had produced spectacular effects by one of his characteristic masterstrokes. Now we were living in hope of seeing his face light up with the same exultation as it used to do in his heyday. But on this occasion we waited in vain. At one moment he moved a little further down the slope and, telescope still in hand, lay in a reclining posture on a bearskin rug. Sometimes he'd walk to and fro, his hands behind his back. Mostly he sat on his folding chair peering through his fieldglass or with a gesture summoning Berthier and exchanging a word or two with him.'

Boulart's querulous and pessimistic colleague Captain Pion des Loches says he can even

'guarantee that from the beginning of the action until 4 p.m. he didn't budge, because all the time I had my eyes fixed on him. More than 100 staff officers arrived one after another; he listened to their reports, then dismissed them with a gesture of his hand, almost always without uttering a word.'

But the scene just behind him is so much the more impressive. Victor Dupuy, on his way back from fetching himself a fresh mount in the rear from among the 7th Hussars' lead-horses, his own being winded, passes close by and sees how

'the Guard was placed behind him, as in an amphitheatre. Massed in columns of battalions, it presented an imposing, magnificent spectacle. The men were all in parade uniforms, as if to march past on the Place du Carousel.'

Dr Flize too will afterwards above all remember 'its bearskins and red plumes'. And Séruzier records that 'despite its privations since Vilna its turnout was as brilliant as in Paris'. Thirion, looking over his shoulder from his place amidst the dense masses of cavalry in the French centre, sees the whole hillock as

'a pyramid of men and bayonets, whose summit was the Emperor. A magnificent and imposing coup d'oeil. At its foot the whole Guard cavalry was drawn up in two lines: the first made up of the Chasseurs, Lancers and Dragoons, the second of the Grenadiers and élite company.'

Immediately below and in front are the three regiments of the Legion of the Vistula. Meanwhile, says Dr Flize,

'the regimental bands were playing military marches, reminiscent of the first marches of the Revolution, when we'd been fighting for Freedom: Allons, les enfants de la patrie.[13] Here the same strains didn't inspire the military; and some of the older officers laughed when they compared the two epochs.'

Earlier Chlapowski has noted how the 'light infantry clarions were choosing the prettiest pieces in the repertoire, because music makes a great impression on hearts before a battle'. – 'I moved a little closer to the Emperor,' Flize goes on,

'who'd not ceased peering at the battlefield through his spyglass. He was wearing his grey uniform and spoke little. Sometimes a cannonball came rolling towards his feet, but he merely stepped aside, as we did who were standing behind him.'

Bausset, who at 10 a.m. serves him a glass of punch, says 'he calmly kicked them aside, as one kicks a stone when taking a walk'.[14] A little farther off Dumonceau is seeing how

'every instant trophies captured from the enemy were being brought to us. Among these some presented the most handsome types you could possibly see, both of men and horses. One of the latter, a superb black courser, was ceded to our Commander Cotti for a 20 fr. piece: then the cuirassier who'd brought it went resolutely back to the scrum.'

At about 11 a.m. everyone notices a kind of lull. It's as if both sides are already showing signs of exhaustion. And Murat sends one of his ADCs, a Colonel Morelli, to Napoleon, urging him to send in the Guard. Arriving at the Schevardino redoubt he hears voices muttering: 'Forward the Guard!' But Napoleon tells him: "And what if there's another battle tomorrow, what shall I fight it with?" Yet goes so far as to give an order for the Young Guard to advance – only immediately to cancel it. And when its commanders, even so, on pretext of straightening its lines, are seen to be 'shuffling' their units in the direction of the firing, sharply orders them to desist. Instead of sending in the Young Guard, and after a renewed attack by Latour-Maubourg's cavalry corps, he orders forward Friant's division. On Dedem's men 'demanding to be sent into the fighting, Napoleon (who he says had 'come up') had replied: "Regiments like this only go into action to decide the victory."

'A moment we remained in column, exposed to roundshot. My two ADCs, General Friant's son and several staff officers were all wounded. Soon we were made to march towards the centre to cover the burnt village of Semenovskaya, several times taken and retaken, and against which the Russians were directing their 20,000-strong reserve.'

Friant, who finds Murat 'all smiles' under furious fire from 100 Russian guns, seizes the burnt-out village; and in the same instant is himself severely wounded.

'Seeing a regiment beginning to give way, Murat runs up to its colonel and seizes him by the collar: "What are you doing?" The colonel, pointing to his hundreds of dead and wounded: "Surely you see we can't hold on here?" Murat: "Well, I'm staying put!" The colonel stares at him: "Quite right, Sire! Let's go and get ourselves killed!"'

Whereupon the remains of Friant's division form two squares, Murat commanding one, and General Gallichet, Friant's chief-of-staff, the other. And under their crossed fire the Russian attack withers away.

At the same time the need for some decisive intervention is clearly growing. Napoleon turns to Lejeune:

'"Go and find Sorbier and tell him to take all the artillery of my Guard to the position occupied by General Friant,[15] and lead him there yourself. He's to deploy 60 pieces at right angles to the enemy line, to crush his flank, and Murat is to support him. Allez!"

'I gallop over to the fiery General Sorbier. Guessing my message, he hardly gives me time to explain it, but replies impatiently: "We ought to have done it an hour ago", and gives the order to follow him at a trot. And at once this imposing mass of "thunderers", drawn by 2,000

horses, gets rolling with a clanking of chains and thudding of horse-
hoofs and goes off down the hillside; crosses the valley; mounts the
easy slope the enemy has covered with trenches, and then breaks
into a gallop to gain the necessary space to deploy on his left flank.'
Boulart, left behind with his battery, is watching his colleagues' fate from
afar:

'For quite a while my gaze followed the three Guard batteries under
a well-nourished fire and covered with a hail of roundshot whose
falls one could only see by the dust they were raising. I thought they
were lost, or at least half so. Happily, the Russians aimed badly, or
too high.'

But Lejeune is accompanying Sorbier into the thick of it:

'In the distance, ahead of me, I see King Murat cavorting in the midst
of the horse skirmishers, surrounded by far fewer of his own troops
and much less occupied with his own cavalry than with numerous
Cossacks. These have recognized him by his panache, his gallantry
and courage, also by his little Cossack mantle of long goat's hair
which he, like they, is wearing. Happy as on a holiday they'd surrounded him and, hoping to seize him, were shouting "Houra!
houra! Murat!" But even at a lance's length none of them dared
attack this man whose sabre, swift as lightning, adeptly evaded every
danger and struck death into the heart of even the boldest. I gallop
up to warn him of what's going to happen [i.e., that the three Guard
artillery batteries are going to open fire from his flank], and Murat,
leaving the line of sharpshooters, comes and gives his orders to make
sure Sorbier is supported. Taking his movement for a flight or a
retreat, the Cossacks pursue us. My horse, not so light as Murat's –
he's riding a beautiful tawny Arab – gets all four feet entangled and
is overthrown by the lashings of a cannon as it makes a 90-degree
turn at the gallop. The furious animal, though hurt by the shock of
its fall, gets up without throwing me, and takes me over to Sorbier in
the centre of the terrible battery which is just firing its first salvo of
grape, shells and roundshot, raking the enemy line throughout its
whole length, every discharge taking effect. In vain the enemy's cavalry tries to destroy this line of guns. Murat's cavalry is giving it too
much to think about; but though it's making brilliant charges, it
can't debouch on to the second line occupied by the Russians on the
plateau, where we're still separated [from it] by a little gentle slope.
We remained the masters of their fortified position. I went back to
the Emperor and gave him these details.'

Now no fewer than 400 guns are bombarding the Russian centre, which
300 others are defending. Ney and Davout mount assault after assault.
Neither Dumonceau, still in reserve, nor anyone else has ever heard anything like it:

'To the stunning uproar of the cannonade close at hand was mingled like a distant echo that of the batteries to our left around

Borodino, and on the right, beyond the woods where Prince Poniatowski was fighting. Then the sonorous vibrations of the atmosphere, like groans, the sharp soughing of roundshot passing through the air produced the effect of someone ripping up pieces of cloth, the cracklings of an intermittent fusillade, sometimes re-animated by lively and prolonged explosions – all these various noises, mixed with clamour of all kinds, formed an infernal din such as the one at Smolensk had only given us a feeble idea of.'

The slaughter on both sides is inconceivable. For two hours Ségur watches the Russians

'advancing in dense masses, into which our roundshot ploughed wide and deep holes. They kept coming on until the French batteries, redoubling their fire, crushed them with canister. Whole platoons fell at once, and we could see the soldiers trying to restore their ranks under this horrible fire.'

'The roundshot and shells rained down like hail,' Planat goes on,

'and there was so much smoke we could only make out the enemy at rare intervals. The Westphalian Corps was massed in close column in front of the [Schevardino] redoubt, and from time to time received shells which, as they burst, sent shakos and bayonets flying up in the air. At each such blow these poor soldiers flung themselves down flat on their stomachs, and not all got up again.'

Planat himself, as he follows Lariboisière about the battlefield, 'not wanting either to quit my post or dismount', is suffering from

'the worst kind of agony one can imagine – from diarrhoea. I daren't describe just how I managed to dispose of what was tormenting me; but in the process I lost two handkerchiefs, which I, as we passed it, threw as discreetly as I could into the trench of the fortification. A serious loss in a country devoid of washerwomen.'[16]

But up there on the plateau Ney is 'animating everybody with his gestures and his fiery manners'. His Württembergers, too, slowly advancing (Suckow supposes as a feint), are being mown down by the Russian cannon when 'Major de Mangold, of the Württemberg staff, arrives flat out at the head of our column and in a loud voice asks for mounted lieutenants who speak French'. Suckow and another present themselves; and are detailed off. But how to stick with 'Ney's too numerous suite'? The two lieutenants'

'wretched little Russian horses have a thousand difficulties in following the Marshal, who was as active as he was mobile. We saw him giving orders at all points, taking his dispositions, and again and again even leading us to within the enemy's musket range. Very frequently he galloped to the hillock on whose summit Napoleon had placed himself. Probably he was reporting to the Emperor or asking for fresh orders.'

On one such occasion Suckow too hears Napoleon, on foot, ask Ney from a distance: 'Well then, Marshal?' But doesn't hear Ney's answer – only sees

'Napoleon very violently lash the air with the riding whip he was holding in one hand.'

Wave after wave, division upon division, is thrown in. The massed green ranks, exposed on their slight forward slope, are mincemeat for the French guns. Soltyk, who is also dashing about on mission, finds Davout, too, directing his troops' movement in the very storm centre of the fighting:

'I told him I was going to return to the Emperor, and asked for orders. He replied: "Since you're going back to the Emperor, tell him there's been a bit of a scrum, as you've just seen; but that just now everything's going all right."'

At the crisis of the struggle, and just as the Russians seem on the point of yielding, Bagration, commanding the Russian left, is badly wounded in the leg. The Russians waver. And 'the French remain masters of the flèches'.[17]

Which however have been designed to be, and still are, open at the rear to Russian counter-attacks. But this time 'the Prince of Eckmühl went on defending the redoubts he'd taken and from which the enemy were trying to dislodge him'. Now Lejeune is sent to him with

'the unpleasant news that Prince Poniatowski, manoeuvring on his right in the very dense or swampy woods, had run into obstacles which were preventing him from bringing the Polish corps on to the Russian rear and doing them enough harm to make a powerful diversion in favour of I Corps. The Marshal's position was at that moment critical, almost untenable. Though he'd been wounded [sic] in the arm, he remained in command. The Marshal, very much annoyed at having to take frontally a position which in his view ought to have been attacked from three sides at once, told me angrily: "He [Napoleon] must have the devil in him, wanting me to seize the bull by the horns!"'

At that moment Davout's chief-of-staff, General Romoef, is hit by a round-shot and, gravely wounded, has to be taken to the rear. But Lejeune hurries

'to King Murat, to explain to him what a critical position Davout was in; and he instantly assembled several masses of his cavalry to support General Friant, to whom I took his order to carry Semenovskaya. An instant later I saw the whole plain covered by innumerable cavalry, Russian, Cossacks, French or Allied, involved in the most obstinate mêlées.'

By now it's getting on for midday; and Le Roy, who's been sent to replace the 85th's Second Major, thinks the fighting on the right flank is slackening. No doubt it's during this lull – but such a vast number of things are of course happening simultaneously as to bewilder all exact chronology – that von Suckow, tagging along on his konya after Ney's splendidly mounted staff, in a moment when they're out of range of the enemy's fire, is amazed when Ney turns to one of his domestics and says: 'Luncheon!' The more so as he's long been living on horseflesh or a bit of black rye bread:

'In the twinkling of an eye the table was laid – it consisted of a big linen tablecloth spread out on the ground, and charged with such appetizing and comforting dishes as butter, cheese, bread, etc. There were even liqueurs in abundance. With a curt "help yourselves, gentlemen!" the Marshal invited us to amply fall to on the delicious things spread out at our feet, and whose very names, so to speak, we'd forgotten.'

Alas, all too little time is allowed for them to do justice to the repast. 'After only a few minutes there was a shout of "To horse, gentlemen!" There was no appealing against it. And again we had to take our places in the scrum.' Everyone, including Ney, has taken fresh horses. Only the two Württemberg lieutenants will have to go on making do with their little konyas. When they point this out to Ney's chief-of-staff they're curtly dismissed and – without having carried a single order.

It's also 'at midday' – i.e., during the same lull – that de Bausset makes so bold as 'officiously' to ask Napoleon whether he'd like to take lunch?

'He signed to me "No." Whereupon I was so unwise as to tell him there was no reason in the world to prevent him from having lunch whenever he wanted to. He dismissed me in a pretty brusque fashion. Later he ate a slice of bread and drank a glass of Chambertin, without diluting it with water.'

But for the two Württemberger officers, only too happy to have at least snatched at so fine a lunch, it's 'no easy matter, dragging our exhausted ponies along behind us, to find our few hundred Württembergers'. And when in the end they do, their comrades are inside one of the flèches, being cannonaded by a battery of 20 Russian guns.

Now a Saxon cuirassier division is thrown in. Climbing up the steep slope of the Semenovskaya, cuirassier lieutenant *von Meerheimb*[18] finds it 'so steep that some of our riders, not realizing it would be better to climb it obliquely, tumbled over backwards and were trampled by the horses coming on behind'. The village on its crest is by this time a mere mass of glowing logs. Beyond it a Russian infantry regiment, caught in the act of forming square, is ridden over; but two others repulse the disorganized cuirassiers with well-disciplined volleys, felling any number of men and horses. Finally a second assault by Friant's division seizes the ground the Russian centre has been holding.

And a gap – at last – opens up in the Russian line.

Through it both Murat and Ney can 'see clearly as far as Mojaisk'. They even make out parts of the Russian baggage train moving off into the woods.

It's the crucial moment.

The moment for the knockout blow.

And this time Murat sends – not an ADC – but his chief-of-staff, to beg Napoleon to send in the Imperial Guard. Belliard rides up, doffs his hat, explains. Napoleon meditates a moment. But temporizes: 'Before I commit by reserves I must be able to see more clearly on my chessboard.' And it's a disappointed Belliard who rides away. Ney too has asked for the Guard. And when it's refused him, exclaims angrily: 'If he's tired, why doesn't he retire to the Tuileries and leave the fighting to the real generals?'

When he gets back to Murat, Belliard is alarmed to see him being pursued by Russian cuirassiers. And where's his suite? All that's left of it, so it seems, 'as extravagantly dressed as himself', is his mameluke Amédé. To escape some Cossacks who're also after him Murat has hastily to take refuge in a square of the Württembergers' 25th division.[19] But Amédé gets left outside:

'The Prince Constantine's cuirassiers's uniform was very similar to that of the Saxon cuirassiers – white tunic and black turnbacks – and their sudden appearance in great numbers had thrown everything into confusion. The Württembergers took them for Saxons and held their fire. But the Negro [*sic*], who hasn't lost his head, keeps shouting: "Fire! Fire!" Placed as he was between the Russians and ourselves, that was magnificent! That "Fire!" could have been the end of him.'

The perilous moment over, Murat remounts, gallops over to Nansouty, and unleashes a new charge; which is also repulsed.

But by now the Russians have plugged the gap in their centre.

And the critical moment has been lost.

There's been a good reason for Napoleon's reluctance to throw in the Guard. A little while before Belliard comes galloping up, begging him to do so, something else has happened.

On the extreme left Ornano's Bavarian Chasseurs have been stolidly suffering under frontal fire from the Russian guns beyond the Kolotchka:

'Packed together, we formed a sure target for the Russian artillery, which had ridden up towards us. As usual the Russian gunners were aiming too high and a lot of their cannonfire passed overhead, so fewer of us in the first line were wounded than might have been expected. But the second line, a brigade of Italian horse chasseurs, were worse off; and the officers were having their hands full getting their men to stay put. Roundshot were falling to right and left, hitting horses and riders. Such a fate struck my sergeant-major Moncrif, a native Frenchman. Our line had become confused, and he'd just ridden along our front to straighten it and had halted in front of my horse to say something to me, when a roundshot suddenly threw him out of his saddle. A few steps away from me lay now only a mutilated corpse, and for the moment we couldn't dismount to drag it aside.'

This has been going on for two hours and the sun is

'high in the sky, when we saw a movement among the numerous Russian cavalry in front of us; and soon it became clear that a considerable mass of it was moving off toward our left wing.'

It is now that Ornano's, or rather Eugène's, negligence in not taking the obvious precaution of placing light infantry in the sparse woods to their left becomes obvious. For it's in this direction, with the overt intention of occupying them, that the Russian cavalry are now moving. Abruptly aware of the oversight, Ornano sends an urgent message to Eugène, who hastily, to make it good, sends him two companies of voltigeurs. But of course they'll take some time to get there. And meanwhile, von Muraldt continues,

'the enemy cavalry, consisting of Guard Cossacks, is implementing its plan. By the time the voltigeurs reach us the wood is already in enemy hands. And hardly have the voltigeurs drawn up to our left, within range of it, than individual sharpshooters from the Guard Cossacks [easily recognizable by their scarlet baggy uniforms] are already visible on its fringe. As soon as the enemy facing us sees we've been outflanked he crosses the Kolotchka, everywhere shallow and easily forded, and, protected by his artillery, attacks our front. Every moment we're waiting for the order to advance against him; but whether our general's attention is mainly directed toward the attack threatening our flank or for some other reasons, no such order comes; and we can only await the enemy, who are coming at us flat out. Not until the Russians are 200 paces away does the order come: "Carbines up! Fire!" And hardly have we fired our carbines – mostly without effect (as is usual with cavalry) – than we're attacked and overthrown by two hussar regiments.'

Disaster threatens. The whole left wing is in instant danger of being driven in:

'At the same time the Guard Cossacks are advancing out of the wood, overriding both our voltigeur companies, and striking into our flank. Attacked from in front and in flank, and on such utterly unfavourable terrain, the whole lot of us take to our heels. For a moment generals, officers and rankers swirl around in a single confused mass. Everyone is spurring his horse to get out of this jam as quick as ever he can.'

Cursing himself no doubt for his oversight in not investing the Lachariska wood with light infantry, Eugène sends off an ADC to Napoleon to notify him of the dangerous irruption. And himself gallops over to the troublespot 'the better to assess the enemy's movement'. Getting there just as the Russians launch their attack, he's

'swept away in this flight and seeks salvation in his horse's swiftness. The best mounted of the enemy follow us with loosened reins and lowered lances.'

The Italian Guard too has been under heavy pressure. Standing there in support of Gérard's and Morand's divisions, 'impassively suffering the losses caused by the guns, powerless to avenge itself and trembling at its own inaction' and sure it's this affray that's going to decide the whole battle, they've been demanding to be allowed to join in. 'Shouting with joy', they've just formed an assault column 'of platoons by the right' – the vélites at the head, then the grenadiers, the chasseurs and the dragoons – and 'joy, pride and hope are shining in all our faces amidst falling shells and grenades and to the incessant whistling of iron and lead', they're just about to attack – when Ornano's staff officer comes galloping up

'to warn the Viceroy, in all haste, that numerous Russian cavalry are debouching from the Lachariski wood to outflank and turn our left. The last adjutant to arrive tells us that Delzons and Ornano have already been crushed and forced to retire on to the Italian batteries, Borodino, the Woina and the baggage.'

About turn! Back across the Kolotchka! 'Annoyed to have our movement interrupted but hoping to be compensated in some other way, we retrace our steps, the tail of our columns leading, and hasten to the threatened point.'

By now the intruders, emerging from the wood, are becoming 'at each moment more numerous'; and already half the Italian guns are having to be turned against them. Colonel Achouard of the artillery is killed and two of his cannon have been taken, when Eugène, arriving on the scene at a gallop and 'promising us that the Guard will be here any moment, has no other recourse but to take refuge inside a square of the 84th, which is instantly charged'. 'At that very moment,' Laugier goes on,

'we're [re]fording the Kolotchka, and, while preserving the greatest calm, are hastening our steps, the more ardent for a rumour that the Prince himself is in danger. Meanwhile the Russian cavalry, all the time growing more numerous, renew their charges against the squares of the Croats' 8th Light, of the 84th and the 92nd. Formed in squares, we advance in échelon to meet the Russians, who by now have reached the Italian batteries, extinguished their fire, and overthrown Delzons' regiments.'

Von Muraldt and his fleeing chasseurs have taken refuge behind the crossed bayonets of the Royal Guard:

'A little way from our infantry, which had formed square behind us, Lieutenant Münch and I were among the first who with our shouts and arguments managed to halt our people and bring some order into them again. Others followed our example. Now the Russians too become aware of our distant infantry square and begin to cease their pursuit,'

driven off 'flat out', says Laugier, by the squares' heavy musketry. And, Muraldt goes on:

'A beginning had been made, and soon we throw the Russians back so violently that they've no time to take away the battery to our front which had fallen into their hands when we'd fled.'

Ornano's light cavalry has regrouped and is thirsting for revenge. Seconded by Italian Guard dragoons and the Guardia d'Onore, it 'flings itself again at the Russians, who hastily recross the Woina and the Kolotchka, and don't dare return' – leaving behind them the two captured Italian guns:

'It's about three o'clock. But the order having come to form up again in our previous positions, we didn't pursue them any further. During this episode, which lasted no longer than ten minutes, many of our people had been wounded with sabre cuts and lance-thrusts, but comparatively few had been killed. After this interesting intermezzo, though all the time fired on by the Russian guns, we didn't budge from the spot.'

Part of Uvarov's improvised, badly carried through, but, as it will one day turn out, decisive intervention[20] – has even caused panic in the baggage train. And the Guard's rearmost units, even though it's only been a question of Cossacks, have momentarily had to about-face to receive them.

But Uvarov's real achievement has been to reduce the French impact in the centre – at the critical moment.

What Napoleon has been thinking about it we don't know. But in the hut behind the Imperial Guard which Larrey is using as his dressing-station for the army's top brass, the wounded generals *Teste* and Compans (doubtless also Dessaix and Rapp) have heard the noise of the fighting coming closer to the left, then dying away again; and that 'panic and confusion' have broken out in the rear.

At about 2 p.m. Girod de l'Ain, in the centre, finds Ney

'more or less alone in command of the whole line. Anyway the firing had begun to slacken on both sides and one would have said the battle was about to end for lack of combatants, so huge had both armies' losses been during the forenoon. Only the batteries, at rather long range, went on replying to each other with frequent discharges. On my way to get to Marshal Ney I found myself following the base of a little earthwork with the sound of roundshot going over my head in either direction. Their whistling and – apparently – the emotions of the forenoon had made such an impression on my poor horse that, though hitherto always a model of docility, he chose this moment to become so extremely restive I had to dismount and lead him by his bridle. And the strange thing is, it wasn't the sound of the guns which set him trembling in every limb, but the whistling of the shot, so well did he understand that it was there the danger lay, not in the guns' detonations.'

Ney has sent Girod de l'Ain to tell General Friedrichs to advance and likewise

'the Duke of Abrantès, who was with the Westphalian Corps on our right. Friedrichs obeyed, taking up a position where he could see the Westphalians behind him, and always in touch with Prince Poniatowsky's Polish Corps, to his right. As for Junot, I found him in a clearing in the wood, dismounted, making his troops pile arms and apparently nowise disposed to budge. Nor did he take any account of what I'd come to tell him: and went on doing, there, what he'd been accused of at Valutina.'

Le Roy, too, who has left Davout's staff to replace the 85th's Second Major, feels that the fighting on the right flank is slackening after the flèches have been turned. Yet no sooner does the 85th, emerging from one of them at about 3 p.m., try to advance across the great plateau, than the storm of grape and roundshot starts up again, as intense as ever.

Nor its chief target is Murat's cavalry masses which, for almost nine hours, have been forming the centre of the French battle line. Hour after horrific hour has passed, as they sit their horses there, immobile under the Russian guns, above all from the 'Raevsky'[21] Redoubt's eighteen heavy pieces. Lejeune sees clearly that, if the Italian artillery had been placed too far from the enemy, Grouchy's, Latour-Maubourg's and Montbrun's three cavalry corps have from the outset been stationed unnecessarily close:

'Out of vanity, or rather, not to give grounds for a false interpretation, they were loth to retire a few hundred paces and take up a less exposed position to the rear. In this way thousands of brave troopers and excellent horses we'd every reason to preserve fell without any profit to the army.'

As the endless minutes pass, then the hours, Colonel *Roth von Schreckenstein,*[22] commanding the Saxon Life Guard Cuirassiers is finding that

'for strong healthy well-mounted men a cavalry battle is nothing compared with what Napoleon made his cavalry put up with at Borodino. To hold out inactively under fire must be one of the most unpleasant things cavalry can be called upon to do. There can scarcely have been a man whose neighbour didn't crash to earth with his horse or die from terrible wounds, screaming for help.'

Captain Aubry sees his colonel's two thighs carried away and two captains and the regimental paymaster killed, apparently by one and the same roundshot:

'The sergeant-major on the squadron's right flank was carried off by a cannon-ball just as I was laying my sabre on his chest to align the front rank, and I was all spattered by his blood. The farrier, who replaced him, suffered the same fate. The brigadier, his neighbour, had three horses killed under him. My turn came soon afterwards. I was hit by a ricocheting cannon-ball or by an exploding shell fragment on the flat of my spur. The blow was so violent that my boot burst open like a sheet of paper torn up by children for their amusement. All that was left was the lining. Fortunately the projectile passed on the side of my instep instead of by the heel – if it hadn't, my leg would have been carried away. I got off with losing all my nails and the flesh of my toes.'

Victor Dupuy had earlier been riding at his general's side

'when a roundshot passed so close to my face I felt its heat. Making an involuntary movement with my body, I gave my horse's bridle a sharp tug. He jerked in the opposite direction and we came apart. Stunned by my fall I lay motionless on the ground. The column halted. General Jacquinot, Colonel Gobrecht of the 9th Lancers and some officers came and stood around me. I heard them saying: "This poor Dupuy has been killed!" A few are already dismounting to give me what help they can, when I suddenly come to myself again, get lightly to my feet, shake my head, and saying "there's nothing wrong with me!", remount my horse. For a few moments this accident, which, most happily for me, was only comic, cheered us all up.'

As the nightmarish hours wear on and on, the 7th Hussars, too, are melting away. Two Russian batteries, one in the redoubt, the other taking them in flank, are slowly decimating their ranks. Dupuy's squadron-leader, Brousselier, comes riding up to him:

'He asked me if I'd anything to give him to drink. I proffered him my flask with a little rum in it. Having taken a swig he said: "Let's go! I'll go back. If I must be killed, it shall be at my post!" Hardly had he got these words out than a roundshot hit him in the chest. He died on the spot. If he'd stayed with me only one minute longer this untoward roundshot wouldn't have been for him.'

All around him, cuirassier Captain Bréaut des Marlots, a man of stoic philosophy if ever there was one, sees only

'dead or dying men. Twice during the battle I went to review the faces of the cuirassiers of my company to see which were the brave ones. I told them so on the spot. Just as I was going up to a young officer, M. de Gramont, to felicitate him on keeping a good countenance and he was telling me he had no complaints to make but would like a glass of water, a cannon-ball comes and cuts him in two. I turn to another officer and tell him how much I regret poor M. de Gramont. Before he can reply his horse is hit and killed by a roundshot. I give my horse to be held for half a minute – the cuirassier who's holding it is knocked over and killed. But though I'm covered with earth the shells are throwing up at me, I don't suffer the least scratch.'

In such dire circumstances he's finding a clear conscience is a soldier's best friend:

'And here's what gave me the calm I needed: "It's a lottery. Even if you get out of this, you'll have to die some day. Do you prefer to live dishonoured or die with honour?" When you're sabring each other you're in motion. The fire which animates you takes away all kind of reflection. But to see virtually certain death, or to put it better, to wait for it, to be surrounded only by dead and dying, this is often beyond human strength, and only philosophy, I do believe, has the power to raise us by showing us the nothingness of our being. The bad man is never a good soldier, remorse stifles his courage. He's only good for some desperate enterprise, charges, etc., and I've often seen this proven. All this proves that all men have a more or less tender conscience, and that no one can wholly stifle it. At the sight of a great danger it's reborn. It's the voice of God, it's the greatest proof of His existence.'

Some people – perhaps their consciences aren't quite so good – are wondering whether it's really necessary to be quite so exposed:

'Shortly afterwards, General Bruyère's horse hurting him in its fall, General Jacquinot, who'd at once withdrawn the 7th Hussars to a less exposed position behind a wood, takes over the light cavalry division.'

Maurice Tascher too will write in his diary: 'Remained for nine hours under cannon and grape.' He's wondering how the many novices 'who could hardly sit a horse' and have fallen by the wayside, would have stood up to this?

For it mustn't be imagined that no one, novice or not, runs away. Vossler sees 'a regiment of Polish lancers break under the fire, passing through us before it could be halted'. There are even general officers who're glad of a pretext, however slim, to quit. General Burot, of the 1st Light Cavalry Brigade (5th and 9th Hussars), known for his cowardice,

'was advancing at the head of his brigade when a roundshot carried away the corner of his hat. As he was retiring he met Marshal Ney, to whom he recounted his mishap. "Are you wounded?" "No, M. le Maréchal, I don't think so." "In that case," the Duke of Elchingen replied ironically, "go back to your brigade, and after the battle you'll have no difficulty in finding something else to put on your head!"'[23]

To the left of this great mass and advanced beyond a deep ravine in front of the Great Redoubt, Griois' guns are firing back at 'the artillery in the redoubts [i.e., flèches] on our right and left, and against the masses of cavalry and infantry facing us':

'All the cavalry reserves have united on this point and formed up in several lines to the right of my batteries. Musket-balls, shells and grape, raining down on us from all sides, were blasting great holes in our cavalry, which stood there for several hours without budging. The plain was covered with wounded men making for the ambulances and horses without riders galloping about in disorder. Close to me I noticed a regiment of Württemberg cuirassiers whom the roundshot seemed to be striking by preference; in all its ranks helmets and cuirasses were flying in pieces. The French Carabiniers, too, placed farther ahead, were also suffering a lot, above all from the musketry, whose balls were ringing out on their armour. My artillery was sorely tried, and soon I'd two guns dismounted and a great number of men and horses dead.'

A shell blows up under Colonel Séruzier's horse and stuns him. 'Just as I was about to mount again, the brave General Montbrun, who'd seen me fall, comes up to me and asks whether I'm not wounded. I thanked him, telling him I'd got off with a mere bruise.' Colonels and generals falling like ninepins. And now it's Montbrun's turn. Riding up to his divisional general Pajol, he

'asks him how he feels, and whether he couldn't move over into a dip in the ground to his left. "But that's where the Vistula Legion are, so I can't. I've already sent someone to look." "Who?" "Biot." "Oh well," Montbrun replies, "let's go and have a look anyway." And there we were, passing along the front of our line. General Montbrun was to our right, flanking us toward the enemy, General Pajol in the middle, and to his left, on a front of three. Behind us came his escort, but none of his ADCs was at his side. Suddenly I hear a dull thud. "Someone's been wounded," I exclaimed. At the same instant General Montbrun rolls off his horse. A 3-pounder had hit him in his left side and remained in his body.'

Roos, working at his surgery only thirty yards away, sees him fall:

'Suddenly I saw General Montbrun turn pale and fall from his horse. I ran to help him. Two French doctors, who were closer than I was, got there first. The wound wasn't bleeding very much. He'd very quickly turned pale and yellow. His very lively look had been extinguished and we saw his strength gradually fail.'

Summoned to the spot, Larrey finds the roundshot has

'passed through the region of his kidneys from side to side. There was little to be done. Death was certain and not far off. I applied a dressing, and had him carried to a little village nearby. I'd run the greatest danger while attending to his wound, a cannon-ball having killed some horses behind us.'

From the dying Montbrun he goes to his colleague General Nansouty, who has 'a musket-ball in his knee'. But the handsome popular Montbrun won't even live long enough to open his wife's letter.

But the hardest nut of all to crack, key to the entire Russian position, is the Great Redoubt. To Dumonceau, waiting by his horse to see what role the lancer brigade is going to play in this murderous symphony, it looks like a 'volcano crowned with vapours, engaged in a violent artillery battle while a compact mob swarms round its base'. Now and then Marshal Bessières, walking to and fro in front of the Schevardino redoubt, comes and asks Pion des Loches whether he can't see a lot of movement there:

'I replied that I saw nothing, didn't even know where what he called the Great Redoubt lay; and His Excellency, I imagine, knew as little about it as I did, because if he had known he wouldn't have failed to indicate which direction it lay in. Each time he withdrew, muttering between his teeth: "We're going to have a lot of trouble to take that big redoubt!"'

Yet now it must be taken.

Although they're immobilizing him physically, neither Napoleon's thudding migraine nor his excruciating dysuria are evidently clouding his mind. For as soon as the threat to the left wing has been staved off he decides on a bold, unconventional stroke.

Its embrasures reduced (as Captain François had found out) to rubble under the crossfire of 170 guns, the Great Redoubt, unlike the flèches, is closed at the rear and in front by great walls of pointed stakes. Also, in front, by a deep ditch and wolfpits. But perhaps it can be carried through its 'throats', left open at each end, by a mass onslaught of heavy cavalry? It's nearly 3 p.m. And an all-out effort is to be launched.

Caulaincourt's brother Auguste having just returned from a mission to the right side of the field, Napoleon, hearing that Montbrun has fallen,[24] summons him and explains his idea.

While the whole of IV Corps, reinforced by Morand's and Gérard's divisions and under cover of maximum bombardment, mount a frontal assault, Latour-Maubourg's IV Cavalry Corps,[25] supported by Montbrun's II Cavalry Corps, are to feign an attack on the infantry masses which are supporting the redoubt on each of its sides. But at the last moment, Auguste Caulaincourt, animating and guiding the cuirassiers' movement, is to swing in at a right angle and try to force a way in through the redoubt's two open 'throats'. A highly unusual, if not unique, way of capturing a fieldwork!

Napoleon tells him: 'Go and do as you did at Arzobispo!'[26] And Belliard tells him to

'seize the moment when he'll see Gérard's infantry column beginning to mount the hill toward the redoubt. Forming a column of four regiments of cuirassiers and two of carabiniers, he's to lead it at a trot toward his right, leaving the redoubt somewhat to one side, as if about to attack the Russian cavalry corps in the plain to his right. Having given the infantry time to mount the slope, he's to turn swiftly to his left and, at the moment when he sees Gérard's troops are ready to storm the parapets, enter the redoubt at a gallop by the gorge, thus taking the enemy between two fires.'

Caulaincourt:

'The Prince of Neuchâtel sent him a written order for the divisional generals to see. My brother seized my hand, saying, "Things have become so hot that I don't suppose I'll see you again. We'll win, or I'll get myself killed."'

At this 'ominous farewell' the Master of the Horse is seized with a dreadful foreboding. But down in the plain[27] Griois, who so far hasn't seen any high-up except Eugène, is relieved to see Murat appear

'with his numerous and brilliant entourage. We were quite sure he'd put an end to a murderous cannonade which was leading to nothing and even slowing down for lack of ammunition, and that he'd dispose of enough troops at one and the same point to make a fresh and decisive attack. And in fact, having examined the situation and ridden over the terrain where, for several hours now, our cavalry was being crushed, he notices that the parapets of the central big redoubt have almost been wiped out by our gunnery.'

Biot has just dismounted to have the dying Montbrun carried to the rear, and Pajol has taken over his command, when one of Murat's ADCs comes galloping up. And gives the order to charge:

'"Let's go," said Pajol, "but someone'll have to make room for me to do so." The king, says the officer, has placed all the cavalry in front of him under Pajol's orders. In the front line, sheltered by a little hill, were the 12th Hussars, a Dutch regiment (Colonel Liegeard) and another chasseur regiment, whose number I don't remember.'

At 3 p.m. 'preparations for a charge,' Tascher notes in his diary. 'La Bourdonnais, etc., etc., wounded'. And Vossler:

'We were on the point of charging, but the enemy recoiled without waiting for the impact, leaving grapeshot from one side and solid cannon-balls from the other to tear through our ranks. In front of us a ravine had been taken by our troops. We followed quickly in their tracks, finding at the bottom of it some brief respite from the murderous fire. But upon breasting the other side we were hit at even closer range and with even greater intensity. For half an hour we were exposed to this murderous fire.'

The Vistula Legion, to the right, is to support the movement. General Claparède is standing in front of the grenadiers of its 1st Regiment in the dip in the ground that Pajol had envied, when an imperial ordnance officer gallops up and orders him forward. Crossing 'a thin rivulet of water [the Kolotchka] that ran across a great part of the battlefield' Brandt sees to his right 'immense struggles going on'; and, to his left, the 'huge mass of halted cavalry files where the enemy fire is making great breaches'. Everywhere the terrain is encumbered by many dead men 'but above all by killed and mutilated horses'. Farther away to his left Brandt glimpses the cupola of Borodino church, the sun flashing on its green tiles. But then the Poles halt again, deafened from all sides by a roar of musketry and artillery fire, and can see nothing.

Now Colbert's brigade, too, which all morning has been in reserve, is moving forward, also to support the movement; and the Red Lancers are beginning 'to be exposed to stray roundshot'. As they cross the Kolotchka they're allowed a moment to water their horses. The Vistula Legion, advancing again, crosses the Semenovskaya:

'Reaching the opposite height we saw an incredible dust. An immense clamour accompanied by an intense cannonade was shattering the air. The roundshot was passing over us and through our columns.'

And now, at last, the vast mass of heavy cavalry, the sun glittering on its plumed and horsetailed helmets and gleaming cuirasses, gets under way. Von Muraldt's men of the 4th Bavarian Lancers, watching from in front of

Borodino, 'can hardly believe their eyes'. In the van, charging up the highway from the village, are the two glamorous Carabinier regiments. After Semenovskaya had fallen Lariboisière and the artillery staff had retired behind Borodino; and as an infantry column comes by – presumably one of Gérard's – Lariboisière's son Ferdinand comes and shakes his hand, saying "we're going to charge". And a few moments later does so.[28]

In front of the village Labaume and the rest of Eugène's staff, too, are watching the mass onslaught. Von Muraldt notices that at this moment the sun breaks through, flashing on the mass of steel cuirasses:

'The whole eminence overhanging us appeared in an instant a mass of moving iron: the glitter of arms, the sun's rays reflected in the dragoons' helmets and on cuirasses mingled with the guns' flashes vomiting forth death from all sides made it seem like a volcano in the midst of an army.'

Lejeune, too, watching from Napoleon's command post, somewhat farther away, is reminded of a volcano:

'I couldn't be a spectator of these beautiful actions without also seeing it with a painter's eye, admiring the effect of these whirlwinds of dust and silvery smoke. A shell having set fire to a barrel of the resin the Russians use to grease their artillery's axles with, instantly purplish flames, coiling along the ground like the threshings of an irritated snake, rose to join the clouds, projecting broad zones of darkness across the sun. If I live to be a hundred, this moving picture [sic] will never efface itself from my thoughts.'[29]

Immediately, says Griois,

'everything opens up. The numerous cavalry forms up in columns, the II Corps' cuirassiers (they were, as far as I can recall, the 5th Cuirassiers) at their head, start to gallop. Overthrowing everything in front of them, they turn the redoubt, entering it by the throat [sic] and by the place where the earth that had rolled down into the ditches made it easier of access. At the same time the Viceroy, with his infantry, attacks the redoubt from the left.'

As the cavalry assault develops, Eugène's three infantry divisions, led by Gérard's, begins struggling up the slope against a gale of enemy grape. Sergeant Bertrand's 4th Carabinier Company of the 7th Light is

'suffering horribly. A roundshot took my captain's head off, killing or mortally wounding four men in the first rank. The lieutenant takes the captain's place; scarcely is he at his post than he's himself stricken by a piece of grape which shatters his thigh. In the same instant the sous-lieutenant's foot is shattered by another shell fragment. The officers hors de combat, the sergeant-major absent, I, as senior sergeant, take command of the company. We're at the foot of the redoubt, two of the regiment's battalions seem to be retiring by échelons, and the two others making an oblique movement. The colonel orders me not to budge. The reasons for his order are beyond me, but I'm proud to be commanding an élite company. My

musket on my shoulder, facing the redoubt and under grapeshot, I'm speaking to my comrades when suddenly a platoon of Russian dragoons emerges from it with a hurrah.'
Bertrand orders his company to form a circle around him,
'which is done in a flash. Without waiting for further orders my comrades open a rolling fire which costs the horsemen, already almost on our bayonets, dear. They vanish, and thanks to my comrades' presence of mind and courage help reached us. The [Russian cavalry] regiment returned toward the redoubt, but again we were forced to retire.'
But just as the leading division (Wathier's cuirassiers) are about to burst in through the northern throat, they're checked by a devastating volley from a Russian infantry formation, 60 yards to its rear. And Auguste Caulaincourt, at the head of the 5th Cuirassiers,[30] falls from his horse, dead, with a musket-ball just beneath the heart. Simultaneously IV Cavalry Corps, led by Zastrow's cuirassier squadrons, are either forcing their way in through the southern throat or else – like the 5th Cuirassiers – which 'because of their position found themselves facing the redoubt' -
'are crossing the ditch, mounting the gentle embankment and crushing the Russian infantry under the weight of its horses and sabring others, then riding against the supporting infantry beyond.'
Colonel von Meerheimb, in Lorge's cuirassier division, makes for the crumbled breastwork, scrambles in, through, and over the shattered embrasures and finds
'the cramped area inside filled with murderous cavalry and Russian infantry[31] thrown together pellmell and doing their best to throttle and mangle each other'.
In the event the leading files of Eugène's infantry, too, are able to scramble in over the shattered embrasures in the cavalry's wake:
'Major Del Fante, on the Viceroy's staff, at the head of the 9th and the 35th Line, turns the redoubt to its left and despite a valorous defence by the Russians, who are fighting desperately, penetrates it; but since the besieged won't surrender, there's the most terrible carnage. Del Fante himself, recognizing a Russian general – General Likatcheff – in the scrum – throws himself at him, disarms him, snatches him from the fury of the men and, in spite of him, saves his life,'
an exploit for which Eugène commends and promotes Dal Fante on the spot – 'a worthy reward', comments Césare de Laugier, 'that honoured at once the prince and the soldier.'
Looking through his telescope, Berthier declares: 'The redoubt's taken! The Saxons are inside!'
Prince Eugène, watching from his vantage point, is heard to exclaim 'The battle's won!' And the whole Italian army cheers. The Grand Redoubt is taken – but which unit has actually captured it? According to Colonel von Schreckenstein (who, being in the struggle himself, must

have heard it from some member of the staff) Napoleon takes 'the same telescope' from Berthier and looking through it declares: 'You're wrong. They're wearing blue, and must be *my* cuirassiers!' apparently forgetting that Laforge's Saxon and Polish cuirassiers also wear blue.

(And so, to the Saxons' and Poles' mortification, the imperial bulletin will determine the matter.)

Still in reserve, the Vistula Legion has halted again. But now it reaches the scene of action. And after the dust has abated somewhat Brandt too sees 'the French had taken the Great Redoubt, and the cavalry were fighting beyond it'. Moving forward in support, Brandt finds scenes around the redoubt that defy description:

'Men and horses, alive, mutilated, dead but lying by sixes and eights heaped on top of each other covered the approaches all round, filled the ditch and the work's interior. While we were advancing they were carrying away General Caulaincourt. He passed in front of us, carried by several cuirassiers on a white cuirassier mantle covered with great bloodstains.'

One of the officers who had brought the news of the redoubt's capture and of Auguste Caulaincourt's death is his ADC, Lieutenant Wolbert 'who'd not quitted his side'. Wolbert, says Castellane, 'came up sobbing'. His chief had been laid low, he tells an impassive Napoleon and a distraught Master of the Horse, 'just as he was coming out of the redoubt to pursue the enemy, who'd rallied at some distance and were rallying to retake it'. Ségur sees how Caulaincourt, is

'at first overcome, but soon steeled himself, and except for the tears that rolled silently down his cheeks, he appeared impassive. The Emperor said "You've heard the news; would you like to retire?" [or Castellane: "go to my tent"] accompanying these words with a gesture of sympathy. But at that moment we were going towards the enemy. The Master of the Horse merely lifted his hat slightly as a token of his gratitude and refusal.'

'He has died as a brave man should,' Caulaincourt will afterwards remember Napoleon as saying, 'and that is, in deciding the battle. France loses one of her best officers.'

But though the success is spectacular, it has a sinister feature. Almost no prisoners have been taken – 'at most a few Russian cavalrymen during our various charges, but I don't recall seeing a single officer taken prisoner,' a Saxon cuirassier will later recall.

Immediately sending several aides to check up on this worrying fact, Napoleon observes to Berthier: 'These Russians let themselves be killed like automata. There's no taking them alive. This doesn't help us at all. These citadels must be demolished by cannon.' But now, says Ségur,

'after the capture of the Great Redoubt he thought he ought to go and see for himself what to do next. I saw him mount his horse slowly and painfully. It was at that moment the old General Likatcheff, the redoubt's defender, was brought to him.'

Del Fante, his rescuer and captor, has brought him in person, 'together with fifteen other prisoners':

'The officer in charge of them [i.e., Del Fante] told the Emperor that they'd put up a gallant defence. The Emperor received the general well. Seeing his prisoner without his sword, Napoleon regretted that he'd been disarmed: "I respect the courage of the unfortunate too much, monsieur", he said, "not to give myself the pleasure of returning his arms to a brave man."'

Dedem – certainly no eye-witness – says that Likatcheff, 'though in his cups, replied with dignity'. But then something goes wrong. Turning to Del Fante, Napoleon asks for Likatcheff's sword – but is given his ADC's instead. 'He took it in his hand, and holding it out to him said: "Here's your sword."' But according to Soltyk, who's there to interpret,

'The Muscovite replied in a dry tone of voice, shaking his head: "Niet, niet", and persisted in refusing it from the Emperor's hands. A cloud passed over Napoleon's face, and turning to me: "What's he saying?" Having in my turn asked Likatcheff to explain his queer behaviour, he replied that it wasn't his sword, but his ADC's, who'd been captured with him; which I hastened to repeat to the Emperor. But already Napoleon's face had resumed its serenity. He smiled disdainfully, handed the sword back to the French [sic] ADC who'd brought him in, and with a gesture ordered the Russian general to be taken away. All this happened in a matter of moments. Only afterwards did I hear Likatcheff had a sword of honour, and didn't want to exchange it for his ADC's.'

In 'a weak and languishing voice' Napoleon tells Ségur

'to take care of him, listen to what he had to say, and then come and report it to him. After which, walking slowly away, he went on, doubtless in the same manner; for ten minutes later I rejoined him at no great distance. All I'd been able to get out of Likatcheff, deeply upset by his defeat, were the following words: "Ah, Monsieur le Général, what a disaster! Do you think your Emperor will let us go on being Russians?" When I repeated these words to the Emperor they made little impression on him, for all their singularity. It's true he'd just heard of the deaths of Caulaincourt and of Canouville, the one the brother of the Master of the Horse, the other of his quartermaster, the former killed by a musket-ball, the other by a piece of grapeshot in the forehead.'

Second-lieutenant *Mailly Nesle*,[32] a 20-year-old aristocrat in the 2nd Carabiniers – being an ADC to General Durosnel (since Witebsk aide-major-général of the cavalry), he hadn't charged with his regiment – is sent by him to General Jeannin, the commander of the Gendarmerie d'Elite, to tell him to get the Surgeon-major to embalm Auguste Caulaincourt's heart.

Although six of the redoubt's heavy pieces, incredibly, had been whipped out of it at the very last moment, not one of the Russian gunners has survived. They'd fought to the death. Not one had abandoned his guns. Inside the redoubt, amidst an incredible wreckage of men, guns and gun carriages,[33] Eugène's ADC Labaume finds

'the body of a Russian gunner decorated with three Crosses. In one hand he held a broken sword, and with the other was convulsively grasping the carriage of the gun he'd so valiantly fought with.'

Heinrich von Brandt, too, notices him – or is it another?

'By the entrance an elderly staff officer was leaning against one of the guns with a gaping head wound. Dead and mutilated men and horses lay six or eight deep. Their corpses covered the whole area at the gorges, filled the ditch and were heaped up inside. Most of the dead along the front of the redoubt were infantrymen. To the right and inside lay the bodies of cuirassiers in white and blue uniforms – Saxon Bodyguards, Zastrow Cuirassiers in yellow and black uniforms, and men from the 5th and, if I'm not mistaken, also the 8th Cuirassier regiments.'

Although the 2nd Cuirassiers, too, have been in the attack, they're one of the regiments which, by-passing the redoubt to its right, have galloped towards 'a line of Russian guns, supported only 60 or 80 metres away by a line of Russian cuirassiers and dragoons'. Sergeant-major Thirion is just wondering why this cavalry doesn't 'move to the front of its artillery to protect it' when his regiment's leading ranks almost come to grief – by tumbling headlong into a deep ravine:

'Typical of the terrain, it prevented us from getting at them. But we gave them proof of our desire to see them at close quarters by going down into the ravine to cross it; but the bottom was so swampy the first horses got stuck in the mud. So we had to get ourselves out again and draw up facing the enemy,'

whose guns are spewing a rolling fire of grape and caseshot at them.

'Rarely, I declare, have I found myself in so hot a spot. Immobile in front of the Russian guns, we see them loading the projectiles they're going to fire at us, can even make out the eye of the pointer who's aiming them at us, and we need a certain dose of sang-froid to stay put. Happily, they aim too high.'

For quite a while Thirion and his steel-clad comrades wait patiently for some infantry to turn up and open a path:

'Finally a Westphalian division puts itself behind us. Separated from the Russians by our two ranks of horses, it imagines itself under cover. But when we, by moving off by platoons to the right, open up a gateway for them to move ahead of us between each platoon, these poor Westphalians, partly recruits, surprised to find themselves so close to thundering guns and to see us making to move off, begin shouting: *"Wir bleiben nicht hier!"* [we're not staying here!], and try to follow our withdrawal, which obliges us to retrace our footsteps to support, or rather comfort, this infantry, at whose heels our horses were marching.'

This pushes the Westphalians down into the ravine,

'where the men's heads are more or less at a level with the terrain in front of them, and thus sheltered from the Russian guns, which can't aim so low. Immediately this infantry opens fire on the artillery and its supporting cavalry. And these troops, 60 metres away from the muskets, have no choice but to make a prompt retreat and are replaced by infantry which skirmish with these Westphalians of ours.'

The 2nd Cuirassiers have just formed up again among the copses when, somewhere behind him, Thirion hears someone plaintively calling out; and together with his adventurous friend Baffcop rides over to see what it can be:

'At the foot of an oak tree we find a young sergeant-major of light infantry who's lost his leg from above the knee and which is only attached to its calf by a little sliver of flesh. This courageous young man tells us he has several times tried to get up and walk, but can't because his foot is so heavy and dragging too painfully at the bit of flesh still attaching his foreleg to his thigh. He insists we shall rid him of this now more than useless limb.'

And so they do, making the best tourniquet they can with handkerchiefs taken from Thirion's knapsack. After fixing the fracture and

'helping the poor fellow to get up, we provided him with two muskets of which he made two crutches and left for the ambulance, saying, "Now I shan't want for courage. I'm saved."'

But Thirion fears he's losing too much blood for lack of a real tourniquet and will never make it. All this is in sad contrast to another death. While the regiment is drawn up there amid the copses, a young conscript falls into a panic and begs Thirion to let him retire,

'assuring me he'd be killed if I didn't. I try to reassure him by placing myself close to him, and more or less succeed. At that moment, exhausted and hungry – I'd eaten nothing since the previous day – I ask one of my comrades for a bit of bread, knowing he still has a little bit on him. He makes haste to share it with me. Just as I'm holding out my arm to take my share, a roundshot takes off my young cuirassier's head: the same shot has hit my left elbow and the bit of bread has fallen to the ground.'

Although his arm hurts dreadfully, Thirion inspects it and finds it's intact. Since it was lower than the poor conscript's head, the flying cannon-ball had passed just above it, and his elbow can only only have been hurt by a bit of his shattered helmet:

'Not wanting to lose my bit of bread, I picked it up on the point of my sword and, finding it soiled by a bit of the dead man's brains, had to remove the wet bit.'

Thirion has often heard of men having presentiments of their own death in battle, but this is the first and only time he'll ever hear a soldier beg to leave his post because he's sure he's going to be killed, and 'if it hadn't been my duty to keep the men in their ranks and encourage the young soldiers I'd have granted this poor young man's prayer'.

Meanwhile a furious artillery duel has begun over the captured redoubt. And very soon what's left of its rear parapet is being carried away 'like a breach'. Not many yards away Claparède's Poles are falling by dozens under the bursting shells and screaming roundshot. Dead and dying alike are being blown to pieces. By and by, though his officers 'naturally awaited death standing', Claparède orders his men to lie down. A grenadier who gets up to help a comrade immediately has his head blown off, spattering brains and blood on Brandt's tunic.[34]

'The battery closest to us had lost all its older officers. A very young one was commanding it and seemed delighted with his task.'

Oddly enough – very oddly, in view of their having lost so many gunners, dead or dying – not one of the French batteries has been silenced by enemy fire. And all, whenever they can distinguish friend from foe, are firing busily into a vast mass of struggling men, gradually melting away into folds in the terrain. All Brandt can see now is an unsupported line of guns 'stretching away as far as the eye could see'. No wonder Sorbier will afterwards remember the battle as a series of more or less unimpeded leaps forward by his artillery.

Each time that Ney or Murat have begged Napoleon to send in the Guard he has refused: 'I'm not going to have my Guard destroyed. When you're eight hundred leagues from France you don't wreck your last reserve.' But now, after stupendous efforts, the Great Redoubt has been captured; and things on the extreme right aren't going too badly either. Soltyk, in his suite, has seen

'a young officer, a Polish artillery lieutenant called Rostworowski, coming towards us. He was pale and his coat was covered in blood. He could hardly keep his horse. Sent by Poniatowski to Napoleon to tell him the village of Utitza had been occupied, one of this brave officer's arms had been broken by a musket-ball on the way, and he was losing a lot of blood. Yet he'd had the courage to carry out his mission. Scarcely had he arrived at the ambulance to have his wound attended to than he fainted.'

Various small trophies have also been brought in:

'A detachment of Polish cuirassiers brought a gun their regiment had captured. But these events were of secondary importance and had in no way drawn the great man's attention.'

What absorbs him now – Pion des Loches sets the time at 'about 4 p.m.' – is the state of affairs in the centre. And Napoleon mounts his third horse to ride forward and study the situation on the spot. After the Likatcheff incident von Roos sees him and his entourage as they approach from the rear and slowly cross the ravine where he has his first-aid station:

'This seemed to us to indicate that he was calm and satisfied. As yet we hadn't learnt to read those severe features which in all circumstances, no matter what, would always seem to us calm and cold.'

While on his way to a dressing-station – perhaps the same, perhaps not – Vossler, too, after having been hit by a ricochet on his 'helmet's brass chin-scale and knocked unconscious', sees him, 'somewhat cold and aloof'.

Meanwhile, on the plateau beyond Semenovskaya, a new and final struggle has started up – a huge and confused cavalry battle. At one moment the Saxon Life Guards go dashing after some Russian dragoons and past scattered Russian infantry who are taking pot-shots at them: and Lieutenant Roth von Schreckenstein, in the thick of it, sees how their colonel can't restrain them:

'I'd almost reached that part of the Saxon Life Guard regiment which was gradually giving up its pursuit of the Russian cavalry when my horse fell back, pierced by several case-shot bullets, fired from somewhere to my left. I looked around for another horse, but the ones nearest me had been wounded. One Russian horse which I did mount refused to move, even when I clapped spurs to it; so I was on the point of moving off on foot, pistol in hand, without really knowing which way to flee. I saw enemies on all sides, either because of an illusion due to fear or because they were really there.'

But again and again the cavalry divisions, with musket-balls 'screeching like rockets around their ears' find themselves up against unshakeable Russian squares. In ever-thickening dust clouds 'and hordes of riderless horses neighing with terror and with streaming manes among the dead and wounded' the struggle goes on and on. Inconclusively. For two more hours.

And still, unknown to the French, the Russians have a large, as yet unemployed artillery reserve. Its commander having been killed, it still hasn't fired a shot.

Neither do the cavalry's attacks and counter-attacks seem to be getting anywhere. At about 5 p.m. Captain Henri Beyle (Stendhal), no doubt well in the rear, out of cannon-shot and amid the baggage train, hears a certain Count Corner, 'a goodhearted man, twice decorated by Napoleon', say: 'Isn't this damnable battle ever going to end?'

But in fact it's dying away of its own accord. 'Only the guns kept firing.' By 6.30 or so a kind of stunned stupor seems to have fallen on both armies.

To straighten their front line, badly mauled but forming an exposed salient on its left, the Russians fall back some 1,500 metres, on to their second. Although 'His Majesty immediately set off at a gallop in front of the [Guard] cavalry to join the King of Naples in following up this success,' the French are in reality too utterly exhausted to pursue:

'The Emperor flattered himself that the Russians were going to hasten their retreat. In order to make out their movements he went with the sharpshooters. Balls whistled around him; but he'd ordered his escort to stay behind. "It's over," [he tells Caulaincourt. And adds considerately:] "Go and wait for me at headquarters." I thanked him, but remained with him. The Emperor was certainly running a great risk, as the fusillade became so lively that the King of Naples and several generals came hurrying up to urge him to retire.'

Although he wants to make a final effort to take the last remaining (third) Russian flèche and a fieldwork commanding the Moscow road, Berthier and Murat try to dissuade him. Besides it's too late in the day. Too many commanding officers have been killed. The Russians,

'though certainly retreating, were doing so in good order and showing an inclination to dispute every inch of the ground, irrespective of how much havoc our guns were wreaking in their ranks.'

Berthier and Murat also stress that

'the only chance of success would be to use the Old Guard, and that in the present circumstances success at such a price would really be a check, whilst failure would be a reverse that would counterbalance the entire success of the battle. The Emperor hesitated; then went forward once more to observe the enemy's movements for himself.'[34]

Caulaincourt, impressed by the 'determined mien of the freshly massing Russians', sees

'the Emperor come to a decision. He suspended the order to attack and contented himself with sending up supports, in case the enemy should attempt something fresh, unlikely as it was; for their losses too were immense. Nightfall put an end to the fighting. Both sides were so tired that in several places the firing ceased without any orders being given.'[35]

As dusk falls, Murat, afraid that his remaining cavalry won't even be up to resuming the battle, has recourse to a *ruse de guerre*. The shattered divisions – Thirion's is one of them – are ordered

'to mount, with a loud din of its trumpets, and when he passed along our front the cries of "Vive l'Empereur!" were to be as loud and strong as if it had been Napoleon himself who was in front of us. Never was real enthusiasm noisier! The aim: to make the enemy believe it was the Emperor who was there with the main body. Afraid we were going to attack them tomorrow, they wouldn't think of attacking.'

By now it's quite dark. A cold damp north wind is blowing over the wreckage of two shattered armies, the thousands of dead and dying. Shocked and shaken in a way they've never been before, the survivors know in their bones that the sacrifice has been in vain. The battle has been neither won nor lost. Which, 3,000 miles from France, is almost as bad as a defeat: 'This victory, instead of arousing any general rejoicing, filled us with grim forebodings.' Half of Vossler's 180 Prussian hussars have been killed or wounded. And he's only one of the many who realize that 'the Russians had withdrawn defeated, but by no means routed'.

During the battle von Muraldt's servant has found him a cow and prepared him a good dinner. But he finds he can't enjoy it. Even the normally sanguine Le Roy is 'so depressed' he can't 'swallow my dram of aquavit' – whether of the French or Russian variety, he doesn't say; but the flèches are strewn with Russian corpses, which Biot sees the French infantrymen 'disembarrassing of the bad brandy in their water-bottles.' Trying some 'of this terrible beverage' himself, he finds 'the pepper and vitriol tore your mouth off'.

Even the bloodsoaked acres that have been gained at such terrible expense are so thickly strewn with dead and wounded men and horses, debris and roundshot, it's virtually impossible to bivouac on them. And many units – for instance the Red Lancers, who haven't come under fire – are retiring behind the Kolotchka. Particularly shocking to Dumonceau as he rides back in the gloaming are the huge numbers of dead and dying horses:

'Some were complaining dolorously or, with no more than a breath of life left in them, giving their death-rattles, every now and again twisting themselves under some convulsive impression. One saw some which, though horribly disembowelled or mutilated, yet kept their legs, motionless, with hanging heads, drenching the ground with their blood, or else, straying painfully about in search of some grazing, dragging beneath them strips of shattered harness, intestines or a broken limb; or else lying stretched out at full length on the ground, now and then lifting their heads to look at their gaping wounds.'

The whole atmosphere is

'in tune with these lugubrious scenes. Sombre clouds spread a melancholy shadow over the plain which that morning had been so filled with uproar, so animated, but was now grim and silent. A few rare cannon-shots were still being exchanged in the distance, but these were only feeble partial engagements, among the dead, strewn all over the battlefield as far as the eye could see.'

The Belgian lancer captain's attention is specially captured by

'a Spanish or Portuguese sergeant, on account of his fine martial air. He seemed to have been shot in the middle of an access of hilarity and his features still bore the impression of it.'

On the fringe of the wood beyond the Schevardino redoubt Dumonceau's servant Jean, too, has as usual prepared him his dinner. Also 'a good bed of moss and leaves with its back comfortably against a tree trunk facing a great flaming fire'. Seen from here

'the army, like the enemy, seemed to have disappeared over the horizon. All we could see now were a few cavalry units on patrol to our right and, at the limit of the plain, facing us, a vast stretch of forest.'

Nearby, the Imperial Guard, bivouacked around its camp fires, is massed around the Emperor's tents. Lejeune sees all five of them have been raised

'at the foot of the field of battle. No doubt this was a token of victory. But the Russian army was still only a musket-shot away from us, and all our superior officers should have been taking measures to be able to begin again. Soon the night became very black, and little by little we saw too many fires being lit on either side not to give us serious preoccupations about another day's fighting on the morrow.'

Having replenished his ammunition and promoted new NCOs, Colonel Griois takes a walk over the battlefield. Most of all he's struck by the numbers of dead Russian cuirassiers:

'The resources of our ambulances, considerable as these were, didn't suffice, and the French wounded had to be given preference. Such wounded Russians as I saw, overcome by their sufferings and by the cold of the night, made no complaint. Nearly every wounded soldier was clasping a medallion or image of St Nicholas, which they kissed eagerly and this helped them to forget their pain.'

Every house still standing is packed with wounded, French and Allied. Labaume sees 'Borodino church, which stood alone and where everyone wanted to camp, filled with wounded whose limbs the surgeons had amputated'. Here as elsewhere wounded highs-ups and other privileged persons are getting priority treatment. And in the darkness Girod de l'Ain – luckily, though he's been as much in the thick of it as Ney himself, he hasn't suffered a scratch,[36] – finds his way back to General Dessaix's bivouac:

'In the midst of his own people and patiently supporting the pains from his wound, he immediately ordered me to draw up the report he had to send in to Davout, and signed it with his left hand.'

Although the spent roundshot which had stricken Davout's chief-of-staff in the lumbar region has left 'no exterior trace', inside, General Romoef – he whose style when writing to divisional generals on the eve of battle was so chivalrous and elegant – is a horrible mess. Larrey realizes the muscles are 'torn and reduced to a mush, the coxal bone and the corresponding lumbar vertebrae broken'. As he attends to him and other top brass he's thinking 'it's impossible to show more valour and courage than these honorable victims'.

At 10 p.m. Planet comes back to a 'tent the gunners had most artistically made of planks for Lariboisière' behind Borodino village. Inside he's horrified to find young Ferdinand lying there groaning. A few moments after he'd come and shaken his father's hand,

'he'd been hit by a mustket-ball while charging down the main Smolensk–Moscow road. After passing through his cuirass and whole body it had lodged itself between his flanks above the kidney.'

Ferdinand has had to wait before being picked up and brought here. Yvan, the Emperor's surgeon, has extracted the missile; but the pain of the operation was and is agonizing. And now he's running a dangerously high temperature.

Yet he's privileged, even so. Where the rank and file are concerned, Lejeune sees

'the wretched wounded dragging themselves toward Kolotskoië, where Baron Larrey had set up his ambulance. Those for whom there were means of being picked up were being carried there. In no time there was an immense number. But everything was lacking at once.'

Captain Francois, among the thousands being taken there – always on the principle 'officers first' – finds himself in the company of

'27 officers from our regiment, five of them amputated, lying on straw or on the floor, lacking absolutely everything. Every room was full of wounded,'

– altogether more than 10,000, he thinks. As for the rest of the 30th's casualties 'they're up there in the redoubt'. In the 7th Light, Sergeant Bertrand's carabiniers have come and presented him with a 'certificate, declaring what I'd done during the battle'. Unlike so many comrades he's counting himself lucky to have got off with a light musket wound in his shoulder 'thanks to the buckle of my pack', when suddenly, though the fighting is over, a musket-ball out of the dark knocks off his shako and kills 'a sergeant, my compatriot, dead. We weren't slow to discover the assassins, hidden in a big hole in the middle of a little ravine. We did justice on them with two balls and our bayonets.'

Lieutenant Maurice Tascher, also miraculously untouched, is spending the night carrying water to the wounded. At one moment he's startled to see a half-buried Russian getting out of his grave. All sorts of gruesome things are happening in the cold wet windy night. Other Russians are roaming about in the darkness. When Colonel von Meerheimb, of the Saxon Guard, who'd been surrounded and knocked unconscious at the storming of the Great Redoubt, comes to, he realizes he's being plundered by some of his Russian colleagues. Fortunately, a French-speaking officer and an elderly grey-haired Russian cuirassier intervene and drive them away:

'The old man bound up my head with a cloth, lifted me on to a second horse, took it by the bridle, and led me carefully and patiently through a birch copse. Whenever he met any of the armed peasants who constituted a reserve militia for transporting, escorting and guarding prisoners, he always made a detour, explaining that it was dangerous to fall into their hands. I became very weak and could barely keep myself up in the saddle. But he kept telling me not to lose heart and frequently called out *Hauptquartieru nie daleku!* which meant, as I later discovered, that headquarters wasn't very far away. He seemed to take special pleasure in my helmet, which he'd taken as booty. The good man probably believed it was made of gold and would ensure him a carefree existence in old age.'

Taken to a Russian field ambulance, Meerheimb is cared for by a Swiss surgeon named Bernhardt, together with many wounded Russian officers. In the middle of the night Brandt's Poles, too, are attacked, this time by some Cossacks. But they're on the *qui vive* and give them a hot reception. Later still Cuirassier-captain Bréaut des Marlots speaks for about two hours with a Russian flag of truce:

'We asked each other what we thought about the war. "We know as well as you do we're going to be beaten," he said. "All we're hoping for is salvation in the winter which will amplify your troubles. Winter and hunger will be the arms against which your courage will give in. Believe me, I know my country's climate, I hope it won't have any malignant effect on you personally."'

As for the Great Redoubt, a Cossack patrol probing about in the darkness is surprised to find it's been abandoned.[37]

At 11 p.m. Napoleon calls for an orderly officer. It's Lejeune's turn. He finds that everyone at IHQ is in 'a heavy sleep. Three hours before daybreak he sent for me and said: "Go and find the Viceroy. Reconnoitre the Russian line to his front with him and come back at once and tell me what's going on."'

It's 8 September.

CHAPTER 22

THE BUTCHER'S BILL

'This theatre of carnage' – Dutheillet misses his Cross – 'Honour his ashes' – an obstinate rearguard – 'The Emperor was very thoughtful and worried' – Dedem distributes brandy – 'Only the Emperor's pen and mallet make themselves heard' – Lejeune's unwelcome promotion – miseries of the wounded – Planat tots up figures – 'he was hardly eighteen years old' – one barrel of flour for 26 wounded generals

Next morning 'under a leaden sky and a cold rain driven by a violent wind' Napoleon rides out over the battlefield. Ségur is in his suite. Slowly they ride over the terrain. It's so thickly strewn with corpses[1] that

'it was impossible, no matter how careful one was, always to walk one's horse on the ground. The Emperor, I saw, was still ill, and the only animated gesture I saw him make was of irritation. One of our horses, striking one of these victims, had drawn a groan from him, alas it was I who'd caused it. Upon one of us remarking that the dying man was a Russian, the Emperor retorted: "There are no enemies after a victory!" and immediately had Roustam pick the man up and give him to drink from his own brandy flask which the mameluke always carried on him.'

Passing at the charred ruins of Semenovskaya, they see how

'the whole ploughed up plain, strewn with wreckage and debris and hemmed in by gloomy dark trees, conspired to give the field a dreadful aspect. Everywhere soldiers were wandering about among the corpses, rifling their dead comrades' packs for food. Russian musketballs were bigger than ours so the wounds of the fallen were terrible. The Russian wounded sat stoically clutching their St Nicholas' crosses as they'd done at Smolensk, or else tried to hobble away in the wake of the Russian army. The Emperor carefully examined every bit of the battlefield, each corps' positions, their movements, the difficulties they'd had to surmount. At each point he asked for minute details of everything that had happened. Arriving at the second flèche, he noticed some 60 or 80 men, with four or five officers. Astonished to find these men still standing there when the rest of the troops had gone on ahead, he asked the officer in charge, an old campaigner, why he was there.

"I've been ordered to stay here," was the answer. "Rejoin your regiment," said the Emperor.

"It's here," replied the officer, pointing to the redoubt's approaches and ditches. Not understanding what he meant, the Emperor asked again:

"I want to know where your regiment is. You must join up with it."

"It's here!" the officer replied, pointing to the same spots, and betraying his own annoyance at the Emperor's failure to comprehend him.'

Only when a young subaltern explains does he understand. The battalions, unable to hold the redoubt they'd stormed so impetuously, had been wiped out. Labaume too is inspecting the battlefield. Everywhere he sees 'mounds of wounded, and the little spaces where there weren't any were covered with debris of arms, lances, helmets or cuirasses, or by cannon-balls as numerous as hailstones after a violent storm.'[2]
But the most terrible sight of all is the interior of the ravines. The wounded who have crawled there to avoid further exposure are
'piled up on top of each other, lacking all succour and swimming in their own blood, groaning terribly. Begging to be allowed to die, they asked us to put a term to their horrible sacrifice. There weren't enough ambulances. There was nothing anyone could do for them.'
As Napoleon enters the Great Redoubt, Bausset notices how 'two of our party, yielding to a very natural grief, aren't following him. 'Tears in their eyes, M. de Caulaincourt and M. de Canouville turned away from the spot that contained the glorious remains of their brothers.' For quite a while Lieutenant Brandt, who's still standing nearby, can observe the Emperor, 'his eyes fixed on this theatre of carnage', at close quarters. On his calling over one of his suite and saying something to him,
'this officer at once went into the redoubt with some chasseurs, whom he arranged in a square, so as to circumscribe a little area within which they counted the dead. The same manoeuvre was repeated at various points; and I realized that by this sort of mathematical operation they were trying to get an approximate idea of the number of victims. During this time the Emperor's face remained impassive, only he was very pale.'

The butcher's bill is horrendous. In a letter to his *belle amie* in Paris – a letter the Cossacks will capture – the 25th Line's clothing officer, a certain Lieutenant Paradis, writes with pardonable exaggeration: 'I've counted 20 Russians dead for each Frenchman. The battles of Austerlitz, Iéna, Eckmühl and Wagram didn't come up to this.' The Russian army has certainly lost a third of its effectives. And on the French side some 30,000 men haven't survived to tell their grandchildren they've been at the great battle 'under the walls of Moscow'.

Never have so many generals been killed in a battle. Inspector of Reviews Deniée, totting up the losses, finds among the casualties no fewer than 49 generals – fourteen generals of division, 33 generals of brigade, 37 colonels,[3] 37 staff officers and 86 ADCs.

The cavalry's losses are especially disastrous. In Maurice Tascher's chasseur regiment 280 men had mounted their horses at dawn yesterday. But after standing motionless for eight hours being slaughtered by cannonfire it has lost ten officers and 87 troopers killed, wounded or dismounted. Heinrich von Roos sees Vossler's regiment ride by – reduced to three officers and 20 men. As Vossler confirms:

'Of the 180 men the regiment had been able to muster that morning half were either dead or wounded. The general commanding our division, General Waltier, and the brigadier of our brigade, as well as their seconds-in-command, had all been wounded and another senior divisional staff officer killed.'

Losses in the infantry regiments are no less appalling. The 7th Light's carabinier company reports 37 men killed, wounded or missing. Many units are all but wiped out. Dutheillet's heroic 57th has lost

'almost 1,400 men, 600 already having been put out of action on 5 September. More than 50 of its officers had been killed or wounded; the colonel had had two horses killed under him.'

Of all the army corps Junot's Westphalians are among the worst hit. Initially 17,000 men and 3,500 horses strong at the Niemen, by nightfall, having lost 59 NCOs and soldiers killed, 580 wounded, five more officers killed – including the officer commanding its infantry, 'a magnificent soldier, a benevolent commander and a gentleman in the real sense of the word' – it has dwindled to a mere 1,300 combatants.

Montbrun's death seems in some way to strike everyone as quite specially ominous – perhaps because it doesn't even figure in the imperial bulletin? Instead it's Auguste Caulaincourt who's been singled out to be the hero of the occasion. Whether to console his grief-stricken brother or because he meant it, Napoleon told him the previous evening: 'He was my best cavalry officer. He had a quick eye and he was brave. By the end of the campaign he'd have replaced Murat.' Once again it's Lejeune who has to arrange the funeral:

'When I climbed up the Great Redoubt to check up on the state of the position which had so occupied us the day before, I found our men working on the burial of their numerous comrades and officers. Caulaincourt was placed in the middle of their entrenchment and I placed the brave Vasserot beside him. All one side of his face had been carried away without destroying or even changing the animated expression on the other part, which still seemed to be ordering his men to fire: "Friends, follow me! We'll be victorious!" I had these two bodies covered with a great number of pieces of the wreckage of armaments, muskets, cuirasses, as I'd already done for General Gudin.'

But Montbrun has many personal friends. And one of them, old Marshal Lefèbvre, commanding the Guard infantry, has a wooden noticeboard erected to honour this man whom Vossler describes as his

'dear and gracious general, a man as kind and considerate to his subordinates as he'd been brave in war, and who, though he'd won all his decorations in battle, had yet miraculously escaped being wounded until the day of his death.'

The noticeboard, 'a rough board, erected on a staff, bore a monumental inscription in his honour, written in ink, after the hurry of the day was over':[4]

HERE LIES GEN MONTBRUN
PASSER-BY OF WHATEVER NATION,
HONOUR HIS ASHES.
THEY ARE THE REMAINS OF
ONE OF THE BRAVEST OF THE BRAVE,
OF GENERAL MONTBRUN.
THE DUKE OF DANZIG
MARSHAL OF FRANCE
HAS ERECTED THIS MODEST MONUMENT IN HIS HONOUR.
HIS MEMORY WILL LIVE FOR EVER IN THE HEARTS
OF THE GRAND ARMY.

Other survivors are interring less illustrious, if not less well-liked comrades. Von Muraldt and his fellow-Bavarians, despite the Russian gunners
having aimed too high, have suffered such losses and their 'officers are so
exhausted' that they find they're being commanded by the brigade
sergeant-major (von Muraldt himself is astounded to hear he's one of six
in his regiment who've been recommended for the Cross, 'a distinction
the more flattering as I was its youngest subaltern'). It is dreadful for
them to have to bury

'the mangled remains of our sergeant-major, whom we'd all been so
fond of. At dawn we dug a hole and laid his mangled corpse in it,
which we after some difficulty had found on the battlefield – an honour admittedly not accorded to many of the innumerable dead lying
scattered in this area.'

Although certainly no necrophile, Boulart too takes a look over the terrible field:

'The ground was piled high, it was hard to move without stepping on
corpses, the ground was so thick with them. Between the redoubts,
the lines of battle, whole squares were traced by the dead or
wounded left there.'

The dead at least are at rest. For the thousands of wounded there's only
suffering. An anonymous officer is appalled to see how there's

'virtually no sanitary service or activity. All the villages and houses
close to the Moscow road were packed full with wounded in an
utterly helpless state. The villages were destroyed by endless fires
which ravaged the regions occupied or traversed by the French army.
Those wounded who managed to save themselves from the flames
crawled in their thousands along the high road, seeking some way to
prolong their pitiful existence.'

Dr Réné Bourgeois is horrified to see that there is

'no real ambulance equipment, no pharmacy where one could obtain
the means of preparing the wounded for their operations or assure
their success. On the battlefield the surgeons had to rip up the
wounded men's own clothes for bandages to give them first aid, after

which they remained all jumbled up and heaped together with several thousand others.'

'Nothing was sadder than other aspects of this battlefield,' Lejeune concludes,

'covered with groups busy picking up 20,000 wounded and taking from the dead such little food as might be left in their knapsacks. The wretched wounded were dragging themselves toward Kolotskoië, where Baron Larrey had set up his ambulance. Those for whom there were means of being picked up were being carried there. In no time there was an immense number. But everything was lacking at once, and they perished, victims of hunger, regretting they hadn't suffered the same fate as those whom death had carried off immediately.'

After Larrey has checked up on the condition of his top-brass patients in the Schevardino Redoubt, Compans and Teste want to get away from there as fast as ever they can – somewhat naturally, since of the 'fourteen of us closely packed in this little redoubt the previous evening, next morning after M. Larrey had been ordered by the Emperor to visit wounded generals, we found ourselves surrounded by twelve corpses.'

Once again everyone is astounded at the enemy's orderly retreat. While realizing that the Russians have 'had no option but to leave many wounded on the battlefield' Colonel Roth von Schreckenstein is 'of the opinion any other army would have left twice as many'. 'A very small number of stragglers had been rounded up; the enemy hadn't abandoned so much as a cart. The enemy had taken with them most of their wounded and we had only a few prisoners, twelve guns from the redoubt plus three or four other pieces taken during our troops' initial assault. The Russians had shown the utmost tenacity. Their ranks hadn't broken. Never had ground been attacked with greater fury or skill, or more stubbornly defended.'

And still, six miles away to the east, can be heard the obstinate rumble of Russian guns.

After completing his survey of the battlefield, Napoleon, with Caulaincourt as usual at his heels, 'galloped off to the advance guard'. Consisting of two cuirassier divisions, several light cavalry regiments and – as always – what had been Friant's infantry, it's advancing slowly through the big forest between Borodino and Mojaisk. On the 'cold windswept battlefield', meanwhile, Colonel Boulart has has taken refuge from this 'first attack of the bad season under my wagon, or rather, in my tent'. There he's sharing a meagre breakfast with d'Hautpoul ('who, though accustomed to a much better one, adapted to it very well') and he's just giving Berthier's ADC some scraps of useful information when the two of them have 'a moment of emotion'. Away to the right a Cossack 'Hurrah!' is heard.

319

Colbert's combined lancer brigade, 'diagonally traversing the battle-field, which was like a desert' and where 'only a few ambulance wagons were busy picking up the wounded and others were being used to carry away a vast quantity of weapons which had been collected', also hear a rumour that a *coup de main* has been attempted against imperial head-quarters, causing the Guard to spring to arms. Alarm over, the Dutch and Polish Lancers resume their way onwards through the 'cold foggy weather' toward Mojaisk, crossing as they do so the scene of Poniatowski's action. 'Not very many dead,' Dumonceau notes, 'and they much scat-tered, compared with what I'd seen on the main part of the battlefield'.[5]

To judge from the distant rumbling of the guns the Russian rearguard is putting up a stiffer resistance than anyone has thought possible.

Friant's division, now shrunk to only two brigades, is still under Murat's orders. Friant himself being *hors de combat* his command has temporarily passed to General Dufour. They've set out in the early hours. And I Corps' other units are following on behind.

Never a man to stay long in the dumps, Le Roy is finding the cool night air is helping him forget his 'sad reflections on the ambition and vanity of conquerors'. At the same time Dutheillet is surprised to find that the excitement of battle, combined with his superiors' praises and his com-rades' esteem, is curing him of his 'dysentery'. Best of all he's been rec-ommended for a full lieutenancy and the Cross. By 10 a.m. the 57th, too, are under arms:

'Each of us is expecting the Emperor, when an adjutant comes to tell our general we're to gulp down our soup and follow the army's movement. So we pocket our ambition until the next opportunity and follow on as cheerfully as may be.'

As usual the 7th Hussars are in the van. The Russian rearguard's sharp-shooters, Victor Dupuy notices, are gradually reducing their fire when

'a musket-ball, striking the boss of Colonel Gobrecht's horse, rico-cheted and struck me on the tip of my right elbow. I felt a very sharp pain, but it was nothing, the skin was hardly broken. But my right arm turned completely black.'

At first Griois, emerging from the 'broad and well-maintained road through the vast forest of pines and birches' which it's taking III Cavalry Corps almost two hours to cross, assumes that Mojaisk, lying on the River Moskova in the centre of a vast 'pronouncedly sloping plain, criss-crossed by ravines', will be a walkover. A view evidently shared by Murat. For with-out properly reconnoitring the terrain, but supporting his gravely dimin-ished squadrons with Griois' gunfire, he throws them forward – only to have them brought up short by some ravines, which force them to retrace their steps under almost point-blank Russian grapeshot:

'The cavalry lost a lot of men in this affair. That of III [Cavalry] Corps, though only in the second line, suffered from the artillery fire it was constantly exposed to.'[6]

But orders are orders. And Mojaisk is to be occupied before nightfall 'because the Emperor wishes to establish himself there'. And now Boulart's guns, too, are moving up, with orders to 'to go and take up position a mile and a half away, toward Mojaisk'. But Mojaisk is proving surprisingly hard to take. Although Dedem's two regiments manage to lodge four voltigeur companies in its suburbs, the Russians are clinging on stubbornly while they evacuate as many as possible of their wounded.

But now night is falling, and Boulart is told to wait until 'daybreak to attack the heights beyond the town'. And Ségur, sent forward no doubt to set up 'the Palace' in the little town, is returning, mission not accomplished, when he narrowly misses being hit by a bouncing roundshot. He's just exchanging some words with Marshal Mortier when he sees

'a solitary person, on foot, in a grey overcoat, on the other side of the road. Head down, he was walking painfully toward Mojaisk. Crossing the road and placing myself in front of him, I observed that it was on fire. Slowly raising his head, he replied: "So the Russians are still holding out in Mojaisk?" Daylight was just coming to an end, and I pointed out to him the camp fires of some 40,000 men, behind the town and dominating it. The Emperor, in a voice as languishing as his whole posture, swung round heavily, as it were all in one piece, and said to me: "If that's the way of it, let's wait until tomorrow!"'[7]

With the same tired dejected air ['*abattement de démarche*'] Napoleon goes back to spend the night in a ruined village called Ukarino, on the forest fringe, 'at the point where the plain opens out in front of Mojaisk'. But when the Guard turns up, it finds Ukarino (or is Deniée right in thinking its name is Starokowno?) already occupied by the 23rd Dragoons who have spent the dreary day 'picking up leaves and cutting pine branches' to give their horses something to eat. After leaving the battlefield at 4 p.m. they're just settling down for the night in the village when the Guard 'which so far hadn't fired a shot' comes and ejects them. 'We were irritated with them and they had to resort to force to make us leave the village; not that they'd profit from it very long,' Auvray adds with relish, 'because it caught fire on all sides'.

Meanwhile a 'hurricane of snow' has suddenly begun to fall. And when Colbert's lancers, too, reach their appointed bivouac they refuses to share their 'sad camp fires' with a regiment of Saxon cuirassiers, even though it was they who'd stormed the Great Redoubt.

At IHQ, with the first light snow whirling around Ukarino's log dwellings, everyone is noticing the Emperor is

'very thoughtful and worried. Yet he kept saying "Peace lies in Moscow. When the great nobles see us master of their capital they'll think twice before fighting on. The battle will open my brother Alexander's eyes, and the capture of Moscow will open his nobles'."'

At the same time he's sure yesterday's battle, unparalleled in his or anyone else's experience, won't 'have any result beyond allowing him to gain further ground. The prospect of entering Moscow still enticed him; but even that wouldn't be conclusive as long as the Russian army remained intact.' And that's the hard fact of the matter, which won't go away. Though he and Berthier have hardly been on speaking terms since their tiff, five days ago, over Narbonne's carriage, since the battle he's spoken to no one else:

'From what the Prince told me, he kept repeating that a large number of men had been killed to no real purpose. No prisoners, no booty – that was what chiefly vexed him and formed the constant burden of his complaints. The state of affairs in Spain, too, was weighing him down just when those in Russia were so far from satisfactory, and he was deeply preoccupied. The condition of the various corps he'd seen was deplorable. All were sadly reduced in strength. His victory had cost him dear. One moment he was imagining signing a peace on the spot, which would give some indication of his victory. The next he wanted to go on to Moscow, stay there a week, then retire on Smolensk.'

But Caulaincourt and Berthier, once again, are agreed: the only thing to do is to quit Moscow 48 hours after entering it and go back to Witebsk.

Although the cold night is marked by 'some sustained firing', Dedem, in the outskirts of Mojaisk, is waiting for dawn to carry out his mission. 'As soon as daylight revealed our bivouacs, a masked battery opened fire from the cemetery'. Hearing Dedem's musketry at first glimmer of daylight (7 a.m.) Boulart's gunners, too, run to their pieces – though as yet they can only see 300 or 400 metres ahead of them, 'only the town, no enemy'. Only to find the Russians have

'retired during the night; their rearguard was still visible on the high ground beyond the town, being followed by our scouts'.

After what Fain calls 'quite a sharp action', Dufour's division advances in two columns, which join up and occupy the town. Part of it is in flames. But not all. And Dedem is happy to find the fire hasn't yet reached 'a big store of brandy' which, despite 'a swarm of Cossacks caracoling about the place', he promptly distributes

'to the advance guard's various units, even though some of Berthier's aides, as usual, had come to order it to be reserved for the Imperial Guard'.

After enjoying their share in the Mojaisk ravine his division debouches on to the plateau beyond the town, and after a mile and a half's march finds itself faced with an 'enemy rearguard in line of battle', whose guns are shelling the burning town to give the Russian baggage train time to draw off. Even so, they're having to abandon 'large numbers of their wounded, both from the battle and from this new action', to perish in the flames in Mojaisk's streets and gardens.

One of the first staff officers to enter Mojaisk with the light cavalry patrols is Planat de la Faye. He has an urgent errand. Not merely to find a house where the artillery staff can do its paperwork – always immense after a battle – but which can also provide shelter for poor young Ferdinand:

'We'd brought him with us, carried in a litter by four gunners. Just as I was writing up General Lariboisière's name on the door of a house in Mojaisk's first side street on the right a shell fell close to me. I just had time to fling myself inside the house – and the shell exploded, but hurt no one.'

What it has done, however, is scatter his competitors, who are 'snatching lodgings from each other. Many ADCs were getting so violent towards one another that anywhere else it'd have ended in duels. The house was very small and rather dirty. But to us, compared with the places we'd lain down in these last few days, and above all with our cold bivouacs at Borodino, it seemed a palace. Ferdinand was given a little room to himself and confided to the cares of our surgeon, a man called Gudolle – quite a good sort of a fellow, but a terrible chatterbox who, I fancy, knew very little.'[8]

Surgeon Trastour, too, working heroically for his wounded, has arrived with Compans, in his carriage, and Teste in his calèche, and manages to find them quarters in a house where Friant, Dessaix and many other wounded generals have already installed themselves.

In the main square, on the left-hand side, is 'a new house, not quite completed, which the palace quartermaster had noticed on reaching the square. It hadn't any doors, but the windows could be closed'. But it has stoves that can be lit. And this, in view of Napoleon's ever-worsening cold, decides the matter. Occupying the upper storey at noon, 'no sooner has he settled into this lodging than he wants to resume the office work, suspended for the past five days'. But here's a contretemps:

'He'd lost his voice completely. In this embarrassing situation he had recourse to his pen. Resigning himself to it, he sat down and began covering sheets of paper with all the orders teeming in his head. His secretaries, Méneval and Fain, the office vassals, d'Albe, Mounier and Ponthon[9] copy at top speed.'

Even Daru and Berthier have to lend a hand,

'but at every line we're held up by some difficulty of decipherment. Yet the Emperor, who minute by minute is finishing one order after another, bangs unceasingly on the table for us to come and take the drafts that are piling upon it.'

Whatever Dr Yvan may say about the usual effects of his bladder complaint, it's obvious that neither his energy nor his clarity of mind are suffering:

'"Reconnoitre the town and trace out a redoubt to cover the defile" – "Have two bridges built over the Moskova river" – "Write to Eugène, ordering him to go to Rouza and build bridges at Sergiewo" – "Collect plenty of cattle and victuals" – "Tell Ney to come here tomorrow with his corps" – "Leave the Duke of Abrantès to guard the battlefield."'

Fain scribbles and scribbles. Even the French bishops aren't forgotten. They're to

'have Te Deums sung for the victory! The whole day passes in these silent labours, where only Napoleon's pen and mallet make themselves heard.'

As always after a great battle numberless promotions have to be approved, at all levels. His chief-of-staff Ramoef having died under the surgeon's knife, Davout has asked for Lejeune to succeed him,

'news which would have flattered anyone else but which I found utterly distasteful. I insisted the Major-General shouldn't follow up this request. But that same evening the Emperor had the commission given to me, signed by himself, and I could only obey. I found the Marshal in his tent on the Moscow road.'

But before Lejeune can take up his new and, as he rightly fears, onerous duties, he has some other writing to do. And goes up into a house

'whose street and courtyard were choc-a-bloc with wounded horses which, though still alive, couldn't get to their feet. When I came down an hour later I was astonished to find all these horses had been dismembered, and their flesh in great part removed. It was the first time we'd seen the men eating horse flesh'

– men from the 23rd Dragoons perhaps, who're beginning to be 'without clothes, without shoes, and without food. Those days we were reduced to eating uncooked cabbages and horse.' But Lejeune goes off to join Davout's headquarters on the Moscow road. One of his colleagues on Berthier's staff has also been promoted. Among the many colonels either dead or *hors de combat* is Colonel Massy, of the 4th Line. Berthier, Fézensac says, was always good to his ADCs.

Up in his first-storey room overlooking the main square, where the Old Guard infantry is bivouacked, Napoleon – however inadequately – is first and foremost occupied with making arrangements for the wounded. A Colonel Bourmont is to remain behind to see to it that they're all picked up. Bourmont will have to search for food for fifteen miles around. And it'll take Dr Réné Bourgeois a whole week and more to help him collect them all,

'both French and Russian, for whom there was, even so, no ambulance equipment and no pharmacy where one could obtain the means of preparing the wounded for their operations or assuring their success.'

There's also a grave shortage of surgical instruments: 'these instruments existed and could have been used, had their transportation and care not been exclusively deputed to individuals wholly foreign to this art'. And in the little house off the main street where Planat and his clerk Cailly are busily totting up

'the all too many items used up, lost or deteriorated after a great battle, putting the matériel into condition again and hastening up the ammunition, replacing killed officers and preparing the work of recompenses and promotions,'
poor young Ferdinand Lariboisière, in the other room, is sinking in agony to imminent death:
'Although I'd known him but slightly, I'd taken a great liking to him. There was something gay, chivalrous and generous about him, which pleased everybody. A charming young man, as frank and loyal as could be. Truly born to the military estate, he'd just come from the pages. I believe he was hardly eighteen years old.'
And when in the afternoon of 12 September IHQ moves on,
'having got certain knowledge of the exact figure of the losses suffered by both armies, the enemy's movements, the quality of the victuals, the state of the administration, of the imminent arrival of the route battalions and Smolensk squadrons, and made quite sure the ammunition consumed was already replaced,'
Lariboisière, together with his chief-of-staff General Charbonnel, lingers for a few hours 'waiting for his son to yield up his last breath'. Obliged at last to tear himself away, he asks Planat to stay
'until his last moment. About 4 p.m. the poor young fellow, who'd been groaning from his wound ever since morning, began to rattle and suffer convulsive spasms that heralded his end. Ferdinand then opened his eyes a moment, put one arm around my neck and, a moment afterwards, died.'
Almost suffocated with grief, the sensitive Planat informs the father. 'The general squeezed my hand and a few moments later left to rejoin the Emperor.' Entrusted with the boy's funeral, that night Planat receives a note written in the handwriting of his friend and fellow-ADC, Honoré Lariboisière. His brother's heart is to be taken out and preserved:
'After allowing twenty-four hours to pass, Gudolle opened up the corpse and, in my presence, extracted the heart, for me a very terrible and dolorous spectacle. This heart was placed in a little beaker of spirits of wine,'
and the corpse itself in a rough-and-ready coffin,
'nailed together by the workmen of the Engineer Corps. In it I enclosed a scroll of strong paper, on which I'd written these words: "The body of Ferdinand Gaston de Lariboisière, lieutenant of Carabiniers, killed at the Battle of the Moscowa, Sept. 1812. His father recommends his remains to the public piety." The funeral took place at nightfall, without any religious ceremony, we having no priest with us.[10] A detachment of 25 gunners commanded by a lieutenant escorted the coffin. To secure it from any profanation we'd dug a ditch in the old town wall, of Tartar construction, which was in ruins. Enormous stone blocks had been displaced and were afterwards put back again on top of the coffin, with such care it was

impossible to see what had been done. Yet if I were to visit Mojaisk I could still point to the spot where Ferdinand is buried.'

IHQ having moved on, Planat sends a lock of Ferdinand's hair to his brother, together with his heart and his belongings.

Mojaisk is indeed full of dead, wounded and dying men, both Russians evacuated from the battle and also an ever-growing number of Frenchmen, notably senior officers. Arriving there on 10 September, the Flemish war commissary Bellot de Kergorre had settled in at first as best he could in the Guard's bivouac on the main square; but has immediately had been detailed off to feed all these sufferers:

'Bandaged with hay and groaning dreadfully, they lived for the first few days on the few grains they could find in the straw they were lying on and the little flour I was able to give them. When soup was made it had to be taken to them, but we'd nothing to put it in! Providentially I came upon a fair number of little bowls intended for lamps, so we were able to give our patients some water. The lack of candles was a terrible privation.'

After distributing a little food that evening by the smoky light of a flaming pine torch, Kergorre is horrified to find he has lost

'some men who, hidden in the straw, had been overlooked. A shocking thing was the impossibility of removing the dead from among the living. I'd neither medical orderlies nor stretchers. Not only the hospital but also the streets and houses were full of corpses.'

One of these wounded is Captain Aubry of the 12th Chasseurs. His boot has been ripped off his leg by the roundshot which has also deprived him of his toes. Little consolation to hear that his wound is unique and that the surgeon at the field hospital has "never seen one like it!" Lying there in the straw in Mojaisk

'I'd quite enough to do driving off people who came too close. The stirring of the least blade of straw around me caused me atrocious pain. The famous Dr Larrey and his surgeons had made so many amputations at Mojaisk that there was a heap of legs and arms so big a large room couldn't have contained them'.[11]

Several days pass before Kergorre can even get hold of some little carts to remove the dead from the improvised hospital: 'I personally took away 128 who'd had been serving as pillows for the sick and were several days old.' As for 600 wounded Russians, abandoned where they'd fallen in the town's gardens, 'they were living on cauliflower stalks and human flesh. Of this at least there was no shortage!'

In blatant contrast to this charnel-house, the wounded Teste sees how the inept and grossly self-indulgent Junot, whose corps is to protect the town, has 'grabbed everything. Junot had occupied the governor's palace with his brilliant staff. There everything was found in abundance and those gentlemen's orgies were in striking contrast to the sufferings and distress of so many wounded.'

Not very far away, at the ruined and deserted village of Elmia, von Suckow, too, has been detailed off to supervise the treatment of 40 wounded Württemberg officers and 500 men. Among them is Lieutenant Vossler, who together with eight others finds himself 'bedded on the floor, which was covered with thatch. Medical supplies were practically non-existent.' Upon the village catching fire and being partly laid in ashes, the survivors are moved to the nearby château of Selso-Karazhin. An hour's march to the rear, it's

'a vast building whose interior offered great comfort. The occupants had fled – precipitously, to judge by the disorder prevailing everywhere, perhaps only a few minutes before we'd got there. In an elegantly furnished room was a fine piano which they hadn't troubled themselves to close. A volume of music was on the desk. What had become of the lady who a minute earlier, perhaps, had been extracting harmonious sounds from this instrument?'

But at least the château abounds in food. 'The sick could be separated from the wounded, and the latter be quartered in lighter and more cheerful surroundings,' though after midnight the cold night air blowing in through the broken windowpanes prevents the patients from getting any sleep. As for the days,

'we spent them either sitting in front of the stove and keeping the fire going or visiting other wounded who were confined to their beds. We spent many cheerful hours with Lieut. von H., who'd lost a foot but none of his gaiety and wit. I whiled away much of my time bringing my diary up to date, though my room mate's garrulous disposition made this something of an effort. The food was as a rule totally inadequate.'

Many of these wounded, too, are dying; some because, like General Dessaix, they've refused to be operated upon. One colonel, 'relying too much on his military authority' tries to counter the pain from his leg by saying over and over again: "Leg, I order you to stop hurting me!"

'We deposited them in the middle of the fields, entrusting the disappearance of their remains to the air and worms, for we'd long lost the habit of burying our corpses.'

For Intendant-General Dumas, it has been a

'painful duty to have to follow on with IHQ and leave behind between four and five thousand wounded in the environs of the battlefield, with so little of what was needed for their relief. Our field hospitals were nearly exhausted, and yet we had to anticipate the results of another battle and be sparing of the scanty means which we still had left to provide for them.'

But Kergorre and his immediate superior, a man called Trussot, move into a little house occupied by a temporary assistant named Ligerot, freshly arrived from Paris. All Dumas has been able to leave him for his 3,000 patients 'in two stone houses, the only ones in town', is 'one barrel of flour, which we distributed to the generals, 4 or 5 pounds apiece. There were twelve divisional generals and 14 brigadiers. As for the other wounded, they were excluded from this issue.'

The scenes at the Kolotskoïe monastery are, if possible, even worse. 'They were daily appealing to us for help. Fortunately,' says Kergorre,

'nature, amidst so many horrors, furthered the cause of medicine. I had very few feverish cases and apart from two or three hundred deaths during the first few days I saved all my patients.'

At first he has heated debates with Superintendent Trussot, who's

'been expressly forbidden to touch the convoys destined for headquarters and ordered to live off the country. But I told him I'd take full responsibility for levying a tithe on the convoys, preferring to be court-martialled for feeding the wounded entrusted to my care than to let them die of hunger.'[12]

He also has to feed 'some *ingénieurs géographes*, among them M. Labaume, busy drawing up his plan of the battle'. He also defies his orders by giving the odd loaf to officers passing through en route for the army; among them the former French consul at St Petersburg, de Lesseps, he who'd been deprived of his job and his expense account for reporting unpalatable facts. He'd been

'on his way home to Paris with his wife and eight children when a courier had caught up with him as he was disembarking at Danzig, and handed him imperative orders to proceed at once to IHQ, then at the gates of Moscow',

whose civil governor he, willy-nilly, is to be. 'He had nothing at all to eat.'

CHAPTER 23

THE LAST LAP

Fézensac takes over the 4th Line – 'even the officer seemed worried' – an unneces-sary engagement -Cossacks and peasants – 'our camp looked like a market' – IV Corps loots Rouza – the splendours of Zvenigorod Abbey

'The road to Moscow is a masterpiece,' thinks cuirassier captain Bréaut des Marlots,
> 'you can march along it ten vehicles abreast. On either side are two rows of very tall trees and between them a path for pedestrians. These trees look very much like weeping willows. In summer their hospitable shade preserves you from the fierce heats and in winter they serve as a guide when the snows fill up the frequent precipices, blending sky with the surface of the ground.'

Riding on from a Mojaisk in flames Le Roy had seen 'our cavalry at grips with the enemy in a superb plain. It was a pleasure to see the way they manoeuvred.' And on 9 September Tascher notes in his diary that his hussars have launched three successive attacks, only for the Russians to retire as soon as [Séruzier's] guns had opened up on them:
> 'In the evening, a charge by the Prussians. Pajol wounded. Sept 10: Same circus as yesterday. But at least at 4 p.m. they halt and stand firm. We get lost and trot until 9 p.m. Bivouac in a wood, without water, or bread, or forage. Ate horsemeat, extreme misery. The regiment reduced to six troops. The Russians are burning everything, even the villages with their wounded in them. My spyglass stolen. Did twelve miles.'

And so on, day after day. Although the Russian is all the time retreating Le Roy sees him
> 'at each position turning about and sacrificing some men to prevent a rout which would have become unavoidable if he'd let himself be pressed too hard. For my part I was surprised to see the discipline, the good order reigning in a beaten army. Being myself in the advance guard, I can affirm that I never once saw a single cart, not a horse, in a word not one single Russian soldier abandoned or straggling.'

For three days Dedem's men go on 'advancing in line, the cavalry occupying the intervals between the infantry'. All the time Colonel Tschudi's Spaniards are
> 'only having skirmishes. We in the advance guard were making thirty to thirty-five miles a day, and in the evening we lay down regularly in square, having two ranks alternately on their feet and one sitting down.'

On 11 September the left wing of Dufour's division is marching in square close to some woods when

329

'three regiments of Russian cavalry charged the 33rd Line's 2nd battalion, its extreme left. No more than 176 men were still present. For a moment the King of Naples thought this little unit had been driven in, and sent me to its assistance. As I approached, the hostile cavalry had surrounded the battalion and were shouting to the French to surrender. But as I appeared they showed signs of retreating. Then a salvo by our infantry at almost point-blank range dismounted more than 76 Cossacks and killed 33 men.'

Murat afterwards asks Napoleon to promote all the dwindled little unit's officers, 'a sergeant-major who'd particularly distinguished himself and the Cross for Captain Callier, commanding the 2nd battalion after the death of its major'.

Now it's Ney who's marching in Murat's wake. Leaving Mojaisk on the morning of 12 September, the newly fledged *Colonel* Fézensac reaches his headquarters in the evening at a village near Koubinoskoië, which he finds surrounded by III corps' bivouacs. It's there he's to take over his regiment. The 4th Line is one of those which had been

'formed in the first years of the Revolution and been through all the German campaigns and it counted Joseph Bonaparte among its colonels. Next day I was received by General d'Henin, the brigade commander. From the very first day I was struck by the troops' exhaustion and their numerical weakness. At IHQ only results counted, without a thought to the the cost; and people had no idea of the state of the army. But when I assumed command of the regiment I had to go into all the details about which I knew nothing and to learn how deep the trouble went. Out of the 2,000 men who'd crossed the Rhine the 4th Regiment was reduced to 900.'

Its original four battalions have shrunk to only two, and each company has a double cadre of officers and NCOs.

'All parts of its clothing and above all its boots were in a bad state. Though we still had enough flour and some herds of bullocks and flocks of sheep, it wouldn't be long before these resources were exhausted. Since twenty-four hours sufficed for us to ravage the country we were passing through we had to keep on the move to replenish them.'

All of which, Fézensac says, was also true of III Corps as a whole,

'and especially of the Württemberg Division, which was almost destroyed. I can assure you there were no more than 8,000 men left of an army corps of 25,000. I noticed the absence of many officers wounded in the last affair, among others, of the 46th, 72nd and 73rd Line. Never had we suffered such heavy losses. Never had the army's morale been in such a sorry state. I no longer found the soldiers gay as they'd used to be. The songs and funny stories which formerly had helped them forget the fatigue of the long marches had given way to a gloomy silence. Even the officers seemed worried, and were only serving out of a sense of duty and honour.'

A general's death, demotion or incapacitation could strip his staff of their privileges.[1] Grouchy being among the many top brass wounded at Borodino, Colonel Griois too finds his situation has changed for the worse. Command of III Cavalry Corps has passed to General Lahoussaye who, if not quite as obtuse as old General St-Germain (he of the rotten bales of hay), is 'far from enjoying our confidence and daily proving how little he merited it'. Although still in command of III Corps' artillery, Griois now finds himself

'without victuals, without provisions, without any distribution at all. I lacked for everything, as did those around me, and we're only too happy when the gunners shared with us the fruits of their maraudings, organized, for the rest, with the best possible order!'

This miserable state of personal indigence he's sharing with his friend Colonel Jumilhac who 'no longer having any troops under his immediate orders, was even worse off'. A scion of the *ancien régime* – Jumilhac is an authentic duke – Griois' friend is

'an arrogant man, violent and choleric towards his inferiors, but amiable, witty and excellent towards his comrades, and we mutually helped each other to put up with our privations and our detestable bivouacs. We were also quite close with Colonel Caumont de la Force, chief-of-staff of the dragoon division – a bon vivant, very gay, altogether original, loving wine and women and seizing every opportunity to get them, without too much care for the quality.'

A few days after leaving Mojaisk, however, III Cavalry Corps is ordered to leave the Moscow highway and follow the Army of Italy as it makes for Rouza.

Just while Fézensac is being received by Ney, Murat is again at grips with the Russians. This time the bone of contention is the charming little château of Fominskoië, 'with a little green dome, and which His Majesty coveted'. Follows what Dedem's men will afterwards call

'the war of the château. We weren't at all pleased about it. With reason – because the King's and his staff's good pleasure were frequently costing the lives of 30 to 80 brave soldiers. I never saw a headquarters that troubled itself so little about its men as that one.'

The Russians, who know the ground, are clinging to their position in front of the château, which has the only stream in the neighbourhood. But Murat, who's in a hurry to get into it to spend the night, takes personal command of the cavalry and orders Dufour to outflank the Russian right, leaving his divisional artillery on the road. Whereupon

'part of the Russian cavalry turned the wood we were to debouch by, fell on a battalion of the 48th and our extreme left and, before it even had time to form up, cut it to pieces at the exit from the forest.'

The French right, meanwhile, is on the highway, and Dedem's two weak infantry battalions, one from the 33rd, the other Tschudi's Spaniards, are being ravaged by enemy grapeshot. Almost the whole Spanish battalion is thrown to the ground and loses all its officers. Tschudi himself has two horses killed under him and his clothes are peppered with musket-balls. In the centre matters are hardly less desperate:

'Not even giving the 15th Light time to form up, His Majesty had the charge beaten, and the soldiers ran at the enemy like so many skirmishers. Having no unit to support them they were cut up by the enemy cavalry, who did real butchery among them. Nothing was saved of this fine regiment except some companies which had got mingled up with the 33rd when crossing the copses and which I'd kept behind me. Upon the 33rd debouching simultaneously with the 15th Light, the King's ADCs had wanted to engage it, too, with the cavalry. But defying these gentlemen's loud-voiced complaints I formed up my battalions before advancing: partly so as to gain time and partly to enable the wreckage of the 48th and 15th to make good its retreat. The King, seeing the outcome of his crazy enterprise, sent generals Déri and Excelmans to me, one after the other, ordering me not to engage. But there was no longer any question of that! The affair was already only too thoroughly engaged. And though the enemy opposed me with three times my remaining forces, I thought it my duty to sustain the combat to give other troops time to turn up and save our retreat from turning into a rout. My skirmishers held the enemy in check; but his artillery, placed in a grove of tall trees, was doing me a lot of damage. All I had to oppose him with was infantry fire.'

Finally the French withdraw, in fairly good order, to 'the position the Russians had allocated to us that morning'. The action has cost the remains of what had once been Friant's crack division the cream of its surviving officers. The admirable Swiss colonel Tschudi has lost one of his two Spanish battalions. And Dedem's ADC Beaucourt, 'an educated officer of great bravery' already wounded at Borodino, has received a musket-ball in his thigh. When it's all over, Dedem annoys Murat by handing in an exact account of the butcher's bill. Worse, he and his officers go to Davout next day and implore him to take them back under his command. Whereupon there's another blazing row between Murat and Davout in front of Napoleon:

'The Marshal could not but be pained to see his army corps' finest divisions being destroyed to no purpose, and a man who he knew was his enemy and who possessed no other military virtue than ebullient courage and great audacity being allowed to commit stupidities with impunity, just because he was the Emperor's brother-in-law. A corporal would have managed the affair better.'

Napoleon, meanwhile, is wholly in the dark, not merely as to Kutusov's intentions, but even his very whereabouts:

'On the 13th, when the whole army was again on the move, the Emperor halted all the columns. Our cavalry were so exhausted they couldn't push their reconnaissance to any distance, and just then we knew so little of the enemy's movements that the Emperor, doubtful as to the direction taken by Kutusov, of whom there was no news, judged it advisable to pause. He hadn't received any reports from Prince Poniatowski on our right and for a moment was uneasy about him, feeling the Russians might have taken advantage of our rest to throw themselves to that side and threaten our flank and rear, in hope of stopping, or at least delaying, our entry into Moscow until they'd had replies from Petersburg,'

i.e., to whatever report Kutusov must have sent to his government after the battle. Perhaps he's even withdrawing, not on Moscow, but on Kaluga, away to the south? Anyway, Colbert is ordered to cut the Kaluga road. Probing in that direction, the lancer brigade finds no trace of the enemy. Sometimes the peasants are even taking his men for Russian Uhlans:

'There were plenty of provisions and forage in these villages, and since our men's discipline was excellent the inhabitants, so far from fleeing, gave us a good reception. Some complained of their own government. Several times these same peasants warned us of the appearance of Cossacks in the surroundings.'

But by no means always. Approaching stealthily, Cossacks nevertheless (again) carry off the Dutch regiment's outpost picket. And again 'only one man escaped flat out at a gallop and brought the news to our camp. Even an hour and a half's pursuit couldn't catch up with the Cossacks.' Mortified by this second surprise of the campaign, Colbert doubles the 2nd Regiment's outposts; and, to make assurance doubly sure, mingles the Dutchmen with his warier, more experienced Poles. And beyond Kijow they capture a mailcoach, one of whose occupants turns out to be one of the Tsar's ministers, a Count Gouriew, whom Colbert sends to Napoleon, no doubt with a request for further orders. Once again he's feeling very much out on a limb: 'Although he had an important cavalry command,' Captain Zalusky of the Polish Lancers is noticing, 'he's not getting any orders, and it even seems his reports aren't reaching the general staff.'

Which is strange. For Caulaincourt is noticing that it's precisely from that quarter Napoleon is all the time expecting Kutusov to attack him. That is, if he doesn't sue for peace. Which he's sure he will, while at the same time offering another battle, for form's sake:

'Officers were sent out one after another in all directions. The King of Naples was ordered to push forward a strong reconnaissance along the Kaluga road. At last the Emperor was reassured, and the army resumed its march. Nevertheless he couldn't explain this movement of the whole [Russian] army on Moscow, as it didn't offer battle.'

Upon Murat reporting that the Russians are neither showing any signs of resistance nor have made any proposals for an armistice, Napoleon is 'amazed. From it he inferred, and he repeated it more than once, that the Russian army had lost far more heavily at the Moscova than had been supposed. He seemed to be in continual anxiety.'

Also probing the countryside over a 12–15 mile front to the right is a strong detachment of Dessaix's division, now taken over by General Friedrichs. Ever since 11 September Le Roy, in command of one of its units, has been 'marching, with no other guide than a bad map that hardly even gave any distances'. Next day – i.e., the day of the Fominskoië affair – his men, without encountering any opposition, enter the pleasant little town of Vereia. But find neither the military stores nor the garrison they've expected. Since all its inhabitants have fled, however, provisions are plentiful:

'An hour later our camp looked like a market: wines, liqueurs, brandy, carboys of crystallized fruits, dragées, hams, sausages, bread, meat, etc., etc. From direst poverty we'd passed abruptly to the greatest abundance. Imagine to yourself a line of 2,000 men, camped in a semi-circle, sitting on the ground, surrounded by bottles, drinking out of them and regaling themselves like millionaires. After the victuals arrived the furs, cloths, silverware, jewels and all the wealth the inhabitants, taken by surprise, hadn't been able to carry off or hide. Terrified to see us coming, they'd only saved their families and some food, retiring into nearby forests, where they were waiting for the storm to pass over.'

And soon everyone, except Le Roy, always alive to his duties, is sleeping off the unwonted feast. The staff having moved into Vereia itself, Le Roy, finding himself in command of the camp, takes care to inspect the outposts before finally returning to sit down to take part in the general jollification, close to the majors and adjutants-major. 'Finally day broke, and revealed to our sight more than half the troops in no state to depart.' Leaving at 6 p.m. the detachment

'destroyed everything they couldn't carry off. It was odd to see the ranker embarrassed to know what to choose as between drink and food. He'd have been only too glad to leave his weapons behind to load himself with provisions.'

Thereafter all the 85th find is a deserted countryside, abandoned villages. Life is less agreeable for the Italians out on the left flank. There too the peasants are fleeing. From a Colonel Asselin, whom Eugène has sent to reconnoitre in the direction of Rouza, Labaume hears how some of them have put up a fight, before being quickly routed by his dozen Bavarian chasseurs – all but the lord of the manor who'd organized this resistance. Despite Asselin's entreaties this nobleman had fought to the death with his dagger, shouting "how can I survive my country's dishonour?" and ended his life on the chasseurs' bayonets.

Beyond Rouza, 'a little town built on a height', the peasants, with their valuables piled on carts, are in full flight – the first time, Labaume says, 'we'd seen such a sight'. The cavalry, of course, easily catch up with them, 'and a very touching spectacle it was to see these carts laden with children and aged invalids. One's heart was ravaged with sorrow at the thought of how our men would share these carts and horses among themselves, laying waste these families' entire fortune.'

Every house in Rouza is pillaged,

'without heed to their owners' cries or a mother's tears as she showed the victors the child in her lap. Wringing their hands, these innocents only begged us to spare their lives.'

Even Labaume exonerates those among the Italians and Bavarians

'who were dying of hunger and only trying to get some food. For them this ardour for pillage was legitimate. Many others under its pretext sacked everything, stripping both women and children, even to the rags they were covered with.'

But then, in a twinkling, everything changes. Some Bavarian lancers come galloping back into town, announcing that whole squadrons of Cossacks are advancing against them. And instantly the pillagers' contentment turns into acute alarm:

'What have we here to oppose them with? Nothing. Only a few wretched soldiers, come to pillage the peasants. Yet it's our only recourse. Immediately they're assembled in the square, hardly 60 of them, half without their weapons.'

Yet when Eugène and his staff ride out to repel this redoubtable foe, they're amazed to see only 'a dozen or so horsemen, so far away they could hardly be made out'. Summoning up two battalions to secure the town, the Italian staff go back to their dinner 'with exquisite wines'.

The pillage of Rouza causes all the 'newly armed' peasants to flee into the forests, having set on fire their villages and the harvest. At the village of Apalchtchouina the Italians find

'the houses abandoned, the château deserted, the furniture smashed, and the provisions wasted, everywhere a picture of terrible desolation. All these ravages showed us what lengths a people can go to if it's sufficiently great to prefer its independence to its riches.'

Just as IV Corps is leaving again, III Cavalry Corps arrives. Although the town strikes Griois as 'rather pretty, it no longer had any inhabitants. Everything was in disorder.' After spending the night there another and different experience is in store for him:

'We came to a vast abbey, a veritable fortress surrounded by high crenellated walls and drawbridges. Only a few leagues from Moscow, I think it's called Zvenigorod. There were still some monks there, whose haggard faces, hidden by a thick beard, expressed hatred and despair. Enormous blue drapes disguised all their figures and gave them the air of veritable phantoms. Seeing us, they withdrew into the most secret recesses of their monastery; and when they couldn't escape us, all we could get out of them was an absolute silence and or a negative sign to all our questions.'

Much of the immense, almost unfurnished abbey, has already been devastated, presumably after IV Corps' visitation:

'but taken as a whole it still looked splendid and magnificent. One hall was wholly embellished with portraits of the ancient dukes of Muscovy, some of them not without merit. Their clothes and their hairstyles, varied as the centuries they lived in, rivalled each other in opulence and singularity, and the long beards enhancing all these faces gave several of them a truly extraordinary expression.'

There's also a small but splendid church, whose many tombs

'of a bizarre and recherché architecture, loaded with inscriptions in Russian lettering and thus illegible to me, were almost all covered in a gilded metal which seemed to me to be silver gilt. The men of IV Corps, who'd got to Zvenigorod before us, had forced their way into the church and taking these plaques of silver or perhaps copper gilt for pure gold, had ripped off part of it. They'd even opened or smashed some tombs in hopes of finding in them precious ornaments or jewels. The disorder in this temple which a whole people had venerated for centuries presented a spectacle as painful to see as to think about.'

Now everyone is noticing how, the closer the army is coming to Moscow, the more opulent is the countryside and its dwellings. Dutheillet, still on the main highway, sees

'châteaux of Asiatic luxury, magnificently furnished with expensive furniture, orangeries and shrubberies of all kinds, splendid stables and, alongside these superb dwellings devastated by both armies' marauders, miserable peasant shacks, built of loam and covered with thatch'.

Still probing towards the Kaluga road under Colbert, the Polish Guard Lancers are 'coming upon all kinds of objects we found extraordinary: palaces housing libraries, greenhouses, gardens'. Squadron-leader Chlapowsky, Soltyk's friend, invites Captain Zalusky to 'a meal so exceptional I could no longer recall a similar abundance'. Between Fominskoïe and Vereia a patrol comes across a large sugar-beet factory, whose store Dumonceau draws on to cure his men's dysentery:

'One night we were surprised to see a great number of little vehicles turn up, loaded with lumps of sugar. From this moment I too began using little britchkas; with my lieutenants I'd two of them, and, behind, two milch cows, a supply of sugar and various victuals.'

Zalusky will afterwards date the final catastrophe from the moment he, too, adopted that bad habit.

CHAPTER 24

'MOSCOW! MOSCOW!'

Another battle? – 'We gazed at the immense city' – 'no chimney smoked' – a parley – von Muraldt's mission – 'all the streets were empty' – amateur heroes – 'Never had I seen him so depressed' – 'I was frozen with terror' – 'to find some humane person' – 'the Tsar won't make peace' – Murat crosses Moscow – 'swans were swimming peacefully' – two dinner parties – 'Fire!, fire!'

Not knowing what's going on to his right, but sure he must at long last be approaching Moscow, Prince Eugène on 14 September

'mounted a hill to our right, and for a long while tried to see if the city of Moscow were visible. Several hills still veiled it from our sight and all we saw were whirlwinds of dust which, parallel to our route, showed the way the Grand Army was marching. From a few cannon-shots fired afar off and at long intervals we concluded that our troops were nearing Moscow without meeting much resistance.'

To get more news of the main column Eugène sends off von Muraldt, the Bavarian Chasseurs' youngest but only French-speaking officer, to Murat. Providing him with a small escort, he urges him not to fall into the hands of Cossacks. It's a brilliantly sunny day. After an anxious half-hour during which his escort kept seeing Cossacks everywhere, Muraldt reaches the Moscow-Mojaisk road, along which he finds 'the Imperial Guard's infantry and artillery advancing rapidly in columns'. Hurrying forward to catch up with Murat, he sees

'only cheerful faces. As the road was very broad, artillery and infantry were marching side by side, and everyone was hurrying on with winged footsteps. Here and there, especially in the Young Guard, the cry "Vive l'Empereur!" was heard. But the old bearskins were quieter and more serious.'

At long last, the Grand Army is nearing its goal. But must it fight another battle before entering it? Napoleon is still sure Kutusov will 'offer battle once again before giving up the capital, but this time with a sword in one hand and peace proposals in the other'. Determined to sign the peace in Moscow, he wants 'to stay there a week and then retire on Smolensk:

"Swords have been crossed. In the eyes of the world honour is satis-fied. And the Russians have suffered so much harm there's no other satisfaction I can ask of them. They'll be no more anxious for me to pay them a second visit than I shall be to come back to Borodino." '

As for himself and Berthier, Caulaincourt goes on, 'we agreed there was no way of finishing this war except by quitting Moscow forty-eight hours after entering it, and returning to Witebsk.' Nor are Griois and his com-rades

'in any way afraid of a new battle. Indeed we wanted one, to put an end to things; but not at Moscow or under its walls, because it was easy to foresee that if we won it, as none of us doubted we would, the town would be put to the sack and perhaps burnt before being handed over to us, and all our hopes were placed in the resources we counted on finding there.'

And indeed that day (14 September) Dedem van der Gelder, advancing along the tree-lined highway behind Murat's cavalry, hears that the advance guard has heard from a deserter that the Russians are fortifying 'a position much more formidable than the one at Borodino'. That morning too the Fusiliers-Grenadiers of the Young Guard enter the last big forest pass 'near a ravine where the Russians had begun to make redoubts for defence'. Emerging from the woods, Dedem sees 'trees cut down, a redoubt, and a line of cavalry crowning the heights'. But just then the light cavalry advance guard – among them Lieutenant Count von Wedel, of the 9th Polish Lancers – reaches a crest of a hill. And there, only a couple of miles away, lies... Moscow:

'"Moscow!, Moscow!" the shout rose from the ranks. We gazed at the huge town, with its golden spires, its red and black painted roofs, its palaces and more modest houses, and the large green parks inside the city, which bears no resemblance to our towns and has a wholly oriental character.'

One only has to peer at the fantastic spectacle through one's telecope to see at a glance that Moscow, the most distant and exotic of all Europe's capitals,[1] is an open city. Only a shallow ditch fronts its suburbs. Otherwise there are no fortifications. Nor is the Russian army deployed in front of it.

But then von Wedel sees something else. And it strikes him as far more sinister:

'On the far side of the city we, through our spyglasses, made out masses of people on foot, on horseback, or in vehicles. They were leaving the town. No chimney smoked. Could the inhabitants have fled? Surely they couldn't be abandoning their homes just as a few hundred people leave a village?'

For three hours the advance guard, ordered onwards down from the Sparrow Hills, is held up by the Russian rearguard. It has rallied 'in little trenches thrown up in front of the town at various distances from each other'. And Murat orders his cavalry and light field artillery

'to deploy in line. The Russians fired three or four rounds. But soon the firing ceased, and the rumour spread that negotiations were being held.'

And in fact Séruzier has seen a Russian general coming towards him, accompanied by an escort. He's been sent by Miloradowitch, commander of the rearguard. Setting his staff at a distance 'in a stentorian voice', Murat rides forward and listens to what he has to propose:

'We should pass through Moscow without halting and go as far as six miles along the Kasan road, our advance guard being preceded at a distance of 200 yards by a squadron of Cossacks.'

If this isn't agreed to, says the spokesman, the city will be set on fire. What to do? After some hestitation Murat replies that he'll have to go and ask the Emperor. Whereupon his interlocutor turns away and begins to go back to the city – but has only gone fifty yards when Murat calls him back and says he'll take it upon himself to agree. Sends off an ADC to tell Napoleon. Dismounts. And is immediately surrounded by admiring Cossacks 'with inverted lances'.

Ever since Tilsit they've remembered him as a giver of lavish gifts. So also now. Lieutenant Tascher sees them clustering around him. Having no other such kingly trifles to give them, Murat, much to that fiery-tempered officer's annoyance, purloins Gourgaud's treasured watch – 'a very fine piece of jewellery' which Gourgaud himself had 'received from an illustrious hand. No one seemed to be making any difficulties. Evidently they'd already decided to surrender the town to us.'

IHQ has passed the previous night at a superb manor-house owned by the immensely rich Prince Galitzin. Lying beside a lake, it was 'the first really fine château we'd seen in Russia. The soldiers of the advance guard,' Castellane had been sorry to see, had 'damaged it somewhat, as was their custom, by slashing the upholstery' of its 'very elegant furniture'. It's also remarkable for 'some very charming sculptures, some of them really good', which Captain Bonnet – at the same time finding its position 'a bit dreary, surrounded by woods pierced on one side by avenues, with a little stream and with lakes, frozen for eight months in the year, and formed with the help of dikes' – will relish, bivouacking there by and by with with Razout's division (III). At 8 a.m. Napoleon has left the château in his carriage for Malo-Wiazma, seven versts from Moscow. And it's there Murat's ADC tells him what's happening. His first words, according to Ségur, are: '"Well then, there's this famous city. And about time too!" His marshals, who'd been discontented since the great battle and held themselves apart from him, now forgot their complaints. We saw them pressing around the Emperor, rendering homage to his fortune and already tempted to ascribe to the foresight of his genius the lack of care he'd taken on Sept 7 to complete his victory.'[2]
Narbonne, a reasonably pacific personage, is sent to Murat to confirm the truce. He's to order him to
'follow the Russians step by step, enter the city, but as far as possible circumvent it, and press them as far as possible as soon as they're outside the barriers. Also to send the Emperor a deputation of the municipal authorities,'
who are to meet him at the city gate. Overtaking Dedem's sorely tried infantry, Narbonne tells him: "And that's the end of it. The Russians are abandoning Moscow and entrusting it to French generosity."
'Soon afterwards the Emperor passed in his carriage, and having called me over to him said: "Get your men on the move. It isn't the end." He seemed worried, I don't know why. Perhaps His Majesty

wasn't pleased with the soldiers' outbursts of joy at the idea that we'd be treating for peace, a sentiment they manifested only too clearly as they saluted the Emperor when he went by them to approach the city.'

Following close on his carriage and entourage – much to I and III Corps' annoyance – is the Imperial Guard. Nor do all the troops break out into cheers, anyway not the 57th Line. 'A few shouts of *"Vive l'Empereur!*, there's the holy city!" were heard, but without much enthusiasm.' It's a 'beautiful summer's day'. Marching swiftly, the Guard infantry is headed by the Fusiliers-Grenadiers. And at *their* head, commanding a posse of fifteen men, marches Vélite-sergeant Bourgogne:

'In my charge I had several officers taken prisoner in the great battle, some of whom spoke French. One of them was a pope, probably a regimental chaplain. He too spoke good French, but seemed much sadder and more preoccupied than his companions in misfortune.'

By and by they, too, halt on the Sparrow Hills:

'The sun was reflected on all the domes, the spires and gilded palaces. The many capitals I'd seen – such as Paris, Berlin, Warsaw, Vienna and Madrid – had only produced an ordinary impression on me. But this was quite different! On me as on everyone else the effect was magical.'

Bourgogne notices how all his prisoners

'bowed and crossed themselves several times. I went up to the priest and asked him why. "Monsieur," he said, "this hill is called the Hill of Salvation, and every good Muscovite must bow and cross himself on seeing the holy city." Soon afterwards we descended the hill.'

Suddenly, much to Lieutenant von Wedel's annoyance,

'one of the Emperor's orderly officers galloped past, and immediately afterwards the order rang out: "Column, halt!" Then the Imperial Guard, in full dress uniforms, went by, as if to a parade. "There's the Guard, who haven't fought once throughout the campaign! They're going to show off in Moscow. As for us riff-raff, we shan't even be allowed to stick our noses inside! It's a disgrace! a scandal!" With suppressed rage we watched this splendid, envied, favoured Guard go past, and already our fine fancies began to evaporate.'

Finally, after a quarter of an hour, Bourgogne reaches the city gate. 'The Emperor was already there with his staff. We halted. And to our left I noticed an immense cemetery.' Soon Boulart arrives and parks there with his guns; 'Everyone was extraordinarily excited.' He and his gunners are dying to make their 'triumphal entry. We were consumed with a curiosity incomparably more devouring than our appetite.'

'At noon the Emperor reached the barrier at the moat and dismounted. His impatience increased with every moment. Every instant he kept sending out fresh orders, continually asking whether the deputation or any notables were on their way.'

He tells Caulaincourt to write to Maret, at Vilna, and to the Arch-Chancellor, Cambacérès, in Paris 'informing them we were in Moscow, and dating my letter from that city'. Shortly afterwards he orders General Durosnel, whom he has appointed military governor, to enter Moscow 'with as many military police as he can muster'. He's to establish order, take possession of the public buildings, guard the Kremlin and keep him supplied with information. But no one else is to go inside the city. Pickets are to be placed 'to prevent any soldier from entering, but there were so many gaps in the walls the precaution was of little avail'.

At the entrance to the suburbs there's a timber bridge. And at 2 p.m. Murat, preceded by the 1st Squadron of the 1st Polish Hussars and followed by Séruzier's guns,[3] crosses it at the head of the 4th Light Cavalry Division and the 2nd and 4th Cuirassier Divisions. Just as he's about to ride into the suburb one of his officers announces a messenger from Prince Eugène. It's von Muraldt:

'I found the King of Naples surrounded by a brilliant and numerous suite and by Cossacks and generals who were flattering him on his bravery. One of the hetmans said: "I've known you a long while now, Sire. You're the King of Naples. The difference between you and me is that I've seen you every day since the Niemen, always the first man at the head of your army. Whilst I, for three months now, have constantly been the last man in ours.'

Like everyone else who sees him for the first time, the Bavarian lieutenant is struck by Murat's theatrical costume:

'It consisted of a short coatee of dark-red sammet with slashed arms. A short straight sword hung from a richly embroidered belt. His boots were of red morocco leather, and on his head he wore a big three-cornered hat, embroidered with gold borders and with a long plume, which he'd put on back to front. His long brown hair hung down in curls on to his shoulders,'

- all no doubt in striking contrast to the ragged and in many cases bare-footed appearance of his troops. A few hundred yards away the Cossacks are already withdrawing into the town. Murat tells the Bavarian officer to go back to Eugène and tell him the city is being evacuated under a truce.

But Muraldt has no intention of doing any such thing. Not until he has seen something of 'this remarkable capital. It was even closer to my heart to take some food back with me.' So mingling with Murat's staff he rides on with them; amazed to see that

'all the streets we rode through were empty, the houses barred and bolted. Not a face appeared at any window. And all shops were shut. This deathly silence and desertedness struck me as rather worrying, as it certainly did many others.'

Pajol's light cavalry division is in the van. Ahead of Surgeon von Roos' 3rd Württemberger Chasseurs are the 10th Polish Hussars and a regiment of Prussian lancers 'commanded by a Major de Werther'; behind them come

341

the 'four regiments of French hussars [5th and 9th] and chasseurs [11th and 12th] which made up our division, and some horse artillery':

'Each of us was feeling more or less deeply the pride of a conqueror. And for any one who wasn't there was no lack of officers and old soldiers to point out, with grave words, the importance of what was happening. It was forbidden, on pain of death, to get off one's horse or leave the ranks, on no matter what pretext. This order applied equally to us doctors, and we submitted. We followed the road as far as to the Moscova without encountering a single inhabitant. The bridge had been destroyed. We forded the river. The water came up to the axles of the guns and our horses' knees. On the far side we saw a few individuals behind their doors and windows. Their curiosity didn't seem very great. There were some gentlemen and ladies on the balconies of pretty stone and wooden houses. Our officers saluted them amiably, and they replied in the same fashion. However, we saw very few inhabitants. By and by we came up with some exhausted Russian soldiers, men straggling on foot on horseback, or in abandoned baggage vehicles, butchers' beef on the hoof, etc. We let them all pass.'

Amazed at so many superb palaces set in gardens, at 'the profusion of churches with their queer architecture and elaborately ornamented towers', Pajol's division debouches into a market place. All its wooden shops are open

'their merchandise scattered in disorder and thrown on the ground, as if pillagers had passed by. We were riding slowly, often halting, and this enabled our men to notice that Russians asleep in the streets had brandy in their water-bottles. It being forbidden to dismount, they got the ingenious idea of using the points of their sabres to cut the cords and so snatched them up.'

Murat, is 'everywhere, supervising everything, and kept passing and repassing our ranks'. After they've ridden for half an hour, the Kremlin comes into view. Hardly is Murat's entourage

'forty or fifty paces from it than a mob of drunken soldiers and peasants comes rushing out from its entrance and from a church opposite, and some shots are fired at us. There were also some officers in the crowd.'

One of these, obviously drunk, rushes at von Muraldt's horse,

'holding a drawn sabre in one hand and a bottle in the other. I receive him with a blow on his shako, which fells him to the ground.'

Now, 'between two rows of ancient buildings', the great Arsenal, a vast neo-classical building, comes into sight. Von Roos sees its doors are

'wide open, and men of all kinds, above all men who seemed to be peasants, were coming out of it with weapons. Inside, others were swarming and jostling. The road and the square where we were were littered with various weapons, most of them new. Underneath the Arsenal gateway some sharp words were being exchanged between the king's ADCs and the men who were carrying off the weapons. Some even pushed their way into the Arsenal on horseback and the quarrel became venemous. Meanwhile the populace had massed in the square. It became impatient and noisy.'

Muraldt goes on: 'Furious at this breach of the terms of the capitulation, the King of Naples orders forward two pieces of horse artillery.' And Colonel Séruzier, who has ridden out ahead, is within an inch of being 'killed by bullets fired from all the Arsenal's windows.[4] Hearing this fusillade I put my artillery to the gallop, surround the arsenal, and send forward a trumpeter with an officer to parley with these sharp-shooters, whom I took to be inhabitants of the town, reduced to despair. My trumpet sounds for a truce, but all we get for a reply is a discharge of musketry. One of my captains, the one accompanying the trumpeter, one of my adjutants and the trumpeter himself have been dangerously wounded. Immediately I give the order to fire – I'd placed my two guns under each of the vaultings serving as an entrance to the Arsenal – and pitilessly rain grape on this troop, who come and fall on their knees in front of my guns, begging for mercy.'

Three salvoes suffice to disperse the crowd, most of which Muraldt sees 'taking to their heels in all directions'. It's then Séruzier realizes who it is he has to do with:

'Not the inhabitants of Moscow, nor soldiers trying to defend the Arsenal and the Kremlin in the teeth of the convention. It was the dregs of society, criminals let out of prison. They'd been promised a pardon and their freedom on condition they revolted against these "dogs" of Frenchmen. I seized part of this scum – galley slaves, there were several thousand of them – and handed them over to our infantry.'

The whole episode has 'only lasted a couple of minutes'. Meanwhile Roos has snapped up a souvenir, suited to the occasion:

'Under the very feet of my horse were various weapons. One of them, a handsome sabre, drew my attention. There was no one there to hand it up to me. And I couldn't use the method invented by our men to get hold of water-bottles. Flouting the ban on dismounting, I quickly got off my horse and in a flash was up again.'

Immediately after Murat had crossed the barrier Napoleon has also sent in several staff officers to find out what's really going on, and above all why no deputation has come out to present him with the keys of the city and implore his clemency. Roman Soltyk is one of them. And he too is alarmed to find the town deserted:

'All doors and windows being closed, I came to believe all the inhabitants had taken refuge in the side streets, and turned off in search of them.'

There the only sign of life he comes across is a group of rich Polish hostages from White Russia – the very ones, perhaps, who'd been carried off from Witebsk? They're guarded, if that's the right word, by 30 Russian stragglers, all very drunk. These are pillaging nearby shops and breaking into brandy stores. Welcomed by his compatriots, Soltyk, despite his Polish uniform, quite simply takes command of their warders:

'It didn't even occur to them to grab up their muskets, propped against the walls of the ground-floor rooms. Instead, seeing my epaulettes and true to the respect Russian troops always have for rank, they doff their forage caps and do their best to scramble to their feet. Their own officer couldn't have been received more respectfully!'

Disarming them, Soltyk loses no time in taking both guards and hostages back to the Dorogomilov Gate, where he finds Napoleon

'at the entrance to the Smolensk district. He was standing on the left of the road. A very large-scale map of Moscow was laid out on the grass in front of him. He was studying it closely and then questioning the people who were being brought to him from the town centre. Obliged to wait for a favourable moment to speak to him, I was present at everything that took place. All reports agreed. Most of the inhabitants had fled.'

At that moment Gourgaud, too, comes back. With him he has '40 fully armed Cossacks he, with the help of a single lancer officer he'd had with him, had captured inside the very Kremlin'.

And now the moment has come for some Guard units to enter. Just as Sergeant Bourgogne has reached the bridge he has seen a third officer – Marshal Duroc – come out through the gate and present 'several of the inhabitants who could speak French. The Emperor questioned them.' 'Most of the people brought to him,' Soltyk goes on,

'were foreigners. One of these, a Frenchman by origin, and director of the Museum of Natural History whose status had given him connections in the highest classes of society, gave the most complete elucidation of the present situation. He assured Napoleon that all the authorities had quit Moscow, or at least abandoned their posts. This seemed to affect the Emperor vividly, and he remained plunged in deep reflections.'

What Soltyk has to report, on the other hand, interests Napoleon as little as his Cossack prisoners,

'nor did I see the cloud that had settled on his brow grow lighter. Doubtless having from this moment a presentiment of the fateful consequences of the system of warfare adoped by the Russians, he didn't even wish to interrogate the Polish hostages I'd brought him. Never had a great capital been delivered into a conqueror's hands in a more extraordinary fashion! How different to his entries into Vienna and Berlin!'

Caulaincourt, too, is observing him narrowly:

'At last reports came in from the King and General Durosnel. Far from having found any of the civic authorities, they hadn't discovered so much as a single prominent inhabitant. All had fled. Moscow was a deserted city, where no one could be found but a few wretches of the lowest classes. His face, normally so impassive, showed instantly and unmistakeably the mark of his bitter disappointment. Never have I seen him so deeply impressed. Already greatly disturbed and impatient at having to wait two hours outside the city gate, this report undoubtedly plunged him into the gravest reflections.'

Mortified he certainly is. But perhaps not quite so surprised as he'd been outside Witebsk. Telling him about the Kremlin episode, Duroc says '"Those wretches are all drunk and can't listen to reason." "Break down the doors with cannon", the Emperor replied, "and drive out all you can find behind them."' Which of course has already been done. But now the Guard's drums begin to roll, and Sergeant Bourgogne gets the order

'*Garde à vous!*, the signal for entering the city. It was 3 p.m., and we made our entrance in compact columns, the bands playing out in front. I was in the advance guard of 30 men, commanded by M. Césarisse, our company's lieutenant. Hardly had we entered the suburbs than we met several of the miserable creatures expelled from the Kremlin. They had horrible faces, and were armed with muskets, staves and pitchforks. As we were crossing the [stone] bridge leading from the suburbs to the town itself, a man crept out from under the bridge and placed himself athwart the regiment. He was muffled up in a sheepskin cape, long grey hair fell down on to his shoulders, and a thick white beard came down to his waist. He carried a three-pronged fork and looked like Neptune rising from the sea. Thus accoutred, he walked up to the drum-major and, taking him on account of his smart uniform and lace for the general, aimed a blow at him with his pitchfork. Snatching the wretch's weapon from him, the drum-major seized him by the shoulders; then giving him a kick from behind, he launched him over the bridge into the water he'd just left. But he didn't get out again. Swept away by the current, we only saw him come up at intervals. Finally he disappeared for ever.'

So much for an amateur hero. And they meet others, some of whom 'only had wooden flintlocks to their muskets. Since they didn't wound anyone we contented ourselves with taking their weapons from them and breaking them. And if they came back for more, got rid of them by blows in their backs with our musket butts. After crossing the bridge we marched along a broad and handsome street. We were astonished not to see anyone come out, not even a lady, to listen to our band playing *La victoire est à nous*. We couldn't understand this total silence, and imagined the inhabitants, not daring to show themselves, were peeping out at us from behind their shutters. Here and there we saw a few servants in livery and some Russian soldiers.'

Pion des Loches' is the first Guard battery to enter:

'At 6 p.m., the Emperor still hadn't made his entry, and he watched us cross the bridge. He was surrounded by generals, but nowhere near him did I see a single Russian. I passed down immense streets in the wake of the infantry. I looked up to the houses' windows to see if I could see any inhabitants behind them. I didn't see a living soul. I was frozen with terror. Sometimes cavalry regiments, galloping hither and thither without meeting anyone, crossed our path. I said aloud the city had been abandoned; and I still laugh at the sententious tone of a Captain Lefrançois as he replied: "No one abandons a great city. These people seem to have hid. We'll find them all right, we'll see them at our knees!"'

Lacking further orders, Boulart forms up his regiment in a square on the road leading to the Kremlin,

'beside the Petrovski family's town palace. On one side was a long straight promenade, planted with trees. On the other a nunnery. I formed my park in square, the guns in battery at the corners, the men and horses in the middle. I forbade the men to absent themselves. Then, having dismounted, I sent my lieutenants with a few gunners to the nearby streets to get some food. Everywhere they found the doors closed and barricaded. So we had to force them. In a trice everything was being pillaged, and doubtless it was the same throughout the city. Afraid of being taken by surprise, I ordered everyone to come back at the sound of a musket-shot.'

Although the Fusilier-Grenadiers, too, have been forbidden to absent themselves, after an hour their bivouac is

'filled with everything we could want, and an enormous quantity of sweet cakes and flour; but no bread. We went into the houses on the square, to ask for food and drink. But as we found no one there, we helped ourselves.'

Outside the Dorogomilov gate the conqueror of Europe is still waiting. Finally, says Ségur, when no deputation appears, an officer

'either anxious to please or else convinced that everything the Emperor desired had to take place, went into the city, caught five or six vagrants, and pushing them before his horse, brought them into the Emperor's presence. From these unfortunates' very first reply Napoleon saw he'd only a few wretched workmen in front of him. Only then did he cease to doubt that Moscow had been evacuated. Shrugging his shoulders he exclaimed with that scornful air with which he crushed everything that opposed his wishes: "Ah! The Russians still don't realize what effect the capture of their capital will produce on them!"'

It had been about midday when Eugène and his staff had sighted the city. And the Italians have nothing of the Germans' phlegm. Up there on the hilltop 'faces light up with joy. The men are transformed. We all embrace each other, we raise our hands to heaven in gestures of gratitude. Many shed tears of joy, and everywhere one hears people repeating "At last! at last! there's Moscow!" We were carried away with amazement at seeing so beautiful a sight, all the more seductive because of all the dreary ones we'd been witnessing. No one could contain his joy, on a spontaneous impulse we all shouted "Moscow! Moscow!". At this name, so long desired, everyone ran up on to the hill en masse. All were struck by the superb picture offered by this great city.'[5]

Césare de Laugier, like so many educated officers, half-consciously re-enacting all sorts of classical paradigms and literary allusions and scribbling it all down in his diary, calls to mind the moment when Tasso's crusaders first caught sight of Jerusalem:

> 'Ali ha ciascuno al cuore ed ali al piede
> Né del suo ratto andar pero s'accorge.
> Ma quanto il sol gli aridi campi fiede
> con raggi assai ferventi, e in alto sorge,
> Ecco apparir Gerusalemmme si vede..., etc.[6]

But to Labaume, Fantin des Odoarts and many others the scene is like something out of the *Arabian Nights*. As Griois' battery reaches the foot of the hill where IV Corps has halted, he joins the Viceroy on top of it,

'together with several of III Cavalry Corps' generals and superior officers. It seems impossible to describe the sensation I felt when, at the summit of this hill, which I was told was called the Sacred Mountain, I heard all mouths repeating the name of Moscow and saw all eyes fixed in the same direction, all spyglasses turned on this city. Sitting down at the crest I contemplated at my leisure, about six miles away, this immense town.'

Although all he gets at such a distance is an overall impression,

'its innumerable bell towers, each of which consists of several cupolas of different sizes and heights and are almost all clad in gilded metal or coloured tiles, glittered most vividly in the sun's rays. In no way did it resemble any cities I'd seen in Europe. As yet nothing was known about what was going on inside it, but the most contradictory rumours were going the rounds.'

The Italians are standing there lost in imagination when, across the intervening plain, they see a solitary figure coming towards them. It turns out to be a ruined merchant who, flouting the government's order to leave, has come out here 'to find some humane person who'll protect his family'. Count Rostopchin, he assures them, the city's governor, has ordered it to be burnt to the ground – 'at which everyone exclaimed it was impossible'. Bursting into tears, the fugitive begs them to prevent such a catastrophe.

Where the Italians cross it, too, the Moscova is only a few feet deep and they don't even wait for their pontooneers to throw a bridge, but fording it skirt the city 'at about half an hour's distance', and leave it to their right. And it's there von Muraldt, back from his mission, finds them, bivouacked on either side of the Petersburg road – and tells them Moscow has been abandoned. He too has quite a tale to tell. Determined to find something to eat, he'd hammered on the closed door of a big house where a German-speaking servant had finally come and opened. Taken upstairs, he'd found a German professor of Moscow University dining with some French ladies, and had been regaled with the best the house could offer; likewise, downstairs, his two chasseurs. His host had told him frankly he didn't think Alexander would ever make peace,

"even if his second capital should fall to the enemy. He doesn't lack resources. And winter, which is approaching, will force the French to retreat. Anyone who thinks the Russians will immediately submit doesn't know them."'

Wined and dined and laden with provisions for his comrades, he'd set out again. Crossing the Dorogmilov bridge he'd seen

'the Emperor, wearing his chasseur uniform, with the usual four chasseurs posted in a square around him, strolling to and fro with his hands clasped behind his back and talking to the Prince of Neuchâtel. Our strange helmets made us instantly recognizable, and the Emperor waved to an officer and spoke a couple of words to him,'

to go over and ask these Bavarian chasseurs what they're doing there. Explaining, von Muraldt is sent on his way. What he has to tell them arouses in his listeners 'many grim forebodings. Not even the most happy-go-lucky saw the future in rosy tints'.

And in fact, no sooner have the Italians bivouacked than they're attacked by Cossacks, 'who set up their outposts under the very noses of ours'. Not far off to their left is a long straight road, 'lined, almost uninterruptedly, by country houses, most of no great size, but all more or less elegant and well decorated' – all of them abandoned by their owners, 'like those in all the other parts of the country we've passed through. Some of us won't even believe it, and laugh at our comrades who're telling them about it.' As for the road to their left, it leads out to a 'curious turretted Gothic-style building in red brick.'[7] It's the Petrovski Palace, where the Tsars reside on the eve of their coronations. Griois and his aristocratic friend Colonel Jumilhac install themselves in one, where they find – oh delight of delights! – even beds. 'For the first time since leaving Prussia I was able to undress and lie down comfortably.'

Since 'the town's surroundings were cultivated in garden plots that offered our men an abundance of those vegetables they'd so long been deprived of, notably enormous cabbages,' all the Germans have immediately begun making sauerkraut – the more welcome as that morning Heinrich von Roos and his men have been reduced to 'devouring juniper berries while our horses ate shrubs'. To its captors Moscow is above all something they're going to eat.

For the third time since leaving Germany the Italians, eagerly awaiting the return of Eugène's adjutant with orders to march in, don their parade uniforms. But alas, Lieutenant Wedel's assessment of Napoleonic priorities turns out to be perfectly correct:

'Stirred by a variety of emotions, we're gazing at Moscow, when a strong force of Cossacks appears away to our left. Good-bye Moscow! The Cossacks ride through the Moscova, we follow them across the river, and soon they're out of sight. We set up our bivouac close to one of the suburbs, on a hill by the main Petersburg road. This time our camp had a peculiar animation. Everyone was excited by the nearness of the town, by hopes of peace, by annoyance over the supposed slight inflicted on us by the Guard, whom we regarded as mere parade ground troops.'

Even the Italian Royal Guard has to cool its heels until the morrow.

Meanwhile Murat's cavalry, preceded at 300 paces by the Cossack rearguard, are crossing the city in the direction of the Kazan Gate. Riding slowly onwards down endless streets of single-storey timber houses interspersed with superb stone palaces, Victor Dupuy and his hussars hardly have time to glimpse the Kremlin's moats and gateways. Even in the remoter parts of the city houses and palaces are all shut up, silent. Claparède's Poles, too, are making very slow progress:

'It took us six hours to do about eight versts [8,800 yards]. During all this time we only met with one inhabitant – a Russian of gigantic stature, who, just as we were passing, came abruptly out of a house so as to cross over to another opposite. In doing so he bumped up roughly against some of the men, and even against an officer, who threatened him with his sword. Immediately this man, who seemed very much lit up, rips open his kaftan and shouts: "Plunge your iron into this Russian bosom!" As we'd been told to treat the inhabitants with the greatest consideration we let the fellow go. "If they're all like that," a sergeant said to me, "we aren't at the end of our troubles."

Brandt has been mysteriously warned by several French residents of 'a fateful plan'. But no more than Maurice Tascher does he see any fires or hear any explosions. But Séruzier, very much on the *qui vive*, has ordered his horse gunners to drag their guns by their bindings, ready for instant action. 'It was the first time I'd passed through a town with my guns on their bindings.' And what a town! Surgeon Roos, still riding on slowly, a little way ahead of them, is realizing that Moscow is

'certainly the biggest city I'd ever seen. Mingled with ourselves, Russians kept passing us on horseback, making for the same gate as we were. We let all that lot pass. Only one Russian officer's orderly, despite his objections, was obliged to decend from his admirable steed.'

Finally, after three hours, the advance guard reaches the Kazan Gate. And there's a small but bloody affray:

'Reaching the gate we were to pass through, we found two Cossacks on horseback who at all costs were determined to bar our way.'

One Russian officer who's lingered behind in hopes of reassuring his relatives that all is well with him, gets a nasty head wound, which Roos has to bind up for him. Otherwise, both sides seem to be joyfully anticipating an end to hostilities:

'Leaving the town, we found several regiments of Russian dragoons, some in line, others riding slowly onwards. We approached each other with the friendliest intentions, which they responded to. Officers and men went up to each other, shook hands, lent each other their water-bottles filled with brandy, and chatted as best they could.'

But then

'a Russian officer of the highest rank, accompanied by his ADC, turned up and very severely put an end to these conversations. But at least we'd had time to notice that peace would be as welcome to them as to ourselves. Their horses were no less exhausted than ours. When they had to jump a ditch many of them fell and only with difficulty got up again. Despite our extreme fatigue, everything was contributing to make us happy, and our camp was unusually animated. No one gave a thought to sleep.'

On the 10,000-acre plain fringed with silver birch woods to the west of the city I and III Corps' bivouacs are spreading out. Strictly forbidden to enter the city, Fézensac's 4th Line, for instance, have been ordered to stay at a distance of three miles. That afternoon Dedem and the Cossacks share

'a numerous herd of magnificent cattle which my soldiers, God knows how, had got their hands on. The Cossacks told us they were theirs, that they'd have nothing for supper if we didn't give some of them back. They weren't worried about the next day and 15 cattle would suffice for them. I had 22 given back to them, and they seemed most content. A secret joy stood painted on their faces, and a malignant smile indicated the hope they already had of punishing us for having got as far as Moscow.'

Delaborde's Young Guard division, which had been left behind at Smolensk, has just caught up, and out of some empty soap boxes 'found in a factory' Paul de Bourgoing and his comrades on Delaborde's staff are making themselves a kind of roofless barrack.

But at the Dorogomilov Gate Napoleon – largely at Durosnel's suggestion – has put off his official entry until tomorrow.

'After pacing up and down in front of the gate for some while, he mounted his charger, rejoined the Prince of Eckmühl a little distance away, and we all went with him to the village near the town,' where he also reconnoitres the surroundings to a considerable distance. Then, coming back, he passes through the suburb, and goes

'as far as the partly demolished [stone] bridge. The river was only a couple of feet deep, and we were able to ford it. The Emperor went as far as the street on the opposite bank, then turned in his tracks to hasten the repairs to the bridge so that the ammunition could cross it.'

Meanwhile Count Daru and his staff have been sent into town at the heels of Murat's advance guard 'to ascertain the state of affairs and make a report the following day'. Penetrating the city's

'vast and magnificent solitude we passed the Kremlin, the square of the Bazaar, and the street leading to the square in front of the governor's palace. The night was fine; the moon's unclouded beams illumined those fine edifices, those vast palaces, those deserted streets, in which reigned the silence of the tomb.'

By and by they too fall in with a professor – whether Muraldt's host or another? – and some French residents

'who'd gone into hiding and couldn't comprehend this sudden disappearance of a population of 300,000 souls'.

And in fact many foreign residents, some of them of many years' standing, fearing or not being allowed to leave with the rest of the population, have remained behind, in terror of being 'massacred by moujiks' – i.e., the common people. Two such are *Madame Louise Fusil* and her friend, both of them actresses in Moscow's French theatre. Earlier that day 'the police had come knocking on every door to urge the occupants to leave, as the city was going to be set on fire and the fire-pumps had been taken away'. But the two Frenchwomen have stayed. Terrified when someone else comes knocking at their door, they're both relieved and amazed when he turns out to be a compatriot, who tells them the French are already in the city. Meanwhile Soltyk and his companions have been entering various palaces:

'All the doors were open. I took up my abode in a palace I was told belonged to the Countess Mackanow, at one of the corners of the square. In its underground kitchens I found two serfs who showed me the apartments. Everything was in as good order as if we'd been expected. In the drawing-room, which had two others opening out from it, there was a round table, on which the ladies' embroidery-work was still lying. Not even the most trifling piece of furniture wasn't in its place. In a very handsome bedchamber the keys were still in the drawers. Afterwards I heard all the linen and most valuable effects had been deposited in a cellar. Among them were two busts of the emperor and empress, concealed in casks of honey. I took the keys of this cellar into my own keeping, so that nothing should be taken away. Five or six new carriages, all in very fine condition, were in the coach-houses.'

Soltyk too, has been sent back into the deserted town. His chief, General Sokolnicki, wants him to find the topographical department some suitable lodgings near the Kremlin, which the Emperor, deputation or no deputation, intends to occupy tomorrow:

'So I re-entered Moscow around 5 p.m., followed only by one muleteer leading a lead-horse. I made for the centre of town. The streets were deserted, and the inhabitants still shut up inside their houses.'

Despite his strong Polish and therefore anti-Russian sympathies, Soltyk can't help being impressed by the architecture of the houses around the Kremlin and their owners' good taste:

'Pushkin's, particularly, struck me by its magnificence. Built in the Italian style and surmounted by a golden cupola from which you could see the whole of Moscow and its environs, it was quite enormous. In the middle of its courtyard was a jet of clear water and a basin where some swans were swimming peaceably. I could even choose from a hundred houses where to spend the night, each wealthier and more magnificent than the next. What a contrast for a man who'd spent several months in bivouacs and the most miserable dwellings! For me they were the enchanted palaces of the Arabian Nights.'

After examining the whole street, Soltyk selects a moderate-sized one, 'yet more than ample to lodge the general and his suite. I was astonished to see a dozen of the Countess Maszenpuszkin's servants hastening to meet me. At their head walked a valet or major-domo, elegantly dessed and in silk stockings. In quite good French he asks me what I want, adding that, when leaving, the Countess had given orders to receive us properly, and has left enough servants in the house to wait on us.'

Her palace is exquisitely furnished, 'marquetry parquet floors, the furniture in walnut or ebony. A little mistress in Paris couldn't have desired anything better.' After an hour a sumptuous dinner is served up, with various wines, even champagne. Still better, the major-domo asks Soltyk whether he'd like to share his dinner with two French ladies whose patriotism has kept them from leaving Moscow until their compatriots arrive, 'the one being the Countess' governess, the other her companion. I conducted them to the dining-room where dinner had been served. And soon there I was, sitting at table between two amiable women whose conversation I found most attractive.'

Elsewhere, Pion des Loches and his fellow artillery officers, too, are at dinner, in the house of a French resident. There the menu is 'vermicelli soup, a whole side of beef, macaroni, some excellent bottles of Bordeaux – perhaps I've never had a better meal in my whole life'.

'But soon gloomy presentiments came to mingle with our pleasant meal,' Soltyk goes on:

'Dinner still wasn't over and daylight was still fading when suddenly one of these ladies, seated facing a window from which much of Moscow could be seen, gets up, runs over to the window and exclaims agitatedly: "There's the fire!" I follow her, and in the distance see a flame of no great size, but clear, rising from the top of a building they tell me is the Bazaar and contains an immense amount of merchandise.'

It's nothing, Soltyk assures them. Just the soldiers' negligence. It'll soon be put out. But the ladies aren't so sure. The feelings of the Muscovite nobles, they tell him, are 'violently aroused against us, and we must expect some great misfortune'.

Misfortune?

They tell him about Rostopchin's project of setting fire to the city (that vague, madcap and apparently self-authorized scheme which Louise Fusil, too, has heard about and now feels ominously confirmed as she hears an explosion, and running over to *her* window sees in the sky something that looks like a 'sword of flame'). But Soltyk gives little credence to

'these scraps of information, based merely on some vague words that had escaped the great lords of the country and been uttered in the intimacy of their homes. Mostly I ascribed them to the timidity of their sex.'

Pion des Loches' amiable host, too, is just saying 'there are so many palaces here, you'll each be able to have one apiece', when they hear that the Stock Exchange is on fire: "Stock Exchange? What's the Stock Exchange?" "A building bigger than the Palais Royal [in Paris]. It's stuffed with works of jewellery, the world's richest artefacts. This night's losses will be incalculable."

'I went outside and saw how the whole horizon really was on fire. I murmured into the ear of one of my lieutenants: "We're lost, the Russians are going to burn Moscow. Let's get back to our park."'

If the Stock Exchange fire, alarming though it is, isn't spreading, it's partly due to the efforts of Major Vionnet of the Fusiliers-Tirailleurs of the Young Guard:

'To prevent it spreading, we brought up 100 men and put the rest of the battalion under arms. Although I'd done this very quickly, on my return I found a house all on fire. Seeing I'm searching for fire pumps, an inhabitant tells me in Italian they've all been taken out of the city at the governor's orders. Worse, the fires have been started intentionally.'

Aided by eighteen Muscovites, however, Vionnet and his men get busy pulling down an adjacent house to contain the conflagration:

'After four hours of wearisome efforts, the little house was demolished. Hardly able to stand on my feet, I returned to my lodging. I'd slept for about an hour and a half when I was awakened to be told the fire had caught another part of the Stock Exchange, in a building exposed to the wind.'

So he turns out again. And by about midnight this fire, too, has been mastered. 'We were dead with fatigue.'

Soltyk and his hosts are relieved to see that no further fires have broken out anywhere else[8] but 'these ladies, even so, remained silent and sad, and our dinner ended less gaily than it had begun'.

As for the always prescient Pion des Loches, he's instantly sure the army will have to retreat. And at his orders his gunners begin getting in some flour, liquor and warm clothes:

'I myself had the doors of a magazine forced and a good number of sacks of flour taken out – not without difficulty – by my gunners, who preferred to go further and search for gold. These sacks once safely in the middle of the park, I went back to my host's house and there spent the night on a chair, clothed and armed.'

After which he installs his men in a magnificent empty palace, without furniture but 'with plenty of rooms where I without loss of time proposed to bake plenty of bread'; installing himself meanwhile in a neighbouring palace which, though fully furnished, has

'no other provisions except some fowl, plenty of oats and an opulent cellar. On forcing the door, I found the prince's servants had spent the night there drinking, the floor being covered with empty bottles and spilt wine. Apart from an enormous, more than 400-bottle tun, all the wine was in bottles laid out on the sand. Glass in hand we identified the most exquisite vintages: Bordeaux, Frontignan, malaga, dry madeira, as well as liqueurs and syrups. Without exaggerating, this cellar was worth more than 10,000 crowns. Still struck with the idea that we'd soon be having to put up with great privations, I then had a barrel placed in my wagon, which was filled with bottles of madeira, some sacks of flour and some salted fish. My gunners too tried to furnish themselves, but without using their intelligence. From a confectionery store they brought me baskets full of dragées, macaroons and grilled almonds. I'd all the trouble in the world getting them to give them up and carry off tuns of excellent porter found in an ice cellar, and a freshly slaughtered ox, hung up in a butcher's shop.'

Dedem, for his part, has just posted sentries in the Kremlin, when he's been recognized by

'the valet of a princess, who'd seen me in Italy. Coming up to me, he begs me to save her house. His mistress has left only an hour ago. I authorize him to break into the writing-desk which he says contains some papers, and promise him a safeguard.'[9]

At first the Dutchman too has thought all these servants' talk of the city being set on fire really only means they're afraid the French will do it. 'But then they explained to me that more than a thousand persons had been left behind as incendiaries, and that M.le Comte de Rostopchin had had all the pumps removed from Moscow.'

Since the Guard are beginning to pillage on their own account, this is a serious matter. And at about 11 p.m. Soltyk, trying to get a night's real rest in his 'good bed', hears someone knock violently at his door:

'It was the two French ladies. They'd come to tell me the house was being invaded by soldiers who were threatening to loot it; that they'd already broken into the wine cellars and right now were busy draining off one bottle after another. The servants didn't dare resist them. I dressed promptly, attached my sabre to my belt, and made haste to go down and repress these disorders. At the entrance to the cellar I found ten or twelve grenadiers of the Old Guard, armed with muskets. Most were completely drunk.'

Luckily Soltyk, as we know, speaks fluent French:

'I reprimanded them sharply and ordered them to get out, shouting at them that they were in the lodging of a general who belonged to the Emperor's household. One of the grenadiers came at me, menacing me with his fist. Several others followed to back him up. Drawing my sabre, I aimed such a blow at the plaque of the bearskin of the soldier who'd threatened me, that I knocked him down to the floor. This demonstration momentarily checked the grenadiers. The ones who were least drunk remonstrated with their comrades, reminding them of the respect they owed to rank and their obligation to observe military subordination. Despite this, after a moment's hesitation, two or three of them flung themselves at me with levelled bayonets. I parried the blows and, remounting the staircase, went back into my room, locking its door and shouting to my pursuers that the first man to try and force the door would get a ball from my pistols in him, because they were loaded.'

At that moment a Russian servant intervenes. And Soltyk's adventure ends peacefully. A moment later the house is 'evacuated by the marauders, who left, taking with them a goodly number of bottles to their bivouac. And the rest of the night passed calmly.'

Earlier, during the afternoon – at 5 p.m., says Fain,

'Napoleon had passed the barrier, gone some yards forward, and taken up his provisional quarters in a big inn on the right-hand side',

an inn Caulaincourt will afterwards remember as 'a mean tavern, built of wood, at the entrance to the suburb', but at the time notes down as 'a little timber house', But which to Bausset, the obese prefect of this temporary palace, seems to be 'a fine wooden house'. Repeated assurances are coming in from Murat that

'numerous stragglers are being caught, that they're all saying the [Russian] army is being disbanded, that the Cossacks are declaring openly they'll fight no more. He confirmed the information we'd obtained inside the city: that Kutusov, until only yesterday, hadn't said a word about having lost the battle or retreating on Moscow. Not until forty-eight hours before we'd entered Moscow had the governor, Rostopchin, even heard that the battle had been lost. The King of Naples was confidently expecting to seize part of the enemy's convoys and was sure he'd be able to break up their rearguard, so utterly disheartened did he believe the Russians to be.' All these details, Caulaincourt sees, 'delighted the Emperor and restored his good cheer'.

Although both Mortier and Durosnel have been sent there, no importance is being attributed to the fire in the Stock Exchange, which they, for lack of fire pumps, aren't able to do much about. Two smaller fires are attributed to the Guard's carelessness in lighting its camp fires. All this in spite of a catch made by interpreter Lelorgne d'Ideville while he'd been in town, trying to rustle up a deputation,

'a police officer, a simpleton, who knew everything that was afoot, and was very candid in all his avowals. At first he became so terrified he seemed to be slightly deranged. Such at least was the impression given by his statements, and no heed was paid to him. Seeing the first small fire break out, he'd declared that before long there'd be many more. Orders had been given to burn down the whole city. His revelations seemed to be delusions of a lunatic. This unfortunate fellow kicked his heels for some time in the guardhouse, where he was left when we had no more use for him.'

Eighty-two days have passed since the Grand Army crossed the Niemen. In that time it has marched some 825 miles, fought two major battles – one of them, the bloodiest in modern times, neither won, lost nor drawn – and several minor ones. Only two-thirds of its effectives are still with its eagles; of the cavalry scarcely half.[10] Yet Napoleon isn't an inch nearer to his objective – to force Russia back into his Continental System – than he was when he'd set out from Paris.

And tomorrow he'll get the shock of his life – as Moscow, as if by spontaneous combustion, bursts into flame.

Fiery prelude to a terrible retreat.

NOTES

Preface

1. All temperatures are in Réaumur. Since water boils at 80° Réaumur, centigrade (Celsius) temperatures will be proportionately higher – or lower.

Chapter 1. Overture to 1812

1 See bibliography under Villemain. Bibliographical references are given for all names italicized when first mentioned in the text.

2. Odenleben writes: 'With incomparable energy and efficiency he provided everything Napoleon needed. Chief among his virtues was an enterprise that knew no limits. He had an ability to say everything in a few words. After passing the night working together with Napoleon, he was the first at his post at dawn, almost always on horseback and constantly present at the Emperor's carriage door. He saw to it that strict economy was observed in all respects.' 'My notes', Caulaincourt himself tells us, 'were made everywhere, at my desk and in camp, every day and at all times of day; they are the work of every moment. I have touched up nothing.' There were moments when he was afraid his master might get to see them. Of this faithful and unusually candid man Napoleon would afterwards say at St Helena: 'He was an excellent Master of the Horse, but couldn't write.' An absurd judgement. Of Caulaincourt's memoirs it has been said that if all others from the period were lost, they alone would suffice to give us an accurate idea of it. Discovered in a locked tin box amid the ruins of the family château after the First World War, there is some evidence that they may have been tampered with; but not in what concerns the Russian campaign. There is no evidence that Caulaincourt's emphatic claims of having been against the war from the outset are an *ex post facto* rationalization. They'll accompany us at highest and most initiated level all the way to Moscow and back to Paris.

3. Since we hear no more of his being in poor health we canonly conclude that it was a pretext.

4. In her *Mes Dix Années d'Exil*, Germaine de Staël, who had sat at dinner with him when he was First Consul, notes that 'his eyes didn't smile'.

5. Like so many others, Constant would quit Napoleon's service at Fontainebleau in 1814, having either been (according to Napoleon) summarily dismissed, or perhaps (according to Constant himself) resigning, in connection with an attempted theft of (or perhaps misunderstanding about) a sum of 100,000 francs. In later years he'd spend his time fishing. After witnessing the Return of the Ashes, he'd say in tears to General Thiébault: 'I don't know how that devil of a man managed it, but he bewitched us all.' Of no man is the saying less true than that of Napoleon's that, 'no man is a hero to his valet'. Although Constant's memoirs, based on his anecdotes, are mainly the work of other pens, the portrait that transpires of a man who, if naturally exigent, was the best and most considerate of masters, is exactly the same as that given by his successor, the transparently honest Marchand, who accompanied Napoleon to St Helena and was rewarded by being made a count. No little melodramatic, the incident seems in its circumstantiality to have the hallmark of truth about it, and as far as I know has never been challenged.

6. Le Roy (or Leroy) says he wrote his memoirs as guidance for his two grandsons who were going in for the military profession. Hence – quite apart from his Lucullan temperament – the circumstantiality with which he describes how he got his dinner each day, sometimes under the most trying circumstances. Although he had a son who was a sergeant in another

357

battalion of the 85th, he had only one friend, his irrepressible adjutant-major Lieutenant Nicolas Jacquet, to whom he gave 'all my confidence and the little friendship I'm capable of. I've been so often deceived and the dupe of my good faith that I regard friendship as something impossible, above all on reaching the age of discretion, leaving aside those childishnesses which, in some people, even so, last longer than the liaisons of their maturity.'

7. Among other things she had recorded in it a visit by Davout: 'and weary work it was, trying to enliven him, for nothing more stolid and uncommunicative can be imagined than this thoroughly unpleasant man. Though neither malicious nor intellectual, his face betrays that he can be very curt and brutal. His aides-de-camp were every bit as disagreeable.'

8. The Coburgers were assigned to the 4th Regiment of the Confederation of the Rhine. They wore a French shako with brass rhomboid plate bearing a hunting horn, white cords, company pompom (grenadiers had bearskins) red cords and plumes, red epaulettes), on a dark-green Prussian-style coat, with two rows of white buttons on the chest, dark-green cuff flaps, yellow collar and cuffs, red turnbacks, three white lace buttonholes on the square cuff flaps, light-blue Hungarian breeches with yellow thigh and side lacing, short black gaiters with a point at the front, white belts.

9. Heinrich von Roos relates that when asked what the imperial 'N's on his men's saddlecloths stood for, they'd reply: *'Noch nur norden!'* (anywhere except northwards!).

10. By 1812 the price of such a substitute – many were professionals, who sold themselves over and over again and then disappeared – had risen to the astronomical sum of 4,000 francs, and few but the very well-off could any longer afford it. This partly explains Caulaincourt's observation to Napoleon, on the banks of the Niemen, that this new war was not regarded as 'national' – i.e., in the inter-

ests of the French middle class (*'la nation'*). It was one thing to draft the sons of the people (*le peuple*) to be slaughtered in their hundreds of thousands; quite another for one's own more or less well-educated son to have to go.

11. Brandt was from that part of East Prussia which Napoleon had sliced off and incorporated in the Grand Duchy of Warsaw.

12. Guitard's proudest boast was that he'd captured 6,000 British troops near Bilbao in 1810.

13. He would serve during the Russian campaign as Assistant Prefect of the Palace, his particular task being to supervise the headquarters mules that carried among other things Napoleon's gold field service.

14. Quoted from Lagerbielke's report to the Swedish Foreign Office.

15. Captain Ross of HMS *Northumberland*, who didn't like Napoleon, describes the ex-Emperor's gait as 'something between a strut and a waddle', partly no doubt because of his having put on so much weight and partly because of the ship's movement.

16. See under Barre de Nanteuil in bibliography.

17. Yet it was this amiable monarch whose ultra-reactionary ideas – or lack of ideas – would most of all be responsible for the massive oppression that would fall on Europe after 1815.

18. Like his assessments of his policies, Méneval's striking portrait of Napoleon's personality, which introduces the third volume of his memoirs – unfortunately skimpy in what concerns 1812 – is wholly positive, yet unquestionably sincere.

19. It would be captured by Cossacks at Krasnoïe during the retreat, together with his marshal's baton.

Chapter 2. The Rape of Poland

1. He had found the gross deceit and official perfidy employed to ruin an honest German merchant particularly scandalous. Like Captain Franz Roeder of the Hessians, he was shocked by the reduced straits of the Mecklenburg fishermen consequent on the Continental Blockade and the ubiquity of Napoleon's customs officers.

2. Heinemann had served in a French line regiment at Wagram, a fact of which he was inordinately proud. This hadn't prevented him from trying to desert while the Brunswick Chasseurs, part of Vandamme's VIII Corps, marched through Germany.

3. Brandt says that in his company, which had been serving in Spain, there wasn't one man who hadn't been wounded since 1809. And when the regiment, en route for Russia, had been been reviewed by Napoleon on the Place du Carousel, expectations had run high: 'One needs to have lived and served in that epoch to understand the importance of such a miliary fete, and what emotions set the heart of the boldest beating at the approach and aspect of this extraordinary man. The upshot of the review, however, didn't come up to everyone's expectations. We were counting on a rain of promotions, decorations, gratifications! In all there were only some 30 for this 2nd Vistula Regiment, which for four years had been living, or rather dying, in an atmosphere thick with musket-balls and grapeshot.'

4. After the Dresden event Marie-Louise had accompanied her father and – violently jealous – stepmother on a visit to Prague.

5. Butkevicius says, most improbably, that Napoleon was 'driving a wagon' – certainly an error in translation.

Chapter 3. Midsummer at the Niemen

1. It seems to have been by no means unusual for Napoleon to disguise himself at the outposts. Corporal Heinemann, then serving in a French Line regiment, was on outpost duty on the Isle of Lobau in the Danube in 1810, when suddenly Napoleon had turned up, borrowed a light infantryman's grey overcoat and shako and, thus attired, had done sentry duty on the river bank to examine the Austrian positions at close quarters. Heinemann relates proudly how his comrades 'elected the Emperor a voltigeur in our company'.

2. The Russian high command at Vilna were still unaware of his proximity, and had no idea of the real size of his effectives. Their latest figures, filched back in February by a Russian officer who'd bribed a French war ministry official in Paris – he'd been arrested and guillotined – were hopelessly out of date. Even the amplest Russian estimates didn't come up to half the Grand Army's real numbers.

3. The only tears this unemotional young man would shed during a campaign that would cause so many would be when Liesje died of exhaustion in a snowdrift, not far from where he was now.

4. Pils was not only a gifted although untrained water-colour artist. He also kept a *journal de marche*, in which he recorded his marshal's – but not his own – doings. Since Oudinot was forever being wounded, Pils always dogged his footsteps with a first-aid box. His son, Isidor Pils, one of France's most famous painters of his day, held his father's oil paintings, based on water-colour sketches made in Russia, in very high esteem. But no amount of research on my part has been able to track them down. What has become of these paintings which, artistic merit apart, must possess first-class documentary value? For example, the one, particularly admired by his son, of the fatal burning of the Berezina bridge during the retreat? – Oudinot's 32 wounds, of which he only considered nineteen to have been grave enough to be worth mentioning in his *états de service*, were by no means untypical. General Houchard had been wounded 48 times, General Achard 28, Rapp 26, Grouchy 25, Junot 18 – and

at the Battle of Heilsberg, Commandant Chipault of the 4th Cuirassiers had received 56 sabre cuts – and recovered perfectly! The account of Oudinot's wedding in his young wife Eugénie de Coussy's memoirs is well worth reading on its own account. See also my short study in Chandler's *Napoleon's Marshals*, Macmillan NY and Weidenfeldt & Nicholson, London 1987.

5. Roustam, an Armenian slave who had entered Napoleon's service in Cairo and on whom he lavished benefits, would also abandon him at Fontainebleau at the time of his first abdication. Hortense Beauharnais painted his portrait.

6. Lejeune had designed his romantic uniform for himself and Berthier's other aides in Spain, where he had been captured by guerrillas and shot; survived; been taken prisoner by the British and taken to England. From there, breaking his parole, he had got back to France thanks to the services of Romney Marsh smugglers, who at one point, however, contemplated cutting his throat. Back in Paris he had immediately reported for duty to Napoleon. Many of his elegant battle paintings are to be seen at Versailles.

7. Thirion, who had joined up in 1805 and been twice wounded, had been in Spain with the 22nd Dragoons. He had once been fined 3 francs by Napoleon for having lost his bayonet. 'I've always thought he wasn't annoyed to be able to show he knew the price of a bayonet.' Thirion died aged 82, in 1869, at Metz.

8. Increasingly faithful to Napoleon as his star waned, Planat de la Faye would volunteer to go with him to St Helena, but was outmanoeuvred aboard HMS *Bellepheron* by Gourgaud. Napoleon's last years might have been very different if Planat, instead of the hyper-emotional Gourgaud, had been in attendance at Longwood. He might even have proved a match for the sinister playboy Montholon. See Forshuvud, Sten: *Who Killed Napoleon?* and Hapgood: *The Murder of Napoleon*, New York, 1981.

9. Berthier's senior ADC had been one of Pauline Bonaparte's lovers. She had given him some priceless diamonds, a gift from Napoleon – who, however, instantly recognized them, sewn into this officer's pélisse, and taken umbrage. Whereupon they'd had to be returned.

10. Gourgaud had two obsessive ambitions: to rise in Napoleon's estimation, and to get married. In the end he succeeded in neither. Gourgaud's father had been a violonist at Versailles and his mother had been the Bourbon Duc de Berry's wet-nurse. In 1815, having betrayed his oath to the Bourbons by weeping, raging and sulking himself back into Napoleon's entourage – at one moment he'd even locked himself up in an attic of the Tuileries and refused to come out until taken back into the Emperor's good graces – he'd escape the firing squad by going with him to St Helena, where his violent jealousy, e.g., of Montholon who while fixing the best accommodation for himself and his wife arranged for Gourgaud to live in a tent in the garden, would finally become the bane of the ex-emperor's existence. Falling violently ill – Forshuvud thinks as a result of Montholon's expertise with arsenic – his mind seems to have become temporarily unhinged and his pathological jealousy made him more and more of a nuisance, so that he finally had to leave. After betraying Napoleon's secrets first to Sir Hudson Lowe, then to Lord Bathurst in London (with the result that Napoleon's confinement was made even more miserable), he would return to Belgium, where he'd pose as the ex-emperor's best friend and finally reinstate himself as a Bonapartist hero of St Helena.

11. Although exceedingly readable, Marbot is always the hero of his own occasion and his memoirs must at times be taken with a fistful of salt. Throughout the campaign he would be the 23rd Chasseurs' acting colonel, its commander Colonel Nougarède being too gouty to sit a horse, 'and this was no way to command a regiment of light cavalry on campaign'. Since the regiment, brigaded with the 24th Chasseurs, formed part of Oudinot's II

Corps, we shall not rejoin it until the Berezina, during the retreat.

12. In the evening of 20 May Coignet had driven his little two-wagon convoy into the Place Vendôme, near the Tuileries cellars, and loaded them with small barrels, each holding 28,000 gold francs. Two others were filled with officers' trunks. Catching up with his regiment at Metz he, at his own suggestion, had gone on ahead to pick up the regimental mail at postes restantes in Germany. On one memorable occasion, when Napoleon, who only measured 5 feet 2 inches, had wished to impress the diplomatic corps and had personally ordered both grenadier regiments' drill movements on the Place du Carousel, little Coignet had had to repeat his orders, making a half-turn and saluting each time as he did so.

13. Throughout the Empire period there were complaints of a shortage of carriages in Paris, the more so as the city only had three cab stands!

14. Unfortunately Stendhal's diary for the 1812 campaign was lost in the retreat. All we have is a few of his letters.

15. Attempts to ignore this regulation could come abruptly to grief. At Elbing, where the 2nd Swiss had bivouacked in a plain outside the town, one of voltigeur Jean-Marc Bussy's comrades, Pillonnel by name, had been detailed off to be batman to that master of the theory if not the practice of warfare, the Swiss General Henri de Jomini. The said Pillonel had been cheerfully on his way into town, when 'an officer, looking out of the window of his lodgings, sees him passing with all his equipment. And calls out: "Swiss, where are you off to?" Pillonel answers: "I'm going to General Jomini." – "Well then, you go straight back to your battalion, and don't leave it again!" It was Napoleon himself, playing the military policeman.'

16. Despite his unsteady seat he had a habit of galloping headlong down ravines so steep his suite hardly dared follow. On one occasion he had ridden from Valladolid to Burgos, a distance of 96 miles, in 36 hours, and none of his staff had been able to keep up with him. Yet the only person who is known to have thought him the 'finest horseman in the world' would be the teenager Fanny Balcombe, for whom he made Admiral Cockburn's horse wheel about on the lawn at The Briars, on St Helena. It was Jardin, the First Groom's, duty to 'throw dogs and pigs between the legs of his Arab greys to accustom them to all kinds of sounds and sights'. Had Jardin neglected his duties, or was Friedland affected by its rider's mood?

17. Caulaincourt's claim that he was always frank with his master is confirmed by a Prussian officer who saw a lot of them in 1813: 'While fully recognizing Caulaincourt's qualities and abilities I think Bonaparte was less reserved with Duroc. The former was no less devoted to his master, but he was too cold and reserved, too bound by etiquette, whereas Duroc knew when to forget formality. On the other hand Caulaincourt spoke frankly to Napoleon and openly discussed matters which others dared not mention for fear of falling into disgrace.' For a striking, and indeed moving short biography of Caulaincourt, see Jean Hannoteau's introduction to the Memoirs.

18. When Philippe de Ségur's – from a literary point of view enthralling – La Campagne de Russie appeared in 1823 it made an immense impression, not least on fervent Bonapartists who accused it of a reactionary tendency. Gourgaud was particularly furious. His scathing – and in points undoubtedly correct – critique led to a duel between the two ex-officers of the Imperial Household. Stendhal too accuses Ségur of currying favour with the Bourbons. Ségur's classical models make him present Napoleon (a) as a victim of hubris, and (b) as suffering from ill-health. While Gourgaud doggedly maintains that he was in the best of health. There is doubtless something in both points of view.

19. But in Stockholm, a couple of hundred miles from Kovno as the crow flies,

Bernadotte, with unusual perspicacity, was writing to the Tsar that Napoleon by invading Russia was 'committing suicide'. Historians have not generally recognized Bernadotte's potentially critical role in 1812. Had he sided with Napoleon and simultaneously attacked Finland and marched on Petersburg, thereby tying down Wittgenstein's corps and so releasing Oudinot's corps, it is just possible that the Russian withdrawal from Vilnius might not have been so successful, and the whole outcome would have been different? This is why Napoleon himself said on St Helena that in 1812 the world's destinies lay in the hands of 'a Frenchman', i.e., Bernadotte. Naturally the remark was also part of his general self-exculpation.

Chapter 4. 'Get into Vilna!'

1. This according to Dr *Heinrich von Roos* of the Württemberg cavalry, III Corps.

2. 'It was only with difficulty that the French could persuade us Poles to take service on their staffs, to replace or supplement "dumb" Frenchmen...' When Napoleon had written to Prince Poniatowski, commanding V Corps, asking for six Polish officers of good family who 'spoke Polish, French, German and (if possible) Russian' to be seconded to imperial headquarters, no one, according to Grabowski, had been very keen. Doubtless, though he doesn't say so, Soltyk had been co-opted as a result of the reconnaissance on the morning of 24 June.

3. In the French army a white plume was the distinguishing mark of a colonel. No regiment, as far as I know – except the 2nd Guard Lancers, which were a new unit – wore them.

4. Cuirassier-captain *Jean Bréaut des Marlots* in a letter home to his sister.

5. He was a brother-in-law of Marshal Lannes. The scene is the one caricatured by Tolstoy in *War and Peace*, obviously on the basis of Ségur's melodramatic account. According to Ségur, Napoleon 'ordered a squadron of Poles to throw themselves into the river. Unhesitatingly these élite troops do so. At first they ride in good order, and when they can no longer touch bottom they redouble their efforts. Swimming, they soon reach midstream. But the current, which is at its swiftest there, scatters them. Their horses panic. Their loss is certain, but it's their own country that lies ahead, their devotion is to the liberator! About to be engulfed, they renounce their efforts, and turning their heads towards Napoleon, shout *"Vive l'Empereur!"* as they drown.' Which sounds dubious, to say, the least of it. As it happens, we've a third account. Marbot says his 23rd Chasseurs, heading II Corps, turned up at the same moment. And certainly he isn't the man to spoil a good yarn. Yet all he saw was *one* man drown: 'I took the man's name. It was Tzsinski.' Gourgaud, too, pours scorn on Ségur's mock-heroics. A Captain *Joseph Zalusky*, he says, commanding the first squadron of the Polish Lancers of the Guard, 'having abandoned his horse, was in danger of drowning. He was saved by some sapper-workmen and light infantrymen' – luckily for us, as he'll have a lot to relate.

6. Blaze explains that in the eyes of the Napoleonic soldier everyone who wasn't a military man was either a 'peasant' or a 'bourgeois'. One didn't steal their property. One simply 'found' and 'took' it: 'No one who hasn't been to war can ever imagine the evils it entails. We officers lived off what our men "found". How could we have done otherwise? Our supplies, even when we had any, couldn't possibly keep up with our rapid marches. In rich countries we would carry into camp twenty times more provisions than we could possibly consume; the rest was wasted. The soldier lives for today. Yesterday he lacked everything. Today he's in abundance. An army's marauders always have this excuse: "I'm hungry, I'm looking for bread." There's no answer to this. The cavalry troopers have a double excuse: they're searching for forage for their horses.'

7. The French armies were unique in having a more or less reliable postal service,

through which anyone could write home to his family or friends. In 1812 the Russians would capture quite a lot of such letters and afterwards publish them.

8. The word 'dysentery' was used indifferently in those days to include diarrhoea.

9. Roeder is absolutely an acquaintance worth making. I am grateful to Miss Helen Roeder, his descendant, for permission to quote from her book, one of the most vivid and personal of all the accounts.

10. Fivaz was Jomini's brother-in-law, and would shortly become his ADC. See: *Soldats Suisses au Service de la France.*

11. It is almost impossible to identify the traditional place-names, spelt differently by various participants in the campaign, on a modern map of Lithuania. Lithuanian place names seem to be as different from the traditional Polish ones as Finnish place-names are from Swedish ones in Finland. Evê is presumably Vievis, Novo-Troki is Trakai, etc.

12. It's Davout who, in Tolstoy's *War and Peace*, orders Pierre Bezhukov to be shot, after he's betrayed his educated status by correctly addressing him as Monseigneur.

13. A privilege Jerome Bonaparte liked to usurp. Sometimes Berthier would be mistaken for his master on account of his hat. Three years later it would be partly for lack of Berthier's routines that Napoleon would be definitively beaten at Waterloo. 'Berthier would have posted an ordnance officer at the Charleroi bridge...'

14. The formerly beautiful Madame Visconti was the passion of Berthier's life. During the earlier campaigns he'd installed a veritable shrine to her in his tent, and the whole army had laughed at him for doing so. The lady had a withered arm. After Napoleon, forbidding him to marry her, had married him off to a German princess, all three lived in a harmonious *ménage à trois* in Paris and at the superb château of Grosbois, whenever Berthier had leisure to be there. Formerly

owned by the guillotined Duke of Orleans ('Philippe Egalité'), brother of Louis XVI, Grosbois had been given to Berthier in his capacity of Master of the Hunt. It was currently occupied by the kidnapped Spanish royal family.

15. Staël, Germaine de: *Mes Dix Années d'Exil.* On 14 July, after escaping from the isolation of her Swiss estate to which Napoleon had condemned her, the most famous novelist and critic of his regime in Europe was also to 'invade' Russia; getting to Moscow before him and leaving for Petersburg before the Grand Army's arrival. Going on to Stockholm to hobnob with and flatter Bernadotte, she would play an important part in stimulating the rising against Napoleon's regime in 1813-14 – and live to regret his fall.

16. According to Dedem it would be his compatriots the Dutch who would be 'least able to stand the privations. Their morale would be quickly affected. We were content with their bravery and their officers' education. But above all the younger men were attacked by depression, becoming discouraged at the idea of being taken so far from their country. They regretted their methodical habits and, for the most part at least, were neither imbued with the spirit of conquest and domination nor with the gaiety characteristic of the French.'

17. The episode is paraphrased from Thomas: *Les Grands Cavaliers du Premier Empire* (nd).

18. Ségur, Philippe de: *Du Rhin à Fontainebleau*, Edn. Nelson, Paris. In his – often very inaccurate – campaign history he writes in the grand heroic style, modelled on classical writers, and makes no mention of his personal actions or feelings. But here, in his personal memoirs, he writes with accents of personal suffering.

19. The Jagellon dynasty (1386-1499) extended the borders of Lithuania to include the whole of Poland.

Chapter 5. Bagration gives Davout the Slip

1. A 'division', in this sense, consisted of two companies.

2. His name was Amédé, and his features are described as 'cherubic'. Napoleon's stepdaughter, ex-Queen Hortense of Holland, who was quite a good artist as well as being perhaps the only really admirable person in the imperial family, had painted his portrait.

3. 'One of the two officers who malingered, Lieutenant Lesueur, who held the Legion of Honour, had to command the laggers and next day got a severe dressing-down from Bessières. Temporarily attached to the Horse Chasseurs of the Guard, they didn't rejoin until later.' – Dumonceau.

4. Allegedly the change was made at the advice of Berthier, his mortal enemy, though it seems unlikely that Napoleon would have taken so important a step at the advice of a man of whose intelligence he had so low an opinion. The three detached divisions were commanded by Count Lobau.

5. In five months' time Smorgoni would become famous as the place where Napoleon, after signing his last bulletin announcing the Grand Army's complete destruction, would quit its last relics to hasten back to Paris.

6. Published in a journal, I have taken this brief résumé from Tarle's more extensive one in *Napoleon's Invasion of Russia, 1812*, London, 1942. At St Helena Napoleon wouldn't even be able to recall the envoy's name: 'Alexander sent someone to tell me that if I'd evacuate the invaded territory and go back to the Niemen he'd treat for peace. But I in turn took it for a ruse. I was swollen with success. I'd caught the Russian army on the hop, had thrown everything into disorder. I'd cut off Bagration. I'd high hopes of destroying him. So I thought Alexander was only hoping to gain time, elude me and rally his forces. No question but that if I'd been convinced of Alexander's good faith

I'd have retired to the Niemen, and we wouldn't have come further than the Dwina. Vilna would have been neutralized; and we'd both have gone there, each with a few battalions of our guards, and treated in person. How many combinations I'd have introduced! He'd only have had to choose. And we'd have parted as good friends.' Napoleon's words, uttered in the presence of Caulaincourt, Duroc and Bessières, gives this retrospective daydream the lie.

7. One of the merits of Curtis Cate's admirable book *The War of the Two Emperors* is that he makes it perfectly plain that it was impossible for Jerome to arrive on time in the theatre of war.

8. Jerome liked to preempt Berthier's privilege, unique in the army, of wearing a Swiss-style civilian hat, of the kind Napoleon had made so famous. A certain colonel Latouche, a Frenchman from the Illyrian provinces, who bore a striking resemblance to Napoleon, was doing so too. According to what Colonel Jumilhac told his friend Colonel Griois, Latouche had been up to his tricks in Warsaw, where he'd pretended to be Napoleon incognito and promised he'd promote Jumilhac to general's rank, which of course he couldn't do. On 25 June, Dessolles, IV Corps' chief-of-staff, had sent Latouche back to France because 'he affects to play on his resemblance to the Emperor and provoke ridiculous misunderstandings, he has been arrested and sent to headquarters'.

9. If Vandamme, instead of the by now sick and supine Junot, had been in charge of VIII Corps at Valutina the Russian army would certainly not have escaped total destruction.

10. Metternich, Napoleon's arch-enemy, would say of Fain: 'Baron Fain is a man of probity, conscientious, who always relates facts as they happened or as they have been presented to him in accounts he feels he should believe. He's a good historian and an honest man.' This, despite the fact that Fain's view of Napoleon is always positive.

11. Alexander had absolutely no illusions as to Napoleon's 'personal friendship' for him. He would write to his sister Catherine in September: 'This spring, before my departure for Vilna, I had been informed on good authority that the constant work of Napoleon's secret agents... if I was with the army, to put all the reverses that might happen down to my account and to represent me as having sacrificed my personal pride by preventing more experienced generals than myself from obtaining successes over the enemy; and, on the other hand, if I was not with the army, to impute it to a lack of courage on my part.'

12. A verst is 1,100 yards.

13. 'Formerly I could keep four or five secretaries busy, but then I was Napoleon. Now it's an effort even to open my eyelids.' – Napoleon in his last sickness, to Dr Antommarchi in November 1820.

14. This could have been as a result of an order from Napoleon to send the gendarmerie to deal with the 33rd Regiment, which was busy pillaging at Voronovo. He'd been told some of Davout's men were making for Lida, on pretext of joining I Corps, but 'really to pillage this valley, which is superb'.

15. Ordered by Barclay to march for Minsk, Bagration had then received another from Alexander himself, countermanding it and ordering him to march north-eastwards for the Drissa Camp, i.e., right across the path of the advancing Grand Army. It had been while trying to cross the Vilna-Minsk road, at Ochmiana, that his advance guard had bumped into Pajol's cavalry. Not knowing that Davout, deprived of Friant's, Gudin's and Morand's divisions, was now at less than half-strength, he'd supposed himself to have to do with 60,000 crack troops – nearly twice his own 35,000. Veering back, he'd made tracks south-eastwards for Slutsk, on the edge of the Pripet Marshes (a vast trackless area dividing the northern from the southern theatres of war). After a 9-day forced march, he'd rested his troops at Slutsk, and was now heading eastwards for Borissow, on the Berezina.

16. One wonders what had become of a certain voltigeur whom Napoleon, when the regiment had paraded in front of him at the Tuileries, had singled out on account of his 'embonpoint, excessive in a voltigeur'; and, turning to General Krasinski, had said: 'Ask that fellow where he's put on so much fat!' And upon the man's replying that it was in France, rejoined smiling: 'Tell him to put himself on a diet, because soon they may well have to fast.'

17. Davout, who in his youth had been a devotee of Montaigne, was nevertheless a convinced atheist.

18. Other eye-witnesses' memories seem inexact. One says it was the 111th Regiment, made up of Piedmontese, that suffered; another, more vaguely, 'a German regiment who'd lost a great many men en route, some of whom had been pillaging and causing disorders'. But that they marched past with dignity, even so.

Chapter 6. Problems at Vilna

1. The Drissa Camp, brain-child of a certain Colonel von Pfull, the Tsar's military adviser, was a system of earthworks on the River Dwina. The idea was that 50,000 men should shut themselves up in it, lure Napoleon to besiege them, and then attack him in flank and rear. Never having been properly completed, it was already being abandoned.

2. 'He understood me in his own way and carried out his task independently,' Napoleon would say of Bacler d'Albe at St Helena. Unfortunately d'Albe's *Souvenirs Pittoresques*, with their admirable engravings of important battlefields, lack a commentary. His son was ADC to Philippe de Ségur. In the rout after Waterloo the valet Marchand would see 'poor little M. d'Albe walking along looking dazed. He'd lost his box of coloured pins.'

3. The day Castellane made his irritated diary entry, Planat had to implement the following:

'Vilna, July 7: I must inform you, *M. le Général*, that General Eblé is being given orders undelayedly to organize a bridging train of thirty-two boats, with two companies of pontooneers and one company of marines, which he will place under the command of General Kirgener [commanding the Guards Engineers], who will take with him one company of the Marines of the Guard, the company of Sappers of the Guard, that of the Grand Duchy of Berg, the three companies of sappers attached to the Guard, two companies of workmen from the Danube Battalion with their vehicles, two companies of miners and two of sappers from the General Engineer Park. This train will march for Widzoni (Vidzeme), where it will be under the King of Naples' orders. However, since the bridging train may retard these troops on the march, the Emperor orders that the pontooneers and one company of sappers be left behind to escort it. General Kirgener will march ahead with the rest of his troops to have all the bridges on the route put back into proper shape. The Emperor demands a detailed report on the bridges.'

Next day comes another letter, no less exhaustive, ordering the bridging trains' successive departures for Sventsiany on 9, 10 and 11 July, each of 30 vehicles. The rigging teams – vital for throwing pontoon bridges across rivers – left behind at Kovno are to be brought up by oxen 'two to each vehicle'. The Intendant-General is to supply Eblé with barley and 200 pairs of oxen.

'The Guard is leaving behind far too many of its guns. Since we have men, and all that is lacking is horses, oxen must be used, these being very suitable for the reserve parks. The Emperor's intention is that you recommend the same method to III, II and I Corps. Since the oxen do not need barley they will infallibly arrive, even if later, but always in time to bring the divisions their replacements.'

Alas, neither oxen, nor goads, nor barley, nor qualified drivers are just now to be

had. This doesn't alter the fact that several major rivers lie ahead; and 12 July brings the wretched overworked Planat two more orders anent the bridging teams: 'Everything must gradually arrive, whether drawn by horses or oxen, but tomorrow it's imperative that the entire personnel shall leave, because without pontoons His Majesty will have to use skiffs and trestles...' Later the same day comes another:

'*M. le Général*. The Emperor orders you to bring 5,000 muskets up to Vilna and as many again to Kovno, and sabres in proportion, to arm the French infantry... Likewise the King of Saxony's 30,900 muskets, which are at Bromberg; the 5,000 new musketoons and 8,000 sabres to arm the insurrection...', etc., etc.

Next day come three more letters. One informs Lariboisière that the siege train has been ordered (apparently over his head) to march for Tilsit, where it's to be embarked to help Macdonald's X Corps invest Riga. Relays of vehicles are to be set up every fifteen miles 'and consist of at least 150 to 200 vehicles'. Two companies, one of naval workmen and one of sappers, are being left at Kovno to rebuild the Niemen and Vilia bridges:

'Construct a redoubt on the high ground on the Niemen's left bank, to defend the bridge. Establish the projected fort on the high ground (right bank of the Niemen, and at the Vilia bridgehead). Each of these works is to have twelve guns. The commandant there will furnish six hundred soldiers to be employed on these works, and twelve hundred peasants...'

(It will be with these guns that Ney with his last rearguard of Bavarians will fire the last shots of the campaign in December.) Gen. Eblé's pontoon bridges 'which are very good' are to be re-utilized at various points along the Vilia as soon as the regular Niemen bridges have been rebuilt.

3. Later, as the summer grew hotter and drier, the whole scheme, so carefully worked out in Paris, would have to be dropped and supplies brought into the town on carts by commercial contract with local Jews.

4. There are vivid accounts of this minor battle by Marbot – who as usual declares himself its hero – by 'grenadier' Pils, and by the Piedmontese *maréchal-des-logis Jean Calosso*. It is in Calosso's account, which in certain points convincingly contradicts Marbot's more vainglorious and self-centred one, that we find the source of the famous incident of the soldier who, having lost his arm in the battle, went back to find it and cut off a finger to recover his treasured ring!

5. Maret had his own secret police, headed by the enigmatic Sémonville, Montholon's stepfather. So did Fouché, and so did Napoleon – all three organizations were busy spying on one another. One of Maret's more ingenious devices was to have his wife, knowing all mail was opened by Napoleon's secret police, insert fictitious bits of gossip into her letters about how devoted her husband was to His Majesty.

6. His violently critical book, in which Pradt writes that 'Bonaparte made himself an imaginary Poland', would be echoed by Sir Hudson Lowe at St Helena: 'Now he's inventing an imaginary St Helena.'

7. Hogendorp had been Governor of Java and Dutch Ambassador to Petersburg. He would end his life in Brazil.

8. It had been Jomini's ambition to write a scientific analysis of General Bonaparte's early campaigns. And Napoleon had personally given orders that he should have access to the War Archives. But the project had been systematically scotched by Berthier, who in this Swiss no doubt sensed a potential rival, and by Salomon, his near relative and chief assistant. Access to all the crucial documents, so necessary to Jomini's great work, had been denied him. It is by no means certain that here Napoleon wasn't playing a double game. Did Napoleon, whose whole empire was in crucial respects dependent on myth-making, really want to have Jomini studying original documents in the War Archives?

9. An idea not altogether unfamiliar to Zalusky. Like many educated Poles he was well up in the history of Charles XII of Sweden, who'd been treated in exactly this manner. In his boyhood he'd also heard an 'Irish doctor Hasselqvist'(certainly a Swede, possibly from Finland) tell his grandmother that if ever the Russians were attacked by a French army this was exactly what they'd do. Brandt, too, had heard his colonel, 'an educated and sensible man', say how afraid he was that 'the Emperor is making the same mistakes. Look how he's forcing his way into the heart of Russia, leaving behind him a disorganized Poland and a Lithuania that's been put to the sack! In this situation the least setback can't fail to have the same consequences. The whole of Germany will revolt and things'll turn out just like they have in Spain, but on quite a different scale. The kings who are just now attached to the Emperor's chariot will hasten to break his yoke.' Of course such memories, wise after the event, can in some degree be filtered through hindsight. But not, one feels, entirely.

10. In a word, exactly the same insouciance that Marbot accuses Oudinot of showing at Wilkomir.

Chapter 7. With the Advancing Columns

1. That is, if he wasn't travelling even more lightly in the calèche which Fain says served to transport him 'from one army corps to another, or to cover in a few hours a road for which the troops needed a whole day. In this way of advancing by leaps and bounds two Chasseurs à Cheval rode a couple of paces ahead of the calèche, with two ordnance officers. At the right door rode the duty stable officer, at the left the Guard general commanding the escort. Around the carriage and behind it pressed the Emperor's ADCs – mostly generals, twelve at most – and the pages; and lastly the escort piquet

of some 24 Chasseurs. Sometimes a second calèche followed, for Grand Marshal of the Palace Duroc, the Master of the Horse, and the duty ADC.' In either case Caulaincourt's office would have placed out 'brigades' of riding horses.

2. The deserters were from the 2nd and 3rd Battalions of the Joseph Napoleon Regiment, commanded by the extremely experienced Swiss colonel Tschudy. Its 1st and 4th Battalions were serving in II Corps and are not recorded as giving any trouble.

3. Jerome had even threatened to abdicate, as his brother Louis had done in Holland. Now he wrote to his wife that he wouldn't submit to such degradation, and hoped to be home within 45 days. When his letter reached his wife on 29 July it would cause her to write in her diary: 'I'm more dead than alive. What will be the results of this action? However unjust the Emperor may be towards the King, he should have bowed to circumstance. Nothing is to be gained by standing up to the Emperor.' Taking the waters at Neudorf, Jerome afterwards tried to make good his blunder by raising a new route-regiment, 800-man strong, infantry, cavalry, guns and train horses, to send off to Russia. Twelve new cannon were to be cast. 'Before 1 Jan, I'll have a small division of 6,000 men: a regiment of the Queen's infantry, a regiment of cavalry, and a battalion of light infantry.'

4 When Rossetti told Napoleon he'd never served against France he wasn't telling the truth. He had in fact served in the Piedmontese army.

5. All quotations from Heinemann's memoirs are translated from an old Swedish translation. Although probably ghost-written and in parts romanticized, the authenticity of most passages is obvious.

6. Madame de Staël, who had been through Austria earlier in the summer when fleeing from Switzerland to Russia – her book *Sur l'Allemagne* (*On Germany*) had given the most profound offence – says the introduction of paper money in

that ruined state had demoralized the population.

On 18 July, the day Napoleon had left Vilna, she had crossed the frontier into Galicia, her goal being Petersburg, which she could now only reach via Moscow. 'Do you imagine, Madame,' Napoleon's Minister of Police had said, 'we've been waging war in Germany for eighteen years in order that so celebrated a person as yourself should publish a book without saying a word about us? This book must be destroyed, and we ought to have put its author in Vincennes!' Published originally only in London, after the Russian débâcle, her book would become a powerful factor in rousing all Germany against the oppressor. On this talkative, talented, plain-looking Swiss woman with a Parisian soul, Napoleon projected all his misogyny and detestation of female emancipation. Hadn't it been an important factor in the *ancien régime*'s undoing? And wasn't this new one directed towards the re-establishment of 'order', after ten chaotic years of Revolution which had finally brought France to a state of complete ruin and threatened civilization itself? And hadn't the Revolution been inspired from first to last by 'ideologists?' of exactly her kind? Their hatred was mutual. Madame de Stael's view of Napoleon was simplicity itself: 'Man is not hindered on his evil course unless by insuperable obstacles or by prick of conscience. Napoleon has not run into the former, and has easily liberated himself from the latter. He stands at the head of a million soldiers, has a hundred millions in income, disposes of all the prisons in Europe and uses its kings as gaolers, a man who uses the printing press when he himself wishes to speak, whilst the oppressed hardly dare confide their reply to the silence of the most intimate friendship.' (If one thinks this an exaggeration, even by the standards of our own time's dictatorships, we should read what Dutheillet has to say about his own childhood in working-class Paris, where 'during the Empire people always spoke of public affairs in hushed voices'.) Madame de Staël goes on: 'In other despotic states there are customs, laws and a religion which the ruler never violates, no matter how sovereign he may be. But in France everything is new, just as France herself is something new in Europe. The limited number of free nations can have no idea of the state of insecurity prevailing there; a state of affairs which has become habitual under Napoleon's sabre. For fifty leagues from the Swiss frontier France is stuffed with lookout towers, prisons and fortresses serving as prisons, and everywhere one sees nothing but private individuals under durance from one person's will or unfortunates held by force in distraint far from the places where they want to live.'

7. Back at the first manor, Legler has just freed the cook – who all this time has had his hands tied behind his back – when 'a beautiful woman, holding two children by the hand and her hair all loose, came rushing toward us and flung herself down on the knees, begging us to help her. During our absence several other units had come to the house and ruthlessly taken away all their animals, 300 in all. "Now I've no food left for my children," she said. "Take pity on us, give us a cow so my children can go on living." "Madame, choose not one, but six, and hide them deep in the forest. I'll stay with you til you've done it." The 'baron', his wife, his cook and two of his servants take the six cows – and six calves into the bargain. Also, 'since I had a rich booty', the 12 sacks of grain and three big loaves. 'I thought to myself, a Christian's duty is to live and let live.' Our memoirists' pages are full of such tales. For another, see Brett-James' (op. cit.) account of Lieutenant Houdart's account of his mission; and, in Helen Roeder's book the very funny story of Lieutenant Grandeville's marauding mission, both omitted here for reasons of space.

8. Labaume, who must also have been present, glosses over the incident, merely saying the Italian Royal Guard co-operated in jealously guarding the biscuit stores against any surprise attack by Cossacks.

9. Even so, Laugier's diary insists, 'these calamities are less keenly felt in the Army of Italy, and least of all in the Royal Guard. Worthy of the name it bears, it wishes above all to distinguish itself by its unremitting discipline, turnout, resignation and firmness of will.'

10. Of all the top brass, says Marbot, St-Cyr was 'the one who best knew how to use his troops on the battlefield; but also incontestibly the one who paid least attention to their welfare. He never asked whether his men had victuals, clothes, shoes, or enquired after the state of their weapons. He never reviewed them, never visited hospitals, or even asked whether any existed! According to him, his generals had to see to all that.' Was this why his Bavarians had arrived at Glubokoïe in such a shocking state? Nor would it get any better, as we shall see.

11. He would soon be able to gauge it and find it shallow. On 22 July Marmont would lose the Battle of Salamanca (which the French called Arapiles) against Wellington. St-Cyr says Napoleon's judgements 'at the head of 500,000 men and seeing the Russians fleeing in all directions' were very different from what he'd later have to say about himself and his colleagues at St Helena.

12. – 'only to be dashed afterwards when I saw Napoleon doing exactly the opposite of what he'd so sagaciously worked out'.

Chapter 8. First Clashes

1. Polotsk was the seat of the Jesuit Order, suppressed by the Pope in 1773 and only surviving in Russia. It was here it had its general, its printing works, 44 priests, 46 novices and 29 assistants. 'These religious', comments Dedem van der Gelder sourly, 'lived up to their reputation by promising us a lot and leaving us in the lurch as soon as we depended on them.'

2. Maurice Tascher was one of three brothers. His diary would be saved by his brother Ferdinand after he'd died in his arms in a Berlin hospital on 27 January 1813.

3. *'Faire la diane'*. The practice dated officially from an order issued at Schoenbrunn on 14 November 1805: 'Before dawn generals and colonels must inspect their outposts, and the line must stand to arms until the reconnaissance patrols have returned. It must always be assumed that the enemy has been manoeuvring during the night in order to attack at dawn.'

4. Of all our eye-witnesses only Dedem has a good word to say for Davout: 'If ever I have to make war again, it's under Marshal Davout I'd wish to do so. The Prince of Eckmühl is the man who best knows how to obey, and thereby has learnt to command. There was never a chief more severe in point of discipline, juster, or who occupied himself more with the welfare of the ranker, his instruction and his needs; and no sovereign ever had a more faithful or devoted servant.'

6. The current year's and the following year's call ups. Napoleon had already ordered the call up for 1813.

7. The Russians had tried the same psychological warfare against Charles XII's Swedes in 1708.

8. D'Hautpoul's instructions are an oft-quoted example of what could be expected of a headquarters ADC on mission. He was to
'go to Beschenkowiczi, where he'll stay until the three bridges have been thrown across and the bridgehead marked out. He'll ensure six ovens are built at those points where they can be erected most swiftly. As there are relay posts between Beschenkowiczi and Kamen, he'll write to me two or three times a day. He'll find out on the spot the whereabouts of Friant's, Gudin's and Nansouty's divisions, Montbrun's cuirassiers and those of Nansouty, and, finally, whether there's any news of the King of Naples. He'll send me all information thus collected. On his way to Beschenkowiczi d'Hautpoul will write me a first letter

from Koszikowa, to inform me of the state of the bridge, the population and that place's resources.'

Chapter 9. Battle at Ostrowno

1. The order to Oudinot, still in the Polotsk area, is that he shall attack Wittgenstein, who is unsupported since Barclay's withdrawal to Witebsk; and the one to St-Cyr is that his VI Corps shall remain at Ouchat to secure the army's communications and go to II Corps' assistance if it's attacked. Having reinforced Wittgenstein with 25,000 of his own troops, Barclay is now left with only 75,000 and therefore more than ever desperately in need of Bagration's forces if he's to be able to give battle at Witebsk.

2. Confirming Marbot on this point. At Wilkomir on 28 June his splendid 23rd Chasseurs, riding on at the head of Oudinot's corps, had all but fallen into the same trap: 'Doubtless you'll be astonished that [Wittgenstein's 25,000 to 30,000 men] had neither major nor minor outposts, nor scouts placed out in front of them; but such is the Russian habit when they're resolved to defend a good position, to let their enemy approach as close as possible without their sharpshooters' fire warning him of the resistance he's going to run into, and it's only when his masses are at close range that they smash into them with their artillery and musketry, astounding and shaking their adversary's men!'

Chapter 10. Fézensac on Mission

1. Van Zuylen would return from captivity but his billiards partner would die, a prisoner, on 17 January 1813.

2. Only a month earlier, on the eve of the invasion, this swashbuckling but effete grandee had been desperately urging his brother to make peace at all costs. During the retreat he'd gratify a dying French officer's last wish by personally cutting his head off.

3. It had been the campaign's second serious battle – depending of course what one means by a battle, as distinct from a mere engagement, 'combat' or 'affaire'. The usual definition of a battle was that a whole corps was involved. On the Grand Army's northern and southern flanks Macdonald, Schwarzenberg and Oudinot had all had serious fights with the retreating Russians which, however, cannot be included within the scope of this book.

4. Faced with the threat of French invasion, a whole series of fortresses were to have been established. Borissow was to have been one of them.

5. Girod de l'Ain also reflects on the difference between Russian and French military psychologies: 'The Russian soldier stands up admirably under fire, and it's easier to demolish him than force him to retreat. But this comes above all of excessive discipline, i.e., a habitual blind obedience to his officers. Usually it's not he who'll lead his comrades, either forwards by his dash or backwards by his flight. He stays where he's been put, or else where he's run into too lively a resistance. This passive and unintelligent obedience is also habitual in officers of all grades. A unit unhappily placed where a battery can enfilade it will remain there, needlessly and profitlessly exposed, as long as the officer commanding it receives no order from his superior to change its position.' All in contrast with the typical behaviour of a French officer, who 'depend upon it, will never hesitate to dispose his unit where it'll suffer as little as possible from enemy fire, and, in order to shelter it, will profit by such facilities as the least bit of space, the least fold in the ground, can offer him, without waiting for orders from above, but always taking care, when changing position, to offer the enemy no advantage.'

6. According to Schuerman's Itinéraire Général de Napoléon 1er, the imperial tents were pitched near a burnt mill, not far from the Luchiesa stream, a little to the left of the main road. Constant describes the layout of Napoleon's own: 'It was separated into three rooms by curtains. The Emperor slept in one of them, the office was in the second, his ADCs and duty officers were in the third. Usually this room served the Emperor to take his meals in, which were prepared outside. I alone slept in the bedroom. Roustam, who accompanied His Majesty on horseback when he went out, slept in the passages of the tent, not to have his sleep disturbed, necessary as it was to him. The secretaries slept in the passages. The grand officers and duty officers ate wherever and however they could. Like simple soldiers, they did not scruple to eat with their hands. Prince Berthier [sic] had his tent close to the Emperor's. He always lunched and dined with him. The meals were served on campaign by M. Collin, the food-taster, and by Roustam or one of the valets.'

Chapter 11. An Army Vanishes

1. My account is essentially made up of Caulaincourt's, Labaume's, Laugier's, Dedem's and Bonnet's.

2. Despite all Gourgaud's urgings at St Helena, Napoleon would never write his own account of the 1812 campaign; so we, too, can only speculate.

3. Straying about for a whole week searching for his own division, Biot had already discovered that in Russia's sandy soil 'footprints of men and horses leave a very feeble mark, and vanish totally at the least breath of wind'.

4. Napoleon could be amazingly quick on the uptake. Others too would notice that the Witebsk people, 'though Polish, no longer cared for the Polish cause'. Soltyk says they had no confidence in a French victory.

5. Lefèbvre-Desnouëttes had been taken prisoner when his Chasseurs of the Guard had been routed in Spain. Like Lejeune, he'd broken his parole (at Cheltenham) and got back to France.

6. Schwarzenberg, in command of the 30,000-strong Austrian contingent, was

defending the Grand Army's extreme right flank in Galicia and Volhynia. See next chapter, when another of his officers arrives.

Chapter 12. Worries at Witebsk

1. After its setback at Babinowiczi Dumonceau's troop had encountered some French chasseurs escorting an officer bearing orders to Davout to rejoin at Witebsk. Just as his regiment was entering the town he'd met with an acquaintance who'd had his arm shattered at Ostrovno, and whose days as a hussar were over. He was looking for another friend, Captain Monceau ('son of the Marshal') to get him a post back in France. This can only be the Captain Monceau of the 7th Light who, Sergeant Bertrand says, had 'just come from the Imperial pages' and would distinguish himself at Smolensk and Valutina.

2. Delaborde's folding campaign desk is to be seen in the museum at Antibes. Whether it's the one he used in Russia I don't know.

3. Only the Guard had a real medical service; otherwise there were only the regimental surgeons, a body of often thinly experienced but intrepid men who tended to be cold-shouldered by their fellow-officers until their services were suddenly needed. Over and over again Napoleon had turned a deaf ear to Larrey's remonstrances and petitions. Back in January an order had been issued that each regiment should bring with it 'eight medical officers, ten mattresses, twelve litters, a box of amputation instruments, 100 kilos of lint, 125 kilos of bandages and a box of medicines weighing at least five kilos' – a risible supply for between 1,000 and 2,500 men, especially as, for every man killed in battle, eight others afterwards succumbed to gangrene – sometimes tetanus, from rusty saws – or typhus. Whatever Gourgaud may say – he can't understand why if the artillery parks could keep up the pace the ambulances couldn't – Ségur is certainly right in regarding the shortage of medical equip-

ment as Napoleon's own fault. After Waterloo Larrey, captured by the Prussians, would be placed in front of a firing squad and only saved in the nick of time by a British officer.

4. Chambray was an artillery officer. He would be the campaign's first objective historian.

5. In 1813 Dedem would serve as *de facto* divisional general under Ney, who would ask for his formal promotion to that rank. But Napoleon had a long memory, and recalling Dedem's critical attitudes in Russia refused it.

6. 'Not Voltaire's,' says Fain, 'which he regarded as unreliable, but Adlerbeth's'. The Voltaire was a little volume bound in green morocco, as we know from Mailly-Nesle who would borrow it during the retreat.

7. His letters to Marie-Louise are the only ones he wrote in his own hand. There is no question of his uxorious devotion to this 20-year-old Austrian princess, niece of Marie-Antoinette's, who after his exile to Elba would capriciously abandon him for the one-eyed Austrian Count Neipperg.

8. Napoleon seems to have had a pathological – but also perhaps justifiable – antipathy to taking medicine of any kind. And indeed, according to the Swedish researcher Sten Forshuvud, it would be through Montholon's 'medicine' he would finally be assassinated. See *The Murder of Napoleon*, by Ben Weider and David Hapgood, Congdon & Lattès Inc., NY, 1982.

9. Napoleon said he took more pleasure in this book, bound in red leather and kept up to date by Hyde d'Ideville, 'than a girl in a novel'. During the retreat it would be captured by the Russians, who were so impressed by its detailed accuracy that they reproached the French with having stolen its contents.

10. This according to Labaume, who however isn't trustworthy in matters he didn't personally witness, and who can only have

been told about this by Eugène. Indeed it's hard to see why Napoleon should have rejoiced at Alexander's rumoured asassination, since he was counting on his own former ascendancy over him to make peace after his 'good battle'.

11. Begos' book, which is also found in *Soldats Suisses au Service Etranger*, Geneva, 1909, was inspired by a need to stress the part played by the Swiss, which he felt Thiers had overlooked.

12. Gourgaud calls him so, and scorns Flahaut's 'pirouettes' at Malmaison in 1815, after Waterloo, when he not merely deserted Napoleon but indulged in sarcastic remarks about the paucity of those who weren't doing so. Flahaut, said to be an illegitimate son of Talleyrand, had an affair with Napoleon's step-daughter, the ill-used Queen Hortense, and is believed to have been the father of her son Napoleon III.

13. A week of exhausting forced marches across endless swamps on roads built on piles or 'here and there crude hides, impracticable either for men or horses' had brought Schwarzenberg's Austrians into Volhynia. On 26 July General Kleingel's advance guard had bumped into Tormassoff's, coming up from the south, and been overwhelmed. After nine hours' bitter fighting, while he'd waited in vain for Reynier to come to his support, Kleingel's 2,500 Saxons, driven back into a convent, had surrendered, together with eight guns. Whereupon Reynier had had to beat a hasty retreat to Slonim and call on Schwarzenberg to come to his support. It was in this predicament that Schwarzenberg had sought orders. Grüber says he saw Napoleon at Minsk. But since Napoleon was never anywhere near that city, he can only mean Witebsk.

Chapter 13. The Great Manoeuvre

1. Since forests in those days were not the object of modern silviculture they were usually impenetrable. Hundred-year-old pines and spruces lay entangled criss-cross and only foresters' and – in ironmaking

districts – charcoal-burners' paths gave uncertain and unmapped access to their depths.

2. Tascher would worry endlessly about the fate of Sergeant-major Lelerc who was 'suffering on his behalf', nor did he cease trying to find out what had become of him. But though he sent a flag of truce and 25 golden louis he never heard from him again.

3. Barclay even seems to have been bewildered by it, marching and countermarching his troops to no purpose until, suddenly he is informed that the Tsar, yielding to popular opinion – which regards his sage withdrawals as mere cowardice, if not treachery – has relieved him of the supreme command of both armies. Naturally this doesn't improve the collaboration with Bagration, who scornfully refers to him as 'the Minister' [i.e., of War, which he also was] and is openly declaring him a traitor.

4. It was by no means an illiterate army. In the 33rd Line, Dedem had found 500 privates worthy of non-commissioned rank, and 'more than 700 who understood the decimal system, the first three rules of arithmetic, the basic elements of campaign fortification; and 300 could have been placed as secretaries in a ministry of state'. Many of the officers were classically educated. Paul de Bourgoing came from a literary family and had a markedly literary sensibility. Captain Faré of the Foot Grenadiers had brought with him La Bruyères' *Charactères*, Fénélon's *Télémaque*, Lafontaine's *Fables* and 'above all' Horace, and was promising himself he'd relearn Latin as soon as he had time, to enjoy him in the original. Napoleon himself had a field-library of a hundred books, among them Voltaire's *Life of Charles XII of Sweden*, a 'little volume bound in green calf leather'. Having carefully perused it, together with a lot of other books about Russia, both old and new – not to mention two as yet unpublished works on the Russian army – he'd declared to more than one listener that he certainly wasn't going to make the same mistake as the Swedish military

hero, whose march on Moscow in 1708 had proved so utterly disastrous and marked the beginning of the end of the Swedish empire.

5. This defile, with steep unscalable sides, was approached by a bridge over a deep ravine, at the foot of a steep slope. Frozen, it would cause the loss of innumerable vehicles and guns during the retreat (15-17 November, the second Battle of Krasnoïe).

6. It would be Dombrowski's division, turned out of Minsk head over heels by Tchitchakoff in November, which would fail to secure the Berezina bridge at Borissow. Dombrowski had served with the French armies since 1796.

7. This suggests that up to 15 August he'd been keeping the exact purpose of his manoeuvre secret, even from his top commanders; which is not impossible.

8. Hastening up to Vilna to nurse her wounded husband at the turn of the month, Oudinot's heroic young duchess will in fact meet Hogendorp's equally young wife at Kovno, on her way back to Germany. She was very ill, and died soon after.

Chapter 14. The Walls of Smolensk

1. Most still stand, despite heavy fighting during the Second World War.

2. Here we can take our choice from other accounts of his costume on other occasions. Was it perhaps a 'hat with turned up brim, garnished with plumes and ostrich feathers'? Or did a 'Polish cap surmounted by an enormous panache' set off a 'goatskin waistcoat à la chevalière, with crimson trousers and yellow bootees'? Or perhaps over his shoulders a 'short gold-embroidered green velvet mantle, or an elegant fur, decked out with gold braidings and bullion, thrown over his shoulders'? Griois doesn't say.

3. It was in fact Bagration's Second West Army. Terrified that Barclay, 'to the ever-

lasting disgrace of the Russian army', would tamely abandon Smolensk, and no longer being his subordinate, Bagration was marching at top speed to prevent the French from cutting the Moscow road.

4. It was actually Neverovski's division, being withdrawn while fresh troops poured into the city to relieve them.

Chapter 15. Smolensk – The First Shock

1. Probably the divisions or perhaps companies forming the column's width had been closed up to two paces from one another. A compact mass, it had little firepower but great weight.

2. Junot's health had been destroyed partly by excessive eating and drinking – he'd swallow 2 dozen oysters before dinner – but also by a sabre cut to his head, a wound, his wife says in her fascinating memoirs, which never quite healed. Junot would in fact become insane and commit suicide in the following year.

3. The nephew of Marshal Moncey's, referred to above.

4. He goes on: 'A mere spectator with no desire to get myself killed to no purpose, I crouch down behind a rampart where the musket-balls go whining over my head. Then ride back into Smolensk. The town seemed to have died. A few drunken or wounded men were staggering about in its abandoned streets. The suburbs were in flames. The military stores and some houses had been looted. Outside, the great battle thundered on. The bloodbath I'd just seen upset me intensely. I felt utterly abandoned. Suddenly I was overwhelmed by a fear so terrible I'd gladly have hid in a mousehole. Every loud explosion made me tremble.'

5. According to G.F. Nafziger's tables, these must have come from the 1st and 2nd Old Guard Foot Artillery (six guns + two howitzers, and the 1st Foot Artillery (six guns + two howitzers). No other corps had more than six 12-pounders. There

were no larger calibre guns, and most of the batteries consisted mainly of 6-pounders.

6. In fact it was a green notebook. M. Dufresne, the First Auditor, had an assistant whose sole business it was to implement all the Emperor's promotions and awards of medals and pensions, etc.

7. Edmund Burke: *On the Sublime and the Beautiful*, 1756.

8. In a letter written a couple of days later to a Parisian friend.

9. Scenes from that terrible night would brand themselves forever on the memory of a certain Ivan Maslow: 'The burning suburbs, the dense and variously coloured smoke, the red glow, the crash of exploding shells, the thunder of cannon, the crackling musketry, the beating drums, the moans and groans of old men, women and children, a whole population falling on its knees, arms upstretched to the skies... Crowds of inhabitants running from the flames without knowing whither... Russian regiments running into the flames, some to save lives, some to sacrifice their own... A long line of carts rolling slowly on, carrying away the wounded. As the twilight deepened, the Holy Mother of God, icon of Smolensk, was carried out of the city, while the dismal tolling of bells merged with the crash of falling houses and the din of battle.'

10. Césare de Laugier had described the scene in his diary: 'From time to time a stir passes through our camp: it's an ADC who's arrived from the battle being delivered under the walls of Smolensk. Eager for news, everyone surrounds the newcomer. Meanwhile the gunfire never ceases making itself heard. All of a sudden we're told a brigade of Italian light cavalry we've long been separated from after leaving it behind at Surash has turned up. Immediately the whole camp is thrown into commotion. Running up to our comrades we all throw ourselves into their arms, embracing them as if we hadn't seen each other for years. Everyone's terribly impatient to get into the

battle and earn his share of distinctions. Pleased as Punch, the newly arrived chasseurs happily accept their comrades' praises, proudly showing off their scars and decorations. They give us some bread, meat and brandy, which we've so long lacked. The evening is all fireworks and bonfires, whose costs are defrayed by the wood where we're encamped.'

11. When, for instance, he'd heard from Napoleon in Madrid that he was offered the choice, not of the Spanish crown as he'd hoped, but between those of Portugal and Naples, he'd fallen ill and taken to his bed.

12. I have been unable to obtain a copy of this very rare book, and I am quoting from a quote.

Chapter 16. Death in the Sacred Valley

1. Barclay's evacuation of Smolensk had been no simple matter. Without so much as a by-your-leave, Bagration, furious to have to abandon the city, had made off along the Moscow highway; and Barclay, to avoid congestion and not expose his columns to possible French gunfire from the southern hills bordering the Dnieper, had therefore opted for a circuitous retreat route. His five divisions were to follow the Petersburg road northwards, then two parallel side roads which would enable them to debouch some ten miles along the Moscow road, the first at Lubino, the second – left-hand column – at Prouditchi. But the scheme had gone agley. Not only had his artillery got stuck in the ravines and bottomless lanes which had proved much less practicable than he'd expected: even his own coachman had gone astray. So that, waking up at dawn, he'd found himself within earshot of French clarions and drums. Not only his carriage, but an entire division had gone round in a circle!

2. Realizing that his entire army was in grave danger of being taken in flank and annihilated, Barclay had ordered young Prince Eugen of Württemberg to stage a diversion so as at all costs to hold up

Ney's advancing column long enough for the Russian van to reach the Lubino crossroads. It was Eugène's fire that was 'ploughing up the plain' near Faber du Faur.

3. It was here that the Russians had withstood the Poles in the 16th and 17th centuries.

4. '...which they'd probably inherited from the Austrians whose subjects they so long have been' von Suckow adds.

5. Oudinot was always getting wounded, more or less seriously. This time a fragment of grapeshot had shattered his shoulder. Of the campaign's premonitions and strange coincidences, the one experienced by his young duchess, whom he'd married just before setting out for Russia, was among the strangest and best authenticated. A bust of her husband, commissioned from a Berlin sculptor, was being unpacked when it fell to the floor and its shoulder had shattered. Shortly afterwards the news came that this was exactly what had happened to the living original! Defying the imperial ban on any woman crossing the Niemen, the intrepid young Duchess of Reggio had immediately set out for Vilna to tend her husband. – Despite numerous first-hand accounts it's impossible for reasons of space to describe in detail the First Battle of Polotsk. Both Colonel St-Chamans and Colonel Sebastien-Joseph de Comeau, the Bavarians' chief-of-staff, were wounded.

6. One of them, newly arrived from Vilna, was Surgeon Déchy, whom Napoleon had reprimanded for bringing his 13-year-old son with him to the wars. After the town's storming, writes Déchy, 'my father and I and other senior officers went and took possession of a superb house, recently abandoned, and which distinguished itself by its sumptuous furniture. Three days after we'd installed ourselves, a large and beautiful lady appeared,' the proprietress. All his life his son would remember her with affection and respect for the kindnesses she showered on him. When his father was ordered back to typhus-ridden Vilna she provided lavishly for their

journey. Was she perhaps the same countess who had befriended Le Roy in 1807?

7. Nine of these patients, Larrey adds proudly, would have completely recovered by the time he got back to Smolensk in November. The two others had died of dysentery. Among the more remarkable wounds 'was one inflicted on a corporal of the 13th Line. A large-calibre roundshot had smashed the head of the left humerus, the clavicle and whole of the shoulder-blade and neck muscles. The bone fragments had been flung on to the back, with the soft parts torn. A wound of terrifying appearance! This soldier, in a state of unbearable suffering, was demanding at the top of his voice that we rid him of the rest of his arm and a mass of bone splinters. Despite the little hope we could hold out for this unfortunate man, I attempted the following operation. Having removed the arm, which clung by a mere few shreds of flesh, and having tied the main artery, I extracted all the detached pieces of bone from the muscles and their periostea. I cut off the the main disorganized shreds. I brought together the frayed edges of this enormous wound and fixed them in place by using a few fascines where the blood had clotted and a large piece of linen soaked in a solution of sodium sulphate, with muriate of soda, some fine cotton pads and the scapular bandage completed the dressing. After the operation was over this wounded man became completely calm. I confided him to M. Sponville, one of the surgeons-major of the flying ambulances.' On the thirty-fifth day the patient would be evacuated from Smolensk back to Poland, 'and was on a good way to being cured. Since then I've had no more news of him, but there's every reason to believe this soldier's life was saved, unless he fell sick in some other way.'

Chapter 17. Stragglers and Prisoners

1. But in fact the sergeant was picked up by an ambulance, his leg was amputated in time, and the first person Heinemann, after his terrible experiences as a Russian prisoner of war, would see when he got

home was the sergeant calmly sitting on his doorstep, having married his girlfriend at Hildesheim.

2. Winzingerode would himself be taken prisoner, having ventured prematurely into Moscow as the French rearguard was abandoning it. Taken to Napoleon, he would be furiously berated and threatened as a 'traitor' since his domains lay within the French Empire. Sent under escort to France, he would be rescued by Cossacks before reaching Minsk.

3. The account of Heinemann's and his comrades' captivity is too awful, too long, and too circumstantial to print. 'Soon our column consisted of a variegated mixture of Spaniards, Frenchmen, Germans from the countries of the Federation of the Rhine, Prussians and Austrians, Hungarians, Croats, Italians and Poles, at nights huddled together in shacks and fighting one another with their fists – for lack of knives'. Particularly painful to the Spaniards and Italians (Heinemann says nothing about any Portuguese) was that the Russian peasants who'd been told they'd come to Russia

'to smash up all images of saints and didn't believe in any God, were real Antichrists. Already we'd burnt down Smolensk and now were going to do the same to Moscow. Curious to see such atheists, the peasants were attracted in droves from far and wide. Also the neighbourhood's superior Russians turned up. For them a kind of gallery of planks had been built for them to contemplate us prisoners from all nations who, beneath them, were lying or standing as best we could on the barn floor. Over our heads we could see broad bearded peasant faces, stupid and curious, peering down through the cracks in the roof. The well-to-do Russians had brought baskets filled with bread and turnips that excited our appetite. But when the hungry prisoners held up their hands and implored to be given some, the Russians were so embittered they couldn't bring themselves to give us any. "Franzus fse propall" ("Frenchmen all kaput"), they

mocked us and spat on us. "They aren't Christians," said others, and only rarely did anyone throw us down a bit of bread.'

And though some of the French, Italians and Spaniards make the sign of the cross in the Catholic fashion, to show what they are, the Russians shout back "Frenchmen not Christians – Frenchmen dogs!" Until a red-headed Protestant Westphalian forces his way forward and crosses himself in Orthodox fashion, 'whereupon they threw him all the bread and turnips he could possibly eat.'

Chapter 18. Dust, Hear and Thirst

1. '*M. le Duc*. You have received orders to leave Kovno and proceed to Vilna. You should march in four columns. At Kovno have ten pounds of rice taken out per man, which the ranker shall carry in his knapsack, and you must see to it that he does not consume more than one ounce a day. You will draw biscuit for six days, irrespective of how much you will be able to have transported behind you in light wagons. At Vilna you will draw food sufficient to reach Minsk, and at Minsk for as far as to Borissow, and at Borissow to Orsha. From Orsha to Smolensk your army corps must march by divisions, so as to arrive within three days: the cavalry shall march first. Exploit your presence to prepare a maximum of supplies along the road from Vilna to Minsk and Orsha. Since the Emperor is directing his march on Moscow, your corps cannot arrive too soon at Smolensk, in order to maintain our communications and form our reserve.'

2. He'd have been still more troubled had he known that it would be here, one frozen November evening amid scenes of horror and despair, that the Army of Italy would lose almost its last guns and the whole of its loot-swollen baggage train.

3. Evidently III Corps was led by the 1st or 2nd Portuguese Regiment. The 3rd was serving with II Corps. The Württembergers would have been part of Marchand's 25th Division. But the Spaniards must

have been those in I Corps, under Colonel Tschudi. Evidently Dumonceau's memory is confused as to the order in which they passed by.

4. This wasn't true. The Poles had suffered heavily, both during their attempts to catch Bagration and at Smolensk, where several generals had been wounded. Zalusky, of the 1st Guard Lancers writes: 'We greatly regretted that the Polish army hadn't been called to form the Army's right wing in Volhynia and Podonia' [instead of Schwartzenberg's Austrians]. 'We couldn't forgive Prince Joseph Poniatowski for having been so soft with Bagration.'

5. Turno's memoir is a particularly important source of information on the campaign, seen from the Polish point of view.

6. 'You have five cavalry depots: Kovno, Merecz, Minsk, Glubokoïe, Lepel. You are to establish march squadrons.'

7. Lossberg's letter is in a collection of letters home.

8. The Viazma, a tributary of the Dnieper, was a river port, with a big barge-building industry.

9. The position had been selected by one of Kutusov's aides, but on closer inspection was found to be unsatisfactory.

Chapter 19. The Gathering Storm

1. Ghjat has been renamed Gagarin, after the first man in space, whose native town it evidently was.

2. Montbrun and Auguste Caulaincourt, leading the Polish Lancers of the Guard, had carried the heavily gunned pass of Somosierra, an exploit which had made the regiment's name.

3. This was a gross exaggeration. Napoleon estimated the true figure at 30,000. In fact it was only 15,000.

4. Although he didn't know it, the *konya* would save his life in the tightest of all spots, at the Berezina.

5. Caulaincourt's daily record, in which he among other things notes the various horses ridden by Napoleon from day to day, is in the *Archives de l'Itinéraire du Général Caulaincourt*.

6. Quoted at third hand from Christopher Duffy's *Borodino, and the War of 1812*, which in turn quotes from P. Holzhausen's *Die Deutschen in Russland*, Berlin, 1912.

7. It is possible that the action may have been screened from IV Corps by a fold in the ground. Laugier makes no mention of it. The idea of fortifying and defending the mound, originally intended only as an observation point, had been Bennigsen's. 'He'd chosen the position and didn't want to lose face. Consequently on 5 September he sacrificed six or seven thousand brave men and three guns.' See Christopher Duffy: *Borodino and the War of 1812*, 1972. I have followed the order of his account of Borodino throughout.

8. Not to be confused with the 2nd Guard Lancers.

9. An anonymous German general calls it so.

10. A contestible statement, as will be seen at Mojaisk on 8/9 September, where Napoleon's mental activity, though he was still suffering acutely from all these symptoms, clearly remained undiminished. Probably it wasn't his cognitive but his conative faculties, his energy, which suffered at Borodino and may well have affected the outcome, or so various generals, including St-Cyr, would afterwards think.

11. Napoleon's heartbeat was extraordinarily slow, only 50. On St Helena he'd tell Gourgaud that he had never felt his own heart beating.

Chapter 20. The Mouths of the Guns

1. 'I spent the rest of this day at this honorable task,' Lejeune goes on, 'which made me make a more exact study of the locality. The Emperor received my sketches, recognized the places he'd seen and seemed satisfied. On his return he'd ordered Bacler d'Albe to demand a similar work to mine from the topographical engineers; and before evening fell an elevation drawing had been made of the Russian positions.' Cf., what Labaume has to say, below.

2. Some writers say 18, others 24 guns, all of heavy calibre.

3. According to Elzéar Blaze, less so than Western European armies.

4. This meticulously revised version is the basis of the earliest known map of the Battle of Borodino, the one Labaume would print in his book two years later.

5. From right to left: Poniatowski (V), Davout (I) supported by Nansouty's, Montbrun's and Latour-Maubourg's cavalry corps, Ney (III), Junot (VIII) (headed by Morand's division and backed up by the Guard artillery, its cavalry, the Young Guard, and Old Guard), and, north of the Kolotchka behind and beyond Borodino, Eugène (IV), supported by Gérard's and Morand's divisions and Grouchy's Cavalry Corps and with extra light cavalry (Otnano's Bavarians and Italians) to guard the army's left.

6. Captured by Cossacks, they are to be read in Holzhausen. See bibliography.

7. The chaplain of the French colony in Moscow, Adrien Suffugé, would be horrified to find that the French army didn't have a single chaplain to show for itself. This single detail, like so many others, seems to show that the Napoleonic military cult should be regarded as a kind of proto-totalitarian religion in itself, forerunner of our modern ones.

8. Gérard's painting wasn't the only portrait of the King of Rome to reach Napoleon in Russia. At Smolensk an auditor of state had brought him a miniature of the little boy seated on a sheep, by Mademoiselle Aimée Thibault. Hung in Napoleon's room in the Kremlin, Gérard's large portrait would be lost during the retreat. Luckily the artist had made several copies.

9. Next day the army would see the bringer of bad tidings 'fighting on foot as a volunteer, to demonstrate that the Army of Spain, despite its resounding defeat, was worthy of the Army of Russia'.

10. At St. Helena, on Saturday, 27 April 1817, Napoleon would tell Gourgaud he'd made a mistake: 'At the battle of the Moscowa I was wrong to attack the Russians' entrenched positions. The fact was, I was thirsting for a great battle, for an army which has plenty of good cavalry and which can manouevre behind a system of good redoubts should never be attacked. One should manoeuvre him out of his position.'

11. Quoted at second hand from Curtis Cate's *The War of the Two Emperors*.

12. Fain, who was passing the night in the company of Caulaincourt's brother, declares explicitly that Rapp's memoirs err.

Chapter 21. Holocaust at Borodino

1. 'The first roundshot he sent in our direction hit Marshal Davout's horse,' Planat goes on. 'It fell at once, dragging under it its rider, whom we thought was seriously wounded. But the marshal got up laughing and had another horse brought to him.' If this is true and Planat's memory isn't confusing the incident of two hours later, then Davout must have lost two horses shot under him at Borodino, a detail no other writer mentions. See Le Roy's account of what happened at 8 a.m.

2. The Jäger regiment had been placed there in the teeth of Barclay's wishes. Césare de Laugier, who was looking on, says there were several bridges. But no

one else mentions more than one in front of the Italians. There were others to their right, constructed during the night.

3. '...delivers the 106th,' Laugier goes on, 'and, obedient to orders, returns in triumph to Borodino'. But as yet Laugier isn't watching, and his account of the outcome differs from all others.

4. Actually V Corps had got off to a slow start. It wouldn't begin seriously to attack the Russian left until about 8 a.m. For events in that sector see Duffy, *op. cit.*, whose lucid account of the battle I shall in the main be following. I've taken the description of what it felt like to be in such an assault column of infantry from Heinemann, *op. cit.* Heinemann, of course, wasn't at Borodino – with his fellow-prisoners he was still being herded on by Cossacks to a camp in the far north. But he describes how the novices in Compans'columns must have felt.

5. Actually it was the 3rd (Dutch) Grenadiers. They would be virtually wiped out during the retreat.

6. 'The outcome justified him,' Girod de l'Ain goes on, 'but it was thanks to a combination of circumstances as happy as fortuitous, and above all improbable. Even so, he was condemned to suffer all his life from his wound, from which splinters kept coming out even ten years later.'

7. How far away was Larrey's dressing-station? No one else makes any mention of Napoleon's leaving his post to visit Rapp there.

8. It was Colonel Achard, it will be remembered, who at Salta-Novka had had to turn Davout round to see how close the Russians were.

9. When Dumont tells this story to Sergeant Bourgogne, just before reaching Moscow, he calls it the 'great redoubt'. Perhaps he in fact thought afterwards that it was the Great Redoubt the 61st had attacked. In fact it can only have been one of the flèches. Florencia of course is the same Spanish cantinière Bourgogne

had met at Witebsk, and the dead drummers the ones who'd entertained him to supper there.

10. General Kutaisoff, leading them, was one of those who fell.

11. Standing on an emplacement 'measuring about 1 square verst' [135,000 sq yds] Prince Nicholas Boris Galitzin, too, was thinking the gunfire 'unexampled in the annals of murderous battles. The fire of our pieces doesn't hold up the French. Scorning danger, they keep closing their ranks as the grapeshot carries them off, and marching to almost certain death they continue to advance at a steady pace, with sloped arms and a remarkable impassivity. Though they can only advance by trampling on their comrades' bodies, they're already on the point of reaching our guns. At this critical moment, at a signal from Bagration, the whole Russian line, headed by its commander-in-chief, advances. Bayonet is crossed with bayonet and a hand-to-hand fight of extermination begins. The cavalry, hastening up from either side into this horrible mêlée, finally climaxes the confusion; and soon infantrymen, troopers, gunners, Russian and French, form only a single confused mass, with everyone dealing out death to whomever falls under his hand.' – Galitzin, Prince Niocolas Boris: La Bataille de Borodino, par un témoin oculaire, St. Petersburg, 1840.

12. This may be rhetorically true, but not factually. Caulaincourt's *Itinéraire* records that the Emperor that day rode three of his horses: Lüzelberg, Emir and Courtois. Pion des Loches even says he 'didn't give a single order', which is certainly absurd and therefore casts doubt on the accuracy of everything else he says. An anonymous eye-witness says about 100 ADCs came and went for orders during the battle. Dedem says he was sitting 300 paces ahead of the redoubt, all the while holding his miniature of his son 'which the Empress had sent him by M. de Bausset. He toyed with it, and often repeated: "he

must see what he'll have to at 25". This sounds apocryphal. Dedem, presumably at the head of his brigade in Friant's division, can hardly have been so close an eye-witness.

13. As far as I know this is the only historical evidence to justify Tchaikowsky's introduction of the Marseillaise into his overture. Otherwise this highly revolutionary and anti-authoritarian ditty was forbidden throughout the Empire period, and Rouget de l'Isle, who in a flash of inspiration had composed both words and music to sing at a salon in Strasburg (not Marseilles!) had remained an obscure and unrewarded infantry captain. Only as an old man did he become famous, but even then hardly outside the confines of his own district.

14. A most dangerous thing to do, if he really did it. One could easily misjudge the force left in a spent roundshot and lose one's foot.

15. This must have been after Friant's division had been flung in, see below.

16. It is a – for us – curious but persistent complaint among our officer eye-witnesses that they had no one to do their laundering for them. To have to wash even one's own handkerchiefs was clearly about the most humiliating thing they could experience!

17. Though Bagration 'at first tries to hide his condition, he's overcome by pain and his wound betrayed by the blood dripping from his boot; and is helped from his horse and laid out on the greensward. Finally he has to retire, his glance still turning back to the battlefield.' – Prince Galitzin's account, quoted in Brett-James, op. cit.

18. Von Meerheimb's account is to be found in Holzhausen's collection of memoirs of the campaign.

19. '... by no means unsteady soldiers (as Ségur falsely says),' writes Faber du Faur indignantly; 'for it was these Württembergers who'd taken the flèche after a bloody fight and would defend it until the end of the battle'.

20. Ouvarov was severely reprimanded for making such a mess of his diversion. It was only years afterwards that he and his fellow Russian generals realized that he had saved Russia from the disaster which would have overtaken its army had Napoleon, in his usual manner, thrown in the Imperial Guard through the hole that, between 11 and 1 o'clock, had been blasted in the Russian centre. Only the Prussians' timely arrival at Waterloo would save Wellington from exactly the same catastrophe.

21. So-called by the Russians, after General Raevsky, who had had it thrown up. He fell in the battle.

22. Duffy calls Schreckenstein's memoir 'probably the most useful account by a survivor of the battle'. He was in Latour-Maubourg's IV Cavalry Corps.

23. There was also M. de St-P***, squadron-leader in the 5th Hussars 'whose colonel had even undertaken in General Montbrun's presence to issue him with a certificate of officerly cowardice any day he asked for it. Several times he'd let his men charge without accompanying them. At Inkowo he'd even slid from his horse and surrendered!' There were also many other strange and idiosyncratic characters, like the one described by Blaze who, being quite exceptionally hirsute, stripped to the waist and at whose furious charge the enemy, as if seeing a bear, as often as not would flee the field. Another regimental officer who admitted to everyone that he was terrified at the sight of the enemy, used to charge them *sitting back to front* on his horse.

24. Dedem says Montbrun had 'just come to ask for the Emperor's orders, and died charging at the head of his cavalry'. The first statement may be true, the second certainly isn't. Indeed much of what Dedem has to relate about the battle seem to be based on ill-founded hearsay. Similarly, Séruzier says Montbrun was 'hit

in the chest and dropped dead at my feet'. And Vossler that he was killed by a howitzer. But Biot's account is the most circumstantial, and anyway Montbrun didn't die until the evening.

25. It was made up of the Saxon Zastrow Cuirassiers, a Polish lancer division, a Westphalian brigade and a Saxon and Polish regiment. The Zastrow Cuirassiers, writes Roth von Schreckenstein, 'wore very heavy, bullet-proof, black iron cuirasses, though only the breast. At that time it was still not considered fitting for a cuirassier to ride a chestnut, or a grey, or a piebald, though the officers rode horses of all colours. The Cuirassiers of the Saxon Guard and the Zastrow Cuirassiers had much smaller, though sturdy horses, either black or very dark-bown, supplied by dealers as Mecklenburgers.'

26. A reference to the occasion three years before when he'd taken some dragoons and forced the Tagus.

27. Only a few paces away from the spot where Montbrun had fallen, Lejeune admiringly saw Ney 'standing there on the parapet of one of the flèches, directing the combatants swarming at his feet, who only lost him from sight when he was enveloped in swirling smoke!' Seeing Grouchy and his staff standing on the edge of the ravine behind Griois' guns, Ney sends for him:

'Hardly am I beside him than the enemy begins firing on our group and a few moments afterwards several ordnance officers and staff officers are killed or wounded by the grapeshot. General Grouchy's horse, stricken in the chest by a roundshot, falls on top of his master, whom we take for dead, but who gets off with a bad bruise.'

28. From Planat's brief account it's not quite clear that the 2nd Carabiniers' charge was part of the assault on the Great Redoubt. But Lejeune has placed the stricken Ferdinand pathetically in his elegant painting, and no doubt for a good reason. Lejeune's painting of the capture of the Raevsky Redoubt is more iconographic than realistic. In the *foreground*

Ferdinand is receiving first aid (which Planat says didn't happen until in the evening after the fighting was over) while a much-slimmer-than-in-reality Napoleon hands back (an equally idealized) General Likhatcheff his sword. Meanwhile in the *background* the Great Redoubt, its height considerably exaggerated, is still being stormed! Although great care has been lavished on details of uniforms, etc., the whole is reminiscent of an ancient Egyptian battle painting, where successive events are shown simultaneously.

29. Griois writes 'at about 2 or 3 p.m.'. We who are used to modern communications and transport can find it hard to realize how much time it took to organize and carry out troop movements in those days.

30. Some historians have questioned whether Auguste Caulaincourt's role in the storming of the Great Redoubt has not been exaggerated, all too naturally, by his brother.

31. In fact they must have been gunners. But there also seem to have been some Russian infantry placed along the front of the redoubt, outside it.

32. Mailly-Nesle was related to, but not a direct descendant of, the illustrious Marshal de Mailly. This kind of preferential treatment of scions of the old nobility with illustrious names (wounded at Tarutino, Mailly-Nesle would spend a large part of the retreat in a comfortable carriage with some ladies and two doctors!) seems to have been a feature of Napoleon's declared policy of integrating old aristocracy in his regime. But Fézensac, who belonged to it, tells us that behind his back and among themselves such privileged officers used to refer to the Emperor as 'M. Bonaparte'. And almost all would desert him in 1814.

33. On the Russian side Prince Galitzin, too, could

'compare nothing to the picture offered by this scene of carnage, whose theatre was the redoubt, at the moment which decided its fate. You'd have thought it was a volcano vomiting flames and smoke from every point in its circumference. This burning mountain, attacked on all sides, thunders, explodes, pours torrents of fire. Then, suddenly, all this uproar is followed by a lugubrious silence. The cavalryman sabring, the infantryman striking out and defending himself by blows of his butt or bayonet, the clashing of weapons, the sun reflected on the steel, the helmets, the cuirasses, the yells coming out of this horrible mêlée – all this made of this terrible scene a picture worthy of the ablest painter's brush. Without fear of contradiction one can say it was one of the most magnificent horrors ever met with in war.'

34. Afterwards whenever he tidied it up and beat it 'the place where the brains had been flung appeared in the shape of a greasy spot like a *memento mori*'.

35. Caulaincourt's account of the battle's closing stages seems rather blurred, no doubt because of the shock of his brother's death. But his testimony concerning Berthier's and, this time, Murat's dissuading Napoleon from sending in the Guard, and of Napoleon's 'hesitation' is of course as crucial as it is reliable.

36. But his 'intelligent horse' has. Along its neck the hair had been shaved as by a razor, without touching the skin, and it had had another such close shave above one hoof.

37. On Kutusov's declaring he'd resume the battle next day, Barclay had even ordered it to be retaken at dawn. After spending the day drinking and eating with sycophantic young officers several miles from the battlefield, Kutusov had sent off the news of his great victory to Petersburg. Later that night, after a council-of-war, he would change his mind and order a general withdrawal. For glimpses of the battle as seen from the Russian side, see Duffy, *op. cit.*

Chapter 22. The Butcher's Bill

1. Next year the peasants would have to bury a total of 58,521 corpses and the carcasses of 35,478 horses.

2. 'Passing behind the Grand Redoubt we saw its broad interior sloping sharply down towards us, all encumbered with corpses and dead horses jumbled up with overturned cannon, cuirasses, helmets and all sorts of scattered wreckage in an indescribable confusion and disorder.' – Dumonceau. Moving forward a month later to a village recently evacuated by a light cavalry unit, Vossler would see how 'the first corpses lay singly, then in heaps. Often my horse couldn't find a way through them and I had to ride over the bodies, the horror of the scene mounting as I passed. Soon I reached the Raevsky Redoubt. Here the corpses lay piled higher and higher. The ditches were filled to the brim with bodies. I found bodies by the hundred in the Württemberg uniform. The top of these fortifications provided a comprehensive view of almost the entire field of battle. Sword and shot had raged terribly everywhere. Men and horses had been gashed and mashed in every conceivable way, and on the faces of the fallen Frenchmen you could still discern the various emotions in which death had overtaken them: courage, desperation, defiance, cold unbearable pain and, among the Russians, passionate fury, apathy and stupor.'

3. One of the colonels killed was the man who'd shattered Robespierre's jaw with a pistol shot.

4. Quoted from J.T. James: *Views of Russia, Sweden and Poland*, London, 1826.

5. For V Corps' contribution to the battle see Duffy, op. cit. Dumonceau may not have been impressed by the Poles' losses, but they'd made a vital contribution by drawing off major forces to the Russian left wing which would have been badly needed in the centre.

6. Among those who were wounded was 'the youthful Colonel Sopransi of the 7th Dragoons, a young Italian, son of Mme. Visconti' – Berthier's adorata. Griois says he was wounded in the ankle, Castellane in the knee.

7. The episode is not to be found in Ségur's impersonally and rhetorically written history but in his autobiography *Du Rhin à Fontainebleau.* Is this one of Ségur's flights of fancy? Why was Napoleon alone? Why on foot? The whole incident seems strange – yet at the same time strangely convincing. A similarly surprising encounter would happen to Dedem outside Smolensk during the retreat.

8. 'But in those huge armies', Planat goes on, 'one didn't enquire too closely into such matters. When twelve or fifteen hundred surgeons have to be appointed one takes what one can find.' Blaze, too, describes these tyros' immense incompetence, how they used rusty saws for amputations, etc., with the result that the ratio of those who died after a battle to those killed during it was usually 8:1. This does not mean there weren't also many well-trained and dedicated men, like Déchy's father.

9. Colonel Ponthon, it will be remembered, was the engineer officer who, brought back to Paris from St Petersburg to join Napoleon's war cabinet, had (according to Caulaincourt) gone down on his knees to beg him not to invade Russia.

10. Planat's categorical statement confirms at first hand the Moscow chaplain Adrien Suffugé's statement. Probably it applies first and foremost to the French units. But I have not found any mention of military chaplains in any of the German accounts either. Nor does Laugier refer to one among the Italians. Almost certainly the Poles must have had chaplains.

11. Refusing to be sent back to Vilna, Aubry would finally reach Moscow thanks to his *cantinière,* who, 'in tears', lent him 400 francs, and to a voltigeur who'd shot a hare. Upon his offering his benefactress a portion she reprimanded the voltigeur for 'paying attention to such useless targets'.

12. Kergorre would afterwards be so fortunate as to have his conduct approved.

Chapter 23. The Last Lap

1. While at the Kremlin, Caulaincourt would have to ask Napoleon to do something for his brother Auguste's ADCs. Strangely, Napoleon had never shown the least interest in their fate after Auguste Caulaincourt's heroic death at Borodino.

Chapter 24. 'Moscow! Moscow!'

1. In the early 19th century very few westerners knew anything about the interior of Russia. It was only after 1812 that such travel books as J. T. James's *Journal* and R. Johnston's *Travels through the Russian Empire and country of Poland* (1815), R. Ackermann's *Sketches of Russia* (1814) and Edouard de Montulé's *Voyage en Angleterre et en Russie* (1825) began to appear. Indeed the first map of Siberia had been made only a century earlier by a Swedish prisoner of war from Charles XII's army.

2. This kind of passage is typical of Ségur, whose vivid account under close examination often tends to fall to pieces. Which marshals? It could only be Davout and Ney; and such an about-face, not to say such adulation, is utterly unlike either of these two men's ways of thinking. On the other hand Ségur may well have been present. Perhaps the wrong word is 'marshals'? From Fain we know that a great deal of flattery and adulation went on from 'courtiers' at IHQ. – Caulaincourt would afterwards remember him as having been 'on the last height overlooking Moscow, called Sparrow Hills' when he got the news. This seems to be an instance of two memories fusing together.

3. According to Roos the first units to enter Moscow were the 10th Polish

Hussars, followed by Prussian Uhlans and the Württemberger Chasseurs.

4. The Arsenal was a large modern building in neo-Classical style. It was found to contain huge stores of British muskets.

5. I have merged Laugier's and Labaume's descriptions.

6. 'All hearts, all feet have wings / How light has now the march become! / How brightly shines the sun on arid fields / and in the zenith stands when now appears / Jerusalem, it's reached, ah yes / Jerusalem, it's there, acclaimed / in unison of voices thousandfold, / Jerusalem!' – Tasso: *Gerusalemme Liberata.*

7. It would remind Soltyk of Hampton Court.

8. The outbreak of fire in the Bazaar – or as others called it the Stock Exchange – on the evening of the 14th remains a mystery. Was it caused by pillaging soldiers of the Guard? Or by civilian looters? Or had one of the incendiaries, drunk perhaps, not waited for the agreed signal at 9 p.m. on the evening of the 15th and jumped the gun? Afterwards, too, many of our eye-witnesses seem very naturally to have confused their memories of the events of the night of 14/15 September with those of the much more terrible night of

15/16th. I have disentangled them as best I can.

9. '...and in fact I sent one. But it couldn't find the palace and for several days went astray in the immense deserted city'.

10. Of Murat's 42,000 horsemen only 18,000 had reached Moscow. Davout's magnificently trained I Corps, originally 79,000, strong, was down to 29,000. Ney's III Corps, once 44,000 strong, was down to a mere 11,000. And of the 50,000 men of IV Corps who had paraded so brilliantly at Glogau in May there were only 24,000 infantry and 1,600 cavalry. (Of Pino's once magnificent 15th Division's 13,000 men, only 4,000.) And of the 39,000 Poles of Poniatowski's V Corps, only 4,844 infantry and a mere 868 cavalry. In worst case of all was Junot's VIII Corps, back at Mojaisk.

Even the Imperial Guard, taken as a whole, had suffered terrible losses, even though, its artillery apart, it hadn't fired a shot. Of an original 50,000 men, 17,871 infantry and foot artillery, 4,609 cavalry and horse artillery had reached Moscow. Although Chambray's figures refer to effectives shortly before leaving Moscow in mid-October, give or take a little they must be approximately valid for arrival there. The campaign's first serious historian seems to have gone to much trouble to check the figures.

BIBLIOGRAPHY

Adam, Albrecht. *Aus dem Leben eines Schlachtenmalers. Selbstbiographie nebst einem Anhange herausgegeben von Dr. H. Holland.* Stuttgart, 1886

Aubry, Capitaine Thomas-Joseph. *Souvenirs du 12ème de Chasseurs, 1799-1815.* Paris, 1889

Augusta, Duchess. *In Napoleonic Days. Extracts from the private diary of Augusta, Duchess of Saxe-Coburg-Saalfeld, Queen Victoria's maternal grandmother, 1806-1821.* Selected and translated by HRH the Princess Beatrice. London, 1941

Bacler d'Albe, Baron Louis-Albert-Guislain. *Souvenirs Pittoresques.* 2 vols., Paris, 1898-92

Barre de Nanteuil. *Le Comte Daru, ou l'Administration Militaire sous la Révolution et l'Empire.* J. Peyronnet & Cie, Paris, 1966

Bausset Joseph, Baron de. *Mémoires anecdotiques sur l'intérieur du palais...* 2 vols., Baudoin, Paris, 1827-9

Beauharnais, Eugène de. *Mémoires et correspondance politique et militaire du prince Eugène, annotés et mis en ordre par A. Du Casse.* 10 vols., Lévy, Paris, 1858-60

Beaulieu, Drujon de. *Souvenirs d'un militaire pendant quelques années du règne de Napoléon Bonaparte.* Paris, 1831

Begos, Louis. *Souvenirs de campagnes du lieutenant-général Louis Begos, ancien capitaine adjutant-major au 2ᵉ régiment suisse au service de la France.* Delafontaine, Lausanne, 1859, and in *Soldats suisses au service étranger.* Geneva, 1909

Belliard, Augustin-Daniel. *Mémoires du comte Belliard, lieutenant-général, pair de France, écrits par lui-même, recueillis et mis en ordre par M. Vinet, l'un de ses aides-de-camp.* Paris, 1842

Berthezène, General Baron Pierre. *Souvenirs Militaires de la République et de l'Empire.* 2 vols., Paris, 1855

Bertin, Georges. *La Campagne de 1812 d'après des témoins oculaires.* Flammarion, Paris, 1895

Bertrand, Vincent. *Mémoires du capitaine Vincent Bertrand, recueillis et publiés par le colonel Chaland de la Guillanche.* Siraudeau, Angers, 1909

Beulay, Honoré. *Mémoires d'un grenadier de la Grande Armée (18 avril 1808 - 18 octobre 1815).* Préface du commandant Driant, Champion, Paris, 1907

Biot, Hubert-François. *Souvenirs anecdotiques et militaires du Colonel Biot, aide de camp du Général Pajol, avec une introduction et des notes par le comte Fleury.* Vivien, Paris, 1901

Blaze, Elzéar. *La Vie Militaire sous l'Empire,* Garnier Freres, Paris, 1837. English editions: 'Recollections of Military Life' in Sir Charles Napier (ed.), *Lights and Shades of Military Life,* Henry Colburn, London, 1850; and *Recollections of an Officer in Napoleon's Army.* Meras, New York, 1911

Bonaparte, Napoleon. *Correspondance de Napoléon 1er*, publiée par ordre de *l'Empereur Napoléon III*. 32 vols., Imprimerie impériale, Paris, 1858-70

Borcke, Johann von. *Kriegerleben des Johann von Borcke, weiland kgl. preuss. Obersteleutnants, 1806-1815, nach dessen Aufzeichnungen bearbeitet von V. Leszynski*. Mittler, Berlin, 1888

Boulart, Jean-François. *Mémoires Militaires du Général Baron Boulart sur les Guerres de la République et l'Empire*. Librairie Illustrée, Paris, 1892.

Bourgeois, Réné. *Tableau de la campagne de 1812, par Bourgeois témoin oculaire*. Dentu, Paris, 1814

Bourgogne, Adrien-Jean-Baptiste-François. *Mémoires publiés d'après le manuscrit original, par Paul Cottin*. Paris, 1898. *The Memoirs of Sergeant Bourgogne, 1812-1813*, Heinemann, London and Doubleday, New York, 1899; and Peter Davies, 1926. Reprinted with a foreword by David G. Chandler. Arms & Armour Press, London, and Hippocrene Books, Inc, New York, 1979

Bourgoing, Baron Paul-Charles-Amable de. *Souvenirs d'histoire contemporaine. Épisodes militaires et politiques*. Paris, 1864; and *Souvenirs militaires du Baron de Bourgoing (1791-1815), publiés par le Baron Pierre de Bourgoing*. Plon-Nourrit, Paris, 1897

Boyen, L.H.C. von. *Erinnerungen aus dem Leben des General-Feldmarschalls Hermann von Boyen*. 3 vols., Hirzel, Leipzig, 1889

Brandt, Heinrich von. *Souvenirs d'un officier polonais. Scènes de ma vie militaire en Espagne et en Russie (1808-1812)*. Ed. Baron Ernouf, Charpentier, Paris, 1877

Bréaut des Marlots, Jean. *Lettre d'un capitaine de cuirassiers sur la campagne de Russie, publiée par Leher*. Chez tous les librairies, Paris, 1885

Brett-James, Antony. *1812; Eye-witness accounts of Napoleon's Defeat in Russia*. Macmillan, London, and St. Martins, New York, 1966

Bro, Louis. *Mémoires du Général Bro (1796-1844), publiés par son petit-fils le Baron Henry Bro de Comères*. Paris, 1914

Bussy, Marc. in *Soldats Suisses au service de la France*. Geneva, 1909

Calosso, Jean. *Mémoires d'un Vieux Soldat*. Gianini, Turin, 1857

Castellane, Victor-Elisabeth Boniface, comte de. *Journal du maréchal de Castellane (1804-1862)*. 5 vols., Plon-Nourrit, Paris, 1895-7

Cate, Curtis. *The War of the Two Emperors*. Random House, New York and Weidenfeld, London, 1989

Caulaincourt, Armand de. *Mémoires du Général de Caulaincourt, Duc de Vizence, Grand Ecuyer de l'Empereur*. Introduction and notes by Jean Hanoteau. 3 vols., Plon-Nourrit, Paris, 1933. English translation in 2 vols.; vol.1 *Memoirs of General de Caulaincourt*, Cassell, London, 1935 and *With Napoleon in Russia*, Morrow, New York, 1935; vol.2 *No Peace With Napoleon*, Morrow, New York and Cassell, London, 1936

Chambray, Marquis de. *Histoire de l'Expédition de Russie*. Paris, 1825

Chandler, David. *The Campaigns of Napoleon*. Macmillan, New York, 1966, and Weidenfeld, London, 1966. *Dictionary of the Napoleonic Wars*. Macmillan, New York, 1979, and Arms and Armour Press, London,

1979; also Simon and Schuster, New York and Greenhill Books, London, 1993. *The Illustrated Napoleon.* Henry Holt, New York and Greenhill Books, London, 1990

Chevalier, Jean-Michel. *Souvenirs des guerres napoléoniennes, publiés d'après le manuscrit original par Jean Mistler et Hélène Michaud.* Paris, 1970

Chlapowsky, Désiré. *Mémoires sur les guerres de Napoléon (1806-1813), publiés par ses fils. Traduits par Jan Celminskiet Malibran.* Plon-Nourrit, Paris, 1908

Clausewitz, Karl von. *La Campagne de 1812 en Russie, traduit de l'allemand par Loredan Larchey, d'après le manuscrit original.* Paris, 1883. Translated from the original 'Feldzug 1812 in Russland' in *Hinterlassene Werke über Krieg und Kriegführung* (1832-1837). Dummler, Berlin. English edition *The Campaign of 1812 in Russia.* 1843; and Greenhill Books, London, 1992

Coignet, Capitaine Jean-Roch. *Cahiers.* Hachette, Paris, 1883. *The Notebooks of Captain Coignet,* Davies, London, 1928; reprinted Greenhill Books, London, 1986.

Combe, Michel. *Mémoires du colonel Combe sur les campagnes de Russie (1812), de Saxe (1813), de France (1814 et 1815).* Blot, Paris, 1853

Comeau de Charry, Sébastien-Joseph, Baron de. *Souvenirs des Guerres d'Allemagne pendant la Révolution et l'Empire.* Plon-Nourrit, Paris, 1900

Compans, Jean-Dominique. *Le Général Compans (1769-1845), d'après ses notes de campagne et sa correspondance de 1812 à 1813, par son petit-fils M. Ternaux-Compans.* Plon-Nourrit, Paris, 1912

Constant, *see* Wairy

Curely, Jean-Nicolas. *Le général Curely. Itinéraire d'un cavalier léger de la Grande Armée (1793-1815), publié d'après un manuscrit authentique par le général Thoumais.* Berger-Levrault, Paris, 1887

Davout, Maréchal Louis-Nicolas, Prince d'Eckmühl. *Correspondance du Maréchal Davout, 1801-1815, avec introduction et note par Ch. de Mazade.* 5 vols., Paris, 1885

Déchy, Edouard. *Souvenirs d'un garde du corps du roi de la compagnie de Noailles, suivis de souvenirs d'Allemagne et de Russie.* Paris, 1869

Dellard, Baron Jean-Pierre. *Mémoires Militaires du général Baron Dellard sur les guerres de la Révolution et de l'Empire.* Paris, 1892

(Dedem) van der Gelder, Baron Antoine-Baudoin-Gisbert. *Mémoires publiés d'après le manuscrit original par Jean Puraye.* 3 vols., Brussels, 1958-63

Denniée, P.P. *Itinéraire de l'Empereur Napoléon.* Paris, 1842

Duffy, Christopher. *Borodino, and the War of 1812.* Seeley, Service, London, 1972. Scribner, New York, 1993.

Dumas, Mathieu. *Souvenirs de Lieutenant-Général Comte Mathieu Dumas de 1770 à 1836, publiés par son fils.* 3 vols., Paris, 1839

Dumonceau, François. *Mémoires du Général Comte François Dumonceau, publiés d'après le manuscrit original par Jean Puraye.* 3 vols., Brepols, Brussels, 1958-63

Dupuy, Victor. *Souvenirs Militaires, 1794-1816.* Calmann-Lévy, Paris, 1892

Dutheillet de La mothe, Aubin. *Mémoires du Lieut-colonel Aubin Dutheillet de la Mothe*. Brussels, 1899

Duverger, P.T. *Mes Aventures dans la Campagne de Russie*. Paris, nd

Faber du Faur, G. de. *La Campagne de Russie (1812), d'après le journal illustré d'un témoin oculaire. Texte explicatif, par F. de Kausler, Introduction par A. Dayot*. Flammarion, Paris, 1895

Fabry, Lieutenant G. *Campagne de Russie (1812). Publié sous la Direction de la Section Historique de l'Etat-major de l'Armée*. 5 vols., Lucien Gougy, Paris, 1901-3

Fain, Baron Agathon-Jean-François. *Manuscrit de Mil-Huit Cent Douze, contentant le précis des événements de cette année, pour servir à l'histoire de l'Empereur Napoléon; par le Baron Fain, son Secrétaire-Archiviste à cette époque*. 2 vols., Delannay, Paris, 1827 and *Mémoires du Baron Fain, Premier Secrétaire du Cabinet de l'Empereur, publiés par ses arrière-petits-fils*. Plon-Nourrit, Paris, 1908

Fantin des Odoards, Louis-Florimond. *Journal du général Fantin des Odoards. Etapes d'un officier de la Grande Armée, 1800-1830*. 4 vols., Plon-Nourrit, Paris, 1895

Faré, Charles-Armand. *Lettres d'un jeune officier à sa mère, 1803 à 1814*. Delagrave Paris, 1863

Faure, Raymond. *Souvenirs du Nord ou la guerre, la Russie et les Russes ou l'esclavage*. Paris, 1821

Fézensac, M. le Duc de. *Souvenirs militaires de 1804 à 1814*. Dumaine, Paris, 1863. *A Journal of the Russian Campaigns of 1812*, London 1852; Trotman, Cambridge 1988.

François, Charles. *Journal du Capitaine François (dit le Dromadaire d'Egypte), 1793-1830*. 2 vols., Carrington, Paris, 1903-4

Fusil, Louise. *Souvenirs d'une Femme sur la retraite de Russie*. 2 vols., Dumont, Paris, 1841. New edn. 1910

Förster, Friedrich. *Preussen und Deutschland unter der Fremherrschaft, 1807-1813*. Berlin, nd. *Napoleons I Russischer Feldzung 1812*. G. Hempel, Berlin, 1856

Giesse, Friedrich. *Kassel-Moskau-Kustrin Tagebuch während des russischen Feldzuges*. Dyk, Leipzig, 1912

Girod de l'Ain, Général Baron. *Dix ans de mes Souvenirs militaires (de 1805 à 1815)*. Dumaine, Paris, 1873

Gourgaud, Gaspard. *Napoléon et la Grande Armée en Russie. Examen critique de l'oeuvre de M. de Ségur*. Bossange, Paris, 1825

Gouvion St-Cyr, Laurent de. *Mémoires pour servir à l'histoire militaire sous le Directoire, le Consulat et l'Empire*. 4 vols., Anselin, Paris, 1831

Grabowski, Jozef. *Mémoires Militaires*. Plon-Nourrit, Paris, 1907

Griois, Lubin. *Mémoires du Général Griois, 1792-1822*. 2 vols., Plon-Nourrit, Paris, 1909

Grüber, Carl-Johann Ritter von. *Souvenirs du chevalier Grüber, publiés par son neveu. Traduits de l'allemand avec des notes par Maleissye*. Paris, 1909

Guitard, Joseph-Esprit-Florentin. *Souvenirs militaires du Premier Empire. Mémoires d'un grenadier de la Garde, publiés pour la première fois par E.H.Guitard.* Paris, 1934

Heinemann, Wilhelm. *Bilder från mina Krigs- och Vandringsår, af Wilhelm Heinemann, enligt hans muntliga berättelser, bearbetade och meddelade af H.E.R. Belani.* Trans. from the German. Stockholm, 1835

Henckens, Lieutenant J.L. *Mémoires se rapportant à son service militaire au 6ème Régiment de Chasseurs à cheval français de février 1803 à août 1816. Publiés par son fils E.F.C.Henckens.* Nijhoff, The Hague, 1910

Herzen, A. *Erinnerungen von Alexander Herzen, aus dem Russischen übertragen, herausgegeben und eingeleitet von Dr. Otto Buck.* 2 vols., Wiegandt und Grieben, Berlin, 1907

Hochberg, Wilhelm, Graf von. *La Campagne de 1812. Mémoires du Margrave de Bade. Traduction, Introduction et Notes par Arthur Chuquet.* Paris, 1912

Hogendorp, Dirk van. *Mémoires du général Dirk van Hogendorp, comte de l'Empire, publiés par son petit-fils.* Nijhoff, The Hague, 1887

Holzhausen, Paul. *Die Deutschen in Russland, 1812. Leben und Leiden auf der Moskauer Heerfahrt.* Morawe und Scheffelt, Berlin, 1912

Jacquemot, Porphyre. 'Carnet de route d'un officier d'artillerie (1812-1813)' in *Souvenirs et Mémoires,* pp. 97-121, 1899

Jomini, Baron Henri de. *Précis de l'Art de Guerre.* Paris, 1838, augmented with appendix, 1855. *The Art of War.* J.B. Lippincott & Co., Philadelphia, 1862, and Greenhill Books, London, 1992

Kergorre, Alexandre Bellot de. *Un commissaire des guerres pendant le premier empire. Journal de Bellot de Kergorre, publié par le vicomte de Grouchy.* Paris, 1899

Kerkhove de. *Histoire des maladies observées à la Grande Armée pendant les campagnes de Russie en 1812 et en Allemagne en 1813.* Anvers, 1836

Kügelgen, Wilhelm von. *Jugenderinnerungen eines alten Mannes.* Ebenhausen bei München, new edn. 1907

Kurz, Hauptmann von. *Der Feldzug von 1812. Denkwüdigkeiten eines württembergischen Offiziers.* ed. Horst Kohl. Esslingen, 1838; new edn. Leipzig, nd

Labaume, Eugène. *Rélation circonstanciée de la campagne de Russie.* Panckoucke, Paris, 1814. *A circumstantial narrative of the Campaign in Russia.* London, 1814. Also translated as *The Crime of 1812 and its Retribution.* Andrew Melrose, London, 1912.

Lagneau, L. A-A, Comte de. *Journal d'un Chirurgien de la Grande Armée, 1803-1815.* Ed. Eugène Tattet, Emile-Paul, Paris, 1913

Langeron, L. A-A-, Comte de. *Mémoires de Langeron, Général d'infanterie dans l'armée russe. Campagnes de 1812, 1813, 1814. Publiés d'après le manuscrit original pour la Société d'histoire contemporaine, par L.-G. F. Picard,* Paris, 1902

Larrey, Dominique-Jean. *Mémoires de chirurgie militaire et campagnes.* J. Smith, Paris, 1812-17

Laugier, Césare de. *La Grande Armée: Récits de Césare de Laugier.* Ed. M. Henry Lyonnet. Fayard, Paris, 1910

Le Roy, C.F.M. *Souvenirs de Leroy, major d'infanterie, vétéran des armées de la République et de l'Empire.* Dijon, 1908

Lecointe de Laveau, G. *Moscou avant et après l'Incendie, par G.L.D., témoin oculaire.* Paris, 1814

Legler, Thomas. *Beresina.* Bern, 1942

Lejeune, Louis-François. *Mémoires du Général Lejeune,* publiés par M. Germain Bapst, 2 vols., Firmin-Didot, Paris, 1895-6

Lettres interceptées par les Russes durant la campagne de 1812, publiées d'après les pièces communiquées par S.E.M. Gorainow, Directeur des Archives de l'Etat et des Affairs étrangères de Russie et annotées par Léon Hennet et le Commandant E. Martin. Paris, 1913

Lignières, Marie-Henry, Comte de. *Souvenirs de la Grande Armée et de la Vieille Garde Impériale.* Pierre Roger, Paris, 1933

Lossberg, General Leutenant Friedrich Wilhelm von. *Briefe in die Heimath geschrieben während des Feldzuges 1812 in Russland.* Cassel, 1844

Mailly(-Nesle), Adrien-Augustin-Amalric, Comte de. *Mon journal pendant la campagne de Russie écrit de mémoire après mon retour à Paris.* Paris, 1841

Marbot, Antoine-Marcellin. *Mémoires du Général Baron de Marbot.* 3 vols., Plon-Nourrit, , Paris, 1891. *The Memoirs of Baron de Marbot.* 2 vols., Longmans Green & Co., London, 1892, and Greenhill Books, London, 1988

Maret, Hugues Bernard, duc de Bassano. *Souvenirs intimes de la Révolution et de l'Empire, recueillis et publiés par Mme Ch. de Sor.* 2 vols., Brussels, 1843

Martens, Carl von. *Dänkwürdigkeiten aus dem Leben eines alten Offiziers. Ein Beitrag zur Geschichte der letzten vierzig Jahre.* Arnold, Dresden and Leipzig, 1848

Martens, Christian Septimus von. *Vor fünfzig Jahren. Tagebuch meines Feldzuges in Russland, 1812.* Schaber, Stuttgart and Oehringen, 1862

Mayer, Louis. *Soldats Suisses au service de la France.* Geneva, 1909

Meerheimb, Franz Ludwig August von. *Erlebnisse eines Veteranen der grossen Armee während des Feldzuges in Russland, 1812, herausgegeben von dessen Sohn Richard von Meerheimb.* Arnold, Dresden, 1860

Méneval, Baron Claude-François de. *Mémoires pour servir à l'histoire de Napoléon I depuis 1802 jusqu' à 1815.* Paris, 1894. English edn., London, 1894

Montesquiou, Ambroise Anatole Augustin, Comte de. *Souvenirs de la Révolution, l'Empire, la Restauration, et le règne de Louis-Philippe.* Ed. Robert Barnaud, Paris, 1961

Murat, Joachim. *Lettres et documents pour servir à l'histoire de la France, 1761-1815, publiés par le Prince Murat, avec une introduction et des notes par Paul de Brethona.* Paris, nd

Nafziger, George F. *Napoleon's Invasion of Russia,* with a foreword by David Chandler. Presidio Press, Novato, 1988.

Noël, Colonel Jean-Nicholas-Auguste. *Souvenirs militaires d'un Officier du Premier Empire, 1795-1832.* Berger-Lerrault, Paris, 1895

Oginski, Michel. *Mémoires de Michel Oginski sur la Pologne et les Polonais, depuis 1788 jusqu' à la fin de 1815.* 4 vols., Ponthieu, Paris, 1826-27

Olivier, Daira. *L'incendie de Moscow.* Laffont, Paris, 1964. *The Burning of Moscow.* Allen & Unwin, London, 1966

Oudinot, Marie Charlotte. *Récits de guerre et de Foyer.* Paris, 1894. Also *see* Stiegler

Paixhans, General Henri-Joseph de. *Retraite de Moscou, Notes écrites au Quartier-Général de l'Empereur.* Metz, 1868

Pelleport, Pierre Vicomte de. *Souvenirs militaires et intimes du général vicomte de Pelleport de 1793 à 1853, publiés par son fils sur manuscrits originaux, lettres notes et documents officiels laissés par l'auteur.* 2 vols., Paris, 1857.

Peyrusse, Guillaume. *Lettres inédites du Baron Guillaume Peyrusse, écrites à son frère André pendant les Campagnes de l'Empire de 1809 à 1814.* Perrin, Paris, 1894

Pils, François. *Journal de marche du Grenadier Pils, (1804-1814), recueilli et annoté par M. Raoul de Cisternes. Illustrations d'après des dessins originaux de PILS.* Ollendorff, Paris, 1895

Pion des Loches, Antoine-Augustin. *Mes Campagnes (1792-1815). Notes et correspondance du colonel d'artillerie Pion des Loches, mises en ordre et publiées par Maurice Chipon et Léonce Pingaud.* Paris, 1889

Planat de la Faye, Nicolas Louis. *Vie de Planat de la Faye, aide-de-camp des généraux Lariboisière et Drouot, officier d'ordonnance de Napoléon 1ᵉʳ. Souvenirs, Lettres, dictés et annotés par sa veuve.* Ollendorff, Paris, 1895

Potocka, Anna. *Mémoires de la Comtessse Potocka, 1794-1820, publiés par Casimir Stryienski.* Plon-Nourrit, Paris, 1897

Pradt, Dominique-Georges-Frédéric de Fourt de. *Histoire de l'Ambassade dans le Grand Duché de Varsovie en 1812.* Paris, 1815

Puybusque, L.-G. de: *Souvenirs d'un invalide pendant le dernier demi-siècle.* 2 vols., Paris, 1840

Rambuteau, Claude Philibert Barthelot, *Mémoires du Comte de Rambuteau, publiés par son petit-fils.* Lévy, Paris, 1905

Rapp, Jean. *Mémoires écrits par lui-même et publiés par sa famille.* Bossange, Paris, 1823. *Memoirs of General Count Rapp.* Henry Colburn, 1823 and Trotman, Cambridge, 1985

Reggio, Duchesse de. *See* Stiegler

Rellstab, Ludwig. *Aus meinem Leben.* 2 vols., Berlin, 1861

Richter, Adrian Ludwig. *Lebenserinnerungen eines deutschen Mahlers, ausgegeben von Heinrich Richter.* Frankfurt-am-Main, 1885

Roch-Godart. *Mémoires du général-baron, Roch Godart, 1792-1815, publiés par J.B. Antoine.* Paris, 1895. New edn Flammarion, nd

Rochechouart, Louis-Victor-Léon, Général Comte de. *Souvenirs sur la Révolution, l'Empire et la Restauration, publiés par son fils.* Plon-Nourrit, Paris, 1889

Roeder, Helen. *The Ordeal of Captain Roeder, from the Diary of an Officer of the First Battalion of Hessian Lifeguards during the Moscow Campaign of 1812-13, translated and edited from the original manuscript.* Methuen, London, 1960. Original German edition is: Röder, Franz. *Der Kriegszug Napoleons gegen Russland im Jahre 1812. Nach den besten Quellen und seinen eigenen Tagebüchern dargestellt nach der Zitfolge der Begebenheaiten* Leipzig, 1848

Roguet, François. *Mémoires militaires du lieutenant-général comte Roguet, colonel en second des grenadiers à pied de la Vieille Garde.* Dumaine, Paris, 1862-5

Roos, Heinrich von. *Avec Napoléon en Russie. Souvenirs de la campagne de 1812, traduits par le lieutenant-colonel Buat. Introduction et notes par P. Holzhausen.* Chapelot, Paris, 1913. And *Souvenirs d'un médecin de la Grande Armée, traduits d'après l'édition originale de 1832 par Mme Lamotte.* Perrin, Paris, 1913. These are translated from the original *Ein Jahr aus meinem Leben oder Reise von den westlichen Ufern der Donau an die Nara, südlich von Moskva, und zurück an die Beresina, mit der grossen Armee Napoleons, im Jahre 1812.* St. Petersburg, 1832

Rosselet, Abraham. *Souvenirs de Abraham Rosselet, lieutenant-colonel en retraite au service de la France. Publiés par R. de Steiger.* Attinger, Neuchâtel, 1857

Rotenhan. *Dänkwürdigkeiten eines württembergischen Offiziers aus den Feldzuge im Jahre 1812. Veröffentlicht durch Freiherrn von Rotenhan.* Berlin, 1892. 3rd edn., Finsterlin, Munich, 1900

Roustam Raza. *Souvenirs de Roustam, mameluck de Napoléon. Introduction et notes de Paul Cottin. Préface de Frédéric Masson.* Paris, 1821

Ruppel, Eduard. *Kriegsgefangene im Herzen Russlands, 1812-1814.* Paetel, Berlin, 1912

St-Chamans, Alfred-Armand-Robert. *Mémoires du Général Comte de Saint-Chamans, ancien aide-de-camp du Maréchal Soult, 1802-1832.* Plon-Nourrit, Paris, 1896

Sauvage, N.J. *Rélation de la Campagne de Russie.* Paris, nd

Scheltens. *Souvenirs d'un vieux soldat belge de la garde impériale.* Brussels, 1880

Schlosser, Ludwig Wilhelm Gottlob. *Erlebnisse eines sachsischen Landpredigers in den Kriegsjahren von 1806 bis 1815.* Leipzig, 1846

Schrafel, Joseph. *Merkwürdige Schicksale des ehemaligen Feldwebels im köngl. bayer. 5te Linien-Infanterie-Regiment, Joseph Schrafel, vorzüglich im russischen Feldzuge und in der Gefangenschaft, in den Jahren 1812 bis 1814, von ihm selbstbeschrieben.* Nuremberg, 1834

Schreckenstein, Roth von. *Die Kavallerie in der Schlacht ander Moskwa.* Schendorff, Münster, 1858

Schuerman, Albert. *Itinéraire Général de Napoléon 1er.* 2nd edn., Paris, 1911

Ségur, Philippe, Comte de. *Histoire de Napoléon et la Grande Armée en 1812.* Paris, 1824. Also: *Du Rhin à Fontainebleau. Mémoires du Général Comte de Ségur (aide-de-camp de Napoléon).* Edn. Nelson, 1910. *History of Napoleon's Expedition to Russia,* 2 vols., London, 1825s. *Napoleon's Russian Campaign,* Joseph, London, 1959

Sérang. *Les prisonniers français en Russie. Mémoires et souvenirs de M. le marquis de Sérang, recueillis et publiés par M. de Puybusque.* 2 vols., Paris, 1837

Séruzier, Théodore-Jean-Joseph, Baron. *Mémoires militaires du baron Séruzier, colonel d'artillerie légère, mis en ordre et rédigés par son ami M. Le Mière de Corvey.* Paris, 1824 .

Soltyk, Comte Roman. *Napoléon en 1812. Mémoires Historiques et militaires sur la Campagne de Russie.* Bertrand, Paris, 1836

Staël, Germaine de. *Mémoires de Dix Années d'Exil.* Paris, 1848. *Ten Years Exile.* London, 1821

Stendhal, M. de. *Journal de Stendhal (1801-1814), publié par Casimir Stryienski et François de Nion.* Paris, 1888. *The Private Diaries of Stendhal.* London, Gollancz, 1955. And *Vie de Henri Brulard, nouvelle édition établie et commentée par Henri Martineau.* Le Divan, Paris, 1953

Stiegler, Gaston. *Le Maréchal Oudinot, Duc de Reggio, d'après les souvenirs inédits de la Maréchale.* 2nd edn., Plon-Nourrit, Paris, 1894. *Memoirs of Marshal Oudinot compiled from the hitherto unpublished Souvenirs of the Duchesse of Reggio by G. Stiegler.* Henry, London, 1896

Suckow, Karl von. *Aus meinem Soldatenleben.* Stuttgart, 1862; French translation: *D'Iéna à Moscou, fragments de ma vie.* Paris, 1902

Surugué, l'Abbé Adrien. *Lettre sur l'Incendie de Moscou en 1812.* Paris, 1821; and *Un Témoin de la Campagne de Russie,* par Léon Mirot. Paris, 1914

Szymanowski, Général Joseph. *Mémoires, 1806-1814. Traduits du polonais par Bodhane Osckinczye.* Lavauzelle, Paris, 1900

Tarle, Eugene. *Napoleon's Invasion of Russia, 1812.* London and New York, 1942. Original edition Moscow, 1938

Tascher, Maurice de. *Notes de Campagne (1806-1813).* Chateauroux, 1938

Thirion, Auguste (de Metz). *Souvenirs Militaires, 1807-1818.* Paris, 1892

Tulard, Jean. *Bibliographie des Mémoires sur le Consulat et l'Empire, écrites ou traduites en français.* Librairie Droz, Genève-Paris, 1971

Van der Gelder, *see* (Dedem) van der Gelder

Vaudoncourt, Frédéric-Guillaume de. *Mémoires pour servir à la guerre entre la France et la Russie en 1812, par un officier de l'état-major française.* 2 vols., Deboffe, London, 1815

Villemain, Abel François. *Souvenirs contemporains d'histoire et de littérature.* 2 vols., Paris, 1854

Vionnet, Lieutenant-Général Louis-Joseph, Vicomte de Marignoné. *Campagnes de Russie et de Saxe, 1812-1813.* Also *Souvenirs d'un ex-commandant des Grenadiers de la Vieille Garde, avec une préface de Rodolf Vagnair.* Paris, 1899

Vossler, Heinrich August. *With Napoleon in Russia, the Diary of a Lieutenant of the Grand Army 1812-13.* The Folio Society, London, 1969

Wairy, Louis Constant. *Mémoires de Constant, premier valet de chambre de Napoléon Ier, avec une introduction et des notes par Arnould Halopin.* Paris, nd. *Memoirs of Constant.* Nichols, London, 1896

Walter, Jakob. *The Diary of a Napoleonic Foot Soldier,* edited and with an introduction by Marc Raeff, Windrush Press, Gloucestershire, and Doubleday, New York, 1991

Wedel, Carl Anton Wilhelm, Graf von. *Geschichte eines Offiziers im Kriege gegen Russland, 1812, in russischer Gefangenschaft 1813 bis 1814, im Feldzuge gegen Napoleon 1815, Lebenserinnerungen.* Asher, Berlin, 1897

Weider, Ben & David Hapgood. *The Murder of Napoleon,* Congdon & Lattès, New York, 1982

Wesemann, J.H.C. *Kanonier des Kaisers. Kriegstagenbuch der Heinrich Wesemann, 1808-14.* Ed: Ho. Wesemann. Verlag Wissenschaft und Politik, Cologne, 1971

Wilson, Sir Robert. *Narrative of Events during the Invasion of Russia by Napoleon Bonaparte, and the Retreat of the French Army, 1812.* Edited by his nephew and son-in-law, the Revd. Herbert Randoph. Murray, London, 1860. Also: *Private Diary of Travels, Personal Services, and Public Events, during Mission and Employment with the European Armies in the Campaigns of 1812, 1813, 1814, from the Invasion of Russia to the Capture of Paris.* Edited by the Revd. Herbert Randolph. 2 vols., J. Murray, London, 1861. Also: *General Wilson's Journal, 1812-1814,* ed. Antony Brett-James. Kimber, London, 1964

Ysarn de Villefort, François d'. *Relation du Séjour des Français à Moscou et de l'Incendie de cette Ville en 1812, par un habitant de Moscou.* Gadárnel, Brussels, 1871

Articles

Auvray, Pierre. 'Souvenirs militaires de Pierre Auvray, sous-lieutenant au 23ème régiment de dragons (1797-1815)' in *Carnet de la Sabretache,* 1919

Bonnet, Guillaume. 'Journal du Capitaine Bonnet du 18ème de ligne' in *Carnet de la Sabretache,* 1912

Butkevicius. 'Napoléon en Lithuanie 1812, d'après des documents inédits', trans. René Martel, in *La Revue de Paris,* 15 August 1932

Everts, Henri-Pierre. 'Campagne et captivité en Russie' in *Carnet de la Sabretache,* Paris, 1901

Kalckreuth, von. 'Erinnerungen' in *Zeitschrift für Kunst, Wissenschaft und Geschichte des Krieges.* Vol. V, 1835

Lyautey, Hubert. 'Lettres d'un Lieutenant de la Grande Armée' published by Pierre Lyautey in *La Revue des Deux Mondes,* 12 December 1962

Pastoret, Amédée-David, Marquis de. 'De Witebsk à la Bérézina' in *Revue de Paris,* April, 1902

Rambaud, Alfred Nicholas. 'La Grande Armée à Moscou. Récits de témoins oculaires russes. D'après l'ouvrage publié par T. Tolytchef' in *Revue des Deux Mondes.* Paris, 1 July 1873

Rossetti, Marie-Joseph-Thomas. 'Journal inédit' published by R. Recouty in *Revue de France,* Sept-Dec 1931, Jan-April 1932

Skalkowski, A. 'Les Mémoires du Général Turno' in *Revue des Etudes Napoléoniennes,* vol.II, pp. 99-116, 129-45, Paris, 1931

Turno, Boris. *See* Skalkowski, A

Zalusky, Joseph-Henri. 'Souvenirs du général comte Zalusky. Les chevaulégers de la garde dans la campagne de 1812' in *Carnet de la Sabretache*, 1897

MAPS

The campaign of 1812 dramatically illustrated in a graph drawn by Charles Joseph Minard (1781–1870) in 1861. The width of the line shows the strength of the army at each location. One can follow the invasion (tinted line) from left to right – Poland to Moscow – and the retreat (solid line) back to the left (west). The latter is linked to the temperature scale below, the temperatures indicated being in degrees Réaumur (in which 80° = 100°C = 212°F).

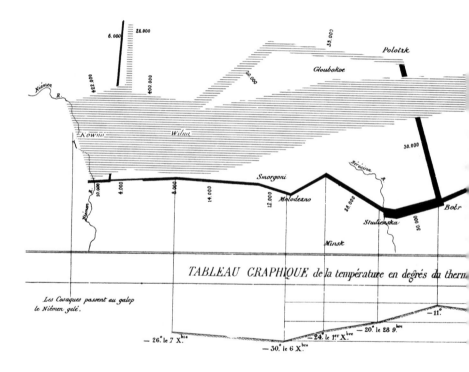

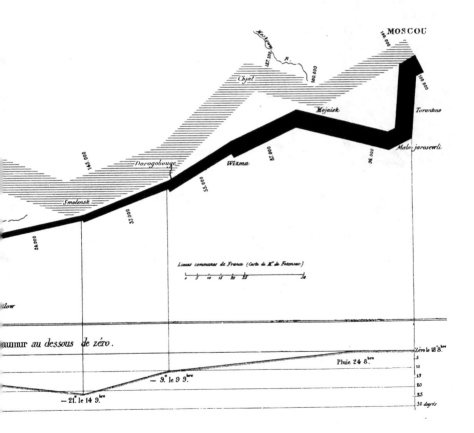

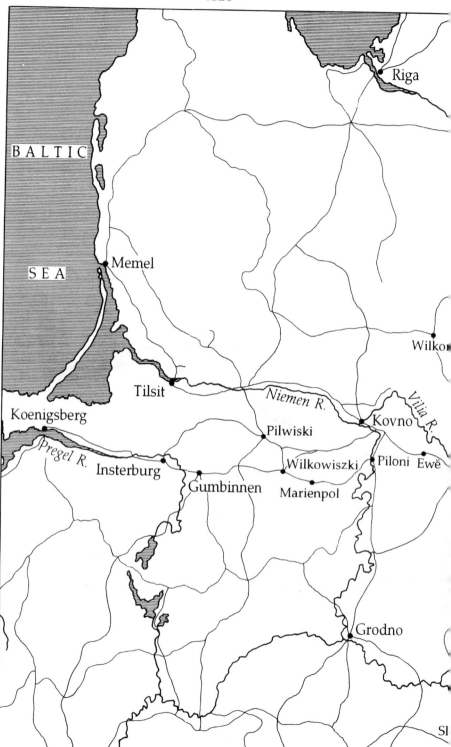

BALTIC

SEA

Riga

Memel

Wilko

Tilsit

Niemen R.

Vilia R.

Koenigsberg

Kovno

Pilwiski

Pregel R.

Insterburg

Wilkowiszki

Piloni

Ewë

Gumbinnen

Marienpol

Grodno

Sl

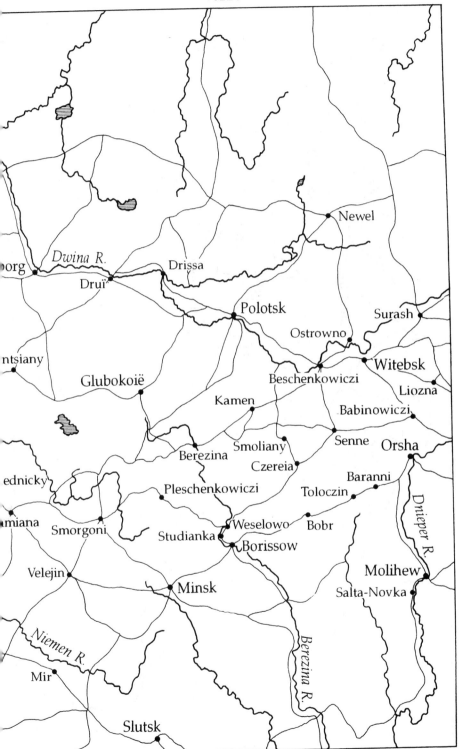

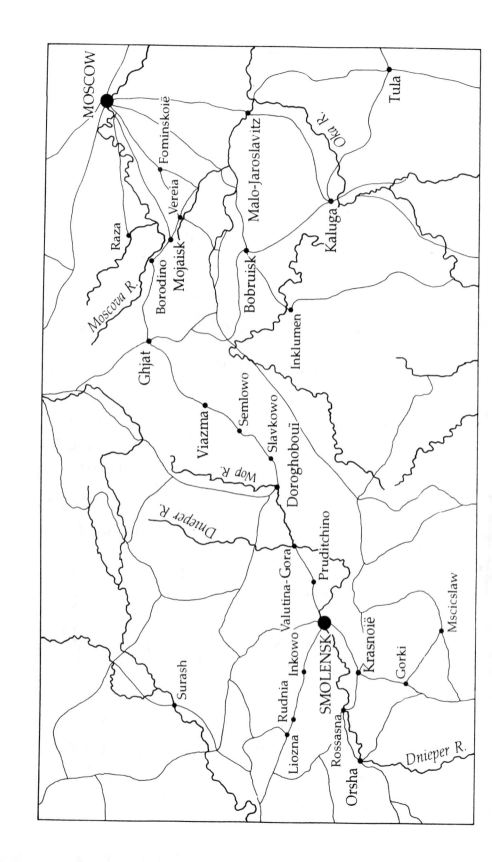

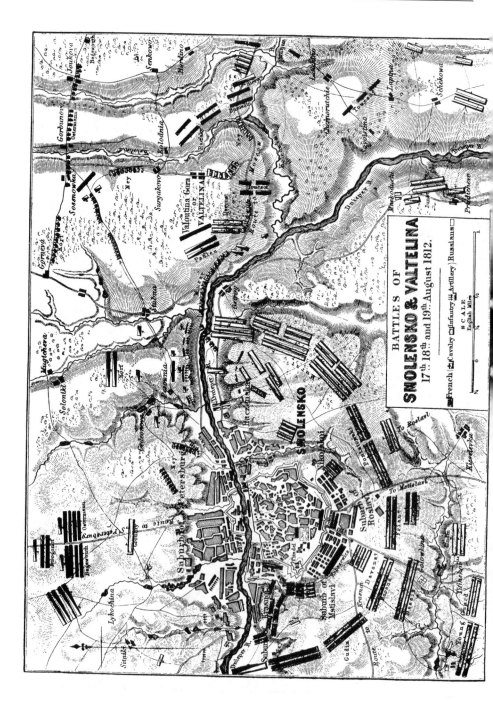

BATTLES OF
SMOLENSKO & VALTELINA
17th, 18th, and 19th August 1812.

French (▲Cavalry ◻Infantry ▦Artillery) Russians ◻

SCALE
English Miles

INDEX

1812

NAPOLEON IN MOSCOW

'True historians aren't those who relate overall facts and limit themselves to general causes; but those who pursue facts down to their most detailed circumstances and reveal their particular causes.'

Giambattista Vico

'Human life is short and fleeting, and many millions of individuals share in it who are swallowed up by that monster of oblivion which is waiting for them with ever-open jaws. It is thus a very thankworthy task to try to rescue something of the memory of interesting and important events, or the leading features and personages of some episodes from the general shipwreck of the world.'

Schopenhauer

1812
NAPOLEON IN MOSCOW

PAUL BRITTEN AUSTIN

AUTHOR OF

1812: The March on Moscow

GREENHILL BOOKS, LONDON

STACKPOLE BOOKS, PENNSYLVANIA

This edition of *1812: Napoleon in Moscow*
first published 1995 by
Greenhill Books, Lionel Leventhal Limited, Park House,
1 Russell Gardens, London NW11 9NN
and
Stackpole Books, 5067 Ritter Road,
Mechanicsburg, PA 17055, USA.

British Library Cataloguing in Publication Data
Austin, Paul Britten
1812: Napoleon in Moscow
I. Title
940.27
ISBN 1-85367-195-9

Library of Congress Cataloging-in-Publication Data
Austin, Paul Britten
1812: Napoleon in Moscow / by Paul Britten Austin.
264 p. 24 cm.
Includes bibliographical references and index.
ISBN 1-85367-195-9
1. Napoleon I. Emperor of the French, 1769–1821 —
Military leadership. 2. Napoleonic Wars, 1800–1815 —
Campaigns — Russia — Moscow. I. Title.
II. Title: Napoleon in Moscow.
DC235.5.M8A87   1995
940.2'7—dc20

Designed and edited by DAG Publications Ltd.
Designed by David Gibbons; edited by Michael Boxall.
Printed and bound in Great Britain by
Creative Print and Design (Wales) Ebbw Vale

Note:
First references to the eyewitnesses
whose accounts make up this 'documentary'
of Napoleon's invasion of Russia appear in
italic

CONTENTS

To my son THOM
and my grandson BENNY
without whose patient encouragement
and computer expertise this work
would never have been possible.

PREFACE

This book is the successor to *1812: The March on Moscow*. A kind of word-film or drama documentary, it's edited, I hope not too inartistically, from the first-hand accounts of well over 100 of the participants, both French and 'allied', in the vast mass-drama of Napoleon's invasion of Russia.

I've resisted the temptation to comment on or evaluate their narratives. All strike me as authentic – if not necessarily accurate, and certainly not impartial. The events, after all, were extraordinary beyond imagining. And allowances must be made for hindsight. It's so easy to be wise after the event!

For reasons of space, I've seen it all from one side only – with a single co-opted witness from the Russian side in the highly critical, not to say caustic, person of General Sir Robert Wilson, the British representative at Kutusov's headquarters.

After the briefest of intermissions I resume in this volume exactly where its forerunner left off: at the gates of Moscow. At the head of his central army, originally some 350,000-strong and made up of Davout's I, Ney's III, Prince Eugène's IV, Poniatowski's V, and Junot's VIII Corps and the Imperial Guard, and spearheaded by Murat's four 'reserve' cavalry corps, Napoleon had crossed the Niemen on Midsummer's Day. But the Tsar's 1st and 2nd West Armies had refused him the pitched battle which, as twice before, would certainly have crushed them, and retreating separately eastwards, forcing him to follow in search of the resounding victory which was to force Russia back into his Continental System and – prime objective of the whole unprecedentedly vast and ever farther-flung campaign – compel Britain to make peace. Far away to the south, meanwhile, Schwarzenberg's Austrians and Reynier's Saxons (IX Corps) had quickly got bogged down manoeuvring against Tormassov's 3rd West Army which, if Russia and Turkey hadn't unexpectedly made peace, should have been fighting the hereditary foe in Moravia. To the northwest Macdonald's X Corps, mostly made up of Prussians, had invested Riga; while Oudinot's II and St-Cyr's VI Corps had pursued Wittgenstein through the blazing summer heats and, ravaged by sickness, also got bogged down at Polotsk.

On 28 July the main body, under Napoleon himself, had again been refused battle outside Witebsk; and after a ten-day pause there to recuperate, the advance had gone on. Napoleon had manoeuvred to circumvent Barclay de Tolly's 1st and Bagration's 2nd West Armies and snatch Smolensk, but failed. There, at last, on 17 August, the pitched battle he had been longing for was fought – indecisively. Smolensk, Russia's third largest city, had gone up in flames; and again the Russians had withdrawn in almost miraculously excellent order, leaving Napoleon no option (in view of the acute political hazards of staying where he was, so remote from his bases, and of the disastrous likelihoods if – after all this marching and fighting – he withdrew) but to push on eastwards and strike for Moscow. Once it had been occupied, he was sure, "his brother Alexander" would have to make peace. On 7 September the Russians had at long last stood and fought at Borodino, one of the bloodiest one-day battles of modern times and of which one could paradoxically say it had 'neither been won, lost nor drawn'. Again the Russian army had retired intact and certainly not beaten. And on 14 September a parley outside the gates of Moscow had led to a brief truce. Under it Murat's advance guard – at least two-thirds of whose horses were either dead of thirst, hunger, overwork or neglect, or had fallen at Borodino – was to follow on at the heels of the Cossacks' rearguard through the eerily deserted city.

It's at this – for all my protagonists – keenly anticipatory moment outside the gates of Moscow – a moment when Napoleon's 'face, normally so impassive, showed instantly and unmistakably the mark of his bitter disappointment [Caulaincourt]' – that they resume, exactly where they finished in the previous volume, their multifarious story.

For the sake of new readers, but I hope without becoming tedious to those who've so patiently read my first volume, I've tried to re-identify, in passing, at least the most important of my eyewitnesses by italicizing their names at their first reappearance. For bibliographical details of these and other sources, see the Bibliography (which, it should be noted, is supplementary to the fuller one in my first volume, which itemizes them all). As in *The March*, there is also an Index, by means of which the reader can, if he likes, follow our protagonists individually. At the same time I have of course tried to keep him informed as to the ongoing military situation.

In the interests of narrative pace, while always preserving my narrators' exact sense, I've sometimes taken liberties with the order of their words, phrases and even sentences. A little reflection will show why I've had to do this. A longish quotation may very well start where I, as 'film editor', want to cut it into my overall narrative; but very likely it will soon stray off into some other direction than the overall one it is necessary for us to follow. Hence my unorthodox use, made in good faith, of some of these translated passages which none the less form the essence of my tale.

Although on occasion I've used the present tense where the original is in the perfect, I've mainly retained the latter, in contrast with my own use of the present. If this – as one unusually militant critic observes – 'sets the pace for a racy tale with reduced regard for the details military history enthusiasts will demand', I can only beg their indulgence and hope my long-dead heroes too would have forgiven me these slight syntactic and grammatical deviations in the interests of the immediacy and vividness which characterizes their writings.

First and foremost my book is a kind of essay in the day-to-day, sometimes hour-by-hour reconstruction of six months of vanished time: a vast historical event which ended perhaps more terribly than any of its kind.

Paul Britten Austin
Dawlish, S. Devon, 1995

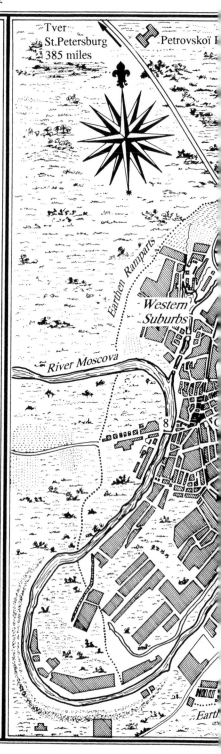

LEGEND

A Kremlin
B German Quarter
C Petersburg District
D Petersburg Suburbs
1 Cathedral of Assumption
2 Magazine
3 Arsenal
4 Kitaigorod
5 Unburnt Quarters
6 Foundlings Hospital
7 Secret Gate
8 Doroghomilov Bridge

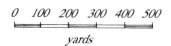

yards

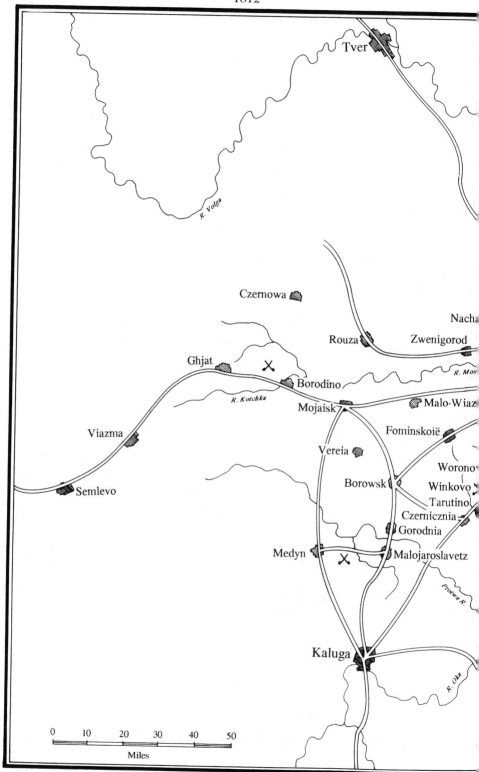

1812

Tver

Czernowa

Nacha

Rouza Zwenigorod

Ghjat

Borodino

R. Mos

R. Kotchka

Mojaisk Malo-Wiaz

Viazma

Fominskoïë

Vereia

Woronov

Borowsk Winkovo

Semlevo Tarutino

Czernicznia

Gorodnia

Medyn Malojaroslavetz

Prolwa R.

Kaluga

R. Oka

R. Volga

0 10 20 30 40 50

Miles

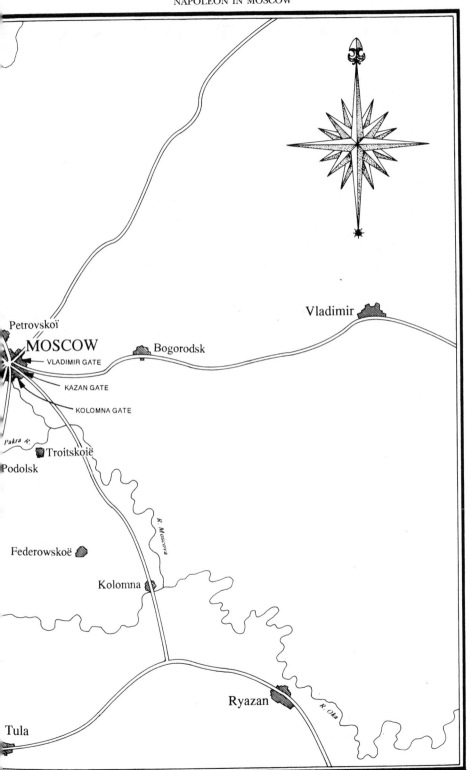

Vladimir

Petrovskoï

MOSCOW

Bogorodsk

VLADIMIR GATE

KAZAN GATE

KOLOMNA GATE

Pakra R.

Troitskoïë

Podolsk

R. *Moscova*

Federowskoë

Kolomna

Ryazan

R. *Oka*

Tula

SOME IMPORTANT EYEWITNESSES

L-A G. Bacler d'Albe, colonel, Napoleon's Topographer-in-Chief and closest collaborator.

A. D. Belliard, general, Murat's chief-of-staff.

V. Bertrand, carabinier sergeant in 7th Light Infantry (Davout's I Corps).

H-F. Biot, lieutenant, ADC to General Pajol, 2nd Cavalry Corps.

G. Bonnet, grenadier captain in the 18th Line, Ney's III Corps.

J-F. Boulart, major of Guard artillery.

A. J. B. F. Bourgogne, sergeant of the Fusiliers-Grenadiers of the Middle Guard.

P. C. A. Bourgoing, lieutenant, interpreter and ADC to General Delaborde, commander of a division of the Young Guard.

H. Brandt, lieutenant in the Vistula Legion, attached to the Young Guard.

A. de Caulaincourt, general, Master of the Horse, responsible for all headquarters transports and the courier service.

V. E. B Castellane, captain, orderly officer at Napoleon's headquarters.

D. Chlapowski, Colonel of the 1st (Polish) Guard Lancers.

J-R. Coignet, sous-lieutenant, formerly drill sergeant of the 2nd Guard Grenadiers, attached as orderly to Napoleon's 'little' or advance headquarters.

Dedem van der Gelder, Dutch ex-diplomat, general of brigade, commanding Dufour's [ex-Friant's] 2nd Infantry Brigade, I Corps.

P-P. Denniée, inspector of reviews, attached to IHQ. In 1842 he would publish Napoleon's day-to-day itinerary.

M. Dumas, general, the army's Intendant-General.

F. Dumonceau, captain commanding 6th Troop, 2nd Squadron of the 2nd ('Red') Lancers of the Guard, Colbert's lancer brigade.

V. Dupuy, major, then colonel of the 7th Hussars, 1st Cavalry Corps.

A. Dutheillet de Lamothe, lieutenant in the 57th Line infantry regiment, I Corps.

B-T. Duverger, Paymaster-captain to Davout's I corps.

G. de Faber du Faur, major commanding III Corps' reserve artillery, artist.

A-J-F. Fain, baron, Napoleon's Second Secretary.

Duc de Montesquiou-Fezensac, colonel commanding 4th Line infantry regiment, III Corps.

C. François, known as 'the Dromedary of Egypt', captain commanding one of the 30th Line infantry regiment's grenadier companies, Morand's division, I Corps.

L. Fusil, actress in the French troupe at Moscow.

G. de l'Ain, staff-captain, ADC to General Dessaix, general of division in I Corps.

G. Gourgaud 1st 'Officier d'Ordonnance' (senior staff officer) to Napoleon.

L. Griois, colonel of horse artillery, 3rd Cavalry Corps.

J. L. Henckens, adjutant-major, acting-lieutenant in the 6th Chasseurs à Cheval, 3rd Cavalry Corps.

D. van Hogendorp, Dutch general, governor of Vilna province.

H. de Jomini, baron, general, Swiss writer on strategy, temporarily governor of Vilna city, then of Smolensk.

B. de Kergorre, administrative officer attached to IHQ.

E. Labaume, captain on Prince Eugène's (IV Corps) staff, author of the first published account of the campaign (1814).

D. Larrey, Surgeon-General, head of the Guard's and the Grand Army's medical services.

C. de Laugier, adjutant-major of the Italian Guardia d'Onore, Prince Eugène's IV Corps.

L-F. Lejeune, baron, colonel, until Borodino one of Berthier's ADCs; thereafter chief-of-staff to Davout.

M. H. Lignières, count, captain in the 1st Foot Chasseurs of the Old Guard.

A. A. A. de Mailly-Nesle, count, lieutenant in the 2nd Carabiniers.

C-F. Méneval, baron, Napoleon's First Secretary.

A. von Muraldt, lieutenant in the 4th Bavarian chevaulegers, attached to Eugène's IV Corps.

A. A. A. Montesquiou, Quartermaster-General, attached to IHQ.

H-J. de Paixhans, inspector of artillery.

P. des Loches, captain, then major in the Guard artillery.

J. Rapp, general, Napoleon's most senior ADC.

Le Roy, major commanding a battalion of the 85th Line infantry regiment, Dessaix's division, I Corps.

P. de la Faye, lieutenant, secretary to General Lariboisière, commander of the Grand Army's artillery.

F. Roeder, captain in the Hessian Footguards, attached to the Young Guard.

H. von Roos, cavalry surgeon, 3rd Cavalry Corps.

M. J. T. Rossetti, colonel, ADC to Murat.

P. de Ségur, count, general, Assistant Prefect of the Palace, author of the famous but far from accurate *Napoléon et la Grande Armée en Russie 1812.*

T. J. F. Séruzier, baron, colonel commanding light artillery of 3rd Cavalry Corps.

R. Soltyk, count, Polish artillery officer attached to Topographical Department at IHQ.

K. von Suckow, captain, Württemberg infantry.

M. Tascher, lieutenant of 12th Chasseurs à Cheval, nephew of ex-Empress Josephine.

A. Thirion, regimental sergeant-major of the 2nd Cuirassiers, 1st Cavalry Corps.

C. Wairy, Napoleon's First Valet.

Sir Robert Wilson, the British government's representative at Kutusov's headquarters.

J. H. Zalusky, captain in the 1st (Polish) Guard Lancers.

CHAPTER 1

"FIRE! FIRE!"

Colonel Griois goes on a shopping spree – 'we take possession of Moscow as if it had been built for us' – a sinister silence – the Italian Royal Guard lodges itself military fashion – Napoleon enters Moscow – fire fuzes in the Kremlin – 'a lugubrious calm, broken only by horses' whinnying' – 'not exactly a spectacle to restore our spirits' – 'a signal like a firework' – 'the whole city was going up in flames'

For the first time since the Grand Army had crossed the Niemen at midsummer, 83 days ago, Colonel Lubin Griois, commanding 3rd Cavalry Corps' horse artillery, and his aristocratic friend Colonel Jumilhac, the corps' chief-of-staff, have slept in beds. It's the first time they've taken their clothes off since leaving Prussia in June. Last night they'd taken possession of a comfortable villa 'said to belong to a doctor' but abandoned by its owner, a couple of miles north-west of Moscow. Not far away Prince Eugène's mainly Italian IV Corps, to which 3rd Cavalry Corps has recently been attached, has bivouacked around the 'the miserable little town of Chorosewo'. Across the plain they can see the city's multicoloured onion spires, gleaming in the autumn sunshine. Since no orders have come, Griois decides to go on a shopping spree.

A keen observer of people and places, a lady's man of the most faithless nature but also a lover of Italian opera and paintings[1] and whose dominant passion is gambling, Griois, above all else in this world, loves Italy – i.e., northern Italy. In the south and Calabria he's had most unpleasant experiences, seen all sorts of horrors and been in the action at Maida in 1806 where Reynier's forces had been repulsed by unexpectedly steady British infantry fire. He's also been in the Tyrol, where he'd offered a pinch of snuff to Andreas Hofer and been desperately sad when that captured hero, at Napoleon's express order, had been shot by firing squad at Mantua. Leaving Verona – how he'd loved Verona! – in advance of his guns with his horses and equipment, 'about all I owned', he'd nevertheless been

'enchanted to do this campaign, whose immense preparations had announced its importance. I hadn't been able to leave Verona and the objects so dear to me without a contraction of my heart, augmented by a virtual certainty I'd never again see this town where at various times I'd spent about three years, where I'd lived so happily, and where I'd tasted every pleasure.'

Unlike Jumilhac, whose wit makes him delightful company for his fellow-officers but whom his friend regards as altogether too hard on the rank-and-file, Griois prides himself on knowing each of his gunners by name

17

and on being so unembarrassed in Napoleon's presence as even to contradict him in technical matters.

Taking his orderly with him, he enters the city, hoping the rumour, which has been going the rounds ever since yesterday, of its being abandoned by its population, will prove to be much exaggerated. And in fact Griois finds there are

'still some inhabitants who'd stayed behind. But almost all were foreigners, Italians, Germans and Frenchmen, who seemed to be delighted to receive their compatriots. I saw a lot of them in the streets.'

That almost every shop is closed he ascribes to

'the merchants' excusable fear during the first moments of the occupation. The order and calm reigning in all the quarters I went through should soon dispel all fear and re-establish confidence.'

An Italian having indicated a 'rather ugly' café, Griois – presumably also the orderly – indulges in the delights of a *café crème*. But above all he craves wine; and an artillery captain of his acquaintance shows him where he can get some, in a Russian merchant's vast underground cellar. There he relishes a bottle of 'a sort of dry Madeira'. Finishing it off, his orderly is of the same opinion. And after loading him down with half-a-dozen more such bottles 'I left my merchant most content, to get in gold what he usually was paid for in paper roubles. Fully disposed to renew our provisions tomorrow and never more lack for any' Griois gets back to his gunners' bivouac outside the city and generously gives the rest of his bottles to his comrades.

Meanwhile, for the third time since entering Russia, Prince Eugène's troops – Italians, Dalmatians, Frenchmen, Spaniards and Croats – have been donning their parade uniforms. To enter Moscow, Europe's second largest and far and away most exotic capital, and march triumphantly down its streets with their bands playing is going to be a *journée* – a great imperial occasion. And IV Corps, headed by the Royal Guard, quits Chorosewo and sets off for the still distant city. At the head of the Royal Guard marches the Guardia d'Onore – a unit made up of 'sons of the best Italian families, each supported by his family with a Line lieutenant's pay'. Its adjutant-major, as Moscow step by step comes closer, sees that it's indeed an open city. Only an old earthwork, broken down in many places, surrounds it. But here, thinks *Césare de Laugier*, is an odd thing. And a very worrying one:

'Nowhere do we see a soldier, either Russian or French. At each step our anxiety grows, and rises to a climax when we make out in the distance a dense column of smoke rising from the centre of town.'

18

Almost more worrying – not a wisp is to be seen rising from any chimney.

Now the head of the column reaches the Zwenigorod barrier. But instead of passing through it, they're ordered to turn left and follow the city limits. Cross another approach road. And reach the Petersburg barrier. This time the Viceroy, followed by the Royal Guard, turns his horse's head to the right and rides between its two stone pillars topped with globes.

Not so IV Corps' other three divisions. To their intense chagrin they have to

'turn their backs on Moscow and go and camp in the plain outside. The 15th Division around the imperial château of Petrovskoï. The 13th at Auksecewskoï. And the 14th at Butyrki, with Ornano's [Bavarian] light cavalry deployed in front of them.'

As they ride in along the Petersburg suburbs' broad well-aligned streets, Eugène's glittering staff find its first houses tawdry and ill-built. But by and by, interspersed with these 'dreary wooden shacks which looked as wretched as the unfortunate people who'd lived in them', come 'others more beautiful ... superb and vast palaces'. Amazingly, not one of them seems to be occupied. And every shop is shut. Obviously the rumour is true. Moscow has been abandoned by its inhabitants!

Never has such a thing happened before.

Nor is there any sign of any other troops, whether Russian, French or allied. Césare de Laugier scribbles in his diary (in the present tense):

'Without uttering a word we're marching down the long solitary streets. The drums are resounding in dull echoes against the walls of the deserted houses. In vain we try to make our faces evince a serenity which is far from our hearts. Something altogether extraordinary, it seems to us, is about to happen. Moscow seems to us to be a huge corpse. It's the kingdom of silence, a fairy town, whose buildings and houses have been built by enchantment for us alone.'

The 'corpse' reminds him ('though here the impression is even more sepulchral) of the ruins of Pompeii and Herculaneum'. For his part Captain *Eugène Labaume*, on the Viceroy's staff, is struck by the extreme length of the streets,

'so long from end to end that the cavalry troopers can't even recognise each other. We saw them advancing slowly towards each other, not knowing whether they were friend or foe, though all were under the same flags.'

At last the order comes to halt. And the Royal Guard draws up in battle – that's to say parade – order on 'a beautiful spacious promenade'. This northern part of the city, they're told, with its 'magnificent and extraordinarily sumptuous timber houses', has been designated for IV Corps' cantonments. The Emperor has already entered Moscow. Unfortunately 'fires have been breaking out on all hands'. For lack of any civil authorities to issue billets,

> 'we're to lodge ourselves military fashion. The Viceroy gives the regiments the order, and the officers who're to implement it indicate the lodgings in charcoal, in capital letters, on each dwelling's front door. Likewise the new name of each street and square, each being known as "such or such company's street", or "such or such a battalion's quarter", "Fall-in Square, Parade Square, Review Square, the Guard's Square, etc."'

At first, in so vast an emptiness, everyone's expecting a trap. But then, insensibly,

> 'we take possession of Moscow as if it had been built expressly for us alone. This singular distribution allows each subaltern, for instance, to have a magnificent palace to himself, through whose sumptuously furnished apartments, no proprietor having put in an appearance to dispute its ownership with him, he strolls at his ease.'

Only in the superb Greek orthodox churches, where the altars are lit up by candles 'as on some religious feast day', are there any Muscovites. But even there the worshippers are mostly of the poorest kind, Russian wounded and stragglers.

No deputation having come out to implore his clemency and surrender the keys of the city, Napoleon has spent the night of 14/15 September in what the Master of the Horse, *Armand de Caulaincourt*, calls 'a mean tavern built of wood' standing to the right of the stone bridge that links the city with its western suburb, but which to baron *Joseph de Bausset*, the obese Prefect of the Palace, seems 'a fine timber house'. The night had passed quietly enough. True, a fire, attributed to the troops' carelessness, had broken out in the Stock Exchange – 'a superb building, larger than the Palais Royal in Paris and packed with exotic goods from all over Asia'; and only with great difficulty been put out – for lack of fire engines. More important, it seems, is that according to the King of Naples' reports from his headquarters in the Balashoff[2] family's palace in Yauza Street, not far from the Bridge of the Marshals and the Kazan Gate, the truce guaranteeing Moscow's peaceful evacuation is still holding. The Kazan Gate lies on the far eastern side of the city and beyond it his 10 to 15,000-strong advance guard is bivouacked. Murat says he's 'confidently expecting to seize part of the enemy convoys and break up the enemy rearguard, so completely disheartened does he believe the Russians to be.'

All these details, Caulaincourt goes on,

'together with the impression sure to be caused in Petersburg by the news of the occupation of Russia's second capital, which must certainly lead to peace proposals, delighted the Emperor and restored his cheerfulness.'

Likewise, albeit perhaps in lesser degree, his own. It's only a week since his brother Augustin was killed at Borodino at the head of the decisive – and unique – cavalry charge that had stormed the Great Redoubt. During the night Caulaincourt has had to interview a Russian policeman who, brought to headquarters, had

'prophesied there'd be many more fires still to come. The entire city was to be burnt down during the night. A simpleton who knew all that was afoot, he'd been very candid in all his avowals. But he was in such a state of terror he seemed a bit deranged. These details were incredible, and we paid no heed to them. We were far from thinking the governor and government had any ambition, as the Emperor said, to go down to posterity as a modern Erostratos.'[3]

At 6 a.m. Napoleon, mounting *Emir*, his favourite Arab grey, has made his triumphal entry, 'unembarrassed by any such tumult as normally goes with taking possession of a great city.' 'No sound', First Secretary Baron *C-F. Méneval* notices from his carriage as it slowly follows in his master's wake, 'disturbed the solitude of the town's streets. Moscow seemed to have fallen into a deep sleep, like the enchanted towns in *The Arabian Nights*.' Probably that intelligent man is as dismayed as Caulaincourt, riding a horse's length behind the conqueror who has already made triumphal entries into all the important capitals of Europe except London, by the 'gloomy silence reigning throughout the deserted city. During the whole of our long route we didn't meet a single soul.'

By and by 'on a hill in the middle of town' a large citadel comes into sight. Surrounded by a crenellated wall and flanked at intervals by towers armed with cannon, the Kremlin reminds Méneval's colleague, Second Secretary Baron *A-J-F. Fain*, of the Doge's Palace in Venice. Its three successive massive gates are 'made up of several vaults closed by barriers and topped by machicolations'. Entering its courtyards. Napoleon goes up the Strelitz Steps (where once Peter the Great massacred his rebellious guards) to the second storey and the great halls of state.

Antique in their splendour, the sparsely furnished State Apartments consist only of three halls and a bedchamber. No Tsar has lived here since the 16th century. But they'll suffice, at least for the time being, for Napoleon's personal headquarters; whether in tent or palace it never consists of more than three rooms.[4] In the Tsar's state bedroom the only other piece of furniture besides the bed, which stands to the left of the fireplace, screened off by an elaborate green tripartite fire screen, is a roll-top desk. And it's presumably at this that Napoleon by and by sits down and – in his own hardly legible handwriting – writes to his blonde young empress Marie-Louise in faraway Paris:[5]

"Mon amie. – I have got your letter of the 31st, in which I read that you had received the letters from Smolensk. I've already written to you from Moscow, which I reached on the 14th. The city is as large as Paris, there are 1,600 steeples and more than a thousand fine palaces. This city is provided with everything. The nobility have left, the tradespeople have been compelled to leave too, the common people have stayed behind. My health is good, my cold has left me. The enemy is retreating, as far as can be judged towards Kazan. This fine conquest is the fruit of the battle of the Moscova [Borodino]. Tout à toi. NAP"

Meanwhile, down in the Kremlin's cellars, that fiery-tempered and – even by Grand Army standards – intensely ambitious staff officer, premier officier d'ordonnance *Gaspard Gourgaud,*[6] tall, brown-haired, thin and muscular and, on so triumphant an occasion, clad no doubt in full sky-blue uniform with silver aiguillettes, is making a startling, not to say alarming discovery. Some powder barrels. Although he'd been lightly wounded at Smolensk on 15 August, he'd been on his feet day and night throughout the campaign, and only yesterday was one of the first officers into Moscow. 'It was I who found the magazines, where there were three hundred kilograms of gunpowder.' An exploit for which he'll shortly be made a baron of the Empire. Other officers of the household are making other sinister discoveries. Hidden in the chimney of the imperial bedroom and elsewhere they're finding 'incendiary fuzes'. Made up of tow, bitumen and sulphur, all are constructed on exactly the same pattern. This causes Caulaincourt and his colleagues to take the 'half-crazed' policeman's nocturnal babblings more seriously. Fetched from the guardhouse, he repeats his story, which is immediately and frighteningly linked up with the disappearance, also allegedly at the orders of the temperamental Governor Rostopchin and his chief of police, Iwachkin,[7] of all the Stock Exchange's fire hoses:

'Search had been made for fire-engines since the previous day, but some of them had been taken away and the rest put out of action. Officers and soldiers were bringing in street constables and peasants who'd been taken in the act of flinging inflammable material into houses to burn them down. The Poles reported they'd already caught some incendiaries and shot them.'

Secretary Méneval, on the other hand, has been exploring the rest of the Kremlin:

'A second city in itself, it encloses the imperial palace, the Arsenal, the palace of the Senate, the archives, the principal public establishments, a great number of churches full of historical curiosities, objects used for the coronation of sovereigns and, finally, flags and trophies taken from the Turks. In one of the principal temples are the tombs of the Tsars. In this imposing basilica reigns a semi-barbarous magnificence, impressive and primitive. Its walls are faced with thick gold and silver plaques on which the principal figures of sacred history stand out in relief. Byzantine-style silver lamps hang from the vaultings and great many-branched candlesticks of similar materials stand on pedestals. In this sanctuary can still be seen a portrait of the Virgin attributed to St Luke. Its frame is enriched with pearls and precious stones. A great bell tower, known as the Ivan Tower, is surmounted by a gigantic cross, in the centre of which is encased a solid gold cross enclosing a fragment of the True Cross. This cross, together with several curious objects from the Kremlin capable of being transported, were to be sent to Paris.'

All this the army is finding very strange, very exotic, very oriental. No other European army has ever been so far east except the Poles a hundred years ago. And indeed very few travellers either.

Apart from its formidable artillery only the Imperial Guard, though it hasn't fired a shot since the campaign opened, is being allowed inside the city – it and the Italian Royal Guard. It's the invariable custom. All I, III, IV and V Corps' Line regiments, which have borne the burden and heat of so many a terrible day, have been ordered to bivouac in the vast 10,000-acre plain, largely covered with immense fields of cabbages and beetroot which 'round as bowls and fiery red throughout' are astonishing Ney's Württembergers, notably Private *Jakob Walter* of General Hugel's 25th Division. As for the cabbages, 'three or four times as big as cabbage heads we'd consider large', they rejoice the hearts of the men of the 57th Line. Evidently they're expecting their stay in Moscow to be a long one, for Sous-lieutenant *Aubin Dutheillet* sees them immediately get busy – at Napoleon's express orders – at making *sauerkraut*, which takes weeks to mature!

A strict order of the day has forbidden anyone to enter the city. But it doesn't apply, of course, to corps commanders or their staffs. One such officer, sent in to secure suitable lodgings for his superiors, is I Corps' paymaster, Captain *B. T. Duverger*. Entering by the Doroghomilov Gate, outside which Napoleon had yesterday vainly waited for his non-emergent delegation, Duverger, with such a plethora of empty palaces at his disposal, is in no hurry to choose; and makes for the Kremlin. Guard Grenadiers and Chasseurs are on duty at its gates, but no one hinders him – or anyone else – from going in. Mounting one of its towers, he looks out over 'the noble city in its whole extent. Far and wide there reigned only a lugubrious calm, broken only by the whinnying of horses and the tramp of troops down the streets.'

Coming down again, Duverger sees how many of the dregs of the populace are venturing out from their hiding places and are already drunk. Near the half-burnt Stock Exchange they're

'beginning to loot shops, and I joined with some soldiers of the Guard to expel them. From time to time an isolated shot rang out, but more as a result of surprise than animosity.'

Although all the magnificent and luxurious palaces have been deserted, in some of them their fabulously wealthy owners have left servants and a French-speaking superintendent behind with orders to make the intruders feel at home. 'On a very large square to the right of and not very far from the town gate, in the great loop in the Moscova between the Kremlin and the entrance by the Mojaisk road,' Major *J-F. Boulart* of the Guard Foot Artillery settles for the Petrovskoï family's great town house, and finds it's an exception. It 'lacked any occupant to do us the honours. Everything was silent around us. This silence had something terrifying about it.' As for his guns, his gun-park and his bearskinned gunners – whose dark blue turnout the Emperor himself on 5 June had found so 'handsome' – Boulart disposes them in the square and in the empty houses round about:

'On one side was a long straight promenade, planted with trees. On the other a nunnery. I formed my park in square, the guns in battery at the corners, the men and horses in the middle. I forbade the men to absent themselves. Then, having dismounted, I sent my lieutenants with a few gunners to the nearby streets to get some food. Everywhere they found the doors closed and barricaded. So we had to force them. In a trice everything was being pillaged, as it doubtless also was throughout the city. Afraid of being taken by surprise, I ordered everyone to come back at the sound of a musket shot.'

Everywhere 'in various private and public buildings' the invaders are alarmed to find fire fuzes identical to the ones found in the Kremlin. General Laborde and a medical officer by name Jeanneau, for instance, have just installed themselves in the Lubiana, Governor Rostopchin's own palace, when to their horror they find some such fuzes in a stove pipe; and hurry off to the Kremlin to tell de Bausset about it.

At 9.30 a.m. Napoleon is just leaving the fortress on foot, when two incendiaries are brought in. Both are wearing police uniforms and have been caught torch in hand. Through interpreter Hyde d'Ideville they tell him 'how houses had been designated for this end, and how in the various quarters everything had been prepared for burning, so they'd heard, in accordance with Governor Rostopchin's orders. The police officers had scattered their men in small detachments and the order to implement their instructions, given yesterday evening, had been confirmed that same morning by one of their officers.'

Officer? Which officer? They're reluctant to name him; but in the end he turns out to be a humble police NCO. Where's he now? They've no idea:

'Their replies were translated to the Emperor in the presence of his entourage. The Emperor was deeply troubled. He couldn't persuade himself that the Russians would deliberately burn their houses down to prevent our sleeping in them, as he'd said at Viazma. He couldn't believe it was the result of a firm resolution and a great voluntary sacrifice. But the successive reports left no further doubt. Some of the arrested policemen were brought to judgement and eight or ten were executed.'

All over town it's the same frightening story. Already, Césare de Laugier goes on, confiding to his diary,

'it's fairly certain the fires aren't to be ascribed to accidental causes. Quite a few incendiaries have been taken red-handed, arrested, and brought before a military commission. It transpires from their admissions that these people have only been acting on orders received from Rostopchin and Iwachkin, the chief of police. Most of them are policemen, disguised Cossacks, employees, pupils at the theological school. Their statements have been collected, and memoranda have been drawn up to be publicized all over Europe. It's been decided to make an example of them by exposing their corpses hung from lampposts in the squares or from trees in the promenades, not exactly a spectacle conducive to giving us back our gaiety.'

Food is everywhere the prime consideration. After spending a chilly night beyond the Kazan Gate, the units of Murat's advance guard, too, are sending marauding parties back into town to find some, both for themselves and their half-starved nags. Meanwhile, in the plain beyond the city, the marauders' comrades are involved in amiable discussions with their Russian opposite numbers, 'both Cossacks and regulars'; how humiliated they're feeling after their endless retreat at the behest of Russian generals they never even see! How much they'd prefer to serve the Emperor of the French and King 'Mourad' of Naples, both of whom – in striking contrast – are always so near the scene of action! Strolling about in his fancy uniform of the day,[8] Murat, vainest of men and cynosure of every eye, is finding in such gratifying talk some small compensation for being in Russia at all, instead of with his adored family in faraway Naples. The golden September morning turns into afternoon; and afternoon into evening. His men are happy to hear the armistice has been extended to 8 a.m. tomorrow. A couple of fires in the distance are ascribed, as usual, to the troops' negligence.

But then something extraordinary happens.

Darkness has fallen and it's getting on for 9 p.m. when Colonel *T-J-F. Séruzier*, whose horse artillery has led the advance all the way from the Niemen, sees

'a signal, like a firework. It went up from a château between Moscow and ourselves, to the right of the town, seen from where we were. And immediately we heard a loud detonation.'

Everyone else notices it too. M. l'Abbé *Surugué*, curé of the French parish of St-Louis-des-Français, is startled to see 'a ball of fire explode over the Yauza' (the tributary of the Moscova which flows into it in the eastern part of the city). And the Württemberger cavalry surgeon *Heinrich von Roos* is standing in his bivouac to the right of the Vladimir-Kazan road, not far from Russian rearguards' campfires which are 'burning admirably', and 2nd Cavalry Corps' gunners and cuirassiers are congratulating one another on the prospect of an imminent peace, when he and his comrades, too, both see and hear the

'terrible explosion.[9] Though hard to be sure of one's sense of direction at night, it seemed to come from the centre of town. So great was its violence, we first thought an ammunition dump or powder factory had blown up, i.e., if it wasn't an infernal machine. At first there was an enormous jet of flames from which balls of fire were coming out in a greater or lesser trajectory as if a mass of bombs and shells had been simultaneously thrown up. This explosion lasted about three or four minutes, and spread veritable stupefaction among ourselves.'

'The generals had just left us,' the Dutch general *Dedem van der Gelder*, commanding the 2nd infantry brigade in Dufour's division which all the way from Vilna has had the misery of being seconded from Davout's to Murat's command, writes,

'when a violent detonation was heard on the side of the Kaluga Gate. It was a powder magazine the enemy were blowing up. It seems to have been an agreed signal, for a moment afterwards I saw several rockets going up, and half an hour later fire broke out in various quarters of the town, notably in the Vladimir suburb where General Dufour and I had taken a house.'

Everyone, Dedem says, saw the explosion. It's Rostopchin's signal:

'It lasted three or four minutes, and put us all in a veritable stupor. As soon as I was sure they wanted to burn down the town for us I immediately decided to join the division, which was bivouacked astride the Vladimir road, underneath the town walls. I set up my headquarters in a mill where I was sure of not being burnt. The wind was very strong and it was very cold. One would have had to be blind not to see it was the signal for a war to the death. Everything confirmed what I'd heard in January at Rostock and Wismar about the Russians' intending to set fire to everything and draw us into the depths of Russia.'

At first, Heinrich von Roos goes on,

'the fire seemed restricted to the area where it had occurred; but after a few minutes we saw flames rising in various quarters of the town. Soon we could count 18 hearths of the fire, then more. We were all stricken dumb with amazement.'

Jerked out of their 'unusual gaiety', his Württemberger troopers are

'all stricken dumb with amazement. We looked at each other, all with the same thought. Staff captain de Reinhardt gave voice to the general feeling: "Here's a bad sign! One that puts an end to our hope of peace, the peace we all need so!" Our camp dominated the town, and we watched this terrible scene without anything of it escaping us. Soon the flames reached the quarters closest to ourselves. The numbers of stragglers and refugees, too, had increased.'

In the extreme west of the city, still bivouacked in the square near the Moscova bridge, Boulart's gunners are looking on from another angle. They see

'a fire, then a second one, then a third, closer and closer, a new one. Though these diverse fires, whose propagation nothing arrested, were in the part of the town furthest away from us, it was easy to read by their light.'

And in the Kremlin itself *Roustam Raza*, Napoleon's Armenian Mameluke servant, asleep with drawn scimitar across the doorway to his bedroom, wakes up to find the whole skyline on fire. Staff captain Labaume is watching from the northern district: 'By now the whole city was only an immense bonfire.'

Until this moment the wind has been blowing from the north-west. But now it too seems to be obeying Rostopchin's order. Césare de Laugier, also in the northern district, feels it 'suddenly veer to the south-west and reach hurricane strength'. So that by 10 p.m. the Italians, too, realise the entire city is going up in flames; and Paymaster Duverger and his comrades at I Corps headquarters in the western district, abruptly awakened in their 'rather fine house by some lamentable cries', dress hurriedly and run out into the street:

'"Fire! Fire!", sinister voices were shouting. The horizon was red. The fire, moving in all directions, sounded like distant torrents. Inhab-

itants and soldiers were mingling in headlong flight. In the light of
the conflagration we read stupefaction and despair in their faces.'
Immediately opposite the Kremlin is the Kitai Gorod, or Chinese quarter.
Many of its exotic commodities, saved from last night's conflagration in the
Stock Exchange, had been laid out in the street and placed under guard.
But now the district's six or seven thousand little shops catch fire again.
Naturally the locals want to grab what they can, and the pickets have to
beat them off with blows of their musket butts. Caulaincourt, deeply asleep
in the Kremlin, is aroused by his valet,

'an energetic fellow who'd been in my service during my Petersburg
embassy.[10] He brought the news that for three-quarters of an hour
now the city had been in flames. I'd only to open my eyes to see it was
true. The fire was spreading with such ferocity that it was light enough
to read in the middle of my room. Jumping out of bed I send him to
awaken the Grand Marshal [Duroc], while I dress.'

From the Kremlin terraces it's possible to survey the whole city and its surroundings. And since the fire chiefly seems to be spreading in the districts
farthest away, Duroc and Caulaincourt, as the imperial household's two
most senior officers, decide

'to let the Emperor sleep a little longer, as he'd been so very tired
during the past few days,'

– largely no doubt because of the acute bladder trouble he's been suffering from ever since Borodino. Nevertheless they send word to Marshal
Mortier – commander of the Young Guard and military governor of
Moscow since General Durosnel has found the task of policing it too much
for him – suggesting he call the whole Imperial Guard to arms. Caulaincourt is himself responsible for all headquarters transport. Since his own
department is already scattered in various parts of the town, he mounts his
horse and rides out to see what's to be done:

'A stiff wind was blowing from the direction of the two points of conflagration visible to us, and it was driving the flames towards the centre. This made the blaze extraordinarily powerful. At about 12.30 a.m.
a third fire broke out, a little to the west; and shortly afterwards a
fourth, in another quarter. All lay in the direction of the wind, which
had veered slightly to the west,'

and is being aided and abetted by any number of incendiaries. At about
midnight Césare de Laugier sees

'incendiary bombs being thrown from the church towers, from the
tops of houses at every moment, and even in the streets. Anyone
caught red-handed is being shot out of hand. Many of these unfortunates are drunk and pass without transition from drunkenness to
death. We've even found several trying to pour out tar to revive the

fire at spots where it seemed to be dying out. Running like convicts, they were carrying incendiary materials hidden under their clothes and throwing them, almost under our very eyes, into the houses we've been occupying.'

By now the extent of the catastrophe is so obvious that Caulaincourt and Duroc can no longer take it upon themselves to let Napoleon sleep. According to Roustam's assistant 'Ali', Napoleon's 'second Mameluke', it's Constant who wakes Napoleon up to tell him Moscow is in flames; but comes out again, 'and since he didn't give us any orders each of us went back to bed'. Looking out of the window, Napoleon had exclaimed:
 '"This exceeds anything one could imagine! This is a war of extermination! Such terrible tactics are without precedent in the history of civilization. To burn down one's own cities! A demon inspires these people! What savage determination! What a people! what a people!"'

Up to now, according to Césare de Laugier, always concerned to defend the honour of the Italian Royal Guard, its rank and file have mainly been
 'carrying out their superiors' orders in the general interest, trying to master the fire and save pieces of cloth, jewellery, cottons, fine materials and Europe's and Asia's most precious items of merchandise.'
But now at the incendiaries' heels
 'come the dregs of the populace who haven't fled, hoping to loot what they can. Locks are being forced, cellar doors bashed in, shops threatened by the fire are being sacked. Sugar, coffee, tea are the first things people are laying hands on; then it's the turn of leather, furs, cloths and all luxury merchandise.'
Whereupon the Italians,
 'excited by the example of this populace pillaging under their eyes, are letting themselves be carried away and putting everything to the sack. First and foremost the stores of flour, brandy and wine are ravaged.'
And indeed why stay outside and starve when food to feed ten armies is being incinerated? One of Major Boulart's subordinates, the always critical, always querulous, Major *Pion des Loches*, a man who always knows best and is cleverer and more farsighted than anyone else, an incurable *Besserwisser*, sees masses of soldiers from the army corps bivouacked outside town on the plain, defying the ban on entering the city, come rushing in – no sentries can stop them. And in no time at all
 'the army was completely disbanded. Everywhere one saw drunken officers and soldiers loaded with booty and provisions taken from flaming houses. The streets were littered with pieces of faïence, with

furniture, with all kinds of clothing. The many women who'd been following the army, meaning to make us pay dearly for the fruits of their pillage during the retreat, were incredibly prompt to supply themselves.'

Everywhere are harrowing scenes, dreadful incidents. On his way to cross the river by a ford, Paymaster Duverger sees one such brawny harridan at work. Ousted from their burning palace, he and a friend are lingering in

'a main street where some poor women and children with hardly any clothes on were coming running from all directions, and already the fire was threatening to cut off their retreat on all sides. An old sutler-ess had placed herself athwart the road. I knew her. That very moment I saw her repulsing with her fist a grenadier who'd tried to stop her from coming into the town. There she stood, her savage green eye on the hurrying fugitives, stopping and searching them.'

So far he's paid no particular heed to her. But now, beside him, he sees another group,

'an old man, two or three children, a girl, beautiful despite her pal-lor, and a woman. Two working men were carrying her on a stretch-er. All were weeping so it broke your heart. The old cantinière flung herself at the sick woman, with a sacrilegious hand searching her clothes to see if they concealed anything of value. That day I was on the verge of fury – heaven forgive me for having struck a woman.'

Pion des Loches, too, sees the army's *vivandières* and *cantinières*

'laden with firkins of liqueurs, sugar, coffee and rich furs. The fire was raging in all quarters of the town and as it reached them the sol-diers were evacuating the places where they'd taken shelter and in turn seeking asylum in the next house.'

Fortunately there are men who act chivalrously. Griois is on his way back to his camp outside the city when he sees running towards him

'a young woman, her hair dishevelled, terror on her face. A nurse-maid was following her, carrying a child. She told me she was the wife of a French businessman whom the Russian army had taken away with it and she'd remained behind, alone with her child and this Russian servant.'

Now her house is on fire and she has nowhere to go. Forgetting to ask her name (can it be Marie-Louise Chalmé, she who'll soon be finding herself in Napoleon's presence?) Griois takes up all three refugees into his car-riage and out to Eugène's headquarters near Petrovskoï.

A man for whom his daily dinner is always of prime importance, the 85th Line's portly 2nd major *C. F. M. Le Roy*, is usually a great stickler for effi-ciency and discipline and always ready to set an example. But now even he, orders or no orders, isn't going to see a whole city roasted alive without res-

cuing some titbits for his ambulatory larder. Accompanied by his bosom
friend Lieutenant Jacquet, 'the only man I ever wholly admitted to my confidence', he goes into town. Advancing down a fine street they find
    'the flames so strong that their force was lifting the metal roofing of
    copper plates which covered most of the houses. Soon they fell back
    with a crash and, thrust sideways by the wind, were as dangerous to
    passers-by as the fire itself.'
For 5 francs the two officers relieve a ranker – he's anyway hugging many
more bottles than he can carry – of a bottle of Bordeaux. After which, out
of sheer curiosity, they enter a palace. Amazingly, all its apartments are
unlocked, all the mahogany furnishings unscathed:
    'The mirrors and pictures ornamenting it, the view out over a superb
    garden, would have made it an enchanting place to linger. I open a
    drawer. Inside are some sticks of sealing-wax, some playing cards, sev-
    eral embroidery patterns, a pretty toiletry set and many other things.
    In the next drawer are a pair of diamond buckles, a necklace of fine
    pearls, two rolls of turbans and two boxes. I'm just about to open
    them when I hear a man come into the room. I assume it's Jacquet,
    who'd stayed outside in the courtyard to try and get us some brandy
    or rum he was thinking he might find in the cellar. I call out to him
    to help me take something from the house. I open a bigger box. It
    contains a game of lotto with ivory markers. In the second I find the
    markers of a game of draughts. I'm just about to open a tallboy when
    I hear Jacquet's voice calling to me to come to his aid. Instantly I draw
    my sword, and rushing out into the corridor, which I find full of
    smoke, I make haste to rejoin my comrade who – the general confla-
    gration being so distant – is as amazed as I am to find the house is on
    fire. From which I conclude that the person who'd come in could
    only have been a Russian incendiary. While we were still expressing
    our astonishment at such a singular fact, a well-dressed man came
    past us, greeting us politely. We returned his salute.'
Roving about the burning streets together with some fellow-Poles trying to
find a way out of the holocaust or, alternatively, something to eat, is Count
Roman Soltyk, an artillery officer who, because he speaks fluent French, has
been attached to IHQ's Topographical Department. He tries calling up, in
Russian, to the shuttered windows of houses where people are begging for
protection:
    'This succeeded several times. But our Polish uniform had already
    revealed us as enemies, and when we asked them what was causing
    the fire they only replied laconically, or else evasively. The principal
    of a college for young ladies who were still in their house pretend-
    ed she knew no French – though to teach her aristocratic charges

this, the second language of the rich, must have been one of her duties.'

And when Soltyk complains that he can't find any food,
'a twelve-year-old girl who'd been looking out of the window and following the conversation turned round quickly and said vehemently: "Food for the French! The putty of these windows is good enough to nourish them!" Though I turned it into a joke I admit I was much impressed. One could hardly hope to get a population to submit when children of twelve were so excited.'

The only Muscovites who seem to be beyond and above their city's trauma are some 'priests who, without distinction of rank or nation, were distributing alms and wine to all who passed in front of their holy retreat'. The scorching air is giving Soltyk and his fellow-Poles a monstrous thirst. 'One of them, as soon as he saw us approaching, offered me a cupful of wine,' which is gratefully accepted. The priests 'were making no distinction between rank or nation.

'Neutral in this great conflict, they were deploring the waywardness of men and had no other aim than to do what they could to assuage their evils.'

Napoleon's favourite ADC General *Jean Rapp*, a veteran who even in middle age walks 'with the jaunty gait of a hussar officer' but has been seriously wounded at Borodino, has already been awakened by his staff at midnight. But now the fire is beginning to eat into the district between the Kremlin and the Doroghomilov Gate; and at 4 a.m. they too are forced out of their palace. 'A few moments later it was turned to ashes.' After making their way to Marshal Mortier's house in the German quarter only for it too to go up in flames a few moments later, Rapp has to climb painfully back into his carriage and make for the Kremlin. Thanks to a shift in the wind it's still unthreatened. Only on his way there does he realize what's happening:

'Russian soldiers and craftsmen were slipping into houses and setting fire to them. Our patrols killed several of them in my presence and arrested an even greater number.'

En route, Rapp's party falls in with the Artillery Staff and its head, General Lariboisière 'and his son, who was sick' (since Lariboisière's elder son Ferdinand had died of his wound after Borodino, this can only be Henri); presumably therefore also with Henri's friend and fellow-ADC, Lariboisière's indefatigable 'man of letters', Lieutenant *Planat de la Faye*.[11] Together they all go and quarter themselves in a house on the river bank:

'My host was an honest hat maker who was sorry for my predicament and gave me all possible care and attention. Hardly was I installed in this kindly craftsman's house, however, than fire broke out in all the quarters around it. So I left in a hurry. If I'd delayed the least bit I could never have got away with my carriage, the street along the river bank being so narrow. We recrossed the river and stopped under the bare sky behind the walls of the Kremlin.'

But all the time the rising gale is bringing the fire ever closer. And finally Rapp's and Lariboisière's party, after again having to move on, settle in the neighbourhood of one of the customs gates, where houses are thinner on the ground and therefore less likely to catch fire. 'I occupied one belonging to a Prince Galitzin.'

Now it's the small hours of this unimaginably terrible night; and Soltyk and his fellow-Poles of IHQ's Topographical Department have finally lain down to rest outside a deserted church, also on the outskirts. By this time

'all the partial fires which were devouring Moscow in the night seemed to have joined together to form only one. The whole horizon was on fire. The church doors were open. As day broke, one of the orderlies chanced to go inside. A moment later he came back, pale, hardly able to get a word out. "Commandant", he said to me, "the church is filled with powder barrels and the windows are smashed." – "To horse, messieurs!" I shouted. "Our heads are lying on a powder magazine ..."

Five times the always amorously inclined General Kirgener, commander of the Engineers of the Imperial Guard, has had to change his lodgings before he and his staff finally ensconce themselves near the Petersburg gate in 'a kind of fortified château surrounded by water'. And there, fire or no fire,[12]

'hard though it is to understand in such circumstances, our dear general had leisure to engage in a love affair. A young slip of a girl found in our fortress was the cause of his little conflagration.'

Like Pion des Loches who, seeing the fire all the time coming closer to his artillery park is doing his best to keep his men from straying too far from it, many an anxious veteran has been asking himself:

'What if a few Russian cavalry regiments should come riding into Moscow tonight? They can easily cut us in pieces. For at the first glow of the flames the troops encamped outside the walls, instead of covering us, were leaving their units to take their part in the pillage.'

If the Russian high command has given no such orders it's because neither Kutusov nor anyone else except Rostopchin's police chief has had any inkling of that erratic personage's – wholly unauthorized – scheme: to evacuate the city and then burn it to the ground. Seeing the city burn from afar, all Russian eyewitnesses are ascribing – and will long afterwards continue to ascribe – the inconceivable catastrophe to the 'atheistic' Frenchmen's negligence, or wickedness. Many decades will pass before it's clearly established that it's all been the work of 'the modern Erostratos'.[13]

CHAPTER 2

NAPOLEON LEAVES THE KREMLIN

His dysuria passes over – 'This exceeds anything one could imagine' – 'the Emperor went to the spot' – Boulart goes to get orders – Napoleon quits the Kremlin – Petrovs-koï palace – Sergeant Bourgogne's and Césare de Laugier's adventures amidst the flames – Murat's advance guard marches east

Moscow's in flames. But Napoleon's dysuria has gone over. At dawn, i.e., at about 7 a.m., he sends for his physician, Dr Mestivier: 'I'd just woken up. Showing me an almost full flask of urine, he told me he thought he was almost clear of the business, he'd urinated so abundantly and freely. But he showed some uneasiness about the sediment, which filled a third of the vessel. I replied that it was the result of a crisis which would quickly help him recover his health.' To be in the imperial presence is to be bombarded by questions.

'His bed was so placed that he couldn't see anything of the city. Whereupon he put his usual question:

"Anything new being said?"

I replied that a vast circle of fire was enveloping the Kremlin.

"Ah, bah!" Napoleon replied. "No doubt it's the result of some of the men's imprudence who've wanted to bake bread or bivouacked too close to timber houses."

Then, fixing his eyes on the ceiling, he remained silent for a few minutes. His features, which up to then had been so benevolent, assumed a terrifying expression. Summoning his valets [sic] Constant and Roustam, he suddenly jumped out of bed. Shaved himself. And quickly, without saying a word, had himself dressed, making movements expressive of his bad temper. The mameluke having by mistake presented him with the left boot instead of the right, Napoleon sent him flying backwards with his foot. As he hadn't made the head movement he usually dismissed me with, I remained there for almost an hour. Some other people came in, and Napoleon went into another room.'

Caulaincourt is certainly also in attendance at the levee. Looking out of the window he sees how the wind is

'fanning the flames to a terrifying extent, carrying enormous sparks so far that they were falling like a fiery deluge hundreds of yards away, setting fire to houses, so that even the most intrepid couldn't stay there. The air was so hot, and the pinewood sparks so numerous, that all the trusses supporting the iron plates forming the roof were catching fire.'

The Arsenal, a fine modern building whose courtyard, Griois will see, is 'ornamented with military trophies, guns and howitzers of colossal dimensions, most taken from the Turks in ancient wars', abuts the Tsars' ancient palace. Already it's being found to contain 18,000 British, Austrian and Russian muskets, 100 cannon with limbers, caissons and harness, as well as 'lances and sabres innumerable' and an immense amount of ammunition useful to the French. And prompt steps are of course taken to prevent the blaze from spreading:

'The roof of its kitchen was only saved by men who'd been stationed there with brooms and buckets to gather up the glowing fragments and moisten the trusses.'

Worse, even more perilous, down in the Kremlin's courtyards dozens of the Imperial Guard's artillery wagons, filled with highly explosive ammunition, are crammed together. And as the forenoon wears on and the fire in the city comes ever closer, the situation is swiftly becoming lethal. Watching from the Kremlin windows, Napoleon breaks out into exasperated ejaculations:

"What a monstrous sight! All those palaces! Extraordinary resolution! What men!"

By noon, despite everyone's efforts, the fire has begun to attack the Kremlin stables, containing 'some of the Emperor's horses and the Tsar's coronation coaches. Coachmen and grooms clambered on the roof and knocked off the fallen cinders.' Of the Kremlin's fire engines only two, put in working order during the night at Caulaincourt's behest, are intact. Everywhere the heat is swiftly becoming unbearable. Secretary Fain sees how the Kremlin windows are cracking as the flames attack the tower that links the palace with the Arsenal:

'Sparks were even falling in the Arsenal courtyard onto a heap of tow used in the Russian artillery wagons. The wagons of our own artillery were also standing there. The danger was immense, and the Emperor was informed. He went to the spot.'

Méneval is alarmed to see such sparks, borne on the high wind,

'setting alight bits of oakum lying on the ground. Not that this danger, which we were so fortunate as to baulk, worried Napoleon, whose soul never even knew what it was to be afraid.[1] As yet he didn't think it necessary to leave the Kremlin. On the contrary, the danger seemed to be keeping him there.'

Now the Master of the Horse, too, is himself in the thick of it:

'I may say without exaggeration we were working under a vault of fire. Everyone was doing his best, but it was impossible to stay more than a moment in any one spot. We were breathing nothing but smoke, and after a while even the strongest lungs felt the strain.'

Even the bridge over the river has become

36

'so hot from the sparks falling on it that it kept bursting into flames. But the men of the Guard and especially the Sappers made it a point of honour to preserve it. The fur on these half-roasted men's bearskins was singed.'

Guillaume Peyrusse is a young paymaster attached to IHQ who has an eye on and is forever scheming to occupy an as yet non-existent post as paymaster to the Emperor on his travels. He sees

'one of our outriders grab a Russian soldier at the moment when he was going to set fire to the bridge, break his jaw and throw him into the river.'

Yet still Napoleon persists in lingering in the Kremlin courtyards, among all those deadly ammunition wagons; and Fain is horrified to see how

'the Guard's gunners and infantrymen, apprehensive at seeing Napoleon expose himself to so great a danger, are only adding to it by their eagerness.'

In the end Lariboisière, whose responsibility all these caissons are, begs him to go away, 'pointing out that his presence is making his gunners lose their heads'. Aided by servants they're also helping Caulaincourt save Prince Galitzin's superb palace, occupied by Rapp and Lariboisière; likewise two other adjoining houses already in flames.

To Major Boulart, the danger to *his* ammunition wagons, parked in the square not far from the Doroghomilov Gate, seems to be becoming from moment to moment ever more imminent:

'While waiting for daybreak, I'd had all hay and straw cleared away from the neighbourhood of my wagons and had posted gunners to see the flaming sparks didn't fall on them, though with the wagons as firmly closed down as ours were and covered in canvas there'd been little to fear.'

But now the vast conflagration is taking gigantic strides toward him. Time's running out. And no one has sent him any orders. Realizing that he must do something before it's too late, he makes up his mind to go in person to the Kremlin, seek out General Curial, his immediate superior, and get his permission to quit 'this hell'. Some time after noon he gives his orders. 'In the event of the fire reaching the only street we could retreat by, they should leave the town in my absence.' Then he mounts his horse. And accompanied by an orderly sets off, hoping to find his way to the Kremlin. Soon, 'with a loud and sinister sound', palaces and iron roofs are crashing down all around them. The gale whistles in their ears. Holding their arms over their eyes, half-deafened by all this rumbling and roaring, they ride slowly onwards through the hot ash and debris falling on their heads. They've no guide, and the distance seems endless:

'Isolated in this desert, my heart shrinks. But soon I get to the region actually being devoured. To right and left flames are rising above my head. I'm being swathed in dense smoke. Further on, the heat is so great and the flames are coming at me so closely, I have to shut my eyes. Can hardly see my way ahead. Often my horse shudders and refuses to go on.'

But then, suddenly, the two men emerge out of this 'fiery zone' into quite another. Almost calm, it consists only of smouldering ashes. Surely they must have gone astray? No. There, rising in front of them, are the Kremlin's crenellated walls! Now it's about 3 p. m. Entering by the great vaulted gate, Boulart finds everyone

'dejected, in a remarkable state of consternation. Fear and anxiety stood painted on all faces. Without a word said everyone seemed to understand everyone else.'

Up in the state apartments he finds Prince Eugène, Marshals Bessières and Lefèbvre (commanding the Guard cavalry and infantry respectively) – Méneval says Mortier too – all vainly imploring Napoleon to leave. But since he seems to be 'afflicted by uncertainty' no one can do anything:

'However, the fire's intensity was growing as it came closer. The windows of the apartment occupied by the Emperor had caught alight and flames were whirling in all directions.'

Also present, certainly, is Berthier, Prince of Neuchâtel, most senior of all the marshals, Napoleon's chief-of-staff, the army's major-general. Now, if ever, he has reason to bite his fingernails to the quick! An orderly officer (Césare de Laugier will afterwards hear that it was Gourgaud)

'having come to tell him the fortress is surrounded by flames on all sides, is ordered to go up with the Prince of Neuchâtel to one of its highest terraces to confirm the fact.'

But so parched and unbreathable is the air up there, they're at once driven down again. And still Napoleon won't budge.

Now it's about 4 p.m. And Caulaincourt sees the Emperor is beginning to wonder whether the burning of the city isn't in some way co-ordinated with the Russians' military operations, 'though frequent reports from the King of Naples had assured His Majesty that they were pushing forward their retreat along the Kazan road'. Gourgaud, too, overhears Berthier point out that "if the enemy attacks the corps outside Moscow, Your Majesty has no means of communicating with them". Only this observation, Méneval sees, makes him decide to leave.

A couple of miles north of the city, not far from where the Army of Italy has its encampment on the plain by the Petersburg road, stands the Petrovskoï summer palace. A large 'Gothick' building, erected toward the end of the last century to celebrate Catherine the Great's victories over the Turks, it's a kind of imperial *pied-à-terre* for the Tsars to stay in on the eve of their coronations. Now one of Gourgaud's subordinates, Major Mortemart, is told to go and reconnoitre the safest way to get there. But he too, unable to get through the flames, soon comes back:

'It was impossible to get there by the direct road. To reach the outskirts we'd have to cross the western part of town as best we could, through ruins, cinders, flames even.'

So at last a decision is arrived at. IHQ will accompany His Majesty along the river bank. Only the 2nd Battalion of the 1st Foot Chasseurs of the Guard is to stay behind in the Kremlin and try to stave off the fire. Inspector of reviews, *P-P. Denniée*, describes the imperial departure:

'He came slowly down the stairs of the Ivan Tower [from where he'd been watching the fire] followed by the Prince of Neuchâtel and other of his officers. Leaning on the arm of the Duke of Vicenza [Caulaincourt], he crossed a little wooden bridge which led to the Moscova Quay. And there found his horses.'[2]

At the stone bridge over the river Napoleon mounts *Tauris*, another of his Arab greys, and, followed by his entourage – Gourgaud of course among them (amidst all this heat, grime and ash his sky-blue uniform can hardly any longer be in the best of trims) – sets off,

'a Moscow policeman walking in front of him, serving as guide. For some time they followed the river and entered the districts where the wooden buildings had been completely destroyed.'

Thereafter 'avoiding streets where the fire was still at its height' the procession passes through 'quarters where the houses were already entirely burnt down. We were walking on hot ash.' Quartermaster-General *Anatole Montesquiou* and his colleagues are obliged 'to protect cheeks, hands and eyes with handkerchiefs and headgear and turn up the collars of our uniforms.' Méneval, Fain and the other secretaries ride slowly onwards in the headquarters carriages. Likewise the treasurers, Peyrusse among them:

'We had all the trouble in the world to get clear. The streets were encumbered with debris, with burning beams and trusses. In our carriages we were being grilled alive. The horses couldn't get on. I was extremely worried on account of the treasure,'

twelve strongly guarded wagons filled with perhaps some twenty millions in gold and silver coin.

But Major Boulart, braving the direct route, has got back to his regiment. He's just getting his guns and ammunition wagons under way and 'the head of my column was just about to recross the Moscova when the Emperor, his march retarded by my long column, appeared with his staff and went on ahead of me'.

A most dangerous moment, says General Count *Philippe de Ségur,* the Assistant Prefect of the Palace and responsible for its pack mules. Some men of I Corps, he says, have guided IHQ out of narrow burning streets; and Marshal Davout

'wounded at Borodino, was having himself brought back into the flames to get Napoleon out of their clutches or else perish with him. Transported with joy he threw himself into his arms; the Emperor received him well but with that calm which never abandoned him in peril.'

Did the Iron Marshal really do that? It's hard to imagine Davout transported with joy in any circumstances. (Nor had be been 'wounded', only badly bruised when his horse had fallen on top of him.) Ségur's dramatic prose must always be taken with a largish pinch of salt. On the other hand he's on the spot, and Davout is certainly devoted to Napoleon's interests. What is true is that 'to escape from this vast region of evils, Napoleon still had to overtake a long powder convoy which was passing through it' – i.e., Boulart's. A single unheeded firebrand or flaming roof-shingle settling on one of his powder wagons and quickly burning a hole, first through its the canvas cover then the lid, is enough to blow the entire Imperial and General Staffs – and indeed the whole Napoleonic régime – sky-high. The sober-minded Boulart confesses to having felt 'gentle satisfaction' at his Emperor's providential escape.

After which the whole procession, Guard artillery and all, winds its way in drenching rain – now it's falling in bucketsful – round the north-western suburbs.

At the Petersburg Gate the ever-prescient Pion des Loches, who since 6 a.m. has had his Guard battery limbered up and ready to leave the city, finds the officer in charge of the picket half-seas under:

'Unable to go a-pillaging, he was levying a tax on all soldiers coming out with booty. He thought he was doing himself an honour in showing me his guardhouse filled with bottles of wine and baskets of eggs. All his men were dead drunk and he himself couldn't stand up.'

If the Kremlin has impressed everyone by its oriental splendours, the Petrovskoï summer palace seems merely odd. To Colonel Griois, who yesterday had had an opportunity to look at it before going on his shopping spree, its

'very antique construction, surrounded by high brick walls and its heavy and severe overall appearance made it seem more like a state prison than a sovereign's palace'.

Reminding Roman Soltyk of Hampton Court, to Captain Count *V. E. B. Castellane,* another of Napoleon's orderlies, its style seems 'Greek, truly romantic'. Just now it's surrounded by an ocean of mud, through which camp stools and beds have to be fetched from Eugène's headquarters nearby. For if the Kremlin's furniture had been sparse, here there is none at all! Even tables have to be improvised. Nor does the Petrovskoï summer palace have any outbuildings; so in no time the entire Imperial and General Headquarters staffs[3] and the Administration, altogether some 700 persons, are trying to squeeze inside out of the rain. The entire artillery staff – Lariboisière, his son Henri, his 'man of letters' and his six 'ill-educated' staff captains who run Planat's errands – all have to cram themselves inside one small downstairs room. At its window Planat reads

'two letters to Lariboisière by the light of the distant fire. We were only some six miles from Moscow, and from there we saw the whole town perfectly. From this vantage point we could assess, better than hitherto, the full extent of the conflagration. The fire seemed to be burning everywhere. The town was no more than a single blaze.'

Is it as fascinating as Smolensk? Somewhere out on the plain with the baggage train a certain dragoon captain Henri Beyle, alias the future great novelist *Stendhal*, thinks not, but is wittily finding it

'the most beautiful fire in the world. Forming an immense pyramid, like the prayers of the faithful it had its base on the ground and its summit in heaven.'

Abbé Surugué, like everyone else, is noticing how the flames' undulations 'whipped up by the wind, are exactly emulating the waves raised by a storm at sea'. After supper Montesquiou and his colleagues at Petrovskoï can't resist going to take another look 'at this fiery spectacle that was doing us so much harm, and to which we nevertheless kept returning'.

But Caulaincourt, who's been on his feet for 21 hours, is too exhausted for any reflections, whether humorous or aesthetic. Just scribbles in his notebook: 'Arrived at 7.30 p.m. To bed.'

Some ten or fifteen miles away to the south-west General Colbert's crack Lancer Brigade, made up of the famous 1st (Polish) and 2nd (Dutch) Lancers of the Imperial Guard, is advancing eastwards. Two thousand men strong, its horses are heavily laden with saddle furniture, including such extras as scythes to cut standing crops and axes to fell trees. The brigade, without news or orders for a week now, has been scouring the countryside in the direction of Borowsk but has found no signs of an enemy. Captain *François Dumonceau's* 6th troop of the Red Lancers' 2nd squadron has probed particularly far afield; but seen 'only a few rare Cossacks'. Now he's on his way back to brigade headquarters, apprehensive that he'll be reprimanded – not for the first time – by his disciplinarian chief for being away too long. Instead he's surprised to be congratulated.

A somewhat cold-blooded young man, the Belgian captain has a keen eye for facts, events and details which he promptly notes down in his diary. Always it's been his ambition to see the Aurora Borealis. And that evening, seeing an immense glow in the sky as the column advances along the Moscow road, he takes it for granted that his ambition is being fulfilled. But his Polish colleague, Captain *Josef Zalusky* of the 1st Guard Lancers, places quite a different interpretation on this glow in the night sky; assumes 'the two armies to be in presence again, preparing for another major battle in front of Moscow. We felt bitterly frustrated at not taking part in it.'

That night the brigade reaches the Sparrow Hill, from which the cheering army had first seen the city, two days ago:

'We found it surrounded, occupied and guarded by our comrades the Horse Chasseurs of the Guard. Together with some other officers I galloped over to our friends, asked them at once: "And Moscow?" "There isn't any Moscow any more." "What d'you mean?" "It's burnt down – look!"'

Poles and Dutchmen gaze out through the darkness over an immense smoking mass:

'Only a little fragment, such as the Kremlin, dominating the town from its height, had been saved. Imagine our terror, from the military, political and personal points of view! We were exhausted by marching all the way from Kovno. Our clothes were in rags, we'd no clean linen, and we were counting on the capital's resources! The Chasseurs interrupted our reflections by offering us Don wine, fizzy like champagne. We drank to the Emperor's health, to the expedition's happy outcome, and, somewhat consoled, resumed our march. We were making for the Kaluga road, to pass the night there. Having immediately supplied ourselves with various things we'd so long desired, above all Turkish tobacco, we spent our first night oblivious of torments. *Jucunda sollicitae oblivia vitae.*' – Happily oblivious of life's cares.

Marshal *Louis-Nicolas Davout*, Prince d'Eckmühl, an even stricter disciplinarian than Colbert, is disliked and feared by almost everybody. Though only some 15–18,000 of his brilliantly disciplined I Corps, originally 69,500 strong, are still under his command, it's not – as is the case with Murat's cavalry – for any lack of care for them on Davout's part. Now he has set up his headquarters in a convent near the Doroghomilov Gate.

There, 26 Muscovites, arrested as incendiaries, have been brought in. Though most of their identities turn out to be fictitious, it's obvious they're men of many civil occupations – farriers, stonemasons, house painters, policemen, a sexton ... and only one, a lieutenant of the Moscow Regiment, is a military man. The first session of the court-martial, presided over by the commanding officer of the 1st Guard Grenadiers, is rather thorough. Though it orders ten of these unfortunates to be shot, the guilt of the sixteen others is found 'insufficiently proven'. And they're sent to prison. But elsewhere many others aren't even being given the benefit of any doubt. Fezensac takes an obviously innocent civilian under his protection but has to hand him over to another officer, to whom he 'recommends' him. The other, mistaking it for a sinister innuendo, has him shot. No wonder Lieutenant *von Kalckreuth*, riding across Moscow with the 2nd Prussian Hussars – a regiment reduced by its long marches from four squadrons to only two – finds

'in the streets many dead Russians, to a great extent old people who, caught red-handed setting fire [to buildings] had been shot on the spot.'

Moscow has two great military hospitals, one of which Napoleon will afterwards declare on St Helena to have been the finest and most commodious he'd ever seen. Both have immediately been occupied by Surgeon-General Baron *Dominique Larrey*'s medical service. Nobly devoted as always to his humanitarian task – overwhelming because Napoleon has repeatedly refused 'the noblest man he has ever met' adequate means for carrying it out – Larrey, together with 'a very small number of my comrades', has remained behind in the burning city in 'a stone house, isolated on the summit of a free-standing quarter near the Kremlin, whence I could observe at my ease all the phenomena of the terrible conflagration'. He and his assistants are doing what they can for their wretched patients, and Larrey himself, as usual, is carrying out many of the amputations and other operations. But as the fire approaches, some 1,000 of them, allied, French and Russian, fall into a panic. Jump out of upstairs windows. And for lack of any means of transport, lie on the pavements with shattered bones and re-opened bleeding wounds, beyond all medical help, and being roasted alive.

But virtually all the other generals have fled. And it's their fault, Labaume thinks, that the pillage is rapidly growing worse. Their absence has unleashed the Furies:[4]

'No retreat was safe enough, no place holy enough, to preserve the Muscovites from the soldiers' greed. They, the vivandières, the convicts and prostitutes, running about the streets, broke into the abandoned palaces and seized from them everything that appealed to their cupidity. Some covered themselves in gold and silver cloths. Others, without the least discrimination, put the most highly esteemed furs on their shoulders. Many covered themselves in women's and children's fur capes and even the galley-slaves hid their rags under fine coats. The rest, going in a mob to the cellars, forced in the doors, grabbed the most precious wines, and staggered off carrying away their immense booty.'

Griois, venturing back to buy some more wine and provisions, witnesses a scene that would be comic if it weren't so horrible. Amid the burning buildings he sees some soldiers emerging from a ladder that leads down to a cellar, where there's a terrible

'dispute, or rather fight, going on among looters who're cutting each others' throats in the dark! Soon emerges from the stairway a dragoon, pale, covered in blood and wine. He took a few steps and, hardly out into the street, fell, expired amidst the bottles he was clutching and only let go of as he died. In the scrimmage he'd had a sabre run through his body.'

At that moment Griois recognizes the army's Quartermaster-General, Count Mathieu Dumas, one of the Emperor's closest collaborators:

'He draws his sword, strikes out to right and left, reaches the stairway and seizing by its hair the first head to present itself he recognizes ... his own cook, who was coming up again laden with bottles, half-drunk, his white waistcoat spattered with wine and blood. It would be hard to imagine anything more comical than the general's astonishment, anger and vexation at seeing his servant emerge among the soldiers' burst of laughter. He gave him not blows of his sword, but kicks, and went away in despair at seeing that the disorder couldn't be mastered and that everyone was mingling in it.'

As they make for the Kazan Gate, Kalckreuth's Prussian hussars are 'often having to trot so as not to be hurt by the debris of collapsing houses or the heat, and braving all dangers and entering blazing houses' to get some food or wine. Kalckreuth and his servant and his friend Lieutenant Manteuffel dismount and can hardly get in through the mob of French soldiers of all arms:

'The first cellar had already been emptied of the wine it had contained, and in the second, several chasseurs were handing bottles to each other. It was impossible to get down there.'

Though other soldiers are shouting loud warnings that the house is about to collapse,

'no one heeded their advice. Fortunately, I mingled with the chasseurs and in this way got a few bottles they handed to me and which they thought they were giving to their comrades. Afraid lest the floor of the first cellar, where we were, was going to collapse under the weight of the mob and that then no one would escape, we contented ourselves with our sparse booty and, not without difficulty, got out of it.'

The gatehouse of the courtyard is already in flames. Only their horses' fleetness can save them. Leaving through the Kazan Gate, Kalckreuth and his comrades rejoin their unit about two miles beyond Moscow.

Even the Kremlin is being pillaged. Rummaging about in its vaults under the church of St Michael and busy rifling the tombs of dead Tsars, some Guard grenadiers are disappointed to find nothing more valuable than the coffins' silver name-plaques. Their only booty is a beautiful young girl who's fled there from her wedding day. Only yesterday she was to have married a Russian officer. Now the grenadiers take her, quivering with terror and praying to the souls of long-dead Tsars to protect her, to their general, 'who immediately forms designs on her virtue'.

Now it's the morning of 16 September. Though the rain's still pouring down, the whole city's one vast blazing pandemonium. Larrey is horrified to see the common people being chased

'howling from house to house. Determined to save their most precious belongings, they'd loaded themselves with bundles they could hardly carry and which one often saw them abandoning to escape the flames. Women with children on their shoulders and dragging others by the hand, were running with their skirts tucked up to take refuge in the corners of streets and squares. Old men, their long beards caught by the flames, were being dragged along on little carts by their children.'

From the 4th Line regiment's camp, about three miles west of the city, its newly appointed Colonel *Montesquiou-Fezensac* – an aristocrat who until Borodino was one of Berthier's ADCs – making a vain attempt to go to the Kremlin, is 'keenly afflicted by this spectacle' and determined to do all he can 'to distract my regiment's gaze from miseries I couldn't alleviate.'

When at about midday yesterday (15 September) the fire had first begun to pose a serious threat to the Kremlin, *François Bourgogne*, a sergeant in the Fusiliers-Grenadiers of the Middle Guard, had been sitting with a comrade with their 'backs against the enormous guns which guard each side of the Arsenal', breakfasting with some friends in the 1st Foot Chasseurs.

'These, I ought to say, had some silver bullion, ingots the size and shape of a brick, taken from the Mint. They were promising to do business with a rabbi whose synagogue had burnt down, and with whom they were amusing themselves by forcing him to partake of a succulent ham.'

Suddenly there'd come a shout 'To Arms!'. Loading a package containing 'three bottles of wine, five of liqueurs and some preserved fruits' on to the poor rabbi, Bourgogne and his friend had immediately gone back into the town to try and find their own regiment and 'staggered through the streets with no worse mishap than getting our feet scorched'. Again and again they'd lost their way. When they'd left the regiment it had been in the main square. But where has it gone? Reaching the Jewish quarter, their beast of burden utters a cry of despair and faints:

'We hastened to disburden him and, opening a bottle of liqueur, we made him swallow a few drops, and then poured a little over his face. By and by he opened his eyes. When we asked him why he'd fainted, he told us his house had been burnt down and that probably his family had perished. With these words he swooned again.'

And there they'd left him. But then one of their own party too had collapsed and had to be left to his fate. Another being half-blinded by flying sparks, they decide to turn back:

'The idea struck us of each taking a piece of iron sheeting to cover our heads, holding it to windward. After bending the iron into the shape of shields we set out, one man leading, then myself, leading the half-blinded man by the hand, the others following.'

There follow endless peregrinations through the burning streets:

'It's 11 p.m. when we at last reach the place we'd left the previous evening. Since I'd had no rest since arriving in Moscow I lay down on some beautiful furs our men had taken, and slept till 7 o'clock next morning.'

While Bourgogne and his comrades had been wandering about in the inferno, a vélite battalion of the Italian Royal Guard had also been called to arms with orders to hunt down incendiaries. Ordering his battalion to fall in, its adjutant-major is horrified at the chaos all round him,

'where the only law is the law of the strongest – soldiers wandering aimlessly about, covered in sweat, smoke-blackened, laden with loot – Russian wounded dragging themselves along as they try to flee from the fire – raving inhabitants, groaning, screaming, yelling, not knowing where to find a refuge.'

All round are only burning and collapsing buildings through which Césare de Laugier and his white-and-green uniformed grenadiers have the greatest difficulty in making their way:

'After innumerable detours we find the road ahead is barred by flames. But we push on. Crossing the ruins of a burning palace at the double, we emerge on the other side into another alleyway, where we again find ourselves blocked by a sea of fire.'

"Go on, go on!" shout the men who're bringing up the rear. "No, no!" cry those at its head, at all costs they must turn back! The one course is as impossible as the other. Stunned by the noise of the madly whirling flames in the roaring hurricane which seems to be blowing from all quarters at once, their situation is becoming untenable:

46

'Blinded by sparks, by burning cinders, by fiery embers, suffocated by this rarified burning air, streaming with sweat, we don't even dare look about us because the wind's blowing a fiery dust into our eyes, forcing us to close them. We're overcome by impatience, almost by madness. Our cartridge pouches, filled with cartridges, our loaded muskets, only increase our peril.'

Another building comes tumbling down just as they emerge from it, injuring several grenadiers. Whereupon the whole battalion panics:

'The earth's burning, the sky's on fire, we're drowning in a sea of flame. Our uniforms are scorched and smoke- blackened, we're having to extinguish the falling cinders with our bare hands. At last the battalion gets moving again. The sappers, by great efforts, cut us a passage leading into a little square where, jammed tightly together, we momentarily recover our breath and our courage.'

They've long ago lost all sense of direction. But what's this? Breaking into the courtyard of a burning palace, they see 'a carriage with its back to the opposite wall' and, inside it, 'a Russian drummer, asleep amidst his loot and dead drunk. Rudely awakened, terrified, he tries to run off.' Though they don't know a word of Russian they try to get him to realise they're only trying to find a way out; and 'he, realizing his fate is tied up with ours, understands. Escorted by sappers and under the adjutant-major's vigilant eye' – Laugier, like Caesar, here writes of himself in the third person – 'he leads the battalion through a little wooden cabin and out into a

'narrow tortuous alley, most of it already in ashes. Under falling tiles, the ground burning the soles of our shoes, the drummers beat the charge with one hand while clinging to each others' jackets with the other, not to lose touch.'

Again the sappers use their axes, this time to demolish a little wall. And lo and behold, after five hours of this 'fiery hell', the vélites of the Guardia d'Onore suddenly find they're

'in a vast field, on the banks of the Moscova! With what joy we gulp in lungfuls of fresh pure air! By now it's 2 a.m. The weather is rainy.'

But where are all those beautiful palaces they'd occupied only yesterday? They've vanished. Instead, ordered out to Petrovskoï, they bivouac there under lashing rain. 'A novel spectacle,' the adjutant-major confides to his diary,

'to see a victorious army encamped around a city in flames, having lost at a single blow the fruits of its triumph and the resources which could have restored its physical strength.'

Neither that day nor the next does the fire abate, or the rain give over. Nor does the looting abate. While his battery had still been parked in the as yet unburned western district it had seemed to Major Boulart there'd been 'a continual procession of our soldiers,' above all from I Corps, 'carrying wine, sugar, tea, furniture, furs, etc., to their camp, and no one opposing it'. But now he reflects that it's just as well something is being saved from the flames, 'and most of what was saved was profitable'. Césare de Laugier:

'Wednesday morning: There's no shop in the town centre which isn't the prey of the flames except a book shop, and another, also in Lupra-va-Blayontence. Resin, brandy, vitriol, the most precious merchandise, all are on fire at once. Torrents of flames, escaping from this immense brazier, are crowned by thick clouds of smoke. The boldest still risk their lives by going into this furnace, then come out again all burnt, but laden with jewels and riches. Seeing this, others try to follow their example; but, less fortunate, don't re-appear.'

Bivouacked out there in the mud near Petrovskoï where they're 'established in English-style gardens and lodged under grottoes, Chinese pavilions, kiosks or greenhouses around the châteaux where their generals were', even staff officers can find no shelter.

'Our horses are tied up under acacias or linden trees, separated from each other by borders and flower beds. A truly picturesque camp, enhanced by the men's novel costumes! Most, to shelter from the weather's insults, had donned garments of the same kind as those we'd just seen in Moscow. Soldiers dressed like Tartars, like Cossacks, like Chinese, were walking about our camp. Here was one wearing a Polish toque; others tall Persian, Bashkir or Kalmuck bonnets. Another, wearing women's clothes, is standing beside one who's dressed up like a pope. And all the while hands, expert or novice, are practising on pianos, flutes, violins, guitars, from which they mostly extort discordant noises. In a word, our army presented the appearance of a carnival.'

Albrecht von Muraldt is a 21-year-old lieutenant in the 4th Bavarian Chevaulegers who, ever since leaving Vilna, where they'd been detached from St-Cyr's VI Corps in July, have been part of the Army of Italy. After Borodino he's been recommended for the cross of the Legion of Honour. To him IV Corps' camp looks like

'a market place. A lot of carriages had been driven out to behind our lines. Somehow or other every officer had got hold of one. Carpets, covers, satin cushions, porcelain dinner services lay scattered everywhere, either offered for sale or used for barter. The ground was so littered with empty or broken bottles one could hardly stand to arms without endangering oneself or one's horse.'

As for the Italians' campfires, they're

'veritable bonfires of paintings and luxurious furniture. All around, officers and men, filthy and blackened by the smoke, are seated on elegant chairs or silken settees. Spread out on the ground here and there in the mud are cashmere shawls, precious Siberian furs, Persian cloth of gold. Over there men are eating around cooking pots off silver plates and cups. What an uproarious carnival!'

Out at the Kazan Gate Sous-lieutenant *Pierre Auvray*'s 23rd Dragoons are sending '40 men to go and pillage the town' while waiting for orders. Auvray himself confesses to have taken 'from an individual a casket of gold, table silver and jewellery, whose value I didn't know'. Also, more excusably, some linen and cloth to clothe himself with. Not many yards away another lieutenant, *Heinrich von Brandt* of the Vistula Legion, sees

'in our bivouac alone a considerable amount of silver, enamelled goldsmith's work, table linen, precious cloths and furs being brought for the men to lie down on. Thereto a mass of such chattels as chairs, torches, etc., which the pillagers were forcing Russians to carry for them. Famine was being followed by excess. All our huts were stuffed with victuals and every kind of liquid, meats fresh and salted, smoked fish, wine, rum, brandy, etc. Around all the campfires people were cooking, eating and, above all, drinking to excess. Each new arrival of pillaged objects was greeted with joyous vivats!'

He's thinking that all this unrestricted looting by both officers and men is 'the logical consequence of the first order to lodge troops in the town military fashion and of the disappearance of the authorities who could have regulated it. It had begun with shops that sold food, wines and spirits, and with lightning swiftness had spread to private dwellings, public buildings and churches.'

The whole flaming city is being rummaged and turned inside out:

'Such unfortunate inhabitants as had remained behind were being ill-treated, shops and cellars forced open. The city rabble, taking advantage of this disorder, shared in the pillage and led the troops to cellars and vaults and anywhere else they thought might have been used to conceal property in the hope of sharing in the pillage.'

By now even Fezensac has been obliged to let the men of his 4th Line Regiment go into town and take whatever they like. For is this really pillage? Gourgaud, at least, doesn't think so. In these extraordinary circumstances to call it 'looting is an abuse of language and an unspeakable harshness'. And one day in a future neither of them can conceive he'll take Ségur physically to task for calling it by that ugly name.

Only Murat's 25,000-strong advance guard, slowly following the 'defeated' and 'demoralized' Russian rearguard eastwards through the steadily falling rain, is having to leave this feast of plunder further and further behind it. Five miles beyond the city, on 15 September, chasseur lieutenant *Maurice*

Tascher – a nephew of the ex-Empress Josephine and like his two brothers who are also in the army a cousin, therefore, of Prince Eugène – has bivouacked 'about five miles beyond the city' amidst 'a dangerous abundance. In Moscow, fire and pillage,' he writes in his lapidary but useful diary.

Made up of some 12,000 infantry and 8,000 cavalry, not all mounted, Murat's force is a small army in itself. Besides the dwindled remains of Nansouty's 1st and Sébastiani's 2nd 'Reserve' Cavalry Corps, it also includes what had been Friant's, but since that general's wounding at Borodino is now Dufour's 1st infantry division, made up mainly of Frenchmen but with a sprinkling of recalcitrant Spaniards. Also the two battle-hardened Polish foot regiments of Claparède's Vistula Legion. In liaison, out on its right wing, is Prince Poniatowski's – also much-reduced – Polish V Corps.

Marching stolidly along the Kazan road, Sébastiani's light cavalry is 'driving before it' the usual swarms of Cossacks who, once again, are up to all the wearisome tricks they'd played on it all the long way from Vilna to Moscow: pretending to mount attacks, then, when the light cavalry has formed up in battle order, vanishing into the woods where they either let their pursuers exhaust their horses or else fall into an ambush. But who is driving whom? Next day (16 September), Sébastiani's leading (2nd) light cavalry division is

'driving them before him for twelve miles through beautiful, well-aligned villages which they're no longer burning',

when it falls into just such a well-planned artillery ambush. Even Murat's life, Tascher sees, is momentarily in danger. And he also catches a glimpse of someone else whose imminent death will also play a certain part in the campaign: General Platov, the Cossacks' supreme hetman's son.

A more feckless, if gallant, light cavalry general than Sébastiani could hardly have been chosen to lead the advance guard. Already, since leaving Vilna, he has twice let himself be surprised – 'I don't know how it is,' his mother-in-law is wittily saying in the Paris salons, 'but my son-in-law goes from one surprise to another.' And in the army he has already earned himself the sobriquet 'General Surprise'. A Corsican relative of the Bonapartes and Napoleon's former ambassador in Constantinople who, among other things, had been the driving force behind the defeat of Admiral Duckworth's squadron in the Dardanelles, Sébastiani is a little man with a dull complexion but a pair of lively black eyes and long curly black hair, who according to Griois 'supplied the want of any education with an astounding self-assurance' – much the same assessment, that is, as Captain Zalusky of the 1st Polish Guard Lancers has already made of him.[5] Coupled with Murat's total insouciance when it comes to his troopers' well-being, or even their horses' survival on the march,[6] it's not surprising if Tascher and his comrades are often going to be in parlous straits.

Also on the march, of course, is Dedem van der Gelder. No one is more critical of Murat's handling of his troops than he; and ex-diplomat though he is,[7] he has been far from diplomatic on that point. Ever since Smolensk he's been suffering from a badly bruised chest – the effect of a spent musket ball that had hit him at Smolensk as he'd led his infantry into action against the city gate. But now, as the blazing city recedes into the distance, the pain's becoming so acute that Dedem finds he no longer can sit his horse. During the night of 16/17 September he feels he's had enough, at least for the time being. And gets Murat's permission – permission doubtless only too readily granted – to hand over his command of Dufour's 2nd infantry brigade and go back to Moscow:

'At a distance of more than six miles the light of the flames lit up the road. Coming nearer, all I saw was a sea of fire, and since the wind was very strong the flames were lashing about like a furious sea. I was happy to find my mill again [near the Vladimir gate], and all night I enjoyed from it this unique spectacle, horrible but majestic and imposing.'

Even if not quite so 'poetical', 'grandiose' or 'sublime' as the burning of Smolensk, Dedem fancies he has before him the spectacle of 'Samarkand taken by Tamerlane'.

CHAPTER 3

THE FAIR OF MOSCOW

The fire abates – Napoleon returns to the Kremlin – horses in churches – the Yellow Palace goes up in flames – rumours in the Kremlin – 'If Your Majesty still retains any of your former feelings for me' – 'famine was followed by excess' – food and furs – Coignet's bad stroke of business – growing shortage of necessities

Not until the third day does the fire begin to die away, for lack of fuel: 'At last, on 18 September, the fire having noticeably died down and the horizon beyond Moscow having cleared, the Emperor re-entered the town. At 9 a.m. he mounted *Moscow* and crossed the town. Our return was no less gloomy than our departure. I can't say how much I'd suffered since my brother's death. The horror of all that was going on around us added to my grief at his loss. Seeing all these recent events broke me down completely. Although one cannot exclusively be affected by one's own personal troubles in the midst of so many public disasters, one is none the less grieved by them. I was over-whelmed. Happy are they who never saw such a grim spectacle!' Reaching the Kremlin, Caulaincourt helps Napoleon change to *Warsaw*, another of his five Arab greys. And on it he rides

'about that part of the city to the right of the theatre. Came to the stone bridge. Went out through the Kolomna Gate. Followed the city moat. Passed in front of the two military hospitals, the Yellow Palace. Returned to the Kremlin at 4 p.m.'

Its antique, not to say uncomfortable, milieu is little to Napoleon's neo-classical taste. Even before the fire had forced him out to Petrovskoï he'd had the town searched for something more up to date, and the luxuriously furnished Yellow Palace of Sloboda, also built for Catherine the Great, had been pointed out. Now his 50-year-old but already white-haired ADC Count *Louis de Narbonne*¹ is ordered to go there with Berthier and see if it'll do. They find all the doors locked, have to climb in through a window. Méneval, who's also one of the party, finds the lamps still have candles in them. Otherwise 'this royal dwelling seemed to be deserted'. Narbonne reports back to Napoleon just as he's reviewing the Fusiliers-Grenadiers in one of the Kremlin courtyards. Whereupon their Sergeant Bourgogne is ordered

'to join a detachment of Fusiliers-Chasseurs and Grenadiers and a squadron of Polish Lancers, altogether 200 men, commanded by a general whom I took to be General Kellermann. We left at 8 p.m., and it was 9.30 before we came to a spacious building at the far side of Moscow. Built of timber and covered with stucco to resemble marble, it seemed to be much the same size as the Tuileries. Our object was to secure it against fire. Guards were immediately posted outside, and, to make assurance doubly sure, patrols were sent out. I was detailed off with several men to inspect the interior, to see if anyone was hidden there.'

Bourgogne searches through its apartments for incendiaries but doesn't find any. Considers himself

'fortunate in having a chance to see this immense building, furnished with all the splendour and brilliance of Europe and Asia. Everything seemed to have been lavished on its decoration.'

But though he and his men take every possible precaution against its being fired,

'a quarter of an hour afterwards it broke out behind us, in front of us, to right, to left, and we couldn't see who'd set it alight. There it was, in a dozen places at once, and flaring from every attic window! The general immediately called for sappers to try to cut it off, but it was impossible. We had no pumps, not even any water. Half an hour after the blaze had broken out, a furious wind had got up, and in less than ten minutes we were hemmed in by the fire, unable either to advance or retreat. Several of us were hurt by falling timbers.'

But they nab the incendiaries!

'Directly afterwards we saw several men, some with torches still burning, coming out from under the grand staircase by some subterranean passage and trying to slip away. We ran after them and stopped them. There were 21 of them, and eleven others were arrested on the other side. These weren't actually seen coming out of the palace, and nothing about them showed they were incendiaries. More than half, however, were obviously convicts. Within an hour the palace was entirely consumed. The utmost we could do was to save some pictures and a few other valuables.'

The blaze has also set fire to the whole surrounding district,

'built of wood and very beautiful. It was 2 a.m. before we could get out of this hell. We set out again for the Kremlin, taking with us our prisoners, 32 in number. I was put in command of the rearguard and of the prisoners' escort, with orders to bayonet any who tried to run away or refused to follow.'

Bourgogne tries to save the lives of an obviously innocent Swiss resident whose home and family have perished in the fire and of a tailor and his son – amidst all the soot and filth only washerwomen are in more acute demand than tailors!

But when Narbonne, next day, gets back 'to take possession of this palace, it had been utterly consumed'.

The Italian Royal Guard, too, has moved back into town. But what a difference in the Petersburg district!

'Only the stone palaces retained some traces of what they'd been. Isolated on this heap of charcoal and ashes, blackened by smoke, these debris of a new town looked like the relics of antiquity.'

Since the churches are built of stone or brick and stand somewhat apart from the dwellings, it's mostly they that have survived. Now they're being used to lodge both men and horses:

'The neighing of the horses and the soldiers' horrible blasphemies are replacing the sacred and harmonious hymns which used to resound under these sacred vaultings,'

the sententious Labaume records in his 'little notebook, no bigger than my hand' in which he's daily jotting down his impressions and experiences.

'All the churches except four or five were turned into stables. They have big iron doors and locks and the French felt safer there at nights. Their horses were covered in cloths made from priestly vestments. In Tchoudov Cathedral we found a dead horse. In another church they were melting down gold and silver and using the images of our saints for firewood. In the church of the Petrovka convent was the big public slaughterhouse.'[2]

What kind of effect such behaviour might be expected to have on pious Russians could have been learnt from experiences in Spain. But evidently hasn't been. Rather the contrary. Everyone is indignant at the Russians for having burnt down their sacred city. Even the usually calm and thoughtful Méneval is so furious at Rostopchin's 'infernal idea of removing the pumps' that he thinks the army should 'march on Petersburg and burn it down. What possible advantage could this monstrous sacrifice be to Russia?'

Naturally all sorts of rumours are going the rounds. At IHQ, back in the Kremlin, 'it's most positively believed', paymaster Peyrusse writes in one of his letters to his friend André in Paris,

'that it's all been a plan proposed by the English to attract us to Moscow and in the midst of the fire and the disorder of a town delivered over to pillage fall on the Emperor's headquarters and the garrison. The General Bacler Tolli [Barclay de Tolly], minister of war, had shared this opinion; but the Emperor Alexander, to whom one can do the justice of believing him a stranger to this terrible attentat, had taken the command of the corps covering Moscow from General Tolli. General Kutusov had disapproved of this ferocious act, and replied that it would be better to defend the town to the last extremity. But nothing stopped the governor. Pressed by the Grand Duke Constantine[3] and incited by some inconsiderable lords, it was he who ordered the town's ruin.'

All of which, if Peyrusse and his colleagues only knew it, is less than half true – Rostopchin's scheme had in fact been quite unknown to the Tsar, to Barclay or to Kutusov, none of whom would ever have acceded to it. IHQ has a few spies who are reporting on the confused brawling relationships at Kutusov's headquarters. One of them is a Captain La Fontaine. Born and brought up in Moscow, he is riding to and fro through the Russian lines, even, when necessary, requisitioning fresh horses in the Tsar's name. Schulmeister[4] isn't here, and wouldn't be any use if he were – Russian isn't one of the languages Napoleon's chief spy commands. One wonders how IHQ has even come by such a mixture of fact and fiction? Can it be thanks to a certain Marie-Louise Chalmé, thirty-year-old wife of the French manager of a large hotel? Herself owner of a milliner's shop on the fashionable Bridge of the Marshals, she'd lost everything except her children and the clothes she stood up in and taken refuge at Eugène's headquarters. Eugène had sent her in a hackney coach to the Petrovskoï summer palace where Mortier had received her and taken her to Napoleon, waiting in a window recess of a large, sumptuously decorated – but otherwise empty – hall. Their interview had lasted an hour, and had evidently touched on political topics, for Napoleon had asked her what she thought of the idea, already dismissed by him at Witebsk in August, of freeing the Russian peasants:

"One-third, Your Majesty," she'd replied, "would perhaps appreciate it. The other two-thirds would have no idea of what you were trying to do for them."

After which she'd been conducted back to IV Corps' headquarters.

Far from wishing to liberate the Russians peasants or anything of that sort,[5] Napoleon's most pressing concern, Caulaincourt sees, is to exculpate both the army and himself of 'the odium of having caused the fire it had in fact done its utmost to put out, and from which self-interest was enough to exonerate it'. And in the streets Pion des Loches reads an order of the day

'in which he accused the Russians of having burnt down their own capital. Any inhabitant who didn't go to register with one of the twelve military commandants was to be killed. For individuals caught torch in hand the punishment was the same. As a result, twelve Russians were hanged in the square where I'd originally stationed myself. Several generals, setting themselves up as judges, had others hanged at the doors of their houses.'

Drastic measures indeed; but not likely to convince the Tsar of the Grand Army's innocence, still less the panic-stricken but furious Petersburg populace. Something more diplomatic is needed. So Lelorgne d'Ideville, head of the Statistical Department, who has lived in Moscow and is acting as Napoleon's interpreter, is ordered 'to find some Russian to whom all the details of the affair could be confided and who'd repeat what he was told in the proper quarters'.

This, it seems, is easier said than done.

Virtually every Muscovite of any social standing has fled. Of the few who've lingered, one is the intrepid if somewhat obsequious governor of the Foundlings Hospital, one of the few large municipal buildings to have survived the fire. Ivan Akinfievitch Tutolmin is also a councillor of state. On the eve of the Grand Army's arrival he'd evacuated all his charges over the age of 15, but himself stayed behind with his 500 younger ones and sent a message to Napoleon, pointing out that his institution was under special protection of the Dowager Empress. Whereupon, at 9 p.m. on 14 September, a picket had been sent to guard it.

Introduced into Napoleon's study, he effusively – doubtless prompted by d'Ideville – expresses his gratitude to the man whom, so he says, he's teaching his charges to call 'their father'. More to the point, he requests permission to write to Petersburg and tell his patroness of her foundation's miraculous escape.

Protected by the etiquette which forbids anyone to speak first when addressing a sovereign, Napoleon, as usual, bombards his interlocutor with peremptory questions. How is Tutolmin's hospital organized? Administered? He wants to know every detail – but just then a new outbreak of the fire distracts, or seems to distract, his attention. Going over to the window, he bursts out into a lacerating indictment of Rostopchin:

"The scoundrel! Fancy daring to add this monstrous, man-made, cold-blooded fire to the calamities of war, which are already so vast! He fancies he's a Roman, but is nothing but a stupid savage!"

Then, interrupting his own peroration, he suggests that Tutolmin – why yes, of course he may write to the Dowager Empress – shall add a few lines. And himself dictates them on the spot:

"*Madame. The Emperor Napoleon groans to see your capital almost wholly destroyed by means which, he says, are not those used in regular warfare. He seems convinced that if no one comes between him and our august Emperor Alexander, their former friendship will soon reassert its rights and all our misfortunes cease.*"

One of Tutolmin's assistants is 'allowed' to take the letter under a flag of truce to the outposts. But will it reach the Tsar, its real addressee?

By next morning d'Ideville has unearthed another putative emissary. This one is received in the vast Throne Room, bisected by a great roof beam supported by two marble pillars and 'gilded and blackened with age', whose only use has been for state banquets.

Ivan Yakovlev, brother of the Tsar's minister to King Jérôme Bonaparte's court at Cassel, is a chronic, almost pathological procrastinator.[6] Although urged by his household to leave town when everyone else had been doing so, he – for quite other reasons than Tutolmin – had dallied too long. His palace burnt down, and with a three or four days' growth of beard, this aged courtier of Catherine the Great appears before the all-powerful Emperor of the French, portent and symbol of the new century, wigless, half in rags, in an old riding-coat, a grubby shirt and two odd and muddy shoes. Flying into one of his theatrical rages which everyone finds so terrifying,[7] Napoleon fulminates again at the 'vandal' Rostopchin:

"This war is fostering a relentlessness stemming neither from Alexander nor from myself. It's the British who're dealing Russia a blow she'll bleed from for a long time to come. Peter the Great himself would have called you barbarians!"

Suddenly he comes to the point. Why does Yakovlev want a passport? Aren't the city's markets being reopened by imperial order? Isn't everything being set to rights? And when Yakovlev replies diplomatically that Moscow just now isn't the most pleasant place for a gentleman and his family to be in, asks him whether in that case, if he's granted a passport, he'll deliver a letter to the Tsar?

But of course.

At 4 a.m. next day the elderly emissary, roused from the temporary lodgings Mortier has found for him, is taken to the Kremlin. This time he finds Napoleon snuff-box in hand, pacing his study in his dressing-gown, looking gloomy.[8] Picking up his letter off the table, he hands it to Yakovlev. Addressed "To my brother, the Emperor Alexander," it's very long; and reads:

"Having been informed that the brother of Your Imperial Majesty's Minister in Cassel was in Moscow, I have sent for him and talked to him for some time. I have charged him to go to Your Majesty and make my sentiments known to you. The beautiful and superb town of Moscow no longer exists. Rostopchin has had it burnt. Four hundred incendiaries have been arrested in the act. All declared they were lighting fires at the orders of the Governor and Chief of Police. They have been shot. The fire seems at last to have ceased. Three-quarters of the houses are burnt down, a quarter remains. This conduct is atrocious and senseless. Is it intended to deprive me of a few supplies? These were in the cellars which the fire could not reach."

And why, Napoleon's letter goes on

"destroy one of the world's most beautiful cities, the work of centuries, to achieve so feeble a purpose? This is the conduct that has been followed since Smolensk, reducing 600,000 families to beggary. The fire-engines of the town of Moscow had been wrecked or removed, and some of the arms in the arsenal handed over to malefactors, who obliged us to fire a few roundshot at the Kremlin to dislodge them. Humanity, Your Majesty's and this great town's interests required that

it be put into my hands on trust, since the Russian army had left it exposed. The administrations, magistrates and civil guards should have been left behind. That was what was done twice in Vienna, in Berlin, and in Madrid. That was how we ourselves acted at the time of Suvarov's incursion.[9] The fires are authorizing pillage, in which the soldier indulges, disputing the debris with the flames. If I supposed such things to have been done at Your Majesty's orders, I should not be writing this letter; but I find it inconceivable that you, with your principles, your good heart and your sense of justice, should have authorized such excesses, unworthy of a great sovereign and a great nation. While having the fire-engines removed from Moscow, Rostopchin abandoned 150 field-guns, 60,000 new muskets, 1,600,000 infantry cartridges, over 400,000 pounds of gunpowder, 300,000 of saltpetre, the same amount of sulphur, etc."

At last he comes to the point:

"I have waged war on Your Majesty, without animosity. A letter from you before or after the last battle would have halted my advance, and in return it would have pleased me to be in a position to sacrifice the advantage of entering Moscow. If Your Majesty still retains some remnant of your former feelings for me, you will take this letter in good part. In any case, you cannot be other than grateful for my having informed you about what is going on in Moscow. Napoleon."

But Yakovlev's mission, too, comes immediately unstuck. The Russian outposts to the north of the city send him sent straight to Winzingerode, a German general in the Russian service, commanding in that sector. As he comes in, Winzingerode is himself sealing a letter of his own to the Tsar. Reads Napoleon's. Is Yakovlev insane? He must be, he tells him, to have made so bold as to undertake such a mission! Sends him under arrest to the Russian Minister of Police.

How unpsychological can one be? As if only too well aware of the inherent absurdity of blending arrogance with humble pleading and that every line of his letter betrays the anxiety over Russian intransigence he's trying to hide, Napoleon only tells Berthier and Lelorgne d'Ideville, 'with whom he discussed it freely', about his letter.

No reply, of course, will ever be received – no more than to his two earlier letters to 'his brother Alexander' from Vilna and Smolensk.[10]

Only about four-fifths of the city is in ashes. Seeking new quarters for Prince Eugène, Labaume hears that 'according to the count of the Engineer-Geographers a tenth of the houses were still standing'. Some 5,000 of its original 30,000 dwellings are in fact found to be still habitable. Already the army corps' staffs and the Imperial and Royal Guards have been ordered to return; and now everyone is installing himself according to rank and dignity. Pion des Loches, for instance, is settling back into Prince Bargatinski's palace and all the time, in view of small fires which keep breaking out here and there, taking great pains to preserve it,

'because of the provisions it contained. Its cellar alone was worth great sacrifices. I was on foot day and night for a week. As the fire had approached, my gunners had pulled down all the palings in the neighbourhood, so effectively that their dwelling – and mine – was among the very few houses of the quarter that had been spared. I'd seen twenty others in its neighbourhood go up in flames together. If M. le Prince Bargatinski found his Moscow palace again it's thanks to me.'

Newly arrived from Spain is Colonel Serran of the Guard Engineers. Since works have been put in hand to update the Kremlin's defences against a *coup de main* – Césare de Laugier hears that the Emperor himself has designed them – they're passed to Lariboisière's department and given to Serran to execute. To be near the works Serran chooses,

'five hundred yards away, the Palace of Prince Kutaisov, barber to the Grand Duke Paul, who by a stroke of good luck rather common in Russia, had acquired immense properties and had his son made a prince. The Prince [Emil] of Hesse [– Darmstadt] was lodged beside us.'

Serran is constantly in touch with Berthier and Duroc, 'whom the Emperor sometimes came and visited'.

As yet – for the first time since crossing the Niemen – there's plenty of food. Moscow, like other cities, is surrounded by windmills; and Caulaincourt, requisitioning one of them, arranges for IHQ's supply of wheat flour – 'which was already beginning to be scarce'. Returning to the city at 6 a.m. on 19 September, Major Le Roy, guided by a soldier of the 85th Line, marches his men along the quay 'where there were some boats laden with grain', and after passing through 'a long suburb, ending at the stream which flows into the Moskova' bivouacks at the foot of a windmill:

'On the other side were two rows of houses flanking the road. The weather having taken a turn for the worse and looking like rain, which in fact fell as night came down, I put my two companies into them and barricaded the bridge. I also managed to put a battalion into shelter in some nearby houses. Next day I visited my sentries. The sergeant placed near the river had found a grange filled with sacks of grain, made of bulrushes, sewn with string, and heaped up to the necks. I told the staff about it, and towards evening the food administration came and took charge of it for the army's benefit.'

Immediately on IHQ's return to the Kremlin a cookhouse service has been organized 'and great activity deployed on building ovens' – whose bread, to judge from earlier instances, will mostly go to the Guard. One of its *can-*

tinières has installed her kitchen behind the high altar of its cathedral. All round the city the immense fields of the huge beets and cabbages, so delightful to the hearts of Private Jakob Walter and Lieutenant Dutheillet, are being carefully cut.

'Numerous stacks of hay were also brought into town, and the potato fields within a radius of six miles were cleared. The transport wagons were in constant use.'

As for potatoes, Regimental Sergeant-Major *Auguste Thirion* and his steel-clad brothers-in-arms of the 2nd Cuirassiers are busy harvesting these 'precious tubers, a piece of gastronomic good luck'. Stendhal, unable even in the most desperate circumstances to restrain his flippant witticisms, writes home that they've become almost sacred: 'We're on our knees in front of some potatoes.'

All this is well and good. In the town's cellars there's no shortage of jams, liqueurs, tea and coffee and other luxuries. Much of the Kitai Gorod has survived:

'It was here that one found products from China. It consisted mainly of a long road, each of whose houses, regularly built in a severe and uniform style, turned out to be a vast shop. I was struck, I'd almost say saddened, by the silent calm which reigned in this quarter whose shops were full of tea.'

But though Paymaster-Captain Duverger is 'rich in furs and pictures, in boxes of figs, coffee, liqueurs, macaroni, salted fish and salted meat' when he entertains his general and ten other officers to a banquet on a leg of beef and they all drink to 'entering Petersburg', he has neither *vin ordinaire* nor – more ominous – any white bread to offer them. After a few days even Caulaincourt is already finding 'wheat beginning to be scarce, so I had a large supply of biscuits baked.'

For once in a very long while the army's horses have plenty of forage, at least for the first week or so:

'The grain and fodder warehouses along the quays had escaped the fire; and between Smolensk and Mojaisk, and since the battle until we'd reached Moscow, the army's horses had been so short of provender that everyone hastened to go foraging to get them some. During the two days of the 15th and 16th they'd got in enough hay to last for several months.'

So it seems. The army's Quartermaster-General, Count Mathieu Dumas (a man with a 'perfect knowledge of facts, an always captivating way of talking and a perfect distinction of manners') estimates there's enough food in the ruined city to feed the army for six months. And Surgeon-General Larrey agrees. Larrey has set up a kind of medical pool where French and Russian surgeons, in a unique collaboration, are working side by side.

Some 5,000 of their patients are either Frenchmen or allies. Himself he's working day and night in 'Moscow's most beautiful hospital' – a building which Boulart, looking out of the windows of 'quite a fine house said to belong to a doctor' out at Petrovskoï (perhaps the very one Griois and Jumilhac had occupied) sees standing up among the smouldering ruins. 'A fine monument of modern construction and grandiose, it was full of Russian wounded, whom it had saved'.

Struggling with overall and indeed overwhelming administrative problems, meanwhile, is the former French consul-general at Petersburg, de Lesseps.[11] Since having to beg a bit of bread for himself from the 20-year-old Breton War Commissary *Bellot de Kergorre*[12] at the Mojaisk hospitals, this 'honest man' whom Napoleon had dismissed for sending in reports that didn't agree with his preconceptions, has covered the 70 miles to Moscow, and immediately on arrival, 'despite his urgent request to be excused all duties,' has been appointed Intendant, i.e., civil governor. De Lesseps hasn't 'forgotten the thirty years of hospitality he'd been met with in Russia'; and his manner of carrying out the task so arbitrarily imposed on him stirs both Caulaincourt's and Méneval's admiration:

'This excellent man was doing all he could to put a stop to many evils, among them the issue of false paper money,[13] the theft of many small sums, as well as the destruction of such archives as had been saved from the fire. He collected, sheltered, nourished and in fact saved quite a number of unfortunate men, women and children whose houses had burned down and who were straying about like ghosts amidst the ruins.'

Many are members of the French colony – for instance the French troupe of actors who, after the Peace of Tilsit in 1807, had settled in Moscow under the Tsar's protection. Its director is one of the notable foreigners who'd been forcibly evacuated by Rostopchin. But most of the troupe had stayed behind. Thanks to Caulaincourt's protection one of them, *Louise de Fusil,* a most resourceful woman of 32, has found shelter in an outbuilding of Prince Galitzin's palace, near the Kremlin. Meanwhile Lieutenant *Paul de Bourgoing*'s kindly and drily humorous General Delaborde, whose division of the Young Guard hadn't been at Borodino and only arrived at Moscow on 14 September, is providing board and lodging for two others, Mesdames Anthony and André, who have also lost everything.

Among Russian 'ghosts' is Count Zagriasski, the Tsar's former Grand Equerry. Like Yakovlev, he'd lingered in Moscow, unable to tear himself away from his palace 'on which he'd lavished a lifetime of care' – only to see it go up in flames. Together with many other homeless and ruined individuals, Caulaincourt kindly takes his ex-opposite number under his wing.

A few – but very few – Russians are allowing themselves to be co-opted into de Lesseps' civil administration.[14] Césare de Laugier hears how 'the town has been divided up into twenty districts, and 50,000 roubles in copper have been placed at the disposition of the syndics to provide speedy help for the indigent. There's only one snag. The difficulty of carrying so much small change about, heavy as it is, renders the execution of this generous action almost impossible.'

While ever fresh fires are breaking out, now here, now there, what's left of the city is being looted, but now not so much for personal consumption as for sale or barter. Even the Kremlin isn't being spared. Though there are Grenadier and Chasseur sentries stationed in its triple vaulted gateway,

'infantrymen were going in, looking for the provisions of every kind it contained in such abundance. But on coming out from the interior courtyard each has to pay 5 frs. to the grenadiers or else abandon his booty – in which case he's treated as scum, stripped, and driven away. They may deny it, these grenadiers who were held up to us as models of courage and honour, but the whole army will certify it for a fact. Marshal Lefèbvre issued an order on the subject and covered the footguards with the most sanguinary reproaches.'

Everywhere markets have sprung up. Not the city's regular ones – no Muscovite is allowing himself to be enticed back into the city by Napoleon's decree. But purely military ones. Of these the great square outside the Kremlin is the scene of only one among many. Thirion accuses the men of the Guard, above all, of this mercantile behaviour, 'so that the army thereafter called them the merchants or Jews of Moscow'. True, old Marshal Lefèbvre, commander of the Guard infantry, has issued the strictest orders. No Russian is to be allowed into the Kremlin. Any found trying to get in is to be shot out of hand. Patrols shall be on the alert day and night at all points, from one end of the Kremlin to the other. And no guardsman is to be allowed to go out without his captain's permission, 'such leave only to be given very rarely.' The Guard, however, always unruly, pays little heed. Newly fledged Sous-lieutenant *Jean-Roch Coignet* sees its rank and file 'roving through the town like wild beasts in a charnel house, seeing to do some stroke of business'.

Who should know better? Coignet's one of them himself. But then, alas, just as he's 'found' a gorgeous Siberian sable fur, he has the misfortune to be detailed off from the Emperor's 'smaller' staff – the only one that's always in attendance – to assist a staff colonel, 'a hard man with a nasty face', who's been entrusted with evacuating corpses from Larrey's two hospitals; but is far more interested in enriching himself:

'We were lodged with an old princess, all four of us with our horses and servants. The colonel alone had three to himself, and he knew how to use them. He sent us into the hospitals to get the sick evacuated. Himself never! He stayed behind to do business. In the evenings he left with his servants, equipped with candles. He knew that the pictures in the churches are relief-work on a silver plate. He had them taken off their hooks to take their silver leaf, put all the saints – male and female – into the melting pot and made ingots of them. He sold his thefts to Jews for bank notes.'

One evening the odious staff colonel shows Lieutenant Coignet his *emplettes* ('little purchases'), and Coignet's so

'imprudent as to show him mine. He insisted I exchange it for a Siberian fox. Mine was sable, but I had to give way. I was afraid of his vengeance. He was so barbarous as to strip me of it to sell it for 3,000 frs to Prince [sic] Murat. This looter of churches dishonoured the name of Frenchman.'

Coignet claims that he and his comrades protected women and children against looters.

Everyone knows that winter's coming daily closer. And anyone who, like Coignet, had been in Poland in 1807 has some inkling of what that will mean. Among the officers, notably, who can afford to pay to get themselves good furs. Russia's famous furs are in high demand. Peyrusse of the Imperial Treasury, however – whether because he's working so very hard or spending so much time worming himself into Grand Marshal Duroc's and Secretary Méneval's good books with a view to his imagined promotion – is finding it singularly hard to find one that's to his taste. Though coffee, tea and sugar abound, he writes home to his friend André ('the men have all taken to drinking sugared water') 'few furs have been found. One sees an immense quantity of ordinary fox. Every ranker has one. But nothing really pretty or rare.'

Well, not quite. In the end he buys himself 'a black astrakhan, which doesn't leave hairs on coats' and three cashmere shawls:

'Two of them are pretty, the man who'd taken them didn't want to sell. The third had been cut in two and shared between two soldiers to wrap stockfish and had cost 40 frs. I bought it off Roustam, the Emperor's valet [sic] for 250 frs.'

If the officers are concerned to get themselves furs, the rankers, who, knowing themselves to be mere cannon fodder, usually live fecklessly *au jour le jour* and jettison or destroy anything they haven't any immediate use for, seem mainly to be dreaming of instant wealth:

'Whilst only few of us thought of providing ourselves with warm clothes and furs against the coming winter, many laded themselves down with a mass of useless things.'

Not so *J. L. Henckens*, NCO and acting lieutenant in the 6th Chasseurs à Cheval, a regiment which has lost *all* its commissioned officers, either killed, wounded or unhorsed at Borodino. Born at Eygelshoven, a few miles from Aix-la-Chapelle, Henckens regards himself as 'almost a Fleming' and besides his native German and French has taught himself to speak Italian – his regiment had long been stationed in northern Italy – and also has a smattering of Polish and Russian. Completely indispensable to Squadron Commander de Feuillebois, commanding the 6th Chasseurs ever since its well-liked Colonel Ledard had died in Henckens' arms of three mortal wounds in the Great Redoubt,[15] Henckens is obviously extremely competent and experienced. When the fire had forced Napoleon out of the Kremlin, each of Grouchy's light cavalry regiments out at Petrovskoï had been ordered to send a party of fifty men and NCOs into town, as an escort for Murat. Instead, Henckens' party, when they'd got there, had been detailed off to protect what he calls 'the Great Theatre', where they'd made the acquaintance of some actors of the French troupe. Saving the surrounding quarter from the flames and sending any soldiers they found straying about in town back to their units, some of Henckens' chasseurs had brought him various useful or valuable objects, saved from the flames –

'one, for instance, a sackful of gold watches. Another had brought me a load of shawls in very striking colours he'd taken off an infantryman who was sent back to his regiment outside the town and asked me to be allowed to carry off his booty to make a shelter for himself at his bivouac. I'd deposited the shawls in the theatre, where the actors told me they were cashmeres of great value.'

One of his patrols, Henckens goes on, had come across a store of furs, and one of his chasseurs had asked him:

"Lieutenant, I've a lot of little packets of furs I've put in a forage bag. What am I to do with those things?"

Feeling the packets, Henckens had decided the furs would come in very handy against the cold, which cannot be very far off. Stuffing as many as he reasonably could into his pistol holsters and coat, he'd taken them back to the regiment to show to Feuillebois and ask his advice. Feuillebois, promotes him acting adjutant-major. Feels the furs. And tells him:

"As far as I can tell, it's the finest petit gris, the rarest and most precious I've ever seen."

One of the chasseurs, a tailor by profession, is set to work to turn them into waistcoats; 'according to his calculations he could make each of us at least two'. And those that are left over he can keep for himself. Henckens and his acting CO themselves sit down and help him: 'though our talents as tailors were limited to sewing on a button or making small repairs, everything went swimmingly.'

Petits-gris are in specially high demand. Engineer-Colonel Serran's travelling companion on his long journey from Spain, a Captain Cornault, also provisions himself 'like a Tartar' with fifty of them. And General Delaborde's ADC and interpreter, Paul de Bourgoing, 'with youthful light-headedness and lack of foresight', provides himself

'not with the amplest and warmest fur, but the one which seemed to me most elegant in shape and colour. Instead of one of the excellent black bear pelts, or wild or white wolfskins, I bought a very pretty Polish-style coat in dark blue cloth, richly adorned with silken fringes and lined with black astrakhan. At that moment I thought much more of my own pleasure, walking about in my general's suite with an elegant garment in the presence of Mesdames Anthony and André than of arming myself against icy winds.'

But when it comes to choosing a fur for his little servant Victor, the Parisian guttersnipe and would-be drummer boy whom he 'out of kindness' has brought with him on the campaign, he wisely buys him a *witchoura* – a heavy Russian wolfskin overcoat. Also a horse. To replace his own worn-out mare, Paul de Bourgoing buys from his brother, one of Ney's ADC's, a mount which had belonged to a Captain du Breuil, killed by a roundshot at Borodino while galloping after his marshal along the flank of the Würtemberg columns. No one but the most feckless is unaware of the threat posed by the Russian winter. Napoleon himself orders Lefèbvre to get fur waistcoats for the Guard to wear under their greatcoats; and Ney is collecting sheepskins. One of his regimental officers, *Guillaume Bonnet*, newly promoted major in the 18th Line – still bivouacked out on the plain – buys himself a fox fur of more modest value than – but equal use to Peyrusse's astrakhan. Only 'by dint of much effort and repeated threats' does von Muraldt, out at the Petrovskoï camp, get *his* servant, 'who was going into town every day, to get me a good fur-lined overcoat'.

For there are much more fascinating objects freely to be had but of much more dubious value. One day, von Muraldt goes on:

'some of our people forced their way into a vault where they found a mass of stamped lead plates – what they were intended for I don't know – which they dragged out to our bivouac in the belief that they were silver.'

Colonel Griois' gunners too, still encamped like Muraldt's Bavarian light horse out at Petrovskoï, discover,

'a considerable mass of metal plates, some of them weighing up to 10 pounds. As far as I could see they were nothing but an alloy of tin and zinc. But they had the colour and brilliance of silver, and had been taken, so it was said, from the stores of the Mint. Everyone was loading himself down with them, by preference over everything else.'[16]

Since these plates bear an official stamp, Muraldt finds it's

'almost impossible to convince the men they're not silver. They filled their kit bags with them and, heavy though they were, loaded them on their emaciated horses. Only by the strictest measures could we prevail on them to let them be or throw them away.'

Everywhere objects of luxury make a strange contrast with the general lack, steadily becoming more noticeable, of the most indispensable foodstuffs:

'It wasn't rare to see soldiers who had no shoes, in tatters, seated amidst bales of rich merchandise, or covered in the most expensive shawls, precious furs and vestments embroidered with gold or pearls. Or else neglecting the masses of tea, coffee and sugar, preferring to them a bit of black bread, a slice of horsemeat and some drops of muddy water.'

Everywhere the precious and semi-precious objects Lieutenant Brandt had seen dragged out to his bivouac outside the Kazan Gate are being 'bought back for a song by those ignoble junk merchants, mostly Jews, who on such occasions seem to rise up out of the ground'. Although as far as Peyrusse can see there's not a single shop open in the whole town, in the markets, 'where most of the rag-and-bone men are guardsmen or the army's employees', Le Roy and his friend Jacquet find

'gold, silver, diamonds, in a word all kinds of expensive luxury items. One gold coin was being bought at twice its value. As for the pearls, diamonds and brilliants, we were all much more on our guard. We knew from experience that Russians love false diamonds. Beside us I saw five silver ingots weighing about 10 pounds sell for 300 frs. A few days later these ingots had fallen to twelve francs apiece, only to be abandoned later on on the highway like petty cash.'

Can it be they're only zinc and tin alloy? Le Roy buys what appear to be packets of Turkish tobacco, only to find they actually contain tea, admittedly 'enough for the rest of the campaign'. And on the three or four occasions when Griois comes back into town to 'lay in a stock of victuals of every kind', though he nowhere sees

'a single inhabitant, the streets which the fire still hadn't reached looked like a veritable fair, all of whose participants, merchants and purchasers, were military men. They'd turned merchant. It was to them officers of every rank came to provision themselves.'

All of which is very bad indeed for discipline. The 26-year-old violin-playing Captain Count *M-H. de Lignières*[17] of the lst Battalion of the Foot Chasseurs of the Old Guard, disapproves intensely; but converts his 'savings', he too, into Treasury bonds and stuffs them 'inside the lining of my waistcoat, the gold cash in my belt'.[18]

At the Niemen the Grand Army had started out with a host of officers' carriages unprecedented in any previous campaign. Coming across 'some shops which contained a great number of carriages which were at the disposal of anyone who fancied them', it has seemed to Griois that the moment has come to replace the light travelling carriage that's brought him all the way from his beloved Verona and which by now is in rather poor shape:

'Several generals and some of my own comrades had helped themselves to these carriages, to replace their own, rendered more or less unserviceable by the road. I went where I was told to, and merely had to choose from among some one hundred new carriages, of the greatest elegance. I took one of the lightest calèches, and as it was already getting late I had it taken to the town house occupied by General d'Anthouard [commander of IV Corps' artillery]. Next day I came back to get it and have it driven to my cantonment. But during the night the fire had made enormous progress and forced d'Anthouard to quit his lodging. My carriage wasn't there any longer. It had been taken away or burnt. I was happy to find my own again, which I'd abandoned the day before.'

Although M. l'Abbé Surugué of the French colony's church of St Louis is astounded and shocked to discover that his post-revolutionary compatriots haven't a single padre in their ranks,[18] he's sure the Frenchmen aren't the worst robbers. And another elderly Muscovite of German extraction, who'd imbibed a hatred for the French with his mother's milk at the time of the Seven Years War, agrees that the damage the Frenchmen are doing isn't usually of the senseless kind:

'Even in the midst of their excesses their courtesy showed through, though not always. While Württembergers and Poles behave like vandals, the French only rob to satisfy life's necessities. The Bavarians leave nothing behind them.'

Unfortunately another French resident, the Chevalier d'Ysarn, gives the lie to these patriotic generalizations. He'd been riding in his carriage toward the Kazan Gate when some French cavalry troopers had forced him to dismount, exchanged his elegant boots for their own route-worn ones, and told him to count himself lucky, as an *émigré*, not to have fared still worse.

Not all the looting is private. Napoleon has plans of his own. 'Guard sappers were being used to demolish the cross of the church of the Kremlin, which was in silver and gold. All was melted down into ingots, a prodigious quantity of silverware, silver and gold.' The cross itself, which orthodox Russians regard as particularly sacred, is to be taken back to Paris to embellish the dome of the Invalides.

'Many generals, officers of all ranks, were buying silver ingots or silverware, jewels and precious stones for a song from the soldiers and putting them in their trunks, the generals in their wagons.'

But at IHQ, where Peyrusse is always hard at work under his chief, General Count Daru,

'all this has given us a very wide berth. I'm clinging to M. Daru who welcomes me very well and whom I, in a moment of famine, have made accept twelve bottles of very good quality Burgundy. He and I paid all the wounded on the battlefield, etc. He's been able to see how active I am. But he has no places at his disposition.'

All Peyrusse is concerned with is to get hold of a few luxuries for the wife of his friend André, with whom he has plans to set up a nice little apartment in Paris.

Bread may be becoming scarce. But wines are abundant. In the house of his aged princess, Coignet and his colleagues have access to

'thousands of bottles of Bordeaux, Champagne wines and Demerara sugar. Every evening the old princess made us take away four bottles of good wine and sugar (the cellars were full of barrels). She often came to visit us. So her house was respected. She spoke good French.'

'We're not dying of hunger, as one might expect,' Césare de Laugier writes in his diary amidst the blackened ruins of the Petersburg district, on 29 September. 'We're swimming, so to speak in abundance, though – let me say in passing – without owing it to the Administration, but to our own lucky discoveries.' And von Muraldt agrees:

'Though there was wine, sugar, coffee, etc., in superfluity, we were still suffering from a lack of bread, meat and fodder for our horses.'

And already the Guardia d'Onore's adjutant-major is seeing 'detachments made up of various arms' having to be sent out to bring back foodstuffs and forage 'even to a distance of twelve miles.'

Meanwhile many officers, as well no doubt as inarticulate rankers, are all too aware that, peace or no peace (and as yet there's no sign of any), they've a very long way to go to get back to the Niemen; still further to Germany, France, Italy or Spain.

CHAPTER 4

A DISCONSOLATE ADVANCE GUARD

Kutusov fools Murat – 'we're beginning to suffer from the cold' – disastrous affair at Malo-Wiazma – redispositions – the Red Lancers lose a troop – 'they buy prisoners from the Cossacks to put them to death' – Lahoussaye's grotesque incompetence – Griois' billet at Winkovo

Meanwhile, day after day, Murat's cavalry, sometimes held up by Cossacks, sometimes not, has been pushing on eastwards down the Ryazan road through 'magnificent countryside, covered in châteaux and villages. Châteaux of remarkable elegance. We come across a few peasants, but many have armed themselves and joined the Russians.'
All the blithe talk of Russian war-weariness is turning out to have been illusory. The Cossacks dodging about ahead of Maurice Tascher's chasseur regiment seem to be anything but demoralized. And on 21 September he notes in his diary: 'It seems the Russian army has taken another route.'
So it has.
That day, leaving two regiments of Cossacks as a cavalry screen to lure the French on as far as possible down the Ryazan road, Kutusov has suddenly switched his main force southwards toward the charming little town of Pakra – situated athwart the River Pakra, its name means 'red', but also 'beautiful'. Justly assessing the strategic situation, Kutusov – in a movement which would have been impossible if Murat had done as Napoleon had recommended when approaching Moscow and skirted the city to the south – has decided to place the Russian army between Napoleon and Russia's two greatest arms factories, at Kaluga and Tula. He'll not only have the rich plains of the Ukraine at his rear but from the whole of southern and eastern Russia also be able to absorb and train the recruits who will soon be pouring in.
A whole day passes in futile pursuits before Sébastiani tumbles to the enemy's manoeuvre; and Murat, crossing the River Moscova on the Kolomna road, again enters into a brief truce. All this means that next day (23 September) Tascher's chasseurs have to make a flank movement towards Podolsk to catch up.

Meanwhile, 30 miles to the west of Moscow, something utterly shocking has occurred.
Napoleon had spent the last night before reaching Moscow in Prince Galitzin's sumptuous country palace at Malo-Wiazma. On the Smolensk

highway, it had been 'the first château really worth the name we'd seen in Russia' – though all its furnishings, Captain Count V. E. B Castellane had been distressed to see, had as usual been smashed up by the advance guard. Since then Malo-Wiazma has been occupied by a squadron of the prestigious Dragoons of the Guard, an élite regiment if ever there were one. Since they're 'daily being bothered by numerous pulks of Cossacks', on 22 September Lieutenant-Colonel Schuurmann, commanding a battalion of the 33rd Line, a regiment largely consisting of Dutchmen whose other battalion had remained in and around Minsk, hundreds of miles to the rear, is

> 'ordered with some fractions of his battalion and those [sailors] of the Danube and Hesse-Darmstadt, together some 300 men strong, and with 200 dragoons, to make a reconnaissance in the enemy's direction. The detachment as a whole, however, was commanded by Colonel Marthod of the Guard. The dragoons formed the advance guard, and the infantry followed in column.'

After a couple of hours this flying column is just reaching a vast forest when pistol shots are heard in the distance. And the column debouches against the enemy:

> 'The latter was disposed in a semicircle in a plain, its two wings supported by the forest. It consisted wholly of cavalry – as far as could be assessed at a distance, a force of some 4,000 men. Reaching the plain, our troops took up their positions. The cavalry drew up in line of battle on the highest point in the terrain. Our lieutenant-colonel received orders to place himself with the infantry about 100 paces to its rear. Meanwhile our skirmishers opened fire in order to make themselves masters of the village situated in front of them. Realizing that the happy outcome of the affair depended on capturing this village, Schuurmann marched for this point at the pas de charge [180 paces a minute] and drove out the enemy that was there.'

While all this is happening, Colonel Marthod and his dragoons have 'made a movement to the front and charged the Russians' left wing. Seeing it, their centre and left wing flung themselves forward at a prolonged gallop, cut off the dragoons' retreat, and in a twinkling of an eye overthrew everything in their path. Meanwhile our infantry had re-emerged from the village, if possible to support the dragoons. But at that moment it was no longer feasible. Within a few instants all [but a few of] the dragoons were sabred. When Lieutenant-Colonel Schuurmann was again more or less in the middle of the plain, all the enemy cavalry, which had finished off the dragoons, made a charge against his men. But the latter, having formed square, were calmly awaiting it.'

No fewer than six charges are made against the square, but each is driven off. In the intervals between them Schuurmann marches his square off the plain to master the wood he must retreat through. Some of the Russian horsemen have dismounted and are firing their carbines at the square, killing or wounding a number of Schuurmann's men. At the same time the Russians have

'placed two of their squadrons in front of the wood to prevent our infantry from getting into it, and furthermore brought up into the gap some artillery, which immediately began firing at the square. The lieutenant-colonel, knowing all too well he was irremediably lost if didn't make himself master of the wood, decided to attack the two squadrons at bayonet point. This movement was carried out so energetically that our men completely routed the Russians and seized the wood, after which they were able to operate their retreat to Galitzin's château.'

The day, Schuurmann will tell the Dutch major *Henri-Pierre Everts* when the 33rd's two battalions are reunited later on, had cost him 120 of his 300 men, and two officers:

'The Dragoons of the Guard were even worse treated. Very few came back, and they only owed their safety to their horses' swiftness. Colonel Marthod, too, was gravely wounded and fell into the enemy's hands.'[1]

In the Kremlin the episode comes as a terrible shock. Kutusov had sent out all his cavalry, and with odds of 20 to one it had celebrated its biggest success. Caulaincourt sees how

'this slight reverse irritated the Emperor as much as the loss of a battle. It made more impression than the loss of 50 generals made hors de combat at Borodino.'

As for the 33rd, it's the regiment which has already been so outraged by Davout's atrocious treatment of it at Minsk in August, when in a fit of fury he'd forced it to march past with inverted muskets for having left behind so many stragglers.[2] And though General Verdun, the commandant at Malo-Wiazma, 'paid warm homage to our troops' conduct', the wretched Schuurmann is so gravely demoralized when he sends in his report on the affair to Berthier that he doesn't even 'dare ask for anything to the profit of anyone in the regiment, no matter how well it had behaved'.

Perhaps they wouldn't have got anything anyway?

The Malo-Wiazma episode, it seems, strikes the whole army as in some way symptomatic.

Immediately orders are given for all the cavalry and other outposts around Moscow to be reinforced. Broussier's division of IV Corps and the three Bavarian chevauleger regiments leave Petrovskoï and move back to a position on the Smolensk highway, some three hours from the city. Ney too has to send units to reinforce the Malo-Wiazma position, among them the 18th Line.

Troops are also sent south of the city to block the Kaluga road which Napoleon had wanted Murat to occupy the day before they'd got to Moscow, but which for some reason he hadn't. In steadily falling rain two of Davout's infantry divisions are sent to contain the enemy and bivouac beyond the forest. One of these is Friedrichs', comprising the 85th Line. On 21 September Major Le Roy had commanded a marauding excursion to the west of the city.[3] That day the regiment, marching south along the Kaluga road, had had a serious brush with Cossack regulars, who'd stabbed twelve of Le Roy's men with their lances. It might have turned into a large-scale affray if the Russians, 'several cavalry regiments and Cossacks, supported by two guns', hadn't retired. Obviously it had only been a reconnaissance in force. Next day, after he has rejoined the regiment in its bivouac behind a wood, his men occupy

'a big, rich abbey, shaped like a citadel. We stayed there. The abbey was pillaged and several of our rankers carried off rare and curious objects.'

On 26/27 September they go on to occupy a château where Le Roy sees 'for the first time, boxed apple and pear trees already shut up in the orangerie, for fear of the winter'. On the 29th they occupy a large village further along the Kaluga road: 'Never in my life have I seen a muddier place, nor wetter mud. We were in it up to the middle of our legs, in the middle of the road, impossible to walk along the roadsides.' And there they stay for four days, until it pleases someone to extricate them from the mud. Then they'd marched hither and thither, to left, to right, to close up on the advance guard, but without seeing any enemy. 'Food was becoming more and more rare.'

The Red Lancers, too, had had to leave their comfortable quarters in 'the large village of Troïlskoïe-Galantschiwo' where they'd confidently been supposing peace must soon follow, 'as on the morrow of Austerlitz, Friedland and Wagram'. On 23 September, joining up with their Polish colleagues, cantoned in a nearby village and 'circumventing the many vegetable gardens the town was fringed with on its south side,' they'd made for Podolsk, which they'd also found abandoned by its inhabitants. 'Thus ended, for us, our stay at Moscow, of which everyone had expected so much.'

Such postings, as Le Roy has already found out, are no sinecure. Two days later the imprudent Lieutenant Doyen lets Colbert's leading troop be inveigled into an ambush by 'too ardently pursuing a few enemy scouts' at the entry to a village. A second troop, sent to its assistance, is also within an ace of being overwhelmed. Surrounded on all sides, it doesn't lose its head. In the nick of time, just as the second rank faces about – a critical moment – Dumonceau's troop turns up on the scene:

'Our unexpected appearance made the enemy relinquish his grip and he withdrew without waiting for our charge, yet continued to harass us to the point where the whole regiment had to be engaged in incessant skirmishes lasting more than an hour, without any ground being gained or lost.'

Suddenly the Russians draw off. Tyskiewicz's brigade of Polish chasseurs, sent by Murat to meet the Guard Lancers, has come up in their rear. But the Red Lancers' entire advance troop has been lost. It's the second such loss during the campaign.[4] Even so, Colbert is 'pleased he'd had a chance to appreciate his regiment's valour and was so good as loudly to express the justice due to it'. Not that General Colbert is a man easily pleased. Next day Dumonceau, too, is reprimanded – not for the first time during the campaign. This time it's for too eagerly following up yet another Cossack force, also withdrawing in front of them.

In a cold rain which will continue falling for eleven days and nights, Murat's force advances slowly south-westwards, with Poniatowski's I Corps marching in parallel a few miles away to the west. Tascher's notebook:

'27 September: beyond Podolsk, snow. We're beginning to suffer from the cold. 28 September: famine. Lack of bread and forage. 29 September: approaching the village of Winkovo.'

There Tascher's chasseurs run into Russian infantry and have to retire behind a ravine, while Poniatowski's guns, still somewhere to the right, seem also to be heavily engaged.

By now, also out on Murat's right flank, Griois and the horse batteries of (Grouchy's) 3rd Cavalry Corps are here too. While still attached to the Army of Italy in the plain north of Moscow, he'd 'changed cantonments almost daily, but always on the Petersburg road and about twelve miles from Moscow,' the last one being in a superb château. But then, in the evening of 21 September, he'd been ordered to move south 'several leagues along the Kaluga road'. Leaving his rather worn-out carriage and his effects – 'almost all I owned' – with his servant in Moscow, he and his friend Jumilhac, 3rd Cavalry Corps' chief-of-staff, hadn't omitted to pay their respects to Grouchy 'who still hadn't entirely recovered from his wound'. The popular cavalry commander had entertained them to

'a very good dinner. At about 10 p.m. we'd got on our horses again, crossed the town by the light of the fire which was still going on, albeit less violently for lack of nourishment, and having marched for several hours halted in an abandoned hamlet until the morrow, when we rejoined our corps, which I didn't leave again.'

Grouchy's good dinner had been the last either Griois or Jumilhac will enjoy for some time; for they're in for a period of 'long and harsh abstinence' they'll not soon forget. Now, in that unusually fierce fight of 29 September,[5] the Russians have occupied a very strong position, and Griois is aiming all his guns at the same point and they're firing as fast and hard as they can when

> 'Murat came and placed himself in the middle of my batteries and from there examined the Russians' movements. At that moment someone brought him a dispatch. He read it and, without getting off his horse, wrote a reply on one of his tablets, with the same sangfroid as if he'd been inside his tent. Yet at that moment a rain of roundshot, shells and grape was falling on us and causing his horse to swerve and make leaps and jumps which he didn't even notice. I forgot the peril to admire the King's perfect impassiveness and martial bearing, brought out even more by his opulent and bizarre accoutrements.'

Murat may fail utterly to look after his cavalry on the march, but Griois, like everyone else, is full of admiration for him on the battlefield:

> 'Never did ADCs or orderly officers bringing him orders or information in battle have any difficulty in finding him. They made for the point where the fighting was going on and on the side where the attack seemed liveliest. They were sure to find him there. It was the *beau idéal* of courage.'

At Russian headquarters, hardly five miles away to the south, there's an Englishman of a very different stamp. Nursing a profound scorn and hatred for 'Bonaparte' and all his works, he desires nothing more or less than his and the Grand Army's total annihilation. General *Sir Robert Wilson* is the British government's special envoy and ever-critical liaison officer at Kutusov's headquarters. Passing through Petersburg with his aide, the young Lord Tyrconnel, he – as the sly and aged Kutusov very well knows – has made good personal contacts with the Tsar, whom he doesn't hesitate to inform of what's gong on at the front. Wilson heartily dislikes the one-eyed, slothful, cunning and aged Kutusov almost as much as the Tsar does. He suspects him, rightly, of having only Russian, not British, interests at heart.[6] Like the Tsar, 'the English general' (as he always calls himself – like Caesar, Wilson always refers to himself in the third person) is determined to scotch any dealings with the enemy – the more so as he clearly sees Murat's troops are in an ever more parlous condition. 'Every day since I've been here,' he writes at the end of September,

74

'prisoners in parties of 50, and even of 100, have been brought in, chiefly wounded. During the five days we remained at Krasnoi Pakra, 1,342 were delivered to the commandant at headquarters. Of course many more are killed, for such is the inveteracy [implacability] of the peasants that they buy prisoners off the Cossacks for several roubles to put them to death. Two guns have been taken by the peasants; vast quantities of baggage, etc., both going to and from Moscow; much melted silver, which I myself have seen:'

Evidently he's met some dragoons of the Guard, captured at Malo-Wiazma, whom he calls simply

'the guards – of whom two [sic] squadrons were taken. [They] told me that they had been obliged to blow up a convoy of 60 powder wagons, rather than suffer them to be made a prize. In brief, the Spanish guerrilla warfare never was more successful, and certainly was not so formidable to the enemy. The prisoners, not French, but foreigners, all hold one language: they all describe themselves as victims to an insatiable ambition and say that privations of every kind have been the prelude to their loss of liberty.'

On 28 September Wilson, who seems to take such Russian reports at face-value, rides out

'to the advanced posts, which remained on the river Pakra. The enemy had lodged themselves opposite, but without any disposition to incon-venience our parties. Five hundred Frenchmen have been taken by the Cossacks as the enemy's column retrograded from the Kolomna road; and yesterday 14 carts, two of which contained gold and silver to the amount of 15,000 ducats, were taken on the Podolsk road.'

Among the Cossacks' captives is a General Ferrier and his two ADCs. Murat tries to get them exchanged; but the offer is turned down. 'The position of the mutual outposts,' Wilson continues, on 1 October, a day when Tascher writes in his diary 'the Cossacks are carrying off a lot of foragers, servants and baggage,'

'was the most extraordinary I had ever seen in war, for they were so interwoven as to present fronts on all points of the compass, and I do not think I ever got so close to an enemy's corps for the purpose of reconnoitring it as I did to Prince Poniatowski's. It was almost the same thing as being in his camp. At night the Cossacks attacked and killed 200 Cuirassiers on a foraging party, and made 85 prisoners.'

By now Tascher's chasseur regiment is reduced to only four troops, his own company to fourteen men. And the cold is becoming 'rigorous'.

Grouchy, one of Napoleon's best cavalry leaders, is still in Moscow, recu-perating from his wound. At Borodino both he and Griois, commanding his artillery, had suffered severe contusions from bits of spent grape – Griois, less severely, in the small of his back. Though this had been very painful – his belt had deadened the shock – Griois hadn't been disabled. But the bit that had hit Grouchy – his 23rd wound – had hit him in the chest, wounding him so severely that he'd had to hand over 3rd Cavalry Corps to his senior divisional commander, General Lahoussaye.

While Grouchy is generally seen as 'brave, prudent, enjoying the confidence of his troops', Lahoussaye is one of those brave but bumbling military men who have the trick of infallibly doing the wrong thing in all circumstances. New to the corps, he's certainly anything but prudent. Indeed the reputation has preceded him of being a complete ass. Some of his officers regard him as a fraud. And no one has any confidence in him. Just now 3rd Cavalry Corps, out there on Murat's right, 'for the ten or twelve days when we were acting in isolation, often without any communication with Murat', is floundering about under its new commander's grotesquely incompetent leadership.

'We did nothing but make marches and counter-marches with no reasonable goal to them and no other result than to put the horses 'on their teeth' and often expose ourselves to shameful scuffles.'

One day, Griois goes on, waxing more and more indignant,

'after we'd been pushed back from position to position, some Cossack pulks which had some guns and were trying to hold up our march, General Lahoussaye, more over-excited than usual, gallops ahead of the tirailleurs and orders the cavalry riding in column on either side of the road and my artillery to follow his movement. Hardly have we reached the top of a hill which dominates the road than we see, a hundred yards or so away, considerable lines of cavalry which, supported by infantry and artillery, seemed to be waiting for us.'

Now the only remedy for such an unreconnoitred advance lies in putting a good face on it:

'Unfortunately the general had lost his feeble head and at the sight of these forces he hadn't expected to run into, he turned tail as quickly as he'd come: "Retreat, at the gallop!" he shouted, giving the example; and ordered my artillery to do the same. In vain I pointed out to him it was the infallible way to lose it, and that it would be much better to retire by echelons, successively taking up position. He wouldn't listen, and went on yelling "At the gallop!" I took care not to carry out his order, and General of Brigade Watier, who was in command of the advance guard's light cavalry, didn't do so either. The dragoon division's good countenance, in line behind us, the fire opened by my guns as we retired from position to position, brought the Russians to a halt and put an end to the combat. We lost quite a lot of hussars and chasseurs in the advance guard platoons, which fell at the first shock, and we were fortunate to get off so cheaply from a scuffle where we could have been crushed.'

Other instances of Lahoussaye's incompetence follow. Having ordered a precipitate retirement down a hill and across a stream, he loses a lot of his baggage train, which promptly takes to flight across the fields. Meanwhile 'without giving any orders, he went from one regiment to another, anxiously asking whether anyone had seen his cook and canteens'. Griois himself is within an ace of being taken prisoner, together with two of his guns, which Lahoussaye has imprudently mingled with his skirmishers and which are suddenly surrounded by a swarm of cavalry:

'On 1 or 2 October we were advancing towards the King of Naples, who was fighting not far away from us. From the liveliness of the firing and the musketry we estimated it to be a hot affair, and our corps' arrival might well decide it to our advantage.'

Everyone urges him to make haste. But Lahousssaye

'remained drawn up in battle order for several hours, close enough to the scene of action for us distinctly to hear the soldiers' shouts and our Poles' hurrahs. Towards evening, however, he decided to plunge into a forest which formed a long defile in front of us. We marched in column along the paved road which passes through the forest, but our movement was becoming pointless. The firing had ceased, we didn't know the outcome, and if it hadn't turned out well for us it had been most dangerous, without infantry, to get ourselves into a defile where the cavalry couldn't act. Night was falling and everyone was feeling amazed that Lahoussaye didn't make us retire, when to our great surprise he ordered us to halt and bivouac for the night. Generals and colonels represented to him that his order was absurd. But he replied drily that his orders must be carried out. General Chastel again insisted on the danger of passing the night in this defile. Then, seeing his observations were useless with such a man, he declared that he took it upon himself not to obey.'

Retiring with his light cavalry division, Chastel leaves Lahoussaye to his

'hardly describable rage, at once risible and insane, at seeing his authority flouted. He became agitated, he lamented, saying since he was taken for an imbecile he didn't wish either to command any more or even be on his horse. Dismounting, he threw away his hat, swearing he'd deal with these mutineers. Meanwhile General Chastel and his troops were on the move. Lahoussaye stayed with the dragoon regiments whose colonels were preparing to follow Chastel. He opted to follow the movement that was flouting his orders and we bivouacked near a little village. The event finally discredited him.'

Another incompetent high-up, strangely enough, both in Castellane's and Griois' opinion, is no lesser a personage than Marshal Bessières, commander of the Guard cavalry.[7] After the Malo-Wiazma affair he'd been ordered to push forward a column in the direction of Podolsk. And for a few days he remains personally on the scene, Griois meanwhile noticing how

'his orders at each moment contradicted each other, I not being able to refrain from pointing it out to him. Most fortunately he left us next day, for there's no doubt I'd have been very much in his bad books, and being the weaker, would infallibly have become his victim.'

Though the two Guard lancer regiments feel Bessières' eye upon them and redouble their discipline, they're shocked to be told to

'suppress all trumpet calls and observe a deep silence in the mornings, so as not to disturb the marshal's sleep. These precautions seemed strange to us. We couldn't conceive that such a chief as the Duke [of Istria], so famous for his military exigencies, could need to be so mollycoddled, while we were still subjected to the dawn regime before daybreak. So we were inclined to ascribe it to an act of courtesy on our general's part.'

Colbert's Lancer Brigade[8] hadn't taken part in the fights of 27 and 29 September near Pakra, near though it had been to 3rd Cavalry Corps, which had. To Dumonceau's regret,

'our brigade didn't budge and from 26 to 30 September we profited from this to form a convoy of wounded and crippled men, who were sent back to Moscow by the direct route we'd just reached.'

Pakra, when the Russians' withdrawal and the reconstruction of bridges over its two rivers enable the Lancer Brigade to reach it at Murat's heels, turns out to justify its name:

'The river flowed gracefully through a verdant valley, at the foot of steep and wooded heights, crowned by a redoubt of considerable appearance. This valley's picturesque aspect and the banks running along the other side were further embellished by the village of Gorki, flanking the river and forming, for once, a group of pretty dwellings, made to look like English cottages, surrounded by greenery and flowers.'

Advancing again, Dumonceau realizes how inadequate Murat's force really is to stand up to the entire Russian army:

'The 1st, 2nd and 4th Cavalry Corps were all no little enfeebled in comparison with their original strength. There was all too little infantry to oppose the entire Russian army.'

But Kutusov has his plan. Dictated neither by demoralization nor enfeeblement, it's to fall back on to an entrenched position in front of the village of Tarutino.[9] On 4 October, pushing on through woods, the light cavalry of Murat's advance guard are 'totally routed', for lack of infantry to support them, and lose about 100 men. Later that day they run into a long line of Russian artillery, supported by Cossacks and any amount of regular cavalry. Wilson:

'The cannonade recommenced about noon, and the French cavalry fell into a Cossack ambuscade – 500 were killed and 180 made prisoners. It was a very gallant affair, most ably conducted.'

And Tascher: 'Our guns retire for lack of ammunition; the lines of cuirassiers advance. All the regiments reduced to 4, 3 or 2 troops; my company has 5 chasseurs. The Russians are burning [villages and crops] again.'

It must be in the midst of this affair that Captain *Victor Dupuy* of the 7th Hussars returns delighted to his own regiment. For many weeks now he's been serving as ADC to his brigade general Jacquinot. But only yesterday he'd been summoned to the 7th Hussars' regimental headquarters, to receive his commission as chef d'escadron. It's under appropriate but utterly exceptional circumstances he's confirmed in his command:

'We were advancing. The enemy soon put in an appearance and put up a more serious resistance than usual. He was supported by a numerous artillery, which inflicted some losses on us. At the moment when it was playing most strongly, Colonel Eulner had me formally recognized in my new rank in front of the regiment, drawn up in line of battle. Never was a reception accompanied by such noisy music! The colonel could hardly make himself heard! For the rest, I was glad to see the end of the ceremony. It would have been cruel to get a cannonball in one's back while it was going on.'

But Bruyères' once magnificent light cavalry division – which had fought at Borodino with barely 1,000 troopers, and which the 7th Hussars belong to – is now down to a mere 400 horses. Yet it has to chase the Russians off the plain beyond a deep ravine. That night it's Dupuy's business to place the outposts and liaise to his left with Sébastiani's light cavalry division – it too, once 3,500 strong, but down to a 'few hundred'. The night's so dark he doesn't manage it.

On a slope down to a lake lies the village of Winkovo. That night Griois and Jumilhac settle in among its ruined timber cottages, 'the first we found vacant', in the lower part of the village, near the lake. Among the miseries of Griois' situation is a minor yet extraordinary one. Earlier, arriving at one of his bivouacs, he's dropped a glove,

'and neither I nor my orderly had been able to get it back out of the mud my horse's foot had trampled it into. This loss, so light in any other circumstance, was for me a very cruel one. I would have no chance to make it good, and throughout the retreat I'd only have one glove. I remember, too, that by a sort of superstitious presentiment I regarded being unable to find this object I'd just seen fall at my horse's feet as a nasty augury of what was to come.'

Though their cottage, like all the others, has only 'one room with a chimney-less stove and several sheds open to all the winds' it does have 'rather a vast courtyard, with shelter for our horses'. Unfortunately, hardly have Jumilhac and Griois lain down to sleep than the building goes up in flames. So do four or five of its neighbours. After vain attempts to put the fire out, the two artillery colonels – the one so culture loving, the other such witty company among his fellow-officers but, in Griois' view, too hard on the rank and file – have no option but to gather up their 'few effects and, laden with saddles, portmanteaux, etc., evacuate our terrified horses'. Outside, in an ocean of mud, they hold a 'sort of council of war' while their orderly officers try to find them some other dwelling. At last one is found in the higher part of the village, and they, 'with a loaf or two of munition bread, already items of luxury', bribe some soldiers to evacuate it. But when this habitation too goes up in flames, they finally settle, most uncomfortably, in a cottage at some distance from the village.

And there, in the wide plain between Winkovo and Kutusov's entrenched camp at Tarutino, the ever-dwindling regiments of Murat's once magnificent cavalry command are going to stay – and starve – until the Russians choose to turn them out of it.

But Colbert's lancers have remained in the rear, at the Woronowo ravine, together with General Friedrichs' infantry division, 'facing a fine big farm of red brick, with two storeys, occupied by the Duke of Istria's staff'.

CHAPTER 5

SETTLING IN FOR THE WINTER?

The pleasures of Moscow – 'a foetid stench impregnates our clothes' – stealing one's enemy's mustard pot – a masquerade – why doesn't the Tsar make peace? – Murat brought to a standstill – Lauriston's baffling mission – 'they'll light bonfires in Petersburg'

'The fire having died down,' writes Boulart, 'we began to enjoy the pleasures of Moscow, i.e., its palaces and what they had to offer.' Does he sometimes play his flute to while away the hours? Or Captain *H. F. Biot*, ADC to the wounded General Pajol, his violin? If so they say nothing about it. 'We had no linen and very little crockery,' Boulart goes on, 'but at the servant's suggestion I had a hole made in a freshly plastered wall and behind it we found prodigious quantities of china, glasses, kitchen utensils, vinegar and mustard, the best China tea and some table linen. In another corner, also walled up, I found a fine library. I shared my riches with my comrades and even some generals. My house became the meeting place for those less fortunate than ourselves who loved good meat and wine. Yet the days passed drearily. We had no other sources of distraction than our libraries, and no one is really tempted to read books who has such reasons for disquietude as we had.'

The shattered city offers other consolations than cultural or culinary ones. Its blackened ruins swarm with prostitutes, by no means all of whom, alas, are professionals. 'Nearly dying of hunger', other wretched women are being

'obliged to surrender themselves at discretion to the first comers. In every house still standing one saw nobody but these creatures, who'd installed themselves as if they owned them. They took possession of ladies' ornaments and in payment for their own favours – often very bitter ones – accepted as presents rich dresses the army had pillaged, and silver bullion.'

It's the wreckage of a world. Walking through the smouldering streets, Major *L-J. Vionnet* of the Fusiliers-Grenadiers of the Middle Guard – Bourgogne's regiment – keeps on coming across 'old men in tears at this appalling disorder'. Everywhere there are great open spaces. But visibility is poor and everything is veiled by a blue haze from the smoke of bivouac fires. Sent from Mojaisk to fetch supplies for Junot's VIII Corps, which is supposed to be looking after the Borodino wounded, a Westphalian bandmaster finds 'all the streets full of French soldiers, who'd lit huge fires beside their pyramids of stacked muskets. A regular camp life had developed. The Frenchmen greeted us in a very friendly way, often calling out to me "Long live the good army of Westphalia! Long live King Jérôme Napoleon!"'

Never has Friedrich Klinkhardt, in a lifetime devoted to teaching his musicians to play the Napoleonic armies' (to our ears) rather dumpy march tunes, even imagined such chaos:

'Here a soldier was holding forth to a circle of attentive listeners. There an affair of honour was being fought out. Now a band played tunes. Now one saw senior officers strolling arm in arm down the streets. Beaming faces looked out from windows of palaces, and some pretty women even nodded to us. Everything was full of life and bustle.'

This in the western, unburned district. But as Klinkhardt comes nearer to the Kremlin and the devastation around it, he and his comrades see 'smoking ruins in which every gust of wind was fanning a bright red flame. Choking smoke was blowing in from all directions.' 'The whole time we were in Moscow,' writes the cavalry surgeon Dr. *Réné Bourgeois,*

'the ashes never ceased smoking and were forever lighting up again from time to time in various places. Truly terrifying phosphoric flames came from amidst these vast ruins. We seemed surrounded by the lava of a scarcely extinct volcano which at every moment threatened to erupt again.'

'So here we are,' Césare de Laugier has written in his diary on 25 September,

'amidst smoking ruins, walls that at each moment threaten to collapse, half-burnt trees. The numerous sign-posts marking the limits of the various districts produce the effect of isolated columns or cenotaphs in a vast cemetery. The mass of ashes exhales a foetid stench that impregnates our clothes. No one knows where the Russian army is, or what it's up to; only that Murat and Bessières, with the Guard cavalry, have been sent to look for it. The most varied rumours are going the rounds.'

Amidst Moscow's blackened skeleton of log-paved streets, its huge but mostly gutted palaces, its great gardens, its vast parks, its churches and its cathedral with nine gilded towers, one pleasure which costs nothing is to go sightseeing. A visit to the ancient palace of the tsars and old patriarchs, standing up starkly on its high ground and within its deep ditch and behind high crenellated walls set with cannon, with its arsenal and six churches, is *de rigueur,* a 'must'. To many who, like Boulart, can only relish the neo-classical style, its architecture which

'has nothing regular about it, says nothing. The Ivan Tower, built beside the cathedral, is remarkable for its dome and the immense silver [sic] cross which surmounts it. At its foot and quite close to this tower, we see, deep in the ground, the biggest bell ever cast, weighing, so we're told, 160,000 kilos.'
Twenty-eight inches thick, it has fallen when the beams supporting it caught fire. The Kremlin's superb crypt 'where one sees the tombs of the tsars', though pillaged, also appeals to sightseers.

The Poles, particularly, are relishing the sweets of revenge. For them it's an important bicentenary – in 1611, after brilliant victories, their ancestors had occupied the Kremlin, but been forced to retreat, leaving their garrison to be massacred. Hasn't Russia within living memory always intervened in the affairs of Poland, and always disastrously? Hasn't she, by inflaming their own internal conflicts, scotched every attempt to update and modernize their grotesquely feudal system, where any landowner can veto any reform? And in the end, though defeated in several pitched battles, participated in the country's successive partitionings and, in 1794, massacred part of the population of Warsaw?[1] One Pole who's taking a special delight in Moscow's occupation – even its destruction – is Captain *Josef Zalusky* of the 1st Guard Lancers. While the Lancer Brigade had been stationed out on the Kaluga road he'd

'as soon as possible got permission from General Krasinski, who was in Moscow in attendance on the Emperor, and gone into this capital where, with pain, it's true, but with even more animosity, I walked about the burnt streets, recognizing there this people who have spread so many fires on our land, from the Baltic to the Tatra Mountains, from the Black Sea to beyond the Vistula, even into Pomerania! Reaching the Moscova bridge beneath the Kremlin, I halted at this point whence the eye embraces so wide a view, and thought how my compatriots, Dmitri's companions, had been executed, and that it was the [bi]centenary of 1612. Thinking also of the Prague Massacres, I told myself "the shade of Jasinski is avenged! From the victims' tomb we can expunge the inscription Exoriare aliquis nostris ex ossibus ultor."'[2]

In the Kremlin the immensely wealthy Polish aristocrat Dominique Radziwill, 'who was, or was soon going to be, a major in our regiment',[3] has found his ancestor's sword. 'Glass in hand' Zalusky and Krasinski examine it 'with emotion'. And more than by the Kremlin's granite hall, its arsenal or ancient churches, Zalusky's impressed by the 'rows of Polish culverins and cannon, stamped with the coats of arms of the Polish kingdom and of various Polish families'.[4] Being a count and a Guards officer, he's given lodgings, 'not in a palace, but in a very comfortable house belonging to a certain Soltykow. Not merely had it not been pillaged, but nothing was lacking and I was treated perfectly by the dvorecki [major-domo]. Despite a courteous reception, I told him I was going to pillage his master's house, and was going to take the mustard pot to make myself a drinking glass out of it, and that I was also going to put the horn tobacco spoon into my pocket to serve me as a camp spoon; and that for his master's sake I hoped no one would pillage his house worse than that.'

Two appeals are made, in de Lesseps' name, on 1 and 6 October, to the legitimate inhabitants, promising them protection if only they'll return to their homes and occupations; and to the peasants to come and sell their produce at market. Both fall on stone-deaf ears. Not one shop is open. And above all there's a desperate shortage, above all, of tailors.

Not quite so desperate, however, in this grim realm of soot and ashes, as the lack of washerwomen. 'Of all the hardships of this campaign,' one officer had written during the long march from the Niemen, 'having to do our own laundry was one of the most humiliating.' Sergeant Bourgogne is therefore particularly delighted when, in an unexplored wing of the provisional guardhouse to which he's been committed for having saved his two tailors from the firing squad, he finds two women sitting on a sofa. With them, dead drunk, is one of the convicts Rostopchin had released with orders to burn down the city and who'd promptly been booted downstairs. The washerwomen – as they're immediately promoted to be – turn out to be no less fond of Danzig gin than Bourgogne himself:

'I stayed for some time with these two sisters, and then returned to my room. I found there an NCO of my company, who'd been waiting for me a long time. When I told him of my adventures he seemed delighted, as he could find no one to wash his clothes.'

Keeping it a secret until 10 p.m., an hour by which everyone else is asleep, Bourgogne and the NCO, who 'seemed to think the two Muscovite ladies would be only too honoured by being asked to wash and mend for French soldiers', together with their sergeant-major, go and fetch them:

'At first, not quite knowing where we were taking them, they made a lot of difficulties, but made me understand I was to go with them. I went to our quarters, where they followed us willingly, laughing as they went. We found a small room free, which we made over to them, furnishing it with whatever we could find – all kinds of pretty things the noble ladies of Moscow hadn't been able to carry away. In this way our friends, though they seemed to be common servants, were transformed into elegant ladies – ladies, however, who had to wash and mend for us.'

Bourgogne hears a 'loud report of firearms' – several convicts and members of the police have just been shot. But his two Swiss tailors, father and son, have been released, and he finds them busy at work

'making some capes out of the cloth off the billiard tables we'd taken to pieces. I went into the room where we'd left our women, and found them at the wash tub and – not surprisingly, being dressed up as baronesses – making a very poor job of it. For want of anything better we had to make do with them.

Dancing is another, if exceptional pleasure. The NCOs of the Fusiliers-Grenadiers organize a ball –

'a real carnival, as we were all disguised. First of all we dressed up the women as French marquises. As they knew nothing of such matters, Flament and I superintended their toilette. Our two Russian tailors were dressed out as Chinese, I as a Russian boyar, Flament as a marquis. Even our *cantinière*, Mother Dubois, wore a beautiful Russian national dress. As we had no wigs for our marquises, the regimental wigmaker dressed their hair. For grease he used suet, and flour for powder. They looked splendid, and when everyone was ready we began to dance.'

They've all been imbibing a lot of punch.

'For music we had a flute played by a sergeant-major, accompanied by the drum to keep time. As the music struck up and Mother Dubois advanced with our quartermaster, our marquises, excited no doubt by the music, began jumping about like Tartars, flying from right to left, swinging their arms and legs about, falling over backwards, getting up, only to fall over again. They seemed to be possessed by the devil. If they'd been wearing their Russian clothes there wouldn't have been anything very extraordinary about it. But to see two French marquises jumping about like lunatics made us nearly die with laughter, and the flautist was obliged to stop playing, the drum filling up the pauses by sounding the attack.'

After the ball is over, Mother Dubois, in her lavish costume – she's perfectly well aware of its value – fails to be recognized by a sergeant of the guard on police duty:

'Seeing a strange lady in the street so early, and thinking he'd found a prize, he went up to her, and tried to take her by the arm and lead her to his room. But Mother Dubois, who had a husband, and moreover had drunk a good deal of punch, dealt the sergeant such a vigorous blow on the face that she knocked him right over. The sergeant was so furious we had our work cut out to din into his head that he mustn't arrest such a woman as Mother Dubois.'

All this is only part of a still vaster masquerade. Though soon in the ninth month of pregnancy, Mother Dubois never walks abroad except in a dress of silver lamé. Another of Bourgogne's comrades appears in the costume of a gentleman from the days of Louis XV.[5] Rummaging in aristocratic cupboards, thousands of men, both veterans and conscripts, many of whom had 'never heard of coffee or white bread except by report' until they'd been conscripted, are decking themselves out fantastically in the contents of the city's surviving palaces.

The rest of the day that Sergeant Bourgogne had set his 'marquises' to work at the washtub he'd been 'busy arranging our quarters and getting in provisions, as it seemed we were to be staying here for some time.' If Major Boulart, too, like Caulaincourt, like everyone else, is

'collecting furniture and all sorts of things abandoned in the city which might come in handy for our domestic arrangements,'
and in general acting as if sure he'll 'have to pass the eight months in Moscow that must elapse before spring,' it's because that's exactly the intended impression Napoleon is giving at the dinners he's inviting his generals to after the daily 1 o'clock Kremlin parades. All his talk is of his glowing prospects; and of the "60,000 Polish Cossacks" which Abbé *D-G.F. Pradt*, his plenipotentiary ambassador in Warsaw, will shortly be sending him:

'He attributed all his difficulties simply to the trouble caused by the Cossacks, for, he insisted, he had more than enough troops to fight off Kutusov and go wherever he wanted to. The rigours of winter, the total lack of precautions against cold, etc., didn't enter into his calculations.'
To stay the winter in Moscow, Berthier and Duroc are now convinced, 'was his favourite idea'. Even Caulaincourt, though sceptical at first and rather sure that all this table talk about wintering in Moscow is

'affected, and merely due to his wish to give a turn to public opinion, to ensure the collection of provisions, and, above all, to support the overture he'd made,'
for a week and more has been listening to

'the Emperor in his intimate circle conversing, acting and issuing orders, all on the presumption that he was going to stay in Moscow.'
Now he's beginning to wonder whether the Emperor doesn't mean what he says,

'and for some time even those most closely in his confidence entertained no doubts on that score. Seeing the season so far advanced without any preparations made for our departure, I too ended by doubting whether we'd evacuate Moscow voluntarily. It seemed to me impossible the Emperor would even think of a retreat when the frost set in, especially as no measures had been taken to protect the men nor any steps taken to enable the horses to cross the ice.'

Even Count Daru, the most experienced, the most loyal and the most indefatigable of all Napoleon's administrators – a man who'd once promised to obey his orders providing he'd always be allowed to speak his mind freely – though at first he'd supported Napoleon's idea of marching northwards 'beyond the 55th parallel' and attacking Petersburg, is now advising him to settle in. Or, alternatively, leave only a strong garrison in Moscow and establish himself at Kaluga, key to the Ukraine, with its milder climate and its vast grain resources. But all the time Napoleon is discussing his plan

'in such positive terms that the most incredulous among us ended by believing he intended to carry it out. Even the Grand Marshal and the Prince of Neuchâtel seemed convinced we'd be staying in Moscow. Everyone was laying plans accordingly.'

And the message is really getting through. Even Césare de Laugier, though on 25 September he'd been struck by 'an outbreak of general rejoicing just caused by orders to leave on 28 September,' is noting that

'the instructions we keep getting seem to indicate that the Emperor intends to spend the winter here, or in the surroundings. The heads of the units have been ordered to provide them with food for six months.'

But why, above all, isn't the Tsar ready to make peace? At Petersburg, to judge by news that's come in, the burning of Russia's 'old' capital has unleashed panic. Even the crown jewels have been put aboard a ship, ready to sail for London. 'On 22 or 23 September,' Napoleon sends for Caulaincourt:

'The Emperor, who for a long time hadn't discussed affairs with me, asked me whether I thought the Tsar would be disposed to make peace if overtures were made to him. I replied frankly that it seemed to me the sacrifice of Moscow argued a far from pacific disposition. It was scarcely probable he'd have set fire to his capital with the intention of signing a peace among the ruins.'

This, while he'd been out at Petrovskoï watching the holocaust, had in fact been Napoleon's own spontaneous reaction. How then has he come to convince himself of the opposite?

Now Napoleon wants to send Caulaincourt to the Tsar, with whom he'd been on such friendly terms, during the four years when he'd been French ambassador to Russia.[6]

'"Will you go to Petersburg?" the Emperor asked me. "You'd see the Tsar. I'd entrust you with a letter, and you'd make peace."'

But Caulaincourt's a man (according to Ségur and others) 'more capable of obstinacy than flattery, endured rather than listened to, and sincere to the point of giving offence'. And he declines:

"It'd be useless to send me on such a mission. I shouldn't even be received." Assuming a jocular and kindly air, the Emperor told me I didn't know what I was talking about: "That fire was the sort of folly a madman might boast of when he kindled the flame, but repent of next day.'"

The Tsar will be all the keener to seize this chance, he goes on, reverting to a notion he'd already entertained even before leaving Paris because his nobles, "ruined by this war and the fire, desire peace. The Emperor Alexander is stubborn. He'll regret it. Never again will he obtain such easy terms from me as I'd have made now. He's done himself so much harm by burning his towns and his capital that there's nothing more I'd have asked of him." All he'll have to do is to impound British shipping. Or if there's a misunderstanding on that point, and the Tsar thinks he, Napoleon, wants to retain Lithuania, he's wrong. He doesn't.

At this Caulaincourt, no doubt remembering the Tsar's words to himself and to Narbonne,[7] says that Alexander won't make peace until the soil of Russia has been evacuated. Even to go and see Kutusov at Tarutino will be useless.

Whereat Napoleon, 'turning abruptly on his heel':

"Very well, I'll send Lauriston. He shall have the honour of making peace and saving your friend Alexander's crown for him."

But what if he won't make peace? Then, Napoleon confides uneasily to Fain in the privacy of his cabinet, the Grand Army will be like "a ship frozen in by the ice. Anyway, Alexander won't let me go so far. We'll come to an understanding, and he'll sign a peace treaty."

Will he? Caulaincourt's scepticism, if better informed than most people's, is by no means unique. Even Paymaster Peyrusse, ingratiating himself with Daru in the Kremlin, is writing home to a friend: 'How can we count on a peace with a people who've nothing to lose, who've chosen to lose everything to save everything?'

A certain Major Fribler of the 85th Line, also has no such illusions. One day before they'd moved to the Kaluga road, he and Le Roy had sat together discussing peace prospects:

"'Ma foi,'" said Fribler, "you who frequent the staffs[8] ought to know more about what's going on than I do. But from the system the enemy has adopted since the campaign opened and which he's persevered in of destroying everything in passing, I think we'll never be able to negotiate with him, not after such a sacrifice, which I regard as a national effort and an act of patriotic virtue. You've too much common sense, my dear major, not to see the trap we've fallen into. He's trying to lure us as far as he can from our reserves, while waiting for the winter. If we're forced to retire by the same road as we've come by, what will it offer us? What to do with an army weakened to less than half its strength, its cavalry exhausted and soon on foot? From all of which I conclude we should retire as quickly as ever we can, having extracted from this town everything we can carry.'"

The portly major had replied uneasily that the Emperor doubtless knows what he's about; but agreed that eight more days in Moscow would suffice. This has been Berthier's opinion from the outset. And Narbonne, at Napoleon's behest daily visiting his wounded fellow-ADC Rapp to inquire after his health, is of the same opinion – and repeats it to his young secretary *A. F. Villemain* – that the Russians, so far from wanting to make peace, are 'entertaining us with pretty talk, so as more easily to prepare the revenge and make it so much the more certain'. Lariboisière, too, goes so far as to tell Planat de la Faye 'during the first fortnight of our stay in Moscow: "If we stay here another fortnight our return to France is really at risk."' Hadn't that been Napoleon's own spontaneous opinion? Hadn't Fain, that first morning out at Petrovskoï, heard him talk of letting the army rest up for a few days and then marching on Petersburg?

Despite the valuable fortnight which has gone by, the option still seems open to him. And around the turn of the month he tells Duroc, who's more of a yes-man than the all-too candid Caulaincourt: 'Moscow's a bad position. We should only stay here long enough to reorganize.'

On October 3, after a sleepless night, he presents the Petersburg scheme to Eugène, Berthier, Bessières and Davout:

"We must burn what's left of Moscow, march via Tver on Petersburg, where Macdonald[9] will come to reinforce us, while the Viceroy and the Prince of Eckmühl secure the vanguard."

Only Eugène, Fain notes, approves of this idea, of which Daru had earlier approved, of marching northwards 'beyond the 55th parallel, attacking Petersburg and so ending the war'. Davout and Berthier, for their part, stress the dangers of such a long march. The intervening country is difficult, often swampy. And they'll have Kutusov and the main Russian army at their heels; all just as winter – the dreaded Russian winter – comes on. That winter which will soon be here.

So the scheme's dropped. Perhaps he hasn't seriously entertained it anyway?

Next day he sends for another of his ADCs, General Lauriston.

Like Caulaincourt, whose successor he'd been at the Petersburg embassy, Lauriston is an aristocrat, of Scottish extraction. A marquis of the *ancien régime*, at the Brienne military school before the Revolution he'd got to know a certain pale-faced lanky-haired Corsican cadet with the uncouth name of Napoleone Buonaparte. Though Lauriston and Caulaincourt don't like each other they're agreed on the futility of making approaches to the Tsar. And Lauriston, too, says he has no taste for such a mission. In his view the army ought to retreat forthwith, via Mojaisk.

"I like simple plans," Napoleon replies. "And the less tortuous a path is the better I like it. But there's one path I won't set foot on again unless peace is signed. And that's the one I've come by."

With these words, without further discussion, he hands Lauriston a letter to the Tsar, and orders him to go to Murat's headquarters, see Kutusov, and obtain a safe conduct:

"I want peace. I must have it. I want it at all costs, providing only our honour is saved."

Already an order has been sent off to Murat, to write to Kutusov as follows:
'It being the Emperor's intention to send one of his ADCs to General-in-Chief Kutusov, he wishes to know the day and hour when, and the place at which, the general is willing to receive him.'
And next morning (5 October) Lauriston's carriage 'accompanied by a numerous suite' rolls out through the Kremlin's vaulted gateway, bound for Winkovo. *En route* it passes through the neighbourhood of the village of Woronowo, where the Guard Lancer Brigade, after various manoeuvrings on Murat's right flank and rear in the Podolsk region, has just arrived. Captain Zalusky and his fellow Poles of the 1st Guard Lancers
'with surprise and regret see him pass through on his way to Kutusov.
In our eyes Napoleon was compromising himself by showing a wish, and thereby his need, for peace, and by extending his stay in Moscow ever longer, hoping for a treaty.'
(But Napoleon can't care less what the Poles think. He's quite prepared to sacrifice them anyway; and has been, since the campaign opened.)[10]

Lauriston's carriage and its entourage rolls splashing down Winkovo's single muddy street. He alights, presents his credentials to Murat and explains his errand – which is certainly very much to Murat's liking. He's never wanted any part of this war anyway; his sole desire is to get back to Naples and his family as quickly as possible. Then Lauriston orders his coachman to drive him to the Russian outposts, and there, under a flag of truce, requests permission for one of his ADCs to present himself at Kutusov's headquarters.

To Wilson's fury, Kutusov, despite his orders from the Tsar – the strictest possible – to have no parleying whatever with the enemy, promptly agrees to meet Lauriston. Not at his headquarters, admittedly. But between the outposts. Wilson, not trusting Kutusov an inch, protests vehemently. And Kutusov, aware that the British general is in personal contact with the Tsar, hastily changes his tune and sends Prince Volkonsky, one of Alexander's own ADCs, instead. This, from Lauriston's point of view, isn't good enough. Refusing even to speak to Volkonsky, he orders his coachman to turn around and drive back to Murat's headquarters.

But Kutusov has other critics and enemies besides Wilson – his headquarters is a hotbed of intrigue and dissension. One such critic and dissenter to the Field Marshal's policies is General Bennigsen, his own chief-of-staff. And that day, Bennigsen, hearing that the King of Naples is at the outposts, has come out to meet him:

'The conversation was very insignificant, Murat's principal remark being "This is no climate for a King of Naples."; but the appearance was pernicious and any unnecessary address of these invaders as a sovereign a wilful piece of base behaviour,'

thinks Wilson. Finally it's agreed that Lauriston shall be received this evening at Kutusov's headquarters, three miles behind the Russian lines. Strictest etiquette is to be observed. And in fact Lauriston gets a firm but most ambiguous reception. At first, Wilson's British uniform doubtless stressing the political aspect, both Volkonsky and Wilson are ostentatiously present 'in council'. After which they both withdraw to the next room, where they wait while Kutusov – devious as can be – and Lauriston – brisk and businesslike – have a private but 'very animated' conversation.

First Lauriston (according to what Kutusov will tell them as soon as it's over) complains of the barbarities being committed by the Russians towards the invaders.

'"Must this strange war," he asks, "this unique war, last for ever? My master has a sincere desire to end this dispute between two great and generous nations and to end it for ever." To this the Marshal answered, that he had no instruction on that point, nor did he wish to communicate any of this to the Tsar, and that he'd be "cursed by posterity if I were to be thought the prime mover of any kind of settlement, such is my nation's present frame of mind."'

As for acts of barbarity, he can't "civilize a nation in three months who regarded the enemy as a marauding force of Tartars under a Genghis Khan."

"But at least there's some difference!"

Lauriston comes back, much upset by the comparison:

"In fact there may be, but none in the eyes of the people: I can only answer for my own troops."

'General Lauriston,' Wilson goes on, 'had no complaint to make against them. He then adverted to an armistice, saying that "Nature herself would, in a short time, oblige it." The Marshal said he had no authority on that head.'

To this Lauriston again ripostes: "You must not think it's because our affairs are desperate. Our two armies are about equal. You are nearer your supplies and reinforcements than we are, but we also have reinforcements."'

He admits that Napoleon's Spanish affairs are just now going badly – as a result of Marmont's stupidities at Salamanca Madrid is temporarily in British hands,[11]

"Doubtless Sir Robert Wilson has his reasons for exaggerating things." Kutusov denies it. But Lauriston persists:

"But numerous corps which are on the march to those countries will soon change the state of affairs. Do not think, Sir, that we're reduced to extremity. Our armies are equally strong. True, you're closer to your reinforcements. But we too are receiving them."

As for the burning of Moscow, it had been "so inconsistent with the French character, that if we take London we shan't set fire to that city".

With these optimistic words Lauriston hands Kutusov Napoleon's letter. Hardly even glancing at it with his one good eye, Kutusov lays it aside on the table. Only at Lauriston's urging does he pick it up again and skim through its contents. Being addressed to the Tsar, he consents to forward it to Petersburg, while pointing out that some time – indeed quite a lot of time – must necessarily go by before an answer can arrive. After half an hour more of talk Lauriston, speaking 'in such a manner that every person was satisfied he'd been disappointed,' takes his leave.

From Wilson's point of view it's Bennigsen's intervention in Lauriston's mission that has spoilt the outcome. According to Murat's 38-year-old Neapolitan ADC Colonel *M-J-T. Rossetti*, too, it had been Bennigsen who'd

'asked for a negotiation and proposed an armistice, which was accepted, the only condition being to give each other twelve hours' warning before resuming hostilities.'

Although Kutusov swears to Wilson on his honour that there's no 'convention' between him and Murat, all firing suddenly and mysteriously ceases. And discussions – what Tascher calls in his diary 'a battle of politenesses between the French and Russian generals, Bennigsen, Kutusov, Minevalovitsch [*sic*]' – follow and continue into the next day.

Naturally all ranks have been eagerly discussing the mission's purpose, which is quickly assumed to be identical with its outcome. As Lauriston sets off for Moscow, Griois, like everyone else, hears that

'a sort of armistice has been agreed, not to be broken without giving each other several hours' warning. For the rest, it was purely local, and didn't extend either on the flanks or the rear of our position. The news spread in our bivouacs and there was general rejoicing. Together Jumilhac and I drained the last bottle of wine we still possessed and had been keeping for some great occasion.'

Among the Lancer Brigade, guarding the Kaluga road twelve miles to Murat's rear, the armistice gives rise to

'various comments, among others to a renewed supposition that peace was near. At all events the immediate consequences were a kind of tacit suspension of hostilities. Each side avoided the other and seemed no longer to wish to get into a fight – '

precisely the result desired, of course, by Kutusov. When one's enemy is gravely short of food and desperate for forage, what's the point of fighting?

But back at the Kremlin Lauriston gives a much more glowing report on his mission than its outcome warrants. And a delighted Emperor exclaims: "When they get my letter in Petersburg they'll light bonfires."

As for his letter, Kutusov forwards a copy of it to the Tsar, with a recommendation that it shall not be answered.

Chapter 6

MARAUDING PARTIES

No hay or straw – Le Roy commands a marauding party – 'every day the circle's being drawn tighter' – Césare de Laugier meets the locals – 'I asked him politely in Latin' – Paul de Bourgoing fights his way out – Ney's reconnaissance in force

Nor is it only Murat's men who are short of essentials. In a Moscow stuffed with tea and coffee, jams and liqueurs, bread and – above all – hay have quickly become rarities. Writing home around the turn of the month (but his letter will be captured by Cossacks) a French NCO tells his sister that 'the horses are gnawing at their mangers for lack of it'. Even a general of brigade like Dedem, nursing his bruised chest in his mill on the outskirts, can't

'get a sack of oats without a permit from the Quartermaster-General, and that was hard to obtain. Only hay and straw were lacking. The Prince of Neuchâtel himself was sending out to the villages to get some.'

Where has it all gone to? Evidently Daru is doing his job of getting in stocks for the winter only too well. By no means all the villagers have fled,

'probably because flight had presented greater difficulties, there being so many of them and the environs of Moscow being so densely populated. Perhaps also because some who'd meant to flee hadn't been able to because the French army, as soon as it had taken possession of Moscow, had spread out in all directions. Finally, it's possible that, being more affluent, they'd found it hard to abandon home and hearth.'

Whether the analysis of the artillery officer, the Marquis *de Chambray*, is right or not, when Dedem sends a sergeant and some men to get him some eggs, chickens, etc., with strict orders to pay for them, 'taking' only some hay, the peasants beg the soldiers to make haste, for fear of the Cossacks; who treat them as an inferior species.

These are everywhere in the town's environs. The very first day after settling at Petrovskoï, Laugier had seen them hovering only a few hundred yards away, waiting to pounce on anyone who strayed from the Italian camp. At dawn on 21 September, notwithstanding Le Roy's well-posted sentries,

'the Guard Chasseurs who'd gone reconnoitring were driven back at the double by enemy cavalry as far as the houses where I'd stationed my two companies. Being under arms, they opened fire and shot down three Cossack regulars. But that didn't mean a dozen of our men weren't stabbed by these gentlemen's lances.'[1]

Dedem makes a pact with the local priest, allowing him to go on ringing his church bell provided his parishioners supply him with necessaries, but the men of the 4th Line, bivouacked with the rest of Ney's III Corps to the west of the city, have all this time been

'so short of almost everything, and only with difficulty managing to get hold of black bread and beer, that strong detachments were having to be sent out to seize cattle in the woods where the peasants had taken refuge, and yet often returning empty-handed. Such was the supposed abundance from the looting. Though the men were covering themselves with furs, they soon no longer had clothes or shoes. In short, with diamonds, precious stones and every imaginable luxury, we were on the verge of starving to death.'

This being the state of affairs, marauding parties are the only solution, not always a very successful one. Simple at first, they've soon become exceedingly problematic:

'Our outposts extended hardly two days' march beyond the town. The Emperor could get no certain information on the Russian army's position. The Russians, on the contrary, were informed about every movement we made; and few days passed without our hearing painful news of their having carried off such or such a battalion, such or such a squadron, sent out to protect our marauders searching for food,'

writes Fezensac. At Davout's headquarters in the monastery at the Doroghomilov Gate his reluctant chief-of-staff General Baron *L.-F. Lejeune* – that future painter of elegant and colourful battle scenes – is daily having to organize ever stronger expeditions. On 17 September, while the fire had still been raging, one of his subordinates had sighted 'a herd of cattle, hidden in a marsh between two forests ten miles away'. And instantly orders had come to Le Roy[2] to take a mixed detachment from the 85th Line and go and grab it. At blush of dawn next day, with a soldier to guide his party, he'd set off:

'At 9 a.m. we got to the edge of the marsh. I had it searched by two detachments of 50 men each and two officers who, each following his own side of it, were to join up at the other side. In the event of their seeing the herd or meeting with any resistance they were to warn me by firing shots or by beat of drum.'

While the remainder of his detachment rests, Le Roy goes up to a nearby isolated church, 200 yards to his right, between himself and the Moskova, and sees, about five miles away on the left bank, in the direction of the city, several foraging horsemen who're returning at a brisk canter, apparently pursued. On his own thickly wooded and deeply ravined river bank he can see nothing. Yet the existence of a church seems to indicate a number of small communities. By and by a Russian peasant appears, but doesn't notice him; and at the same moment a drum roll tells him someone – or something – has been captured without resistance. Half an hour later the head of a very variegated herd of animals appears – oxen, cows, little ponies, sheep and pigs. 'Having massed them together, we set out to our left and followed a track which the livestock seemed to follow of their own accord.' Sure enough, it leads to a village by the river, and into the court-yard of a 'pretty château no Frenchman from the Army had as yet visited'. Deciding to halt for a couple of hours to rest his men, he notes that he's now about seven and a half miles from his camp. He's just starting to count the captured herd when his son, a sergeant in the 85th, brings him one of the château's inhabitants.

'He'd arrested him just as I, together with three others, was getting out of a ferry. He tells the major he has evacuated his family to anoth-er of his properties and has come to see whether the invaders have any knowledge of it, and if not, to rescue some of his possessions. "Monsieur," I told him, [says Le Roy pompously, stretching truth fur-ther than it was ever stretched before] "The French soldier only makes war on armed men. You have nothing to fear. And if all Rus-sians had done as you have, the countryside our army has passed through wouldn't have been ravaged."'

With these words he sends off 50 men to explore the other part of the vil-lage on the far bank of the river, which laps the edge of the château's gar-den. Muskets and lances have been found in the village – the former of Russian manufacture, the latter simply long rods with a long nail or knife blade at the end, the kind the Cossacks are using:

'I assumed they belonged to peasants who were being incited to rise against us, and that the persons we'd just arrested were leading the insurrection. I tacitly decided to take these gentlemen to Moscow: and, what strengthened me in this resolution, two of them seemed to be disguised Russian officers. The elder was about forty, the youngest about twenty. They were wearing French-style tail-coats, hussar-style boots with spurs, had little moustaches and round hats. The other individual had a serious air, a malicious eye, and the muscles in his face never stopped twitching. He was dressed like the first ones, in French clothes, a furred cap, big and roomy trousers strapped under-foot. I was going to question them when the master arrived. I was astonished to hear him speak Russian to the fellow with the sinister face and to hold his cap in his hand, while the other didn't take his hat off. His son said: "This gentleman has just had a meal prepared and we've stewed it up."'

And in fact the Russian invites all the detachment's officers to refreshment, 'apologizing for not being able to treat us as we deserved. He'd also provided beer for the men.' Le Roy – with his embonpoint, he's a man who relishes his victuals – thanks him and orders an officer to follow him to the table of a pretty room which seems to have lost half its furniture.

'There's an old cooked ham, a quarter of cold mutton and sausages, two dishes of dessert, wine and liqueurs. At first, having decided to leave in good time, I was loath to depart. But unable to resist our host's insistence I took my place at table opposite the eldest of them, and didn't lose sight of a single one of his movements. I kept an eye on him like a cat watches a mouse, without his noticing it; because the main door of the dining-room, which was behind him, had been left open and to all appearances I was watching what was going on down in the courtyard. So I had one eye on him and the other on the château's courtyard. Beside this man sat an old tippler of a captain of the 33rd Regiment, who got thoroughly tipsy. Next was the young man with the little moustaches, speaking German to his neighbour. Then another Russian, all of whose manners struck me as military. From time to time he looked at the man sitting opposite me and smiled.'

Le Roy also notices that the number of servants waiting on them is steadily growing. Some have moustaches, while others are bearded peasants. His neighbour tries to reassure him by saying they've come bringing more provisions in case the French would like to stay the night. At 4 p.m. Le Roy goes down into the courtyard and orders a captain of the 17th Light Infantry – his party, regrettably, has been taken from several regiments – to form an advance guard with the herd and not leave the road. Vodka in great bowls has been served to the men and by now many of them are drunk. Going back into the dining-room, Le Roy peremptorily asks the four Russians to be so good as to accompany him to Moscow. 'The poor devils seemed thunderstruck – and this confirmed me in my idea that they all spoke French.' He threatens to use force if they resist. 'The first young man asked if he could go into the next room and get his clothes. I consented, ordering the drunken captain to go with them.'

Now Le Roy assembles his detachment, meaning to place his four prisoners in the middle of it, and calls up to the officers he's left in the dining-room to bring these gentlemen, whether they like it or not.

'I was just about to mount my horse, when the sergeant of the Moscow outpost came and told me he'd seen a couple of groups higher up river, which some horsemen were fording. He was sure they were Cossacks. I was just going to go and see, when the officers came out of the château and approached me, laughing. They told me the Russians, having gone through several rooms, had asked the old drunk to wait for them while they went into the little room – saying they'd only be long enough to fetch their coats. Of course they'd escaped by another passage that lead out of it into the garden.'

Le Roy, furious, decides to ask permission to return next day with a battalion of his own regiment – the 85th – to search the château and capture its occupants. Guided by the flames and smoke of Moscow 'the detachment, having doubled its advance guard, returns to its encampment at 9 p.m. with its herd of cattle, sheep, pigs and ponies.'

But were those four Russians newcomers who'd come to fan the flames of an insurrection? Or were they in charge of one that's already been organized? He can't be sure. 'In either case the hidden weapons would have justified my arresting them,' he concludes. And the moral? 'Always prefer a detachment made up of men from your own company or regiment to ones supplied from different units.' But he'd accomplished his most important task: to get his lowing, mooing, bleating, neighing booty back to camp before nightfall. General Friedrichs comes and promises him a light cavalry escort and men from his own unit to return next day and wreak vengeance on the fugitives and their château,

'not because they'd run off, but for having assembled a lot of men strange to the village, as well as some soldiers. If I'd let myself be lulled by their fine promises what happened two days later to a detachment of the 108th regiment would have happened to me.'

Luckily, next day (19 September) he's suddenly ordered by Davout to take his battalion to the outskirts to support the Chasseurs of the Guard on the Kaluga road:

'"I'm sorry, my dear Le Roy", he said, "you can't go back to look for what you left behind out there either on the road or in the marsh. Soon we shan't have any meat, even for our sick and wounded. I'm going to send a detachment of 300 men from the 108th under a bright and efficient captain called Toubie."'

Le Roy hands over the livestock to his general's ADC, 'keeping only two pretty little Russian horses to carry my baggage'. But Toubie and his party aren't sufficiently on the *qui vive*, and are massacred.

As the days pass, then weeks, such marauding expeditions are having to range ever farther afield and be provided with ever heavier escorts. Far from responding to de Lesseps' appeal to 'come out from the woods where terror retains you' and sell their 'superfluous' produce to market, the peasants are (as Le Roy had suspected) forming themselves into efficient guerrilla bands. Hardly a day goes by without at least 300 French or Allied soldiers being snapped up by the Cossacks or by bands of guerrillas. 'The circle is daily being drawn tighter around us,' a French officer writes home,' – but his letter too is intercepted by the Cossacks:

'We've having to put 10,000 men with artillery into the field outside Moscow to forage, and still can't be sure of success unless we fight. The enemy is gaining the energy we're losing. Now audacity and confidence are on his side.'

A despondent General Gelichet, posted at a point some forty miles from the city, writes that every order he gets is only making him

'want to resign my command. As for the victuals you ask from me, the thing's impossible. The 33rd would be helping us out if it still had the horses killed the day before yesterday. As it is, it has only two head of cattle left.'

Even on 30 September Césare de Laugier has written in his diary that 'the colonels of the Royal Guard are taking turns with the Army of Italy's generals of brigade to direct and command such flying columns. The good and intrepid Colonel Moroni, the vélites' colonel, being more than once detailed off for this kind of job, I, by virtue of my rank, am having to go with him.' And goes on:

'So yesterday about 1,000 infantrymen, 200 troopers and two pieces of cannon were placed under Moroni's orders, to attempt a reconnaissance along the Tver road, as well as to protect numerous Saccomans' [Sacs-au-mains = bagmen] bringing with them carts and pack horses. The greater part of the villages we passed through were totally deserted, and had been searched from top to bottom by earlier reconnaissances. Between Czerraio-Griaz and Woskresensk, about 28 versts [20 miles] from Moscow, we'd reached the extreme limit of our earlier excursions. In the plain a few sparse villages and country houses which, albeit abandoned, were still completely intact and witnessed to the sudden flight of the inhabitants. There we camped for the night.'

The Italian vélites realise that they're in the presence of enemy troops. But at dawn they form two columns and pursue their way without troubling themselves:

'And in fact the enemy withdrew as we advanced. We passed through more villages without trouble, guaranteed as they were by the chain of posts set up by cavalry and infantry. The heat was excessive, and a magnificent forest spread out beyond the advanced posts to the right, where I was. Accompanied by some NCOs, I wanted to push on that far.'

But then something surprising happens:

'I'd only gone a few paces when I heard voices. Alone, I walked calmly over to the side the noise was coming from. There I saw through the trees, in the middle of the wood, a clearing where there was crowd of people, men and women of all ages and kinds. I came a few steps closer. They looked attentively at me, but without being either scared or surprised. Some men, whose manners and faces didn't augur any good to me, came toward me.'

The vélites' adjutant-major signs to them to keep their distance, but calls over

'the one of them I'd recognized as one of their priests. Then, using Latin, I asked him politely to tell me whether this was the population of the villages just now occupied by our troops. "We are", the pope replied gravely, after looking closely at me, "part of the unfortunate inhabitants of the Holy City whom you've reduced to the state of vagabonds, of paupers, of desperates, whom you've deprived of asylum and fatherland!" As he said this, tears ran down abundantly from his eyes. At that moment his companions began advancing with threatening gestures. The priest managed to calm them and ordered them back. Whereupon they remained at a certain distance, to hear what we were saying.'

The priest says he cannot conceive what 'barbarous genius, what inhuman cruelty' can have animated Napoleon to set fire to their venerable capital. Césare de Laugier says he's got it all wrong ... No, no, says the priest. It's he who's deceiving himself. There's no question but that Napoleon was the author of the fire:

'While we were talking I was able to examine at my leisure this crowd of unfortunates who were gradually coming closer to us. The men's masculine, energetic, bearded faces bore the impress of a deep, ferocious, concentrated pain. The women's air was more resigned, but it was easy to guess what anxieties they were going through. Untroubled by my paying so little heed to what he was saying, the pope went on with his sermon. Swept along in some line of reasoning, he happened to touch my horse and lay his hand on the pommel of its saddle. Seeing how moved I was, he redoubled the violence of his words. For my part I was lamenting the fate of so many unhappy families, women, old men, children, who, because of us, were in such a pitiful state. And this thought made me forget the danger I was so imprudently exposing myself to.'

Suddenly one of the Russians comes up to the 'pope' and, 'with a look of sovereign scorn' says something in his ear. Suspicious, the Italian officer begins to walk away:

'But then the pope asked me whether I was a Christian, a question which only half surprised me, as I knew we'd been represented to the Russian people as a band of heretics. The moment everyone knew I'd said I was, I saw all the faces looking at me with greater interest, and the conversations grew more animated. Then the pope took my hand, pressed it affectionately, and said: "Get going as fast as you can. Ilowais-ki, reinforced by the district's militia and some completely fresh caval-ry, is advancing to attack you. By staying here you're exposing yourself to every danger. And do what you can to prevent the acts of impiety your leader and your comrades are making themselves guilty of!'"

Before going back to his men, de Laugier makes a last effort to convince the kindly priest of his error; tells him that he and all his flock can come back to Moscow without the least risk. But his interlocutor accompanies him to the fringe of the forest, 'and didn't leave me until he saw the NCOs appear, who'd come to look for me'.

The priest's warning turns out to be correct. 'A long column of cavalry had appeared near the Liazma. Other Cossacks and armed peasants were coming up along the Dmitrovo road.' Some foragers are running back to the Italian lines as fast as their legs can carry them. Many of the them, pur-sued by Russian scouts, have abandoned their carts or horses, already laden with plunder:

'The Dragoons of the Royal Guard advanced. The Marienpol Hussars made ready to receive them but, disturbed by the artillery fire, beat a retreat, carrying away the Cossacks, who'd imprudently advanced and had exposed themselves, not without some rather serious losses.'

By now it's 4 p.m., too late in the day to come to grips with this enemy. So Colonel Moroni, his foraging operation – apart from the few carts and horses the foragers had abandoned – being completed, gives the order to march off home:

'But being followed closely by the enemy and forced to escort a numerous convoy, he thought it dangerous to make the whole move-ment en bloc. First the wagons and other impedimenta filed off as far as a wood to our rear, then the troops followed in the best order.'

This is the signal for the Russians'

'best horsemen to attack, uttering shrill cries, and firing some shots, but without daring to come too close. Hardly was the convoy lined up properly along the road which passes through the forest and the sharpshooters had been placed on its flanks to protect it if attacked, than our columns abruptly faced about, and marched against the enemy. Seeing this, the many groups of armed peasants soon began to flee, throwing away their weapons as they crossed the fields. The cavalry followed their example. Night was already falling. Then two vélites rejoined the detachment. They'd got lost in the woods while looking for me, and the pope I'd spoken with had saved them from the hands of the Cossacks by hiding them until we'd come back.'

Not all foraging expeditions, the vélites' adjutant-major adds sombrely, operating under the same conditions, are being so successful.

Young Lieutenant Paul de Bourgoing, he of the fancy fur, has to interrupt his struttings to and fro in front of the two actresses General Delaborde has taken under his wing, and sally out with some wagons and 50 men of his own regiment, the 5th Tirailleurs-Fusiliers of the Young Guard, to see what he can find in a village on the left bank of the Moskova – its right bank has already been occupied by the various Guard cavalry regiments. He's just entering a village dangerously close to the Russian outposts when the tocsin sounds and a fusillade breaks out between his men and some peasants who 'aided by some Russian soldiers lodging with them, defend their cows and sheep'. Seeing one of his officers and five men beat a hasty retreat, dragging a cow with them and followed by a compact mass of peasants, he orders his men to fire. The Russians reply with well-nourished musketry. A corporal falls wounded in his arms, spattering him with his blood. From all sides armed peasants and Cossacks come running or galloping across the plain. Now the whole detachment, carrying its badly wounded corporal on a cart, has to beat a hasty retreat. Already night is falling, and it's necessary to find the bridge across the river. Which they do – receiving timely support from a company of voltigeurs. The corporal dies on the forage cart.

Altogether, such sorties are producing less and less. By the second week in October no escort under brigade strength, or stronger, has much chance of bringing in a convoy of foodstuffs. Baron Lejeune, struggling with all the paperwork needed to reorganize I Corps and set it to rights, is finding

'these last days very hard. Our foragers no longer brought us anything back, either for the men or the horses. Their accounts of the perils they'd run were scaring, and to listen to them it seemed we were surrounded by a network of Cossacks and armed peasants who were killing all isolated men and from whom we ourselves would only escape with difficulty. These perplexities made the task of restoring order as soon as possible in the army's organisation extremely laborious, both for the corps commanders and their chiefs-of-staff. The days and nights were all too short to cope with so many difficulties and I hardly had time to see anything more of Moscow than the very long street leading from my suburb to the Kremlin.'

War Commissary Kergorre puts the matter in a nutshell:

'Even if we had had enough provisions to spend the winter here, we should still have had to retreat, for absolute lack of forage. What would we have done without cavalry, without artillery, in winter quarters in the land we'd conquered, without communication with France?'

Large-scale reconnaissances are being made, some even at divisional strength. On 27 September the 18th Line, part of Ney's III Corps, had moved into town to occupy the German quarter, where there are 'still some good houses left standing'. Though Captain Bonnet finds himself poorly lodged, this inconvenience is more than made up for by his being promoted *chef-de-bataillon*, i.e., major. But on 3 October, III Corps, too, has to send out a

'strong reconnaissance of élite companies. I'd a command. The marshal led us to Bogorodsk, a little town 48 versts [35 miles] north-east of Moscow in the direction of Vladimir.'

And there, for four days, they 'lodge in the houses, a trifle anxious for the strong point we'd set up, and without news of the army. The road being intercepted, we guarded ourselves with greatest care.' But next day (6 October) they hear that the rest of III Corps is now on the same side of the town. All Ney's units except Colonel Fezensac's 4th Line have marched as far as Bogorodsk. On about 10 October Fezensac hears that

'a division of IV Corps made a movement on Dmitrov on the Tver road. Meanwhile Marshal Ney seized Bogorodsk, 36 miles from Moscow, on the Vladimir road. We spent several days erecting huts around this little town, as if to spend the winter in it. This pretence was perfectly useless. It fooled neither the enemy nor our own men. I didn't go to Bogorodsk. At that moment I was in an expedition commanded by General Marchand on the banks of Kliasma between the Vladimir and Tver roads. Part of my regiment went with me. The rest had followed Marshal Ney. The enemy, faithful to his system, withdrew as we approached. General Marchand had a blockhouse constructed at a point where a detachment had been carried off by a regiment of Cossacks. The command of this little fort had just been entrusted to a very intelligent officer when suddenly Marchand received the order to return with his whole detachment. Anyone could see that the army was about to quit Moscow, since it had ceased to defend the approaches.'

Not until 13 October will Bonnet leave Bogorodsk and get back to Moscow the following morning – only to go down with a fever.

CHAPTER 7

LOVELY AUTUMN WEATHER

A theological assumption – 'so this is the famous Russian winter?' – parades and promotions – a mortifying setback for Lejeune – a fragile courier service – Abbé Pradt's difficulties in Warsaw – Muraldt visits Berthier – the Canaries at Smolensk – trophies – evenings at the theatre

Although the nights are becoming chilly, the weather's beautiful. Golden autumn days succeed one another, with the clear blue skies one only finds in the far north. Stopping briefly at the 4th Bavarian Chevaulegers' bivouac out at Petrovskoï for a visa, a Russian who's obtained a permit to visit his estate tells von Muraldt, 'The weather's so lovely for the time of year, one is tempted to believe God is with the Emperor Napoleon' – 'a theological assumption', von Muraldt remarks, 'belied by the outcome'. Unless, that is, illness is a mark of divine favour. For it's now, he sees, men are beginning to fall ill:

'Sicknesses, particularly dysentery,[1] appeared ever more violently. Few of our men were spared, and even among the officers only the youngest and strongest escaped this torment.'

Again and again Caulaincourt, who after all has spent four winters at Petersburg as French ambassador, warns Napoleon of winter's imminent onset. In vain. And his frankness gains him no thanks. Napoleon makes mock of Caulaincourt's fears. Even after the third week has passed without the least sign of any reply arriving from the Tsar, he's exclaiming: 'So this is the terrible Russian winter M. de Caulaincourt frightens the children with!'

'The weather was so fine and the temperature so mild, even the locals were amazed. On his daily rides His Majesty remarked very pointedly when I was present "the autumn in Moscow is fine and even warmer than at Fontainebleau."'

As for notions that the Russian army is disintegrating or demoralized, 'he continually ridiculed the stories told by the King of Naples, even though they fed the hopes he wanted to entertain, in spite of the reflections he must have had.'

Each day at 1 p.m. there's a splendid parade in the Kremlin courtyards. Reviewing the Old Guard infantry on Thursday 6 October, Napoleon turns to Narbonne:

'Well, my dear Narbonne, what do you say about such an army manoeuvring in bright sunshine?'

'I say, sire,' replies that gentleman of the *ancien régime* and one-time minister of war to the Republic, 'it's had a good rest. Now it can take the road so as to occupy its quarters in Lithuania, leaving the Russians their capital in the state they've left it in.'

Promotions and decorations rain down. Pion des Loches, promoted major, is overjoyed when two brother officers bring him his commission, the more so, he says, as their compliments are obviously sincere. Now he's to command the 1st Company of the Old Guard's Foot Artillery together with the 2nd Company of Foot Artillery of the Young Guard, plus a park and its train. 'It was mainly from this time I kept open house. We were rarely fewer than seven or eight at dinner.'

Next day Roguet's Young Guard division is reviewed. On 8 October there's a 'general parade'. On the 10th the turn comes to Compans' division of Davout's I Corps; and Sous- Lieutenant Dutheillet of the 57th Line is promoted full lieutenant[2] for his heroic assault on the first of the Bagration *flèches* at Borodino. Also, he says, because Compans' division is suffering from a general shortage of officers.

(In sharp contrast to the state of affairs among Ney's Württembergers, where *Karl von Suckow*, rejoining divisional headquarters in the Kazan district, with his convoy of 400 more or less recovered Borodino wounded, finds there's such an excess of them that any number have to be detailed off to follow the army 'as amateurs'. There are, in fact, very few Württembergers left. The day before Compans' division goes on parade one of its generals, Scheler by name, writes home to his king from the Kazan suburb:

'the infantry in a state to bear arms number no more than 490 men, but we're expecting a convoy of convalescents. The artillery still has 385 men. The four cavalry regiments together 444 men. General Breuning's condition is hopeless. The extraordinary homesickness so many people have been stricken with and which there is no medicine for is consuming his strength. All we're getting from the French administration is some ammunition. What we're above all short of is vigorous horses. The French have taken no measures for subsistence or to renew the equipment, or else only bad ones. Nor is anything being done for the hospitals.')

Best of all, Pion des Loches' promotion entitles him to a wagon of his own for the homeward journey:

'As captain I'd had one wagon for myself and my lieutenant, half filled with my troops' effects and reserve shoes. Now I was major I had a wagon to myself, smaller it's true, but sufficient for my victuals for a retreat of three to four months [which he immediately gets busy filling with], a hundred cakes of biscuit a foot in diameter, a sack holding a quintal of flour, more than 300 bottles of wine, 20-30 bottles of rum and brandy, more than 10 pounds of tea and as much again of coffee, 50–60 pounds of sugar, 3–4 pounds of chocolate, some pounds of candles. Then, against the event of a winter cantonment on the left bank of the Niemen, which I regarded as inevitable, a case containing a rather fine edition of Voltaire and Rousseau, Clerc and Levesque's History of Russia, Molière's plays, the works of Piron, [Montesquieu's] Défense de L'Esprit des Lois and several other works such as Raynal's Philosophical History, bound in white calf and gilded on the spine. Further, for 80 frs I'd bought myself one of the most beautiful furs that have been brought back from Moscow.'

Alas, for at least one superior officer that day's parade of 10 October is far from being a happy one. Lejeune, the future painter of battle scenes, a man who on occasion can find that 'in war a heart moved by bellicose exaltations is endowed with a sensibility more exquisite than at any other instant in life,' has wearied of the unending paperwork involved in being Davout's chief-of-staff, an appointment he'd never wanted and even begged to be excused from. Until Borodino Lejeune, like Fezensac, had been one of Berthier's 'lady-killers' – prancing about in the gorgeous uniform he'd designed for his colleagues. But Berthier, Fezensac tells us, never fails to help his staff officers up the ladder. And now – apparently without waiting for the Emperor's signature – the army's Major-General has presumed to give Lejeune command of the 57th Line. The upshot, as witnessed by Lieutenant Dutheillet, is utterly painful:

'Candidates for the cross of honour were very numerous. I recall that the Emperor, coming to the regiment's front – it was very much reduced – saw at its head, in command of it, Colonel Lejeune, from his [sic] staff.[3] Having asked Berthier how it came about that Colonel Lejeune was in command of the 57th, in advance of his signature, he said: '"Colonel, I haven't taken the command of the 56th from you, I fancy, so as to give you the 57th. Return to the staff, that's where you belong." And to General Compans: "Who's the division's senior major?" "It's Major Duchesne of the 25th." "Have him immediately recognised as colonel of the 57th." Which was done. And in front of the division Colonel Lejeune got the most humiliating of affronts an officer can experience.'

Berthier takes him back and consoles him, Dutheillet supposes. Actually, as Lejeune himself laments – though he makes no mention of this no doubt extremely painful incident – he has to resume his arduous duties under Davout. But young Dutheillet must have known who his colonel was, and there can be no reason to doubt his account of an episode altogether characteristic of Napoleon's drastic ways at parades or his phenomenal photographic memory for who's who in the army.[4]

These parades, of course, although perhaps primarily designed to keep up morale in a situation everyone knows is more and more worrying, are more than ceremonial events. Though Napoleon is being lavish with rewards, as Césare de Laugier notices, he's also scrutinizing each division with a view to its efficiency in a nearer future than his dinner guests suppose. Nor is he deceived by his own praise of the fine weather.

At first communications with France and western Europe have functioned well:

'The post-houses were fortified. The courier service, which I'd organised at the campaign's outset, was given special attention. The despatch case containing despatches for the Emperor was arriving regularly every day from Paris in 15 – often in 14 – days. The service's punctuality was truly astonishing.'[5]

Even so, though he won't admit it, Napoleon's concern for the mail's daily arrival shows how aware he is of being out on a limb:

'He was always impatient for his courier's arrival. He noticed the delay of a few hours, and even grew anxious, though this service hadn't ever broken down. The Paris portfolio, the packets from Warsaw and Vilna, were the thermometer of the Emperor's good or bad humour. It was the same with all of us. Everyone's happiness hung on the news from France. Small consignments of wine and other objects arrived. Officers, surgeons and administrative officials also came to join the army.'

The service, Caulaincourt goes on,

'was carried on by postillions relayed from post to post between Paris and Erfurt, from Erfurt to Poland by couriers stationed in brigades [teams] of four at every hundred miles; in parts of Poland by relays of postillions, across the frontier and through Russia by French postillions personally selected by Count Lavalette [head of the post office]. They were mounted on the best post-horses, and placed at my service. There were four to every relay, and each relay covered from 15 to 21 miles.'

Engineer-Colonel Serran, covering all the hundreds of miles through Lithuania and Russia on his way to Moscow from Spain, had been less impressed; he thought that

'nothing would be easier than to intercept them, leaving us isolated, very much weakened, with rather a lot of cavalry in a pitiable state, an enormous amount of artillery matèriel, 600 miles from any friendly country.'

He'll turn out to be right. 'A few isolated men,' Caulaincourt hears one day, have been 'chased or captured. One courier was delayed almost 15 hours, which worried the Emperor extremely. Every quarter of an hour he asked me, also the Major-General, whether we'd heard anything about what had caused the delay.'

Caulaincourt profits by the occasion to

'renew the demand I'd been making ever since we'd got here for an escort for the courier, even if only a couple of men. But to establish this at all the relays would have entailed a considerable detachment of troops, and the cavalry was already considerably reduced in strength. So the Emperor dismissed the matter, saying it was an unnecessary precaution as the road was perfectly safe.'

Well, it isn't.

'Three days later the postillion driving the courier to Paris escaped several gunshots beyond Mojaisk and was chased for a couple of leagues. Whereupon the Emperor lost no time in sending out the detachments I'd asked for.'

Even so, Caulaincourt's initial self-congratulation that it 'was as easy to travel from Paris to Moscow as from Paris to Marseilles' is rudely disturbed when Cossacks capture the courier returning from Moscow for Vilna and Paris:

'Other points along the Smolensk road were similarly intercepted by enemy parties, with the result that all sure communication with France was cut off. Vilna, Warsaw, Mainz and Paris were no longer daily receiving their orders from the great Empire's sovereign master.'

And back at Gumbinnen, the last town on the Prussian frontier before Kovno and Vilna, where a courier should pass through daily, the district governor Schön has just reported on 7 October to the Prussian chancellor Hardenberg in Berlin that

'since 1 October not one courier has arrived here from the general headquarters, nor any official news of the capture of Moscow, nor even a letter from Moscow.'

All he has to go on are rumours from Vilna that the city had been set on fire. 'According to these the misery reigning in the army is beyond any idea. Already people are talking of the Emperor Napoleon's coming back.' And when on 10 October the Vilna courier at last arrives, after taking five days, he brings news that 'the fire of Moscow is a lie'. Not until 15 October will any official news, despatched on 17 September 'not from Moscow, but from a bivouac in front of Moscow, arrive from IHQ. 'That the journey has taken so long is said to be due to the lack of horses between Moscow and Smolensk and to the Cossacks who are troubling the road.' The very first despatch from Moscow itself won't pass through Gumbinnen until 24 October, having 'taken four weeks because it has had to be escorted from Moscow as far as Smolensk'.

Napoleon's choice of *D. G. Dufour de Pradt*, Bishop of Poitiers and Archbishop of Malines, for the post of ambassador plenipotentiary at Warsaw – a post, one would think, of utmost importance – had been so odd as to be inexplicable. Ever since July, when he'd thought of sending the pro-Polish Narbonne from Vilna to replace him because of his blunderings with the Polish Diet, Napoleon has been bitterly regretting it. According to Mme de Rémusat, that acute observer of human nature, Pradt

'had intelligence, and knew how to intrigue. His language was at once verbose and piquant. He had some humorous small talk, held liberal opinions and too cynical a way of expressing them. He was mixed up in many matters without achieving much success in any. He even managed to wrap up the Emperor in his words; perhaps gave some good advice; but when he'd managed to obtain the right to implement it, spoiled everything.'

That Pradt's an intriguer, Napoleon – who'll describe him afterwards as 'my spy on the clergy' – knows very well. Hadn't he caught him out, reprimanded him at a levee, but pardoned him? 'I made a mistake, but God protected him.' Yet it's this weak reed Maret, at Dresden[6] in May, at his orders had suddenly been ordered to go to Warsaw as minister plenipotentiary. Whereat, Pradt says, he'd felt 'a mortal chill in my veins. There I was, ambassador in spite of myself.' His task had been 'to push the Poles into transports [of enthusiasm], avoiding delirium'. And above all to produce '16 million Poles on horseback' to fight their arch-enemy – a task which, as Napoleon sees it, should have been as easy as putting a match to a barrel of gunpowder. But ever since the July day at Vilna[7] when he'd refused to re-establish the Kingdom of Poland, and even told one of the Diet's emissaries, in confidence, that he might 'at any moment make peace with Alexander', his Polish affairs have been going agley. Such blowing hot and cold had

'produced exactly the opposite effect of what he'd hoped it would. They'd gone there all fire, and come back as ice. Their coldness had spread to Poland and since then no one has managed to set fire to it again.'

Pradt, uncomfortably resident in a Warsaw more astoundingly poverty-stricken than anything he'd ever imagined, has found Poland 'foul and primitive' and the Polish administration no less so:

'I was bewildered by the gap I found to exist between the real state of Poland and the picture I'd been given of it. Anyone who'd wished to follow Napoleon's line of march had seen him create for himself an imaginary Spain, an imaginary Catholicism, an imaginary England, and an imaginary nobility, even more so an imaginary France; and now he'd made himself an imaginary Poland.'[8]

Since 1806 the Poles have been supplying the French armies with thousands of men. Currently, Pradt estimates, 85,700 of them are serving in various corps – a figure utterly out of proportion to a poor duchy, of Napoleon's own creation, with only five million inhabitants and whose trade, consisting almost entirely of fat grains that couldn't be stored very long and whose outlets – Turkey, Danzig and Russia – are being strangled by Napoleon's invasion of Russia together with the detested Continental System and the British blockade:

> 'The Duchy's revenues amounted to 40 million francs. Its expenses exceeded 100 million. The deficit for 1811 and the first few months of 1812 amounted to 21 million.'

No one in Warsaw has a penny to bless himself with. Every day Pradt is keeping open house – without ever being invited back, for the simple reason no one can afford it. Vandamme's[9] name, particularly, is hated throughout Poland. His Westphalian troops of VIII Corps, and the Saxons of IX Corps, passing through in June and July, had murdered and pillaged and ravished:

> 'All these horrors had their roots in the system, as absurd as it's inhuman, of waging war without magazines. This system has become the flail of the armies as of the peoples, has killed the art of war and relegated almost all those who follow this once so noble profession to the category of ferocious animals. He who in this way has depraved the generous hearts of warriors and by so doing has multiplied a hundredfold the calamities inseparable from war, has merited the curses of the human race.'

Jérôme[10] had been as endlessly loquacious as – and no less demanding than – his imperial brother. As for General Dutaillis, the French commandant at Warsaw, Pradt regards him as a ruthless brute. Even back in October 1811 there'd been talk of reducing the Polish armed forces by a half, and a great review fixed for 7 November had had to be cancelled – 'because the soldiers had no shoes'. Yet, though everywhere in Europe the harvest has failed, with starvation as the result, the Duchy has already provided 25,000 horses for the campaign. Ordered, via Maret at Vilna, to get hold of 10,000 more cavalry horses, Pradt tried to – 'I say tried, because that number of horses suitable for cavalry didn't exist.' Maret, Duke of Bassano, is Pradt's *bête noire*. Every day he's sending him peremptory letters from Vilna – in the seven months of his so-called embassy Pradt says he got 400 of them – telling him to

> 'keep out of politics and supply the army's needs. I was delighted whenever a day passed without one arriving by the post. The Duke of Bassano [Maret, Napoleon's foreign minister and plenipotentiary at Vilna] was the Emperor's monkey, one of the flails of our age. Every-

thing about him has to be flattered, admired, even down to the duchess's little dog, of whom it's been said "that dog has made many an auditor, many a prefect".'

Maret, Pradt says, 'didn't have the art of abbreviating interviews or discussions', of sitting too long at table; of wasting hours chatting up the ladies while men with urgent business have to sit outside for three or four hours waiting in his antechamber; of 'turning night into day and day into night', and never getting down to work in his office until midnight 'amidst an infinite number of portfolios without order or classification'. In a word, he detests him. Otherwise Maret's reputation is of quite another order than Pradt's. According to the young Duchess Marie-Charlotte Eugénie de Reggio, who has just joined her severely wounded husband Marshal Oudinot at Vilna, Maret

'like Count Louis de Narbonne, wore his hair in the old style. He carried himself and his well-powdered head very straight. He was tall; his manner was grave; his movements were slow, his words rare and always well-considered. Taken as a whole, he was imposing.'

Particularly so, perhaps, to the ladies on whom he, according to Pradt, lavished so much time in long chats.

The farther away any corps or unit is, the less the words of the master are likely to be put into effect. One day von Muraldt, the youngest of the 4th Bavarian Chevaulegers' officers and the only one to speak good French, is sent into town to Prince Eugène's headquarters in

'one of the few surviving palaces. It was situated in a street that hadn't suffered as much as most from the fire.'

While there he's sent in the middle of the night to the Kremlin, not very far away, with a despatch to Berthier. What Eugène wants to know is how he's to send letters and despatches to General Wrede, commanding the Bavarians of St-Cyr's VI Corps, at faraway Polotsk, whose excellent cavalry had been seconded to Eugène at Vilna in July. Though Muraldt doesn't realise it, he's exceedingly lucky the Bavarian chevaulegers aren't with their wretched compatriots who, Wrede has reported back to Maret at Vilna in September, have 'a perfect mania for deserting' and are dying in large numbers from typhus. The night is pitch black. Though he takes a French chasseur to guide him, Muraldt soon gets lost among the ruined streets. The chasseur pretends to know his way about, but after half an hour of straying hither and thither the young officer realizes he doesn't, and that they're lost. Now and then they bump into marauders, who've also lost their way. 'We'd wandered about for a couple of hours when we at last met a patrol of Guard Horse Grenadiers, who put us on the right track.' So they reach the Kremlin, 'brilliantly illumined by the campfires of the Imperial Guard all about'. One can just walk in. On the main stairs he encounters Roustam,

> 'who very politely gave me the information I desired. An adjutant announced me. I found Berthier writing at a little table in the centre of the room. In all its four corners secretaries sat similarly writing, and only the scratching of quills disturbed the profound nocturnal stillness in this high-ceilinged, spacious, faintly lit hall. The Prince seemed tired and strained, and only glanced through my despatch.'

So, in his excellent French, Muraldt repeats its question *viva voce*. To this Berthier replies

> 'that no definite information had been recently received from Marshal Gouvion St-Cyr's army corps. Nor were those communications wholly secure. And anyway he'd inform the Viceroy at the first suitable occasion. This answer wasn't at all to my liking. It indicated all too clearly that things weren't as they should be to our rear, as we already partly knew.'

On the other hand Eugène's emissary is delighted when Berthier tells his adjutant to give him some supper,

> 'for just then one could show no greater politeness than to offer someone something to eat. On a big table lay the remains of an evening meal, to which I did all honour – in those days one always went hungry.'

Equally uncertain, even worrying are the behaviour and secret dispositions of Prince Schwarzenberg and his Austrian corps, in faraway Galicia. On the same day that Napoleon had entered Moscow, in that southern theatre of war, Tchitchakov, coming up with his Army of Moldavia – an army which, if French gold had been a match for British, should still have been fighting the Turks – had absorbed Tormassov's force and taken the offensive against Poland. Whereupon an outnumbered Schwarzenberg had retired behind the Bug and, together with Reynier, had forced Tormassov to retire. One day Berthier gets a personal letter from Schwarzenberg whose very politeness seems worrying. On that Caulaincourt, Duroc and Daru are all agreed:

> 'In brief, its sense was the following: "The position is already embarrassing, may become graver. Anyhow, whatever happened, the Prince assured Berthier of his personal sentiments and the value he placed and always would place on him."'

He expresses no such devotion, either real or feigned, towards Napoleon; and certainly feels none.[11] Napoleon sees through Schwarzenberg's letter. Tells Berthier:

"This gives warning of defection at the first opportunity. It may even have started already. The Austrians and Prussians are enemies in our rear. This letter is sentimental twaddle."

Foreign Minister Maret, however, who is keeping an eye on Schwarzenberg's movements, seems perfectly satisfied, as he has reason to be. Napoleon writes to his all-important father-in-law, the Emperor Francis in Vienna, asking him to promote Schwarzenberg field marshal and send him 10,000 more men. He's also beginning to worry about Macdonald's mostly Prussian X Corps and its immense siege train, investing Riga. As for St-Cyr's operations around Polotsk, Napoleon directs Victor to divide his attention between Vilna and Minsk, where he is to liaise with the extremely experienced Polish General Dombrowski, a veteran from '96 and Italy.

Everywhere the Russian numbers are growing.

Smolensk, however, is Napoleon's nearest base and is now becoming the prime object of his attention. It's in that wreck of a burnt out city that such sapient regimental officers as Le Roy and Fezensac are looking forward to going into winter quarters. These, according to Napoleon's new plan, will be taken up along the Molihew–Smolensk–Witebsk line, where the stores assembled at Smolensk, together with yet more supplies being collected at Witebsk, Vilna and Minsk, should be sufficient to feed the army through the winter.

At Smolensk immense food convoys and fresh units have been arriving almost daily from Germany. One such unit is Berthier's own Neuchâtel Battalion. Marched – at his express order not too ruthlessly – from their depot at Besançon, 'the Canaries', as they're universally called in the army because of their yellow coats, are doubtless unique in not having lost a single one of their 666 men *en route*. When they get to Smolensk they're overjoyed to find that their own well-liked commander Colonel Jean-Henri Borset – a middle-aged man of cheerful spirit who loves to join in amateur theatricals, 'especially comedy' – is already installed as the city's *commandant d'armes*; and – again at 'their' prince's special behest – are housed 'as comfortably as possible'.[12]

Not all regiments are being treated so considerately. When the 129th Line staggers into Smolensk on 13 October it will number only 724 men and 40 officers, i.e., be hardly a battalion strong. As for the food convoys, few if any can go a step further. After dragging their wagons so many hundreds of miles their scraggy oxen drop dead and aren't even worth eating.

Indeed the position at Smolensk is far from rosy. That once prosperous city, abandoned by its populace at the time of the battle and the fire,[13] is hardly recognisable. When its new governor, General Charpentier, arrives from Witebsk (where, much to his successor's distaste, he's being replaced

113

by the wounded General *F-R. Pouget*, he finds he hasn't a single mason to 'put the hospitals into good repair, to rehabilitate buildings which could be of the greatest usefulness for troops passing through and the garrison and, in a word, to procure objects of prime necessity'.

Where's the company of artisans, Charpentier writes to Berthier: the one, he suddenly seems to remember, that had accompanied Imperial Headquarters (but his memory is failing him, it was Davout's I Corps) at the campaign's outset? He needs them so badly:

'We could do with 10 locksmiths, 10 masons, 10 joiners, 10 carpenters, 2 coopers, 2 tinkers, 1 hatter, 4 edge- toolmakers, 2 tinsmiths, 2 cutlers, 2 cordwainers, 4 saddlers, 8 shoemakers, 8 tailors.'

In the burnt out houses of the upper town are tile stoves which could be dismantled and re-erected elsewhere. But above all it's becoming difficult to increase the stores. All around Smolensk, as around Moscow, Cossacks are so terrifying the peasants that they won't sell the troops their wares any longer. Charpentier urges upon Berthier his imperative need to keep the '160 mounted men of the 1st Polish Horse Chasseurs' who speak Russian, or anyway the local dialect (a blend of Russian and Polish), in order to keep the Cossacks at bay and deal with the population.

In Moscow Colonel Serran's works on improving the Kremlin's fortifications have largely been carried out by 5 October, for on that day Césare de Laugier has already seen there '12 heavy- calibre guns in battery, while 18 others are ready to be placed beside them.' For their part the Italians have converted

'the prison known as the Ostrorog, situated in the suburbs, into a kind of fortified citadel. The two convents occupied by I and III Corps' depots are to be used for an identical purpose.'

Yet all these fortificatory works, it seems, are at least in part a blind, intended to throw dust in the army's – perhaps also Russian – eyes. For at about that same date, 'at the time he'd decided to send Lauriston to the Russian camp', Secretary Fain, taking down letters and orders to Berthier in his self-invented shorthand, has already realised that Napoleon is already beginning to plan the army's departure:

'From then on he'd been incessantly busy. We'd seen him imperatively assign 15 October as the last date for evacuating the wounded. As early as 9 October the trophies he wanted to honour France with had been packed up and loaded. Among them were the flags taken by the Russians from the Turks over a hundred years ago, some ancient armour, a madonna which the devout had enriched with diamonds, and the gilded cross from the belfry of Ivan Veliki, which had so long dominated all the domes of Moscow and which the Poles had

often mentioned as the object of the Russians' devotion, even super-
stition.'
Caulaincourt will afterwards seem to recall a report coming in that the Russian authorities had declared the recovery of the gilded iron cross to be the
first goal of all orthodox Russians, and it had been this which had 'fixed the
Emperor's determination' to take it back to Paris and place it on the dome
of the Invalides. Unfortunately, as treasurer Peyrusse either sees or hears,
    'one of the cables of the crane broke, and the weight of the chains
    dragged down the cross and part of the scaffolding. The ground was
    shaken by the enormous weight of this falling mass, and the cross was
    broken in three places,'
shattering the cathedral dome in its fall.

More important than trophies are the wounded. That same day, 5 October,
Fain hears Napoleon tell Daru:
    '"I want to preserve my freedom to choose my line of operation. How
    many days do you need to evacuate the hospitals?" "Sire, forty-five
    days." "That's far too long. Your calculations are exaggerated. Expe-
    rience shows that three months after a battle not a sixth of the wound-
    ed are still at the ambulances. So first separate out your wounded into
    two classes – those who a month from now will be able to march
    unaided, and those whose trouble would be aggravated by being
    moved. There's nothing you need do about either of these cases. But
    into your second class, on the contrary, you'll enter those invalids who
    can conveniently be transported. These are the only ones you need
    worry about, beginning, as is only right, with the officers. You see, if
    you rectify your calculations in this way you'll come to quite a differ-
    ent result, and we'll gain precious time."'

Meanwhile appearances must be kept up. As the French had penetrated
ever deeper into the soil of Holy Russia, the actors and actresses of the
French troupe, though still under the Tsar's patronage, had felt themselves, like all other foreign residents, being regarded with ever deeper suspicion. Not even an attempt to stage an anti-Bonapartist show had saved
them. Their director had been one of a party of foreigners whom Rostopchin had rounded up and deported by barge to the interior. While
some of the company's actresses had followed their gentleman friends to
Petersburg, the homes of those who'd remained had first been pillaged by
the departing Russians, then looted by the French. Her house burnt down,
the 38-year-old *Louise Fusil* has been left with nothing and has only survived
thanks to the asylum given her by Caulaincourt. Certain others of her colleagues likewise.[14]

Another, much more famous, artist who has survived the fire is the Italian tenor Tarquinio. Summoned to the Kremlin to sing to Napoleon, who's fond of Italian music, he's being accompanied on the piano by the son of Martini (composer of the ever popular *Plaisir d'Amour*). Is it he, Tarquinio, who now first mentions to Napoleon the presence in Moscow of the remainder of the troupe? Or Bausset, the Prefect of the Palace? Bausset at all events takes

'the opportunity of mentioning the matter to the Emperor during lunch. He distributed some immediate reliefs, appointed me to superintend them, and ordered me to find out whether, given their present composition, it would be possible to stage a few performances and so provide some slight entertainment for the army lodged in Moscow.'

Though no professional singer, Louise has a pretty voice and has sometimes even sung duets with Tarquinio. Ordered to seek her out, Bausset finds her and one of her fellow-actresses, almost in rags, in some outbuildings of the Galitzin palace. But Louise absolutely declines the honour of singing before His Majesty 'who's a connoisseur'. What she and her colleagues can do perhaps, providing Bausset can find them a theatre and costumes, is to stage some plays and vaudeville pieces.

Fortunately a theatre has survived – evidently not Henckens' 'big theatre', but the one in Count Posniakov's palace. One of the most beautiful in town until the catastrophe, it had been the scene of the city's best productions. Found to be still serviceable, its auditorium is hastily whitewashed, its boxes magnificently draped, and a 1,700-candle candelabrum, brought from some church, is hung from the ceiling. Here, rigged out in the strangest fragments of clothing, the company rehearses in front of an astounded Bausset. The male lead, otherwise naked except for a Russian militiaman's cap, appears in a military greatcoat. Enter the young lover in a seminarist's cassock and a Russian general's plumed hat! The *père noble* at least has some trousers, albeit badly patched. Alas, the Villain of the piece, though shod in superb boots from the days of Louis XIII and a grey Spanish coat he'd saved from the troupe's burning wardrobe, hasn't. Though wearing a red fur-lined jacket which reaches to her knees, Mme Burcet, who seems to be in charge, has neither skirt nor petticoat. The overall effect? In Louise Fusil's eyes, it's as if they're 'dressed up to attend a masquerade ball for lunatics and beggars'. Bausset, shocked, immediately asks Daru to get them something better. Which is done. 'We drew up a sort of repertory,' Bausset, Ségur's superior, goes on:

'In the unhappy situation in which the actors found themselves, nobody had any pretensions. The distribution of parts was very easily done. Never was there a cast more united, more flexible, or easier to manage. Besides, Mme Burcet had a strong influence on them and knew their talents well. I wasted no time in obtaining costumes and suitable premises for their performances. In the Mosque [sic] of Ivan the military authorities had collected everything that had been rescued from the flames, and there, thanks to the kindness of Count Dumas, the army's Quartermaster-General, I found all sorts of costumes. The French actors took velvet dresses and clothes which they fitted to their figures and to which they fastened some broad gold braid which was to be found in quantities in these stores. In fact, they were dressed in great style, though several of our actresses, such was their distress, barely had the necessary linen to wear under these beautiful velvet dresses – at least,'

the over-plump Prefect of the Palace adds hastily, 'that's what Mme Bursay told me.' The actors' ludicrous rags and tatters replaced by odd – if more seemly – costumes, the theatre opens to a packed, virtually all-male, not to say all-military, audience 'at 6 p.m. precisely' on Wednesday 7 October, with a double bill:

LE JEU DE L'AMOUR ET DU HASARD

The Game of Love and Chance, Marivaux's famous comedy of 1730, is followed by

AMANT, AUTEUR ET VALET

Lover, Author and Valet, a one-act comedy by Ceron. 'This was a brilliant début,' Bausset goes on:

'The pit was filled with soldiers, while the two rows of boxes seated officers of all arms. Only a small charge was made at the doors and this was shared among the actors, with nothing but the cost of lighting deducted.'

Audience enthusiasm knows no bounds. The actors forget all their usual rivalries. The orchestra consists of the Guards bands' finest soloists. Mlle Lamiral's Russian dance number – she's been a teacher of dancing and deportment at the Catherine Institute for daughters of the Russian nobility – takes the house by storm. And for eleven successive evenings a very good time is had by all. 'We went on acting', Louise will afterwards remember, 'right up to the eve of our departure, and Napoleon was most generous to us. He rarely came to see the play.' That excellent actor – in his own role[15] – prefers to listen to Tarquinio in the Kremlin. One day when he does come, the Emperor goes on talking through a pretty air Louise is singing and which is making 'a kind of a sensation'. Yet no one claps, because the Emperor is there. Such is the etiquette:

'Napoleon asked what the matter was; and M. de Bausset came and told me to begin again. I was so overcome with emotion I felt my voice was trembling and thought I'd never get through it. I managed to, though; and from this moment this romance became so fashionable that people never stopped asking me to sing it. The King of Naples even asked me to give it him for his band:

> '*With fond farewells a handsome knight*
> *Consoled his sword as he flew to the fight:*
> *"On honour's field love guides my course,*
> *Puts arms in my hands, o'er my life decides.*
> *When victory's mine I'll soon return,*
> *And seek the prize whereto I yearn.*
> *My heart's the gauge of thy constancy,*
> *Thy love proves valour's faith in thee."'* [16]

Such were the pretty sentiments that could move the hearts of Napoleonic warriors amidst Moscow's blackened ruins.

CHAPTER 8

A LETHAL TRUCE

Talking to the enemy – 'the peasants are buying them at 2 silver roubles a head to kill them' – 'we were getting absolutely nothing from Moscow' – Mme de Staël at Woronowo – Wilson helps Rostopchin burn down his château – 'the law of cuckoldom, from which no one's exempt' – a bad joke – a march on Turkey? – bright frosty weather – 'our enfeebled arms turned the millstone' – 'How will it all end?' – Le Roy loses his son to the Cossacks – 'Bah, they won't attack you'

Hardly less fantastical, perhaps even more so, are the theatrically glamorous costumes of King Joachim I of Naples as he gallops about the disconsolate plain beyond Winkovo, letting himself be admired and chatted up by the Russians. Between him and them there's 'a kind of tacit agreement'. At outposts 'placed a mere 50 yards from each other' Victor Dupuy of the 7th Hussars even sees

'the King of Naples, finding the Cossacks too close to us, go among them, and make them withdraw their sentries and show them where they ought to be. The Russians obeyed. Their generals, even those of the advance guard, whom we'd often had a chance to see, made no difficulties about yielding to the King's least requirements. He really had an air of commanding the whole lot of them.'

On 6 October, the day after Lauriston had gone back to Moscow, Griois had been present at the first of these strange encounters:

'The enemy had come closer and closer to us and his scouts were at pistol range from our own. Murat, informed of this, had the signal to mount sounded all down the line. He summons one of the commanders, asks him in an imperious tone of voice by what right the Russians are occupying ground they'd been repulsed from during the affair of the 4th, and orders him instantly to retire.'

The Russian officer declines, saying he must refer the matter to his general; who soon turns up. And is reproached, even more arrogantly, by Murat:

'His anger no longer knows any bounds when the general answers him, in the calmest and most respectful tone, that the space separating the two armies after the affair of the 4th not being occupied by our troops, nothing prevented him from putting his outposts there with orders not to commit any hostile action.'

"This ground belongs to me; I'd driven your troops off it. You should have stayed in the position I'd driven you back to, and you've broken your word by leaving it after the suspension of hostilities. But you're not to be trusted. You respect nothing. Yesterday, when I was visiting my

outposts, one of your Cossacks was so insolent as to fire at me. If my officers hadn't restrained me, I'd have killed him on the spot. What's
more, I summon you to instantly withdraw your posts to their first position, or I'll oblige them to." And at the same time he orders the cavalry to advance and my artillery to arrive at the gallop. "Your Majesty",
the Russian general replies, "is free to do what he likes. I cannot withdraw my outposts, and if they're attacked, they'll defend themselves. As
for the offending Cossack, he'll be severely punished, and I beg Your
Majesty to accept my excuses for this act, which I wholly disavow.'"

Griois and the other officers, much pained to see how violent Murat has
become, are even afraid it may lead to negotiations being broken off
because of 'a misunderstanding that had no importance'. After remon-
strating with him, the generals in his suite interpose themselves *vis-à-vis* the
Russian general,

'who relaxed his pretensions. After an hour of debate and at the
moment when our troops, arriving on the scene, were only waiting for
the signal to attack, everything arranged itself amicably and we went
back to Winkovo. I was close to the king throughout this scene which,
if the possible consequences hadn't been so grave, and but for the
king's martial air, which gave dignity to his wrathful disorganised gestures and his Gascon rodomontades, Murat's rage would have been
really funny.'

All this and much else is being reported back to the Kremlin, where Ségur
is hearing how the King of Naples is

'enjoying the admiring glances which his good looks, his reputation
for bravery and his high rank were attracting. The Russian chiefs took
care not to upset him. They overwhelmed him with every mark of def-
erence that could sustain his illusion. If he took a fancy to some bit of
ground they were occupying, they made haste to give it up to him.'

'This inoffensive behaviour', Dupuy goes on, 'led us to believe peace was
very near. We ardently desired it, for every day our ranks were growing
thinner.'

The magnificent cuirassier companies, for instance, which had entered
Russia 130 troopers strong, are 'now only 18 to 24, so that a division didn't
even reach regimental strength'. Everywhere it's the same story. Arriving
from Moscow, Lieutenant *Mailly-Nesle*, a young aristocrat at IHQ, whose
only notable deed so far has been to be ordered to get Auguste Caulaincourt's heart embalmed after Borodino, is shocked to find his own regiment, the prestigious 2nd Carabiniers, have

'lost so many horses I think we weren't more than 100 men in the two
carabinier regiments all told. We'd left France 1,400 strong, and several detachments had joined us.'

For five days the Carabiniers, in their brass-coated breastplates and superb Grecian-style helmets, have only been eating horseflesh. Though 1,500 troopers are daily being sent out to forage, all they're bringing back is 'a few bales of hay'.

How different from the situation near the village of Woronowo where, twelve miles behind Murat's lines, Zalusky has been given the duty of providing a special escort for the Emperor should he suddenly turn up. There the Lancer Brigade is in clover. Each day they're breakfasting on

'polewka [rice wine] and rice cooked in milk from our own cows, and dining on whole roast pigs or chunks of beef roasted on wooden spits, and then taking coffee from iron pots hung up over an enormous fire, kept up from morning until late at night by the cantinière, or rather several cantinières at once. On the four sides of the hearth, on rugs or bits of canvas, heaps of roasted coffee, of raw coffee, of crushed sugar mounted up. And beside them cups, glasses, goblets – from the most sumptuous in gilded porcelain to earthenware mugs, Muscovite wooden drinking bowls and white metal campaign gourds. Against payment, the cantinière, sugaring it amply, poured out mocca to amateurs of all ranks assembled there and seated on canapés and satin divans with gold brocade, morocco leather, or simply on planks which supported trestles and barrels.'

Alas, nothing of all this, nor anything like it, applies in the Winkovo camp. There the Line cavalry regiments are literally starving. Each time the 7th Hussars have to 'do the dawn'[1] there are

'unfortunate horses which, lying down and worn out, could no longer struggle to their feet and died on the spot. Though Moscow was stuffed with victuals, the men were in the greatest need. The King wrote to the Emperor to inform him of our truly calamitous situation. The Emperor interrogated the ordnance officer carrying the despatch who, to play the courtier, replied that we lacked for nothing – and that was a word too much! The Emperor even got angry with the King of Naples for sending him a pack of lies. This became quickly bruited abroad and the officer received all the reproaches and all the curses he deserved. I shall abstain from giving his name.'

Murat's opposite number on the Russian side is a man who cuts hardly less glamorous a figure than himself. No one, in Wilson's view, is better matched to deal with him than General Miloradovitch, whose

'manner, his tone of voice, gestures, etc., render him superior to Murat in fanfaronade, while his singular courage and the unbounded confidence of his soldiers secure him every respect from the enemy'.

On one such occasion Miloradovitch airily tells Murat:

'Really it's an outrage, letting so many of your dead remain unburied, and your wounded lie in that wood. I'll give permission to come within my posts and remove them.'

Other generals, too, are talking to their French and Polish opposite numbers. The Russian

'General Korf, a most excellent man, with a fund of dry humour, met General Amande at the advanced posts. Soon the conversation turned to peace. And Amande observed: "We're really quite tired of this war: give us passports and we'll depart."

"Oh no, General," said Korf. "You came without being invited; when you go away you must take French leave."

"Ah!" said Amande. "But it's really a pity two nations who esteem each other should be carrying on a war of extermination. We'll make our excuses for having intruded, and shake hands upon our respective frontiers."

"Yes," replied the Russian, "we believe you've lately learnt to esteem us. But would you continue to do so if we suffered you to escape with arms in your hands?"

"*Parbleu!*" sighed M. Amande. "I see there's no talking to you about peace now and that we shan't be able to make it."'

Peace! It's what everyone's waiting for. And, in the Kremlin, Napoleon is still making a confident outward show of expecting it. Can it be he's really deceiving himself, and thus endangering the army and his empire? Everything possible, Caulaincourt is dismayed to realise, is 'being done to prolong the Emperor's fatal feeling of security and feed his hopes of an arrangement'. Not that he's really taken in by Murat's reports of the Russian army being demoralized or disintegrating:

'He continually ridiculed the stories told by the King of Naples. Yet they fed the hopes he wanted to entertain, in spite of the reflections he must have had. "Murat's the dupe of men far more astute than himself. All this talking under a flag of truce serve no purpose except to those who send them, and they invariably turn out to our disadvantage."'

Indeed Murat's position at Winkovo is utterly precarious. Ahead of him, based on its entrenched camp at Tarutino, some three miles ahead of his outposts, he has an ever-growing Russian army, while a couple of miles behind him the road to Moscow runs through a long, deep defile that has a stream running through it and can only be crossed at one point. In the event of a sudden reverse that ravine can be deadly. Furthermore, it's a very strange kind of a truce which only applies 'to the front between the two camps. At least that's how the Russians were interpreting it. We could neither bring in a convoy nor go foraging without fighting. So the war went on everywhere except where it could be favourable to us.'

Not that Murat, any more than General Amande, lacks for warnings:

'Colonel Neninski, whom he'd sent to the Russians, had talked to Platov and other senior officers, who'd said quite openly: "You're tired of the war. For us, on the contrary, it's just beginning. We'll strip you of everything: your wagons, your baggage, your guns."'

And when on 8 October Murat personally asks Miloradovitch to let his cavalry go foraging to right and left, the Russian answers bluntly:

'Why, would you wish to deprive us of the pleasure of taking your finest cavaliers of France like chickens?'

MURAT: "Oh! then I'll take my measures: I'll march my foraging columns with infantry and artillery on its flanks." MILORADOVITCH, ironically regretting not having an occasion to see the French cavalry make a real charge:

"That's just what I want, so I can order my regiments to face them."

Murat galloped off, and instead of his marching the columns to protect his foragers, the Cossacks last night took 43 cuirassiers and carabiniers, and 53 this morning,' probably another example of Wilson's implicit trust in Russian claims. In his lapidary diary Lieutenant Maurice Tascher is noting the

'extreme poverty of the army, which is living off vegetables, horsemeat and unground rye. In the forests the peasants are defending themselves against the soldiers when they try to get some food and forage.'

And not only defending themselves but also avenging themselves on the invaders. Wilson hears how they're 'buying French prisoners from the soldiers for a few francs a head, to kill them'. Himself, though suffering from a painful leg caused when his carriage overturns but in piquant contrast to conditions in the French camp only a few hundred yards away, 'the English general' is relishing 'sturgeon, caviar and large barrels of red and white grapes' given him by Platov's newly joined Don Cossacks. One day he forwards a letter to the ambassador of the Spanish government in exile. Found in the pocket of a French officer of the Swiss Colonel Tschüdi (commanding the 2nd Battalion of the Spanish Joseph Napoleon Regiment in what had been Dedem's brigade), it begs permission to be transferred to the 57th Line (Dutheillet's regiment, still back in Moscow), as he's sure 'his honour will be ruined by the desertion of his men on the first occasion.'[2] Like everyone else, Wilson is by now certain that French morale is at a complete ebb. His only wish is that Bonaparte would 'attack our camp, but I fear he won't. Yesterday 200 French cuirassier foragers were made prisoners. A general came with a flag of truce to remonstrate against the cruelty of the Cossacks in falling upon "poor men only going in search of a little hay!" Sweet innocents! How tender! How humane! how considerate these myrmidons have become!'

And all the time, as Murat's forces are dwindling away, Kutusov's are growing stronger. Each day that passes, no matter how fine the weather, has brought winter a day nearer.

On 9 October Wilson, who has hurt his leg and just heard that yesterday, though the King of Naples commanded in person, 'the French lost 4 caissons on the ground, and a wood and plain covered in dead', takes his carriage and rides out to Woronowo, twelve miles to Murat's right rear. At the junction of the 'fine, broad, well-maintained old Kaluga road' and another that leads westwards to the little town of Vereia and to the 'new' Kaluga road, Woronowo is of strategic importance. Though French troops are probing toward 'this pretty village, bisected by a stretch of water, the village on the hither side, the château and its outbuildings on the other', they've so far not occupied it.

But that's not why Wilson's carriage is taking him there. It's at Woronowo that Rostopchin has his unusually superb country residence. And he has invited 'the English general' over ... to help him burn it down.

Back in August, while everyone had been trembling for the fate of Smolensk, it had been at Woronowo that the governor of Moscow and his countess had received Europe's most famous novelist. Napoleon's most inveterate enemy and leader of the intellectual opposition to his military dictatorship, on 10 May Mme *Germaine de Staël*, had flouted his Geneva prefect's express orders that she be kept under house arrest in her home at Coppet,[3] and taking her courage and her nerves in both hands and, accompanied by her daughter and her lover *Albert Jean Michel de Rocca*, had fled to Bern. There she had taken the German philosopher Schlegel into her carriage and, passing through the recently insurgent Tyrol, had arrived in Vienna. There, though feted as usual – no woman in Europe is as famous as the author of *Corinne* – she'd been horrified to find that, as a result of three successive defeats at Napoleon's hands, the easy-going Austrian regime had been replaced by a quasi-Napoleonic police state of the kind she most utterly detests. Her plan had been to go on to Petersburg, thence to Stockholm, to see her old friend, the former Marshal Bernadotte, now Crown Prince Elect Karl Johan; and thence to England, the country which, next after her beloved France, she most ardently admires for its parlia-

"What a monstrous sight! All those palaces! Extraordinary resolution!
What men!" But of Rostopchin, who'd ordered his police to set fire to the city:
"He fancies he's a Roman, but is nothing but a stupid savage!" The marshal
standing behind Napoleon is Ney.

Moscow in flames, seen from the riverside. It was along this road that Napoleon and IHQ escaped from the Kremlin, passed round the west side of the town and went out to the Petrovskoï Palace.

V. V. Verestchaguin imagines Napoleon being guided through the flames by Davout's grenadiers. In reality it's doubtful whether he ever came so close to the fire. But Quartermaster *Anatole Montesquiou* and his colleagues had 'to protect cheeks, hands and eyes with handkerchiefs and headgear and turn up the collars of our uniforms'.

The Petrovskoï Palace, occupied for three days by Napoleon and IHQ when
the fire was at its height. Its 'Gothick' style reminded Roman Soltyk of Hampton Court and
to Castellane seemed "Greek, truly romantic". It hadn't a single stick of furniture.

Return to the Kremlin from Petrovskoï, 19 October. Caulaincourt found
the scene utterly depressing. The Guard Dragoons' breeches can hardly have been so
white! A few days later one its squadrons was annihilated at Malo-Wiazma.

Incendiaries, real or imaginary, were shot by firing squad in the monastery by the Doroghomilov Gate where Davout ('the Iron Marshal') and his reluctant chief-of-staff, the future battle-painter Baron L-F. Lejeune, had their headquarters. – Oil painting by V. V. Verestchaguin.

'Moscow, September 24, 1812' – one of the scenes drawn by Major Faber du Faur on his unit's arrival on 24 September. 'In this labyrinth of devastation' he saw remains of the iron-plate roofings whose fall had been so dangerous to many of our eyewitnesses.

Moscow seen from the south-west by the Württemberger Major G. de Faber du Faur. His fine engravings, based on drawings made on the spot, cover the whole campaign. Left: the River Moskova. Middle ground: remains of half-burnt monasteries.

'Moscow, October 8.' One of the many intact monasteries, whose brilliant colours contrast vividly with the ruins of houses, Faber du Faur noted, was a depot for the 4,000 dismounted cavalry. View 'from the north-west bastion of the powder magazine,' to the east of the city, where III Corps was quartered.

Right: Baron A-J-F. Fain, Napoleon's hard-worked Second Secretary, kept a private journal. Metternich admired him for his probity and intelligence.

Below: Captain Boniface de Castellane, one of Napoleon's orderly officers, was 'so so used to the Emperor's infallibility and his projects succeeding' that he was prepared to march on India.

Below right: Colonel Bacler d'Albe, Napoleon's chief topographer, was, physically speaking, his closest collaborator. Sometimes as they lay stretched out over the map table fixing Bacler's coloured pins they would 'let out loud cries as their heads bumped together'.

Above: Rostopchin was an unbalanced personality. As he left the city, which at any moment would burst into flames, he told his son to look at it for the last time. He and his pious wife had recently entertained Mme de Staël at his château at Woronowo, which he also personally set fire to and which General Wilson thought 'could not be replaced for £100,000'.

Above right: Colonel Lubin Griois, commanding 3rd Cavalry Corps' light artillery, conversed familiarly with Napoleon on ballistics, prided himself on knowing each of his gunners by name and on never ducking when roundshot came whizzing overhead.

Right: General Jean Rapp, Napoleon's battle-scarred and most senior ADC, though many times wounded and aged 41 in 1812, he 'still walked with the jaunty gait of a hussar officer'. Although not recovered from his four wounds at Borodino, he insisted on serving during the retreat.

Far left: The Dutch ex-diplomat and general of brigade Dedem van der Gelder was too critical for his superiors' liking. – From a miniature painting.

Left: Major C. F. M. Le Roy, promoted Lieutenant-Colonel of the 85th Line at Moscow, wrote his memoirs to show the importance of getting one's daily dinner. His son, a sergeant in the 85th, was captured by Cossacks and never heard of again.

Opposite page, bottom: Césare de Laugier, Adjutant-Major of the Italian Guardia d'Onore, an Elban whose diary is always concerned to defend the honour of the Army of Italy.

Below: 'Over 100 ammunition wagons' assembled in October in the open area to the east of the Kremlin's two spectacular churches were so thick on the ground that Faber du Faur found it hard to find a spot from which to draw them.

Davout at the Doroghomilov monastery, in the western part of the city.
Presumably it's his reluctant chief-of staff, Baron Lejeune, the future painter of
battle scenes, who is talking to him.

The Battle of Tarutino where Murat's starving advance guard was only saved by his personal intervention and the Polish Legion of the Vistula. 'Seeing Bagavout's infantry advancing in three squares to cut off our retreat, the King of Naples put himself at the head of some carabiniers and the 5th Cuirassiers, charged and sabred them to pieces.'

Prince Eugène Beauharnais, Viceroy of Italy, commanded the Army of Italy.
He was, said Napoleon, "The only member of my family I've never had to complain of."
But his attitude to his Italians was arrogant.

Right: Leaving Moscow, midday 19 October. Napoleon at the Kaluga Gate. 'The crush in the streets was terrific. The units were crossing each other's path in all directions... more than 500 guns, 2,000 ammunition wagons with their half-starved teams, the endless train of vehicles of all kinds and nations laden with booty and foodstuffs...' All would by and by have to be abandoned.

Right: Marshal Mortier's mines were partly defuzed by rain. But when the others went off they blew part of the Kremlin sky-high and made the 'loudest bang' Lieutenant Paul de Bourgoing would ever hear in his life. Lieutenant-Colonel Le Roy heard it from fifty miles away.

Bringing up the rear on 23 October and turning off from the old Kaluga road to reach the new road, III Corps had to blow up any number of its ammunition wagons, their teams being already utterly exhausted. This one was casually exploded by a gendarme who fired his pistol at it while it was having its load lightened!

Advance or retreat? "That's enough, gentlemen. I shall decide." The scene in the weaver's cabin at Gorodnia. In fact he did not do so until next day, when he was sure the Russian army had once again eluded his grasp. – Oil painting by V. V. Verestchaguin.

Borowsk, 26 October. Ney's III Corps being attacked by masses of Cossacks. "A brief discharge of artillery and a charge by the cavalry of the Royal Guard sufficed to drive them off. At Borowsk our luck seemed to turn. In the afternoon of the 26th we began our retreat." – Engraving by Faber du Faur.

mentary form of government. For a moment, while anxiously waiting in Vienna for her passport to arrive from Petersburg, she'd even contemplated braving the hazards of travel through Turkey and getting to London that way. But then the Tsar's passport had come; and on 14 July , anniversary of the fall of the Bastille and the same day as Napoleon had left Vilna for Glubokoïe, she too had – it's the only appropriate word – invaded Russia. How frustrating that her arch-enemy's armies and their thousand cannon should have placed themselves between her and Tsar Alexander! It had added 800 more miles to her journey, a wide detour via Moscow – still supposedly far outside the theatre of war. In fact she'd probably been the last western European to see the ancient city before it had gone up in flames.

Driving out to Woronowo, she'd been entertained by the Rostopchins. Not that the city governor is in the least degree a liberal. A week or two later, to save his own skin he wouldn't hesitate to throw a journalist who'd been disseminating French ideas to be torn to pieces by an infuriated mob. What Rostopchin's 'pious' countess (one day to be the author of the century's most sado-masochistic novel) or their daughter (one day to wed Philippe de Ségur) had thought of their garrulous visitor, we don't know.

From Moscow she'd gone on to Petersburg, and there still more deeply imbued the reportedly liberal-minded Tsar with her ideas. And thence to Stockholm, where her brilliant garrulity is fast wearying the taciturn Swedes as she makes propaganda for their new ruler as putative successor to a defeated Napoleon.[4]

'Situated by the roadside', Rostopchin's château will appear to Dumonceau, that sober-minded and meticulous observer, as

'an ordinary country house, of modern architecture, plastered on the outside and having two storeys, four or five windows in its façade, with a door in the middle, enhanced with an attic portico supported by two columns.'

But by then it'll be in ruins. To Wilson, as his carriage approaches it, the still intact château seems very much more impressive, irreplaceable for less than £100,000:

'The very stabling was of rare grandeur, surmounted over the gateways by colossal casts of the Monte Cavallo horses and figures which he had brought from Rome, with costly models of all the principal Roman and Grecian buildings and statues that filled a large gallery in the palace, the interior of which was most splendidly and tastefully furnished with every article of luxurious use and ornament that foreign countries could supply.'

Unfortunately Friedrichs' division is fighting its way towards it. And to Wilson Rostopchin's sacrifice of his lavish residence seems a 'magnificent act, executed with feeling, dignity, and philosophy. The motive was pure patriotism. Rostopchin, on hearing the pickets commence skirmishing, and seeing the enemy in movement, entered his palace, begging his friends to accompany him. On arriving at the porch, burning torches were distributed to every one. Mounting the stairs and reaching his state bedroom, Rostopchin paused a moment, and then said to the English General: "That's my marriage bed; I haven't the heart to set it on fire; you must spare me this pain."

'When Rostopchin had himself set on fire all the rest of the apartment then, and not before, his wish was executed. Each apartment was ignited as the party proceeded, and in a quarter of an hour the whole was one blazing mass. Rostopchin then proceeded to the stables, which were quickly in flames; and afterwards stood in front contemplating the progress of the fire and the falling fragments. When at last the Cavallo group was precipitated, he said: "I am at ease." And as the enemy's shots were now whistling around, he and all retired, leaving the enemy the following alarming and instructive lesson affixed to a conspicuous pillar.'

Written in charcoal and afterwards to be read, not to say differently remembered, by many French and Polish eyes and quoted with various pathetic embellishments, it reads, according to Heinrich von Brandt, who'll be arriving in a minute with his voltigeur companies of the 2nd Vistula Legion:

I'VE SET FIRE TO MY CHATEAU, WHICH COST ME A MILLION, SO THAT NO DOG OF A FRENCHMAN SHALL LODGE IN IT. [5]

Dumonceau sees it attached to the left-hand pillar. Beneath it, some French soldier, 'also in charcoal, but illustrated with a drawing' has proffered his (probably obscene) comment. Le Roy, arriving on the scene with the 85th Line, proffers others, expressed with greater elegance and innuendo:

'The newly built château of cut stone, constructed in the Italian style, had a fine appearance, though since the morning it had been on fire. Since it hadn't been able to bite into the walls the fire had concentrated on burning the panelling, furniture and floors. The grand staircase was almost wholly reduced to quicklime. However one of the regiment's captains, Souvigny by name, risked going up to the upstairs apartments and brought back some curious belongings and a roll of letters written in French.'

These, Le Roy goes on gleefully,

'were nothing but the correspondence of Rostopchin's daughter with a certain cousin who hadn't always respected the bonds of relationship, at least so one could suppose from the free and familiar expressions in this correspondence.'

All of which will delight Le Roy, that great hater of aristocrats the more when, many years later, he comes to write his memoirs:

'I'll wager a hundred to one the little cousin is a friend about the house of M. le comte de Ségur, and count though he be, neither intelligence nor wealth, as our good Lafontaine wittily puts it, protect anyone from the law of cuckoldom, before which all ranks are on the same level. And it's not certain it's he who has carried on the direct line of Asia's greatest conqueror.'[6]

Evidently the same notice, also scribbled in charcoal, has also been nailed up on the doors of the parish church, where Le Roy's bosom friend Lieutenant Jacquet, bivouacking there, points it out to him as the battalion's staff settles for the night in the porch:

'But the French had been politer than that boyard. They'd left the two marble statues above the main door standing on their bases. With my own eyes I saw them still there when I left. As for the park and its embellishments, everything had been spoiled by the artillery and its vehicles which had camped in the gardens and occupied the kiosks. The trees had been cut down for the men to warm themselves, since the nights were beginning to be cold.'

When Griois sees

'this stroke of patriotism, so little in our own style and whose heroism has something barbarous about it, it gave us food for thought and a glimpse of what we had to expect in such a country.'

But that isn't how it's received in the Kremlin. Declaring Rostopchin's defiant notice 'ridiculous', Napoleon sends it – presumably in a copy – to Paris, to be printed in the newspapers, where, according to Caulaincourt, 'it made a deep impression on all reflective people, and, in respect solely to the sacrifice of his house, found more admirers than censors'. But Gourgaud[7] fancies he can detect Rostopchin's true motives. Hadn't this Russian count, he asks, burnt down his château simply to escape the reproach of not himself having lost anything in the great disaster he had precipitated?

Bored by having nothing to do in Moscow as the days and weeks go by, Captain Biot, ADC to the wounded General Pajol, offers his services to Murat's chief-of-staff General *A-D. Belliard*. The wise and efficient Belliard, 'the only man who had a hand with Murat', has just been appointed Major-General of the Cavalry, as successor to Auguste de Caulaincourt, killed at Borodino. Now he sends Biot with a despatch to Murat, possibly to inform him of this fact. On the way Biot falls in with a certain General Dumont, who generously gives him his card to take to his valet who, he says, will give him a bottle of wine and a beefsteak; but before he goes on to Winkovo Dumont also takes him to Prince Poniatowski, who sends him on his way.'

The hitherto well-fed Biot is appalled at the state of affairs in the Winkovo camp. He has brought his comrades of the 11th Chasseurs some Moscow chickens, bread, rum and wine. And well he has done so. For by now they're very hungry indeed. The state of things at the Winkovo camp worry him so that he's 'unable to get a wink of sleep' at the 11th Chasseurs' bivouac. 'Men and horses were dying of hunger. Literally. Never any distributions.' Rather than stay there he prefers to accompany Murat on a reconnaissance, where, almost more alarming, he sees at a glance that the over-confident Sébastiani[8] is still being guilty of all sorts of negligence: 'His favourite occupation, Colonel Meuzian of the 5th Hussars told me, was uttering declamations.' Murat sends Biot back to Moscow with a despatch, and probably a letter to Belliard, for they are in frequent correspondence.

Honours, at least so it seems, are flying to and fro between Moscow – where Biot finds his conduct at Borodino has made him a chevalier of the Legion of Honour – and Winkovo. A similar one reaches Griois – but in circumstances that nullify its effect. At a musket shot's distance outside the village, he and Jumilhac and their orderlies are almost daily having to use the flats of their swords to fight off insubordinate soldiers who want to grab their timber cottage and burn it down for firewood. Driven off, they swear they'll come back in the night. But now something much worse befalls. Immediately after Lauriston's visit, Griois, taking advantage of the unofficial truce, has sent his empty ammunition wagons back to Moscow to be replenished from 'the great artillery park'; and with them his orders to his servant Batiste, also left behind in Moscow, to join the returning convoy and bring him his own wagon, his carriage, worn though it is from its long journey from Italy, his victuals and his horses, all of which he'd also left behind:

'Several days had passed since I'd sent off my order; but everything in front of us being calm, I assumed the same state of affairs prevailed between Winkovo and Moscow, and wasn't at all worried that the convoy was delayed. But then, one day at dinner, Lahoussaye, with a laughing air, announced that he'd just received my nomination to the Legion of Honour.[9] At the same time he had some annoying news for me. My vehicles had been carried off by Cossacks.'

At first Griois thinks the idiotic Lahoussaye is only joking. He isn't:

'A quartermaster sergeant of the Train, who'd just arrived, told me that on the second day out of Moscow the convoy had been assailed by Cossacks, whom the escort had prevented from doing it any great harm, they'd only smashed up some wagons and made off with the horses. But just as they were going off they'd caught sight of my carriage, with my wagon and lead horses, quite a long way from the convoy's rear, seized it without anyone resisting them,' and made off into the forest. His carriage is worth 'at least 20,000 frs. The loss in my situation was irreparable.' It's a stunning blow:

'All I had left was what I was wearing, a shirt in a portmanteau, the horse I was riding, and another I'd brought with me. But what I regretted most was my papers and some other objects of little value; and, above all, my faithful servant Batiste, who I feared had probably succumbed to fatigue, chagrin and maltreatment.'[10]

His adjutant-major Lenoble, too, had had all his effects in Griois' wagon, 'so we could only console each other. He even went to the place where the "hurrah"[11] had occurred; but returned with the sad certainty that all was lost. By some kind of fatality this was the only event of this kind that occurred while we were at Winkovo. Every day unescorted convoys were arriving without accident from Moscow.'

Not all promotions to the rank of chef d'escadron are as straightforwardly due to experience and merit as young Victor Dupuy's. For years now – Henckens had seen it start as early as 1806, in Italy – experienced regimental officers who've risen from the ranks have had to get used to seeing blue-blooded youngsters from ancient military families advanced over their heads. Now the 6th and 8th Chasseurs, in Chastel's light cavalry brigade of 3rd Cavalry Corps, is no exception. On 6 October Lauriston had brought out with him in his suite two such newly fledged colonels – the young Belgian count de Talhouët for the 6th and Talleyrand's son, Count Talleyrand de Périgord, for the 8th Chasseurs, both, 'though still in their twenties, orderly officers to the Emperor:

'It seems the Emperor had found his dead colonel's temporary successor, Squadron Commander de Feuillebois, a trifle on the elderly side. It's true young colonels with experience of the great staffs are necessary for light cavalry regiments,' and young Talhouët, though he knows 'virtually nothing about what goes on inside a regiment, had been to a good school to learn the profession,'

sighs Henckens, on poor Squadron-leader Feuillebois' behalf. Swallowing his cruel disappointment – short of performing some spectacular feat under the Emperor's very eyes, it's good-bye forever to further promotion or a colonel's epaulettes – Feuillebois at once recommends to young Talhouët that he avail himself of the 34-year-old but highly experienced Henckens' services. Talhouët, who since being wounded in the shoulder at Mojaisk on 8 September has been resting in Moscow, turns out to be a young man with a lot of good sense, and confirms Henckens, though still not commissioned, in his post as acting adjutant-major to the 6th Chasseurs.

Cuirassier-captain *Bréaut des Marlots* too rejoins his regiment, bringing with him a wagon laden with coffee, sugar and wine:

'The wine was soon drunk up, but I still had nearly 600 pounds of sugar and coffee, which was a fine stock even after giving some of it to my comrades. I drank it day and night.'

On one occasion – but only one – some tuns of wine arrive 'without escort and without accident' for 3rd Cavalry Corps from Moscow. And here's a really big surprise for Surgeon *Heinrich von Roos* and his 3rd Württemberger Chasseurs, in the nearby village of Teterinka, occupied by Sébastiani's light cavalry division. At the campaign's outset huge herds of sheep and cattle, prodded on across Europe – some from as far afield as Italy and Hungary – by 'frighteningly inexperienced drovers', had accompanied the regiments; but of course had immediately fallen far behind. Now, all of a sudden, the Württemberg chasseurs and Prussian lancer units are rejoined by

'the remains of herds of cattle, cows and sheep we'd assembled at the Niemen. I can leave it to your imagination what state these beasts were in. But they were no less welcome for that.'

Even Murat comes and asks for some proper meat.

'We sent him now a sheep, now a haunch of beef or cow. As for ourselves, we made broth of sheep or beef, like tea or coffee. Sometimes it happened, but rarely, that one of the Moscow regiments, knowing how badly off we were, sent us some real tea, some coffee or sugar.'

But the men who've brought the herds have terrible things to relate about the state of affairs in the rear; how on the Borodino battlefield there are

'still wretched mutilated creatures crawling about, living off rotting horseflesh with their teeth and fingernails, all black, like wild animals, having nothing human about them but their shape.'

Similar horrors are related by two troopers who'd been taken prisoner at Inkowo[12] on 8 August and who, to von Roos' and their comrades' amazement, turn up disguised as peasants.

One day a begging letter is received via the outposts from five officers who've been captured by the Russians. They want some money. The cash is raised and sent to the outposts. But is never received. This is war *à outrance*. Nothing so stimulates the imagination as hunger! Remain only its imaginings. In the Kremlin the younger officers, always the most optimistic, are discussing how, peace once made, in the spring the French and Russian armies will be marching southwards together against Turkey – or possibly even India.[13] 'We're so confident,' Captain Castellane writes in his journal,

'that we aren't discussing the possibility of such an enterprise succeeding, but how many marches will be needed and how long it'll take letters to reach us from France. We're used to the Emperor's infallibility and his projects succeeding.'

Can it be an echo of these fancies that reaches the 2nd Cuirassiers out at Winkovo and causes Regimental Sergeant- Major Thirion's imagination to sprout erotic wings?

'We imagined we'd be taking up winter quarters in the Ukraine, and in the spring the Russian and French armies would march together to conquer Turkey. Each of us already saw himself as a pascha. We made it a duty in advance to restore their liberty to numerous victims shut up in harems. Instead of being herded together waiting for their despotic shepherd to select a favourite, it'd be they who'd toss a handkerchief amid our squadrons. Each of us wanted to bring a beautiful slave back to France. One fancied a Greek, another a Circassian. This one a Georgian, that one a daughter of the Caucasus. These castles – not in the air but in Turkey – helped us to pass a very dreary, very painful time in this camp we'd named The Camp of Famine, a title it merited all too well, since we lacked for everything. No tents. No shelter. Sleeping under the open sky on a little straw, eating horseflesh, drinking river water from the infected stream.'

Surely this disastrous war must soon be over? Is as good as over already? Topics of conversation vary, but are never gay. Some of the officers try to cheer their men up by reminding them it's the great, the hitherto never defeated, Emperor Napoleon who's still in charge. Others are sceptical, accuse these optimists of not revealing their true thoughts:

'The women accused Napoleon of not keeping his promises, "he who lives well-off in Moscow with his Guard and sends us here to die of cold and hunger!" We let these women relieve their feelings by such words, but none of us would have permitted himself to express himself in that fashion.'

Only the weather's superb. Since settling into their cabin Griois and Jumilhac have 'only had two days of rain. On the other day the air is steadily getting colder. By now the 3rd Württemberg Chasseurs are burning down Teterinka's barns, one by one, for firewood. Soon there's

'nothing left of the village but a few rooms for the senior officers and invalids. We only had enough straw to feed the horses. We used it for sleeping on at night and then gave it to the horses to eat. Often the nights were so cold we hid under straw to sleep. And next morning this straw was so sticky with hoar-frost we had to break it to get out. The cadaverous horses and the saddles were white with it.'

Fortunately the sun comes out in the daytime and melts the hoarfrost:

'We cooked what grain, barley, buckwheat we could get hold of. We boiled them until the grain swelled, burst and softened. Then we removed the husk and made soup and thin broth. Part of these grains were reserved to make bread of, after we'd ground them. This work was most arduous for our thin and enfeebled arms. Officers and men alike, we took turns at turning the millstone. Those who wouldn't put their hand to it had to go hungry. For more than three or four days my arms refused to do this milling work.'

Von Roos must be wondering what good he'll be for carrying out amputations after a fight. And goes on:

'The saltpetre of our gunpowder, dissolved in the soup, gave it a bitter taste, caustic, disagreeable. It also caused diarrhoea. So we had to abstain and give up using any kind of salt. For fat we used candles.'

The 7th Hussars, 'very badly established in the utterly ruined village of Winkovo' are

'living off leaves of tea or cabbage, grilled horseflesh or chicken. Food and forage were utterly lacking. Strong detachments, taken from our division and that of General Saint-Germain's cuirassiers [2nd, 3rd and 9th, 1st Cavalry Corps], went searching for it at distance of 5 or 8 miles, but brought back very little.'

In one of these forages Dupuy loses a horse and a servant, taken by the enemy:

'The grand'gardes needed more than a third of the men available in the division. The saddle was hardly ever off our horses – only for a moment during the day, to let them drink. Yet the Russians were leaving us in peace. Between us there was a kind of tacit agreement.'

As the cavalry's horses dwindle and die, Griois is hearing from the Russian camp

'musketry fire by sections and platoons, which told us new recruits were being hurriedly trained. The King of Naples, no doubt warned of Russian preparations for a new offensive, had ordered all baggage wagons, horses and anything else that might hinder a night action should be sent back to a village less than three miles to our rear. Next morning, if nothing happened in the interim, they were to be sent forward again. For the first few days this order had been punctiliously obeyed; but when it was seen the enemy hadn't attacked and that the only effect of this precaution was to wear out the horses, it was relaxed.'

Frequent convoys of sick men, too, are leaving for Moscow. 'A month more of this, and the whole reserve cavalry', says Griois bluntly, will be 'annihilated without even fighting'.

On 10 October the volatile Murat, always capable of falling ill merely from disappointments or frustration,[14] writes again to Belliard:

'My position is terrible; the entire enemy army is in front of me. The advance guard's troops are reduced to nothing. And it's no longer possible to go foraging without incurring the virtual certainty of being captured. Only two days ago we lost 200 men in this fashion. How will it all end? I'm afraid to tell the Emperor the truth; it would pain him. Won't there be officious persons who'll poison my reports? Ma foi, so much the worse. Tell the Prince of Neuchâtel something of this. If only I could see the Emperor! My health isn't at all good, and I'm sure to get ill at the first rains, but let God's will be done. Doesn't the Emperor want to do anything for the advance guard? Send us some flour, or we're going to die of hunger. Give me some news, I know nothing.'

For his part Napoleon is intending to use Murat's cavalry – what's left of it – for a screen to hide a sudden march on Kaluga, taking Kutusov off guard. And His Majesty is becoming exasperated by all the quasi-fraternizations. Now he renews his orders to inhibit all truces or discussions with the Russians, and even orders "any general having intercourse with the enemy to be shot". Though addressed to his distant relative Sébastiani, to spare his brother-in-law's feelings, the order naturally also reaches its real addressee, on whom – Murat writes again to Belliard, the only effect of such a ban on chats at the outposts is to cause him even greater worry:

"For to me they've been an assurance that the Russians won't attack me without warning. This has facilitated our foragings. How unhappy I am, adieu! When will the Emperor make up his mind? What will become of his army this winter?"

Among the infantry regiments supporting Murat at Woronowo is the 85th Line. Its First Major having just died, Le Roy is notified on 10 October that he's been promoted – certainly at Davout's behest – lieutenant-colonel, and is to succeed him. His first duty in his new capacity is to go to Moscow and report to Davout on the regiment's condition. For seven or eight miles Lieutenant Jacquet accompanies him along the Moscow road; but then returns to the regiment. The deserted highway is dangerously exposed. So is a convoy of vehicles coming toward him in the distance.

And now Le Roy, riding along with his trusty servant Guillaume, is in for a terrible shock.

The convoy, bound for Woronowo, turns out to be commanded by the 85th's baggage-master. Its escort, Le Roy sees at a glance – and tells him so – is utterly inadequate. Well, the baggage-master's all too well aware of it: '"You're right. Yesterday evening I was attacked in the forest and was so unfortunate as to lose four sergeants, on their way to rejoin. They'd laid their weapons on the vehicles and were marching at some little distance from the convoy when some armed peasants and Cossacks carried them off. The worst of it all – for you – is: your son's one of the prisoners. Of course we opened fire. But not being in sufficient strength to pursue the pillagers we decided to guard the vehicles as far as to the next post."'

Stricken to the heart, Le Roy pursues his way. What can be happening to his son?

'I still had five more miles to go before I got to the wood where they'd been captured. I realized all too well it was too late to help my child. Even so I had hopes of learning something about these unfortunate men's fate. What stupidity! Ah, young people, young people! Soon I reached the fatal spot. The wood was too dense to penetrate. Seeing a road to my right, I told Guillaume to go on along the highway; I wanted to see where this track led to.

"It can lead wherever it likes," the brave lad said to me, "but I'm not leaving you."

"Very well then, come along with me."

'We put our horses to a gallop and soon we saw a big plain. As this track took us not very far from the town, I decided to follow it. Hardly had I done half a mile or so than I came to my senses, saw what danger I was exposing myself to, also my devoted companion. Halting in my tracks I turned to Guillaume and said:

"You've just heard me saying how imprudent my son's behaviour was. Yet here am I, making the same mistake! What are we looking for? Where are we going? What can we do if we're attacked? We'll only get ourselves killed without any chance of avenging ourselves."'

Guillaume points out that it's safer to be out in the plain where any enemies will be visible at a distance, and that they still have every chance of reaching Moscow before nightfall. By and by they see some infantrymen running toward a tree. Challenged, Le Roy and Guillaume declare themselves. The infantrymen belong to an outpost of the 108th. Lodged in a windmill, they're grinding corn for their division. Their captain, all sympathy for Le Roy's terrible loss of his son, invites them to stay the night.

'We spent a large part of the night chatting together. To avoid any surprise half the troop were under arms, the other rested with their backs against their packs. As dawn was breaking I dropped off a moment.'

Despite all the grinding noises in the mill Le Roy doesn't wake up till 10 a.m. And immediately – extraordinarily, but true to his Lucullan character – he feels

'revived and disposed to have breakfast. My head had cleared of all the bleak notions it had been overcharged with since yesterday. I gave no more thought to what I was leaving behind in Russia. All my wishes turned toward my family, whose sole breadwinner I was.'

Even so, the shock has had a profound effect. For here's a strange thing. All Le Roy's military ambitions have vanished overnight! From now on his only wish, like so many thousands of others', will be to get back to France, and 'on grounds of long service to get a retirement pension ample enough to keep me from poverty, and to which I felt I had a most legitimate right.'

On 13 October Castellane, in the Kremlin, notes in his journal that the eleven regiments of Grouchy's 3rd Cavalry Corps, together, only add up to 700 horses. Griois takes up the refrain. 'Under pain of dying of hunger' his horse gunners are still having

'to off and search for some kind of nourishment, since one wouldn't have found a blade of straw for 30 miles around and since – either because of transport difficulties or the insouciance of the administrations – we were getting nothing, absolutely nothing, from Moscow. There our comrades had an abundance of everything, were living in magnificent palaces, eating succulent dishes, drinking the best wines, while we were having to sustain ourselves on a crude broth, rye cakes baked under ashes, muddy and marshy water. Our foragers were having to go 9 to 12 miles to bring back a little crushed straw or even a little of half-rotten thatch from roofs. Many were killed or captured, and these losses were happening over and over, every day, though we were taking care now to have them escorted by numerous detachments.'

One such foraging expedition, on a very big scale, has gone quite exceptionally far. Colonel *T-J-J. Séruzier*, commanding 2nd Cavalry Corps' horse artillery, had been 'given orders to take command of a strong detachment, taken from all our light cavalry regiments. To these forces I was to unite half my squadron of horse gunners.' But though his column marches for 120 miles and even pushes

'into the Ukraine, it wasn't until in the surroundings of Poltava[15] I found any inhabited countryside. This country is very fertile. I found remounts for the whole of my cavalry and assembled a considerable number of wagons, which I loaded with grain, flour and forage.'

They all get back without being molested; and Séruzier, already rewarded after Borodino with a 4,000 francs pension, finds he's been nominated, not a Chevalier, but a Commandant of the Legion of Honour. 'I was as happy as a brave military man can be.'

By now Murat's situation has become so desperate that he sends his 36-year-old Neapolitan ADC, the newly fledged Colonel *M-J-T. Rossetti*, to Moscow to

'tell the Emperor how compromised his advance guard was, and how impossible it would be for him, should he be attacked, of successfully resisting a much stronger enemy. "Tell the Emperor," the King added, "he shouldn't count on our suspension of hostilities. It's illusory, since on either side we can attack each other after giving only a few hours' notice.'"

The King had only agreed to it, Rossetti's to explain, in order to give his men a few days' rest. But it's

'"solely to the Russians' advantage, since it in no way changes my position, whilst every day the enemy is being reinforced and all day long I hear from my camp the shots of their recruits' target practice.'"

At 10 p.m. on 12 October Rossetti sets out with his despatches

'for the Emperor and for Berthier. I reached the Kremlin at 8 a.m. At 10 a.m. I was introduced into the Emperor's office. As he had already informed himself of the contents of the King's despatches, which I'd handed to Berthier, I no sooner appeared than he says to me:

"Well! So Murat's complaining, is he?"

"Sire," I replied, "it's because he's in a very critical situation."

"Bah! With light cavalry one can live anywhere. Not all the surrounding countryside has been devastated. He can draw resources from it.'"[16]

Rossetti points out that the countryside is entirely occupied by Cossacks, and that even marauding parties commanded by generals are only bringing back a few bales of hay 'not sufficient for one-fifth of our horses'.

'"Where's Poniatowski?"

"On the other side of the ravine, between Pictrowo and Kroueza."

"Show it to me."

'I showed him on the map the position of V Corps. Having examined the map for ten minutes, the Emperor says to me brusquely:

"What an idea of Murat's, to put himself in a ravine! It's on the Nara he should have established himself.'"

Rossetti explains that that's exactly what they'd been intending to do on 4 October, but that the enemy had prevented it with his whole forces, obliging Murat to withdraw to the Winkovo position:

'While the Emperor was walking to and fro, I expounded to him in greatest detail what the King had told me to say. He wore an air of not entirely giving faith to my report. Often he interrupted me, saying:

"Bah! They won't attack you. They're in more need of rest than we are. My army's finer than ever. A few days' rest has done it a lot of good.'"

But when Rossetti reiterates that the advance guard is in a 'state of *dénuement* [utmost destitution]', he says:

'"Assure the King that tomorrow I'll be sending him a convoy of flour. Tell him he must absolutely hold his position. Anyway, he won't be attacked; but in any case he must halt and retrench himself at the Woronowo defile.'"

Rossetti's account seems circumstantial enough. But we've caught him out telling fibs before.[17] Can the greatest soldier of the age, emperor though he be, be so preoccupied with other matters that he only now bothers to check up on the exact position of his only major field force, facing the entire Russian army?

Certainly he seems to have left it very late to give Murat any real orders; and even then they seem too vague to be addressed to a field commander of Murat's wavering temperament and fluctuating strategical ideas. At 2 p.m. Napoleon dictates a letter, as always via Berthier:

"On the basis of your reports and the reconnaissances which have been sent in to him, the Emperor thinks the Woronowo position is a fine one, reserrée [compact] and able to defend itself with infantry, which would easily cover the cavalry. If you think so too, you are authorized to take up that position. The Emperor has sent off his horses, and the day after tomorrow the army will reach you to attack the enemy and le chasser [drive him off]. Three days will be needed for the army to reach your level; thus you will only have to spend four or five more days [where you are]; and if you think the enemy's going to attack you or that the nature of things is making it impossible for you to avoid the losses you've been sustaining these last eight days, you have the recourse of taking up the Woronowo position. All the vehicles which you have sent [to Moscow] are laden with victuals. Those being sent off this evening will also leave [again] tomorrow."

The long rambling letter goes on with that air of vagueness which can characterise Napoleon's orders at critical moments, as if partly dictated by a need to pass the buck. And this one will certainly need reading twice. As Napoleon himself, on second thoughts, seems to realize. Has Murat enough sense to adjudge his own situation aright?:

'Make sure to reconnoitre the outlet which could lead you toward Mojaisk, so that if you have to make a retreat in front of the enemy, you would thoroughly know that road. The Emperor supposes that your baggage, your park, and the greater part of your infantry could disappear without the enemy noticing it."

As if still bothered by uncertainty, he asks:

"Is it true that your cavalry when moving back through the Woronowo defile could be covered by your infantry and in a less fatiguing position than the one where it is [now], in flat countryside that obliges it to be always on the qui vive? At all events it is very [surely?] important

to procure your troops food for several days. In Moscow are 1,000 quintals of flour and plenty of brandy at your disposition."
If the advance guard had been commanded by Davout or Ney it's just possible such fuzzy instructions might have sufficed. To Murat, whose cavalry screen is going to be crucial if Kutusov is to be outflanked by a sudden drive southwards to Kaluga, it can only give an uneasy feeling that, no matter what happens, it'll be he who'll get the blame if things turn out badly.

Even Henckens, from his on-the-ground viewpoint as adjutant-major of the 6th Chasseurs, is seething with irritation to see the Russian army becoming steadily reinforced and the attack on Kaluga delayed until the season for it has passed. Say Gourgaud and other apologists what they will, Napoleon's incisiveness at this moment is far from what it used to be, and will be again.

While Rossetti is talking to Napoleon in the Kremlin, Murat is lodging a formal complaint with Kutusov. Cossacks have carried off some of his muleteers which have accidentally crossed the agreed demarcation line. If he doesn't get them back, he says, he'll raise the cease-fire.

That day too Sous-lieutenant Pierre Auvray of the 23rd Dragoons, foraging at a distance of nine miles from his bivouac, runs into Cossacks:
'Hardly have we had time to put ourselves in a state of defence by forming up a troop of officers and NCO to contain them, while the dragoons were making off with their loads, than a fight started. We charged the Cossacks in force to be able to get across a little stream, where we were mixed up pell-mell with them. Almost all our officers were wounded. I received two lance-thrusts in my left arm. One young officer was killed.'

That same day (13 October) Wilson hears more good news. On the Mojaisk road a convoy of
'350 wagons, laden with Buonaparte's plunder, was proceeding under the escort of four cavalry regiments and two battalions of infantry. Three hundred Cossacks charged at night, killed all the wagons' horses, rendered the column immovable and have given advice to 3,000 men under General Docturov, who has marched to profit by the occasion.'

Three days later at roll-call Surgeon Heinrich von Roos finds his regiment of Württemberg chasseurs consists of one major, five lieutenants, four sergeant-majors, five NCOs, a handful of medical personnel ... and only sixteen chasseurs. Next day (17 October) Wilson and Murat both get off their horses at the outposts 'to have a fairer gaze at each other'. But on Murat sending an officer, 'I desired Captain Fanshaw [his ADC] to request that he would return to his line.'

Between this true-blue English officer and gentleman and an upstart king who was born an inn-keeper's son, at least, there are to be no dealings.

And anyway the time for parleying is past.

CHAPTER 9

PREPARATIONS FOR DEPARTURE

Napoleon reads a novel – 'They even said he was mad' – convoys go astray – too many cannon? – handmills – reconnoitre another return route – the wrong François – a first fall of snow – 'in twenty days' – Napoleon's concern for the wounded – rules for the Comédie Française – what are the poets doing? – 'an officer arrived post-haste'

Do Napoleon's orders to Murat betray a lack of inner certitude? Perhaps. Ségur, always concerned to give a critical turn to his drama, describes, doubtless exaggerates, his state of mind:
'In the midst of that terrible storm of men and the elements massing all round him, his ministers, his ADCs see him spend these last days discussing the merit of some new verses he'd just received, or drawing up regulations for the Comédie Française in Paris, which took him three whole evenings to complete.[1] As they know perfectly how anxious he is they admire the force of his genius and the ease with which he shifts his attention and fixes it on whatever he chooses. All one noticed was that his meals, until then so simple and brief, were taking longer. He was trying to numb himself. Then they saw him, to satisfy a craving [*s'appetissant*], pass long hours in a half-reclining position, as if stunned [*engourdi*] and, a novel in his hand, waiting for the dénouement of his terrible history.'
But Caulaincourt belies all this. And so does Gourgaud. Though no less critical than Ségur will be, the Master of the Horse is finding
'the Emperor's activity to reorganise his army and prepare it for new combats really extraordinary and it was giving the heads of each arm a lot to do.'
A lighted candle in his first-storey window assures the army that its all-puissant emperor is ceaselessly busy. Any number of his orders are in fact dictated in the small hours. In Prince Baratinsky's palace Planat de la Faye hardly has a moment to leave his desk, has to sleep on the floor at nights on a catskin fur, explaining to his six ill-educated artillery captains, feverishly transcribing and delivering Lariboisière's orders, that, in Russia, proper beds are rare luxuries. On one of his daily tours of inspection, Napoleon suddenly appears in Lariboisière's 'light and smoke devices' department. He's been informed that its personnel have only been able to produce 10,000 rounds during the last fortnight. Peremptorily he orders them to step up their output to 6,000 a week, 'and send them to the Kremlin for storage as soon as they're ready'. Cannonballs picked up on the field of Borodino, too, are arriving by the

cartload. "*Mon Dieu,*" sighs the depressed Lariboisière who, after his son's death at Borodino,

'no longer uttered a word at table. "Haven't we already much too much for our teams? And what does the Emperor think we'll bring it all back with?"'

In Caulaincourt's, Pion des Loches' and many other people's opinion, too, the army already has far more guns than it has horses to drag them. But when someone, probably Lariboisière, suggests 'part of them should be left behind', the ex-gunner emperor explodes:

"No. The enemy would make a trophy of them!"

Altogether he's very touchy about trophies. After all, *something* must be brought home from this unexampled but so far fruitless campaign. As to leaving some of the guns behind, Gourgaud scorns the idea:

'At the time when it was getting ready to leave, the army still had 600 pieces of artillery and their teams, fully supplied. They had been reinforced by the horses of the Bridging Train which it was intended to leave behind in the Kremlin [in fact, they weren't left behind]. So it couldn't enter the Emperor's head to abandon part of his artillery to the Russians. It would have been a mistake so much the greater as he was expecting a new battle.'

By now, not everyone is as confident in the Emperor's judgement as Gourgaud. Planat hears other generals besides Lariboisière, whose 'gaiety, full of good-nature and seasoned with a light dose of the malice we'd known in him, had totally disappeared',

'expressing these fears openly and in a fashion less respectful toward the Emperor. They even went so far as to say he was mad and wanted us to perish to the last man. On this occasion, as later, I noticed that the most injurious remarks against the Emperor always came from the Prince of Neuchâtel's staff. The Emperor wasn't ignorant of this, and didn't like them'

– the blue-blooded young gentlemen, that is, who form an aristocratic little club of their own, whose members refer to him in private as 'Monsieur Bonaparte' and, it's felt, look down on the rest of the army. 'The most one could expect of them,' writes Count *J-C. Beugnot* in another context, 'was they weren't insolent to you.' Major *Marcelline Marbot,* currently serving with Oudinot's faraway II Corps near Polotsk, is even more sarcastic. They did nothing all day, he says, but play cards and dice, 'winning or losing several thousands of francs with utmost indifference'. Nor is Fezensac, who until after Borodino had been one of them, much impressed by all this administrative activity:

'Nothing much was being sent to the advance guard, either. Yet every day the Russian army on the banks of the Nera was getting stronger.'

As for chronically overworked Berthier himself, Ségur sees he isn't 'doing much to second his chief in this critical circumstance. He didn't recommend any new precautions and waited for the least details to be dictated to him by the Emperor.'[2]

The daily parades, of course, have continued. On Sunday 11 October it was the turn of Gérard's [formerly Gudin's] division to be reviewed in the Kremlin; on the 12th Morand's. Certain of its officers, commanding its quarters of the town, fail to turn up. Likewise their detachments 'not knowing where to go'. By now Captain *Charles François'* leg wound, sustained on the eve of Borodino, has healed sufficiently for him to burn one of his crutches – no matter what heroic acts men have performed, only the crutchless may appear on parade before the Emperor:

'For the sixth time I was proposed for the Cross and another reward. The regiment took up arms, went to the Kremlin where the Emperor reviewed it, along with the other regiments of the 18th Division.'

Five lieutenants are promoted captains, six sous-lieutenants are made lieutenants and ten NCOs sous-lieutenants:

'Three officers' crosses and 40 crosses of the Legion were accorded and a grant of money to the regiment's worst battalion commander, obtained by dint of sheer importunities. Not that it did him any good, because he left his bones behind in the retreat. Colonel Bouguet was promoted general and replaced by a major from the Young Guard. The Emperor asked Colonel Bouguet where I'd been wounded. "At Schevardino, and he's one of our old dromedaries from Egypt." The Emperor came up to me and said: "What are you asking for?" My colonel didn't give me time to reply, and declared "The Cross!" "Granted," replied the Emperor. Having done so many campaigns, I'd been going to ask for a money grant, which would have been granted. But my colonel, though wishing me well, did me wrong.'

And even then François' nomination somehow gets overlooked – or rather, is sent to the 13th Light by mistake, where there's another Captain François, and is only retrieved after much trouble. (What the other Captain François felt history doesn't relate.) That day, it seems, one whole regiment has been late on parade; for on the morrow Davout writes apologetically to Berthier, wanting to know whether this was really so, and if so which regiment it was, 'so that I can punish the colonel'.

Three days later, on 13 October, there'll also be an oversight, presumably in 'Monsieur' Salomon's department.[3] Only 185 letters notifying Davout of the promotions made at the parade of two days earlier are sent him, instead of 187, and 'immediately forwarded to the military men they're intended for'. Perhaps His Serene Highness the Prince of Neuchâtel will look into the matter, try and find out what the difference is due to? But one of these commissions, anyway, is 'for an officer of the 85th'. Who can he be, if not our friend Le Roy? For Sergeant *Vincent Bertrand*'s regiment, the 7th Light, there are seven promotions and no fewer than 32 crosses – the 12th Line gets what must be an all-time record of 37.

What state is the army in? What kind of an army is it now? Artillery-inspector *H. J. de Paixhans*, one of Lariboisière's ADCs, is one of the many individuals who've been turning up in Moscow during the last few weeks, a delay due in his case to a gammy leg. The first thing that's struck Paixhans is the army's youth, even in the cavalry and artillery, and the large numbers of merely nominal Frenchmen:[4]

'Dutchmen of all ranks had come to poison the artillery units. All had been poorly and hastily trained. As for the NCOs who'd been promoted 2nd lieutenant, they'd come from a class become too feeble for its proper functions, as a result of the enormous consumption of men during the previous years.'

In the artillery train, four horses, their harness and a load of ammunition are being entrusted to two feeble conscripts. Most divisions, Paixhans notes, are only at quarter strength, a mere two to three thousand men, 'the other three-quarters dead, prisoners, marauders or stragglers [he makes no mention of the all-too-numerous wounded]. There were altogether too many administrators'.

As for the army's morale, Caulaincourt is troubled by the effects of a cult of glory, as opposed to efficiency:

'Our men were doubtless very brave, but they were careless and lacking in vigilance, which arose as much from their character as from lack of order and discipline. This was often a subject for serious reflection on the part of the Prince of Neuchâtel and other generals around the Emperor. There were too many young regimental officers. Dash and courage were valued above all else. At all his reviews the Emperor made everything of audacity, courage and luck. No commanding officer was ever brought to account for losses due to his negligence, his lack of order and discipline, even if it had caused the loss of two-thirds of his force.'

Despite the evidently satisfactory appearance of Davout and Delzons' crack divisions when on parade early in the month, Césare de Laugier has already made his own worried assessment:

'The many sick and wounded who've come back into the ranks, the new march regiments that have turned up, have more or less given the infantry the same numerical force as they had before the battle [of Borodino]. But the cavalry – and above all the artillery – are in a deplorable state. I won't speak of the horses of the Guard, which have fought and suffered less than the others and preserved a better aspect; but those of Murat and the light cavalry attached to the infantry units! The poor animals are painful to look at, their end isn't far off. None of them have been able to profit from a moment's rest since the hostilities began! As for artillery's guns, even though their number is already out of proportion to the forces at our disposal, more of them are turning up every day. Just now the army counts 501 cannon, but drawn by scraggy horses incapable of making a long journey. And the same can be said of the horses of the baggage train, ambulances and others. We're asking ourselves how we're going to transport the precious booty assembled in Moscow and already loaded on to wagons; that is, if the Emperor doesn't order them to be abandoned.'

Typical of the whole equine situation, no doubt, is von Suckow's little Russian horse – the one on which he'd tried to keep up with Ney's staff at Borodino. Hardly does it reach Moscow than the poor little animal simply drops dead of starvation. 'For several days it had been impossible to feed him. There wasn't a blade of forage anywhere in the town or its surroundings.'

Not every convoy that leaves Smolensk is reaching Moscow. In late September Napoleon had ordered that no more artillery should advance further than Smolensk, and all artillery and cavalry between Smolensk and Moscow were to be concentrated at Viazma, Ghjat or Mojaisk. After an affair during which some artillery coming up from Viazma has lost its guns, a furious Emperor even cashiers one of the majors commanding it, who promptly blows his brains out. Another artillery convoy, coming from Italy and commanded by a Major Vives, is abandoned by its escort; and Labaume says the guns would have been lost if General Ornano and IV Corps' Bavarian chevaulegers hadn't caught up with the Cossacks as they were carrying them off in the middle of a forest and retaken them. Its commander, too, is arrested.[5] And at Vereia, the 'pretty little town' where Le Roy's men had enjoyed a vast meal just before reaching Moscow, the garrison is suddenly attacked and massacred. Everywhere the peasant bands are becoming more and more active.

The far rear, as usual, is essentially beyond Napoleon's control. There a host of oversights are being committed. Words and acts go their different ways. Where, for instance, are the great stores of rice and other foods which should be arriving at Minsk, but evidently aren't?

"*October 9:* To Berthier: Haven't I said and said again a thousand times to bring up to Kovno and Vilna all the clothing which is at Danzig? So write to Danzig that my orders shall be carried out."

160

Minsk, with its huge and ever-growing stores of food and clothing, is obviously going to be crucial to the army's survival during the winter. Why hasn't a great mass of clothing for which he has 'paid out at least several hundreds of thousands of francs' reached Minsk from Kovno? "Explain this mystery to me." Two days later (14 October) he will order Maret at Vilna to send the rice he's had collected from all over Europe "even from Trieste" to Minsk via Grodno: "Two thousand four hundred and fifty quintals of rice, sent off from there, have arrived at Cracow. They should have been embarked on the Vistula on 12 September."

An instance of his attention to details – a detail one would have thought, in this case, should have been the business of Dumas or Daru – is his almost obsessive preoccupation with some handmills, ordered for the army, and long awaited.[6] On 6 October he'd dictated:

"*The Emperor to M. Maret, Duke of Bassano.* Forty portable mills left Paris by post on 6 September. It is now 6 October. So they should have passed through Vilna. I have exhorted you to inform yourself on the progress of this convoy. It is my intention that you shall withdraw one of these mills to serve as a model. Have it operated under your eyes, and let me know how much [corn] it has ground in 24 hours and how many men successively have done this work. I want you to have 50 of these mills constructed at Vilna on the basis of the one you use as a model. As soon as you have had two or three made, you will send one by post to Warsaw for Durutte's division, and one to Königsberg for Loison's division. In the same way you will send one to Minsk for 50 to be made. I assume there are workmen in the countryside who will do it promptly. You must also send one to the Duke of Tarente [Macdonald] to have some made on this model at Mittau.'[7] For the rest, having taken this model, you will let this convoy continue its march, for it's getting very late for me to receive it. A second convoy of 160 of these mills, loaded on four ammunition wagons, left Paris by post on 16 September; it must arrive before long. If the first one has already passed through [Vilna], you will carry out this operation on the second. From this second convoy I authorize you to hold up six, which you will send by post coach to Marshal St-Cyr; perhaps he'll be able to have some made at Polotsk. Anyway he will be receiving a greater number on the third and fourth convoys."

On 10 October Davout acknowledges the letter Berthier 'at the Emperor's orders' had done him the honour of writing him, to the effect that

'portable mills have left by post from Paris for the army, where they should arrive any time now, and that it was His Majesty's intention that, on these handmills' arrival, ten should be distributed to each of the five divisions of I Corps. I have informed the troops under my orders of this mark of the Emperor's solicitude.'

No detail is too small to escape his photographic memory. In a list of officers who have died of typhus in the Vilna hospitals he spots a certain artillery surgeon by name Déchy. Hadn't he, en route for the Niemen in June, severely reprimanded that dedicated officer for bringing his 14-year-old son to Russia?[8] True. And straightway an order goes off to Berthier to give the orphan a grant and arrange for him to be escorted back to France, where he's to get the best possible education.

What Napoleon is envisaging isn't a retreat ('a word', Dedem has been reprimanded when he'd used it, 'unknown in the French army'); or if there is to be one, it must be heavily disguised as a new offensive. His plan – confined no doubt as usual to himself and Colonel *Bacler d'Albe* ('and perhaps to Berthier') sticking his coloured pins into the great map laid out on the big table in the middle of his office – is as follows. Marching out southwards, he'll either strike at Kutusov or bypass him; march on Kaluga and Tula; destroy the arms factories there ('the largest in Russia'); and, passing through the Ukraine, meet up with a column, made up of 'march regiments, isolated and disbanded men, men who've recovered their health' and amounting to '12,000 infantry and 4,000 cavalry, to which have been attached 12 cannon' coming out to meet him from Smolensk. Commanded by the veteran general Baraguay d'Hilliers, the column is to be held ready to leave at a moment's notice. Falling back on Smolensk and its huge stores – supplies which, if the Emperor's orders have been properly obeyed, should be enough to sustain the Moscow army throughout the winter – he'll put the army into winter quarters 'along the Molihew–Smolensk–Witebsk line'.

Secret orders are drawn up for a departure on 20 October.

"*M. le Prince de Neuchâtel*. The Smolensk highway being exhausted, it's necessary to reconnoitre routes parallel to it at two or three leagues into the countryside, where there should be resources, villages, at least some shelters. These deviated routes must be tangent with the central points of Doroghoboui, Viazma and Mojaisk."

And the same day, again, to Marshal Victor, at Smolensk:

"Retain at Smolensk all infantry, cavalry, artillery detachments, the convoys, vehicles, and in general everything that presents itself in isolation to pass through. With all you've thus retained you'll immediately form a column of ten to twelve thousand men. Give it twelve cannon and victuals for ten days. Summon General Baraguay d'Hilliers to Smolensk and put him in command of this division. Place under his command and protection all the vehicles accumulated for the army, and hold this column in readiness to leave by the new route which is to be reconnoitred. Thereafter other columns will be formed. Six thousand men can pass everywhere."

From now on it's his intention, the Emperor goes on, that

"only despatch riders, the army's trunks, staff officers on mission, and certain urgent objects, such as the 500 portable handmills arriving from Paris, the first delivery of which should have reached Smolensk, shall reach us by the old route. Thus relieved, the old route will remain open for evacuating the wounded and for everything returning from Moscow to Smolensk. None of the heavy convoys from Smolensk to Moscow are to pass that way."

For weeks now Fain has been hearing 'everyone telling the Emperor the temperature didn't usually fall below zero in Moscow before mid-November.'[11] Evidently he believes them; or anyway wants to; for he still won't listen to Caulaincourt, wise from his winters at the Petersburg embassy. But on 13 October (the day of Davout's polite little reprimand to General Headquarters), there comes a first light fall of snow, which, to Caulaincourt, 'seemed to bewilder him':

'After a few excessively hot and fine autumn days, the weather has changed abruptly and turned cold. Today the first snow has fallen,'

Césare de Laugier notes in his diary. And Fain hears the Emperor exclaim: "Let's get a move on. In twenty days we must be in winter quarters."[12]

Is it the nightly performances at Count Posniakov's refurbished theatre, or a calculated impulse to let Paris – and Europe – know that, though so far away, he's still fully in control of everything, that causes Napoleon, despite all these more urgent demands on his time, to devote two (not, as Ségur says, three) whole evenings to drawing up new statutes for the Comédie Française?[13] – and theatrically address them from Moscow? The regulations (which are still in force) run to 100 paragraphs. On that ominously snowy morning of 13 October he signs them. And next day, in front of his generals – who, Narbonne notices, 'either out of modesty or indifference listened without saying anything' – holds forth at length on literature and the drama.

'The Kremlin's drawing-room occupied by the Emperor, underneath the Tsarina's state apartments, was illumined by great chandeliers. The Emperor was striding to and fro. Everyone around him was silent. M. Daru, the intellect most apt to [discuss] all topics but also the gravest and the one most attentive to the army's serious needs, was just then overwhelmed by a thousand cares; and wasn't present.'

But Narbonne is, and will immediately afterwards dictate it all to his secretary Villemain:

'Doubt and worry were obviously weighing heavily on all minds, hardly leaving them the strength for such mental relaxation.'

Suddenly Napoleon turns to Narbonne, that courtier of the *ancien régime*, and says:

'"I ought to have consulted you, my dear Narbonne, before sending off my decree of this morning, about the very matter we're talking about. I'm sure you greatly loved theatre in your youth and were a great connoisseur. It's true, I believe, it was above all comedy, the manners of the great world, Célimène, Mlle Contat."'

Which is true. 'As he quickly threw out this last name a faint twitch of a smile seemed to mask the Emperor's grave features'.[14] His own preference, he goes on seriously, is for Corneille and high tragedy, where:

'"at the moments of supreme decision great men are truer than the crises which develop them, we aren't burdened down with all the preparatory details and conjectures, often false, which historians give us. But the gain to glory is so much the greater. For, my dear fellow, there are any amount of miseries in a man, fluctuations, doubts. All these should vanish in the hero.'

For his own part, he goes on, amidst his generals' glum or perhaps faintly shuffling silence, he's

'"grateful to Tragedy for making some men grow, or rather giving them back their true stature of superior beings in a mortal body."'

But what, he'd like to know, are the poets of his own reign doing? Where are their modern heroes? Why aren't they bringing Charlemagne on stage, or Saint Louis? Or, above all, Peter the Great,

"that man of granite, hard as the stone courses of the Kremlin, who founded civilisation in Russia and who a century after his death forces me to this terrible expedition."

The assassination of the rebellious Strelitz guards only a few yards away from where he's speaking had been like his own 18th Brumaire. There in Peter the Great, if they like, was a genius!

"People haven't realised that he gave himself what even the greatest man born to a throne lacks: the glory of being a parvenu. Peter the Great voluntarily turned himself into an artillery lieutenant, like I've been, to learn about ordinary life and rise by degrees to greatness. Even so, what setbacks there were to that fortune and that genius! Can you conceive how such a man, at the head of the army he'd created, could let himself be invested on the banks of the Pruth, starved out and almost captured by a Turkish army? Such are the inexplicable eclipses in even the greatest men. Yet the man of genius always recovers himself after a mistake, as after a misfortune."

Amidst this tumult of ideas, Villemain scribbles that night,

'M. de Narbonne hesitated to reply. In it he saw, among the dreary realities of the moment, a shock effect of speculative attention and free reverie taking command of this powerful intellect; or perhaps an illusion of security which he, in his disquietude, wanted to extend to the minds of the others.'

With an effort Narbonne replies that ever since Peter the Great Russia has been full of tragic memories. Napoleon ripostes:

'"Let's act in such a way as not to augment them."'

Peter had lifted Russia out of chaos, but not provided it with an intellectual tradition. He'd found it barbarous, and it was still semi-barbarous. By force of numbers he'd defeated Charles XII of Sweden at Poltava,

"but less by his own genius than by that king's own fault. If Charles XII, that prince who was more a soldier than a general, hadn't advanced so far into Russia, or had retired in time and gone on carrying out his invasion manoeuvres even in the depths of winter, he'd never have been defeated."'

It hadn't been Tsar Peter's tactics, Narbonne boldly points out, that had been victorious. But the climate. The innuendo isn't lost on Napoleon, who replies with alacrity:

'"I see what you're driving at, my dear Narbonne. Talked to about theatre, you reply with politics. For the rest, the two things do sometimes touch each other. But don't worry. We shan't make Charles XII's mistake. It's been written in history to preserve us."'

He's been obliged to wait awhile here in Moscow to see what effect 'those two thunderbolts, the battle of the Moscova and the taking of Moscow would have. I had reason to believe in a peace. But whether it comes or not, there's a limit for us.'

Either he'll take the army "which by and large has rested up" back to Smolensk and while the fine weather lasts put it into winter quarters in Lithuania and Poland: or else he'll follow Daru's advice

"which I call a lion's: collect provisions here, kill and salt the injured horses and pass the winter in Moscow which is still a town, and in the spring resume offensive warfare – though I don't incline to this project. One can go far. But one mustn't be away from home too long. I feel Paris calling me even more than Petersburg tempts me. So, my dear fellow, you can be content. With or without a peace, we'll soon be leaving."

Next day he sends for Mathieu Dumas and asks him whether most of the wounded aren't already on their way to Smolensk. And when he hears they aren't, realises 'how much time has already been wasted, and that he must make haste to cope with the innumerable cares of so perilous a retreat'.

On one of those days, if Ali's memoirs are to be trusted, Napoleon falls to 'discussing with Duroc the best sort of death. The best, according to Napoleon, was to "die on the field of battle, struck down by a bullet". For his part he feared he wouldn't be so happy. "I'll die", he said, "in my bed, comè un' coglione."' On St Helena, where he will, he'll say: "I should have died after entering Moscow."

In fact the evacuation of the wounded – according to a recent report there are still 12,000 in Moscow – is a major problem. The medical administration, Caulaincourt sees, has 'ceased to exist except on paper'. But transport wagons must be found for all but the most severe cases, who are to be gathered together in the main hospital, with their surgeons, and be left to the tender mercies of the returning Russians. Altogether Napoleon estimates he has only 800 to 900 wagons in Moscow, and he has no intention of sending them to the rear filled with the sick and wounded. "The walking wounded can conduct their comrades." But any wagon arriving from Smolensk may be used for the purpose; and I, III, IV and VIII Corps are ordered to drum up between them a further 200. The 60 furnished by I Corps and the 40 from III Corps

'are to leave tomorrow and the day after. They're to be loaded with flour, brandy, wine, medicines, which are to be sent to Mojaisk and above all to the convent,'

i.e., the great Kolotskoië Abbey, three miles from the field of Borodino, where the wounded had been assembled, and where – so Césare de Laugier hears – a secret order has been given for all the muskets assembled after the battle to be burned.

"General Ornano will have them escorted. Arrange for these convoys to leave in a regulation manner and carry to those hospitals the help they so badly need. Begin the evacuation with the officers. Express my dissatisfaction to the pay commissioner in charge at Mojaisk,"

he adds. Also to his war commissaries (among them no doubt the hardworking Bellot de Kergorre) and the Administration's agents at Kolotskoië,

"for never writing to let me know the state of affairs in their hospitals. Lastly, send an officer and an agent of the Administration to find out exactly how many sick there are at Mojaisk, at the monastery, and as far as Viazma, so that I can in all circumstances know what sacrifices would have to be made should our operations mean we must abandon those establishments."

As for the large numbers of wounded still in Mojaisk itself, he writes sharply to Berthier that, having provided Junot and his VIII Corps and "the other route commanders with the men they've asked for to be able to master their surroundings", he intends that his intentions shall be carried out:

"Therefore the commandants shall have the countryside scoured for thirty miles around and in this way collect a good number of peasant carts to serve for the evacuation of our wounded. You will render the duc d'Abrantès [Junot] responsible for having all the wounded evacuated to Viazma, and the commandant at Viazma [Poincaré] to have them evacuated to Smolensk. In a word, whatever happens, my intention is that eight days from now there shall not be a single one of our wounded at Mojaisk, Raza, the Kolotskoïe abbey, or at Ghjat."

Davout, who has already written to Berthier on 10 October pointing out that despite the 'great number of weapons existing at the abbey and Mojaisk, the commandants at those places are still letting unarmed men pass through', is having difficulty in supplying enough wagons for the wounded. On 13 October, however – the day of the first snowfall and after 'a detachment of the 108th Line in General Friedrichs' division has been attacked by Cossacks and armed peasants in the village of Cigadaiewo' – he has given orders for all his sick and wounded to leave;

'and I hope those of the 1st, 3rd and 5th divisions will be able to be transported by the means at our disposal. But it is indispensable that the Intendant-General shall supply transportation for those of the 2nd [Dufour's] and 4th divisions, detached with the advance guard, who are much more numerous than the others, and have no means of being brought here.'

A recommendation which causes Berthier to write on the morrow to Belliard, telling him the wounded are to set out 'for Vilna or Smolensk'. Those who after resting up a few months at Vilna find themselves in a state to go on campaign again will report to IHQ. Those others who, by reason of the nature of their wounds, aren't in so favourable a state, will be authorized to go back to France. 'This arrangement, however, only applies to generals, colonels and battalion commanders.' What is to happen to the irreparably wounded subalterns, NCOs and rank and file he doesn't say.

There are also the army's cadres. At Smolensk some officers – even some of the Canaries' rank and file who've served out their time – are being sent back to France to form them for the new units to be raised from next year's recruits.[15] On 12 October Lieutenant Dutheillet of the 57th Line has heard that each regiment has been

'ordered to send a battalion of cadres to each corps' depot, to train the recruits who'll be coming in. As lieutenant I was included among the officers to be sent off, even though my commission still hadn't been sent to me. All these cadres hardly added up to 700 or 800 men. We left Moscow on 14 October, I think, taking with us General Nansouty, who'd been wounded and was in command of us. There were also a great number of generals and officers of all ranks, sick or wounded, whom we were charged with escorting.'

One of the convoy's wounded, Lieutenant Brandt of the Vistula Legion, will suppose afterwards that

'if I hadn't left a few days in advance but been forced to make the retreat with the regiment, I've every reason to believe I, in the state of weakness I was in, would have succumbed to its fatigues, if I hadn't been killed by the enemy's iron.[16]

Another – unwounded – member of the convoy is Daru's cousin, dragoon captain Henri Beyle, of the Food Administration. As yet the future novelist Stendhal's sole ambition is to write comedies – while in Moscow he's been labouring over one more called *Letellier*, as unactable as all the others – live in Paris and keep mistresses. But now, as the long train of jolting and groaning wagons, laden with its cargo of sufferers, sets off down the Mojaisk–Smolensk highway, all he has to keep his spirits is his (to us rather irritating) gift for persiflage.

On the day when it had snowed, Césare de Laugier and his comrades, still out at Petrovskoï, had begun asking one another which route they'll be returning by, 'will it be the road we came by, or will we pass through the south-western parts of the [Russian] empire?'. He has heard that 'only staff officers on mission, and *estafettes* [express couriers]' are to leave for Smolensk by the Mojaisk road'. Now he hears that

'in the evening of the day before yesterday, the Emperor's horses left for an unknown destination. All the wagons are laden with food. Yesterday General Borelli, ADC to the King of Naples, left again with the Emperor's secret orders for his master.'

Next day he hears that the convoy carrying the trophies is leaving, escorted by a force under the wounded general Claparède. And during the night of 15/16 October Laugier writes in his diary:

'The Italian detachment at Czernaiagriaz has been ordered by the Emperor to come back to Moscow, but without its cavalry. Broussier's division, the Dragoons of the Royal Guard, placed out along the Smolensk road, are moving towards Fominskoië.' 16 October: Orders to Marshal Victor to send some artillery horses to Viazma 'to collect the ammunition wagons and artillery vehicles abandoned along the road and take them back to Smolensk.' 17 October: Today, general distribution to the whole army: leather, linen, bread and brandy. This wise measure, which would have been most useful if it had been taken a little earlier, comes too late. The ranker is throwing away everything he can't use on the spot; and anyway, he's

already too heavily laden and I'm afraid this distribution may be a pure loss.'
But then, on the 18th, something dramatic happens.

The usual parade, this time mainly of Ney's III Corps, is to be held at 1 p.m. Lieutenant-Colonel Le Roy, as he now is, has given up his original intention of asking Davout to let him stay with the regiment for the rest of the campaign. At 10 a.m., after drawing his march orders to leave for the 85th's depôt at faraway Coblenz, he goes to the Kremlin to say goodbye to some friends in the Imperial Guard:

'Many units had already assembled there. They seemed to be dismounted cavalry.[18] I asked to speak to Captain Gouttenoire of the Chasseurs of the Old Guard, who'd come from the 108th and who was a close friend. I found him on guard at the entrance to the palace where the Emperor was lodged.'

Gouttenoire tells Le Roy the Guard's under orders to be ready to leave within 24 hours. And that all the sick and wounded have left for Smolensk. 'As I've said already,' Le Roy goes on,

'there were dismounted troops marching in two ranks, portmanteaux on their backs, wearing big boots, armed with reserve muskets, carbines, musketoons and pistols. All these men seemed to me very heavy and in no state to sustain an action, being entirely foreign to the new service being exacted of them. It was even likely that instead of being of any use they'd end up by embarrassing us.'

"You can see from this movement they're thinking of retreating," Gouttenoire tells him. "This morning we've heard gunfire in the direction of the advance guard on the Kaluga road. And we're waiting impatiently to hear what's happened. So, old comrade, if you leave for France it'll be with us.'"

Le Roy replies that this will be much more to his liking than running all the risks of travelling on his own. He's just listening to local gossip and looking at the big Ivan Bell, lying there in three pieces after its fall from the tower, [19] when

'the Emperor came out of the palace to go on parade. He was walking by himself, eight to ten paces ahead of his staff. His expression was preoccupied. Coming out of the castle courtyard, he turned left and went towards the troops assembled a few paces away. I slipped in among the officers of his suite to watch the parade, which began at once. The troops were ordered to make several forward movements.'

Unfortunately, Major Guillaume Bonnet, as he now is, still suffering from the after-effects of the fever he'd contracted out at Bogorodsk and unable to keep his legs. So though the 18th Line, also part of Ney's corps, are being reviewed and the usual expectations are running high, he has to ask his colonel for permission to withdraw. 'My absence was the reason why he couldn't get me the cross.'[20] General Pajol, on the other hand, commander of the 2nd Light Cavalry Division, has more or less recovered from his broken arm; and together with Captain Biot, his ADC, has just attended Napoleon's levee. Also present on parade is Cesare de Laugier with

'some battalions of the Imperial Guard, the Royal Guard, and Pino's Division. We were drawn up in battle order in the Kremlin's first courtyard. The Emperor was passing us in review. The time was perhaps around 2 p.m. They were about to distribute the rewards the troops are so avid for, when suddenly Colonel Béranger, ADC to the King of Naples, turned up, chapfallen [*les traits décomposés*] and with a worried air.'

As Béranger demands to speak to the Emperor, Biot too recognizes him:

'He hardly took time to shake my hand in passing, and said to me in a low voice: "Things are going badly!"'

Instantly

'the review stops. The Emperor withdraws into Peter the Great's apartments.'

What has happened?

CHAPTER 10

BATTLE AT WINKOVO

*Sébastiani surprised – 'They halted not four paces from us, uttering wild shouts' –
a wounded Murat saves the situation - Bréaut des Marlots' single-handed fight –
'This spoils everything' – immediate departure – a merry dance – Wilson is furious
– dead cats in Murat's kitchen – Louise chased by starving dogs – a parting shot*

Among the first to feel that something serious was in the wind had been
the 7th Hussars' Victor Dupuy:
> 'With the grand'garde on 17 October I had under my orders Captain
> Decalonne of the 8th Hussars and 100 men from the division's various
> units. Having relieved the old outposts, placed my own, and visited the
> line of scouts, whence I could see nothing out of the ordinary, I
> reported to General Bruyères. He recommended the greatest vigi-
> lance, and told me that, by all appearances, we would be attacked dur-
> ing the night. I went back to my post. I had half the horses constantly
> bridled up by turns and didn't neglect my patrols. The night passed off
> quietly. At dawn I again visited my whole line with Captain Decalonne.
> Everything was in order on our side, and we saw nothing on the
> enemy's to make us fear a sudden attack. I left the mounted guard and
> reported to General Bruyères, as was the practice each morning.'

At first light of dawn on that misty morning of 18 October, Griois,
'stretched out alone on a bench in our smoke-filled room,' is
> 'deeply asleep when I was awakened by the noise of firing. To begin
> with I assumed this must be the Russian recruits practising. But soon
> the noise seemed to be closer than usual. I open the window beside me
> – i.e., push up a little wooden shutter like the ones used in hen-hous-
> es. And on the ravine's further side see our sentries exchanging shots
> with enemy sharpshooters. Everything was lying in a dense mist.'

Perhaps it's just some Russian patrols who've approached too closely in the
fog? Hardly, because
> 'from other points, too, the firing could be heard; and all over camp
> the trumpeters were sounding 'To horse!' So it must be serious. I
> order my artillery to harness up, send my servant and vehicles to the
> rear, and with my adjutant and orderly officers go to the camp's for-
> ward edge. Already our pickets are falling back on their regiments,
> formed up in battle order.'

Dupuy finds the rest of Bruyères' light cavalry division outside his bivouac:
> '"Go back quickly," he said as soon as I approached him. "This is the
> critical moment. Stand your ground as well as ever you can!" And, in

fact, at that moment we heard some carbine shots in the distance.'
Dupuy immediately sets off again as fast as his horse can carry him:
'When I got to the middle of the plain I saw my grand'garde being vigorously driven in by Russian dragoons. I flung myself into the middle
of the scrum, trying to rally my men. Deceived by the Russians' white
mantles – our Prussians and Poles had similar ones – I'm in the midst
of them, shouting at the top of my voice: "Halt! Rally!" when a Russian trooper, letting his sabre dangle by its strap, tries to seize my
horse's bridle, saying to me in French: "Surrender, Monsieur!" At the
same moment Brigadier Wolf of the 7th Hussars came rushing toward
me, shouting: "They're the enemy!" Wolf and I let our sabres play on
the man who'd attacked me and on other enemies who were coming
on the scene. Then, thanks to our good horses, in three bounds we
were out of reach and amidst some of our own men who'd come up
at the sound of my voice! Whereupon I rally my men. Then our
defence gets organised. We begin firing in an orderly fashion, only
yielding ground yard by yard, thus giving the division time to fall back
on General St-Germain's cuirassiers beyond the ravine.'

But Griois ('happily for us Lahoussaye was so ill he wasn't able to mount
his horse') is having trouble with his horse-gunners:
'I don't know how they'd chanced to get hold of some brandy that
day. But I noticed it as, at the first musket shots, I went to the park,
assembled my companies and ordered them to mount. Already that
corn-brandy [vodka], a veritable poison, was affecting several of the
men. Even the officers were tipsy. One of my best captains, usually a
model of sobriety, fell almost senseless at my feet as he was speaking
to me. Another was in more or less the same state. How to get my
orders understood, still less carried out, by men who'd lost their presence of mind?'

Despite Murat's anxieties and warnings the sudden onslaught has taken
Sébastiani completely by surprise. At 6 a.m. 'just when we least expected it'
Sous-lieutenant Pierre Auvray of the 23rd Dragoons sees,
'roundshot, fired at the chasseurs camped in front of us, come bouncing into our shacks. We were still abed. Our horses were unsaddled.
In the midst of the roundshot, which were causing havoc, each of us
rushes to mount his horse, and we abandoned some of our possessions.'

And still Dupuy, out there in the plain, isn't out of danger. His horse, shot
in the right shoulder by two Russians from behind a thicket, falls, with him
beneath it:
'The animal expired with a plaintive sound. The Russians rush to
grab me, but I get up promptly. Some of my hussars surround me.

One of them dismounts and helps me unsaddle and unbridle my unfortunate horse, while the others keep the Russians at bay. This done, I order the hussar to mount his horse again, give him the furniture of mine to carry off, and keenly regretting the loss I'd just sustained of my good old companion, leave on foot to go and get another. For me this was an immense loss, above all in these circumstances – at the moment when we were about undertake so long and arduous a retreat and it was utterly impossible to make it good!'

The signal for the Russian onslaught, writes Séruzier, commander of 2nd Cavalry Corps' horse artillery, had been

'a shell fired at my bivouac. I'd ordered the "To Horse!" to be sounded, the officers struggled to get to their posts. But each of them was surrounded on all sides by a cloud of Cossacks. One could hardly see a thing, and at that moment I'd hardly 15 men around me. My foot and horse gunners, unable to get my orders, set about defending themselves with their usual courage. But this time, lacking co-ordination from a commander-in-chief, for a long while it was nothing but a mêlée, where in the end we were overwhelmed by superiority of numbers.'

To his surprise Séruzier keeps hearing his own name being shouted among the Russians all around him:

'Afterwards I've come to know that Count Orlov was in command of the part of the attack aimed at my troops. Furious at the success of my expedition into his domains as far as the surroundings of Poltava, he'd sworn to get me, and given the Cossacks orders to capture me alive. In my first despair at having let myself be surprised I tried to get myself killed. Not succeeding and seeing my men gradually rallying, I began to hope of escape if I managed not to be recognised. So I got someone to give me a neck-band to cover my decorations, and managed to reach a mass of gunners who'd got together and were looking for me.'

Putting himself at their head, he drives off the Cossacks, and is glad to find the fright they've given him is worse than the damage inflicted.

The Russian attack by Bennigsen, who, supporting Wilson's insistent demand for action, has carefully if not brilliantly planned a surprise led by Bagawout, Dupuy sees, is being made 'simultaneously all down the line'. It all but succeeds. Bennigsen's idea is to march his infantry divisions to the defile at the French rear and, while Davidov's cavalry engages Murat's, cut it off. This is why, behind the line of light cavalry, Captain Bréaut des Marlots of the 3rd Cuirassiers (2nd Cavalry Corps) has just been about to go off foraging when

'a cloud of Cossacks fell upon us. The 4th Cuirassier Division, the whole of Segin's troops, were already overthrown and were retiring in disorder. My lieutenant said to me: "See that, Captain? But look! They're quite close." My horses were unsaddled and I told my servants: "Quick, get my horses ready. I'll deal with this one," – the one I meant to mount. And, against my better knowledge and knowing nothing can be done properly in a hurry: "Don't be scared, they won't get this far." Finally we formed up in line of battle. The guns are firing grapeshot at us, nothing stops them. I'd had my lead horses hurriedly taken to the rear. We're forced to retire, but in good order. Musket balls are falling among our ranks like hail.'

'By and by', Griois goes on,

'the mist lifts and allows us to see Russian masses advancing on us, manoeuvring as they come. I aim my gunfire at them, the Russian gunners reply; and the battle is raging all along the front.'

Dupuy: 'The 2nd Cavalry Corps, camped to our right, didn't get off as lightly as we did. It lost all its vehicles and a lot of men. Above all my old regiment, the 11th Chasseurs, was very badly cut up.' And Bréaut des Marlots:

'An hour later we were being taken in the rear, from the front and, shortly afterwards, from the flanks. We had to fire on all sides. Everywhere we saw only Cossacks, the earth groaned under them. But their great numbers didn't intimidate us, and if we saved ourselves in this encounter we owe it to our staunchness. We retired in good order.'

By 10 a.m., Auvray of the 23rd Dragoons goes on, other troops have come to their assistance,

'and about time too, because by then we were in so difficult a position that the roundshot and shells were enfilading our ranks from both sides, and we were on the point of giving way.'

But Orlov hasn't only been trying to capture the depredator of his estates. At the head of the first Russian column – there are three – he's been ordered to turn a wood on Murat's left, the one held by Sébastiani. Murat's right flank, against the banks of the River Nara, consists of Poniatowski's Poles; and Murat himself, in the centre, has been dangerously cut off from both forces by the steep Winkovo ravine, with the Czernicznia stream flowing through it. The whole position, as Rossetti had pointed out to Napoleon in the Kremlin, is utterly precarious. Séruzier goes on:

'Sébastiani's troops managed to form up on the Woronowo road. Immediately the enemy cavalry, supported by infantry, tried to cut him off. But the King of Naples, jumping on his horse, arrived at the head of his reserve. Twice he charged with his usual dash and forced the Russians to leave him master of the battlefield. Six battalions of Russian grenadiers tried to support their cavalry, but a second charge decided the matter.'

Murat's 'reserve' seems to consist largely of the tiny relics of the 1st and 2nd Carabiniers, which Lieutenant Mailly-Nesle had been dismayed to find added up altogether to no more than 100 mounted men:

'The 1st Regiment charged this cloud of cavalry very valorously, despite several batteries which were taking it in flank. But as the regiment's horses could only trot and were in no greater strength than an ordinary company, they were repulsed, lost a lot of men, and came to rally behind us. But then we were completely surrounded by enemies who flung themselves at us, brandishing their Cossack lances and uttering savage shouts. However, though we were perhaps not more than 60 men, we remained motionless, shouldering our sabres. This countenance astonished them and they halted not four paces from us, uttering a thousand insults, roaring like wild beasts and firing at point-blank range. So enraged were they with us that after firing them they flung their carbines and pistols in our faces. General Sébastiani and our colonel were out in front of us, their horses' rumps in our ranks.'

Suddenly the young aristocrat finds his arm is paralyzed. He's been shot in the right shoulder. And is ordered to retire – and his withdrawal from the ranks causes a supporting body of cuirassiers to do likewise! By and by he's joined by other wounded officers, among them 'the colonel, peppered with bullets, sabre cuts and lance-thrusts, but happily without having received any mortal blow'. Shedding his heavy cuirass, with its distinctive yellowish copper overlay, Mailly-Nesle receives from two Poles 'a sky-blue pelisse lined with white hare skin, and under a red velvet bonnet lined with astrakhan, dressed like a Cossack, makes off peacefully' to the rear.

But the carabiniers have put up a resistance that's prevented the Russians from cutting the Moscow road. Rossetti sees 'repeated charges by General Müller's cavalry on our left flank driven off and put to flight' thanks to Murat's personal intervention, and Müller himself is killed:

'Then the King, seeing Bagawout's infantry, too, advancing formed up in three squares to cut off our retreat, puts himself at the head of the Carabiniers, commanded by General de France, and of the 5th Cuirassiers, and charges the squares and sabres them completely. Bagawout himself remained on the battlefield, mutilated by sabre cuts. The King is wounded, but doesn't leave the fighting. My friend General Gry, captain in the Guards, is killed; Colonel Bonafoux and Captain Bauffremont, ADCs to the King, are wounded. I have my colback sliced in two by a sabre cut.'

Murat, so inept in so many other respects, is more than justifying his reputation as an incomparable leader of cavalry on the battlefield.

'Murat's charge,' writes *M. R. Faure*, 1st Cavalry Corps' medical officer, 'which the King of Naples led in person, was so impetuous that in an instant two of the enemy columns were broken and cut to pieces, while the [Polish] Zayoncek Division attacked the enemy from the other flank with the bayonet and drove them off.' At one moment Murat himself has been within an inch of being captured by some Cossacks but in the nick of time managed to take refuge in a Polish square:

'A mass of heavy cavalry was coming toward us at the gallop, as if to charge. But about 50 paces away it halted abruptly. There was a moment of terrible silence, during which all we heard was the panting of their horses. Then the Russians, no doubt seeing from our attitude that they'd do themselves no good, turned bridle and went off in as good order as on parade.'

A Pole, a cousin of Brandt's colonel, having saved his life, Murat instantly rewards him with a barony and a life pension.

Auvray goes on: 'Such carriages and ambulance wagons as might get in the way were burned, and once the passage was free we carried out our retreat towards Moscow.' Griois sees Murat laughing at the haste with which some soldiers, 'after first sharing the contents', are burning, at his orders, two of his own carriages which 'not having retired quickly enough' are jamming the road.

At about 3 p.m. Sébastiani's badly mauled cuirassiers notice that the cannon fire is abating, and 'the enemy didn't seem to be so intent on following us'. But now Bréaut des Marlots' blood is up. Being humiliated by a lot of Cossacks is something that's half-turned his head:

'I'm at the rear of the regiment which, at no more than company strength, is marching in column of troops, and I no longer even have a company to command. I'm chatting to my comrades about all these things, stressing my disgruntlement at seeing brigands like Cossacks putting the wind up a lot of soldiers. The whole division is marching en bloc. At that moment, 200 yards off, I see four Cossacks pillaging a vehicle. I seize my chance. Say to the commandant: "I want to prove that four Cossacks are nothing to one good soldier." Galloping over I manage to put them to flight, pursue them for 300 yards and challenge the officer, who speaks German, to cross swords with me. He swears he'll kill me. I laugh in his face. I run at him. He throws himself among his Cossacks. The commandant (a brave soldier) comes to my aid. Since he's not well enough mounted to stand a charge, which can't be long in coming, I beg him to retire. He believes me, and retires. As soon as I see he's out of danger, sure my horse will move faster than theirs and without consulting my courage, I fling myself among the Cossacks to get them to charge and, as they do, retire.

When I've retreated for 200 yards, I look behind me and see they're advancing in file and at a distance of nearly fifteen yards from one another. I turn about, fall on them, slash up the face of the first and, without pausing, do the same to the second. The third takes flight. I pursue him, the point of my sword at his back. But unfortunately my sabre is worthless, can't even pierce the sheepskin he's wearing. Others come and surround me. One thrusts his lance at my head, shattering my helmet and knocking it off. I catch it by its mane, just as another passes his lance through my thigh. I'm so excited I feel no pain, am only furious with my sabre. Again I throw myself among them. Already I'm being seconded by other men who're coming to my rescue – by now there are some fifteen Cossacks. We force them to retreat for almost a mile, and night comes down.'

In his private battle Bréaut des Marlots has lost one of his best friends, a captain who wasn't sufficiently up on the Cossacks' mode of fighting:

'The colonel reprimanded me, saying I always wanted to play the hussar. My wound, though deep, turned out very well. I tore off the front of my shirt to bind it up.'[1]

The 6th Chasseurs, in the 3rd Cavalry Corps, have also defended their 'position foot by foot, hoping to be supported by the cuirassiers, our reserve, but in vain. After the very indecisive fight we'd seen to our amazement the Russian army take up its position again at Tarutino, so that we were free to go and look for our cuirassiers.' But when Henckens and his comrades get to Woronowo, 'to our great surprise there they were, in great disorder, having been taken by surprise by Cossacks that morning two leagues to our rear'.

There or some other 'village ten or twenty leagues from Moscow' Coignet, sent from the Kremlin with despatches for Murat, also sees:

'some routed cavalry. Our men, mounted bareback, had been surprised while attending to their horses' sores. I couldn't see Prince Murat. He'd escaped in his shirt. It was pitiable to see these fine cavalrymen running away. I asked where the Prince was. "If he's been captured," they said, "they've taken him in his bed." And I could find out nothing. The Emperor heard about it afterwards from Nansouty's ADC.'

For the fourth time during the campaign Sébastiani, above all, has lived up to his nickname. As for the French right, Griois thinks the Russians could easily have turned it 'if they hadn't aimed their opening effort at the left, held by Sébastiani's Cavalry Corps'. Grouchy's 3rd Cavalry Corps, stationed on the right, hasn't fared quite so badly.

By evening various people and units are claiming to have saved the situation. Hearing about the affray, Dedem in his mill near the Kazan Gate even gets the impression that it's all been the work of the feeble remains of Dufour's infantry division. And others will claim it was the Poles of the Vistula Legion. Otherwise the King of Naples has been in his element, and is very definitely the hero of the otherwise miserable occasion. He has even been wounded, for the first time since Egypt in 1799. A lance, says Thirion,

'pierced his side and Tartar-style pelisse, which however covered his clothes and prevented anyone from seeing they were stained in blood. He didn't speak of this wound, which was anyway a light one, and only at the day's end did he have it examined by his doctor.'

The advance guard's losses have been more than considerable. Biot's first glance had seen everything in its true light. From the nearby wood, which Sébastiani hadn't bothered to occupy, the Cossacks had been able to watch everything that had been going on 'even in his headquarters'. Besides 38 out of 187 guns, lost largely for lack of horses to draw them off, Sébastiani has lost some 1,200 to 1,500 men killed and as many again made prisoner – all chiefly, so it would seem, because of his fecklessness; but also because Murat had delayed until that very morning his permission to withdraw in good time to Woronowo. To all intents and purposes it's the end of 1st Cavalry Corps; and though Grouchy's and Latour-Maubourg's two cavalry corps are still in order, their horses are on their last legs. Several generals, too, have been killed, among them General Déri, Marshal of Murat's Palace, 'and General Baltier, chief of Poniatowski's artillery, had been taken'. Poniatowski himself has been hurt in the knee. No one doubts that it's been Murat's presence of mind and physical energy, together with Claparède's and Latour-Maubourg's divisions, that has saved the situation: 'We were saved,' writes Surgeon Roos, whose 3rd Württemberg Chasseurs have been annihilated (a shell had burst beside the place where he'd been getting a night's uneasy sleep under frost-packed straw),

'thanks to the ability and resolution of Murat, who put the cuirassiers and other debris of the cavalry to admirable use. If the Russians, instead of attacking us at dawn, had waited until 10 a.m. or midday, by which time half our troops would have been away foraging, they could have seized our camp without firing a shot.'

Russian losses are about equal to those of the French. Bagawout, who'd executed the entire attack, is dead. Wilson, beside himself with fury at what he regards as Kutusov's lackadaisical way of seconding it,[4] is at the same time delighted at Murat's discomfiture. 'All his silver, equipage, bed, etc., even his plume, seen flaunting in the fight where it had been hottest, were taken,' he crows delightedly into his diary that evening:

'The French camps were quite disgusting. They were full of dead horses, many of which were prepared as butcher's meat.'

Even dead cats, he hears, have been found ready for the cookpot in what
had been the King of Naples' headquarters. But all His Britannic Majesty's
representative himself picks up among the debris are 'a few amusing letters', chiefly from the fair sex. Among the prisoners is a nephew of
Napoleon's War Minister Clarke. Wilson does what he can for them. And
goes on, not a little smugly:

> 'Elliott, Gen. Clarke's nephew, assures me that for the last twelve days
> he has been living like the rest of Murat's army on horseflesh without
> salt, and without any bread. As Elliott was plundered of all his money,
> etc., I gave him a hundred roubles, had his wounds dressed and filled
> his vacant interior with a good dinner, breakfast, etc. I know that Gen.
> Clarke had been very civil to many English prisoners, and perceive
> that he is a friend of Lord Hutchinson's. I was therefore moved to
> show kindness to Elliott, as well on public as on private grounds. The
> Cossacks are now so rich they now sell the most valuable articles for a
> little gold, as that alone is portable in addition to their stock. They
> must have gained yesterday an immense booty.'

And here comes another source of satisfaction. Earlier that day – presumably before Béranger's arrival – Napoleon had sent Lauriston back to
Murat with a new letter to be forwarded to Kutusov. It reads:

> "General Lauriston has been charged to propose to Your Highness
> that arrangements should be reached that would give to the war a
> character conformable to the established rules of warfare, and ensure
> measures that shall minimise the evils the country must suffer such as
> are inevitable in a state of war."

This time it's another of Murat's ADCs, Colonel Berthémy, who – rather
unseasonably – has to deliver the letter in Kutusov's camp, where everyone's celebrating what they will claim as 'a great victory'. According to
Anstett, an *émigré* who'll report the conversation to the Austrian chancellor
Nesselrode, whose agent he is, when Berthémy presents himself before
Kutusov (who 'has the upper hand in the conversation') he doesn't so
much as let him open his mouth.

Cossacks are an unpredictable people. That evening, Griois will hear later,
they invite Sébastiani's wretched gunners, whom they've captured with
their guns, disarmed and bound, to a grand party:

> 'In joy at their triumph and already drunk as lords, they wanted to cel-
> ebrate with national dances. They wanted everyone to take part and,
> remembering their prisoners, invited them to join in the general
> rejoicing. At first our poor gunners had no idea of anything but
> refreshing themselves; but little by little, restored by the good treat-
> ment lavished on them, they joined in the dancing. This conduct

drew upon them the Cossacks' esteem and tender feelings, and upon the reciprocal benevolence reaching its height, our Frenchmen again donned their coats and shakos as well as their weapons, shook their new friends warmly by the hand, who embraced them, and each took leave of the other in a friendly spirit certainly not shared by their sovereigns. And that was why the gunners rejoined their division.'

By no means are all the French and Polish prisoners as fortunate. And Wilson, who's been on horseback for eighteen hours, adds a terrible postscript:

'More prisoners are momentarily brought in. Above 1,500 are now before our eyes, in wretched condition, with teeth chattering, etc. The peasants have bought numbers from the Cossacks, at two silver roubles a head, to kill them ... Another general is killed. Five guns and two standards are among the trophies, but the most consolatory is the rescue of 300 wounded Russians, in a church which the enemy had just fired.'

This, then, is what, in essence, Murat's downcast ADC Colonel Béranger has to report to Napoleon at the Kremlin. News which causes him instantly to advance the Grand Army's departure from Moscow, planned for 20 October, by twenty-four hours:

'"*Moscow, 18 October 1812. Mon cousin*, give the order to the Prince of Eckmühl to move his headquarters this evening to beyond the Kaluga Gate, and there place his infantry, his artillery and all his military equipment, as well as his baggage, in such a fashion as to leave tomorrow at daybreak for *une forte journée* [a hard day's marching]. He is to leave a guard at the entrenched convent [by the Doroghomilov Gate] until the Duke of Treviso [Mortier] has relieved him, should there be reason to."'

Ney gets exactly the same order. So does old Marshal Lefèbvre. He's to have the Guard infantry bivouac outside the Kaluga Gate "in a square around the Emperor's lodgings". Likewise Eugène, together with an extra instruction: He's to "place himself *une lieu* [an hour's march] ahead, so as to be able to leave first."

First and foremost this insult to French arms must be wiped out. On no account must Europe think he's fleeing from Moscow after an ignominious defeat. His plan now, Napoleon writes to Maret, Duke of Bassano, his Foreign Minister and plenipotentiary at faraway Vilna, is to march southward towards Kaluga; defeat Kutusov or push him back; and then march via the Ukraine "into the square which lies between Smolensk, Molihew, Minsk and Witebsk. The operations will then be directed on Petersburg and Kiev" in the spring. "In affairs of this sort," he adds in a wry postscript, "the outcome often turns out very differently from what has been envisaged."

In a flash everyone's preparing to leave. 'A moment after' Béranger's arrival, the Guardia d'Onore has been

'ordered to return to our respective quarters and get ready to leave on the spot. So it's good-bye, doubtless, to the last hopes of peace! Hastily, we return to our quarters, fold up our gala uniforms, and with pleasure put on our marching coats. Everything's topsy-turvy. Joy at leaving can be read in all faces. Only one thing troubles us: to leave behind us some comrades who're no longer able to walk. Many of them are gathering up all their strength to follow us.'

Le Roy goes to Davout's headquarters in the convent by the Doroghomilov Gate

'to take his orders and thank him for the protection he'd given me by having me promoted lieutenant-colonel. I found him just as he was mounting his horse to go to the Emperor.'

Davout tells him:

'"Oh, my dear captain," (that's what he called me) "go and make haste and rejoin your regiment. Tomorrow it'll receive orders to march for Malojarosl-la-Wetz [Malojaroslavetz] on the Kaluga road. I hope we'll go a fair part of the way in each other's company."'

Davout wants to send him back to France to take over the 85th's depot and train its cadres. Which suits Le Roy down to the ground. The lingering thought that his son is being dragged away, maltreated by Cossacks, perhaps being tortured to death by enraged peasants, has cured him of all thirst for promotion; even if, as Caulaincourt puts it,

'those who trained the men at the bases and kept things going obtained no recognition if they weren't with the Grand Army or hadn't taken part in such or such a battle and a brave lieutenant-colonel who, after fighting twenty campaigns, was back in the depot was forgotten, just because he'd had no chance to contribute brilliant deeds to the successful affair of the moment.'

Le Roy has had enough of brilliant deeds. Major Pion des Loches, too, had been at the parade where

'III Corps was reviewed by the Emperor at the same time as a great number of dismounted men of all arms. After an orderly officer had brought some news, the review ceased and Marshal Lefèbvre enjoined me to prepare to leave, following on after the [Foot] Chasseurs of the Guard. Such an order made us wonder what its cause could be, and we soon heard that the King of Naples had been vigorously attacked in the neighbourhood of Moscow and lost what little cavalry remained to him.'

At 4 p.m. the newly promoted artillery major marches out:

'Under my orders I had the 1st company of Old Guard foot artillery, commanded by Captain Lavillette, with Messieurs Dumas-Catturet and Aubertin under him, and the 2nd Company of Foot Artillery of the Young Guard, a park, a train, and a medical officer, and a sergeant-sous-aide in the Train.'

The Army of Italy, too, is marching out:

'At 5 p.m. drums beating and to noisy music, we pass through the streets of Moscow ... Moscow! Which we'd so longed to get to, but were now leaving without regret. All we thought of was Italy, our own folk, whom we were going to see again after such a glorious expedition. On the Bridge of the Marshals, the sight of the Kremlin and the fine buildings on the Moskova's banks that had been saved from the fire drew a last glance. Finally, the troops, laden with loot, leave Moscow and take the Kaluga road. Soon the silence is broken and, at a marching pace, we begin singing, telling stories. Everyone's happy.'

Bourgogne and his fellow-sergeants of the Fusilier-Grenadiers had been 'reclining like pashas on ermine, sable, lion skins and bearskins amid clouds of East Indian tobacco and rose petal smoke and enjoying a flaming punchbowl of Jamaica rum'

when the duty clerk had entered and told them to prepare for instant departure next day:

'We gave the Muscovite women and the two tailors their share of the booty we couldn't carry away. They threw themselves on the ground to kiss our feet twenty times – never had they imagined such riches.'

Captain François of the 30th Line, though still limping about badly on one crutch with two musket balls still in his left leg and any number of bruises (fortunately, though he can mount neither of them, he's got two horses), defies – wisely as it'll turn out – the regimental surgeon's wish to send him to hospital; and prepares, he too, to leave for ever this Moscow they should have left at least three weeks ago.

Superintending at dinner that evening, Bausset sees that the Emperor's so agitated he can hardly sit out his meal. Has he only now, the obese Prefect of the Palace wonders, tumbled to the real nature of his predicament? Various reports are coming in of the Winkovo affair and causing him – evidently in front of Caulaincourt, Berthier etc. – to criticise himself 'for having stayed in Moscow without inspecting that position:

'"It means I must see everything with my own eyes. I can't rely on the King. He trusts in his own bravery. He leaves things to his generals, and they're careless. The King performs prodigies of valour. Without his presence of mind and courage everything would have been lost."'

Above all he's determined to

"wipe out the effects of this surprise. It mustn't be said in France that a check like this has forced us to retire. This upsets all our plans. It spoils everything. The honour of our arms must be re-established on the battlefield."

On no account must it seem – least of all at Vienna and Berlin – that the Grand Army is being forced to retreat as a result of this skirmish, as he calls it in his letter to Marie Louise.

In Moscow the evening is warm and beautiful – so warm and pleasant that Dedem van der Gelder, in his mill near the Kazan Gate, dines with some fellow-officers 'in front of open windows'. But all over the ruined city some 3,000 foreign residents, as well as Russians who feel they've compromised themselves by collaborating with the invaders are piling every transportable chattel on to carts and carriages and making for the Kaluga Gate.

Getting home late to her lodgings in the outhouse of Prince Galitzin's palace, after a successful performance of *Les Amants Protées* ('Lovers in Their Various Guises'), Louise Fusil has just sat down to repair her 'Petronilla' costume for a forthcoming production, when a fellow-lodger, a French officer, enters. 'Armed from head to foot', he advises her and her friend to get going. In two hours, he says, the army'll be leaving Moscow. Other French officers have already pointed out to her how furious the Russian soldiery will probably be with all foreigners who remain behind – 'the women above all aroused their compassion, because some couldn't find any horses and others had no money to pay for any'. Though this is exactly her own predicament she decides to leave. She'll go as far as Minsk or Vilna, she thinks, and there await calmer times before returning to Moscow. Hurrying through the already deserted streets, she's 'examining with a sort of fright this town, where I saw only ruins,' when

'suddenly a pack of dogs threw themselves at me. They were so hungry they ran after me to devour me, flung themselves at my shawl and tore it to pieces; also my dress which, however, was wadded and of rather strong material. My screams drew the attention of a peasant armed with a thick stick. I still shudder when I think those dogs might have been rabid.'

Everyone who has a carriage is setting out in it. War Commissary Bellot de Kergorre, for instance, who's come up to Moscow from Mojaisk and has filled his with

'bread, wine, sugar, everything we could carry away, even a mattress – it was so full only one person could get inside. I was far from expecting the host of miseries we were going to suffer; but I was sure we'd lose our horses from fatigue and hunger, and from the first day I meant to get used to walking. Nothing was more fearful than the crossing of this great city, in the midst of its ruins and by the light of

a few stars and of a few dying fires vaguely illuminating the remains of palaces. Only the noise of our wheels broke the silence.'
But then Louise has a stroke of luck:
'One of the Emperor's orderly officers, a nephew of M. de Caulaincourt, put his servants and carriage at my disposal. It was a very fine dormeuse [a light carriage in which one could sleep]. I also kept my furs, knowing very well I might need them. It was beautiful weather and I was far from foreseeing the disasters to follow: because if I had, nothing would have induced me to leave Moscow.'

But for ten Russian soldiers it's the end of life's road. Obviously innocent of any part in burning down the city, they've been 'left in prison, hapless victims of their obedience to their superiors and the orders of a madman, as the Emperor said,' where Berthier has been sparing them. Now, evidently without a thought as to what effect it must have on the fate of the 4,000 non-transportable wounded assembled in the Foundling Hospital,[5] Napoleon vents his frustration by ordering the hapless ten
"to be shot as incendiaries. Let the execution take place in the morning, without drawing attention to it."
– a written order which, to Wilson's intense fury, will be found left lying in a cellar in the 11th *arrondissement*; and become the basis, perhaps, of the execution scene in Tolstoy's *War and Peace?*

CHAPTER 11

TAKING FRENCH LEAVE

A lovely sunny day – a host of vehicles – the loot of Moscow – effectives – a crawling army – a bizarre spectacle – Bourgogne lightens his pack – 'the Romans gave civic crowns' – why no courier? – 'the loudest bang I've heard in my life' – Griois gets a fresh wardrobe – the rumble of the guns

At 2 a.m. on 19 October the exodus begins. It's just such another golden autumn day as the one, 35 days ago, when they'd first gazed in amazement from the Sparrow Hill at the still intact city. Prince Eugène, who has 'given himself all possible trouble to reorganize his corps' ('but Davout too had given himself a lot of trouble on I Corps' behalf, to prevent the catastrophe he'd begun to foresee') is in the van:

'The Italian Guard was superb. The Emperor has sent it off first, with orders to take the Mojaisk road, then throw itself to the left and get to Malojaroslavetz by the Old Kaluga Road.'

After the Army of Italy comes I Corps. The crush at the Kaluga Gate is stupendous. Slowly, chaotically, throughout the forenoon, IV and I Corps surge out between its twin stone pillars: 'All day it was as much as we could do to get out of town,' Le Roy will recall, 'so encumbered was the road.' After Davout comes Ney. His reserve artillery only reaches the Kaluga Gate at about 1 p.m., just as Napoleon appears.[1] Major *G. de Faber du Faur*, commanding III Corps' 12-pounders and artillery train, promptly sketches the scene – a grenadier grabs a private carriage's startled horse – Caulaincourt, Duroc and Berthier in immediate attendance – surely that's Duroc to whom a plumpish Emperor, apparently imperturbable, is talking as he walks one of his Arab greys forward through the throng? A few yards behind, to add a touch of lighter blue amidst the Imperial Staff, under the warm hazy sky, Gourgaud's uniform gets him into the picture, as it will into so many others.

All day the divisions move slowly out between the Kaluga Gate's monumental pillars. Last out is the Imperial Guard. Surgeon Roos sees it go by, both foot and horse:

'The men marched past in columns, well aligned, proud and handsome, alert and smart like troops leaving their winter cantonments. Each of them carried three or four white loaves attached to his knapsack and a bottle of brandy hanging from strap of his sabre or cartridge box. They were followed by a convoy of baggage such as has never been seen in any war.'

Though Pion des Loches' two companies of Young Guard foot artillery leave in the afternoon, the Foot Chasseurs won't get out of the gates until midnight.

If the army had been characterized at the Niemen by the 'vast, the unprecedented host of vehicles it was dragging after it', the evil is now many times worse. Assembling the 1,100 men of his 4th Line in a sandy space beside Prince Galitzin's huge town palace 'as big as the Tuileries', Fezensac has already been shocked to see some overladen carts and carriages being abandoned:

'They were burning such foodstuffs as we couldn't take with us, and we saw provisions being burnt under our eyes that perhaps would have saved our lives.'

And Dedem is no less shocked to discover that

'when we left there was enough of it left in the stores to nourish 20,000 horses for six months. Leaving Moscow I saw a storehouse whose immense long vaults were filled up with sacks of fine flour. It was left to be looted. And yet eight days previously I'd had difficulty in obtaining a sack of crude flour.'

Now, reaching a hilltop outside the town, Fezensac looks out over

'the immense caravan, reminiscent of the conquerors of Asia, marching several vehicles abreast. The plain was covered with these immense baggages, and on the horizon Moscow's bell towers bounded the picture. We were ordered to halt at this spot, as if to let us contemplate a last time the ruins of this ancient city, which soon disappeared from our sight.'

The caravan is indeed immense. It strikes Davout's paymaster Captain Duverger as

'a bizarre spectacle: this disorderly caravan of every kind of vehicle, military carriages, little carts, calèches, droshkis, most of them attached to little Russian horses, painfully dragging themselves across a sandy plain – this hotchpotch of individuals from all countries and both sexes isolated in the crowd by completely different interests and languages, mechanically following the impulse given them by necessity. The French who lived in Moscow, even the Germans, had left the city – they were afraid to expose themselves to the barbarians' reprisals if they remained. So they'd fled, taking with them wives and children and a few fragments of whatever they'd possessed.'

The Kaluga highway is broad, but not broad enough. An otherwise anonymous Captain von Kurz sees the vast baggage train crawling along it and beside it in no fewer than ten parallel columns:

'Most officers owned a cart, but the generals had half a dozen. Supply officials and actors, women and children, cripples, wounded men, and the sick were driving in and out of the throng in kibitkas and droshkis, accompanied by countless servants and maids, sutlers and people of that sort. The columns of horsemen and pedestrians broke out on either side. Wherever the terrain permitted they crossed the fields flanking the road, so as to leave the paved highway free for those on foot. But the enormous clutter of transport got jammed up, even so.'

So vast is this host of vehicles, Major *L-J. Vionnet* realizes,

'that their column, alone, took up a space of eighteen miles. It's impossible to imagine what disorder this caused. The soldiers fought to get ahead of one another; and when, sometimes, by chance, a bridge had to be crossed, they had to wait for twelve hours. The vehicles had been well numbered, but even by the second day their order had been turned upside down, so that those whose rank entitled them to a carriage didn't know where to find it and consequently couldn't get at its contents. From the first days of the retreat we already began to lack for everything.'

The strategic and logistic implications of this ball and chain of impedimenta clinging to the army's heels just when every effort should be being made in true Napoleonic style to steal two or three marches on the Russians, certainly aren't lost on Davout's unwilling chief-of-staff. Not that Lejeune isn't himself one of the officers responsible for it:

'I'll give you an idea of my own position in this respect – I who was one of the officers most interested in travelling without impedimenta! I still had (1) five riding horses [essential for a staff officer]; (2) a carriage drawn by three horses and carrying my belongings, as well as furs to wrap round me at our bivouacs; (3) the wagon laden with staff documents, maps, and the kitchen utensils for the officers and clerks – this was pulled by four horses and weighed down by the clerks, the cook, the oats, sugar, coffee, flour, and some scarce bales of hay; (4) the secretary's horse; lastly (5) the three horses which I'd harnessed to my sister's carriage: she'd gone on ahead. All this made a clutter of six vehicles and twenty-five horses, and yet they scarcely carried the essentials! The traces kept on breaking. Halts held up the march. Sand, defiles, marshes – all caused delays. And the army took twelve hours and often longer to cover the distance that one vehicle on its own would have covered in two. The Emperor was very much upset by these delays, and ordered that every vehicle not essential for transporting the few provisions we carried should be burnt and the horses be used to pull the guns. This very wise but severe measure was but feebly enforced. The Emperor had one of his own carriages burnt, but the example wasn't compelling enough and found no imitators.

There were too many people who had an interest in evading it.'
'Despite our foreboding of the mischief awaiting us,' Fezensac goes on,
'each of us was determined to carry off his own part of the trophies –
there was no employee so insignificant he hadn't taken a carriage and
packed up some precious objects. For my part I had furs, paintings by
the great masters (rolled up for easier transport) and some jewellery.
One of my comrades had loaded up an enormous crate of quinine.
Another a whole library of lovely books with gilded spines and bound
in red morocco, including Demoustier's *Letters to Emilia*. I hadn't forgotten my comforts either: rice, sugar, coffee. In my reserves I counted three great pots of jams, two being cherries, a third of currents.'
Even such a veteran as Major Boulart of the Old Guard artillery is
'carried away by the mania for having a carriage. In my wake I had a
very fine brand-new coupé, given me by a general who didn't know
what to do with it! Didn't I even commit the same folly of buying horses to harness it to? This elegant coupé contained sugar, tea, furs and
some magnificent editions of books, and in my delirium I supposed
I'd be able to bring part of those objects back to France.'
Marching on his own at the Italians' heels, Lieutenant-Colonel Le Roy too
sees how
'most officers were having themselves drawn along like Russians do,
in light carriages with four horses abreast. Each carriage had to keep
its rank on the road and was unable to change direction, that is unless
the drivers wanted to take off at a cross-roads to rejoin their army
corps. But the road only had to narrow in a defile for these gentil-
lesses [pretty toys] to turn over and get left behind.'
The 28-year-old war-commissary Bellot de Kergorre, walking along beside
his heavy-laden carriage in the wake of IHQ, notices that 'to the tilt of their
light cart the troupe of actors who were following us had affixed the words:
"First actor to S. M. I. R." [His Majesty the Emperor and King] ... "First
valet" ... Sad recourse against accidents en route!' For his part, Kergorre is
marching with the Intendant-General's headquarters, where, to add to all
the private plunder, General Count *François Roguet's* three regiments of
Guard Grenadiers are escorting the Treasury wagons, including the imperial loot. Bellot de Kergorre:
'I was carrying away trophies from the Kremlin, including the cross of
Ivan, several ornaments used at the coronation of the tsars, and a
Madonna enriched with precious stones, which had been given by the
Tsarina Anna in 1740 in memory of the victories won over the Poles
and the capture of Danzig in 1733. The treasure comprised silver
coins or bullion melted down from the large amount of silverware
found in the ruins of Moscow. For nearly 40 miles I had to pick my

way through the army's procession of horse-drawn vehicles. Every one was laden with useless baggage.'

And Planat de la Faye, marching with the artillery staff, notices in particular how 'the number of *cantinières* with carts had grown enormously'. Their vast pillage isn't merely bogging down the army 'just when it most needed to be mobile'. It's also

'beginning the army's demoralization, or, more correctly, that of the French troops – the German and Dutch troops had already commenced their career as pillagers and scroungers at Viazma'.[2]

Though it may not seem so, a certain priority has in fact been given to foodstuffs. Most of the baggage train, Biot realises, is transporting 'farinacious foods, biscuit, rice, wine, coffee, tea, sugar and rum'. And Dr René Bourgeois, too, is glad to see that all vehicles except the artillery wagons are carrying forage for the horses and victuals, 'flour, wine, sugar, coffee, tea and liquors'.

Even so, the stupendous caravan reminds Captain Labaume, riding onwards with Prince Eugène's staff, of Virgil and Livy's descriptions of 'the destruction of Troy or Carthage'. And Boulart, consoling himself that this isn't a retreat but an offensive towards the south, is reminded of 'the ancient Persian armies in their expeditions against the Greeks'.

But how strong are the army's actual effectives? Prince Eugène is in the van with 20,000 infantry but only 2,000 cavalry, less than half the effectives that had started out from Glogau in May. His once 13,000-strong 15th Division, for instance, now numbers only 4,000. The marquis *de Chambray*, marching with his guns, will afterwards go closely into the matter and give the army's effectives as:

I Corps 29,000 (originally 79,000)
III Corps 11,000 (originally 44,000)
IV Corps 25,600 (originally 42,400)
V Corps 6,000 (originally 30,000)
VIII Corps perhaps 1,500 (originally 18,700)
Imperial Guard 22,480 (originally 51,300), the original figures being Labaume's. Caulaincourt sets the total at 102,260 and 533 guns.[3]

For the time being Mortier is to stay behind in the Kremlin with Delaborde's division of the Young Guard, Carrière's brigade of 4,000 dismounted cavalry (organised in four battalions), two companies of sappers, four of artillery and a brigade of 500 cavalry. He's to collect all sick and wounded who can't be evacuated and leave them in the Foundlings Hospital:

"After the army has left, the Duke of Treviso will tomorrow cause the municipality to make a proclamation, warning the inhabitants that rumours of evacuation are false: that the army is moving on Kaluga,

Tula and Briansk to seize those important points and the arms factories they contain, and obliging the inhabitants to maintain order and
prevent anyone from trying to complete the town's destruction."
Any destruction that's to take place, notably of the Kremlin and the Arsenal, which is expected to be total, is to be at Mortier's hands.

A great deal of the army's superfluous plunder is already having to be left
behind. Disgusted at having to march at such a snail's pace, 2nd Lieutenant Coignet puts all his little party's possessions and equipment on their
horses and burns their wagon. 'After that we could go anywhere.' The
Fusiliers-Grenadiers of the Middle Guard are bringing up the extreme rear.
And all that first day Sergeant Bourgogne is amazed to see what the army's
leaving behind:

'Being at the very rear of the column I was in a position to see how
the disorder was commencing. The route was cluttered with precious
objects, such as pictures, candelabras, and many books. For more
than an hour I picked up volumes which I leafed though for a
moment and then threw away again, to be picked up by others, who,
in their turn, threw them away. They were editions of Voltaire, of Jean-
Jacques Rousseau and Bouffon's *Natural History* bound in red Morocco and gilded on their spines.'

Ahead of him is a vast mob:

'This crowd of people, with their various costumes and languages, the
canteen masters with their wives and crying children, were hurrying
forward in the most unheard of noise, tumult and disorder. Some had
got their carts smashed, and in consequence yelled and swore enough
to drive one mad. This was the convoy of the whole army, and we had
any amount of trouble getting past it.'

Even by this first evening Bourgogne's pack is beginning to seem much too
heavy. So leaving at dawn next morning and overtaking

'a large part of the fatal convoy, which had passed us while we were
asleep and where we could hear screams in French, oaths in German,
entreaties to the Almighty in Italian, and to the Holy Virgin in Spanish and Portuguese,'

he decides while waiting 'for the left of the column' to lighten it:

'I found several pounds of sugar, some rice, some biscuit, half a bottle of liqueur, a woman's Chinese silk dress embroidered in gold and
silver, several gold and silver ornaments, amongst them a little bit of
the Cross of Ivan the Great – a piece of its outer silver-gilt sheath,
given me by a man who'd helped take it down. Besides all this I had
my [parade] uniform, a woman's large riding cloak (hazel colour,
lined with green velvet. As I couldn't figure out how it was worn, I

imagined its late owner to be over six feet tall), then two silver pictures in relief, a foot long and eight inches high, one of them representing the Judgement of Paris on Mount Ida, the other showing Neptune on a chariot formed of a shell and drawn by sea-horses, all in the finest workmanship, and several lockets and a Russian prince's spittoon set with brilliants. These things were intended for presents, and had been found in cellars where the houses were burnt down.'

First and foremost Bourgogne, 'feeling pretty certain I shouldn't be wanting them again just yet', jettisons his regulation white knee breeches.[4] What else he throws out he forgets to say. But he does tell us what he's wearing:

'Over my shirt a yellow silk waistcoat, wadded inside, which I'd made myself out of a woman's skirt; over it a large cape lined with ermine, and underneath the cape a big pouch hung at my side by a silver cord. This was full of various things – amongst them a gold and silver crucifix and a little Chinese porcelain vase.[5] Then there was my powder-flask, my firearms, and sixteen cartridges in my cartridge case. Add to all this a fair amount of health, good spirits and the hope of presenting my compliments to the Mongol, Chinese and Indian ladies, and you'll have a very good idea of a vélite sergeant of the Imperial Guard.'

Hardly has Bourgogne relieved himself of his unwanted loot than

'ahead of us we hear firing, and are ordered to set off at the double. Half an hour afterwards we got to a place where part of the convoy, escorted by a detachment of the Red Lancers of the Guard, had been attacked by partisans. Several of the lancers had been killed, also some Russians and many horses. Near a cart was a pretty woman stretched on her back on the ground, dead from shock.'

Why does Dumonceau make no mention of this? The Lancer Brigade, detailed off to 'provisionally form the army's extreme rearguard' and cover its flank in the direction of Podolsk, has come back from Woronowo to meet it. Soon isolated outriders had approached,

'and once well on our way it wasn't long before we ran into IV Corps, marching in files on either side of the road and leaving its centre to us. We saw they were thoroughly refreshed. The men seemed gay and in good fettle.'

The rankers of the Line don't hesitate to poke fun at this Guard regiment[6] which, no more than the others, hadn't been thrown into the action at Borodino – and get as good as they give. Then comes

'the immense mob, bigger than ever, of parks and baggage of all kinds, marching on a front of several files, covering the whole road and wrapped in a cloud of dust.'

191

Not to get entangled in it, the Red Lancers take off to the right of the road. And now, on the second day of the march southwards, Dumonceau is sent off to reconnoitre two or three leagues from the highroad – which is perhaps why he'll afterwards forget to mention the affray of the 20th:

'It was recommended to me that I should march prudently, explore the countryside thoroughly and not let myself get pinched. I got back by evening, not having seen a soul. The population of the villages seemed to have returned to their homes, but kept themselves hidden, so that it was impossible to make them appear to obtain any information.'

Griois, too, withdrawing 3rd Cavalry Corps' light artillery after the affair at Winkovo, sees the Moscow army come by:

'Dense columns made up of troops of the different arms, marching in disorder; the horses weak, emaciated, hardly dragging the artillery. The men, on the contrary, having had an abundance of victuals for the last six weeks, were full of strength and health. Carriages of the greatest elegance, peasants' carts, wagons pulled by little country horses and overladen with baggage, were marching in the middle of the columns, pell-mell with the saddle and pack horses. The rankers were crushed under the weight of their packs. To abandon their booty would have been too cruel. Yet already that day baggage was being thrown on the road and vehicles abandoned. This mass of men, horses and vehicles seemed more like an emigration of a people changing its country than an organized army.'

It must have been Ségur who, as usual, in his capacity of Assistant Prefect of the Palace, has gone on ahead of IHQ and fixed on the 'mean' manor house of Troilskoïe, about fifteen miles from Moscow, for its first overnight stay. Nearby is concentrated the Italian Guard cavalry and almost the whole army, except Delaborde's division, left behind in Moscow, and what's left of Murat's cavalry – still retreating from Winkovo towards Woronowo and the main column. Already IHQ has met with 'many of the wounded from the Winkovo affair, of which the Emperor only now heard the details'.

Making his way on a *teleg* [Russian four-wheeled cart] to Moscow to be bled, his thigh shattered by a lance-thrust, is an aristocratic youngster of the Carabiniers: Prince Charles de Beauveau. Son of one of Napoleon's chamberlains, 'he was smiling as though his wound was causing him more pride than pain'. Sure they'll never see Moscow again, Caulaincourt sends one of his father's colleagues, the one-eyed chamberlain Count Turenne, hurrying after him. Turenne brings the boy back. And Caulaincourt obtains permission to place him in one of the imperial carriages.

His arm still paralyzed by that lance-thrust in his shoulder, Mailly-Nesle, too, has been making for Moscow in a carriage in which there are some ladies. But knowing the last convoy of wounded has already left, a gendarme named Gimblaut advises them to go no farther. So their comfortable carriage joins the throng. After the miseries of the Winkovo camp the Moscow army, despite all its loot and the snail's pace it's proceeding at, makes a 'magnificent' impression.

'Almost all the staff officers had dressed themselves in the Russian style. Only the artillery was in a bad state. The good horses had been replaced by wretched little konyas, harnessed up by dozens to each gun. The soldiers had provided themselves with gold and silver. They were clad in the most precious furs. Each officer had a little loaded cart in his suite. The most elegant and opulent carriages were following their convoy of immense spoils. Each soldier was carrying at the hilt of his sabre some silver or at very least silver-gilt cutlery. Most of them had silver ciboria or chalices, which they used with inappropriate familiarity. In their knapsacks others had little statues of Muscovite saints, or a silver egg which they scraped or broke up for their transactions with the cantinières. They marched gaily, singing at the tops of their voices, and their full rubicund faces were evidence enough that they lacked neither for bread nor wine.'

Rapp, reporting fit even though his Borodino wound still isn't completely cured, declines Caulaincourt's offer of one of the Emperor's own carriages and mounts his horse, 'to see if I could stand its movement'. As he does so he sees Napoleon talking to Daru who – in addition to his own duties, that highly cultivated and immensely hard-working man, has just taken over those of Chief Commissary Mathieu Dumas, who's gone down with influenza, worsening to pneumonia. Calling Rapp over, Napoleon says:

"Well then, Rapp, we'll withdraw toward the Polish frontier via Kaluga. I'll provide us with good winter quarters, and let's hope Alexander will make peace."

"Your Majesty seems to have waited long enough," Rapp replies. "The inhabitants of the country are predicting a severe winter."

"Bah, bah – always going on about your inhabitants! Today it's 19 October. Look what lovely weather we're having! Don't you recognize my star? Anyway I couldn't leave until I'd got the sick and wounded evacuated. I couldn't leave them to the fury of the Russians.'"

Rapp replies respectfully that in his opinion he'd have 'done better to have left them in Moscow. The Russians wouldn't have done them any harm, whereas now they'll be running the risk of perishing on the country roads.'

But Napoleon, more realistic, won't concede this. As for the climate and winter's imminent onset, 'regardless of what he said to contradict me, his obvious worry showed he hadn't convinced himself.'

Next day Castellane watches Dr Yvan set Beauveau's thigh, an operation the youngster bears with great courage. After which Caulaincourt places him in Mailly-Nesle's carriage, which the two young aristocrats have to share with two ladies, three doctors and a footman.[7]

All that day, the second of his march southwards, Napoleon lingers at Troilskoië, waiting for the huge numbers of stragglers and vehicles to catch up. Roman Soltyk, waiting there with IHQ's topographical department, thinks the infantry is

'in good shape; the cavalry that had been camped near Winkovo in truth much reduced; but that of the Guard, as also that of the three corps which had been in Moscow, still quite well mounted.'

But here comes a nasty reminder of Russian intransigence. Kutusov's reply to Berthier's – i.e., Napoleon's own – letter of 16 October, delivered to him by Colonel Berthémy on the evening of the Winkovo fight, and suggesting that the laws of 'civilised' warfare be better respected, comes in via Murat's outposts. In it Kutusov "emphasises a truth" whose scope, he's sure Berthier (i.e., Napoleon) will undoubtedly grasp, and which he'd already enunciated to Lauriston at Tarutino:

"However keenly one may desire to do so, it is difficult to inhibit a nation that is embittered by all it sees, a people who for three hundred years have never known war within their frontiers,"

[which is going it a bit strong – the Poles had been in Moscow in 1611-13],

'who are ready to immolate themselves for their country and who are not susceptible to those distinctions as to what is or is not usual in ordinary warfare."

No question, that is, of the "polite political war" Napoleon had intended to wage on his "brother Alexander", to be decided by "a good battle". But a war à outrance, an all-out war, a war to the death.

Both Caulaincourt and Berthier have been noticing a peculiar reluctance on the Emperor's part to give up Moscow for good. But now, as if reminded by Kutusov's letter that, as he himself has earlier said, "Moscow is no longer a military, only a political position" and 'forced to it by the losses incurred at Winkovo, by the reports on the state of our cavalry, and the realisation that the Russians wouldn't come to terms', he reluctantly makes up his mind to do so. Relinquishing his dream of signing a peace there, he dictates an order to Mortier to evacuate the city. After blowing up the Kremlin and the Arsenal, he's to leave, "either at 3 a.m. on the 22nd or at the same hour on the 23rd, whereby he'll become the army's rearguard".

As for the remaining wounded, "I cannot sufficiently urge upon him," he goes on,

"to have all the men taken with him who are still left in the hospitals, and to do so he can dispose of and make use of all vehicles he can lay his hand on, such as the wagons of the Young Guard and the dismounted cavalry. The Romans gave civic crowns to those who saved citizens. The Duke of Treviso will deserve as many such as the soldiers he rescues. He should let them use his own and all available horses. That's what the Emperor himself did at St Jean d'Acre. He has so much the more reason to take this measure, because the Emperor promises that as soon as the sick-convoy has caught up with the army, all horses and vehicles free because their loads have been consumed will be sent to meet this need. The Emperor hopes to be able to show the Duke of Treviso his satisfaction at his having saved five hundred men. Naturally he should begin with the officers, then the NCOs and give preference to Frenchmen. He is to assemble all generals and officers under his command and impress on them the importance of this measure."

Thereafter Mortier shall join Junot at Mojaisk where, after picking up all the surviving Borodino wounded, he's to follow on behind the army as its rearguard.

Farther on, ahead of IHQ, some 30 miles from Moscow, Davout's headquarters have halted at another country house, built, 'up to its first storey on a base of cut stone. Having many orders to write out,' his chief-of-staff Lejeune mounts

'a magnificent staircase to some apartments which seemed to have been only recently deserted and without having been voided of their piano, harp and numerous chairs, on which lay scattered a guitar, some violins, music, embroidery designs and other lady's needlework. Hardly had I been writing for ten minutes than we felt the smell of smoke. Soon it was so strong it distracted us from our work.'

Leaving hastily again, Lejeune hears 'the window frames crack' and sees the whole building collapse in flames.

Once again the Cossacks are burning everything they can. And not merely burning. They've also developed an alarming swiftness – as Sergeant Bourgogne has already seen – in raiding convoys. After leaving Fominskoïë – IHQ's next objective – Prince Eugène's Bavarian cavalry are 'riding along the Kaluga road through a wood and General Ornano was riding at the head of the 2nd Chevaulegers at rather a brisk canter, and the baggage and lead-horses, including the general's own, were following on behind the regiment,' when they have a first taste of it. Partly because Ornano is setting such a brisk pace, and partly so as not to get mixed up with IV Corps' disorderly baggage train, a considerable gap has opened up between the 4th Chevaulegers, some 160 to 200 horse, following on, and their commander and his staff:

'Suddenly a hurrah rings out, Cossacks come dashing out of the forest and fling themselves on the baggage and lead- horses. In a flash they've plundered some wagons, seized a couple of loose horses and stabbed down others – all so neatly and swiftly that almost all of them have vanished into the forest before we've even had time to ride back and draw our swords.'

But they do catch one Cossack. And Ornano – he who'd already given proofs of his incompetence at Borodino – makes himself ridiculous by galloping back,

'shouting and swearing and heaping reproaches on us, and claiming that the captured Cossack's nag, at least, was his. We couldn't help laughing as the wretched nag was led out to him. Hardly had he caught sight of it than, with an oath, he put spurs to his horse's flanks and dashed off swearing.'

By taking the cross-country roads that link the old and the new Kaluga roads, Napoleon's idea is to steal a march on Kutusov. And indeed it's only after he's been marching for three days, on 22 October – four days that is – since Bennigsen's half-successful action, that the first news of the French having left Moscow reaches Russian headquarters.[8] Wilson hears that,

'a French officer, brought in as prisoner, admitted that Moscow was evacuated, that Napoleon was with the column at Ignatowo, but stated that he, the officer, knew nothing of the army's movements except that it was leaving Russia. Messenger after messenger then poured in from all quarters with similar intelligence.'

Wilson says nothing of Kutusov falling on his knees and thanking the Almighty for Russia's deliverance.

But though news of his enemy's movements has taken three days to reach Kutusov, Napoleon's plan of outflanking him and striking for Kaluga still calls for speed. Unfortunately that same day, 22 October, the gorgeous weather, with its golden autumn sun shining down out of pellucid blue skies on the evergreen forests and silver birch woods, suddenly breaks. And by morning next day the ground is 'so sodden we'd great difficulty in making Borowsk in two cross-country marches'. For the first time – but not the last – an abrupt change in the weather has come at a most inconvenient moment:

'Making our way across ploughed land and not everyone being well harnessed up, some 1,500 vehicles had to be abandoned. The winding of the road made it impossible for us to assess the innumerable quantity of vehicles making up the headquarters. The rises in the ground, the ravines, were covered with them over a surface of more than twelve miles. There must have been at least 25,000. We were keeping a width of a couple of miles on either side of the main road, a contour clearly traced by the burning villages.'

The steadily falling rain is rendering the side roads utterly unsuitable for the guns and heavy vehicles. What's even worse, the massive downpour has 'done for the draught-horses', and a good number of ammunition wagons and transports are having to be abandoned:

'We set fire to at least 20,000 sutlers' vehicles and others overloaded with sugar, coffee, etc., which were encumbering the road and hindering our passage.'

That day Kergorre finds his chief, the army's Chief Commissary, 'bivouacked in a swamp. M. le comte Dumas had left suffering from pneumonia. Feeble and old, he was exhausted by his work.'[9] That day Count de Lobau exchanged his carriage for a little one I had. His was superb. It had cost at least a hundred louis; but he was finding it too heavy, and as I had some strong horses it suited me perfectly. I filled it with coffee and sugar, pieces of cloth and cashmeres, etc.'

Much of the day is spent building a bridge over the Nara at Fominskoië while the army – disastrously as it'll turn out, in view of its urgent need to strike south – is given a day's rest. Unfortunately, the ranker, Dr Réné Bourgeois 'not having been able to equip himself with food like the officers, had none at all.' This, only four days out of Moscow, and with at least a fortnight's march ahead of them!

Perhaps even more alarming, Kergorre and his comrades are beginning 'to hear the explosion of artillery wagons being blown up, for lack of horses to pull them. The further we advanced the more frequent these explosions became.'

Already Napoleon's obsession with saving his guns is becoming a handicap. That day the Italians, marching doggedly on ahead,

'cross the Nara. The rain keeps falling, the country roads are bad and it's impossible to get on any faster. At each bridge there are blockages, of men, horses and baggage. Most of these bridges are narrow, hardly solid. Often they sag under the vehicles' weight. Added to the slowness of our march, all these obstacles are tiring the men and finally exhausting the artillery horses. A mass of light carriages are getting broken or unable to follow on.'

As a result of all this, Césare de Laugier, sitting for a moment somewhere out of the rain, concludes in his diary, 'a certain feeling of sadness is hanging over the army'. It has also been this drenching cold night, Caulaincourt sees, that has 'really opened Napoleon's eyes and finally convinced him that he must abandon Moscow' – his original idea having been to retain it as a base while occupying the 'fertile Kaluga province, as he called it'. Now he must above all attack and defeat Kutusov.

And still he won't admit, even to Berthier, that he's retreating.

For three days now the courier has been interrupted and there's been no news from Paris. For Napoleon, with all the affairs of Europe centred in his own brain, its arrival, Caulaincourt sees, is each day's most important event. How eagerly he awaits the leather despatch case, how impatiently he opens it – even, if the key isn't instantly to hand, slashes it open with a knife! The three-day gap, due, Caulaincourt has to explain to an irritated Emperor, to Cossacks having seized the second post-station from Moscow, has been the campaign's longest so far. 'This worried and annoyed the Emperor more than I can express.' And it sets him complaining bitterly, first to Caulaincourt, then to Berthier, about the "lack of foresight, the incompetence and negligence" being shown by Foreign Minister Maret, at Vilna, and by Abbé Pradt, his ambassador plenipotentiary at Warsaw.

As if realising that the army is soon going to be surrounded by swarms of Cossacks who can't be driven off for lack of light cavalry, Napoleon has got it into his head that it's Pradt's job, so far from being an ambassador as he understands the word, to squeeze thousands of non-existent "Polish Cossacks" out of the bankrupt duchy – a job of satrap for which the slippery archbishop is singularly unqualified. In the rain near Borowsk, he's complaining to Caulaincourt that "all his present difficulties and any that might arise from them" are due to the Russians having made peace with Turkey,[10] thus freeing Tormassov's Army of Moldavia to come up in his rear and attack Schwarzenberg and Reynier in Volhynia; also to the Russians' alliance with Sweden, both of which happenings he regards as being Maret's fault.

At 1.30 a.m. on 23 October, the air's shaken by an immense distant explosion. Le Roy is riding along the Kaluga road to rejoin the 85th when[11] 'we hear a violent explosion from the direction of Moscow.' What can it be? Three more follow, the last at 4 a.m. Following an unfamiliar road out of Moscow with Delaborde's Young Guard division, miles away to the west, Lieutenant Paul de Bourgoing, his ADC, hears it too. It's the loudest bang he'll ever hear in his life ...

Only later next morning does Le Roy learn what it was.

Mortier has done his best to carry out Napoleon's instructions. His two companies of sappers have done their work and the Kremlin – or at least part of it – has been blown sky-high. The four stupendous explosions have caused many of the city's surviving houses to collapse from the shock-waves – and the few remaining inhabitants to think it's the end of the world. If the Kremlin as a whole hasn't been wiped out it's been thanks to the drenching rain, which has dampened the fuzes. One French officer who'd approached to find out why the explosion wasn't even greater has been stunned by falling masonry:

'By the first two explosions part of the walls and one of the towers toward the river were destroyed; by the third, the church of St. Nicholas and Moscow's four great bell towers were blown up with tremendous violence; at the same moment the lofty tower of Ivan Veliki, the first of the Czars, was rent from the top to its base, and the cross of the cupola, crowning its summit, buried in the ruin below. The fourth shock,'

the anonymous officer goes on,

'had been by far the most dreadful. The walls of the Arsenal, which were upwards of three yards in thickness, together with a part of the gate of St. Nicholas and several adjacent pinnacles, were blown into the air and shook the whole city to its foundations.'

'The most peremptory orders were given to the detachment occupying the Kremlin,' *J. T. James*, visiting the scene of the explosions next year, will be told:

'With unutterable malignity he had marked out for devastation some of the fairest portions of this proud citadel, that had stood uninjured amidst the times of the conflagration. The barbarous fury of Buonaparte attacked whatever Russian piety had spared, the most after his departure. The mines were prepared, and at two o'clock on the last night of their [i.e., Mortier's] stay this horrid purpose was carried into execution. The ground where we stood was strewed with the relics of the church of St. Nicholas: the great bells that were its chief boast (one of which weighed more than 200,000 pounds) lay scattered in different directions, as they chanced to have fallen at the time; and of the celebrated bell cast by the Empress Anne nothing was discoverable but the ring of the top, so deep was it buried in rubbish.'

Hearing the distant noise of the immense explosions, 'though we were hardly astonished by anything any longer, and expected everything,' Pierre Auvray remarks, 'the army was astonished.'

'When the Russian General Ilowaiki re-entered Moscow on 23 October, he found in the three existing hospitals some 1,400 Russian sick or wounded and 650 French sick or wounded who'd been too weak to be transported with their comrades. Even so, part of these latter were thrown on to carts to be dragged to Tver; but they all perished from cold and misery or were assassinated by the peasants charged with taking them there, who cut their throats to get their coats. The rest were left in the hospitals with French surgeons who'd remained behind to look after them, but they were given neither food nor medicines,' writes *Frédéric-Guillaume de Vaudoncourt*,[12] a staff officer who will himself be captured during the retreat.

That day the Italians 'pass through a deserted Borowsk and bivouac an hour's march further on, near the village of Uvarovskoië'. There Césare de Laugier hears that:

'instructions have been sent off at 5 this morning by the Major-General [Berthier] to the Duke of Abrantès [Junot, at Mojaisk]. He's to burn everything he can't take with him and be ready to leave at the first signal for Viazma. The heads of all units as far as Smolensk are being forewarned of the army's movement and General Evers is ordered to leave Viazma with 4 to 5,000 men to open the army's communications with Smolensk via Juchnow.'

It seems to him that the Emperor, after his sweep southwards and giving Kutusov a bloody nose in revenge for the Winkovo affair, is planning to rejoin the devastated Smolensk road at Viazma.

Leaving Fominskoië at 9 a.m. IHQ marches all day. And at 7.30 p.m. it too reaches Borowsk – where a courier finally arrives. Always Napoleon's first act at such moments is to study the covering sheet, giving hours of arrival and departure at and from the various post-stations. This one gives an even more serious explanation of the long delay:

'A body of Cossacks, together with great numbers of peasants armed and organised as a militia, are cutting off communications beyond Ghjat – a complication which seems to be spreading.'

He observes to Caulaincourt:

"We're going to be without news from France. But even worse, France won't be getting any news of us."

Everything's still going at a snail's pace. Nor is the stopover at Borowsk a happy one. Depressed by the dreary landscape and "these slaves' [Slavs'] wild and terrible appearance which must offend any eye used to other countries", Napoleon tells Rapp:

"I wouldn't wish to leave a single man here. I'd sooner sacrifice all the treasures of Russia than a single wounded man. Horses, pack wagons, carriages, everything must be used to save them."

And sends off another letter to Mortier to that effect. 'But of course he was confusing words and his own will with facts and possibilities.'

A few miles beyond Borowsk is a village that's been occupied by Prince Eugène and part of IV Corps. Bivouacking his artillery there, Griois is invited to dinner by General *C. N. Anthouard*, head of IV Corps' artillery, whose acquaintance he had presumably made during the last days of the advance on Moscow, when the wounded Grouchy's guns had been placed at Eugène's disposal. It's several days now since Griois, horseless and carriage-less and, lacking all his captured equipment ('almost everything I pos-sessed') has had anything to eat except 'bread and whatever I'd been able to buy from the *cantinières* one rather rarely ran into and who were regard-ed as well supplied if they could offer a bit of cheese and ham'. But now, at Anthouard's headquarters, plenty of good wine raises his spirits. Even bet-ter, all his fellow artillery officers there, no doubt lit up by the good wines, want to help him make good his loss of all his effects back at Winkovo:

> 'On getting up from table each wanted to contribute something to re-establish my wardrobe. Colonel Berthier [Berthier's 38-year-old son] gave me some cloth for a pair of trousers; another a shirt; another a cravat; the general a pair of completely new boots which seemed to be made to fit me, in the circumstances a gift beyond prize. At nightfall I decided to rejoin my artillery and left, taking with me a most agree-able memory, which I'll never forget.'

But a cold rain is falling,

> 'and when I hid myself away, wrapped up in my greatcoat, under one of my batteries' ammunition wagons, I regretted the warm and well covered resting place I'd just left.'

By now it has taken the army six days to cover the 100 kilometres that sep-arate Borowsk from Moscow – mainly because everyone's clinging to the plunder. But now, what's that in the distance? A vague rumble of gunfire? No matter, it's time for a halt. And Surgeon Roos – no more than anyone else who'd been at Winkovo – he has had a chance to participate in the city's plunder – is amazed by what he sees. That evening there's a sort of fair. Valuables are taken out and displayed, the heavier items for exchange for less heavy ones. A gaping Roos gazes at

> 'the most beautiful carpets I've ever seen, tapestries and wall-hang-ings and cloths embroidered with gold and silver, pieces of silk of every colour, men and women's clothes, embroidered and brilliant such as are only seen at the courts of princes. One heard it being said: "Such or such a one has so or so many precious stones, another has a case filled with diamonds, another rolls of ducats." I listened astound-ed.'

And still, somewhere ahead, through the rainy weather, the guns are rumbling.

CHAPTER 12

"WHERE OUR CONQUEST OF THE WORLD ENDED"

Two armies race through the night – 'the only member of my family who's never given me cause for complaint' – Malojaroslavetz – Delzons makes up for lost time – Wilson in action – 22,000 Italians fight 70,000 Russians – Soltyk repeats Napoleon's exact words – Malojaroslavetz lost and retaken six times – Séruzier's exploit

A bare day's march south-south-west of Borowsk the new Kaluga road is crossed by a deep gorge and the River Luja, beyond which a long ravine leads up to some heights and the little town of Malojaroslavetz. It's the only point at which the Russian army has a chance of holding up the French lunge southwards. And it's there Eugène's three divisions are making for.

To the ever-critical eyes of Dedem van der Gelder, the 32-year-old Eugène de Beauharnais, Viceroy of Italy, seems

'almost childishly afraid of the Emperor, whence his need to do even more than he wished him to. He was rude both to and about his Italians. For all his excellent and cautious qualities as a general his haughty tone had soon lost him their affections.'[1]

Planat de la Faye, less critical, sees Eugène as a man

'full of uprightness and loyalty, without political initiative, calm, gifted with consistency and sound judgement. All these qualities made him an excellent instrument in the Emperor's hands, whom he always served with fidelity and exactitude and a devotion without limits.'

"In all my family," Napoleon himself had said of him, "only Eugène has never given me any subject for complaint." And afterwards, to Count *Mathieu Molé*, he'd describe him as "less brilliant than the King of Naples. In one aspect he's less eminent. As a whole he's even a mediocre man, though there's more proportion and harmony in him." If Murat hates Eugène, it's also because of the remorseless feud between Josephine's family and the Bonapartes, to whose coterie Murat belongs by marriage.

Such is the man whose corps is leading the Grand Army. Marching along the Malojaroslavetz road, his 22,000-strong IV Corps is headed by the fourteen French and two Croat battalions of Delzons' 13th Division, reviewed only a week ago, on 17 October, by Napoleon in the Kremlin. The 37-year-old Delzons has a long fighting record that goes back to Lodi; and it had been he who'd launched the initial assault on the village of Borodino. Behind his division comes the Italian Royal Guard, followed immediately by what's left of Grouchy's 3rd Cavalry Corps: its artillery consists of Griois' own regiment's 4th and 5th Companies, attached to the imbecile Lahoussaye's dragoon division, and its 6th Company, attached to Chastel's 3rd light cavalry division (6th, 8th, 25th Chasseurs, the 6th Hussars, a regiment of Saxon dragoons and two regiments of Bavarian chevaulegers). All Grouchy's units, except the artillery, are by now reduced to riding mere nags.[2]

'I'd left my bivouac early, and was making for Malojaroslavetz, which was only three leagues away. The Viceroy's army corps had taken the same direction, and most of the units that made it up must already have been close to that town when a cannon shot, coming from that direction, hastened the columns' march. The noise grew louder as we came nearer and announced a serious affair.'

At a certain distance behind him Griois knows Broussier's 14th Division (French and Spaniards) is following on; and, bringing up the rear, Pino's 15th Division (Italians and Dalmatians).

It had been late in the evening of 22 October that a message had reached Docturov, commanding the 2nd Russian army corps, that the French have switched their direct line of advance down the old Kaluga road and are making for Malojaroslavetz. An excited Wilson had pointed out to him the importance – rather evident, one would think – of concentrating there and barring Napoleon's passage. Docturov, however, had irritated him by wasting a lot of time in sending a messenger to Kutusov to get permission to move. But now, all day during the 23rd in drenching rain and during the night, Docturov's 70,000 men have been

'straining every nerve to reach Malojaroslavetz before the enemy, whose lights were frequently visible during the night, as the columns occasionally approached within a mile or two of each other, through flat meadow lands country full of brooks and broad ditches, unprovided with any pontoons or other means, except such as could be found on the spot.'

Many of his leading units are being transported in wagons. And soon they've

'crossed the Protwa at Sparskoië and gained the plain which lay in front of [i.e. from the Italians' point of view, beyond] Malojaroslavetz. Everyone was ignorant of the location. There were five main roads out of Malojaroslavetz. And the Russians placed outposts on them all.'

Already, late yesterday evening (22 October), Chastel's light cavalry, Henckens' 6th Chasseurs among them, have entered the town and found it abandoned by its inhabitants. Spreading out on the plain beyond 'in the directions of Tourantina and Kaluga, we here and there ran into regular enemy troops, who were falling back in front of us'. Now, also late in the evening, Delzons' division is approaching Malojaroslavetz. Ordered to march at midnight to get to the bridge at dawn, Delzons – if we're to believe Dedem van der Gelder (but the Dutchman is back with IHQ at Borowsk and so doesn't actually see what's going on, and anyway has a strong tendency to criticize on slender grounds of hearsay) –

> 'thought he had time to let his troops have their soup and didn't get going until 2 a.m.[3] It was this two-hour delay' [Dedem goes on] 'that changed the face of affairs, and decided the fate of the army and the peace. If he'd carried out his orders punctually he'd have seized the position without firing a shot.'

Dead beat from their forced march, Delzons' two leading battalions cross the gorge in the darkness – Cossacks have already demolished the bridge – and struggle up the long narrowing ravine, flanked by rocks, which leads up to Malojaroslavetz. Malojaroslavetz, Wilson will see when he gets there at dawn, 'is built upon the side and summit of a lofty hill, rising immediately above the Luzha (which the enemy called the Lutza)'. Somewhere out in the dark plain Delzons' men can hear the voices of Docturov's scouts, being held off by Chastel's light cavalry; but otherwise see no sign of any enemy troops. Placing outposts and sentinels out in the direction of the surrounding plain, they lie down to snatch a couple of hours' sleep;[4] and Delzons sends back an ADC to notify Eugène, who of course notifies Napoleon, spending the night at Borowsk, that the town has been occupied.

Now it's the early hours of Saturday morning, 24 October. 'Over the river', Wilson sees,

> 'is a bridge. Between the bridge and the beginning of the ravine is a distance of about a hundred yards. The ground on both flanks of the town, ascending from the river, is woody and steep, and the ground on the left is intersected with very deep fissures and ravines, so as to be impracticable for artillery movements from the bank of the river. The whole town is built of wood. Near the summit of the hill there is an open space like a grande place. And near the ravine, at the bottom, are a church and a couple or more houses that command the approach.'

Arriving on the scene Docturov orders

> 'two regiments of chasseurs, supported by two more, to dash into the town and drive the enemy (whom some fugitive inhabitants had reported to have reached and entered it) out of the place, and over the river, which ran immediately below, and to destroy the bridge.'

In Delzons' camp everyone's

> 'asleep except the sentinels, when suddenly, four regiments of [Russian] chasseurs come rushing out of the woods which crown the heights, cause the sentinels to fall back hastily on the outposts, the outposts on the battalions, which taken by surprise, were forced after

putting up a certain defence to abandon the village [sic] and go and join the rest of the division down in the plain.'

Meanwhile, Delzons or his subordinates have fortified the bridgehead on the south bank, using the church and some large houses. At the first alarm, Césare de Laugier goes on, Delzons – whose sappers have also been busy re-establishing the bridge – has called his division to arms 'and runs to his men's assistance'. While it had still been dark Wilson has himself taken command of a couple of Russian guns, brought them forward and aimed them at the bridge:

'Already the Russians had deployed their artillery on the heights and on both sides of the town, so as to fire on the bridge below them [sic] and prevent any new offensive. Finally, the Russian cavalry deployed to the right of the infantry.'

As day dawns Wilson sees

'a large body of the enemy descending the lofty hill on the left bank of the river to pass the bridge and enter the town. This dense body was flocking forward as if quite at ease and unconscious of any serious opposition being designed to the passage and occupation.'

Reporting back to Docturov, he goes on,

'the English General galloped with a battery of light artillery placed under his directions to an elevation which he had selected for its site, and opened its fire almost within grapeshot of the mass. At the first discharge there was a general halt. On the second a wavering. On the third a total dispersion, and every one flew forward or scrambled up the hill to get out of the reach of this unexpected cannonade. The movement of the advanced guard was thus checked.'

And indeed Delzons' position is critically exposed. Obviously Docturov's corps – perhaps the entire Russian army – is coming up to defend Malojaroslavetz and block the Grand Army's advance southwards. 'New Russian columns,' Césare de Laugier goes on,

'were emerging in compact masses out of the woods beyond Malojaroslavetz and coming up to range themselves in battle order. And in no time at all we saw forts being raised behind their front that they were putting in a state of defence even during the fighting, with a parapet and a ditch.'

His own action, Wilson claims, has

'gained nearly an hour before the Viceroy could arrive in person, bring up his artillery, and re-establish order: an essential hour for the Russians.'

Delzons' ADC has of course long ago reached Eugène, who,

'escorted by the Dragoons of the Royal Guard and the Queen's Dragoons, had already got going when he'd heard the sound of the guns.

We were to stand to arms immediately.'

'In about an hour' Wilson again sees 'the enemy, under cover of a heavy fire, recommence the descent of the hill and join the two battalions defending the bridge.' Laugier:

'The Russians' plunging fire was raining down in this funnel where Delzons was immobilized. The Viceroy ordered him to get out of this position at once, cost what it might, and to advance. The road onwards from the bridge follows the bottom of a ravine between great stone blocks, whose summits were occupied by numerous Russian sharpshooters, supported in turn by the masses already encamped on the hill.'

The 'brave and heroic' Delzons, who'd fought at Lodi, Rivoli and the Pyramids, hardly has a moment more to live. Colonel Séruzier, whose guns, standing in reserve and unable to reply because of the degree of elevation required, sees him

'rush to the middle of the mêlée, rally his division and try to repulse the enemy. He was just beginning to resume the offensive when some sharpshooters, ambushed behind a wall, fired at him. He fell dead.'

As do his two brothers, 'one his brigade commander, the other his ADC'.[5] Immediately Eugène sends his chief-of-staff to take over. 'Like the experienced soldier he was, Guilleminot occupied and fortified the church and two houses' at the bridgehead. And when 13th Division is again thrown back this at least enables them to enfilade, at point-blank range, any Russian attempts to counter-attack. It also gives Broussier's 14th Division (18th Light, 9th, 35th, 53rd Line plus the remains of his two Spanish battalions) time to arrive on the scene:

'Each time the Russian troops passed these advanced posts they were fired at from behind, fled in disorder, and ours resumed the offensive to thoroughly repulse them. Prince Eugène keeps demanding the arrival of new troops; but no matter how much these hasten their steps, it seems they'll never get there in time.'

By now the battle for Malojaroslavetz and the French army's advance on Kaluga is becoming a very serious affair indeed. More and more of IV Corps' units are arriving on the scene; and again 13th Division, commanded now by Guilleminot and supported by Broussier's 14th, is trying to force its way up the ravine. Despite all Wilson's firing,

'the enemy pushed up through the streets of the town to the outskirts, when the battle began with a violence which corresponded with the magnitude of its objects and the resolute determination of each party to achieve its own. The enemy was infuriated by despair, the Russians by 'the Moscow cry of vengeance'.

Each repulse suffered by Guilleminot's men leaves the 13th Division's leading units cut off. And from the plain behind Malojaroslavetz, more and more of whose timber houses are in flames, one Russian division after another is turning up and deploying. 'Even the militia who'd just joined,' Wilson goes on,

'(and who, being armed only with pikes, formed a third rank to the battalions) not only stood as steady under the cannonade as their veteran comrades, but charged the sallying enemy with as ardent ferocity. Docturov, under cover of his powerful artillery, which poured shot, shell, and grape on the advancing columns, re-entered and repossessed himself of the whole town as far as the ravine, except the church and adjoining houses which the enemy had garrisoned, and which commanded the ground beyond, so that the Russians could not remain under their fire to contend for the ravine and seizure of the bridge,'

and are therefore thrown back again. Dalmatian and Spanish obstinacy equals that of the Russians:

'The roar and crash of the guns, the rattle of light firearms, the whining and sighing of bigger and small shot, the laments of the wounded and dying, the curses in all languages that were heard during bayonet charges, words of command, horn signals, fifes and drums, and added to all this the wavy motion forward and backwards of the masses in gunpowder smoke that hid friend and foe in so secret a darkness that one could often only make out the enemy positions from the lightning flashes or the advancing batteries – all this made an impression that went through the marrow of one's bones. Anyone who says he goes under fire without an oppressive feeling is an idiot. But the danger being shared, it seems less apparent to the individual. Seeing one's comrades falling to right and left, one offsets it by accustoming oneself to the danger which for every minute that passes drives out all fear, also in the increasing rage that takes pleasure in avenging ourselves on our murderers.'[6]

Not until 10 a.m. has Napoleon first heard the distant sound of the guns. At IHQ's 'first halt' outside Borowsk – probably at the village of Ouvarovskoië – he's taking a light breakfast by the roadside together with Murat, Berthier and Lariboisière and questioning two captured Cossacks. Calling for Gourgaud, he sends him off to Eugène to order him to seize Malojaroslavetz and hang on to it until Davout can come up with I Corps. But already Eugène, before flinging in his third – and last – infantry division (Pino's 15th), has sent back Roman Soltyk, evidently on mission to him from IHQ, to ask for prompt supports. Twenty-two thousand Italians, Dalmatians, Croats, Frenchmen and Spaniards are at grips with seventy thousand Russians; but "all these troops won't be enough to hold Kutusov's army at bay". Somewhere along the twelve miles of road between Ouvarovskoïe and the heights above the Luja gorge the two staff officers, galloping in opposite directions, probably run into each other, exchange information.

After successive attempts, however, Guilleminot at last regains the town square. But though Broussier's 14th Division reinforces him he still can't establish any lodgement beyond it. Séruzier, who's been on the scene for some time with the 2nd Cavalry Corps' light artillery and witnessed 'the town being taken and retaken several times by our troops', is beginning to be seriously worried:

'Nothing was decided and we were losing a lot of men. Wanting to put an end to it, the Prince ordered General Pino's [15th] Italian Division to cross the bridge to support Broussier's and Guilleminot's. He asked for my artillery, of which he had utmost need, and he'd placed the Royal Italian Guard and General Ornano's light cavalry in reserve behind the riverbank, at the entrance of the forest.'

And now here's Soltyk, the Polish patriot, expert on ballistics and speaker of fluent French, after galloping into Ouvarovskoïe, standing in front of his idol – who promptly sends him back to Eugène:

"He's begun to drink the cup," Napoleon tells him to tell Eugène, "and he must drain it. I've ordered Davout to support him."

On his way back Soltyk overtakes the heads of Davout's column, which he sees are forcing the pace. Finding Eugène – who tends to be as calm and imperturbable in battle as Murat is excitable – exactly where he'd left him, amidst all the shot and shell, he sees that by now 'all of IV Corps except the Italian Royal Guard' are 'heavily and inextricably engaged'. Napoleon's orders seem so abrupt – not to say self-evident – that Soltyk hardly likes to repeat them verbatim to the Viceroy,

'because they seemed to express some dissatisfaction. I just told him the Emperor ordered him to press the attack with vigour. I was about to go on when Eugène turned away with a gesture of marked impatience toward his chief-of- staff beside him, and spoke to him in a low voice. Then, turning to me again, he said with vivacity: "But what did he say, then, when you'd explained to him the difficulties of the position and the enemy forces' superiority?"'

Respectfully, Soltyk this time repeats Napoleon's exact words.

'This energetic order produced the effect Napoleon had expected. The Viceroy went in person to meet the Royal Guard, which at this moment was debouching from the wood, gave it the order to cross the bridge and charge the enemy. And in fact, this force advanced at the double and flung itself at the bayonet point on the position already

seized by the Muscovites. Thus the electric spark I'd brought set fire
to the troops and victoriously carried the day,'
concludes Soltyk, and adds: 'From then on I decided never to alter a word
of Napoleon's orders.'

Césare de Laugier says nothing about charging the Russians at bayonet
point, but leaves us in no doubt as to the Italian Guard's morale:

'It's then he sends Colonel Labédoyère to accelerate our march, and
at the same time to inform the Emperor of events. The Royal Guard
meets this distinguished officer[7] as it comes down the hillside that
dominates the Luja.'

Labédoyère encourages them with flattering words, telling them their comrades are in danger, and they'll miss their chance to demonstrate their own
bravery:

'At these words, repeated from mouth to mouth, all the battalions
utter joyful shouts. The columns no longer march, they fly, and
despite the speed with which our chiefs lead us on, we don't seem to
be going fast enough. Military songs are struck up. Joy seems to forget fatigue.'[8]

Reaching the Luja and following its bank they see 'on the left- hand side of
the road the Italian reserve cavalry encamped [i.e., General Guyon's 9th
and 19th Chasseurs] near the pine wood':

'We hadn't seen our brave comrades since the last days of September.
But we knew of their exploits and made haste to hold them in our
arms and equal them. The encounter couldn't have been more à pro-
pos. Hardly had we spotted them than they come to meet us. They
blend themselves with our ranks. Everyone is looking for a friend, a
relative. They bring us liqueurs, victuals. We shake hands, we weep
with emotion. The idea of the fatherland transports us![9] It's about 10
a.m., perhaps, when we finally join our own men, engaged since early
morning.'

Well, perhaps a bit later than that – it must have taken Soltyk at least half
an hour to reach Eugène from the point on the hither side of
Ouvarovskoië where he'd taken Napoleon's orders.

At last, after furious struggles in the ravine and the town, Guilleminot has
managed to bring all three divisions of the Army of Italy into line facing
the Russian position at the crest of the hill,

'the 13th's first and the second [Pino's 15th] division in Malojaroslavetz and one in front of the town, and part of the 14th in the
suburb, beyond a deep ravine which extends for more than 300 yards,
along and parallel with the Kaluga road.'

But not for long:

'Seeing the day's success depended uniquely on the possession of this important point, Kutusov sends the whole of Raevsky's corps to Docturov's assistance. The town is taken, then retaken, even up to three times, Guilleminot and Broussier, obliged to yield to force of numbers, fall back to the bridge, where the Viceroy is, to keep account of the overall movement and prepare reserves. He immediately sends them Broussier's second brigade. Then the action seems to move on. Hardly have the battalions left the houses behind them, hardly have they set out from the central point and appeared in the plain, where they're exposed, than they weaken. Overwhelmed by the fire of an entire army, they become demoralised and fall back. The Russians are being incessantly reinforced. Our files yield and break up. The obstacles of the terrain only increase the disorder. Shells fired from both sides have set fire to the town, built of wood. And this circumstance finally puts paid to the two divisions' evolutions and assaults. For the fifth time they have to fall back. The Russians gain ground, and for a moment the defence is paralysed.'

It's then, Césare de Laugier goes on, that the Viceroy sends in Pino's division.

'The troops, led by their chief, march in closed columns, in good order, silent, unquiet, avid for glory. As for ourselves, all the infantry of the Royal Guard, we're made to remain in the little town to the left of the Luja.'

The fire of a Russian battery on a hilltop to the left of the advancing columns isn't merely causing havoc in their massed ranks; it's also forcing the Royal Guard to keep changing its position. Some of its light artillery is 'as much exposed as any sharpshooters to the enemy fire, and are themselves firing upwards'. Its gunners draw Césare de Laugier's admiration as they force the Russian battery off the hilltop. Crossing the bridge again, Pino's Italians 'get their breath back' and form up again:

'Then the first brigade, Generals Pino and Fontana at its head, move towards the right of the town, to protect the 13th Division; the second, led by the Corsican General Levier, climbs up the other side to take the Russian columns which have repulsed the 14th in the rear. And we're overjoyed to see our Italians seize all the positions indicated to them by the Viceroy, and by General [sic] Gourgaud, the Emperor's ADC [sic], who's turned up on the scene. The 1st Brigade forces its way into the town and drives out the Russians. A horrible mêlée ensues amidst the flames that are devouring its buildings. Most of the wounded who fall are burnt alive, and their corpses, soon calcinated, present a horrible sight. The second brigade follows the ravine under terrible artillery and musketry fire. The suburb is retaken and so are the heights.'

Any number of senior Italian officers are being killed or wounded. By now it's about 1 p.m. And already at around midday Napoleon has arrived on the scene

'and placed himself with his staff on a mound facing Malo-jaroslavetz, above the Luja, to the left of the road and perfectly placed to observe the enemy's movements. He spent more than an hour looking through his telescope, penetrating the enemy's intentions.'

Now Eugène's artillery, two-thirds of it French, with the assistance of men from the Royal Guard, reaches the heights, gets through the town, 'crushing dead and dying men heaped up on the roads, mutilating them horribly'. Though the grenadiers of the Italian Guard remain down by the suburb, its foot chasseurs advance and, reinforcing Pino, dislodge the Russians from the houses at bayonet point and drive them back to the junction of the Marina and Czurickowa roads – a charge which, however, brings them up against a deep ditch out on the plain, concealed by hedges. Shattered by fire from the Russians' right-hand batteries and, charged by cavalry that's 'causing them grave losses', they're driven back into the gardens of the suburbs, where that half of them who have survived dig in. But Pino's 2nd Brigade reinforces them, and a new assault is launched, and this time, avoiding the ditch, they establish themselves in a wood beyond the burning town.[10]

At about 11 a.m. Lejeune had received orders from Napoleon, already within a mile or two of the town,[11] for Davout to quicken his march and move up to Eugène's right. And by now I Corps is beginning to turn up on the heights overlooking the Luja,[12]

'and take up position to the right facing the enemy, all of whose cavalry was spread out over the plain and observing our movements'.

The problem, however, is that there's no room to deploy across the bridge – or rather bridges, for by now Davout is throwing a second – into the confined space beyond. But his artillery is soon in action from the north bank.

Every one of Docturov's regiments, like Eugène's, is heavily engaged; and on the Russian side, too, officer after officer has been despatched to hasten the arrival of reinforcements from Kutusov's main army:

'The killed and wounded exceeded 5,000. The troops, exhausted by their previous marches and seven hours' combat, could scarcely continue the action. At that anxious moment Raevsky's corps came within view and, as soon as it reached the position, was ordered to penetrate into, and carry the town by storm. The "huzzas" of the columns announced to the enemy that they were about to be assailed by fresh troops, whose impulse they quickly found they were unable to resist. The Russian grenadiers carried all before them, and for the sixth time the Russians became masters of every post but the fortified church and buildings adjacent. The Viceroy, alarmed for the safety of the troops left within them and in the ravine, as well as for his bridges, urged forward Pino's division to rally the fugitives and lead another onset. The Russian grenadiers, notwithstanding its impetuous efforts and the flames raging around them (for the town was on fire in all parts), tenaciously maintained their position: and the Viceroy was compelled to send across the river all his corps, except the cavalry, to preserve his têtes de pont.'

As wave after wave is thrown in, Lejeune sees how the formidable Russian artillery,

'sited on the heights in the town's gardens, was sweeping from top to bottom the whole of the road along which we were arriving, without our guns being able to gain the upper hand by firing from below upwards, because they could only be placed in the meadows along the Luja. So all efforts had to be made at bayonet point, on a point so narrow as to permit no flanking movement. All the advantages of numbers and terrain were on the enemy's side. I Corps went into the line at about 2 p.m.'

'Debouching by the village of Maloczina,' Séruzier goes on, 'Davout immediately ordered Gérard and Compans' divisions to cross the Luja,' – Gérard's division deploys to the right of the enemy position, Compans' to the left. Lejeune can

'see the Russians' movements perfectly. We expected Kutusov would take full advantage of his very strong position to block our advance and himself take the offensive.'

'Of all I Corps' regiments,' carabinier-sergeant *Vincent Bertrand* claims, 'only the 7th Light's élite companies came under fire, the rest of the regiment manoeuvred all day.'

But Séruzier's horse artillery has been playing so much the more important role. Immediately upon Eugène's calling for his guns,

'I'd had the trumpeters sound "To horse!". Wishing to turn the Russians' flank, I'd started searching for a ford to get my guns over.'

Finding one, and quite a broad one too, Séruzier carefully reconnoitres it in person, then goes back to his gunners. Since the opposite bank is very steep, he hastily sends across eighteen men,

'each armed with a shovel or a mattock, with orders to flatten it enough for a wheeled vehicle to pass. Ahead of this ford was a little forest, and it was this which had made me choose this ford rather than another.'

In a jiffy they're in the wood; then out of it again and flying 'at a full gallop towards the enemy's rear. And there I am, in battery, sending shells and grape at the enemy.' Even if the Russians weren't already so heavily engaged with the Italians, says Séruzier, they could hardly have seen him coming. And are taken utterly by surprise. Deploying undisturbed in their rear, Séruzier's guns do such 'terrible damage' to their centre that it half-paralyses their resistance to IV Corps, pressing them from the town.

Even so, more and more fresh Russian troops are being thrown in, and the Italian chasseurs' Colonel Peraldi,

'who'd taken over from General Levié, who'd just been killed, supported himself on the little wood, covered against the Russian cavalry. At that moment I redoubled my fire and in less than three-quarters of an hour the victory was ours.'

Finally Lejeune sees how

'Guilleminot and Broussier's combined efforts and, coming up behind them, those of Pino's Italian grenadier division, boldly directed by Prince Eugène, forced the Russians to withdraw into the plain and abandon the town to us, in flames. At once our artillery was able to climb the hill and debouch into the plain; and so it did, while crushing thousands of the wounded, the burnt and dead who were encumbering the street.'

And in fact, Séruzier proudly remarks,

'the Viceroy with about 18,000 men had beaten more than 80,000 Russians; the enemy lost 8,000 men in this fight, and the French [sic] some 4,000. The affair was one of the most brilliant of the campaign.'

Wilson is dismayed to see how 'the Russians in their turn, yielding to the new pressure, retired from the town, and took post at half-cannon shot distance'.

Yet Davout's corps, unable to deploy fully because of the narrowness of the bridgehead, has hardly played any part at all. Not, for instance, the 85th:

'Davout had hastened the march of his corps toward the sound of the guns. But having marched all night we'd got there when everything was over.'

'The day', writes Planet de la Faye, presumably looking on with the Artillery Staff,

'belonged entirely to the Italians [sic] 'and justified the Emperor's praises, which more than once irritated and wounded the pride of the French military men. The French [sic] troops only arrived in the line when the Russians were already in retreat.'

But Guilleminot hastens to reward Séruzier for his special contribution by obtaining for him the Italian medal of the Iron Crown and 'anything else he wanted for his brave gunners'. Thus finished, writes Césare de Laugier proudly,

'an 18-hour battle during which a handful of Frenchmen and Italians, at the bottom of a ravine, had stood up to a Russian army, whose positions seemed impregnable.'

In fact about 16–17,000 French and Italians have been engaged, against seven Russian army corps with their reserves, i.e., sixteen divisions, or nearly 100,000 men, of whom some 70,000 were actually in the firing line. 'The Army of Italy', Berthier will write at 9 p.m. tomorrow evening to Junot at Mojaisk, 'has lost some 2,000 men killed or wounded [probably an underestimate] and the Russians 7 to 8,000 [certainly an over-estimate; each side probably lost some 6,500 men]. 'Two Russian generals' corpses have been found on the battlefield and 2–300 prisoners taken.'

From the outset, Dedem will afterwards hear, Kutusov had regarded himself as defeated. 'Kaluga's going to suffer the same fate as Moscow,' he'd declared.

The little timber-built town of Malojaroslavetz certainly has. All that evening and into the night it smoulders and blazes, burning to death the wounded. Its centre, so far as there still is one, cannot even be occupied by the victors. Russians and Italians alike hear the screams of those who are perishing in the flames.

CHAPTER 13

"THAT'S ENOUGH, GENTLEMEN. I SHALL DECIDE."

A cold night – a crucial council-of-war – 'Fetch the horses, let's be off!' – Napoleon almost captured – 'Napoleon's star no longer guided his course' – an affair on the Smolensk road – 'He was astonished at the wild fury of the fighting' – 'the Emperor wavered for some time' – decision to retreat – Italian exploits rewarded – Dumonceau in action – a pyramid of fire – Griois brings up the rear – a phial of poison

Night falls. Another very cold one. No one is getting much sleep. Least of all Napoleon. After carefully going over the ground with Caulaincourt he has established his headquarters

'in a weaver's hut only a few paces to the right of the main road, at the bottom of a ravine, on the bank of the stream and village of Gorodnia – a wooden house, old, dilapidated, stinking, and divided in two by a piece of canvas.'

'Almost all of us', says the Master of the Horse, 'bivouacked in the open air.' He'll remember the hut as standing 'a couple of miles from Malojaroslavetz, at the entrance of the bend in the Luja'; Ségur as being half as far away. What is certain is that it stands at the cross-roads of the Emperor's destiny.

Kutusov, in trying to overrun the Army of Italy, has had to throw in almost everything he has; but even so, has been fought to a standstill. Loath initially to force a pitched battle, and not turning up with his main army until 4 p.m., the limit of his effort has been to try, unsuccessfully, to drive the Italians out of Malojaroslavetz.

'We blamed him for sacrificing a great number of his men, only to be beaten in the end, and fail of his object. Nor had the Viceroy's success gained our objective for us. We held the field, but Kutusov had given us the slip. So there was no change in our situation. The Emperor spent the night in receiving reports, issuing orders, and, on this occasion, discussing his difficulties with the Prince of Neuchâtel.'

Several times during the night he summons Caulaincourt, Duroc and Bessières to the weaver's hut. Asks them

'whether he should pursue Kutusov, who'd abandoned an impregnable position and probably eluded us? And if he didn't find the enemy drawn up beyond Malojaroslavetz, what route should he take to Smolensk? He had to make up his mind.'

It's perhaps the most difficult and, as it'll turn out, most fateful decision of his career. Shall he *(a)* push on with his original scheme and make for Kaluga, on the correct assumption that Kutusov has no desire whatever to fight another Borodino and will merely go on retreating? Or *(b)* make for Smolensk via Medyn, along a route neither army has yet devastated, but with a repulsed but not defeated Russian army at his heels? Or *(c)* do what he's sworn he'll never do: retreat by the same devastated route he'd come by – a route which offers neither men nor horses anything whatever to eat?

According to Gourgaud it's Count Lobau who, asked for his advice, is the first to offer an opinion. In his view the army must retire as promptly as possible to the Niemen, and by the shortest route – i.e., by the ravaged Mojaisk road. 'He repeated this several times.'

Unwelcome advice! And others disagree. Later Napoleon will disclaim it as his own view – and all the disasters of the retreat came of following it. As mere Assistant Prefect of the Palace Ségur certainly isn't present; and as usual it's impossible to know how much substance there is in his dramatised dialogue. But, outside the weaver's hut, he may well be hearing what's passing inside it. Murat bursts out that 'if he's only given what's left of the cavalry and that of the Guard he'll overthrow everything and re-open the Kaluga road'. But the Emperor,

'raising his head, knocked over this wild talk, saying: "We've had enough of temerities. We've done only too much for glory. The time has come to think of saving what's left of the army."'

Bessières, 'his pride trembling at the idea of having to obey the King of Naples and feeling himself supported' by the others, declares that the transports won't suffice for a further advance. 'And finished by uttering the word *retreat,* which the Emperor approved by his silence.'[1] This is followed by a heated discussion between Murat and Davout, who declares for taking the Medyn road, through unravaged countryside. Bessières and Berthier intervene to calm the two enraged marshals. And Napoleon cuts short the discussion with the words:

"That's enough, gentlemen. I shall decide."

It's the crisis of the campaign. The most crucial decision, perhaps, he's ever had to make.

Although the roads are 'in such a bad state that only part of the artillery had been able to reach their position, and that only with difficulty', nightfall had found both IV and I Corps drawn up beyond the burning town. Sergeant *Vincent Bertrand's* carabinier company is with the rest of the 7th Light

'in our bivouac on the Kaluga road. In the night a sutler's horse ran away, drawing many others after it. Terrible panic. Even generals ran after their mounts; even our stacked muskets are overthrown, many men hurt, or burnt by falling into campfires. All the pickets and first lines flew to arms, so did the Russians facing us.'

Stationed not far away with the 23rd Dragoons, Sous-lieutenant Pierre Auvray[2] certainly isn't the only man to assume they've been attacked. And Bertrand, for his part, has to 'spend the rest of the night standing to arms, pack on back, without even enjoying an hour of the sleep we so badly needed'.

The Russian army may be slipping away, but Cossacks, Caulaincourt goes on,

> 'were swarming everywhere. If we heeded them less than we might
> have done, it was because about noon in the same area, but to the left
> of the road, we'd chased away some new ones wearing crosses on their
> caps, modelled on those of the Don Cossacks.'

Having just received some reinforcements of Don Cossacks, Zalusky (who should have been in Napoleon's escort, but since yesterday evening he's not been feeling well and has attached himself to another squadron of the Polish Lancers, also at Zielonka, and commanded by Janowski) notices that Platov (who's bitterly mourning a favourite son killed in a skirmish) is

> 'flattering himself he'd take Napoleon prisoner. He'd surrounded
> the entire French army, and wasn't always being victoriously
> repulsed.'

That dark night on the heights above the Luja, everything's confused and uncertain. A little after nightfall the Imperial Guard had withdrawn a little, so as to be closer to IHQ and cover both its rear and its left flank. But having bivouacked in the dark its units hardly know anything about their surroundings.

Towards 4 a.m. an orderly officer named d'Arenberg, one of Gourgaud's subordinates, enters the hut and warns Napoleon that 'in the shadow of night and taking advantage of folds in the ground some Cossacks were slipping in between him and his outposts'. 'An hour before daybreak,' Caulaincourt goes on,

> 'the Emperor sent for me again. We were alone.
>
> "Things are getting serious," he said. "I beat the Russians every
> time, and yet never reach an end."
>
> After a quarter of an hour of silence, during which he walked to
> and fro in his little shelter, he went on:
>
> "I'm going to find out for myself whether the enemy are drawing
> up for battle, or whether they're retreating, as everything suggests.
> That devil Kutusov won't ever join battle! Fetch the horses, let's be
> off!" As he spoke, he picked up his hat to go.'

All the clock round, Caulaincourt explains,

> 'there was always one troop of horses bridled and saddled; and the
> duty picket, which consisted of 20 light horse, was saddled and bri-

dled too. The squadrons in attendance provided the picket and relieved it. On the other campaigns there'd been only one squadron in attendance; but in Russia there were four[3] – half of them light cavalry, half grenadiers and dragoons. The picket never left the Emperor, the squadrons followed in echelon, and saddled up when the Emperor called for his horses. As he did so in haste and without warning, he always set out with only two or three other people; the rest caught up. After Moscow, and indeed since Smolensk, the same squadrons had remained in attendance for two or three days running. Men and horses were worn out.'

Napoleon's just picking up his hat to go when Bessières and Berthier come in. They point out how dark it still is outside, and that, with the Guard having taken up its position after nightfall, no one knows the other corps' exact whereabouts. Caulaincourt, who as always is responsible for Napoleon's personal safety, urges him to wait until dawn. So do Bessières and Berthier. But he's impatient to be off.

Then one of Eugène's ADCs comes and says nothing can be seen of the enemy. Only swarms of Cossacks everywhere. Some of them, not very far away, are thought to have lost their way and blundered into the outposts. Gourgaud and d'Arenberg too, the two *officiers d'ordonnance* on duty, assure him noises of horses on the march have been heard all night. So Napoleon agrees to wait. But 'after half an hour' – Rapp gives the time as 7.30 a.m. – 'his impatience drove him to set out' without waiting for his escort.[4] But what's going on? The road, Ségur sees, is

'encumbered with ambulance wagons, artillery and luxury carriages. It was the interior of the army, everyone was marching on, suspecting nothing. At first, far away, to the right, some platoons were seen running, then great black lines advancing. Then shouts were raised. Already some women and a few camp-followers were running back, paying no heed to anything, answering no questions, with an utterly terrified air, speechless, and all out of breath. At the same time the carriages, unsure of themselves, became troubled. Some wanted to go on, others to turn back. They crossed each other's tracks, jostled each other. Soon it was a tumult, everything was in an utter disorder. The Emperor, always advancing, looked on and smiled, assuming a panic had broken out. His ADCs suspected Cossacks, but they saw them coming on in such good order, that they were still in doubt.'

Rapp resumes:

'Dawn was hardly showing. The Emperor was placed between the Duke of Vicenza [Caulaincourt], the prince de Neuchâtel and myself. Hardly had we left the cottages where we'd spent the night and gone a mile or so than we caught sight of a swarm of Cossacks. They were

coming out of a forest ahead of us, to our right. Since they were in quite good order we took them for French cavalry.'
Naturally so, since they're already in the midst of the Guard's bivouacs. One of the three Grenadier regiments is only 300 yards from the road. Rapp hears Caulaincourt recognize the Cossacks for what they are:
'"Sire, they're Cossacks."
"It's not possible," Napoleon replied. Shouting their heads off, they flew at us. I grabbed his horse by its bridle and myself turned it about.
"But surely they're our own lot?"
"They're Cossacks, hurry up!"
"They certainly are!" Berthier said.
"No doubt about it," Mouton [Lobau] added. Napoleon gave a few orders and moved away'
– on to some high ground, 'to be able to see more clearly'. Roustam, as always only a few paces away, sees Napoleon 'draw his sword and await the Cossacks' – out of pride, says Ségur who, despite Napoleon's notorious impassivity at moments of crisis, is a considerable expert at penetrating it:
'So did the Prince of Neuchâtel and the Master of the Horse, and, placing themselves to the left of the road, they awaited the horde. At the same moment, crossing the main road, the horde overthrew everything in their way, horses, men, carriages, wounding and killing the soldiers of the Train whom they dragged away to strip them; then, turning away the horses harnessed to the guns, they carried them off across the fields.'
Soltyk, too, is in the Emperor's suite and reports 'these eye-witness details'. He sees how
'Napoleon, as soon as he heard the enemy were so close, had turned his horse's head and at a gallop rejoined the service squadrons marching behind him, while the generals and officers accompanying him drew their sabres, formed a cavalry troop together with their escort, and without hesitation charged the first Cossacks to approach and halted them.'
Ségur sees
'the chasseurs (only ten or twelve had as yet joined us) already moving forward unbidden to join the advance guard. The light was still so poor we couldn't see further than 25 yards. Only the clash of arms and shouts of men fighting indicated where the skirmish was, or even that we were already at grips with the enemy.'
Rapp says he himself
'advanced at the head of the service squadron. We were flung into disorder. My horse received a lance-thrust six inches deep. He fell over

on top of me. We were trampled at the feet of these barbarians.'
Rapp's horse isn't the only victim. So is Berthier's duty ADC, Captain
Emmanuel Lecoulteux:

'At the exact moment when he'd killed a Cossack, having snapped off
his sword in a Cossack's body and grabbed his lance, he was pushing
back other enemies with it. A green overcoat covered his uniform,
and together with the lance in his hand it made him look like a Russian officer. A dragoon of the Guard,[5] taken in by this fatal resemblance, plunged the long blade of his sabre into him so deeply that its
whole length came out through his chest. Seeing this terrible blow, we
all thought we'd lost an interesting [sic] friend.'

Fortunately the Cossacks, who're only interested in plunder, haven't
realised who they have to do with:

'Some little way off they caught sight of an artillery park and rushed
toward it. Marshal Bessières had time to arrive with the Horse
Grenadiers of the Guard, charged them, and took back the wagons
and guns they were carrying off. I got to my feet again, someone
helped me back into the saddle and guided me back to our bivouac.
Seeing my horse covered in blood, Napoleon fearing I'd been hurt
again, asked whether I was wounded. I replied that I'd got off with a
few bruises. Then he began to laugh at our adventure, which I didn't
find funny.'

'If these wretched fellows hadn't yelled so as they attacked, as they always
do, to dull their minds to the danger,' Ségur says, 'perhaps Napoleon
wouldn't have escaped them. It was Platov and 6,000 Cossacks who, behind
our victorious advance guard, had tried to cross the river, the low plain and
the main road, carrying away everything as they passed.'

From only a few hundred yards away, Sergeant Bourgogne, too, has witnessed the episode: 'A moment after their scuffle the Emperor, chatting
with Murat, laughed at his having nearly been captured.[6]

But though the Guard recapture the guns and the few gunners in Cossack hands, and force them to recross the river, 'we were left with many
wounded' besides the unfortunate Lecoulteux. General Pajol, his arm still
in a sling – Napoleon had suggested he leave for Minsk with Nansouty's
convoy of sick and wounded, but he'd declined – had been riding along on
his horse when Captain Biot, his ADC, who, having suddenly fallen sick is
riding in their carriage in a kind of torpor, suddenly feels its horses bolt,

'so it seemed to me, in the opposite direction. Only by breaking one
of the windows did I manage to get the door open. When I'd got into
the carriage I'd kept my sabre by me. As I got out, it got caught in the
door, forcing me to run beside the coach. However I managed to get
clear. But there I was, all of a sudden, alone at the roadside.'

Fortunately Pajol's lead-horses come along and Biot manages to mount one and re-assemble some scattered infantrymen. Someone tells him a sergeant-major of the horse chasseurs, whose job it is to carry the imperial portfolio and who 'usually rides very close to the Emperor, has received a lance thrust that went through both case and portfolio'.

By now other squadrons of Guard cavalry have come up, including two of the Polish Lancers. Zalusky's squadron commander, Kozictulski, too, has been stabbed by a lance 'for which the Emperor promoted him major in our regiment'.[7] Being Janowski's senior, Zalusky had immediately taken over his squadron when the 'hurrah' had occurred:

'We met a regiment of [Line] dragoons, deployed on a broad front and pushing some Cossacks in front of them. Elsewhere we saw a squadron of the Mamelukes hastening up. In the twinkling of an eye, after coming to an agreement with Elie, head of the Mamelukes, we decided to attack the Cossacks through the intervals of the line of dragoons. We pushed them back beyond the Luja until we ran into the regiment of Horse Chasseurs of the [Russian Imperial] Guard.'

Boulart too has passed a bad night:

'I hadn't slept much and my head was full of sinister forebodings. Suddenly – it's one or two hours before daylight – terrible shouts are heard in the direction of headquarters, the ear is stunned by them.'

His gunners have jumped to their pieces:

'The Guard is ready to level its bayonets on the side the noise is coming from, and I have my artillery in a circle to be able to fire in all directions. However, the noise begins to diminish, becomes more distant, and soon can't be heard at all.'

The fleeing Cossacks, Lejeune sees, have also run into a battalion of the 3rd (Dutch) Grenadiers of the Guard, who open fire on them. 'This tall black line of bearskins made such an impression on the Cossacks that they fled into the forest.'

The Italians' baggage train, too, has 'received a dawn visit from Cossacks'. But they'd been driven off by 'a detachment of the Dragoons of the [Royal] Guard, which sabred and dispersed them'. Among other exploits General Joubert, commander of the IV Corps' baggage train, seated in his light carriage, 'with happy presence of mind had the courage to draw his sword and fight off the Cossacks surrounding it until help arrived'. And Griois' horses, watering down at the Luja in the morning mist, had luckily escaped as the Cossacks had swept through the camps. – Their victory, Ségur concludes,

'was short-lived, due to mere surprise. The Guard cavalry came galloping up: and at the sight of them they let go, fled, and their torrent poured away, leaving, it's true, some nasty traces, but abandoning all it had been carrying off.'

To his life-long satisfaction Rapp will be rewarded for his presence of mind during the affray with a mention in the Bulletin of "the imperturbable courage this general has so often shown". No question, says Caulaincourt, but that if Napoleon had set out earlier, as he'd wanted to, he'd have

'found himself in the midst of this swarm of Cossacks with only his picket and the eight generals and officers who accompanied him. Doubtless we should have sold our lives dearly as one can by hitting out blindly in the dark with light swords. But the Emperor would certainly have either been killed or captured within musket shot of the road and the Guard.'

Among the woods and bushes in the far-flung plain 'no one would have known where to look for him'.

But above all the Master of the Horse attributes the whole terrifying episode to the paucity of the army's light cavalry and its wretched condition:

'In general our men fought well, but were keeping a poor lookout. In no army were the reconnaissance duties so neglected. We seldom covered rear or flank. One Guard battalion was bivouacked barely 300 yards from the spot, and on the same side of the road as where the Cossacks had spent the night.'

Nor is it only at Malojaroslavetz that the Cossacks are swarming in such huge numbers. The previous evening, Captain Henri Beyle, *directeur des approvisionnements de réserve*, escorting his convoy of 1,500 wounded along the desolate and ravaged Moscow–Smolensk highway with 'two to three hundred men' under Claparède, has also been in serious trouble, and expecting the morrow to be his last:

'Just as we were lighting our fires, we were surrounded by a swarm of men who opened fire. Complete confusion reigned. The wounded cursed. We had the greatest difficulty in making them take up their muskets. We repulse the enemy, but we believe ourselves destined for great adventures. We had a gallant wounded general named Mounier, who elucidated the affair. Attacked as we were at that time of evening by a horde of infantry, it seemed probable we were facing 4 or 5,000 Russians, partly soldiers of the line, partly indignant peasants. We were surrounded, and it was no safer to retreat than to advance. We decided to spend the night on our feet and next day, at first light, to form square, put our wounded in the centre, and try to break through the Russians. If hard-pressed, we'd abandon our vehicles, form a small square, and fight to the last man rather than let ourselves be captured by peasants who'd kill us slowly with knife-stabs or in some other pleasant fashion. Having made this resolve, we took the necessary steps. Each man made up a bundle of what he regarded as his least essential belongings, ready to jettison them at the first attack so as to lighten the vehicle. I shared a room with five or six wounded colonels, who'd been unknown to me a week earlier but who on the march had become intimate friends. All these men agreed we were done for. We distributed our napoleons to the servants in an attempt to save a few of them. We'd all become close friends. We drank what wine we had left.'

This is evidently not the same convoy as the one commanded by the wounded Nansouty, in which, says Lejeune,

'we'd already sent back our prisoners, those of our wounded who could be transported and much of the army's clutter to Smolensk. I profited from these convoys [sic] to have my sister sent back to France. I installed her in one of my carriages which I'd had harnessed to three good horses with good grooms, taking care to furnish it with food and furs. She was going to travel under the protection of some of our wounded generals and, even more, under the aegis of providence.'

Nor is it clear which convoy had left first, Nansouty's or the one Lieutenant Brandt is in, with 400 sick and wounded officers and 12,000 men, from the Hospital of St Paul. 'I was with the first convoy, a circumstance to which I probably owe my life.' But it's exposed to the same dangers. This same murky misty morning on which Napoleon has so narrowly escaped the Cossacks, and which Stendhal and his comrades are fearing will be their last,

'we set off on foot, walking beside our carriages and armed from head to foot. There was such a mist that one couldn't see four yards ahead, and we kept on halting. I had a book by Madame du Deffand, and read almost all of it.'

Luckily just then the enemy has other matters on his hands: 'The enemy didn't consider us worthy of their anger.'[8]

Meanwhile, beyond the heap of ashes and calcinated corpses that 24 hours ago was the town of Malojaroslavetz, a kind of tacit armistice prevails. Henckens' chasseurs had earlier been withdrawn to the bridgehead so as not to get in the way of the combatants in what had been almost an infantry battle. But Griois' guns, also linked with Chastel's brigade, have

'taken up position at the town's exit in a plain where there were already several infantry units. We were facing the Russian army, from which only the line of outposts separated us. Only a score of paces separated theirs from ours. Sabre in hand, carbine raised, they were in each other's presence without firing.'

Somewhere out there in the plain Kutusov is giving an order which makes Wilson and almost everyone else at Russian headquarters utterly furious. The Russian army is to withdraw two or three miles along the Kaluga road. In that moment – if he hasn't realised it before – Wilson sees definitively that Kutusov has no interest whatever in what he, Wilson, in his despatches is calling 'saving the universe' – i.e., in British interests. Nor in destroying the Grand Army by force of arms or capturing the Emperor of the French. Only to provide him with 'a golden bridge' – or rather, a bridge of ice and snow – back to the Niemen, 500 miles away. With winter only a week or two off, the best way of getting rid of unwelcome intruders is surely to freeze them out?

Nor is that sly and cynical old roué so lavish of Russian lives as is General Guyot, commander of the Horse Chasseurs of the French Imperial Guard, with those of Frenchmen and Poles. Drawn up near a wood, Zalusky's lancers are being fired on during the forenoon by Russian infantry, and men and horses are being needlessly sacrificed. But when Zalusky suggests they move a little further away, Guyot replies astonished:

'"What's that you say? Don't soldiers only exist to be killed?"

I realised I'd spoken out of turn, and stayed beside him until he chose to move away from the spot.'

Never before has Napoleon been so near to being captured, least of all by a bunch of 'barbarians'. 'As soon as he had a few men around him,' Caulaincourt goes on,

'he went on quickly to reconnoitre the enemy's position beyond Malojaroslavetz. He made a very close inspection of the formidable defences which had been carried yesterday, and realised with regret that the enemy had indeed retreated, leaving only a few Cossacks behind.'

Captain Labaume and the rest of Eugène's staff see him,

'arriving with a numerous suite, coldly pass over the battlefield and without emotion hear the dolorous cries of the unhappy wounded calling out for help. Yet, though accustomed from twenty years' experience of the evils of warfare, to which he was so madly attached,9 he couldn't help being astonished at the wild fury of the fighting.'

As Napoleon and Murat arrive on the scene,

'the King of Naples galloped up to our outposts and energetically gave vent to his dissatisfaction. Why weren't we firing? And he ordered the first vedette he met to fire at the Russians. This signal was repeated all down the line. The "To horse!" was sounded. Our cavalry, which had dismounted, put itself back into the saddle, and we went forward, pushing the enemy's skirmishers and light cavalry in front of us.'

During the whole of the rest of the day, Griois goes on,

'there were several fairly lively engagements. Although surrounded by swarms of Cossacks we always had the advantage. The very fine but cold weather favoured this little war which our cavalry carried on ardently.'

The more so as the handsome, popular and capable Grouchy, though scarcely recovered from his Borodino wound, is again in command, relieving 3rd Cavalry Corps of Lahoussaye's ineptitudes.

Rapp too notices how amazed Napoleon is that the Russians should have withdrawn from such a strong position; and how impressed he is by the courage of 'the militiamen he found mingled with the dead and wounded regulars'. The carnage is immense. The Army of Italy has lost some 2,000 men, or a tenth of those who only a week ago had marched so cheerfully out of Moscow. Ségur is horrified:

'No battlefield was ever of a more terrible eloquence! Its pronounced forms, its sanguinary ruins, the streets, all trace of which had been obliterated except the long trail of dead and heads crushed by the cannon wheels, the wounded still to be seen emerging from the ruins, dragging themselves along with their coats, their horses and their limbs half burnt, uttering lamentable cries: and, finally, the lugubrious sound of the last sad tributes the grenadiers were paying to the remains of their dead colonels and generals – all bore witness to the most furious shock of arms.'

At the entrance of the forest near the battlefield Captain Lignières sees

'an ambulance set up. There was an enormous quantity of amputated arms and legs, tossed hither and thither and also in heaps.'

One of the legs heaped up there probably belonged to Colonel Kobylanski, Davout's Polish ADC: 'having had a leg smashed up to his haunches he'd had to suffer amputation.'[10] Le Roy, also visiting the battlefield, is more horrified by the carnage and destruction than impressed by the victory:

'Everything topsy-turvy. Not a house standing. The dead and wounded all heaped up on top of each other, Russians and French [sic] pell-mell. The first men to be wounded had tried to take refuge in the houses and were all burnt or crushed in them. It was a heart-rending sight, enough to make one detest heroes and conquerors.'

And indeed to what purpose? After putting up a fierce resistance, the Russians have once again made off. Napoleon's 'first impulse was to follow Kutusov, but along the Krasnoïe road.'[11] But by now Eugène and Davout have joined the imperial party. Both, like Berthier, point out

'how exhausting this change of direction would prove to cavalry and artillery already in a state of exhaustion, and that it would lose us any lead we might have over the Russians. The Emperor wavered for some time. As he saw it, the fight at Malojaroslavetz wasn't enough to offset the King of Naples' defeat.'

What one of Docturov's staff officers, a prisoner, has to say, may also be a factor in his fateful decision. The Russian tells not only of Kutusov's dilatory march to Malojaroslavetz, but also repeats what – he claims – the Tsar had said when he'd received Lauriston's peace proposals:

"This is where my campaign begins."

All the night's debates when Napoleon 'had resisted every conceivable argument adduced to decide him' still haven't really led to a decision, Caulaincourt realizes, but 'merely postponed it until he could see for himself whether the enemy had really eluded him'.

By now, it seems, Bessières has joined the party, which is unanimously in favour of a retreat. Caulaincourt too seems to have given his opinion, for he uses the words 'we' and 'us'. Only after the others have repeatedly pointed out that

'if Kutusov wouldn't stand and fight in such an excellent position as Malojaroslavetz he wasn't at all likely to join battle sixty miles further on,'

does Napoleon 'in this unofficial council of war' let himself be convinced. And decides to retreat via Borowsk, 'where part of the troops, most of the artillery, and all the vehicles already were. In view of the state of the horses,' Caulaincourt adds, 'this was a weighty consideration.' But is Napoleon really convinced he's doing the right thing?

'Did the Emperor wish it to seem he was only yielding to the convictions of others?[12] Or did he really believe he might still crush the Russian army and at long last turn the campaign to his advantage before deciding on his winter quarters? I can't say.'

It's certainly the bitterest decision Napoleon has ever had to take. None of his campaigns has ever ended with a retreat.

'Napoleon's star,' says Wilson,

'no longer guided his course. For after the [Russian] rearguard had retired, had any, even the smallest reconnaissance, advanced to the brow of the hill over the ravine – had the slightest demonstration of a continued offensive movement been made – Napoleon would have obtained a free passage for his army on the Kaluga or Medyn roads, through a fertile and rich country to the Dnieper; for Kutusov, resolved on falling back behind the Oka, had actually issued the orders "to retire in case of the enemy's approach to his new position".'

Once clear of Moscow, Ney's orders had been to make a feint with his 11,000-strong III Corps to the left of the Kaluga road, as if coming to

Murat's support; but also, in the event of Kutusov moving faster than the main French column, to fend him off. Now he has closed up behind it as its rearguard and is at Borowsk. At 10.30 a.m. Berthier writes to him:

'It is the Emperor's intention to get back to Viazma via Vereia and Mojaisk, so as to profit from what is left of the fine days, to gain two or three marches on the enemy's light cavalry, which is very numerous, and finally to take up winter quarters after so active a campaign. Consequently His Majesty orders you, M. le Duc, without delay to direct toward Vereia and thence to Mojaisk escorted by one of your divisions, the Treasure, the headquarters of the Intendance, the military carriages, the parks of the army's artillery. With your other divisions you will form this convoy's rearguard and you will leave troops at Borowsk until they are relieved by Morand's division.'

Thus, writes David Chandler in his *The Campaigns of Napoleon*, 'after winning a small tactical advantage, Napoleon in effect conceded a huge strategical victory to Kutusov, who had no wish to fight a further action.'[13]

*

Meanwhile the Italians' exploits must be rewarded. 'The Emperor reviewed us,' Laugier goes on proudly, 'and turning to the Viceroy told him: "The honour of this fine day belongs wholly to you."'

Though Le Roy thinks IV Corps is 'in a pitiful state' he's glad to see Napoleon being 'very generous in rewarding the brave men of this corps, as they deserved.'

For once the Imperial [27th] Bulletin isn't lying, exaggerating or censoring, when it declares:

"This feat of arms is to the greatest credit of the Viceroy and the IV Army Corps. The enemy used two-thirds of his army to sustain his position: it was in vain. In the fight at Marojaroslavetz the Royal Italian Guard, highly distinguished itself."

Lieutenant-colonel de Baudus on the IHQ staff[14] hears for example of

'the admirable conduct in this encounter of General Letort, colonel-in-second of the Dragoons of the Guard. For six weeks this intrepid officer had been sick and was so weak he could only follow the army in his carriage. As soon as he hears his regiment is marching against the enemy he calls for his horse, has himself fixed on to it and once facing the Cossacks, gets back all his energy, follows and directs the movements of his brave dragoons and doesn't relapse into the deplorable state where his illness has put him until the guns have fired their last round. His fiery soul re-animated his dying body, suddenly gave it back the strength his long sufferings had gradually taken from it.'

At 5 p.m., Laugier goes on,

'having visited everything and pushed reconnaissances along the Kaluga road, the Emperor returned to Gorodnia. His discontented air as he went off made us think he was in disagreement with his principal generals and that, if only he were listened to, the battle would begin again. However that might be, we anxiously prepared ourselves for a new fight, and impatiently awaited the signal for it. To our great astonishment, the whole day passed without any order coming.'
Caulaincourt returns with his master to the weaver's hut; 'and from there he issued his orders'. To all who understand their implications – and that's more than a few – they come as a nasty shock. Lejeune and I Corps' staff are

'impatiently awaiting the order to advance, when a most unexpected order struck us with surprise and consternation. The Emperor saw himself reduced to order the army to abandon the Kaluga road and again take the one to Mojaisk we had taken when coming. Napoleon was going to throw us, without any food, back into a desert and on to the ashes we'd left behind us. It was to take from us all hope of finding a scrap of nourishment. This decision afflicted us cruelly.'

The news of the Emperor's close-run brush with the Cossacks has spread like wildfire throughout the army. Already it had reached Colbert back at Ouvarovskoïe at midday, where his Lancer Brigade has arrived from the rear and is guarding the Malojaroslavetz road. The lancers had just 'done the dawn' that morning, and the enormous baggage train from Moscow they'd overtaken yesterday was crawling past them through the mud, when they'd been assailed by the very same Cossacks, Chlapowski says, that had just been driven off by the Dutch Grenadiers of the Guard. At about midday Dumonceau has seen them come back, this time in force:

'They flung themselves at us on our brigade's flank. One of the Cossacks, doubtless an officer, shouted out to our lancers, in good French: "Come on, come on, you Parisian fops!"'
But Colbert, all too well aware of Cossack tricks, forbids anyone to take up these challenges. Ordering both his regiments to mount, he makes immediate and judicious dispositions. Whereupon the Cossacks vanish into the forest – only to re-appear suddenly at its fringe on the brigade's right. The Dutchmen's own right is resting on Ouvarovskoïe village, with the Poles in echelon to their left rear. Chlapowski gathers some straggling infantrymen of the 300 or 400 'who were all the time passing among us' and ranges them behind a hedge, in a hut, ready to manoeuvre the Cossacks into their zone of fire. 'The lead horses were sent to the rear and drawn up prominently on a slight rise in the ground so as to seem to be a reserve.' After which a troop of the 2nd Regiment is sent out ahead in open order.

They're protected by

'a ravine, parallel with the road and only crossable at a very few points, which separated us from the enemy, with another to the rear of the village. In view of the distance at which they'd first appeared and would have to cross in order to come to get at us, the various dispositions had been taken in good time, the more so as the multitude in question was advancing at a walking pace, with hardly ordinary calmness, on a broad front, like a threatening storm.'

Dumonceau estimates their numbers at between three and four thousand, 'over two-thirds more than we had to oppose them'. Suddenly, finding themselves held up by the ravine, the Cossacks throw themselves *en masse* to their own right; and outflanking the lancers' advanced party 'fling them back with savage howlings'. So suddenly do they surround the supporting squadron it hasn't time to fall back on the infantry ambush. Colbert promptly sends the 2nd Squadron – Dumonceau's – to rescue the 1st, who charge home,

'dispersing or overthrowing anything that tried to resist us, and thus joining the endangered squadron. But at the same moment the flood of Cossacks had closed behind us.'

Whereupon Colbert throws in the Red Lancers' last two squadrons, all that's left of the regiment:

'The general shouts "Half-turn about, left, by fours!" – and all the survivors gallop flat out to the rear, where they execute another perfect turn, the concealed infantry at the same moment firing volley upon volley from behind its hedge and taking the Cossacks in flank.'

The ambushers, for once, have been ambushed. Even so, Dumonceau finds himself fighting for his life with his sabre against Cossack lances:

'This time the struggle was brief, and wholly to our advantage. In a flash the whole of the regiment's front was freed. But then the field of combat appeared in its sad aspect. Our losses were unveiled. More than 150 of our men, recognizable by their red uniforms, were lying on the ground, among them one of our cantinières. Half were dead or dying.'

Some, still in their death-throes, are being stripped by Cossacks, whom their comrades are prompt to drive away. One lancer, pierced through by seventeen Cossack lances, 'survives for the time being'. Although the Poles of the 1st Guard Lancers, the élite of the élite, the heroes of Somosierra,[15] had witnessed this terrible scrimmage, they'd 'only advanced at the last moment to protect us as we rallied'.[16]

Meanwhile 'the remnants of the 1st and 2nd Cavalry Corps, which had been on observation on the right bank of the Luja' have 'crossed the river and the battlefield, and, passing along the faces of redoubts covered with Russian corpses, taken up position about six miles from the town to observe and cover the Kaluga road and mask the retreat. We were in this position until evening,' an anonymous officer of the 16th Chasseurs will recall. Griois, too, has been summoned to Grouchy's headquarters, 'where I found Marshal Davout'. The retreat via Mojaisk, the two corps commanders tell him, is to start at midnight. The enemy mustn't suspect it. And part of his artillery is to form the rearguard. Griois suggests it might be a good idea

'to take out a dozen guns in front of our line and with them, at night-fall, direct a well-nourished fire at the Russian camp. The marshal accepted my advice. And when night fell I aimed my gun [sic] at the enemy fires they, to my great astonishment, replied only feebly.'

The reason, though he doesn't know it, is that Kutusov, too, has begun his precipitate retreat.

That evening no one is more astonished, or dismayed, at the order which has just reached them than the Italians. Instead of attacking again, they're to retreat to Borowsk:

'This very night we're to reach Uvarovskoïë, regulating our move-ments on those of Davout's corps, which is to be the rearguard. Departure has been fixed for this evening at 10 p.m. An order to burn everything we find along the road,'

reaches Césare de Laugier. On the plain beyond Malojaroslavetz Pierre Auvray's 23rd Dragoons are doing outpost duty when an order comes for 'every soldier to light a fire'. 'At nightfall', the anonymous captain of the 16th Chasseurs goes on,

'each of us had just found some spot where we could get a little rest, when our attention was re-awakened by a brilliant light produced by a tall pyramid of fire. Seemingly hovering in the air, it lit up the plain at a distance. Surprised, we watched this singular spectacle and were losing ourselves in speculations as to what it might be, when a violent detonation at a great distance reached us and increased our disqui-etude. We were told this pyramid of fire, which went on burning through a good part of the night, was the spire of a church tower we'd seen far off during the day and which, like the explosion we'd just heard, was a signal for our army. At midnight, the order being given in a low voice, each of us silently got ready to leave. Great numbers of fires were lit to impress the enemy. At various times during the night loud explosions were heard in the distance. At midnight, sadness in our souls, we mounted our horses in the deepest silence, and set off, the left leading. Crossing the plain we saw at intervals in the distance scattered soldiers who were busy keeping fires burning, and who fell back on us as our rearguard passed them. In this way we marched for two or three hours, always by the light of the pyramid of fire, as far as the Luja bridge, thrown over the fairly broad river that was mirroring it. Finally distance and heights covered with forests hid it from our view.'

'At midnight,' Auvray's dragoons too retire across the Luja: 'Any guns lacking teams were thrown into the river.'

What was this 'signal' or 'pyramid of fire'? No one else mentions it. But that the scene was lit up far and wide is certain:

'Hardly had the first troops of our rearguard marched than a mass of flames rose from a village they'd just left. The fire spread in a few instants, and I was afraid the clarity it was spreading might wake up the Russians and cause them to discover our movement, for the village lay on the line of our advanced posts. But the enemy himself was in full retreat, and we left last without being interfered with.'

Last of all to cross that bridge are two of Griois' guns, supported by some troops of cavalry and voltigeur companies. In this way, he concludes,

'towards midnight the two armies turned their backs on each other, marching in opposite directions, each being as anxious as the other that its movement shouldn't be disturbed! It even happened that the roundshot I'd been sending to the enemy with no other idea than to fool him had chanced to fall in a defile he was having to pass through and thrown a kind of disorder into the crowd pressing together there, as I read in Ségur's History of the Grand Army.'

And indeed Ségur's rhetoric, for once, isn't exaggerated when he exclaims:

'My companions! Do you remember it, this sinister field, where the conquest of the world came to a halt, where twenty years of victories were undone, where our good luck began to crumble away?'

Has his own near-capture affected Napoleon's judgement? Or even his nerve? Certainly he too has had a shock; for late that evening, in strictest confidence, he sends for Dr Yvan. Asks him to make him up a phial of quick-acting poison he can wear 'in a little leather bag round his neck', to be taken if he should be captured.[18]

NOTES

Chapter 1. 'Fire! Fire!'

1. In 1815, after Waterloo, Griois would run to the Louvre to have a last glimpse of its 'trophies' – art treasures pillaged from all over Europe, notably Italy, the ones that had so delighted William Hazlitt's heart and eye during the Peace of Amiens in 1802. His memoirs were written in 1827–31. Grouchy's 3rd 'Reserve' Cavalry Corps, only 6,800 strong at the outset of the campaign but by now, like the rest of Murat's cavalry, reduced to scarcely half its effectives, should have been commanded by Kellermann, if that veteran had not been ill. It consisted of a division of dragoons (7th, 23rd, 28th and 30th Dragoons) under Lahoussaye – whom many officers regarded as a fraud – the brigades of Seron and Thiry, a division of light cavalry, the brigades of Seron and Thiry, under Chastel (6th, 8th and 25th Chasseurs and 6th Hussars). Its cuirassier division, commanded by the 'not very intelligent' 45-year-old Doumerc, was serving with Oudinot's II Corps at Polotsk and had never joined the main body, but would do so, memorably, at the Berezina.

2. Readers of *1812, the March on Moscow* (hereinafter referred to as *The March*) will recall that it was Count Balashoff, the Tsar's police minister, who had been sent to negotiate with Napoleon at Vilna in June/July. See *The March*, p. 78 et seq.

3. Erostratos was the ancient Greek incendiary who burned down the temple of Diana in order to achieve immortal fame.

4. For Napoleon's headquarters arrangements, see p. 93.

5. This letter is dated 16 September. Evidently he had written one either on the 14th or 15th, but if so it has disappeared. If this letter was really written on 16 September it is strange that he makes no mention in it of the fire.

6. In *The March* I incorrectly translated Gourgaud's rank as 'First Ordnance Officer'. As critics have pointed out, 'Officier d'Ordonnance' has nothing to do with ordnance (artillery), but should perhaps be translated as First Orderly Officer. I was led astray by the circumstance of Gourgaud's having come from the artillery.

7. Police Superintendent Voronenko would afterwards report officially to the Moscow Administration: 'On 14 September at 5 a.m., Count Rostopchin ordered me to go to the Wine Arcade and the Custom House ... and in the event of a sudden entry by enemy troops, to destroy everything by fire, which order I carried out in various places as far as it was possible in sight of the enemy until 10 p.m.' The previous afternoon a depressed Barclay de Tolly, now commanding the 1st West Army under Kutusov, had been unhappily watching his troops march out of Moscow, when he had noticed the city's fire engines being dragged away by the fire brigade. Rostopchin happening to be nearby, he had asked him why this was being done. To which Rostopchin replied enigmatically: 'I've my good reasons.'

8. For some samples of Murat's fancy uniforms, see *The March*, pp. 125, 128, 178, 189.

9. Roos places the explosion and the great outbreak of the fire late in the evening of 14 September, i.e., the day of the army's arrival. Like some other eye-witnesses who do the same, his memory is almost certainly telescoping the events of the two evenings. The balance of the evidence seems to indicate that Rostopchin's rocket went up at about 9 p.m. on 15 September.

10. Caulaincourt had been Napoleon's ambassador at St Petersburg for four years. See *The March*, p. 16.

11. For the nepotism by which Planat de la Faye, a mere lieutenant in the Artillery

233

Train, had come to be Lariboisière's 'man of letters', see *The March*, p. 44.

12. This according to Colonel *Serran* of the Engineers, who had just arrived from Spain 'having done a thousand leagues from Vittoria to Moscow' – *Histoire de ma Vie.*

13. Tsar Alexander had always disliked Rostopchin, who had secretly regarded him as party to the assassination of his father Paul I. Afterwards he would detest him. The 'modern Erostratos', however, would remain enigmatic and self-contradictory about his key role in the destruction of Moscow. He would end his days in Paris, where his daughter married *Philippe de Ségur*, the campaign's second historian after Labaume.

Chapter 2. Napoleon Leaves the Kremlin

1. This isn't strictly true. Nor would Napoleon, no matter how adeptly he always feigned total impassivity at moments of crisis, have made such a claim. He was also secretly very much afraid of being poisoned. Justifiably, in the closely researched and reasoned view of the Swedish researcher Sven Forshuvud. In 1814, *en route* for Elba, the Austrian commissioner saw him fall into a panic and, for lack of his own cook, refuse to eat with him and his colleagues.

2. In his melodramatic but rhetorical account it seems that the Assistant Prefect of the Palace, *Philippe de Ségur*, afterwards gave especially free rein less to his memory than to his 'creative imagination'. He says that Napoleon 'after several *tâtonnements* [gropings about] left the Kremlin over some rocks, by a postern overlooking the Moscova'. This is directly challenged, like so much of his history, by Gourgaud, who says that Napoleon left by a main gate.

3. See *The March*, pp. 96, 97.

4. We must always remember that Labaume's account, the first to appear in

print, came out in 1814, while Napoleon was on Elba. How much of its moralizing was a condition for passing the Bourbon censor? Not that his indignation is necessarily insincere. The book would afterwards go into many editions, both French and English, and was only slowly supplanted by Ségur's powerful if often inaccurate masterpiece, published in 1824.

5. See *The March*, pp. 105, 106.

6. See *The March*, pp. 123, 124, 125.

7. See *The March*, p. 32.

Chapter 3. The Fair of Moscow

1. See *The March*, Index.

2. From Rostopchin's official report to the Russian government after the departure of the French.

3. The Tsar's brother, who of course had had nothing at all to do with it.

4. The biography of Charles-Louis Schulmeister, Napoleon's arch-spy, makes fascinating reading. See Alexandre Elmer, *L'Agent Secret de Napoléon*, Fr. trans., Paris, 1932.

5. See The March, p. 162.

6. Yakovlev had an illegitimate son. In his memoirs the future great socialist Alexander Herzen would afterwards describe how his forever tergiversating father had got left behind in Moscow when everyone else had left. The account by Herzen's nurse can be read in Daria Oliver, *The Burning of Moscow*, London, 1966, p. 106, from which I have taken some of these details.

7. For other examples of this, see *The March*, pp. 26, 79.

8. I have summarised my account of the Yakovlev interviews and his mission from Olivier's imaginatively written book. Not being able to read the original documents,

I am not sure how far the details are authentic.

9. The veteran – but ferocious – Russian general Suvarov had invaded Italy and retrieved all Bonaparte's conquests there before being driven out of Switzerland by Masséna in 1799.

10. The same day (19 September) as Yakovlev took Napoleon's letter, a Piedmontese officer in the Russian service, a Colonel Michaud, reached Alexander with the appalling news that Moscow had been reduced to ashes. Alexander, shaken, told him (so he will later relate): 'Colonel Michaud, don't forget what I say to you here. Perhaps a day will come when we shall enjoy recalling it: "Napoleon or I; he or I". Now we can no longer both reign. I've come to know him. He'll not deceive me any longer.'

11. See *The March*, pp. 19, 328.

12. In *The March* I erroneously called Kergorre a Fleming. In fact he was born at Nantes.

13. Unbeknown to Caulaincourt, Napoleon, while planning the campaign in Paris, had had a huge issue of forged rouble notes of every denomination secretly printed, with the express purpose of devaluing the Russian currency.

14. The collaborators would in fact be very leniently treated after the war.

15. Chastel's light cavalry division of 3rd Cavalry Corps had followed up the cuirassiers' assault and for a while held the captured redoubt under massive Russian artillery fire. Every single one of its officers had been killed or wounded or lost his horse, and many men had been out of action for a considerable time to come. Henckens is utterly critical of cavalry having been used to carry the Great Redoubt. Henckens would never know whether it had been Napoleon's or Murat's idea. 'For a commander it's glorious to carry out heroic actions with a minimum of losses; but whoever ordered the cavalry to carry out this extraordinary attack when the enemy hadn't yet begun to waver made an unpardonable error.' Unknown to him, they had. On the eve of the battle Colonel Ledard had told Henckens that he had a clear premonition it would be his last evening, and had asked him to bury him 'as deeply as possible with my decorations, my sabre and all,' having first taken out his pocket book from his left-hand pocket with his portrait of his wife, 'and when you get back to France give it all to my wife with my adieux. He said all this with admirable composure and after asking me "have you understood?", said, "Let's talk about something else."' – Henckens had served in Italy and Hungary and had been wounded by a bayonet in the stomach at Wagram, but recovered entirely.

16. 'It was the last thing', Griois adds, 'they abandoned during the retreat. Several times I saw this kind of ingot fall from the packs of unfortunates succumbing *en route*, their weight having doubtless hastened their death by increasing their fatigue.'

17. 'Most of the gold cash', he adds, 'I spent for myself and my company and some officers during the retreat. One of these gold coins would save the life of General Gros at the Polish frontier.'

18. Ney's Württembergers, however, had six padres, three Catholic and three Protestant. So did Oudinot's Swiss regiments, the Polish Vistula Legion, and other Polish units. In fact Allied units usually had them.

Chapter 4. Murat's Disconsolate Advance Guard

1. The 41-year-old Marthod would die in captivity on 5 October, presumably from his wounds.

2. See *The March*, pp. 90, 239.

3. For once I am breaking my rule of as far as possible relating events in chronological order. For Le Roy's marauding expedition see Chapter 6, Note 2.

4. See *The March*, pp. 104, 168.

5. Or possibly another, two days later; Griois isn't quite clear.

6. Even in 1813 Kutusov would maintain that the total destruction of Napoleon was undesirable, as it would only serve British interests. He saw the campaign from a purely Russian point of view. The covert power struggle between Britain and Russia would continue right up to the Crimean War.

7. 'A good cavalry officer,' Napoleon would say afterwards of Bessières on St Helena, 'but a bit cold. He had too little of what Murat had too much of,' namely dash and audacity. See also, p. 58.

8. Dumonceau gives an extensive account of his regiment's movements, too long to be quoted here.

9. In his valuable documentary work *Napoleon's Invasion of Russia* (Presidio Press, Novado, CA), George F. Nafziger prints a map of what he calls 'the Battle of Czernicznia or Trautino', and dates it to 6 October – when, as we shall see, there was already an unofficial truce and Murat was talking to the Russian outposts. Presumably this refers to the head-on collision between the Russian army and Murat's advance guard of 4 October. By the Battle of Tarutino is usually meant the battle at Winkovo of 18 October. See Chapter 10, Notes.

Chapter 5. Settling in for the Winter?

1. Although many Poles, particularly of the officer class, had volunteered for service with the French armies in Italy in 1796, Kosciuszko, the hero of the 1794/5 uprising, who had vainly tried to modernise the country, had never trusted Napoleon, rightly as it would turn out. In 1812 he was living in retirement at Fontainebleau.

2. In 1610 the Poles had occupied the Kremlin for a while and they laid siege to it again in 1617. This was before the establishment of the Romanov dynasty, but the wars had ended with Smolensk becoming Polish. The Latin words mean 'May someone arise from our bones to avenge us'.

3. In June 1812 Prince Dominique Radziwill had offered the Polish Diet a whole regiment of cavalry to be raised at his own expense 'on the sole condition of commanding it himself'. After the Tsar had ordered him back to Vilna, on Napoleon's arrival there he had assumed command of the regiment and lavishly provided the French with much-needed supplies. Later he was transferred to the command of the Polish Guard Lancers. He was to die in battle in 1813.

4. The guns would still be there when he visited Moscow many years later.

5. Here, as elsewhere, Bourgogne's vivid account should be read *in toto*.

6. See *The March*, Chapter 1.

7. See *The March*, p. 30.

8. See *The March*, p. 142 et seq. After his initiative and efficiency at the Molihew battle in July, Davout had been so pleased with Le Roy's behaviour that he had attached him to his staff. Evidently Le Roy is now back with his regiment.

9. Marshal *Macdonald*, commanding the mostly Prussian X Corps, sent in late June to invest Riga, represented the Grand Army's extreme left wing.

10. See *The March*, Index.

11. On 22 July Wellington had routed Marmont at Salamanca and on 11 August he had re-entered Madrid. This meant that on 25 August Soult had had to abandon the siege of Cadiz.

Chapter 6. Marauding Parties

1. Surgeon Heinrich von Roos says that Cossack lances (which he calls pikes)

rarely caused wounds that were dangerous or penetrating. 'For that they would have to be caused with unusual force and flung [*sic*] by a horseman at a gallop.' But they were also a cutting weapon, 'penetrating cavities, damaging important organs, severing blood vessels and often causing a mortal wound.' At night, they had the careless frontiersmen's habit of sticking their lances point down into the ground, which dulled them. Several Frenchmen noted this. Although they used lances skilfully, they caused many minor wounds.

2. For once, against my usual principle in this documentary, I'm backtracking chronologically. Le Roy had led his marauding party before the 85th had been ordered out on the Kaluga road with the rest of Friedrichs' division.

Chapter 7. Lovely Autumn Weather

1. As explained in *The March*, the word 'dysentery' was used indiscriminately to cover all types of diarrhoea.

2. The regiment's new colonel, however, would fail to forward Dutheillet's promotion to its depot at Strasburg, 'with the result that later, the army's baggage having been captured by the Russians and the notifications of these nominations being intercepted by the partisans, I wasn't inscribed as lieutenant at the War Ministry, and could only obtain that grade at another review by the Emperor, at Magdeburg in 1813. Thus, in returning to the Strasburg depot, I lost all the fruits of this campaign.'

3. For the structure and functioning of the General Imperial Headquarters Staff, see Elting, *Swords Around a Throne*, p. 83 et seq. which is more accurate than my own account in *The March*. For Lejeune's adventurous career and artistic achievements, etc., see *The March*, Index. Napoleon's moods and reactions on parade were always unpredictable. The day in Prussia when he had chatted with Major Boulart, a subaltern had taken advantage of his sunny mood to request a

post in the civilian administration for a relative. This, thought Boulart, was going it a bit strong. But the request had been granted. Gouty old Colonel Nougarède of the 23rd Chasseurs had not been so fortunate and had come in for a nasty shock. At the Tuileries the Emperor had told Marbot that he 'loved' the old man, who had been with him in Egypt, but now could no longer mount a horse and had to use a carriage – 'a sad way of commanding a light cavalry regiment on campaign'. As soon as a post became available, he had told Marbot, he would promote Nougarède general of gendarmerie; after which Marbot could take over the regiment. So far so good. But at Insterburg Nougarède, failing to notice Napoleon's tetchy humour, had made so bold as to ask a favour for a relative who hadn't served the required time. Whereupon Napoleon had 'flown into a most violent rage, ordered the military police to eject the officer in question from the Army and galloped off, leaving him stunned,' and Marbot to serve until 15 November as acting colonel.

4. See also Brandt's account, *The March*, pp. 214, 215, and Marbot's memoirs.

5. At St Helena Napoleon would say, having evidently forgotten certain contretemps: 'I had no worries about my communications. In reality I had only 80 leagues of communications. In 40 days not a single *estafette* was taken from me. I lost more in France.' For further fascinating details of the courier service see *Memoirs of Caulaincourt*, vol. 1, p. 278, ed. Jean Hanoteau, Cassell, London, 1935.

6. See *The March*, pp. 28, 29, 30.

7. See *The March*, p. 100.

8. Since, as Aristotle points out, 'everything has the defects of its qualities' and this applies as much to character as anything else, no one is so well qualified to 'see through' us as a percipient enemy. Pradt was a prelate of the *ancien régime*. In March 1814, on the eve of Napoleon's first abdication, he would write a book about his experiences at Warsaw. Published in

September 1815, after Waterloo, it would run into at least six editions. Hudson Lowe and the ex-emperor would both read it at St Helena, and the exasperated Lowe would comment that 'after making himself an imaginary Poland, Buonaparte is making himself an imaginary St Helena'. Pradt sees in Napoleon nothing but a quasi-psychopathic adventurer, a megalomaniac, more and more carried away by his own imagination and less and less capable of seeing anything inconvenient to it:

'The Emperor is all system, all illusion, as one can't help being when one is all imagination. He Ossianizes [romanticizes public] affairs. It's enough to have seen him leaf through a book to gain an idea of how much he can acquire from it. The pages fly between his fingers. His eyes run down each page. And at the end of very little time, the hapless piece of writing is almost always rejected with a sign of scorn and generally disdainful formulae: "There's nothing but stupidities in this book; the man's an ideologist, a constitutionalist, a Jansenist." This last epithet is the *maximum* of insults. His head is always in the clouds, always carrying his flight toward the Empyrean, from this elevated point he pretends to skim the earth with an eagle's eye and, when he deigns to tread on it [to do so], with giant strides. With Napoleon it's agitation, extreme agitation, that is the basis of existence. He lives in the bosom of hurricanes as others do in the bosom of peace. Nebuchadnezzar the Superb must have been a model of humility beside a man impregnated with such a dose of self-love.'

That Napoleon was in highest degree what today is called a narcissistic personality is beyond question. Pradt seems to have been one too, although infinitely less intelligent. The sensible administrator Count Beugnot, who was in the 1814 provisional government, a Bonapartist but not a fanatical one – he too went over to the Bourbons – tells a funny first-hand story of how he and his colleagues played a practical joke on Pradt which, if true, shows that that prelate had little sense of political realities.

After his dismissal at Warsaw in December, Pradt will hear that Napoleon, fixing responsibility for the Russian catastrophe on him, had said of him 'One man less, and I'd have been master of the world.' 'Who was that man?' he goes on sarcastically, 'who, sharing in a way the power of the Divinity could have said to this torrent *Non ibis amplius?* [Thou shalt go no further]. This man was myself. Looked at like this, I'd saved the world. But far be it from me to arrogate any such [achievement] to myself!'

An acute observation on what she regarded as Napoleon's weakest point is to be found in the memoirs of Mme de Motteville: 'The closer one came to the Emperor's person the more disagreeable life became. It was always better to have to deal with his intellect than his character. What he feared most in the world was anyone in his proximity simply exercising or bringing him [*qu'on apportât*] the faculty of judgement.'

9. See *The March*, pp. 23, 40, 81.

10. See *The March*, Index.

11. On 11 June Schwarzenberg had written to Metternich: 'We are still very angry with the French. No one wants to get used to fighting alongside them. However, out of *esprit de corps* we are loath to expose ourselves to [a charge of] dishonouring the uniform.' John Elting has a high opinion of Schwarzenberg; and considers his Austrians' management of the campaign 'a better job in 1812 than either before or after'.

12. Between 1807 and 1814 the little principality of Neuchâtel, formerly with its parliament's assent belonging to the King of Prussia but arbitrarily given by Napoleon to Berthier, telling him he would be able to get twice as much income out of it as the King of Prussia had done, contributed about 2,250 men to its yellow-coated battalion. There was no conscription, as elsewhere; but the swift ruin of the principality's economy after Oudinot had occupied it in March 1806 with seven battalions of French infantry, 100 gunners and 250 horses in the depths of winter, caused many young men to accept the recruiting sergeant's offer of 180 francs,

and there was pressure on each village to provide a certain number of recruits. Almost none ever saw their native land again. For the detailed history of the Neuchâtel Battalion, see A. Guye's painstaking study, to which I also owe the following statistics on Smolensk before the fire, which he obtained from the late Soviet Government.

13. Before the disaster Smolensk had had 12,599 inhabitants: 505 merchants, 2,015 workmen, 249 officials, 248 coachmen and carters, three monasteries, 21 stone and five timber churches (orthodox, Catholic and Protestant), sixteen 2-storey official buildings, 54 stone dwelling houses, 30 factories, 2,400 timber yards, two glove factories, four furriers, 27 butchers, 60 stone shops and 230 timber ones and twelve asylums. All this had been ruined.

14. Mme Burcet, who would afterwards falsely claim to have been the troupe's director, had long been mistress of the Duke of Brunswick, mortally wounded at Auerstadt in 1806, and later, also according to Dedem, an intimate of Prince Henry of Prussia (in whose hussar regiment Lieutenant Vossler is currently serving). She had known all the top people in Moscow and been familiar with what had been schemed against Napoleon.

15. 'The trouble with Napoleon', Caulaincourt thought, 'was that he never for a moment ceased playing the great emperor.'

16. '*Un chevalier qui volait au combat*
Par ces adieux consolait son arme:
Au champ d'honneur,
*   l'amour guide mes pas,*
Arme mon bras, ne ceaine rien pour ma vie.
Bientôt vainqueur, je viendrai vers toi.
Et j'obtiendrai le prix de ma vaillance
Mon coeur sera le gage de ta foi
Et mon amour celui de ta constance.'

Chapter 8. A Lethal Truce

1. For the cavalry's dawn routine, see *The March*, pp. 123–4.

2. Tschüdi's Spaniards, though at first strongly inclined to desert (see *The March*, p. 107), had fought valiantly at Borodino (pp. 267, 329).

3. Since her banishment there, among other things for refusing even to mention French conquests in Germany in her book on German culture, few of her friends had dared visit her. Her daughter's tutor had even been forcibly dismissed for unpatriotically preferring the original Greek tragedies to those of Racine and Corneille. See *The March*, pp. 357, 363, 368. Her no doubt exaggerated picture of Napoleonic Europe as a prison house is confirmed by what an eye-witness to the execution of Malet and his fellow-conspirators writes of working-class life in Paris at that time: 'Everyone kept his mouth shut; one did not dare speak, for fear of being compromised. As long as the Great Empire lasted I always heard people talking in low voices, even in the family, about political events. Any individual who spoke aloud, without being afraid, was assumed to be a spy.'

The father of Germaine de Staël's daughter Albertine was none other than Narbonne, now Napoleon's ADC, for whom in the early stages of the Republic, when her salon had still been immensely influential, she had obtained the post of Minister of War. Rocca, a wounded and retired officer, also one of her party, was her second husband and father of her son.

Her book on Germany, published in London in 1813, would set its seal on its war of liberation. But when the tide went against France and Napoleon she would experience nothing but horror: 'I hate the man, but I blame events which make me wish him success.' His final overthrow shook her to the core of her being.

4. See *The March*, p. 201.

5. 'All the other versions', writes Brandt, 'are incorrect. I can vouch for this because a long while afterwards I saw this bit of writing again in the house of a former officer of my regiment, Malinski, who had carried it off and preserved it.' Caulaincourt's version of the text of Rostopchin's notice, presumably based on what was reported to Napoleon or on what was printed in the

Paris papers, is more extensive: 'For eight years I have been embellishing this country [house] and have been living happily in it in the bosom of my family. The inhabitants of this property, to the number of seventeen-hundred and twenty, are leaving it at your approach and I, I am setting fire to my house so that it shall not be soiled by your presence. Frenchmen, I have abandoned my two Moscow houses, with furniture worth half a million roubles; here you will only find ashes.' Caulaincourt doesn't usually embellish his texts; and in the light of Brandt's sober statement and claim afterwards to have seen the preserved original, one wonders where the more extensive version has come from?

6. Evidently gossip had it that Rostopchin claimed to be descended from Genghis Khan.

7. One hysteroid person usually sees through another. For Gourgaud's hysterical behaviour in 1815 and on St Helena, see Frédéric Masson and Sten Forshuvud's accounts. Also *The March*, p. 360. This does not mean of course that Gourgaud was not an excellent staff officer, a pertinent critic of Ségur's romanticized text, or, apparently, a better mathematician than Napoleon, to whom, he says, he – on St Helena – vainly tried to explain the duodecimal system. That Rostopchin was the very type of a hysteric is beyond question.

8. See *The March*, pp. 105–6, 168. In 1813 Sébastiani would cap his achievements by losing his entire corps' artillery.

9. Griois had first been recommended by King Joseph for his services in Calabria, then, by Grouchy, commander of 3rd Cavalry Corps, after Borodino. His nomination dates from 11 October 1812.

10. Luckily, Griois adds, it wasn't so. 'And it was better for him to spend a forced stay in Russia than this fateful retreat, which would probably have been too much for him.' Murat promised to indemnify Griois, 'at least in part'. But the disasters which followed would make it unthinkable for Griois even to remind Murat of his promise.

11. The Cossack word 'Hurrah' means 'death'. The army called their wild assaults 'hurrahs', and scornfully referred to the Cossacks as *hourassiers*, cf. cuirassiers.

12. See *The March*, pp. 168, 381.

13. There is no question but that Napoleon from the outset had had such a march in mind, perhaps on India. See *The March*, p.20. The French historian *Emile Bourgeois* has even traced in Napoleon a lurking lifelong obsession with the Orient, derived partly from his youthful readings of the classics and partly from his correct insight that much of Britain's power rested on the gold it was getting from India and using to finance the successive coalitions against him. While envisaging his Egyptian expedition in 1798 he had declared: 'This Europe of ours is a molehill. Only in the East, where six hundred million people live, is it possible to found great empires and realise great revolutions.' And seeing St Helena rise out of the sea he would say to Gourgaud: 'I'd have done better to stay in Egypt. If I'd done so I'd have been Emperor of the Orient by now.' – Pietr Geyl (*op. cit.,* pp. 241–9) outlines and criticises Bourgeois' thesis.

14. See *The March*, p. 201.

15. Scene of Charles XII of Sweden's decisive defeat. See *Peter Englund*'s admirable documentary.

16. The eminent historian Gabriel Hanotaux marks it as one of Napoleon's cardinal faults, mostly in civil government but also in military matters, that while he
'Always demands of his servants forcible and immediate execution, he generally places only moderate means at their disposal, and those in a niggardly fashion. Meanwhile he purposely mistakes their available resources, grudges them in fact, to show surprise when finally results do not come in. This, the greatest defect of all that can mar a man of action, the maladjustment between the imagination and the reality, is to ruin him.'
See Pieter Geyl, *op. cit.,* p. 414. This would seem to be a case in point.

17. See *The March*, pp. 110–11.

Chapter 9. Preparations for Departure

1. Actually two. Unlike the great body of our writers, Ségur is fatally given to exaggeration and inexactitudes. 'But M. de Ségur looks for every opportunity to make Napoleon look more like a man out of his wits than an able general,' Gourgaud would write in his *Examen critique* ... which would give rise to a duel between them and is certainly very much more objective than Ségur's romanticised and 'literary' masterpiece.

2. For Berthier's declining powers and Napoleon's paralysing influence on his subordinates' initiative generally, see *The March*, pp. 65–6. Berthier, though ageing and sick, would nevertheless be an efficient aid to Eugène in gathering the remnant of the shattered army in 1813. Allowance must of course always be made for subjective and retrospective assessments, especially in Ségur's case. There is also contrary evidence that Berthier tried to get Napoleon moving. As for Berthier's glamorous, aristocratic aides, as Edmund Horton says, 'They were acknowledged to be frequently insufferable, but arrived always where they were intended to arrive, never got lost, knew how to speak high and low, even to marshals. A message entrusted to them was always delivered,' which was not invariably the case with other ADCs, sometimes with fatal consequences, as we shall see at Witebsk.

3. Salomon, was Berthier's chief assistant. See *The March*, p. 94.

4. See *The March*, pp. 46–9.

5. 'And he was going to be punished', Ségur adds, 'when the retreat began. The loss of the army would be his salvation.'

6. At St Helena Napoleon would point out to Gourgaud that such handmills had been used by the ancient Romans and ought to be an important logistic feature of any modern army.

7. It was at Mittau in Estonia that Macdonald's mostly Prussian X Corps had been held up in its march to invest Riga. But not for long. They had occupied Mittau and come up to Riga by late July.

8. See *The March*, p. 36.

9. Excerpts from Roeder's detailed account of the Hessians' experiences should be read in Helen Roeder's book. Roeder's memoirs are among the most living and vivid of any. Since the book is obtainable in English I refrain from quoting as exhaustively as it deserves.

10. This was exactly what had happened. See *The March*, p. 240.

11. Afterwards Napoleon would say frankly at St Helena: 'I didn't believe the winter could be like that. I imagined the one we had had at Eylau.'

12. Weatherwise Napoleon would turn out to have misjudged the situation by about a week. Had the whole army got to Smolensk by 1 November the outcome might have been considerably different.

13. The statutes still apply. Oddly enough the stage-struck Gustaf III of Sweden, another 'enlightened' dictator, had done exactly the same thing for his newly founded national theatre, whose statues he modelled on the original ones of the Comédie Française, during his almost equally disastrous Finnish campaign of 1789.

14. Mlle Contat, like Mme de Staël, had been Narbonne's mistress.

15. For a picture of how they were received, see *The March*, pp. 22–3.

16. '*fer*', perhaps a misprint for '*feu*'.

17. Stendhal's diary, unfortunately for us, would be lost in the retreat; only a few flippant letters have survived.

18. As happens with our eye-witnesses now and again, Le Roy's memory seems perhaps to be confusing the events of two

separate days. For according to Schuer-
man/Caulaincourt it was on Wednesday
15 October that the dismounted cavalry
were reviewed. This would agree with
Gouttenoire's telling Le Roy that all the
sick and wounded are leaving the same
day for Smolensk.

19. 'It was covered in gold plate to the
thickness of a sou. The architect charged
with getting it down had done his business so badly that the ropes had broken
and the cross was broken into several
pieces as it fell on the pavings, having
made several holes in the church tower. It
seems it had never been able to be used
without breaking all the windows and
bringing the town's pregnant women to
bed.'

20. No doubt the reader will have already
gained the impression from *The March*
that no regimental officer ever got decorated or promoted if he couldn't appear
on parade. In fact, as John Elting points
out, Napoleon's correspondence shows
that he periodically checked up on deserving officers who were not with the Grand
Army (*Swords*, op. cit., p. 600).

Chapter 10. Battle at Winkovo

1. 'But I always kept my horse,' Bréaut des
Marlots adds, 'and at the end of ten days I
was cured.'

2. Thirty guns, according to Lejeune, who
hears about it in Moscow. But Wilson, who
was on the spot, says 36, whereof, Zalusky
hears to his indignation, '18 not even
taken by the Russians but purely and simply abandoned'.

3. The final loss of the cavalry at Winkovo,
from starvation and the battle, added to all
the losses during the advance on Moscow,
was the last straw, and was decisive; not
only for the retreat, but also in the longer
term, when, together with all the other
losses, lack of cavalry would prove crucial
at Leipzig in 1813. Cavalry took much
longer to train than infantry. See *The
March*, p. 49.

4. So was Kutusov's chief-of-staff Bennigsen, who wrote to his wife: 'I can't get
over it! This magnificent, brilliant day
could have had incalculable consequences
if only I'd been reinforced. But Kutusov
had forbidden it.' No doubt wisely – for
the Grand Army, its cavalry apart, was considerably restored and Kutusov wanted to
avoid another head-on confrontation. His
plan, as we shall see, was to see it off Russian soil, leaving its destruction to 'General
Winter'. – Kutusov's motives for his Fabian
tactics, romanticized by Tolstoy and
approved by *Tarle*, are in fact very difficult
to assess. Virtually all his contemporaries,
like Bennigsen and Wilson, criticised him
violently for his *fainéantism* and for not
seizing opportunities for momentary
advantages. Did he really realise that only
time – and winter's inevitable approach –
would do the job more efficiently for him
than any amount of battles?

5. A report drawn up in October for
Napoleon had revealed that in Moscow
there were about 12,000 French and allied
sick and wounded, few of whom were fit
enough to stand the rigours of a journey.
Captain T-J. Aubry of the 12th Chasseurs
was one of the few left behind who did survive – but only after spending eight horrible months in the typhus-ridden hospital:
'We'd been 43 officers in our hall. All
died one after the other and in the delirium of this disease, most singing, some in
Latin, some in German, some in Italian,
psalms, canticles, the Mass ... It was almost
always their death-throes. Only three of us
were left, among us a cuirassier officer
who'd been amputated at the thigh. Mortality was in the same ratio among the rank
and file, more than 1,800 dying out of the
1,850 shut up in the hospital. Finally we
were moved, and the mortality ceased at
once.'

Chapter 11. Taking French Leave

1. Napoleon had left the Kremlin at 7
a.m., after writing to Marie-Louise to tell
her he's been thinking of asking her to
come and meet him in Poland: 'We've had
no cold weather at all, we haven't yet had

any experience of the rigours of the northern climate.' The Winkovo setback he had written off as 'a vanguard skirmish with Cossacks'. One must remember that all his letters to Marie-Louise, gossip being what it is, really had an eye to public consumption in Paris, therefore in Europe. Their propaganda value was important.

2. Opinions seem to differ sharply as to whether the French or their so-called allies were the worst plunderers. One of my critics writes in the margin: 'Disagree totally! Discipline in the German regiments was *always* better than in the French! The French [had] pillaged and scrounged on a professional level everywhere they went since 1796.' This is certainly true; and indeed not only since then, but since the revolutionary armies' very first campaigns. *Xavier de Vernères'* first experience of pillage, in 1792, shocked him deeply. The town of Menin having just been taken by storm from the Dutch, out of sheer curiosity he got permission to walk some 3 or 4 miles to view what was going on there:

'My first instinct was to turn back, not to be counted among those who were dishonouring the laurels they'd just won. But my curiosity got the better of me, and I stayed in this desolate town, most of whose inhabitants had fled. Soon I repented of yielding to this impulse when, upon seeing the commander-in-chief [Houchard] and terror-stricken at this apparition, I thought he'd have me arrested as one of the authors of this pillage. But I was quickly reassured and, let me say, indignant, when I saw him, with no sign of discontent, watching the excesses being committed under his eyes, by his indifference even seeming to encourage them. Delivered from this fear, I did none the less hasten to leave behind me a town whose disorder I didn't view with the same apathy as General Houchard.'

But again young Xavier's curiosity had got the better of him. Entering a grocer's shop he went into the house at its rear:

'There I saw a mob of soldiers smashing the furniture to remove their contents and linen. Immediately I quit this painful scene of pillage, admittedly not without yielding to its evil influence, for in again passing through the shop I couldn't resist a strong

temptation to take something myself; and seeing a stove-in barrel full of Corinthian raisins I complaisantly plunged my hand into it to fill my pockets; then, encouraged by this first attempt, I provided myself with pens and further appropriated two clay pipes to the value of two centimes apiece, to teach myself to smoke.'

Everywhere, for the next fifteen years, it was to be the same story. Xavier Vernères' filched clay pipes and raisins could stand for the ruin and pillage of Europe. Anyone who still has a sentimental or merely colourful view of the Napoleonic wars should read Jean Morvan's *Le Soldat Impérial, 1800-1814, 2 vols., Paris,* 1904. If the British and German troops could sometimes be restrained from committing rapine and pillage it was merely by fear of the lash. When France was invaded two years later the French would be horrified at Prussian and Russian retribution. 'One notable phenomenon,' Volunteer Janke of Breslau – who would notice how the ubiquitous scenes of pillage 'knocks all the gaiety out of me' – observes 'is the fact that the Prussians enter houses from the front, whereas the Russians always go in from the back, thus proclaiming their thievish character.'

3. Chambray's book, the first 'serious' history of the campaign, came out in 1825, a year after Ségur's, and he seems to have gone to some trouble over facts and figures, but to have taken his figures here from Labaume, whose book had come out in 1814, while Napoleon was on Elba. Wilson estimated the retreating Moscow army at 'about 90,000 effectives mostly infantry, 12,000 men under arms in artillery, gendarmerie, staff, equipages and commissariat, and more than 20,000 non-combatants sick and wounded ... altogether about 140,000 individuals.' Recent historians give the total effectives leaving Moscow as about 108,000, plus several thousand Russian prisoners and civilians, and 569 guns.

4. E. Blaze, in his *La Vie Militaire sous l'Empire,* relates how at the outset of a campaign the infantry regularly went through the ritual of throwing away their knee-breeches 'which constricted even the stoutest marcher'. Next day these

would be picked up by the commercial suppliers, and stored away until after the campaign was over. Whereupon they would be sold back to the colonels who had already paid for them perhaps twice over! But for the Guard to throw them away must have been unusual. At any moment they could be called upon to wear them on some *journée* – e.g., at Borodino, or marching into Moscow. Presumably the Guard, being among other things 'parade troops', did not – they might be needed for triumphal entries into conquered cities. On the other hand they did *not* normally march in their bearskins, which were carried from the waist belt in oilcloth bags or, more usually, in a ticking bag on top of the pack.

5. 'These objects seem to have escaped the general ruin and I still keep them as relics,' Bourgogne adds at the time of writing.

6. Henckens was certainly not the only member of the army to be extremely bitter about the privileged status of the Old Guard in 1812. 'Its only role was to *impose on* the enemy'. And in fact its 1st and 2nd Grenadiers and 1st and 2nd Chasseurs would be virtually unique among the army's regiments in not losing a single officer killed and only five wounded. On the march any Guard unit took precedence over any Line unit. Elzéar Blaze tells a funny story, no doubt endemic in the Napoleonic armies, of how,

'A wagon belonging to the Old Guard, harnessed up to four mules, tries to cross my regiment's path, and the men, crossing under the noses of these poor beasts, took a malicious pleasure in preventing them from getting on, because they belonged to the Imperial Guard. One of them called out in a mocking voice: "Come on, soldiers of the Line, give way to the Mules of the Guard." "Bah!" replied another, "They're donkeys." "I tell you they're mules." "And I that they're donkeys." "Very well, but even if they're donkeys, what of it? Don't you know that in the Guard donkeys have the rank of mules?" – Each man in the Guard rated one rank higher than he would in the Line.'

7. Caulaincourt says that both the privileged young gentlemen got safely home to Paris. Abandoning Napoleon in 1814 like many of the aristocratic party, Mailly-Nesle would become ADC to the Duc de Berry – who in 1814 had taken his foster-brother Gourgaud under his protection – and in August 1815 be made a peer of France. Such behaviour would be characteristic of virtually all the aristocratic officers Napoleon had promoted and favoured.

8. For reasons known only to himself but probably quite simply out of fear of Napoleon's counter-action, Kutusov had never whole-heartedly approved of the so-called Battle of Tarutino, at which he hadn't even been present in person, and to Bennigsen's fury had refused point-blank to send in reserves thereby risking the entire Russian army with its thousands of raw recruits, who so far hadn't been in a battle and of whom Murat's exasperated troops might have made mincemeat. After it was over Kutusov had again withdrawn his army into the entrenched Tarutino camp.

9. Mathieu Dumas was in fact 49. 'In Paris,' Kergorre observes, 'with every medical art to help him, this sickness would have been the end of him. In the retreat, having no other room or other bed but his carriage, or other remedy but a little wine and broth, nor other doctor than Desgenettes, he arrived at Vilna cured.'

10. See *The March*, p. 100.

11. Le Roy would remember it as happening 'just after 2 a.m.'

12. Gourgaud regards Vaudoncourt as a particularly reliable historian and eye-witness. Many other first-hand accounts agree. The prisoners were treated atrociously. See also *The March*, p. 377, note 3.

Chapter 12. 'Where our Conquest of the World Ended'

1. See also *The March*, p.119. Many years later at Munich Planat would see Eugène,

who 'in 1812 had been as thin as a pin', and find him 'big and fat, full-faced with a high colour, his eyes shining and to all appearance in excellent health'. But with the years, from being the firm and enterprising man of 1812, he had become 'apathetic and circumspect. Except in a *tête-à-tête* one could only get an insignificant word out of him. The fall of the imperial regime and the humiliation he had been obliged to submit to in his children's interests had broken down his spirit and seemed to have taken all the bounce out of him.' He had become dependent on his wife, the Bavarian princess whom Napoleon had married him off to, and on the good graces of Tsar Alexander, against a promise never to get mixed up in political intrigues 'and I shall keep my promise'. He also told Planat he would have liked to have been a sailor, and that he was sure he would have succeeded in that career. A private person in the Europe of the Great Reaction, he would marry off his daughter Josephine, named after her grandmother the Empress Josephine, to Bernadotte's son Oscar, so that in due course she became Queen of Sweden.

2. Doumerc's cuirassier division, which had been split off at the campaign's outset, was serving in II Corps.

3. 'It was this two-hour delay that changed the face of affairs,' Dedem goes on, 'and decided the fate of the army and the peace. If he'd carried out his orders punctually he'd have seized the position without firing a shot.' Actually, Delzons and Eugène seem to have been loath to send in a full division at night on the far side of a tricky river crossing. The thought that Delzons' leniency decided the fate of Europe is certainly dramatic, but must be written off as coming within the teasing category of great matters hanging on tiny threads.

4. David Chandler says that they didn't. But Césare de Laugier, who's at pains to defend the Italians' military honour on this as on every other occasion, says that they did. On the other hand the Italian Guard had not reached Malojaroslavetz,

so neither can he have known at first hand.

5. Césare de Laugier, who can only have heard about, not witnessed Delzons' death, gives a slightly different version, according to which 'a discharge of grapeshot throws him down. His brother, who was also his ADC, tries to run to his aid and falls into his elder brother's arms, stricken down by a second gunshot.'

6. No more than any others of Junot's Westphalians was *Wilhelm Heinemann* at Malojaroslavetz – he was with his fellow-prisoners being driven like harassed cattle to Archangel – See *The March*, pp. 275, 377. Heinemann scorns as 'madness' the notion – advanced by both Wilson and Césare de Laugier – 'of deriving the ranker's courage from any independent self-confidence or from feelings of national honour. And should anyone have such higher ideas, or at least wish to boast about it [the fact is], the mass goes into battle animated by a kind of despair which nevertheless not uncommonly does wonders of bravery.'

7. In 1815 Wilson would save Lavalette's life by helping him to escape from prison in Paris after he, like Ney, had been condemned to the firing squad for his role in the Hundred Days. Labédoyère was executed.

8. Like Zalusky, the glory-seeking Césare de Laugier wrote his memoir to stress the exploits of their respective armies, which until then (in the opinion of Italians and Poles) had been under-estimated by French historians, notably Thiers. The naïve military enthusiasm of at least some Italian units, repeatedly described by Laugier, should not, I think, be written off as romantic hindsight. See also *The March*, pp. 126, 152. IV Corps' performance at Malo-jaroslavetz shows what remarkable *esprit de corps* the Army of Italy still had.

9. For similar scenes of Italian cordiality, see *The March*, pp. 126, 183.

10. I'm taking Laugier's account of the battle, partly because it's the only more or

less complete and coherent one from the French side, and partly because it would seem to render the Italians' greatest exploit of the campaign as they would afterwards remember it.

11. According to Denniée's *Itinerary* he had left 'the first bivouac' after Borowsk at 11.30, and only at 1 p.m. 'arrives on the plateau which fringes the valley of the Luja, goes on to Gorodnia, goes forward half a league in the direction of Malo-jaroslavetz, and gets there as the combat between Prince Eugène and Docturov is ending.' Denniée is usually correct on such matters, being himself at headquarters as Inspector of Reviews.

12. Séruzier will afterwards remember, almost certainly incorrectly, I Corps as arriving on the scene at 'about 10 a.m.'

Chapter 13. 'Enough, Gentlemen. I Shall Decide.'

1. To judge by what would afterwards occur at Smorgoni, Napoleon may have used Bessières as his stool-pigeon to make a suggestion he wished to avoid making himself. This would accord with his way of keeping up a façade of infallibility, necessary to the whole imperial regime.

2. In *The March* I inadvertently promoted Auvray to captain's rank in the 21st Dragoons. In fact he was a sous-lieutenant of the 23rd Regiment.

3. In fact the escort had been doubled after the Cossacks' attempt on IHQ on the morning after Borodino.

4. Analyzing the causes of the near-fatal episode that was to follow, Caulaincourt explains (as Castellane had done at Vilna in July) how 'by day or night the Emperor would mount his horse without warning; he even took pleasure in going out unexpectedly and putting everyone at fault'.

5. Lignières says that it was a horse grenadier who ran Lecoulteux through. 'But God preserved him for us, he's still

alive.' Zalusky too says that he had never heard of the Guard Dragoons forming part of the imperial escort. But according to John Elting all four Guard cavalry regiments did so ordinarily in rotation.

6. All this has happened so suddenly and quickly and in such a bad light that different eye-witnesses would afterwards have different memories of it. Lignières, for instance, entirely disapproves of both Ségur's and Rapp's accounts:

When I saw how far away the Cossacks were, I began crossing the plain to rejoin the regiment. I passed through an artillery park. Some of the horses had been killed, others carried off. The soldiers of the Train and other combatants had been killed. A *cantinière* was dead as result of ... She was in a horrible state.'

7. Zalusky dismisses Gourgaud's statement that the 3rd Troop of the Dragoons of the Guard had been in the advance guard commanded by Lieutenant Joachim Hempel:

'That's as may be. I wasn't there. But I've never seen a troop of dragoons figure in the advance guard marching ahead of the Emperor.'

8. And ends: 'And we weren't attacked until the evening, and then by some Cossacks who stabbed 15 or 20 wounded men with lances. There, Madame,' concludes the future novelist and Napoleon-worshipper, with a Stendhalian flourish:

'is the best episode of our journey. It was proper that I should render you an account of it. Although I always remain hopeful, during the night I did what I believe everyone else did: I drew up the balance-sheet of my life and reproached myself bitterly for not having had the sense to tell you just how devoted to you I am.'

9. Once again we must remember that Labaume's book was published in 1814 during the first Bourbon restoration, and heavily slanted against Napoleon – perhaps had to be, to pass the censorship; but is not necessarily insincere for that. His

Relation circonstanciée would be republished in numerous editions, both French and English, during the next thirty years.

10. Zalusky says Kobylanski 'afterwards carried off by the French grenadiers, happily reached Poland'.

11. That is, from Kaluga via Yelnia, the route Kutusov would in fact take, tracking the retreating army. Clausewitz, who was serving with the Russian army, regards the notion of marching through the Ukraine with the Russians at their heels, making it impossible really to exploit the countryside, as utterly impracticable. Naturally the pros and cons of Napoleon's fateful decision have been endlessly discussed by historians. As *Tarle* explains, Clausewitz 'was the first military writer to explode the widespread opinion that' the decision to retreat via Mojaisk 'was a blunder. 'Where could Napoleon have found provisions for his army, if not in the stores he had prepared in advance? What good was an "untapped region" to an army which had no time to lose and was constantly forced to bivouac in large masses? His entire army would have been starving within a week. A retreating army in enemy territory needs, as a rule, a previously prepared route. By "prepared route" we understand a route secured by garrisons along which stores required by the army have been organised.'

12. Afterwards (according to Gourgaud) Napoleon was several times heard to regret aloud having taken others' advice instead of relying on himself alone.

13. Later, at Mantua, Labaume would hear Wilson say that Eugène, with 20,000 men, had stood up to nine Russian divisions of 10,000 men each.

14. Quoted in Bertin, *Etudes sur Napoléon*, pp. 161–2.

15. It was the Polish Guard Lancers, led by Auguste de Caulaincourt (hero of Borodino), who in an 'impossible' feat of arms had forced the Somosierra Pass in the teeth of an entire Spanish army and opened up the road to Madrid.

16. Chlapowski, of the Polish Guard Lancers, had a very low opinion of their Dutch colleagues' ability to defend themselves. Certainly the two regiments forming Colbert's brigade were of very different calibre. Though exposed to the same dangers and vicissitudes, none of the Poles' officers would be killed although six were wounded, while the Dutch regiment lost ten killed and four wounded. Chlapowski was unusually chauvinistic, even for a Pole, but these Poles were picked veterans and this war was the first campaign for most of the Dutch.

17. It would be the contents of this phial that Napoleon, according to Caulaincourt, would swallow after his first abdication, at Fontainebleau in April 1814; but by then 'the poison had lost its force' and merely made him vomit.

BIBLIOGRAPHY

This bibliography is supplementary to that given in *1812: The March on Moscow*, (Greenhill Books, London, and Stackpole Books, Mechanicsburg, Pa., 1993). For the sake of convenience I have reiterated all authors whose memoirs are here important.

Anthouard, Charles-Nicolas. 'Notes et documents du Général Anthouard', published by F. Masson in *Carnet de la Sabretache*, 1906, pp. 286–307, 337–54, 386–409, 452–69

Aubry, Capitaine Thomas-Joseph. *Souvenirs du 12ème de Chasseurs, 1799–1815*. Paris, 1889

Auvray, Pierre. 'Souvenirs militaires de Pierre Auvray, sous-lieutenant au 23 régiment de dragons (1897-1815)', *Carnet de la Sabretache*, 1919

Bausset, Joseph, Baron de. *Mémoires anecdotiques sur l'intérieur du Palais et de quelques événements de l'Empire, de 1805-1814*. Baudoin, Paris, 1827–9

Beauchamp, A. de B-Ch. *Histoire de la destruction de Moscou, en 1812 et des événements qui ont précédé, accompagné et suivi ce désastre* (trans. from German), Paris, 1822

Beaulieu, Drujon de. *Souvenirs d'un militaire pendant quelques années du règne de Napoléon Bonaparte*, vol. I, Paris, 1831

Begos, Louis. *Souvenirs des campagnes du lieutenant-général Louis Begos, ancien capitaine adjutant-major au 2ème régiment suisse au service de la France*. A. Delafontaine, Lausanne,1859

Belliard, Augustin-Daniel. *Mémoires du comte Belliard, lieutenant-général, pair de France, écrits par lui-même, recueillis et mis en ordre par M. Vinet, l'un de ses aides-de-camp*. Paris, 1842

Bertin, Georges. *La Campagne de 1812 d'après des témoins oculaires*. Flammarion, Paris, 1895

Bertrand, Vincent. *Mémoires du capitaine Vincent Bertrand, recueillis et publiés par le colonel Chaland de la Guillanche*. Siraudeau, Angers, 1909

Beugnot, Jean-Claude, comte. *Mémoires du comte Beugnot*. Paris, 1866, Librairie Hachette, Paris, 1959

Beulay, Honoré. *Mémoires d'un grenadier de la Grande Armée (18 avril 1808 – 18 octobre 1815), Préface du commandant Driant*. Champion, Paris, 1907

Biot, Hubert-François. *Souvenirs anecdotiques et militaires du Colonel Biot, aide-de-camp du Général Pajol, avec une introduction et des notes par le comte Fleury*. Vivien, Paris, 1901

Blaze, Elzéar, *La Vie Militaire sous le Premier Empire, ou Moeurs de Garnison, du*

Bivouac et de la Caserne. Paris, 1837. Translated as *Life in Napoleon's Army: The Memoirs of Captain Elzéar Blaze*, with commentary by Lieutenant-General Charles Napier, and introduction by Philip J. Haythornthwaite (Greenhill Books, London, 1995); and newly translated as *Military Life under the First Empire* by John R. Elting (The Emperor's Press, Chicago, Illinois, 1995)

Bonnan, C-A. *Mémoire sur la Russie 1812*. nd

Bonnet, Guillaume. 'Journal du capitaine Bonnet du 18ème ligne', in *Carnet de la Sabretache*, 1912, pp. 641–72

Boulart, Jean-François. *Mémoires militaires du Général Baron Boulart sur les guerres de la République et l'Empire*. Librairie Illustrée, Paris, 1892

Bourgoing, Baron Paul-Charles-Amable de. *Souvenirs d'histoire contemporaine. Épisodes militaires et politiques*. Paris, 1864

– *Souvenirs militaires du baron de Bourgoing (1791–1815), publiés par le baron Pierre de Bourgoing*. Plon-Nourrit, Paris, 1897

Brandt, Heinrich von. *Souvenirs d'un officier polonais. Scènes de ma vie militaire en Espagne et en Russie (1808–1812)*, ed. Baron Ernouf, Charpentier, Paris, 1877

Bréaut des Marlots, Jean. *Lettre d'un capitaine de cuirassiers sur la campagne de Russie, publiée par Leher*. Paris, chez tous les librairies, 1885

Bussy, Marc. in *Soldats suisses au service de la France*. Geneva, 1909

Calosso, Jean. *Mémoires d'un vieux soldat*. Gianini, Turin, 1857

Castellane, Victor-Elisabeth Boniface, comte de. *Journal du maréchal de Castellane (1804–1862)*, 5 vols., Plon-Nourrit, Paris, 1895–7

Caulaincourt, Armand de. *Mémoires du Général de Caulaincourt, duc de Vicence, Grand Ecuyer de l'Empereur*. Introduction and notes by Jean Hanoteau. 3 vols., Plon-Nourrit, Paris, 1933. English trans. vol. 1 *Memoirs of General de Caulaincourt*. Cassell, London, 1935; vol. 2 *With Napoleon in Russia*. Morrow, New York, 1935; vol. 3 *No Peace with Napoleon*. Morrow, New York, and Cassell, London, 1936

Chambray, marquis de. *Histoire de l'Expédition de Russie*. Paris, 1825

Chandler, David. *The Campaigns of Napoleon*. Macmillan, New York, 1966, and Weidenfeld, London, 1966

– *Dictionary of the Napoleonic Wars*. Macmillan, New York, 1979, and Arms & Armour Press, London, 1979; Simon and Schuster, New York, and Greenhill Books, London, 1993

– *The Illustrated Napoleon*. Henry Holt, New York, and Greenhill Books, London, 1990

– *On the Napoleonic Wars*. Greenhill Books, London, and Stackpole, Mechanicsburg, Pa., 1994

Chevalier, Jean-Michel. *Souvenirs des guerres napoléoniennes, publiés d'après le manuscrit original par Jean Mistler et Hélène Michaud*. Paris, 1970

Chuquet, Arthur. *1812, La guerre de Russie, Notes et Documents.* 3 vols., Paris, 1912

Clemenso, H. 'Souvenirs d'un officier valaisan' in *Annales Valaisannes*, 1957, Ch. 5, pp. 12–110

Coignet, Capitaine Jean-Roch. *Cahiers.* Hachette, Paris, 1883, English trans. *The Notebooks of Captain Coignet.* Davies, London, 1928, reprinted Greenhill Books, London, 1986

Curely, Jean-Nicholas. *Le général Curely. Itinéraire d'un chevalier léger de la Grande Armée (1793–1815) publié d'après un manuscrit authentique par le général Thoumas.* Paris, 1887

Dedem van der Gelder (see Gelder)

Denniée, P. P. *Itinéraire de l'Empereur Napoléon.* Paris, 1842

Dumas, Mathieu. *Souvenirs du lieutenant-général comte Mathieu Dumas de 1770 à 1836, publiés par son fils.* 3 vols., Paris, 1839

Dumonceau, François. *Mémoires du général comte François Dumonceau, publiés d'après le manuscrit original par Jean Puraye.* 3 vols. Brépols, Brussels, 1958–63

Dupuy, Victor. *Souvenirs militaires, 1794–1816.* Calman-Lévy, Paris, 1892

Dutheillet de la Mothe, Aubin. *Mémoires du lieutenant-colonel Aubin Dutheillet de la Mothe.* Brussels, 1899

Duverger, B.T. *Mes Aventures dans la Campagne de Russie.* Paris, nd

Elting, John R. *Swords Around a Throne.* London, 1989

Englund, Peter. *Poltava.* London, 1994

Everts, Henri-Pierre (1777–1851). 'Campagne et captivité en Russie, extraits des mémoires inédits du général-major H. P. Everts, traduits par M. E. Jordens' in *Carnet de la Sabretache*, 1901, pp. 620–38, 686–702, Paris, 1900

Faber du Faur, G. de. *La campagne de Russie (1812), d'après le journal illustré d'un témoin oculaire.* Texte explicatif, par F. de Kausler, Introduction par A. Dayot, Flammarion, Paris, 1895

Fain, Baron Agathon-Jean-François. *Manuscrit de Mil-Huit Cent Douze, contenant le précis des événements de cette année, pour servir à l'histoire de l'Empereur Napoléon; par le baron Fain, son secrétaire-archiviste à cette époque.* 2 vols. Paris, 1827

– *Mémoires du Baron Fain, premier secrétaire du cabinet de l'Empereur, publiés par ses arrière-petits-fils.* Plon-Nourrit, Paris, 1908.

Fezensac, M. le duc de. *Souvenirs militaires de 1804 à 1814.* Domaine, Paris, 1863

– *A Journal of the Russian Campaign of 1812.* London, 1852; Trotman, Cambridge, 1988

Franchi. *Récit de Franchi, sous-officier dans la compagnie d'élite des 8ème Chasseurs à Cheval, Loisirs d'un soldat.* Etienne et Beauvoir, Le Mans, 1861

François, Charles. *Journal du Capitaine François (dit le Dromadaire d'Egypte), 1793–1830.* 2 vols., Carrington, Paris, 1903–4

Freytag, Jean-David. *Mémoires du général Freytag, ancien commandant de Sinnamary et de Conamama dans la Guyane française, accompagnés de notes historiques, topographiques et critiques par M.C. de B.* Nepveu, Paris, 1824

Fusil, Louise. *Souvenirs d'une Femme sur la retraite de Russie.* 2 vols., Dumont, Paris, 1841

Gelder, Baron A-B-G van der. *Mémoires publiés d'après le manuscrit original par Jean Puraye.* 3 vols., Brussels, 1958–63

Geyl, Pieter. *Napoleon, For and Against.* Jonathan Cape, London, 1949, 1964, 1968

Gourgaud, Gaspard. *Napoleon and the Grande Armée in Russia.* A critical examination of Count Philippe de Ségur's writings. Anthony Finlay, Philadelphia, 1825

Griois, Charles Pierre Lubin. *Mémoires du général Griois, 1792–1822.* 2 vols., Plon-Nourrit, Paris, 1909

Grunwald, Constantin de. 'L'Incendie de Moscou, mystère de la campagne de Russie' in *Miroir de l'Histoire* 68 (1955), pp. 287–95

– *La Campagne de Russie.* A collection of excerpts from the participants' memoirs, etc. Julliard, Paris, 1963

Guye, A. *Le Bataillon de Neuchâtel, dit les Canaris, au service de Napoléon à la braconnière.* Neuchâtel, 1964

Henckens, Lieutenant J. L. *Mémoires se rapportant à son service militaire au 6ème Régiment de Chasseurs à cheval français de février 1803 à août 1816.* Publiés par son fils E. F. C. Henckens. Nijhoff, The Hague, 1910.

Herzen, A. *Erinnerungen von Alexander Herzen, aus dem russischen übertragen, herausgegeben und eingeleitet von Dr. Otto Buck.* 2 vols., Wiegandt und Grieben, Berlin, 1907

Holzhausen Paul. *Die Deutschen in Russland, 1812. Leben under Leiden auf der Moskauer Herrfahrt.* Morawe und Scheffeldt Verlag, Berlin, 1912

– *Ein Verwandter Goethes in russischer Feldzuge, 1812.* Berlin, 1912

Jacquemot, Porphyre. 'Carnet de route d'un officier d'artillerie (1812–1813)', in *Souvenirs et Mémoires,* pp. 97–121, 1899

James, J. T. *Journal of a Tour through Russia.* London, 1813

Kalckreuth, von. 'Erinnerungen' in *Zeitschrift für Kunst, Wissenschaft und Geschichte des Krieges,* V, 1835

Labaume, Eugène. *Relation circonstanciée de la campagne de Russie.* Paris, 1814 and successive augmented editions. A new translation by T. Dunlas Pillans, with an introduction by W.T. Stead, appeared as *The Crime of 1812 and its Retribution.* Andrew Melrose, London, 1912

Langeron, A.-L. Andrault comte de. *Mémoires de Langeron, général d'infanterie dans l'armée russe. Campagnes de 1812, 1813, 1814. Publiés d'après le manuscrit original pour la Société d'histoire contemporaine par L.-G. F. Picard.* Paris, 1902

Larrey, Baron Dominique-Jean. *Mémoires de chirurgie militaire et campagnes.* J. Smith, Paris, 1812–17

Lassus-Marcilly, F.N. 'Notes sur la campagne de Russie', in *Carnet de la Sabretache*, 1914, pp. 86–92

Legler, Thomas. *Beresina.* Bern, 1942

Lejeune, Louis-François. *Mémoires du général Lejeune, publiés par M. Germain Bapst.* 2 vols., Paris, 1895–6

Lemoine (-Montigny), E. *Souvenirs anecdotiques d'un officier de la Grande Armée.* Firmin-Didot, Paris, 1833

Le Roy, C. F. M. *Souvenirs de Leroy, major d'infanterie, vétéran des armées de la République et de l'Empire.* Dijon, 1908

Lignières, Marie-Henry, comte de. *Souvenirs de la Grande Armée et de la Vieille Garde Impériale.* Pierre-Roget, Paris, 1933

Lorencez, Guillaume Latrille de. *Souvenirs militaires du général comte de Lorencez, publiés par le baron Pierre de Bourgoing.* Paris, 1902

Macdonald, Marshal J.-E.-J.-A. *Souvenirs du maréchal Macdonald duc de Tarente.* Introduction par Camille Rousset. Paris, 1892

Mailly(-Nesle), A.-A.-A., comte de. *Mon journal pendant la campagne de Russie écrit de mémoire après mon retour à Paris.* Paris, 1841

Majou, L. J. L. 'Journal du commandant Majou', in *Revue des Etudes Historiques*, 1899, pp. 178–202

Méneval, Baron Claude-François de. *Mémoires pour servir à l'histoire de Napoléon I depuis 1802 jusqu'à 1815.* Paris, 1894; English trans., London, 1894

Merme, J. M. *Histoire Militaire.* Paris, 1852

Molé, Mathieu, comte, marquis de Noailles. *Le comte Molé (1781–1855). Sa vie, ses mémoires.* 6 vols., Champion, Paris, 1922

– *Souvenirs d'un témoin de la Révolution et de l'Empire (1791–1803). Pages inédites, retrouvées en 1939, publiées et présentées par la marquise de Noailles.* Le Milieu du Monde, Geneva, 1943

Muraldt, Albrecht von. *Beresina.* Bern, 1942

Nafziger, George. *Napoleon's Invasion of Russia.* Presidio Press, Novato, Ca., 1988

Ney, Maréchal Michel, prince de la Moskova, duc d'Elchingen. *Mémoires du Maréchal Ney. Publiés par sa Famille.* Fournes, Paris, 1833; English trans., Bull and Churton, London, 1833; Carey, Pa, 1834

Nottat, N. 'Souvenirs de la campagne de Russie', in *Revue du Train*, 1953, pp. 35–41

Paixhans, General Henri-Joseph de. *Retraite de Moscou, Notes écrites au Quartier-Général de l'Empereur.* Metz, 1868

Pastoret, Amédée-David, marquis de. 'De Witebsk à la Bérézina' in *Revue de Paris*, April 1902, pp. 465–98

Pils, François. *Journal de marche du Grenadier Pils (1804–1814), recueilli et annoté par M. Raoul de Cisternes. Illustrations d'après des dessins originaux de PILS.* Offendorff, Paris, 1895

Pion des Loches, Antoine-Augustin. *Mes Campagnes (1792–1815). Notes et correspondance du colonel d'artillerie Pion des Loches, mises en ordre et publiées par Maurice Chipon et Léonce Pingaud.* Paris, 1889

Planat de la Faye, Nicolas Louis. *Vie de Planat de la Faye, aide-de-camp des généraux Lariboisière et Drouot, officier d'ordonnance de Napoléon 1ᵉʳ. Souvenirs, Lettres, dictés et annotés par sa veuve.* Offendorff, Paris, 1895

Pouget, François-René (known as Baron Cailloux). *Souvenirs de guerre du général baron Pouget, publiés par Mme de Boisdeffre.* Paris, 1895

Poutier, R. *Souvenirs du chirurgien Poutier sur la campagne de Russie.* Brive, 1967

Pradt, D.-G. Dufour de. *Histoire de l'Ambassade dans le Grand Duché de Varsovie en 1812.* Paris, 1815

Prétet, Ch-J. 'Relation de la campagne de Russie', in *Revue Bourguignonne*, pp. 419–51

Puybusque, L.-G. de. *Souvenirs d'un invalide pendant le dernier demi-siècle.* 2 vols., Paris, 1840

Rapp, Jean. *Mémoires écrits par lui-même et publiés par sa famille.* Bossange, Paris, 1823; English trans., Henry Colburn, 1823; Trotman, Cambridge, 1985

Réguinot. *Le Sergeant Isolé.* Paris, 1831

Renoult, A. J. *Souvenirs d'un docteur.* Paris, 1862

Rigau, Dieudonné. *Souvenirs des Guerres de l'Empire, avec reflexions, etc.* Paris, 1845

Rocca, A. J. M. de. *In the Peninsula with a French Hussar.* Greenhill Books, London, 1990; Presidio Press, Novato, Ca., USA

Roeder, Helen. *The Ordeal of Captain Roeder, from the Diary of an Officer of the First Battalion of Hessian Lifeguards during the Moscow Campaign of 1812–13.* Trans. and ed. from the original manuscript. Methuen, London, 1960.

Roguet, François. *Mémoires militaires du lieutenant-général comte Roguet, colonel en second des grenadiers à pied de la Vieille Garde.* Dumaine, Paris, 1862–5

Roos, Heinrich von. *Avec Napoléon en Russie. Souvenirs de la campagne de 1812, traduits par le lieutenant-colonel Buat.* Introduction et notes par P. Holzhausen. Chapelot, Paris, 1913

– *Souvenirs d'un médecin de la Grande Armée, traduits d'après l'édition originale de 1832 par Mme Lamotte.* Perrin, Paris, 1913. (These two books have been translated from the original *Ein Jahr aus meinem Leben oder Reise von den westlichen Ufern der Donau an die Nara, südlich von Moskva, und zurück an die Beresina, mit der grossen Armee Napoleons, im Jahre 1812*. St. Petersburg, 1832)

Roustam Raza. *Souvenirs de Roustam, mameluk de Napoléon*. Introduction et notes de Paul Cottin, préface de Frédéric Masson. Paris, 1821

Saint-Chamans, A.-A.-R. *Mémoires du général comte de Saint-Chamans, ancien aide-de-camp du Maréchal Soult, 1802–1832*. Paris, 1896

Sayve, A. de. *Souvenirs de Pologne et scènes militaires du campagne de Russie 1812*. Paris, 1833

Schuerman, A. *Itinéraire de l'Empereur Napoléon 1ᵉʳ*. Paris, 1911

Schumacher, Gaspard. *Souvenirs*. Paris, nd

Séruzier, T.-J.-J, Baron. *Mémoires militaires du baron Séruzier, colonel d'artillerie légère, mis en ordre et rédigés par son ami M. Le Mière de Corvey*. Paris, 1823

Soltyk, comte Roman. *Napoléon en 1812. Mémoires historiques et militaires sur la campagne de Russie*. Bertrand, Paris,1836

Staël, Germaine de. *Mémoires de dix années d'exil*. Paris, 1848; English trans., London, 1814.

Stendhal (Henri Beyle). *Journal de Stendhal (1801–1814), publié par Casimir Stryienski et François de Nion*. Paris, 1888, Gollancz, 1955

– *Vie de Henri Brulard, nouvelle édition établie et commentée par Henri Martineau*. Le Divan, Paris, 1955

Stiegler, Gaston. *Le Maréchal Oudinot, duc de Reggio, d'après les souvenirs inédits de la Maréchale*. 2nd edn., Plon, Paris, 1894; English trans, Henry, London, 1896

Suckow, Karl von. *Aus meinem Soldatenleben*. Stuttgart, 1862; French trans. *D'Iéna à Moscou, fragments de ma vie*. Paris, 1902

Surugué, l'Abbé Andrien. *Lettre sur l'Incendie de Moscou en 1812*. Paris, 1821, and *Un Témoin de la campagne de Russie, par Léon Mirot*. Paris, 1914

Tarle, E. *Napoleon's Invasion of Russia, 1812*. Moscow, 1938; London and New York, 1942

Tascher, Maurice de. *Notes de campagne (1806–1813)*. Châteauroux, 1938

Tchitchakov (Tchitchakoff), P.V. *Relation du passage de la Bérésina*. Paris, 1814

– *Mémoires*. Berlin, 1855

Teste, François-Antoine. 'Souvenirs du général baron Teste', in *Carnet de la Sabretache*, 1906, 1907, 1911, 1912

Thirion, (de Metz), Auguste. *Souvenirs militaires, 1807–1818*. Paris, 1892

Trafcon, J. *Carnet de campagne*. Paris, 1914

Turno, Boris. 'Les Mémoires du général Turno, par A. Skalkowski', in *Revue des Etudes Napoléoniennes*, vol. II, pp. 99–116, 129–45. Paris, 1931

Van Vlijmen, B. R. F. *Vers la Bérésina*. Paris, nd

Vaudoncourt, F.-G. de. *Mémoires pour servir à la guerre entre la France et la Russie en 1812, par un officier de l'état-major français*. 2 vols., Deboffe, London, 1815

– Quinze années d'un proscrit. 4 vols., Paris, 1835

Victor, Claude Perrin, Maréchal, duc de Bellune. *Mémoires*. vols., V and VI, Paris, 1847

Villiers, C. G. L. de. *Douze ans de campagnes.* Paris, nd

Villemain, Abel François. *Souvenirs contemporains d'histoire et de littérature.* 2 vols., Paris, 1854

Vionnet, Lieutenant-Général Louis-Joseph, vicomte de Marignoné. *Campagnes de Russie et de Saxe, 1812–1813.*

– *Souvenirs d'un ex-commandant des Grenadiers de la Vieille Garde, avec une préface de Rodolf Vagnair.* Paris, 1899

Walter, Jakob. *The Diary of a Napoleonic Foot Soldier,* ed. Marc Raeff, Windrush Press, Gloucestershire, and Doubleday, New York, 1991

Warchot, R. *Capitaine au 8ème chevauxlegers polonais. Notice biographique sur le général-major Edouard de Mercx de Corbais.* Namur, 1855

Ysarn, François-Joseph d': *Rélation du sejour des Français à Moscou et de l'incendie de cette ville en 1812, par un habitant de Moscou annoté et publié par A. Gadaruel.* Brussels, 1871

Zalusky, Joseph-Henri. 'Souvenirs du général comte Zalusky. Les chevaulégers de la garde dans la campagne de 1812', in *Carnet de la Sabretache,* 1897, pp. 485–95, 521–33, 601–15

A work I would particularly recommend to all students of the period is Jean Tulard's admirable *Bibliographie critique des mémoires sur le Consulat et l'Empire.* Librairie Droz, Geneva and Paris, 1971. This, although confined to memoirs written in or translated into French, is exhaustive and useful for evaluation.

INDEX

257

1812
THE GREAT RETREAT

'The habit of victory cost us even dearer in retreat. The glorious habit of always marching forwards made us veritable schoolboys when it came to retreating. Never was a retreat worse organised.'

Caulaincourt.

'Extreme misery knows not the law of humanity. One sacrifices everything to the law of self-preservation.'

Louise Fusil, at the Berezina.

'I have never, to this day of writing in 1828, seen an account of the retreat that could be described as exaggerated. Indeed I'm sure it would be impossible to exaggerate the misery endured by those who took part in it.'

Lieutenant Vossler.

'For the honour of humanity, perhaps, I ought not to describe all these scenes of horror, but I have determined to write down all I saw. And if in this campaign acts of infamy were committed, there were noble actions, too.'

Sergeant Bourgogne.

1812
THE GREAT RETREAT
told by the survivors

PAUL BRITTEN AUSTIN

GREENHILL BOOKS, LONDON
STACKPOLE BOOKS, PENNYSYLVANIA

1812: The Great Retreat
first published 1996 by
Greenhill Books, Lionel Leventhal Limited, Park House,
1 Russell Gardens, London NW11 9NN
and
Stackpole Books, 5067 Ritter Road,
Mechanicsburg, PA 17055, USA.

British Library Cataloguing in Publication Data
Britten Austin, Paul
1812: The Great Retreat
1. Napoleonic Wars, 1800–1815—Campaigns—Russia
I. Title
940.2'7
ISBN 1-85367-246-7

Library of Congress Cataloging-in-Publication Data
Austin, Paul Britten
1812 : The Great Retreat / Paul Britten Austin
464 p. 24 cm.
Includes bibliographical references and index.
ISBN 1-85367-246-7 (hbk)
1. Napoleonic Wars, 1800–1815—Campaigns—Russia
—Personal narratives, French 2. Russia—History, Military—
1801–1917—Sources 3. Napoleon I, Emperor of the French,
1769–1821—Military leadership 4. France. Armée—History—
Napoleonic Wars, 1800–1815—Sources. I. Title.
DC235.A86 1996
940.2'7—dc20   96–29074

Designed and edited by DAG Publications Ltd.
Designed by David Gibbons; edited by Michael Boxall.

Printed and bound in Great Britain by
Creative Print and Design (Wales) Ebbw Vale

CONTENTS

To the English-speaking world's
two greatest Napoleonic scholars of our century,
Professor David Chandler, D. Litt. (Oxon)
and
Colonel John R. Elting (USA. Rtd)
this volume is dedicated in admiration and gratitude
for all their kindness and generosity.

PREFACE

I have really nothing to add to the prefaces of the first two volumes of this work: *1812 – the March on Moscow* and *1812 – Napoleon in Moscow* – except to say that this volume completes the drama of the Russian disaster, as experienced by the invaders and described by them in their own words. For my translation and other methods of presenting my 'word film' the patient reader should turn to the prefaces of those volumes.

The story has of course been told innumerable times. But apart from Sergeant Bourgogne's immortal classic, whether the sheer magnitude of the event has wearied authors or their publishers, it has always been, for understandable reasons, in résumé. As the reader will see, there are many first-hand accounts; indeed the body of material I've drawn on, some 160 participants, has been almost too great, and the fewer the survivors the more detailed their narratives become. First and last my project has been to reconstitute, in maximum close-up, a fragment of past time. Even this, of course, is an illusion. The most objective and circumstantial account adds up to only a millionth part of the reality. Hundreds, perhaps thousands, of other participants must have kept diaries that perished with them in the snows. The mind boggles at the task that would have presented itself if they hadn't! The relevant surviving details have been what has fascinated me. If some are too gruesome for the tender-minded reader I can only suggest he – or she – skip them; but not their implications. To have omitted them would have been intellectually dishonest. *Bellum dulce inexpertis*, says Erasmus: 'How charming is not war to those who've never been in it!'

Despite the ever-growing mass of first-hand material (I've used no others, and new memoirs are always being unearthed), I've tried to let the whole compose itself into what is, I hope, a kind of outsize symphony, whose first brilliant bars were struck by all the trumpets and drums of the Imperial Guard at the Niemen on that Midsummer's Day of 1812 – only to end in the few survivors' frozen 'cello tones of horror and despair.

Lastly, on a personal note. My book has taken almost 25 years to compose. If I've persisted – I might almost say had the fortitude – long enough to complete it, it's not been because of any abiding obsession with military history as such; but because of the striking and manifold glimpses into human nature it affords, until at times the 1812 story has even seemed to be a tragic paradigm of human existence: – the outset's overweening optimism, not to say arrogance – the flawed calculations – the horrific results – the raw egoism of survival – the staunchness of some, the cowardice and fatuity of others, the heroism and true greatness of a few – the friends left by the wayside ... *Homo lupus hominem* – the leopard, alas, hasn't changed its DNA, as our own 'unforgivable century' has all too amply shown. No philosopher of the pessimist school could want a better

7

instance of what Dr Johnson called 'the vanity of human wishes', here geometrically demonstrated by what might be called the aesthetic of its own historical logic. I've had to make nothing up.

My gratitude goes to my publisher Lionel Leventhal for his devotion to a project which in the upshot has run to as many words as there were men in the Grand Army. It was in his office, long ago, our project was conceived. And with it – and with me – he has had almost half a working lifetime's patience. We are both of us grateful to three experts who have given the text their critical attention: namely, Philip J. Haythornthwaite, Digby Smith and John R. Elting, all themselves distinguished authors in the Napoleonic field. Their keen eyes and immense knowledge have eliminated many an error, larger or smaller. I should also particularly like to thank Assistant Professor Algirdas Jakubcionis of Vilnius University for his ready help in suggesting and providing illustrations; and, once again, Peter Harrington of Brown University, Providence, Rhode Island, USA, for helping with the illustrations.

Dawlish, S. Devon, 1996

SOME IMPORTANT EYEWITNESSES

Pierre Auvray, captain, 23rd Dragoons.

Louis Begos, captain adjutant-major, 2nd Swiss Infantry Regiment.

Vincent Bertrand, carabinier sergeant, 7th Light Infantry, Gérard's division, I Corps.

Honoré Beulay, sous-lieutenant, 36th Line, Partonneaux's division, IX Corps.

Hubert Biot, captain, ADC to General Pajol.

Guillaume Bonnet, captain, 18th Line, Razout's division, III Corps.

Jean-François Boulart, major, Guard artillery.

A.-J.-B.-F. Bourgogne, sergeant, Fusiliers-Grenadiers, Young (Middle) Guard.

Paul de Bourgoing, lieutenant, 5th Tirailleurs of the Guard, interpreter to General Delaborde, Young Guard.

Heinrich von Brandt, captain, 2nd Regiment, Vistula Legion.

Jean-Marc Bussy, voltigeur, 3rd Swiss, Merle's division, II Corps.

Jean Calosso, regimental sergeant-major, 24th Chasseurs à Cheval, Castex's brigade, II Corps.

V. E. B. Castellane, captain, orderly officer at IHQ.

Armand de Caulaincourt, general, Master of the Horse, responsible for IHQ transports and the courier service.

Désiré Chlapowski, colonel, 1st Polish Guard Lancers, Colbert's lancer brigade.

Jean-Nicholas Curély, regimental sergeant-major, 20th Chasseurs à

Cheval, Corbineau's brigade, II Corps.

Dedem van der Gelder, general of brigade, ex-diplomat, attached to IHQ.

François Dumonceau, captain commanding a company of the 2nd ('Red/Dutch') Guard Lancers, Colbert's lancer brigade.

Victor Dupuy, colonel, 7th Hussars, Bruyère's division, 1st Cavalry Corps.

B. T. Duverger, captain, paymaster to Davout's I Corps.

Henri-Pierre Everts, major, 33rd Line, Dufour's division, I Corps.

Baron A.-J.-F. Fain, Napoleon's Second Secretary.

G. de Faber du Faur, major, commanding reserve artillery, Ney's III Corps.

Raymond Faure, surgeon, Grouchy's 3rd Cavalry Corps (prisoner).

Fezensac, duke, colonel, 4th Line, Razout's division, III Corps.

Charles François, 'the Dromedary of Egypt', captain commanding the 30th Line's grenadier company, Morand's division, I Corps.

Jean-David Freytag, general of brigade, III Corps.

Louise Fusil, actress, travelling with IHQ.

Gaspard Gourgaud, baron, colonel, 1st *officier d'ordonnance*, IHQ.

Lubin Griois, colonel of horse artillery, 3rd Cavalry Corps.

J. L. Henckens, NCO, acting adjutant-major to the 6th Chasseurs à Cheval, Chastel's division, 3rd Cavalry Corps.

Dirk van Hogendorp, baron, general, ADC to Napoleon, governor of Vilna province.

Porphyre Jacquemot, lieutenant, 5th Company, 5th Artillery Regiment, at Vilna.

Henri de Jomini, baron, general, military theorist, governor of Smolensk city.

von Kalckreuth, lieutenant, 2nd Prussian hussars, Niewievski's brigade.

Bellot de Kergorre, war commissary in charge of a Treasury wagon, marching with IHQ.

Captain Eugène Labaume on staff of Prince Eugène's IV Corps, author of the first published account of the campaign (1814).

D.-J. Larrey, baron, Surgeon-General, IHQ.

Cesare de Laugier, adjutant-major of the Guardia d'Onore of the Kingdom of Italy, IV Corps.

Thomas Legler, lieutenant, 1st Swiss Regiment, Merle's division, II Corps.

L.-F. Lejeune, baron, general, until Borodino one of Berthier's ADCs; thereafter chief-of-staff to Davout.

C. F. M. Le Roy, lieutenant-colonel, 85th Line, Dessaix's division, I Corps.

M.-H. de Lignières, count, captain, 1st Guard Foot Chasseurs.

G. L. de Lorencez, general, chief-of-staff to Marshal Oudinot, II Corps.

J.-E.-J.-A. Macdonald, marshal, Duke of Taranto, commanding X Corps.

A.-A.-A. Mailly-Nesle, count, sous-lieutenant, 2nd Carabiniers, riding with IHQ.

Marcelline Marbot, colonel of the 23th Chasseurs, Castex brigade, II Corps.

Albrecht von Muraldt, lieutenant, 4th Bavarian Chevaulegers, Ornano's light cavalry brigade, attached to IV Corps.

Amédée de Pastoret, marquis, war commissary at Witebsk.

Pierre Pelleport, viscount, colonel, 18th Line, Razout's division, III Corps.

François Pils, 'grenadier', artist, batman to Marshal Oudinot, II Corps.

A.-A. Pion des Loches, major, Guard foot artillery.

Planat de la Faye, lieutenant, secretary to General Lariboisière, artillery staff.

F.-R. Pouget, baron, general, governor of Witebsk.

D.-G.-F. Dufour de Pradt, bishop, ambassador at Warsaw.

Jean Rapp, general, ADC to Napoleon.

Roch-Godart, baron, general, governor of Vilna city.

L.-V.-L. Rochechouart, émigré count, serving under General Langeron in Tchitchakov's army.

Franz Roeder, captain, Hessian Footguards.

François Roguet, baron, general, commanding 2nd Division, Imperial Guard.

Heinrich von Roos, surgeon, 3rd Württemberg Chasseurs.

Abraham Rosselet, captain, 3rd Swiss Regiment, Merle's division, II Corps.

M.-J.-T. Rossetti, colonel, ADC to Murat.

N. T. Sauvage, lieutenant of the Train, VIII Corps.

Philippe de Ségur, count, general, assistant prefect of the Palace, in charge of IHQ's mules.

T.-J.-J. Séruzier, baron, colonel of horse artillery, 2nd Cavalry Corps.

Roman Soltyk, count, captain, attached to IHQ's Topographical Department.

Karl von Suckow, captain, Württemberg cavalry, III Corps.

Maurice Tascher, lieutenant of chasseurs à cheval.

F.-A. Teste, baron, general, governor at Viazma.

Auguste Thirion, regimental sergeant-major, 2nd Cuirassiers, Saint-Germain's division, 1st Cavalry Corps.

L.-J. Vionnet, major, Fusiliers-Grenadiers, Young (Middle) Guard.

H. A. Vossler, lieutenant, Prince Louis of Prussia's Hussars.

Jakob Walter, private in a Württemberg infantry regiment, III Corps.

R. Warchot, captain, 8th Polish Lancers.

C.-A.-W. Wedel, count, general, VI Corps.

Sir Robert Wilson, general, the British government's liaison officer at Kutusov's headquarters.

J.-H. Zalusky, captain, 1st Polish Guard Lancers.

For bibliographical details of these and other sources I refer the reader to the comprehensive bibliographies in *1812 – The March on Moscow* and *1812 – Napoleon in Moscow.* Any additional sources are given in the Notes.

Note:
First references to the eyewitnesses
whose accounts make up this 'documentary'
of Napoleon's retreat from Russia appear in
italic.

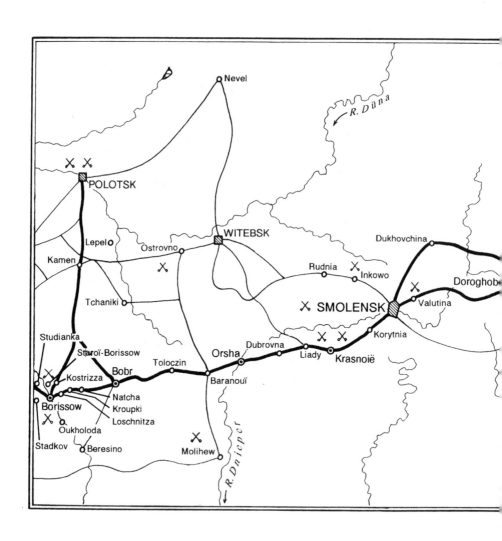

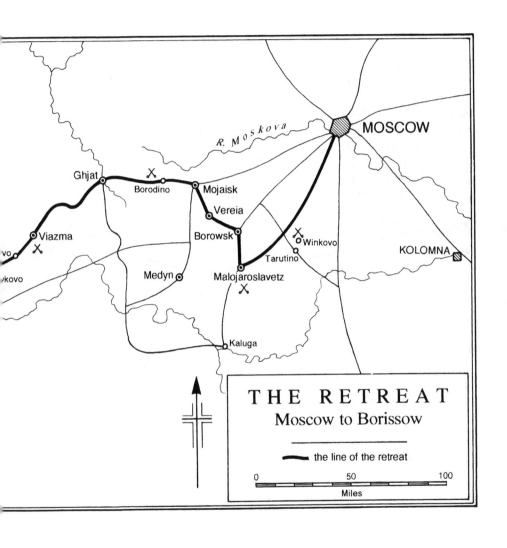

R. M o s k o v a

MOSCOW

Ghjat
Borodino
Mojaisk
Vereia
Viazma
Borowsk
Winkovo
vo
Tarutino
KOLOMNA
kovo
Medyn
Malojaroslavetz

Kaluga

THE RETREAT
Moscow to Borissow

━━ the line of the retreat

0   50   100

Miles

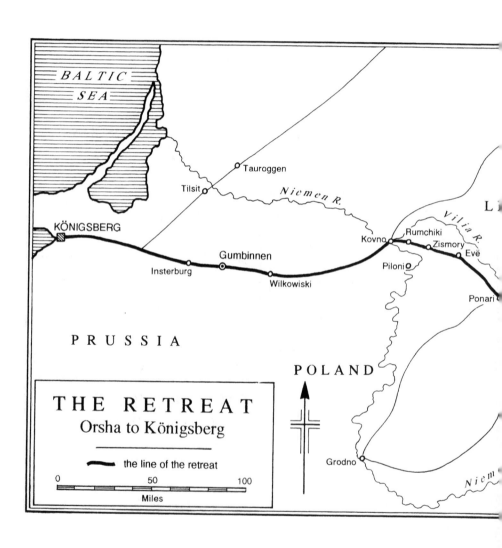

BALTIC
SEA

Tauroggen

Tilsit

Niemen R.

KÖNIGSBERG

Rumchiki

Kovno

Vilia R.

L

Zismory

Evë

Gumbinnen

Piloni

Insterburg

Wilkowiski

Ponari

PRUSSIA

POLAND

THE RETREAT
Orsha to Königsberg

the line of the retreat

Grodno

0   50   100

Miles

Niem

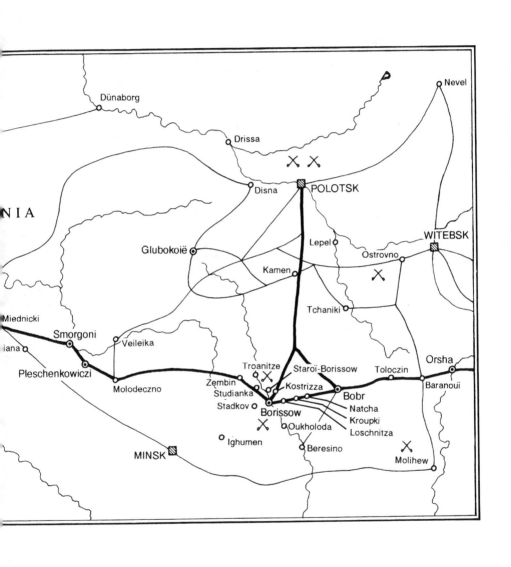

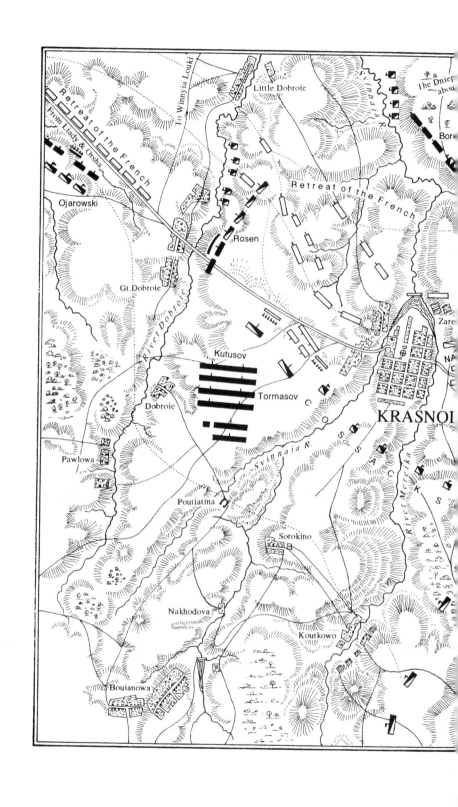

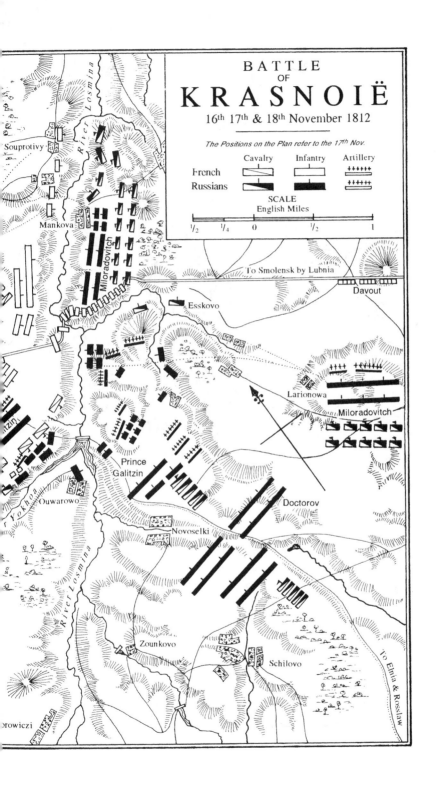

BATTLE
OF
KRASNOIË
16th 17th & 18th November 1812

The Positions on the Plan refer to the 17th Nov.

	Cavalry	Infantry	Artillery
French			++++++
Russians			+++++

SCALE
English Miles

$1/2$ $1/4$ 0 $1/2$ 1

Souprotivy

River Losmina

Mankova

Miloradovitch

To Smolensk by Lubnia

Davout

Esskovo

Larionowa

Miloradovitch

Prince
Galitzin

Ouwarowo

Doctorov

Novoselki

River Losmina

Zounkovo

Schilovo

To Elnia & Rosslaw

rowiczi

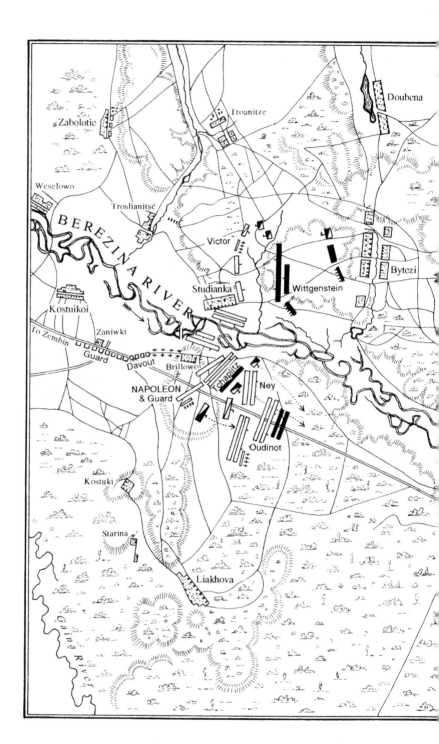

THE CROSSING
OF THE
BEREZINA
26th 27th & 28th Nov! 1812.

	Cavalry	Infantry	Artillery
French			+++++
Russians			+++++

SCALE

1   ½   0   1   2

English Miles

Vougly

To Orsha

Platov

BORISSOW

Zasténok

Staroi Borissow

enstein

Nowoi
Stakhov

BEREZINA RIVER

Bridgehead
Dymki

To Bobr

khov

Tchichakov

Stakhov

Brodnia R.

akov

THE EVENTS SO FAR

In the midsummer of 1812 Napoleon had crossed the Niemen with nine army corps: a third of a million men, the largest and most redoubtable, not to say multi-national, army in European history. To effect liaison between their two corps the Russians, refusing him the battle he sought, had hastily withdrawn into the interior until, on 14 August, they'd stood and fought at Smolensk, which had gone up in flames. A pyrrhic victory for the French. The main 'Moscow' army had already lost so many men and horses en route that what should have been the crucial battle (Borodino, 7 September) had been indecisive. Moscow, evacuated by Kutusov and occupied by the French (14 September), had been set in flames by its governor Rostopchin.

For five illusory weeks Napoleon waited in the Kremlin, hoping that the Tsar would make peace, while his advance guard at the Winkovo camp had literally starved. On 18 October the Russians attacked it, and only Murat's prompt action had saved it from annihilation. Next day Napoleon had marched out southwards for Kaluga and the unravaged Ukraine with some 110,000 men and a vast baggage train glutted with the spoils of Moscow. On 24 October 22,000 Italians, Frenchmen and Croats of Eugène's IV Corps ('The Army of Italy') had run into and defeated 70,000 Russians at Malojaroslavetz. Once again Kutusov withdrew, and in the dawn mists next day Napoleon himself was within an ace of capture by Cossacks. Reluctantly deciding the Grand Army had 'done enough for glory' he'd ordered a retreat via the devastated Mojaisk–Viazma road to Smolensk, where he hoped to go into winter quarters before fighting a second campaign in the spring of 1813. 'Towards midnight the two armies turned their backs on each other, marching in opposite directions.'

PHASE ONE
TO SMOLENSK

'A WORD UNKNOWN IN THE FRENCH ARMY'

'Suddenly everyone seemed indifferent' – 'the retreat of the wounded lion' – the Cossacks – the loot of Moscow – contents of a wagon – plight of the wounded and prisoners – Mailly-Nesle keeps singing – Ney's corps at Borowsk – Dumonceau sacrifices his cart – a cock goes into Le Roy's cookpot – Davout's protest – Napoleon as seen by Dedem – growing food shortage – an imperial outburst – plight of the Mojaisk wounded

After a second night in the weaver's cabin Napoleon rides out again toward Malojaroslavetz. Looks out over its smoking ruins and, through the smoke-haze, to the plain beyond. Has Kutusov really retired? The reports are confirmed. And this, his Second Secretary A.-J.-F. Fain notices, removes his final objections to a retreat via the main Mojaisk–Smolensk highway. At least Kutusov's withdrawal will give the army a chance to get clear away. And at 9 a.m. 26 October, 'beside a fire lit at the roadside, he sends the order to everything left at Gorodnia to retire on Borowsk,' a dozen or so miles to the rear; and at 11 a.m. himself turns his back on this foe who has so long and so successfully eluded him.

Only once before has he ever retreated. It is an operation of which he has little or no experience. Everyone knows instinctively what it means. And is depressed by the insight. Hadn't he sworn he'd never retire by the route he'd come by – through 'the desert we ourselves created'?

Between Moscow and Smolensk, as the self-appointed war artist *Albrecht Adam*, who's had his bellyful of campaigning and gone off home, already knows,

'everything was devastated for more than 300 miles. The villages were ruins. The towns were starving hospitals. The few barns or houses were filled with corpses of men and domestic animals, some half-rotted. You only had to follow the cadaverous stench to be sure you were on your right road.'

The few men the ex-cakemaker and his travelling companions had encountered, 'stragglers following the army and lacking all nourishment, were straying hither and thither in utmost distress' in a countryside 'infested with Cossacks and peasants'. Several times they'd 'only escaped them by a miracle'.[1]

Morale is low. Everyone knows how the Emperor, in that hut at Gorodnia, had 'sat for a whole hour pondering his fateful decision'; and how, at dawn yesterday, he'd blundered into a swarm of Cossacks,[2] and could easily have been captured. Though IHQ has done its best to hush up the shocking episode 'by evening next day the whole army knew about it, and was retrospectively trembling with fright'. Also at a rumour that Platov, the Cossacks' supreme hetman, has been 'seized with such violent hatred of the French after his son had been killed in an affray between Cossacks and Polish Uhlans at Vereia that he'd ordered all short fat Frenchmen to be brought before him for special viewing, and even promised his daughter's hand in marriage to anyone – be he only a simple Cossack – who brings Napoleon before him, dead or alive.' This rumour the Dutch ex-diplomat and general of brigade *Dedem van der Gelder*, who'd incurred Berthier's dislike for the way he'd stood up for foreigners and been told curtly at the Kremlin 'if you aren't satisfied you can go home', is sure 'disquieted Bonaparte'. Though how he knows it he doesn't say. At all events the word 'retreat', which this scathing critic of military behaviour had been told at Witebsk in July 'didn't exist in the French army', has become the grim reality.

Hardly have the units about-faced and marched off one after another down the Borowsk road than it seems to Major *A. A. Pion des Loches*, of the Guard Artillery, that 'everyone seemed seized with indifference'. The newly promoted major, too, is a chronic dissident and a considerable know-all. And to him the 'indifference' already seems to be 'turning our retreat into a rout'. In charge of the Guard Foot Artillery's 1st Company, the 2nd of the Young Guard's and a part of the Train, he's deeply shocked when the Guard Artillery's chief-of-staff General Lallemand comes riding up and orders him

'to abandon the ammunition wagons by preference and destroy the ammunition as I lost horses. In vain I put it to him that it was useless to keep the guns without their supplies: "The Emperor", he said imperiously, "doesn't want a single gun abandoned." What wisdom! Did that man think the guns falling into the enemy's hands would be the only witnesses of his retreat? But his order was carried out.'[3]

As it is, they're already 'abandoning the ammunition wagons, and this without any formal instructions. Each of us was following his own whims.' It doesn't occur to Pion des Loches that while Napoleon will be able to replenish his ammunition at Smolensk, with its immense stocks of everything, cannon are another matter. Lallemand's order will be almost the last he'll receive in Russia.

Naturally not everyone loses heart. Colonel *Lubin Griois* is filled with admiration for the 'rare cool-headedness and courage' of his corps commander General Grouchy, whose 3rd Cavalry Corps is covering the army's rearguard, formed by Davout's I Corps. Griois' horse artillery was the last to cross the bridge over the Luja Gorge:

'Present everywhere, with a serene calm air, he inspired so much confidence, so much assurance in such mounted troops as still remained that the enemy, despite reiterated attempts, could neither overcome nor discourage him. It was the retreat of the wounded lion.'

Yet he has hardly recovered from the wound he received at Borodino. And of his cavalry, after starving for a month at the Winkovo camp,[4] all too little's left. It's a brilliant sunny day. Griois' horse-gunners are having incessant brushes with ever-growing numbers of Cossacks:

'They came and caracoled around us, at times even to within pistol range. Whenever they put too much liveliness into their attack, we halted; and several discharges or a charge by a few platoons sufficed to drive them off. But this meant slowing down, and did them too great an honour. So we limited ourselves to making them respect us by sending them some grape and musket shots as we went on marching.'

Easy enough to identify, even from afar, 'from the disorderliness of their masses, the obscure colour of their horsemen's clothing and the motley of their piebald horses', the Cossacks too have artillery:

'They were crowning all rises in the ground, debouching from all roads, and advancing in all directions. So we faced to all sides. Our guns replied to theirs. And at all points a minor war commenced between our light cavalry and theirs.'

No one's the least bit intimidated by these 'barbarians', whom the troops scornfully refer to as '*les hourrassiers*' (cf. cuirassiers) on account of their 'hurrahs'[5] as they brandished their lances.

'Now and again some of our platoons charged through these clouds of horsemen, who dispersed in front of them, to return at a gallop at some other point to recommence their howlings and provocations.'

There are even single-handed combats,[6]

'a veritable jousting. Each combatant tried to show off his brilliant courage and skill in the eyes of his comrades. Above all our Poles distinguished themselves. Their way of fighting and their shouts, very much the same as their adversaries', added something more lively and picturesque to the noise of the cannon or exploding shells. Alternately pursuing and pursued, depending on whether some comrades came to join them or they had to do with new assailants, they caracoled in little troops between the two armies,'

a truly superb spectacle, Griois thinks, which recalls what he's read about ancient wars. But some of his men are wounded. And these, the first to fall, he puts on to his ammunition wagons:

'But the more gravely wounded, who couldn't keep up with us with their comrades' aid, them we had to leave behind to the Cossacks. Their entreaties, their cries, pierced my heart. But there was nothing else we could do, short of carrying them on our shoulders.'

Cossacks are indeed everywhere. Dedem van der Gelder, relieved of his command since Moscow and attached to Imperial Headquarters, is remembering how, as he'd galloped along this same road 'carrying the Emperor's orders to the Viceroy' during the Malojaroslavetz action, they'd 'put paid to two of my hussar orderlies and I'd only owed it to my horse's swiftness that I hadn't suffered the same fate'. Now he hears they've even surprised Dufour's (ex-Friant's) division and 'taken some cannon'.

Autumn days in Russia aren't meant to last. By and by the sky clouds over, and the weather turns to a depressing drizzle. Through a rain-sodden, heavily wooded countryside of oaks, ashes and silver birches almost stripped of their last leaves and a sombre background of conifers deep green against all these tones of brown and grey, the army rides, trundles or trudges back along the Borowsk road it has just advanced by. Soon the leading units run head on into its grossly swollen baggage train,

'a disorderly caravan of every kind of vehicle, military carriages, little cars, *calèches, kibitkas, droshkis*, most of them attached to little Russian horses ... most opulent and elegant carriages, sutler carts, wagons, barouches, diligences, coaches of every variety, including state coaches,' that until yesterday had brought up the rear, but now are forced to turn their horses' heads and become its van. Already, en route for the unattainable Ukraine, some 20,000 of its vehicles have either broken down, tangled their spokes with one another's wheelhubs, lost their horses or, getting in the way of the guns, have had to be burned. Whereupon their

'precious objects, pictures, candelabras, whole libraries, gold and silver crucifixes, ciboria or chalices, beautiful carpets, tapestries and wall-hangings and cloths embroidered with gold and silver, pieces of silk of every colour, embroidered and brilliant clothes, both men and women's, such as are only seen in the courts of princes ... precious stones, cases filled with diamonds or rolls of ducats'

in a word, all the fantastic loot of Moscow – have been tipped into ditches.[7] Yet there are still masses of vehicles jamming up the road.

If there's one man who's utterly furious with Kutusov for missing out on the 'glorious golden opportunity' he'd been offered at Malojaroslavetz and, in general, for the one-eyed Field Marshal's sloth and *fainéantise*, it's the British government's special envoy and liaison officer at his headquarters, General *Sir Robert Wilson*. The Russian army, he's noting in his *Journal*, so far from being weakened, has actually 'been reinforced by numerous militia and all had fought with determination'. And now here's its senile, or perhaps even treacherous commander letting Bonaparte, that enemy of mankind, give him the slip!

It's enough to drive any right-thinking man mad.

To the retreating army, however, more important by far than its booty are the foodstuffs also stored in its baggage train. And many a foreseeing officer has his well-stocked wagon jolting along with the regimental ones. En route for Moscow, as a mere captain, Pion des Loches had had to share one 'half-filled with my company's effects and reserve shoes' with his lieutenant. Now, promoted major, he's entitled to one of his own, 'smaller, it's true, but sufficient for my victuals for a retreat of 3 to 4 months'. Among other things it also contains a singularly fine Chinese porcelain dinner set which had taken his fancy, and,

'against the eventuality (which I regarded as inevitable) of a winter cantonment on the left bank of the Niemen, a case containing a rather fine edition of Voltaire and Rousseau; Clerc and Levesque's *History of Russia*; Molière's plays, the works of Piron; Montesquieu's *L'Esprit des Lois* and several other works such as Raynal's *Philosophical History*, bound in white calf and gilded on the spine.'

His no less ample larder consists of

'100 cakes of biscuit a foot in diameter, a sack holding a quintal of flour, more than 300 bottles of wine, 20–30 bottles of rum and brandy, more than 10 pounds of tea and as much again of coffee, 50–60 pounds of sugar, 3–4 pounds of chocolate, some pounds of candles.'

For 80 francs he's also bought himself 'one of the most beautiful furs that have been brought back from Moscow'. This chilly day his foresight is seeing itself rewarded: 'I was keeping open house. We were rarely fewer than seven or eight at dinner.' One of his subalterns even has a tent,[8] to which he has access in exchange for sharing his provisions:

'Before leaving we had copious boiling hot soup. I'd put some bread and sugar in my pocket. On me I had a bottle of rum. At the midday halt some glasses of wine; in the course of the day some bits of chocolate, of biscuit, to keep our strength up.'

Surgeon *Louis-Vincent Lagneau* of the Fusiliers-Grenadiers of the Young Guard, too, has a tent, 'very likely', he thinks (erroneously) 'the only one in the army'. He'd had it made at Moscow of striped canvas and got his men to make its pegs and poles:

'My ambulance wagon was big and very heavy. We'd loaded it with wine, rice, biscuits, sugar, coffee and many other supplies, either in small casks of the kind carried by our *cantinières* or else in large sacks. This was to be our viaticum for the retreat.'

Neither has I Corps' paymaster, Captain *P. T. Duverger*, forgotten to look after Number One:

'I had a fortune in furs and paintings. I had any number of cases of figs, of coffee, of liqueurs, of macaroni, of salted fish and meats. But white bread, fresh meat and *vin ordinaire* I had none.'

He too can give a dinner for sixteen of his comrades, among them a general: 'We solemnly toasted the success of the coming campaign and our entry into St Petersburg.'

All this is in crude contrast to the plight of the ordinary ranker. Unless he's a free-enterpriser who's 'hired a retinue of others to care for themselves and their horses and the handling of as many as four carriages in their train', all he has is what he can carry on his back.[9] And Smolensk, with its huge magazines, filled with supplies brought up from the distant rear, is at least ten days, perhaps a fortnight away. Yet even the ranker is to be envied, compared with the sick and wounded. After his narrow escape during yesterday's Cossack flurry – where Napoleon could so easily have been captured – General Pajol's normally healthy ADC Captain *Hubert-François Biot* had been overcome with faintness and collapsed in a ditch. Luckily Pajol had found him there and had him put into 'a wagon driven by the wife of one of his orderlies, a trumpeter of the 11th Chasseurs'. And now Biot's jolting along on top of some sacks of flour.

Even this is to be preferred to the fate of the 2,000 or so Italians, Spaniards, Croats and Frenchmen who'd been wounded at Malojaroslavetz. For, General *Armand de Caulaincourt*, Master of the Horse, sees there's no longer any medical service, except perhaps residually in the Guard. Dr *Réné Bourgeois*, also of 3rd Cavalry Corps, had seen the wounded being

'hastily laden on to ambulance wagons and their belongings passed to the *vivandières*. Deprived of all help or food they painfully followed the army.'

Still worse is the plight of the Russian prisoners, of whom several hundreds, too, are being herded along. Yet not quite so brutally, perhaps, as are the tens of thousands of French and allied prisoners who are being herded eastwards: those of them, that is, who've been lucky enough not to have been sold off 'at 2 frs a head' to be tortured and killed by enraged peasants. Of the 1,400 sick and wounded Marshal Mortier's had to leave behind in the three Moscow hospitals as 'too weak to have been transported with their comrades', some have been

'thrown on to wagons to be taken to Twer. All perished from cold and misery, or were assassinated by the peasants charged with driving them who cut their throats to take their coats. The rest were left in the hospitals with the French surgeons who'd stayed to look after them, but were given neither food nor medicines.'[10]

At least one Frenchman, however, is glad he's fallen into British hands. For a mixture of family and political reasons, Wilson has offered to get the nephew of Napoleon's war minister Clarke exchanged. But the young man, realising what would be in store for him, has declined

'until the French were out of their present embarrassments, as he'd "had enough of horse-flesh and Cossack iron". I then despatched him, with a very strong letter of recommendation to all Russians, a good cloak and two hundred roubles.'

Few prisoners have either. Fezensac's dictum about how 'for a prisoner the difference in the way officers and the rank and file are treated can be the difference between life and death' is applying in all its rigour. A few miles away to the south-east Surgeon *M. R. Faure* of the 1st Cavalry Corps, captured in the desperate mêlée at Winkovo,[11] is noticing – with winter coming on any day now – how sure his guards are that the Grand Army's hated *sabacky franzusky* are doomed. At first the officers, at least, aren't being too badly treated:

'A prisoner chief-of-staff came and brought each officer of his corps [the 2nd Cavalry Corps] six ducats from Prince Kutusov, who was acting towards the prisoners with all the generosity and all the greatness of soul to be expected of a man of superior merit. Among all the Russian officers we saw a kind of fraternity reigned that witnessed to a good spirit in an army, and which should be conducive to beautiful actions on campaign.'

Faure's party had left the Winkovo battlefield 'satisfied with the Russians' conduct, under the orders of an officer we had no reason to complain of.'

En route southward for Kaluga they'd found the roads congested with transport vehicles making for the Russian army:

'All day on the third or fourth day we'd heard a cannonade which lasted until ten or twelve that night. It was the Malojaroslavetz affair, three or four leagues [9–12 miles] distance from us.'[12]

They also see masses of peasants who've been forced to evacuate their villages. Reaching Kaluga, 35 miles beyond Malojaroslavetz, Faure sees all its well-to-do inhabitants have fled, just as they'd done at Moscow:

'Those merchants who hadn't yet left were ready to do the same. The governor had made all preparations, in the event of our army threatening it, to set it on fire. He came to feast his eyes on the prey being brought to him. He complained loudly that we wore an air of being in good health. He'd been told the French army lacked victuals, and to have satisfied him we'd have had to be as thin as he was.'

The governor 'abuses' a Pole who'd had a leg carried off at the thigh at Winkovo, and this causes the common folk to follow suit. But Faure forgives them, blames only the governor. Most shocking of all at Kaluga is the brutality being shown to some wounded soldiers who've 'fallen into very bad hands' and are herded together into a filthy building:

'Battered and bruised and no longer having the strength even to cry out, they're wrenched off the carts. A wretch, an inferior officer, charged with conducting them, had had two or three shot en route because they'd seemed to want to escape.'

Only when a superior officer turns a blind eye and lets Faure's comrades go shopping do they momentarily forget their indignation. But even then two or three of them are insulted by 'a Russian wearing a sword'. All this, however, is only the beginning of the prisoners' sufferings.

As always, privileged connections make all the difference. Almost optimally comfortable (apart from his wounded shoulder) is a certain aristocratic sous-lieutenant of the prestigious 2nd Carabiniers, the young Count A.-A.-A. *Mailly-Nesle*. If he and Prince Charles de Beauveau, son of one of Napoleon's chamberlains, are swaying along (none too strongly escorted against Cossacks, he thinks) ahead of the imperial baggage train in one of the Emperor's own carriages, it's because he's a relative of the once famous Marshal Mailly.[13] Like so many other 'whites', Mailly-Nesle has rallied, at least temporarily,[14] to the new regime. But he 'hates the despotism and tyranny weighing on France' and 'sees himself condemned to lead this soldier's life':

'So here I am in an excellent carriage with one of my friends, a footman at my orders, and what's more with three doctors to care for us and bandage our wounds. We had six horses to pull us, with two postilions. I thought I'd got myself out of trouble.'

Since being wounded at Winkovo, the insouciant Mailly-Nesle has bought himself 'a fox pelt, which was very useful to me'. He also has

'a certain plank which was serving us as desk or dining-table by day and

28

for a chandelier in the evening, and which, by placing it across the two seats, served me for a bed'.

From a 'M. Lameau, attached as a geographer to the Emperor's cabinet' he has borrowed Voltaire's *History of Charles XII* of Sweden – the very same 'pretty little volume, morocco gilded on the spine' Napoleon had been reading in the July heats at Witebsk and kept on his bedside table in the Kremlin. In it Mailly-Nesle can read all about how that royal hero's entire army had been wiped out at Poltava, not very far from here, in 1709. Between chapters he sings lustily, to keep his own and his friend Beauveau's courage up. But who's this now, coming toward them – in the wrong direction – if not

'L——, radiant and smart as if he'd just come out of the Tuileries. I asked him why he hadn't stayed on his estates, shooting hares. He replied he'd had to do *his duty*.'

Italics for irony! Snug Mailly-Nesle may be in his comfortable if overcrowded carriage – the only flies in his and his fellow-passengers' ointment are some bugs that are causing them to itch and scratch. Yet 'many of us were badly dressed, still wearing summer trousers. There was a lack of gloves and other items of clothing.'

After spending three days at Czsirkovo, at the junction of the Podolsk and Fominskoië roads, Ney's III Corps have left that village at midnight, 25/26 October, to bring up what they're still assuming is the army's rear. Struggling on through bottomless lanes is newly-promoted Major *Guillaume Bonnet*. He'd gone down with a fever on the eve of leaving Moscow and on the morrow of III Corps' departure had 'left the city, alone, in a *droschka* through streets where no Frenchman was to be seen' but fortunately caught up with his regiment some fifteen miles along the Kaluga road. Now he's noting in his diary how the Cossacks, who're prodding at them to see how they'll react, keep their distance 'with 2 bad cannon, firing 20 roundshot, which as yet haven't hit anyone' – perhaps thanks to 'Guardin's and Beurmann's light cavalry, who've been ordered to set fire to all the villages'. When Ney's men reach Borowsk in the evening they find it too in flames.

A link between III Corps and the main army, these last few days, has been Colbert's Guard Lancer Brigade, consisting of the 1st (Polish) and 2nd (Dutch) Regiments. Himself also ordered to fall back six miles to Borowsk, Colbert has sent his young Belgian Captain *François Dumonceau*, commanding 6th Troop of 2nd Lancers' 2nd Squadron, on ahead to tell Ney about his regiment's near-disastrous affray with a huge horde of Cossacks at Ouvarovskoië.[15] Outside Borowsk he finds

'the head of the Marshal's column peacefully bivouacked. The general in charge there was little moved by my account, and, despite my remonstrances, only slowly got his men under arms to receive us.'

At 8 a.m. on 26 October the always efficient Colbert has sent out a reconnaissance southwards toward Malojaroslavetz. No Cossacks has it seen. But instead, to its dismay, run into a 'long convoy of wounded coming toward us'. Its conductors' statements make it seem likely that the entire army is following in their wake:

'We were all painfully affected. After the success of the day before yesterday we couldn't conceive that it could be a question of a retrograde movement.'

Only now, in the evening, do Ney's men learn that the army's retreating. The news comes as a considerable shock to Bonnet and the Württemberg Major G. *Faber du Faur*, in charge of the 12-pounders of Ney's reserve artillery. And orders come for III Corps to leave for Vereia, the next town along the Mojaisk road. Just as the units are getting ready to leave the Cossacks attack. And Ney's men have to face about and 'in very open country and the plain, stripped [of everything]' draw up in line of battle. Not that Cossacks are anything for an entire army corps to worry about: 'A brief discharge of artillery and a charge by the cavalry of the [Württemberg] Royal Guard sufficed to drive them off.' How many vivid close-ups do we not owe to Faber du Faur's engravings! 'At Borowsk', it seems to him, 'our luck seemed to turn; and in the afternoon of the 26th we began our retreat.'[16]

Bonnet's diary is always succinct. That evening he makes one of his cursory jottings: Though only 1,100 men of its original strength are still with the colours, the 18th Line is still two battalions strong. Only at 7 p.m., as Ney's regiments are leaving their campfires, does the situation dawn on him:

'We must give up [the idea of] marching south. Doubtless we've been repulsed, or the Emperor is manoeuvring – I don't know how.'

At this moment Colbert's men arrive, ride up on to a plateau near the burning town, and bivouack in the midst of 'several infantry units and various parks' squatted around the thousands of campfires. Out there in the darkness Cossacks are still hovering about at the foot of the hill. Yet no one bothers – only his Dutchmen are jittery, so it seems to Dumonceau: somewhat naturally so after their private battle of the 25th: 'We were all more or less demoralised by our setback.' Only when IHQ and the other Guard regiments come marching into Borowsk does a staff officer come and tell Colbert to prepare for an immediate departure for Smolensk. 'News that fulfilled all our wishes. It soon effaced the impression of a retreat.' Perhaps quite a few of Dumonceau's Dutchmen, too, have had their bellyful of campaigning? At least in Russia?

After the Ouvarovskoïe affray they've a lot of wounded to take with them. Keen observer and recorder of events though he is, the 26-year-old Dumonceau is neither emotional nor very tender-hearted. Nevertheless he distributes his food between his favourite mare Liesje,[17] his second horse and his servant Jean's rough-haired '*konya*' (Russian pony), and sacrifices his cart and other contents. And when, next morning, when the Lancer Brigade rides off to its usual position at the head of the Guard column, the cart, with three wounded lancers on it, moves off escorted by a corporal.

Only for safety's sake is the 85th Line's newly promoted Lieutenant-Colonel *C. F. M. Le Roy*[18] travelling with it and I Corps. Promoted by Davout for his efficiency, he's going back to France to the regimental depot. With him, meanwhile, he has his best friend, Lieutenant Jacquet, the only confidant he's ever had, and his ugly-faced but devoted servant Guillaume. Their treasured iron cookpot, which has followed them all the way from Glogau in Prussia, turns this trio into a quartet. The portly Le Roy's abiding concern, namely, is to secure his dinner each day.

What's sauce for the goose is sauce for the gander. Ever since Smolensk the Russians have burnt down their villages, and in the end even their sacred capital. To delay Kutusov's pursuit Napoleon has ordered every village, every house, every cottage, every barn along the route to be fired. Nothing's to be left standing for his men to take shelter in, should they too follow this already devastated route. Strictly speaking it's I Corps, bringing up the rear, that's to carry out this order. But it's being anticipated by the Imperial Guard, heading the column. That night the bald-headed, bespectacled Iron Marshal and his staff sleep

'in a big timber château, furnished and adorned with mirrors and which seemed to offer its proprietor everything desirable and agreeable.'

And in the evening Le Roy joins his men in a hunt for wildfowl. He needn't have troubled himself. Finds his dinner under the straw he's sleeping on in the shape of 'a big cock'. But though it 'begins to raise the devil's own shindy' its protests avail it nothing. It goes straight into the iron cookpot. As for the château, when they wake up next morning 'all that had vanished. Like the village, it was put to the flames. It was the matter of an instant.'

Davout, some people are thinking, is being altogether too methodical with his routines. Should be moving faster. After resting there all day, not until evening are the 85th:

'ordered to advance near a wood where we lit big fires to deceive the Russians. Just before midnight we retired and recrossed the river at the same point as had served us the previous day. Our march would have been concealed had it not been for the imprudence of our scouts who, in withdrawing, set fire to two large villages and so displayed all our movements to the enemy. So closely were we pursued by Cossacks, we were able to fire a few shots at them.'

Shelter's important. Waking up that morning at Borowsk, Dumonceau had found it was snowing. As yet only lightly. Even so, he's been sleeping under

'a thick layer of snow. It was the beginning of winter, which had come to stay. Our march, resumed this time at the head of the whole Imperial Guard, went on under a sombre and misty sky across snowy morasses of mud.'

Now Borowsk, where 'the several bridges over the Protwa had been finished too late', a big traffic jam has been left behind for Davout to cope with. Four miles further on Dedem's called for. He finds Napoleon 'warming his hands behind his back at a bivouac fire made up for him beside a little village on the Vereia road'. With him is Marshal Berthier, his chief-of-staff and the army's major-general. Napoleon orders Dedem to go back and direct both IV and I Corps to take a parallel road to the left of the main column:

> 'He personally expounded his intentions. While the Prince of Neuchâtel was explaining His Majesty's intentions to me I had a chance to study the face of this extraordinary man. Then, suddenly turning to the Prince of Neuchâtel, he said: "But he'll be captured." And this in a tone of indifference which struck me, for it wasn't a question of myself but of a general movement of the whole army. Napoleon had the air of one of those chess-players who, seeing the game is lost, finish it honestly and say to themselves: "Now let's have another".'

Dedem doesn't like Napoleon,

> 'because he'd ruined my country. At Borodino I'd witnessed his indifference and terrifying stoicism. I'd seen him furious and taken aback when entering Moscow. Now he was calm, not angry, but also not depressed. I thought he'd be great in adversity, and this idea reconciled me to him. But here I found in him the man who sees disaster and realises the whole difficulty of his position, but whose soul isn't a whit put down, and who tells himself: "It's a setback, we must clear out. But they'll meet me again."'

Dedem evidently carries out his mission; for after riding onwards for two or three hours Dumonceau's surprised to see the head of another column appear to his left 'beyond a little stream'. And Colbert sends an adjutant to find out who they are. Yes it's IV Corps. following a cross-country road, doubtless the one Napoleon has indicated. Coming back, the adjutant tells Dumonceau how the Army of Italy had been saddened to see dead lancers from the 2nd Regiment lying on the ground at Ouvarovskoïë 'but been cheered to see so many Cossacks among them'. By then Ouvarovskoïë itself, like all the other villages, was in flames. And in its ashes Captain *Eugène Labaume* on the Viceroy's staff, had been shocked to see

> 'the corpses of several soldiers or peasants, children whose throats had been cut, and several girls massacred on the spot where they'd been raped'.

As for Ouvarovskoïë's magnificent château 'although of timber, of a size and magnificence equal to the most beautiful ones of Italy and full of exquisite furniture and chandeliers', Eugène's gunners had placed some powder wagons on its ground floor and blown it sky-high. Then, marching for Borowsk, IV Corps had left behind it the whole of I Corps and Chastel's cavalry division, which Griois' artillery belongs to, to cover the army's retreat at the distance of a day's march. Some of IV Corps' artillery having got stuck in a ford at Borowsk, it had been necessary to march with the rest of it – and its powder wagons – through the burning town. But, says Adjutant-Major *Cesare de Laugier* of the Italian Guardia d'Onore, 'we got through without incident. Everywhere we'd seen ammunition wagons abandoned for lack of horses to draw them. Such losses at the very outset of our retreat gave us a premonition of the future in the most sombre colours. And those who were carrying with them the loot of Moscow trembled for their booty.'

After being seriously held up by the immense baggage train, Razout's division of III Corps reaches Vereia, 6 hours' march from Mojaisk, at about midday on 27 October. Following closely in the wake of IHQ are 25 Treasury wagons, stuffed with the imperial spoils from the Kremlin, but also with millions of gold '*napoléons*' (20-franc pieces). The one in the care of the 28-year-old Breton war commissary A. *Bellot de Kergorre* is heavily laden. In a ravine just before Vereia he has to put the brakes on all its four wheels. But this doesn't prevent it, no more than all the other vehicles, from rushing down the steep slope, blocked by the artillery. 'Other carriages, even ammunition wagons, followed our example.' Vereia itself turns out to be

'a pretty little palisaded town which, apart from a fight between Poles and Russians' [its Polish garrison had been taken by surprise and massacred], had only faintly suffered the horrors of war. It was the more unfortunate in that it lay a little off the main road and had momentarily flattered itself it would escape them.'

Its fields haven't been ravaged at all. 'Its well-cultivated gardens were covered with all sorts of vegetables, which in an instant were carried away by our soldiers.' Bonnet's men instantly baptise it Cabbage Town.[19] But Kergorre is upset to see

'men stealing the timbers from barns where generals were sleeping, so that the latter awoke to find themselves under the bare sky'.

Although the weather's decidedly chilly, Napoleon declares: 'The winter won't be on us for eight more days.' But how to gain the shelter of winter quarters at Smolensk before then?

Warming his hands at a campfire that evening is one of Napoleon's aristocratic staff officers: Squadron-Leader Count *V.-E. B. de Castellane*, ADC to Count *Louis de Narbonne*, who in turn is ADC to the Emperor. The day after the army had marched out from Moscow Castellane had been sent off on mission to the 1st and 2nd Battalions of the Spanish Joseph-Napoleon Regiment, stationed at Malo-Viazma,[20] on the main Moscow–Mojaisk highway. And it had been Castellane's business to liaise with them at Prince Galitzin's superb country house, where their task had been to protect the convoys of wounded retiring westwards from Cossack incursions. After doing '40 miles by cross-country roads' he'd found

'adjutant-commandant Bourmont, a very amiable man, the one who'd served with the Chouans. But for the last two years he'd been serving with the Emperor's army and as yet hadn't been given the cross, though it had been requested for him. Under his orders he had two battalions of the Spanish Joseph-Napoleon Regiment and two of Bavarian chevaulegers.'

On 22 October they'd left Malo-Viazma and marched to the village of Koubinskoë:

'Soon after we'd got there the Cossacks appeared and carried out a hurrah against a convoy of wounded. The isolated men escorting it had behaved badly. Colonel de Bourmont called his men to arms, I carried the order to the Bavarian colonel to charge with his brigade. He answered that his horses were too exhausted to gallop. During that expedition the only use he was to us was to exhaust 50 infantrymen a day to protect his forage and, to the Spaniards' great annoyance, to eat sheep from the flock they'd collected. I asked the Joseph-Napoleon regiment to provide me with 50 men of goodwill to go on ahead a couple of miles and save more of the [wounded] men. Those 50 grenadiers marched at the double toward the enemy. We rescued 100 well-armed men who'd hidden in the woods, without firing a shot.'

Now five days have gone by. After hearing about IV Corps' exploits at Malojaroslavetz, Castellane and the Spaniards' Major Doreille are talking over their own experiences. With some difficulty. Doreille, namely, is a native of Tarascon, and 'can't speak French', only Provençal. The 39-year-old Doreille tells the handsome young aristocrat from Napoleon's staff how

'he'd had six brothers killed since the beginning of the revolutionary wars. He was the sole support of his old and poverty-stricken mother.'

On this snowy morning of 27 October even the *Intendance-Générale*, escorting the Treasure, has to depart in a hurry. 'The Cossack guns were at half-range.' But his servants having found a chicken and some onions, Belot de Kergorre, loth to abandon his stew, delays departure until the last possible moment. And indeed, though it's only a week since the army left Moscow, food's beginning to be in short supply. As yet Colonel *Montesquiou de Fezensac* of the 4th Line (III Corps) is noticing there are large discrepancies between various units:

'One regiment had kept some oxen and had no bread; another had flour but lacked meat. In the same regiment some companies were dying of hunger while others were living in abundance. And though the superior officers ordered them to share and share alike, egoism employed every means to outwit their supervision and escape their authority.'

I Corps' horses, Paymaster Duverger is distressed to see,

'always on the march, had nothing to eat and were collapsing from fatigue and abstinence. The collapse of a horse was our good fortune. The poor beast was hacked to pieces. Horseflesh isn't bad for the health. But it's hard and fibrous. Some preferred the liver. The nights were beginning to be long and cold. We were sleeping on a damp and frozen soil. The ideal bivouac was one in which we could stretch out softly on a little straw in front of a fire of dry wood, sheltered by a pine forest. If there was horse stew, some wheatbread, and a flask of aquavit to pass around, it was a feast.'

34

'From the second day of the retreat,' Davout's reluctant chief-of-staff, the future artist Baron *Louis-François Lejeune,* says:
> 'a cold fine drizzle came to add itself to our mental torments, the diffi-culties of the route and the inconveniences of the bad weather. The cold damp nights spent in bivouac, the inadequate nourishment from unleavened munition bread or badly cooked broth began to give the troops dysentery.[21] The sick no longer had the strength to keep up with their units and were falling behind.'

Even the 7th Hussars' new colonel *Victor Dupuy* is having to subsist all day on a cup of sugared coffee for breakfast. All the long way from the Niemen to Moscow his regiment had been in the extreme van. Then they'd starved in the Winkovo camp. Had no share in Moscow's culinary riches. Now Roussel d'Hurbal's brigade of Bruyères' light cavalry division of Nansouty's 1st Cavalry Corps is forming IV Corps' rearguard. Arriving at the regi-ment's bivouac Dupuy walks to and fro beside the road,
> 'waiting until some Polish marauders should pass. I bought some rare and furtive provisions for their weight in gold. A bit of pork grilled on charcoal, or some fistfuls of flour dipped in melted snow helped me and my companions to believe we weren't hungry.'

Unfortunately this windfall only upsets their stomachs. But then Dupuy has a real stroke of luck:
> 'I saw my former farrier of the élite company of the 11th Chasseurs, Bou-ton by name, and now sergeant-major of the Chasseurs of the Imperial Guard. He was escorting a wagon. He offered me some sugar and cof-fee. I emptied all my dirty linen out of my portmanteau and furnished it with these provisions, very useful to me thereafter. Having taken a good dose of coffee in the morning, I didn't feel hungry all day.'

Everyone's feeling more and more miserable. Particularly so sous-Lieutenant *Pierre Auvray* of the 23rd Dragoons, escorting the baggage hour after hour,
> 'without any rest from 2 a.m. to 11 p.m. and at each moment being attacked by peasants dressed as Cossacks who charged the column to get hold of the superb carriages many officers had supplied themselves with in Moscow. These carriages, laden with gold, silver and victuals, drew the attention of peasants whom the fires had deprived of their asylums. Every day they took some, along with their drivers, whom they stripped and sent back again.'

Mailly-Nesle hears a new word in the French language, '*se démoraliser*'. Defines it as 'a kind of nostalgia'. Another officer who dates its first out-break from this second day of the retreat is Lieutenant *N. L. Planat de la Faye*, general factotum and 'man of letters' to General Lariboisière, supreme commander of the army's artillery. IHQ and the artillery staff has just got to Vereia when
> 'after dinner an officer came in who'd had nothing to eat since morn-ing. Though by nature compassionate and disposed toward everything called sacrifice and devotion, I myself hadn't been exempt from the bar-barism and brutal egoism,'

now beginning to prevail. 'We had nothing left to give him except a little bread or biscuit and a glass of bad brandy.' Irritated, the officer lodges a formal complaint. Since it's Planat's comrade and friend Honoré de Lariboisière, the general's surviving son, who's responsible for distributing rations, he goes to his father to explain. But ever since his other son Frédéric's death after Borodino[22] old Lariboisière has been deeply depressed. And all Honoré gets is a furious upbraiding. That day, too, Planat loses – for all futurity – another friend, on account of a 'little piece of meat not quite equally divided'.

IV Corps headquarters has spent the night in a hut in the miserable hamlet of Alféréva. Only Prince Eugène and his divisional generals have been able to get some shelter. His staff-captain Labaume, too, dates the disintegration of morale from that day. Any army – as Napoleon had memorably pointed out but seems temporarily to have forgotten – marches on its stomach. And Lieutenant *Albrecht von Muraldt* of IV Corps' 4th Bavarian Chevaulegers is shocked to notice how quickly the spreading food shortage is affecting obedience and military discipline:

'Men were beginning to leave the ranks without permission, and anyone who wasn't present when the others bivouacked was hardly asked after when leaving next morning. Yet this was only the beginning!'

Two days later Lieutenant *Louis-Joseph Vionnet*, also of the hitherto so well-disciplined Fusiliers-Grenadiers of the Young Guard, will be noting how

'the habit of stealing was establishing itself in the army. From now on nothing was safe except what one wore on one's own person. Men were taking portmanteaux from horses and pots off fires,'

placing Le Roy's and Jacquet's great iron cookpot in perpetual danger. Already men are withdrawing into the forest to eat such little bread as they still have left. Here and there a unit seems to be miraculously intact. From his carriage Mailly-Nesle admires a regiment of Portuguese light cavalry as it comes trotting across the fields. 'Their excellent condition, the rested air of these men in chestnut brown uniforms, their handsome faces, serious and brown, provoked our admiration.'[23] Only the exiguous Pion des Loches, it seems, is snug:

'In the evenings we raised our tent. I undressed, I lay down on bearskins and there, in my sleeping-bag, covered by my fur, slept as soundly as at any bivouac. My servant Louvrier, a strong robust man, looked after my horses. Thanks to the precautions I'd taken at Moscow I had less to suffer from than anyone.'

Just outside Vereia the retreating army runs into Marshal Mortier's two Young Guard divisions. They'd left Moscow, four-fifths of it in ashes, at 7 a.m. on 22 October, with orders to march for Borowsk via Vereia, after blowing up the Kremlin. Not until 11 p.m. that evening had the last unit left the city. While Mortier had been making his preparations something extraordinary had happened. Curious to see what was going on, General

Winzingerode, the commander of the Russian forces north of the city, had taken it into his head to walk into it dressed in a civilian overcoat. Upon his trying to chat up a post of the 5th Tirailleurs,[24] its lieutenant, who'd had his wits about him, had arrested him despite his 'vain attempt to save himself by pretending he'd come to parley and waving a white handkerchief,' and sent him to Mortier. Winzingerode's ADC, a Captain Narishkin, wondering what had become of his chief, had insisted on also being taken prisoner.

Mortier's force consists of General Delaborde's Young Guard division with its artillery, some sappers, a brigade of 500 cavalry who still have their mounts, and Carrière's scratch brigade of 4,000 troopers who haven't. As they join the column, Dr *Heinrich von Roos* of the 3rd Württemberg Chasseurs notes these provisional units are

'armed like infantrymen with muskets from the Moscow arsenal. This armament was so little to their liking that when they saw the great disorder prevailing among us they threw away both muskets and ammunition and each went aside on his own, his portmanteau on his back and holding the ramrod in his hand like a stick, without any officer being able to prevent them.'

Just as Napoleon's getting off his horse Winzingerode and Narishkin are brought before him. And instantly he's anything but the calm self-possessed person Dedem had seen. The Emperor of the French has a long memory.

'"Who are you?" he shouts at Winzingerode, unleashing on him all his frustration at the turn the campaign has taken:

'"A man without a country! You've always been my personal enemy. You've fought with the Austrians against me, then asked to serve with the Russians. You've been one of the greatest perpetrators of this war.[25] Yet you were born in the kingdom of Württemberg, in the states of the Confederation of the Rhine! You're my subject! You aren't an ordinary enemy, you're a rebel, and I've the right to bring you before a court. Do you see this desolate countryside, Monsieur, these villages in flames? Who ought to be reproached with these disasters, who are they due to? To fifty adventurers like yourself, suborned by England, which has thrown them on the Continent. You've been taken with weapons in your hand. I've the right to have you shot!"'

Winzingerode tries to explain that since the French had anyway been on the verge of evacuating Moscow there'd been no point in further hostilities. His attempted parley had aimed at avoiding useless bloodshed and above all at preventing any further damage to the city. He denies he's one of Napoleon's subjects, not having been in his native country since he was a child. If he's serving Tsar Alexander it's out of personal devotion.

'The more M. de Winzingerode tried to justify himself, the angrier the Emperor became, raising his voice so loud that even the picket could hear him.'

Present at the stormy interview are Caulaincourt, for four years ambassador at St Petersburg and explicitly against the war from the outset. The middle-aged Berthier, who's beginning to have had enough of wars of any kind. And, at a more respectful distance, other staff officers.[26]

'At first the officers of his entourage had withdrawn a little. Everyone was on tenterhooks. Glancing at each other, we could see in every eye the distress caused by this painful scene.'

Berthier, standing closest to his master, is most distressed of all, as the others can

'see in his expression, and his remarks confirmed it when, on some pretext, he was able to join us. The Emperor called for the gendarmes to take M. de Winzingerode away. When no one passed on this order, he repeated it so loudly that the two men attached to the picket stepped forward. The Emperor then repeated to the prisoner some of the charges, adding that he deserved to be shot as a traitor.'

Stung by this word Winzingerode,

'who'd been listening with eyes lowered to the ground, drew himself up, raised his head, and looking straight at the Emperor and those standing nearest to him, said loudly:

'"As whatever you please, Sire – but not as a traitor!"

'And walked away of his own accord, ahead of the guards, who kept their distance.'

Now Murat arrives on the scene and tries to calm his raging brother-in-law who's

'walking to and fro with nervous hurried steps, summoning now one of us, now another, to vent his anger. He met only with silence.'

Caulaincourt, who has witnessed many an imperial rage, has 'never seen him so angry.' Clearly Winzingerode's life's in danger. General *Jean Rapp*, Napoleon's favourite ADC, 'is sure he'd have been in despair if this order, obviously dictated in a furious rage, had been carried out'; and joins with others in begging him to postpone it. This only sets Napoleon off inveighing against the Russian nobility 'which had dragged Alexander into making war:

'"The weight of this war is going to fall on those who've provoked it. In the spring I'll go to St Petersburg and throw that town into the Neva."'

Berthier, 'beside himself', sends an ADC to the headquarters élite gendarmes, ordering them to treat their prisoner with consideration. 'Everyone,' says de Ségur,[27] 'hastened to wait upon the captive general to reassure and condole with him.' But neither Berthier nor Caulaincourt have

'ever seen the Emperor so completely lose control of himself. A little way off we could see a fine large house. The Emperor sent two squadrons to sack and fire it, adding: "Since these barbarians like to burn their towns we must help them."'

An action which strikes Caulaincourt as peculiarly shocking:

'It was the only time I'd ever heard him give such an order. As a rule he tried to prevent such destruction as only harmed private interests or ruined private citizens. He returned to Vereia before nightfall. Not one inhabitant remained.'

To Bessières' ADC Major Baudus, too, the scene has come as 'one more proof that the Emperor perfectly realised the depths of the abyss to whose edge he'd let himself be drawn'. The wounded Rapp and all the staff are sorry for the 'traitor' and do what they can for him and for his loyal and self-sacrificing ADC. Narishkin, says Dedem, 'was shown more consideration'.

Napoleon usually doesn't give a fig for Berthier's views – his job is simply to implement the commander-in-chief's orders. But now even Berthier makes so bold as to point out that Winzingerode *isn't* in fact one of the Emperor's subjects. Together with Caulaincourt he urges Murat to have another word with him. By now Caulaincourt's anyway becoming easier in his mind about the outcome 'in proportion to the Emperor's annoyance. Princes, like other men, have a conscience which bids them right the wrongs they've done.' And by and by he's sent for.

'"Has the courier arrived?"' Napoleon asks.

The question's a good omen. Napoleon knows very well it's still too early in the day,[28] and is already 'much quieter'. But still needs to vent his spleen. Winzingerode's behaviour, Caulaincourt hastily agrees, has been 'most irregular'; but surely His Majesty has 'used his prisoner so sternly in words that no further punishment is needed?' Won't further severity only look like an act of personal act of malice against the Tsar, whose ADC Winzingerode is? Rulers, Caulaincourt makes so bold as to observe,

'"have no need, after so many cannonballs have been exchanged, to come personally to grips with each other".

'The Emperor began to laugh, and affectionately pinched my ear, as was his habit when he tried to coax people.

'"You're right. But Winzingerode's a bad character, a schemer, a secret agent of the London government and Alexander's been at fault in making him his ADC."'

But he, Napoleon, won't be equally at fault in treating him badly:

'"I'd rather they'd captured a Russian. These foreigners in the service of the highest bidder are a poor catch. So it's for Alexander's sake you're taking an   interest in him? Well, well, we won't do him any harm."

'The Emperor gave me a little tap on the cheek, his signal mark of affection. From the outset I'd seen he only wanted an excuse to go back on his words.'

And in fact Napoleon tells Caulaincourt to 'try to persuade Narishkin to dine with us'. As for Winzingerode,

'"I'll send him to France, under a good escort, to prevent him from intriguing throughout Europe with three or four other firebrands of his sort."'

At dinner Napoleon turns to Narishkin:

'"What's your name?"

'"Narishkin," the young officer replied.

39

'"Narishkin! With a name like that one is too good to be adjutant to a defector."'

'This piece of rudeness upset us extremely,' Rapp says, 'and we did all we could to make the general overlook it.' Still speaking to Narishkin, Napoleon tells him what an excellent moment it is for making an honourable peace, "the French army's movement being in some sort a retreat". Evidently he's intending to send Narishkin to Alexander.

Was the calm feigned, and the rage a real explosion of fury and frustration? Or vice versa? 'The trouble with Napoleon', writes Caulaincourt, 'was that he never for a moment stopped playing the great emperor.' In what concerns Narishkin, he changes his mind. For next day both men are sent to the head of the column to set out for France with an officer and an élite gendarme. Caulaincourt, who's already given Narishkin some money, sends his valet after him with one of his own overcoats, against the increasing cold.

In sharp contrast to the indiscipline prevailing among the 4,000 dismounted cavalry, Delaborde's division is in good shape. But his well-educated interpreter Lieutenant *Paul de Bourgoing* is oddly hatted; having unaccountably lost his own hat on eve of quitting Moscow, he's had to replace it with a doctor's head-dress. With him he still has his faithful and enterprising servant Victor, the plucky 13-year-old Parisian street-urchin who'd so dearly have liked to enlist as a drummer-boy, but been found too puny of stature, and whom Bourgoing out of pure kindness had taken on as his 'philistine'. Delaborde's nature, too, is generous and hospitable. His little household has grown to include four French civilians from Moscow and two actresses from the French Theatre in Moscow. Also a painter named Lavanpierre, and a tutor ('a learned grammarian') named Lardillon. Mme. Anthony, one of the actresses, is sure she'll never see France again, and is often in tears.[29] 'The day we left Vereia,' Planat de la Faye goes on,

> 'began our embarrassments caused by the quantity of useless vehicles encumbering the army. In the defiles the military police and artillery officers overturned and smashed several of these carriages to right and left of the road. Above all they were pitiless toward such sutlers' wagons as didn't belong to any regiment. One of them being overturned, a magnificent harp and books bound in morocco and gilded on the spines fell out, to a great burst of laughter from all present.'

More and more guns and ammunition wagons are having to be left abandoned. All their horses have to eat is mouldy thatch off the one-storey timber cottages. Pion des Loches is shocked to see how

> 'superior officers first had the abandoned ammunition wagons parked, then burnt. The men were throwing away their weapons and packs to march more easily.'

Soon, he thinks, the army won't even be able to defend itself.

Terrible things happen in the evening of 28 October as Davout's corps reaches Vereia, greatly upsetting the cultured and humane Griois:

'At the entrance to the town some infantry battalions had halted to the left of the road. In front of them I saw their divisional general Friederichs, telling his men to take three Russian peasants they'd just seized to a certain distance and kill them. I trembled when I heard this order given at the top of his voice. The peasants thought they were being taken to some post to be guarded – I can still see them with their great overcoats and their cloth caps on which was sewn a Greek cross, impassively walking to their deaths as they didn't know what their fate was to be.'

Does such a cross worn on the headgear of the *opolchni* conscripts make them liable to pain of death if captured? Evidently Friederichs thinks so. They only have to go 40 paces from

'the general, who was following them with his eyes. I heard their cries. All three had had a bayonet thrust into the small of their backs just as they were entering a little straw hut. There they all fell down together, and the fire being put to it stifled their groans. I only knew this General Friederichs by sight. He was certainly one of the handsomest men in the army. But this abominable trait ever afterwards made me regard him with horror.'[30]

Although marching on ahead, even the Guard is obeying the order to burn everything, leaving it to III, IV and V Corps to 'set fire to the few houses that had been left'. This of course is leaving no shelter at all for I Corps. That evening Davout writes to Berthier from Vereia and asks His Serene Highness

'to give such orders as may be needed so that the troops marching ahead of the advance guard shall not burn the villages, thus destroying the resources the rearguard has such great need of.'

He even makes so bold as to point out that 'it alone should be charged with burning the villages it abandons'. And adds: 'The Emperor's army will have great benefit of this.' The order, Griois says, was rescinded. But the practice went on.

Not entirely, it seems. A big village has been left for the 85th to set fire to: 'Though it had offered us good shelter, it was none the less delivered over to the flames. As it lay in a dell we remained on the other slope while it burnt. On the far side was the enemy, indifferently watching this act of destruction.'

The same day 'some ammunition wagons were set fire to and blew up. In the distance the hollow projectiles, bursting one after another, emulated the sound of a battle.'

As for Vereia itself, that little palisaded town of muddy streets whose culinary delights Le Roy had earlier sampled when he'd visited it under more idyllic circumstances with a large detachment just before reaching Moscow,[31] 'though its gardens still offered us some vegetables the town itself no longer existed'.

I Corps is on its way from Vereia's blackened ruins towards Mojaisk where everyone knows they'll be rejoining the main Moscow–Smolensk highway, when suddenly the 85th are 'almost surrounded by enemy cavalry who seemed disposed to disturb us. It was then we, for the first time, made use of our regimental 4-pounders, which kept the enemy at a respectful distance.'

After Vereia comes Mojaisk. 'We'd passed through it 51 days ago as victors.' Since then it's been occupied by the sorry remnant of the Westphalian VIII Corps. Its commander General Junot, having lost the campaign for Napoleon at Valutina,[32] had been forbidden to show his face at the Kremlin. At Mojaisk, despite Commissary Kergorre's heroic disobedience to orders in his efforts to feed them and the plentiful harvest, the insouciant and selfish attitudes of Junot's staff had let any number of the Borodino wounded starve to death.[33] But now room must be found on the army's transports for the 2,000 or so who've survived and fill Mojaisk's remaining houses. What about the 200 wagons that have been brought from Moscow expressly for the purpose?

'Having left Moscow already full of refugees, women and children, the vehicles had had to take up the men wounded at Winkovo and Malojaroslavetz. And now these at Mojaisk!'
Hastily carried out and put on carts and carriages
'drawn by men from the hospitals, they were placed on the top-seats, on the fore-carriages, behind on the trunks, on the seats, in the fodder-carts. They were even put on the hoods of wagons if there wasn't any room underneath. One can imagine the spectacle our convoys presented. At the smallest jolt the least securely placed fell off. The drivers took no care. And the driver who followed after, if not distracted or in a stupor or away from his horses, or even for fear of stopping and losing his place in the queue, would drive on pitilessly over the body of the wretch who'd fallen.'
The weather's fine but chilly. 'Fortunately the keen frost preserved us from the infection the great numbers of dead men and horses would otherwise inevitably have caused.' Even so, IHQ skirts the town at a distance, for safety's sake, and presumably neither Planat nor Honoré Lariboisière visit the 'spot in the ruinous town wall' where they'd placed the mortal remains of young Ferdinand.[34] Do they cast a glance in that direction? Never, says Planat, will he forget its exact location.

When on the morrow Davout's regiments also 'skirt Mojaisk to avoid the last houses which had just been set fire to', they see how in the end only the church tower 'white amid black swirling smoke' is left standing, 'its clock still striking the hours after the town no longer existed'.

CHAPTER 2

BORODINO REVISITED

At Napoleon's bedside – the grim field of Borodino – 'cursing warfare, he predicted the Emperor himself would be abandoned'– ruthless vivandières *ditch the wounded – who shot the Russian prisoners? – Lejeune saves his sister – Davout's rearguard at Kolotskoïë abbey – a windfall at Ghjat – a heroic carabinier – Griois defends his cart – a devastated countryside – Colonel Chopin's robber band – a helpful Russian*

Spending the night of Wednesday, 28 October (the one Davout spends at Vereia) in the ruined château of Ouspenskoïë, just beyond Mojaisk, Napoleon, at 2 a.m., sends for Caulaincourt. 'He was in bed.' Telling the Master of the Horse to make sure the door's properly closed, he says he's to sit down at his bedside. 'This wasn't habitual with him.'

A long conversation follows. He asks Caulaincourt to speak his mind frankly about the situation. Wise from his four winters as ambassador at St Petersburg, Caulaincourt predicts the effects of extreme cold, and reminds him of 'the reply Alexander was said to have given when he'd got the peace proposals from Moscow: "My campaign's just beginning."'[1] The allusion irritates Napoleon, as does any reminder of Caulaincourt's personal knowledge of, and friendship with, the Tsar:

'"Your prophet Alexander's been wrong more than once," he retorted. But there was no lightness in his reply. His troops' superior intelligence would somehow enable them to protect themselves against the cold – they'd be able to take the same precautions as the Russians did, or even improve on them.'

And then there are the 'Polish Cossacks' that Ambassador Pradt's[2] certainly been drumming up in Warsaw. Any day now he's expecting to run into 1,500 or 2,000 of them. They'll change the situation entirely. Flanking the army, they'll enable it to rest and find food. Caulaincourt notes Napoleon's – as it seems – incurable optimism. After talking for an hour about one thing and another, he comes suddenly to the point. As soon as he has 'established the army in some definite position' it's 'possible, even likely' that he'll leave it and go back to Paris. What does Caulaincourt think about the idea? What effect will it have on morale? Caulaincourt, who's least of all a yes-man, agrees that it's an excellent idea, the best way of re-organising it and keeping a firm hand on Europe. He should date his orders of the day, like his decrees, from the Tuileries; but be careful about choosing the right moment to leave.'It was 5.30 when the Emperor dismissed me.'

If only they'd left Moscow a fortnight earlier, instead of hanging about waiting for peace overtures from the Tsar! That's what many people are thinking as they slowly pull out on to the main Smolensk road. Then they'd already be ensconced behind those medieval walls on which even the Grand Army's 12-pounders had made no impression, living off the well-stocked magazines and protected by Marshal Victor's IX Corps! True, the frozen Dnieper will no longer provide a line of defence. But, welcomed by its light infantrymen lining the surrounding hills, no one doubts the army's ability to hold out until the spring, far off though it be, five or six months away! And by then Marshal Augereau's XI (Reserve) Corps and Schwarzenberg's Austrians, together with many thousands of 'Polish Cossacks', will have come up and re-established the situation. And if the Tsar still doesn't make peace – why, then they'll march on Petersburg. It too is inflammable!

But from Mojaisk to Smolensk is 80 leagues,[3] well over 200 miles.

Meanwhile where's Kutusov? Fastest melting away of all is the cavalry – Lieutenant *von Kalckreuth*'s regiment, the 2nd Prussian Hussars, for instance, which had performed so brilliantly at Ostrovno in July,[4] now counts only twenty troopers and officers. And without cavalry reconnaissance an army's blind and deaf. So it's impossible to know. In fact Kutusov's main body is some 30 to 40 miles away to the south, following the road to Medyn (where Wilson's diary will rejoice on 30 October, 'The Cossacks have defeated the advanced guard of Prince Poniatowski.'). By now 'the English general', as Wilson always styles himself, is beside himself with fury at Kutusov's sloth, his indifference to his opportunities to annihilate the infamous Buonaparte, once and for all; and by making 'a false movement, occasioned by his personal terror rather than by an error of judgement', having made 'a circuit of near 80 versts [50 miles]' and losing sight of the French:

> 'I can scarcely behave with common decency in his presence. His feebleness outrages me to such a degree that I have declared, if he remains Commander-in-Chief, that I must retire from this army.'

Probably nothing would please Kutusov more. Pestered by all and sundry, he's beswarmed with intrigues. And his army too is extremely short of rations as it struggles along the Medyn road.

At least the Smolensk road is better. 'Leaving the ploughed fields which had cost us more than 10,000 vehicles', the army begins moving off down it. First, the pitiful remains of Junot's (Westphalian) VIII Corps. Then the Imperial Guard. Then III Corps. Then Eugène's IV Corps. Last – a day's march behind – Davout's once so formidable I Corps. Each in turn crosses the broken ground beyond Mojaisk – those ravines where, on 8 September, Murat's impulsiveness had thrown away the lives of so many of his troopers – and plunges into the forest beyond. Beyond that, everyone knows, lies the terrible battlefield.

There have been others where Napoleon has held commemorative parades – Austerlitz, for instance. No one thinks of holding one here.

Emerging from the forest they first see to their right 'the remains of the cabins where Kutusov had camped' and where he'd made his fateful decision to retreat and, if necessary, even abandon Moscow. But most of the mournful scene is spread out to their left: 'It was a cold day,' Lieutenant von Muraldt of IV Corps' 4th Bavarian Chasseurs will always remember, 'and a furiously whirling snow, whipped up by an icy wind, did nothing to dispel our gloomy thoughts.'

Dumonceau, riding on as usual ahead of the rest of the Guard and 'crossing the Borodino bridge where so many had fallen',[5] can just make out

'the former redoubts, covered in snow. Standing out white against a murky horizon, they were no longer visible except as shapeless hillocks. This plain, once so noisy and animated, was now only a vast solitude.'

The sole sign of life he can see is 'a horseman, doubtless looking for some souvenir or memento'. Also, 'the immense flocks of carrion crows which for several days now had constituted our habitual cortège, as if following a prey they could be sure of' and whose sinister activities are marked all along the roadside 'by messy reddened snow from which protruded the hideous remains of half-eaten corpses'.[6] Mailly-Nesle and his favoured companions, looking out of their carriage, notice that many of the dead are

'as yet hardly decomposed, and had kept what one might call a physiognomy. Almost all had their eyes fixedly open. Their beards had grown out of all measure for this epoch. And a bricklike and Prussian-blue colour, marbling their cheeks, gave them an abominably filthy and messy aspect.'

Following immediately behind with IHQ, another aristocratic officer, Quartermaster *Anatole de Montesquiou*, is horrified to see

'a Frenchman wounded at this battle who'd been left without help. He'd sat down with his back to a tree beside the road and was waiting for the Emperor to pass. As soon as he recognised him he advanced on all fours and reproached him for all he'd suffered by being so cruelly abandoned. He went on cursing war and predicting that the Emperor himself would be abandoned and forgotten. The Emperor showed only pity. Turning to his officers who were following him he said: "Have this poor fellow put in a carriage and lavish every care on him."'

Captain *K. F. E. von Suckow*, who'd had to leave his dead Württembergers unburied, finds

'the famous battlefield in exactly the same state as we'd left it in on 8 or 9 September. More than 20,000 corpses of men and horses in a more or less advanced state of decomposition were lying where they'd fallen'.

The only difference, Surgeon-Major von Roos of the 3rd Württemberg Chasseurs notes, is that 'the grass had grown since that sanguinary day'. Not far from the Great Redoubt, the bloodiest spot of all, von Suckow sees an object sticking up. Curious, he rides over to take a closer look. It's

'a simple pine trunk stuck in the earth, and bearing a noticeboard, on which was written in ink already half-effaced by the rain, these words, which I've faithfully preserved: *"Here lies General Montbrun. Passer-by, of whatever nation you may be, respect these ashes! They belong to the bravest soldier in the world. This feeble monument has been raised to him at the orders of his faithful friend the Marshal Ney."'*[7]

Farther on the Italians see 'rising up like a pyramid in the midst of a desert' the famous Great Redoubt.[8] Leaving Eugène's staff, Labaume too rides over and climbs what can only be a heaped up mass of corpses. From the summit of the so fiercely contested redoubt he sees a solitary soldier whose 'motionless figure produced in the distance the effect of a statue'. But he also hears unfortunates crying out for help:

> 'One of these was a French soldier who'd lost both legs and for two months been living off the stream and herbs, roots, and a few bits of bread he'd found on corpses, and at nights had been sleeping in the bellies of eviscerated horses. A general took pity on him and placed him in his carriage.'

Reaching the Kolotchka stream, IV Corps crosses it at least as precipitately as it had done when moving in the opposite direction to storm the Great 'Raevsky' Redoubt, at first ineffectually, then with success:

> 'The slope down to the little river was so steep and the soil so slippery that men and horses instantly fell on top of each other. On all sides were only horses' carcasses and half-buried corpses, blood-stained coats, bones gnawed by dogs and birds of prey, and the debris of arms, drums, helmets and cuirasses. There we also found the shreds of standards. From the emblems on them one could judge how much the Muscovite eagle had suffered on that sanguinary day. Crossing the theatre of their exploits our men proudly showed the places where their regiments had fought.'

'Yet', reflects von Muraldt, grimly contemplating the scene,

> 'the masses of blood that had flowed on this soil and the advantage gained by such convulsive efforts hadn't led to anything except a retreat, with unexampled difficulties and sufferings!'

The dead at least are at rest. A couple of miles farther on beyond these scenes of horror comes another, in its way even more ghastly. The enormous walled and turreted edifice of the Kolotskoië monastery which the Italian Guardia d'Onore's Adjutant-major *Cesare de Laugier*, when he'd first glimpsed it in the distance on 5 September, had taken for a whole town and which during and after the battle had been the army's hospital where Surgeon-General Baron *Dominique-Jean Larrey* had made so many amputations, strikes Colonel Fezensac as 'nothing but a vast cemetery'. All its monks had fled. Only some 2,000 of the 20,000 wounded collected there have survived. Though Larrey finds the dressing-stations he'd set up there,

> 'no one had bothered to use the fine weather to evacuate the wounded. They were squatting in a stinking infectious barn, surrounded on all sides by corpses, almost never receiving any rations and obliged to eat cabbage stalks boiled with horseflesh to escape the horrors of famine. Because of a severe shortage of linen, their wounds had seldom been dressed. The surgeons were themselves having to launder the bandages and compresses.'

The Belgian surgeon *D. de Kerkhove* is so horrified that his 'pen refuses to describe the sufferings the sick and wounded had been reduced to'. What's become of the supplies of medicines and food, etc., sent back from Moscow? He's sure those who'd already died are happiest. As III Corps arrives in the wake of the Imperial Guard, Napoleon immediately orders a brigade of 200 Württemberg chasseurs and light infantry to lift all the wounded on to sutlers' carts. Surgeon Roos sees his Württembergers carrying them out and their officers indicating where they're to be placed. Although the men complain of this imposed fatigue,

'the order was carried out in the most punctilious fashion, and all was finished in an hour and a half. Every carriage, whether it belonged to a marshal or a colonel, every wagon, every *cantinière's* cart or *droschka* had to take one or two.'

Even the fastidious Mailly-Nesle and his fair companions have to move over: 'One of the Emperor's footmen, Mouet by name, had been detailed off to take care of them, which he did meticulously.' Dumonceau, waiting a long time outside the main gate, sees Larrey himself standing there, 'presiding over their departure and reassuring them with encouraging remarks'. Although most have to 'to drag themselves along on foot, some on crutches', all strike the Belgian captain as 'joyful and resolute to resume their journey'. Perhaps they realise instinctively that they're luckier, at least for the time being, than those placed on carts?

For these the journey's going to be short. 'However good the Emperor's intentions,' the mild and pious Surgeon Roos exclaims, horrified,

'it turned out badly for the poor wounded. They fell into the hands of crude-minded coachmen, insolent valets, brutal sutlers, enriched and arrogant women, brothers-in-arms without pity, and all the riff-raff of the Train. All these people only had one idea: how to get rid of their wounded.'

From the inept cavalry general Lahoussaye – travelling along in his carriage and apparently doing nothing to help Grouchy, his superior, at the rearguard – Murat's Neapolitan ADC, Colonel *M.-J.-T. Rossetti*, hears that 'the *vivandières*, whose carts were laden with the loot of Moscow and who hadn't accepted them without murmuring at this extra weight' are deliberately falling behind and letting the column overtake them. 'Then, waiting for a moment when they were alone, they threw all these unfortunates who'd been confided to their care into the ditches. Only one survived sufficiently to be picked up by the first carriages to pass.' Never has the Master of the Horse seen, nor will ever see,

'a sight so horrible as our army's march 48 hours after Mojaisk. Every heart was closed to pity by fear of starvation, of losing the overladen vehicles, of seeing the starving exhausted horses die. I still shudder when I tell you I've seen men deliberately drive their horses at speed over rough ground, so as to get rid of the unfortunates overburdening them. Though they knew the horses would mutilate them or the wheels crush them, they'd smile triumphantly, even so, when a jolt freed them from of one of these poor wretches. Every man thought of himself and himself alone.'

47

It's Mojaisk all over again. When Larrey hears about wounded men being dumped in ditches he complains to Napoleon. Who has some of the worst offenders shot.

All that 'long and painful day' Rossetti and others at IHQ are 'hearing detonations at every instant. It was ammunition wagons that were being blown up for lack of horses to pull them.'

Somewhere towards the head of the column 3,000 Russian prisoners are being herded along, though no one has any food for them:

'Parked like cattle, they weren't being allowed to go a yard from the spot. Laid out on the ice [*sic*], all those who didn't want to perish were eating the flesh of their comrades who'd just expired from their miseries.'

And now, 'three miles before reaching Ghjat', here's another terrible sight, heavy of sinister import:

'Lying to the left of the road were about 200 Russians, who'd just been killed. We noticed that each of them had his head shattered in the same way and his bleeding brain was spread out beside him.'

They've just been shot by their Spanish and Portuguese escort. 'Each of us, depending on his character, approved or remained indifferent. The Emperor kept a sombre silence.' Not so Captain *Josef Zalusky*, who's already seen them as he's riding along at the head of the Polish Guard Lancers beside their CO, General Krasinski:

'We were horrified. Indignant, Krasinski galloped forward to the officer in charge at the head of the column, a Portuguese colonel. Krasinski reproached him for his barbarous cruelty that nothing justified. The Portuguese took these observations very much amiss and replied in an improper manner. It was neither the moment nor the place for a discussion. Krasinski hastened to the Emperor's staff and told them how the prisoners had been treated. The Emperor immediately sent his *officier d'ordonnance* Gourgaud to obtain clarification of this incident.'

The Polish count and artillery officer *Roman Soltyk*, marching with IHQ's Topographical Department, has actually heard the shots:

'To my horror I'd been told straggling prisoners were being shot by their Spanish escorts. In vain the Spanish soldiers had pushed them on with blows of their musket butts; in the end they fell down exhausted. Whereupon these barbarians fired bullets into their ears to finish them off.'

Roos counts 'eight of these corpses' and on reaching Ghjat is told the cold-blooded massacre had been the work of 'some Baden grenadiers'[9] who'd been cruelly ordered to kill 'all prisoners who might become exhausted and unable to go on'. Fezensac, too, hears they'd been shot by troops of the Confederation of the Rhine:

'I owe the men of my regiment the justice of saying that they were indignant. They realised too what cruel reprisals the sight of such barbarism would expose any of them to who might fall into the enemy's hands.'

Soltyk, a fervent admirer of Napoleon, is clearly unable to believe his hero can condone such murders: 'As soon as he was told of these horrible executions he showed his extreme displeasure and put an instant stop to them.' And both Rossetti and Roos notice that 'these executions ceased from the next day, when the Cossacks began to harass us between Ghjat and Viazma.'

Everyone feels that the retreat, crawling along at a snail's pace, is going far too slowly. And it's the unpopular Davout who gets the blame – though others, Labaume says, defended his method:

'Too hasty a retreat would have redoubled the enemy's audacity. If the rearguard had refused to stand and fight, their light cavalry would have been able to cut it to pieces.'

Actually I Corps has left Mojaisk this morning, followed by ever-increasing swarms of Cossacks, who're trying delay if not actually cut it off. Just after leaving what's left of Mojaisk, its chief-of-staff Lejeune sees them

'trying to force a passage across our path, but without success. They had to restrict themselves to pursuing and briskly cannonading one of our big convoys which, considerably delayed, had to pass across their front as it emerged from the town. Their roundshot was doing horrible work among the convoy, several hundred ill-harnessed vehicles, carrying many wounded as well as the wives and children of French businessmen resident in Moscow who'd been pillaged and were obliged to flee from the Russians. There was even the personnel of the Moscow French theatre.'

In that convoy, he knows, is his own half-blind sister. The carriage in which he'd sent her on ahead from Moscow was one of his own; and he'd

'taken care to furnish it with food and furs and harnessed it to three good horses with good grooms and under the protection of some of our wounded generals and, even more, under the aegis of Providence'.

Now he's so lucky as to be able to snatch it – and her – out of the panicking convoy:

'Her coachman assured me the three horses were still excellent and full of vigour. So I asked my sister: "Are you up to braving the guns?" Trembling she replied: "I'll do whatever you wish." At once I told the coachman: "Cross this plain at the gallop, the cannonballs will pass over your head. In this way you'll reach the head of the convoy, after which you can get on unopposed and without stopping." My advice was good and he succeeded.'

Hearing Cossack cannon for the first time during the retreat, Le Roy, marching with the 85th Line, knows how to interpret the sound:

'We were going to be relentlessly pursued by the enemy's army and by the entire population of this savage countryside. We'd only be able to count on our own courage and tenacity to escape out of the hands of these barbarians.'

Coming to the Kolotchka stream with the extreme rearguard, Griois finds the 'fragile bridge we'd built over it[10] broken. We ourselves forded it easily. But it wasn't the same for the guns. They had a lot of trouble getting clear of its muddy bed and climbing up its steep banks. Several vehicles remained there. Only when we were out of this fix did we realise we were on the battlefield we'd left seven weeks ago. No more illusions now!' Running his glance over the 'ravines still covered with weapons, roundshot and debris', he too has some

'sad reflections. The future had darkened. I recognised the various positions I'd occupied during the battle. Silence, solitude reigned, replacing the noise of the thousand guns and innumerable masses which had smashed into each other there two months ago.'

While waiting for his artillery to ford the stream – 'but fatigue and the draft horses' bad nourishment didn't allow us to do so very promptly' – he hears less ghostly guns firing to the rear. It's the rearguard (evidently he's been relieved) 'standing firm to halt the enemy who was pressing us too hard, and to give the artillery and baggage encumbering the ford to get clear of it'. A little way away he sees Davout himself, on foot, urging on 'the isolated units preceding his rearguard'. Davout tells him to get a move on. It's easier said than done. But by and by he and his friend the witty if not exactly amiable Colonel Jumilhac bivouac in a ravine near the monastery walls, which protect them from the biting wind. 'Not far from there General Grouchy had established himself under a tent. It was the last time I saw him during the retreat. The ground was completely frozen over.' Griois too sees the abandoned wounded – 'some who'd been evacuated from Moscow; also those who'd been brought there after the battle'.

Le Roy, Jacquet and Guillaume bivouac on the actual battlefield. 'The famous redoubts were on our left. Of Borodino itself only the church was still standing.' So does the Dromedary of Egypt. The 30th's passage across the Kolotchka is particularly dreadful. 'After a slow painful march of eighteen miles across the snow that everywhere covered the ground' Captain François and his men haven't

'a blade of straw to lie down on. Nor could we make up a fire, the wind being so violent it put it out as soon as we tried to light one. My horses were still carrying a few victuals for me, but there was no longer anything to feed them on except the few rotten leaves they nosed about for under the snow. The French cursed their sad destiny and impatiently waited for sunrise to get on the march again, without having taken the least nourishment to restore their strength.'

Next morning Davout's last unit, the 7th Light Infantry, crosses the battlefield and Carabinier-Sergeant *Vincent Bertrand* finds:

'thousands of bits and pieces of weapons and *matériel* belonging to both armies under our feet. Here and there the remains of our comrades fallen on the field of honour. The redoubts, though breached, were still standing, and we recalled the alternative options in that battle of giants. This one we'd taken at bayonet point, that one over there had repulsed us. Glorious but dolorous memories!'

And when, an hour later, he too reaches the abbey, the 7th Light take up position there. 'The enemy attacks us in force.' In fact there's a sharp engagement. The whole of Platov's force, with cannon, falls on the 30th Line. Captain François' men

'can't go a thousand paces without having to halt and face about, albeit without firing – the mere movement's enough to send these fanatics flying. They come up till they're a hundred paces from us and deafen us with their hurrahs. Sometimes we fire a few salvoes of cannon fire at them. As we approach the village of Kolotskoië,[11] they unite themselves into a vast body and attack our army corps. We fight them off, after they've killed a few men and taken five ammunition wagons.'

The fight costs the 7th Light

'a few killed and wounded. The latter no longer re-appeared with the flag. The few wounded in the abbey, [although] almost cured, were abandoned too.'

(Did it perhaps cost more than that? Or is the 'the agreeable news' that reaches Kutusov's headquarters of Platov's men having captured '20 cannon and two standards and the destruction of two battalions at the convent of Kollodiy [sic] near Borodino' exaggerated, as so many Cossack claims turn out to be?)

Anyway it's the end of the 2nd Prussian Hussars. Under the monastery walls its officers are told that their regiment's dissolved. Erased from the list of combatants, they're free to proceed as they like, each take his own orderly or, if he prefers, attach himself to some general of his choice. Before quitting the position Lejeune wishes,

'to find out how many of the enemy were turning up in the plain. So I went forward and stood on a terrace of the monastery, and found myself in the presence of 100 or so Cossacks who were approaching to reconnoitre. Seeing me, they took to their heels; but realising I was on my own, soon came back, and I, in my turn, hardly had time to rejoin our own men who'd left and were already far off.'

'From Borowsk to the main Smolensk highway there'd been no real road. We'd made our way across forests, fields and swamps.' But the Moscow highway's both broad and well-paved. Yet now they've reached it, Cuirassier Captain *Bréaut des Marlots* is distressed to see everyone beginning 'to march more or less on his own account'. First Corps' Paymaster Duverger sees 'all the villages within our reach are burning. We moved toward Smolensk between hedges of flame – a measure necessary, it was said, to slow the enemy's pursuit.' Nor can the abandonment of so many wounded be helping morale. Each unit', Ségur confirms, 'seemed to be marching on its own. There was no staff, no order; no common knot to bind all the units together.' 'There's not a man isn't terrified at the thought of what awaits him,' Captain *Charles François* is thinking as he limps along in the rear with the 30th Line:

'Here we are, only 120 miles from Moscow, in the middle of a devastated countryside where we fight only by the light of burning buildings. Today, the ranker, if he has anything to eat and who used to share his

morsel of bread with his comrade, is carefully hiding the little he has.'
Murat's ADC Rossetti is certainly not the only one to be feeling a nip in the
air. Winter's on the way:

'A mere gust of wind lasting a few minutes is enough to bring it on,
rough and biting. In an instant everything changes – roads, faces, men's
courage. The army's becoming sombre, its march painful, and consternation's beginning to spread.'

Lejeune orders those horses which, on a highway littered with vehicles,
have dropped from sheer inanition and can be put on their feet again to
be

'immediately harnessed up to carts laden with the wounded. But
scarcely had they dragged themselves a few paces than they died. So our
wounded remained there, abandoned. And as we went off and left them,
averting our glances, we had to harden our hearts to their cries. This day
[30 October] was very long and dreary. We had to march all night long,
in a cold that was beginning to feel very keen, because we had to get to
Ghjat before the enemy, who was forcing his marches by cross-country
roads to get there first.'

Until two months ago, 'one of the most flourishing commercial towns in
Russia, where leathers, canvas, tar and ropes needed by the navy were
manufactured', Ghjat has already been reached by IHQ yesterday evening
– only to find that all its timber houses, carelessly reduced to ashes on the
eve of the battle, have 'vanished almost without trace. One would have
thought one was on the site of a forest fire.' Only its main street of stone
houses still stands. The weather may be cold, but it's brilliantly sunny.
Caulaincourt, who ever since Vereia has been marching on foot 'and finding it to my advantage, as I didn't suffer from the cold', notices how the
temperature has fallen:

'At Borowsk we'd begun to feel the cold. Only the surface of the ground
had been frozen. The weather had been fine, and the nights quite
endurable in the open if one had a fire. Here at Ghjat the winter was
already more noticeable.'

But here at least is an unexpected windfall, if only for IHQ. Part of a convoy partly pillaged by Cossacks 'in charge of two footmen, are the remains
of a consignment sent from France for the Emperor's household'. Since
the horses are beginning to fail and they've no means of taking its surplus
with them, they distribute it among themselves, 'and there was abundance
at headquarters. Clos-Vouillet and Chambertin were the commonest wines'
– luckily for Napoleon, who drinks nothing else:

'We stored up our strength and a sense of well-being against the days of
real privation ahead. Everyone still had a few provisions. A small biscuit
ration was issued. In spite of the cold nights and several patches of
ground where a brief thaw had made the going difficult, the men were
standing up well to the long marches.'

But it's different with the horses. Caulaincourt's prime duty is to keep
them operational:

'They were worn out by having to go six miles from the road to forage and because of the wretched quality of what, at cost of so much danger and exhaustion, was being brought back. All but the strongest were dying. The reserve horses were being harnessed up: but since they no longer sufficed, we were already beginning to abandon some of the vehicles.'

One of Ghjat's still standing stone buildings has been used as a hospital; and when III Corps gets there its colonels are ordered to go and identify any wounded from their regiments. 'The sick', Fezensac is shocked to see, 'had been left without medicines, without food, without any help. Amidst all the refuse of every sort encumbering the stairs, the corridors, and the centre of the halls,' he can hardly get inside, but is 'delighted to be able to save a few men' of the 4th Line. But what's the good? Shortly afterwards Dr Réné Bourgeois, too, is horrified to see no one's really bothering about these sick men. Already it's as much as a healthy one can do to stay alive, and the *vivandières* and officers' servants driving the carts and wagons

'soon got rid of them either by offloading them by the roadside or intentionally forgetting them at the bivouacs. Not one of them would reach Smolensk.'

Wounded generals, of course, are another matter. Never has Rapp never seen so many:

'General Friant, whose wounds still hadn't healed, General Durosnel, who was almost all the time suffering from nervous fever and delirium; General Belliard [Murat's chief-of-staff], who'd been hit by a musket ball at Borodino ...'

or, more exactly, at the Mojaisk ravines. To his list Rapp could have added Dedem, whose chest bruise, dating from Smolensk in August, still hasn't healed properly and is causing him ever worse pain.

And here's something shocking, that bodes ill for the future. Invited by some grenadiers of the Old Guard to share their campfire beside a half-demolished wall, von Suckow witnesses something that not only astounds but also deeply worries him:

'Hardly had I installed myself than one of those staff officers in such an elegant uniform – blue with red waistcoat and silver hussar-style aiguillettes – came up to my grenadiers and invited them to leave their nice warm spot and cede it to General NN and the officers of his staff. How stupefied was I – a German officer used to the severest discipline – to hear one of the grenadiers, getting up, say in a loud voice:

'"*Mon officier*, there are now no longer any generals. There are only unfortunates. We're staying where we are."

'The other retired without a word.'[12]

That evening Surgeon Roos is surprised to bump into an officer who – quite voluntarily – has collected a party of his chasseurs and, wanting to see Moscow, brought them all the way from the Niemen:

'But he'd arrived too late. We were still gathered around our fire when we heard that our king had arrived from Stuttgart, bringing money for

the rank and file, decorations and sabres of honour, gold medals and money for officers and men who'd distinguished themselves.'
All of which may be gratifying but in the present circumstances isn't the least use. By contrast Roos sees that many men are belatedly trying to rough-shoe their horses against the winter. But within a 6 or 7-mile band of devastated countryside on either side of the route there's 'not a straw of hay' to feed them with. Though Major Bonnet, getting to Ghjat, is sent out with 300 men of the 18th Line to maraud, he finds not a grain or any forage in the villages: 'The inhabitants and quadrupeds had decamped. We brought back absolutely nothing.' Ghjat is 'surrounded by small streams flowing through lakes.' The 85th Line, getting there next day with I Corps, finds

'the bridge badly rebuilt and we'd a lot of trouble getting across, because of the congestion of teams and vehicles. The jam and the lack of order at the rivers soon caused the two wretched hastily reconstructed bridges to cave in. The swampy ground around them couldn't support the vehicles' weight. A great number got stuck there.'

Among them Le Roy sees to his dismay 'a wagon belonging to my former battalion, with my trunk inside it'. But the resourceful Guillaume rescues much of its contents.

By now III Corps' Württemberg infantry division is reduced to only two platoons. Next morning it leaves what had once been the 'pretty little town of Ghjat' and until late in the evening manages to hold off the Cossacks until the panicking mob of stragglers have passed on. One of von Suckow's feet is becoming frost-bitten. Wearing 'a red velvet dressing-gown with rabbit skin linings' he hitches a ride in a yellow carriage led by a barefooted Russian girl and driven by a French businessman with a blunderbuss across his knees. Inside are two young French ladies.
Then the ruins of Ghjat, too, are left behind.

Riding ahead with Prince Eugène's staff, Labaume sees a
'countryside trampled by thousands of horses, which seemed never to have been cultivated. The farther we advanced the more the earth seemed to be in mourning.'

The marching regiments are all jumbled up with convoys of various kinds. The Prussian lieutenant *Heinrich August Vossler*'s convoy of 100 Württemberg wounded from Borodino ('including some 50 fit for duty') had almost reached Moscow when they'd had to turn back and been caught up in the retreat's chaos:

'Day by day the column was growing, for anyone travelling along that road was seeking safety in attaching himself to our contingent, whose defensive strength increased proportionately. In a matter of days we found ourselves in the company of generals and officers of every rank, and every arm of the service was represented. Few were fully equipped. Some carried an odd assortment of weapons. Most were unarmed. But all, without exception, were burdened with a rich collection of loot, ranging from worthless rags to finest shawls, from tattered sheepskins to costly furs, from rickety carts to gilded coaches. For the rest, certain distinctions still prevailed. The infantryman was still marching on foot, the trooper either rode a *konya* or shared some kind of vehicle with several others, or at least as long as it could keep its feet drove in front of him his galled nag, loaded with his weapons. Apart from Frenchmen there were Spaniards, Portuguese, Germans, Poles, Dalmatians, Illyrians, etc.' Now Sergeant Bertrand is realising that not all wounded who fall behind are reappearing, 'something which from this moment onwards was becoming the invariable rule'. 'Right now', Captain François goes on,

'the army's position is horrible! As for me, since leaving Moscow, despite my two bullet-holes in my left leg and several other wounds which still haven't formed scabs, I've been marching all the time with my right foot in a down-at-heel shoe. But like all my brothers-in-arms I foresee such ills, and don't dream of bothering about my wounds. I no longer dress them, and my good leg goes on as if it were a machine.'

And always there are

'cannon at our heels, as well as irregular Cossacks, barbarians, who were joining up with the peasantry to do us as much harm as possible. The latter, riding lamentable nags, were armed with a long stick at the end of which they'd fixed an iron lance point or a long nail. From this moment we had to fight one against ten. A carabinier of my regiment, grievously wounded in the head during our defence of the Kolotskoïe abbey, was marching on his own to the left of the column formed by our [Gérard's] division. Assailed by three Cossacks, he's stricken by several lance thrusts and falls. These savages were trying to carry him away. But he, having held on to his sabre, gets up and puts himself on guard, intending to resist to the death. An unequal combat starts. Happily the Cossacks' yells reach his comrades who're flanking the column. A corporal goes back to help the wounded man. Tries to shoot. His musket misfires. So he attacks with the bayonet, and, seconded by the carabinier, soon puts one of these Cossacks *hors de combat* and takes the other two prisoner.'[13]

At one moment Griois, too, has to defend himself almost single-handed. All his remaining possessions, notably 'the little food we still had, and our kitchen outfit, a stew pot, a mess-tin and a camp-kettle' are 'in a little Russian go-cart I'd found en route'. But he's wearing a bearskin coat, the second he has bought en route, his first having been stolen – it's still possible to buy one for 30 or 40 francs. Having gone on ahead of his artillery, he's riding along together with his 'adjutant-major, two gunner orderlies, my Bavarian servant and a soldier of the Train' who's leading the cart some 500 or 600 paces ahead of them; when across the plain they catch sight of some horsemen, whose 'irregular way of riding and lances' show they're Cossacks:

'As soon as the soldier of the Train caught sight of the enemy he tried to turn back. But either this cart didn't turn easily or he was too precipitate, the pole-bolt holding the front carriage broke, and our baggage rolled out in the middle of the road. However little the booty tempted them, the Cossacks advanced. But it was our last resources which were in question! My adjutant and I draw our sabres and grasp our pistols. We place ourselves in front of our overturned cart, thoroughly determined to defend it, and I order my servant and the soldier of the Train to at least save what was most precious, i.e., the food; which they did with ardour and not letting themselves be intimidated by the presence and shouts of the enemy. It wasn't the same with the gunner orderlies, on whom I was counting even more. One went off on the pretext of finding help; the other fled.'

But though there are now only two of them, and they poorly armed, Griois and his adjutant-major show themselves so self-assured that, together no doubt with the sight of 'some infantry platoons that appeared in the distance', the Cossacks are sufficiently impressed, after 'prancing about in front of us and threatening us with their shouts and lances', and clear off. By and by, after taking the best of the cart's contents on to their horses for a while, Griois and his adjutant-major find an abandoned empty ammunition wagon to replace it:

'That evening my two gunners rejoined me, very much ashamed of themselves, and I treated them according to their deserts. However, I kept them by me, because one did the cooking and the other served me as secretary.'[14]

Others are in no position to defend themselves. Lieutenant Auvray of the 23rd Dragoons, for instance, is suffering

'from dysentery caused by the bad things we were being forced to eat so as not to die of hunger. We couldn't have passed along a stream, a pond or a ditch without drinking from it. To cap it all, I had a boil as big as an egg on my right thigh, which gave me great pain for eight days. Neither able to walk nor sit my horse, I had to lie across its saddle.'

Dedem, 'still living off the provisions we'd brought with us from Moscow', notes how troublesome any little stream can be:

'Since it hadn't been intended to take the Smolensk road again, no one had given a thought to rebuilding the little bridges the Russians had destroyed while retiring on Moscow and which we, during our advance, had passed by quite easily thanks to the drought and the summer heats.'

But now these bridges are a repeated source of ill-affordable delays:

'Now that the rains had begun again they'd become indispensable for the artillery and carriages; and all the time our march was held up by the need to rebuild them. It was frightening to see the immense quantity of carriages parked *en masse* and which could only get over one by one and very slowly. Woe to those vehicles which got stuck in the mud! They were promptly turned over and the owner, who had all his resources in them, thereafter saw himself exposed to lacking his basic needs!'

There are resourceful and not always scrupulous officers who're determined not to so expose themselves. Colonel Chopin, for instance, commander of 1st Cavalry Corps' artillery, whom Griois knows slightly and at whose bivouacs he, together with his friend Jumilhac and his adjutant-major, can be sure of enjoying some good soup,

'a bit of meat, and to round it off some coffee, a rarity, and, something even rarer, a bottle of hydromel a drink [made from honey] which, without being the equal of wine, is drinkable. A true devil-may-care of a fellow, persuaded that the vital thing is to stay alive and that one must above all think of oneself, since the retreat had started Colonel Chopin had gathered round him a dozen of his most alert gunners, most fertile in resourcefulness. A well-harnessed wagon followed him, and every evening it was the place of assembly to which each of his gunners brought whatever he'd managed to get hold of, either in the villages or, or at the expense of isolated men whom they, by force or persuasion, had stripped of part of their provisions. Thus the colonel's robber band (the only name one can give to it) lacked for nothing. The wagon was well-filled, and to see or listen to its purveyors, it'd never be empty. Chopin himself gave me these details. I hadn't the courage to blame the way in which he'd acquired the dinner we were eating, but could never make up my mind to resort to the same methods on my own account.'

But the best-stocked wagon can break down – indeed, the more heavily laden the more it is likely to do so. As Surgeon Lagneau's now does. Before leaving it behind, his party load their provisions on to the ambulance horses, 'in sacks suspended on either side'. Even his famous tent is

'loaded, together with its pegs, etc., on a little Cossack horse which was gallantly living on pine or willow bark and went up and down the ravines just like a little dog. His unshod hoofs had grown down so they had a very good grip on the ice.'

Reaching each night's halt, the party pitch their tent. To get out of the icy north wind 'which took our breath away', everyone – the general, the adjutant, the quartermaster, the paymaster and Lagneau himself – lends a hand. 'This done, we unloaded the provisions and stored them in the tent.' Some sappers under their command are good amateur cooks and have their share of the soup. While it's getting ready 'we sheltered in our tent and were as snug as in some billet in Germany'.

Almost no one else is. A captain of the 18th Line, Viscount *Pierre de Pelleport*, seeing wagons and carriages of every kind being abandoned because their hungry teams can't take another step on a road covered in ice, has the 18th Line's battalion wagons opened:

'The officers could do what they liked with their effects. I had the military chest counted. It contained 120,000 gold francs. I divided it up into several parts. Each of the officers, NCOs and men received a small sum, promising not to abandon this deposit confided to his honour, and to hand it over to a comrade if about to succumb.'[15]

When Delaborde's Young Guard division had left Moscow the weather had at first been so pleasant that young Paul de Bourgoing's little servant Victor had laid his overcoat on his horse and tied it to Delaborde's carriage. Suddenly both are stolen. 'All Victor now had against the winter was a waistcoat of grey broadcloth.' But Madame Anthony, following on in a calèche, takes pity on her little compatriot. In her theatrical baggage she finds Victor a triple-collared greatcoat, one of the garments perhaps Prefect of the Palace de Bausset had provided for the troupe's performances in Moscow. Paul de Bourgoing too is shivering by their bivouac fire. How cold the nights are getting! What a fool he'd been, instead of one of 'the excellent black bear pelts, or wild or white wolf skins' which, after the Moscow fire, had been so plentifully available to anyone who could pay for them, to buy himself a pretty – but pitifully ineffectual – fur-lined hooded cape,

'a very pretty *polonaise* in dark blue cloth, richly adorned with silken fringes and lined with black astrakhan, most elegant in shape and colour'.

Also of the party is a Russian who'd stayed behind in Moscow and been Delaborde's guest but is fleeing from what he imagines will be his compatriots' vengeance. Bourgoing's just cursing himself for a vain young fool when the Russian comes up and offers to swap the *polonaise* for his own thick red fox fur:

'Believe me,' he said, 'You won't be able to stand our 25 degrees of frost.'

Gratefully but reluctantly, Bourgoing accepts. 'What a difference in warmth!' Next morning the Russian has vanished. Had he been a spy? Anyway they'd been good friends, and he'll owe him his life. As for the two women, they're rarely getting out of their carriage except to join the circle at Delaborde's fireside in the evenings:

'We heard their voices, often trembling with disquietude, calling out to us from afar. Anyway they were accompanied by one of our group, whom they'd had fallen in with on the march.'

Already the column looks more like a masquerade than a retreating army. And Paymaster Duverger too wraps himself up 'in a woman's fur, lined with yellow taffeta. The sleeves were too long for my arm. The surplus served me as a handkerchief.' Now anything in the way of a fur is in acute demand and will command almost any price. Among the Württembergers everyone's envying von Suckow his rabbit-lined dressing-gown:

'An eminent Westphalian general, obliged for the time being to hoof it like a mere lieutenant, several times returned to the charge and offered me fantastic sums for it. But by this time money no longer had any value, seeing we found nothing to buy.'

Even at IHQ, with its dozens of horses, mules and carriages, all traces of imperial splendour are vanishing. At nightfall, 5 p.m., on 30 October Napoleon reaches 'the pretty château of Weliczewo:

'Not a window frame remained. With difficulty, enough of its debris was assembled to make one passable room for the Emperor and another for Berthier. The woodwork of the billiard table was the only intact piece of furniture.'

CHAPTER 3

GETTING THROUGH AT VIAZMA

Apprehensions – Teste at Viazma – shooting of Russian prisoners – Captain Roeder mounts guard outside Napoleon's office – the Guard loots the magazines – 'I'm no ordinary general' – Miloradovitch attacks – the Battle of Viazma – Ney takes over the rearguard

By now, as the van approaches Viazma, that 'newly built city of 15,000 inhabitants, remarkable for the elegance of most of its buildings' where the army in late August had feasted so plentifully on geese and fish, everyone who remembers its topography is getting apprehensive. Viazma, namely, lies at the junction of the Mojaisk and Medyn roads. And since Napoleon's rejection of the latter for his retreat, the Russians are certainly following it, aiming to cut him off. Leaving Rouibki in the afternoon, Fain hears en route that

'our advance guard still hasn't reached it. It seems that Konownitzin, who's just replaced Platov, has been trying to gain a few hours on us. We're hoping Viazma will offer us some resources. But the enemy is being so slow in yielding it to us we fear he's preparing another fire.'

At 5 p.m. IHQ halts 'at the nearest château [Weliczewo], on the heights three leagues in front of the town.' To the south, with 30 miles more to go, Wilson's hopping mad at Kutusov's sloth:

'We have 50 versts to reach Viazma and I fear much that we shall not arrive there in time. Had we moved on Jouknow after we had quitted Malojaroslavetz, as we all besought the Marshal to do, we should have been now in an impregnable position facing Viazma, and the golden glorious opportunity lost at Malojaroslavetz might have been retrieved.'

General Baron F. A. *Teste*[1] had been wounded at Borodino. Relieved of his brigade, he'd presented himself at the Kremlin with his arm in a sling and been amiably received:

'I'm going to assign you a post well worth a brigade,' the Emperor said. 'Make yourself ready to leave for Viazma, where you'll replace Baraguay d'Hilliers as governor. There you'll find 8,000 men of all arms.'

Arriving with a convoy of wounded at this town 'surrounded by ravines and situated on a fine plateau which equally dominates the plain and the mouth of the defile traversed by the Smolensk–Moscow road' on 12 October, Teste had found

'not a single inhabitant. Before we'd appeared there in August,[2] it had counted 20,000 souls. Out of 20 houses which had escaped the fire, only five or six are at a pinch inhabitable.'

Keeping one as a hospital, he'd turned all the others into stores and sent out large marauding parties, protected by cavalry. All had returned without mishap. And even after most of this cavalry had suddenly been taken from him, on 16 October, he'd gone on industriously filling up his magazines with 'a great amount of foodstuffs, destined for the numerous detachments we were told should be coming from Smolensk to join the army'. One of his marauding parties had been commanded by Major *H.-P. Everts.* Getting there as recently as 22 October, Everts' battalion of the (mostly Dutch) 33rd Line[3] had escorted a convoy of the Imperial Treasure to Doroghobouï – the next town along the Smolensk highway – and then come back.

All this time Teste had heard nothing from Moscow. And not a word about the army's retreat; only from a convoy that had passed through on the 18th 'that communications were becoming more and more problematic'.

Also at Viazma are the Hessian Footguards. A month earlier, at 6 a.m. on 21 September, they'd marched out from Witebsk,[4] bound for Smolensk, to form part of its garrison. Captain *Franz Roeder* had taken with him his cart and pony, 'two servants, a dog and two goats, one black, one white with crooked horns' to provide milk for his coffee. Gradually, much to the temperamental Roeder's fury, starvation, exposure to bad weather and – not least – incompetent officers who thought the lash the answer to everything and who constantly incensed the humane but fiery-tempered Roeder by their indifference to their men's welfare, had begun to dissolve the crack regiment's discipline. Reaching Smolensk they'd still numbered 'about 600 combatants, including bandsmen, the 1st Battalion of the Prince's Own about 500, the 2nd Battalion a third less'. But from there they'd been ordered forward to Viazma; and on 7 October to their surprise had met

'a munitions convoy escorted by the Flanker Regiment returning to Smolensk. The commander told us that all the convoys had received or would receive orders to turn back, and this would be the case with ourselves.'

The Flankers[5] belong to the Young Guard, to which the Hessians are also attached. Roeder, a man for whom campaigning is a veritable passion, hungering as he always is for new experiences, had found it 'vexatious' not to have a chance to see Moscow, that legendary city. On the other hand he'd long ago become pessimistic about the campaign's outcome, and therefore seen the convoy's return as

'good news, for it must either signify a cessation of hostilities with the possible hope of peace, or that the Emperor is returning to winter quarters in Poland and doesn't intend to expose us all to the winter at a point so far forward in Russia.'

But then something more sinister had begun to happen. Roeder's diary, 9 October:

'Today we found on the road a Russian soldier who'd not long been shot – a prisoner who, from weakness, illness, or perhaps only a wounded foot, had been unable to go further and so, in obedience to orders, was shot by the escort!'

The previous day the Hessians had met the unit that had carried out these executions:

'400 Italians of the 2nd Regiment. The commandant at Doroghobouï allowed 30 prisoners to be shot while we there because, being ill, they could go no further.'

Roeder, like any other officer in his senses, had immediately realised the implications. 'That the Russians would be justified in taking reprisals upon the prisoners they take from us appears to have struck nobody.' Yet another such massacre of prisoners had taken place at Viazma on the 10th. And on the 16th

'news went round that a few hundred armed peasants and Cossacks who had their base of operations five leagues from here had seized the baggage of a Westphalian regiment and murdered the escort. Captain von Storck was sent out to reconnoitre with two officers, eight NCOs, eight Schützen and 120 men.'

Next day – with understandable haste – this commando had returned without having seen either Cossack or armed peasant. Finally, on 24 October, Teste had received an urgent order to

'inspect the highways northwards as well as southwards and to seek out roads running parallel as far as Doroghobouï, along which an army or great host might pass, see what accommodation there was for troops suitable to the cold season and such sustenance as the country may provide.'

It had been left to him to figure out why he should do all this. But his report was to be sent in to Berthier by 30 October at the latest. Whereupon a detachment of four companies of the Hessians, with no fewer than 300 armed men and 50 troopers (20 French dragoons plus 30 Portuguese chasseurs) had been detailed off. After escorting the elderly Baraguay d'Hilliers – sick, mean and talkative – to Doroghobouï, the Hessians had carried out their reconnaissance. The main road has been stripped of everything edible; but some distance away from it they'd found plenty of everything that farms could provide or forests conceal. Safely back at Viazma, Roeder's half-witted and irascible Colonel Follenius had wanted him to write out his report in quadruplicate. But Roeder, who's not feeling very well, had refused. More important, it seems to him, is to lodge a violent protest against some Portuguese chasseurs who, though themselves utterly scared of Cossacks, had maltreated some villagers. This done, Roeder's just about to turn in for the night, when suddenly – at 4 p.m. on 31 October – the whole situation changes.[6]

Who's going to get to Viazma first, the French or the Russians? An ADC of Caulaincourt's dead brother Auguste, official hero of Borodino, has been sent ahead to order Junot and his Westphalians 'to carry the town at daybreak, taking all possible precautions to preserve it'.[7] Eugène, too, a few miles to IHQ's rear, is worried. And has sent one of his ADCs, Squadron-Leader Labédoyère, on ahead. Also, to make assurance doubly sure, Staff Captain Labaume. Overtaking IHQ, Labaume's surprised to see Napoleon, in lieu of his famous Swiss-style civilian hat, wearing a fur-trimmed bonnet.

Evidently Eugène's as anxious as anyone else to get to Viazma before the Russians do. And in fact Labédoyère only gets back to his headquarters after running into all sorts of dangers. That morning at Weliczewo will stand out in Planat's memory as

'one of the pleasantest of the retreat. There was only a single hut [*sic*] occupied by the Emperor. We were bivouacked a little way off, sleeping as best we could, around a fire of green wood. That morning, before daybreak, I heard the *diane* being beaten. It indicated the existence of a regular service in the midst of the army's commencing disorganisation. The drum I'd heard was that of a battalion of the Old Guard, bivouacked in square around IHQ. Daylight was just beginning to appear, and I saw that battalion under arms, splendidly turned out and with a good countenance.'

And at crack of dawn Napoleon himself goes on ahead. At 2 p.m. Teste's 'on horseback inspecting my outposts on the Ghjat road' when 'an ordnance officer presents himself and announces to me the Emperor's arrival'. Teste gives all necessary orders to the Viazma commandant (orders apparently not passed on swiftly enough to reach Roeder two hours later) and, as protocol requires, rides out eastwards to meet the Emperor,

'whom I wasn't slow to recognise, though contrary to his habit he was wearing a tunic of green velvet with gold brandenburgs.[8] He was advancing at the head of a group, where Murat and Berthier were in the front line. "There's Teste!" exclaimed the King of Naples. – "Well, Teste," said the Emperor, "what's new here?" – "Sire, nothing, absolutely nothing" – "Have you got some food for us?" – "Our magazines are provided with everything we've been able to collect from 8 to 10 leagues around."'

Pleased, Napoleon tells him the Guard's following on immediately behind him:

'"It's been given food for five days. See to it that it doesn't get any distribution at Viazma. Keep everything for the wounded, who should be reaching you the day after tomorrow."'

And with these words he rides on into the town, and 'at 4 p.m. dismounts at my predecessor's former lodging'.

Of all the Hessian officers Roeder alone can speak fluent French. Sick or not, he's ordered to take 100 of his best men, augmented by those of the Lifeguards' 2nd battalion, and mount guard over 'the Palace', Napoleon's lodgings:

'I posted two grenadiers in the antechamber, in accordance with the adjutant's orders, and stationed the smaller posts as I thought fit. I'd stationed six sentries in pairs in the antechamber and at the head and foot of the stairs, but didn't let them load, like outdoor sentries, partly because such a sentry can't make immediate use of such a shot anyway, and partly because one might go off by mistake. The adjutant observed this and remarked that with such strong fellows the bayonet was the best and only weapon of defence. I also saw to the barricading at all points with such reinforcements as might be necessary, especially at the rear of the house, sending out patrols to watch and listen, doubling the sentries, etc. In short, everything was done to render impossible any surprise attack by an intrepid enemy who might have been informed by the locals.'

All of which is rewarded by the duty adjutant with a curt 'good' and a 'very good', and even by a few words from Berthier himself, 'whom I hadn't seen since Tilsit' [in 1807]. As he posts his sentries in front of the audience chamber, Roeder hears Napoleon's 'loud voice'[9] ordering all sick and wounded to be instantly evacuated to Smolensk – and having himself so recently come from Smolensk along a road no one's done the least thing to keep up, he reflects privately that none of them will get so far. Soon, from that upstairs room, he hears His Majesty dictating other orders. One, to be carried by one of the officers who come stumbling downstairs between Roeder's pairs of sentries, is to General Charpentier, governor of Smolensk, to tell him that 'on 3 November the army will be at Doroghobouï':

'Full details of all stores at Smolensk are to be forwarded thither. Other orderlies and ADCs are being sent off to Witebsk and Molihew, with orders to bake every loaf of bread those towns are capable of.'

A courier, too, has arrived. Bearing letters, Fain sees, posted from Paris (on 14 October), Vilna (26 October), and two more from Saint-Cyr (19 and 20 October) in charge of II Corps and his own Bavarian VI Corps at Polotsk, as well as from Victor, 'the most recent being dated 24 October'.

In a flash everyone from Berthier down to the sentries knows that Victor, so far from being at Smolensk, as everyone's been assuming, and ready to come to their aid, is marching northwards to support the long-suffering but still intact II Corps which, if Napoleon's orders have been obeyed, is withdrawing inwards from the Polotsk region on to the Moscow army's line of retreat.[10]

During the early part of the bright cold night, with -3° to -4° Réaumur (-2° C) and some ice on the Viazma river where it flows through the town, and fields covered with thick frost, Roeder and his sentries hear and see some Guard artillery and cavalry come marching straight through the town without halting. Since they're commanded by Murat this makes them wonder just what's going on. But Napoleon just works on:

'Reports kept on going in to him. He was still busy at midnight. It wasn't quiet in his room until 1 a.m. and I saw him up again at 3.30.'

Then, at 9 a.m., the Old Guard arrives. The Emperor stands on the balcony, watching it march past. Obliged to cede their barracks to it, the Hessians have to go out to the western suburbs and bivouac out in the icy cold.

All that day [1 November] Napoleon spends at Viazma dictating orders as he waits for what he, with increasing annoyance, regards as Davout's dilatory rearguard and for the rest of the army to catch up. As usual if he has a spare moment he reads the newspapers, brought presumably by the courier. But what's this? His kid brother Jérôme, King of Westphalia[11] has gone and turned Cassel's principal Protestant church into a Catholic one!

– Write! And at top speed Fain, sitting in a corner of the room at his little portable desk, takes down in his scribbled shorthand a letter to Vilna, for Maret to forward to Cassel. He's to tell Jérôme

'it's very dangerous indeed to touch matters of religion and that it only embitters the population. That Cassel's a Protestant town and he must leave its Protestants in peace.'

At about midday on 2 November it's up and off. Grooms and escorts dash for their horses. Caulaincourt appears with the imperial riding whip; Napoleon stumbles down those narrow steep stairs; the sentry at the door shouts '*l'Empereur!*'. The brown imperial berline draws up outside. And IHQ leaves 'for Semlovo, where he was to set up his headquarters'. Teste continues,

'I joined the escort for as far as a league from the capital of my government, where I got my last orders from the Emperor's mouth.

'"You'll tell Marshal Ney that as soon as I Corps has passed through Viazma he's to be responsible for the rearguard. Davout's to support him."'

But when Teste gets back to Viazma he's met by a sight so shocking that for him it will be

'the cruellest memory of my career. During my two-and-a-half hour absence, the [rest of the] Imperial Guard, which had only been expected that evening, had entered Viazma, forced the sentries, and pillaged all our magazines. In a few instants the provisions we'd had so much trouble to gather in were dissipated, dispersed, annihilated by men who, though already supplied with food for five days, were acting like starving lunatics.'

All Teste can do that evening is to send on an indignant report to Berthier, protesting at the Guard's abominable – but customary – behaviour. And when,

'in the morning of 3 November, the big convoy of wounded reached us, it went straight on towards Smolensk, since we'd no more distributions to give it. That evening[12] the Guard followed this convoy in the same direction, and I appealed to the gentlemen, its officers, to act so that their troops should hand over some small part of their provisions to come to the aid of these brave men.'

When the Young Guard turns up the Hessian Footguards are rejoined by the other battalion of the Prince's Own, returning from Moscow with clothing, coffee, sugar, tea and food – some 80 head of cattle! After which they too are swept up in the retreat.

The crush outside the town gate is immense. As the Old Guard leaves the town Commissary Kergorre, who's had to bivouac beside the gate, has the headquarters police place a wounded Dutchman on his Treasury wagon,

'to serve us in certain circumstances as a safeguard. The road being blocked by the Guard and its teams, we had to pass through Viazma by impracticable paths, cross deep ditches, wells and courtyards and gardens, and even clamber over demolished houses.'

Fortunately Kergorre's horses are still in good nick, and he even regains the Smolensk road to find

'the Old Guard passing by. But this road being very broad the greater the jam inside Viazma became the better we marched. Marshal Lefèbvre was in command of it. Seeing me on foot beside my wagons, he called me over and chatted a long while with me. I walked on beside his horse. We spoke at length of the present circumstances, of the Administration at such moments. He was full of consideration and politeness.'

But the language of the miller's son who'd risen from the ranks in the old Royal Guard to be Duke of Danzig is by no means that of the drawing-room.

'That morning he'd expected to be attacked by Platov, and had made this harangue to his troops, drawn up in the square:

'"Grenadiers, Chasseurs! The Cossacks are over there, and there, there and there [pointing to the four points of the compass]. If you don't follow me the whole lot of you are done for. I'm no ordinary general, and it wasn't for nothing that the Army of the Moselle called me the Eternal Father. Grenadiers, Chasseurs, I tell you again: If you don't follow me you're all f....d. For the rest, I don't give a damn, go and get f....d!"'

The ex-hussar Marshal Ney also has a blunt way of speaking – sometimes, Teste thinks, a good deal too blunt. During the morning of 4 November, the ex-Governor's preparing to depart when he sees

'III Corps arrive, with its chief, to whom I transmitted Napoleon's orders. When I told him it was Davout who was to support his rearguard, Ney said to me: "Oh? As for that, we know what kind of support *he* provides." He deplored, in terms I shan't reproduce, the Guard's conduct.'

IHQ reaches Semlovo at 7 p.m., followed by the Guard. 'An hour's march from the spot where we were to spend the night', one of Pion des Loches' gunners comes to tell him his wagon's axle is broken.

'My officers' desolation was even greater than mine. It was carrying all our provisions and the axle's specification wasn't the same as those of our other vehicles. What was to become of us? How begin repairs, at night, in the extreme cold. Where find some workmen even? Fortunately Levrain, the best sergeant of our company of workmen was marching with me at the head of the Train. He ran back to the tail and we'd hardly reached our bivouac before he brought me my wagon, fitted with an ordinary axle.'

Pion des Loches rewards him with six bottles of Bordeaux. 'It would give him life for several days.'

But though IHQ bivouacks at Semlovo, and next morning (3 November) marches on towards Slawkovo, which it reaches at 3 p.m., Poniatowski, Eugène and Davout's corps are all still on the wrong side of Viazma. And Kutusov's van is still nearing that 'highly defensible position'. This time it's Planat de la Faye who's sent back to tell Davout to stir his stumps. In Moscow, Planat, that man of a delicate constitution, had been so taken up with his duties that 'unlike so many other officers I hadn't been able to get myself either a fur or double shoes'[13]. Now, shivering in his inadequate clothing, he sets out. Finds Viazma, so far from being congested, utterly deserted. Mission accomplished, he halts there 'to find something to eat, for I was dropping for hunger' – evidently Davout, as usual, hadn't shown any normal hospitality:

'Having strayed about awhile among the ruins without finding a living soul, I spotted, in the corner of a tumbledown cottage, a man squatting in front of a small fire.'

Planat's astonished to find that it's a Captain Burgstaller,

'whom I'd been much attached to in Berlin, a true philosopher, without a care in the world, taking things as they came and men as he found them. Burgstaller had lost nothing of his good humour. In his pot he was cooking a bit of horsemeat, seasoned with some gunpowder, and for half an hour he entertained me with his striking buffooneries and gay reminiscences from the past.'

Then he rejoins de Lariboisière's headquarters at Slawkovo.

Since before dawn, the Army of Italy, preceded by the Polish V Corps, and followed by I Corps 'albeit at a distance', has been pursuing its march in a dense fog. Near the demolished village of Tsarewo-Simiche it has to cross 'an earthen causeway over which the main road used to pass, but which the guns' passage has deteriorated to a point where it was no longer practicable. And to continue on our way we had to go down into a swampy plain, bisected by a broad stream. Although the first only crossed it thanks to the ice, they broke it in doing so, and then one either had to expose oneself to wading the river or else wait for wretched hastily constructed bridges to be finished. From the moment the head of the column had got there more vehicles were constantly arriving. Thus the artillery, carriages and *vivandières*' carts were all spread out on the road, while their drivers, as their habit was, took advantage of this moment to light fires and warm their numbed limbs.'

Everyone's in this seemingly secure state when suddenly,

'out of a thick wood to our left, Cossacks yelling frightfully, came out and fell on this unfortunate mass. At this sight, each man, driven by fear, acts on impulse. Some take refuge in the woods, others run to their vehicle and whip up their horses, and without knowing where they're going disperse over the plain; and there, stuck in the swampy ground, fall an easy prey to the Cossacks.'

The more fortunate entrench themselves behind the mass of vehicles and await deliverance, 'which duly arrived with the infantry'. Meanwhile the employees of IV Corps' baggage train are beginning to pillage it. 'Now one was no more in safety even among one's own people,' Labaume will remember bitterly, 'than one would have been among enemies.' Theft, indeed, is becoming endemic. Last night even Sergeant Bertrand 'driven by hunger' has indulged in it. On reaching the 17th Light's bivouac and seeing some men of the Train sleeping under shelters around a rousing fire, he had 'profited by their cook's absence to jump over these sleepers and make off with one of their well-filled pots, which comforted us, my comrades and me'. Now, at about 8 or 9 a.m., through the 'cold, very dense fog, which prevented us from seeing ten paces ahead, but in greatest safety' Griois and his witty friend Colonel Jumilhac are still riding on some distance ahead of his artillery, somewhere ahead of I Corps and IV Corps' rear,

'when some roundshot whistled past our ears. After a few moments an extremely lively fire of guns and musketry started up on our left.'

That first shot makes Prince Eugène (he'll tell Wilson one day) 'start with more alarm than he'd ever felt in his life, as he instantly foresaw the fatal consequences'. The neighbouring infantry units come to a bewildered halt:

'The generals didn't know what to do or which way to face. We were being blasted by an enemy we couldn't see. Finally a few battalions deployed. Others formed squares against cavalry, which soon fell on us, and our fire answered the enemy's. Little by little the fog broke up under the guns' detonations, and at last we were able to see who it was we had to do with. It was the entire advance guard of the Russian army, led by Miloradovitch, whose masses, protected by the thickets of wood and the fog, were bordering the road we were following. They'd waited to attack us until the greater part of IV Corps had already passed through Viazma, or anyway reached it, and until I Corps offered them its flank.'

Both IV and V Corps have left the troublesome Tsarewo–Zalomitsch defile behind them when

'a strong detachment of Cossacks suddenly throws itself on to the highway, momentarily cutting us off from Poniatowski's corps. The Royal Guard, in the van today, loses no time in putting them to flight. But at the same time the cavalry of the enemy's advance guard attacks the left flank of our last columns and tries to bar the road to them. The Guard forms column, makes a bayonet charge and frees our companions.'

Preyssing's handsome Bavarian cavalry brigade, attached to IV Corps ever since June, and whose elegant manoeuvrings the Italians had so admired in July[14] but is now 'reduced to about 200 horses', is approaching the town when

'ahead of us cannon suddenly began banging away, and on some high ground in the town's vicinity we spotted some troop masses firing several guns at an enemy still invisible to us. They belonged to Poniatowski's corps, and the Russians were trying to cut communications between it and our own. But since they were rather low down we couldn't see them.'

As soon as they do, von Muraldt goes on, IV Corps – 'not without noise and confusion' – draws itself up in line of battle to the left of the route. The victors of Malojaroslavetz, Frenchmen and Italians, are in an increasingly desperate state. More and more of their men have been straggling, and Cesare de Laugier, throwing anxious glances over his shoulder, has been seeing how

'a great number of sick or wounded or men too feeble to keep up with their units are just throwing away first their packs, then their muskets, hoping to march better and rejoin their regiments. Pell-mell, In disorder, they're still struggling on, making superhuman efforts not to lose sight of the rearguard. Finally they fall. God knows what will happen to them!'

Twelve or even fifteen emaciated horses, he sees, are now being needed to pull even one cannon. I Corps, which consists of only 11,000 or 12,000 of its original 79,000 combatants, is in no better state. It's just about to pass through the Tsarewo defile when Miloradovitch 'taking advantage of the gap between I and IV Corps' attacks with swarms of light cavalry:

'It came and fell on the column of unarmed men and passed through it several times, without however doing much harm to this dense mass which had huddled together like a flock of sheep at the approach of a wolf. Only a few isolated men were stabbed by their lances.'

For a while Davout's rearguard clings to the village of Federowskoï, but Paskewitch's cavalry finally drive it out and are pursuing it along the Viazma road. And for a while the whole of I Corps is in danger of being overwhelmed by Miloradovitch's 19,000 men.

While all this is going on, another Russian corps, approaching by the Medyn road, is trying to seize Viazma itself. But since the town's defended on that side by two rivers in a semi-circle, and Ney's leading divisions are already in occupation, this isn't easy. Fezensac sees how

'Ledru's division took up position on the plain dominating these streams, and prevented the enemy from forcing a passage, while Razout's division fell back to help I and IV Corps force their way through.'

Things aren't going well for Davout,

'who's being attacked by considerable forces. The Viceroy, informed of the danger he's in, orders our columns to fall back, assembles them and forms them up to fly to the Marshal's assistance. Poniatowski too retraces his steps and takes up position in front of Viazma, to the left of the road.'

Placing Ornano's Bavarian chevaulegers – 'the few cavalry still available' – to the Poles' right, Eugène has to withdraw his divisions quite a long way before they can take up a position on some high ground and threaten Miloradovitch's left flank in rear:

'We position our artillery, and our sharpshooters, under the protection of hedges, attack the enemy lines. At the same time Davout's main body goes into action to open a passage.'

After the Italian light infantrymen have forced the Russian gunners to clear off at a gallop 'the Viceroy sends a column of infantry through the brushwood to the Russian left'. This forces them to face about and, attacked on all sides, to relinquish their position astride the road. But just as the two corps, in contact again, are about to resume their march toward Viazma, Lejeune sees some 50 Russian guns 'again open up a very keen cannonade'. The Italians resist with courage; 'but Davout's corps,' Laugier's alarmed to notice, 'demoralised by the fatigues and all kinds of privations endured since Malojaroslavetz, no longer has the fine bearing it's had since the campaign's outset'. Labaume and Eugène's staff notice it too:

'The men were observing but little discipline and most were wounded or sick with fatigue and swelled the mob of stragglers.'

Griois, meanwhile, has been cut off from his guns and obliged to take refuge in a square formed by a regiment of General Nagel's brigade of the Italian 3rd Division, the 92nd Line. At every instant he sees how difficult the ever-growing mob of civilians and stragglers is making it even for orders to be heard, let alone carried out:

'This mass of isolated men, recognising neither chiefs nor discipline and only heeding its thirst for pillage, was sorely tried. At the first cannon shots it had halted, not knowing where to go in the fog that surrounded it. Swollen by the greater part of the employees whose administrations no longer existed, by *vivandières* and a multitude of little carts laden with children and foodstuffs, it was throwing itself now to one side, now to the other, according to where the last projectile to strike in its midst had come from. This flux and reflux of roundshot, ploughing furrows in every direction and from which arose screams of despair, presented a horrible spectacle. For very good reasons the units that were fighting repulsed these fugitives who were trying to take refuge in their midst, so that the poor wretches found themselves exposed to the enemy's fire and sometimes to our squares' too. They floated in disorder over terrain littered with dead, wounded and shattered vehicles.'

Seeing all this, Laugier goes on,

'the enemy become bolder, redouble their gunfire. On our side the wretched state of our horses delays the artillery's manoeuvres. Sure of his superiority, Miloradovitch tries another vigorous attack to outflank us. But the Italian chasseurs, the Bavarians, and the Polish [line] lancers (though very badly mounted) face the Russians boldly and put them to flight. At long last, thanks above all to our cavalrymen, the infantry reaches the high ground covering Viazma town.'

By now it's about midday and the fog has cleared. For two days Victor Dupuy has 'only taken coffee and some grains of gruel, which some hussars of the 8th had invited me to eat with them'. General Jacquinot sends him to halt and reunite all scattered officers or troopers of what had been his light cavalry division who may already be passing through Viazma. 'I fell in with a light artillery captain, Crosnier by name. He told me to follow him.' Crosnier introduces him to

'one of the French families who'd fled from Moscow, whom the Emperor had told him to take back to France. It consisted of a mother and her two daughters, aged twelve and fourteen.'

But Dupuy's too hungry to be sensitive to their charms, 'A leg of mutton hung up over a rousing fire drew my attention more particularly. What a long time it had been since I'd been at such a feast!' Crosnier even fills Dupuy's pockets with bread and rum, which he duly shares with Jacquinot and Tavernier, his chief-of-staff. In the midst of all the hurly-burly von Suckow, too, has two strokes of luck. Not only does he fall in with some of his armed companions, but he buys a pot of jam from a Jew which, he suspects, has come from some marshal's wagon – 'but we didn't demand a certificate of origin' – and a cake of the kind for which Viazma is noted.

East of the town, meanwhile, the fighting's still heavy. IV Corps' 13,000 men are drawn up at right angles to the road, more to its right, now, than its left, 'with its left flank forming a hook to face the Cossacks all round us'. I Corps is on its right. At last Griois' artillery – he's been worried for its safety – turns up, but at I Corps' extreme rear. Ney, too, has sent back a brigade to flank Davout on his other side, the whole positioned 'at a very acute angle to the post road'. A second line is formed by Poniatowski's 3,500 Poles and the remainder of 1st Cavalry Corps. Although the French side outnumbers Miloradovitch's 19,000 men, the weather's getting colder every minute, and in the ranks of the Guardia d'Onore – any number of its wounded officers have 'bandaged heads or arms in slings' – many men who haven't eaten for days are fainting and collapsing; 'others, hardly able to carry their weapons, are keen to fight to warm themselves or are hoping for death to deliver them from this long agony'. Griois sees the redheaded Marshal Ney

'coming back at a gallop. I can see him still, at the spot where the fighting was hottest, speaking to the men, indicating to the generals what dispositions they should take up, animating all hearts with the confidence that flashed from his glances. He made an effect on me I don't know how to describe. The King of Naples in the thick of the fire had never seemed to me more handsome.'

And indeed it's Ney who, by coming back to the other corps' assistance, has stabilised the whole situation:

'Throughout the action he was present in person and for a long while marched with the Viceroy and the Prince of Eckmühl to confer with them on what dispositions they should adopt.'

But then, just as Cesare de Laugier is staring at 'all three of them together on some high ground near the Royal Guard to the right of the post road, trying to concert their operations', the Russian columns again renew their attack. 'All along the line the firing resumes with extraordinary vigour,' so that among other things the 85th's 2nd Battalion, in square near a forest where there's a fresh clearing, is driven in by combined Russian cavalry and artillery. 'One minute,' Le Roy sees to his horror,

'sufficed for it to vanish. Its commander, whose name was Centenier, had called on the 1st Battalion to support it. It was 200 yards closer to our cavalry and under its protection. Otherwise it would certainly have suffered the same fate. It received into its square the wreckage of the 2nd Battalion which, though most of its men were wounded, had escaped from the enemy's hands. The 1st Battalion's commander had his throat cut by a piece of grapeshot which laid him out dead, while each man, after firing his musket, was trying to flee and escape this massacre. Only our obstinacy got us as far as the town, so as to give the vehicles and the column of disarmed men time to pass through it and gain the protection of III Corps, drawn up in line of battle at the town's exit.'

Preyssing's light cavalry brigade is ordered to charge the 'numerous Russian guns, if possible seize them, or at least reduce them to silence.' An impossible task. But

'regardless of our weakness and the exhausted state of most of our horses, we carried out our order with such determination that the Russians were put to flight, yet without our being able to take any of their cannon. On our exhausted steeds we were only able to attack them at a trot.'

At about 3 p.m. the light begins to fail, and the rest of the 85th, after being blasted by heavy-calibre roundshot, withdraw slowly, Le Roy says, towards the town. So, just before 4 p.m., does IV Corps. Marching through its flames, Le Roy sees III Corps drawn up in line of battle on the plateau beyond.

The 85th may have withdrawn slowly. Not so many of Davout's other units. Watching the battle from the Russian positions Wilson sees how I Corps, though covered by Ney's corps,

'broke and rushed to the points of passage in great confusion. A regiment of Russian grenadiers charged his rearguard into the town, bayoneting all who resisted.'

And all the time, Lejeune says, 'the Russians hadn't ceased to aim 50 guns on our unfortunate convoys, which kept moving on during the battle.' To Major Bonnet, whose 18th Line, part of Razout's division, has been protecting I Corps' retreat, it's the Italians' retirement that's looked more like a rout, and I Corps to have retreated in somewhat better order. If so, it's partly thanks to the staunchness of the 7th Light, which for part of the day has been engaged with regular Russian cavalry. Sergeant Bertrand's had two muskets shattered in his hands, 'one while I was charging it, the second when priming'. Now, at nightfall, the regiment's been ordered to cover the bridge over the steep-banked, swift-flowing river:

'Menaced by cavalry, the four battalions form a massed close column by divisions, our effectives by now being much weakened. Towards 9 p.m., at the moment when, seated on our packs, we were taking a well-earned rest, we were warned of the enemy's attack by the firing of our outposts, one of which was carried off. It was cavalry. Colonel Romme closed us up on the head of the column, the last division [i.e., two companies] faced about, the files of the wings to right and left, and thus we had a full and compact square, in complete defiance of all regulations, but well suited to the circumstances. The firing began immediately from all its four faces, and more than one Russian trooper met his death under our musket balls or on our bayonets. Only a few men were wounded by pistol shots.'

Colonel Romme is complimented by Gérard, his divisional general. But still their job isn't finished. An hour later they march for the bridge, and the first battalions cross. But Bertrand's own carabinier company is ordered to guard the river bank on the far side until the whole column has got over:

'My captain Moncey (son of the Marshal)[15] sends me upstream to reconnoitre with a few men of my choice. After 20 minutes I'm fired on. I establish myself on the fringe of a wood to reply and send a corporal to warn the captain. The whole company, and even all who hadn't crossed the bridge, come running to my aid. But the enemy have disappeared. And we cross to the other bank. It was already well into the night.'

The Italian Royal Guard has bivouacked 'about two and a half miles from the town' near a convoy of sick and wounded in the vast forest beyond which is 'serving them as a hospital and a tomb. The difficulty of making the horses move had forced their drivers to abandon everything'. Facing the enemy, on the left of the highway and finding any amount of firewood, the Italians 'light enormous fires', which burn through the night. 'The Viceroy had his tent in the middle of the regiment of Vélites, who in front of the prince tried to put on a pretence of gaiety very far', their adjutant-major notes, 'from everyone's hearts'. Now and again he hears Ney's guns banging away at the Russians across the river and, looking back, sees what's left of Viazma's houses going up in flames. In the flaming horror of Viazma as 'the Russian general Tschlogokoff marches into it, drums beating and flags flying'[16] several hundred French sick and wounded are being burnt to death in a church after some abandoned shells have exploded in it – the very same church, perhaps, where in August Napoleon had ordered a posse of the Imperial Guard to complete the funeral obsequies of its venerable bishop?[17] But Wilson's gratified to see 'a Swiss family, consisting of a mother with her two daughters, most beautiful girls, saved, and honourably conducted in safety to a sheltering post'.

In 'the English General's' embittered opinion Miloradovitch's failure to cut Davout off has been entirely due to Kutusov's having stacked arms at Biskowo, where he'd 'remained inflexible, saying "the time has not yet come",[18] and to his consequent failure – or even lothness – to hasten on beyond Viazma and cut off all three corps, as Miloradovitch had suggested. 'Had the Marshal marched at 8 a.m. or even 10 or 12, Viazma might have been seized, the bridges destroyed, and the corps of the Viceroy, Poniatowski, Davout and Ney would have had no alternative but dispersion, ensuring destruction or surrender.' But he hadn't. And Ney had been free to stabilise the situation.

In Colonel *T.-J.-J. Séruzier*'s view the struggle to get through Viazma has 'cost the French 4,000 men, and the enemy twice that number'. Wilson, who thinks the French have lost 6,000 men, says the Russians took 2,000 prisoners, – the Russians themselves will afterwards estimate them at 3,000 – one standard and three guns.[19] Thousands of stragglers and vehicles have had to be abandoned for lack of horses. And any number of officers have fallen. Cesare de Laugier admiringly records their names. 'It was in this engagement', writes Lejeune, 'that Colonel Banco, the Viceroy's ADC, commander of the 2nd Italian Horse Chasseurs, had his head carried away by a cannonball.' Among the Russians' prisoners is the 35-year-old General Pelletier, commander of Poniatowski's artillery. He's of the same opinion as Pion des Loches, de Lariboisière and other gunners, and tells his captors so:

'Napoleon's made a great mistake in keeping more than 100 pieces of artillery. He'd have done better to discard 500 cannon to get to Smolensk with the whole of his army. Instead of which he's been obliged to remain in support during the daily brushes he's no longer able to escape, his cavalry being as exhausted as his teams.'

Von Muraldt's 4th Bavarian Chevaulegers' last charge has cost them nine-tenths of their men and horses:

'Our brigade, bivouacked by a wood by the wayside, had been so badly mauled, we counted only 30-40 horses left. Over and above the dead and wounded we also lacked some officers who'd gone off during the battle to find a place of safety or fodder for their mounts. Now, next morning, these reappeared; and our general, Preyssing, now surrounded mainly by an insignificant group of officers, saw himself obliged to report to General Ornano that from now on his brigade must be regarded as dissolved.'

But Ornano, a divisional general who so far has inspired but little confidence, either in young von Muraldt or in anyone else,[20] just shrugs:

'"What d'you expect me to do about it? Everyone's got to get out of this affair as best he can." This consoling observation freed us from further duties. The common bond which had assembled officers and men under the same flag and placed on them their mutual duties, was dissolved. But there was some consolation in the thought that the regiment had asserted itself in its last fight.'

Von Muraldt's is by no means the only cavalry regiment that no longer exists. In Laugier's eyes, too, 'the saddest result' of the battle for Viazma 'was that almost all the cavalry's horses succumbed, not being up to such fatigues'. The numbers of Italian infantrymen who've thrown away their muskets, too, are greater than ever. The battle has also cost Le Roy his last few possessions, including his portmanteau, which he'd entrusted to his batman, who now doesn't even dare appear before him. But as usual Le Roy is philosophical. Tells his faithful Guillaume:

'Oh well, you see, my friend, I've not long been encumbered by my most precious possessions, which would have caused me a lot of worry and which I'd anyway have had to get rid of later on. That fellow's done me a great service. If you see him again, give him a 5-franc piece to drink my health.'

From now on, he decides, he'll dispense with all personal aids and accessories. And begins by making 'two big pockets which I crudely fitted inside my greatcoat', and also in the tails of his uniform coat,

> 'putting into them a razor, a well-stocked travelling case, some thread, some buttons, a box of tea and my knife. Sometimes I stuffed it all inside my shako. The greatcoat's pockets did duty as a larder. It took me several days to fix things up in my own way; and when all was ready I waited to see what would happen next.'

CHAPTER 4

HANDMILLS AT DOROGHOBOUI

Fezensac's strictness with stragglers – retreating chesswise – 'naked wretches flying from the peasantry' – a ridiculous masquerade – end of the cavalry – the loot of Moscow – handmills but no corn – how the Polish Lancers coped – playing the Cossack – Napoleon waives protocol – Le Roy's walking wardrobe – boeuf à la mode – destroying guns

Although Ney has taken up a good overnight position at the edge of the great Viazma forest with the river in front of him, and is fending off the Russians coming from Medyn, Fezensac's deeply shocked at the demoralised state of I and IV Corps: 'The Italian Royal Guard was almost alone in marching in good order.' As for the stragglers, of whom there are thousands, it's more than he can do to persuade them to go on ahead:
'It was important to them to gain a few hours' march; and anyway we couldn't allow them to mingle with our ranks and hinder our movements. I did my very best to persuade them to leave without waiting for the rearguard.'
All in vain:
'Weakness or laziness made them deaf to our advice. Hardly had daylight appeared than III Corps took up its arms and got going. At this moment all the isolated men quit their bivouacs and came to join us. Those who were sick or wounded stayed by their fires, begging us not to abandon them to the enemy. We had no means of transporting them and had to pretend not to hear these plaints we could do nothing about. As for that flock of wretches who'd abandoned their flags though still in a state to fight, I ordered them to be repulsed with blows of musket butts. If the enemy attacked us, I warned them, I'd fire on them at the least embarrassment they caused.'
'Massed at 200 to 300 pace intervals' Ney's battalions 'march off down the road'. Taking turn and turn about with the 4th and 7th Light, it's Major Bonnet who's commanding this 'rearguard of the rearguard' retreating by stages '*à reculons*' or 'chessboard fashion'[1] – 'a new experience' for his men as they 'fall back by battalions 100 or 150 paces. So as to alternate defence with offence the even battalions of the second line, instead of falling back at the same time as the even battalions of the first line, may form columns by divisions, at either close, half, or whole distance behind the first division, the right in front, and then advance outside the right of the first line's even battalions as they retreat and form up into line a few fathoms to the rear of the left of the first line's uneven battalions.'
Is the 18th Line actually manoeuvring, over and over again, in this intricate fashion? Bonnet doesn't say. Neither does Bertrand, nor Fezensac, who of course take all such matters for granted. But it can hardly be the most habitual of drill movements?

Stragglers! By now there are so many thousands the Cossacks aren't even bothering to take prisoners, a task they're leaving 'to the peasants and the militia', who're carrying it out with extreme cruelty. Wilson, who at Viazma has just seen how 'fifty French, by a savage order, were burnt alive' and heard how 'fifty more from another village' suffered the same fate, even sees a brave French drummer boy leap first among his comrades into a common grave where furious peasants are burying them, too, alive. 'The English general', ordinarily so smug and self-satisfied, witnesses horrible scenes as he follows on with the Russian advance guard, and 'as a man and an Englishman' does what he can to help

'a French woman, naked to her chemise, with black, long, dishevelled hair, sitting on the snow, where she'd remained the whole day and in that situation had been delivered of a child, which had afterwards been stolen from her. This was the extreme of mental anguish and bodily suffering.'

He even sees scenes of cannibalism where stragglers, before dying, have tried to eat a dead comrade; and among the starving

'a veteran French grenadier. I was just putting a bit of biscuit into my own mouth when I turned my eye upon his gaze. It was too expressive to be resisted; I gave him what I designed for myself. The tears burst from his eyes, he seemed to bless the morsel, and then, amidst sobs of gratitude, expressed his hope that an Englishman might never want a benefactor in his need. He lived but a few moments afterwards.'

Sentiments unknown either to the peasants or to their other enemies, the Cossacks. In 'the air enveloped in flame and smoke' he sees how all prisoners are being

'immediately and invariably stripped stark naked and marched in columns in that state, or turned adrift to be the sport and the victims of the peasantry.'

He also hears

'the prayers of hundreds of naked wretches, flying from the peasantry whose shouts of vengeance echoed incessantly through the woods; the wrecks of cannon, powder-wagons, military stores of all descriptions, and every ordinary as well as extraordinary ill of war combined with the asperity of the climate, are forming such a scene as probably was never witnessed to such an extent in the history of the world'.

Meanwhile the stragglers' column 'marked by flocks of black crows, forever circling overhead, pursued by hordes of dogs which had been following them all the way from Moscow and were living off the dead and dying' is plundering the wagons that are continually being abandoned:

'They took the horses and ate them and dressed themselves in whatever warm garments they'd found in the wagons. Here began the ridiculous, terrible masquerade into which the entire French army was soon transformed. Yet this was only the beginning. Such was the army's condition as we approached Doroghoboui.'[2]

Once out of the forest, with Razout's 2nd Division still forming the rearguard and 'each division's left at its head', III Corps marches all day westwards. 'The officers and generals, all at their posts, directed its movements.' Only of the cavalry hardly any are left:

'Already half destroyed by our stay at the outposts at Winkovo,[3] a fortnight of marching and fighting had finished off its disorganisation. Almost all the horses were dead of starvation or fatigue. Such feeble troops as were still left and whose number was daily dwindling were marching in isolation, no longer forming either divisions, or brigades, or regiments, and hurrying on, as far as their mounts' weakness permitted, to cover the distance between one bivouac from the next.'

Even the admirable Grouchy[4] 'who alone would have been able to keep a certain order in 3rd Cavalry Corps' but still hasn't recovered from his Borodino wound, is unable to prevent it dwindling away. As for his inept subordinate Lahoussaye, who has replaced him, 'ill, almost speechless', he's incapable of restoring order or inspiring confidence. So its dismounted troopers, unable to follow their units, 'went to swell the flock of unfortunates who were marching in disorder, without discipline or commanders'. And Griois, 'getting no orders from anyone, having to take everything on to myself, march and choose direction as I thought most advantageous,' is on his own. As for the isolated groups of troopers,

'we didn't usually ride along the road, but a bit to one side of it, where we still found farms whose inhabitants had fled, leaving some grains of corn for our horses. Besides, the highway, from being so marched on, had become so slippery it looked like a skating rink. Even the most insignificant slopes called for trouble and effort. Often both men and horses slipped backwards, and that several times over. This was particularly the case with the French horses which, as is known, have no frostnails to their shoes, and which were therefore incredibly wearied. There you have the explanation why the French cavalry melted away so quickly.'

Lieutenant von Kalckreuth of the Prussian hussars again falls in with

'a Horse Grenadier of the Guard. At Viazma his handsome regiment had seemed rather strong to me. But a few days later he assured me it was already wholly dismounted. The Cossacks' repeated attacks, too, were doing much to ruin the French cavalry. One only had to say the word *Cossack* rather loud for everyone to look behind him and trot on ahead, even though no Cossack was to be seen.'

Caulaincourt too is dismayed to see how the army's horses are falling like flies for lack of winter shoeing. Only the Polish Guard Lancers, familiar with winter campaigning conditions in the north, are 'always managing well' as they ride on ahead of IHQ. At least their wealthy colonel Count *Désiré Chlapowski,*[5] scathing though he is about his colleagues of the Dutch Lancers' ability to defend themselves, is satisfied with them:

'Our lancers always rode the little peasant horses we kept with us, so as not to fatigue our own. The officers always slept amidst the lancers. Those ordered to find forage in neighbouring villages rarely returned empty-handed. Since we were always near IHQ and kept running into convoys of cattle coming to join the army, provisions sufficed. When we got to the place where we were to pass the night our lancers occupied some building or other and kept a lookout to see the French didn't set fire to it to warm themselves.'

Von Muraldt's little group is far from being the only one to go marauding. Leaving a road incessantly blocked by fallen horses, broken wagons, carriages and guns, they're

'free to settle for the night wherever they like. For the most part men left the road (particularly if they were mounted), and found their way to some village or farm as yet unoccupied that might offer them a roof over their heads and fodder for their horses. Even so it often happened that after riding far afield we had to camp under the bare sky. If, on the other hand, one did get under a roof, one was in danger of being attacked and taken prisoner by the Cossacks. Very often, too, one had to defend one's night quarters, fruit of such a search, sabre in hand against similar little units. Those who were more numerous or stronger showed no pity to the weaker, but thrust them out into the cold, and on top of it even seized such victuals as they might have with them.'

Some groups even

'play the Cossack. Spotting at a distance some village others have already occupied, they began shouting 'Hurrah!' and in this way frightened them away, and then took their places. It was the boldest who were generally managing best.'

It's every man's hand against his fellow. The Polish Lancers' foraging expeditions, however, are being organised in collaboration with those of the Vistula Legion,

'most often of its 2nd Regiment, under the orders of Malczewski, and a detachment of our cavalry. Spreading out over the neighbourhood they brought back some food for the men and forage for the horses.'

Above all the regiment is guarding Chlapowski's cook

'like the apple of its eye. Helped by a dozen troopers, Garolinski got busy preparing our food as best he could. Our men undertook to find some meat and flour. He had the meat cooked, and with the flour made various kinds of biscuits which he grilled slightly. Unfortunately there was a grave shortage of salt. Almost every morning before leaving each horseman got one of his Garolinski's hot *galettes* and a bit of meat, which had to suffice for the day.'

But Zalusky has had to sacrifice, one after the other, the two cows he's been bringing along to provide cream for his coffee. Certain precautions are still being taken. The Young Guard, Sergeant *A.-J.-B.-F. Bourgogne* of the Fusiliers-Grenadiers is noticing, is 'almost always being made to march behind the cavalry and artillery' so that there shall be some horseflesh for them, as for other Guard units, to eat at the day's end:

'Always there were always plenty of dead and dismembered horses. A still greater number, though still alive and on their feet, but stupefied, had been left behind and were letting themselves be killed without flinching.'

Although platoons of Russian cavalry and infantry are marching parallel across the immense plain, nothing happens until the evening of 3 November, when the Russian units try to prevent the rearguard getting through a defile. But Fezensac's regiment, supported by two guns, defends it and gives the others time to get through, leaving behind two voltigeur companies, who only retire after nightfall. But hardly have Bonnet and his men

'begun to get some rest than the Russians threw some shells at our bivouacs. One hit a tree at whose foot I was sleeping. No one was hurt, and there were a few moments of confusion in some of the 18th's companies. I've always noticed that shots fired at night do little harm; but they strike the imagination and give the men the idea that the enemy are being prodigiously active.'

Next day – not a very cold one, Pion des Loches is glad to find – Ney resumes his methodical retreat:

'The Emperor wanted to march slowly to preserve the baggage. In vain Marshal Ney wrote to him that there was no time to be lost, that the enemy were pressing the rearguard hard, that on our flanks the Russian army was making long days' marches, and we should be afraid he'd get to Smolensk or Orsha before us. For the rest, the weather was fine and fairly mild for the season, and we were hoping to arrive safely at Smolensk, which should be the term of our wearisome efforts.'

Bridges are still among the most serious obstacles. Coming to one which, like so many others, has collapsed under the vehicles' weight, notably of course of the ammunition wagons, the nimblest men of the 85th

'jumped it easily, the stream being no more than 4 or 5 feet wide. But the pedestrians spread themselves upstream and downstream, so as to cross more easily without having to take their shoes off. Yet this crossing held us up almost all day! Fortunately several wagons got bogged down and broken. They served us as a support to cross this gutter.'

And all the time, on either flank, Lejeune too, also marching on ahead with Davout's headquarters, sees

'many columns of Russian cavalry and artillery trying to overtake us and wait for us at the defile beyond Doroghoboui.'

Sometimes they see a break in the column or some convoy, and pounce. Even IHQ's baggage, though it's going on well ahead, isn't immune. Among vehicles which aren't going to make it to Doroghoboui are all Murat's remaining carriages and wagons – among them no doubt the one containing his many perfumes. Already on 18 October, seeing that his carriages were holding up the chaotic retirement from the Winkovo battlefield, Murat had ordered the men to burn them and 'laughed at the urgency they, having emptied them of their contents, put into carrying out his order'. This loss of his remaining carriages is more problematic. Yet his spectacular wardrobe seems to have survived it, for Surgeon Roos sees him wearing

'over his French general's uniform a Spanish cape, sometimes red, sometimes green, with silver tassels. His hat was ornamented with several white plumes, and he was wearing Hungarian boots, red, green, or yellow.'

Duroc, Grand Marshal of the Palace, has been exigent, so Castellane's thinking, in his choice of employees for the imperial household. 'Thanks to the constant efforts of the *maîtres d'hôtel* and the cooks' everyone at IHQ is 'almost always getting something to eat, better or worse. Not on a par with our hunger, it's true, but no less astonishingly for that.' Normally, only Berthier dines at Napoleon's table. But now Murat, no longer having a table of his own to dine at, also takes his place at it. But 'his ADCs and all the officers of his suite' including Rossetti, are 'obliged to take pot luck elsewhere.' Not too disastrously that first day. However ill-seen by the imperial devotees Dedem van der Gelder may be, his culinary status is still excellent:

'The King went to dine with the Emperor. In the evening, since I was still affluent and well provided for, I offered his staff officers a splendid supper, with Madeira and Bordeaux wines, and an abundance of mocha coffee and liqueurs from the isles of the Indies! My cook, who'd stayed at Drontheim, prepared horsemeat marvellously and all my guests thought I was serving them beef!'

Alas, it's the swan-song of Dedem the diplomat's career as a host:

'Next day my *calèche* was crushed by the artillery; and a nice little well-harnessed *droshka* well supplied with provisions and belonging to the Count de Castel-Bajac, one of my ADCs, was carried off by the Cossacks, who thereupon tasted our wine, carried off the carriage and drove away the coachman, telling him to tell his master they'd found our wine excellent.'

But he still has his wagon left 'and my mobile kitchen. My ADCs escorted it.' Otherwise

'only the Emperor was well served; that's to say, he always had white bread, linen, his Chambertin, good oil, beef or mutton, rice and beans or lentils, his favourite vegetables.'

Caulaincourt notices how few are the Emperor's personal demands.[6] A lieutenant of the 1st Company of the Chasseurs à Cheval, *J. M. Merme*, who'd served in Egypt and has 'the privilege of lighting a fire for him at each of his halts', notices it too:

'One day as I was preparing to make up the Emperor's fire, I put my handkerchief over my busby to keep the cold out a bit. Seeing him approach, I made to take it off. But he said to me: "We aren't at the Carrousel here. It's colder than usual today, so keep the handkerchief on your head!"'

Merme himself is making a point of never warming himself at a fire and 'consequently never had a limb frost-bitten'.

As the years have gone by it has progressively been the practice for regiments, particularly cavalry regiments, to leave their regimental Eagles at home. The danger of these sacred objects being captured by France's enemies is too great. The flags are less sacred. Leaving Viazma with a party of his wounded Württembergers, surgeon von Roos has had his taken off their poles and wrapped around the bodies of the strongest marchers (a 'precaution thanks to which I'd afterwards discover the Württemberger troops hadn't lost a single one of their flags in Russia'). Also in the endless column a dwindling group of dismounted 2nd Cuirassiers are escorting Sergeant-Major Thirion, who's carrying their eagle on its blue pole. 'Having had nothing to eat for two nights except bark off the trees it had been tethered to,' his poor horse, which he's been dragging behind him, has dropped from hunger and fatigue:

> 'I'd cut short this good companion's agony with a shot through its head. Not wishing to leave my cuirass and sabre to the enemy, I'd thrown them under a bridge; shouldered the standard and a double-barrelled shotgun I'd bought in Moscow; and continued the retreat on foot.'

At every step the 'bronze eagle with spread wings, at the end of a rather long staff' is getting heavier:

> 'Under the eagle, nailed to the staff, was a square flag of white satin surrounded on three sides by a gold fringe of heavy gold, the length and thickness of one's finger. It was embroidered with the words: The Emperor to his 2nd regiment of Cuirassiers. The reverse bore the names of all the battles the regiment had been in, and on every square inch of satin left blank by these inscriptions was a swarm of bees half the size of one's thumb. A white satin cravat was tied to the eagle's feet. It hung down for a foot and a half, and at each end had a tassle made from twisted fringes larger than a finger, all in gold. The whole was furled in a morocco sheath.'

All this has long been cutting into Thirion's shoulder. So he points out to Colonel Dubois that even if he sacrifices his life defending it, there's a danger of it being captured by Cossacks. And is given leave to hide it. 'I unscrewed the eagle, which was placed in Adjutant Millot's portmanteau. Flag and cravat were folded and put in the colonel's. And the staff was burnt.' Thus relieved, 'both morally and physically', Thirion, that man of steel, trudges on.

At last Doroghoboüï, in its 'vast amphitheatre overlooking the Dnieper' comes into sight at the end of the long straight highway – the one the army had advanced along in open order through the terrible August heats.[7] A mile or two before reaching it its van runs into a Dutch unit, marching for Viazma. After escorting a treasury convoy from Smolensk to Doroghoboüï, Major *Henri-Pierre Everts'* battalion of the 33rd Line is marching eastwards – how keenly he's looking forward to seeing Moscow! Instead what he sees – 'I'd never seen so striking an example' – is a 'confused mass of all units, prey to an extreme panic and disorder'. Someone assures him the 33rd's other two battalions under his Colonel de Marguerye will be arriving that very day with the Emperor and the entire Moscow army! 'It was superfluous for me to go any further. I made an about turn and waited for the Emperor at Doroghoboüï.' When IHQ turns up he goes to Jomini,

> 'who was responsible for directing troop movements. From his adroit and judicious questions I realised immediately that this was an officer

81

absolutely equal to the situation. He seemed to me to be a most reflective person and very calm. It's absolutely impossible to give any idea of
the way in which at each moment everyone, prey to the most intense
over-excitement, was coming to ask him questions.'

Advised by Jomini to wait for de Marguerye, he also meets
'our brigade's former general Barbanègre who, despite his character of
officer of a crack regiment, was also marvellous at playing the role of
courtier, a bit to please the Emperor, a bit to encourage the troops'.

Over and over again Barbanègre assures Everts 'that this flight (taking place
amidst the most utter disorder) was a beautiful, remarkable retreat'. At
about 10 o'clock next morning, amidst utter disorder, all jumbled up with
'generals, wounded officers and men, commissary wagons and other
employees, the wreckage of the corps' ammunition trains, the carriages
of COs and everything else of the sort one can imagine ...'

the 33rd's two other battalions arrive, escorting a big artillery park. The first
thing de Marguerye asks Everts is, has he any food? Everts shows him his carts
full of barrels of rice, bread and salt, and a small supply of *votki* [*sic*], which
Marguerye delightedly distributes to the whole regiment 'as promptly as ever
possible. It went without saying', and the colonel tells Everts all about the
fight at Malo-Viazma in September,[8] when a squadron of the Guards Dragoons had been wiped out but most of his Dutchmen had survived.

Waiting there with a convoy of wounded, Lieutenant Vossler, too, is
astounded to see 'the first trickle of retreating soldiers', i.e., the army's
monstrous vanguard of loot and looters from Moscow:

'We were amazed at their appearance. Many carried no weapons. Others were armed after a fashion, but either their muskets were unserviceable or they'd run out of ammunition. These men were no longer
soldiers, but marauders and camp followers, mostly burdened with bales
of wool, linen, silk of every colour and description, with men's and
women's furs ranging from sable to sheepskin, hats and caps of every
shape and size, fashionable boots and shoes, kitchenware of copper,
brass and iron, silver and tin cutlery, pewter plates and dishes, glasses,
goblets, scissors, needles, thread, waxed twine, and so on and so forth.
In short, with every kind of object which the well-equipped peacetime
traveller, on horseback or on foot, whether gentleman, journeyman,
merchant, artist or whatever, could possibly require. Most were
mounted, usually on wretched little Russian ponies, others on carts,
barouches, diligences and coaches of every variety.'

Even the captured state carriages are still rolling along, having evidently
got through at Viazma.

Orders have been given that Doroghobouï, too, shall be burnt to the
ground; and no sooner has the Guard entered it than it tears down its houses
to make up its bivouac fires. By the time the other corps begin to arrive,
'nothing was left except a house or two. Its stores had been pillaged, the
brandy there'd been so much of was flowing in the streets, while the rest
of the army was dying for lack of *spirituosa*.'

III and IV Corps have been attacked by Miloradovitch while still two miles outside the town. When Eugène's men get there Labaume's shocked to see men

'straying about like cattle, sleeping under vehicles, or setting fire to the few remaining houses where generals are trying to warm themselves'.

The weather's horrible. 'As yet we hadn't had such bad weather since leaving Moscow,' thinks Griois, arriving soaked to the skin by a 'cold and humid wind and clouds of sleet which, piercing our clothes, numbed all our limbs'. Bourgogne's comrades are in like state – he particularly so, being bitten all over by lice, which he gets rid of by shaking out his garments over a fire. But what's this, arriving from the opposite direction? If not the long-awaited convoy bringing the handmills on which Napoleon had lavished so much detailed attention in the Kremlin?[9]

'Early next morning [5 November] before setting out, a distribution of handmills was made in every regiment of the Guard, in case we found any corn to grind.'

All the other corps, too, are exhorted to take their share. 'This offer of mills, when there wasn't a single grain at our disposition' seems 'a bitter mockery' to Griois: 'So all these useless pieces of furniture remained stored, at the disposition of the Cossacks.' Bourgogne's men find 'the mills very heavy; we got rid of them before twenty-four hours were over.'

Before leaving again, Le Roy, methodical as ever, passes his wardrobe in review. It consists of

1 pair of string shoes
1 pair of linen underpants, same length as my trousers
1 pair of trousers of blue broadcloth
1 pair of stable boots over the trousers
1 flannel waistcoat against my skin
1 shirt and a knitted woollen waistcoat over it, given me by Colonel
  Schultz at Vilna
1 waistcoat of blue cloth, with gold braid on front and pockets
1 blue frock coat and my epaulettes hanging down on my chest
1 strong broad cape collar hanging down over its shoulders
2 capacious pockets sewn into the interior 'serving me for a larder'. Two
  cords prevent the collar from being whipped up by the wind: it's also
  attached by two brandenburgers.
2 black silk handkerchiefs, the sturdier one protecting my ears and
  nose. To this end I had lined it with furs; the other served as a necktie.
1 shako, covered over with oilskin cover, containing needles, thread,
  scissors, soap and razor
1 sabre in its sheath, the handle resting under my left armpit
1 strong knife, with an ivory handle, with a pocket knife and corkscrew
1 notebook and pencil
1 black silk bonnet under the shako
1 bottle sheathed in wicker
Finally, as pocket handkerchiefs, my two hands.[10]

But Griois' amusing comrade and fellow artillery colonel, the aristocratic Jumilhac, 'violent and choleric towards his inferiors, but amiable, witty and excellent towards his comrades', wanders away into the night and doesn't come back.

When I Corps gets under way early next morning, Lejeune has to leave behind the cows that have so far been traipsing along with Davout's headquarters:

'Leaving Doroghobouï, we made a long march, and at nightfall halted in a big forest where General Jouffroy had been forced to halt with the many ill-harnessed guns he was in charge of. This night was employed to fill the ammunition wagons which could still be put in motion, blowing up those we were abandoning, and burning the wheels and carriages of guns we couldn't drag any further.'

To Davout's unwilling chief-of-staff and future painter of elegant battlescenes, who has found in the excitements of warfare a unique sensation of pleasure beyond all others, there's something tragic about these

'ever-multiplying explosions, the signals of our catastrophe. They tore at our heart just like a mother's is torn by the knell of a church bell sounding for her child's funeral.'

To console him General Jouffroy has a tent put up and invites Lejeune to supper – 'A supper! Oh God, what luxury in our misery!' Which among other things acquaints him with curry – something he's never tasted before:

'So far I hadn't been reduced to eating horsemeat. But the only dish the general could offer me was spiced horseflesh, a stew known as *boeuf à la mode*. This flavouring made this black, insipid, scraggly meat, full of sinews that resist even the sharpest incisors, very edible. An insipid yellow fat, saffron-coloured, gives this dish a repulsive appearance. Yet we were very happy to eat this excellent meal, washed down with a bottle of good wine taken from some great Muscovite lord.'

In vain, in a temperature which is falling sharply – Larrey, wearing a thermometer attached to his buttonhole, sees its mercury's at -16° Réaumur (-10° C) – Captain François, the 'Dromedary of Egypt', exhorts his men to 'remember' the Egyptian campaigns where I'd suffered even more acutely', and tells his comrades:

'"One can be even worse off! Here we've horseflesh to eat. In the deserts of Syria we often hadn't anything at all! You're complaining how cold it is, but I suffered more from the heat in the middle of Arabia's burning sands. Patience and courage!"'

But, he adds sadly,

'they scarcely listened to me, and we marched a whole day in deepest silence. Many of our guns and almost all our baggage were being abandoned along the road. The cavalry, so beautiful six months ago, being almost wholly without mounts, the men disperse and have no more discipline. Subordination is despised, the military hierarchy comes to an end. The general officer's no longer able to occupy himself with the soldiers who've made his glory for him, and the misery of these brave fellows causes them to despise their commanders' voices. They just wander away from them or ask them to kill them. This request was made to me several times! What could I say to revive their courage?'

But though he himself and some others are keeping up an unbroken morale, this doesn't prevent them from being tortured by hunger:

'A horse falls, they throw themselves on it, quarrel over strips of its flesh. To find firewood to cook this meat we have to go deep into the countryside, at risk of being massacred. Thus our rest halts are consumed by finding something to cook this disgusting food with.'

The oft-wounded François, marching with

'a boot and slipper on my feet, a crutch in my hand, covered in a pink fur lined with ermine and the hood over my head, with my faithful batman and my two horses who went on as they liked, without losing sight of us,'

pays a grenadier of the Guard a gold napoleon.[11] Otherwise he's eating only

'half-cooked horseflesh, in such fashion that the fat and blood spattered me from my chin to my knees. My face was blackened with smoke, my beard long, and I looked like a Mayence ham, and despite my situation I often laughed both at my costume and at that of my brothers-in-arms. We walked on with long icicles hanging from each hair of our beards, the skins that covered us half-burnt at such rare campfires as we were able to light. Those who had neither knife, sabre nor axe and whose hands were frost-bitten couldn't eat. I saw soldiers on their knees and others seated near shacks biting at horseflesh like famished wolves. Thanks to my batman I never lacked this resource, and each day I ate two or three pounds of this meat without salt or bread.'

But the result is 'dysentery'. Melted snow, which is all most men have to drink, is as bad for them as it is for the horses. Larrey, agreeing with Caulaincourt that it's hunger, not cold, that's killing the army, explains why:

'The little heat left in the viscera was absorbed. In particular it killed those who'd grown thin from abstinence and lack of nourishing food. In such people death was preceded by constrictive pains in the epigastric region, by sudden fainting fits, by a painful constriction of the throat, and by obvious anxiety – all symptoms of hunger.'

Even the Surgeon-General himself will have to march for the next three days on only 'two or three cups of pure coffee without sugar'. Then a friend gives him 'a glass of Bordeaux which I drank with indescribable pleasure'. And is immediately quit of his hunger pangs.

More and more, Smolensk is the magic word. There, everyone's saying to encourage himself as much as his neighbour, 'there's any amount of stores. Victor's IX Corps, fresh from Germany, is waiting for us', and will form the army's rearguard, enabling it to go into winter quarters in Poland. 'At least,' writes that amateur soldier, the sapient Dedem van der Gelder, 'that's how the multitude reasoned. Those who saw farther took care to keep their wisdom to themselves.'

That morning Wilson's Cossack escort, coming on the site of a French bivouac, see

'a gun and several tumbrils at the bottom of a ravine, with the horses lying on the ground. Lifting up the feet of several they call out, run and kiss the English general's knees and his horse, dance about and make fantastic gestures, like crazy men. When the delirium had somewhat subsided, they pointed to the horses' shoes and said: "God has made Napoleon forget that there is winter in our country." It was soon ascertained that all horses of the enemy's army were in the same improperly shod state, except those of the Polish corps, and the Emperor's own, which the Duke of Vicenza [Caulaincourt] with due foresight had kept always rough-shod.'

CHAPTER 5

SNOW

'We were assailed by whirlwinds of snow' – 'their limbs gradually stiffen' – doing a bear – Ney at Doroghobouï – Malet's conspiracy – Mother Dubois gives birth – plight of the amputees – Bourgogne hides nine potatoes – 'very well, I'll wait' – eating live horses – importance of cookpots – why southerners survived better – a grotesque masquerade – 'the way the Russians defreeze fish' – Louise Fusil kisses a gendarme

For several days the landscape's been 'swathed in cold vapours'. Le Roy, approaching Doroghobouï and bivouacking in a barn (sole relic of a hamlet) is sure 'everything boded snow for the morrow'. And sure enough, on 5 November

'the mists get thicker. An immense cloud, pressing down, falls in huge snowflakes. In the great black forests the wind begins to whistle and howl. It's as if the sky were coming down. Suddenly everything becomes confused, unrecognisable. Objects change their aspect ...'

The Russian winter Napoleon had so trivialised in spite of Caulaincourt's warnings yet whose onset he'd almost exactly predicted at Viazma, blasts the army with its icy breath. Scarcely have Dumonceau's men installed themselves in a hamlet on the forest edge than 'the temperature becomes glacial and a furious wind pounces' on them, driving before it thick whirlwinds of snow:

'No shelter protects us. Our fires could no longer warm us. The harsh north wind pursued me even in under my bearskin coverlet. Frozen on one side, grilled on the other, stifled by the smoke, agitated by the tempest's roarings as they violently shook the dense woods,'

he has to get up and run about all night, gets no rest. Already two nights before, on 2 November 'this suffering of a kind we'd so far not experienced' has already stricken I Corps' rearguard. Its chief-of-staff, spending it with Gérard's division in a big forest where the thermometer was showing -8° to -9° Réaumur (-10° to -11°C), had seen

'what a disastrous effect the snow was already having. When the moment came to leave, many men, stunned by the cold, couldn't get to their feet. We had to leave them where they were.'

In the most frightful cold Lieutenant Vossler sees

'men only lightly clad, without fur or overcoat, toiling along the road. It's visibly overpowering them. Their limbs gradually stiffen. They fall. Pick themselves up painfully, stagger on a few paces and fall once more, never to rise again. Some were showing their naked toes through their torn shoes or boots, first purple, then frozen dark blue or brown, and finally black.'

Dumonceau sees men sit down to rest by the roadside with their backs to trees or a heap of stones:

'At first they seem merely drowsy. But soon they become agitated, make futile efforts to get up; struggle convulsively, eyes haggard and glazed, the mouth fringed with froth, intelligence visibly extinct.'

Even veterans who've taken 2,000-mile marches from Spain and Italy in their stride and marched through many another blizzard – but then they hadn't been starving – are 'doing a bear'. Going suddenly headlong they fall on their faces. Or else death announces itself

'by strange symptoms. Here you're approached by someone with laughter in his eyes, his face beaming. He shakes you effusively by the hand – he's a lost man. Here another looks at you gloomily, his mouth uttering words of indignation and despair – he's a lost man.'

For Ney's rearguard to traverse Doroghoboüï's blackened ruins is far from easy. Although he has 'managed to reach the town and blow up the bridge', and is all the while heavily engaged, he knows that half-way to Smolensk the army must cross a bridge over the Dnieper; and it's his intention to hold up the Russians all day on 8 November, to enable it to do so in some kind of order. But the night is

'the coldest we'd had so far. Snow was falling in abundance, and the wind's violence prevented us from lighting fires. Besides which the heaths we were encamped on offered few resources for our bivouacs.'

Next morning, in a thick mist, the 4th and 18th Line (Joubert's brigade) withdraw into the remains of Doroghoboüï, closely followed by Cossacks. Fezensac details Joubert's dispositions for holding up the Russians:

'Doroghoboüï is situated on a height, has its back to the Dnieper. The 2nd Division, ordered to defend it, was disposed like this: two cannon in battery at the end of the lower road, supported by a post of the 4th Regiment. To the left, a company of the 18th on the Dnieper bridge; to the right, on high ground, in front of a church, 100 men of the 4th, commanded by a major; the rest of the division in the courtyard of the castle, on the same height; the 1st Division in reserve, behind the town.'

But all these sage dispositions come to nought:

'The Dnieper bridge was captured, the church post thrown back. General Razout, shut up in the castle courtyard with the rest of the division and delivered over to his habitual indecision, was going to be surrounded when he, at long last, gives us the order to march. There wasn't a moment to lose. I carried off my regiment at the *pas de charge*, and we threw ourselves at the enemies occupying the town's heights.'

Up to their knees in snow which breaks up their formation, the 4th attack in open order with the bayonet, fighting the Russians man to man:

'The Russians' progress had been held up, but soon the enemy penetrated into the lower part of the town, and General Razout,[1] afraid of being cut off, ordered the retreat. I fell back slowly, reforming my platoons and always facing the enemy. The 18th, which had seconded our efforts, followed this movement. Leaving the enemy masters of the town, the two regiments came and reformed behind the 1st Division. Marshal Ney, dissatisfied with the ill success of his plan, took it out on Razout, on Joubert, on everybody. He maintained that the enemy forces hadn't been big enough to have driven us out of Doroghoboüï, and asked me how many I'd seen. I permitted myself to reply that we'd been too close to count them.'

Nor does Ney succeed in recapturing two ammunition wagons which have accidentally been left in the town. No sooner has the 99th Line, under Colonel Henin, set off to do so, than it's forced back by Russian cannon fire. And Ney angrily 'resumes his retreat in good order'. Rapp:

'The army recrossed the Dnieper, the Emperor took up his headquarters in a ravaged château 120 kilometres from Smolensk and fifteen beyond the river. At this point its banks are rather steep and it was covered in ice-floes.'

Does he have any idea how many of his guns, 'not a single one of which was to be abandoned', are all the time having to be blown up or left behind? There are moments when Captain François, limping about on his one good leg, is even having to 'harness up fifteen horses to pull one field-gun'. And when the Württembergers have to spike eight of Faber du Faur's 16-pounders, von Roos sadly, for the last time, contemplates their gun-carriages:

'Everyone present was deeply moved. It seemed we were abandoning a parent or a friend in distress. These were the first guns the Württemberger troops had lost since the beginning of the war.'

Worried how the artillery will get across the Dnieper, Napoleon sends Rapp to Ney, telling him to hold off their pursuers until it's all across:

'All night we were busy getting the guns over. The last was still being pulled up the slope on the other side when the enemy came into view.'

In the ensuing fight several hundred men are wounded and have to be left behind:

'They bemoaned their lot, uttered pitiful cries, begging us to kill them. But what could we do? It was a heart-rending sight. Each of us was staggering under the burden of his own life. One could hardly stand upright. None of us had the strength to help anyone else.'

And all the time it's getting colder.

A few hours after IHQ has left Doroghoboui at 8 a.m. on 6 November and is nearing the village of Mikhailowska, it's met by a courier 'at a gallop, asking for the Emperor'. He has frightening news from Paris. Count Daru, the army's *Intendant-Général*, brings the locked leather portfolio to Rapp, who's on duty:

'A long time had gone by since any dispatches had come – and I opened these for the Emperor. He ripped open the packet, glanced at its contents, and lit on a number of the *Moniteur* which he glanced through. The first article he read contained an account of Malet's *attentat*; but since he still hadn't read the dispatches, he couldn't make head or tail of it.'

'"What's this? What plots, which conspiracies?"'

'He opened the letters. They contained all the details of the attempted coup. He was astounded. This police which is aware of everything, guesses everything, had let itself be fooled. It was more than he could explain:

'"Savary in the La Force prison! The Minister of Police seized, arrested!" 'I went out to distribute some orders. The matter was already known. Amazement, dismay, was written on every face.'

And in fact the news seems to be instantly known even to the Fusiliers-Grenadiers, who've seen the courier arrive. And to everyone else. Halting at a house in Mikhailowska which has been serving as a posthouse, Napoleon exclaims again and again to Caulaincourt and others that Savary should rather have let himself be killed than seized. Most alarming of all is that during the brief episode – it had only lasted from 4 a.m. to 11 a.m. on 23 October – no one had evidently given a thought either to the Empress or his son the infant King of Rome. So frail, at the political level, is his regime![2] Truly, as Talleyrand had whispered to the Tsar at Erfurt in 1910, the colossus has feet of clay – a realisation which certainly strengthens his intention to quit the army as soon as possible.

But there's also more urgent news. Marshal Victor's IX Corps, for instance, instead of attacking Wittgenstein, has been withdrawing in front of him. Two letters are swiftly dictated and sent off, urging Victor to resume the offensive and save the Moscow army's communications.

All day long on 6 November the snow falls heavily, freezing damp clothes to marching bodies:

'An envelope of ice seizes their bodies and stiffens all their limbs. A sharp violent wind grabs their breath even as they exhale it. Cutting it short, it forms icicles which hang by their beard around their mouths. Everything's becoming an obstacle.'

Many tumble into the unparapeted wells typical of Russian villages, and now invisible in the snow. Muskets are becoming

'insupportably heavy to their numbed limbs, slip from their hands, break, or get lost in the snow. Others' fingers freeze fast to them. The poor fellows drag themselves along, shivering, until the snow, clinging to their feet like a stone, or some bit of debris, a branch, or the body of one of their companions, causes them to trip and fall. There they groan in vain. Soon the snow covers them. Slight mounds show where they lie. There's their tomb! The whole road is strewn with these undulations, like a churchyard.'

Few, in this blizzard, have the strength to heed a fallen comrade. 'Even the most intrepid or the most indifferent', Philippe de Ségur sees as he plods on with IHQ's mules, covered with their purple horsecloths,

'are affected. They hurry by, averting their glances. In front of them, around them, all is snow. Their gaze loses itself in this immense dreary uniformity where the only objects that stand out are the great pines, funerary trees, with their funereal verdure, and the gigantic immobility of their black trunks and huge sadness. The whole army's being swathed in an immense winding sheet.'

It's so cold no one's riding a horse. Mailly-Nesle's companions, male and female, get out of their fine carriage and to keep warm 'walk onwards bent almost double, with our hands thrust in under our armpits, the part of the body we notice stays warmest'.

As in June's summer heats³ there are many suicides. Lejeune keeps hearing 'musket shots on either hand, men were shortening their sufferings'. Some even do a friend the same service. Hearing a shot ring out behind them, Dumonceau's company turn their heads. It's a Württemberger who's blown his friend's brains out. And then 'without even a backward glance' trudges on.

If the day's terrible, the night's worse. After making only seven miles or so the men of the 85th discover how hard it is to set fire to living pine. 'This wood only burns as long as there's resin in its branches, after which it turns black and gives off a thick suffocating smoke.' Von Muraldt's party too are finding it

'slow and wearisome work. First you had to fell a tree with your sabre (axes were rare or non-existent), or at least lop its branches, for no dry wood was to be found. And even then, for hours on end, you had more smoke than fire. Only when it had at last begun to burn and we'd cleared away the surrounding snow could you begin making your wretched meal. Horsemeat was grilled at sabre-point and then eaten half-raw and bloody and without salt.'

Anyone still possessing a modicum of flour tries to make 'galettes, a kind of thin cake we kneaded together with icewater and tried to bake over the fire' to go with their horsemeat. 'But usually we were so tormented by hunger we couldn't wait until they were thoroughly done, but ate them up much too soon.' With stomach ache and diarrhoea as a result. Duverger takes up the miserable tale:

'After we'd restored our stomachs a little we chatted for a few moments. Each talked of his ambitions and while doing so sleep came to numb our limbs.'

Captain Count M.-H. Lignières of the 1st Foot Chasseurs of the Guard describes his night:

'There was scarcely any fire. The snow built up on one's back. When you quit your place to heed a call of nature or warm yourself by walking about a bit, you saw in front of you a mountain of snow, from whose midst emerged a scarcely perceptible cloud of smoke. When you went back to take your place again it was thick with snow you had to get rid of.'

Sleeping beside such a campfire, the staff of the Imperial Household find 'the snow, melting on our bodies, seeped into our furs and then, freezing again, turned them into heavy mantles of ice, comparable to those horrible leaden capes described by Dante.'

The Fusiliers-Grenadiers have bivouacked near a wood. All that 'sad day' its sick have been making 'supernatural efforts' in hopes of reaching Smolensk, only to die in the evening.

'A moment after, our *cantinière*, Mother Dubois, the wife of our company's barber, was taken poorly. Our Colonel Bodel did all he could, lending Mother Dubois his own mantle to cover the shelter where she was courageously putting up with her trouble. The regiment's surgeon spares no efforts. And in the end all turns out happily. In a jiffy, while the snow's falling, she gives birth to a big boy – unhappy predicament for a woman.'

'That night', Bourgogne adds, 'our men killed a white bear, which was instantly eaten.' The bivouac is also fatal to the horses:

'One usually had to go some distance and break the ice to water them. Then one needed a bucket to draw the water. Arriving at night, where find a river or a well? A surface of water was indistinguishable from the surface of the ground. Ice, broken only with difficulty in the evening, would be frozen hard again in the morning. Furthermore, even to break it we needed an axe or iron rod, and all implements were scarce. A driver, arriving half dead with cold in the evening and scared of getting lost, would try to find some way of lighting a fire, finding some shelter and getting something to eat. More often than not he just left the horses where they were.'

Tethered to snow-laden pine or silver birch trees, the wretched animals try desperately to break the ice with their hoofs; can't, and die of thirst and cold. And when morning comes their drivers 'set out without even having unharnessed' the survivors. Those without horsecloths, Larrey sees, are the first victims. 'It was above all at night they perished, mostly for lack of water, trying to make holes in the ice with their hoofs.' Thanks to Caulaincourt's foresight, however, the hundred or so drawing IHQ's carriages are 'still numerous and in tolerably good condition' – proof to the Master of the Horse that it's not cold that's killing army's horses, 'but lack of proper care, food; and above all drink.'

After that freezing horrible night the Fusiliers-Grenadiers are on their feet long before dawn. 'As yet the *diane* ['dawn' = reveille] hasn't been beaten'; but Bourgogne, who's come by a whole bear skin, is

'already awake. Seated on my pack I foresee a terrible day from the wind that's already beginning to whine and whistle. I make a hole in my bear skin and put my head through it, so that the bear's head dangles on my chest. The rest covers my pack and back, but it's so long its tail drags along the ground.'

Frozen to the bone and aching all over, Paymaster Duverger and his comrades don't want to get up. 'The heat of one's body had melted the ice on the spot where one had slept, and you could count our places.' When they do get up,

'many just went on sitting there. Thinking they were asleep, we gave them a shove. They were dead. At first we only thought they were drowsy, stunned by the cold. But then, shaking them to wake them up, we found they were dead or dying.'

Every unit's bivouac is

'marked by rings of soldiers lying stiff and dead. The surroundings were encumbered by the bodies of several thousand horses.'

After spending the night in a barn, General Kerner of the Württembergers wakes up to find *all 300* of his men frozen stiff around their campfires. 'No help could save them,' Dumonceau goes on:

'We had to leave them lying there, beside the fires. There could be no question of burying them. Time and means were lacking, and the frozen ground too hard. In this way I lost my chief sergeant-major. We'd found him dead with his feet burnt up to the ankles and the upper part of his body frozen.'

But at last the *diane* is beaten, then the *grenadière* ['stand to arms'!]; and though it's not daylight Bourgogne's comrades set out. 'We got up,' Duverger goes on,

'and like the old nags who'd been condemned to drag numbered carts and the cuckoos[1] from Paris, hesitantly put one foot in front of the other. With oblique and uncertain step we move on.'

Dumonceau's lancers, too, resume their march on foot, 'dragging our horses by the bridle, to warm ourselves by the exercise'. Likewise the Fusiliers-Grenadiers: 'Then the blood begins circulating again. We get warmer as we march, and begin living again.' This morning Mother Dubois, 'covered with the greatcoats of two of the company's men who'd died in the night', is riding on Colonel Bodel's horse, holding her baby wrapped in a sheepskin. After marching for about an hour in the dark and catching up with the unit ahead of it the regiment makes a brief halt:[5]

'Mother Dubois wanted to use this moment of repose to give her newborn the breast. Suddenly she gives a cry of pain. Her babe is dead, hard as wood.'

The men try to console her by saying it's a blessing both for the baby and for herself, and

'despite her groans and though she's pressing it to her breast, take it from her; place it in the hands of a sapper who, together with the child's father, goes a few paces aside from the road and with his axe digs a hole in the snow, the father meanwhile on his knees, holding his child in his arms. When the hole's ready he kisses it, lays it in its tomb. Then they cover it, and all is over.'

Many much longer lives are being granted no such obsequies.

Now the Young Guard's column, its 'lips glued together' as it follows on behind the Guard Artillery, is marching through a thick fog:

'Our nostrils or rather our brains froze. We seemed to be walking on through an atmosphere of ice. All day the snow, blown by an extraordinary wind, was falling in flakes so big no one had ever seen the like of them. Not merely could we no longer see the sky, we couldn't even see the men ahead of us.'

Already in this struggle to survive

'there were no more friends. We looked suspiciously at each other, even became ungrateful toward one's best comrades.'

Near the 'wretched village' of Mikhailowska there's a dispute over a loaf of newly baked bread Bourgogne's obliged a surgeon-major to sell him for 5 francs, only to have it grabbed by his comrades 'leaving me only the bit I was holding between my thumb and two first fingers of my right hand'. Now everyone's only thinking of himself. Seeing a man surreptitiously boiling some potatoes for his general, Bourgogne forces him to sell him nine of them. And slips them – no less surreptitiously – into his cartridge pouch.

'To let oneself be affected by pity at the deplorable scenes one witnessed was to doom oneself. Those who were so fortunate as to find enough strength in themselves to resist the many evils were the ones who developed the coldest sensibility.'

Duverger sees what's happening to those who don't:

'They fell on the road and didn't get up again. We saw their legs begin to tremble, and their body leaning forward augured death. Their companions followed them with their eye and speculated on how soon they'd fall. Still alive, they were stripped naked. We quarrelled over their clothing, snatching from them what feeble resources they still had left.'

A ranker begins pulling the clothes off his general who's collapsed and is dying by the roadside. The general begs him weakly at least to wait till he's dead: 'Very well, *mon général*,' replies the grenadier stolidly. 'I'll wait.'

Hard-heartedness is going to incredible lengths. Réné Bourgeois sees[6] a captain of engineers who's fallen by the wayside appealing to the passers-by for help:

'"I'm an engineer captain, help me!" A grenadier turns round, stops in front of him, and in a voice half-serious half-mocking, says, "What, you're an engineer captain? Well, then, draw up your plan."'

The cruel iron law of survival is the order of the day. And Napoleon's order from Doroghobouï for the army to march

'as we did in Egypt, with the baggage in the middle, a half-battalion in front and at the rear, and battalions in file on either flank ... units at short intervals, with artillery between',

is falling on snow-filled ears. Likewise the order: 'No man may leave his unit or lack a musket.' All around, Cossacks and armed peasants, dodging about in the steadily falling snow, are

'pushing their audacity to the point of penetrating our ranks, carrying off pack horses and wagons they suppose to be loaded with the greatest treasures. Our men haven't the strength even to resist these abductions'

and are too busy trying to steal from one another. Only the horses of the wounded, Victor Dupuy's glad to see, are still being respected by 'soldiers of all ranks'. Not that their owners can use them. It's too cold. 'They'd have frozen within a few hours.' He leaves to our imagination

'the plight of the sick and wounded, more especially of amputees. Piled up pell-mell in wagons whose horses were succumbing to fatigue and inanition, the unfortunates were abandoned in the bivouacs and on the roads, and died raving. Those who had the strength to do so killed themselves. Their companions, the friends of these sad victims, couldn't help them. They averted their eyes.'

Fezensac sees an exception is still being made for women and children:

'Everyone was doing his best to succour them. For a long while our drum-major carried a child in his arms. Officers who still had a horse shared it with these poor people.'

Perched on a gun-carriage Le Roy recognises a commissary's wife who'd been most theatrically attired in Moscow but has lost her husband:

'The silk shawl she was wearing was all scorched, her eyes dulled and red, her face fallen, witnessing to this poor woman's physical and moral sufferings.'

Even veterans for whom comradeship is the one great ethic of a military life are failing to honour it. During that second icy night in the snow, Sergeant Bourgogne, so far from telling his starving comrades about his treasure trove of potatoes, has slept clutching them tightly. And at the next halt 'like an egoist' goes aside into the thickest part of the wood, takes some out – only to find they're

'just ice! I try to bite into them. My teeth slip on them without being able to detach the least bit. It's then I regret not having shared them yesterday with my friends.'

He goes and rejoins them, shamefacedly,

'still holding in my hand what I'd tried to eat, all red with my lips' blood. They ask me what I've got. Without replying, I show them the potato and the ones in my cartridge case.'

Where's he found them? He gestures toward the wood. They run into it, hoping for more. In vain. And Bourgogne's potatoes, when boiled, just melt away like ice. His comrades however, who've cooked a whole pot of horse's blood,

'invited me to have my share. Which I did without being asked twice. I've always reproached myself for acting like that,' he confesses. 'They've always thought I'd found my potatoes in the wood, and I've never disabused them.[7] But all this is only a sample of what we'd see later.'

Cold and hunger have made everyone so insensitive to others' suffering that not even the horses are being allowed to expire before being torn to pieces. Those left behind or killed during the night

'were frozen so hard it was impossible to cut anything from them. As soon as a horse dropped, no one tried to help it to its feet again, but instantly we saw the soldiers throw themselves at it, open up its flanks to tear out the liver, the least repulsive part; and without having bothered to kill it before sacrificing it like this, we saw them, I say, get irritated over the animal's last efforts to escape its executioners.'

Lejeune sees some men hitting a dying horse and shouting as they try to dismember it: '*Coquin!* [Rascal!] Why can't you lie still?' Kergorre too sees how horses 'still alive, from which a large part of the rump had been removed, were weeping as they watched themselves being dissected, and no one thought of finishing them off!' Captain François, who's marching with IV Corps, sees a young woman rush in among some soldiers who've just disembowelled one. Though she's wearing a marten fur lined with white satin she plunges her hands into the animal's belly to tear its liver out. But having no knife has to put her head inside and use her teeth instead. Sergeant-Major Thirion's little party of dismounted cuirassiers cut slices from the horses' rumps as they trudge on through the snow:

'It was too cold to kill them and cut them up. Our hands would have refused to perform this service, they'd have frozen. The wretched animals gave not the least sign of pain, proof positive how numb and insensitive they were from the extreme cold. Under any other conditions these slices of flesh would have brought on a haemorrhage and death. But with 28 [*sic*] degrees of frost this didn't happen. The blood froze instantly and arrested the flow. We saw some of these poor horses walking for several days with large pieces of flesh cut away from both thighs.'

The sergeant-major himself has a little pannikin

'which I wouldn't have exchanged for a fortune. Inserting a knife blade as gently as possible between the ribs, I held up my little casserole to catch the blood, and then cooked it – a black pudding I'd nowadays consider insipid, but which I thought delicious.'

Born survivors like Thirion have their own techniques:

'When I halted with my dismounted cuirassiers at the place where we were to spend the night, I unclasped my cape and threw it on the snow, laid my carbine and helmet on it and, very tired though I was and suffering from a wound in my foot, I started dancing what in choreography is called "pigeon's wings". My comrades thought I'd gone mad, but I reassured them by saying it was to keep my spirits up; or rather, to prevent them from weakening.'

Others, like Commissary Kergorre, are applying no less sophisticated survival techniques:

'As long as I'd any boots I never failed to take them off in the evening and don a pair of linen slippers, which in the daytime I put in my pocket. When morning came I was a great deal less exhausted, my feet not being swollen, and thus I preserved my footwear which otherwise I might have burnt while asleep at the bivouac.'

As for Pion des Loches, he's positively smug about his elaborate arrangements. And who cannot but admire the sangfroid and sagacity of a certain general G***,

'who'd no one left of his brigade, had lost all his horses too, whose servants all had frost-bitten limbs, and who'd lost all his remaining baggage. Out of all his possessions he took a simple cooking pot. Armed as he was with this modest and precious utensil, everyone who had nothing to cook their food with wanted him to join them.'

Installing 'the owner of this treasure in the best spot close to the fire,' they give him a good part of its contents 'and return it him, well cleaned. The gallant general loaded it on his shoulder again and continued on his way, not worrying about his night or his supper, thus always assured to him.'

As for Le Roy and Jacquet's treasured iron cookpot that had so nearly gone missing at the Niemen in June, their ugly-faced young servant Guillaume is guarding it jealously . 'Anyone', says von Muraldt, 'who still owned a little flour, rice, coffee or sugar, and thereto any vessel to cook with, was a millionaire. Everyone fawned on him.' His own 'most precious treasure' too, is 'an iron pot, which never left me. Not many had anything of the kind with them, or else had lost it.' At I Corps' headquarters Duverger and his comrades are

'taking turns at the cooking. It wasn't my kind of task. My stew always smelt of the pot. It wasn't always we had some horsemeat or aquavit. Often no pure water. It was then we prepared our thin Spartan broth. Here's the recipe: Melt some snow – and you'll need plenty to get only a little water. Put in some flour. Then, for lack of salt, some gunpowder. Serve up hot and only eat when you're really hungry.'

Observant individuals like Thirion are noticing how some types and nationalities – Frenchmen, Spaniards, Italians and Portuguese – are, most unexpectedly, surviving better than others:

'Brown subjects of a bilious-sanguine temperament, almost all from southern countries of Europe, put up a better resistance than blond subjects, almost all from the northern countries – which is the opposite of what is usually supposed.'

Dupuy too thinks the southerners are surviving better, and ascribes it to their livelier temperament. An idea also shared by Larrey.[8] 'The former's circulation', he explains,

'is doubtless more active. Their vital forces have more energy. It's also probable their blood, even under the influence of extreme cold, retains much better the principle of the heat identified with its colorative part. From the same cause the moral strength is so much the better sustained. Courage doesn't abandon them, and by understanding how to care for their own preservation they know better than the usually apathetic inhabitants of cold and humid climates how to avoid pitfalls.'

His theory is that southerners have a more vigorous circulation and are therefore of a darker complexion and by the same token have greater moral resources. 'Thus we'd see Dutchmen of the 3rd Grenadiers of the Guard, 1,787 men strong, both officers and rankers, perish almost to a man. Only 41 got back to France.'[9] Surgeon Roos, for his part, is convinced from experience that those who seem to be surviving best tend to be those who're

'best at muddling through, and those most used to privations, no matter what nation they belonged to. Young men, on the other hand, inexperienced, feeble or lazy, or simply spoiled children used to being waited on, who from the outset had been unable to stand the summer heats and most of whom had remained in the rear, were the first to succumb.'

Sometimes there are unburnt houses along the way. Woe betide anyone who sits too long in an overheated room! Soon he finds his limbs swelling, due – Larrey supposes – to

'an expansion of the capillary blood vessels of the interior members, to which the latent heat and life seemed to retreat. The meninges becoming similarly inflated results in heavy headaches, lesion of the mental faculties and an alteration in those of the sense organs. The individual was stricken with general weakness and an extremely painful anxiety. He started a cough, which grew quickly worse. More or less violent, it was accompanied by mucous, sometimes bloody expectorations. Often a diarrhoeic flux occurred at the same time: a desire to vomit, with colic pains. The pulse became feverish, the skin dry. The sick man felt a painful swelling in his members, cramps, fits and starts, and a prickly heat in the soles of his feet. Sleep was laboured and accompanied by sinister dreams. The vessels of the conjunctive injected themselves. Fever developed, with aggravations in the evening. The beatings of the carotids and of the temples became noticeable to the naked eye. Delirium or lethargic drowsiness set in, and danger was imminent. Such were the main symptoms that accompanied his affliction, which could be called *catarrhal ataxia from congealment*. Its course was more or less swift, according to the subject's constitution, his age and his degree of vigour.'

Nor is it only the landscape that's changed its aspect. The army itself has become a grotesque masquerade. Everyone, from generals down to privates, has donned whatever costly silks and furs he's brought from Moscow. 'Each soldier was wearing whatever he'd found in the pillage,' Louise Fusil, *soubrette* of the former French theatre in Moscow, notes with expert eye, as her carriage (property of Caulaincourt's nephew) rolls slowly onwards through the blizzard under its owner's protection:

'Some are covered with a moujik's caftan or some plump kitchen wench's short fur-lined dress. Others a rich merchant's coat and – almost all – in the fur-lined pink, blue, lilac or white satin mantles of the kind all the common people here make into articles of luxury (respectable Russian women wear black ones).'

Nothing would have been funnier, the intrepid actress goes on,

'if the circumstances hadn't been so sad, than to see an old grenadier, with his moustaches and bearskin, covered in a pink satin fur. The poor fellows protected themselves as best they could against the cold; but even they laughed at this bizarre spectacle.'

The staff of 5th Division, I Corps, have christened General Compans, its commander, 'the Tartar' because of his 'cap of crimson velvet edged with sable' given to him at Hamburg by his new wife. Now he's wearing it over

'a dress coat without embroidery or epaulettes, blue breeches, top boots, and an ample greatcoat lined with very good fox fur and trimmed with sable tails. Its collar covers my ears and, reaching down to my ankles, lets nothing be seen except my cap and my booted feet. Over this

I'm wearing my sword, hanging from a gold-embroidered crimson velvet belt. Only the triple stars on the sword-knot indicate my rank. Such is the full-length portrait, my dearest, of Compans the Tartar,' he'll shortly be writing to his bride.[10] As for the rank and file, some are making themselves boots out of old hats:
'Very few had any furs, mantles or greatcoats, so as soon as they took the least rest they were overcome with stupor. The young men, being the most inclined to sleep, succumbed in great numbers. Most of our men would be mutilated by gangrene due to coming too close to the fires.'
The only cure for frost-bite – a remedy Larrey repeatedly applies to himself – is to rub the white numb skin areas with snow,
'or, if these means didn't suffice – the way Russians defreeze fish – to plunge the affected part into cold water, soaking it until air bubbles are seen rising from the frozen part.'

'It was a Friday [6 November] and we were almost at Smolensk,' Louise Fusil goes on:
'The officer in the coach by which I'd left [Moscow] had ordered his coachman to get there by evening. This latter was a Pole, the slowest and clumsiest I've ever come across. He spent all night – as he maintained – searching for forage. In the meantime he'd let his horses freeze at their leisure, with the result that they could no longer move their legs when he wanted to get them moving again; and we lost two. Those two once dead it was impossible for us to make headway with the two others. We got stuck at the entrance of a heavily encumbered bridge until Saturday the 7th. I was wondering what to do, and made up my mind to abandon the *calèche* as soon as day dawned and cross the bridge on foot to go and ask the general in command at its far end for help or a seat in some other carriage. But just then the Pole returned with two horses he said he'd "found". Of course I realised he'd stolen them; but nothing was commoner.'
Theft, particularly of horses, has become universal:
'Everyone was robbing everyone of everything with perfect impunity. The only risk was to get caught red-handed, because then one risked a thrashing. All day long one heard "*Ah, mon Dieu*, someone's stolen my portmanteau! Someone's taken my pack! Someone's stolen my bread, my horse!" – and this from the general officer down to the ranker. One day Napoleon, seeing one of his officers wearing a very fine fur, said to him, laughing: "Where've you stolen that?" – "Sire, I've bought it." – "You've bought it from someone while he was asleep!" The witticism was repeated throughout the army.'
A joke to Napoleon perhaps, not to the lone straggler, for whom it can mean death. Only because Lariboisière, seeing her in tears, tells a gendarme to include her *dormeuse* among Davout's carriages does Louise get across a congested bridge:
'This gendarme – I don't know why – took me for the wife of General Lauriston and lost himself in beautiful words. As we finally crossed the

bridge it was lined on either side by generals, colonels and an officer who'd long been waiting there to hasten the march. The Cossacks, as I've heard later, weren't far off.'

Alas, a quarter of the way across the horses go on strike:

'Any carriage blocking the route in a difficult passage – the order was positive – was to be burnt. I saw myself worse off than I'd been the day before. On all sides the shout went up: "this carriage is preventing us from passing, it must be burnt!" The soldiers wanted nothing better – because they'd loot it. They too shouted: "Burn it! burn it!" But then some officers took pity on me and shouted: "Come on, men, put your shoulders to the wheels!" And so they did, and they themselves were so good as to hustle them into doing so.'

Once in the clear, a laughing Louise rewards the gendarme with a kiss – 'and he was most content'.

Today the Red Lancers, still riding ahead of IHQ, are taking a pause when desperate shouts arouse them from torpor. A 'hurrah' of Cossacks has attacked the mob of stragglers – presumably from VIII Corps. The Dutchmen mount hastily, gallop forward, form up in line – but don't bother to try and recover the few wagons the Cossacks are making off with. 'Hands and feet numb with cold and hardly bellicose,' they just sit there shivering on their horses. But the Cossacks are circumspection itself, 'and this helped to guarantee us against their undertakings'. While 'skirmishing' in this lackadaisical manner, the Red Lancers are overtaken by IHQ,

'and for a few moments its numerous escort was a powerful support to us. Instead of his usual grey overcoat the Emperor, riding his usual beautiful white horse and imperturbably preserving his calm serenity, was wearing a green velvet pelisse with a rich fur lining and enhanced with gold brandenburgs. Near him we spotted the brilliant King of Naples, wearing his Polish sky-blue tunic, also fur-lined and decorated with gold tresses, both otherwise having his neck and the lower part of his face wrapped up to the nose in a broad Indian shawl, and on his head, as always, his Polish toque surmounted by a bouquet of floating feathers. After him came the Duke of Istria [Duroc], always white-powdered and his long stock wig immaculately set, as if to appear in a drawing-room. He was simply dressed in a deep blue mantle, maintaining his strictly regulation appearance.'

After them come Berthier and various generals and orderly officers, uniformly dressed in mantles, 'the only non-regulation feature being turned up collars and scarves around their noses'.

Surprisingly, no one, or almost no one, as far as Kergorre can see, is overtly accusing Napoleon of the disaster that's obviously overtaking the army:

'It's been said that the soldiers insulted Napoleon during the retreat. I, who saw His Majesty in the most painful circumstances, think I can assure you it's not true.'

Dumonceau, unemotional as ever, agrees:

'A few higher-ranking pessimists in fits of bad temper might reason differently; but instances of this among the rank and file and the subalterns were rare, and our devotion remained absolute. Our confidence in him was still intact. No one among us dreamed of reproaching him for our setbacks, and in our eyes he still retained the prestige of a supreme arbiter.'

'The rank and file, it's true,' Kergorre adds, 'were no longer shouting "*Vive l'Empereur!*" But they said nothing.' 'Such was the respect the Emperor was held in and the devotion to his person that no one in his suite,' Caulaincourt affirms, 'not even his servants were ever insulted.' His testimony, he claims, is 'worth something' because ever since Vereia he's always been marching on foot,

'sometimes with the Emperor, sometimes ahead of him, sometimes behind; but always among groups of uniformed men, without my riding-coat and wearing my uniform hat. Unquestionably any discontent among the soldiers would have shown itself in the presence of a general in uniform. The behaviour of the unfortunate men freezing to death by the roadside, I admit, often amazed me. But I wasn't alone in admiring it.'

Even Dedem – critical though he is and though he's beginning to hear the rank and file swear at their officers – never hears

'any soldier swear at the man they owed all their ills to. All I heard was men of the Old Guard saying; "Ah, Moreau[11] would have led us better!"

Is this really true? Of the soldiers perhaps. Perhaps not of the Administration, etc. Cavalry surgeon Réné Bourgeois sees one such employee

'who'd had both legs crushed by the wheels of a carriage that had knocked him down. There he lay on the road, prey to terrible pains, at the moment when Napoleon passed by at the head of his Guard. Seeing him, he raised himself up, and gathering all his strength to make his voice as loud as possible, overwhelmed him in abuse:

'"There he is," he said, "that miserable puppet who for ten years has been leading us about like automata. Comrades, he's mad! Don't trust him! He's turned into a cannibal. The monster will devour you all!"'[12]

If there are angry feelings, they're among the top brass. Caulaincourt's shocked to see,

'they were so weary of warfare, had such a craving for repose, for the sight of a less hostile country, for an end to these far-flung expeditions, that most of them let themselves be blinded as to the present fruits and future consequences of our disasters by the thought that they'd prove a useful lesson to the Emperor, and cool his ambition. This was the common view.'[13]

The diary of Secretary Fain, that student of human nature, confirms it:

'Around the Emperor the courtesan's smile has fallen from those lips most accustomed to wearing it. All faces have fallen. The strong minds, which have no mask to lose, are the only ones whose expression hasn't changed.'

Caulaincourt's for instance. Or Duroc's. Dumonceau's men having found a ford,

'the Grand Marshal of the Imperial Court joined us to profit from it. He was riding a very fine horse, was dressed as if for a parade, in white breeches, well-waxed stable boots and all the rest of that kind of costume, only wearing over it neither mantle nor greatcoat, but only a spencer [short-tailed jacket], tight to the body, indifferent to the cold. Otherwise he seemed cheerful. Most amiable to all who approached him, he was on his way to go and prepare the Emperor's lodging, accompanied by some officers and élite gendarmes. All had been provided with horses in good condition.'

Thanks to Caulaincourt's foresight at Moscow, as Wilson will afterwards hear, all the 73 headquarters horses are rough-shod – an obvious precaution that's otherwise only been taken by the Poles. As soon as Duroc's party have crossed the ford he leaves with it 'at a gallop'.

The Guard Horse Chasseurs, too, still have 600 men mounted. And when 300 fresh horses are 'sent forward by a Polish nobleman "to help the Emperor during his retreat"' they're sent to the senior cavalry regiment as remounts. IHQ's spirits also rise during its last day's march before Smolensk when a convoy of provisions intended for Ney's rearguard is seen coming toward it.

'Recalling other times and other ideas, it raised the morale even of the most despondent. Everyone believed in abundance and thus in reaching his goal. The Emperor flattered himself on it more than anyone, and said so several times.'

But when the Red Lancers rejoin the column shortly thereafter they have to come to the rescue of the

'infantry escort who're being attacked and their convoy pillaged by the mob of disbanded men. There was a lot of vociferation on our account but most of the convoy was saved and able to go on its way.'

Did any of its contents ever reach Sergeant Bertrand and his men, executing their chequerboard retreat for four days on end?[14] These two blizzard-stricken days (6–7 November) have destroyed one-third of the Moscow army. 'From this day onwards,' Labaume will write in his history of the campaign,[15]

'it lost its strength and military bearing. The ranker no longer obeyed his officers, the officer abandoned his general. Disbanded regiments walked along any old how. Struggling to keep alive, they spread out in the plains, burning and sacking everything they came across.'

Yet all the time Lejeune sees men like Captain François who 'though riddled with wounds remained full of energy' never lose their morale. And if there's one thing Thirion's noticing it's that

'any man who thought it impossible for us to make the remaining 100 or 150 leagues [3–500 miles] to get out of Russia was a man lost. Two or three days later he'd disappeared.'

CHAPTER 6

DISASTER AT THE WOP

Griois buries two guns – 'winter had fallen on us in all its severity' – IV Corps marches for Witebsk – a new command – Del Fante plunges in – the guns are lost – a day's rest

On 7 November, while still at Doroghobouï, IV Corps has been ordered to leave the main column and march for Witebsk. Witebsk, 'an infinitely important strategic point on the Vilna–Petersburg road at a distance of 24 leagues [75 miles] from Polotsk and 30 from Smolensk' where Napoleon had left a weak garrison in August, but where large stores have been accumulated, is known to be under threat. Crossing the Dnieper by the pontoon bridge at 6 a.m., Eugène's men[1] have peeled off to the right along the Witebsk road. Along this less devastated route, they hope, there'll at least be more to eat.

Grouchy's 3rd Cavalry Corps no longer exists – the 'inept, almost dazed' Lahoussaye[2] is just riding along in his carriage, indifferent to everything' and Grouchy himself seems to have 'disappeared', and for several days now Griois' horse artillery has been marching on its own. Having friends among Eugène's artillery staff[3] he decides to follow on after IV Corps. That night, after crossing the Dnieper, he bivouacs

'under a mere roof on four posts, a sort of barn, open to every wind, but a fine lodging, even so, compared with the ones I'd so long been occupying'.

After his gunners have made up a big fire in the middle of it he lies down to sleep, surrounded by his horses. Waking up at daybreak he finds he's

'covered in thick snow, likewise the whole landscape. It wasn't falling any longer; but the cold sky was icy. Everything was frozen. The mud had frozen hard during the night. Winter had fallen on us in all its severity.'

It's almost impossible to get his guns and ammunition wagons moving:

'In vain our poor exhausted horses tried to drag them out. Only after doubling the teams, using levers to prise the wheels loose, and by joining their efforts to those of the horses, did our gunners and the men of the Train succeed in getting part of the artillery on the move.'

Griois has to triple his teams. And to do this – each caisson now only having four horses to drag it – two guns and two wagons have to be abandoned. All the woodwork is stacked up in a hangar and burnt, and the

'guns entombed in the ashes. It was the first time I'd left behind loaded wagons and guns. So it was with sadness in my soul I got going again on 8 November, to catch up with IV Corps.'

But even then the snow, icy and hardened, frustrates the horses' hooves:

'We had plenty of ice-nails in reserve, but as yet hadn't used them to shoe the horses. Yet even this wouldn't have been enough. After a few hours march their diamond-shaped heads would have been worn down, and they'd have become utterly useless – as we soon found out.[4] Calkins are a lot better, but we'd have needed more time and resources than we possessed.'

The bad road surface still further slows his march. And all the time Cossacks, flanking his column with light guns mounted on sledges, flit from one bit of high ground to the next; fire at his men; kill a few; and then, when his guns laboriously begin to reply, move on to the next eminence. Ahead of him, but steadily nearer as the whole procession slows down, is IV Corps' reserve artillery:

'Our sixteen 12-pounders had long been trying to climb a long and steep hill, surfaced with thick ice. In vain we doubled and tripled the teams. Some of the vehicles had managed to take a few steps, but then come to a halt. The drivers' whiplashes and oaths, the efforts of the gunners putting their shoulders to the wheels, were of no greater avail. Only with greatest difficulty had part of the divisional artillery, lighter and better harnessed up, been able to surmount this obstacle.'

Griois has just caught up with it when its commander, General C.-N. Anthouard, is hit by a roundshot which 'after killing the orderly officer at his side' (von Muraldt hears) has 'fractured his thigh'. 'If it hadn't been for his chief-of-staff Colonel Berthier,'[5] Griois reflects, 'who carried him to his carriage on his shoulders, he might have stayed there on the snow, like most men wounded that day.'

Only after 'infinite toil and reinforcing the teams with the horses of four wagons' which Griois again resigns himself to abandoning, does his artillery get up the hill 'and reach the château of Zazelé' whose 'charming position, vast and opulent outbuildings' he'd admired when coming this way before, en route for Moscow:

'Now, covered in snow, shrouded in a dense fog which hardly enabled us to make out its walls, it was encumbered with troops and carriages and looked very different. Happy the first-comers! No shelter remained for anyone else.'

Himself being one of them, he's looking for some nook or cranny where he can get out of the cold and make up a fire, when he hears the seriously wounded Anthouard is asking for him. He finds him lying on some straw in a peasant's hut. A certain Colonel Fiéreck (Anthouard tells him) should normally succeed him. But the elderly Fiéreck just now evidently having no taste for command and also, in Eugène's opinion, 'not being active enough', he has proposed to the Viceroy that Griois should take over IV Corps' artillery. In this new capacity he joins Anthouard's adjutant-commandant[6] in a little low room in the château.

The Italian, Spanish, Croat and French regiments' hopes of finding better conditions along the Witebsk road have been cruelly dashed. But their baggage train is still considerable and 'as yet we didn't feel our losses in this respect'. But ruin and Cossacks are everywhere. 'Everywhere during that night at the château of Zazeló [sic] von Muraldt's party of disbanded Bavarian officers, clinging to the Italian Royal Guard, see 'people dying of hunger and cold, and horses, tormented by thirst, trying to break the ice with their feet to find water'. And just ahead, he knows, barring tomorrow's march, 'a little river,' von Muraldt remembers, 'so inconsiderable that we hadn't even noticed it when we'd crossed it during our advance.'[7]

The Wop.

Like many others, Cesare de Laugier's certainly reflecting, as he approaches it, how swiftly it flows between its steep and marshy banks 'and is difficult to ford'.

Already Eugène has sent on a party of engineer-geographers under General Sanson, accompanied by some cannon, to find out what state it's in and seize the bridgehead. Sanson sends back a report that they've already found Cossacks 'infesting all its banks' – and himself is immediately captured. So that evening Eugène sends on General Poitevin with 'the company of sappers that's marching with his headquarters' to throw a bridge. 'We left at first dawn [9 November),' Griois goes on:

'The weather was cold and a thick mist prevented us from hardly seeing anything ten paces ahead of us. We didn't even see the Wop until we'd reached the deep ravine which it flows at the bottom of. A considerable crowd, pressing together at the same point, indicated that the bridge was on that side. I dismounted and went on in that direction. Soon I was sorry I had. But it was too late. I had to follow the crowd I was entangled in. Finally I got to the entrance of the bridge, a frail planking.'

After a few paces everything comes to a halt. Shouts are heard ahead, but no one understands why;

'until the terrifying news is passed from rank to rank that the far end of the bridge is broken, or rather has never quite been completed. The unfortunate first-comers, fooled by the fog, had tumbled into the torrent.'

And in fact the Viceroy's sappers,

'either for lack of time or *matériel* and workmen, exhausted or hungry and cold, had had to leave the bridge as they'd found it. There was no time to think of re-establishing it. We had to make up our minds to ford the river.'

The pursuing Cossacks, with their sledge-guns, promptly open fire on this confused mass. And Eugène, after sending out some fresh troops to support the light infantry that's trying to stave them off, realises 'someone from his household will have to set an example of courage by being the first to cross'. And orders his *officier d'ordonnance* (senior staff officer) Colonel Del Fante[8] to do so at the head of the Royal Guard. Flowing swiftly between its steep banks of frozen mud, the Wop's covered by 'a thin layer of ice'. Up to his waist and almost swept off his feet by ice-floes, Del Fante struggles across to the far bank, followed by Guilleminot, Eugène's staff and the Guard.

'General Pino, wounded and on horseback, Adjutant-commander Del Fante, General Théodore Lecchi, turn to the grenadiers of the Vélites who, formed up by platoons at the head of the columns, were anxiously awaiting their orders on the steep river bank. "Let's save the army," they shout. "Follow us!"'

These 'young men from the best Italian families, each being supported by his family with a Line lieutenant's pay,' their Adjutant-Major goes on,
'needed no further exhortations. The drums beat the charge, and the Royal Guard, followed by other regiments, throws itself into the river. The men have water up to their shoulders and break the ice-floes as they cross over. But many get stuck in its mud and disappear. The blood of others, gripped by the cold, freezes.'
Some perish under the weight of their weapons. As for those who do get over,
'their feet slip on the icy bank. The men roll down over each other. Some fall back into the river. Lastly, those who reach their goal, streaming with water, pierced with cold, their only thought is to hold out their hands and their musket to their comrades coming on behind them. It's impossible',
writes Cesare de Laugier, his pen refusing 'to depict the troops' situation after this crossing, either the physical torments they endured, or the pains caused by this bath of ice.' The river not being all that deep, the first vehicles don't manage too badly. But their wheels churn up its muddy bottom, and their successors are soon in trouble:
'Only by taking time and at the price of great efforts, by doubling and tripling the teams, could a gun or caisson be got over.'
The carriages are another matter. The ford has been
'reserved for the artillery. Repulsed from it, they were trying to cross at other points. But there the river was even more steeply embanked. They got stuck deep in the mud, where their horses remained motionless, half-frozen.'
Griois, on horseback, crosses and recrosses 'at least ten times, keeping the gunners and soldiers of the Train at their pieces, calling, shouting, swearing encouraging some, inciting others'. His trousers are soaked through,
'but I was so agitated I didn't even notice it. I still see those brave soldiers of the Train – they had to begin by breaking the ice-floes all round them – having to remain for hours together with their teams in the middle of the water, and then, having dragged out a gun or an ammunition wagon, having to begin the same efforts all over again, endure the same fatigues. Their horses' traces, stiff with ice, were scarcely pliable.'
Finally, by dint of endless effort, four guns are got across. But then everything gets stuck. And in no time, on the left, eastern bank,
'a mass of cannon, powder wagons, vehicles of every kind, had piled up, covering the river bank farther than the eye could see. Sutlers, everyone who owned any kind of vehicle, were running hither and thither with anxious shouts, trying – if possible – to find some way across. Gunners, seeing no hope to get the heavy pieces across the swampy, ice-covered river, begin blowing up their caissons and spiking their guns. Everyone who hasn't a horse has to plunge into the water. The broken ice-floes can scarcely be thrust aside, and men have the icy water up to their bellies –'

Griois says to their armpits. His four cannon, once across, have been 'immediately ranged in position on the far bank to keep the Cossacks under control and secure the crossing for the troops, the numerous marauders and non-combatants still on the other bank. But the muddy bottom is all churned up and makes it impossible to proceed. One vehicle gets stuck. Others add themselves to it. And everything comes to a halt. Instantly this, the only practicable ford, is encumbered with ammunition wagons and all kinds of vehicles carrying the little that's left of our provisions from Moscow.'

The Viceroy, seeing there's not a ghost of a chance of getting the bulk of his artillery across – some 70 guns and their trains – orders it all to be abandoned. Officers, too, realise the last moment's come for their carriages and wagons. Extracting their most precious contents – i.e. any foodstuffs – they hastily load them on to their horses – that is, if their men give them time to do so:

'The ground was littered with portmanteaux, war chests and papers. A quantity of objects hidden away in Moscow and which a justifiable sense of shame had kept hid, again began to see the light of day.'

In the gloaming Staff-Captain Labaume's shocked to see how the Italians have begun pillaging their officers' carriages and wagons – but only 'surreptitiously' Griois says, 'under cover of dark' – 'hardly giving its owner time to select what he wants from it'. Labaume, like Griois, like everyone who hears it, is appalled by

'the shouts of those crossing the Wop and the consternation of those about to do so, whom we at each moment see plunging with their mounts down the steep and slippery bank. A *vivandière* had five small children and all the fruits of her industry. Reaching the Wop, she looks with stupor at this river which is forcing her to leave her whole fortune on its banks and her family's sole means of subsistence. A long while she runs to and fro looking for a new way across. Finding none, she comes back, much depressed, and says to her husband: "*Mon ami*, we'll have to leave it all behind. Don't try to save anything but our children."'

Which they do:

'The women's desolation, their crying children and even the soldiers' despair turned this passage into a heart- rending scene, the very memory of which strikes terror into all who witnessed it.'[9]

The Viceroy himself sits his horse until nightfall, superintending the crossing. Only then does he cross over. That freezing night Griois is horrified to see

'nothing but people, desperate at having lost everything, frozen to the bone by the ice which covered their soaked clothing, having neither shelter to repose their head, nor the tiniest spark to warm themselves with. Shivering with cold, the soldiers, who'd all forded the river with water up to their shoulders, went off in all directions to find some food they could carry off or a house to pull down [for firewood].'

Himself, all things considered, he's not too badly off. His artillery staff, 'after walking a long while across the fields, were so fortunate as to find an isolated cottage, where we settled in. Part of it we demolished for a fire which dried our clothes.'

Two or three bottles of wine that have survived from an abandoned carriage, together with a few fistfuls of flour and 'some sauerkraut we were so lucky as to find in the cottage' make up their dinner and 'in the end we fell asleep. Yesterday, certainly, we'd been badly off for victuals. But now it was a lot worse.'

At dawn on 10 November Eugène sends Labaume back to Broussier's 14th Division, left to cover the crossing, to see what's going on the far bank and save whatever can be saved:

'For more than three miles all one saw was ammunition wagons and guns. The most elegant calèches from Moscow were piled up on the road and along the river bank. Objects taken from their carriages but too heavy to carry off had been scattered far and wide over the countryside, where they stood out only the more boldly for being scattered on the snow. There one saw costly candelabras, antique bronze statues, original paintings, the richest and the most highly esteemed porcelain. A porringer caught my eye. It was of the most exquisite workmanship, painted with the sublime composition of a Marcus Sextus. I took it, and out of this cup drank the muddy icy waters of the Wop. Having used it, I indifferently threw it away near the spot where I'd picked it up.'

Captain François, whose 30th Line forms the rearguard, sees 'the Cossacks laughing like madmen at all this confusion'. For Broussier it's no laughing matter. He's 'obliged to spike 60 guns, which were left behind, together with a mass of artillery vehicles'. 'Except for the four guns which had got across,' von Muraldt sees,

'not merely was the whole of IV Corps artillery lost, but all the vehicles of every kind we'd been dragging with us, as well as a lot of prisoners. All became the Cossacks' prey.'

Some of Broussier's gunners, says Ségur,[10] echoing Griois' account,

'laid a train of powder up to beneath the ammunition wagons that had come to a halt at a distance behind our baggage. Waiting until the greediest Cossacks came running up, as soon as they saw them in numbers, all maddened with pillaging, they flung a flame from a campfire on to this gunpowder. The fire ran, and in an instant reached its goal. The wagons are blown up, the shells explode, and those Cossacks who aren't annihilated scatter in terror!'

How many guns does Broussier really save? Some sources say twelve, others fourteen; but none say how he got them across the Wop. 'Together with those the prince still possessed, these sufficed to keep the Cossacks at bay.' Like everyone else Labaume is full of contempt for the 'cowardice' of the Cossacks, who

'never attacked able-bodied troops. Though surrounded with loot, they still stripped their prisoners, leaving them naked on patches of snow.'

And Broussier can no longer prevent them from flinging themselves on the many sick, feeble and wounded who've got to be left behind.

IV Corps' condition as it resumes its march is now utterly deplorable,
'the men without shoes, almost without clothes, exhausted and famished, sitting on their packs, sleeping on their knees and only rousing themselves out of this stupor to grill slices of horsemeat or melt bits of ice.'
But Eugène himself, 'the most perfect model of military behaviour', never loses his head. The 14th Division brings up the rear and the Royal Guard is vanguard. With them are only 'some armed platoons, the feeble remains of 13th Division and of the Bavarian chevaulegers and a mob of employees and *vivandières*, to whom yesterday had added a terrifying mass of soldiery marching in hurrying waves, without weapons or order.'
That day (10 November) the village or 'small town' of Dukhovchino comes into sight, the way to it barred by a broken bridge and more Cossacks besides those who're at IV Corps' heels,
'walking their sledge guns from position to position. So we were attacked from ahead and behind. Any hesitation would have been fatal. But the Prince Viceroy made haste to form up the Italian Guard in square and press forward,'
together with what Cesare calls 'the Bavarian dragoons and lancers'. 'The mounted officers,' Griois goes on,
'some orderlies on horseback, even the servants, formed a squadron, commanded by General Guyon, and supported the Guard's movement. This squadron's composition was as ridiculous as could be. One saw horses of every height, men in all sorts of uniforms, mostly without weapons. I'd joined it, as had several of my comrades. To close my file I had my Bavarian servant armed with a riding whip, and myself I only had a sabre with a broken blade. But seen from afar this troop gave the effect of the light cavalry we lacked; and after a few unsuccessful hurrahs and discharges of their guns the Cossacks vanished.'
To set an example to his by now thoroughly demoralised troops, Eugène even puts his own hand to the work of rebuilding the bridge. 'Towards 2 or 3 p.m. we entered Dukhovchino in peace.' Up to now the small town of wooden houses has
'only known the passage of Grouchy's cavalry corps and Pino's division during the advance; and hadn't suffered greatly. It was in much the same state as when I'd left it six months ago. As then, the inhabitants had fled at our approach. But their houses were at our disposition, and to us these furtive little timber cabins seemed to be palaces raised by good genies in the midst of these frozen deserts. Each of us got hold of whichever lodging seemed best to him. To cap our happiness we also found some potatoes which had escaped the Cossacks' greed. To us Dukhovchino seemed a land of Cockayne.'

Better still, though the corps is expecting to continue its march on Witebsk tomorrow morning, Eugène orders a day's rest. And Griois and his companions make up a raging fire in their stove:

'These stoves, seven or eight feet square, are built of timber faced with argil clay, and shouldn't be fuelled without care. But we who'd got there pierced through with cold, we had no thought to anything but stuffing it with everything that could burn – doors, shutters, three-legged stools, ladders ...'

The artillery staff sit or lie down around their cookpot, waiting for it to boil. 'The conversation wasn't in the least degree coloured by our sad situation – so quickly do a few moments of well-being make one forget past miseries! A military man's adventurous life makes him so trust to luck and bother so little about the future!'

But there's another reason for Eugène's halt. What's the state of affairs at Witebsk? He has sent off a Polish spy to find out.

CHAPTER 7

HOW WITEBSK WAS LOST

Pouget hops about on one leg – an impatient Jomini – pretty but exalted Polish châtelaines – 'what a garrison!' – Witebsk's indefensibility – countermanded orders – flagrant disobedience in the face of the enemy – Pouget fights a single-handed battle – Eugène's night march for Smolensk – 'Each night she belonged to anyone who'd feed her'

A former colonel of light infantry, the 45-year-old Baron *François-René Pouget*, newly promoted general of brigade, has only one complete foot. In 1809 he'd lost most of the other at the Isle of Lobau but – like his colleague Teste and 'though M. Larrey's opinion in surgical matters should be regarded as final' – had refused to have it amputated. In August, at the First Battle of Polotsk, he'd been wounded again, this time in the leg. After which he'd followed the – also wounded – Oudinot's example; handed over his command and gone back to Vilna. Although he adores only two objects in this world – the Emperor Napoleon and the 26th Light, whose colonel he'd been since 1805 – he'd written to Berthier at Moscow for permission to go to take the waters in France

'this having been prescribed for me, on pain of always having one leg bent behind me without being able to straighten it'.

At the same time he'd confided to Oudinot he was afraid of missing out on any further rewards or promotion:

'I knew any officer, no matter what his rank, who left the army's cadres, even on account of his wounds, was totally forgotten.'[1]

The good-natured Oudinot had comforted him, saying he'd already written him down for a 20,000-franc grant. While waiting for Berthier's reply Pouget had presented himself to the province's governor, the Dutch General *Dirk van Hogendorp*, and also made the acquaintance of his sparring partner, the Swiss General *Henri de Jomini*, governor of Vilna town.[2] Jomini, 'young, full of talents and ardour' and one day to become the age's most eminent military theorist, had 'seemed greatly preoccupied' at being left so far to the rear while great events were going forward. But then Napoleon's peremptory order had come that he should second Charpentier[3] as governor of Smolensk city, pending Marshal Victor's arrival in the theatre of war.

Temporarily out of cash but impatient to be off, Jomini hadn't known where to get hold of a wagon for his and his ADC's effects. Pouget, hopping about Vilna on one leg, prides himself on his habit of trusting fellow-officers; and against a mere verbal promise of future payment 'without even a receipt' sells Jomini his own. So Jomini, certainly to Hogendorp's intense relief, had departed.

Berthier's reply to Pouget's application, on the other hand, had come as a shock. One foot or two, wound or no wound, he was instantly to take over from Charpentier the governorship of Witebsk. After some thought he'd 'decided to obey'. And though his ADCs are still having to half-lift him into and out of his carriage, he and they had woven their way from one Lithuanian château to the next, where the party had found all the Polish *châtelaines* – each prettier and more 'exalted' than the last – passionately devoted to the 'national' cause.

'September 27, dined and slept at Bogdanow, in the home of Madame the widow Omoliska, who had two big beautiful daughters. I think it was the most exalted family in all Poland. I can still see the mother getting up at table to drink to the Emperor's health and the re-establishment of the Kingdom of Poland, adding that she was prepared to shed her blood for her country. One of her girls told me: "Yes, *M. le Général,* if we have to make war to reach this goal my sister and I will take up arms in man's clothing."'

Why, they all ask, hasn't Napoleon restored the Kingdom of Poland? A question Pouget naturally can't answer.[4] Only at the deserted château near the Ostrovno battlefield[5] do he and his aides, instead of wrestling with political matters and fervent protestations, have to wrap themselves up in their mantles and sleep on straw. Reaching Witebsk on 30 September they'd found Charpentier[6] so eager to be off as to begrudge his successor even one more day to initiate him into his functions. Next day Pouget, almost fainting with pain from his wounded leg tendon, had mounted his horse to inspect the town and found it 'divided into two unequal parts by the Dvina, the less considerable of these, situated on the right bank, almost exclusively inhabited by Jews'. But here's a shock:

'Open on all sides like a village, this town, the most important in White Russia, hasn't even the resource of some gardens surrounded by walls or hedges which, at a pinch, could favour its defence.'

To guard it he'd need 6–7,000 cavalry and infantry. As for its garrison ... what a garrison!' All he has are

'some 900 isolated men, made up of all the marauders, stragglers and men who'd come out of hospitals, the refuse of all the armies, the most furtive, dirtiest and worst soldiers in the world. Clad in rags and shreds of clothing, without either officers or NCOs, most of them had straggled ever since crossing the Niemen and never seen the enemy.'

Absent as they are from their units, they're getting neither clothing nor pay, 'not a kopek for a shave, for their laundry, to set themselves to rights, nor even for a glass of brandy. Their hosts had to feed and wash for them.' Pouget doesn't know which is worse, the pain in his leg or this monumental pain in the neck:

'No one ever saw anything provide a worse service than these isolated men. Each time they mounted guard one had to create a commandant for it, a sergeant, a corporal, and take even *them* at face value. No tasks done properly. No reconnaissances carried out. Rounds at a standstill. The sentinels just sat around their fire with the *chef de poste.* Their weapons were in a bad state, and as for what might happen in the vicinity they couldn't care less. Such were the troops charged with the defence of an administrative capital, one of the most important points in our line.'

All of which confirms Major Everts' experience from the Minsk area: 'A great fault of this campaign was to leave too few troops in the rear and on the flanks, the more so as we knew the Russians there were still in force.'[7] Fortunately Pouget also had 300 men 'from various detachments, made up of Hessians[8] and other men of the Young Guard, sixteen military policemen commanded by an officer, two 4-pounders, a section of gunners and one of pontoneers'. But indifference to the Russian army's propinquity is massive:

'We were only five leagues [fifteen miles] from the Russian advanced posts at the little town of Gorodok, who often pushed parties to within sight of Witebsk, where we were on the *qui vive* day and night.'

And there's nothing Pouget can do about all this – except to profit from an order received by Charpentier, and evacuate 400 men towards Moscow, keeping only the élite. 'My God! what an élite! I'd have needed one.'

Ten days had passed. He does his best to ingratiate himself with the locals. 'I raised no contributions in my own personal interest.' All he asks the magistrates for is some furniture for the timber residence on the main square that Napoleon in August had found utterly bare of any:

'In the name of the town they offered me a basket of French wines containing 20 bottles and ten of liqueurs, which I'd thought I shouldn't refuse.'

None of these amiable measures, however, bring him much help. The administrative commission 'richly composed of princes and counts' set up by Napoleon during his 8-day stay has evaporated. The man whose job it is to get in provisions from the province is Pouget's 29-year-old Intendant *Amédée de Pastoret*.[9] 'Of all the intendants I know,' Pastoret will write on 28 October to his friends at Vilna,

'I am the unhappiest. The Emperor of the French has given me twelve districts to govern, but the Emperor of Russia has thought fit to administer eight of them himself or through his generals, and, what's worse, isn't leaving me in peace in the others. M. de Wittgenstein, whom you certainly know of, has outposts six leagues away from me. Quite near me, it's true, I've two Marshals of France and three army corps. But judge for yourself how much they must consume of all sorts of things. My brave subjects haven't the least desire to fight, nor are they much inclined to give away their money. So I can expect little help. From another aspect, the administrative commission the Emperor made me president of has vanished away like a vain cloud that passeth and cometh not back. Imagine a poor young man',

the letter goes on (only to be intercepted by Cossacks),

'all alone in a country virtually unknown to him. Put enemies ahead of him and nothing behind his back. Suppose him to have neither money nor military forces; suppose him to be finding neither zeal nor goodwill around him – and you'll have a faint idea of our situation. *Ma foi!* I'm

not exaggerating, but I'm having a lot of trouble putting up with it.'
Even before Pouget's arrival most of the local officials, knowing what's in
the wind, have already quit. Prompt suppression of unruly peasants earns
him the gratitude of local Polish landlords and he fancies he can rely on
their sentiments. With the Witebsk Jews, on the other hand, 'always', as he
puts it sarcastically, 'on the side of the stronger' (somewhat naturally, they
having no political power to protect themselves in any other way) he has a
lot of trouble. Notified by Berthier in October of the Moscow army's
retreat, he's ordered to construct '36 ovens and provision the town with
corn, barley, oats, hay and straw' – something he does

'with all speed. Soon the requisitions filled the magazines, and the ovens
were built.'

And all the time he's keeping Saint-Cyr (at Polotsk) and Victor (at
Smolensk) informed of Russian movements around Gorodka, whence
two squadrons of Russian dragoons and Cossacks keep reconnoitring in
his direction. One day, with his sixteen gendarmes, he even has to fight
a little battle with them in the town's outskirts. 'The other day,' Pastoret
writes, 'some Cossacks came and dined for the third time in Witebsk's
suburbs.'

Then, on 19 October, had come a dispatch from Saint-Cyr, under heavy
pressure from a reinforced Wittgenstein. He's obliged, the newly fledged
Marshal writes, to evacuate Polotsk. And a messenger instantly goes off
from Witebsk to Smolensk to notify Victor of Saint-Cyr's urgent need for
support from IX Corps:

'So as not to attract attention my Polish messenger travelled on foot. He
was so energetic he covered the 30 leagues [90 miles] separating me
from Smolensk in 30 hours. But got there too late, even so. II Corps had
already carried out its withdrawal, during which – as General *Lorencez*[10]
put it when he informed me of this beautiful retreat – the French hadn't
lost "a single nail from any of its vehicles". Nevertheless it exposed my
left flank.'

However, here comes a reinforcement in the shape of Daendels' division
of Victor's IX corps. For a while Daendels takes over responsibility for
defending Witebsk and advises Pouget to send 400 of his ill-organised men
to Surash and Veleiz to gather in more supplies. By and by Daendels leaves
again, for Sienno. All he has to bequeath Pouget as garrison is his weakest
battalion,

'conscripts who'd never fired a shot or seen an enemy, soldiers from
Berg who, even so, lacked their grenadier battalion, which was guarding
Victor's carriages!'

On 4 November an order comes from Victor. Obviously there's been a
scare. Pouget's to evacuate Witebsk and march his garrison to Smolensk:

'I began by evacuating the hospitals and sending off the administrations,
giving them a 200-man escort, with orders to wait for me at Falkowitz, 20
versts [12½ miles] from Smolensk, and if I myself didn't get there next
day, to keep going.'

But they've only been gone four hours when a new order countermands. Now, Victor writes, he's *not* to evacuate the town, 'or, if I'd already done so, to get back into it, even by force, because it seemed the enemy had no designs on Witebsk.' Congratulating himself on already having shed his lame ducks, Pouget orders

'the pontoneers to prepare combustible materials to burn the bridge. I took out of the gymnasium 24,000 pikes deposited there by the Russians, had them burnt and their iron points thrown into the Dvina's deepest depths. And waited to see what would happen.'

First and foremost he's anxious about the Ostrovno road, leading to Beschenkowiczi.[11] And here comes the Beschenkowiczi commandant, an officer named Descharmes, bringing a second letter from Lorencez, telling him to evacuate his administration to Smolensk and cover their retreat. From its date Pouget can see it's been delayed several days. Since only one is needed to get to Witebsk from Beschenkowiczi, Pouget wants to know the reason why. Oh, replies a nonchalant Descharmes, surely the matter isn't all that important? An irate Pouget sends him back with a flea in his ear, four chasseurs and a corporal, to Ostrovno, twelve miles down the Beschenkowiczi road, to keep an eye on the enemy's movements. To his amazement Descharmes refuses. Not until 'I threatened to send him to the Marshal, bound hand and foot, to have him brought before a court-martial and punished for disobedience in the face of the enemy' does a disgruntled Descharmes get going.

Next day, to Pouget's amazement and even greater fury, here's Descharmes back again, having simply ignored his mission:

'How can this man have merited the confidence of the army's Major-General and been put to command at Beschenkowiczi? He was a traitor who was losing everything for me and for everything military and patriotic at Witebsk.'

Pouget instantly orders him back to Ostrovno. Next day two squadrons of light cavalry – Pouget, still painfully moving about on his unhealed leg, has every need of them – turn up from Smolensk. But by now Victor's 'putting eighteen more leagues [50 miles] between himself and me. I saw I had nothing more to hope for.' And here in the evening comes a letter from General Castex, commanding the light cavalry of Victor's rearguard[12] – with news which Pouget communicates to, among others, Intendant Pastoret. His outposts, Castex writes, are currently between Ostrovno and Sienno. If he, Pouget, doesn't hear anything more from him by morning it'll mean he has retreated.

The night, though it lasts until 7 a.m., passes quietly – 'except for a timber house catching fire, whether by malevolence or to serve as a signal to the Russians, or in hopes that I'd send some troops to put it out', Pouget can't judge. But then, at dawn, just as he's telling Rollin, his reliable gendarme officer, he has nothing to fear from the Ostrovno road,

'the barrier at the bridgehead opened to let through the fifteen men who were guarding it, and whose captain was sending them to occupy the Riga Gate during the day. Hardly had they been replaced by two sentries than the latter found themselves surrounded by Russian infantry. They retreated quickly to inform me. One of their horses fell and its rider was taken prisoner. The other escaped and warned the big post at the bridgehead, who had the barrier closed. The enemy, who'd known all about our movements, were waiting for the fifteen men who'd been sent to the Riga Gate, turned them and, without a cartridge fired by either side, made them lay down their arms. At the bridgehead were 50 men. Their captain had orders to have all the bridge's timbers that formed its floor on the right bank thrown into the river, and to stand firm, retiring to their left. I had them replaced by the Berg voltigeurs.'

Now a lot of firing breaks out among the houses, and Pouget withdraws to the town castle. It's there, in its courtyard, he has his two 4-pounders:

'They fired a few shots at the columns arriving by the Gorodok road. But now the enemy skirmishers were so close that they kept hitting the gunners at their pieces. The left bank, where my guns were in position, was a steep gradient 20 feet above the right bank.'

So his two cannon are anyway useless. 'Their projectiles couldn't make any hits there except by passing over the roofs of the houses on the left bank and firing at maximum range. So I had to order a retreat.' Pouget sends to inform Rollin, in command of his sixteen gendarmes, and Colonel Chavardès on the Surash road, that he's fixing a point on the Smolensk road outside the town where everyone's to rally:

'I was still greatly astonished and most worried not to hear anything from M. Descharmes at Ostrovno. Because that was where the real danger was coming from. So far I'd only been attacked from the front. I got out of the town in good order, didn't leave a man behind.'

Not thinking that there was anything definitive about the situation and that 'the *Grande Armée*, as it fell back on Witebsk, might still profit from them, I'd forbidden any of them to set fire to any of the magazines' which Amédée de Pastoret's emissaries had so diligently wrested from the peasantry, doubtless condemning them to starve during the winter. Now they'll be consumed by Wittgenstein's troops.

A mile and a half outside the town Pouget orders a halt, assembles all his men, and waits for his rearguard. But as he does so sees Russian units, appearing along the Surash and Ostrovno roads, who're engaging his men. His two cannon are playing on the Russian cavalry when their commander comes and begs him to cease fire – for lack of matches. 'It wasn't the moment to reproach him for having deceived me.' And besides

'the men of the Train were such bad horsemen they couldn't even handle their guns without dismounting. I'd never seen the like of it. They needed ten times more time than anyone else to execute the least movement.'

Chavardès and a dozen men are captured, but the rest of his rearguard rejoins:

'I got going by platoons in double column, my artillery in the middle. For my rearguard I'd a few brave fellows of the Imperial Guard, who'd arrived three days ago. I'd done my four last campaigns as a colonel of light infantry, and was so used to seeing, being charged by and repulsing enemy cavalry, that I thought I could succeed again. More than once I've seen and found by experience that it's good troops which make their generals famous,'

observes Pouget, thus contradicting – very naturally in the circumstances – his adored Emperor's famous dictum that 'there's no such thing as bad troops, only bad officers'. But though he detaches skirmishers to keep off the Russian cavalry that's now appearing on all hands,

'these wretched soldiers from Berg knew no better what they were doing than their officers did. Instead of dispersing and spreading out, they were marching *en masse*, at one moment too close to my column, at the next too far from it. I had to send one of my ADCs to direct and command them.'

Knowing full well that there must also be Russian infantry and artillery in the offing, he tries to hasten his pace. But can't, because

'half the men in my column were convalescents who could only walk with difficulty, but whom I didn't want to abandon. At each instant I was seeing them being sabred or captured by the enemy. Nevertheless I made 20 versts [12½ miles] or four leagues, always firing and always closely pressed and harassed. The Russians saw what kind of troops it was they had to do with, and became steadily bolder. I was everywhere, at the head, at the tail, encouraging and calming these conscripts, telling them I'd get them to Smolensk providing they obeyed me and kept calm.'

But that's just what they can't do. Finally, charged on all sides at once, he has to form square. But its badly aimed volleys don't add up to 50 shots and despite his orders won't even present its bayonets to the enemy,

'so it was easily overwhelmed. Most of it threw itself into a forest clearing. If it had gone on firing from there it could still have done the cavalry a lot of harm and dispersed it. But it took good care not to. Furious at such conduct, I resolved to defend myself personally. I passed my sword between my thigh and my saddle so as to draw my pistols and break out through the cavalry. First I killed a dragoon. A second presenting himself with raised sword, I fired off my second shot. I saw him put his hand on his chest, like a man who's been severely wounded. I flung my excellent horse into the mêlée to break through sword in hand, but in the same instant saw I was surrounded by more than 30 dragoons, and felt a sabre blow on my left shoulder. I saw all their swords pointed at me. One of these men grabbed me by my left wrist and wrenched my arm up so sharply it put my shoulder out of joint. Others dragged at me by one of my cloak's multiple collars and tore it.'

Realising that it's all up with him – the Russian troopers are infuriated by their two comrades' deaths – he does what many a senior officer would do in such a crisis:

'I let them know who I was by opening my cloak and showing them my gold lace. I was wearing a fatigue cap garnished with martin, not quite so tall as those worn by our chasseur officers. It could be the enemy had taken me for a mere subaltern. The sight of my uniform impressed them. I asked in German to see the troop's commander.'

He sees several, among them a German-speaking Livonian RSM, who takes him under his protection: 'The dragoon who'd put my shoulder out of joint ripped off a gold star of the Legion of Honour of the smaller format' and the sergeant-major makes him give his captor his

'purse, two watches in gold watchcases and their chain, my pocket handkerchief and my portfolio; but not finding anything valuable in it, gave it back.'

Although his 'protector' keeps searching him anew for more possessions and relieves him of his two gold rings, 'one my wedding ring, the other given me by a Witebsk lady whose château and village I'd saved' they don't treat him too badly as they set off back to Witebsk, holding his horse's bridle. But as they pass through the town

'my escort shouted hurrahs that were only repeated by some Jews. The old Poles, Russian subjects since the First Partition [of Poland in 1772] didn't respond.'

All this has happened on 7 November, some twelve miles from Falkowitz. Reaching Witebsk, Pouget is much better treated than his miserable garrison:

'The Russian general Tscharba, who'd been in Witebsk while we French had been there, came and embraced me and with permission of the general in command offered to take me to his house.'

Which he does. And gets back his two watches and his Cross for him. Whereon Pouget, seeing the miserable look on the Livonian's face, presents him with one of the watches, keeping 'the one my wife had given me before going off on the first Austrian campaign'. Altogether Pouget ascribes his good reception at Witebsk – by everyone except its Jews – and 'the sympathy of its inhabitants to the memory of the gentleness with which I'd treated them during my governorship'.

Five days go by. Then, just as he's to leave by sledge to be taken to Wittgenstein's headquarters, a local lady bestirs herself to buy back his Cross 'for 50 roubles, which was more than it was worth'; and the Russian commandant grants his request that his departure shall be 'at night, so as not to be a spectacle a second time for the Witebsk populace, which is the same in Russia as it is in all countries'.[13]

Obviously there's no sense in IV Corps' struggling on to Witebsk and trying to save its stores, which have fallen to Wittgenstein. When Eugène's Polish spy gets back to Dukhovchino and tells him all this, he at once sends off an officer to Smolensk 'to inform Napoleon of the disasters at the Wop' and notify him that IV Corps, less its artillery and baggage train, is rejoining the main army. That evening his artillery staff are

'sitting or lying around our mess tin, watching our pot boil, and cooking some bits of meat we (most exceptionally) had been able to get hold of, and whose unaccustomed odour flattered our sense of smell,'
when Griois hears shouts and shots:
'It's those devils of Cossacks who, repulsed at midday, are reappearing at 3 p.m., hoping for better luck as it gets dark! They're attacking our posts at the end of the town, close to our house.'
They all rush out. As ever, a few musket and cannon shots suffice to drive off 'the barbarians'. But when, three-quarters of an hour later, Griois and his comrades get back to their snug fireside it's to find the house 'thick with smoke from the stove which, too vigorously heated, had caught fire'. Officers and servants try to 'master the flames, which finally split the stove apart. In no time the wooden walls, the thatch and wattle roof, had all caught fire.' Only in the nick of time are they able to free their horses from the outhouses. 'But what was irremediable was the loss of our good soup.' Similar fires are breaking out elsewhere; and when, that evening, the march is resumed – toward Smolensk – even those of Dukhovchino's houses that aren't on fire are 'set in flames before departing'. Captain François and his comrades of the 30th Line, though accustomed to such sights, can't help being astonished at
'the horrible but superb spectacle a snow-covered forest produces in the shadows when lit up by torrents of flames. All the trees, wrapped in a bark of ice, astounded our eyes and produced, as if in a prism, the most vivid colours and subtlest nuances. The silver birch branches, which are like weeping willows, bent down to the ground in the shape of garlands, and all round us the icicles, stricken by the light, offered a rain of diamonds, rays and sparklings.'
Now all that is left behind, and the night, by contrast, is pitch black, 'only illumined, as by the Aurora Borealis, by the light of other burning villages'. Only a few such villages, 'black spots against a white surface', lie too far from the road to be safely approached, and aren't molested.
That black night many a frozen and starving veteran feels he can go no further. A grenadier of the Royal Guard, collapsing by the roadside, hands in his Cross of the Iron Crown of Italy to his officer. 'Disdaining, like many others, to ask for any other help and stoically seeing death approach, he says to one of his comrades who wants to try and pick him up: "It's no use. All I desire of you is that you'll do me the pleasure of handing my Italian decoration to my captain. I won it fighting against them at Austerlitz and don't want it to fall into their hands."'
Already Cesare de Laugier, concerned as he'll always be for the honour of the Army of Italy and more especially for its Guardia d'Onore, has
'five of these decorations, belonging to as many vélites, in the leather bag I'm wearing round my neck, and General Théodore Lecchi has several more in his keeping that have come to him in the same way'.
But not everyone's being so heroic. Trudging on in the midst of his little column with one of his gunners holding his horse's bridle, Griois is horrified to see for the first time

'an act of barbarism which later would so often be repeated and in so many guises that I paid no more attention to it, but whose atrocity struck me during that night march. A Bavarian chevauleger, overcome by fatigue or weak from his wounds, fell almost senseless in the middle of the road. Not merely did his comrades, his friends, not try to help him up. One of them who'd been throwing a covetous glance at the poor fellow's boots, and despite his complaints and his *"Mein Gott!"*, uttered in a supplicating voice, halted to wrench them off him. I saw it and I shuddered. But all sensibility was already so emulsified [*sic*] among us that I didn't say a word, and 20 other officers, many Bavarians among them, contented themselves, like I did, with hurrying on so as not to hear the unfortunate man's groans.'

'Nothing's so sad or sinister,' Griois is thinking,

'as a night march during a retreat. Taciturn, discouraged, the men march painfully on. All one hears is their oaths and the monotonous sound of their footsteps in the snow.'

Staff-captain Labaume, who is feeling particularly sorry for

'the Frenchwomen who'd come with us from Moscow, mostly on foot in cloth slippers, dressed in wretched silk or cotton cambric dresses and who'd covered themselves in furs or soldiers' greatcoats taken from corpses',

is shocked to hear an unnamed general cruelly abuse a wretched Russian girl, Pavlowna by name, whom he'd callously seduced under promise of marriage. Although she's pregnant and loyal to him, he tells her to

'go back to Moscow, because he's married already anyway, and there perhaps find the husband her parents had destined for her. The girl fainted, and the general marched off into the night toward Smolensk.'

Labaume is especially touched by the plight of the

'young and touching Fanni. Pretty, sweet, amiable, witty, speaking several languages – in a word, possessing all qualities seductive to the most insensitive man – she was reduced to begging for the slightest service, and usually the bit of bread she obtained obliged her to requite it in the most servile way. She implored our help and we abused her. Each night she belonged to anyone who undertook to nourish her.'

As they approach Smolensk he sees her again,

'but no longer, alas, able to walk. The unfortunate girl was having herself dragged along behind a vehicle, and when her strength gave out she fell down into the snow, which no doubt became her winding sheet, without her having aroused anyone's compassion nor anyone throwing her so much as a pitying glance, so brutalised were our souls and so extinct our sensibility. Misery no longer had any witnesses. We were all its victims.'

CHAPTER 8

SMOLENSK AGAIN

A fire-blackened ruin – Napoleon: 'Stop shoving!' – 'Their eyes, sunk in their orbits, were melancholy and motionless' – 'If I dared to I'd have them all shot!' – the Old Guard's jumble sale – IV Corps arrives – Murat 'a friend nursing a friend' – 'now I've nothing, not even hope' – the Hessians wait in the cold

On the day of the Wop crossing, a day so cold no one had been able to sit a horse or ride in a carriage, IHQ had 'painfully circumvented the slopes at Valutina and in the distance caught sight of the high walls of Smolensk. Napoleon, Fain had noted in his diary, 'was walking, and so were all his lot'. Ahead of them the fire-blackened skeleton of Russia's third largest city lay covered in snow:

'The heights it stood on showed the domes of the venerable cathedral majestically over their summit. But this building stood almost single amidst heaps of ruins.'[1]

Outside the Dnieper Gate there's soon a huge, ever-growing crush. Paymaster Duverger, sent on ahead by I Corps' chief-of-staff to get hold of some horses and victuals and bring them back to Davout's headquarters, finds the Treasury and trophies convoy – 25 wagons, according to Vionnet – 'stretching right up to the gates'. Its officials are under orders 'to prevent any kind of vehicle getting in among our wagons. A magnificent berline, harnessed with four horses, advances swiftly.' Kergorre signs to the coachman to halt.

'He refuses and goes on. My comrades and I seize his horses' bridles and the carriage is already at the edge of the ditch when a woman appears at its window. She's young and beautiful. Her clean costly garments, the luxury surrounding her, indicate her as being the object of some mysterious protection, exempting her from the common misery. In the name of the Emperor, of the Major-General, she signs to us to let her pass. We refuse. She insists. Has to step down even so, and is reduced to walking. What was the lady's name, her status? I don't know.'

Certainly it isn't Louise Fusil, though a Guards colonel holds up her carriage, too:

'It was holding up his regiment. My servant did his best to convince him the carriage belonged to M. de Tintignier, nephew of the Master of the Horse. "D'you think that worries me?" he replied. "You'll go no further." The noise of this discussion woke me up and doubtless it was at this moment that the colonel caught sight of me; for he said: "Oh, I'm sorry, I didn't realise there was a lady inside." I looked at him and, seeing him covered in a blue satin fur, began to smile.'

This reminds the colonel of his odd appearance, for he bursts out laughing:

'"A colonel of grenadiers dressed in blue satin," he said, "is certainly comically got up. But *ma foi!* I was dying of cold and bought it off one of the men." We chatted for some while and he ended by inviting me surreptitiously to share some provisions still left to him. A fire was lit, spruces cut, and what he called the cabin of *Annette and Lubin*[2] was erected. Alas, its dreary verdure didn't do much to help the "shepherds" occupying it to get out of the cold, and the song of the nightingale was replaced by a crow's lugubrious croaking.'

But in the end Louise too has to abandon her carriage and, never expecting to see it again, at 3 p.m. she finally gets through the Dnieper Gate. Even Napoleon himself it seems has some difficulty in getting in. Dedem's struggling in the crush when 'a man in a grey overcoat' just in front tells him sharply to stop shoving – turns round – and he sees who it is!

'As soon as the Emperor had entered, the gates were shut and the army was forced to camp under the town walls.'

Passing through the 'entirely demolished' New Town, Dumonceau sees many new bivouacs and carriages and 'preceded by a mob of disbanded men, clamouring to be let in' reaches the hard- frozen river and its bridge, only to find the gate closed in his face. No one's to be allowed in, the military police are insisting, except the Old Guard. Its infantry are to preside over the distributions. No one's to get any who doesn't first rejoin his unit. Colbert's lancers cross the Dnieper over the ice and in a freezing mist that seems to promise a thaw, follow on downstream in the gloaming behind some dismounted Guard Dragoons:

'Scattered and covered in their big white mantles, they seemed like so many phantoms. Although hardly able to drag themselves along and visibly overwhelmed with weariness they none the less marched on with exemplary perseverance.'

After following the left bank for six miles, Dumonceau cantons in a fully intact village.

The Hessians too have been among the first units to arrive. Franz Roeder, who's been 'remembering the armies at the Berezina and on the Dvina – 80,000 combatants with newly arrived reserves – and still believing in good winter quarters in Poland', is instantly disillusioned:

'In the bitterest cold we stood about until 10 p.m. on a bit of ground in front of the bastion, as though no one knew what the Young Guard's first division was supposed to do next. At last word came that every man was to fend for himself. Everybody rushed off and I crowded my entire company into one small house.'

Pion des Loches, who'd 'left Moscow with 101 vehicles, and only had 24 left, but faithful to my orders' has kept 'all his guns'. But even the Young Guard artillery isn't let in and he has to bivouack outside the city walls.

All these units have of course had to cross the Valutina battlefield of 19 August. To Dumonceau's eyes it was only marked by snow-covered mounds. But the Fusiliers-Grenadiers have to bivouack there on the ground,

'still covered with dead and debris of all kinds, and out of which legs, arms and heads stuck up. Almost all were Russians, for we'd done what we could to give burial to our own.[3] But as it had been done in haste the subsequent rains had uncovered part of all this. We made up our fires with the debris of weapons, caissons, gun-carriages.'

The stream's water still being putrid with corpses, Bourgogne has to go back almost a mile to 'the very spot where on the morrow of the battle King Murat had aligned his tents' to get some that's drinkable; then, with a friend, 'as far as the ravine to visit the battlefield. As at Borodino, a legless French grenadier is rumoured to have survived inside a dead horse.'

Napoleon meanwhile is in a furious bad temper. The news of Malet's conspiracy is still festering. But something more immediately worse has happened. While obeying his order to march out along the Medyn road to meet the retreating army, one whole brigade of Baraguay d'Hilliers' scratch infantry division, 3,000 men newly arrived from France and commanded by General Augereau, brother of the Marshal, has just surrendered. Assailed by 5,000 Russian cavalry and the villagers of Yazvino, Liakhovo and Dolghomostoë, Baraguay himself – he who'd entertained Roeder with his reminiscences en route for Viazma – had been nine miles to the rear with his guns and convoys. And Augereau, unable to hold out until Baraguay could come to his assistance, had simply capitulated. Whereupon Baraguay, old and sick, had promptly retreated head over heels to Smolensk. Everyone agrees that his behaviour had been utterly incompetent. And a furious Napoleon places him under arrest and sends him back to France under escort.[4] He also, most unjustly, makes him scapegoat for an insufficiency of supplies.

Even worse news is the fall of Witebsk. Informed of it by Pastoret who, unlike the captured Pouget, has managed to reach Smolensk, Berthier exclaims 'three or four times: "not possible!"' And sends him to Napoleon, whom he finds alone with Murat. Pastoret assures Napoleon that there'd been supplies enough at Witebsk to feed the entire army for ten days or maintain a whole army corps for the rest of the winter. Abandoned by his Polish aides, he'd had no little difficulty in gathering them in.

'"What! You were all alone?"

"All alone. And I beg Your Majesty to excuse me if I for this reason haven't carried out your intentions."'

At the time of Witebsk's hasty evacuation, he tells Napoleon, Saint-Cyr had at most 30,000 men. Napoleon retorts that he's got at least 50,000 and Wittgenstein only 20,000. But Pastoret replies 'firmly' that 'from spies and frequent reports' he knows that Wittgenstein has 50,000. He also feels obliged to tell His Majesty of what seems to him to have been Victor's sloth and failure either to support Oudinot or save Witebsk. Whereupon Napoleon bursts out:

'"No, that Victor fellow isn't in a state to command even a division, a regiment!"' Approaching the map on the table, he bursts out in a tirade against his marshals:

'"See how they sacrifice the safety of my armies to themselves! All of them, you see? Davout's half-mad and no further use. This Victor comes to Smolensk to destroy to no purpose the stores prepared here. Augereau [in

Germany] hasn't wanted to move, and thinks he's doing me a favour by obeying me. Yet obey me they shall, even so! They know who I am and I know what they are. No, no, there isn't one of them one can entrust with anything. Always, always I have to do everything! Very well, I *shall* do everything. But let them execute it, let them obey! They'd better take care, I'll know very well how to dispense with them!'"

To the Polish General Krasinski he says:

'"If I dared to, I'd have them all shot." He was particularly furious with Davout.'

'Fortune had so long showered her favours on him,' Caulaincourt reflects, 'he couldn't believe she'd deserted him.'

But where are all the 'immense supplies' that should be here at Smolensk? The officer responsible tells him – what *Honoré de Beulay* had seen in September how

'the bands of stragglers left behind by the advancing army had enveloped Smolensk in terror and destruction and intercepted many of the convoys en route. Finally, the heads of long food convoys, assembled in Germany, had appeared – all those that had managed to cross the sands of Lithuania – but as yet had only brought 200 quintals of flour and rice.'

And how on arrival several hundred German and Italian cattle, dying of hunger and fatigue and 'loth either to march or to eat' had had to be slaughtered:

'Their eyes, sunk in their orbits, were melancholy and motionless. They'd let themselves be killed without trying to avoid the blow. At Krasnoië a park of 800 cattle had been carried off by the Russians.'[5]

Then Victor had had to supply IX Corps before leaving for Polotsk to support Oudinot.

None of these excuses are accepted. And in fact Fain notices 'a big discrepancy between what had been ordered and what had been done'. Larrey, too, is furious with the dishonest war commissaries who've intercepted reports from his officers on the peculation of medical supplies. And when *Henri Jomini*, the city's newly arrived governor under Charpentier, governor of Smolensk province, excuses Commissary Siaufat on grounds that armed peasants have made foraging impossible, Napoleon orders Siaufat to be shot. Which, according to Jomini, he is (though no records confirm it).

But worst of all is the strategic situation. Victor's failure to hold Witebsk, Napoleon declares, has wrecked his plan of putting the army into winter quarters. The simple fact is the Moscow army is in no condition to maintain itself at Smolensk or anywhere else. The retreat must go on ...

"Wittgenstein has everything to gain by remaining where he is," Napoleon tells Fain afterwards in his office, "and the Duke of Bellune everything to lose." Just as he's dictating the second of two notes to Victor, one of his ADCs, a Colonel Château, is announced. What His Majesty has just ordered, he explains diffidently, is precisely what his chief's trying to do. Without even being given time to rest up Château is sent back to tell Victor the army will shortly be marching for Orsha, i.e., be keeping to the Dnieper's south bank. Two hours later, in a third dispatch, Napoleon assures Victor it's mostly only militiamen he has to deal with behind the Dwina: 'You haven't a moment to lose!'

Fain, certainly familiar with Napoleon's anxieties, notes in his journal: 'We're even fearing for our main road to Vilna!' And Generals Eblé and Chasseloup of the Engineers are sent on ahead with a strong detachment to check up on road conditions and the state of the bridges between Smolensk and Orsha and report back to Berthier on what supplies are available at depots en route. Likewise on alternative roads. Jomini can keep them company.

That first night, Daru tells Dedem, 'the Emperor had no other lights but some wretched candles stuck in a bottle'. And another officer, E. *Lemoine-Montigny*, only has to

'push the door ajar to contemplate this man who'd made so many kings tremble, asleep, almost alone, hardly even guarded. The room he was resting in was at many points exposed to the open air. Lauriston, on duty that day, was stretched out on a *chaise longue*. It's not there you meet with a double row of courtiers.'

After pillaging the Viazma stores, the Old Guard isn't sparing the far larger ones at Smolensk. It's looting them. Several of the magazines around the main square, Major *von Lossberg* sees to his own satisfaction, 'contain enough flour and fodder for a fortnight'. Planat de la Faye, who's been starving on a handful of rice for breakfast and a biscuit for the rest of the day, sees

'immense resources in provisions of every kind; and if anyone could have put any order into the distributions the men would easily have been able to provision themselves for 15 or 20 days'.

But now, after turning up at 9 a.m. on 10 November and again ousting the Hessians from their lodgings, the Old Guard is turning everything upside down:

'Already the disorganisation, despite the Emperor's presence, was so great that the magazines were pillaged. The corps coming on behind us wouldn't be able to find anything.'

'With the help of our servants and four gunners' one of Planat's fellow-officers manages 'to get hold of a little most intelligently selected supply, made up mainly of rice, biscuits, salt and fat, plus a little barrel of brandy'. The artillery staff place them, together with their cookpot and kitchen utensils, on a very light little Muscovite *teleg* (two-wheeled cart) ready to resume the long icy march.

Down at the Dnieper Gate, meanwhile, only one fatigue party from each line or Young Guard regiment is being allowed in at a time to get its share.

Colonel de Marguerye details off Major Everts and 'a sous-adjutant of the 33rd Line, all the quartermaster-corporals and such rankers as were needed' to go and get what they can. They're

'to calm the monstrous famine, which had gone beyond the uttermost limits. The distribution was being made during the night and since we could foresee the many difficulties and ill-will it would be carried out with, a senior officer from each regiment was charged with presiding over it. When I got to the town gate there were already men from some other units there, and every instant their number was growing. Not merely was each party doing its best to get in first; all this led to a general mêlée which we all, senior officers and adjutants, sabre in hand, had to contain.'

Finally the 33rd's emissaries come across a church where a commissary and his employees are distributing sacks of flour

'in the midst of such an effervescence that not being able to stand his ground he had another replace him. They had a numerous guard to protect them, yet it was only with great difficulty the commissaries were to some extent able to keep the upper hand.'

Everts' group of Dutchmen get eight sacks of flour and two small barrels of vodka:

'As we came out of the church, other starving men tried to snatch them from us. The adjutant and the sergeants-major stood up to them with drawn sabres, all of us hitting out to right and left as I cleared a way for us. You'll easily conceive,'

Everts ends, all out of breath and 'harassed and exhausted by this troublesome stint', how when they get back to the 33rd's bivouac outside the walls, 'that this feeble distribution could only bring slight relief'. No one, for lack of the famous handmills, even has means of turning the flour into an edible paste; and the Cossacks, who've left the column in peace for several days, are already in presence again and firing at them from several sides

'with our own artillery, which they'd picked up on the roads, and were promptly using to dispute our stay in Smolensk and the positions around it'.[6]

The 33rd are sent to a hilltop on the city's western side where, despite a plethora of firewood, some 60 of them succumb during the night. 'At daybreak they looked to our eyes like stone statues.' So Everts is sent to General Friederichs to deplore their exposed position. He finds that general, so merciless to Russian peasants, with his headquarters staff in a pig-sty which 'had escaped the fire and was fortunately still standing'. Friederichs takes pity on his Dutchmen, lets them move down to the foot of the hill, leaving only pickets at its summit.

Not even all Guard units are being allowed in. Like Colbert's lancers yesterday, Major *J. F. Boulart*'s artillery, attached to the Chasseur brigade, has to pass under the great walls along the river bank between the Old Town and the New. After which, 'turning left, with much effort we climbed the heights and passed underneath the citadel – where Gudin's corpse was resting in one of the ramparts'.[7]

There Boulart's guns and wagons go and place themselves

'on a kind of esplanade near the Krasnoïe gate, whose trees were almost as useful in providing shelter from the snow as they'd been in summer against the sun. We received a ration of bread, biscuit and meat.'

Out in their populated village[8] Colbert's men, well away from the crowd, are freely entertained to 'several delights we'd lost the habit of', and in the cellar of a barn Dumonceau and two of his lieutenants light a nice fire of the kind which 'according to the custom of the country with their smoke help dry or finish ripening the harvest hung up under the roof'. Thereto abundant 'bread, flour, grain, salt and brandy' reach them from the Smolensk stores. Dismounted troopers find remounts and his regiment is even joined by 100 fresh lancers, who'd just arrived from France with Baraguay d'Hilliers' division. But back in the ruined city even the 1st Foot Chasseurs get 'almost nothing'. And on the field of Valutina Lejeune spends the night

'on the banks of the Dnieper beside the bridge where General Gudin had died. Soon our campfires were surrounded by the stragglers, turning up without their weapons, covered in fur-lined silks and women's clothes, ampler than men's and of every colour. Many were wearing what they'd stripped from their comrades en route. Stunned by hunger and cold, they came to ask for a little place at the fires of those who'd still enough strength to light one.'

But the latter begrudge them even 'the tiniest bit of these rays of reviving warmth' and the newcomers, standing perforce behind them, soon

'sag under the weight of fatigue, fall to their knees. Then we see them sit down, and then, involuntarily, lie down. This last movement is the harbinger of death. Their colourless eyes open to the sky. Their lips contract in a happy laugh – one might have thought some divine consolation was softening their agony, indicated by an epileptoid spittle. None of these stragglers hesitated to sit down on the chest of some man lying on the ice until the latter breathed his last.'

None will ever enter Smolensk:

'In the same instant as he stretched out his limbs with an appearance of being in heavenly bliss, the man who was still standing made himself a seat out of the dead man's panting chest and remained like that, reposing his whole weight on him in front of the fire, up to the moment when he himself, unable to get up again, soon ceased to live. The snow only partially covered the terrors of this spectacle!'

Kergorre's convoy has been two whole days in the rear but has halted

'by a big artillery park, where we found Colonel Neigre, our director-general, who was having his horses rough-shod for ice and had the goodness to tell his farrier to do the same for ours.'

Reaching the city gate on 11 November,

'the Dnieper bridge kept being repeatedly blocked by the jam and the gates closed, we had to turn to the right with the rest of the army. Bivouacking at the foot of the wall we were given biscuits, rice, flour and even a sack of oats for our horses.'

When at last the Young and Middle Guard are allowed in, Sergeant Bourgogne wanders about all night in search of food. Loses his footing as he follows a Badener who's clutching a brandy flask, flies down an icy slope and tumbles into a cellar occupied by

'one of those gangs which, multiplying as they went, had been prowling about ever since the great cold had begun'.[9]

In an urgent whisper a poor woman the gang's been forcing to keep them company ever since Viazma tells him how they particularly hate men of the Imperial Guard. So he leaves in a hurry, wanders about among the walls of ruined houses and is within an inch of falling 50 feet from the ramparts into eternity. Everywhere he stumbles over 'corpses which, even two and a half months after the disaster, we saw still lying all over the place in the streets and a great number of others heaped up to a height of one metre at the foot of the town walls' – though Berthier, on 16 August, had asked Napoleon to let him use Russian prisoners to get them all buried he hadn't succeeded in his task. Around a church they're lying particularly thickly. And what's that – if not organ music? Wherever Bourgogne turns it haunts him so that he assumes he must be hallucinating. But upon entering this church he's actually been circling around all the time he finds it's filled with

'the men of my company. Some of them were singing, and others, several of the regiment's musicians, were playing on the organ. They were all dreadfully drunk!'

Next morning Bourgogne remembers his promise to go back to the cellar to rescue his benefactress. 'But the birds had flown.'

In the main square the Old Guard, whose pillage has been less inspired by necessity 'than of greed and arrogance', is holding – as at Moscow – a gigantic jumble sale, 'a veritable bazaar of everything one desires in the way of luxury and demanded by necessity, an incredible quantity of things.' Major Lossberg, buying 'half a pound of butter for a five-franc piece' from one of the Smolensk Jews who're 'pushing in most impudently and buying as well as selling', wonders whether they'll be able to keep their profits:

'Hundreds of soldiers, most of them from the French Guard, were dealing in plunder they'd got hold of during the campaign, particularly in Moscow. It consisted mostly of clothing, women's shawls and scarves of all kinds, as well as articles stolen from churches. An NCO in a green uniform – probably Italian to judge by his looks and way of speaking French – asked 2,000 francs of me for a church ornament which – if he was telling the truth (he talked knowledgeably about diamonds, explaining the various stones' value) – was worth at least ten times as much. The throng of soldiers of all nationalities was so great that one had difficulty in pushing through them. For 20 francs I bought a yellowish brown beaver cloak with a double collar, and put it on at once.'

Slipping into a house that's still standing, Captain Lignières of the 1st Foot Chasseurs gets 'for a gold napoleon and 20 francs some 20 loaves of bread, which I distributed to my company'. And indeed food is really the only thing anyone's interested in. That jovial giant of a man, Marshal Mortier, makes General Pajol a present of a sack of wheat and half an ox.[10]

'Here a *vivandière* was offering watches, rings, necklaces, silver vases and sometimes precious stones. There a grenadier was selling brandy or furs. Farther on, a soldier of the Train was trying to sell Voltaire's *Complete Works* or Emilie de Desmoustier's *Letters*. A voltigeur was exposing some horses and carriages for sale, and a cuirassier kept a shoe and clothing shop.'

The imperial vintner, 'having speculatively imported a great quantity of wines and liqueurs into Smolensk' is selling off his entire stock for its weight in gold. 'Even the rank and file spent all they had to get hold of a bottle of brandy.' All of which, thinks a shocked Amédée Pastoret, horrified to see 'officers treating the men they did business with as equals', must surely be inimical to discipline? 'Having discussed or shared profit and loss with them, it caused them to lose all respect.' But though the men are beginning to take liberties with their officers – yes, and even swear at them – Dedem never hears them 'swear at the man to whom they owed all their ills'. Dedem himself, spitting blood and still suffering from the chest bruise from a spent musket ball that had hit him as he'd marched up to the Malakhofskaia Gate at the head of his brigade on August 18, is being personally cared for 'as a child' by Daru, who's 'working ceaselessly and showing much energy and courage'.[11] In Moscow, Dedem had taken on an intelligent and resourceful stable-hand who,

'full of zeal, had been driving my carriage, gone off foraging with rare boldness and with no fear of the Cossacks, and sometimes cooked my supper'.

In a word, another Victor. 'Everybody admired my little gunner's intelligence and energy.' But now here's a quandary, a real surprise:

'In a moment of impatience I struck him, and he revealed his identity. It was girl of fourteen or fifteen, of good family and education, but with a marked taste for horses. She'd left her parents' home to go off with a French artillery officer she'd fallen in love with.'

Dedem buys her a horse of her own on which to continue the retreat.

Greatly to Louise Fusil's surprise, her carriage does turn up after all; but not unlooted by its owner's servants:

'Everything I possessed and my trunks, which I'd placed on wagons belonging to officers, had been taken by the Cossacks. All that was left me was a chest containing shawls, some jewellery and silver.'

Captain *Bréaut des Marlots* of the cuirassiers still has all his steeds with him, 'the finest in the army, and certainly the best. I'd made great sacrifices to save them'. Now, ousting some Polish hussars from a house in the outskirts, he has

'plenty to eat and drink for two days, and so did my horses. It was a great blessing for me, as at that moment my feet were rather frost-bitten. The colonel's cook waited on me. She was a very beautiful woman. However, she made not the least impression on me, my heart was of ice.'

Vossler, the wounded Prussian hussar lieutenant, has no such female attendant. His servant has thought him dead en route. However, he joins some other Württemberg officers who're burning furniture from neighbouring empty houses to warm themselves. 'By now the city was little more than a heap of rubble, for not a night passed without several houses going up in flames. Not a single inhabitant was left.'[12]

Mostly demoralisation reigns. True, one of Mailly-Nesle's fellow-officers of the 2nd Carabiniers has turned up 'exhausted by fatigue' but with the regiment's standard in his pocket. But his aristocratic friend Louis L****, he who'd preferred campaigning to partridge shooting, and who'd been so bright and lively on his unexpected arrival from France, is suffering from

'the dreary silence all round us, the apathy of some and the agony of others, and lastly this snow enveloping all the earth and seeming likely to engulf us. All this concurred to induce lugubrious thoughts and carry fear and terror into the most resolute souls. I'm happy to be able to say, however, that Beauveau and I didn't lose an opportunity to laugh and from time to time sang full-throatedly. To bear the misfortunes of war with courage and gaiety there's nothing like being a Frenchman, being young and, perhaps, also being a gentleman?'

Particularly, perhaps, the last. The ugly little dragoon captain *Henri Beyle*, one day to become known as the great novelist Stendhal, is at this time only a commissary of foodstuffs and certainly no gentleman – at least not in Mailly-Nesle's sense of the word. But he's no less certainly a Frenchman, despite his criticisms of his compatriots. On 2 November, after 'three or four times a day swinging from extreme boredom to extreme pleasure' he'd reached 'attractive Smolensk, a trifle spoiled by snow' with the rest of his convoy of 1,500 wounded, or as many as had survived. His normally rather comical appearance hadn't been improved by the journey; for when he'd knocked at his hosts' door and on entering had held out his hand to a colleague of the Administration, he'd been

'taken for an insolent lackey. We're far removed from Parisian elegance. I'm reckoned to be the most fortunate because I've saved my carriage by means of money and by flying into a rage with any wagons that came close. That is, if one can call having only four shirts and one greatcoat 'saved'. Those who aren't stout-hearted are full of bitterness. But the ranker lives well. He has cups full of diamonds and pearls. They're the happy ones in the army, and as they're in a majority, that's as it should be.'

All this persiflage he'd sent off in a letter to a Parisian lady friend. His diary will be lost in the snows.

If Heinrich von Roos is feeling more cheerful it's partly because the weather's momentarily not quite so cold, partly because a decoration awarded him by the King of Württemberg has unexpectedly reached him. Anyway, pious and resourceful, he's finding his three-day stay at Smolensk 'very supportable'. The third night, after dining on kidneys given him by a Pole who firmly believes the French will be victorious again, he 'for the first time since the war started' even sleeps – luxury of luxuries – in a bed.

Although ill-housed Napoleon certainly isn't idle.[13] 'The Emperor rode out each day, visiting the town and its surroundings as though he'd have liked to keep them too.' Caulaincourt thinks that 'the state in which he saw the army during its march through the town convinced him that our plight was worse than he'd been willing to admit to himself.' Optimistic as usual, though, he doesn't doubt he'll be able to go into winter quarters as soon as he's joined up with Schwarzenberg, Oudinot and Victor:

'He was expecting the arrival of the Polish 'Cossack' levies he'd announced we'd find near Smolensk. Was he misled in this respect, or did he announce this reinforcement to create an illusory hope in everyone else's mind? I don't know.'

Attempts, mostly fruitless ones, are being made to reorganise the army. And certainly there are reinforcements. Fezensac finds his 4th Line 'reinforced by the 129th Line and a regiment of Croats'. Pion des Loches runs into Colonel Pelgrin, commanding his artillery park, who'd come no further than Smolensk and whose *matériel* is under the walls:

'I received 27 loaded ammunition wagons, and sufficient horses in a very good state to draw them were fetched for me from distant villages. They bivouacked beside my park, but the cold was so fierce they were visibly perishing.'

By 12 November everyone's getting ready to leave. Hoping for the remount price of 15 gold louis/napoleons, Franz Roeder sends his horse to the artillery – 'a pony will serve me as well'. But his horse can't get through the press and comes back to him. Those of the 'cuirassiers and the heavy cavalry generally' fill Dedem with horror:

'The French cavalry horses were in a frightful state, whilst those of the Prussians, Saxon and Württemberg regiments were still in quite good shape. Their horses' wounds were being regularly attended to, and their superior officers never left their units.'

Caulaincourt himself is 'employed day and night in reorganising the Emperor's carriages. I'd sent orders ahead to forge shoes with three calkins for all the horses'; and he bribes the arsenal workmen, who're working for the artillery by day, to work for him by night. Although Napoleon can hardly be brought to consent to it, he consigns a lot of superfluous vehicles to the flames but stocks the rest 'with all the provisions I could obtain for cash'. The only carriages he conserves are 'those of Messieurs de Beauveau, de Mailly, and de Bausset', the fat major-domo, who's suffering from gout.

Of the 11,000 men of III Corps who'd left Moscow hardly 3,000 are left. 'What Frenchmen there used to be in our army corps are reduced to one quarter,' Major Bonnet writes in his newly resumed diary. 'The foreigners have vanished. Not one left.' Fighting their everlasting rearguard action on the Dnieper's bank, Ney's men, who're 'devilishly cold', are feeling they've been forgotten by those they've been protecting. 'No question of relieving us as rearguard. While we were staving off the enemy, the other corps had finished off the magazines and pillaged them.' All that reaches them is 'a few biscuits'. Inside the town Mailly-Nesle can hear 'the cannon firing all the time' as Davout throughout 12 and 13 November has to help Ney fight off the Russians, 'a sound repeated by the echoes from these huge old walls'.

By the time the already depleted 111th Line, having helped Ney hold the bridgehead, withdraws into the city it has lost 20 officers and 449 men and both the 15th Light and the 33rd Line have been reduced from 4 battalions to one, i.e. from 4,500 to 450 men. In the morning of 13 November I Corps,

'with Marshal Davout at its head, passes through Smolensk in considerable numbers and takes up position beyond it in the western suburbs, bivouacking in gardens where the assault had taken place'.

But though Sergeant Bertrand's young Captain Moncey sends him back 'into town to find some victuals' he too finds that 'the Emperor's foresight in accumulating food, clothing, linen and shoes' has been made nonsense of by

'the employees who've abandoned their posts. It was a mob of wounded from all arms, frozen men, stragglers going on ahead of the column, who, in inexpressible disorder, were pillaging all these resources. And the cold was at -23° !'

(Larrey's thermometer, more accurate no doubt, is registering between -19° and -20° Réaumur [-24° to -26° C) Nevertheless Bertrand gets hold of '5 to 6 kilos of flour and some broken biscuit' and putting himself at the head of his two carabiniers and sword in hand 'defending these meagre provisions against those who, with the most horrible threats in their mouths, wanted to wrench them from us,' takes them back to 60 surviving grenadiers.

But what's this – if not the head of Eugène's bedraggled column appearing over the hills along the Petersburg road? After a 50-mile march some 4,000 men, all that's left of IV Corps, are arriving by the icy road from Dukhovchino. Sliding down the last steep slope, Griois and his party joke at their 'long skids and frequent falls. The idea that the term of our ills was close to hand had given us back a kind of gaiety.' Luckily the gate just then happens to be open. Climbing the steep icy main street to the main square they everywhere see groups of men and packed houses – and realise they haven't a ghost of a chance of finding any shelter. So going straight through the town and out by the opposite gate they find the

Guard Artillery bivouacked on its 'esplanade' and their 'little caravan' is promptly established in 'a kind of half-roofed hangar' its horses have been occupying. 'For us it was a veritable palace.' Whereupon Griois goes to see

'Colonel [*sic*] Boulart, commanding a battalion [*sic*] in the Guard, who'd invited me to supper. He was under a tent, and I enjoyed a meal I'll never forget as long as I live: wine, bread, meat, coffee, all things I'd long lost the habit of. So I did them every honour, despite the extreme cold [-28°]. It was so great we had to break our wine by hitting it with a hatchet and putting it over the fire.'

This gives the hospitable Boulart – who's under orders to leave tomorrow morning – 'the satisfaction of entertaining some of my comrades to some passable cooking'. Griois goes back to his hangar, where his comrades 'at risk of being suffocated by the mob' have procured some food from one of the magazines. 'Without having supped as well as I had, they'd shared with some friends in the Guard.'

He has, however, an uneasy conscience. Not merely has IV Corps lost all but four of its last remaining guns – should he, who really belongs to Grouchy's 3rd Cavalry Corps, ever have joined it with his own horse artillery at Doroghoboui? Feeling he must justify himself to Grouchy's superior, the inspector-general of cavalry, he asks the whereabouts of General A.-D. *Belliard's* headquarters. Climbing the little staircase of 'a rather vast building destroyed by the fire before it had even been completed', Griois, 'without meeting either servants or orderlies' pushes open a half-shattered door, and in front of him sees the King of Naples and Belliard, his former chief-of-staff,

'chatting joyously. Belliard, still suffering from the wound he'd got at Mojaisk [on 8 September], was lying on a wretched pallet, part of which was occupied by Murat. The picture wasn't uninteresting. A king – for that, after all, is what he was and was recognised as such – in the company of one of his wounded generals, in guise of a friend who nurses a friend.'

That, he thinks, 'is a rarity, and I confess I felt touched by it'. But since his bad news is

'agreeable neither to tell nor hear, and anyway no longer had any importance at all, I retired without them noticing me. Murat merely asked who was there. I didn't reply.'

After a lot of searching about among the benighted crowds he finally locates Eugène's headquarters, only to hear he's with the Emperor. Eugène's report on the state of IV Corps, Caulaincourt notes, comes as a considerable shock. So Griois has to wait:

'The session in Napoleon's room was a lengthy one, and to me seemed all the longer as the hall where I was open to all the winds, and the cold glacial despite the fire the officers were carefully keeping up. At last the door opened, Eugène appeared and with him Murat. Murat seemed extremely gay, and no one would have divined our sad situation from his noisy guffaws [*ses bruyants éclats*]. Parting from him, Eugène came over to me.

'"My dear Griois," he said, "before daylight you must be out on the road we've just come by. I'm going there too. Broussier's division, which I've left in position, is surrounded by the enemy. We must clear a way for him. See you tomorrow!"'

Dismayed by this unexpected order Griois goes back to his hangar, rouses his chief-of-staff. 'It was about midnight. And at 5 a.m. we had to be on our feet. Wrapping myself in my mantle I threw myself down on the straw and fell asleep.'

That cold blustery night the whole of the 85th Line lodges in two or three of the suburb's remaining houses. A howling gale's battering the window panes (amazingly, some are still intact) of Le Roy's tiny room. The regiment's ever-cheerful, ever resourceful *adjutant-sous-officier* is an NCO who's always been equal to all thinkable situations. Long ripe for promotion, Sergeant-Major Ballane has already bought a gold epaulette, gold lace and all the other accoutrements proper to a *sous-lieutenant* from a lacemaker who's followed the army. These precious symbols of his future commissioned self he keeps wrapped up in a little bag

'which he never allowed out of his sight, hung it round his neck with a good rope and several double knots, containing as it did all his fortune, all his happiness'.

Alas, how easily snatched from us are our symbols of promotion! Bellane's just been doing the cooking in a room occupied by the officers of the 85th Line, Le Roy has just shaved Jacquet, and their precious cookpot – that more than symbolic means of survival they've been keeping their eyes on ever since the Niemen – is bubbling on the stove, when Ballane, laying his bag on the window sill, goes off to fetch them some stores and some rum. Alas the windowpane is one of the many thousands the glaziers of Davout's corps[14] have lacked time or inclination to repair; and window there is none. Suddenly Ballane notices his bag's gone. And rushing outside sees some remnants of IV Corps marching by. But, alas, no sign of his bag! Stricken, he comes back into the room. *Sic transit gloria mundi.* Though everyone tries to console him, this exemplary soldier cracks. Bursts into tears: "Now I've nothing left me," he sobs, "not even hope."

'He began weeping, and lay down. Despite all our entreaties and arguments he ate nothing all day. From this time onwards we'd notice how he lost his activity, became indifferent and in the end succumbed to his chagrin.'

Back at his bivouac in the western suburb, Sergeant Bertrand sees all the neighbourhood's houses packed with officers and men who've lit fires in them to warm themselves. Among them is one of his comrades. 'Foreseeing what's going to happen, I implore him to come out.' But though the officers and some of the men 'already stupefied by the heat and incapable of a decision' do as he says, his comrade won't:

'Soon a mob throws itself on these houses. The ones inside try to defend their repose. A horrible fight starts up, and the weak are pitilessly crushed. I run to the bivouac to register these atrocious scenes. I've hardly got there before the flames devour these houses and everyone inside.'

But the carabinier company bivouacs apart

'with the colonel and other officers. We set fire to ambulance wagons abandoned for lack of teams, and passed a good night of sleep and happiness, which however wasn't complete, since we had to defend ourselves, musket in hand, against those accursed Cossacks, even around our nice bright fire.'

When morning comes nothing's left of the houses. 'We see only ruins and corpses.' But the trio from the 85th have passed the night with Le Roy's friend Captain Gouttenoire of the 1st Foot Chasseurs:

'The Guard was lodged beside us, in houses near the rampart. The wind was very strong, the cold excessive and the snow went on falling in big flakes.'

Le Roy also pays a visit to another friend, Colonel Schmidt of the Illyrian regiment [III Corps], whom he finds has been charged with the task of blowing up the Smolensk fortifications before Ney's rearguard leaves:

'When we parted he took me aside and confided to me several thousand-franc notes and 150 francs in silver to give to his wife. He foresaw a catastrophe which, he said, couldn't fail to happen to him while blowing up the fortifications at the enemy's approach.'

Schmidt also gives him food for several days, including 'a little sugar loaf which I hid in one of the pockets of my greatcoat, as well as part of the rest of our breakfast,' *inter alia* a chicken.

At 5 a.m. Griois and Colonel Berthier, both frozen to the bone and unable to ride their horses over the ice, have gone back through the city and 'not without several tumbles' descended the slope to the Dnieper Gate. Mounting 'with even greater difficulty, in 25-28 degrees of frost', the even steeper gradient they'd so cheerfully slithered down yesterday, they've found it 'lined with dead men from IV Corps 'covered in wounds and frozen solid, who'd yesterday been attacked by Cossacks' and reached the hilltop at dawn. There they find the Royal Guard facing to the rear – it too has been closely followed by 'numerous regiments' of Cossacks, who've thrown themselves on the stragglers, the remains of IV Corps' baggage and on Broussier's rearguard.

Eugène's men have absolutely no idea of the state of affairs in Smolensk, and from moment to moment Laugier's comrades are

'expecting Victor's troops to come out and replace us. Completely ignorant of what's been happening in the rear, we're amazed they're taking so long to do so.'

Already the indomitable Eugène is standing there to the right of the road with some of his staff officers. Griois goes up to him:

'The weather was superb; but the sun's pale rays only seemed to make the cold more piercing. The prince had detached some troops to protect the retreat of Broussier's division and was awaiting the outcome'. For to the rear a minor battle has developed around a chapel on the hilltop. Broussier, together with 'the few Bavarian horse still with us', is fighting a heroic rearguard action. Pino's division too, marching after the rest of IV Corps, has had to 'fight its way through Grekoff's division, near Kamenka'. Although the Cossacks have massacred the stragglers, 14th Division has established itself in a village, with a nearby palisaded château as a kind of entrenchment. There Broussier, 'resigned and generous,' says Cesare de Laugier, has awaited his fate:

'Late into the night we'd had to stay put in the position indicated to us. Imagine these soldiers standing completely immobile on very high freezing ground where the wind buffets them furiously, in -29 degrees [-36° C], without food, without hope, and their only prospect to freeze to death rather than abandon the flag – and all the while seeing Smolensk far off in the distance!'

Isn't that a scene, he asks, that Plutarch would have preserved for posterity? 'Honour to so many illustrious warriors who there sleep their eternal sleep!'

Already Eugène has sent '50 soldiers, skeletons of two companies, to attack a hillock crowned by Cossacks'. Scorning the grapeshot and lance-jabs, this handful of brave men 'reaches the height like a troop of lions'. And in the end Broussier retires 'in good order but with extreme difficulty' from the village, now in flames from Platov's shellfire, and manages to cover the withdrawal of what little remains of IV Corps' baggage and its stragglers.

But the cold's so intense that 32 of the Guard grenadiers have dropped dead in the ranks while awaiting the order to leave. Perhaps at the terrible, the shattering, news Eugène has told them: *There's to be no halting at Smolensk.* At 8.30 that same morning 'the Emperor has left, accompanied by the Old Guard and preceded by three hours by the Young Guard'. It's a stunning blow. At least the sweet Fanni has been spared the horror of this final, most cruel disappointment. 'If lightning had struck at our feet we couldn't have been more stupefied.' For the first time the Adjutant-Major sees men who simply 'refuse to believe' it leave the ranks and go down to the town to find out the truth of the matter for themselves. But then, by the Dnieper, 'a horse lying in the ditch, strips of whose flesh were being fought over by some soldiers, destroyed or at least reduced to very little the hopes we'd been flattering ourselves with' and they return and confirm the ultimacy of the disaster.

'At that moment a new scene of horror presents itself to our eyes. Any number of soldiers belonging to the rearguard division, lots of employees, servants, disbanded men who've fallen behind, try to rejoin us and go down into Smolensk. Wounded, streaming blood, pursued by Cossacks, they run toward us howling and imploring us to help them. The road's thick with these unfortunates.'

So steep is the slope and so dangerous the ice that

'all these unfortunates, hardly able to stand up, let themselves roll down it, most of them only to perish in a veritable lake of blood and render up their last sigh under these walls which have been the unhappy object of their longings'.

Although poorly mounted, some cavalry officers and some remaining dragoons of Eugène's escort, unable to contain themselves at the sight, throw themselves at the Cossacks – luckily its commander General Lecchi has had the Guard infantry fall back for the best part of a mile – put the Cossacks to flight and rescue some men of their prey. Only then, leaving Broussier's and Pino's divisions on the heights of the Petersburg road,[15] do the Royal Guard and the dismounted cavalry at last march down towards Smolensk.

They meet Ney's men at the junction of the Doroghoboüi and Valutina roads, and envy them for

'not having crossed the Wop and having kept a large part of their artillery and vehicles. The numerous baggage, flowing in from all directions, mingled with the cavalrymen and infantry and caused so much confusion that people were cutting each other's throats to get in.'

The Italians have to wait for three hours. And when they at last reach the charred remains of Smolensk's suburbs it's only to be told that 'all the stores had been consumed'.

To get up the main street, where officers like Dumonceau had gone sightseeing in the August heats, Staff-Captain Labaume has to 'get down on all fours and hang on to the points of rocks jutting up out of the snow'.

And it's a fact. Napoleon and the Guard have left that morning (14 November). After Roeder's men – nominal members of the Young Guard – have been belatedly issued with some flour and rice – certainly not enough for the six days it's supposed to last – that irritable officer's been kept awake until midnight by noisy distributions of 'shoes, leggings, shirts and wicker brandy flasks, but, alas, no bread!' Up at 2 a.m. after only two hours' sleep, the Hessians, though told they'll march out at 4 a.m., have to draw up in the main square and wait and wait. Berthier, whose pampered Neuchâtel 'canaries'[16] are also to leave with the Young Guard, takes pity on them:

'Seeing no orders for departure come from the Emperor he assembled some men from the bands under the Emperor's window and told them to play the air *Where Can One Better Be than in the Bosom of One's Family?*[17] They'd scarcely begun, when the Emperor appeared on the balcony and ordered them to play *Let's Watch over the Safety of the Empire.* The men had to play it, in spite of the cold, and immediately the order to leave was given.'

Just as Napoleon's about to leave, Lejeune goes in to him and again begs to be relieved of the onerous job he'd never wanted in the first place:

'The Emperor agreed and nominated General Charpentier, no longer governor of Smolensk, to relieve me. But although I no longer either had the title or the salary I still went on with the work, as this general, by no means anxious to come and take up a post of whose difficulties he was only too well aware, managed to evade reporting for duty.'

137

Finally the Hessians, consisting now of eight sergeants, one drummer, seven *Schützen* and 42 guardsmen (ten of them sick), get the order to march. 'Of course,' Franz Roeder caustically concludes in his diary,
'we didn't march out until 9 a.m. in -18° [-22.5° C], the men with empty stomachs and no sleep. This is wreaking terrible havoc. We might have been able to get our strength back here if only we'd been given enough to eat and hadn't had to observe that murderous vigil.'
In a freezing wind the Italians wander about the streets, looking for something to eat. Evidently the magazines still have something to offer, for the pillage follows as before:
'Men flung themselves on the food stores. These were smashed in, looted. There men were killing each other, suffocating each other. As for ammunition, there were no horses to carry it. At least weapons could have been given to this mob of soldiers who'd thrown their own away or lost them. They took good care not to come and find some more. A small number were being distributed to some men of good will and to gunners whose cannon had been left behind in the ice. I had some carbines given to all from IV Corps who formed a kind of battalion.'
That evening of 14 November 'having had a dinner at Lariboisière's which was far from coming up to Boulart's', Griois, returning to his hangar, is told that IV Corps is to leave tomorrow morning.

The 'hospitals', now to be abandoned, are full to overflowing. Because of the failure of this promised land that was to have been Smolensk, writes Labaume,
'despair seized our hearts. Each man, thinking only of his own existence, became oblivious of honour and duty or, more properly, no longer let it consist in submitting to the orders of an improvident leader who hadn't even thought of giving bread to those who were sacrificing their lives for him.'
Although Cesare de Laugier certainly wouldn't agree with such treasonable sentiments, even he, with ice-cold fingers, writes in his diary:
'Assailed by terrible doubts, but determined at all costs to survive, many of us are losing what's left of our military bearing.'
Invited by Sébastiani's ADCs to share a piece of roofing, Victor Dupuy ties up his horse with theirs. Passing 'in front of the house the Emperor had occupied' and seeing 'the remains of his stocks of wine being sold off' he buys 'two bottles of wine, and for 12 francs a soldier sold me a munition ['issue'] loaf pillaged from the magazines.'

PHASE TWO
TOWARDS THE BEREZINA

CHAPTER 9

THE ICY ROAD TO KRASNOIE

An icy day – courageous women – 'she came back, caressed me, went away again and disappeared' – Roeder loses his inkpot ... and Napoleon his maps – Cossacks outside Krasnoië – Boulart forces his way through – Louise leaves her carriage – Prince Eugène's bivouac

Junot's 1,800 Westphalians had marched out early in the morning of 14 November at the heels of the dismounted cavalry, followed by the Poles of V Corps and the 900 men of the Vistula Legion escorting the Treasure, IHQ's baggage and the trophies. Now, on the 15th, the Guard, amounting to upwards of 9,000, leaves behind it the city's fire-blackened skeleton and marches for Krasnoië, 35 miles away. In hopes of avoiding confusion and retarding Kutusov, IV, I and III Corps have been ordered to follow on, in that order and at one-day intervals – a plan, as we'll see, fraught with dire consequences. To bring news, likewise at one-day intervals, of how the city's holding out, IHQ has left behind four of its staff officers.[1]

Hearing that 350 guns have so far been abandoned, Cesare de Laugier, in an off-the-cuff estimate of the state of the army, thinks that more men than not are still under arms. But Secretary Fain, better informed, notes that 50,000 men under arms are now protecting 60,000 without any.

Leaving under a sombre sky – to Planat it looks 'completely black against the snow' – Larrey consults his little Réaumur thermometer dangling from his coat lapel and sees it's fallen to -19° (-23.75° C). And Planat's comrades' hearts, hearing 'the rearguard's guns rumbling in the distance', ache 'at the thought of so many brave fellows getting themselves killed for our sakes, perhaps never to rejoin us'.

Outside the town gate this freezing morning Mme Domergue, wife of the producer of the French theatre at Moscow (whose husband is currently enjoying himself in captivity with sundry Russian ladies,[2]) is sitting dejectedly on a gun-carriage with her little son 'feeling sad and trying to calm my son's crying' when she sees Napoleon

'now on foot, now on horseback, giving orders to his ADCs. He came up to me and said:

'"You're suffering a great deal, aren't you, Madame? But take courage, you'll see your husband again, and I'll recompense you for your misfortunes."

'"Sire," I replied, "at this moment your goodness makes me forget them."

'He was always as much master of himself as when things were going well. His attitude was calm and his face serious.'

On the other hand she's upset to see the Emperor is unusually clad:

'Over his grey overcoat he was wearing a kind of Polish pelisse, trimmed with marten. His little hat had been replaced by a green velvet bonnet also trimmed with fur, from which a gold tassel escaped. This head-dress was fixed by two black ribbons under his chin.'

This she, 'being a woman and superstitious', feels is a sinister portent:

'I was struck by the sight of these ribbons of lugubrious hue and at not seeing his hat on his head, that talisman which seemed to protect his brow and his genius.'

Roustam, always in close attendance, sees two more of the troupe's actresses, 'one old and one young and pretty', warming themselves by a fire, made up by some Sailors of the Guard who're 'using the most virulent expressions' as they 'impute all their ills to the Emperor for bringing them to this infernal country'. The older woman exhorts them to

"Show more courage, have more energy. Brace yourselves against adversity. Remember you're soldiers and Frenchmen."

Duverger sees yet another actress, Madame Adnet, 'weeping for her family, killed by the cold'. And remembers how in Moscow she and Louise Fusil had taken the lead roles in *Marton et Frontin*, a performance he'd found 'a sad parody of our Parisian theatres'.[3]

Only Mailly-Nesle, riding on ahead as usual in his carriage, seems to take any interest in the grisly relics of the battle of 16/17 August,[4] lying 'in fragments in a terrible pell-mell so that one couldn't walk without sending bones rolling or crushing rotting flesh'. After 'spending a few nights under a roof, something that hadn't happened since time out of mind and a trifle' compared with the snug winter quarters they'd been looking forward to, Colbert's lancers have emerged in the early hours from their village and been delighted to see the road 'clear of the mob which had previously been encumbering it'. Yet it's already littered with fresh corpses, presumably Westphalian or Polish. Flanking the Guard again, the Lancers

'ride alongside over the fields. The Emperor was marching on foot at the head of the column of his old grenadiers, followed immediately by his travelling *coupé*, harnessed to four bays.'

Three or four times he and Berthier get into it, 'but without going on ahead, and after getting some rest' get out again. But the road's a sheet of ice, and Napoleon has to 'lean now on Caulaincourt's arm, now on Berthier's, now on someone else's.'

Everything that depends on horsepower is in a very bad way: 'Neither the artillery nor the cavalry had a single rough-shod horse – most of our losses,' Dedem sees,

'must be attributed to want of shoeing: i.e., to our lack of foresight. The gunners had been warned in vain. The forges had been abandoned on the road. Our farriers had no nails, and could lay their hands neither on iron nor coals.'

No sooner has Pion des Loches helped to their feet the fine new horses he's just been given in Smolensk, than their hoofs slither beneath them and they slip and fall again:

'I harnessed up as many as 20 to save one of my field-forges, and still didn't succeed. That day I lost 27 of my ammunition wagons.'

Only Private *Jakob Walter*'s *konya* can 'always help itself up again', even has 'the good custom, when we went downhill, of sitting on its rump, bracing its forefeet forward, and sliding into the valley without my dismounting. The other German horses' shoes were ground entirely smooth. Nor could those irons be torn off, since no one had a tool for that.'

'If my officers had been as zealous as myself,' Pion des Loches goes on, he'd have saved a good part of the ammunition wagons. 'But what could one expect of depressed men who'd no longer any authority over their subordinates?' Dreadfully upset and shamefaced, he goes and tells Sorbier. But all the commander of the Guard reserve artillery, 'seeing how embarrassed I was, most obligingly' says is:

'"That's desolating for you. I couldn't give a damn. It makes little odds whether you lose your ammunition wagons today or tomorrow. The sooner you lose them, the more the gunners are worth who're killing themselves trying to save them. You won't get a single vehicle to go as far as the Niemen, no matter what trouble you go to. Not", Sorbier adds, "that I'd say that to everybody."'

If whole teams of horses are dropping dead between their traces and the steep gradients are 'littered with abandoned horses that hadn't been able to scramble to their feet', Dedem sees it's 'not for lack of food, since we still had oats to give them. It was due to their own unavailing efforts' to drag guns and caissons uphill. But above all, Caulaincourt's thinking – agreeing with Pion des Loches – it's due to Napoleon's obsession with keeping every gun, whether or not there are any horses to draw it:

'The sensible thing would have been to distribute a certain amount of artillery to each corps before leaving Smolensk; make sure it was properly mounted, even supply it with reserve horses; and sacrifice all the rest. As it was, the tiniest frozen slope in the undulating road was fatal.'

Lariboisière, supreme commander of the Grand Army's artillery, his surviving son Honoré and the latter's close friend Planat de la Faye have every reason to 'follow the route in silence'. The Guard Artillery 'which is mounted best' is crawling along at hardly more than one mile per hour. And despite Lariboisière and Chasseloup's strict orders that all abandoned guns are to be burnt, nothing's being done about it. Everywhere Mailly-Nesle sees:

'guns piled up on top of each other. The frost had glued, or rather cemented, the wheels to their axle-trees. On the detestable surface ice the wheels slid without being able to turn. From this came a continual groaning noise, produced by the rubbing of the iron of the felloes,'

so that the Guard Artillery takes thirteen hours to cover the fifteen miles between Smolensk and its next bivouac, at the 'miserable hamlet' of Korytnia.

More tragic than guns, many of the women are being abandoned – for instance a commissary's wife Dedem had seen clinging to a gun-carriage shortly before reaching Smolensk:

'Their sufferings only added to those of the men. Whilst that sex, much more humane than ourselves, gave evidence of compassion and interest in the midst of indescribable sufferings, I saw distinguished officers heartlessly and barbarously abandon amiable and interesting women. In this way a *vivandière* of the 9th Hussars fed me for several days, and the wife of one of the Emperor's coachmen, whose husband had served me at Mecklemburg, often brought me supper and even wine.'

Otherwise masculine egoism, already rife, has become worse. Having come from Witebsk, Intendant Pastoret has not yet seen anything of the retreat and is deeply shocked at the way privileged persons' carriages and other vehicles are always pushing ahead of the guns, which 'should have had right of way; but no one was respecting it'. On the other hand Franz Roeder is appalled to see

'how little protection is being given to the carriages, the baggage trains, the artillery, even the Imperial Treasure – how bridges are never being repaired, even when this could be done in a couple of hours – how no detachment is ever being stationed to cover the defiles and crossings – how men are being stricken down and murdered on the least pretext – how everyone's riding or driving through the troops, whilst these, never for a moment safe from stumbling, must toil and struggle on in the press.'

After having been ridden through thick snow inside one of the Young Guard's squares, Roeder's own horse finally collapses on the highway, 'a victim to my batman's monstrous negligence, to thirst, hunger and fatigue'. To make matters even worse, he hears to his dismay that 'the wagon with the officers' effects has sunk in a swamp at almost exactly the same moment!' But here at least is a bit of luck. His Sergeant Bruck, whom he'd saved from a flogging back in July, has snatched his valise from the sinking wagon – one of only two survivors. Roeder rewards Bruck with a *louis d'or*; but, just as he's giving it to him, here comes another Cossack 'hurrah'. So, hastily saving 'the writing case with Sophie's letters, my sash and orders, uniform, spyglass, epaulettes, money and a few eatables such as coffee and sago' – he flings his valise back to his sergeant, and trudges on.

No one knows where Kutusov is, or what the Russians are doing. 'Not a single cavalry brigade' apart from the Guard Lancers and fragments of its other

'much reduced regiments remained in a state fit to cover our movements. Unless we took horses from the Guard we weren't strong enough even to make a reconnaissance at a distance or bold enough to get definite news of the enemy's whereabouts. Indeed we weren't even trying to.'

With Napoleon leaning on his arm, Caulaincourt sees all his direst prophesies about the Russian winter being fulfilled.

Le Roy, Jacquet and their Guillaume have gone on ahead, 'being no use to the regiment, where there were already as many officers as rankers'.

Besides, the 85th's newly fledged lieutenant-colonel has orders to return to its depot in France. Tramping onwards through the frozen wreckage of men and horses, caissons and field-forges with his Guillaume beside him 'holding my horse tied to his arm ... the poor beast gnawing such pine branches as came within his reach' Le Roy has reason and enough to reflect on his favourite philosophical theme – the vanity of life. Even his bitch quits him. 'I whistled. She came back, caressed me, went away again and disappeared.' This, in their present circumstances, is enough to make the usually so unemotional Le Roy, a man for whom a good night's sleep and a hearty breakfast had sufficed to get him over the shock of his son's death,[5] begin to wonder whether he too soon won't be 'a little hump, barely perceptible under the snow'. Won't 'some observer soon be saying "there's another fellow who'll never see his family again."?' So forcibly does the thought strike this highly professional soldier who'd begun his military career 'by chance but continued it by taste' that, despite stoic efforts to restrain his tender feelings, he begins 'sobbing silently, but so strongly that my poor Guillaume, thinking something must be amiss with me', tugs at his waistcoat, asks what's up:

'"Nothing," I said. "I'm done for [*rompu*]. Let's get going."'

Overtaking IHQ, he notices its personnel are expecting an enemy attack; and decides to make tracks for Krasnoïe – and Vilna – as fast as ever he can.

Cossacks are at everyone's heels. Even of the Guard Artillery. One of Pion des Loches' subalterns, who'd lingered in company with another to 'drink a few glasses of hot wine' while he lightened his wagon 'his horses no longer being able to pull it', only rejoins his unit thanks to the fleetness of his steed and to report that his comrade has been 'Cossacked'; likewise that

'Captain Lavillette, marching at the convoy's tail to get two inadequately harnessed guns to follow on, had succumbed to the same fate. Thus in one day I lost two good officers, one for his having given in to a gourmand's temptation, the other for having been zealous in his duty.'

So hilly is the road and so far have the imperial carriages fallen behind Claparède's advance guard that IHQ overtakes them as they're struggling on at Korytnia. Three miles and an hour farther on they hear that the expected attack has materialised – against a small artillery park and the convoy that's been bringing back the Moscow trophies, together with

'the Emperor's carriages, which had just joined this park. The Cossacks had taken advantage of the moment when the column had halted to double up its teams so as to get up one of the steep icy slopes, thus opening a gap between the head and the rear, with the result that the small detachments guarding it hadn't been able to defend it as a whole.'

Kergorre's Treasury wagon is mixed up in the affray but escapes:

'A defile, approached by a narrow road across a little frozen lake, was blocked by the baggage train. Some vehicles had tried to get through it. The first had got across, but the others had fallen into the water. One of them was the wagon with trophies, among them the famous cross of the church of St John which Rostopchin had said Napoleon must never set eyes on, and which the latter had therefore had taken down from its bell tower.'[6]

Not merely do the Cossacks make off with upwards of a dozen horses, they even loot some of the imperial transport vehicles, whose terrified drivers upset them into the ravine and 'dropping everything that hampered their flight' have simply taken to their heels. 'The Cossacks scattered everything but took little,' Caulaincourt hears. 'It could almost all have been recovered if there hadn't been a second flurry at the column's head.' Among the wagons lost is 'the one containing the maps'. Likewise a not inconsiderable amount of the Imperial Treasure. Kergorre, who's already given up his own carriage to save a friend who'd straggled, estimates 10 millions – Denniée, doubtless more accurately, 1,294,000 gold francs. The artillery park has 'lost half its teams, and most of the IHQ officers their personal effects – myself', Caulaincourt adds succinctly, 'among them' – all this a mere six normal hours' march out of Smolensk.

Napoleon, the Master of the Horse notices, shows no annoyance with his servants for losing his maps. And the incident at least has one good effect. Everyone at once becomes

'more cautious. For 48 hours or so it brought back many who'd left the road. But such was our situation, one can't help asking oneself whether it was really a good thing to rally in wretches we couldn't feed' and who still further slow up the march. 'And we had to hurry.'

That morning Franz Roeder loses something – to him – far more precious. His inkpot. Relic of his beloved and deeply mourned Sophie, it has frozen and broken. 'So writing, too, will soon be at an end.'

If Napoleon and the Guard have left Korytnia precipitously and before daybreak (leaving a surprised Colbert to follow on with his lancers), it's been because of some alarming news. Fifteen hundred Russians under Ojarovski have just occupied Krasnoië and 'carried off the remains of an Italian battalion and some dismounted troopers of Sébastiani's corps'. But then better news comes back. The Vistula Legion has flushed them out and secured the little timber-built market town of narrow streets perched on a hilltop.

Nowhere between Smolensk and Krasnoië does Larrey see 'a single habitation. Everything had been burnt down.' But thanks to the Poles' prompt action Krasnoië itself is intact. So, no less important, is the 'narrow trembling bridge' over the Krasnoië ravine. Approached by a 'steep, boxed-in road with sharply sloping sides even more difficult because of the ice' – a serious bottle-neck – the ravine is only 30 paces wide.[7] As General Count *François Roguet*, commander of the Young Guard's 2nd Division, sees at a glance, 'no more favourable point could be imagined for holding up a retreating army'. Why hadn't Ojarovski blown it up?

Marching towards it the Guard encounters no opposition. But the IHQ carriages, going on ahead all too lightly escorted, do. As Mailly-Nesle's – the only one apart from Napoleon's own and those of a few other high-ups to have got so far – has still about a mile and a half to go to reach the ravine, its occupants see Russian light cavalry, 'with guns mounted on sledges, which helped them to aim at us':

'The Cossacks' hurrahs, the disorder being caused by roundshot and shells, the postillions' and drivers' shouts and the *cantinières'* shrill screams were causing everyone to lose his head. Everyone wanted to get away. The wheels get hooked into each other. Horses struggle. Carriages turn over.'

To Dedem's admiration his little female groom attacks a Cossack single-handed and grabs back his loot. But soon afterwards disappears for ever. Planat, following on with Lariboisière's remaining son Honoré in charge of his carriage and wagon, runs on

'ahead of the stragglers, who'd taken to their heels but some of whom had kept their muskets. I exhorted them not to scatter and to march slowly. As long as the Cossacks saw a gun or a bayonet, I said, they wouldn't attack. My efforts were fruitless. Each man sought his own safety in flight. This was the signal for the Cossacks' hurrah.'

Mailly-Nesle sees 'the enemy cavalry cross the road at a gallop, killing everything it meets with'.

'Honoré had already ordered our carriages to turn off by themselves to the right. Being well-harnessed, they quickly – by driving across country – reached a little village on the Krasnoië ravine. The little stream was completely frozen. The carriages crossed it easily. But the wagon, being much heavier, broke the ice and fell into the water to above its axles. Two of its four horses were drowned, and the lead horses were only saved by cutting the traces. All the artillery's papers were in this wagon and were lost.'

So are all Planat's personal belongings, all his diaries and years of corre-spondence. Mailly-Nesle is more fortunate; his carriage isn't attacked:

'A few infantry had come to our aid, restoring order among us and forc-ing the enemy to retire. M. Montaigu, an *officier d'ordonnance*, had climbed into our carriage. The Emperor and his Guard came up, and together we arrived in Krasnoië, where we parked in the square oppo-site the church. The air inside the carriage was so cold that our breath was falling in icy flakes.'

By the time the Lancer Brigade approaches Krasnoië in a 'calm and lumi-nous evening' Dumonceau sees in the distance away to his left something more serious than Cossacks: namely, heads of Russian infantry columns debouching on to the high plateau that slopes toward the Losima stream. 'Already Ojarovski's corps was threatening the left of the Maleiwo road.' Napoleon, of course, has seen them too. Halting on the highway as the Guard's leading infantry units cross the shaky bridge and march up the icy incline toward Krasnoië, he orders Roguet

'to put his grenadiers into the houses of the town's eastern suburb. Leav-ing the road, the Emperor assembled the Old Guard's officers and NCOs and told them he wasn't going to see his grenadiers' bearskins in

146

the midst of such disorder: "I'm counting on you to do great things, just as you can count on me.'"

When Rapp arrives. his head bruised by one musket ball and his horse having been killed by another, he tells him: '"Now you can stop worrying. You aren't going to be killed during this campaign."

"I hope Your Majesty's prophecy comes true. But you assured poor Lannes the same thing, yet he had to go to it."

"No, no, you won't be killed.'"

All Krasnoië's inhabitants have fled, and the Guard infantry packs itself into their houses. But the cavalry's sent off to find night quarters in the environs, and Dumonceau finds himself in the very same hamlet, six miles outside Krasnoië, that his men had occupied on 14 August.

At the bottle-neck at the ravine, meanwhile, a 'prodigious blockage of all kinds of vehicles' is piling up. Escorted by Kirgener's engineers, Boulart's Guard batteries reach it at nightfall and have to park and 'wait for three hours while men and horses ate what they could'. Time passes. Nothing budges. Only the Cossacks are still pressing in from the left. Finally Boulart, exasperated, quite simply decides to

'force my way through this disorderly mass of vehicles. Ordering all mine to follow, tightly closed up and leaving no gaps so as not to be cut off, I place myself at the head of our column. By dint of my men's main force I either straighten out those vehicles which are in my way or else overturn them. Moving slowly, either smashing or crushing everything in our way, and without for one moment allowing cries, shouts, tears or groans to arrest our march, after a thousand evils, the head finally reaches the bridge and gets through to the head of the jam.'

But even this isn't the end of his troubles:

'The road, it's true, is free; but thereafter it climbs sharply and the surface is icy. I have the ice spiked, some earth taken from the embankments of the road, which is here hollowed out of the hillside; throw the soil down in the middle of the road; manhandle the wheels, myself setting the example; and by hook or by crook get the vehicles one by one to the hilltop. Twenty times, going either up or down this hill, I fall heavily. An hour before dawn all my artillery's up there.'

For Pion des Loches, too, it's a terrible night:

'The guns could only pass one after another down the very steep slopes. We were on our feet all night; and it was morning before the turn came to my batteries.'

But Colonel Séruzier's already inside the town and has posted his horse artillery at the exit to every main or side street. By the time Boulart reports to a delighted Sorbier he's been given up for lost.

For Louise Fusil getting into Krasnoië is a traumatic experience. Caught outside with some of the other headquarters vehicles – among them, just ahead of her own, Narbonne's famous yellow carriage[8] – an officer advises her:

'"I fancy, Madame, the Cossacks are very close to us. Just now an officer came and spoke in a low voice to a wounded colonel who's been in my calèche. After stammering out his excuses he's got on horseback, even though he can hardly stay in the saddle."'

So Louise and her fellow-actresses have to get out of their carriage: 'Cannon balls were crossing the road, so we made up our minds, got on the horses and for lack of beaten paths made our way across country in the snow. The poor horses, who hadn't had anything to eat all day, were in it up to their bellies, and had no strength left. So here I am on horseback, at midnight, no longer owning anything but what I have on me, not knowing which road to follow, and dying of cold. At 2 a.m. we reached the column [Boulart's?] that was dragging along some cannon. I asked the officer in command whether we had far to go to rejoin imperial headquarters. "Oh, easy on!" he said, annoyed. "We shan't be rejoining it, because if we aren't taken prisoner tonight we shall be tomorrow morning. We can't escape."

'No longer knowing which way to go to get on, he halted his unit. The men wanted to light some fires to warm themselves; but he wouldn't let them, saying their campfires would give them away to the enemy. I got off my horse and sat down on some straw they'd laid out in the snow. There I experienced a moment of discouragement. But the coachman having recovered our carriage, we went on very slowly all night by the light of burning villages and the sound of gunfire. I saw unfortunate wounded men leaving the ranks. Some, exhausted by hunger, asked us for something to eat. Others, dying of cold, begged us to take them into the carriage, implored any help we could give them. But there were such a lot of them! Camp-followers implored us to take the children they no longer had the strength to carry – it was a desolating scene. One suffered both from one's own miseries and others'. When we were in sight of Krasnoïe the coachman told me our horses could go no further. I got out, hoping to find IHQ in the town. It was just beginning to grow light. I followed the road the soldiers were taking and came to a very steep slope. It was like a mountain of ice, and the soldiers went sliding down it on their knees. Loth to do the same, I made a detour and got there safely.'

The decision to have IV, I and III Corps leave Smolensk at one-day intervals, Caulaincourt's thinking, 'shows how far the Emperor was deluding himself as to the army's situation and the dangers menacing it'. Above all the scheme is causing dangerous gaps to arise between the various corps. Already a first gap has opened up between the Guard and the Army of Italy. Leaving Smolensk in the early hours of 15 November, Eugène had delayed IV Corps' departure 'a good hour' by gathering all his non-walking wounded into one place and providing them with victuals. 'A wise measure', in Cesare de Laugier's eyes; but one that gives rise to an agonising scene. The non-leavers had 'clenched their fists in despair, flung their arms round our legs, sobbed, screamed, clung to us, begged us to find them some means of transport: '"For pity sake don't leave us to the Cossacks, to be burnt alive, be butchered as soon as they come in. Comrades, comrades, friends, for pity sake take us with you!"

'We go off with heavy hearts. Whereupon these unfortunates roll on the ground, lashing about as if possessed.'

Staggering to his feet before dawn after a sleepless night even colder than yesterday's, Griois had been horrified to discover he was half-blind from the smoke of his campfire. And when his last handful of guns had left the shattered city he'd been 'obliged to take the arm of a gunner' – he knows them all by name – 'who guided me'. After a while his sight had cleared, but he's still feeling very weak: 'the reverberation of the [light on the] snow and the prickings of an infinity of little needles of ice filling the air' make his eyes smart.

IV Corps too has abandoned most of its women 'whose sufferings only augmented our own'. And the groans and screams of deserted comrades, resounding in Cesare de Laugier and his comrades' ears 'a good part of the route', will only be forgotten 'at the thought of the new perils already surrounding us on all sides'. Pursuing its way in silence along the icy Krasnoië road, all he hears is

'the sound of blows to the horses or their drivers' curt oaths, frequent when they find they're on an icy slope they can't cope with. Again, despite the drivers' admirable zeal, were having to abandon vehicles, ammunition wagons and guns. Expiring horses covered the road, and entire teams, succumbing to exhaustion, fell all at once on top of each other. All the defiles the vehicles hadn't been able to get through were filled with arms, helmets, shakos and cuirasses; stove-in trunks, half-open valises, and clothes of all sorts were scattered in the valley.'

Laugier's shaken to see how the whole Krasnoië road is

'littered with ammunition wagons, carriages, abandoned guns no one has thought of blowing up, destroying, spiking or burning. Here and there, dying horses, weapons, all kinds of effects, pillaged trunks, eviscerated packs are showing us the road followed by those ahead of us. We also see trees at whose foot men have tried to light a fire; and around their trunks, transformed into funerary monuments, the victims have expired after futile efforts to get warm.[9] The waggoners are using the corpses, numerous at every step, to pave the road by filling in ditches and ruts. At first we shudder at the sight; then we get used to it. Anyone who hasn't good horses and faithful servants with him will almost certainly never see his own country again. Far from exciting our sensibility, such horrors just hardened our hearts.'

The Guardia d'Onore's Colonel Battaglia having died on the eve of leaving Smolensk, Major Bastida has detailed Cesare de Laugier to the 'dangerous and most painful task of bringing up the regiment's rear and making sure no one straggles' – a task which 'furthermore made me a spectator of all our column's misfortunes'. Leaving Smolensk at the very last moment to chivvy on his vélites,

'and mounted on my exhausted horse, I'd hastened to rejoin. But not being rough-shod against the ice he kept falling. I saw Cossacks appearing to the left and on the heights around Smolensk and was afraid I'd become their prey.'

One of these falls dislodges the entire saddle and saddlecloth, but with 'hands numb with cold and freezing feet' he manages to fix them as best he can and starts 'running, holding my horse to get warm'. At every step the poor beast slithers on the ice which drags him this way and that and opens sores on his swollen feet. Catching up at long last with the column, Laugier entrusts his horse to a sapper named Maffei, with orders not to let him out of his sight. And that's the last Laugier sees of his horse or his few possessions.

Bivouacking for the night at 'the miserable village of Lubnia' where Napoleon, during the advance, had celebrated his 43rd birthday,[10] Eugène's staff occupy one of its two remaining half-demolished shacks, the Viceroy the other:

'Under a wretched shed, hardly covered, a score of officers, jumbled up with as many servants, crouched around a little fire. Behind us all the horses were ranged in a semi-circle to serve us as a shelter against the furiously blowing wind. The smoke was so thick we could hardly even see the faces close to the fire, busy puffing at the cinders where their food was cooking. The rest, wrapped up in furs and mantles and flat out on their bellies on the ground, were lying on top of each other so as not to feel the cold so much, and they only stirred in order to abuse anyone who trod on them; to curse the horses, which were moaning; or snuff out a fire some sparks had lit in their furs.'

Griois sees Eugène's hardly better lodged than his officers, and respects him for it:

'I found him lying on a wooden bench in a little partly destroyed cabin, the best preserved even so in the village. We passed a terrible night. An icy wind and whirlwinds of snow nothing protected us from kept us awake all the time; anyway the terrible cough Colonel Fiéreck was being tormented by would have been enough to prevent us from getting a wink of sleep.'

In the early part of the night they hear a man groaning outside the shack, 'but not one of us gave a thought to alleviating him by bringing him closer to our fire. To make a place for him would have been to disturb ourselves. And why take pity just on him, rather than on so many others no less wretched?'

MOVEMENTS OF THE VARIOUS CORPS, 13–20 NOVEMBER

Date	Guard	IV Corps	I Corps	III Corps	VIII Corps, V Corps and Vistula Legion
13	In Smolensk	Reaches Smolensk	Enters Smolensk		Leave Smolensk
14	Leaves Smolensk	Rearguard action on heights north of Smolensk	At Smolensk	Fights rearguard action east of Smolensk	At Korytnia
15	At Korytnia	Leaves Smolensk	At Smolensk		Vistula Legion ejects Russians from Krasnoië
16	Evening: reaches Krasnoië; Young Guard fights night action	At Korytnia Breaks through to Krasnoië at night by *ruse de guerre*	Leaves Smolensk		At Krasnoië
17	Young Guard's battle to defend Krasnoië	In support of Young Guard	Breaks through to Krasnoië and forms new rearguard	At Kortynia	Leave Krasnoië with Treasure followed by Guard
18	Marching for Orsha	Marching for Orsha	Marching for Orsha	Ney, held up by Russians, marches for Dnieper and crosses by night	Reach Orsha
19	Marching for Orsha	Marching for Orsha	Marching for Orsha	Rearguard actions against Cossacks	At Orsha
20	At Orsha	At Orsha	Reaches Orsha	Early morning; Ney reaches Orsha	Leave Orsha for Toloczin and Bobr

CHAPTER 10

THE GUARD STRIKES BACK

A crucial decision – the Young Guard's night action – 'he was the worst man I've known, and the cruellest' – Eugène refuses to surrender – Colonel Klicki has his wits about him – the Iron Marshal loses his bâton – 'a snail, carrying my all on my back' – 'how about some apricots in brandy?' – the Young Guard's heroic battle – Davout breaks through – François saves the Eagle – 390 heroic Dutchmen – a courteous captor – massacre of the wounded – Kutusov talks to Intendant Puybusque – 'the baggage taken was enormous'

Having failed to exploit Napoleon's five-day halt at Smolensk, Kutusov is belatedly lining up some 90,000 men 'including 500 guns, well-mounted like their cavalry in strength'[1] along the low hills south of the Krasnoïe road. A totally out-matching force, that is, to cut off IV, I and III Corps.

Napoleon is faced with a crucial choice. What shall the Guard do? Abandon the rest of the army, hurry on to Orsha and seize the Dnieper bridges? Or make a stand that'll give Eugène, Davout, perhaps even Ney, a chance to catch up? Not once during the campaign has the Guard 'given' (*donné*), as the expression goes. Some people like von Kalckreuth are even wondering whether by dint of almost never fighting its pampered regiments haven't become 'mere parade ground troops'. Their 'only achievement in this campaign', Hencken thinks, has been 'to impress the enemy' – for instance at Borodino. Even there it hadn't been unleashed.[2] This is why the Young and Old Guards together still have upwards of 20,000 men,[3] and it's against just such a moment as this they've been conserved. They're going to teach the Russians a lesson.

Evidently Napoleon's plan is to stake all on a lightning blow with the entire Guard:

'Drouot's strong batteries had been placed in position, and everything was prepared for battle and he didn't doubt he'd succeed, believing, as in happier times, that his luck would hold. He was full of confidence in his veterans, whom he'd doubtless been keeping in reserve for just such a desperate venture.'

But prudence prevails. Caulaincourt sees him return to what, apparently, has been his original plan. A two-phase operation, more efficacious and less risky, especially in view of the hazards of a night operation. 'There's nothing more terrible than a battle at night,' Bourgogne knows, 'when fatal mistakes can often occur.'

That evening Napoleon sends for Rapp. Tells him:

'"We've Russian infantry quite close. So far they've not been so audacious. At midnight you must attack them at bayonet-point. Surprise them, and take away their taste for coming so close to my headquarters."'

Rapp has all the Young Guard[4] placed at his disposal. He returns to his headquarters 'a miserable house in the town, thatched with straw' and is just about to plan the movement when Narbonne appears; 'His Majesty doesn't want you to get yourself killed in this affair,' he tells him.

Mortier, the Young Guard's commander, is evidently more expendable. And it's he who's to take over in chief, while Roguet executes the actual movement. On guard outside Roguet's headquarters with fifteen Fusiliers-Grenadiers, Sergeant Bourgogne is congratulating himself on his 'luck to be under cover and near a fire we'd just lit' and has just put his men 'into a stable' when everything 'turns out quite otherwise'. The regiment is to take part in the night operation, together with Roguet's Grenadiers, the Fusiliers-Chasseurs, Voltigeurs and Tirailleurs. Although the Young Guard includes many veterans like Bourgogne and Paul Bourgoing of the 5th Tirailleurs, very few of its 18-year-old conscripts have ever been under fire before; and en route for Moscow thousands, for instance from the Flankers, have died of sheer physical exhaustion.[5] But at 9 p.m. comes the order to

'surprise and seize the villages of Chirkowa, Maliewo and Bouianowo, about three miles along the Smolensk–Krasnoïe road and occupied over a distance of 400 *toises* [about 800 yards][6] by sizeable forces of infantry, artillery and Cossacks.'

'At 11 p.m.,' Bourgogne goes on, 'a few detachments were sent ahead to find out exactly where the Russians were. We could see their campfires in the two villages they were holding.' At about 1 a.m. Roguet comes to him and says 'in his Gascon accent:

'"Sergeant, leave a corporal and four men here in charge of my quarters and the few things I still have left. Yourself, go back to the bivouac and rejoin the regiment with your guard." To tell the truth I was very much disgusted at this order. I don't mean I was afraid of fighting, but I terribly begrudged the time lost for sleep.'

It's a pitch-black night. But Roguet's able to adjudge the enemy's position 'by the direction of his fires. The villages,' he'll recall, 'crowned a fine plateau behind a deep ravine. I formed up three columns of attack.' Some time between 1 and 2 a.m.[7] they get the order *'En avant! Marche!'*

'We began to move forward in three columns – the Fusiliers-Grenadiers and the Fusiliers-Chasseurs in the centre, the Tirailleur and Voltigeur companies to right and left. The cold was as intense as ever. With the snow up to our knees we had the greatest difficulty in marching across the fields.'

Trudging through it at the end of his rank Bourgogne hears several of his men muttering that they hope this'll be the end of their sufferings – they can't struggle on any longer. Roguet goes on: 'Noiselessly, the units to right and left got as close as they could to the enemy masses. Then, at a signal given by me in the centre, we, without firing, flung ourselves on the Russians at bayonet-point.'

Evidently the surprise isn't complete, for Bourgogne sees some Russian units have had time to form up:

'On our right a long line of infantry opened a murderous fire on us. On our left their heavy cavalry was made up of cuirassiers in white uniforms with black cuirasses. After half an hour of this, we found ourselves in the midst of the Russians.'

Roguet:

'Immediately the two wings engaged toward Bouianowo and Chirkowa. In the middle of the night it was so intensely cold that the Russians were exposed even in their shelters.'

The Fusiliers-Grenadiers, it seems, have no experience of Russian 'resurrection men'.[8] As the Young and Middle Guard move forward they pass over several hundred 'dead or seriously wounded' Russians lying on the snow:

'These men now jumped up and fired at us from behind, so we had to about-face to defend ourselves. Unluckily for them, a battalion in the rear came up from behind, so that they were taken between two fires. In five minutes not one of them was left alive.'

But neither are the Fusiliers-Grenadiers by any means unscathed:

'Poor Béloque was the first man we lost. At Smolensk he'd foretold his own death. A ball struck his head, and killed him on the spot. He was a great favourite with us all, and in spite of the indifference we were now feeling about everything, we were really sorry to lose him.'

'The fleeing Russians,' Roguet is noticing, 'though surprised and not knowing where to defend themselves' are 'moving from their right to their left.' As for the cuirassiers to Bourgogne's left,

'though they howled like wolves to excite one another, they didn't dare attack. The artillery was in the centre, pouring grapeshot at us. All this didn't in the least hold up our impetus. In spite of the firing and the number of our men who were falling, we charged on into their camp, where we made rightful havoc with our bayonets.'

By now, Bourgogne goes on,

'the Russians who were stationed farther off had had time to arm themselves and come to their comrades' help. This they did by setting fire to their camp and the two nearby villages. We fought by the light of the fires. The right- and left-hand columns had passed us, and entered the enemy's camp at its two ends, whereas our column had taken it in the middle.'

Divided and in disorder, the Russians have only had time to throw down their arms and fling their guns into the lake at the head of the Krasnoïe stream. And Roguet, judging it unwise to pursue the mass of fugitives too far in the dark, orders a cease-fire. But to order it in the darkness and confusion is one thing, to obtain it another. By now the Fusiliers-Grenadiers, in one of the burning villages the Russians are trying to get out of but can't, and 'blinded by the glare of the fires' have lost all idea of their whereabouts. And when some Russians who're on the verge of being roasted alive in a burning farmhouse offer to surrender, the Fusiliers-Grenadiers' adjutant-major, too, orders the cease-fire. But French blood is up, and a wounded sapper, 'sitting in the snow all stained with his blood', refuses:

'He even asked for more cartridges when he'd fired his own. The adjutant-major, seeing his orders disregarded, himself came over with a message from the colonel. But our men, now frantic, took no notice, and still went on firing.'

The trapped Russians, no less desperate, attempt a sortie,

'but our men forced them back. Unable to endure their situation, they made a second attempt. But scarcely had a few of their number reached the yard than the building collapsed on the rest, and more than 40 perished in the flames, those in the yard being crushed as well. When this was over we collected together our wounded and with loaded weapons gathered round the colonel, waiting for daybreak. All this time the rattle of musketry was going on continuously all round us, mingled with the groans of the wounded and dying.'

In the grey dawn Bourgogne helps a dying Russian to a more comfortable position. The man had tried to kill him, but in the nick of time he'd shot and badly wounded him, after which he'd been run through by adjutant-major Roustan's sword:

'All the houses in the village and the entire Russian camp were covered with half-burnt corpses. The Tirailleurs and Voltigeurs had lost more men than we had. After this bloody contest the Russians abandoned their positions, and we remained on the battlefield, but all the time staying on the *qui-vive*, unable either to get a moment's rest or even warm ourselves.'

Then, in the Fusiliers-Grenadiers' freezing bivouac, something very odd happens:

'After daybreak, while we were all talking together, Adjutant-Major Delaître came up. He was the worst man I've ever known and the cruellest, doing wrong for the mere pleasure of doing it. I don't think there was a man in the regiment who wouldn't have rejoiced to see him carried off by a bullet. We called him Peter the Cruel.'

But now Delaître begins to talk, and

'greatly to our surprise, seemed much troubled by Béloque's tragic death. "Poor Béloque!" he said. "I'm very sorry I ever behaved badly to him." Just then a voice said in my ear (*whose* voice I never knew): "He'll die very soon." Others heard it too. He seemed sincerely sorry for all his nasty behaviour to those under him, especially to us NCOs.'

It's this shock that is enabling Napoleon to wait for Eugène, for Davout, and – hopefully – even for Ney. It has also served notice on Kutusov that the name he's so afraid of is still really to be feared. The Imperial Guard, at least, can still bite back.

At crack of dawn IV Corps – 'scarcely 4,000 men under arms' – but 'in hope of being better off tomorrow night'[9] – makes haste to leave its icy bivouac at Lubnia. All Griois now possesses is his sole surviving change of shirt and, as a last possible recourse, a precious loaf of white bread given him at

Smolensk by General Desvaux, commander of the Guard Horse Artillery. Cesare de Laugier's doing his best to keep up with the slowly trudging column, when

'a man, passing close at a canter, knocks me over, and in my fall my cold sores open up. There I lie, stunned by the shock, mad with rage and realising how powerless I am, unable to stir. Two Italian soldiers who've fallen behind pick me up and lay me on the bank to the right of the road. I feel all my blood freezing, see death approaching, and gradually lose consciousness.'

But his luck holds. A Frenchman named Dalstein, also a captain-adjutant-major and serving with the Italians, sees him lying there; brings him to; encourages him; forces him to get up and come along with him.

All that morning IV Corps marches slowly on without meeting any particular obstacles. 'The weather was fine,' Griois goes on,

'the cold less keen, and the sun, despite the pallor of its rays, was cheering up the snow-covered countryside a little. It was about midday. I'd dismounted at a place where the debris of carriages, weapons and effects showed there'd been a recent hurrah, and while walking onwards I was running my eye over some papers I'd picked up, when two or three roundshot whistled past my ears. They came from a little wood, not far to our left. We saw the puffs of smoke but as yet no unit had appeared. At this unexpected attack everyone rallied to the nearest platoons – but just at the moment no one was expecting to run into the enemy. There was little order in our column, which was widely spread out over the terrain.'

Griois immediately jumps on to his horse and joins Eugène, 'who was quite a way ahead of his troops and waiting for them', accompanied, Labaume says,

'by his staff, some companies of sappers and some Sailors of the Royal Guard who were going on a couple of miles ahead of the divisions.'

Soon Cossacks appear from the woods and cover the high ground to right and left. The gunfire multiplies. Then – Labaume gives the time as 3 p.m. –

'the Viceroy catches sight of the disbanded and isolated men who've been marching ahead of him and occupying the road for a great distance running back. They're being attacked by Cossacks.'

Among those who come galloping back is General Count Ornano, now without any of his Bavarian cavalry, but who's 'been wounded or thrown off his horse'.[10] They'd found the road barred by a body of troops. Eugène turns his horse, gallops back to his main body, halts its column and, haranguing it, explains what a critical position it's in. Immediately, says Cesare de Laugier,

'all who've a weapon, though devoured by fever or annihilated by the cold, come and take their place in the ranks. And the Viceroy deploys his battalions.'

He also does what he did at the Wop, but this time with greater difficulty:

156

namely, scrapes together some ranks of mounted officers to look like cavalry, von Muraldt among them:

'But a few roundshot falling among us broke us up. After which, in open order. we rode over the snowy icy field, trying to find a hollow to protect us from the enemy's fire.'

Meanwhile chief-of-staff Guilleminot has assembled into companies all the advance party of isolated men who still have weapons, so that together with his sappers and sailors they add up to 1,200 men. 'The disbanded men, administrators and even the women' – evidently some haven't been left behind at Smolensk – 'come pressing in on them from all around. Superior officers who have no men are seen proudly joining the ranks.' The sailors insist on being commanded by one of their own officers, 'but every other platoon is commanded by a general'. One against ten, they're being bombarded by Russian guns and musketry from the surrounding high ground.

What to do? To press on is impossible. After a council of war, Guilleminot, seeing no sign of the main body yet coming to his aid, decides to fall back on to it. Forms up his little force in square – and marches straight through the intervening Russians!

'At first the Russians, stupefied, open up a path for them. Then call out to them to halt. Their only reply is resolutely to continue their march in a disdainful silence, only presenting the points of their weapons. Whereupon all the enemy fire opens up on them at once; and after a few paces half this heroic column litters the ground. The remainder pursue their way in good order – a truly incredible outcome for a force composed of such heterogeneous elements.'

They're welcomed with the Italians' joyful shouts. Seeing that the road passes through a wood, Eugène, to fend off the Cossacks, orders Guilleminot to collect the disbanded men in it, together with his sapper companies and the marines. At that moment, according to Laugier and Ségur,

'a Russian officer, Colonel Prince Kudacheff, Miloradovitch's ADC, preceded by a trumpeter sounding for a parley, comes forward towards the Viceroy's group. The Emperor and the Imperial Guard, he tells them, have been defeated the previous evening:

'"You're surrounded by 20,000 Russians, supported by Kutusov's entire army," he says. "Nothing remains for you but to surrender on the honourable conditions Miloradovitch proposes."

'Already several officers, to prevent the Viceroy being recognised, are going forward to answer. But he thrusts them aside:

'"Hurry back to where you've come from," he tells the spokesman, "and tell whoever's sent you that if he has 20,000 men, we've got 80,000!" And the Russian, at the sight of this handful of such proud men, astounded at such a reply, retired.'[11]

'At the sound of the guns,' Griois goes on,

'the troops hastened their steps, and as they turned up the prince formed them up in line of battle. Detached, my gunless gunners act as tirailleurs and draw up the guns which still remained to IV Corps – i.e., the two or three belonging to the Broussier division, served by my regiment, and six or eight of the Italian Guard's.'

Meanwhile Eugène has placed the Royal Guard in the centre of IV Corps, the 2nd [14th] Division (comprising what's left of the 2nd and 4th Battalions of the Spanish Joseph-Napoleon Regiment)[12] to the left of the road, and the 1st [13th] Division to the right, with Pino's [15th] Division in reserve, all in squares. Attacked first by cavalry, then bombarded by a much stronger artillery than he can muster – by now Eugène only has two guns left – he 'sends the Royal Guard to attack the Russians' right flank'. Repulsed by 'terrible' grapeshot, decimated and forced to retire, it again forms square to drive off an attack by dragoons against its left flank. The Russian masses are far too great to be fought off without artillery. Even the two Italian guns only manage to fire a few rounds 'for lack of ammunition'. Whereupon Eugène 'orders [his ADC] Adjutant-Commandant Del Fante, followed by 200 volunteers, to advance along the highway to rejoin and cover the retreating 1st Division.' Del Fante succeeds, but falls, seriously wounded:

'M. de Villebranche, an auditor of the Council of State, seeing him get up all covered in blood, offers him his arm and helps him drag himself to a wood where there are some disbanded men. At that moment a roundshot hits the brave Del Fante, shatters his shoulders and decapitates M. de Villebranche.'[13]

All his men are massacred. 'As for the gunners, they let themselves be killed at their guns rather than surrender.' Having run into such a wall of fire, Labaume says, Eugène is forced

'to pretend to wish to prolong the fighting on our left by re-animating and uniting the 14th [Broussier's] Division. And upon the Russians concentrating the greater part of their forces to roll it up, the Prince ordered all who remained to profit by the failing daylight to slip away to the right with the Royal Guard.'

Despite the Russians' huge numerical superiority and considerable losses, IV Corps flushes them out of the woods.

'We gained ground against them. But new enemies appeared, outflanking us on all sides. Their crossfire and the charges of their cavalry, which we had none of our own to oppose, caused us to suffer a lot.'

But November days are short, and by 4 p.m. the light is failing:

'We kept up the fight until nightfall without being driven in. It was high time. One more hour of daylight and we'd probably have been wiped out.'

All this happens so near to Krasnoïe that Napoleon, 'uneasy at IV Corps' delayed arrival' but hearing the gunfire, has ordered his ADC General Durosnel to take 600 men – two squadrons of the Polish Guard Lancers and a battalion of Old Guard light infantry, with two guns, and facilitate

Eugène's breakthrough. Just outside Krasnoië Durosnel runs into Cossacks and sees masses of Russian cavalry 'marching to the left of the road to manoeuvre more easily'. Forms square. Fires a few shots. Sends off three of his Polish lancers to circumvent the Krasnoië ravine and tell Eugène to do the same. And marches on. But then he too runs into such massive opposition that, realising he's done all he can, he beats a retreat back to Krasnoië:

'The Emperor was perturbed at the thought of part of his Guard being in action and cut off from the main body of the army.'

Durosnel gets back just as Latour-Maubourg and all that's left of the cavalry is about to set off to his relief. Delighted at this detachment's safe return, Napoleon invites Durosnel to supper.

By now some of Pino's Italians and Dalmatians, waiting behind as rearguard, are feeling so discouraged that they refuse to leave their campfires. So do the fragments of the improvised 'cavalry':

'In vain we were told the crucial thing was to try to deceive the Russians as to our camp's position – our most urgent need was for fire to protect us against the biting cold. Our situation was desperate anyway. We were expecting to be taken prisoner on the morrow and our only hope lay in a reasonable capitulation. Our despondency was also the worse for a rumour that the Emperor had left Krasnoië with his Guard, abandoned us to our fate.'

The order goes round: 'No campfires!' Even so, IV Corps is soon in trouble again with Cossacks who can easily pick out its black mass against the snow. And fires, though forbidden, glimmer faintly, so that in the grim freezing night one or another roundshot keeps falling among them. 'The enemy', Griois resumes,

'was only 600 yards off. He was occupying the road we must follow and was only waiting for morning to bring about our final defeat. Overwhelmed by cold and hunger, regarding retreat as impossible and our loss as certain, we were anxiously waiting to see what course the Viceroy would adopt, when, towards 10 p.m., the order was passed down *sotto voce* to form the ranks and get going, and Prince Eugène, at the head of the Royal Guard, followed by some debris of [the other] battalions, marched off into the night. There was no need to recommend silence; each of us realised it unbidden.'

Eventually the secret night march gets under way:

'In this march across the fields, over thick snow, in profound darkness, one hardly heard some raucous but stifled coughs the men couldn't suppress, and the clickings of their weapons against each other during their frequent falls.'

For the second time in two days the Italians have to leave their wounded behind, this time lying on the blood-stained snow:

'A former vélite named Vignali, whose comrade I'd been when I'd entered that unit, had had his side shattered by a roundshot. I'd have given my life to save him, but there was no vehicle nor anyone willing to help me carry him. Each movement I made to help him caused him a frightful spasm of pain. "It's impossible," he said. "I'll never move again. Do me the kindness of finishing me off with a shot, or pass your sabre through my body so I die instantly."'

But this is more than Cesare can bring himself to do. Exhausted by his efforts, he's obliged to leave him: 'My eyes close as I remember it, I still fancy I can hear his sad complaints, his voice which broke my heart.'[14] By now almost nothing is left of those 'scions of the best families in Italy', the once ardent Vélites of the Guardia d'Onore. Griois too has to 'abandon the little baggage and artillery we still possessed'. The column hasn't gone very far when

'an enemy sentinel, placed at some distance to our left, gave us the *Qui vive?* in Russian. We'd been detected, and each of us made ready to give a hot reception to the hurrah which would doubtless soon fall on us.'

Labaume – he can only have been a few feet away – takes up the thread of Griois' account:

'Colonel Klicki,[15] who knew Russian, was marching at the head of our column when he was halted by an enemy scout who, in Russian, called out to him *"Qui vive?"* This didn't trouble this intrepid officer in the least. Going straight up to the sentry, he said to him in his own language: "Shut up, you fool. Can't you see we're Ouvarov's corps and that we're off on a secret expedition?" At these words the soldier fell silent and let us pass under cover of night.'

But now the moon's up, brightly illumining the wide snowy expanses. Griois and everyone else is sure the Russians must see them:

'In its bright light, which in any other circumstances would have been so useful to us but was increasing our perils, didn't the enemy easily see our column standing out against the snow's whiteness?'

In fact, Cossacks do approach, but 'probably believing we were troops of their own nation' don't interfere. And in the dim dawn light the Italian infantry again sets off, 'without knowing whither'. Hurriedly its few remaining mounted officers attach themselves to it,

'following the dark line winding away across the snow. For a while this march went on in perfect silence. After an hour or two we, after a left turn, rejoined the main Krasnoïe road, leaving the enemy behind us. A discharge of musketry received us at the town's approaches. It was an outpost placed out ahead of the Young Guard's bivouac that, taking us for an enemy, had fired at us. We declared ourselves and reached the foot of the rather steep hill where Krasnoïe's situated.'

The weather, it seems, is thawing slightly – the ice on the Losima, flowing through the ravine, keeps breaking. Although Griois' horse gets across all right, his adjutant-major Lenoble's doesn't:

'The ice broke beneath him and the poor animal, stuck in the mud up to his breast, struggled for over half an hour, and after we'd tried in vain to save him we had to abandon him, to the great regret of his master, who lost in a puddle of water a handsome and good horse which the

Above: A Cossack *pulk* prepares to swoop from high ground. Their blood-curdling 'hurrahs!' (the Cossack word for 'death') caused the French to call them sarcastically '*les hourrassiers*'. Though the least show of resistance sufficed to drive them off, they starved the Grand Army to death by forcing it to keep to the road. Lithograph by Engelmann after a drawing by Lebach.

Below: Nothing had changed on the field of Borodino except the aspect of the dead. The Belgian captain François Dumonceau saw that the former redoubts, 'covered in snow and standing out white against a murky horizon, were no longer visible except as shapeless hillocks. This plain, once so noisy and animated, was now only a vast solitude.' Engraving by Faber du Faur.

Above: The Battle of Viazma, 3 November. Carabinier Sergeant Vincent Bertrand of the 7th Light Infantry was in Davout's rearguard, seen in the background. The church [right] must have been the one where Napoleon, during the advance, had insisted on Guard grenadiers attending the bishop of Viazma's funeral obsequies. Oil painting by V. Adam.

Opposite page, top: Witebsk. Hopping about on one leg, its governor, F. R. Pouget, found it impossible to defend, certainly not with the 900 'marauders, stragglers and men out of hospitals' at his disposal: 'the refuse of all the armies, the most furtive, dirtiest and worst soldiers in the world. Clad in rags and shreds of clothing, without either officers or NCOs, most of them had never seen the enemy.'

Right: 'En route near Pnewa, 8 November. Do you recognize the man in the grey coat,' the artist Major Faber du Faur asks us in doggerel verse, 'that gleaming meteor who so often had led us to war and victory and who alone was wearing a fur-brimmed cap? It's the Emperor!' – 'Yesterday I'd been the conqueror of the world', Napoleon would tell his Council when he got back to Paris, 'and commanding the finest army of modern times. Next day nothing was left of all that.'

Opposite page, top: Smolensk: 'The heights it stood on', J. T. James would see in 1813, 'shewed the domes of the venerable cathedral majestically over their summit. But this building stood almost single amidst heaps of ruins. The main street, the great square, all had suffered the same destruction.' *Views of Russia, Sweden and Poland,* 1824.

Above: Württemberg gunners destroying most of the cannon that by dint of great efforts they had dragged as far as Smolensk (12 November). One of Smolensk's 32 towers can be glimpsed in the background. Next year J. T. James would see French and allied artillery of all calibres 'beginning with the heaviest' on display outside the Kremlin. Engraving by Faber du Faur.

Left: 'Between Korytnia and Krasnoïe, 15 November.' After spiking their last four 6-pounders, the remains of the 25th (Württemberg) division and a horde of unarmed men and women forced their way past Miloradovitch's 'dark lines' to join the Imperial Guard at Krasnoïe. Engraving by Faber du Faur.

Right: The second battle of Krasnoïë, 17/18 November. The anonymous artist has focused on the wreckage of the baggage train, pillaged by Cossacks. It was here Davout lost his bâton – only for someone to filch it mysteriously during the victory celebrations at St Petersburg! Nineteenth-century steel engraving.

Below: Grenadier Pils' on-the-spot watercolour of Marshals Oudinot and Victor on a gloomy overcast November afternoon as they try – but signally fail – to coordinate II and IX Corps' movements.

Right: Portrait, painted on a mug, of Captain Franz Roeder of the Hessian Footguards. A temperamental stickler for justice and humanity, he wrote the most vividly personal of all surviving diaries. By kind permission of Miss Helen Roeder.

Opposite page: Marshal Oudinot, Duke of Reggio. On St Helena, Napoleon would call him *"un buon' uomo ma po di testa"* ('a decent sort of a fellow but not much brains'). He received his second wound of the campaign at the Berezina. Already his young duchess had defied the imperial ban on any woman crossing the Niemen and had come to Vilna (Vilnius) to nurse him.

Left: As a prisoner-of-war in England, little voltigeur Jean-Marc Bussy had nearly been sent to serve with the British army in India but escaped back to France, only to be sent to Russia in the 3rd Swiss Regiment.

Above: Another Swiss, the famous military theorist Henri de Jomini. Briefly town governor of Smolensk, he was regarded by his superior at Vilna, the Dutchman Dirk van Hogendorp, as an insufferable popinjay. Another Dutchman, Major H. P. Everts, however, regarded him as 'an officer absolutely equal to the situation'. Berthier disliked him. Miniature by Migneret.

The émigré Count L. V. L. Rochechouart served with Tchitchakov's army. He played a part in wresting the Borissow bridge from Dombrowski's 17th (Polish) division, only to be almost trapped in Borissow town by Oudinot's advance guard and swept away by Doumerc's Cuirassiers on 18 November.

Marshal Michel Ney, Duke of Elchingen, Prince of the Moscova, hero of the retreat. By rejoining at Orsha with the remains of his rearguard 'he had executed', wrote Captain François – the 'Dromedary of Egypt' – 'one of the finest and most courageous movements ever attempted by so feeble a corps. It would be to show oneself lacking in the esteem every military man ought to have for Marshal Ney not to recognize his rare talents.' But Colonel Montesquiou de Fezensac was shocked at his lack of feeling for others' sufferings.

Below: Marshal Macdonald, commander of X Corps, two-thirds of which were Prussians. He was of Jacobite ancestry. In late December his Prussian subordinate General Yorcke signed a convention of neutrality with the enemy that triggered off a Prussian rising against the French.

Above: General Count de Lorencez, Oudinot's chief-of-staff. They had married two sisters on the eve of the campaign. Lorencez strongly defends Oudinot's strategies and handling of the preliminaries to the Berezina crossing.

enemy's fire had so often respected. Half way up the hill we met the Guard artillery, Colonel Drouot at its head, on its way to take up position on the Smolensk road we were arriving by.'
General Triaire, commanding Eugène's rearguard, keeps halting and facing about. As usual, the Cossacks don't dare attack. Half an hour after the wreckage of IV Corps has joined up with the Young Guard a mile and a half outside Krasnoïe, Triaire's men finally catch up,
'and you can imagine our joyful surprise, when without realising how it had happened, we suddenly caught sight of a town lit up by bivouac fires and immediately afterwards of the Imperial Guard's familiar bearskins.'
In fact the whole market town's a blaze of light:
'There were twenty times as many people in it than it could contain. Also, the brightness of the lights shining out through each house's doorways and windows, the noise the soldiers were making, the considerable number of those less happy ones who had had to camp out of doors,'
all this at once removes any thoughts Griois and three of his fellow-officers may have had of finding shelter. Worn out, shivering to death, they slip in among the crowd on the market place
'near a bivouac of élite gendarmes [headquarters police], where several assembled beams of wood made up a sparkling fire. The expression on the faces of the gendarmes as they saw four obviously suffering and needy officers approach was hardly encouraging. But it wasn't the moment to be sensitive, and despite their patent ill will we occupied the ends of the beams. We could hardly even see the fire, but in revenge the wind blew all its smoke at us.'
How inhospitable can one be? The gendarmes spread out and consume whole cooking pots full of soup, round off their meal with ample coffee, tea and wine. 'Such was the degree of insensibility we'd reached,' adds Griois forgivingly, 'we, in their place, would probably done the same.' Only when his servant turns up with a *konya* can they mix themselves some rye flour and scarcely boiled water before wrapping themselves up in their ragged furs and getting a little sleep.

Davout too must be rescued. Perhaps also Ney. But just how far in the rear is I Corps and how big is the gap between them? No one knows.
Davout too had delayed leaving Smolensk at dawn on 16 November. Adjudging it 'vitally important to provision his troops in order to prevent them deserting, he hadn't regarded it as his duty to hurry'. And when I Corps had marched out it, too, had dragged with it masses of stragglers. Outside 'the same ramparts as earlier had witnessed our triumph' Lejeune had seen 'an immense quantity of guns, all parked and having to be abandoned to the enemy' – those taken from Sauvage's regiment perhaps among them. Along the road to Lubnia 'entirely covered with guns and ammunition no one had had time to spike or blow up', through the cluttered defiles, marching, riding, slithering or trundling over the corpses of predecessors which would 'have entirely obstructed the road if they hadn't

so often been used to fill up ditches and ruts' its chief-of-staff Lejeune sees 'trees receding into the distance, at which soldiers had tried to light a fire' but died while doing so. 'We saw them in their dozens around some green branches they'd vainly tried to ignite.'

Once I Corps had been 'a rival to the Guard'. But since the Viazma débâcle its morale is prey to 'an egoism not yet seen in the French armies'. And when a swarm of Don Cossacks swoops on its baggage train its drivers do as IHQ's had done – 'unharness their horses and make off with the most precious contents'. Among vehicles lost in this way is Davout's personal wagon, containing his Marshal's bâton, clad in purple velvet and beswarmed with imperial gold bees. Also a now wholly redundant map of India.[16]

One of the fugitives who tries to rejoin 'across fields, woods and precipices', with his two remaining wagons ('naturally enough, seeing they each contained part of my resources') – one his unit's accounts wagon, the other the property of his colonel – is Lieutenant *N. J. Sauvage*, of the Train.[17] After an hour and a half he meets up with his 'most zealous protector and most faithful companion' Captain Houdart:

'Like many others he'd been relieved of the vehicles he'd been trying to save. All his booty was his two horses and a little portmanteau. More fortunate than myself, he'd extracted from one wagon a little barrel containing almost a gallon of brandy I'd been keeping in reserve since Moscow. At our first encounter we looked each other in the eye without knowing what to say. Each looked to the other like a fox who'd eaten his hen.'

Ever since Doroghobouï Sauvage has foreseen that he'll lose his effects . So he too is troubled. What upsets him most is 'the loss of victuals all the gold in the world couldn't replace'. After a couple of swigs the two Train officers have just joined the ever-swelling column of isolated men when, noticing that the plain to their left is covered with Russian cavalry, they, 'like everyone else who'd just abandoned more than 80 vehicles of all kinds containing a large part of the staff's treasures' hurriedly join 'two companies of engineer sappers, 140–150 men in all' already drawn up to the right of the road.

'Already formed up in square, they were being charged by four strong columns of Cuirassiers of the Russian Guard.'

Houdart manages to get inside the square with his two horses, but Sauvage has to abandon his *konya* Coco, counts himself lucky to get in at all, even though he's half crushed to death. Attacked on all its four faces, the gallant sappers fend off the four cuirassier squadrons,

'at the front rank's bayonet tips, which remained immovable, whilst the second and third ranks, though their muskets often misfired, kept up a well-nourished fire, flinging their murderous lead at the Muscovite troopers. These, unable to penetrate the square, and after briefly slashing at the defenceless mass, have to retire, leaving more than 50 of their corpses along the square's faces.'

Sauvage is just getting out of the square again when, 25 yards away, he sees his Coco calmly nibbling at a few blades of straw sticking up through the snow half way between it and the rallying Russian squadrons. He's just making a dash to grab her when he hears the order given for a new charge – thinks better of it – and nips back into the square, which had already got under way again. 'So in less than two hours I'd lost horse, portmanteau and trunks, and found myself reduced to the lot of the snails, unembarrassed and carrying my all on my back.'

Not all Davout's men are as resolute. Some individuals in a detached body that's making its way back in hopes of joining up with Ney even let themselves be enticed with the spoils of the Korytnia affray, 'brandy, peaches and liqueurs, biscuits from Reims, apricots in brandy, and spiced bread, all destined for the Emperor's table'. Among the happy captors of 'a wagon containing 60,000 gold napoleons' are four Russian officers – 'one had got drunk and lost all his share during the night!' But though some of Davout's men are enticed to lay down their arms, the head of the column, 'consisting of 300 or 400 officers' goes on its way 'to shouts of *'Vive Napoléon!'* The Russians couldn't help admiring their devotion, for their loss was certain.'

But it takes all sorts to make a world. Ever since Mojaisk, von Roos has had his eye on a certain German light infantry officer who, though dragging with him a whole wagon-load of tea – 'as one transports grain' – has only been letting his batman brew it out of used tea leaves! But now, Roos is glad to see, poetic justice is done: the Cossacks take both the German and his tea.

At Krasnoïe, meanwhile, the Guard has fallen in, ready to fall back at first glimpse of I Corps coming down the Smolensk road. This makes accommodation suddenly available for Griois and his three friends, who're able 'to enter one of the houses they were abandoning and get warm'. But the Red Lancers, ordered to be at Krasnoïe before daybreak, have left their hamlet, reach their rendezvous on the town's eastern outskirts, and find

'the Imperial Guard already drawn up under arms. Its fires had been doused. All we could make out in the profound darkness was confused crowds, motionless. A lot of men seemed to have caught colds, because all round us we heard dull coughing. Riding past them we were led ahead to the left of the town; then drew up in line of battle, facing the enemy, whose fires could be seen afar off on the other bank of the Losima stream.'

It's the whole Russian army, Dumonceau hears, that's in presence, outflanking the French position, whose front is the frozen brook. He also hears how yesterday, thanks to the Middle Guard's night action at Kontkovo, Eugène had broken through. It's still pitch dark.

The Hessian Footguards have been standing to arms since 3 a.m. Franz Roeder sees his own company (originally 442 men and 26 officers) is now down to only seven sergeants and 27 men, and the Prince's Own to 450 men and 23 officers. 'What a brigade of Guards, of only four battalions!' Yet, he consoles himself, 'we're much stronger than the French units!' And now the great moment – the climax, from his point of view, of the whole voluntarily undertaken campaign – has come. With the rest of the Young Guard the Hessians are to fall back along the Smolensk road and form Napoleon's battle front. Taking his personal dispositions Roeder writes a brief farewell letter to Sophie, his second wife, who's providing a mother for his and his deeply loved Mina's children. Generously he presents Prince Wittgenstein with a Göttingen sausage he's come by, 'so that he might have something for [the 20-year-old] Prince Emil[18] in the impending battle.' Then Roeder too, with many of his men dropping from fatigue, trudges back out into the snow along the Smolensk road, and 'after two hours', drawing up by battalions in line of battle to the left of the highway and suffering terribly from the cold and feeling drowsy 'probably from hunger' stands there until 8 a.m.

Paul de Bourgoing has fought in Spain and witnessed the appalling vestiges of Borodino. But this, he realises, is going to be his first real battle. And as ADC to General Delaborde, commander of the Young Guard's 1st Division, he must live up to his romantic role.[19] Before riding out of Krasnoïe on a captured mare he has re-christened Grisélidis, he has therefore shed his thick fox fur and entrusted it to his plucky little servant Victor:

'The battlefield was an immense snow-covered plain, crossed by a long and deep ravine, almost parallel with our front. On this escarpment's very steep bank, fading away in the distance, were placed, to our left, a Hessian brigade, by now reduced to 500 or 600 men. Our line extended for about a mile and a half almost parallel with this ravine, its right resting on Krasnoïe. In the centre, two regiments of the same strength, the 1st Tirailleurs and the 1st Voltigeurs. Then, to our right, a battalion of the Dutch [3rd] Grenadiers. Mortier, his staff, his escort of Red Lancers and his squadron of Portuguese cavalry commanded by the Marquis de Loulé had placed themselves out in front of this long line of infantry.'

To impress, if possible, the Russians the front has been

'extended out of all measure by placing our men in two ranks instead of three, thus presenting to the enemy a line of battle lengthened by one-third, but proportionately weakened in the event of a hand-to-hand fight'.

A few yards away from the Hessians are the Fusiliers-Grenadiers:

'To our left and behind us a ravine lay athwart the highway. This hollow sheltered all those who were near it. On our right were the Fusiliers-Chasseurs, with the head of their regiment a gunshot from the town. In front of us, 250 yards off, was a regiment of the Young Guard commanded by General Luron. Still farther to our right were the Old Grenadiers and Chasseurs, commanded by the Emperor, on foot.'

Chlapowski too, in his escort, sees how

'the whole mass was commanded by the Emperor himself, on foot. Walking with firm steps, as if on a grand parade day, he placed himself in the centre of battlefield, facing the enemy's batteries.'

Always, on days of battle, Dumonceau seems fated to enjoy some perfect vantage point. As it has grown light he has seen how the Young Guard's regiments, 'supported by a few guns' already in position, are fringing the Losima's semi-circular valley. And how, somewhat nearer the town's exit, the heads of the Old Guard infantry columns are drawn up. Out ahead of them, 'detached at the bottom of the ravine, at the village of Ouwarowo, whose defence had been confided to it and recognisable by their sky-blue greatcoats' over their white and scarlet uniforms, are the Dutch (3rd) Grenadiers.

Now an hour has gone by. And at about 9 a.m. Roeder sees some Russian units, mostly artillery, approach and draw up in front of his Hessians. All along the line it's the same. Artillery, artillery, artillery. The Russian plan is simply to wipe the Young Guard out with cannon fire. And after half an hour more the Russians open up at the Hessians across the snowy plain with 'about ten guns and two howitzers. We were especially exposed to the fire of a battery of some six pieces lying a little to the left, which never stopped firing at us and with great violence.'

Within half-range of the Russian artillery almost the first Fusilier-Grenadier to fall is the man who's always enjoyed making life hell for everyone else – the sadistic Adjutant-Major Delaître. 'He was leading his horse, the bridle over his right arm' and Bourgogne and two of his friends are immediately behind him:

'A roundshot had taken off his legs just above the knees and his long riding-boots. He fell without a cry. Didn't utter the least sound. We halted. Since he was blocking the path we were walking on we were forced to step over him to get on at all. I, the first to do so, looked at him as I passed on. His eyes were open and his teeth were chattering convulsively. I came closer to listen. Raising his voice, he said: "For God's sake take my pistols and blow my brains out!" No one dared do him this service. Without replying we went on our way – most luckily, as it happened: for we hadn't gone six yards before a second discharge carried off three of our men behind us, and killed the Adjutant-Major.'

Of all the cavalry regiments, the Polish Guard Lancers, Zalusky notices, are the most numerous. The rest, all that still have mounts, are standing beside their horses, 300–400 yards away behind them and their Dutch colleagues, 'in columns of fours. Like ourselves they were on the crest of the plateau, so as to stand out at a distance. Seen in flank they seemed to be a considerable mass of cavalry. Finally, ahead of them, to our left rear, was the Viceroy's corps, massed at the limit of the plateau, facing the point at which the road debouched along which the retarded corps should be arriving. All we could see of the enemy was some isolated horsemen in the distance, criss-crossing the vast snowy plain that spread out in front of us like an amphitheatre. As yet their masses were hidden from our gaze by some folds or other accidents of the terrain.'

It's on the Smolensk road and the high ground in front of Krasnoïe, of course, that Napoleon's and his staff's telescopes are focused. Surely the head of Davout's column must soon appear?

165

'But instead of seeing the Marshal arrive all we saw in the direction of Smolensk were deep columns of the Russian army. They were beginning to surround us to the south, while the Russian cavalry was already showing itself beside and behind us.'

'Under a sombre sky' Dumonceau sees the fighting commence over at Ouwarowo, 'against which the enemy directed reiterated efforts'. Now the Russian sharpshooters are 'advancing in great numbers toward the ravine, and they'd already carried a small village on our right flank'. At this Murat – he no longer has so much as a brigade of cavalry to command – rushes up to Chlapowski and orders him

'to follow with one squadron at the trot. The snow being deep, it was hard for our horses to do so. Halting with us in front of the little village the Russians had occupied, the King of Naples said to me: "Get into it!" This was an extraordinary order to give to cavalry, but we had to obey. As you'll believe, I didn't stroll through the village! Yet the snow, which almost came up to our horses' girths, didn't enable them to gallop.'

Chlapowski enters the hamlet by its main street:

'Russian chasseurs fired at us point-blank out of the houses' courtyards. Four lancers fell – Murat has them on his conscience. We also had six wounded. The Russians didn't flee, anyway they couldn't get out of the courtyards quickly enough to escape behind the hedges.'

The Polish lancer squadron emerges on its far side. Reforming his squadron in front of the Russian line 'about 600 paces away', Chlapowski notices

'a company of Guard Grenadiers that the Emperor, probably in view of Murat's extravagant order, was sending to seize the village. They occupied it without firing a shot. The Russians hardly had time to fire once. Some of them managed to withdraw by crossing the ravine. The others were taken prisoner.'

Returning to his starting-point, he finds Napoleon still

'on foot in front of his Guard. I came back to take my place near him. He was furious with Murat. Addressing me, he said: "How could you listen to that fool?" At each moment the shells were beginning to fall more thickly and were throwing several of our men to the ground. The Guard stood immobile as a wall. Our guns placed on the ravine's edge were hardly replying. The Emperor wasn't allowing them to, saying that the Russians were firing from too far off. But their *unicorns* were reaching us.'

If the Russian 'unicorns' – howitzers (Chlapowski explains) 'whose axle trees are decorated with unicorns' – are striking at unusually long howitzer range, it's thanks to their long barrels and 7–10-pounder calibre. Dumonceau, now standing by his horse, now 'running to and fro to keep warm', notes how much of the Russian artillery though 'mounted on sledges and manoeuvring swiftly' is, as usual, firing too high. Even so

'the Russians were smothering us with projectiles. Fortunately most of them ricocheted on some slight undulation of the terrain and then bounced well over our heads, or else, merely rolling up to us, were spotted and easily avoided. His shells exploded with a crash the more sonorous for the repercussions from the frozen ground.'

Having stood his youngsters up in a thin wall against this storm of shot and shell, Mortier has promised Napoleon to hold up the Russians until nightfall. Then, if Davout still hasn't appeared ...

More and more enemy guns, 'hastening to line the slope of the high ground opposite', are being brought into action. Never have the Hessian Footguards

'had to stand up to a cannonade of such long duration, not even at the great battles of Wagram and Aspern. I left my place for a moment to have a word with Captain Schwarzenau, and just before I got back to it a ball passed terribly close to Lieutenant Suckow,[20] who'd stepped in, killing outright the men who were standing in the second and third rank to the right. The first of these was my old cook, Heck, an honest fellow, who died a noble death. Another shot, passing close to my eyes, passed through a gap in the ranks without doing any damage but struck the hand off a drummer in the 4th Company. Unfortunately the Prince's Own, which was close to the Russian cavalry, had to form square, and in a short time it lost ten officers and 119 men dead and wounded.'

The French are utterly outgunned. And even some of those guns they do possess, Bourgogne says, 'were soon dismounted'. Everyone agrees that to stand up to short-range cannon fire without being able to reply is worst of all. Yet the Young Guard's 18-year-olds, now undergoing their baptism of fire, are suffering terribly: 'Our men died without budging.' At first the Russians bombard Delaborde's division with 30 guns; then with more and more:

'It was the first time our young soldiers had heard the sharp snoring sound of roundshot and the more accentuated sound of shells, ending their flight with the crash of an explosion. My old general passed slowly down the battle front saying: "Come on, my children, noses up! Now we're really smelling powder for the first time." Joyful shouts and *vivats* met these words.'

Yet despite his notable sangfroid in critical situations, even Delaborde's evidently beginning to be a bit worried. And rides over with his staff to join Mortier's:

'One of the old captains said that the three regiments placed out on the ravine had been put there "like a bone for the enemy to gnaw on".'

Feeling the battle must soon reach its crisis, Delaborde gallops off again across the snow and places himself in the midst of the Hessians, who're still receiving the full force of the enemy fire. Paul de Bourgoing follows him. Finding 'the young prince [Emil], then 20 years old and of heroic valour, surrounded by dead and wounded', Delaborde congratulates him on his men's staunchness. Gallant compliments are exchanged, Delaborde declaring – somewhat gratuitously – that 'complete equality between French and allies is the custom on the battlefield'.

After a couple of hours a third of the Fusiliers-Grenadiers have been killed or wounded:

'But the Fusiliers-Chasseurs were worst off of all. Being nearer to the town they were exposed to a deadlier fire. For the last half-hour the Emperor had drawn back to the high road with the Old [Guard] Grenadiers and Chasseurs. We [the Young Guard] remained alone on the field, with a very few men from various corps, facing more than 50,000 of the enemy.'

But what's this? Dumonceau pricks up his ears. Beyond the roar of the Russian guns battering away at the long thin infantry line he hears another more distant, more feeble but more welcome sound. It's the 'intermittent cannonade, coming ever closer' of Davout's few and Miloradovitch's many guns exchanging salvoes. And at about 11 a.m. Reviews Inspector Denniée sees Napoleon, 'confident that his repeated orders had reached Davout and Ney and they they'd be joining us that evening or night', get into his carriage. 'Ordering the Old Guard to resume the retreat toward Liady', he returns to Krasnoïe.'

It had been shortly after dawn that the 30th Line, advancing along the Krasnoïe road, had run into Russian guns mounted on sledges, and after losing several officers and 82 other ranks had beaten a hasty retreat. Captain François' left arm, badly bruised by a shell-burst, aches horribly:

'At 6 a.m. we advance slowly, because the Russians are cannonading us from all sides at once. At the village of Katowa a Russian corps debouches and comes marching down on us. A moment later three other enemy units appear in front of Waskrenia. The Guard is opposite this village, which gives us some hope. Marshal Davout prepares us for a fight. Despite the enemy grapeshot, we take up position to the left of Waskrenia, and the engagement becomes brisk. Our regiment's out in front, only 600 feet from the Russian batteries.'

Lejeune sees General Compans, commander of the 5th division, in the thick of it. He's

'as smiling and cheerful as if in his own garden, where he liked to take long walks. His cheerful face was making his men forget the danger they were in.'

The forenoon wears on. Doesn't the Russian command realise how frail are the Young Guard's thinning ranks as they stand staunchly to be decimated in the snow? Why don't the Russians launch a general attack? 'While we stood thus exposed to the enemy's fire,' Sergeant Bourgogne goes on, 'our numbers continuously diminishing, we saw to our left the remainder of Marshal Davout's army corps calmly marching toward us, in the midst of a swarm of Cossacks.' Calmly? They may look calm at a distance. In reality they are anything but.

Finally, at about midday, François catches sight of 'several French divisions being sent to our aid'. General Friederichs, halted to the right of the road at the head of his division's column, orders it to form up in half-companies. Since roundshot are already rolling among them from the Russian batteries on the high ground to the left, he tells Colonel Marguerye of the 33rd to send out two companies of voltigeurs to clear a path:

'But these two companies not being numerous enough, Lieutenant-Colonel de Jongh, commanding that Dutch regiment's 1st Battalion, is sent to support them. Then the entire regiment has to do so, with orders to charge the artillery in open order. We were fortunate enough to be able to carry out this order so completely that we made ourselves masters of the highway.'

Whereupon the Russian guns withdraw to almost harmless distance. 'In this fight our regiment had two officers and some 60 men wounded or killed.' And now here are some 'divisions' coming to meet them, among them the pitiful remains of IV Corps, with the 'debris' of the Guardia d'Onore, 4,000 bayonets at most, so François thinks. But it's enough. And I Corps breaks through, taking the rest at a run:

'We joined up with them; but having to march in square and close columns and under the enemy's roundshot and grape we'd lost a lot of men.'

From his unchanged vantage point Dumonceau sees Davout's men 'pour past [s'écouler] in a compact mob [foule] – François says 'en masse with IV Corps' which, its mission accomplished, no doubt also hastily retreats to the town. Wilson is there:

'The enemy passed like flocks of sheep without even offering to fire at us. It was then the Cossacks came to us and said: "What a shame to let these spectres walk from their graves!"'

What neither Dumonceau nor Wilson see is the much-wounded Dromedary of Egypt

'unable to march as fast as the others on account of my wounds in the confusion of this precipitate retreat [sic]. Suddenly I can't see the flag in the middle of the regiment. Can the man who'd been carrying it have been killed? No question but that our standard's been left behind on the battlefield! No sooner has this thought struck me than, without a thought to the danger or bothering about the Russian sharpshooters who're advancing on the line just abandoned by our division, I about-face and hobble back. At last I see the Eagle; pick it up; and, walking as fast as I can, carry it off, despite the shots being aimed at me. Several musket balls pass through my fur! The Russians too are hastening their march, all the while firing grape. In the end I'm hit by a piece of shell which carries away the skin on the back of my right hand and gives me a nasty scar on my right buttock.'

Luckily François still has

'the strength and presence of mind not to succumb to this accursed misfortune of war. My left arm's in a sling, my crutch has been shattered, but I don't abandon the Eagle. So absorbed have I been in saving it I get into Krasnoïe without even feeling any pain.'

But now he does. Since there's neither water nor linen to dress his wound he asks a comrade to 'snap off the flagpole, lay the Eagle in its tasselled cravat, and hang it around my neck'. Then he rejoins the 30th in the rear of Krasnoïe, where he finds his batman and his two horses.

But all's far from well with the heroic – but by now badly mauled – Dutch Guard Grenadiers. No sooner have Davout's units broken through than Dumonceau sees they're abandoning

'the important position entrusted to them, which the Russians instantly occupy with their artillery, and direct its fire against us. After this our own position was untenable. A regiment sent to recover the ground is forced to retire. Another moves forward as far as the foot of the batteries, but is stopped by a regiment of cuirassiers. Retiring to the left of the battery, the 3rd Dutch Grenadier regiment forms square. Again the enemy's cavalry come on to the attack, but are received by a heavy fire, which kills a great many. A second charge meets with the same reception. But a third, supported by grapeshot, succeeds. The regiment's overwhelmed. The enemy breaks into the square and finishes off the remainder with their swords. Powerless to defend themselves, these poor fellows, nearly all very young, having their hands and feet mostly frostbitten, were simply massacred. We witnessed this scene without being able to help our comrades.'

Among the few survivors 'flowing back to us' Dumonceau recognises an old friend, Captain Favauge, 'supported by a grenadier'. Hit in the small of his back, he's suffering so terribly Dumonceau fears he won't survive:

'Only eleven men came back. The rest had all been killed, wounded or, if taken prisoner, were being driven away by sword-thrusts into a little wood opposite. Colonel Tindal himself, covered with wounds, was taken prisoner, with several other officers.'

But in all essentials the operation has succeeded. And at long last as the daylight fades Mortier gives the long-awaited order to retire. As the intrepid Delaborde's surviving youngsters about-face and march for Krasnoië he says to them:

'Do you understand, soldiers? The Marshal orders you to march at the usual pace. *At the usual pace!*':[21]

All his life Bourgogne will broken-heartedly remember

'the terrible and sad scene as we left the field and our poor wounded, surrounded by the enemy, saw they were being abandoned, above all those of the 1st Voltigeurs, some of whom had had their legs shattered by grape'.

After making several probes near a wood to see if the Russians are strongly supported (they are), the Hessians, too, retire, 'covered by one weak division'. Only at 4 p.m., just as the last light fails, do the Russians launch a truly furious onslaught. The 1st Tirailleurs, who've lost two-thirds of their men and are still out on the crest of the ravine, are also ordered to retire. In the end only the 1st Voltigeur Regiment's still out there. Paul de Bourgoing can distinctly hear its 20-year-olds, now bearing the whole brunt of their first and last battle, shouting "*Vive l'Empereur!*" as they're scythed down by Russian grapeshot. And when at last another ADC is told to 'make for a white-ish point where the smoke of the combat can scarcely be made out in the evening mist' and order them to retire, all he finds when he gets

there are 'a few scattered groups here and there, still resisting the Cossacks and the Novgorod Dragoons'. Where are all the rest, he asks one of their lieutenants whose face is covered in blood:
'They no longer exist.'

Lieutenant Vionnet, who's had two horses killed under him but escapes with only two light bruises and five Russian musket balls in his greatcoat, sees that the 'first two regiments of Tirailleurs and Voltigeurs had been entirely wiped out. Of those two units not 120 men were left.' The Fusiliers-Grenadiers see

'many of them painfully dragging themselves along on their knees, reddening the snow with their blood. They raised their hands to heaven, uttering cries which tore at one's heart and imploring our help. But what could we do? At each instant the same fate awaited us too; for as we retired we were also having to abandon those who were falling in our own ranks.'

But Delaborde, sitting his horse at the town gate, goes on 'encouraging and directing the men who were defending the entrance'. As he's waiting to retreat through the gateway 'with the last companies to pass through Krasnoïe', Bourgogne sees

'some pieces of artillery on our left, firing at the Russians for our protection. They were being served and supported by about 40 men, gunners and light infantrymen – all that was left of General Longchamps' brigade. He was there himself with the remnant of his men, determined either to save them or die with them. As soon as he caught sight of our colonel he came to him with open arms. They'd been through the Egyptian campaign together. They embraced as two friends who hadn't met for a long time and perhaps wouldn't ever meet again. The general, his eyes full of tears, showed our colonel the two guns and the few remaining men: "Look," he said. "That's all I've left!" General Longchamps, with his poor remainder, was forced to leave his guns, all the horses being killed, and follow our retreat, taking advantage of what cover he could find behind houses or earthen banks as he went.'

Soon the Russian roundshot, fired at close quarters, is 'going through this little country town's wooden houses, killing several soldiers of our rearguard. Shortly afterwards,' Paul de Bourgoing goes on, 'the main street is swept by musketry, and it's at this moment I come across Victor, no less exposed to the keenest fire than the most valiant of our infantrymen'. All this time his faithful 'guttersnipe' has been admiring his lieutenant as he'd galloped about out there on the snowy plain!

'He'd been waiting for me to give me my fur, which he hadn't wanted to leave behind.

"Quick, lieutenant, take your fur. I can't march as fast as the rearguard and we'll have to get a move on if we're not to be left behind."'

But 'the officers of the 30th, assembling in Krasnoïe, are regarding Captain François as 'a lost man, so covered am I with wounds. However, I don't despair. I've still got a good appetite, little though it's excited by any succulence in the dishes making up my meals.'

Although his exploit's been quickly reported to his colonel, who reports it to General Morand, and he to Davout,

'who engages my colonel to write him a report on my conduct, and though the report was written, certifying my feat of arms and telling me I'm being recommended for the Cross of the Legion,'

nothing, sighs François, ever comes of it.

All day Boulart and his gunners and men of the Train, parked beside their lake, have been listening to the sounds of battle,

'all in a state of acute anxiety, an anxiety aggravated by the incessant passage of non-combatants and vehicles through the town'.

After what seemed an interminable waiting with his slimmed down artillery, Boulart had seen the head of the Guard column appear: 'Debouching from Krasnoïe and without halting, it continued its march towards Liady. I followed its movement.' Every house in Krasnoïe and its big monastery have been filling up with the Young Guard's wounded. But now Larrey sees his surgeons, too, falling under the roundshot or Cossack lances. And not only his surgeons, either. But also women:

'The Frenchwomen who'd left Moscow with us were carrying their devotion to the point of heroism. They came out and bandaged our wounded under the fire of the Russian guns. Above all the directress [sic] of the Moscow Theatre, Mme. Aurore Bursay, distinguished herself.'

As usual the Surgeon-General has himself been operating on many of the gravest cases. To Lejeune, coming in with I Corps,

'nothing was more afflicting than to see all these rooms encumbered with fine young soldiers aged 20 to 25, who'd only recently joined and who'd seen action for the first time that day, and who, within the hour, were going to be left in the enemy's power. All who could walk after their wounds had been attended to were making haste to leave. All the others stayed there without surgeons and without help. There were perhaps 3,000 of them.'

As evening has come on, 1,200 others have been evacuated from the town. Krasnoïe itself is 'intersected by a deep hollow' crossed by another 'little trembling bridge'. Going on ahead in his carriage Mailly-Nesle has seen men who'd fallen from the bridge lying dead in the half-frozen river, at the bottom of which Bourgogne is astonished to see

'a herd of oxen, dead of cold and hunger. Only their heads were visible, their eyes still open; their bodies were covered in snow. They belonged to the army, but hadn't been able to reach us. They were frozen so stiff our sappers could hardly cut them up with their hatchets.'

But now Larrey even has to leave behind the 1,200 he'd evacuated from the battlefield amid Krasnoïe's splintering and crumbling timber houses – 'for lack of transport we could only take a very few with us'. And the deepening dusk is rent by the 'piercing cries of hundreds of seriously wounded youngsters' as they realise they're being abandoned to the 'brutality of a savage and pitiless enemy, who were already stripping them without regard to their situation or their wounds'.

I Corps' rearguard consists of 390 Dutchmen of the 33rd Line. Davout, on the spot, orders its Colonel de Marguerye to send a strong detachment to occupy some ruined houses to the left further along the Liady road. But then, just as all the rest of I Corps is already crossing a street to his right, the Marshal comes back with a new order: to draw off the whole regiment 'broken up into echelons'. Major Everts listens

'attentively to the Marshal's orders. For many years his military reputation had stood on solid foundations. But on this occasion experience once again told me that in unforeseen situations even great men of that stamp can make mistakes.'

If they remain scattered like this among houses so widely detached, Everts sees, they'll neither be able to keep on the move nor put up a resolute or vigorous rearguard action. 'We'd be beaten in detail at all points.' Already the rest of I Corps is more than 300 yards away and the Russian cavalry's coming on quickly toward them. So he advises de Marguerye to ignore Davout's orders, concentrate his men, get out into the plain, and form square. All the 33rd's other senior officers agree:

'But having advanced a few hundred paces in column, we heard a vigorous hurrah behind the regiment. At which the colonel ordered us to halt and form square to sustain the Russians' charge. But the mass of Cossacks noticed our movement and faced about. A few moments later four hostile squadrons of Cuirassiers of the Guard appeared and flung themselves flat out at us.'

Although the 33rd's muskets are 'in bad shape after the bivouacs', they keep up a well-nourished fire, killing or wounding a lot of the cuirassiers. A second charge also fails, and the survivors make off to attack isolated men and units. But then, seeing Friederichs' division has now left the 33rd behind, Everts realises his men are isolated:

'The cuirassiers came and drew up in front of our square's left face. While they were doing this, six guns were placed to their left and in front of them. They opened up a heavy fire of grape at us. The colonel still wanted to send some skirmishers against this artillery. But the regiment's effectives were too reduced. It could do no more.'

Once again the Russian cuirassiers attack. Once again they're repulsed. But then two battalions of Chasseurs of the Russian Guard come on in open order, keeping up a well-nourished fire, and by now very few of the Dutchmen are still on their feet, 'least of all on our left face, the one facing the artillery'. Colonel Marguerye orders all his officers to take up muskets and do what they can to fill the gaps:

'At that moment he himself was hit by two musket balls in his neck, and began losing a terrible lot of blood. I quickly handed him my pocket handkerchief to stem it.'

A third time the Russian cavalry charges – and this time breaks into the shattered square. Just as Everts is about to take command, the 33rd is charged by Russian infantry,

'furiously striking with bayonet and sword, pointing and slashing in all directions, and terribly augmenting the numbers of our killed and wounded. The colonel suffered two more wounds in the lower part of his body. Fifteen officers were killed, 20 wounded, some very gravely. In all, only six officers remained unscathed. I was one of these privileged men. Of our rankers only 66 were still on their feet. Thus the square was as it were framed in corpses.'

Taken prisoner, all the survivors are 'stripped of everything we had on us or in our clothes'. Violent rows break out among the Russians, accompanied by fisticuffs, 'because each wanted to take everything. As I personally experienced. Having taken everything off me, down to my shirt', two Russians dispute the capture of Everts' gold watch. Even so, he counts himself lucky not to be among the wounded:

'Thus undressed, they took me to General Roozen [sic] who was so courteous as to believe what I told him of my rank, etc., and spontaneously even had the goodness to have me at once given an old Russian overcoat and something strong to drink. In addition to all this, at my request he had the humanity – most essential of all – to order an end to the massacre of my unfortunate comrades. To do this he sent an adjutant and two drummers, who made a roll, and put an end to it. At the same time several of our officers, who were in a most precarious situation because of their wounds, were being carried to the general. One of them, Captain von Ingen, made him a Masonic sign. At which the general gave him a few paper roubles, which he took out of his portfolio. From every point of view I cannot pay homage enough to the generous and loyal conduct of the enemy general who'd commanded there. May Heaven reward this brave man!'

While their former subordinates are marched off naked into captivity, some senior officers are even buried with military honours. 'The unit was led to the grave (in which the officer was to be placed without any coffin) by a platoon of their men, escorting it with reversed arms, and a drum beating a kind of funeral march.'[22]

Only after they've left Krasnoïe a quarter of a league behind them do the surviving Fusiliers-Grenadiers

'calm down a bit, sad and silent at the thought of our own position and of our unhappy comrades we'd been forced to abandon. It seemed to me I could still see them begging us to help them.'

Looking behind they see some of the least severely wounded, almost naked, coming after them, and hurriedly give them whatever can be spared to cover their nakedness.

But back in Krasnoïe after Davout had left, they're being told, some 3,000 unevacuable wounded are simply being thrown out of the windows into the streets and (so Chlapowski'll hear) being massacred by the returning inhabitants.

CHAPTER 11

MARCHING, MARCHING, MARCHING ...

Getting out of Krasnoïe – Louise nearly dies – the cavalry's last charge – 'As long as your sacred bloody persons get through' – 'the Old Guard passed through like a 100-gun battleship through fishing boats' – Napoleon skids into Liady – live Jews and chickens – where's Ney? – 'We must get to the Berezina as quickly as possible' – 'For the first time he struck me as worried'

For the thousands of stragglers getting through Krasnoïe has been a nightmare. Carriageless, all alone in the mob, Louise Fusil had asked an officer how she was to join IHQ.

'"I think it's still here," he said, "but that won't be for long. Because the town's beginning to burn." The fire was spreading fast – the little town was all of timber and its streets exceedingly narrow. I ran through it, burning beams threatening to fall on my head. A gendarme was so kind as to help me as far as to the exit where a dense crowd was jostling one on all sides.'

'"The Emperor left long ago," he tells her. "You'll never be able to catch up with them again."

'"Very well, then," I said. "I'll just have to die, because I haven't the strength to go any further."

'I felt the cold was numbing my blood. This asphyxia, they say, is a very gentle death; and I can believe it. I heard someone or something buzzing in my ear: "Don't stay here! Get up!" Someone was shaking me by the arm. I found this disturbance disagreeable. I was experiencing the sweet self-abandonment of someone who's falling peacefully asleep. In the end I understood nothing, lost all sensation.'

But when she comes out of this benumbed state she's in a peasant's cottage, with a lot of officers standing around her. 'They'd wrapped me up in furs and someone was feeling my pulse.' It's Napoleon's personal surgeon Desgenettes:

'I thought I was coming back from a dream, but was so weak I couldn't stir. I scrutinised all these uniforms. General Bourmann, whose acquaintance I so far hadn't made, was looking at me with interest. Old Marshal Lefèbvre came forward and said: "Well, how are things with you? You've come back from very far away." They told me they'd picked me up out of the snow.'

Only Desgenettes has saved her from being placed close to their big fire. "Don't do anything of the sort!" he'd shouted. "You'll kill her on the spot! Wrap her up in all the furs you can find and put her in a room where there isn't one." By and by she begins to thaw out and Marshal Lefèbvre brings her 'a big mug of very strong coffee. "Keep the mug,"' he tells her. "It'll be historic in your family." But adds more softly: "If you ever see it again." And takes her into his carriage, which is soon rolling on behind a Guard detachment. Her fellow-actress Madame Bourcet hasn't been so fortunate. Dedem sees her perched on a gun-carriage in the costume she'd worn in the comedy *Ma Tante Aurore*, 'the only one she'd saved from the pillage'.

Griois hasn't a single gun left. On its way down the slope out of Krasnoïe behind IV Corps, his group (Berthier's son among them) see 'our troops at grips with the enemy'. It's Davout's rearguard.

Now all sorts of people have neither horse, cart, carriage nor wagon to carry their effects. Von Muraldt's horse has given up the ghost, leaving him to struggle on under the weight of his iron cookpot. After grabbing a riderless one and 'galloping' into Krasnoïe, Lieutenant Sauvage joins I Corps just as it's 'descending the slope' beyond the town. But the horse is recognised as belonging to a Polish general. And he has to dismount and walk.

Once again guns are being left behind – even the Guard's. General Lallemand approaches Pion des Loches and authorises him in the Emperor's name to abandon any he must, but on one condition: that he bury them deep in the ground and burn their gun-carriages,

'though to do that we'd have needed spades and pickaxes, and they'd been lost with the ammunition wagons. I left four pieces on their carriages, had the lashings cut, and some spokes broken.'

But Boulart's guns are rolling along down 'the great broad road straight to the horizon and planted on both sides with three rows of magnificent silver birches' that had provided shade against the appalling August heats. 'An hour and a half beyond Krasnoïe' some Cossacks, pressing in from the left, carry off General Desvaux's wagon, and Boulart's guns, preceded by a horse battery, have to fire some shots at them.

'Three miles beyond Krasnoïe, a new ravine, a new mêlée. My first gun gets jammed in it, I can't get it out. So, even though it brings me close to the Cossacks, I direct the rest of my column a little further to the left. To avoid breaking up the ground I recommend that no vehicle shall follow in the tracks of the one ahead. This succeeds admirably, and I have the happiness to get back to the road without being held up at all, and leave behind me all this scrum the Russians are already firing their guns at.'

Once again Boulart, by superior management, has saved his guns – all except one. Regretting its loss, he goes back to see whether anything can be done about it. Just as he's deciding it can't, he witnesses a painful scene. A Russian roundshot carries away the jaw of a fractious donkey, ridden by well-dressed young woman, a fugitive from Moscow. Although he realises this means she'll soon be the Cossacks' prey, probably their victim, 'my artillery was already beginning to be far away, and I'd no means of saving this unhappy woman'. Farther on, at a new jam where the road narrows to cross a swamp and is only viable to one vehicle at a time, he's shocked to see even superior officers – 'almost all stripped of any resources and reduced to an extremity more painful than the men's' – pillaging the bogged-down vehicles.

For still the Russians aren't giving the column any peace, and the survivors of the Young Guard (Vionnet contradicts Pastoret) haven't so much as a single gun to oppose them with:

'We had to pass through a hollow road under the fire of four guns and two howitzers, which made extraordinary ravages. Not a shot failed of its effect. One can imagine the carnage caused by this battery.'

To keep the Russians at a healthy distance on a line of high ground to the left, Colbert's lancers are riding across thick snowy fields, flanking the Old Guard. Just then a cannonball from that quarter kills an infantryman at Dumonceau's side, causing his horse to shy and fall on top of him. 'The shells which went beyond us were bursting around the Emperor without his even appearing to notice them.' Suddenly Pastoret's group see

'the enemy unmask a battery he'd been concealing on our left flank. He sends some parties of cavalry to support it and lets his cavalry appear on our right and ahead of us. At the same time he attacks our rear on the paved highway. Instantly the Emperor changes his battle front, and to keep the Russians at bay throws the Young Guard and the heavy cavalry to the right, leaving the stragglers, whose numbers make them look like a considerable corps; sends a reinforcement to the rear; and with the Old Guard marches in line to the left. At a signal the officers gather and form a circle. Napoleon tells them "it isn't me you're to serve. It's us. It's the Empire, it's France. Remember, the safety of one is the safety of all."'

The column advances to the attack. Colbert's lancers and the rest of the Guard's light cavalry under Lefèbvre-Desnouëttes, called in, charge together and disperse the Russians. Now only some 2,000 cavalry are left. And when another Russian battalion makes a determined effort to come down from the high ground and block the road, it's ordered to stem it. The charge is hit by a storm of fire. The relics of the 23rd Dragoons, says *Pierre Auvray*, are

'obliged to charge home. So great was the mêlée, not to be stabbed by their bayonets we could only get clear by separating their weapons with our hands. In that moment, just as I'm about to sabre my Russian, he jabs his bayonet at my left side. My sabre belt parries the blow.'

Holding his horse's reins with his right hand Auvray tries to fend the man off with his left. 'His musket shot goes off in my hand, taking off my forefinger and the ball ripping the front of my coat.' And that makes one more non-combatant to add to all the thousands of others. He has great difficulty in finding the 23rd Dragoons' surgeon to amputate the stump of his finger. Very few of his comrades return from that charge.

Meanwhile the Russian gunners, it seems to Pastoret, are aiming directly at Napoleon:

'Upon a shell falling quite close to the Emperor, he struck it with his riding whip saying: "Ah! What a long time it is since I've had a shell between my legs!" The shell exploded, covering the Emperor in snow, but without hurting anyone.'

Berthier urges him to leave the spot and move further off to the right. As he's doing so, an officer who's just stepped forward to take orders – he's standing exactly where Napoleon was a moment ago – is hit and killed by a roundshot. A French battery unlimbers and silences the Russian fire. Noticing that fresh Russian troops – far too numerous for Davout to contain – are all the time being thrown in, Napoleon concludes that III Corps has probably been forced to capitulate 'or perhaps is making a great detour around the Russian army to rejoin him'. This time there can be no turning back. 'We marched,' says Chlapowski,

'in close columns headed by the service squadrons, the Guard artillery on the road, then the infantry, and finally all the Guard cavalry'.

Pastoret sees the Guard's close-packed column go by:

'To right and left rode the cavalry, with orders to scout for us. In front of us two battalions of infantry with two guns formed the usual advance guard and preceded the Emperor's carriage, under the Master of the Horse, that of the Prince of Neuchâtel, and that of Count Daru. All the others had been consigned to the rear. After this advance guard came the combat corps.'

It's a sight he'll never forget. Nor will the Russians:

'The Emperor was marching first, alone, followed by the Major-General [Berthier] and the *Intendant-Général* [Daru], walking together, and by the Grand Marshal of the Palace [Duroc], who was driving his own sledge. Behind him, sword in hand, came the Marshal Duke of Danzig [Lefèbvre] commanding the Guard; and after him the Guard itself, as if on parade. Each divisional general was at the head of his division, each brigadier at the head of his brigade; each colonel led his regiment, and each captain his company. No officer could under any pretext whatsoever quit his particular post. The men, brought back to discipline, marched in their ranks and in perfect order. A uniform and equal step seemed to unite so many movements into one, and the deep silence reigning in this immense body of troops was only disturbed by the firm curt cry of command, repeated by the officers at regular intervals from rank to rank, and which, from the Guard, passed on down to the various corps following it. The enemy observed us from afar.'

In his place at the head of his company of the 1st Foot Chasseurs, 'marching almost all the time in square' is Captain Lignières:

'In the middle of the square the Emperor marched with his staff, his carriage, his wagons, the artillery. We were forbidden to let anyone, no matter whom, enter the square. All round us was a mob of stragglers, an innumerable mob we rejected with blows of our musket butts. Each time we changed direction we had to pass through this mob. Marshal Lefèbvre, in command of us, said: "Chasseurs, you must pass. I insist your sacred bloody [*sacrée*] persons shall be respected. As long as your sacred persons get through I don't give a damn for the rest."'

178

Never as long as he lives will Denis Davidov, head of a band of Russian partisans, forget that sight. As 'the Old Guard, with Napoleon himself in its centre' approaches,

'we jumped on our horses and placed ourselves close to the main road. Noticing our noisy bands, the enemy cocked his muskets and proudly continued his march, without hastening the pace. All our efforts to detach a single soldier from his closed columns were in vain. The men, as if carved out of granite, scorned all our attempts and remained intact. I'll never forget the free and easy air and the menacing attitude of those warriors who'd been tried by death in its every aspect. With their tall bearskins, their blue uniforms with white belts, their red plumes and epaulettes, they looked like rows of poppies in a field of snow. Our Cossacks were in the habit of galloping around the enemy, snatching his baggage and guns if they straggled, and circling scattered or detached companies. But those columns remained unshakeable. In vain our colonels, our officers, our NCOs or simple Cossacks thrust themselves at them. The columns advanced, one after the other, driving us off with musket shots and scorning our useless raids. The Guard with Napoleon passed through our Cossacks like a ship armed with a hundred guns passes through fishing boats.'

'This calm regular march so impressed the enemy,' Pastoret is no less amazed to see, 'that for several days he no longer attacked us.'

That evening Sauvage strays from one bivouac to another, vainly searching for his Captain Houdart. But what's this? An abandoned wagon, full of shoes! Nearby, lying on the snow, is a Polish lancer's portmanteau. Taking out several pairs, he puts them into it; and shortly afterwards has the luck to fall in with – though not exactly be welcomed by – the officers of his division's artillery train, who've still got their wagon and are making some soup. Sauvage is just turning in for the night when the enemy guns open up again. And all the French scatter, despite their officers' attempts to hold them together. At that moment Davout

'hastening to the danger point, managed by his example and exhortations to gather round him those who scorned the Russians' 20 or 25 shots at us. In this way the Marshal hid his army corps' disorder from the enemy and prevented them from attempting any other movements.'

From Smolensk to Orsha is 123 kilometres. From Krasnoïe to Orsha some 50 miles. Half-way between them, everyone remembers, is the little town of Liady, the first in Lithuania. How long they seem, these sixteen leagues! Mailly-Nesle, no longer singing as he walks along beside his imperial carriage, is feeling sad:

'Each of us, his head lowered, his hands hidden in his clothes and his eyes fixed on the ground, sombre and silent, was following the unfortunate man in front of him. The plaintive cry of the wheels on the hardened snow, and the croaking of constellations of rooks, the northern crows, and other birds of prey which always followed our army, were the

179

only sounds heard, unless the Cossacks came to shake our poor French soldiers out of their melancholy apathy.'

Today (18 November) a thaw has set in; and the fog's 'so thick we could see nothing'. Sergeant Bourgogne is

'terribly tired. Our men were still in some sort of order. But the previous days' fighting and having to abandon their comrades had demoralised them. They were thinking the same fate no doubt was in store for them.'

Towards nightfall it begins freezing again

'and the roads were so slippery we kept on falling over, and many were seriously hurt. I marched last of the company.'

As darkness falls they drive some German, Italian and French stragglers out of a church:

'Unfortunately for them the night grew much colder, with a high wind and a fall of snow, and when we came out next morning we found many of the poor wretches dead by the roadside. Others had dropped farther on, while trying to find somewhere to shelter. We passed by these dead bodies in silence. No doubt,'

he goes on, with a retrospective twinge of bad conscience,

'we ought to have felt guilty at this sad sight, of which we were partly the cause. But we'd reached that point of indifference to even the most tragic events that we told each other we'd soon be eating dead men, as there'd be no more horses left.'

This is one hour before reaching the village of Dubrovna. Until now I Corps, too, has been marching in quite good order; but partly as a result of that night when the officers had pillaged the abandoned vehicles, it's become 'almost completely disorganised'.

And now and again everyone looks back over his shoulder.

What's become of Ney?

At first, while Davout had still been at or near Krasnoïe, Napoleon had told Berthier to order him to fall back to Ney's assistance. But then thought better of it:

'For Davout to have lingered at Krasnoïe would have jeopardised the army without serving any useful purpose. To return there, as certain persons proposed, was quite pointless. Ney's fate was already sealed, one way or the other.'

Caulaincourt forbids us – his future readers and armchair strategists – to pass judgement as between Ney and Davout. Still less so on Napoleon. But his own verdict is unequivocal:

'The fact is, of course, the pace ought to have been accelerated all along the line, and Ney should have left Smolensk on 16 November. But the Emperor could never make up his mind when it came to ordering a retreat. We knew nothing definite about III Corps, of which I Corps had had no news since the 16th. Not a single officer had returned.'

Altogether communications have virtually broken down:

'The dispatch of orders and reports was all but impossible, or else so slow they were rarely arriving in time to be any use. Staff officers, having mostly lost their horses, were on foot. Even those who still had them couldn't make them walk on the ice, and so got there no sooner than the others. Braving every kind of danger, they were often captured. To make any progress at all they had to attach themselves to some unit, halt when it halted,, and advance to join another unit when it advanced. Had those sent with messages even reached their destination? The Emperor was lost in conjectures.'

When he'd left Smolensk he'd believed for some reason the Russian army was to his right. Now, hearing from a peasant and from contingents familiar with the locality that there's a lot of Russian cavalry to his left, he realises it must be Kutusov trying to steal several marches on him.[1]

Cold and sunny the weather may be, but the whole landscape's an ice-rink. Just before Liady, eleven miles from Krasnoïe, the great plateau comes abruptly to an end; and there's a steep descent. How is IHQ to get down it? Eblé's three companies of sappers are already at Orsha, having made 'all necessary repairs to the bridges along the road'. But evidently Jomini's report hasn't come in yet. If it had, Berthier's headquarters guides would know that the slope

'can be turned by a road to the left. I've got the commandant of that place to promise to point it out to the whole Train. The two slopes between Dubrovna and Orsha, of which one goes up and the other down, are no less bad and will cause a great delay in the march. There are two or three very steep slopes and very dangerous to the artillery teams. It seems to me there's nothing to do about it, except the descent at the entrance to Liady.'

where Eblé, he says, has thrown down some fascines so as to be able to turn it a bit further on. From the sublime to the ridiculous – Napoleon will soon be telling Caulaincourt, is but a step:

'It descended so steeply, and a large part of its frozen surface had been so polished by all the horses and men that had slipped on it that we, like everyone else, we were obliged to sit down and slide on our backsides. The Emperor had to do the same, as the many arms proffered him didn't provide enough support.'[2]

After a few miles the Russian pursuit has faded away. The Lancer Brigade's been able to leave the fields' deep snow and – Dumonceau says nothing about the slope – ride straight along the road and, wary – as back in August[3] – of its single street's transverse logs, so dangerous to their horses' legs, right through it.

Amazing! Not since leaving Moscow has anyone seen any inhabitants. But here they are:

'Almost all Jewish, they'd stayed behind their filthy window panes, with an air of consternation watching us pass. From the lights in the windows we realised the houses were full. A profound calm reigned everywhere.'

Castellane, arriving with IHQ, is delighted to see them. Perhaps even more so the chickens and ducks, real live ones, which 'to everyone's great astonishment are running about in the town's streets and yards!' 'Every face cheered up, and everyone began to think that our privations were at last at an end. Liady's modest resources, combined with such things as money could buy in its neighbourhood, enabled a fair number of men to take the edge off their appetites.'

Caulaincourt adds these details, he says, somewhat solemnly, 'because small things have great influence on Frenchmen, whose spirits are quick to rise and fall'. There's even wine to be had, at least for the first comers, and 'a good bedroom with windows, a wooden floor to sleep on and a stove to heat the air'.

Boulart says nothing about chickens or ducks – perhaps by the time he gets there they've all found their way into IHQ's cookpots. Nor about how his guns and caissons have negotiated the slippery slope – perhaps Jomini's report has caused them to take the circuitous road to the left. But at the bridge at the town entrance reasonably good order prevails, for once. Boulart is standing there with his batteries, 'shivering and impatiently wait-ing my turn' to cross it, when he's summoned to Davout – who tells him I Corps, too, is to march straight through without halting. Since some Cos-sacks – evidently they've appeared again – are being supported by infantry he needs Boulart's guns to disperse them. Boulart waits until 4 a.m. – all he gets to eat is some biscuit and sugar 'hard as stone, which spoiled my teeth and lacerated my gums' – before he can get moving again. Then he puts his guns into battery, and drives off the Cossacks.

Griois and his friends have done considerably better for themselves. Arriving at Liady towards nightfall 'at about the same time as the Emperor' they've found

'this little town's houses full of military from all corps, pressed together there *en masse*. An emotion [*mouvement*] reigned there which, without being one of gaiety, had something less lugubrious about it than the usual sight presented by our bivouacs. It's true' [he goes on som-brely] 'the inhabitants were all Jews whose hideous squalor in any other circumstances would have shocked us. But by dint of threats and blows we, for gold, were able to get some potatoes out of them.'

Louise Fusil is more considerate, more humane: 'They were Jews, but at least living beings. I'd gladly have embraced them!' Squeezing himself into a room 'which was already housing more people than it could reasonably contain' Griois sees Dr Desgenettes, who'd saved her life. Luckily, one of Griois' party finds another, less crowded house to spend the night in, and they 'replace the insipid and detestable broth by our potatoes'. Franz Roeder, now feeling very ill, gets here too, and Prince Emil gives him back a slice of his Göttingen sausage, which is so much the more welcome as he has lost his boy-batman Dietrich; and notes in his diary: 'Musketeer Alt, with the furs, fodder and cooking pot, may well be utterly lost.' Next morn-ing, finding his feet so swollen he can't pull his boots on, he has to turn to one of his Hessians to lend him a pair of soldier's shoes, even if they're two sizes too big for him.

But for 300 men of I Corps that night Liady is the end of the road. In the cold foggy morning Fezensac sees how

'all had perished, burnt to death in a barn, blocking the doorway as they'd all tried to rush out at once. Only one was still breathing, and to finish him off he had to be shot twice.'

Now 'the weather, which had been cold but very beautiful' suddenly changes. And there's a thaw, so that 'a thick damp fog enveloped us' and Griois' group march on

'through melting snow. The dampness of the air and the water running away from the surface of the layer of ice covering the silver birches along the road pierced our clothing; and the cold we were exposed to, though a great deal less sharp, was more inconvenient and above all less healthy than that of the preceding days. I was promptly seized of a fierce cough, accompanied by a sore throat.'

Doubtless he isn't the only sufferer. Everywhere Castellane sees sledges being abandoned in the slush. Liady being a Lithuanian town and therefore on 'liberated' territory, the officers of the Italian Guard have assumed

'it'd be respected. But even after seeing a good part of its houses demolished to feed the bivouac fires yesterday evening and last night, we were most surprised and pained to see, as we left, what remained – sad and hard necessity – being given over to the flames to slow down the enemy's pursuit!'

Possibly only Roeder, who has a special respect for them, gives a thought to its poor Jews. They'd been right to be apprehensive.

'All eyes were now turning to Orsha, which the Emperor, like everyone else, regarded as an important base.' Halfway, 30 kilometres further on, lies the village of Dubrovna. After leaving Liady at 5 a.m., IHQ has to march for twelve hours to get there. When it does it installs itself in Princess Lubomirska's château. Like all Lithuanian villages Dubrovna is mainly Jewish. Le Roy's little group, hurrying on to keep ahead of the mob of disbanded men, have already passed through on 16 November and found

'all the inhabitants in their homes. We'd halted in my former billet where there were already two superior cavalry officers. Neither had a horse. For a while we'd chatted about our miserable state. They told me we were in danger of being cut off at the Berezina, at the big Borissow bridge. This news had made me hasten my march to Orsha.'

At Dubrovna Griois' 'little caravan' is 'happier than it'd been so far, in the fairly spacious house' of some people who provide them with 'wonderful fresh bread and a little honey and not too dirty a floor to sleep on in front of the fire'. By now Griois has run a high temperature. In the middle of the night a Cossack 'hurrah' disturbs his sleep – at the first shots all but two or three of the armed pontoneers he has placed at the door have rushed off to join the troops in the market place. But the Cossacks find they've bitten off more than they can to chew. It's Napoleon's headquarters and the Imperial Guard they've tumbled on.

By dawn it's freezing again. As Dedem sets out along the Orsha road that morning (19 November) he sees

'the Emperor trying to reorganise the Guard. He was walking along, preaching discipline. Marshal Duroc and the other generals with him had tried to halt the soldiers and incorporate them. But their efforts had been unavailing.'

Von Muraldt – his memories from Krasnoïe to the Berezina will be fuzzy – will nevertheless remember one thing very clearly:

'At a fire by the roadside I saw the Emperor. He was wearing a fur-lined dark green coat and as far as I could judge doing his utmost to restore some kind of order among the pitiable mass. Yet no one was paying any attention any longer either to his commands or of his orders of the day.'

The only person in his entourage, Griois thinks, who seems to be perfectly cheerful is Murat, whom he sees arm in arm with Napoleon, who's walking with a 'long stick':

'Neither the cold nor our sad situation had taken away the air of self-assurance and gaiety natural to him. He smiled as he spoke with the Emperor, and the numbed faces of the others provided stuff for facile jokes. Walking in front of him was Marshal Berthier, wearing a blue over-coat. He seemed to find nothing amusing about his present situation. A fur, a toque and fur boots *à la polonaise* made up Murat's costume, whose elegance contrasted with everything around him.'

Where's the enemy. What's Kutusov doing? For four days, someone tells Cesare de Laugier, 'we've known nothing of what the Russians are up to. Jews, though promised rewards, can say nothing.' From Dubrovna on, Dedem thinks, it's become clear to Napoleon there's

'no salvation for him or ourselves except in the enemy's lack of audacity. He realised that sooner or later the few men under arms would melt away.'

But Pastoret notices something else:

'Having realised what a catastrophe had followed from lost time, he was now the first to insist on keeping going.'

That day the young Intendant falls in with the remnant of the Witebsk garrison. Among them are some of his own employees, with whom he offers to share his remaining 100 roubles. 'Almost all refused. Afterwards I only saw six men out of all those who'd made up the administration of a large county.' Marching on between the endless double alley of silver birches, one of his companions is kicked by a horse,

'which could have broken his leg, and in our situation this accident could have been mortal. At that moment it happened that M. Larrey had just passed us on horseback, and immediately declared: "Nothing broken. I heard the blow."'

But from then onwards Pastoret has to give his arm to his bruised friend.

As for Cesare de Laugier, he's learning a 'magic lesson about the heart of man!' He's finding it very remarkable

'that in the regiments where the colonels have shown themselves just but severe the officers are firmer in maintaining the bonds of discipline. These superiors are always respected, and above all always helped with their needs – in sharp contrast to the regiments where there reigns softness, condescension and a generous negligence. There the men refuse respect, first in little groups, then in a great number and more and more often. Only a few units can be excepted from this rule, where the chiefs' vigilance is extreme. Yet even they can't prevent it altogether.'

He jots down the various corps' strengths in his diary:

'Of the Imperial Guard's original 35,000 remain only 7,000
'Of I Corps' 67,000, only 5,000
'Of IV Corps' 41,000, only 4,000
'Of VI and VIII Corps' 86,400, only 2,000'

perhaps as many or more disbanded men. 'As far as Smolensk,' he's thinking, 'the number of combatants had exceeded those of the disbanded. Since Krasnoïe it's been the other way round.'

At Orsha someone, for once, has really done his duty. This big town, lying in a bend in the Dnieper, is stuffed with supplies of all kinds: food, guns, bridging equipment, and, most important of all of course (Jomini has reported back to Berthier when he's got here on 20 November) 90,000 food rations. They've been assembled, says Pastoret – who'd had a corresponding task at Witebsk – by the Portuguese Marquis d'Alorna, 'a scion of the royal house of Braganza, governor of Molihew province and well-liked by its inhabitants, adored by his men and well-seen by the Emperor.'[4] If Molihew can be guarded and the convoys protected against the soldiery by the élite gendarmes he'd met on the Liady road and brought back to Orsha, there's some hope – so Jomini has reported to Berthier – of their being properly distributed. The survivors of the Guardia d'Onore gape at the gendarmes, freshly arrived from France,

'as at something novel, extraordinary. The cleanliness of their equipment, their gleaming weapons, the splendour of their strappings are all in most singular contrast to the rags and tatters and the filthy state displayed by ourselves.'

Already they'd stopped Le Roy as he'd reached the first Dnieper bridge – there's one on each side of the town – and taken him to the town's military governor:

'He put me a lot of questions, to which I replied, concealing part of the truth. But I fancy he knew more or less what was going on and what straits the army was in. But he was far from imagining how demoralised it was.'

But falling in with a friend who knows nothing of the disastrous retreat, he'd told him about it: 'He soon left me under pretext of letting me get some rest, and ran to the general to pass on the information I'd just given him.' Le Roy had just been about to stretch out on some straw when Jomini[5] had come into his room. For lack of any other superior officer, the Swiss had wanted Le Roy to take charge of a strong detachment:

'You're to take it to a point an hour's march from here on the Dnieper to defend the river passage, which, only at this point, is probably frozen over. You'll have a village on your right and a forest in front of you. But above all you must concern yourself with the passage, which must be strictly guarded. I've just got news that the Emperor's going to halt here. As soon as the Guard arrives I'll immediately have you relieved and I'll be sure to let the general staff know of your great devotion.'

So Le Roy, irritated – yet content, even so, to have got six days' rations out of the inhabitants – had left . His detachment comes from every thinkable regiment – all convalescents, a captain tells him, who've been halted and assembled at Orsha to police the town and guard its food stores:

'Having sent the town governor and the general heartily to the devil, I thought of nothing except the punctilious execution of my orders. I had my whole wardrobe on my back. I was leaving nothing in the rear. My faithful Guillaume was going with me. And, lastly, I had enough food for several days. So I wasn't worried.'

Taking up his position overlooking the Dnieper, he places lookouts. 'At about 9 a.m. the corporal in charge of an outpost on the river comes and tells me a flag-of-truce wants to speak with me.' He turns out to be 'a Russian officer, very well horsed and speaking fluent French'. Le Roy hears his proposal:

'"We're on both flanks of your army, which has just been crushed at Krasnoïe. The Imperial Guard is blocked at Dubrovna. We've just cut communications between that town and Orsha. So your Emperor can retreat no further. So, go and see if you wouldn't like to surrender. In that case you'll be received as prisoners of war and well treated in Russia." He paused a moment, and seeing we were making ready to drive him off with musket shots, vanished into the woods. But during the forenoon, fearing I'd be forgotten, I sent back an old sergeant to the main headquarters to remind them of our existence. The river was frozen hard enough to support men and horses, but Cossacks were beginning to appear on the other side. Towards evening I went up on to the high ground dominating the village to try and see what was going on around Orsha, only five versts or a good hour's march from me. I saw fires all around it and could even make out the sound of vehicles crossing the river,'

presumably Boulart's cannon. Le Roy's about to fall back when

'my old sergeant returned with verbal orders to abandon my post, retire on Orsha, and send back the men in my detachment to their own regiments'.

But having already sent out a patrol over to the opposite bank he has to await its return.

That afternoon (19 November) IHQ has installed itself in the town's big Jesuit building. En route Pastoret has seen

'the Emperor, indignant to see so many of our guns and ammunition wagons being abandoned for lack of horsepower, while a multitude of infantrymen and stragglers were insolently riding the horses they'd stolen from them'.

Now he sees the Emperor station himself at the bridgehead, where he

'for two hours, a stick in his hand, functioned as a baggage master-general. One by one the carriages reached the bridgehead. He asked who they belonged to, with his inconceivable memory remembered how many belonged to each, let some go on, had others burnt, and sent the horses to the artillery. There a Marshal was allowed two vehicles, a general officer one, M. le Prince de Neuchâtel six, and so forth with the others. All men who were on horseback but had no right to be were obliged to dismount.'

This piece of accounting, Pastoret thinks, if rigorously carried through, would be almost enough to rehorse the artillery. But at the end of two hours Napoleon

'found it tedious, went off and left it to the Prince of Neuchâtel, who even more quickly became bored with this novel occupation. This task descended from one level to the next, until in the end it was confided to a staff officer. Night came down. Everyone passed unhindered. And the disorder began afresh.'

There are fierce disputes over lodgings. Entering a house, Captain Lignières of the 1st Foot Chasseurs finds his way blocked by an ADC who claims it's his general's:

'He was a foreigner, and so was his general. We replied that there was room for everybody. There were about 30 of us, officers and chasseurs. The ADC tried to prevent us staying. One of our officers fell into a violent dispute with him. I kept on telling him: "Oh, my dear fellow, let Monsieur alone, if he troubles us too much we'll put him out of the door."'

Finally the two officers call each other such names they've no option but to fight it out with cold steel:

'It was evening, very clear because of the snow. They went behind the house. Our comrade passed his sabre through the body of the ADC, who fell on the snow and stayed there. We hadn't so much as seen his general. Several generals were far too egoistic.'

For his part Boulart has been assigned a place on a bearskin

'in a vast courtyard of an immense building on the left as you come in. I was on the snow, but two walls were sheltering me, and I wasn't too badly off. I had the pleasure of again meeting Lieutenant Lyautey.[6] In a word, our position seemed to be improving. But we were intensely worried over the fate of Marshal Ney and his corps, whom we believed had been captured.'

Lieutenant Sauvage gets to Orsha at about 2 p.m. and finds the town

'already encumbered by the Imperial Guard and the various corps trying to reunite all the isolated men. Distributions of bread, meat and brandy were being made there. There I again find M. Mabru, Captains Houdart and Bergeret, as well as a dozen gunners of the company. From Captain Houdart I hear that after unheard of efforts the two sapper companies have been almost totally destroyed by the Russians' ball and grapeshot.'

Parked on some high ground are 36 new guns. Elsewhere there's a bridging train.[7] Even in the best of circumstances each of its pontoons needs a dozen big cart-horses to pull it. Surely they can be put to better use? Seeing it's freezing again, Napoleon, concerned as always for his artillery, makes what will turn out to be a near-fatal decision. To burn the Bridging Train.

On the other hand Fain notes that

'everything that may be useful for constructing trestle bridges – tools, iron clamps, nails, forges, coal, ropes – are being loaded on to the carts, passably well teamed, that are to go on with General Eblé.'

Like Jomini, Colonel Séruzier of the horse artillery finds himself attached to Eblé's party and from now on 'with what remained of my guns' is

'at the head of a body of pontoneers, charged with the task of securing the crossings for the army's return, just as I'd had to during our victorious march on Moscow!'

Nor is it only pontoons that are to be abandoned here at Orsha; but also 500 sick, 25 (presumably less serviceable) cannon, and several hundred Russian prisoners. In the morning Griois is sent for by Prince Eugène:

'He received me with his usual kindness. He told me the Emperor was going to divide up several batteries that were at Orsha among the various army corps, and he ordered me to distribute them to IV Corps' artillery companies, adding that it was crucial to the army's salvation to keep these guns until the moment, not far off but decisive, when they'd have to be used.'

Going up to some high ground

'where the park was set up, I found the Emperor's first *officier d'ordonnance*, Colonel *Gourgaud*, who gave me the guns allocated to IV Corps. I gave some to the Italian Royal Guard's gunners, and the rest to the French companies. These guns had no horses; and to harness them up we had to take those of a bridging unit, whose vehicles and boats were being burnt.'

Napoleon will soon be wishing he'd kept his bridging equipment, no matter how many horses would have been needed to draw its pontoons on their massive drays, and had jettisoned some of his guns instead.

A few futile efforts are being made to reform units or build new ones out of the human debris. Lefèbvre tells Pion des Loches – over and above his well-stocked wagon he only has four guns left – to join them up 'with those of Colonel Drouot, commanding the Guard reserve batteries', collect all the gunners and any Line and Guard pontoneers who no longer have any *matériel*, form them into a battalion and continue the march at their head, behind the Old Guard infantry:

'"There are 1,500 of them," the Marshal said, "all armed. You'll form them up in companies and you'll be commanding a tiptop infantry battalion. Do you really know your infantry drill?" I knew them better than His Excellency, and that wasn't saying much,' claims Pion who always knows everything better than anyone else, but forgets that Lefèbvre had risen from the ranks of the old Royal Guard. 'Yet I didn't manage to bring up a single one of those 1,500 men.' V Corps, too, is reinforced by 'garrisons from Orsha and its surroundings, among them a depot of Polish cavalry, a most useful help in our pressing state of equine penury'.

The Dnieper being very wide, everyone's astounded that the Russians haven't even tried to bar it. 'In our disordered state,' Labaume sees, 'the most formidable of armies would never have been able to force it without exposing itself to total ruin.' Dedem too notices:

'the whole army's surprise at the Russians' complaisance. So we crossed the Dnieper on two hastily constructed bridges. Marshal Kutusov had left us with the flattering prospect of seeing Victor's and Oudinot's corps turn up.'

This puts Napoleon into a good mood – the least thing, Caulaincourt's noticing, suffices to spark off his optimism. On the other hand, Rapp sees, he's 'lost all hope of seeing the rearguard again'. There's a massive distribution of food and new clothing, at least to the Guard, which by this time, according to Bourgogne, consists 'only of 7,000 or 8,000 men, the remnant of 35,000'. 'We've said good-bye to the Dnieper,' Fain jots down in his journal, 'by burning on its banks[8] carriages, baggage, papers, and everything we could lighten ourselves of to double up the teams we were conserving.'

Now it's the morning of 20 November. After waiting for his patrol to return from the Dnieper's far bank and having heard 'from the old sergeant that the Emperor, the Guard and several corps were already setting out for Borissow', Le Roy, judging he has no time to lose, has reunited his detachment and marched it back to town, where he finds I Corps has arrived – but not before the wretched and heroic 30th Line has lost three more officers and seventeen men before getting to the bridgehead and the protection of some guns placed on a hilltop. Sending his men back to their units, Le Roy finds the 85th

'bivouacked on the crest of a hill dominating the town, where it had taken shelter against the walls and gardens which in happier times had been Orsha's ornament'.

Sad news. Poor resourceful Sergeant-Major Ballane – he who'd pinned all his hopes on his officer's insignia but had them stolen at Smolensk – has died the previous day. The 85th's Major Frickler, too, seems to be sickening after stilling the pangs of hunger with hemp seed. None of this prevents the lucullean Le Roy and Jacquet – presumably Guillaume too – from sharing 'a well-cooked ham'. That morning, after marching for an hour and a half with the Hessian Footguards, Roeder ('very ill') too arrives and rides

'straight over the Dnieper bridge, 125 paces long. On a hill on the far bank I found Colonel Follenius. Mustered all those of our men who'd gone on ahead. On this hill we were told the army was to take three routes: via Minsk, Vilna and Witebsk. We were to take the first route.'

Just as Roeder's jotting these words down in his diary, Berthier, perhaps, is reading a report which, dated that same day, is from Jomini and mainly concerns the state of the routes westward,[9] particularly to Minsk. But his letter opens, almost offhand, with a rumour which, if true, is devastating indeed:

'*Monseigneur. I heard yesterday that the enemy has occupied Minsk with a corps of regular troops. Because of this I feel I must remind Your Highness, who has not followed that route, that from Bobr to Minsk there are 34 leagues of continual forests, constituting a defile where a little infantry troop with cannon could hold up the march of an army. Throughout the whole extent of this road it is impossible to pass either to right or left of it.*

'There is also an error in the distances marked on the map. Semolevice is eleven leagues from Minsk and ten from Borissow ... The map shows five to six leagues less. That road is bare of everything except woods and swamps.'

Minsk – with all its stores, enough to feed 100,000 men for six months, clothe and rearm them – taken? It's incredible. Even more than incredible, it's terrifying. Surely it can't be true? How can Schwarzenberg, whose prime task has been to keep it secure, have been so remiss?

No sooner has IHQ tumbled to the disaster which must be befalling III Corps than everyone from Napoleon down sets about washing his hands of it:

'The Prince of Eckmühl [Davout] wasn't generally liked. The Prince of Neuchâtel [Berthier], rather as if he wanted to clear himself in advance, was showing everyone the General Staff's orders to the Prince of Eckmühl. He showed them to me. The outburst of fury against Marshal Davout was the more general in that the Emperor publicly charged him with being responsible for all the dangers that might overwhelm III Corps. Great and small alike seized the opportunity of casting their stones at him, without finding out whether the orders he'd received, the advice he'd given to Ney, or the circumstances of the moment, didn't justify him.'

Yet in some obscure way everyone's pinning his faith on Ney. 'To his everlasting glory', Caulaincourt goes on, the army has only one opinion about him:

'To catch up with us on the Krasnoïe road was regarded as an impossible task. But if anyone could make the impossible possible, Ney was the man. Every map was in use, everyone pored over them, tracing out the route he'd follow if courage could open a way for him. "He'll retreat through Kiev rather than surrender," was the general view.'

The only fear is that at the sound of IV Corps' guns at Krasnoïe Ney may have got himself killed while trying to fight his way through. As IHQ leaves Orsha at noon on 20 November, the Master of the Horse observes Napoleon,

'dressed as usual in his chasseur officer's coat and a great overcoat, on foot at the head of his guards, surrounded by a numerous staff. He seemed to be most uneasy, and was marching hesitantly. At each moment he halted, and only after doing so for a quarter or half an hour did he resume his march. Doubtless the purpose of these repeated halts, which seemed to surprise everybody, was to wait for the rearguard, of which we still had no news, and give it a chance to rejoin us. Consternation stood painted on every face.'

Some twelve miles further on IHQ halts again, this time in 'a miserable peasant village', before finding lodgings in Baranoüi manor house, a couple of miles from the road.

For several days now there's been no courier. No news from Victor's operations on the Dvina. Or from Schwarzenberg, who should be making Tchitchakov's presence on the Berezina impossible. Napoleon speculates:

'"No doubt Tchitchakov intends to join up with Tormassov, and they'll send an army to the Berezina, or rather to join Kutusov in this hilly country. As I've always thought, Kutusov's leaving us alone now so as to get ahead, and is going to attack as soon as these reinforcements have reached him. We must hurry. If my orders have been carried out I too will have my forces assembled on the Berezina. We've got to get there as fast as possible, because great things may happen there."'

'For the first time,' says Caulaincourt, 'he struck me as worried about the future.'

As for what's happening to Ney, that's anyone's guess.

CHAPTER 12

NEY'S AMAZING EXPLOIT

Ney leaves Smolensk – a naked man runs twelve miles – 80,000 Russians to 6,000 Frenchmen and Württembergers – 'we marched across ploughed fields, suffering horribly from hunger' – General Henin's obstinacy – 'We were still eight leagues from Orsha' – 'Our position isn't brilliant, Marshal' – 'Go and tell your general a Marshal of France never surrenders' – a tragic lieutenant of Voltigeurs – 'Ney's calmness kept the men to their duty' – 'Qui vive?' – 'France!' – 'there was a joy hard to describe'

Of the 11,000 men of III Corps who'd left Moscow only 3,000 had reached Smolensk. 'Nothing was left of the Württemberg division or the cavalry. The artillery had only retained a few guns.' Fezensac had admired his men's staunchness as they'd slowly withdrawn through the eastern suburbs into the Old City. His 500 men of the 4th Line had been the last to withdraw from the burnt-out ruins beyond the Dnieper. 'During the three days this affair had lasted,' he assures us, 'no notice had been sent to Ney of the danger' about to engulf him.

In the city, reinforced by the 129th Line, the Illyrians and I Corps' 2nd Division – of which the 2nd and 3rd Battalions[1] of Joseph-Napoleon's Spanish Regiment form part – Ney had 'assembled all the isolated detachments and united them with his own corps, reorganising a battery of six guns' (to which 20 men of Lieutenant Sauvage's company have been attached, though Sauvage himself, as we've seen, had marched on ahead with I Corps). Then, in the afternoon of 16 November, one of Davout's ADCs, a Major de Briqueville, had come back to tell Ney that I Corps was ordered to hasten its steps and recommended he do likewise. Ney – according to Caulaincourt, who'll hear about it afterwards, presumably at the Baranouï manor house – receives Briqueville

'ungraciously enough. The two marshals didn't like each other. They'd just had a difference of opinion about the pillage of Smolensk.'

In fact there'd been a blazing row. Ney had accused Davout of stripping the magazines, leaving nothing for III Corps. ('When I in my turn entered the town,' Bonnet had written in his diary, 'I could find nothing for my regiment or myself.')

In the evening a second messenger had arrived. Since he, Davout, was going to force the pace to support Eugène, who was at grips with the Russians outside Krasnoïe, he advises Ney to leave forthwith. To this Ney, who only has a few hours to provision his corps and is forced to choose between starving en route and being cut off, replies arrogantly that 'all the Russians on earth and all their Cossacks won't be strong enough to prevent me passing through them'.

'Of the last orders sent to him, one never reached him, and the other only arrived in the evening of 16 November, when it was too late. These delays were due to the state of our communications.' Communications now so bad as to be non-existent:

'A lieutenant and twelve men who'd been sent back to Smolensk for food were all captured by the Cossacks as they tried to return. Only a drummer got back – leaving 43 of the 67 men to answer roll call that morning.'

That evening, as he retires through what's left of this city which he (like Le Roy) had known as a prisoner of war in 1807, Fezensac sees

'the doors and windows of what remained of its houses shattered, the rooms full of corpses, in the middle of its streets carcasses of horses, all of whose flesh had been eaten by the soldiers and even by some of the inhabitants.'

Major Bonnet realises that the town's 'on fire for the second edition [*sic*]'. 'The fire', says General *J.-D. Freytag*, whose division leaves at midnight, 'was so violent that the bright light of its flames in the midst of a very dark night lit up our way for us for 12 miles.' Fezensac will

'never forget the impression of sadness I felt that night, in the deserted streets by the light of the fire reflected in the snow and contrasting singularly with the soft clarity of the moonlight'.

Colonel Schmidt of the Illyrians is carrying out his orders to blow up the medieval walls and ramparts, and as Bonnet marches out with Razout's division at 3 a.m., he sees

'one of the towers of the rampart, standing up on the horizon against the glow, leap up and lie down, overthrown by the mine laid underneath it'.

It's the so-called Royal Citadel.[2] Just as he's leaving, Fezensac hears 'several strong explosions'. But then Miloradovitch's Cossacks come bursting in and prevent his men from doing more damage: 'Their many guns killed or wounded more than half his Illyrians.' Luckily Schmidt himself, against his own gloomy forebodings, finds he's unscathed.

Ney's battalions are now massed in bodies 'three or four times greater than before Smolensk'. And march on, undisturbed by Cossacks. Major de Briqueville is with them, but his message, it seems, has been forgotten. No one realises that III Corps is cut off. But when Freytag's division is 'half-way to Krasnoië' and has 'halted briefly to wait for daybreak' something astounding happens:

'We saw running toward us a man who'd been stripped of all his clothes, having absolutely nothing on but his shirt. It was a sergeant-major who'd been in hospital at Smolensk. At the height of the fire this unfortunate man, forgetting his sickness and the terrible cold then prevailing, had run through the flames and ruins, and having done twelve miles, he'd reached us, still running. Unfortunately we couldn't lend him the least scrap of clothing, we had none ourselves.'

Tragically the sergeant-major 'having escaped from the enemy, the flames and his fatigue after covering such a distance at such a speed' expires of cold 'in the midst of his own men'.

All day their march goes on. And when, as they're advancing quietly along the Krasnoïe road at dawn on 18 November, they 'hear a lively cannonade' in the distance ahead of them, everyone assumes it can only be Victor's IX Corps, sent to their assistance. On the other hand they keep seeing 'traces of bivouacs obviously not French'. Between 1 and 2 p.m.

'we were approaching Krasnoïe, when, as a tailpiece to these reflections, some roundshot reached us from our left; and soon we were filing past some rather well-nourished gunfire. Colonel Reissenbach was sent forward with some voltigeurs in line of skirmishers against these pieces.'

But what unit is this in the morning fog 'to the right of the road, less than a league from Krasnoïe' which Bonnet sees 'rallying, not having been able to force its way across the Krasnoïe ravine'? It's Ricard's brigade[3] – seconded from I Corps at Smolensk – that's run into

'the enemy drawn up in battle order not far from that town. Now it was our turn. He presented long lines of cavalry, several infantry corps, and his left extended to a short distance from the highway. A rather deep ravine separated us from the Russians, who were opening a cannonade and deploying some formidable artillery.'

Major Faber du Faur, commanding the remaining three 12-pounders of Ney's reserve artillery, sees

'swarms of Cossacks approaching to within 4,500 paces and crossing the road in all directions. Their artillery saluted our column with a murderous discharge of roundshot and grape. Scarcely had we made the painful attempt to take the guns off their limbers than most of our teams were blasted to pieces by the enemy fire, and we saw ourselves unable to advance our guns.'

So they spike them and leave them to the Cossacks. After which his surviving gunners, 'the armed men at our head', join the compact mass of unarmed men.

Only now, it seems, as Ricard's survivors come staggering back to the right of the road to take refuge with Ney's three divisions, do they realise that it's not Marshal Victor's army corps that's come to meet them:

'It had been the Prince of Eckmühl who'd come to grips with the Russian army and tried to force his way through to Krasnoïe. The enemy had been waiting for us on the heights, to cut off our retreat. The Russian army, ranged in line of battle, was barring the route.'

Ney, in observation on the other side of the ravine, has only 6,000 combatants, six cannon and his personal escort of 'two squadrons of Polish lancers' plus the usual horde of stragglers and camp-followers to embarrass his movements. There's a thickish morning mist. But through it he sees he has against him Miloradovitch's 80,000 men, drawn up in front of the forests away to the left and across the road. Forming up his line of battle in the plain, Ney assembles 'all the sappers, and adding to them 100 of the most determined men,' entrusts their command to Colonel Bouvier of the Engineers:

'Supported by a few guns and the rest of our rearguard, he had to attack and punch a hole in the enemy; but at the height of the action this brave officer was felled by a roundshot and his troops were repulsed by cross-fire from an enemy anyway vastly superior in numbers.'

At this moment one of Miloradovitch's ADCs approaches under a flag of truce. He tells Ney he's confronted by an army of 80,000 men. If the Marshal wants to convince himself of the truth of this statement he can send an officer to see with his own eyes. Miloradovitch, he says, admires his talents and courage; and this doesn't permit him to propose anything unworthy of so great an officer as Marshal Ney. But the fact is he's been abandoned by the rest of the French army. And has no option but to surrender. – 'For sole reply, taking a few salvoes of gunfire as a pretext, the Marshal took the spokesman prisoner,' confiding him, says Tschudi, to the 48th Line.

Bonnet's colonel, commanding the brigade that's come to include the 'Illyrians, the 4th Line's two battalions, and ourselves, also two battalions strong', leads the attack and charges with the 4th Line. To the right, Ricard's already in action again:

'The 48th were ordered to cross the ravine, follow the highway in closed column and then abruptly change direction to the left, to charge the Russians with the bayonet as soon as parallel with their flank.'

But the moment the enemy see what they're about, the 48th are

'crushed by the Russian artillery. No one had ever seen such dense or continuous grapeshot. Even so, these soldiers, dying of hunger and cold, charged so vigorously that we twice saw the enemy's guns beat a retreat and form battery again. Both the general of brigade and the colonel, several paces ahead of the first platoon, were gravely wounded.'

His arm shattered by a fragment of grape, the 48th's colonel realises that

'this rumour, spreading through the ranks, seemed to be worrying the rank and file, but went on marching at the head of his unit, and didn't leave the field of battle until he'd been hit in both legs by two pieces of grapeshot. The regiment, which had only 650 men under arms, lost 550 of them and had to recross the ravine.'

Fezensac, marching at the head of the 4th Line along the road criss-crossed by cannon fire, sees how every cannon shot is

'carrying off whole files. At each step death was becoming more inevitable. Yet our march wasn't slowed down for a single instant.'

'Favoured by the fog,' says Bonnet, the 18th Line cross the ravine,

'but amidst a hale of grape. Climbing up its other side I was hit in the cheek by a fragment which almost made me lose consciousness. I left my rank. The regiment impetuously continued its charge and, taking off to the right, threw back a line of infantry; but enveloped by numerous cavalry it was itself annihilated, except for two or three officers who'd been wounded early on, and the colonel, Reissenbach, the officers of his company and myself. The Eagle was left there.'

The leading 'division'[4] of Fezensac's regiment, 'utterly crushed by grapeshot,' is thrown back on to the one behind it,

'carrying disorder into its ranks. The Russian infantry charged us, and the cavalry, falling on our flanks, threw us into a complete rout. For a moment a few well-placed skirmishers halted the enemy's pursuit. Ledru's [10th] division was put into the line, the six guns replied to the numerous Russian artillery. During this time I rallied what was left of my regiment on the highway where roundshot was still reaching us. Our attack hadn't lasted a quarter of an hour, yet the 2nd Division no longer existed. My regiment was reduced to 200 men. The Croat [Illyrian] regiment and the 18th, which had lost its eagle, were even worse treated.'

For the 2nd Division, which also includes Colonel Tschudi's Spaniards, 'it had been impossible to reconnoitre the enemy lines because of the fog,' its Commandant Lopez will remember:[5]

'We'd crossed the ravine, swept by grape from the enemy batteries, of which we captured two guns. General Ricard, wounded in the head at the action's outset, had still gone on giving orders. He was everywhere at the same time, electrifying the men with his shouts of *"Vive l'Empereur!"*'

By now the Joseph-Napoleon's two battalions are 'only 35 files strong, having had 76 men killed or wounded in this affair, eight of them officers'.[6] More than half the Croats, too, have been put out of action, and Colonel Schmidt's been wounded in the leg. Ricard's men have made

'an impetuous attack without artillery, unsupported by I Corps' other divisions and, despite the fire of 50 pieces of cannon placed in an advantageous position, had thrice overthrown the Russian line.'[7]

It's also been the end of the 18th Line. 'So,' Bonnet, his cheek streaming with blood, realises, 'the road to France was cut off for us.' 'While we were ranged in order of battle in the plain,' Freytag goes on,

'all the time standing up to a terrible and continuous fire, our carriages, our horses, part of the artillery and all the unarmed men, the stragglers and the sick who'd remained on the road, fell into the power of a "hurrah" of Cossacks. All the food and the few resources still remaining to us were lost. Marshal Ney gave orders that if possible the fight should be sustained until dusk, in order to retreat by the Dnieper.'

Thus begins Ney's ever-famous night retreat.

At first he thinks he'll make a detour southwards and aim for Molihew. But the wounded Colonel Pelet of the 48th Line (so Captain François will hear), points out to Ney (who'd 'bitterly' complained that the Emperor 'was abandoning the rearguard, what will become of us?')[8] that the Russians are stronger on that side. So perhaps it'll be better to cross the Dnieper on its ice and get to Orsha that way? The Dnieper lies only nine miles away; but to find a road to it means retracing their steps for three miles. Fezensac relates 'verbatim, a singular dialogue':

'Ney's self-confidence equalled his courage. Without knowing what he meant to do nor what he could do, we knew he'd do something. The greater the danger, the prompter his determination; and once having made up his mind, he never doubted he'd succeed. His face expressed neither indecision nor disquietude. All looks were fixed on him, no one dared interrogate him. Finally, seeing an officer of his staff beside him, he said to him:

'"We're in a bad way."

'"What are you going to do?"

'"Cross the Dnieper."

'"Where's the road?"

'"We'll find it."

'"And if the river isn't frozen?"

'"It will be."

'"*Well, the best of luck to us!*"'

It's about 4 p.m. and dusk is already falling as Fezensac's men, 'suffering horribly from hunger', march off

'across ploughed fields. I was on foot, like any ranker. At the beginning of our attack on Krasnoië I'd had a horse killed under me and it was impossible to find another.'

'At about 9 p.m.' Freytag goes on, 'we reached a village on the banks of the Dnieper. All we found in the way of food was a drink made of beetroot.' The village's name is Danikowa. Pretending to bivouack there for the night, Ney lights fires and places outposts. Meanwhile a lame peasant is 'found and used as a guide to tell us where the Dnieper's most likely to be frozen. Led by this peasant we set off.' By and by they come to a second village – François calls it Gusinoë – where the Dnieper has steep banks.

'It was Marshal Ney's intention to wait for dawn before crossing the river. Since it wasn't entirely frozen over despite the extreme cold, it was crucial to be able to see clearly so as to find those points along it where the ice was thick enough to bear the weight of men and horses.'

While the surgeons give what first aid they can to the wounded, Ney snatches some sleep.

'Ney alone, oblivious of the day's and morrow's dangers, slept deeply. But at midnight a message arrives of the enemy's approach. Cossacks have even been seen in the village. Marshal Ney at once ordered the crossing to begin – the guns and their ammunition wagons were abandoned.' Likewise the non-walking wounded.

'Disorder and confusion were extreme. Everyone tried to get across first. We slid down very gently one after another, fearing we'd be swallowed up under the ice, which was cracking at every step we made. At every moment we were between life and death. But apart from the danger to ourselves we had to witness the saddest spectacle. All around us we saw unfortunates who'd fallen into the ice with their horses up to their shoulders begging their comrades for a help they couldn't give. Their complaints tore at our hearts, already overwhelmed by our own perils. Reaching the other side we had to clamber up a very steep bank, twelve feet high. It was all slippery from those who'd gone before us and made the ascent impracticable'

– in a word, the same situation as at the Wop.

'Three times I'd reached the top, and three times I fell back into the river. My strength was beginning to desert me when I heard the voice of Marshal Ney telling me to make haste and come up. "I can't", I said, "unless someone helps me." Instantly the Marshal used his sabre to cut a branch off a tree, reached it down to me and in this way pulled me up. Without his aid I'd infallibly have perished.'

So thin is the ice that 'very few horses were able to get across'. Fezensac confides 'the Duke of Piacenza to two sappers, who finally saved him and M. de Briqueville who'd been dangerously wounded the previous day and who crossed the Dnieper by dragging himself on his knees. The troops formed up again on the other side of the river.' 'In the midst of such disorder', Freytag goes on,

'it was very hard to rally the scattered troops, discouraged as they were and almost succumbing to the intense cold. The cavalry, above all, delayed us. It was impossible for it to cross at the same point as we had. So it had to go a long way to find a more solid passage. At last it rejoined us, and we set out.'

But Fezensac sees little if anything of it:

'Success had already crowned the Marshal's first plan. We were over the Dnieper. But we were more than 15 leagues [45 miles] from Orsha. And must get there before the French army had left it. We were going to have to cross unknown districts and stand up to enemy attacks, with only a handful of exhausted infantrymen, without either cavalry or artillery.'

Next day, surprisingly, those who've got across find themselves unmolested. They pass through a village full of sleeping Cossacks, whom they take prisoner:

'At first daylight on 19 November we took the Liubavitschi road. Only for a few moments were we held up by a few Cossack outposts, who fell back as we approached. By midday we'd reached two villages on high ground, whose inhabitants hardly had time to flee and abandoned their provisions to us. The men were falling into the joy caused by a moment of abundance when we heard the shout: "To arms!"'

The Russians are pushing back their outposts:

'The troops came out of the villages, formed up in a column, and got going again, the enemy being in presence.'

Even if it's only Cossacks there are entire squadrons of them

'manoeuvring in an orderly manner, and commanded by General Platov himself. Our sharpshooters contained them, the columns quickened their pace while preparing themselves to meet cavalry.'

If Ney's men aren't afraid of them it's because 'Cossacks never dared drive home against an infantry square'. Much more serious, Platov has some guns on sledges. At 3 p.m., just as the few survivors of the 18th Line are halting in a village, they see some Cossacks:

'Three masses appeared, of about 100 horses. We took up our weapons and marched against them. As the hostile cavalry retired it led us on to a dozen guns which briskly saluted us. By marching to the left through shrubs and bushes we supported ourselves on the bank of the Dnieper.' They manage to march past them. 'Until nightfall Marshal Ney fought unceasingly against so many obstacles, availing himself of the least accidents of the terrain.' But as darkness falls he has to turn his column off to the left, 'along the woods which fringe the Dnieper. The Cossacks had already occupied them.' The 4th and 18th Line, led by General Henin, are ordered to throw them out. 'Meanwhile the enemy artillery took up position on the other side of a ravine we'd have to cross. It was there Platov was counting on exterminating the whole lot of us.'

Fezensac leads his regiment into the wood and the Cossacks withdraw; but so dense and black is the forest his men have to face in all directions at once:

'Night came down, we heard nothing from around us. Ney, as likely as not, was still marching on. I advised Henin to follow his movement. To avoid being reproached by the Marshal for leaving the post he placed him in, he refused.'

At that moment they hear loud shouts at some distance, indicative of a charge being made: 'So it became certain our column was continuing its march and we were going to be cut off.' Fezensac assures Henin

'that the Marshal, whose way of doing things [*manière de servir*] I knew very well, wouldn't send him an order. It was up to each unit commander to act according to circumstances; and anyway he was by now too far off to be able to communicate with us. The 18th had certainly left long ago.'

So he should follow on. But all Henin agrees to, at the utmost, is to join up with the 18th and so re-unite the two regiments. But the 18th has already left the scene, and 'instead we ran into a squadron of Cossacks'. But though Henin, too late, tumbles to his situation, and 'though we searched the woods in all directions' they can no longer find their road:

'The fires we saw lit on various sides still further helped to bewilder us. The officers of my regiment were consulted, and we went in the direction the majority suggested.'

With only 100 of his men left to him, Fezensac is more than an hour's march behind the column. He has to march as fast as possible, while fighting off Cossacks

'who kept shouting at us to surrender and firing point-blank into our midst. Those who were hit were abandoned. A sergeant had his leg shattered by a shot from a carbine. He fell at my side, and said coldly to his comrades: "Here's a man done for; take my pack, it'll be useful to you." Someone took his pack, and we left him in silence. Two wounded officers suffered the same fate. Yet I noticed uneasily the impression this state of affairs was making on my regiment's men, and even on its officers. Then so-and-so, a hero on the battlefield, seemed worried and troubled – so true it is that the circumstances of danger are often more frightening than the danger itself. A very small number preserved the presence of mind we were in such need of. I needed all my authority to keep order as we marched and to prevent each man leaving his rank. One officer even dared give it to be understood we'd perhaps be forced to surrender. I reprimanded him aloud, so much the more sharply as he was an officer of merit, which made the lesson more striking.'

Finally, after over an hour, they see the Dnieper to their left. Fezensac's men recover their spirits. And Henin makes them march along the river bank, so the Cossacks shan't outflank them. And though Platov's cannon open fire at them, their aim in the darkness is chancy. Over the plain, over ravines whose sides are so steep they can hardly clamber up them, wading half-frozen streams up to their knees, they march on. Not a man quits the ranks:

'General Henin, hit by a fragment of casing from a bursting shell, wished to say nothing about it, for fear of discouraging the men, and went on commanding with the same zeal. Doubtless he could be reproached with obstinacy for defending the Dnieper wood too long; but at such difficult moments error is pardonable. What no one will deny him, at least, is the bravery and intelligence with which he guided us as long as this perilous march went on.'

At last, just as Ney's about to set out again, they see, ahead of them, his campfires. So, though utterly exhausted, the men of the 4th march for yet another hour, until they come to a village where there are some provisions and they can rest up. Yet

'we were still eight leagues from Orsha, and Platov would unquestionably redouble his efforts to carry us off. At 1 a.m., the fall-in was beaten.'

Freytag, too, though with the main body, has been having a nightmarish night. Forced to cross a swamp where the rearguard was being ravaged by grapeshot, he'd only managed to do so by clinging to a horse's tail:

'Although it was the darkest of nights we rallied and formed up in line of battle. A senior Russian officer came quite close to shout to us: "Surrender, surrender – all resistance is useless." "Frenchmen fight but don't surrender," replied General Ledru des Essarts, and ordered us to fire by platoons. We'd shared out the cartridges left after the battle at Krasnoïe. We marched on, always harassed by the enemy. The third day [20 November] at about 3 p.m., Marshal Ney made us take up a position with our backs to a forest.[9] We had a great deal of difficulty in scraping together 1,500 men who were in a state to hold their arms. But the monstrous cold made them incapable of using them.'

'To present a more imposing front we formed up in two ranks. All who'd lost their weapons or thrown them away when crossing the Dnieper were placed behind them. In front of us we saw a swarm of Cossacks, whose skirmishers came to within pistol-shot range. Nevertheless our troops stood with arms shouldered, and for lack of cartridges only pretended to fire when the Cossacks advanced by troops. Whereupon they retired and contented themselves with manoeuvring in front of us.

It was at that moment that Marshal Ney came up to me and said:
'"Well, Freytag, and what d'you think of this?"

'"That our position isn't brilliant, Marshal. But even that wouldn't be too bad if we only had some cartridges."

'"True; but it's here we must know how to sell our lives dearly."

'At nightfall the Marshal had fires lit at distances, to make the enemy think we were going to spend the night in the forest. At the same time he told us unit commanders to prevent our troops from giving themselves over to sleep, because at 9 p.m. we'd be breaking camp. In this interval the Russian general commanding-in-chief sent a flag of truce to summon Marshal Ney to surrender with his feeble army corps which, he said, couldn't fight the 100,000 Russians who surrounded it. I was present at the interview, and this was Ney's reply to the spokesman:

'"Go and tell your general a Marshal of France never surrenders."

'An hour later a second came to us, with the same purpose:

'"As for you, monsieur," the Marshal told him, "you'll stay with us. I'd very much like you to see for yourself how French soldiers surrender."

'At 8.45 a third came to claim his predecessor, and put the same proposition to the Marshal.

'"That makes two of you", he said again, "to see for yourselves in what fashion I'm going to surrender to the Russians."'

'While this flag-of-truce was speaking to Marshal Ney,' (Captain François will hear afterwards),

'the Russian kept throwing glances in all directions. The Marshal had him blindfolded and put him under guard of a few troopers. The officer's protests were of no avail. Yet it was true. The Russians surrounded us on all sides. At 9 p.m. exactly the Marshal gave the order to fall in without making the least noise. He advised us[10] to make our troops march in close formation and without uttering a word. We set off and with the greatest sangfroid and in the deepest silence passed through the Russian camp. However, the enemy noticed it. But before they could start shouting their hurrahs we were out of their camp. It was so dark and we marched so fast they couldn't get at us. Not that they didn't send many cannon shot after us or capture some stragglers, if one can apply this name to unfortunates who'd have needed supernatural strength to escape their destiny.'

By this time Henin's brigade has rejoined. The column trudges on undisturbed until daybreak. Then the Cossacks re-appear, taking advantage of its having to cross a plain,

'Platov advanced on sledges the artillery we could neither avoid nor get at. And when he thought he'd thrown our ranks into disorder, ordered his Cossacks to charge home. Marshal Ney swiftly drew up each of his two divisions in square. The 2nd, commanded by Henin, being the rearguard, was the first to be exposed.'

Fezensac has to use the strongest threats to force all isolated men who still have a musket to join the ranks. The Cossacks, 'feebly contained by our sharpshooters and driving before them a mob of unarmed stragglers, tried to reach our square. At their approach and under the gunfire the men forced the pace. Twenty times I saw them about to disperse and run on all sides, deliver themselves and us to the Cossacks' mercy. But Marshal Ney's presence, the confidence he inspired, his calm at so dangerous a moment, kept them to their duty. We reached some high ground. The Marshal ordered Henin to make a stand there, adding that it was a question of dying for the honour of France. Meanwhile General Ledru was marching for Jokubow [Teolino], a village with its back to a wood. When he'd established himself there we went and joined him. The two divisions took up position, each flanking the other. As yet it wasn't midday and Marshal Ney declared he'd defend this village until 9 p.m. A score of times General Platov tried to carry it. His attacks were constantly driven off and, in the end, weary of so much resistance, he took up position facing us. Already that morning the Marshal had sent off a Polish officer to Orsha.'

When the time comes to resume the march Ney's men are so weary he has to set fire to the 'big village' to get them to leave its houses. In the fire's lugubrious light Fezensac contemplates the spectacle of Ney's rearguard:

'The previous day's fatigue and the water filling my boots had brought back all my previous sufferings. Hardly able to march, I leant on the arm of M. Lalande, a young voltigeur officer.'

Earlier, Fezensac has had occasion to reprimand him. But now, very pleased with him,

'I felt the moment had come to promise to make it up for him, and promised him he'd be the first in the regiment to be promoted captain.'

Tragically, the voltigeur lieutenant too falls; 'but I like to think that the hope I'd given him sustained his courage for a while and perhaps softened the horror of his last moments.' 'But the enemy wasn't in force,' Bonnet sees, 'and despite their demonstrations, their bivouac fires, which seemed to have been lit by 10,000 men, we passed through their lines at 9 p.m.'

It's a bright moonlight night. At Orsha, Davout's been ordered 'incessantly to send back scouts along the Smolensk road' and Eugène too has been told to wait for Ney until midnight. 'If we didn't get any news of him by then we must go on our way and give up all idea of ever seeing him again.' But who's this officer coming across the endless expanse of snow towards the 1st Guard Lancers' outposts, commanded by Chlapowski?

'In the distance we take him for a Russian. But soon he's recognised as a Frenchman [sic]. We go to meet him and are overjoyed to learn that Marshal Ney and his men have escaped by a miracle and are only a league away.'

By and by Chlapowski and his Poles make out

'the brave Marshal himself, riding a wretched horse, followed by a few hundred men under arms, and an almost equal number of disarmed soldiers who'd thrown away their muskets out of exhaustion. The Marshal's officers told us what had happened during their painful march.'

The incredible news is sent instantly to Eugène, some of whose units have already set off down the Bobr road. Griois, with his fresh artillery from the Orsha depot, is

'already at some distance from Orsha when Prince Eugène, retracing his steps, told me we were going to turn back to meet Marshal Ney, of whom there'd just been news, after several days of cruel anxiety'.

Other units of IV Corps, after being regaled to something so rare as a distribution of rations, superintended by the Royal Guard, 'which had produced a better effect than threats, also – rare indeed – a roof to sleep under,' are 'reposing calmly in the warmth. At the news of Ney's being in peril,' Cesare de Laugier goes on, 'everyone's on his feet'. 'Nothing less than this motive,' Griois confirms,

'was needed to make us, without regret, turn back in the middle of the night and in a very sharp cold mount the Dnieper again without even knowing how far we'd have to go.'

Laugier:

'Retracing our steps, we did two leagues [eight miles] in the dark, often halting to listen. The Viceroy, for lack of any means of communication in this sea of snow, had a few cannon shots fired.'

Griois:

'then we drew up in position, and at the Prince's order, I had my guns fire three shots, to notify III Corps where we were'.

Laugier:

'to which Ney's force replied with some platoon volleys. From that moment the two corps marched to meet each other.'

Thus it comes about that Freytag, Fezensac and Bonnet are struggling over the last lap towards Orsha and 'the Cossack posts along the road are falling back before us' when they see 'a division' of IV Corps, led by the Viceroy himself, has come out 'a whole league' to meet them:

'After the "*Qui vive?*", to which the answer was "*France*", he and the Marshal embraced. Immediately there was a joy hard to describe, which somewhat revived our flagging morale.'

Laugier:

'Ney and Eugène were the first to meet, and threw themselves into each other's arms. At this sight everyone broke ranks. Without recognising each other, everyone embraced everyone else – Württembergers, Illyrians, Frenchmen, Poles, Tuscans, Genoese, with Italians clustering around the newcomers, we listened to their Odyssey. We overwhelmed them with our praises, our attentions, and in this moment forgot past ills, men's egoism, the cruelty of fate and future perils.'

Among joyful reunions those of the fourteen officers and 50 other ranks of the 2nd and 3rd Battalions of the Joseph-Napoleon Spanish Regiment – all who're left – are probably not the least emotional. For the first time during the campaign they meet their slightly more fortunate compatriots of the 1st and 4th Battalions. Even Le Roy, five versts [more than three miles] away, hears the shouts of joy coming from Orsha. Laugier writes in his diary that morning:

'Pell-mell, forming so to speak only a single family, we've come back to Orsha, where we're helping these unfortunate men to restore themselves and rest, guarded by ourselves.'

The news, of course, has been instantly transmitted to Napoleon at Baranouï – by Gourgaud, who's been left behind at Orsha to supervise the town's evacuation, probably also its destruction. Reaching the Baranouï manor house, he finds Napoleon dining with Berthier and Lefèbvre. Breathlessly he announces the splendid, the amazing news. 'At once,' says Fain, 'the Emperor got up, and grabbing both his arms said with emotion: "Is that really true?"' Several staff officers are sent back to 'tell the Marshal to hasten his steps'. And by and by 'Major de Briqueville, who'd been wounded by a roundshot in the thigh when fighting with III Corps', arrives with all the details. Never has the Master of the Horse known

'a victory in the field cause such a sensation. The joy was general. People were drunk with delight. Everyone was on the move, coming and going to tell of this return. It was impossible to resist repeating it to anyone one met. Such a national occasion had to be announced even to the grooms. Now officers, soldiers, everyone was sure we could snap our fingers at misfortune, that Frenchmen were invincible!'

By and by Ney himself appears. 'Never', Chlapowski notices,

'was the Emperor more expansive than in this interview. Going to meet him, he told him "I'd have given everything not to lose you."'

But at first Ney, Planat de la Faye notices, is

'in a very bad humour, complaining that we'd abandoned him. But when he knew the details of our retreat, he saw very well we'd done everything humanly possible. His gaiety returned, he jokingly uttered one of those soldieresque wisecracks which ran through the army like a powder train: "Anyone who gets back out of this'll need to have his balls tied on with iron wire."'

'Thus,' Captain François, the Dromedary of Egypt, concludes proudly,

'was executed one of the finest and most courageous movements ever attempted by so feeble a corps. And it would be to show oneself lacking in the esteem every military man ought to have for Marshal Ney not to recognise his rare talents; also those of Colonel Pelet, who together saved the debris of twelve regiments and a great number of wounded, of employees and non-combatants in the army's extreme rear.'

CHAPTER 13

THE TERRIBLE NEWS AT TOLOCZIN

'We had to keep marching, marching' – good-bye to the Dnieper – the unspeakable Drouot – terrible news at Toloczin – 'this is beginning to be very serious' – 'never was there a more critical situation' – 'people recalled the long wooden bridge at Borissow'

'No more rearguard duty for us,' Bonnet observes with relief at 8 a.m. on 21 November, as he makes ready, despite all promises of ample rations, to leave Orsha without any. All that's left of III Corps,

> 'some sappers, one or two battalions of Poles and the fragments of 30 different regiments who, unwilling to be captured, have melted together like a snowball',

are being hustled on ahead by Davout's rearguard. Awakened at dawn by the sound of Russian guns – 'the storehouses, very much exposed', have become targets for Russian artillery fire – Lejeune has his pockets filled by a young cousin who's been in charge of the Orsha hospital,

> 'with sugar and ground coffee. I urged him to flee, go on ahead of our retreat. But he wanted to go indoors again to fetch his money and his overcoat, probably got delayed, disappeared in the crowd, and I've never seen him again.'

As Fezensac marches down the 'fine broad highway, one of the loveliest one can imagine' with its 'magnificent avenues' which Dedem has found 'so beautiful at other times' but where the birches' filigree hangs down in silver veils of icicles, he's wondering how he's going to conserve 'this little handful of men who couldn't be granted a moment's rest'. Only 80 of them are still under arms. 'I was pained to see what a bad state their equipment and shoes were in, how thin they were, and the air of dejection on their faces.' His only consolation, if it is one, is that 'III Corps' other regiments were perhaps in an even worse state than mine'.

Le Roy, who'd woken up in the small hours and, fortified by a 'well-cooked ham', had left with Jacquet and their trusty Guillaume, after cleansing Schmidt's leg wound sustained at Krasnoïe with 'brandy and salt mixed with luke-warm snow water'. At all costs 'they're determined to get to the head of the column.' Oddly enough, Schmidt's wagon – it must have been marching with I Corps – has turned up, and they've been treated to some of its contents. Just beyond the town is the bridge over the Dnieper – 'the natural frontier', Pastoret thinks, 'between Poland and Russia'. As Daru crosses over he remarks to him: 'I've crossed many rivers in my life but never one with such pleasure as this one!' But for much of the day Bertrand's battalion of the 7th Light Infantry remains

> 'in position on the Dnieper's left bank, our mission being to hold up a cloud of Cossacks as long as possible. Their cries and gallopings hardly scared us. We made this mass respect us until the few guns found at Orsha and the other troops had crossed the bridge. Then it was our turn

to cross over, and the Marshal [Davout] didn't do so until after the battalion's very last voltigeur.'

Once again the straight broad highway with its double lines of silver birches stretches interminably ahead. 'Beyond the town,' Bertrand goes on,

'the road was solid ice. We could no longer stand up. Anyone who fell over dragged down others with him. Many, not being able to get up again because of the atrocious cold, were left behind at the discretion of our barbarous adversaries. Sometimes we heard these unfortunates calling out to us, but couldn't go back to help them. All the time we had to keep marching, marching, to avoid the cannon and irreparable losses.'

Fain and IHQ may have 'set off more cheerfully, the name of Marshal Ney on everyone's lips'; for Labaume and the rest of Eugène's staff the fine highway is

'only a place of tears and despair. All we heard on all sides was complaints and groans. Some declared they could go no further, lay down on the ground and with tears in their eyes gave us their papers and money to give to their family. A little further on we saw a woman who'd fainted; others were holding children in their arms, imploring all the passers-by to give them a bit of bread.'

Colonel Drouot, commander of the Guard's reserve artillery, will one day impress Napoleon.[1] But just now Pion des Loches is discovering he's 'a kind of military Tartuffe. Cold and reserved, he's sacrificing everything and everyone to his own promotion', and taking care neither of his men nor his *matériel*. Pion knows he's got some supplies hidden away in his light travelling carriage and invites him and his officers to set up a joint mess with the 'ten or twelve around the fire'. Drouot turns up alone. Where are the others? His officers, Drouot replies, aren't in the habit of eating with him. And when Pion suggests he take some of his provisions into his carriage, Drouot says he has no room for them. Anyway he still has a keg of wine intact, and doesn't need them, 'and that'll be enough for the two of us':

'A few paces away I saw Adjutant-Major Bitche and Surgeon Aide-Major Boileau sitting near a campfire with a depressed air of "supping by heart". These poor devils, belonging to no company, ought to be eating with their colonel.'

So Pion calls them over and promises to feed them daily as far as the Niemen if they'll guard his wagon with their lives.

Ever since Smolensk Maurice Tascher has been looking after his younger brother Eugène, a 20-year-old *sous-lieutenant* of artillery, wounded in one foot near Kolomna, but now with both feet frost-bitten. Eugène – it's his first campaign but his brother's sixth (the two brothers are nephews of the ex-Empress Josephine) – is riding on Maurice's sole remaining horse. During the course of the day, as they and everyone else make for Toloczin,[2] the tiny relic of Maurice's chasseur regiment sees a Cossack 'hurrah' carry off two companies of cuirassiers.

Before getting there IHQ halts briefly at the village of Kamienska. While trying to find quarters for some wounded men Daru has bumped into a Polish officer who has some news. News which, if true, is very worrying indeed. 'Admiral' Tchitchakov and his part of the Army of Moldavia, which should have been fighting the Turks[3] or at very least Schwarzenberg's Austrians, is in fact advancing on Minsk – with its immense stores of food, clothing and weapons. How can that be? What's Schwarzenberg doing?

Napoleon's plan now, protected by II and IX Corps and with the great Minsk depot as his supply base, is to halt the retreat behind the Berezina. But he's worried. As well he may be.

Toloczin, reached at nightfall, turns out to be
  'a country town of 250 timber houses on a little river crossed by a timber bridge. Two windmills. Continuous plain',[4]
– 'quite a defensible town', Maurice Tascher thinks it when he gets there. The morning's ice has turned to a thaw and hundreds of heavily laden sledges which have gradually been replacing carts and wagons are getting stuck in the slush and having to be abandoned. Here too are stores. Thanks to his commissary's uniform Kergorre, conducting a Treasury wagon, gets hold of a sack of flour and a huge bottle of brandy:
  'By gathering all my strength and despite the crowd of bayonets I managed to drag a sack as far as our house. But General Lefèvre-Desnouëttes had expelled our comrades and put his horses in the barns. Fortunately our industrious friends, profiting from whatever lay to hand, the many wooden fences and a little straw, had prepared the best bivouac in the world. There we found an excellent fire, beds prepared on the snow, but under shelter; the whole as well-arranged as a bivouac can be. The joy was general when they saw our flour and enormous bottle of vodka.'
Kergorre has even obtained some bread. Among the masses of men who've been fleeing on ahead he finds two Königsberg peasants. They have a sledge and two good horses, and are making tracks westwards, having been forced to follow the army all the long way from Königsberg. He and his friends bribe them to take them along with them.
  'Never would they have consented to let us get on to it for mere gold! We had to give them a bit of bread. All the debris of the Polish army were fleeing in sledges. There were several thousand of them, each containing two, three or four officers or soldiers. Soon the crush was such that we had to abandon our Prussians and resume our way on foot.'
IHQ itself lodges in 'some kind of a convent'. And it's here that Napoleon gets some very terrible news indeed. The worst possible news.
  Minsk has fallen!
  All its immense stores 'which the Emperor had been counting on since he'd left Smolensk to rally and reorganise the army' are lost. Its garrison, 4,000 Poles, mostly Lithuanians, under General Bronikowski, have been turned out head over heels by Tchitchakov's 30,000 Russians.

The French *émigré* General Lambert had captured '5,000 invalids and any amount of gunpowder and cannon barrels'. Even more disastrously, the Russians had seized two million rations (40 days' supplies for 100,000 men), 30,000 pairs of shoes and any amount of clothing – everything, in a word, the retreating ragged army's in such desperate need of. How can such a thing have happened? Haven't a total of 80,000 allied troops, notably Schwarzenberg's Austrians and Reynier's Saxons, been more than enough to prevent such a catastrophe?

'It also meant that he must face the disturbing certainty that the Moldavian Army might already be massed in our rear, instead of, as he'd all along been hoping, trying to join forces with Kutusov on our flank.'

Caulaincourt can't help admiring the way Napoleon takes these shocks: 'The Emperor's character, like steel by fire, was tempered anew by these reversed circumstances, this vista of danger. He immediately made up his mind to hasten the retreat, reach the Berezina if possible before Kutusov, and fight and vanquish whatever stood in his way. He was sure he'd find the Berezina bridge well guarded. That was the main thing. On that point he had no qualms.'

Yet waking up suddenly after a brief doze while keeping Daru and Duroc beside him to chat with him, he 'asks these gentlemen, waiting to withdraw till he was asleep', what they're saying.

'"We were wishing", Daru replies, "we had a balloon."'

'"What ever for?"'

'"To carry off Your Majesty."'

'"Heaven knows, things are difficult enough. So you're afraid of being made prisoners of war?"'

'"No, not prisoners of war. They won't let Your Majesty off as lightly as that."'

In the small hours he sends for Caulaincourt. Says:

'"This is beginning to be very serious."'

The Master of the Horse has spent four winters at Petersburg as his ambassador. Does he think it's cold enough for the rivers and Berezina marshes to freeze hard? Ney had had to abandon his guns. Yet he'd crossed the Dnieper on the ice? And he goes on 'jokingly':

'"Their balloon isn't to be laughed at. Here's an occasion when only brave men will have a chance of saving their skins."' Once across the Berezina, he assures Caulaincourt, he'll again be able to control events:

'"Together with my Guard the two fresh corps I'll find there'll be enough to defeat the Russians. If we can't, we'll have to see what our pistols can do. We must be ready to destroy everything, so as to leave no trophies to the enemy. I'd rather eat with my fingers for the rest of the campaign than leave a single fork to the Russians. We should also make sure my weapons and yours are in good condition, because we'll have to fight. But are we going to get to the Berezina in time?"'

he muses, asking rather himself (Caulaincourt thinks) than his interlocutor.

'"Will Victor have resumed the offensive in time to drive off Wittgenstein? If the Berezina passages are closed to us, we may be forced to cut our way through with the Guard cavalry."'

Almost more than by the military situation he's worried by the lack of any news. Malet's conspiracy is still festering in his mind. Is France aware of the disaster that's befallen the army? And he repeats his idea of Caulaincourt and himself leaving for France. Meanwhile everything superfluous, everything that can bog them down – forks for instance – must be got rid of. Caulaincourt has a word with Daru, and they agree that

'henceforth everyone who fed in the Emperor's mess should be responsible for his own cup, plate and cutlery if he wanted to keep them'.

The pretext they'll give is that Ségur's canteen mules are giving out.

Morning comes, and Jomini and Eblé hear the terrible news confirmed. Soon similar details are reaching Labaume at IV Corps headquarters:

'Dombrowski had been ordered to raise the siege of Bobruisk, go to Minsk and hold it. But the bad dispositions taken by the governor of that place caused it to be surrendered before help could come. Whereupon Dombrowski had moved back to Borissow, where he'd found the debris of the Minsk garrison.'

Secretary Fain reflects in his journal:

'The army is cooped up in a cramped space of fifteen leagues, between Kutusov, Wittgenstein and Tchitchakov. We're encircled by 140,000 Russians, who hold almost all the outlets. Never was there a more critical situation! Some high-ups are murmuring about memories of Toloczin and Charles XII. Some are even speaking in low voices of capitulating.'

Nor can the situation be concealed from the troops. An ADC to General von Ochs of the Westphalians, a Captain Johann von Borcke from Magdeburg, hears a dark rumour spreading that

'two new armies were threatening our line of retreat. On the march these rumours steadily gained substance, and the names "Tchitchakov" and "Berezina" were passing from mouth to mouth. At the time of our advance, four months earlier, the river had looked very insignificant to everyone. But now it seemed possible that the crossing might be fiercely contested. People clearly recalled the long wooden bridge at Borissow and the black marshy bank. And these recollections were enough to make us shudder at the prospect of having to fight our way across in the teeth of a fresh Russian army.'

Cesare de Laugier, too, hears how

'Generals Zayoncek, Junot and Claparède are to burn half the wagons, luxury carriages and all kinds of small vehicles which have accompanied us this far, and send the horses to the Guard Artillery. A staff officer and 50 gendarmes are seeing to it that this operation is carried out, on pain of death.'

Anyone under colonel's rank is only allowed to keep one vehicle. The horses of the Train, too, are to be sent to the artillery. Evidently it isn't only the horses pulling the guns and caissons of the Guard Artillery that are giving out, but also those drawing its treasure chests. Its paymaster Eggerlé opens them and gives everyone advances. Pion, in his turn, opens his wagon and has all his 'candles lit'.

But IHQ's 24-hour halt at Toloczin, Fain notes in his diary, has done its 'men and horses the greatest good'. Just as Pion and his group are about to set off again,

'an *officier d'ordonnance* comes to tell us His Majesty's finding the conduct of his Guard's artillery officers scandalous, abandoning guns and ammunition wagons and harnessing their best horses to their wagons to save their personal effects'.

But Pion replies abrasively that *his* officers aren't undressing at bivouacs, like Gourgaud's subordinates are. As for his wagon, it contains food, and 'we prize our lives more than our guns, which are useless anyway, for lack of ammunition wagons and gunners'. But when the *officier d'ordonnance* warns them that the Emperor's just had the wagon of an officer of the Train burnt 'without letting anyone extract any of its contents', second thoughts prevail. Pion's party realises that the same thing can happen to their own wagon. Anyway its horses are obviously unlikely to drag it much further. So they off-load its most valuable foodstuffs on to the animals' backs:

'"It's all over with us," said Bitche. "In a week we'll all be dead." I emptied my trunk into a travelling-bag I'd had made at Moscow out of one of Prince Bayetinski's tapestries. I gave my sword to Lagrange, who'd lost his. I put about 100 pounds of biscuit and a loaf of sugar into my sack, and four bottles of rum into my canteen, loading myself with a fifth. I distributed a quintal of very fine flour to my comrades, together with my supplies of tea and coffee and the rest of my sugar. There remained more than 150 bottles of wine and liqueurs which we drained off during a large part of the night. Thus a few hours destroyed resources which would have kept us alive a fortnight longer.'

In his much regretted wagon – the one he'd filled so methodically with victuals in Moscow but which they now leave standing by the roadside – Pion also says adieu to

'a magnificent spyglass, a pretty little mahogany desk and my box of books. But I kept another box containing a superb Chinese porcelain dinner service which I placed in an artillery wagon.'

Drouot's egoism appalls them. 'Pretending to eat a bit of biscuit and then slipping off aside to drink a few gulps out of a bottle that he was carrying between his greatcoat and his coat', he's not sharing anything with anyone:

'Bitche and I never took our eyes off him. More than once we caught him red-handed. I admit he once offered me a long sausage. I cut it into two parts: one very small, which I gave him back, the other very big, which I shared with Bitche and Boileau. I was delighted by my prank,'

but he doesn't get a chance 'to commit a second mistake'. Drouot's superior, 'Old Thunderer' General Sorbier, commander of the Guard artillery, isn't exactly a charming character either. 'A man of medium height, thin and sallow', the sensitive Planat de la Faye finds his face 'cantankerous and repulsive'. He too is 'what's called a bad bedfellow'. Yet even he scorns Drouot, keeps on sending him back to make sure their rearmost *matériel* is keeping up, etc. And finally tells him not to present himself before him unless summoned.

After 'marching with great difficulty along a thawed, muddy road' the Fusiliers-Grenadiers had reached Toloczin at about midday on 22 November and have been 'halting on the far side of the town, drawn up by the roadside'. Alas, Bourgogne's pack – so weary or thoughtless he's becoming – has been abandoned on a sledge to the Cossacks:

'So good-bye to my knapsack and its contents, which I'd so set my heart on taking back to France! How proud I'd have been to say "I've brought this back from Moscow!" I saw Cossacks in the distance carrying off their prisoners – and no doubt my poor knapsack too.'

All of a sudden who should he see in the crowd, a basket on her arm, if not the very woman who'd saved his life in that den of thieves at Smolensk? And she too recognises him – 'by my bearskin'. Yes, she tells him, all the brigands who'd beaten her for refusing to do their washing had been killed at Krasnoïe, 'fighting desperately to save their money, for they had a lot of it, above all gold and jewels'. Now she's all on her own:

'But if I'd take her under my protection she'd take good care of me. I consented at once, never thinking of the figure I'd cut in the regiment when I turned up with a woman.'

If only Bourgogne can find a house or a stable to change in, she'll give him some fresh linen out of her basket. 'I accepted joyfully. But as we're looking for a suitable place I hear the drums beating.' So telling his new-found 'wife' to follow on and wait for him on the road, he falls in:

'Just then the Emperor came past with King Murat and Prince Eugène. Placing himself among the Grenadiers and Chasseurs, the Emperor made them a speech. He told them the Russians were waiting for us at the Berezina, and had sworn that not one of us should get across. Then, drawing his sword and raising his voice: "Let us all swear to die fighting rather than never see our country again!" The oath was taken. Bearskins and shakos were waved on the points of bayonets, and shouts of *"Vive l'Empereur!"* were heard. Marshal Mortier made us a similar speech, received with the same enthusiasm, and similarly with all the regiments. It was a splendid moment, and for the time being made us forget our miseries.'

As for his 'wife', she's been

'engulfed in the torrent of Prince Eugène's thousands. They and the corps belonging to Marshals Ney and Davout were in complete disorder. Three-quarters of them were sick or wounded, and the rest utterly demoralised and indifferent to everything.'

Only the Poles of V Corps – after a fall from his horse at the beginning of the retreat Prince Poniatowski's had to hand it over to Zayoncek, a senior guards officer – and Claparède's Vistula Legion seem to be coping.

Claparède himself – his Poles don't like him a scrap – has fallen into despondency. Dedem van der Gelder, indeed, is often finding the Poles so obliging as to 'swap my horsemeat for mutton cutlets and *kacha* soup'. In general, he says, 'the allied troops were finding them much more amiable than the French'.

Amazingly, Le Roy, who's glad to find 'the road firmer than it was yesterday, though the wind and snow seem to want to bring us to a standstill', has a bit of luck. While passing through a hamlet, what does he see abandoned in the middle of the road but a big bear's skin! Picking it up, he puts it on his horse and tells Guillaume to take good care of it. Once again he and his friend Colonel Schmidt of the Illyrians are keeping each other company. Yes, Schmidt agrees again, they're worse off as superior officers than they'd ever been as subalterns. But to Captain François, aching from his multiple wounds, in Davout's rearguard, it's obvious all such distinctions have long ago been lost:

'For a long time now officers of all ranks and the men had the same accoutrements. Nothing more extraordinary than our half-burnt sheepskins and greasy leather garments. Our long beards had icicles hanging down from each hair. Everyone was walking along, speechless, haggard-eyed, stunned. Whenever a man fell, those who could open their mouths said: "There's yet another who's *done a bear*" – *faire l'ours*, such was the expression. And a few instants afterwards one of those who'd just said this *did a bear* in his turn. Some were wearing a beggar's scrip or haversack with a little flour in it hung over their shoulders, with a pot hanging at their side by a bit of string. Others were leading shadowy horses by the bridle, carrying a few victuals and kitchen utensils. If one of these horses fell, we sliced it up and put the flesh on the backs of those that remained, to nourish us.'

Private Jakob Walter, trudging onwards with a *konya* whose unshod hoofs, he's pleased to see, aren't having any trouble with the ice, is noticing that hardly one man in a hundred has a cookpot. To belong to a group, now, is a man's only salvation:

'The units were more or less dissolved. Their wreckage had formed a great number of corporations of six, eight or ten men who marched on together, having their reserves in common, repulsing all outsiders. All these unfortunates walked huddled together like sheep, taking the greatest care not to break up amid the crowd, for fear of losing their little group and being maltreated. Did a man get lost? In that case another corporation took any victuals he might have and pitilessly drove him away from all the fires – if the wind allowed any to be made up – and from any spot where he wanted to take refuge. He didn't cease to be assailed until he'd rejoined his comrades. These men passed in front of the generals, and even of the Emperor himself, without paying more heed to them than they would to the least man in the army.'

Images of ontological catastrophe which will fix themselves in François' mind forever:

'Our heads were hideous, our faces yellow and smoke-begrimed, filthy with the soil of our bivouacs, blackened by the greasy smoke from conifers; eyes hollow, our beards covered with snot and ice. We couldn't use our hands or button our trousers, which many had fastened with a bit of string. Like my comrades, I'd opened mine at the back, but often did my business in them. On all the roads we heard the sound of corpses being ground to pieces under the horses' feet or the vehicles' wheels. On all sides we heard the cries and groans of those who'd fallen and were struggling in the most terrifying death-throes, dying a thousand times while waiting to die.'

Where the route crosses the Molihew road, surgeon von Roos sees

'a Westphalian soldier sitting on the ground. He was holding a big ingot of silver in the shape of a rectangle. Weighing 15–20 pounds, it probably came from a church ornament. He was offering it in exchange for food. But no one wanted it.'

Returning from Molihew whither he'd been sent from Smolensk to order the units stationed there to fall back on Borissow, *Roman Soltyk* of the Topographical Department rejoins the column; and is devastated to see how things have changed in the meantime:

'The infantry, accompanied by the little country horses the French called *konyas*, laden with various objects, was marching all pell-mell with them. The cavalry was almost wholly dismounted, and our troopers were walking painfully on foot. In general the men's clothing was in the worst of states. Their torn coats didn't keep out the cold. Some were covered in women's opulent furs; others in velvet mantles looted from the Kremlin. Others had found nothing to protect them against the rigours of the season but cloth-of-gold or silver chasubles. The men's footwear was in an equally wretched state. Many had wrapped their feet in linen and the bark of trees, tied with bits of string.'

As the cold becomes more severe he often sees

'soldiers, stupefied – or, rather, inebriated by the freezing weather – fling themselves headfirst into a campfire and so die consumed by its flames, without it even occurring to their comrades to drag them out'.

Only when he catches up with IHQ does Soltyk see

'the units we'd rallied in Lithuania and the Guard, above all, marching in good order. The latter was setting an example of devotion and subordination. Harassed by such long marches and such severe privations, its men were marching and dying in their ranks. Although bent under their weight, all were carrying their weapons and packs,. Frequently one saw one totter, fall and expire on the road.'

Next comes Bobr. En route for it, Schmidt, realises his wagon is no longer an economic way of transporting his provisions; and distributes

'biscuit and rice for two days to each man who'd been escorting it, which, with the bread they should have received at Orsha, should suffice for them for several days'.

He also makes them a present of the wagon and its horses. The rest of its contents are distributed among the party and its servants. Le Roy's pickings are some clean underclothes, a shirt and 'a brand new flannel waistcoat, mine being in shreds' – to keep his *embonpoint* warm. Also a couple of pocket handkerchiefs to protect his ears from frost-bite. Le Roy's amazing memory of every meal he has ever eaten will recall that evening's

'rice and a bit of beef, the last we still had, and which we ate with pleasure, despite the mob of people who were resting up and warming themselves in the room. After we'd dipped into the pot, spoonful by spoonful, we gave the rest to our servants.'

But only a bit of a wall of a burnt house provides shelter against the wind. That night (23 November) he and his friend and his servant lie down

'on some still warm cinders. The bearskin sheltered us. We lay pressed against each other to avoid a cold which had resumed with new strength.'

Upon the Illyrian regiment's surgeon suddenly appearing, Schmidt decides to travel on in his cabriolet. And Le Roy returns to him the notes and silver he'd entrusted to him at Smolensk,

'though he made difficulties about taking them, saying that being wounded he was afraid he mightn't get out of the danger we were all in'.

Having no taste for painful *au revoirs* that may turn out to be *adieux*, Le Roy leaves early next morning. And Franz Roeder, sick but no longer able to ride in Colonel Follenius' chaise because of the extreme cold, has to walk for seven hours to get to Bobr. 'Searching for water, my horse broke the ice, stumbled into a water hole and I fell in up to my stomach.' And the horse drowns. The dysentery-ridden Roeder studies his frost-bitten feet, but sees he

'must go on stoutly or perish. I pulled myself together with all the strength of my body and soul and did seven or eight hours on swollen feet.'

Once again his Sergeant Vogel has disappeared. The Hessians' neurasthenic Major Strecker has had some kind of stroke. Only Mailly-Nesle still rides on in his carriage

'in a very sad state of mind. The discouragement was growing daily. They told me they were going to burn our calèche and that I'd have to make do with a horse.'

So taking with him the basic necessities – they include 'one spur' – he too tells his servant Louis to do what he likes with the rest.

Marching for Bobr, Napoleon sends off an order to Oudinot. While Victor goes on manoeuvring his IX Corps to stave off Wittgenstein, II Corps is to come and form the column's rearguard. Clearly, now, only one thing matters. The bridge at Borissow. At all costs the army's last link with France must be saved.

PHASE THREE
ACROSS THE BEREZINA

CHAPTER 14

STRUGGLES FOR THE BORISSOW BRIDGE

Oudinot resumes his command – 'the very type of a light cavalryman' – 2nd Battle of Polotsk – two Marshals at loggerheads – how Minsk was lost – 'they lay down on their faces and no one could lift them up from that position' – Corbineau's long march – racing for 'that accursed bridge' – 'come and take coffee tomorrow at Minsk' – could Marbot have done better?

It had been in the last days of September, while being nursed back to health by his young wife at Vilna, that Oudinot had heard about the burning of Moscow and immediately 'realised what a catastrophe must ensue. All these items of news, his indefatigable artist-batman, Grenadier *François Pils*,[1] saw, had thrown him 'into a state of indescribable agitation'.

Although the doctors had done all they could to keep him there a fortnight longer, on 28 October he'd left to resume command of II Corps. From Borissow, where those wounded generals in Nansouty's convoy able to do so had come to pay him their respects, he'd gone on to Orsha. And on 9 November, in wild country overrun by Cossacks, his party had been met by a detachment of Colonel *Marcelline Marbot*'s 23rd Chasseurs,
'waiting on the road to escort him. The day was so sombre one could hardly see any longer. But since the Marshal didn't want to hang about,' they'd pushed on to Czéreia to reach Partonneaux's division, IX Corps' largest. And it had been 'at the gates of that town we met a courier bringing the bad news from Borissow' – i.e., of the loss of Minsk.

After the First Battle of Polotsk (18 August), when Saint-Cyr had taken over, II Corps had at first done very little fighting.[2] But its French, Swiss and Croat regiments, almost as much as the Bavarians of Wrede's VI Corps, had been terribly ravaged by sickness. Of the 12,626 Bavarians – half of Saint-Cyr's VI Corps – whom Wrede had mustered on 15 June before crossing the Niemen, only 4,557 were alive in September; and on 15 October only 1,622. Forced marches, typhus, homesickness and, above all, dysentery had killed most of the rest; likewise any number of men in II Corps. The Swiss Lieutenant, *Thomas Legler*, smitten like everyone else, had had to relieve himself 'up to 60 times a day. The doctors were invisible.' He'd been so weak he'd had to cling to the walls of the Jew's house in Polotsk which served for a hospital for himself and five other officers. Finally he'd cured himself by putting hefty doses of 'pepper, cinnamon and nutmeg in my soup'.

From time to time reinforcements had arrived. For instance to the 20th Chasseurs in Corbineau's light cavalry brigade. On 21 August their highly efficient little major *Jean-Nicholas Curély*, fresh from France, had turned up with some 100 troopers. Three days ago the regiment had even fled from the enemy, leaving some Bavarian gunners to be sabred by Russian cavalry, and Curély had had to bear the entire army's reproaches. Self-educated son of a labourer, a real republican of the old stamp who (like Le Roy) regards Napoleon's self-coronation as 'an act of weakness', in the eyes of his comrade de Brack[3] the 38-year-old Curély is 'the very type of a light cavalryman'. His party had formed a brilliant contrast to the rest of the regiment, most of whose horses had no shoes and whose harness was all in pieces. Instantly he'd deployed an activity worthy of Napoleon himself in his best days. The regiment's Colonel Legrange having been sick almost throughout the campaign, Curély had taken over as its effective commander: set the 20th Chasseurs' bakers to baking, its shoemakers to making shoes, and those men who couldn't do anything else to taking turns at grinding corn in a nearby mill. Meanwhile, as always, he'd been tirelessly making good the gaps in his own education, both practical and intellectual, each evening copying out what he'd read during the day. Soon each trooper had his four spare horseshoes and 50 nails. 'As for meat, there was no shortage, the countryside having an abundance of cattle.' So the 20th Chasseurs, at least, hadn't starved.

More substantial had been the 5,000 newcomers, among them 1,000 more recruits, which the four Swiss regiments of the ailing II Corps, now only some 6,000 strong and forever manoeuvring and fighting Wittgenstein's Russians, had received on 12 October. Three days after their arrival, the same day as Murat 500 miles away had been fighting to rescue his advance guard at Winkovo,[4] Wittgenstein had begun his general offensive. The Second Battle of Polotsk had been a most sanguinary affair. To his intense chagrin Legler, though recovered from his dysentery, hadn't been allowed to take part – it had been his day for police duty:

'The enemy column marching at us was said to consist of 20,000 men, the one aiming at our right wing of another 20,000, and the one which on the evening of 17 October had crossed the Dvina at Drissa, of 8,000 men. Thus we had to do with 40,000 men in whose camp there'd been no lack of anything, while a third of us looked like skeletons, and we could only put up 25,000 men to resist them. "Now at last the turn has come to us," everyone was saying, squeezing each other by the hand. "We'll resist to the last man. *Schweitzertreu ist alltag neu* [Swiss fidelity renews itself daily]."'

At nightfall the Swiss grenadiers had broken out from a surrounded churchyard at bayonet point, but when they'd got back to their camp

'150 grenadiers were missing at the roll-call, among them our Captain Gilly, whose corpse was buried with military honours at 11 p.m. in front of his battalion and all the brigade's officers'.

But Curély had been the hero of the occasion, momentarily even capturing Wittgenstein himself. By the end of the day, when Saint-Cyr, himself wounded in the knee, by an elaborate feint managed to evacuate his hospitals, all his provisions, artillery and parks from Polotsk and cross the Dvina, both II and VI Corps had suffered terribly. Of the 2nd Swiss' 1,200 men, for instance, 37 officers had been killed or wounded and 600 other ranks had been left on the battlefield. But it had also been largely Swiss staunchness that had secured the corps' retreat – the one Pouget had been notified of at Witebsk. In one of the three Swiss light infantry companies that have also been covering the heroic retreat is little voltigeur *Jean-Marc Bussy*.[5] Saint-Cyr had told them:

'I know you Swiss. For the attack Frenchmen are brisker. But if it comes to a retreat we can certainly count on your courage and coolheadedness.'

At the Bononia defile Wrede's Bavarians, too, had made a heroic stand, preventing a Finnish-Russian corps from taking II Corps in the rear. 'They showed great bravery,' thought Curély, who'd also participated in the fight with 50 of his 20th Chasseurs and himself been wounded by a lance-thrust in the shoulder. 'We killed all the horses drawing the enemy's guns and caissons, not being able to carry them off.' Even if these Swiss are largely conscripts[6] they have a military tradition all their own. Used to selling their superfluous young men dear (*'pas de l'argent, pas de suisse!'*), they've always been famous for their loyalty to their employers.

Meanwhile Victor's IX Corps, '30,000 strong and consisting of Germans' – apart, that is, from Partonneaux's division, which is mostly French – 'had come up from Smolensk' though not in time to hold the Dvina line. Among its German units are the conscripts – if any are still alive – whom the kindly Duchess Augusta of Saxe-Coburg with heavy heart had seen march out from Coburg last summer.[7]

'For the first time since 17 August we now also saw Marshal Oudinot again, who'd resumed command of II Corps. With this reinforcement we'd have thrown the enemy back over the Dvina if Victor hadn't had other orders in his pocket. These, to us, were an enigma.'

So far Victor's corps hasn't been in any battle. As for what's left of VI Corps, with his wounded knee as 'pretext' (Marbot) Saint-Cyr has handed it over to General Count Wrede.

From the moment when Oudinot had resumed his command he and his fellow-Marshal, the 47-year-old *Claude Perrin Victor*,[8] Duke of Belluno, have been at loggerheads. 'The great fault,' Oudinot's chief-of-staff and newly fledged brother-in-law Lorencez is seeing,

'had been not to give superior command of all the corps on the Grand Army's flanks to one Marshal alone. The Duke of Reggio had tried to get the Duke of Bassano to adopt this measure, but that minister hadn't dared to.'

And from the moment when Oudinot's resumed his command there's been trouble. 'At that epoch,' writes Marbot,

'all the Marshals of the Empire seemed determined not to recognise any rights of seniority among themselves, because none of them was willing to serve under one of his comrades, no matter how grave the circumstances'.

Victor isn't one of Napoleon's favourite marshals. A jaunty perhaps rather shallow personality with a baby mouth, his sunny nature has earned him the sobriquet *Beau-Soleil* ('beautiful sunshine'), causing Napoleon, so it's rumoured, to give him his ducal title (lit. 'beautiful moon') in mockery of his slightly bandy legs. But he's an efficient field commander. Pils goes on: '*M. le Maréchal* went to see Marshal Victor, whose seniority had given him command of both corps. On 13 November the two Marshals spent two hours in conversation to decide on a common course of action against Wittgenstein.'

That day it's bitingly cold – for the first time Pils and his *patron* have just seen 'a man drop dead not far from a bivouac fire'. But evidently it isn't cold enough to freeze Pils' water-colours, for his brush memorably captures the two marshals' postures where they sit their horses amid the gloom of the Russian winter afternoon, trying to concert their incompatible plans.

Both II Corps and IX Corps, however – some 25,000 Swiss, Portuguese, Illyrians, Bavarians and Frenchmen, all in fairly good fighting trim – are intact fighting forces. II Corps' morale, perhaps, is the better of the two – they've even added twelve captured Russian guns to their own '60 well-harnessed pieces'. But Victor is far from pleased with his.[9]

The two marshals' failure to see eye to eye is causing a serious lack of co-ordination.[10] Marches and counter-marches have followed, which neither Legler nor anyone else among the Swiss can see any sense in. Nor do they see any more of Victor's men – though on one occasion, at least, they've had to come to II Corps' assistance. But II Corps' retreat south-westwards, albeit arduous, has been nothing to compare with the Moscow Army's sufferings. Of *that* neither Oudinot, Victor nor anyone else has the slightest inkling.

But now Minsk has fallen. And the bridge at Borissow must at all costs be secured.

It hadn't only been Bronikowski, the Minsk governor, who'd been in complete ignorance of Napoleon's and the Moscow Army's whereabouts, still less its dilapidated state. So were the Russian commanders in the south. It had been in the first days of October that the fetchingly handsome young French *émigré* Count *L.-V.-L. de Rochechouart* (yet another of the Tsar's many ADCs) had joined Tormassov in Volhynia. A month later it had been decided to split the so-called Army of Moldavia in two:

'The first part, 40,000 men strong under the orders of Admiral Tchitchakov, was to take the road for White Russia and recapture Minsk and Vilna. The second, with the remaining 30,000 men, commanded by General Count Sacken, to stay where it was and go on playing at prisoners' base with Schwarzenberg. We were in utter ignorance of what had happened since the French had evacuated Moscow. Our continual marchings and counter-marchings had deprived us of all regular communications and we were far from envisaging the enemy armies' deplorable condition.'

Tchitchakov's men, on the other hand, are in a 'magnificent state'. Kossecki's Polish brigade, reinforced by 300 troopers of the 18th Dragoons under their Colonel *Lafitte* – a man Bronikowski will afterwards praise for

his singular presence of mind – had made a 4-day fighting withdrawal in front of Lambert's advance guard until, on 15 November,
'assailed in open country by cavalry very numerous compared with our own, and ten pieces of artillery, we ended up by suffering considerable losses. Two battalions of the new Lithuanian levy threw down their arms and refused to fire; or rather, they lay down face to the ground and nothing could lift them out of that posture.'
This left Kossecki with only
'a very small battalion of the 46th and about 250 troopers still left to myself. After surrounding the 46th's little square the enemy charged. I hurried to its assistance, charged three times. The mêlée lasted more than ten minutes.'
All in vain, Colonel Lafitte will write three days later from Borissow: 'I've only saved about 100 of my cavalry.' 'Our advance guard', Rochechouart goes on,
'was commanded by Lieutenant-General Count Lambert, a French gentleman who'd come to Russia with his brother. After several wearisome marches and a few days rest,'
Lambert's force had suddenly appeared in front of Minsk, taking Bronikowski, governor of the province,
'wholly by surprise. Amazingly, even one day before we got there, Bronikowski didn't even know our army was at his gate.'
This in spite of several warnings from both Dombrowski and Oudinot. Bronikowski's unpreparedness, not to say nonchalance, had amazed everyone at Tchitchakov's headquarters. Having 'hardly 2,000 men to oppose to 30,000 Russians,' Rochechouart goes on,
'not merely had he not organised any defence. He hadn't even tried to put up any resistance, which anyway would have served no purpose. Why hadn't he foreseen our army corps' march? Why hadn't he sent out a few scouts, if only to know what Prince Schwarzenberg was doing and where he was, etc., etc.?'
Rochechouart (writing in 1842) hazards an explanation; ascribes
'without a doubt Bronikowski's sense of security to the mendacious reports inserted into the Grand Army's bulletins, announcing victory after victory on all sides and at all points, also the annihilation of all the Russian armies. Hence, apparently, his confidence, his easy-going attitude which would cost Napoleon so dear.'
In fact it's cost him the 'immense stores of clothing, equipment, provisions and all kinds of ammunition' he at such vast expense and trouble has accumulated there. Fleeing from Minsk, Bronikowski has
'withdrawn in all haste toward Borissow, in hopes of defending the bridgehead on the Berezina. There he was met by the remains of Dombrowski's division, with some soldiers from the Spanish and Portuguese depots who were in that little town.'
Part of Nansouty's convoy of wounded officers had just left Borissow when it had been obliged to turn back; and Artillery-Inspector *H.-J. Paixhans* had

actually been on his way to Minsk when he'd met 'several couriers coming back in all haste' who'd told him it had fallen into the enemy's hands. Leaving him, too, no option but to turn back.

In Minsk, 'after spending two days resting up the troops and supplying them suitably, even lavishly, with anything they might need,' Tchitchakov holds a council-of-war to decide what to do.' March on Vilna, which will probably fall into his hands no less promptly then Minsk has? Or on Orsha and, after destroying the Dnieper bridges, join up with Wittgenstein? The choice falls on Vilna,

'but only after we'd have seized Borissow and its bridgehead. The operation was entrusted to General Lambert, colonel of a superb 800-strong regiment of Russian hussars, whose five squadrons were on full war footing. He was given a few heavy-calibre guns, thus raising the number of troops under his orders to about 10,000 men.'

Lambert's own ADC having fallen dreadfully sick at Minsk, he's only too happy to accede to Rochechouart's request to be taken on instead:

'I'll be needing an infantry officer on hand to direct this army, which isn't my own.'

And next day Tchitchakov's advance guard had begun its march on Borissow.

Bronikowski, says General *Guillaume de Vaudoncourt*, 'had drawn up no plan of retreat, given no orders, so most of the garrison troops, without either a general or any orders, had moved mechanically toward the main army, which by this time we knew was retreating.' Seeing some 1,500 men bivouacked at nightfall at the corner of a wood on the Borissow road, Vaudoncourt takes charge of them. 'In two days' march we reached the Berezina. Rejoining us at Borissow, Bronikowski, who'd lost his head,' (but not to the point of omitting to take a roundabout route via Molihew to put his wife in safety)

'wanted to leave again [for Bobr] next day, thus abandoning the bridge. The Portuguese General Pamplona and I were opposed to this; decided to wait for General Dombrowski, and send word to Oudinot.'

In Nansouty's convoy there the 2nd Vistula Regiment's wounded adjutant-major Captain *Heinrich von Brandt* sees how the town's least corners are

'full of riffraff – people of all kinds in the most varied costumes – debris of troops chased by the enemy – cadres of regiments which were just getting themselves organised – fugitive patriots, and those good-for-nothings who make a vile business out of the finest sentiments, and under the most noble appellations make a habit of following armies and fouling them, everywhere causing pillage and theft. The ragtag and bobtail of gentlemen, scribes, servants, cooks, bailiffs and gardeners who've gathered here from Warsaw and the neighbourhood, with the old Polish nobility's gilded ideas of liberty, its ferocious indocility. All the tobacco shops and inns are full of these men who, day and night, are playing cards and drinking.'

The town itself, whose 300 houses are 'built on an amphitheatre against a hill dominating the whole of the Berezina's left bank', is easily defensible, especially from the west. Less so from the east. 'The long bridge crosses over lake and swamp, and at the entrance of the town are two marshy rivers.' When Dombrowski gets there with his intact division he occupies 'as best he can' the fortifications on the right bank – one of a chain begun but not finished under threat of a French invasion. Dombrowski himself is one of Napoleon's oldest officers, having served under General Bonaparte in Italy in 1796. Major Everts of the 33rd had seen him

> 'very simply dressed in a middle-class overcoat, with a wretched cap on his head, but on his chest the great star of the Order of Poland, surrounded by a brilliant escort of Polish lancers. The general's tall stature, together with a certain dignity and his way of speaking to me, made a good impression.'

However, Brandt goes on, 'since no staff officer had been sent to mark the position, the result was that Dombrowski didn't cover the bridge.'

And now it's the evening of 20 November. Reaching what Rochechouart calls 'the entrenched camp' on the right bank, Lambert's force bivouacs

> 'in front of the enemy's outposts. During the night Lambert made his preparations for a dawn assault. As soon as we could see to put one foot in front of the other we took up arms to form assault columns, throwing out skirmishers to reconnoitre the position and our adversaries' strength.'

'Shortly before daybreak', Vaudoncourt goes on, 'the enemy attacked us briskly,' quickly driving in Dombrowski's outposts,

> 'who promptly fell back on the small number of men they had in line. These troops, we could see, belonged neither to the same corps nor to the same nation. This cast doubt on their ability to put up a defence and deprived it of the redoubtable dash of French troops. Thus no sooner had a few squadrons of our numerous cavalry deployed in the plain than it was abandoned to us, and the enemy all fell back into the entrenchments at the bridgehead. Whereon artillery fire began that cost us some men and several horses.'

The first volley shatters the arm of Lambert's Piedmontese chief-of-staff, whose wound is 'so serious they had to amputate on the spot, cutting off the arm as close as possible to the shoulder'. Rochechouart has been given the extreme right. 'On that side the entrenchments, which seemed to me to be in a very bad state of repair, abut on the river's very steep banks.' Lacking men to storm them, he leaves his men under cover in a dip in the ground and, unscathed by a volley of musketry from the entrenchments, gallops over to Lambert and asks for a battalion of infantry. Having very little of it, Lambert orders 300 of his hussars to dismount, take their carbines and 'pretend to be grenadiers'. Then, after giving Rochechouart and his three troops time to get back, he orders an attack all along the line. Everyone's in a state of high excitement. But 'a few cannon shot aimed by the guns on top of the entrenchments sufficed momentarily to calm the general impatience.' On the extreme right Rochechouart has no difficulty in storming

'the badly defended barrier. Our skirmishers, followed by a few other soldiers, got in through this egress. Thus we were the immediate cause of the bridgehead being abandoned. For the enemy, finding themselves subject to an improvised attack from within their entrenchments, fled by the long bridge that leads over to Borissow, hoping to be in time to burn or cut it.'

But victors and vanquished entered the town pell-mell, and this, for the moment, saves the bridge. That, anyway, is how Rochechouart will remember things. For Vaudoncourt they're all a good deal more complicated. The fight has lasted all day:

'A French battalion guarding the bridge had been overwhelmed and the Russians were already masters of it when a German battalion, close at hand and under arms, drove them out.'

Shortly before dusk Dombrowski, who 'together with the Minsk garrison had about 7,000 men against Tchitchakov's [total of] 30,000', finds he has more than 2,000 men out of action, is himself almost out of ammunition, and has to think of retreating.

'He did so in good order. The valorous Poles crossed the bridge in closed ranks and sustaining the enemy's reiterated attacks. Dombrowski took up a position immediately behind Borissow on the high ground on the river's left bank. The enemy tried in vain to dislodge him, and night put an end to the fighting. Thus was lost the bridge over the Berezina.'

Lambert himself has been shot in the shoulder at the head of his hussars. 'As soon as a modicum of order had been restored in the little town, which the French had precipitately evacuated' Rochechouart installs himself in a house 'of good appearance on the square, which had just been occupied by the Minsk governor'. There the two French émigré officers get the shock of their lives:

'In this house there was – an extreme rarity in Russia – a fireplace. It was in the drawing-room. I shouldn't mention this detail if it hadn't had a most extraordinary result. A good fire was still burning in the fireplace, which had doubtless been lit so as to hastily throw various papers into it. Among those not yet consumed I noticed a letter signed *le Maréchal le duc de Bellune* and addressed to Bronikowski, governor of Minsk.'

The letter – which Rochechouart will always remember verbatim 'because of its being so interesting to us' – had been brought by one of Victor's ADCs and been on its way to Bronikowski at Minsk with various orders that its bearer, a Prince Sulkowsky, was to have supervised. It contains some shattering news:

'His Majesty the Emperor Napoleon should arrive the day after tomorrow, 23rd, at Borissow, and on the 25th will be at Minsk.'

And they, who've been assuming the Grand Army is hundreds of miles away! 'Judge our surprise at learning we'd tomorrow have to deal with the entire French army!' Victor's next sentence is even more puzzling:

'The long marches his army has had to make, together with the numerous and glorious combats it has delivered, make rest and food imperative.' Lambert instantly sends Rochechouart to Tchitchakov with the letter, telling him to point out how small his detachment is to be able to defend Borissow. Since he no longer can walk, let alone mount his horse, he has entrusted the vanguard to General Count Pahlen[11] 'one of the bravest and most intelligent of officers. All the rest will immediately advance along the Orsha road.' Leaving his Cossack servant, his carriage and all his equipment in the town, Rochechouart dashes off and 'at the bridgehead with his whole headquarters staff' finds Tchitchakov who naturally hurries to Lambert to discuss the alarming situation. And Rochechouart goes off to get some much-needed sleep.

Vaudoncourt, meanwhile, aware that the fate of the bridge and therefore of the Grand Army is in his hands, is spurring for Bobr,

'to try to get some reinforcements to Dombrowski during the night. Not having occupied Borissow until after dark, the enemy hadn't been able to distinguish one thing from another, or establish himself in solid military fashion. The Poles were still masters of the windmills and the narrow paved road which crosses the bank of the stream and by means of which one could easily debouch on to the castle. A brisk attack, made a little before daybreak, could still chase the Russians back over the bridge and regain possession of it.'

A mile and half before reaching the village of Natcha he bumps into II Corps' artillery park,

'camped end to end in column. Its guard had been confided to a Portuguese regiment, and I'd reached it without noticing any sentries. II Corps was turned to face the Grand Army as it arrived, with its back to the enemy, who were only nine miles away!'

He hastens to warn the park's commanding officer – according to the army list a Colonel Levavasseur – 'of the danger he was in of being surprised if, at daybreak, any parties of Cossacks, after overtaking Dombrowski, should throw themselves upon him'. But the officer's sceptical:

'He seemed extremely astonished at an event which apparently didn't trouble him greatly, and on which he even seemed to wish to cast doubt. Anyway he hadn't been notified of it, he said. Nor had he heard the gunfire (of 100 guns nine miles away and for eleven hours on end!) and was awaiting his Marshal's orders. I confess that if he hadn't been commanding Frenchmen [sic] I'd liked to have seen Tchitchakov turn up at that very moment. We'd have had a pretty collapse!'

When an exasperated Vaudoncourt finally gets to Natcha and passes on Dombrowski's message to Merle, Merle too, surprisingly – according to Napoleon he's 'worth four Marshals'[12] – is sceptical. Hurrying on to Bobr, where he knows Oudinot to be, Vaudoncourt's aghast to see the first fugitives from Moscow,

'some pale and exhausted cuirassiers walking painfully on bare feet in the mud. A stick in their hand they were driving their horses on before them, laden with their cuirasses and hardly even able to support so slight a burden.'

Nor is he even immediately admitted to Oudinot:

'At 9 a.m. someone came and told me the Marshal was expecting me. It was certainly high time. I couldn't contain my indignation, and replied by sending both the messenger and his superior to the devil.'

Despite Oudinot's at times leisurely way of making war,[13] the news is at least not lost on him. Is the bridge still intact? Can it be recovered? Perhaps. And when, later in this morning of 22 November, at Natcha, the 46-year-old Portuguese general-of-brigade Emmanuel-Ignace de Pamplona confirms the same dire news, Oudinot takes energetic action. Riding forward, he meets Dombrowski with 'only 300 infantrymen and 500 cavalrymen' at the village of Kroupki a little further on, and forms – and personally accompanies – a powerful advance guard. Placed under the command of General Legrand, it consists of Corbineau and Castex's light cavalry brigades

'together forming about 800 horses, reinforced by Dombrowski's 2nd and 7th regiments of Polish lancers, and two battalions of the 26th Light Infantry,'

supported by Doumerc's division of cuirassiers. Its orders: 'March against Pahlen and recapture Borissow!' The rest of Legrand's own division and of II Corps are to follow after.

That Corbineau's 6th Light Cavalry Brigade happens to be available is a story in itself and an important one.

After the Bavarians' heroic fight at the Bononia defile, Saint-Cyr had ordered VI Corps' new commander, Count Wrede, to retire to the large town of Glubokoië, not far from Vilna.[14] And though Corbineau's brigade (7th and 20th Chasseurs, 8th Lancers 'mostly Poles') actually belong to II Corps, he'd assigned it to Wrede as a rearguard. Lorencez had countermanded the order, but Wrede

'turning a deaf ear refused to rejoin us, manoeuvred as he thought fit, and made his retreat in the direction of Vilna'.

When Corbineau and his officers reach Glubokoië (according to Curély) they feel they've had enough. And when moreover on 17 November an order comes from Oudinot for them to return to II Corps, Curély tells Corbineau:

'"With 800 sabres one can go anywhere. Let me have the advance guard and we'll march over the enemy's stomach and rejoin the Grand Army."'

Reluctantly ignoring other and more senior officers' advice, Corbineau says he 'wants to share II Corps' great dangers' and obtains the permission of Wrede 'who'd just been reinforced by both infantry and cavalry' from Vilna, to leave him:

'With his brigade, still 1,500 men strong we crossed a countryside unknown to us but swarming with enemy troops, a twelve days' march, that separated us from II Corps.'

En route for the small town of Pleschenkowiczi, not far from the Berezina, they nearly bump into a Cossack regiment on its way to join Wittgenstein –

and which, incidentally, has just freed Winzingerode and another captured Russian general, on their way to captivity in France.

'Arrived on the banks of the Berezina, we hear a violent cannonade coming from the direction of Borissow. The enemy were attacking and seizing the bridgehead occupied by Dombrowski's 4,000 Poles. This disagreeable event we learned of from fugitives who joined us. But the news didn't deflect Corbineau from his project of joining up with II Corps and either conquering or dying with our brave comrades-in-arms.'

Spotting a peasant riding a horse that's 'wet up to its belly', Curély deduces the existence of a nearby ford, and sends him to Corbineau to guide them to it. By now, Curély goes on, Corbineau, regretting having taken his advice, has become extremely disgruntled:

'Usually he sent for me to give me his orders himself. But since the moment when he'd decided to fall back he hadn't spoken a word to me.'

The ford lies opposite a hamlet named Studianka. Near its 25 timber cottages on a low hill stands the even smaller hamlet of Weselovo. Reaching the ford 'in faint moonlight' at midnight of 21 November, Corbineau's chasseurs and lancers form up 'in close column, eight men abreast' on the low marshy ground:

'At the moment before crossing, faint-hearted men embraced one another, said good-bye and drank a drop together, they said, for the last time, adding that Curély would be the death of them.'

At 2 a.m. they splash out into the Berezina's darkness and force their way through 'ice floes 20 feet in diameter'. Luckily, even in mid-stream, the water, flowing rather slowly, is only 3½ feet deep. 'The horses only swam twenty paces' before struggling up the steep eastern bank, 'without losing a horse or a man'.[15] Riding on towards Kostrizza, (a pleasant surprise) they run into the 6th Polish Lancers 'apparently part of Bronikowski's command, who presented an effective of almost 500 men'. Only then does Corbineau come riding up to Curély, still commanding his advance guard:

'"Brave men never perish, do they, Curély?" he says, half-apologetically.
'"No, never."'

After which they speak of other matters. Crossing the small Natcha stream, they suddenly emerge on to the main Smolensk road, where Oudinot welcomes them with open arms. Lorencez also hears Oudinot

'praise the resolution, the presence of mind, of the 6th Lancers' Colonel Sierawski in having successfully got out of so delicate a scrape. This unit had also profited from the Studianka ford pointed out to us that very morning by Corbineau, and where he'd crossed the Berezina en route from Veleika via Zembin. It was the concordance of these reports which decided the Marshal to propose that point to the Emperor for the army to cross at, in the event of the more direct Minsk route being shut off.'

So perhaps the discovery of the Studianka ford won't have all been Corbineau's – or Curély's – doing?[16]

But now it's Corbineau and Castex's brigades who're leading the dash for Borissow. Not that Oudinot has many illusions about the outcome. Already he has written to Berthier:

'*Monseigneur*. Unless ordered to the contrary, I shall attack the enemy at Borissow tomorrow. Yet I must draw Your Excellency's attention to the fact that, even if I should manage to drive him out of the town, it's probable he'll burn the bridge, whose re-establishment would be absolutely impracticable. This will be confirmed to you, Monseigneur, by all who know the Berezina's swampy banks and Borissow's formidable position.'

Having himself crossed over the long wooden and easily inflammable bridge in early November and just listened to Corbineau's account, Oudinot's already searching the map for some alternative crossing:

'To find a ford one has to go four leagues upstream abreast of Weselovo. The road that crosses that ford leads to Zembin. I impatiently await new instructions. For the rest, the road from Zembin to Pleschenkowiczi and Veleika or Smorgoni is itself very good. I speak of it as one who has twice passed along it.'

Legrand's advance guard is marching at top speed for Borissow when 'at three-quarters of a league from Loschnitza' he runs headfirst into Pahlen's men. 'He was immediately attacked.' Marbot, prancing about at the head of his 500 chasseurs, is in the thick of it:

'It was at nine miles from Borissow, in the plain of Loschnitza, that Lambert's advance guard ran head on into our cuirassiers, who, having fought very little during this campaign, had solicited the honour of being placed in the front line.'

At the sight of Doumerc's

'magnificent and still strong regiments, the sunshine sparkling on their cuirasses, the Russian cavalry stopped dead. Then, getting back their courage, they were just advancing when our cuirassiers, charging with fury, overthrew them and killed or captured a thousand of their men.'

According to *Drujon de Beaulieu* it's at 4 p.m. that 'the 8th Polish Lancers and [Berkheim's] 4th Cuirassiers make their brilliant charges' and take all these prisoners. The 24th Chasseurs' Piedmontese regimental sergeant-major *Jean Calosso* says they and Marbot's regiment, too,

'fell furiously on the enemy. Having sabred some squadrons of dragoons with the aid of a light battery which was following our swift movements, the regiment fell on the regiment of Finnish foot chasseurs,[17] defending the town's approaches, rolled it up, and with no very great losses to ourselves took them all prisoner.'

After 'less than two hours' marching' Legler sees the Swiss infantry, coming on behind, who've been surprised to hear

'sudden musketry. One or another gun, too, was being fired. At first we didn't know what was going on, or whether it was we who were being attacked. Suddenly the order "At the double!" was given behind us. We began to run, while some light cavalry, riding past our flanks at their fastest trot, as it were dragged us with it.'

After running for a quarter of an hour they're ordered to halt in a clearing:
'In front of us on the ground lay 600 captured Russians, many of them wounded. We also saw some dead. We couldn't grasp what had happened until the enigma was solved for us. As soon as we'd got our breath back, curiosity attracted us to the prisoners.'
One of them's a captain who speaks good French:
'He told us we were cut off and that he belonged to Admiral Tchitchakov's army that had come up from the Turkish frontier and occupied the Berezina's right bank at Borissow. They'd been its advance guard. He added that this was the second time he'd been a prisoner of the French, but this time he didn't think he'd have to go to France.'
Tchitchakov's officers meanwhile have spent the day
'assembling the troops and discussing what was to be done. We were impatiently awaiting news from our advance guard, which must have spent the night at Loschnitza, six versts away. After which it was to march for Bobr.'
When a messenger comes and tells him that Pahlen's men have run into superior forces just beyond Loschnitza, Tchitchakov simply doesn't believe it. To make things worse, his baggage train, glutted with the spoils of Minsk, has already gone on across the bridge and is packing the town's streets. Marbot goes on excitedly:
'Not merely had Tchitchakov made the blunder of going on ahead and running into Oudinot's corps. To it he'd added another – of having all the vehicles of his army follow him.'
Unlike the French and their allies who'd been strictly forbidden to bring any woman of higher social status across the Niemen, Tchitchakov's Russians have been marching in almost 18th-century fashion. This afternoon Rochechouart's dining lavishly with the wife of his supplies Intendant Rochmanoff 'in charge of our army's provisions', who had filled at least 300 carts with the fruits of Minsk. Marbot continues:
'Everyone knows that after delivering a charge the heavy cavalry's big horses, and above all those of the cuirassiers, can't go on galloping very long. So it was the 23rd and 24th Chasseurs who got the order to pursue our enemies while the cuirassiers, at a moderate pace, came on in the second line.'
Oudinot, meanwhile, hurries off another dispatch to Berthier:
'The enemy's been pushed back from one position to the next as far as Borissow, where our light cavalry, supported by a regiment of cuirassiers, made an extremely brilliant charge. Upon which he withdrew in disorder into the town, which we'd have entered together with him if he hadn't set fire to a bridge which lies at its entrance.'
This, however, makes all the difference. Lorencez:
'Wishing to put the river between himself and us, the enemy didn't dispute the entrance to the town. He hastened to get over the little bridge, which he blew up, leaving a few hundred prisoners and some of his baggage in our power. This obstacle[18] made us lose precious minutes wondering what to do, just when the least instant was so precious!'

The disorder during the Russians' precipitate retreat onto Borissow,' Marbot goes on,

'was so great that the two regiments of Castex's brigade often found their march entangled in these abandoned carts'.

'Two marshy streams' at the entrance to the town are also holding things up. And together with the enticements offered by the carts cause the whole prompt action to go agley.

The handsome young Rochechouart's making pleasant small talk with Mme Rochmanoff when

'In the middle of dinner we saw some Russian hussars, part of the advance guard, their horses bathed in sweat, so fast had they galloped. Shouting "The French are here!", they were making for the bridge. Luckily for herself Mme Rochmanoff took fright, wanted instantly to recross the river and make for Minsk; and despite all I could say to reassure her, she put this project into immediate execution. I remember I insisted on having some coffee.'

'Come and take it tomorrow at Minsk!' cries his fleeing hostess. The fugitives' numbers are growing every minute and out in the street Rochechouart tries to question some. In vain. 'Yet these were the same soldiers who'd behaved so bravely the day before yesterday!' Whatever can have happened?

'Prey to what's called panic fear, all these men could say was *"Frantzousi! Frantzousi!"* They were drunk with fear, if I so may put it. Some guns, followed by their caissons, passed through the town flat out, overturning and crushing anything in their way.'

Moving with the tide toward the bridge, Rochechouart catches sight of Lambert's Russian wife. Bareheaded, she's appealing to some of his hussars: "Lads, are you going to abandon your wounded commander?"

'Being Russian, she'd been able to make herself understood. They dismounted and lifted him on to their shoulders. Four mounted hussars, leading their comrades' horses by the rein, put themselves at the head of this cortege to clear a path for it as far as the end of the interminable bridge. Tchitchakov, too, who'd just been about to sit down to table with all his officers, had been obliged to leave his dinner there, ready to be served up and, like myself, cross that accursed bridge on foot.'

'Within the space of half-an-hour' Rochechouart realises it's all over:

'Of the advance guard of 6,000 men with twelve guns, only about 1,000 and two cannon had recrossed the bridge. All the rest had been dispersed or captured. The wretched Pahlen had never been able to get 100 men together. Having only yesterday taken over command, he was unknown to the men under his orders. Nothing equalled his despair.'

As a party of Calosso's chasseurs enter the town, dismount, establish themselves in its first houses, and wait for the light infantry to arrive, Calosso sees how Pahlen's men have 'abandoned to our advance guard a great number of wagons laden with victuals. In view of our penurious state, this was truly a windfall.' He even sees Pahlen's own abandoned carriage

'fully harnessed up. I let my troopers pillage it, reserving for myself some biscuit, salt meats, tea, rum and other delicacies. Unfortunately the Russian infantry, protected by some houses from which was coming an incessant and well-nourished fusillade, had halted us, and were having time to prepare the bridge's destruction, meanwhile sending enough shells to dislodge us by setting fire to the houses we'd occupied.'
Marbot, this time, really is at the hub of events. A charming, handsome self-centred braggart he may be; but he's also a very capable and intelligent officer:[19]

'As soon as we'd got into the town the confusion had become even worse. Its streets were encumbered with baggage and draught-horses, and the Russian soldiers, having thrown away their weapons, were slipping by between them as they tried to rejoin their units. Nevertheless we reached the town centre, albeit only after losing precious time which the enemy had profited from to cross the river. The Marshal had ordered his light cavalry to reach the bridge and try to cross over it at the same time. But to do that he'd have had to know where this bridge was.'

Surely, one thinks, it can't be all that difficult for a colonel of light cavalry, formerly ADC to Marshal Lannes, to find his way down to a river bank? Can he be unaware of so elementary a piece of topography? 'None of us was familiar with the town.' And hasn't Oudinot himself only recently spent four days here? Can it be that Marbot, in his vivid and circumstantial story, is trying to explain away why the bridge's seizure, the whole point of the operation, is coming unstuck?[20] At length Marbot's troopers bring him a Jew:

'I questioned him in German, but either because this joker didn't understand that language or pretended not to, we couldn't get anything out of him. I'd have given a lot to have my servant Lorentz by me, who habitually served as my interpreter. But as soon as the fighting had broken out that poltroon had stayed in the rear. Yet it was necessary to get out of the impasse the brigade was in. So we had the streets swept by several platoons, who at long last caught sight of the Berezina.'

To carry it they need infantry. Just then Oudinot himself appears on the scene and orders Castex to dismount three-quarters of his two regiments' troopers and with their carbines attack the bridge:

'Leaving our horses in the charge of a few men in the neighbouring streets, we hastened to obey, led by Castex, who, in this perilous enterprise, wanted to march at the head of his brigade.'

On the far bank Marbot sees

'masses of fugitives fleeing into the countryside. Although it's virtually impossible for dismounted cavalry to carry a bridge and establish a bridgehead without bayonets, I was beginning to have hopes things would turn out all right, since the enemy was only opposing us with a few skirmishers.'

The 'interminable ... accursed' bridge, as Rochechouart calls it, is about 180 feet long and commanded from the right bank by 18–20 Russian can-

non, 'which looked decidedly impressive'. Marbot has just ordered his chasseurs to seize the first houses to left and right at the bridge's far end and hang on until some infantry turns up, when suddenly
'the guns of the fortress roar out, covering the bridge's surface with a hail of grapeshot. This throws our feeble battalion into disorder and momentarily forces it to fall back. A group of Russian sappers carrying torches profit from this instant, and set fire to the bridge. But as their presence prevented the enemy artillery from firing, we threw ourselves at them! Most are killed or thrown into the water. Already our chasseurs have put out the fire that's hardly been lit; but a battalion of grenadiers, arriving at the charge, force us at bayonet point to evacuate the bridge, which in no time, covered with flaming torches, becomes an immense brazier, so hot that both sides have to withdraw to a distance.'
'Able to contain us at his leisure,' Calosso sees, 'the enemy had been able to set fire to the bridge.' While Pils is making the sketch of the fateful conflagration which he'll one day turn into a much-admired oil painting, Calosso, less interested in the aesthetic aspect, is relieved to see
'the 11th Light Infantry turn up and replace us; and we made our bivouacs to the rear of the main road and astride it'.
With II Corps surrounding Borissow on three sides and the uncrossable river on its fourth, Castex's men are free to attend to provisioning their wagons and saddlebags:
'By the usages of war the enemy's baggage belongs to its captors. The officers of Tchitchakov's corps had done themselves handsomely. So Castex authorised the chasseurs of my regiment and those of the 24th to possess themselves of the contents of the 1,500 carriages, wagons and carts abandoned by the Russians.'
(Marbot multiplies the number by five. Legler, a matter-of-fact Swiss, sees only 200.)
'The booty was immense! To forestall all discussion Castex had planted alignment posts dividing the immense quantity of captured carriages into two portions. There was a hundred times more than the brigade could carry off. Never has such a profusion of hams, *pâtés*, saveloys, fish, smoked meats and all sorts of wines, plus an immense quantity of hard tack, rice, cheese, etc., etc., been seen in an army's rolling stock! Furs and shoes abounded, which would save many a man's life'.
Not to mention horses:
'Almost all were good ones. We selected the best to replace those our troopers were complaining about. The officers also took them to carry the foodstuffs. Each took an ample provision.'
Efficient regimental officer that he is, Marbot assembles his men and stresses to them that with a long and arduous retreat ahead of them what they'll be needing is food and warm clothes, and warns them
'overladen horses don't last long; furthermore I'd be holding a shake-down inspection and everything that wasn't food, footwear or clothing would be pitilessly thrown away'.

Is it Mme Rochmanoff's dinner, getting cold but still on table, or Tchitchakov's, that *maître d'hôtel* Roget takes over as Oudinot sets up his headquarters in the house on the main square? Aware of the danger of packing the town with his troops, he sends back an order for his other divisions

'to bivouac between Loschnitza and Nemonitza. Only Castex's brigade remained in Borissov, forbidden to communicate with the other units, so as to hide the fatal news from them as long as possible.'

Which certainly won't be very long – for all news spreads like wildfire – especially as Oudinot (says Marbot, contradicting himself) allows each regiment to send in a party to take its share of Pahlen's victuals. And 'at dinner-time' the Swiss come marching in. Their prisoners join others 'huddled together in abandoned houses' whom Oudinot – the temperature falling sharply – has ordered 'to be assembled around great fires in the main square' in the custody of 100 Württembergers of Bronikowski's division 'who can't be better employed'. ADCs are sent off into the night to check on the state of the roads up and downstream.

But what to do now? Chief-of-Staff Lorencez goes on:

'We had three crossing points reputed to be fordable: Oukholoda, two miles[21] downstream; Stadkov, one mile upstream; and lastly Studianka. We had these points reconnoitred as far as the night's darkness permitted. We found them all guarded. Anyway, the first two were too easily seen by the mass of the enemy's forces to tempt Marshal Oudinot, who never varied in his preference for the last.'

Already Oudinot has sent off two officers to Berthier. At 4.45 a.m. on 23 November, he sends off a third, with a new message. The concentration of the enemy at Beresino, he writes, is partly due to Tchitchakov having been reinforced there. He, Oudinot, has been intending to commence operations at Studianka at 6 p.m., 'but this seems to me to be of too serious consequence not to defer it and await His Majesty's orders'. So deferred it has been. 'As was his duty,' Lorencez goes on, 'he let the Major-General be aware of this danger. As we know, when it came to obstacles, the Emperor wanted to hear of none except those that appeared to himself.' It's only three leagues to Studianka, so Oudinot thinks he can afford to wait a little longer. One league further upstream from Studianka there's yet another ford, deeper and less practicable, it too guarded by Russian cavalry and infantry. At 5.30 a.m. he sends Corbineau's report on to Berthier, saying he has sent him to Studianka to seize the ford there. And writes:

'There are two more passages: one at Stadkov, a mile upstream, and the other at Oukholoda, two miles downstream from Borissow. The aim of the movements noticed yesterday evening on the enemy's two flanks was to occupy these crossing points, which are all guarded. During the night it has not been possible to carry out any reconnaissances exact enough to be sure which is the most favourable point for throwing a bridge.'

He's going to probe them all and

'during the night throw my bridge at the one I shall have chosen. I have 20,000 men in front of me which will no doubt move to the point where I try to make my crossing. So I do not dare guarantee the success of this enterprise, though thoroughly resolved to try everything to make it succeed.'

Next day, Lorencez goes on,

'the whole of the cuirassier division marched off pompously toward Oukholoda, where the ford had been ostentatiously sounded and materials amassed. None of these movements could escape the Russians' notice.'

To reinforce the feint

'we assembled some Jews in the town and interrogated them minutely on the road between Borissow and Beresino and from there to Ighumen and Minsk. We pretended to be convinced that this route was the one that presented the fewest obstacles. Some of the Jews we kept by us to serve as guides. The others we let go and had them taken beyond our outposts, making them promise to come back from the direction of Beresino to inform us of the enemy's movements. We knew enough of their evil [sic] dispositions to flatter ourselves they wouldn't be discreet.'

At 1 p.m. Oudinot sends off a new dispatch to Berthier saying he has in fact decided on Studianka, but that 'the enemy, on his side, isn't ignoring the strong demonstrations' he's making at Oukholoda and Stadkov. 'His troops are in continual movement. But the most pronounced of these, though we all think this is concealing some other project, is the one he's making on his right, toward Beresino.' (Beresino, where Kutusov thinks Napoleon will try to cross so as to recapture Minsk, lies downstream at a distance of 42 miles from Bobr.) Upon his artillery commander returning from Studianka at 4.45 p.m. Oudinot writes again:

'"*Monseigneur.* Your Serene Highness will see from the report of General Aubry who at this moment has just got back from Studianka at the moment I've received your latest dispatch, that the passage is far from being assured. The enemy doesn't seem to be at all being put off the scent and it is certain it's Steingel's troops, coming via Beresino, who are facing that ford. This explains the movement to the right made by the enemy yesterday. A peasant who yesterday served as guide to a column of about 6,000 Russians and who escaped from their hands, has told us that column has today made a movement in the opposite direction. But despite the obstacles presented to crossing at Studianka I think we should manage to overcome them provided I am promptly supported, for, within a few hours, I shall find myself between two hostile army corps. The river at that point is deeper than it was three days ago,"'

i.e., when Corbineau had forded it. Aubry, however, has already begun making his preparations for a crossing at Studianka. 'By 9 p.m. twelve trestles will be ready, with timber collected for the table'. Rising ground on the left bank is enabling him to do this out of sight of the Russians:

'The river is 35 to 40 *toises* [70 to 80 yards] wide at the ford, which three days ago was at most 3½ feet deep, but is deeper now, if the inhabitants are to be believed, who assure me the waters have risen. The access on this side won't be difficult. When one reaches the other bank there's a straight paved road which crosses a marsh that's impracticable except during times of hard frost. It's still broken at a few points because of the very nature of the ground."

But a few fascines will fix that. Aubry has seen cavalry and infantry on the move in the village which is in the centre on the far side, and seen cannon being established on the paved road,

'or at least in its direction and on the village's flanks, to cover the bridge. The right bank slightly dominates this one and above all has the advantage of thoroughly concealing our works when we begin them. There's no doubt that during the course of the day it'll be covered by numerous artillery which will make the passage very difficult,'

the more so as Corbineau has seen some 8 to 9,000 men arriving on the scene from Lepel and lighting their fires. Aubry adds a PS to his sketch, detailing the positions of the Russian guns, 'both on the low ground and in a clearing in the forest, between the road and the village'. He's sure the plateau to the left of the village will soon also be covered with them.

To tell Berthier, i.e., Napoleon, verbally about all this, Oudinot sends off another of his ADCs, a Major Lamarre.

Whose fault is it the Russians have had time to burn the bridge? Jean Curély, that exemplary light cavalryman, wasn't on the spot – he was pursuing Pahlen's 7th, 14th and 38th Jäger Regiments, cut off while foraging, in the direction of Staroï-Borissow. But when he hears about it all he's sure Castex's chasseurs can't *really* have charged home. Not as *he'd* have done! On the other hand, if the cavalry hadn't been in quite such a hurry to intervene or if the supporting infantry hadn't been left so far in the rear – and above all if Castex's chasseurs hadn't been so greedy – crucial minutes could have certainly been saved:

'If it had charged home, it would have prevented the bridge being burnt. It wasn't its fault, but when it's a question of saving an army one must do more than we dared at that moment.'[22]

CHAPTER 15

'HOW EVER SHALL WE GET THROUGH?'

'Burn all the documents of State!' – the Sacred Squadron – Oudinot utters only one word: 'Poltava!' – 'Then came the Emperor, a stick in his hand' – 'our soul was invaded by an infinite sadness' – 'they passed us pell-mell in their thousands, didn't even dare look at us' – 'they were alive, we were shadows' – 'it had never crossed our minds that the Emperor could be defeated' – 'The Emperor walked to within 50 paces of the Russian sentry' – 'our position was horrible, perhaps unexampled'

At all hours of day and night anyone with a dispatch from another corps is always instantly admitted to Napoleon's presence. Major Lamarre finds him 'alone in a timber hut' not far from Toloczin, en route for Bobr,
> 'with only one grenadier sentry outside. He was asleep on a map of Russia spread out on a table.'

Awakened abruptly by Oudinot's ADC, his first words are:
> '"How shall we get through? How ever shall we get through?"'[1]
> 'Then, wide awake, while consulting his map, the Emperor made his interrogations and calculations, and gave his orders with his usual lucidity.'

Everyone at IHQ instantly grasps the full horror of the situation. Among them Rapp:
> 'Napoleon had every reason to worry. We had neither bridging equipment nor food. The main Russian army was advancing. Wittgenstein was coming closer, and the Moldau troops were barring our way. We were surrounded on all sides. Our position was horrible, perhaps unexampled. Nothing less than the Emperor's head and strength of character was called for to get us out of such a fix.'

Anyone else, Caulaincourt is thinking, would be shattered:
> 'But instead of making him lose heart, these misfortunes brought out the energy so characteristic of him. Hope, the merest suggestion of success, raised his spirits higher than he was disheartened by the worst setbacks.'

Clearly the crisis is at hand.

That 'Admiral' Tchitchakov should be at the Berezina is no surprise. But Wittgenstein's presence seems inexplicable. What's Victor doing? Next day several staff officers are sent off to locate him. When one finally returns, it's to report that instead of heading Wittgenstein off 25 miles away to the north, he's at Lochnitza, not far from the Berezina. Opening the dispatch, Napoleon declares: "The evil's irremediable. And it'll only increase the crowding." And Victor receives an angry reprimand. Various officers are sent for and consulted. Among them Pajol, whose light cavalry division had formed I Corps' advance guard in this area in August. He recommends that II, VI and IX Corps shall fling themselves on Wittgenstein and defeat him, thus leaving the army to retire unmolested to Vilna by some circuitous northern route. But his ADC, Captain Biot, hears 'Napoleon, after reflecting a moment', say:

"That could be done if all my Marshals hadn't lost their heads."
Which is hardly fair. It's the Russians who'll shortly be losing theirs. [2]
Jomini too is sent for. Not so much, as he'll claim, for his strategic
insights, as for his supposed knowledge of the area. He finds Napoleon in
the same wretched room where the big campaign map, stuck with
Berthier's black and red pins, lies spread out. Murat, Eugène and Berthier
are likewise present. As Jomini enters, Napoleon even comes a few steps
towards the door to meet him. Says:

"We're in a tight spot. When one isn't used to setbacks they seem heavy.
But I still have high hopes. The enemy's divided. I'm going to manoeuvre as I did in Italy. The troops I've brought from Smolensk are going to
join Victor's corps on the Dvina. First we'll fall on Wittgenstein, then
turn back and attack Kutusov. What do you say to that?"

Upon Jomini pointing out the grave dangers involved in this plan,
Napoleon (no doubt cutting short his sententious and generally superfluous remarks)[3] goes back to the map table and together with Berthier again
studies the position:

"At all events we must shake off Wittgenstein. If we wait for him, he
could interfere with us on the Vilna road."

What to do?

Jomini credits himself with having closely reconnoitred the district
during the summer and autumn, and also recommends the Studianka
ford, already chosen by Oudinot. At that moment one of Victor's staff
officers, a General Dode, is announced. Like Jomini, he declares
Napoleon's plan of attacking Wittgenstein to be impossible. Victor, he
says, has had no option but to fall back in front of the Moscow army. With
the result that Wittgenstein is now safely ensconced behind the Tchaniki
marshes.

Dode too watches as Napoleon studies the map. In the Kremlin de Bausset had always seen *The History of Charles XII* lying on his desk and even on
his bedside table. Now, as Dode sees him searching for a suitable crossing
point, he hears him mutter:

"Podoli! Ah yes! The Podoli! Charles XII!"

Then, after throwing Dode a look of consternation, he stares up at the ceiling and begins whistling to himself. Coming up to Jomini, Murat,
delighted with his advice, takes hold of his side-whiskers, embraces him
and says in his cordial way:

"Thank you! Oh, what good you've done! You'll save us all if you can
deflect him from this fatal idea."

All according to Jomini. Caulaincourt too sees Napoleon hesitate about
where to cross the river:

'Minsk attracted him more and more because he hoped Prince
Schwarzenberg would have made his way there, and that, by means of a
double manoeuvre, the Russians wouldn't have been given time either
to evacuate the town or destroy its supplies. He'd also made particular
inquiries about the route through Oukholoda [south of Borissow]. But

the reports of General Corbineau, who'd arrived in person towards 1 p.m. [23 November] decided him.'
Writing his orders in the shorthand of his own devising, Fain sees his plan is to cross at Studianka, march down the Berezina's right bank, chase Tchitchakov away from the Borissow bridge, restore it, and then march for Minsk. Alternatively, he'll follow the Studianka–Zembin road to Molodeczno, where it joins the Minsk–Vilna highway.
At 4.30 a.m. Eblé receives orders to leave at 6 a.m. for Oudinot's head-quarters and
'work on establishing several bridges over the Berezina for the army to cross. You will divide yourselves in two, and if all your men can't leave promptly enough, you'll take with you the best marchers, so as to get there during the night and be at work tomorrow at daybreak, while the other party can be at work tomorrow before midday. Take care to leave working groups along the route to repair bridges and the worst bits of road. I'm giving the same order to General Chasseloup',
commander of the Engineers. Possibly as an afterthought he tells him to 'take Jomini along' with him. And shortly thereafter Cesare de Laugier notes in his diary that
'they've left at 6 a.m. with all their sappers and such tools as they still possess, to proceed at once to Borissow and re-establish various bridges over the Berezina at points to be shown them by the Duke of Reggio'.

And here's another dispatch come in from Oudinot. He's had the ice – presumably on the marsh opposite Studianka – tested: "Infantry will undoubtedly be able to act and deploy on either side of the road after crossing the river." But he'll need to be supported at the very moment when the bridges – he's planning to throw three – are ready, and has sent Corbineau to Napoleon to describe everything in detail and the various approach roads. These supports will have to deploy to the right of the road while II Corps attacks the plateau to its left. And where's his ADC, Colonel Hulot, who'd carried his second dispatch informing Napoleon that he's waiting for orders before setting the movement on Studianka in motion? Has he reached IHQ? If so, why hasn't he come back? He's beginning to be worried, Oudinot's written again at 2.30 a.m. (25 November): "Meanwhile the troops are standing by, ready to march."

But what's Schwarzenberg doing, away to the south-west? For four days there's been no news of him. All that's known for certain is that on 12 November he'd been at Slonim. Surely he must be drawing closer, is even perhaps hot on Tchitchakov's heels?

Wherever the Austrian corps may be, Napoleon is only too well aware of his own desperate situation. Alone again with Berthier, he tells him to order *Intendant-Général* Dumas to 'burn all my papers without any exception whatsoever, to abandon my wagons and send the horses to the artillery'. Zayon-cek, the senior Guards officer commanding V Corps, is to burn half of all the carriages, 'before 9 a.m. this morning, so as to give General Sorbier 120 horses and about 80 *konyas*, and more if he can.' A staff officer is to employ 50 gendarmes to ensure the order's carried out. A similar one is sent to Victor, who's to report back on how many horses he can provide Sorbier with: "No individual of colonel's rank or higher may have more than one vehicle, whether carriage, cabriolet, chaise or wagon."

Not only are all IHQ's remaining papers to be burnt, but also all the State papers. If there's to be a *Götterdämmerung*, nothing, nothing at all, must remain for the Russians to publish![4]

Dedem van der Gelder, sent with a message to Berthier and recognising some carriages as belonging to General Daendels, commander of Victor's 26th Division, realises it can only mean that IX Corps is somewhere close at hand. He notices an officer whisper something in another's ear. And hears the reply: "So we're cut off on all sides."

That evening Dedem sees his friend Daru burning the Emperor's papers, 'even including the most secret treaties'. Showing Daru one of these documents in a beautiful silver-gilt case, one of the four secretaries says mournfully: "There's no copy in Paris." "That's all one," Daru replies. "Burn it!" Still later that evening Daru tells Dedem in confidence that tomorrow will decide their fate: "Perhaps I'll never see France, my wife or children again." As for his friend, the former Dutch diplomat, Daru says he's sure his Russian connections will stand him in good stead: "For my part, the fate of Count Piper awaits me." Taken prisoner at Poltava, Charles XII's prime minister, who was with the Swedish army, had died miserably in Siberia. 'Yet no one could have shown more calmness or activity in his master's service than M. Daru did in these circumstances.'

Still doing his best for his poor brother Eugène, Maurice Tascher that night hears an appeal go round. 'All officers who've still got horses are to form a guard for the Emperor.' Still having his, he puts his brother in his servant's care and joins what will be known as The Sacred Squadron. François, who's just sold off one of his two to one of General Morand's staff officers for 120 francs, sees

'such officers as had retained their horses assemble and form into four companies of 150 each, to escort the Emperor. The King of Naples commanded in chief,'

anyway nominally. Actually Grouchy.[5] Belliard, Murat's chief-of-staff, notes and will preserve their names. The Squadron, says acting-adjutant-major *J. L. Henckens* of the 6th Chasseurs, had first been formed at Orsha by Berthier who

'in the Emperor's name had charged Grouchy to collect all the cavalry officers who hadn't lost their horses into a squadron of four troops, in cadres, and commanded by generals and colonels.'

'Of my regiment,' Henckens goes on,

'only Colonel Talhouët[6] and Lieutenant Berger were still horsed and therefore entitled to belong to it. Colonel de Talhouët, who didn't want to be separated from me, presented me to Marshal Berthier, explaining that I was acting as adjutant-major.'

Berthier had accepted him despite his non-commissioned rank and notified Grouchy. Thirion of the 2nd Cuirassiers is among those who're immediately sceptical about its value:

'Doubtless it was good to watch over the Emperor's safety as head of the army. But it was to take the superiors he was used to from the already demoralised ranker – men who'd led him under fire, with whom he'd been victorious, and who enjoyed his confidence. This measure could only increase the demoralisation and be harmful when we had to fight.'

Henckens disagrees. Reminds us that

'Platov, commanding the Cossacks, was said to be extremely rich and to have promised his only daughter in marriage to anyone who seized Napoleon's person, and we were so to speak surrounded by Cossacks. I believe few people have understood or wanted to understand its great value. A special guard was more than necessary.'

But it's immediately 'the object of jealousy, especially on the part of the Guard'. Also invited to join are the group of officers from the 2nd Pruss-ian Hussars. 'But no one could make up his mind to leave his comrades to get himself admitted into a circle of officers wholly foreign to him.' But their major points out that they're the only Prussian unit in the army, and such a refusal may be prejudicial to their future. So next morning, at the village of Kroupki, Kalckreuth and two other lieutenants present them-selves to Grouchy:

'All the officers, from all the cavalry regiments – French, Bavarian, Würt-temberger, Poles and others, some still in uniform, others dressed like peasants – were drawn up in a single rank on some flat ground. A gen-eral passed along the front, which was rather long, counting it. Only when he'd got to the middle did he begin a second rank, to place itself behind the first.'

The three Prussians stick together, in the second. Then the squadron's

'divided up into four troops. Generals commanded them. The colonels, in the guise of NCOs, rode on the flanks. The remaining officers, of all ranks, were the troopers, simple soldiers.'

Ordered to count themselves off by fours,

'our companions being Poles who knew little French, we had to do so several times before things were in order. Finally, at the signal "By the right, march!", we left in a column of fours and took the Borissow road.'

After kicking their heels for six days at Borissow, Nansouty's convoy of wounded officers have retreated precipitately to Bobr. And it's there, to his dismay, Brandt sees 'the first bizarre phantoms' of the Moscow army. Out-side his lodgings, though the Emperor hasn't arrived as yet, he notices two headquarters gendarmes and a lot of men without weapons. For a while he and his comrade gape at the painful, desolating spectacle:

'Lieutenant Gorszynski said to me: "Most of these stragglers are strong and healthy. I don't get it. They must have been sent on ahead from the camp on some fatigue duty. So certainly it's somewhere in the offing." While giving free rein to our observations, we see groups gathering at street corners to read some placards. We go closer. An order of the day has in fact been stuck up which most energetically blames the stragglers' and isolated men's behaviour and orders them to rejoin their units and their division without delay and tells them where these are. The military police are ordered to intervene resolutely to restore order and discipline. Finally, mutineers are threatened with a drumhead court-martial.'

But the placard doesn't seem to make the least impression on its readers. Only one thing consoles the two Polish officers:

'In this Babylonian disarray there wasn't a single soldier from the Vistula Legion. What was really terrifying was that these men, the Grand Army's strange advance guard, lacked weapons. Yet most of them didn't seem to have suffered much from exhaustion or hunger!'

In fact it's the army's huge van of stragglers, those bands of marauders who

'without attaching themselves to any definite unit and seeming to have no other goal but to get back safe and sound, only using their weapons to pillage with. A long while I wandered about among this mob, vainly asking for news of the army and above all of my own division. Finally I got hold of an officer of the Guard, who told me Claparède's division was escorting the Treasure and the trophies, and he supposed he'd soon be here.'

In return Brandt tells him that to all appearances the Russians are masters of the Borissow bridge.

Then, suddenly, an assortment of officers of every rank turn up, with pretensions to clear out the inn and its stable for Berthier and his suite, even threatening to throw out the wounded by force:

'But the Frenchmen among us refused to submit. "You're being cruel," they shouted. "We're poor wounded men and we'd sooner be killed than thrown out of our lodgings."'

In the midst of this odious scene Berthier arrives, says one room's enough for him, and a corridor for his staff. Napoleon, meanwhile, has occupied a

'low, one-storeyed building, our former shelter, with a small porchway held up by two wooden columns. On each side of the door is a vast room with a chamber. They've wanted to lodge Berthier in a neighbouring house, but have had to give up the idea since the roof has fallen in and made it uninhabitable. It's thanks to this circumstance we have the honour of having him as our neighbour.'

Not a very agreeable honour, even so. 'Continual comings and goings are preventing anyone from getting a wink of sleep.' But in the morning some officers of the Vistula Legion appear, announcing its imminent arrival. Outside the Emperor's lodging Brandt sees 'some 40 to 50 soldiers bivouacking. A picket's encamped in the market place. In front of the house two Old Guard grenadiers, musket on shoulder. How everything's changed since I last saw the Guard in the Kremlin! Then it was in all its strength and splendour. Today, decimated by its marches and sufferings, its coats torn, it has lost a lot of its self-assurance.' Yet, he notices,

'the old browned faces still present a quite special and martial imprint, and these men, who are anyway always surly, are more laconic, more scowling than usual. Nor have they been forgotten at distributions, as can be seen from their well-garnished cookpots and full water-bottles. We don't see the Emperor.'

That evening there's a sudden severe freeze-up after the thaw, and a heavy snow begins falling. As the Lancer Brigade reaches Bobr the mush is turning into 'rough-surfaced ice which tore at our feet and in which we often sank so deep as to be utterly weary, and made worse by a fresh thick layer of snow'.

Leaving Bobr at 8 a.m. on 24 November, IHQ marches for Loschnitza, 32 kilometres away. The ever-privileged Mailly-Nesle's beginning to feel quite *démoralisé*, but before leaving is given one of the Emperor's stable horses. Reaching Loschnitza 'a village of 30 houses in dense forest' at 6 p.m., Napoleon is met by a 'Polish gentleman from Vilna' bearing a letter from Maret, Duke of Bassano, who describes him as

'"very wealthy, head of a distinguished family, a man wholly devoted to Your Majesty's service. I've already entrusted him with a similar mission to Oudinot and Victor. He has successfully carried it out and at peril to his own life. He has been captured and maltreated by Cossacks, but still he got there. Despite his own wishes the Emperor of Russia had nominated him gentleman of his chamber. He would be the happiest of men if Your Majesty would attach him to your person."'[7]

Count Nicolas Abramovitch, though 'hardly recovered' from his rough treatment at the hands of the Cossacks, and disguised as a peasant, has brought a coded letter dated 22 November which when deciphered announces what at first glance seem happy tidings. The day he'd left Vilna everyone had been rejoicing. Schwarzenberg has beaten the Russians! 'News of this victory', Caulaincourt notes,

'has at once spread among our bivouacs. Yet from the date [16th] and place of the battle on the Bug it's instantly obvious it's irrelevant to the present situation.'

All Sacken's 25,000 Russians have done is lead Schwarzenberg a wild-goose chase to the Bug – in exactly the wrong direction – thus freeing an unthreatened Tchitchakov to advance on Borissow. 'Schwarzenberg', a depressed Fain notes in his journal, 'has made a thorough cock-up of everything, exhausting his 50,000 men in marches and counter-marches'. On the other hand Tchitchakov's force is thought to amount to no more than 20,000 and thus be insufficient to man all the Berezina's possible crossing points.

But miracles do happen. If not big, then little ones. That day (24 November) 'an officer I hardly knew by sight' runs up to Lejeune,
 'begging me, with a gracious smile, to accept a parcel about the size of two fists. And refusing to explain himself, ran off again. Intrigued and mystified, I put the parcel to my nose. I felt how it gave off a delicious smell of truffles. In effect it was nearly a quarter of a pâté of duck's liver from Toulouse or Strasburg! I never saw this officer again.'

In view of the sudden urgency of reaching the Berezina, the Lancer Brigade has been ordered not wait for the rest of the Guard, go to the head of the column, and march out from Bobr forthwith. Colbert orders the 'trot', but Napoleon soon overtakes them at a gallop with his usual chasseur escort. And at about midday, in a field in the forest to the right of the highway, Dumonceau's men, catching up, see him standing by a fire. Called over, Colbert paces to and fro with the Emperor. Both lancer regiments have dismounted and are awaiting further orders. Although at the time they'd hardly even noticed so trivial an obstacle, and Dumonceau doesn't know it, what Napoleon's asking Colbert is, exactly where his Red Lancers had forded the Berezina on 13 July. At the same Weselovo ford, Colbert tells him, as Corbineau had used. Evidently Napoleon explains the exact situation; for going back to his men Colbert has the word passed round that a new Russian army has come up from Moldavia under Tchitchakov, and that worrying circumstances lie ahead. After which, still at a trot, the Lancer Brigade pursues its way westwards. Only later in the day, hearing that the Borissow bridge has been broken and that all their haste has been in vain, does it fall to 'a more ordinary pace'.

At nightfall IHQ reaches Loschnitza where it's 'very badly lodged', and where Oudinot has come to meet Napoleon. 'The sight of the disorder, which hit his eyes for the first time,' Lorencez sees,
 'but even more so Napoleon's state of mind and the Prince of Neuchâtel's tears, told him what he must reckon with. He saw only too clearly he'd just have to shut his eyes and abandon himself to Fortune! On his way back from this visit he clapped me on the shoulder, and said this one word: "Poltava!"'

For several days Sergeant Bourgogne's been straying about in the forests.[8] But now, on the morning of the 25th, after meeting up in the most extraordinary circumstances, fighting a single-handed battle with Cossacks and being sheltered by Lithuanian peasants, he and his fellow-sergeant Picard emerge unexpectedly on to the main road:
 'It was maybe about 7 a.m., not yet quite light. I was deep in my own reflections when I saw the head of the column approaching. I pointed it out to Picard. The first men we saw seemed to be some generals, a few still on horseback, but mostly on foot, as were many other superior officers. They were the debris of the Sacred Squadron, formed on 22 November [sic], but which after three days so to speak no longer existed.[9] The

ones on foot, virtually all of them with frost-bitten feet wrapped up in cloths or bits of sheepskin, and dying of hunger, were dragging themselves painfully along. After that we saw some cavalry of the Guard.'
But then he and Picard see a sight they'll never forget:
'The Emperor, on foot, a stick in his hand. He was wrapped up in a fur-lined greatcoat and had a puce-coloured velvet cap with a band of black fox fur on his head.[10] On his right, also on foot, walked King Murat. On his left, Prince Eugène. Then Marshals Berthier, Ney, Mortier, Lefèbvre and other Marshals and generals whose corps had been partly wiped out. Hardly had the Emperor passed us than he mounted his horse, as did some of those who were with him. Three-quarters of the generals no longer had one. My poor Picard, who hadn't seen the army for a month, looked at all this without saying a word. But it was all too obvious from his convulsive movements what he was feeling. Several times he struck his musket butt on the ground and his chest and forehead with his fist.'
Bourgogne sees
'great tears running down his cheeks and falling on his moustaches, hung with icicles. Then, turning to me: "In truth, *mon pays*, I don't know whether I'm asleep or awake. I weep to see our Emperor marching on foot, a stick in his hand, he who's so great, he who has made us so proud!" As he said these words Picard raised his head and struck his musket, as if to give more expression to his words. And went on: "Did you notice how he looked at us?" And in fact, as he'd passed, the Emperor had turned his head in our direction. He'd looked at us as he always looked at the men of his Guard when he met them marching alone, and above all in this moment of misery, when he seemed by his look to inspire you with confidence and courage. Picard alleged the Emperor had recognised him, which is quite possible.'
The whole, Bourgogne concludes,
'was followed by 700–800 officers, by NCOs marching in order, and in the greatest silence, carrying the eagles of the regiments they'd belonged to and which had so often led them to victory. These were the debris of more than 60,000 men. After them came the Imperial Guard on foot, always marching in order.'
'Gloomy, silent and with downcast gaze,' writes General *von Borcke*,
'this rabble of dying men walked from Orsha to the Berezina like a funeral procession. Preoccupied only with oneself, feeling the seeds of death in one's enfeebled body, and only reminded that one was a human being because of one's instinct of self-preservation, one was no longer capable of conversation. We'd sunk to the level of beasts.'
'Imagine', says Le Roy
'a mass of individuals traipsing along without any order, like a flock of sheep urged on by a shepherd to avoid a storm, saying nothing, or very little. Our hair, side whiskers and moustaches were frozen and glued to the cloths and furs we'd wrapped our face and ears in. We couldn't help the tears running from our eyes and down our nose, where they mingled

with the aqueous humours coming out of it, ran down together on to the chin, and there congealed, forcing us to hold our necks stiffly. If any of us said anything, it was without looking at each other, the least movement being difficult. The wind and the snow prevented us from turning our heads.'

Anyone who's so strong, healthy or warmly clad that he's 'spared the torture of walking in a single block' can count himself happy.

And yet – now and again amazing things can happen. Straying from the highway, von Muraldt and his little group of 12–15 Bavarian chevauleger officers have 'the unexpected luck to find a big house no military had yet visited and whose proprietor was still at home'. Astoundingly, he 'serves them all a splendid meal of bread, meat, chicken, etc!' Is it all a hallucination? No. And if they want further proof – they've only got to feel its 'disastrous effects' on their weakened stomachs.

That afternoon Victor's IX Corps debouches on to the main Orsha–Borissow road, 'goal of all our efforts'. Hardly has the 36th Line's newly promoted Sous-Lieutenant Honoré Beulay of its 4th Battalion (Partonneaux's division) ordered his grenadiers to stack their muskets than

'we're ordered to take them up again. The main army's advance guard, on its way back from Moscow, was announced. At its approach an enthusiastic shout of *"Vive l'Empereur!"* went up from all our regiments, expressing our joy at feeling ourselves so close to Victory's favourite.'

Surely their troubles are at an end? Surely luck's going to change and smile on them again?

'At last we were going to avenge ourselves on the these accursed Russians who'd been giving us such a tough time! In the Emperor's stores we were going to find new clothes, soft and warm, to replace our coats, full of holes.'

Soon they'll be eating flour bread again, the very taste of which they're beginning to forget!

'Our joy grew as our comrades came nearer. We had all the difficulty in the world to keep the men in the ranks. Every one of them would have liked to run to meet the men of the Grand Army from Moscow, press them to their hearts, carry them in triumph!'

Marching down the highway with Murat's staff, Rossetti hears Victor's men shouting as they come closer:

'Some of us thought we were being attacked. But it was Victor's army corps. It was waiting for Napoleon to pass. Seeing its Emperor again, it was receiving him with long-forgotten acclamations.'

'When they were no more than a few hundred metres away,' Beulay goes on, 'all the shakos were on our musket barrels. It was a delirium!' – But then they get a horrible shock:

'What wasn't our stupefaction when, instead of the haughty, vigorous, disciplined army we were expecting to see, all we saw was a mob of stragglers – emaciated, in shreds, without weapons, marching any old how,

with a ferocious and desperate air. We stood rooted to the spot.'
Are these men with hardly human faces really Frenchmen?
'Most were got up in strange tatters. Some had brilliant- coloured oriental carpets hung round their necks. Others were invisible under rich
furs. The infantrymen had taken dying troopers' great white or blue
mantles. Many heavy helmets had been thrown away and replaced by
Cossack or peasant bearskin or dog-skin caps, or even by cotton bonnets
or common handkerchiefs. Most of these poor devils had wound bits of
cloth or sheepskin around their feet, so as not to walk barefoot in the
frozen snow. Ashamed and confused they didn't dare halt, or say one
word to us, or even look at us. Nor did it occur to us to put them any
questions, or ask for explanations.'
Although Beulay sheds a tear at the sight of 'an old white-haired general,
dragging himself painfully along on an officer's arm, exhausted, his face
contracted with pain', soon he's 'no longer counting the degraded generals being swept along by this human torrent.
'In the presence of this shipwreck we forgot our own ills and our soul
was invaded by an infinite sadness. So when the Emperor appeared,
framed by the remains of his Guard, which no longer formed more than
a handful of men but which had at least kept their weapons and military
air, our regiments were struck dumb; and it was only with great difficulty
we made them, by order, utter a few cries of "Vive l'Empereur!"'
It's the first time Beulay's ever set eyes on
'this hero, this demigod, who'd made the world tremble. Poor man, it's
not with this worried brow, this extinguished glance, this back bent
under the weight of bad luck, I'd imagined him!'[10]
To Caulaincourt, marching at Napoleon's side and staring back at Victor's
men, it seems he's never seen what a proper army looks like before, or has
totally forgotten it:
'Our men, though vigorous on the march and full of dash when under
fire, were emaciated, bloodless, filthy as chimney-sweeps, and as feeble
as spectres. To us these others, less exhausted and better nourished, less
begrimed by bivouac fires, seemed like men of another race. They were
alive. We were shadows. The contrast in the horses was even more striking.'
Victor's men are particularly aghast to witness something never before
seen in a French army: senior officers being jostled in the mob and not
even protesting! Also to see 'the mob, not to have to step aside, trampling
on those who fell, without heeding their groans'. But most perhaps of all
to see
'the Emperor himself turning his back to the enemy. Then we too
became demoralised. The monstrous disaster had been hidden from us.
The idea had never crossed our minds that Napoleon could be
defeated.'
To offset, if possible, the effect of this nightmarish scene, General de Blamont, commanding the 12th Division's 2nd Infantry Brigade

[125th/126th Line], 'seeing consternation on every face' has the presence of mind to harangue his officers. Then he orders them to go back to their units and 'tell the cowards to join the runaways and stragglers, but the brave men to prepare to show the world what a French soldier is capable of!' These rousing words, Beulay sees, do the trick:

'That evening the veterans, having seen Napoleon go by, felt themselves cheered up. While savouring a beefsteak of dead horse, they joked into their moustaches: "The Emperor's got more than enough men to play these Russian rascals a trick or two! Just let him get busy and you'll see!"'

But they've also heard from fugitives how 'since Moscow they'd lost more than 100,000 men, all the baggage, almost all the artillery, a number of flags, and that the Emperor, a few days before, had collected on to one bonfire all the Eagles that had escaped the enemy and burnt them.[11] Only seven or eight thousand brave men remained to assure the Emperor's safety.' And Beulay, like Oudinot, knows enough history to compare the army's predicament with 'Charles XII's a hundred years ago, on the eve of Poltava', where the Swedish army of 25,000 men had been wiped out, all save 1,200 men.

The contrast may even have affected the Guard. For shortly after this Lignières is among a group of its officers who've bivouacked for the night:

'The Emperor was on horseback. We were scarcely a dozen officers in a circle around him. This, more or less, is what he said: "It pains me to see that men of my Old Guard are straggling. Their comrades should bring them to justice [*les claquer*]." And he repeated: "*Les claquer!* I'm counting on my Old Guard. It should count on me and the success of my projects." He repeated the same words several times, looking at us with a sad face which had lost its composure. Few grenadiers or chasseurs heard this discourse. The men of the Old Guard who were falling behind were those who, really sick from hunger, their wounds and cold, absolutely couldn't keep up.'

Caulaincourt sees how its veterans cheer up 'as soon as they saw the Emperor, and each day the duty battalion was maintaining an astonishing standard of smartness'. As for the Sacred Squadron, Lignières sees it's becoming scattered:

'Those officers having no units, marched in isolation, trying to find themselves and their horses something to eat. I never saw them united. I knew many of them. I always met them alone. This squadron never figured except on paper.'

Captain François agrees: 'They didn't respond to the confidence placed in them. In a few days they'd melt away.'[12] 'Since Toloczin,' Maurice Tascher, who still belongs to it, scribbles in his diary,

'we've been marching through a continual forest. Today, having done three leagues, we've halted in a hamlet close to road. Cruel situation of my brother Eugène, whom I'm obliged to leave alone with a chasseur, close to the Emperor's château. Slept on the snow, no fire, extreme cold. Left at 4 a.m.'

Besides the Guard certain other units are retaining a modicum of morale. Colonel Dubois is constantly and energetically urging on his dismounted cuirassiers – of Thirion's regiment – carrying

'carbines, to which was attached a bayonet as long as on a voltigeur's or dragoon's musket. Every morning he put his feet on men who wished for nothing better than to go on sleeping, beginning with myself, who always slept next to him.'

Lejeune and Haxo, commander of I Corps' engineer corps, spend the night in a forest, both rolled up together in their bearskin 'which was rather more than 3 square metres in extent'. The Lancer Brigade has just occupied a large, long village, to the right of the highway beyond Loschnitza, 'a village of 30 houses in the depths of the forests', when IHQ turns up there and establishes itself there for the night – so that Dumonceau's men have to give up half their 'excellent shelter' to the *Chasseurs à Cheval.* 'The whole population was there and keen to succour us.' Next day, en route for a rendezvous farther on, Dumonceau's shocked to see

'in a field to our right a fine battery of artillery, seemingly brand-new, so well was it preserved. Though parked in perfect order, no personnel or team was with it. It seemed to have been abandoned.'

But shortly afterwards he's encouraged to see one of Oudinot's regiments march by in good order. Compared with the Moscow army its turnout is 'a delight to behold'. And Le Roy, marching with Davout's 1,200 men between Natcha and Kroupki, is struck by the good shape II and IX Corps seem to be in, and above all by their

'numerous and well-horsed artillery. Unfortunately they had too many vehicles in their wake and were jamming up the road.'

At 4 p.m. on 25 November 'before nightfall', Napoleon enters Borissow, whose '350 timber houses' are packed with Oudinot's troops. Seeing the Emperor get out of his carriage and mount his horse to reconnoitre, Intendant Pastoret, sits down dejectedly in the main square and contemplates

'the horror of our situation. Our men were ready to drop with exhaustion, discouraged by hunger. Half of them no longer bore any weapons. The cavalry was destroyed, the artillery altogether lost, and there was no gunpowder. It was in these circumstances we, after a five weeks' march, were going to have to cross a difficult swift-flowing river, carry positions, and triumph over three armies who were waiting for us, sure they could give us the *coup de grâce.*'

A few moments later Regimenttal Sergeant-major Calosso, with the 24th Chasseurs down by the broken, still smouldering bridge, sees the Emperor halt

'a few paces away from us without dismounting, and train his spyglass on the enemy camp. Its various arms could be made out by the naked eye on the high ground opposite, where there was considerable activity.'

Dumonceau, who's also there, notes their 'considerable state of agitation' on the high ground on the other side. 'Our own bivouacs were peacefully concentrated around the town.' Thomas Legler too is driven by curiosity to

247

'follow his staff, which halted about 60 paces from it. Alone, the Emperor walked along it as far as to our farthest sentry, who was standing hardly 50 paces from the Russian one.'
The bridge, he sees, is broken
'in three places, the Russians not having been able to destroy it in its entirety. On their side only about 40 feet of it had been torn up.'
So fascinated is Legler to see Napoleon out there on the bridge, he fails to notice that Caulaincourt's there too. Obviously what Napoleon is contemplating is whether 'a straightforward attack might enable him to get control of the bridge and thus more easily cross the river' – an idea he's earlier discussed with Caulaincourt.[13] But, like Legler, both Napoleon and Caulaincourt are impressed by the
'18–20 cannon commanding it from much higher ground on the far bank. The Russians could easily have reduced the town to a heap of ashes,'
thus obviating, before it can even be organised, any chance of being outgunned by Oudinot's 60 cannon, whose ammunition wagons would be blown sky-high in the ensuing inferno. But though Borissow's so packed with men and weapons that 'one could hardly find one's way about', the Russians, oddly enough, aren't firing a single shot. Calosso can only conclude that Tchitchakov's waiting for Kutusov to come up and take Napoleon in the rear.

The Studianka ford – if still fordable – lies a little over six miles upstream; and Corbineau has already seen some of Tchitchakov's units lining its western river bank. Only a large-scale feint can save the situation. A few moments later Calosso sees
'ADCs taking fresh orders to the various divisions. The 1st Cuirassier Brigade, which had bivouacked behind us, mounted and took the road that follows the Berezina downstream. A few battalions, followed by a lot of military baggage, marched off in the same direction.'
Seeing these 'detachments and various transports moving off to the left', Dumonceau naturally assumes – as Tchitchakov, too, hopefully does – that this betokens some projected operations on that side.[14] And in fact the cuirassiers have been ordered to halt with their baggage train at Oukholoda village, where there's another ford, and there 'make a great deal of noise' as if preparing for a crossing. Meanwhile all Oudinot's other units are to march for Studianka. But before they do so Napoleon makes no bones about granting all his requests for promotions,
'something that had rarely been the case in earlier wars where the Emperor himself hadn't been present, so that many desserts had gone unrewarded'.
Legler himself gets the Cross. For the 1st Swiss there are thirteen more Knight's Crosses; the 2nd get eight; and the 3rd and 4th Regiments six apiece. As the scarlet ribbon and heavy gold epaulettes are being attached to one of his comrades in a room at Borissow, the recipient remarks:
'It all looks very pretty. If we were at home one could just be proud of it, but we aren't there yet. There'll be many empty shakos before then.'

CHAPTER 16

TWO FRAGILE BRIDGES

Who's to build them? – Dumonceau sleeps under a snowdrift – 'We're all dead men' – 'His eyes lit up with joy and impatience' – 'the bridge wasn't particularly solid' – 'his velvet mantle was flung carelessly over one shoulder' – 'he looked tired and worried' – 'the horses sank up to their knees in mud' – 'You shall be my locksmith' – 'it was like being in a wine press'

Already at nightfall on 24 November Castex's brigade had 'silently left our bivouacs and marched up the left bank', followed by Oudinot and his staff. Like most Lithuanian country roads this is 'a difficult one' of transversely laid logs, now knee-deep in snow. For a guide Oudinot's taken one of the local Jews he'd 'retained'. Half-scared out of his wits, no doubt, they can't get any sense out of him; and the usually so bluff and good-natured Oudinot suspects him of trying to lead them astray. Loses his temper. And sends him 'to General Aubry, who immediately had him shot'.

When Castex's men get to Studianka at daybreak they find Corbineau's already there. After defeating the Russians at Loschnitza at 9 p.m. on 23 November and, pursuing them, they'd

'ridden as far as to a hillock near Weselovo and heard the Russians swimming the Berezina to rejoin their main body on the right bank'.

Curély had been all on fire to pursue them; 'but Corbineau had just made himself comfortable in an old hut and wouldn't allow it'. Ordered to take a look around in the immediate neighbourhood, about six miles from Borissow, some fifteen of his troopers had come upon a big farm still occupied by some Cossacks, the manor house of Staroï-Borissow. Lying a couple of miles east of the river, it belongs, like many other estates in this area, to the immensely rich Prince Radziwil, currently serving with the Polish Guard Lancers. Turning the Cossacks out head over heels, Curély's men had seized ten of the Cossacks' horses and found 'victuals of all kinds, more than 200 sacks of flour, and brandy for the whole brigade. I had some bread baked and took away some of the flour.' Back at Weselovo in the morning Curély had seen, on the far bank, 'considerable numbers' of Russians, passively looking on. A little way downstream, on some high ground overlooking the ford which at every moment is becoming less fordable, stands Studianka village. Since a bridge was obviously going to be needed, and so as not to signal his presence to the Cossacks – prowling about on and beyond the marshes, Corbineau had hidden the bulk of his brigade behind a fold in the ground near some woods half a mile to the east. They'd 'destroyed several ammunition wagons to provide clamps and nails, and pulled down several huts' to provide the necessary planks:

'Hidden inside the houses, they were beginning to work on the construction of materials for trestle bridges. Our chasseurs made bread out of the flour we'd taken and the pontoneers worked ceaselessly all day and night.'

Just now, with the cold severe if not yet intense, the Berezina should be freezing solid. But when Calosso gets here with Castex's brigade he sees 'only a few rare ice-floes'.

At this point, Marbot notes, the river's no wider than 'the Rue Royale in Paris, opposite the Ministry of the Marine, i.e., about twelve *toises* [24 yards]'. But because of the flat and marshy right bank the flood waters have effectively increased it to 40 [200 yards]. And if the half-frozen marshes are added, the obstacle it now presents is even greater. Not that it's particularly deep – about the same as the Wop. But at least at the steep left bank its waters are swift-flowing. And in mid-stream the flood has doubled its normal 3½-foot depth.

Which makes all the difference.

Meanwhile, throughout the moonless night, the rest of II Corps has been marching for the crossing point. Among other things little voltigeur Jean-Marc Bussy and his comrades in the 3rd Swiss have seen 'a lot of carts, halted at the roadside, their shafts in the air,' captured by Pahlen's men, but

'the first troops to arrive from Polotsk had retaken them. We're told they'd been made in Switzerland to bring us some effects. Each of us is given two pairs of shoes and two pairs of gaiters.'

The march along the 'hardly distinguishable track being followed by a long file of wagons and stragglers', Legler's finding, is taking four hours. Captain *Abraham Rosselet* of the same regiment, is impressed by the

'strictest order and profound silence this movement upstream was being made in, in closed ranks, and without permitting anyone, on any pretext, to leave them. Although we were all shivering under the rigour of an icy temperature, we were forbidden to light fires.'

Now it's the early hours of 25 November, and the first of Oudinot's infantry and his pontoneers are beginning to turn up. En route, too, Bourgogne and Picart have seen a detachment of about 30 of Eblé and Chasseloup's pontoneers and engineers, under three officers: 'Having formed part of the Orsha garrison, they looked strong and well.' During the forenoon Calosso sees the rest of II Corps' infantry and artillery arrive:

'Without delay we got busy demolishing the best preserved houses to obtain the materials needed to build a bridge. The Sailors of the Guard and the Pontoneers got to work on it. Whereupon we were allowed to light fires.'

Soon Eblé and Chasseloup's men appear on the snowy scene. With them, snatched from the premature burning of the bridging train at Orsha, they've brought six wagons full of tools, nails, iron clamps, plus two campaign forges and all the iron items needed for constructing one or more trestle bridges. Likewise two carts loaded with coal. For appearance sake Chasseloup has left one of his pioneer companies at Borissow. But the others have been marching non-stop for 48 hours. Eblé examines Corbineau's construction and finds it's not solid enough. Although Oudinot's pioneers have also made a few trestles, their work too is found unsatisfactory. So all has to be begun again. There's even a professional flare-up, Marbot says, between Oudinot's gunners and Eblé and Chasseloup's men:

'Unable to moderate or even bury their differences in difficult circumstances, each came with pretensions to build the bridges unaided, so that they mutually brought everything to a standstill and nothing was getting on.'

But it's Eblé's pontoneers, most them Dutchmen,[2] who're the experts at making trestle bridges. At first the plan is to throw three bridges. But then it's realised the available materials won't suffice for more than two. One for the infantry. The other, the left-hand one, some 200–300 yards downstream, for the cavalry and wheeled vehicles. Each is to consist of 23 heavy trestles of varying height, placed in the river at 12-foot intervals:

'All the works were being done with timbers from the demolition, already carried out during the night of 25 November, of the houses of Weselovo. The trestles' height was from 8 to 9 feet, and the length of the caps 14 feet.'

Soon, the pontoneers know, they'll have to go down into the icy water to plant them in the soft muddy bottom – something which will become progressively harder because of the 'immense ice-floes' swirling downstream from right to left. Though half of Eblé's men are allowed to get some sleep, the others have to busy themselves immediately.

For time presses. At any moment Tchitchakov may appear in force on the opposite bank. Pils – equipped as usual with his sketchbook and watercolour box – sees

'the preparatory work and the trestles' construction hastened on by Eblé being done behind a fold in the ground encasing the river and so preventing enemy scouts from seeing the workmen as they moved about'

– the same hollow, that is, that has been hiding Corbineau's men. Opposite.

'On the right bank, the very swampy terrain was frozen, and it was thanks to this the vehicles would be able to get across.'

Fortunately the thermometer's still falling. But it'll only have to rise a couple of degrees to melt that thin crust of ice. And then anything that moves on wheels will sink into the morass.

Napoleon had left Borissow at 10 p.m. yesterday evening. As he'd reached the town's outskirts on the Orsha road, Fain had noticed how he followed the 'first cross-country road to the left, the one leading to Studianka'. Some way from the town the road forks. Both branches lead to Weselovo and Studianka; but while the left-hand one follows the river

251

bank, the other climbs upwards towards Staroï-Borissow. Earlier in the night Colbert's lancers, going on ahead, have recognised its great barns as the same ones they'd occupied on 13 July after fording the river at Weselovo, en route from Zembin to Borissow. Now, in pitch darkness and the icy wind, Dumonceau finds the great farm (already visited by Curély) deserted, and under thick snow. Why doesn't Colbert allow his lancers inside its buildings, Dumonceau asks himself. Doubtless to save the contents for IHQ, the Sacred Squadron and the rest of the escort. 'This was discouraging. Even so, we killed some cattle and had a distribution of fresh meat. It was a detestable night,' for Colbert insists on reserving 'the farm's abundant resources' for IHQ 'and only accorded us strict necessities'.

At about 11 p.m. IHQ turns up. But even Rapp and Mouton, still suffering from their Borodino wounds, only have a little straw to sleep on: 'We were thinking about the troubles of the morrow, and our observations weren't cheerful.'

The army's chances of getting across, they realise, like everyone else who still has his wits about him, (but thousands, like Griois, are too stunned and exhausted even to think about the matter) are slim indeed. There's no longer any likelihood of Schwarzenberg coming up behind Tchitchakov's army – perhaps he's even joined forces with Wittgenstein? A report even comes in – happily it turns out to be false – that 'due to Victor's negligence' one of Tchitchakov's units has crossed the Berezina and already made liaison. With one army ahead of them, ensconced behind a river, and another – soon two others – in their rear, only IX and II Corps, the Poles and the 8,500-strong Imperial Guard are still capable of putting up a substantial fight in this desperate situation.[3] At 4 a.m. Berthier sends off a dispatch to Davout, still at Loschnitza, telling him that the enemy's on the right bank at Studianka, and that the Emperor's going to have to 'carry the passage by main force'. 'Ney took me aside,' Rapp will remember:

'We went out, and he said to me in German: "Our position's unheard of. If Napoleon gets away with it today he's the devil himself." We were no little worried, as we unquestionably had every reason to be. The King of Naples came up to us. He was no less worried: "I've suggested to Napoleon," he told us, "that he save himself and cross the river a few miles away. I've got Poles who'd answer for his safety and take him to Vilna. But he won't hear of this proposal. For my part I don't believe we can escape." All three of us had the same thought. Murat went on: "We're all dead men. Because there can be no question of surrendering."'

By now the moon's come up and the night's cold and clear. Crossing fields to attend to some wounded men, Larrey notices

'how serene the sky was and the cold rather sharp. I couldn't help being struck by the appearance of a comet, situated due north. It seemed to be going down toward the Pole.'

While Berthier's been writing his dispatch to Davout the Sacred Squadron is passing through Borissow in pitch darkness. On the far bank Maurice Tascher sees 'the whole line of Russian campfires. Turned off to the right,' he notes in his diary. 'Followed the Berezina. Bivouacked at Klein [*sic*] Borissow.'

'For greater safety,' Mailly-Nesle sees, 'the Emperor's horses had been sent off early in the morning.' But at Borissow, to his exasperation, IHQ's cooks are still asleep:

'I left without getting anything to eat. It was infinitely painful to go about among all Bonaparte's domestics like a beggar, asking for something to eat. Overwhelmed by the importunities of all these unfortunates perishing from hunger around the kitchen whose exhalations filled the bivouac, they took me for a simple soldier and sometimes let me go away empty-handed.'

But his footman Mouet's in worse case – his carriage burnt, he's been 'put on foot'.[4] And Private Jakob Walter, like thousands of other conscripts wandering about in the chaos, is in still worse – 20 dead cows he's found in a yard at Borissow are so hard-frozen nothing at all can be got off them. And everywhere slivers of half-frozen horseflesh have to be fought for and cut off amidst 'scuffling and slugging'.

By the time Tascher gets to Staroï-Borissow Rapp and Mouton have already left:

'Before long, riding in one of the Emperor's carriages, we came within sight of the enemy's camp fires. They covered the far bank. Forests and swamps swarmed with them, as far as the eye could see. The Emperor conversed with Ney awhile, had something to eat, and gave his orders.'

As it begins to get light Napoleon arrives at Studianka.[5] 'Hearing guns firing at Borissow' at dawn, the 20th Chasseurs assume it's a feint attack. 'A moment later we saw the Emperor and his staff arrive, followed by a column of infantry.' Napoleon goes straight to the timber cottage at Weselovo where Oudinot has his headquarters. And 'between 7 and 8 a.m.' just as Pils is

'opening its door, which was fixed by a tourniquet, the Emperor bumped up against me and said: "Is Oudinot there?" Recognising Napoleon's voice, *M. le Maréchal* came hurrying out. His Majesty was wearing a fur and a green velvet cap, lined with furs which came down over his eyes. The Prince of Neuchâtel, who was with him, was wearing the same costume, albeit of a violet colour. The Duke of Reggio took them down to the Berezina's banks. After going upstream as far as Studianka, the Emperor examined the area, visited the works, and asked what state II Corps was in.'

Oudinot tells him he still has all his artillery, 'thereto the fourteen [*sic*] guns he'd taken from the Russians on the banks of the Drissa'. His men are raring for a fight as soon as they've crossed over. 'Napoleon rubbed his hands together, and said: "Very well! You'll be my locksmith to open the passage."'

And now, as if by magic, something utterly improbable happens.

'While we were talking in this way,' Rapp goes on,
  'we saw the enemy march off. His masses had vanished. The fires were
  going out. All we saw were the tails of his columns losing themselves in
  the woods, and 500 or 600 Cossacks spread about the fields. We examined the matter more closely through our spyglasses, and became convinced he'd really broken camp.'
To Lieutenant Thomas Legler, rejoining Oudinot's other divisions with the
1st Swiss at dawn, it seems as if
  'they'd had orders to let us pass unhindered; the building of the bridges
  could have been put paid to without firing a single shot. On the opposite bank I saw with my own eyes some 1,500 infantry filing by, taking
  with them two field guns and between 600 and 800 Cossacks. The Russians seemed to be nothing but passive spectators.'
What's Tchitchakov doing?

On 24 November few of Lambert's Russian hussars, Rochechouart says,
had failed to reply at the roll-call on the west bank at Borissow:
  'But even when a big detachment that had been posted along the left
  bank as far as the little town of Beresino, where there was a bridge, had
  rejoined, six of our twelve guns hadn't reappeared.'
Then, towards evening, one of Kutusov's officers, Colonel Count Mikhail
Orloff, had turned up. With him he'd had the young and strikingly handsome Lord Tyrconnel, Wilson's ADC, newly arrived from England. Also a
letter from Kutusov containing 'all sorts of details about the French effectives' and describing the appalling state they're in. It had urged upon
Tchitchakov the importance of 'putting every imaginable obstacle' in
Napoleon's path, in order to prevent him from getting 'as many of his men
as possible across the Berezina. But take care.' (Rochechouart will always
remember the exact words)
  '"You have to do with a man as clever as he is cunning. Napoleon will
  make a demonstration that he is going to cross at one point, to draw
  your attention to it, while most likely doing it on the other side. Prudence and vigilance!"'
And this, Rochechouart goes on, was why Tchitchakov, when he'd been
warned by a
  'detachment of light troops sent upstream on observation and to try to
  establish contact with Wittgenstein had sent to warn him that the French
  were preparing to throw a bridge at Studianka, had assumed – the place
  being so swampy and thus ill-suited to throwing a bridge – it was a feint;
  and that the French would profit by it to make the true crossing at some
  opposite point. At Beresino, for example.'
Eblé's bridge-building operations at Studianka, so far from alerting
Tchitchakov to what was really going on, have caused him to give 'the
whole army the immediate order to march for' Beresino. Only
  'Count Langeron was sent with 4,000 men and eight guns to a point facing Studianka, to observe the enemy's movements. Another detachment

under that general's orders had been left to guard the [Borissow] bridgehead and prevent any attempt to re-establish the broken bridge.' Between them Napoleon and Kutusov have really and truly '*donné le change à* [bamboozled] Tchitchakov!' So that in the dawn light Calosso's troopers of the 24th Chasseurs, 'massed in a fold in the ground between the river bank and the village, but in full view of an enemy who didn't pursue his march the less for that', see

'the Russian columns on the opposite bank marching for Borissow. Over and over we said to each other: "We'll just have to believe those imbeciles don't grasp the advantages of their position."'

Rapp goes to Napoleon,

'whom I found deep in conversation with Marshal Oudinot: "Sire, the enemy has quit his position." "It can't be possible!"'

Ney and Murat – Rossetti presumably with him – come and confirm the incredible report:

'Whereon Napoleon rushes out from Oudinot's headquarters. He looks and can still see the last files of Tschaplitz's column moving farther away and disappearing into the wood. Transported with joy, he threw a glance to the other side of the river. "I've fooled the Admiral" (he couldn't pronounce Tchitchakov's name).[6] He thinks I'm at the spot where I've ordered the feint attack. He's hurrying off to Borissow!" His eyes lit up with joy and impatience.'

Soon all they can see – and hear – on the far side are a few Cossacks who've come out of the forest to

'gather some forage from the hay stacks scattered about the meadows. He gave orders to drive them away. And immediately some Polish lancers swam the ford',

with voltigeurs riding up behind them:

'Colonel Jacqueminot, ADC to the Duke of Reggio, and the Lithuanian Count Predzieski were the first to throw themselves into the river and reach the opposite bank despite the ice-floes which cut and bloodied their horses' chests.'

'The Emperor passed close by us,' Calosso goes on,

'to mount a small hillock that dominated the river on our side. All our eyes were fixed on him. Not a sigh, not a murmur arose from our ranks. The pontoneers throwing the bridge were up to their necks in water. They were wholly unopposed. It was exceedingly cold. The Emperor was generous with encouragement.'

Now the Lancer Brigade, too, has reached the river bank. Zalusky, feeling hungrier than any day since the campaign opened ('unless it had been at the battle of Mojaisk' i.e., Borodino), watches as

'under our eyes the Berezina ford was tried out by an officer of the 8th Regiment, aided by a few lancers,'

– 'about 60 of them,' Rapp specifies, from the 8th Lancers of the Vistula, under Colonel Thomas Lubienski. With them, Calosso sees, are the debris of the 7th Polish Lancers,' 'who knew the neighbourhood better than we did. As the Emperor wanted some prisoners to be brought to him for questioning, our brave allies flung themselves on the tracks of the Cossacks and, seizing two of them, brought them to headquarters.'

Rossetti sees 'Squadron-Leader Sourd and 50 chasseurs of the 7th carrying some voltigeurs on their cruppers followed them. Likewise two frail skiffs, which in 20 voyages carried over 400 men.' When 50 of Curély's chasseurs, too, are sent swimming across, each trooper has an infantryman riding up behind his saddle: 'These few infantry were put into a wood to drive off the few Cossacks who'd been left to observe,' and who're seeking refuge from the chasseurs and lancers behind bushes. All, however, escape: 'Except one,' says Rapp, 'whom M. Jacqueminot took prisoner and brought before His Majesty.' A young artillery lieutenant in Merle's division, *F.-N. Lassus-Marcilly*, has been standing there admiring General Jacqueminot as he

'having left his horse, had reached the far bank and seized a Russian infantryman [*sic*], whom he brought back at a gallop on his crupper to the Emperor's bivouac. I'll live for centuries before I forget that brief apparition. Clad in his brilliant uniform, Jacqueminot halts his horse and dumps his prisoner, just like a horseman might throw a truss of hay to the ground, and then went off, doubtless to change his clothes. Stupefied, the wretched soldier has difficulty in getting up, and blinded by the brightness of the fire puts his hands in front of his eyes. "How many men in your battalion?" the Emperor asks, a question translated by Prince Poniatowski or General Krasinski. Someone replies: "He doesn't know." Same answer when he asks: "In your company?" Finally, "In your squad."'

Dumonceau, too, can scarcely believe his eyes. All he sees on the far bank, 'a low-lying marshy swamp rising farther off to slightly higher wooded ground that bounded it a thousand paces away, were some groups of our horsemen who had just swum the river and were moving about in the distance to reconnoitre its limits. All eyes were fixed on them, anxiously waiting to see what they might find, for each of us appreciated the importance of the enemy not being there to dispute our crossing.'

Rapp, however, disapproves of all this 'unnecessary chasing of Cossacks', because one of the lancers, too, is taken prisoner;

'and it was when examining him that the Russians tumbled to Napoleon's whereabouts.'

Calosso, though no Napoleon-worshipper, confesses that:

'In such critical circumstances we still had faith in his genius. On his way back, his reconnaissance over, he passed close to us. We thought he seemed more satisfied. He was chatting and gesticulating vivaciously with his generals. We couldn't hear what he was saying, but we realised he was congratulating himself on having lured the Admiral into making a mistake. Shortly afterwards a double battery was set up on the hillock the Emperor had just left. And we were allowed to go there to see the march past of the enemy whose rearguard frequently kept turning round to keep an eye on our operations.'

Seeing '30 pieces of artillery retreating' on the high ground beyond the marsh, Rossetti reflects:

'A single one of their roundshot would have been enough to annihilate the single plank we were going to throw to join the two banks and save ourselves. But that artillery was falling back as a battery of ours was being set up. Farther off we could see the tail of a long column which, without looking back, was moving off toward Borissow. However, a regiment of infantry and twelve guns still remained in presence, but without taking up any position, and we saw a horde of Cossacks wandering about on the forest fringe. It was the rearguard of Tschaplitz's division which, 6,000 men strong, was thus moving off, as if to make us a gift of our crossing.'

The French artillery commanding the river and the marsh from either side of the bridgehead, Legler sees, consists of 'two batteries of twelve guns each to left and right'. 'At that moment', Rossetti goes on, 'two enemy guns reappeared and opened fire.' As it happens we know who they're commanded by. Seeing the bridge-building operations commence and 'hoping to fire on the workmen as soon as they reached the middle of the river' *Ivan Arnoldi*, an officer of the Russian horse artillery, has sited his four guns in the marshy terrain, as close as he can bring them:

'But hardly had we fired our first salvo than we were saluted from a hillock by a battery of 40 guns. I saw my men and horses falling in a whirl of dust.'

Faced with such heavy calibre long-range artillery fire, Arnoldi has to beat a hasty retreat. Whereon Rossetti hears

'the Emperor order the guns to remain silent for fear of their recalling Tschaplitz, as the bridge had hardly been commenced. It was 8 a.m., and the first trestles were still being sunk.'

The French battery, Rapp will afterwards remember[7] is 'commanded by a brave officer with a wooden leg' – doubtless Captain Brechtel, 'who did the whole campaign with a wooden leg, which didn't prevent him from mounting his horse'.

'During the action a roundshot' (evidently from one of Arnoldi's guns) has 'carried it away and thrown him over. "Fetch me another leg out of wagon No. 5," he told one of his gunners." Strapped it on, and went on firing.'

Among the units standing by the river bank waiting to cross are the 500 troopers of Marbot's handsome 23rd Chasseurs – 'the colonels of our corps' other regiments could only muster 200' – and it must be about 8 a.m. For he, like Pils, is admiring the pioneers as they 'throw themselves completely naked into the Berezina's cold waters, though we didn't have a single drop of brandy to give them' and begin

'placing out their trestles at equal distances in the river, with its huge ice-floes, and with rarely exampled courage going out into the water up to their shoulders. Some fell dead and disappeared, carried away by the current; yet their comrades' energy wasn't the less for seeing them come to this tragic end. The Emperor stands watching these heroes; doesn't leave the river bank.'

Dumonceau, who reckons the distance between the two bridges as being about 200 yards, sees him 'walking to and fro along the shore from one bridge to the other'. Of the two it's the left-hand bridge, designed to carry artillery and vehicles, that must be the more stoutly built. Oudinot, Murat and other generals are standing there with him,

'while the Prince of Neuchâtel, seated on the snow, sends off the correspondence and prepares the army's orders. Since the engineers didn't suffice for such gigantic work, General Aubry sends for men from several infantry regiments to make fascines to support the bridge's table.'

The bridges have

'the structure of sloping saw-horses, suspended like trestles on shallow-sunk piles; on these lay long stringers and across them only bridge-ties, which were not fastened down'.

Progressively as the left-hand bridge is completed its table is strewn with straw and horse dung to minimise the wheels' bouncing and bumping. While waiting for it to be completed so that II Corps can cross, Marbot too sees Napoleon walking about talking both to officers and men, with Murat at his heels. Just now that glamorous personage seems 'eclipsed' – but brightens up at the sight of Oudinot's cavalry, which is still in such excellent order. Napoleon too is 'delighted [s'extasia] at the fine state of preservation of these troops in general' and, Marbot preens himself, 'of my regiment in particular.' But who's this he, overjoyed, sees coming toward him, if not his brother Adolphe's devoted servant Jean Dupont?

'His zeal, courage and fidelity had stood up to all tests. Left alone when my brother had been captured at the campaign's outset, he'd gone with the 16th Chasseurs to Moscow; done the whole of the retreat while looking after my brother's three horses; and despite the most seductive offers had refused to sell any of them. After five months of fatigues and miseries this brave lad was coming to join me, bringing back all my brother's effects. But in showing them to me he told me with tears in his eyes that, having worn out his footwear and seeing himself reduced to walking barefoot on the ice, he'd permitted himself to take a pair of his master's boots.'

For a moment Napoleon also halts in front of the 20th Chasseurs. And Oudinot wants to present – the desperately shy – Curély to him. And Corbineau tells him he's promoted colonel.[8]

While all this is going on, thousands of individuals are still struggling on towards Studianka, alone or in groups. Griois, like Le Roy, keeps falling in – for the last time, as it'll turn out – with acquaintances. Is it these chance encounters that will have some sinister influence on his friends' fates? For most will perish. And Le Roy and Jacquet, struggling to catch up with the Guard where they feel they'll be safer, try to save an officer who's lost all his horses, wants to go no further, and is obviously at his last gasp. He turns out to be a man named Albitte, who during the Revolution had been a member of the Convention and one of its most zealous commissioners, 'which by no means diminished his merit in my eyes'.[9]

'A little sooner, a little later,' Albitte tells them, 'there must be an end to it. In France I'll leave a name,' he murmurs as they leave him to die, 'that'll one day be appreciated.'

Farther on, propped in a seated position against a pine tree, they come across the 85th's Major Frickler: Le Roy goes up to him, asks: 'What the devil are you doing there beside a fire that's gone out?' But Guillaume tactfully plucks at his sleeve: 'Leave him, he's dead.'

'I had to put my hand on his face. Found it cold and frozen. The eyes were open. As yet the snow, because of the fire, hadn't covered him. He'd died for lack of food. I still seem to see that unfortunate young man, with ebony black side whiskers, ivory teeth, the most robust, the most handsome man in the regiment. "Poor boy, may God comfort him,"'

says the deistic major, weeping. 'He'd just been pillaged. His pockets were turned inside out.'

Struggling on among III Corps's stragglers and amidst this vast swill of a stunned and disintegrating humanity toward Studianka 'where the indescribable horror of all possible plagues awaited us', Private Jacob Walter, buffeted like thousands of others by the icy swirling snow and all alone in this vast but ever-dwindling host, can only trust to his own resourcefulness. Not that he isn't still always keeping a weather eye open for his Major von Schaumberg, whom he has lost, then – to the latter's great joy – found; but will lose again. By now Walter's had to leave his horse behind; likewise the sledge in which, ever since Smolensk, he'd been dragging the major's possessions. And when he does find a friend, what does the latter do – if not accuse him of stealing a bit of his bread. 'Which broke my heart.' But now here's another fellow-Württemberger coming toward him. Outside Smolensk he'd nobly shared a 2-pound loaf with him: 'Laying it on the ground, he'd cut it in two with his sabre'; and Walter had been so moved that he'd said he'd never forget it as long as he lived

'because you've treated me like a brother. This second meeting, with both of us in the most miserable condition because no aid was available, caused a pang in my heart which sank in me unforgettably.'

But soon they too are separated – for ever.

Jakob Walter's recently published account, though often hopelessly confused as to times and places, is in some ways the most affecting of all. Like most conscripts who'd been torn from their homes all over Europe, he has no emotional investment whatever in politics, military glory or strategies. Only in survival, to which he is helped, he says again and again, by his trust in God. In general the Germans are religious, the French not.

Now it's broad daylight and only three of Studianka's 25 timber houses are still standing. At 9.30 Pils returns with Napoleon and Oudinot to II Corps' headquarters cottage:

'He was served a cutlet, which he ate standing. When the *maître d'hôtel* presented him with the salt cellar, which consisted of a screw of paper, His Majesty said to him: "You're well mounted. All you lack is a white saddle,"'

a pun on the words *sel* (salt) and *selle* (saddle). Oudinot shares 'his few remaining provisions' with the top brass, 'who'd been putting up with great privations for several days now'. For II Corps still has lots of the loot from Minsk taken, first by Pahlen, then by itself. It's even for sale. Here are some victuals for Captain Josef Zalusky and two of his lieutenants

'which helped me and provided me with provender for a long time to come. We bought a pig, some geese, and had eleven big round rye loaves baked. For a gold coin, a napoleon or a ducat, one could purchase a lump of sugar, a packet of tea and a litre of rum.'

Ever since Smolensk Victor Dupuy's shoulder bag has been hoarding a deep-frozen chicken. Now he too decides to contribute it to some other officers' rice stew. Paul de Bourgoing (his general, like many another middle-aged man, is on the verge of despondency) has been 'present at a village's complete demolition'. On the high ground where it had stood Fain sees how the 'double battery' commanding the marshes on the opposite bank now consists of 40 guns. And Dumonceau how 'the parks and baggage, arriving incessantly from Borissow' are building up. Hearing that 'the Emperor was by the riverside' and despite the strict orders against leaving one's unit, Captain Rosselet wants 'to see the great man at close quarters in the situation we found ourselves in'. Slipping along past the Swiss he gets down to the waterside:

'I saw him at close quarters. His back was resting against some trestles, his arms were crossed inside his overcoat. Silent, having an air of not paying attention to what was going on, only fixing his glances from time to time on the pontoneers a few paces away, sometimes up to their necks amidst the ice-floes, busy placing the trestles, which they seemed to have the greatest difficulty in fixing deeply, while others, as soon as they were in place, were laying the planks on them.'

General Roguet sees him 'put his foot on each plank as it was laid'. All Rosselet hears him say for quite a while 'in a bad-tempered impatient tone to the superior officer in charge of the works' is that 'all this was taking too long'. Captain *Louis Begos* of the 2nd Swiss, who hears it too, thinks he's no longer

'the great Emperor I'd seen at the Tuileries. He looked tired and worried. My friend Captain Rey of our 1st Regiment was in a good position to study him at his leisure, and like myself he was struck by his worried expression. Having dismounted, he was leaning against some beams and planks, looking down. Then, with a preoccupied impatient air, he lifted his head. Turned to General Eblé and said: "It's taking a very long time, General. A very long time." "You can see, Sire", replied Eblé in a vivacious and self-assured manner, "that my men are up to their necks in the water, and the ice is holding up their work. I've no food or brandy to warm them with." "That'll do," the Emperor replied. He stared at the ground. After a few moments he began complaining again. He seemed to have forgotten what the general had said.'

This must have been at the left-hand, larger bridge. For at about 11 a.m. Pils sees an officer come and tell him the other one is ready: 'His Majesty immediately gave his orders.' First to cross is the 1st Battalion of Albert's brigade:

'Placing himself at its head, M. le Maréchal directs the advance guard. Napoleon, who'd placed himself at the bridgehead, his feet on an ice-floe, tells him: "Don't go over yet, Oudinot. You'll only get yourself captured!"'

But Oudinot points to his men:

'"Amongst them, Sire," he replied, "I'm afraid of nothing;" and, his horse being led by a chasseur, he set off quickly, with General Albert at his side.'

Is Albert's brigade really the first to cross? Or has Pils overlooked Castex's 23rd and 24th Chasseurs? Or is Marbot's memory determined to take pride of place? Anyway Castex hastens to join up with Corbineau:

'We in our turn followed the Polish cavalry. The 23rd Chasseurs followed next. The bridge wasn't particularly solid, so we had to cross it on foot, and, to be on the safe side, preserve a certain distance between one horse and the next. This slowed down the brigade's crossing. Once on the right bank each of us mounted independently, and each squadron, as soon as it was assembled, advanced along the Borissow–Vilna road, which wasn't far away.'

Scarcely are the scouts across than carbine shots are heard on various sides:

'Then the voltigeurs deployed in open order and, marching straight ahead, had to cross a marshy area before reaching the hillside, which they climbed. One by one the Cossacks, protected behind some bushes, were flushed out. During this fusillade the Marshal was on foot, the horses sinking up to their knees in the mud; but as soon as he'd reached more solid ground he galloped off to rejoin the voltigeurs who were reaching the Minsk road, in the forests,'

i.e., the 'long road, straight as an avenue' over to the left, down which Tschaplitz's rearguard has disappeared:

'During this short ride he met with the corpses of many Cossacks. All had been shot through the head.'

Aware of the extreme danger of an enemy unit seizing the series of highly inflammable little bridges between the marsh and Zembin, chief-of-staff Lorencez has sent Marbot there to seize them. Nothing, Chambray realises, 'was more important than to occupy the road leading us to Zembin because six miles from Studianka it crosses a marshy woodland, impracticable for vehicles except when frozen hard or in very hot weather.' Unbelievably, it's wholly intact.[10] Pils goes on:

'As soon as the whole of the first brigade had reached the Minsk road, M. le Maréchal ordered it to halt and wait for the rest of Legrand's division.

He placed himself in observation with General Albert, following the movements of a strong party of Cossacks. In the same moment two roundshot flew by to his right. One of them knocked General Albert over. Jumping up at once, he exclaimed: "That scum haven't any good powder, or I'd have been cut in two!'"

After Albert's infantry comes Legrand's; then Maison's French division; then Merle's Croats and Swiss. Two guns are also 'very carefully taken across' the infantry bridge. When at 1 p.m. Caudras' brigade begins crossing over, Napoleon is 'still in the same position where I'd left him, just as taciturn, with the same pensive air'. The Swiss shout '*Vive l'Empereur!*' as they go by, but without Napoleon 'paying us the least attention'.

Not until about 3 p.m. is the artillery bridge almost ready. And still there's no sign of Tschaplitz coming back! Among Merle's divisional artillery, queued up at the bridgehead, are two guns commanded by Lieutenant Lassus-Marcilly. Who's in a state of ecstasy: 'My captain had brought me, together with a little bit of ribbon, the news of my nomination to the Legion of Honour.' Standing by his bivouac fire only a few feet away, Napoleon tells Lassus-Marcilly they must hurry up:

'I replied that we were waiting our turn behind the other batteries. And as he turned to go back to the fire, a clumsy gunner trod on his foot. The Emperor gave him a gentle shove between the shoulders, saying calmly: "What a clumsy b*****r he is! [*Que ce bougre-là est lourd!*]"'

What in fact are the Russians up to? Caulaincourt is one of those at IHQ who're lost in speculation:

'The Admiral's inaction baffled everybody. Why hadn't he, who'd been able to observe our tactics for the last 36 hours, burnt or dismantled the Borissow bridge, so as to be easy on that score? How come he hadn't made a quick sally with perhaps 80 guns and blown us to smithereens while we were crossing the river? Was he waiting for Wittgenstein? Nor was it any easier to understand the slow pace of Wittgenstein's pursuit. Had Kutusov joined forces with him? Was he manoeuvring in our rear?'

No one knows, or can even guess, the answers to these questions. It's all a riddle – but one that Rochechouart could answer: 'Reaching Beresino in the morning of 25 November we'd seen no trace of the French army, and this had begun to make us fear we'd made a very false move, as useless as it had been wearisome.'[11] And this is why the day, Pils notes in his diary,

'is passing in great tranquillity. The army's gone on crossing. The snow's falling so thickly the daylight's obscured by it.'

Back from their feint in the direction of Beresino, even Oudinot's magnificent cuirassier regiments have crossed over 'without any difficulty – even our sutlers were getting across with their carts'. This gives Marbot an idea. Why not unharness a few such carts, tie them together and fix them in midstream? Wouldn't it make an extra bridge for the infantry?

'This idea seemed to me such a good one that, though soaked through up to my waist, I re-forded the river to pass it on to the generals at IHQ.

My project was found to be good, but no one lifted a finger to go and put it to the Emperor. Finally General Lauriston, one of his ADCs, said to me: "I charge you with carrying out this footbridge, whose usefulness you've just explained so well."'

But of course Marbot has neither sappers, infantrymen, tools, stakes, nor ropes to do it with. Nor can he leave his own regiment, already on the right bank. So nothing's done about it.

Late in the afternoon the last of the red-coated Swiss arrive. As the 'little élite battalion of united grenadiers and voltigeurs (four companies, of which two of the 3rd and two of the 4th Regiments) crosses the left-hand bridge' Jean-Marc Bussy notices that Napoleon's wearing *both* his hat *and* 'a fur cap under it'. At this critical juncture that potent symbol, unique in the army, is obviously needed.[12] 'Wretched though we are,' Bussy goes on, 'we don't give it a thought. We shout "*Vive l'Empereur!*" at the tops of our voices.' 'As soon as our horse artillery had reached the right bank,' Legler goes on,

'a considerable swarm of Cossacks came out of the wood where they'd been hiding, intending to cut it up. But the chasseurs quickly formed up and opened fire in two ranks, which our two batteries on their flanks could support with no danger to themselves. Whereupon the Cossacks fled. Meanwhile the general crossing had begun, and there'd begun to be continuous shouts of *"Vive l'Empereur"*. When the turn came to us, and we had to halt near the bridge, some words from the Emperor's mouth reached our ears, directed to General Merle:
'"Are you pleased with the Swiss, General?"
'"Yes, Sire. If the Swiss attacked as sharply as they know how to defend themselves, Your Majesty would be content with them."
'"Yes," Legler proudly hears Napoleon reply: "I know they're a good lot [*des braves gens*]."'

Just how brave they'll shortly have to show, as they're the army's prime bulwark. 'When we'd crossed the bridge at last,' Legler goes on, 'we sent up a ringing cheer for the Emperor.' Then they too turn off left 'if possible to throw the enemy back on to his fixed position opposite Borissow.'

At 4 p.m. Oudinot's guns begin to cross the left-hand bridge – Rossetti says 4.30, Denniée, 5 p.m. The captured Russian ones are left behind on the left bank. As each 12-pounder crosses over, what Caulaincourt calls the bridge's 'matchwood' construction sways and shakes wildly, and the weight thrusts its trestles ever deeper into the river's muddy bottom. Soon both bridges' platforms are hardly a foot or two above the swirling waters. Neither has a rail. Gourgaud, who'd been one of the first officers to swim his horse across the river and back, sees how everything's being promptly repaired under the Emperor's eyes by the pontoneers, sailors and sappers. And Fain, also standing near the bridgehead, notes in his journal:

'Braving the cold, fatigue, exhaustion, even death, they're working ceaselessly, water up to their shoulders. The death they must find under the ice-floes is not less the death of brave men for that.'

Ahead of II Corps lies a pine forest – the Brill Farm Wood. Through it runs the main Borissow–Zembin road, down which Tchitchakov's army, estimated by Napoleon as only about 25,000 men but in reality some 35,000, will surely at any moment come hurrying back to remedy its disastrous mistake.

'However, our division didn't see the enemy that day. The first two divisions drove him back without loss. While marching for two hours along the country road at the first division's heels we didn't even see a single wounded man coming back.'

By and by an orderly officer comes riding up, orders them to form up in assault columns to left and right of the road. And there, with Legler's regiment to the rear, they make ready to spend the night.

Meanwhile, on the left bank, the Guard has turned up. And after it III Corps – 900 men all told, so Major Bonnet estimates. Ney's men are immediately sent across to support Oudinot. As soon as the 4th Line has bivouacked as best it can in the Brill Wood beside fires that 'scarcely served to warm us' Fezensac decides to count his effectives. 'Since Smolensk I'd had neither the time nor the courage to study my regiment's destruction at close quarters.' Summoning his officers he compares the roll-call with

'the list I'd brought from Moscow. But what changes since that time! Of 70 officers hardly 40 were left, most of them ill or exhausted. I spoke with them at length about our present situation. I praised several whose truly heroic conduct deserved it. I reprimanded others who were showing more weakness, and above all I promised always to try and encourage them by my example.'

Worst of all,

'almost all the company cadres had been destroyed at Krasnoïe, which made it much more difficult to maintain discipline. Of the remaining men I formed two platoons, the first made up of grenadiers and voltigeurs, the second from the centre companies. I designated officers to command them, and ordered each of the others to take a musket and always march with me at the head of the regiment. I was myself at the end of my strength. I'd only one horse left. My last portmanteau had been lost crossing the Berezina. All I possessed was what was on my back – and we were still 50 leagues from Vilna, 80 from the Niemen! But in the midst of such sufferings I counted my own privations for nothing.'

Even Ney himself has

'lost everything. His ADCs were dying of hunger, and more than once, I remember, they had the goodness to share with me what little food they'd been able to get hold of.'

But what's that up there in a tree? Honeycombs!

'Difficult and dangerous though they were to get at, some of the men, thinking they might as well die of a fall as perish from hunger, managed to reach them with the aid of a rod. They threw that honey down bit by bit and their comrades threw themselves on it like famished dogs. The cold had started up again, the snow was falling furiously.'

Late into the freezing night the icy north wind, sweeping ever more fiercely across the marshes, whines and soughs in the Brill Farm Wood's conifers. Having 'established its outposts at nightfall' Castex's light cavalry brigade, too, joined after dark by the 1st Infantry Brigade and by Doumerc's cuirassier division, bivouac

'in the great forest. The rest of II Corps, by now reduced to about 12,000 men, camped in the little plain, around a hamlet. The thatch of the roofs served our poor horses for nourishment.'

When men from the Moscow units come begging the Swiss for 'something to relieve their sufferings' in the intense cold, all they have for them is 'a little food, to save them from starving to death'. Regimental Sergeant-Major Calosso's comrades want to drive away a wounded Italian officer 'wrapped up in a little fur, partly grilled by the camp fires and belonging to some Russian peasant', from their big camp fire; but he manages to obtain a place for him. 'Observing him closely' as the Italian uses his sword for a skewer, he notices the bullion of its sword-knot:

'This detail enabled me to recognise in this unfortunate man a senior officer. All I could see of his uniform was a filthy collar, turned down, and of doubtful colour. On his head he had a grey astrakhan cap.'

The officer turns out to be a colonel of one of the regiments of the Italian Royal Guard. Oudinot himself, sheltering from the gale in a shack where he has set up his headquarters, sends off a report to Berthier. He has thrown the Russians back, but at a village whose name he thinks is Stakhov he's run into the enemy ensconced 'behind a ravine, where he has placed some more cannon this evening, over and above those he'd shown during the day'. And it's been impossible to drive him out. 'If I'd had some cuirassiers we'd have done something brilliant.' Meanwhile he must have some orders for tomorrow. If he attacks in the morning and drives the Russians still further back, how far is he to pursue them?

'On this point I should observe to Your Highness, that if we get engaged in the Minsk road, which is a continuous defile through forests, we shall absolutely lack for everything, and the enemy will be able to hold us up at each step.'

Precisely as Jomini had reported at Orsha. Oudinot adds in a PS that he hopes the rumour he's heard of his Polish supports being taken away isn't true? Or anyway not the lancers 'because I need them'. Yes, and then there's the 124 of his men he'd left at the Borissow bridge. He'll be needing them too. And even the 150 Württembergers in charge of the prisoners (who, like his captured Russian guns, have been left on the eastern river bank). Captain Begos of the 2nd Swiss will never forget that bivouac, 'which did little to restore us, as we'd had practically nothing to eat all day, and above all because the Russians were so close. The forest consisted of full-grown trees, rather dense, both the ground and the pines being thick with snow. At nightfall, each soldier took his pack as a pillow and the snow for his mattress, with his musket in his hand. An icy wind was blowing hard. To keep each other warm our men lay closely huddled together. The biggest pines weren't shedding their snow, and under this kind of umbrella we suffered less. Our vedettes were at their posts, and the officers, most of them leaning against a tree for fear of a surprise, didn't get a wink all night.'

Legler counts only 300 men still under arms in his company. But they're raring for a fight. To its intense regret the 1st Swiss have had to leave their Colonel Raguettli at Borissow:

'several of us had offered to stay behind and help him, but he'd rejected all such offers. "Gentlemen, other duties call you. You must attend to them first, and if you manage to get across – as I hope you will – we'll soon see each other again."'

Raguettli's place has been taken Commandant Blattmann, the elder of his majors: the other, Commandant Zingg, 'as we didn't need two commanders', remains in the rear:

'Having crossed the Berezina and thrust back the enemy we breathed more freely. Now the road to Vilna was open – even if it wasn't the right one.'

Conditions on the left bank are no more comfortable. Getting there earlier in the day, von Muraldt's little group of a dozen Bavarian light horse officers had found the terrain

'covered as far as the eye could see with cannon, ammunition wagons and all kinds of vehicles, where fires had been made up, and a variegated mass was crowding together. Among this mass of warriors of all ranks and arms one seldom saw anything reminiscent of a complete uniform.'

Arriving at Weselovo in Follenius' carriage, Franz Roeder has rejoined his company of the Hessian Guards. Although they've brought some meat and flour from Borissow, they've only one cookpot between them; so it's impossible to cook it all, and 'my turn never came'. More and more irritable as he grows weaker, Roeder has to lie down supperless for the night:

'In the darkness my greatcoat was stolen from me by one of my batmen, my jar of honey was pilfered by another, and my coffee got left behind.'

The crossing's still going on when, at 8 p.m., three of the left-hand bridge's trestles collapse and are carried away, together with such vehicles as are just then passing over them. So in the darkness and icy gale the heroic pontoneers have to wade out into the river again, smash the ever thickening ice-floes with their axes and, in 4 to 5 feet of water, reset the trestles to a depth of 6 to 8 feet. Fortunately the right-hand bridge, not having to support such weights or sustain such shocks, is still intact. And the thousands of disbanded stragglers who've already assembled in the bridgehead area are free to cross over.

But few do.

Why leave their camp fires? Even if II and III Corps' fires are beckoning to Mailly-Nesle 'like an illumination at the château of the Tuileries', the rest of the swamplands beyond the river are a pitch-black icy darkness swept by the freezing wind. How hope to survive in such a night without a fire? So almost everyone stays put. Von Muraldt's group force their way into a half-demolished barn that's already packed full with shivering men and have to defend themselves all night against 'those outside, who were trying to carry away the beams still left, to keep up their fires'.

Now it's 27 November. At 1 a.m. Oudinot sends off a new dispatch to Berthier. He's just heard that 'the enemy has placed six more guns in front of his position'. His units are asking for more ammunition, which can't be supplied: 'the main bridge not having been repaired at all, the caissons can't be brought across. The same is true of the rest of the artillery.' The forest being 'very sparse', he's had to extend far to his right and left. After the Croat regiment's losses yesterday Merle's division has only 800 men left. And from what prisoners have said he'll shortly have 40,000 Russians to deal with. Oh yes, and in his first report he'd forgotten to mention that he'd sent a reconnaissance party out along the sensitive causeway that leads to Zembin, 'which I only found occupied by a few Cossacks'.

An hour passes. At 2 a.m., the artillery bridge again begins to give way, this time in mid-stream. Even the half of Eblé's men who've had the chance of a little sleep are getting to the end of their tether. Eblé, though himself a man of 50, hasn't slept at all; but encourages them by himself several times going down to the river. And by 6 a.m. the bridge has been repaired.

In the grey dawn light 'the Sacred Squadron again assembles and remains in battle order, close to the bridgehead'. Beyond the Brill Wood the Swiss, too, have been standing to arms since dawn. But today, '27 November, everything was quiet on our side. The cannon's thunder was only heard in the distance,' Legler will recall. Le Roy, who has a fever, has spent the night in a ditch on some high ground, wrapped in his great bearskin. Only at 9 a.m. does he wake up. Feeling very poorly, he climbs up to the brink of the ditch, and finds

'the cold very sharp. We had a perfect view of the troops as they were crossing over, slowly, because of the jam of men who, loath to cross during the night, had come rushing in a mob at the bridgehead and all wanted to get across at once. They were shoving and crushing one another. It was the beginning of that disorder that reigned and would only go on getting worse until next day.'

Seeing the Old Guard still bivouacked where it was yesterday evening, he and Jacquet decide to wait until it stands to arms and then cross over in its wake.

At daybreak the Vistula Legion arrives. Ever since he'd been picked up at Bobr by his comrades of its 2nd Regiment, the wounded von Brandt has been riding in a carriage drawn by 'mouse-sized horses' and is

'in paradise. What joy to find oneself among regular troops again! The regiment's surgeon's been taking care of our wounds. We've been getting plenty of bread and gruel and tea morning and evening.'

Claparède's Poles, at least, are in good fettle:

'I can't say I found any difference between the Old Guard's and our men's turnout. On the contrary, they were more cheerful – when a Pole sees his superiors sharing his difficulties he doesn't become so easily downcast.'

Not that any one likes Claparède himself – arrogant, heartless, always look-ing for someone to blame,[12] the Polish officers had quickly come to detest him 'as had their forerunners in Germany and Spain': Relieved only yester-day from having to escort the Treasure – a burden that's been hanging round the Vistula Legion's neck since Smolensk – his men are going to be badly needed in the coming fight on the right bank. Now, after a difficult, frequently impeded night march they 'halt by the forest fringe' at Studianka:

'In front of us and to our left we saw some bivouac fires. Then, as soon as we could look around, on the slope of some high ground that sur-rounds it like an amphitheatre, a miserable village of about 25 houses – Studianka – and around it several units. We also saw a bridge had been thrown and that some of our lot were already over on the other side. Our mood changed as if by magic. The battalions drew up alongside one another in battalion columns. We must have had a good 1,800 to 1,900 men under arms.'

After a while Brandt sees

'the Emperor suddenly came out of a house. He was surrounded by a crowd of Marshals and generals. He was wearing a grey pélisse which he threw back with his left hand, and we could clearly see his shining boots and white breeches. As always, he was wearing his little hat. His face betrayed no sign of any emotion. He was talking to old Eblé who was respectfully holding *his* hat in his hand. Beside him, unless I'm mis-taken, was Murat, wearing a grey fur cap surmounted by a heron plume, a pelisse and a sabre hung by the kind of cord known as Egyptian. Berthier and Eugène were wearing furs.'

Near the bridge Brandt also sees many others of the top brass:

'the excellent Duroc, whose life presents the image of a perfect knight – Ney, *figura quadrata firmisque membris* [with his firm square-set features], in a light overcoat, of sombre green – Mortier, *ipse inter primos prestandi corpore* [standing out among his peers by dint of sheer physical size] – the noble Narbonne with his bizarre, old-fashioned hairstyle, and many more. Most of the adjutants and senior staff officers only had riding-coats or light overcoats. That morning the temperature could have been between 2 and 3 degrees. The snow was no longer falling, and it looked as if we were going to have a fine day.'

The Vistula Legion having done much to pull Murat's chestnuts out of the fire at Winkovo on 18 October, the King of Naples comes over to speak to Brandt's colonel,

'whom he'd taken a liking to ever since the Tarutino affair. Exchanging a few indifferent words with him and pointing to us he said: "What are you thinking of doing with your wounded?" "Faith!" the colonel replied, "they'll follow on behind us as best they can."'

Brandt notices how 'a wound Murat had sustained at Aboukir' [in 1801] 'and which had broken his jaw at the moment when he'd captured the Turkish army's *seaskier* but which usually was hardly visible' is reddened by the cold. '"I present you," said my colonel, indicating myself, "the commandant who valiantly led the attack at Winkovo. I've done all I can to bring him with me." "It was a fine feat of arms," replied the King, "a heroic attack, and I shan't fail to remember it. Meanwhile I grant him the decoration of the royal order."'[14]

At about 10 a.m. the order comes for Claparède's men to cross over, 'the baggage, the wounded, etc.' – Brandt among them – to stay where they are to await instructions – 'naturally that pleased us no end.' Claparède's men will bring Ney's effectives up to about 6,000. As Brandt approaches the bridgehead he sees Napoleon still standing there,

'as impassive as at the Kremlin or the Tuileries. He was wearing a half-open grey overcoat, through which one could see his ordinary campaign uniform. That day Murat, whom no circumstance prevented from showing off the effect of *his* uniforms, was wearing a fur bonnet with a big heron's plume in it.'

'The élite gendarmes,' Brandt goes on,

'in full uniform and thereto clean, but mounted on very emaciated horses, had formed a wide circle around the avenue leading to the bridge, and weren't letting any unarmed man through. Between the battalion's intervals we had plenty of time to view the entire scene. It must have been about 10 a.m. when the division was ordered to cross the bridge. Yet the gendarmes still repulsed us: "Only combatants to pass!"'

Since no carriages are being allowed over, Brandt and Lichnowski ('we'd been expecting this') have already got out of theirs 'and abandoning our vehicle and the mouse-sized horses which had brought us from Smolensk, followed the regiment on foot'. Brandt protests furiously but in vain at being taken for a mere straggler. Luckily, at that moment, a superior officer comes to his aid by pointing out that he belongs to the corps that's just crossed over. So the gendarme lets him through. The river, 'flowing very fast in a swampy bed', Brandt estimates, is '150 to 160 paces broad' and 'in certain places a good 8 to 10 feet deep:

'There'd been a massive thaw, and many an ice-floe must have measured 10 to 15 square feet. Nowhere did the bridge's surface offer a perfect surface. Little by little the planks were being pressed down; above all at the end near the other bank, part of the bridge was even covered in water which wetted us up to our ankles.'

As to its construction and solidity, Brandt as he crosses over thinks

'it certainly wouldn't have found grace from an expert. But if one bears in mind that there'd been no materials at all, and that of the entire [bridge-building] equipment only a few wagons filled with clamps and nails, two campaign forges and two coal carts had been saved, that the neighbourhood's houses had had to be demolished and trees felled to get the necessary timber, that the pontoneers were working with the water up to their necks while the cold formed crystals all over their bodies – then one will certainly regard this construction as one of the most glorious of all warlike actions in this campaign which counted so many.' 'Not far from the bridge on the far side' the Legion halts in a small wood where it's 'superbly sheltered'. Some time during the forenoon Napoleon – accompanied by Caulaincourt – crosses provisionally to reconnoitre the position on the other side, particularly 'the road leading to Borissow'. Altogether he's going to have some 11,000 Poles, Swiss, French and Croats to stave off Tchitchakov's 35,000 Russians until the rest of the army and its 20,000 stragglers, protected by Victor's IX Corps, have crossed over.

Alone, IX Corps hasn't as yet been in a full-scale battle. En route from Borissow with the Treasure, now being escorted by some men of IV Corps, Kergorre admires

'the Duke of Bellune's guns, these ammunition wagons drawn by fine horses, their harness in good condition. It was a long time since we'd seen anything of the kind – such of our own few caissons and baggage wagons as still existed being drawn by wretched little horses with their ragged rope harness.'

But when some of Victor's men, halted near a little village before reaching Borissow, stare at Griois and his friends, the latter, so far from blushing with shame at own ragged appearance, had smiled 'at the thought that they'd soon be on the same level as ourselves'.

Of his three divisions Victor has left the largest – Partonneaux's 12th, 4,000-strong – at Borissow, with orders to stay there at least until IV Corps and the huge mass of stragglers and wounded have got across the Studianka bridges.

Which makes Partonneaux's division the army's extreme rearguard.

Some time during the forenoon Victor's other two divisions – Girard's 28th (Polish) and Daendels' 26th (Berg, Badener, Hessian, Dutch, etc.), adding up to some 9,000 infantry and the 7,800 troopers of Fournier's cavalry division – begin to turn up at Studianka and crown the high ground to the east of the bridgehead. And Napoleon, feeling the situations on both banks to be reasonably well established, and having ordered IHQ to be set up near the hamlet of Brillowo, about a mile from the river, has come back to the left bank. And immediately the Sacred Squadron, after hanging about near the bridgehead until 2 p.m., gets the order to 'see whether the bridge was free enough to allow the Emperor to get across if we cleared a path for him'. Like so many others, von Muraldt's little group, riding down from their barn, see him 'standing by the left-hand bridge, surrounded by his suite, personally to supervise the crossing.' Inching her way forward in Lefèbvre's carriage, Louise Fusil, too, is able to

'examine him closely, standing at the entrance to the bridge, to hasten the march. To me he seemed as calm as at a review at the Tuileries. The bridge was so narrow our carriage almost touched him: "Don't be frightened," Napoleon said. "Go on, go on. Don't be frightened." These words, which he seemed to address more particularly to me – no other woman was present – made me think there must be some danger.'

Murat is looking his usual spectacular self:

'Holding his horse by the bridle, his hand was posed on the door of my calèche. He looked at me and said something polite. To me his costume seemed utterly bizarre for such a moment and in -20 degrees. His neck was open. His velvet mantle was flung negligently over one shoulder. His hair was curly. His black velvet toque was adorned with a white feather. All this gave him the air of a hero in some melodrama. Never before had I seen him at such close quarters and I couldn't take my eyes off him. When he was some distance behind the carriage I turned round to look him in the face. He noticed it and saluted me graciously with his hand. He was a real flirt and liked women to notice him.[15]

Louise goes on:

'Many superior officers, too, were leading their horses by the bridle, because no one could cross this bridge on horseback. It was so fragile, it trembled under the wheels of my carriage. The weather, which had grown milder, had somewhat melted the ice on the river, but that only made it more dangerous.'

Roustam, standing as usual a few feet away from Napoleon with his immediate necessities, sees Caulaincourt

'getting the Household carriages and the artillery over one after another. He was recommending to their drivers to go gently and keep their distances, so as not to fatigue the bridge excessively. At the same time he was making the Grenadiers and Chasseurs of the Old Guard cross in single file on either side.'

Fain sees Marshal Lefèbvre,

'that old warrior, who hadn't shaved for several days, adorned with a white beard and leaning on a traveller's knobbly stick, which in his hands had become a Marshal's baton, tirelessly active.'

And at the far end of the bridge Pion des Loches sees him

'transformed into an overseer, between two hedges of the Old Guard, directing the carriages of the Imperial Household, close to their owner, who that day were judging it prudent to do a few more leagues than the rest of us,' –

i.e., to make for Zembin as fast as ever they can go. Colonel Victor Dupuy, in the Sacred Squadron, is told by Squadron-Leader Offier of the 1st Carabiniers that its members are to try to cross individually. Offier himself, riding a big powerful horse 'still very vigorous', tells Dupuy to hang on to him:

'Reaching the level of the bridge, he made a right turn with his horse and continued advancing. Rather slowly, amidst curses and shouts flung at us, we managed to reach the bridge to safety. The access to it was so blocked that the bridge itself was almost wholly free. Near it and on either hand many unfortunates were still struggling in the river and it was impossible to help them! Once we'd got across we found an officer stationed there to indicate to survivors the place where the Sacred Squadron should muster.'

Evidently Maurice Tascher and some others of its mounted officers 'go off on their own'. The crush, not only at the bridgehead but even on the bridges themselves, is stifling. Lariboisière's inspector of reviews Paixhans gets across among the Grenadiers 'without touching the ground'. The Sacred Squadron pushes its way through the mob, 'even a trifle roughly, being nervous ourselves'. As nervous, Henckens thinks, as Napoleon is: 'He realised that each moment lost could mean utter complete ruin.' As soon as the Squadron's on the other side, says Henckens, 'the Emperor crossed over with his suite'.

There's nothing of imperial etiquette about Napoleon's crossing of the Berezina. All ranks are confounded. Mailly-Nesle, himself following on 'after them as closely as possible'- with his companions in their carriage as usual – sees even Caulaincourt 'shoved and hemmed in on his horse, having the greatest difficulty in getting the Emperor's horses over'. Crossing in the crowd at the same time as Napoleon is one of Captain von Suckow's Württemberger friends, a M. de Grünberg:

'Under his coat he was holding a little greyhound bitch that was shivering piteously. Napoleon offered to buy it. M. de Grünberg replied that the animal had shared all his sufferings, but of course he'd place it at Napoleon's disposition. The Emperor, visibly very much moved, replied: "I understand your attachment to this animal. Keep it. I wouldn't want to deprive you of it."'

Henckens sees 'several women crossing over with their children, of whom I recognised some as the ones I'd seen at the theatre in Moscow.' And reflects sadly: 'They'd have done better to have stayed in Moscow instead of following the army. The Russians wouldn't have avenged themselves on them for the Emperor Napoleon's mad enterprise.' 'A short while afterwards,' Dupuy goes on,

'the roll-call was called in each company [of the Sacred Squadron]. No one was missing.[16] Formed up in close column of companies, we were placed in front of the cavalry of the Imperial Guard. The Emperor was between the two bodies. It was in this order, it was being said, we were going to pass through Tchitchakov's army. Resolute as we all were, no one doubted we'd succeed.'

After he'd crossed over,' Henckens concludes,

'we surrounded him, both when he was resting and when he was on foot or horseback, watching the troops cross, which was going on in a fairly orderly fashion'.

At about 2 p.m. it's the turn of the Guard foot artillery. Pion des Loches has to set his remaining gunners to the task of removing, by brute force, the file of carriages and carts that are keeping the head of his column from the bridgehead. But so compact is the mob that neither Muraldt nor anyone else can move an inch forward:

'A few élite gendarmes who still had horses had been ordered chiefly to turn away non-combatants (a description applicable to almost everyone) as they swelled forward, so that the Guard could pass unhindered. A task they flung themselves into heart and soul, without distinction of rank or person, receiving all who tried to thrust themselves forward – efforts which for every moment that passed were becoming less and less fruitful – with violent blows of the flats of their swords.'

Despite the appalling jam and 'although mishandled by the headquarters gendarmes', von Muraldt and his sick friend Knecht – who'd given him his second horse at Krasnoië – manage to squeeze in between two of the Guard's cannon. By now Pion des Loches' first vehicle is 'at the tail of Boulart's teams, whose head was at bridge's abutment'. The odious Drouot 'like many others' has gone on ahead and crossed on his own account, leaving his carriage in the care of the resentful Pion, who has it immediately behind him. 'Despite the press of soldiers of the Train and gunners trying to get over', he's obliged to get it across for him. Just ahead of him Boulart, busy getting his teams methodically across one by one, is finding the bridges 'not very solid' and having to be 'incessantly repaired' by the indefatigable Eblé's pontoneers 'who had the courage to put themselves into the water and work there despite the cold. They behaved admirably.'

But November days are brief. By 3 p.m. dusk has begun to fall. From a few hundred yards away on the hillside Le Roy, Jacquet and Guillaume, seeing the Guard's preparations to cross over and 'fearing with reason that in such a mêlée as we were going to find ourselves in we might become separated or stifled', have divided up their 'remaining assets'. Le Roy exacts a promise from Guillaume that, if he himself doesn't get across, he'll go home 'to our beautiful country' and tell his family what became of him. But if they should both get home, then, he promises, Guillaume will always find in him a good friend:

'We embraced, weeping, and together made for the bottom of the slope where the Guard must assuredly pass by to present itself at the river crossing.'

For a while they stand warming themselves at a fire beside four cavalry troopers who seem to be waiting for someone whose orders they are under and who, Le Roy assumes, belongs to the Guard. But though one of them has seen the Emperor himself having the devil's own job getting through the crowd, they themselves, one of the troopers explains, belong to Fournier's cavalry division of IX Corps. They're going to rejoin it and stave off the Russians.' It'll be another story tomorrow morning,' one of them adds grimly, 'when we have to evacuate our position and retire, burning the bridges.' That, for Le Roy, is enough:

'I didn't listen to any more. My legs gave way beneath me. A cold sweat rose from my feet to my head, and I felt a strangely violent thudding in my chest and around my ears. I fell, rather than sat down. My eyes filled with tears and I could no longer see clearly. All these symptoms gave me a presentiment that my end was at hand. I sat there as if turned to stone, my head on my knees.'

Only Guillaume can shake him out of his stupor.

Zaniwki, about a mile and a half from the river, is a hamlet of three cottages. And it's here, in a 'little white house', IHQ installs itself as best it can. The 'Palace', Secretary Fain notes, has only two rooms:

'The inner one's been reserved for the Emperor; the other's been instantly occupied by his suite. There we lie down pell-mell on top of one another, like a flock herded together in the narrowest of sheepfolds.'

Since the three troops of the Sacred Squadron are surrounding it, the Guard has bivouacked at the village of Brillowo, a little to the south. Its last unit to cross the river has been the Lancer Brigade. After a forenoon idled away in their comfortable billets upstream at Troanitze, they'd been briefly disturbed at about midday by Cossacks and ordered to stand to arms. Then the regiment's silver trumpets had cried 'To horse!' And the two Guard lancer regiments had moved off down towards the bridge:

'Most of our various army corps had crossed already, likewise the whole Imperial Guard. Only part of the parks and vehicles had remained to follow on with us; but the mob of disbanded men were creating an obstacle to this by turning up from all quarters, interfering everywhere, encumbering the terrain over a considerable extent and refusing to let us through. The detachments of pontoneers and the military police at the bridgeheads were struggling violently with them to contain and regulate their passage.'

By now the confusion and attendant struggle is beyond belief:

'We saw there a compact agglomeration of several thousand men of all arms, soldiers, officers, even generals, all jumbled up, covered in the filthiest rags and grotesquely disposed to protect themselves against the freezing weather, swarming with vermin and – over and above these accoutrements indicative of their extreme misery – faces downcast by exhaustion, pale, sinister, smoke-blackened, often mutilated by frostbite, the eyes hollow, extinct, hair in disorder, the beard long and disgusting.'

In the end the Red Lancers have to draw their sabres to force a way through and

'behave like lunatics, knocking down anything in our way and, striking out with their flats, thrust back all those who, pushed by the multitude in the opposite direction, were hemming us in from all sides, as in a wine press. In this way we managed to get through, followed by thousands of enraged yells.'

Zalusky's memory of the 1st Regiment's passage will be less ferocious. But even they have to

'turn our lances point downwards. In this way our regiment, by dealing out harmless blows to right and left, slipped through softly and easily.'

274

Do they cross on horseback, or on foot and leading their mounts by the bridle? Zalusky won't afterwards be able to remember. But Dumonceau will. When at last his Dutchmen get to the bridge itself they're
'ordered to dismount and cross over, one by one, holding our horses, to avoid shaking the bridge. It had no rail, was almost at water level, covered with a layer of horse dung. It was already badly damaged, dislocated, in parts weakened and swaying in every direction. Some pontoneers, in the water up to their armpits, were busy restoring it. Among them were some Dutchmen who welcomed us and made haste to ease our passage by tossing into the river a broken cart, some dead horses and other debris of all kinds that were obstructing it.'
After debouching from the bridge and remounting, Colbert's men ride across the marsh:
'We found it broken up in several places, so that despite the freezing cold we got bogged down. Then we mounted the high ground bordering the forest and, facing left, were placed in support of the whole Young Guard infantry, united in a massed column and still forming an apparent body of three or four battalions along the roadside. The rest of the Imperial Guard could be seen farther off, formed up behind us in reserve.'
Finding that his two servants are missing, Zalusky 'with some difficulty' goes back and fetches them across the river while the Young and Old Guard, drawn up in that position, hear Oudinot advancing – evidently against the first units of Tchitchakov's army to be returning to the scene –
'by the echoes of his fusillade, witnessing to his successes. As night began to fall this noise ceased little by little. Then we got busy making our bivouacs. The Emperor, who until then had remained near a fire at the head of the infantry of his Guard, retired and went to lodge in an isolated farm, the hamlet of Zaniwki, situated behind us by the roadside, at the entrance to the woods.'
Only the Lancer Brigade is 'led about three miles from the rear to Kostuikoi', where Colbert hopes to find some forage. Unfortunately that village has already been 'invaded and demolished by the multitude' of stragglers clustering round IV and VIII Corps. 'We could hardly even find any stakes to tether our horses to. Nor was there any firewood.' So Poles and Dutchmen have to lie down in the freezing mud beside smoking fires of snow-laden green conifer, with nothing to protect them from either mud or wind. Already, during the forenoon, Caulaincourt has
'personally examined all the paths through the marshland. The soil was marshy, trembled beneath one's feet. If the cold, which had grown less during the three preceding days, hadn't yesterday become very much keener again we shouldn't have saved a single gun or its carriage.'
Now it's on this trembling surface of 'marshy but frozen ground' that Boulart, reaching the western bank apparently without mishap, 'has the good sense' (the usually so self-complacent and critical Pion des Loches amiably concedes) to park his artillery, about three-quarters of a mile from

the river. 'We had no firewood. The night was cold and hard.' Caulaincourt sees how

'the last ammunition wagons cut or broke through the crust of hard-frozen grass which served as a sort of bridge, and got bogged down. Their wheels had nothing to get a grip on and sank into the bottomless mud.'

Arrived at this disconsolate Slough of Despond, where his gunners are bivouacking in the thickening darkness beside damp smoky fires that merely blind them, Pion listens sardonically as Drouot, 'a trifle ashamed of himself, tried unsuccessfully to get us to believe he'd done his best to get back to us'. This, as far as Pion's concerned, is the end of the man who will seem to Napoleon in retrospect to have been his 'incomparable' artillery officer. But at least 'no fewer than 300 vehicles belonging to General Niè-gre's main park, among them 50 reserve cannon' – i.e., 12-pounders – have crossed over in the wake of IHQ and the Old Guard. This, Fain notes, means that altogether 250 guns with their equipment are on the right bank. 'As for the carriages and light carts piling up around Studianka, their number is incalculable.'

Eugène, ordered to cross over with the remains of IV Corps, leaves I Corps to follow on at daybreak tomorrow. But though the pitiful remains of the Army of Italy have been ordered to cross at 8 p.m., Labaume hears their officers think it'll be easier to cross by daylight tomorrow morning; and remain squatting beside its fires:

'Only Prince Eugène and some staff officers crossed the river at the hour they'd been ordered to.'

What an accusation! The loyal-hearted Cesare de Laugier indignantly and circumstantially refutes it:

'The debris of the Royal Guard, about 500 men, follow immediately behind the prince. Hardly has Eugène set foot on the right bank than, turning to General Théodore Lecchi, its commander, he tells him: "Leave an officer here to show Broussier and Pino's divisions the way to follow so as to reach that burning village where we're going to bivouac." In my capacity of adjutant-major, I've been detailed off by that general for this painful task.'

Will he be able to rejoin his comrades in the darkness?

'The bridge remained free about twenty minutes. Then the 1st and 2nd Divisions arrived together. They crossed the bridge by sections of five to six men abreast, and after a quarter of an hour, during which the bridge was free again, Pino's division arrived.'

Only IV Corps' artillery, such as it is, has been intentionally left on the eastern bank to reinforce Davout's. At the Viceroy's bivouac in a burnt out village Labaume finds

'the darkness horrible, the wind frightful. Blowing violently, it flung icy snow in our faces. So as not to freeze, most of the officers, chilled to the bone, ran or walked to and fro, stamping their feet. Wood was so hard

to come by, we could hardly light a fire for the Viceroy. To obtain a few sparks we had to remind some Bavarian soldiers that Prince Eugène had married their king's daughter!'
It's a veritable swamp. IV Corps' Italians, Frenchmen, Croats, etc. seek out frozen patches to lie down on. Then fresh orders come. Tomorrow, still escorting the Treasure and the convoy of wounded generals, they're to form the army's advance guard and, after occupying the vital little bridges of the long Zembin causeway, be at Zembin itself (nine miles away) at dawn.

Once again nightfall clears the bridges. And anyone can walk over who cares to. Although Claparède's men send back for their vehicles and find one of them quite clear, 'the carriages were so entangled and the men so closely squeezed together, there wasn't the least hope of extracting the platoon that was escorting them'. Once again most of the crowd on the left bank prefer to remain where they are – among them von Suckow. Almost unable to walk because of his frost-bitten foot, and though he realises he'll have little chance of surviving in the mob tomorrow, he prefers to pass the night's freezing gusty hours in the company of a small party of French stragglers beside camp fires 'abandoned by some Bavarian light horse' – von Muraldt's perhaps?

'Suddenly my attention was distracted by a cannon shot which had gone off at a certain distance from us. Who were these people announcing their approach? Immediately, thousands of men rushed toward the bridges, shoving and crushing each other to get across that same evening. Seeing this happen, I decided to remain that night near my fire with the Frenchmen, and I soon saw we had plenty of emulators. As night fell thousands of fires were lit and the cannon fell silent.'
So grateful is one of the Frenchmen – the young son of a Lyons master-tailor attached to the military bakery – to von Suckow for assuring him that Napoleon won't be marching on Petersburg in the spring that he gives him half a piece of bread.
Not until 9 p.m. – and by now of course it's pitch dark – has I Corps got to Studianka. 'The mass of vehicles encumbering the road', its chief-of-staff sees,
'was immense. There were all those that had escaped the order that they should be burnt, plus all those of Marshals Victor and Oudinot's corps, which had joined us.'
Lejeune spends the night
'putting things in order, first, to get the ammunition wagons across, then to repair the bridges, which were frequently breaking down under theirs and the guns' weight. The night was black, and at each step they took in this village, Dutch, French, Spanish or Saxon officers and men'
keep tumbling into those insidious Russian and Lithuanian wells which, lacking parapets, for weeks have spelt death to the unwary. 'Their cries of distress called out to us to help them, but we had neither ropes nor ladders

to get them out.' I Corps too remains on the left bank to support Victor in tomorrow's struggle with Wittgenstein. After 'exchanging a few shots with the enemy' – i.e., with its most advanced units – the relics of the 7th Light Infantry have lit their bivouac fires 'on the fringe of a big wood. There we had some big old oaks to heat us, but nothing to eat.' Whereupon Sergeant Bertrand, 'as my habit was', goes off to take a look around. He knows that 'in the neighbourhood of the *cantinières* one could often come across a "Jew"[17] who only sold between four eyes and secretly; but at this moment I couldn't find one.'

Instead, his 'good star' arranges for him to fall in with 'a friend I hadn't seen since Wagram, a sapper sergeant-major of the Engineers, who was working on the bridges'. After he's told him how hungry he is his friend gives him a biscuit, saying:

'"It's been cooked in fat, you'll find it's good." I found it delicious, and didn't fail to give part of it to Sergeant Durand, my *alter ego*. Just as I was getting ready to sleep in front of a good fire, they tell me Louise, one of our *cantinières*, is on the point of giving birth, and is suffering badly. All the regiment is moved and finds ways of running to this unfortunate woman who under a sky of ice has nothing to eat, has no shelter. Our Colonel Romme sets the example. From everyone's hands our surgeons – their ambulance stretchers had been left behind at Smolensk for lack of transport – are receiving shirts, handkerchiefs, everything we could give.'

Although Bertrand himself has nothing to contribute,

'close to us I'd noticed an artillery park belonging to the Duke of Bellune's corps. I ran to it and taking a blanket from a horse's back ran back as fast as ever I could go to carry it to Louise. I'd done a bad deed, but I knew God would forgive me in view of the motive. I got there at the moment when our *cantinière*, under an old oak, brought into the world a shapely male infant.[18] Thus – in one of the debris of the Grand Army's most critical moments – our brave Louise gave the Fatherland one more defender. Marshal Davout distributed praise to everyone for our generous behaviour, and especially to our surgeons.'

Those who cross the bridges in the darkness and swirling snow this second night – and many isolated men do – are wise. For the congestion at the bridgehead is only growing worse. Yet the day, from a military point of view, Pils notes in his *Journal de Marche*,

'has passed in great tranquillity. The army has moved onwards. The snow's been falling so thickly that the daylight's been obscured by it. The paths traced yesterday by the infantry and artillery have been covered over again to a depth of a foot and a half.'

And all this time the Russians have hardly been heard from! But tomorrow?

CHAPTER 17

PARTONNEAUX SURRENDERS

Where's Partonneaux? – a letter of resignation is ignored - 'it's as if they were mad-dened by the gleaming gold' – a coward – 'standing out all round us in sombre lines we saw the enemy masses' – 'since we were as incredulous as St Thomas' – Beulay's last fight – Castellane at Zaniwki – Marbot is indignant

At the Zaniwki cottage, meanwhile, some worrying news has come in. Kutusov's advance guard has just appeared on the Orsha road.[1]

Other news, still more worrying, follows.

Wittgenstein isn't where he ought to be. Already he's somewhere between Borissow and Studianka!

But it can't be true! Hasn't Victor left Partonneaux's division, his strongest, at Borissow to hold him at bay? At once, as if by premonition, everyone at IHQ feels extremely anxious. And Gourgaud's sent back across the river to find out what's afoot. Two and a half miles from Studianka on the Borissow road he runs into one of Partonneaux's units, the 4th Battalion of the 55th Line, under its Major Joyeux. Where, he asks him, is the rest of his division? Joyeux's reply makes Gourgaud's blood freeze:

'It can only be somewhere ahead of me.'

Ahead? But it can't be! Hasn't he, Gourgaud, just come down a road where he's seen nothing but stragglers? The 55th had been left behind to be chopped to pieces if necessary, an embittered Joyeux explains, until a staff officer should come and relieve them. The officer had come. And here they are, en route for Studianka. Reaching the fork in the road and unsure in the darkness which way to go, he'd heard some vehicles moving along the road branching off to the left:

'I spurred my horse, and caught up with them. Asked the men around them what division or army corps they belonged to. None of them wanted to reply. The whole lot were stragglers.'

Whereafter some peasants 'who hadn't even wanted to be paid' had guided him this far along the road that follows the river line:

'"We're the last rearguard", says Joyeux. "We've only Russians behind us."'

How can a whole division of 4,000 men, artillery and 500 cavalry, have vanished? Yet it has. Partonneaux's division, the whole army's rearguard, can only have branched off to the right, up toward Staroï-Borissow! And what's happened to it since is anyone's guess. Dashing back to Studianka, a panicky Gourgaud crosses the empty bridge. His return, Fain sees, 'throws the Emperor into a great perplexity'. And Rossetti hears him exclaim:

'"Why, just when by a miracle everything has seemed to be saved, does this[2] have to come and spoil it all?"'

If there's one man who understands instinctively what's happened it's Rossetti – yesterday he'd made the same mistake himself. Left behind at Borissow with 'two horses from the Emperor's stable' and orders, after he'd

279

picked up any of Murat's other staff officers who might turn up, not to leave until nightfall on 26 November,

'my route illumined by the enemy's fires which covered all the high ground on the right bank, I'd set out at the prescribed hour, taking with me the ADCs Pérignon and Bauffremont and all members of the King's household who'd managed to get as far as Borissow. After an hour the road divided and as the Berezina flowed on my left I didn't hesitate to take the road on that side. But after marching for a while I'd noticed that this road wasn't trampled down and that the snow covering it was virtually intact. So I turned back and took the right-hand route. The night was very dark; yet I'd noticed that it was insensibly bending to my right and that I'd necessarily turn my back on the river.'

Whereon Rossetti had halted his 'little column. At about 2 a.m. the sound of wheels heralded an artillery park coming up behind me.' Part of Victor's corps, it too was supposed to be making for Studianka. Its colonel, having closely studied the map before leaving Borissow, is sure he's on the right road, and refuses to turn back. 'At dawn he stumbled on the Russians. As for me I lit a fire, and at first light, having realised I was on the wrong track, I'd reached the bank of the Berezina cross-country.'

Surely Partonneaux can't have done the same?

Ten days have passed since 17 November when the 42-year-old Partonneaux had written a despondent letter to Berthier, asking to be relieved of his command:[3]

'"Up to now courage and zeal have kept me going. But my physical strength has abandoned me. I can no longer stand up to the pains being caused me by the rigour of the season and my wounds. The very service of the Emperor may be compromised by my no longer being able to be as active as before."'

Although originally 'made up of young soldiers, many of them refractory conscripts', his division – his letter had gone on – was now in excellent shape, though like himself it needed to rest.

Berthier hadn't replied.

Perhaps things would be turning out differently now if he had?

At Borissow Sous-Lieutenant Beulay and his 36th Line had managed to save 'a long file of stragglers whom we afterwards had all the trouble in the world to prevail on to evacuate Borissow, where they'd been retained by hope of sleeping in the warm under a roof'.

For Borissow, as yet, has plenty. When the artillery staff had got there Planat de la Faye's servant,[4]

'a big Hamburger, very soft and very heavy, though very clean and very meticulous on the job, had lain down in the house of some Jews, and refused to leave it. He seemed neither to be sick nor suffering from frost-bite. But he was beyond measure demoralised and in a state of terrifying stupidity.'

Griois too might easily have ended his life at Borissow, if the newly promoted Squadron-Leader Bonnardel of the 1st Horse Artillery 'more fortunate than I and in the best of health' hadn't seen his house was on fire in
the small hours and raised the alarm. 'Could anyone who'd seen us breakfasting together have guessed it would be Bonnardel, so robust and full of
life, who'd succumb that very day and I, whose pale and cadaverous face
heralded my approaching end, who'd survive?' When the time had come
to leave, Griois had urged him to get going. But Bonnardel, 'confident in
his strength and his horse's health, preferred to stay and rest a little longer
and let me leave on my own. It was these short moments of repose that
caused his loss.' Bonnardel and 'his gunner, who cooked for him' had
fallen to the Cossacks.

It's to prevent this sort of thing that Victor had entrusted the rearguard
to Partonneaux when he'd left for Studianka with his two other divisions in
the afternoon of the 27th. That afternoon Honoré Beulay had seen something strange, novel and upsetting

'beside the Studianka road where it comes out of Borissow. Several
wagons filled with gold and silver coins had been abandoned, either
because their horses had been killed or because the Emperor, afraid
his military treasure might profit the enemy, had preferred everyone
to take a fistful as he passed by.'

It can only have been left there by Claparède's '50 most reliable' Poles or
by Eugène's men who'd taken over from them:

'The wagons had been opened, revealing their gold, brilliant as a sun.
At once all these unfortunates who hadn't strength enough to carry
their weapons flung themselves on the spoils. Men who hadn't even
been able to drag themselves along became as agile as monkeys, strong
as bulldogs disputing a bone! There was a senseless shoving and pushing, a general battle. Everyone wants some of this gold, plunges his
hands into it, fills his pockets. And all those who've managed to clamber
up on to the wagons are loth to cease dipping into them as long as
they've a pocket left. It was as if the gleaming gold had driven them
mad.'

Even when the Russians bring up some cannon and fire on them at short
range – so that Partonneaux orders one of his battalions to drive them off
with volleys of musketry – it makes no difference.

'We were counting on rejoining the Marshal that same evening. It had
been agreed. Alas, Providence had decided otherwise.'

Then something even more unusual had happened. 'After coping with the
stragglers', the division had just been forming up to march for Studianka,
and Beulay's battalion was

'just coming back to resume its place in the column, when we heard
some veritable howls coming from the town side. Everyone spun round,
expecting an attack. We were mistaken. The mob of defeated men was
still trailing miserably by. But in their midst two horsemen who seemed
to be warmly wrapped up in numerous greatcoats were emerging; and it

was at them the men were shaking their fists, a gesture they accompanied with a flood of insults.'

Their officers try to restrain them, but mingle their shouts with their men's. One of the horsemen is their own lieutenant-colonel, who on some pretext had deserted them earlier in the campaign. The other's his batman:

'He seemed less then enchanted to see us again and was trying in vain to hide under his hat brim and pull up his collars to his nose.'

When they'd seen the colonels and generals of the Moscow army stumbling along behind carts on the Orsha road they'd been

'seized by compassion, even to the point of tears. But now, seeing this coward who'd run away at the first cannon shot and abandoned a still intact regiment, a shiver of rage ran from one end of the column to the other.'

With the word 'coward' and sarcasms of every kind hailing down on him 'like the rumbling of thunder', the wretched lieutenant-colonel, 'livid as an exhumed corpse, with haggard eyes lost in the distance, without trying to defend or excuse himself' trots on past the column, 'thinking only one thing: how to save a life he'd degraded'.

But then something very unfortunate had happened. At 4 p.m. (according to Beulay) Berthier's ADC Mortemart had arrived with orders to Partonneaux

'to spend the night at Borissow, to continue to draw Tchitchakov's attention and facilitate the passage of as many victims of the rout as possible. Tails between our legs, we went back into Borissow just in time to catch Tchitchakov's chasseurs, who were trying to cross the Berezina, one by one, on the bridge's half-charred timbers.'

After which the division, always on the *qui vive*, had spent a last miserable night there. At crack of dawn Partonneaux had sent

'several companies toward the Orsha road. But now the stragglers were only turning up in dribs and drabs, at wide intervals. Impatient, M. Partonneaux went on ahead of them, leaving our battalion's voltigeur company at the Borissow bridgehead. He led his division on to the main road, trying to collect the 5 or 6,000 stragglers the Emperor had specified.'

The cold, Beulay goes on,

'was becoming intolerable. Our men could hardly load their weapons, so painful was the contact with the iron. It was snowing. Great flakes were mercilessly swirling round our faces and blinding us. We couldn't see so much as 50 metres ahead of us. But in front of us we could hear musket shots which told us Kutusov [*sic*] was approaching with giant strides.'

Seeing no more fugitives coming down the Orsha road, Partonneaux had withdrawn the battalion into Borissow:

'Hardly have we got back there than General Platov's cavalry, detached by old Kutusov, charged our rearguard. On another side Wittgenstein's men, profiting by our absence, had slipped into the suburbs and, hidden in enclosures, were attacking us with a well-nourished fusillade. Without replying to this musketry, we put our bayonets on our musket-barrels and butchered our adversaries.'

Unfortunately, Beulay goes on,

'even before we'd left Borissow, their regiments had got ahead of us and were occupying the slopes which dominate the road we were to follow. We cross the town at the double in the direction of the Studianka road. But so encumbered is this highway with wagons, corpses, stragglers, we can hardly get on. The wind, whistling from the North Pole, pierces us. The snow never ceases falling. There are hardly 3,000 of us left, and we've only three guns to face the entire Russian army, united against us!'

Yet they've no alternative but to advance. Now the division, reduced to three-quarters of its strength, is marching in brigade columns. Partonneaux himself is with the right-hand, i.e., most exposed one. The Russians, who've crowned the heights towards Staroï-Borissow, open fire. By now they're too numerous even to reply to:

'We move on at the double, always hoping Marshal Victor, attracted by the crackling of the fusillade, will hasten to our assistance. We've not gone very far when it seems to us heaven has heard our prayer. Straight in front of us, athwart the road, we see a major troop movement. Alas, it isn't Victor. It's the Russian artillery taking up position to bar our path. As soon as they're within easy range, all these guns converge their big mouths on to the middle of the road, and let fly at us a discharge which wipes out our leading ranks. After the first, a second; then a third. No sense in being stubborn! The Russian infantry to our right, too, had maximised its fire. To the left we were hemmed in by a river we couldn't cross. Ahead, a cloud of roundshot was crushing our column from one end to the other. So we'd have to retreat. But just as we're about-facing, Platov's 10,000 horsemen fall on us like a hurricane, sabring everything that comes to hand.'

'The situation,' Beulay goes on with dry understatement,

'was becoming complicated. More than half of us were reddening the snow. Night was falling. We didn't know where we were. General Partonneaux hastily assembles a council-of-war. It's decided we're to break up into brigades and, silently, under cover of darkness, try to slip between the enemy units. It was excessively audacious. There was little chance of success. But what else could we do?

'The general took command of the first brigade and went off to our right. The second brigade, which I belonged to, remained in the middle. The third moved off to the left, on the river side. 'M. Partonneaux tried to climb the hillsides, hoping to find a break in the mesh of light infantrymen that was tightly hemming us in. But he ran into an enemy force which threw him back into the valley. Wherever he presented himself he was hemmed in in the same way. Suddenly, there's a free space opening in front of him. Overjoyed, he enters it. But the ice breaks under the weight of his men, and while they're trying to get out of the swamps they've been pushed into, the Russians take them prisoner. The third brigade, on its side, ran into the deep masses which were pressing down on us, thus opening the banks of the Berezina.'

It was this movement, Beulay supposes, that allows his battalion's voltigeur company, left behind at Borissow, to slip through:

'At nightfall these brave fellows, realising no one was bothering about them, had finished off burning the Borissow bridge's half-burnt girders, and set off, without drums or cornets, along the river, just in time to find the road open,'

and – evidently unnoticed by Gourgaud – reach Studianka. After it had left Borissow, Beulay goes on, 'the fire put to the bridge, aided by the wind, had spread to a whole quarter' of the town:

'Soon, against the vague glow of this distant fire, we saw the enemy masses standing out all round us in sombre lines. At the same time it gave the Russians an exact idea of our position and our formation. For three hours Wittgenstein, thus informed, pierced us through and through with projectiles. M. de Blamont had sent several patrols to try and find a way out. All had come back empty-handed. But one of them told our general that a short way away, behind a little wood, there was a fold in the ground where we could take cover. M. de Blamont took all that was left of the 2nd and 3rd Brigades there. Only my regiment stayed on the plateau to keep the Russians at a distance and prevent them from setting up their batteries on the edges of that ravine. At about 10 p.m., while we were still serving as a target for the enemy, my battalion commander, who was commanding the regiment since the disappearance of M. W***, asked me to go and find the general and tell him there was only a handful of us left; that we'd run out of ammunition, and ask him to relieve us, if possible.'

The Russian outposts fire several salvoes at Beulay's 'thin figure' as he runs, 'but not a musket ball hit me'. Soon he's with the divisional staff. Alas,

'in the midst of the senseless disorder reigning at the bottom of this hole it was impossible to reconstitute any unit whatsoever, regiment or battalion, to take our place. "If you can't hang on any longer," the general replied, discouraged, "come down to us. As for relieving you, you see it's nothing to count on." As he said these words he gave a cry of pain. He'd been hit in the knee by a stray musket ball. We no longer had any generals or colonels. From that moment it was some rare commandants and captains who took over their functions.'

On his way back Beulay runs into his comrades 'running like a flock of sheep' at the edge of the plateau and thus increasing the confusion down in the hollow. Whereon the Russian guns approach and level themselves at what's left of the brigade:

'It was a veritable butchery! I was spattered from head to foot in my neighbours' blood. Maddened, stunned by this horrible uproar, by the cries of the wounded, the rattle of the dying, the whistling of musket balls, the snoring of roundshot, the roaring of the guns,' he wonders whether he's still even to be numbered among the living. Forming a kind of square, the 36th throw themselves at the Russians. By now it's about 10.30 p.m. Except for the flash of firearms and the distant glow of the Borissow fire it's pitch dark:

'Finally Wittgenstein, ashamed of this slaughter, ordered a cease fire and sent a flag of truce, charging him to tell us that Partonneaux and the 1st Brigade had laid down their arms; that it was madness to try and resist hundreds of thousands [sic] of men; that we'd given sufficient proof of our valour; and that the time had come to stop getting ourselves massacred to no purpose. But no one believed our divisional general had capitulated, so, without our listening to any more the Russian officer was sent back where he'd come from.'

Beulay's account becomes more and more tragic:

'We'd had nothing to eat since yesterday, our clothes were in shreds and the temperature was so cruel that those who escaped the bullets were succumbing to the cold if they remained immobile even a few instants. Marvelling at such courage, the Russian general lost no time in sending us a second flag of truce. Since we were as incredulous as St Thomas, this officer invited us to send one of our own people to assure himself that M. Partonneaux had in fact been taken prisoner. It was my friend M. Taillefer, the lieutenant of grenadiers who'd been promoted at the same as myself, who was charged with this mission. He went to the Russian headquarters, where in fact he found General Partonneaux in a state of utter despondency. When he asked him for orders, the general replied that he had no more orders to give, he left it up to us what to do. Then Wittgenstein summoned M. Taillefer to him and told him that if we didn't surrender instantly he'd kill the whole lot of us to the last man. He declared we'd violated the laws of warfare, that it was inadmissable that 200,000 men [sic] should be held up in their pursuit by the shadow of a brigade, that such a thing was folly on our part to attempt, and a culpable weakness on his own part to tolerate.'

Taillefer comes back. A new council of war is held. And it's generally agreed that Wittgenstein's right:

'Only eight or ten men were left per company. Even so, we decided to temporise, wait for daylight. We couldn't believe that the Emperor, who'd been so concerned over the fate of some miserable stragglers, should have allowed Marshal Victor to consent to sacrifice a whole division without trying to do something to save it from the trap they'd sent it into.'

The Russians, sure of their prey, also cease firing. Many of Partonneaux's men die of despair and inanition the moment they've nothing more to do. Beulay himself, stumbling about among the corpses and wounded, only survives by resisting a longing for sleep. Meanwhile his enterprising batman is determined to make him some breakfast. Rifling a nearby abandoned wagon, he finds in it

'something more precious than all the gold we'd seen glittering yesterday: a superb loaf of delicious barley bread, which we shared secretly
with a few intimate friends'.
The batman also roasts some horse steaks over a fire made of the butts of
the muskets everywhere littering the ground. One of the muskets is loaded,
goes off as he breaks it, and the ball passes so close to Beulay's ear that it
begins to bleed:
> 'Then the dawn appeared on the frozen horizon. Soon reveille's sound-
> ing on all sides in the enemy camp. A great movement begins. In the
> front rank we see the mouths of the guns of the [Russian] Imperial
> Guard trained at us. The gunners were lighting their matches, ready for
> the first order. Instinctively the few brave survivors form square. But
> while they're feeling for ammunition in their empty pouches the Rus-
> sians fling themselves on us from both sides. We're prisoners!'[5]

At Zaniwki, meanwhile. Castellane – like other staff officers – isn't being
allowed a moment's rest. 'Since no one foresaw this fight,' he'll jot down
in his diary eventually, 'several officers of our staff have gone on ahead.'
All the time, this horrible night, he's being sent on mission to the various
corps. Lots of IHQ's horses have been stolen – including six of Lobau's and
his wagon:
> 'Our men have [got into] a horrible way of stealing things. At our
> bivouac someone steals Chabot's hat. He had his head lying on it. A fur's
> been taken from one of my horses. More than one officer, believing his
> horse is following him, is getting here with only its cut reins around his
> arm. If he turns round, it's to see his horse already killed, cut up and
> shared out.'
At 'the Palace' Napoleon never ceases 'asking each officer arriving from
Studianka whether the poor people and baggage were still crossing'. And
is told, correctly, that the bridges are free, but that few if any of the estimated 20,000[6] wounded, *cantinières*, women, camp followers and refugees
from Moscow huddled there around their campfires are in a hurry to
profit from it. 'All night and until daybreak,' says Lejeune,
> 'the army's passage over the bridges had been going on without too
> much disorder, and I myself had been able to cross to and fro several
> times to place those things which were most in the army's interests in
> safety on the right bank'.
Marbot, going back to fetch 'the horse which carried the war squadrons'
little cash box and accounts' is utterly critical of the general staff's failure
to exploit these night hours:
> 'Having well and truly established my regiment at the Zaniwki bivouac,
> I galloped back. And imagine my amazement when I find the bridges
> completely deserted! Just at that moment no one was crossing over! Yet
> only a hundred yards away, in beautiful moonlight, I see more than
> 50,000 [*sic*] stragglers or isolated men of the kind we called roasters
> [*rôtisseurs*] seated in front of immense fires, calmly grilling horseflesh, as

if unaware they've a river in front of them they could cross in a few minutes and finish preparing their supper on the other bank.'

It's his first sight of the debris of the Moscow army, and it comes as a terrible shock:

'Not one officer of the Imperial Household, not an ADC of the army's Major-General [Berthier] nor any Marshal was there to forewarn these unfortunates and, if need be, drive them toward the bridges.'

What Marbot evidently doesn't notice is the heroic Eblé going about in the moonlight among the torpid stragglers, trying to get them to bestir themselves while there's still time.[7] Another officer who, half-dead from hunger, crosses unhindered is the Polish Captain *Boris von Turno*:

'A vague instinct, one of those prophetic impulses one has in one's youth, turned my thoughts to General Dombrowski's division. His troops, who had come from Molihew, might have some provisions. By giving me hope this idea gave me courage. I went to the bridge, where all I heard was the monotonous bumping together of the ice-floes being carried along by the Berezina. No one was going over it.'

Reaching the other side Turno finds he's in luck. Turning left toward the Brill Wood, where little voltigeur Jean-Marc Bussy and his colleagues of the Swiss infantry are doing 'nothing but run about in the forest, in the snow, to pick up firewood and keep our fires alight for the sake of the poor wounded, who've all been attended to by our surgeon,' Turno chances upon

'four Polish artillery officers gathered around a big fire. The captain, who recognised me, exclaimed: "My dear friend, you're in luck! He offered me his water-bottle, whose contents I swallowed at a single gulp. Galvanised by this dose of alcohol, like a man waking up, I looked around me. In front of their hut a really nice-looking duck was turning on the spit, the bubbling of two saucepans emitted to my ears a culinary harmony which was making our eyes shine with savage brilliance.'

And he quotes to his 'Amphytrion' the words of Sancho Panza, 'greatest of philosophers: "It's not the man who makes the stomach, but the stomach that makes the man."' But not very far away Brandt and the Vistula Legion's other wounded have heard

'late into the night the cannon thundering on the other bank. It was the fighting that was deciding the fate of Partonneaux's division.'

CHAPTER 18

HOLOCAUST AT THE BEREZINA

'Throughout this horrible day we saw the human heart laid bare. We saw infamous actions and sublime ones, according to differences in character.' (Rossetti) – 'Napoleon was never better served by his generals than he was that day.' (Caulaincourt)

Some time after midnight, Fain has noted in his journal:
'The day now beginning is likely to be a tough one. But we hold the passage.'
And Napoleon has sent off the devoted Abramovitch to Vilna, to tell Maret the army's across the Berezina; though not all of it is. 'More than 60,000 men,' Rossetti realises,
'properly clad, well-nourished and fully armed, are about to attack 18,000 half-naked, ill-armed ones, dying of hunger and cold, divided by a swampy river and embarrassed by more than 50,000 stragglers, sick or wounded and an enormous mass of baggage.'
Already on his feet at 5 a.m., Oudinot, wearing a 'brown fur *witschoura* and an astrakhan bonnet turned down over his ears', shares some onion soup with his staff, Pils among them:
'Each of these gentlemen were placed under contribution so that the cook could do his business. One supplied the bread, another the onion, a third the fat. It didn't take long to share it out.'
Pils, no doubt savouring his share, is thinking that if his *patron*'s
'two motley legs sticking out of the *witschoura* weren't sheathed in a special pair of boots, well-lined with fur on the inside but on the outside only revealing striped blue and white feather-lined drill, he'd look like a well brought up bear'.
Tchitchakov's attack is expected at dawn. And sure enough, at 7 a.m. the 'the sound of the guns in the direction of Borissow' tells Fain he's 'attacking II Corps in the woods. The Emperor mounted his horse and galloped off.' Castellane, in his suite as it passes 'in front of Razout's division in reserve behind III Corps', sees that it amounts to perhaps half a battalion; Fezensac's regiment to a platoon. And that Ney's been 'reinforced by Claparède's division, by 12,000 men of the 15th Polish Division and by some other troops of Zayoncek's.'

A moment later Wittgenstein's guns too begin firing from the direction of Staroï-Borissow. 'At about 7 a.m.' Pils, at the shack which has been Oudinot's headquarters, sees
'Captain Cramayel arrive at a gallop to warn us that the enemy's attacking and that the Cossacks are already at blows with the outposts. This officer has hardly said what he had to when a shell, passing through the pine branches, falls noisily on the shack and shatters it. At once *M. le Maréchal* mounts his horse and orders Merle's division to advance. The

2nd Swiss Line marches at its head; a second shell carries off eleven of its men. The 11th Light and 124th Line follow on.'

So begins the Battle of the Berezina.

Thomas Legler is noticing that 'a little snow was falling', and at about 7.30 he and his Commandant Blattmann are strolling to and fro on the road and Blattmann reminds him of 'a favourite song of mine, "*Our Life is like a Journey*"' and asks him to sing it for him. 'I started to at once, and when I'd finished it, he heaved a deep sigh. "Yes, Legler, that's how it is. What splendid words!"' Other officers join them and spend 'the morning's early hours singing and chatting'.

Evidently Tschaplitz's attack is taking some time to materialise. Because it's already '9 a.m. when suddenly a roundshot passes overhead with a horrible loud noise' startling Legler's colleagues:

'We couldn't understand how we could have been standing so near the enemy without any outposts. Now we heard heavy cannon fire in the distance; and to our right musketry seemed to be coming closer. An orderly officer came galloping up from that direction: "Our line's been attacked!"'

Hardly have the group of Swiss infantry officers taken 100 paces to their right than 'to our great astonishment an enemy came forward'. The Swiss scouts 'quickly spread out backwards and sideways', keeping the enemy at a distance by a well-nourished fire until the regiment has rejoined 'the division that united us to our brigade's two other divisions, which we'd lost sight of. On the road both sides' artillery were facing each other, but the enemy's so much aslant it we could now and again trace the damage their roundshot were doing.'

The Croat Regiment having been stationed elsewhere, Merle's four Swiss infantry regiments, 'these four units together perhaps amounting at most to 2,500 men', only have the French 123rd Line to support them. 'Behind us a few small Polish infantry units, a squadron of chasseurs and one of lancers formed a second line.'

By now it's growing light and the 3rd Swiss, with the 4th Swiss to their right, are firing volley after volley, 'fighting without budging'. Yet all the time

'it seems to us the enemy's being reinforced. His firing's becoming livelier. Suddenly we're thrown back, we retreat some 50 paces. The chiefs shout: "Forward!" Everywhere the Charge is beaten. We're flung at the enemy, cross bayonets at point-blank range. Slowly, the Russians retire, still firing.'

Soon the Swiss are held up by cavalry, 'which makes a charge through the sparse snow-laden pines. But all this has been no more than a *passade*. In no time our battery and the 4th's dismount the Russian battery, which is abandoned on the road.' But the Swiss are suffering heavy casualties. The 2nd Regiment, only a few yards away, is

'the most advanced of all. After a first, very successful charge, our commandant Vonderweid, from Seedorf, was following it up vigorously', and Captain Begons orders his adjutant, 'an NCO named Barbey, to go and get some cartridges. He was obeying when he was hit mortally. I gave the same order to a certain Scherzenecker. He too was hit, in the right arm. I was just going to send a third officer, when I saw that the Russians, protected by numerous light infantry, were still coming on ever more thickly. Although our regiment scarcely had 800 men, it was well-equipped and aware of the importance of the position entrusted to us. We heard a formidable noise of gunfire and hurrahs. It was the Russian army which, knowing our army corps had crossed the river and to dispute the passage with us, was coming on in ever greater numbers.'

Now the Swiss – the 1st Regiment has spread out *en tirailleurs* – are beginning to run out of ammunition:

'On both sides the firing was murderous. It wasn't long before General Amey and several staff officers had been wounded and several killed, among them our commandant Blattmann. A bullet went through his brain. General of Brigade Canderas and his adjutant had fallen too; a roundshot had taken off the latter's head.'

By now Legler – he's taken cover behind a tree – is estimating the number of men – 'it was growing every minute' – standing idle for lack of cartridges to be at least 300. 'All these were coming and placing themselves calmly behind the line of officers.' When he asks them what they're doing there, they simply reply "give us cartridges". What can he reply to that? At that moment he sees Merle 200 yards away. Runs over to him. Asks leave to attack the advancing Russians at bayonet point. Merle tells him to run back and, in his name, order the firing to cease and to charge with the bayonet. Legler insists that the drummers 'since we'd ceased fire' shall take the lead:

'But this they all refused to do. So in the heat of the moment I seized the first one to hand – a Swiss from the Glarus canton, by name Kundert, living at Rüti, something I didn't notice in the heat of battle – by his collar and threatened to run my sword through him if he didn't follow me. After which I, at a run, dragged him behind me to the front line, while he beat the attack with one hand. However, just as I let go of him a bullet hit him in the right jawbone.'[1]

All his long life[2] the 23-year-old volunteer *Louis de Bourmann* will remember and celebrate the 2nd Regiment's homeric struggles. He too has seen 'the intrepid Fribourgeois' Vonderweid fall:

'He'd just given his horse to his adjutant, who'd been wounded in the leg, and was fighting on foot at the head of his braves when a Russian musket ball went through his throat. He gave a cry, stifled by blood, and fell backwards into my arms. After the first moment had passed, he, without losing consciousness, said these simple words to his fellow-citizen: "Bourmann, I've died here as a Christian."'

And is carried to the rear by his men, 'hardly to survive for forty-eight hours'. At last cartridges have arrived and been distributed to Legler's men. Not enough to keep up a heavy fire however. So a second bayonet charge is launched. 'Twice at a hundred paces' distance we forced him to retire.' With some grenadiers Legler goes to the rear to get more ammunition, 'but had to search about for a powder wagon for a good half hour before we found one'. Just as they're going back to the firing line with as many cartridges as they can carry, they see Commandant Zingg, who insists on taking over now that Blattmann is dead. But as they approach the regiment they see, 'about 300 paces to the left of the road', another Russian column advancing and outflanking them. 'Already it could take us in the rear.' Being only a cannon-shot from the bridge on the forest fringe, the Swiss can't see very far ahead. And Begos assumes the 3rd and 4th Regiments must be somewhere to his right,

'almost opposite the bridge. For the rest, it was hard to grasp the army's overall movements. In such moments each man feels how important it is to stay at his post. It was a question of preventing the Russians from approaching, so what was needed was a heroic defence, no more, no less! Not for a single moment had we nothing to do. Swarms of Russians were aiming such a well-nourished fire at our regiment that after an hour of combat we'd lost quite a lot of ground.'

Legler's men, however, have been following up their bayonet attack 'for the best part of half an hour', and the Russians have turned and fled – as troops almost always do when seriously threatened by a bayonet charge –

'when we were swept up in the flight of the lancer squadron on our right flank. Looking back as we ran, we saw Russian dragoons at our heels, and some enemy infantry advancing with them. Again I yelled out to halt and form up. Those who heard me did as I'd ordered, and our well-aimed shots at the nearest dragoons, felling them from their horses, had such a good effect that the others galloped back, leaving the infantry standing.'

By now, through thickly falling snow, the Russian artillery's enfilading the road at short range. It's causing such slaughter among the Swiss that Oudinot, sitting his horse amidst the swirling snowflakes, orders Merle's division to move off to its left. Thus placing it under cover of the forest, he brings up two of his own guns. And Pils, in the saddle beside his Marshal, and clasping his first-aid box, sees how,

'before they've had time to be ranged in battery, one of them is carried off by the Russians, whom we hadn't realised were so close. We couldn't see farther than 30 paces for the snow.'

For all their staunchness the Swiss, Fezensac realises, are losing a lot of ground:

'Only three weak battalions placed on the road – all that was left of I, III and VIII Corps – served as their reserve. For a while the fight was sustained; under pressure from superior forces II Corps was beginning to sag. Our reserves, hit by roundshot at ever closer range, were moving towards the rear. This movement put to flight all the isolated men who filled the wood, and in their terror they ran as far as the bridge. Even the Young Guard was wavering. Soon there was no more salvation except in the Old Guard. With it we were prepared to die or conquer.'

But then, in a jiffy, everything changes aspect. 'What were to have been the scenes of the Grand Army's tomb became witnesses to its last triumph.' Oudinot, 'indignant at such audacity' on the Russians' part, 'remains in the middle of the road without bothering about the bullets whistling by on all sides.' The moment has come, he decides, to send in his heavy cavalry; and sends his last ADC, M. de la Chaise, to General Doumerc, ordering him to advance his cuirassiers' – the 4th, 7th and 14th Cuirassiers, that is, who've already done such splendid service after Polotsk and in front of Borissow. So impatient is Oudinot 'while waiting for his order to be carried out that he stamps his foot', asking Pils as he does so whether he hasn't got a drop of brandy to warm him:

'I'm just searching for it in my bag, paying no more heed to what's going on, when, having found some dregs of brandy, I offer them to him. In the same instant I see *M. le Maréchal* put his hand to his side and fall from his horse, which instantly bolts,'

dragging with it its rider (according to another eye-witness) hanging upside down. Pils, 'alone beside him' struggles to dismount,

'but couldn't extract my right shoe from the stirrup. The illustrious wounded man gave no more sign of life. But then a young voltigeur whose right fist had been carried away and who was holding his musket in his left hand came to my assistance, freed me and helped me to lift *M. le Maréchal.* We raised him to a sitting position.'

At this moment Captain de la Chaise comes back to report his mission accomplished:

'Supposing his chief to be dead, he threw himself upon him and embraced him. Between the three of us we placed him on the voltigeur's musket and took him away from this spot where the musket balls were still whistling. Then Lieutenant-Colonel Jacqueminot appeared, bringing back a Russian officer, whom he was grasping by the collar. Finally General de Lorencez, chief-of-staff, and some other officers had rejoined us. We got busy making a stretcher out of pine branches.'

Napoleon, meanwhile, has returned to his headquarters at the Zaniwki hamlet, only a cannon shot away, and is standing

'on foot at the forest fringe on the right of the road, surrounded by his staff. Behind him the Imperial Guard, drawn up in battle order,'

amounts in all to some 5,500 men – Mortier's Young Guard (2,000) Lefèbvre's Old Guard Infantry (3,500), and Bessières' 500 Chasseurs and a handful of Horse Grenadiers:

'Informed of the Duke of Reggio's condition, the Emperor immediately sent his own carriage, escorted by some Horse Grenadiers. But *M. le Maréchal,* who'd recovered consciousness, declared he couldn't stand the jolting, and so we went on carrying him.' Bonneval, sent with a dispatch to Ney to take over command of II Corps as well as his own, sees 'Jacqueminot following after, all in tears.'

As the men carrying Oudinot pass before him, Pils goes on, 'His Majesty took a few paces toward us and said:

'"Well, Oudinot, so you no longer recognise me?"'
Seeing that Oudinot has fainted again, he turns to Corvisart and Larrey and tells them to attend to him.
'The Horse Chasseurs of the Guard were drawn up to the left of the road. Captain Victor Oudinot, the Marshal's son, sees the convoy passing, has recognised his father, jumped the ditch and come to him. We laid *M. le Maréchal* down on a mattress in the Emperor's hut. There he was given first aid. Some linen, eau de cologne and Bordeaux wine had been put at his disposal, rare though such things were at that moment.'
Coming to, Oudinot says he has every confidence in his own chief surgeon. It's he – Capiomont, not Desgenettes – he wants to operate on him; indeed Bonneval, returned from his mission to Ney, hears Capiomont insist on it 'as his right and privilege'. Upon his 'refusing to be tied down', Pils gives him a napkin to bite into. And the operation begins. 'If he vomits,' opines Desgenettes, 'he's a dead man.' But though the probe goes in 'to a depth of 6 or 7 inches', he doesn't; and 'the ball was never found or extracted'. Desgenettes asks Intendant-Général Dumas, himself ailing, to look after him. And Pils, with an obviously very agitated pencil, captures the moment when Napoleon is informed that his Marshal's condition isn't desperate. Bonneval, coming with the order to Ney to take over, has found him
'on a little white horse, surrounded by his whole staff. There he was, in the midst of a very well-nourished fire, as calm as at the Tuileries. He had, I remember, a singular habit. Each time musket balls or a round-shot whistled in his ears, he shouted: "Go past, rascals! [*Passez, coquins!*]"'
The Brill Wood's pine trees, though heavily snow-laden, are 'very sparse'. And upon Doumerc's 3rd Heavy Cavalry Division coming up, Ney orders Colonel Ordener of the 7th Cuirassiers, supported by the 4th, '200 cuirassiers at most', to charge through it. Within sight of Thomas Legler and his men – they're about to be taken in the rear by yet another Russian column which 'advancing with loud shouts' – has just forced some French or Swiss infantry to give ground', the cuirassiers are ordered to charge:
'The brave cuirassiers of the 4th and 7th Regiments, who were standing only 1,000 paces away from us, had seen the enemy too. We clearly heard the word of command: "Squadrons, by the left flank, march!" As soon as the cuirassiers had crossed the road they went in to the attack.'

In front of them is a huge Russian square. Nearby is Rochechouart, who's 'marched for the Studianka ford with everything we could collect'. Langeron has invited him to come with him
'into the forest with the grenadier battalion and a good regiment of Don Cossacks. No sooner have we got into the said forest than we're vigorously charged by a regiment of cuirassiers, such as we certainly didn't expect to meet with on that kind of battlefield'.
Legler sees only 'four shots fired; then the enemy fled'. The great Russian infantry square is shattered and dissolves:

'Our grenadiers, taken by surprise, were sabred and routed, while our Cossacks made a show of resisting, which thanks to our horses gave us time to escape.'

No sooner have Legler's Swiss seen the cuirassiers charge than

'we threw our ammunition to the ground and all ran forward with a single shout: "The cuirassiers are attacking the enemy in the wood to our left! Forward at the bayonet!" Some were shouting *"Vive l'Empereur!"* and I myself, *"Long live the brave men from Polotsk!"* The assault was general and this time succeeded so well that we took 2,500 [*sic*] prisoners, two-thirds of them wounded. Many dead and badly wounded men were lying on the ground.'

After this catch, says the breathless Legler,

'followed a calm that lasted for a quarter of an hour at least. Now, at long last, our other column, the Poles, advanced, and we were issued with cartridges, which had finally arrived in sufficient quantity. The oddest thing about this bayonet attack was that though we'd lost many dead and wounded during the firing, we ourselves hardly lost anyone at all. The enemy's second line, which now engaged us, hadn't been firing at us for half an hour before the Poles were forced back on top of us. We absorbed them into our line and resumed our firing. We were amazed how accurate the enemy shots were; if it had been sharpshooters we'd had in front of us they couldn't have done us worse damage.'

But Tschaplitz's men are falling back head over heels onto Stavkowo. Rochechouart the émigré is half shattered by his compatriots' achievement, half proud of it: 'The French and Polish infantry seconded the cuirassiers' efforts. The prize of their victory was 4,000 [*sic*] prisoners and five guns.'[3]

As they come back, driving before them 'a long column of prisoners, most of them slashed by sabre cuts', Doumerc's victorious cuirassiers are welcomed by Fezensac's men 'with transports of joy'. Rapp sees them ride past in front of the Guard 'still beautiful and to be feared, in battle array at the forest's edge'. And Fain hears how the Russian square had consisted of no fewer than 7,000 infantrymen. From a Russian officer he interrogates through his Polish interpreter Napoleon hears that all 'are from Army of Moldavia'.

It's been the battle's turning-point, at least on the right bank. 'Tchitchakov, who hadn't expected to come upon such redoubtable enemies, didn't renew his attack.'

Castex's light cavalry brigade is pursuing the enemy toward Stavkovo, when another of Berthier's ADCs arrives with an order – addressed presumably to Castex but which Marbot claims was to himself.[4] Its bearer is a young aristocrat of a very fine family indeed. Alfred de Noailles, 'heir to the Dukes of Noailles', is 'a fine officer', cherished by his ex-colleague Lejeune 'for his virtues and fine character' and 'esteemed and respected by everyone', including Bonneval, as 'a loyal and brave officer, infinitely religious and charitable'. On top of his splendiferous uniform[5] Noailles is also wearing a pair of Napoleon's own epaulettes, given him only three days ago 'at the Borissow bivouac by Angel, the usher of Napoleon's office'. Before reporting back to Berthier, he feels he ought to take a quick look at what's going on at Stavkovo. He's approaching the village and chatting with a certain Sous-Lieutenant Hippolyte Dessailles, commanding a party of II Corps' skirmishers, and Dessailles is exhorting him not to needlessly expose himself under fire – ('he'd do better to go and look for the Marshal') – when 'a ball hit him in the head. The French skirmishers, forced to withdraw from the position, abandoned M. de Noailles.' He was at once surrounded, Marbot goes on,

'by a group of Cossacks who, having thrown him off his horse and seized him by his collar, dragged him away, hitting him! The superb furs and gold-covered uniform he was wearing had probably tempted their cupidity. I instantly sent a squadron to rescue him, but this effort was fruitless, as a lively fusillade from the houses prevented our troopers from getting into the village. He was probably massacred by those barbarians.'

But soon Dessailles' light infantry, 'reoccupying the high ground, find his body again, stripped and motionless'. And when young de Noailles doesn't re-appear at IHQ, Berthier sends de Courbon, yet another of his ADCs, to look for him. And here accounts begin to differ:

'Near our tirailleurs I found a dead man, bearing a strong resemblance to M. de Noailles. He'd been hit in the head by a bullet.'

Since it's disfigured him, Squadron-Leader Courbon needs other items of evidence:

'I looked for them in a mark on his shirt and a professionally made cotton waistcoat, the only clothing left on him. But as I took them off I noticed that this dead man had a cauterised wound on his arm.'

Having lived with Noailles, but never noticed such a scar, he goes on looking elsewhere. But finding no other suitable corpse, returns to IHQ, where, however, he's told about the cauterisation. 'Others who knew him more particularly and said that he'd had just such a mark' regard it as proof positive. Lejeune will hear he'd been 'disfigured under the horses' feet and could only be recognised by his tall stature [5 feet 8 inches], the whiteness of his linen and its mark.'[6]

And still everyone's expecting Partonneaux to turn up.

'Even his rearguard battalion had arrived without any difficulties. No sounds of any fighting had been heard. The road, according to a reconnaissance party which had come back, was still free'

– a road, Captain *Roland Warchot*, bringing up the extreme rear with only a single company of the 8th Polish Lancers, is finding

'paved with transversely laid tree trunks. Under my orders I had some 500 horse. Against me I had perhaps about 10,000. But the accidents of the terrain were making it impossible for the Russians to deploy into columns of platoons, but obliged them, much to their annoyance, to

stick to the timber road. This enabled me, with a single troop of twelve to sixteen files, to contain them and bar their passage.'
'Up to now,' Warchot goes on,
    'they'd not had any guns with them, and I wasn't afraid of their charging me as long as I didn't find myself obliged to beat a retreat. But from the moment I had to retire and thus lose some ground I suffered considerable losses. Generally the Russians are terrible the moment one no longer stands one's ground. They fall on you like madmen. My horses were poorly shod, or not shod at all. Finally, quite close to the village of Weselovo, I had to abandon my lieutenant who had at least 30 sabre cuts and lance thrusts.'
At that moment Warchot – the lances are jabbing at his left shoulder – sees a barrier across the road. Tries to leap it. Fails. And has to leave his horse astride it – but not before repaying another lance stab in his back with a sabre slash across his enemy's face. But then another lance thrust goes through his chest 'and came out between my shoulders'. And he loses consciousness. 'The 20 or 30 lancers still with me shared my ill fortune and were either killed or taken with me.' (Not surprisingly the rest of Warchot's account is rather confused!)

But where is Partonneaux? Surely a whole division simply can't vanish, least of all on a day of battle?
    'The uncertainty had only increased at about 9 a.m., when Wittgenstein's force was seen to be preparing an attack.'
Always it seems to be Dumonceau's singular good luck to be able to view great actions from some optimal vantage point. Before dawn Colbert had led the Lancer Brigade back to the same position behind the Young Guard as it had occupied yesterday. 'We dominated, as in an amphitheatre, the entire intervening plain, so we could see what was going on,' on both banks. At about 8 a.m. he'd heard the fighting start up again,
    'this time not merely ahead of us but on both banks of the Berezina. The sky was sombre. At first, as yesterday, a compact crowd had accumulated at the bridges and was causing a dreadful tumult without being able to cross them in an orderly manner. All the while it was being swollen by a broad column intermingled with carriages or carts which we saw still turning up over the hills there. Behind it Marshal Victor's IX Corps, our rearguard, its right leaning on a wood which it doubtless still occupied throughout its entire extent, and its left extended by some cavalry squadrons in the direction of other woods as it arrived fighting at the hill's crest, was occupying them along its whole length and maintaining itself there all day long. Now our eyes were being drawn to this line, now to the bridges. Through the smoke we confusedly made out the former's successive movements, marked by the direction of the firing, at times flinging itself down the reverse slope in front of some enemy assault; then, having repulsed it, returning to re-occupy its former position.'
The sky is sombre; but the situation of all the thousands still on the eastern bank is even more so. A dawn fog has played its part,

'causing the crowd to take the wrong direction, force it to retrace its steps and form a kind of reflux that augmented the confusion.'
Several times during the night the wounded Lieutenant Auvray had gone down toward the crowd at the bridgehead, only to give up, dismayed at its size. But then,

'at about 3 a.m. I'd heard a murmur that the enemy was attacking the tail of the column. Despite the pain my wound was causing me, I'd thrown myself into the crowd; and there I'd stayed for three hours without being able to get on. However, at 6 a.m. I'd managed to reach the far bank; and two hours later, in a village where they were waiting for me, was so fortunate as to meet my dragoon Ducloux and Médard Chagot, who'd got across the previous evening together with my horse and effects.'

Franz Roeder, desperately ill now with dysentery and pleurisy, has been hoping to cross over in Colonel Follenius' chaise; but found it already occupied by Captain Schwarzenau – an officer who always arouses his special antipathy. Stamping off in a violent rage, he'd mounted his pony, which he'd found 'without a bridle and with one stirrup two spans too long'. But though he'd got to the bridgehead early, he too had been dismayed at the size of the terrible throng already jammed there. Just as he'd been about to give up in despair he'd heard a familiar voice shouting to him through the throng:

'"Cap'n Roeder, Cap'n Roeder, Sir. Don't you worry, Cap'n. Leave it to me, Sir. Just you lean on me, Sir."'

It's his Sergeant-Major Vogel, an ex-tailor whom he, on the outward march, at Vilna, had stood up for against the insults of his good-for-nothing popinjay of a lieutenant and saved from a lashing. Now justice and humaneness have their reward:

'He led my horse by the mane and forced his way through, while I, like a poor sinner, clung to its neck.'

Half an hour farther on from the bridge Roeder bivouacks, always in the terrible freezing wind. 'Fortunately,' he scribbles in his diary, 'I've got some good hay for bedding. The right side of my chest is giving me great pain each time I cough.'

'At about 8 a.m.,' writes Lejeune who's there with I Corps,
'when the return of daylight had enabled us to see spread out before our eyes the immensity of everything that still had to cross over, each man had hastened to get closer to the bridges, and the great disorder had begun.'

Bidding a little group of Frenchmen a curt adieu, von Suckow, who has been on his own since the dissolution of III Corps' Württemberger division, is one of thousands who suddenly decide that if he isn't to suffer all the horrors of imprisonment in Siberia the time has come to try to get across.

Le Roy is another. Though near despair, his Guillaume is sure le bon Dieu will help them get across and back to la patrie. But this morning it's taken him all of three hours to get his master even to wake up. Though it's no longer snowing, the cold's very keen. Already, Guillaume points out, all the camp fires have been abandoned, and everyone's rushing towards what seems to be the sole remaining bridge. Le Roy rubs the sleep from his eyes. Much as he hates 'theologians', he hastily agrees about *le bon Dieu* 'because we're really in a very tough spot'. And though both Guillaume and Jacquet try to support him, it's as much as the fanatical deist can do to totter two or three steps. Where have the cavalry troopers they'd seen the previous evening gone to? They've rejoined the rearguard, Guillaume says, which at any moment now will be cutting its way through the struggling mass beneath them! At this terrible news Le Roy falls on his knees:

"You know what calamities are crushing me just now," he admits silently to the God he has 'often offended but always honoured'. "Be favourable to me, and I'll do my best to improve. Or else strike me down in this moment when my repentance is sincere!" 'During this fervent prayer,' he goes on,

'I'd fallen to my knees, my arms stretched up toward the sky, my face turned toward the side where the crossing was painfully proceeding. This black mass, mobile as the waters of the sea lashed by an impetuous wind – this sight brought me to my senses. One can smile even at the grave's edge! At this supreme moment the smile on my lips seemed to censure my lack of courage since yesterday. What had really been going on in my furtive individuality, for it to be making me, all unbeknown to myself, so timid and pusillanimous? Me, an old soldier who'd stood the test of twenty battles! The lion had become a miserable roe-deer! Could the devil, or rather my good angel, have been meddling in my business? If so, they could clear off and leave me in peace.'

He doesn't need Their Lordships, he tells himself, to take so much trouble over him and make him

'commit stupidities, to spy on my actions and be my accusers and informers at the sound of the famous trumpets, so promised by Christian preachers and so little desired by their flock. I blushed with shame at all these theatricals before God and this one man who'd been witness to them. At all costs I wanted to repair my mistake. So I immediately quit my chicken-hearted cowardice.'

Whereupon, head held high and 'mounted on my spurs like a village curé's cock', he braces himself for the ordeal ahead. Before he does so he makes Guillaume a present of his silver watch, tells him to secure it under his greatcoat and advises him, if their pony should become an embarrassment, to abandon her; 'likewise my gun and the precious possessions from Moscow'. All he asks of Guillaume, should he survive him, is to tell his family how he'd perished.

The basic trouble, Sergeant-Major Thirion sees, is that

'as only the first ranks could actually see the two bridges, the mass behind them, who couldn't, was pushing and shoving for all it was worth and thrusting the first ranks into the river'.

Thirion himself, with the 2nd Cuirassiers' Eagle still in his pocket, crosses by the right-hand bridge with his back to the mob, 'the better to resist any shove from behind which might have flung me into the water'. At the same time he's 'half-carrying, half-pushing' a comrade named Liauty,

'wounded in the night by a sabre cut near his buttock, and, I fancy, in the joint, which he'd sustained while struggling to demolish a hut where some other men had taken refuge'.

Grabbing a horse from a recalcitrant soldier, Thirion loads Liauty on to it and gets across.[7] Many are unable to so. One of them is IV Corps' elderly inspector of reviews, M. de Labarrière, who's come the hundreds of icy miles from Moscow in a sledge. Seeing a friend, a wounded officer, he runs up to him. 'Leaning on each other,' Labaume sees, 'they got lost in the mob, and he's never been heard of since.'

Griois too will soon be in the thick of it. With the rest of IV Corps' officers who've just spent a comfortable night in their barn

'we'd ridden down as quickly as our horses' sad state permitted towards the bridges, which we couldn't see because of the mist but which were no more than two miles away. The weather was sombre, the cold piercing, and some snowflakes were falling.'

At first they suppose the vast jam is due to some temporary hold up; and wait for it to clear:

'But fresh masses of isolated men are arriving on every hand, and only swell it further. No more movement. No one can budge. At each instant the obstacle's growing. After waiting for three-quarters of an hour we decide to go ahead; and do so, albeit slowly, thanks to our horses which strike and overthrow the wretched footfolk.'

To Griois it seems the disorder's beginning

'with the retrograde movement of some horsemen of II or IX Corps, who cut their way through, overthrowing everything before them. Doubtless it was some ill-conceived order, too strictly enforced, that caused much of the day's disasters.'

The distinction between the two bridges' purposes avails nothing without proper military order:

'vehicles, horses, pedestrians were following the same route. Getting to the bridge, vehicles and horses were refused access. An attempt was even made to send them back. The thing was impossible, and soon the paths were obstructed.'

Griois is riding a little two-year-old Polish pony he'd bought on the way to Moscow but which has become so weak it can hardly carry him. And in no time his companions have left him behind. Soon he's regretting even plunging into this ocean of desperate human beings. How dearly he'd like to get out again! 'Not to be thought of.' As yet it hasn't fallen prey to panic – not as a whole – though the weaker are crying out against the stronger, who're everywhere using brute force. As before, certain hardy individuals are trying to swim the river. And one or another even succeeds. Fain and his colleagues see them among the bushes and 'scarcely recognise Colonel

V***t in his savage nakedness'. Another is a comrade of Pion des Loches named Béranger. Fezensac has seen

'a *cantinière* of the 33rd Line, who'd given birth to a girl at the campaign's outset and carried it all the way from Moscow, cross the river with water up to her neck, leading her horse with one hand and with the other holding her baby on her head'.[8]

Others, less resourceful or more patient – or despondent – or less conscious of the impending danger – are just sitting there on the snow, head in hands, waiting to see what'll happen. Rossetti, no doubt on mission to Victor, sees 'above all the sick and wounded renounce life, go aside and resignedly sitting down stare fixedly at this snow that was to be their tomb'. Everyone who's on his own is having similar experiences. And by no means all are even getting as far as the bridge. At last, getting into the column, von Suckow finds he's

'surrounded on all sides, caught in a veritable human vice. The moments I spent after entering this *closed society* until the one when I set foot on the right bank were the most terrible I've ever known. Everyone was shouting, swearing, weeping and trying to hit out at his neighbours.'

Himself struggling in the mob, he sees a friend, wounded at Mojaisk, on a *konya*, being attacked by a French infantryman

'with formidable blows of his musket butt; but though only a few paces from him I could do nothing to help him. So tightly pressed were we one against another, it would have been impossible even to reach out my hand to him. Again and again I felt myself lifted off the ground by the human mass, squeezing me as in a vice. The ground was littered with men and animals, living or dead. Every moment I found myself stumbling over corpses. I didn't fall, it's true. But that didn't depend on me. I know no more horrible sensation one can feel than treading on living beings who cling to your legs and paralyse your movements as they try to get up again. Still to this day I recall what I felt that day as I stepped on a woman who was still alive. I felt the movements of her body and at the same time heard her calling out, croaking: "Oh! Take pity on me!" She was clutching my legs when, suddenly, as a result of a thrust from behind, I was lifted off the ground and freed from her grasp. Since that time I've often reproached myself for involuntarily having caused the death of one who was so close to me.'

'Up to now,' Cesare de Laugier assures us,

'the crossings over the bridges had been made with the greatest regularity. But as soon as the guns were heard again and with the Partonneaux battalion's arrival it had become known that his division had fallen into the enemy's power and that Wittgenstein was advancing, then men, women, baggage, light carriages, guns, ammunition wagons, heavy coaches – all rushed toward the bridges' narrow approaches.'

These first roundshot are being fired by a Russian battery which is boldly advancing 'under cover of some light infantry amidst the snow-covered bushes' along the Borissow road. At this moment the vehicular bridge breaks and has to be repaired. Which of course causes a panic rush toward the other one.

After striking his miserable bivouac in the marsh 'not everywhere equally frozen' at daybreak, Major Boulart, on the western bank, has had to abandon quite a few of his vehicles,

'and with them a good number of gunners who'd only been able to keep up with our march thanks to the vehicles (each time a vehicle was abandoned we reckoned that six times as many men perished with it)'.

After this he has 'gained the neighbouring high ground, where I was placed in battery on the Borissow road where it emerges from a wood'. From there, looking out over the situation on the far bank, he realises almost at once that things over there are likely to get desperate:

'Everything indicated I'd have to open fire. I entrusted Captain Maillard with 2,000 francs in banknotes, which I asked him to keep for my wife in case anything should happen to me. I was ready for anything, though not without turning over sad thoughts in my mind. The Emperor was near my artillery almost throughout the day.'

By and by Napoleon, who seems to Boulart to be in low spirits ['abattu'], orders him to open fire across the river at the Russian battery that's unleashing panic at the bridges. Depressed or not, Boulart's relieved to see that the ex-gunner emperor makes nothing of a little incident which might normally have unleashed his wrath:

'This is what happened. Though we didn't realise it, one of my guns was loaded. Assuming it had some stones at the bottom of its barrel, I ordered them to be burnt out by putting some powder into the vent. But a violent detonation and the whistling of the roundshot showed we'd been mistaken. The Emperor merely said, with a kindly air: "What a nuisance. That could give the alarm where they're fighting, and above all in front of us."'

All this Captain Dumonceau, that predestined observer of battles, also sees from a distance:

'Napoleon had ordered a battery of the Imperial Guard to take up position on our left near the river bank. By aiming its fire across it, it took the enemy battery on the other bank obliquely, thus forcing it to withdraw to a distance. At the same time it turned back a column that was preparing to deploy from the wood on which IX Corps' right was resting. Then we saw infantry skirmishers who'd just been driven out of the wood return with élan, throw out the enemy's, who in their turn emerged from it and thus under our eyes restored IX Corps' support. On the far left we could see repeated cavalry charges which didn't cease to maintain their superiority there.'

No doubt the four troopers Le Roy had spoken to yesterday are playing their part in them. For it's Fournier's cavalry which, flinging itself repeatedly at far superior numbers, is holding Wittgenstein's right wing in check.

301

'In the distance away to the right, a slight depression in the terrain exposed part of the Russian army, deployed in front of ours. From there it in turn could see our multitude gathered at the bridges, at which it had begun to aim the fire of one of its batteries.'

It had been 'shortly before dawn' that the remains of I Corps had also deployed. Coming out of their wood on the left bank, the 7th Light had formed up in line of battle. Even at that early hour Sergeant Bertrand had noted that Russian roundshot was beginning to fall on them. 'We go into action, and, a strange thing, we beat the Russians, taking from them some guns and prisoners.' But it's not until now, some time between 10 and 11 a.m., that Wittgenstein, with some 30,000 men and 'numerous artillery', as well as Miloradovitch's, Platov's and Yermolov's 10,000, sent on ahead by Kutusov, unleashes his first real attack on Victor's remaining two divisions, deployed on the low line of hills. Against him Victor has hardly 11,000, mostly Poles, Bavarians and Dutchmen, plus – to his left – Fournier's 800 cavalry, facing much larger numbers of Russian horse. To strengthen his line Daendels' 26th Division – men from Berg, Baden and Hesse – after crossing the river, has been ordered back again.

At 11.30 a.m. Tascher sees the first cannonball come rolling along the ground. And it instantly unleashes panic. 'To escape this artillery fire,' Dumonceau sees how

'the multitude rushes in all directions – running from bridge to bridge in hope of getting across – being thrown back by those who're flowing in the opposite direction, and thus forming two opposed torrents, clashing against and violently repulsing each other. Then we see the shells bursting among them – the roundshot tracing broad holes in this compact mass – new torrents being caused by their terror. One of the bridges, foundering under the mob that's flung itself on to it and carried away by the waters, was gradually vanishing into the depths. Other unfortunate individuals were risking their lives in the river to find a ford, or save themselves by swimming. Together with all this we heard, like the roaring of a distant storm at sea, cries, yells, the crashing of vehicles, an undefinable uproar. It filled us with horror. And with all this we heard, like the distant roarings of a tempest at sea, cries, yells, wagons exploding, an undefinable uproar which filled us with terror.'

IHQ's watches are showing 1 p.m. when Napoleon at last learns that Partonneaux has surrendered. No details of course are known. But it comes as a great shock. An 'infuriated' Emperor inveighs against Partonneaux's 'cowardice':

'If generals haven't the courage to put up a fight, they can at least let the grenadiers do it!' he declares. 'A drummer could have saved his comrades from dishonour by sounding the charge. A *cantinière* could have saved the division by shouting "Every man for himself!" instead of surrendering.'

At the same time he orders the news to be kept secret – or rather, only com-municated officially to the hard-pressed Victor. But soon even Labaume, marching for Zembin with IV Corps headquarters and the Treasure, hears that the army, at the critical moment, has lost its rearguard:

'3,000 infantry and two squadrons of cavalry had surrendered after run-ning towards the Russian campfires which they'd taken for our own. Everyone was furious with Partonneaux for his "cowardice", which was contrasted with Ney's brave resolution.'

At the bridgehead, meanwhile, the crush is becoming more and more nightmarish. Everyone who'd been making for the broken bridge now turns and makes a rush for the other. But though everyone's having simi-lar dreadful experiences by no means everyone's getting as far as the bridge. Nor is it the Russian roundshot that's causing the worst slaughter. 'The enemy', Kergorre and his companions, who're also there, realise,

'was aiming at this mass, but, true to his habit, was firing too high. The danger from the projectiles was the lesser. No one bothered about them. The most dreadful thing was what we were doing to ourselves. For a dis-tance of more than 200 paces the bridge was ringed around by a semi-circle of dead or dying horses and by several layers of men who'd been thrown down. One couldn't afford to make a false step. Once you'd fallen, the man behind would put his foot on your stomach and you'd add yourself to the number of the dying. Forming a platoon to help one another, and holding our horses by the bridle, we'd hardly launched out into the mob than we were scattered like sand before the wind. I was car-ried off my feet and lost my horse.'

Having weighed up his chances of swimming the river, but reflecting that he hasn't any change of linen or a fire to dry himself 'so I'd indu-bitably perish when I got to the other bank' – as against being stifled in this crush, von Suckow too, recommends

'my soul to God, gave a last thought to my own family, and braved all the perils. Behind me as far as the eye could see was a column of fugitives, every moment being joined by more. In front of me was a carriage which in the present circumstances could be described as elegant. Drawn by two horses, it had reached the end of the queue and was trying to pass through it. Inside was a lady and two children. Suddenly a Russian roundshot, falling in the team, smashes one of the animals to pieces. The mother jumps out of the post-chaise, and holding her two little ones in her arms begs those who are passing to come to her aid. She prays, she weeps, but none of these fugitive passers-by, prey of panic terror, bothers about her, wants to listen. I've just left her a few paces behind me when I no longer hear her groaning voice. I turn round. She and her children have disappeared; or rather, she's been knocked down by the human flood, crushed and pulverised by it.'

Quite close at hand and 'not far from the bridge we were to cross by' Sur-geon Roos, also of the Württembergers, sees on a horse another 'beautiful lady of 25, wife of a French colonel who'd been killed a few days ago. Indifferent to everything that was going on around her, she seemed to devote all her attention to her daughter, a very beautiful child of four, whom she was holding in front of herself. Several times she tried to reach the bridge, and each time she was repulsed. A grim despair seemed to overcome her. She wasn't weeping. Her eyes fixed now on the sky, now on her daughter, at one instant I heard her say "O God, how unhappy I am not even to be able to pray!" Almost instantly her horse was hit by a bullet and another shattered her left thigh above the knee. With the calm of silent despair she took her crying child, kissed her several times and then with her bloodstained skirt, which she'd taken off her broken leg, she strangled the poor little girl; and then, hugging her in her arms and pressing her to herself, sat down beside the fallen horse. Thus she reached her end without uttering a single word and was soon crushed by the horses of those pressing forward on to the bridge.'

Several hours of this Dantesque nightmare must be endured if one's to get across. But slowly, very slowly, Commissary Kergorre sees, the bridge is coming closer:

'My two furs had been torn off in strips, only my greatcoat remained. Three times it was taken off my shoulders. It was my salvation. I kept it at peril of my life. Three times I halted to put my arms back into it. A few people in the midst of this crush were still holding on to a horse.'

He too loses a friend – a Monsieur Pichault – in the mob. They can only exchange a last parting glance. From time to time great surges go through the crowd. A series of shocks turns Griois' pony round so that it's facing in the wrong direction; and there – so it seems, for more than an hour – he sits with his back to the bridge 'in this desolating position which finally took away all hope'. But then he catches sight of his regimental sergeant-major, a man named Grassard. Tall, young and vigorous, he no longer has either horse or effects, only a *konya*. But when, finally, he hears his colonel shouting, he turns it round, gets to him, and 'bridle in one hand and sabre in the other, he began pushing forward, shoving aside or overthrowing everything in his way'. Griois' own sabre has snapped in half. But though he's 'a miserable scarecrow' with hardly strength enough to hold it in his hand, he does his best to co-operate:

'The crowd was so dense one couldn't see the ground, and it was only from how my beast, more or less sure of itself, was putting its feet down that I could judge whether it was walking on earth or corpses.'

Suddenly he's thrown off into the wreckage of an overturned wagon. But, to his own amazement, by a convulsive effort finds himself back again in the saddle, unharmed! As they at last approach the bridge

'the overturned or abandoned vehicles, the horses raising their heads amid the debris that was crushing them, the corpses – all this seemed like an entrenchment impossible to surmount'.

But then some of the pontoneers, still faithfully at work repairing the bridge, notice his gunner's uniform and help him to get up on to it. And

Napoleon and Caulaincourt walked out along the long timber bridge over the Berezina at Borissow to within 50 paces of the Russian sentry. Not all Marcelline Marbot's dash had been able to prevent the Russians from firing it in three places – his 23rd Chasseurs had been too busy looting Count Pahlen's 300 carts, filled with provisions taken from the immense stores captured by Tchitchakov at Minsk. Copper engraving from Lieutenant Honoré de Beulay's memoirs.

Without exaggerating the length (about 72 feet) or fragility of the improvised Berezina bridges – their tables were hardly a foot above the water – this anonymous artist's picture of the troops crossing the infantry bridge shows the appalling crush on the eastern bank.

Above: 'Around 10 a.m. the cavalry and artillery bridge caved in under the latter's weight. A number of men sank with it, and most of them perished. This led to a rush for the other, infantry bridge', seen in the background. Nineteenth-century steel engraving.

Below: The Berezina's flood waters, swept by ice floes, had effectively increased the passage to 'well over 200 yards' and doubled its normal depth of 3½ feet in midstream – which made all the difference. V. Adam's famous lithograph of the scene from the high ground where Lieutenant-Colonel Le Roy woke up on the morning of 27 November, considerably exaggerates the overall effect.

Opposite page, top: The heroic General Eblé vainly exhorting stragglers to bestir themselves in the night of 27 November and cross the remaining bridge before it is too late. Pils' untutored watercolour brush captures all the drama of the scene. On 30 December the middle-aged Eblé, 'no more than a shadow of himself' and 'in a state of utter dejection and exhaustion', would die at Koenigsberg.

Above: Standing up to the Cossacks 'in the outskirts of Ochmiana, 4 December 1812'. By now almost everyone had several weeks' growth of beard. Like thousands of others, the dying man in the foreground has already been stripped of his shoes and greatcoat. Engraving by Faber du Faur .

Left: At Zaniwki hamlet, Napoleon's headquarters on the Berezina's right bank, III Corps headquarters staff assembled for the night of 27/28 November. Note the infantrymen stripping the three houses' roof timbers: 'Next day Zaniwki had almost wholly vanished, having been taken away for the bivouac fires.' Faber du Faur.

Above: 5 December at Smorgoni. Of the 266 troopers of the prestigious Polish Guard Lancers who escorted Napoleon's 'hermetically sealed' carriage on runners as he left the army, only 36 would reach the first staging post; and only 8 of Murat's Neapolitan Guard Lancers who took over from them would get as far as Vilna. Staff captain Eugène Labaume would see their bodies littering the route, 'showing Napoleon had passed that way'.

Below: Vilna's 'long, low and narrow' Medyn Gate where thousands of survivors trampled each other to death on 9 December and 'for ten hours on end and in -28° of frost thousands of soldiers who'd thought they were saved fell frozen or stifled while other entrances were completely free' – Cesare de Laugier. The gate still exists. Sepia drawing, 1785.

Above: Governor Hogendorp's placards – or were they Roch-Godart's? – tried ineffectually to direct each corps to one of Vilna's huge monasteries, which had all been earlier converted into hospitals. 'No one could stay in those halls without fumigating them,' writes the 13-year-old son of artillery surgeon Déchy who died of the typhus while heroically tending his patients there, 'so fetid was the air. There was no bedding'. Reaching this 'Tartar hell' on 12 December, Rochechouart would try to save some of his compatriots from being thrown out of the windows to make room for Russian sick and wounded. Nineteenth-century engraving.

Below: Lieutenant-Colonel C. F. M. Le Roy's new shoes hindered him from keeping up with the scanty remnants of the 85th Line as he slithered along this road out to Ponari Hill. It was here the Fusiliers-Grenadiers' 'handsome poodle' Mouton stood up to a Russian cuirassier and Sergeant Bourgogne admired Ney's adroit handling of the rearguard. Nineteenth-century lithograph.

Vilna's Lichtenstein Coffee House, invaded by famished survivors. During the night of 9
December the Württemberger Captain Karl von Suckow was aroused by a violent kick in
the ribs 'from Monsieur Lichtenstein in person, who'd earnt so much money from us and

who'd always received us with the deepest and humblest bows. Now he shouted at me: "Get up, you dog of a German! And get the hell out of here!'"

'From all the town's streets and alleyways people were already crowding across the square en route for Kovno.' A nineteenth-century artist's impression of the chaos outside Vilna town hall in the evening of 10 December, after Murat had given orders for the retreat to go on. Captain Josef Zalusky of the Polish Guard Lancers (left), assuming it to be at an end, had even donned his new parade uniform. But had to take it off again. Lithograph by J. Damelis. By kind permission of Vilnius Museum .

Above: Ponari Hill, about 5 km long and 2 km wide, rises some 160–180 metres to the plateau leading to Kovno and the Niemen. The road's gradient in those days was much steeper than it is today and nothing that moved on wheels could get up its 'icy slope... polished like marble'. At its foot, friend and foe together pillaged the Imperial Treasure's gold millions, and all the remaining guns were lost. No one mentions the chapel at its base. Sepia drawing, 1786.

Right: The news reaches Paris. Having crossed Europe with unprecedented speed in the company of his Master of the Horse, Armand de Caulaincourt, Napoleon got there only two days after the publication of his ever famous and unusually truthful XXIXth Bulletin. Engraving by Opiz, 1814, Bibliothèque Nationale.

his pony, in turn, is the means of helping a *cantinière* who's carrying her child in her arms, and who clings to its tail:
'What a weight fell from me as I crossed it! My feeling was like that of a condemned man who'd been pardoned on his way to execution. On the bridge itself I was almost alone, so congested was its access. It was hardly above the water, in such fashion that the corpses being carried by the current were held up there among the ice-floes. A great number of horses whose riders had drowned came and leant their heads against its table and stayed there as long as they had strength to. They garnished one side of the bridge for almost its whole length.'
At the far end Griois is effusively thanked by the *cantinière*, who insists on sharing her last remaining bit of sugar with him. 'I reproach myself for having accepted it.'
For their part Le Roy, Jacquet, Guillaume and their *konya* Bichette have been making for the upstream edge of the struggling mass. Reaching it, Le Roy notices that the hard-frozen river bank, being 'a little higher than the current, could bear the weight of a man'. And standing with his right shoulder against Bichette's left, and holding the bridle short at her mouth, he mutters in her ear:
'"Come along, my beauty. Maybe today means eternity for both of us. Who knows where we're going? Neither of us. But we mustn't let this painful uncertainty scare us!"'
He's counting more on her, he confides to the mare, than on either his guardian angel or his patron saints, 'who, I fancy, are wringing their hands very little over my cruel plight'.
To reach the bridge has taken Kergorre two hours and now his last strength is giving out:
'If the struggle had lasted another quarter of an hour I'd have gone under. Despite the cold my face was bathed in sweat. I was no more than two paces from the bridge. I put out my hand. I begged those in front of me to lend me theirs. I gripped one of the trestles ... but I'd overlooked human egoism. People just looked at me and passed on. A raging horse which had been thrown down was the last obstacle. Finally Providence came to my aid. A violent shock threw me over this horse. And in an instant he had ten people on top of him, pounding his head and belly. As for me, I was thrown between him and the bridge. I was saved. The bridge was a bit higher than my stomach.[9] Gathering the little strength I had left, I threw myself at it and managed to clamber up. Since there were no dead men or horses on it, people were passing along it in an orderly fashion, like a big crowd does when it's in a hurry.'[10]
There, at the far end of the bridge stands Sergeant Bourgogne, shivering with fever. Ever since yesterday evening he's been stationed there by his colonel to direct any of the Fusiliers-Grenadiers' stragglers:
'At its outlet was a marsh, a slimy, muddy place, where many of the horses sank and couldn't get out again. Many men, too, who were being

dragged into the marsh by the weight of the others, sank down exhausted when left to themselves and were being trampled by others coming on from behind.'

Bourgogne tries to dissuade a corporal named Gros-Jean from going back to the left bank to look for his brother. Points out

'how many dead and dying were already on the bridge and preventing others from crossing by clutching their legs, so that they were all rolling together into the Berezina, appearing for a moment amid bits of ice, only to disappear altogether and make way for others.'

But Gros-Jean won't listen. Handing Bourgogne his pack and his musket, he says 'there are plenty of muskets on the other side'. At that moment he fancies he sees

'his brother on the bridge, struggling to clear himself a path through the crowd. So, listening only to the voice of despair, he climbed over the dead bodies of men and horses which blocked the way from the bridge and pushed on. Those he met first tried to thrust him back; but he was strong, and succeeded in reaching the unfortunate man he'd taken for his brother.'

But alas, it isn't. Nothing daunted, Gros-Jean reaches the far end only to be knocked down at the water's edge; trampled on; almost falls in. He clutches a cuirassier's leg,

'who, in turn, grabbed another man's arm. Hindered by a cloak over his shoulder, he staggered, fell, and rolled into the Berezina, dragging after him Gros-Jean and the man whose arm he was holding.'

Even so, Gros-Jean manages to clamber up by his knees on to a horse that's floating against the bridge; and by and by some engineers, hearing his shouts, throw him a rope,

'and thus from one support to another, over dead bodies and lumps of ice, he was drawn over to the farther side. I didn't see him again.'[11]

Although an hour has passed since Le Roy's got to almost within reach of the bridge, he hasn't advanced ten paces. But then 'some very lively firing started up on the right bank, causing the bridge and what was going on on top of it to stand out starkly against the flashes'. Jumping on to Bibiche, he finds the half-frozen water only comes up to her hocks. Yet between them and the bridge there's still a 'hole or ditch, whose depth I don't know, filled with ice-floes'. He tells Guillaume, who's still just behind him, to pull the horse out of this hole if he should drown in it. At that moment a shell falls into the water beside him:

'Fortunately it didn't explode. But my God! what an uproar this projectile caused in this confused mass of men from eighteen different nations, each swearing in his own language. The most vigorous grabbed the bridgehead, having crushed the feeblest, and got across first.'

The ditch isn't deep 'but the bottom not being firm, Bibiche was plunging about in the mud, shoving aside the ice-floes and all the while getting nearer to the bridge'. Suddenly, just as Le Roy's about to undertake the perilous leap from her back on to its timbers, 'my poor beast, finding some firm ground under her hoofs, leaped in one jump out of the hole and fell like a second shell into the mob around the bridgehead, and, guided by instinct, followed some horses pulling a gun – so that I crossed this dangerous passage as if by magic. Whew!'

Once on the bridge's timbers men are finding that it's not too difficult to get to the other side, albeit followed by 'benedictions' from the less fortunate ('kill him' – 'stick a f*****g bayonet in that brigand's guts!' – 'fire a shot into his arse!' 'chuck that f*****g mongrel into the water!' etc.). Von Suckow too is getting close:

'Hardly had I climbed up on this mass of men and horses than I saw at a glance there were a few corpses that had been thrown down on to the first ice-floes. Anyway those poor fellows had all been drowned.'

The bridge itself, he sees, is

'built of such pitiable materials that it was swaying to and fro in so terrifying a fashion that at any moment one expected to see it collapse. I despaired utterly of being saved. It was my first and only fit of discouragement throughout the campaign.'

And still, as they'd done yesterday and the day before, the military police are striking out to right and left with the flats of their swords. Finding himself standing on a horse – 'it was a chestnut' – that's lying on its side, panting convulsively, von Suckow gets another violent shove from behind, and almost falls to

'share the fate of this poor beast. At that moment I mentally said good-bye to the joys and sufferings of this earth, yet involuntarily stretched my arms out before me. My hand desperately clutched the collar of a blue cape. The man who was wearing it – a French cuirassier officer of prodigious stature who still had his helmet on his head – was holding an immense cudgel and using it with utmost success, pitilessly striking out at all who came too close to him. After long admiring this man's efficiency in shaking off all troublesome neighbours, I had only one thought: "You're not going to quit this fellow." And not relinquishing my lucky hold on the collar I let myself be taken in tow by its wearer.'

But the cuirassier notices what's happening:

'To get rid of me he had recourse to his cudgel, whirling it about behind him. But his efforts were to no avail. Seeing the blows as they came, I did my utmost to avoid them without letting go of his collar – so adroitly, he didn't once touch me. Seeing he wasn't getting anywhere like this, he ceased whirling his stick and adopted a new tactic, letting out formidable oaths. And when this didn't work either, he says to me: "Monsieur, I adjure you, let go of me, for if you don't we're both lost."'

But Suckow only holds on all the tighter. And, with the cuirassier swearing and cursing and trying to shake him off, reaches the bridge. Finally, realising they'll never get on to it like this, von Suckow lets go of the cuirassier's mantle – jumps for it, and finds himself up to his knees in the icy water.

'Even today, sitting by my stove, I shiver when I think of it.' By and by he too scrambles up on to the bridge.

Le Roy too struggles over the sharply tilted bridge, only pausing at its far end to see what's become of Guillaume. But there's no sign of him. Exhausted and frozen, Le Roy warms himself at a fire fuelled by several looted wagons, abandoned – like Boulart's – for lack of teams in the frozen swamp. But still sees no sign of the irrepressible, the devoted Guillaume! So, hearing a drum beating not far off and suspecting frost-bite in one foot, Le Roy makes off, alone, in that direction. 'You couldn't see ten paces ahead of you, the snow was coming down so thickly.'

But now the short day's ending. Dusk has put an end to the fighting along the eastern ridge. All that remains now is for Victor's men to effect their retreat. At about 8 p.m. 'illumined by the enemy's shellfire' Eblé – it's his *sixth* night without sleep – and his pontoneers and some gunners (among them Chambray's unit) begin clearing 'a kind of trench' through the rampart of corpses and dead horses encumbering access to the bridge. While the military police stave off the mob, Captain François, approaching with the 30th Line, now numbering only 143 men, sees

'horses, baggage, artillery trying to cut a path. A terrible struggle begins among these despairing men. I, who love extraordinary things, was horrified by this scene. To all the noise was added the whistling of roundshot, the explosion of shells and ammunition wagons.'

As the 7th Light cut a way through the mob and approach the bridge, Sergeant Bertrand too sees 'a spectacle of such horror' as his pen, even after half a century, will almost refuse to describe: 'scattered heads, arms, legs, a bloody slush!' What's more, such survivors as are closest to the 'trench' try to thrust themselves in among the ranks. But to yield to them out of mere humanity, the officers realise, will be to wreck everything:

'First and foremost we had to save everyone still grouped around the flag. Our salvation lay at the tips of our bayonets. Just as our column is passing very close by this mass of victims, I hear my name being called out, and in this sad confusion see the wife of one of the regiment's NCOs, holding her dying child in her arms. This sight made the most atrocious impression on me I've ever felt. Always I shall have before my eyes the expression on this mother's face, with her lost and supplicating look. But my duty as a soldier, though it tore my heart in two, came before all feelings of commiseration. In any other circumstance I'd have given my life to save this woman and her child. May God be my judge! All these unfortunates remained in the enemy's power.'

Ordered to take the place of the NCO bringing up his company's rear, he's just hurrying back to do so, when one of General Gérard's ADCs, taking him for a runaway, smacks his face. Bertrand raises his musket to his cheek and his finger's on the trigger, when he tumbles to the misunderstanding. Even when they get to the bridge his men see two horses are blocking it and want to heave them into the water:

'But being told they belonged to superior officers, we didn't; but the poor beasts were driven on with bayonet jabs. At last here we are on the bridge. The flooring having given way on one side, we were marching along a very steep slope. Several of us fell into the water. I saw some of them going by on enormous ice-floes, trying to reach the other shore, among others an officer who, stricken by another ice-floe, vanished under the waves. However, some others were luckier.'

A staff officer has indicated the assembly point on the other side; but at roll call the 7th Light have trouble lighting their fires. Bertrand goes to his colonel to report the smack in the face he'd received:

'He'd already been informed about it, and sent me, together with an adjutant-major, to the ADC who, having said how sorry he was, shook my hand, saying: "let's forget it, my old comrade, and let's close our ranks, because tomorrow we'll be needing them."'

Although Captain François' wounds have 'reopened and begun to bleed again', he too manages somehow to get through and rejoin his division:

'My comrades had thought I was one of those crushed underfoot. They made me share their black soup and the regimental surgeon-major dressed my wounds for the first time since I'd left Moscow.'

On the bridge, without even noticing it, he has lost his blue cape with silver clasps. And even when his servant – for 48 hours they've lost touch – turns up and 'bursts into tears, seeing me saved yet again' he's failed to save any of his horses,

'which didn't surprise me. But one of them had been carrying twelve soup spoons, thirteen forks, a ladle for stew, a soup ladle, a pair of silver spurs and a large sum in roubles. In the morning a soldier brought me my *konya*, albeit stripped of its bags.'

Even when they've got across, the refugees are by no means always out of trouble. At Brillowo, Castellane, on mission as usual, sees

'men of I Corps using violence to strip them of their packs. I forced two of them to cough up. They'd taken a straggler's portmanteau. The latter told me what was in it. Making them open it I furiously hit the thieves, who pretended the portmanteau was their property, with the flat of my sword.'

By about 5 or 6 a.m. all of Victor's IX Corps has crossed, except for Fournier's cavalry, now only 200 out of 600 troopers, mostly Baden hussars, who're to bring up its rear. Eblé's been ordered to fire the bridge at 7 a.m. or even earlier, and has already had inflammable materials placed on the bridge's transverse logs, ready to be ignited at the first sign of the Russians approaching. An order he has passed on to Colonel Séruzier,

'to break the bridges and blow them up as soon as Victor's corps and such vehicles as had been preserved should have reached the other side. I was charged to hasten the latters' crossing; and I put all possible firmness and celerity into this mission.'

Eblé pays a last visit to the stragglers huddled or asleep round their bivouac fires. Urges them for the last time to bestir themselves while there's still time. During the night Roman Soltyk too had seen

'staff officers being repeatedly sent to these unfortunates to urge them to cross the bridges at once. But these orders and threats were in vain. No one stirred. Most had fallen into such apathy that they listened indifferently to the words being addressed to them.'

'We knew the Russians were getting close,' Séruzier goes on,

'but I couldn't get the drivers of the baggage, the *cantinières* or the *vivandières* to listen to reason. In vain I told them everyone would be saved if only there was a little order; that their safety depended on crossing at once, and that our troops' salvation would depend on the bridges being broken. Only a few crossed with their light vehicles. The greater number lingered on the left bank.'

Some distance from the other bank Le Roy pauses to bind up his frost-bitten foot in some rags and bits of string:

'Daylight appeared on the horizon. The wind was still very strong; but the snow wasn't falling any longer. A few cannon shots and a fusillade were heard to our left, on the side where the Emperor and his Guard were. I was surprised by the deathly silence reigning on this side of the river.'

The musketry volleys are coming from the Brill Farm Wood, where Tchitchakov's men are tentatively – very tentatively indeed – returning to the attack. 'Seeing the dense line of marauders hastening on up the hillside,' Le Roy, not doubting that the 'rearguard was at grips with the enemy', gets going again.

Now it's past 7 o'clock. And still Eblé hasn't given the order. His tendermindedness is saving many a life. Among others Jomini's. Suffering, like Griois, from bronchial fever, he'd managed yesterday evening to squeeze himself and his two ADCs, Liébart and Fivaz, into one of Studianka's three remaining timber cottages, occupied by Eblé and his staff. And found some straw to sleep on. But now morning – in the shape of a Russian shell[12] – awakens Jomini by setting fire to it. Where's everyone gone? Where's Eblé? Have they abandoned him? Held up under his arms by Fivaz and Liébart, the future great writer on the so-called art of war, too, makes for the bridge. And already the crush has recommenced and when at last Jomini reaches it he's pushed off into the ice-floes. In front of him a cuirassier's riding a *konya*. Gaining sudden strength from some quinine he's been taking, Jomini clambers up on to its rump and seeing some Bavarian infantry crossing, calls out to them – in French – in German – but is ignored by everyone – until an NCO he'd known at Smolensk reaches him down his musket and hoists him up, enabling Liébart to help him over to the opposite bank.

Séruzier's position is becoming anguished. Eblé has waited and waited. Now it's long past 7 a.m. Eight o'clock passes, and still he waits: 'Again the enemy appeared, the danger was growing from minute to minute.' The

first enemy units, even so, are only Cossacks, and they, as usual, are much
more interested in plunder than in forcing the bridges:
'It was then the drivers of the vehicles still on that bank realised what
danger they were in. But it was too late! The carts, carriages and artillery
wagons carrying the wounded got jammed at the bridge's entrance.
Men began cutting their way through at bayonet point. Several men
flung themselves into the water to swim across – and perished. The
enemy, who was saluting us with cannon fire, sent us any amount of
shells and put the finishing touches to the disorder. The jam destroyed
all hope of getting across. A mob of men and women were going to be
sacrificed. But it was certainly their own fault.'
Already Bourgogne, at the bridge's western end, has seen
'numbers jumping into the water, but not one was reaching the shore. I
saw them all in the water up to their shoulders. Overcome by the terrible cold, they were all perishing miserably. On the bridge was a sutler
carrying a child on his head. His wife was in front of him, crying bitterly.
I couldn't stay any longer, it was more than I could bear. Just as I turned
away, a cart containing a wounded officer fell from the bridge, together
with its horse.'
Eblé can no longer put off the fatal moment. Séruzier:
'It was only at the last extremity, i.e., when the Russian guns were harass-
ing me from all sides, that I, with keen regret, decided to carry out General Eblé's order, which was the Emperor's.'
Fuzes and powder trains under the transverse planks are fired. And the
bridge bursts into flames. Bourgogne turns away from the scene of horror
that follows. As the flames leap up a howl goes up from the far bank, the
like of which no one who hears it will ever forget. Even on the Zembin
road, several miles away, Louise Fusil hears
'a scream, a single cry from the multitude. Undefinable, it still resounds
in my ears every time I think of it. All the unfortunates who'd been left
on the other bank were falling, crushed by the Russian army's
grapeshot. Only then did we grasp the extent of the disaster.'
Tragically, ironically, the Berezina – at last, but too late – has begun to
freeze over:
'But the ice not bearing, it broke, swallowing up men, women, horses,
carriages. A beautiful woman, caught between two ice-floes as in a vice,
was seen clutching her child in her arms. A musket butt is held out to
give her something to hang on to. But soon she's swallowed up by the
very movement she's making to grasp it. General Lefèbvre [the Marshal's son], who wasn't exactly tender-minded, was pale as death. Kept
repeating: "Oh, what a dreadful disaster! And those poor people who've
been left there under the enemy's fire."'[13]
To Colonel Séruzier it's
'the most afflicting spectacle anyone could see. The Cossacks flung
themselves on these people who'd been left behind. They pillaged
everything on the opposite bank, where there was a huge quantity of

vehicles laden with immense riches. Those who weren't massacred in this first charge were taken prisoner and whatever they possessed was falling to the Cossacks.'

From somewhere in the vicinity of the Brill Wood, the Polish Captain Turno, no less appalled, sees 'whole ranks of desperate men being pushed onwards by masses of other unfortunates coming on behind', hears 'their piercing screams' ... witnesses

'the terror of those being hit by enemy roundshot ... ammunition wagons and shells exploding in the midst of this shouting, groaning mob. My heart was torn with grief. The Russians, who've crowned the high ground beyond, are sowing terror and death amid the 10,000 sick or wounded soldiers and a multitude of carriages or wagons, most thrown on top of one another and broken.'

Looking back from the high ground towards Zembin, Le Roy sees the guns' smoke as they fire, but – so violent is the whining of the north wind – hears no explosions. Taking refuge in a half-demolished house, he looks out over the 'narrow space of a mile and a half, half of it taken up by the river, and is sure

'a clever painter, had he been at my side at that moment, could have made a beautiful picture! He'd have painted a still-life [*une nature morte*]. Trees laden with hoar frost, snow and icicles. In the foreground the village of Weselovo. In the background, between white-powdered conifers, would be seen perfidious Bashkirs,[14] waiting keenly for a favourable moment to throw themselves on their prey. The river itself would play the chief role and, at a pinch, could represent Acheron, the river of Hades in the fable. The damned on the left bank. The elect on the right.'

Yet the elect, Le Roy muses, are hardly happier than the damned, except insofar as 'the latter have the repose of nothingness, while a large part of the elect would succumb to the same fate'. Even as he drags himself toward Zembin, looking everywhere for Guillaume and Jacquet, no other sound strikes his ear except that terrible howl of despair. And there it'll go on resounding, he says, 'for thirty years; and, I feel, until my natural heat is extinguished'.

CHAPTER 19

TWO PRISONERS

Surgeon Roos seeks another way over – a Cossack – 'we're going to take the bird with the nest' – 'screams, lamentations, tears, supplications made themselves heard' – 'men were praying in all languages' – Beulay is driven like a beast back to Witebsk

Among 'the damned' left on the eastern bank is Heinrich von Roos. Having taken one look at the struggling masses at the bridges and seeing no chance of getting across, he and several others – like Muraldt's group before him – have wandered off upstream. Perhaps, after all, there's another, more practicable ford higher up? The results are fateful. Seeing a group around a campfire, he'd approached them

'with a view to warming myself and drawing up some new plans. They were Polish grenadiers, guarding some bits of rotten butcher's meat. They confirmed for a fact that there was no bridge higher upstream. After resting up a little, we decided to go back to the village, no matter what fate might be waiting for us.'

Emerging from the woods, they come across a flock of soldiers of all arms being driven to the rear by a swarm of Cossacks:

'I was turning off to my left to get back into the wood when a Cossack grabbed the collar of my cape: *"Tu officier?" "Oui!"* No matter how great my terror, I felt truly relieved not to feel his iron pike instantly penetrate my body. As is often the case with prisoners, I, who thought that after coming so far I could courageously and coolly face all the evils that were threatening us, felt very humble. The Cossack, a young beardless man of about 24 years, was pocked with smallpox, yet was neither ugly nor was his face disagreeable. Taking me aside, he made me understand I must empty my pockets and share with him everything I owned.'

It takes Roos a certain amount of time to get at his pocket under cape and overcoat.

'But at length I pulled out a piece of paper containing fourteen ducats, which I handed over to him. He contemplated them with pleasure, pocketed them, and by putting his two fists against his right ear and clucking with his tongue got me to understand he wanted to know whether I had a watch. I shook my head. Without showing any anger, he took the musket that was hanging from his shoulder, cocked it, and aimed it at me. This time both courage and sangfroid deserted me completely. I fell on my knees, and involuntarily, trembling all over, cried out: *"Pardon!"* I don't know whether he understood. Anyway he didn't fire. He uncocked his musket and I got up. He searched me in the region where he'd seen me take out the ducats, found my Leipzig watch, and immediately put it to his ear. Despite the joy he was getting from his catch, he went on looking at me with a threatening air.

'Not content with ducats and my watch, he searched me again and found my decoration, wrapped up in some paper. As yet I'd never worn it, because with us Württembergers decorations are worn on the uniform jacket but not on the greatcoat. Seeing it, he was delighted and seemed to regard me with greater goodwill. From my cartridge pouch he took the thalers which I'd been keeping ever since the battle of Borodino,' [on the eve of which the Württembergers had received arrears of pay], 'together with the silver roubles the Poles had given me at Ljasna. Finally, he took my instrument case. In vain I implored him to give it back. All he left me was my pipe, some scissors, some first-aid things and my powdered coffee. The Cossack was already wearing a Cross of the Legion of Honour on his chest. He immediately added my decoration. Then, without doing me the least harm, he took me to the rear. To our right a serious engagement was going on; and I soon realised I was behind the Russians' battle line. They were assembling prisoners, and among them I recognised a young officer of our Württemberger infantry regiment. I beckoned to him. He came over. I took him by the arm and from then on we never separated. He'd been treated worse than I had. But they'd left him his uniform, his boots, and his trousers, but taken his hat, his cape, and everything he had on him. He told me his name was Schaefer, and he was a clergyman's son. I, in turn, told him my story while we were being put together with another group of prisoners. My young Cossack rejoined his detachment and we were confided to others to be transported.

'We were made to march forward behind the Russian battle line. To our right the cannonade was violent. The road we were following went through a wood. Schaefer wanted to take his own life. He suggested I should buy some brandy, drink ourselves asleep with it, and then lie down in the snow, never to wake up again. I found his project good, but replied that neither of us having any money, nor any other means whatever of getting hold of any brandy, we'd have to try and replace it with water – in our exhausted state, and with the cold getting worse, it would produce the same effect.

'We met many Russian troops belonging above all to the militia, in great greatcoats and round hats ornamented in front with a yellow cross. The men had muskets and black belts and straps. The officers were wearing a green and red uniform, with caps of the same colour. We admired these peasant-like soldiers' thoroughly military order as they marched in closed columns. Many of the French, above all some officers, wanted to complain to the Russian officers of having been despoiled; but the officers they spoke to just went on marching by, and the Cossacks, with blows of the knout, forced back into the ranks anyone who'd left them.

'Still holding on to each other's arms Schaefer and I walked on without anyone doing us any harm. The order was given: "Officers to the front!" We obeyed promptly, and didn't budge again from the place

314

assigned to us. But the French malcontents drew fresh blows on themselves.

'Some women were weeping and lamenting. Either because of our obedience or disciplined spirit, or for some reason to be explained by events still to come, an old Cossack came and offered to let me mount a horse he'd taken from the enemy. I got on to it, and the Cossack led me by the bridle. Schaefer had the same good luck.

'However, my Cossack who, despite his grey hairs and beard, looked every inch a military man, wanted to get into conversation with me. To everything he said I replied yes or no, in German, accompanying this word with a gesture of approval or negation. I think I got the sense of some of the words he was addressing to me: "Isn't it true the Cossacks are a decent lot?" He proffered me his water-bottle of brandy. He'd already given me some bread, and later he even gave me some sugar.'

But there's a reason for such generosity:

'He thought I had some money in my black silk cravat. Twice he probed my neck, and ended by appropriating it. He also exchanged his crude cape for mine, which was more refined. He'd also taken a great liking to my velvet-lined boots, and made me understand he'd give me his own in exchange. But things went no farther.

'However, we'd reached a village where there were already a lot of prisoners. Some Russian troops were drawn up in lines. To our right the musketry and cannonade was still going on. There was a Russian officer on horseback there who seemed to me to be of German origin. I asked him where this road led to. "To Borissow!" After an exchange of questions and answers, he said to me: "Probably this war will end today. We're going to take the bird with the nest."'

'It was getting colder. It was snowing. Soon the snow was coming down in whirlwinds. Then night fell. Schaefer, without hat, without gloves and without cape, felt so cold that he dismounted. He preferred to walk. Gradually our Cossack detachment dwindled. My old Cossack, in his turn, pushed off, and I had to start walking again.

'We'd passed through some woods where, here and there, some abandoned fires were still alight. The road wasn't clear, the cold was atrocious, and a violent wind was blowing. The snow got thicker and thicker. Enfeebled and starving as I was – I hadn't eaten anything all day except what the second Cossack had offered me – worried about the future and without any money, I felt utterly demoralised and thought I was going to die.

'In the distance, on some high ground, we saw an enormous conflagration. We supposed it must be Borissow on fire. It was late at night when we got there. We'd reached the goal of our day's march and were going to be able to rest, but were asking ourselves what fate was reserved for us.

'For a long while they marched us through the streets until the Cossacks had found the man who was to take command. Finally, we halted in front of a little house. One of our guides went inside, another stayed outside the door as sentinel, and the others surrounded the group of prisoners, which might well have totalled three to four hundred men. Some French officers wanted to enter the house, but were forced back into the ranks by blows of the knout.

'After an hour's wait we were directed towards a row of houses that were on fire. At once the rumour went round that we were going to be thrown into the flames. Immediately screams, lamentations, tears, supplications made themselves heard. The women were particularly vehement. "If we're to die by fire, let God's will be accomplished," I told myself, joining my fate to that of my companions.

'Utterly exhausted, shivering with fear and the cold, we were being guarded by some infantry from the Tobolsk Regiment. We lay down on some ground the fire had dried out. At first our guards, wanting to appropriate whatever the Cossacks might have left us, prevented us from going to sleep. Those men who still had their packs were obliged to hand them over; if they didn't they were crudely reprimanded. I noticed that these packs, after a hasty examination, were often being handed back to their owners. One of the Cossacks came up to me: *"Tu Capitan?"* "Yes," I replied. But even if I'd answered No, it wouldn't have helped. This time I was stripped of everything the Cossacks had left on me, though – I must say – without their using any brutality.

'The loss of my pipe caused me as much pain as the loss of my instrument case. I'd bought it at Vienna, after the battle of Wagram. It was decorated with an image of Emma of Falkenstein at the moment when she pours oil on the wounds of her knight, who's taken refuge in the cloister, where they've recognised each other by their rings.

'Separated from everyone I loved and belonged to, stripped of everything that could have been any use to me, alone amidst thousands of unknown people, I, like them, felt poor, poverty-stricken, and deeply unhappy. All round us the silence was profound. And for the first time in my life I heard soldiers praying. There was so little space, we were lying on top of one another, in an inexpressible confusion. A Pole was stretched out on my legs, I had an Italian to my right, a Spaniard or a Portuguese to my left, and my head was resting on a Frenchman. Men were groaning and praying in all languages. Catholics from all countries were saying the *Ave Maria*. Certain passages from Gellert's *Canticles* came to my mind and brought me some consolation. Finally I fell asleep.'

But after only two hours von Roos wakes up again. From among the sleeping prisoners he seeks out four chasseurs of his Württemberg regiment. He also sees men of Partonneaux's division 'who'd been allowed to keep their baggage and packs'.

Among them is Lieutenant Beulay: 'So it's been to end up like this,' he's thinking to himself,

'we left France, crossed Europe and, for several months now have been putting so much energy into fighting a conspiracy of men and the elements! We were prisoners of people we'd ruined, exasperated ...'

He wonders why Partonneaux's officers have been singled out and brought into town, the men having been abandoned out in the fields. Why this apparent favour?

'They parked us in the heart of the town, like a vile herd of cattle inside a big hovel whose roof and all doors and windows had been devoured by fire. Between these four walls, because of the draughts, it was colder than out in the countryside, and we didn't even have the recourse, left to our men, of cutting themselves beefsteaks from dead horses.'

Towards dawn several NCOs, who've managed to join them, are horrified to find their superiors in such abject misery. Discovered, they're sent back, escape, are recaptured and slaughtered. For five days Partonneaux's officers won't be given a mouthful of food. Then a tender-minded sentry lets Roos slip out to buy himself a bottle of brandy and some biscuit. 'All down the street Russians wearing the most varied uniforms were walking about.' Some hit him with the flats of their swords. But he gets what he's looking for. Others follow his example. They've just finished their 'feast' when

'in a temperature of -33°, with the north wind cutting our faces and our moustaches bristling with icicles, a Frenchman, completely naked, presents himself at our door. He claimed to be an adjutant-major. For a lark some Russians who'd been drinking had burnt down the hospital where he'd been left, stripped its patients to their shirts and thrown them, dressed like Adam, into the street. He begged us to give him something to put on against the cold. In vain. We ourselves were shivering under our threadbare clothes with holes everywhere! To rid ourselves of his useless tears and supplications we put him out of the door. After ten minutes his complaints had ceased. Death had put an end to his misery. So exasperated by suffering were we that none of us, alas, felt any remorse at this abominable behaviour, nor did it in the least degree trouble our digestion.'

On the fifth day, 'at 4 p.m.' the Cossacks come and haul them out of their prison, where the French and their allied prisoners are leaving behind so many dead comrades it's more like a cemetery. Then they're driven on by blows of the Cossacks' *nagaïkas* (leather knouts) along an icy road through the freezing night – 'we'd never known such cold'. When the whips don't suffice

'the Cossacks took their lances, as if they had to do with cattle. But at the end of a few hours neither whip nor lance availed. Many of us, exhausted by cold and fatigue let ourselves drop and were crushed under the escort's horseshoes.'

Beulay only survives by staying in the thick of the column and taking tiny sips of his brandy.[1]

Surgeon Roos has been much luckier. Typhus is raging at Borissow and after some days he's allowed to report for medical service. Wittgenstein isn't accepting any French medicos – only Germans. Roos, taken on in that capacity, sees 300 women and girl prisoners shut up together in a freezing cold storehouse for their protection. Perhaps some of Louise Fusil's fellow-actresses are among them? Not all of them have managed to get across – Langeron and Rochechouart have 'captured actresses of a troop of the *Comédie Française*' meaning certainly the Moscow troupe. 'Also Italian singers belonging to Murat's musicians.'

PHASE FOUR
BEYOND THE BEREZINA

CHAPTER 20

CORTEGE THROUGH THE SNOWS

The Zembin bridges – 'a single bale of straw and a spark from a Cossack's pipe...' –
Victor reprimanded – where's Guillaume? – plight of the women – Ney's hard-heart-
edness – Oudinot's private battle – 'Good-bye, my friends, you must march as far as
you can' – Shedding the prisoners – Bausset's gouty leg at 'Miserowo' – Marbot
fights the Cossacks – the Poles feel at home – IHQ no longer recognisable

From the Berezina to Vilna is 54 leagues, to the Niemen, 80. Which is a
long way still to go.

Tchitchakov, repulsed by Ney, had quite simply given up. And in the
evening of the 28th Fain and the rest of IHQ had moved from the Zaniwki
hamlet,

'almost completely destroyed during the day. In the evening we only
found three barns standing, of which two were occupied by the Emperor
and his household, the third by the King of Naples and Prince of
Neuchâtel's officers.'

But now a new day's dawning. It's 29 November:

'We left the banks of the Berezina, pushing in front of us the crowd of
disbanded men and those marching with Victor's already disorganised
corps.'

For disorganised it is:

'Yesterday evening, together with II Corps and Dombrowski's division, it
had still presented 14,000 men. But already, except for some 6,000, the
rest no longer had the shape of a division, brigade or regiment.'

Evidently Victor feels he's done enough. Half his men have been left
behind, dead or wounded. A brigade of light cavalry which Napoleon has
demanded and been duly sent on ahead to IHQ, 'consists only of 60 troopers'. Yet all the thanks he gets for his resolute stand (Deniée is shocked to
hear) is a severe reprimand for not having attacked Wittgenstein at
Tschereia and so perhaps have made

'the fateful crossing unnecessary. It had reduced our reserve corps to
the same state as those which had gone all the way to Moscow. Hardly
had the march been opened than Victor declared he could no longer
form the rearguard. He even tried to pass on ahead and leave III Corps
exposed to the Russian vanguard's attacks. This led to a rather brisk
exchange of words between him and Marshal Ney.'

Both marshals appeal to Napoleon, who tells Victor to do his duty. But the
demoralisation's already beginning to spread to

'these fine troops, who're beginning to feel the effects of our propinquity. The unlucky carry misfortune with them! Only a few regiments of
German cavalry preserved the most exact discipline, at least as far as
such a thing was possible at this fatal moment when all subordination
was extinct, even among officers.'

The army may have won a tactical victory, but not much of it is effectively left. It's being seen off by all three Russian armies: Tchitchakov's, as advance guard, following along the same main road. By Kutusov, somewhere on its left. And, by Wittgenstein marching parallel to its right. Both at Chotaviski and Molodeczno, Fezensac will hear, the rearguard, Victor's IX Corps, is energetically attacked and completely routed. Riding on with Murat's staff, Rossetti sees Victor's men

'amid the mass of disbanded men who'd come from Moscow. There were still 60,000 men, but without any cohesion. All were marching pell-mell, cavalry, infantrymen, French, Germans, Italians. There was no longer either wing or centre; the artillery and the vehicles rolled on through this confused mass, their only orders being to get on as well as possible.'

Long before dawn Le Roy has woken up under six inches of snow, but found himself 'sound in mind and body'. Just as he's searching about him for his Bibiche – he finds her nibbling at some fruit trees – someone seizes his arm. What joy! It's Jacquet. Immediately Colonel Piat of the 85th invites them 'to share their soup *en famille.*' Then, at 4 a.m., the remains of I Corps – according to Captain François' probably exaggerated estimate, 8,700 men – 'led by the Duke of Eckmühl in person, had set off via the village of Zawitchin to march for the little Jewish town of Kamen' via Zembin. The Swiss have left the battlefield with particularly heavy hearts:

'We took our farewells of the poor friends from the homeland who had to be left behind by the fires, awaiting their fate. We got under arms without tap of drum, the enemy was too close. Nor had we noticed the Russians taking any of us prisoner.'

Marc-Bussy's Major Weltner, his thigh carried away by a roundshot, had been carried to

'a little house close to the Berezina. At all costs he'd wanted to leave with us. So we, six voltigeurs, are sent to look for him. He wants to get on horseback. Impossible to remain in the saddle with the newly operated stump of a thigh half a foot long! So he has to stay where he is. A trumpeter of our company was also left on the battlefield.'

'So here we are on the road,' voltigeur Bussy goes on,

'in a tightly closed up column. It'll make a very small square, all that's left of our two [3rd and 4th] regiments. We daren't speak to each other, for fear of hearing of our comrades' deaths. Yesterday morning we were 87 voltigeurs in the company. This morning we only find seven safe and sound! And everywhere it's the same tale, more or less.'

With IX Corps, II Corps is making up the rearguard, Castex and Corbineau's light cavalry brigades bringing up the extreme rear.

But where's Guillaume? Is he one of the 'damned', Le Roy's wondering – pillaged, stripped, being driven along stark naked, with a Cossack lance at the small of his back or even killed by those 'archers of death' the Bashkirs? That his Guillaume, so young, so lithe and vigorous, hasn't got across the river somehow is more than he can believe. So great is his faith in him, he keeps turning round to try and make out

'the ugly face of this poor fellow I was sending to all the devils each time my hopes were disappointed. In the fierce cold wind we didn't *march* to Zawitchin; we ran, without halting. My foot was painful, my hand cured – by rubbing it with snow.'

'The Borissow–Molodeczno road via Zembin', Lejeune knows,

'was the only one we could hope to take. A very narrow paved road, it was raised above the water, and at every step cut by little bridges to allow the waters of the immense marsh it crosses to flow away. These little bridges are thrown at quarter-hour intervals across broad and deep streams with muddy banks; and the Cossacks would only have had to break one of them, to bring the entire army to a halt.'

How is it possible they haven't? 'The army,' Rossetti goes on,

'crossed over three consecutive bridges 300 fathoms long with an astonishment mingled with terror. A spark from a Cossack's pipe would have sufficed to ignite them. And from that moment all our efforts, our passage of the Berezina, would have been in vain. Cooped up without food, without shelter, between these swamps and the river, in the midst of an insupportable hurricane, the Grand Army and its Emperor would have been forced to surrender.'

One of the longest of the '30 or 40 little wooden bridges' is more than ¾ of a mile long. Caulaincourt, crossing it with IHQ and Napoleon, has the same thought: 'A match set to a bundle of straw would have been enough to cut off our retreat.' 'If the Russians had been in our position and we in theirs,' Boulart reflects grimly, trundling his guns and ammunition wagons along the Zembin causeway, 'not a Russian would have escaped.' Nor, if Junot had had his way, would a single Frenchman or ally, nor even the Emperor himself. Having himself crossed this long bridge yesterday with his advance guard of 800 Westphalians – so Intendant Pastoret's shocked to hear – Junot had ordered the bridges

'to be burnt. Grouchy had been sent to prevent him. The Duke of Abrantès had replied coldly that it'd be safer for himself that way, and he didn't give a damn for anything else. M. de Grouchy insists, and while they're discussing the matter the first men of the fighting corps arrive; and at the Emperor's approach the Duke of Abrantès gives way. One trembles to think of the horrible disaster such an action would have caused. It'd have been all up with us. Not one of us would have seen France again!'

That the Cossacks haven't set fire to what Dumonceau calls this 'long dike across swamps covered with a vast forest of conifers' seems miraculous.

Somewhere towards the rear of this Dantesque procession across the swamps ,the Grand Army's official historian[1] is struggling along. That morning Jomini, all his precious campaign notes lost in the Berezina's waters, has woken, coughing and spitting blood, in one of the three remaining Zaniwki huts to find himself alone. Once again he's been abandoned. Evidently even his ADC Liébart has given him up for dead. Luckily, just then, Victor's chief-of-staff General Château had come in. After sharing some *pâté de foie gras* with him and washing it down with a bottle of Bordeaux, Château had placed him in Victor's carriage. For a while this had been fairly comfortable. But upon its being threatened by Cossacks, Jomini's had to bundle out again into the icy north wind, trusting to his Astrakhan fur – soaked in the Berezina but dried out at Berthier's campfire – to serve him as a cuirass against it. After a while, again, he drags himself over and seats himself on one of the rearguard's gun-carriages, jolting on along the log causeway. But then the gun has to be placed in battery, and he has to move over to an ammunition wagon's canvas cover. But the cold's getting worse and worse and, in the end he has to get down and walk. Jomini's by no means the only invalid in the throng. Wracked by coughing but supported by Sergeant-Major Vogel (someone's just stolen their horse), Franz Roeder too is stumbling along the Zembin causeway:

'I can hardly walk for the pain in my right lung. Found a wretched pony by the roadside. Was lifted on to it and so rode on for about an hour and a half on the beast's jagged back. My sergeant-major is making himself of indescribable service to me. Am I going to get as far as Vilna?'

Le Roy and Jacquet, meanwhile, have soon found Colonel Piat's and his entourage's company disagreeable and pushed on by themselves:

'For vigorous individuals the weather was supportable. As we marched we talked of the perils and privations that had overwhelmed us. We were sure we'd be finding food and reinforcements at Vilna that would enable us to resume the offensive.'

Then, halfway to Zawitchin, Le Roy feels a clap on his shoulder. And there he is – his Guillaume, but without the pony. He'd lost her at the bridgehead. When Fournier's rearguard cavalry had come slashing their way through the crowd he'd waited for a gap to arise between it and Victor's slower moving artillery horses, and slipped in between. What's more important, Guillaume has a bottle of wine and a little rice and biscuit: 'I knew you'd be needing them,' he says. So delighted is the once so portly Le Roy, he tells him to his face, in front of Jacquet:

'"Since you've been with me I've never had the least reason to complain of you."'

The bottle, opened with his penknife's corkscrew, is found to contain excellent Madeira.

The Zembin causeway is 6½ miles long. So narrow and so crowded are its bridges and everything's going so slowly that some impatient individuals are trying to outflank them and are getting stuck in the marshes. General Preyssing, von Muraldt's former brigade commander, is one of them. Heedless of his subordinates' warnings, Preyssing leaves the causeway – and both horse and rider sink into the swamp. Unable to extricate him in the biting cold, everyone passes on, leaving him to his fate. But 'Old Thunderer' Sorbier, commander of the Guard Artillery, resorts to a more effective way of getting ahead. Although he has managed to get most of his artillery across the Berezina, he's had to leave his own effects on its left bank:

'Whereupon he'd taken out his handsomest uniform, with gold lace on its every seam, and donned it. Trotting along on a little Polish horse, without overcoat or fur, but armed with a long rod with which he pushed aside the stragglers, he kept shouting "Out of the way! Out of the way!". And everyone mechanically stood aside! In this way he got as far along the road in two hours as was taking us all day.'

In similar vein, Berthier's ADC Bonneval finds himself walking along beside Marshal Lefèbvre:

'Like all the rest of us he was on foot, a long stick in his hand, and we were pushing on side by side. Arriving at a bridge encumbered with baggage and troops that were making it virtually impossible to pass, the Marshal sees a huge figure of a man, 6 feet tall, in front of him, wearing a cuirassier's cloak,'

– the very man, perhaps, who'd involuntarily been of such help to von Suckow on the Berezina bridge? But no – 'Administering two or three blows of his stick on his back, Lefèbvre shouts in his German accent: "Co on, zen, co on, vot ze tevil, you're in my vay!" The other man turns quickly.' And who should it be if not his fellow-Marshal Mortier!

'"Ah! my gomrade," Lefèbvre says, confused, "if I't known it vos you, I vouldn't have hit zo hart!"'

Pausing after the first of these bottle-necks to rally his few men, Fezensac is shocked to see

'officers of all ranks, soldiers, servants, a few troopers scarcely able to drag their horses along, wounded and cripples mutually supporting one another, all pell-mell. Each was telling of the miraculous way in which he'd escaped the Berezina disaster and congratulating himself on having saved his own life by abandoning everything he'd possessed.'

Even more pitiable, as usual, is the women's plight. One wife is walking along beside her husband, an Italian officer who, carried by two soldiers, is obviously breathing his last:

'Acutely touched by this woman's trouble and the care she was lavishing on her husband, I gave her my place by a fire we'd lit. She needed every illusion bred of tender feeling not to perceive how futile her cares were. Her husband was no longer alive, but she went on calling to him up to the moment when, no longer able to doubt her misfortune, she fainted across his corpse.'

Corbineau, Castex and Séruzier aren't being guilty of the same oversight as the Cossacks. Curély – his inept and ailing Colonel Lagrange has found himself a sledge and has handed over to him – is making sure the 20th Chasseurs burn each little bridge as they leave it behind. Useless, says Marbot:

'The burning of these bridges served no purpose at all. The rigorous cold which, at this time of year, so easily could have turned the Berezina into a highway, had come down and frozen the waters hard enough to support cannon!'

At the bridge over the Goina stream Dumonceau's men are overtaken by the Sacred Squadron, 'assembled under the pretext of guarding IHQ, but in reality to provide a refuge for isolated officers, 200 to 300 cavalry officers under General Grouchy's orders'. Among them Dumonceau espies three old comrades. One, Sloet by name,

'officer of the 11th Hussars, was walking alone at the foot of the dike among the trees, in a state of complete marasma, foaming at the mouth. A mere shadow, he was carrying a phial of I don't know what elixir with which he kept trying to revive himself.'

Dumonceau gives him a piece of biscuit, is thanked profusely – and never sees him again.

Zembin, where Napoleon is meaning to spend the night, is reached by IHQ at about 10 a.m., and turns out to be a village swarming with people. After breakfasting 'in the neighbourhood of the Russian prisoners' he changes his mind and goes on to Kamen. IV Corps, escorting the Treasure, has been at Zembin since yesterday evening. Only after nightfall does Griois get this far and find

'an agitated multitude moving in all directions. The bivouac fires touched one another and were being fed by the village's houses, almost all of which had been demolished.'

But he's lucky. Falling in with one of his group who've already been there a long time, having probably arrived with Eugène's staff last night, he lets them take him to a still intact cabin. 'I was received like a friend everyone had thought was lost. They embraced me, tears in their eyes.' Griois' group of officers even accept his RSM – who'd saved his life – as one of themselves. Everyone's been telling everyone else of how he got through across the Berezina:

'On a spontaneous impulse we were embracing those who'd come back and whom we'd never expected to see again. We congratulated each other in the most natural way on having escaped from a day more terrible to us than the bloodiest battle.'

Bourgogne, who can only be kept from falling asleep by kicks to his behind from an officer named Favin, who also pulls him by the hair, sees

'many whom we thought had perished coming on from the Berezina. They were embracing and congratulating one another as if it were the Rhine they'd crossed, still 400 leagues away.'

On the other hand, Griois is astounded to find he's been robbed en route:

'When I, on getting there, wanted to take the bread and tea I'd bought yesterday out of my saddlebags, I found there was nothing in them. To empty them someone had cut them open from end to end, even while I'd been on horseback, under my eyes, without my seeing it.'

All he now owns is a little portmanteau 'which I lost soon afterwards'. There's the usual struggle for lodgings. Some infantrymen who try to demolish their cabin for firewood and smash its doors are supplanted by some grenadiers who declare it's needed by General Friederichs' staff. Griois' group, 'though numerous' offer to accommodate them 'even if we should suffocate'. In vain. The pitiless Friederichs chucks out the first comers and even orders his grenadiers to put a wounded officer out of the house 'despite his groans and our remonstrations. Doubtless the night and the cold put an end to his sufferings.'

The plight of the women is really piteous. Most, like Louise Fusil, have got here last night. Among them is the beautiful blonde wife of the French librarian in Moscow 'whom Rostopchin had taken away to send to Siberia'. She's in despair. One after another the generals' carriages she's been travelling in have broken down and since the Berezina she's been walking on foot and had to carry her child in her arms. Wrapping them in a wolf skin and several lengths of silk, Lejeune seats her on one of his horses.[2] Kergorre, too, sees

'some beautiful women who'd all the while been under Marshal Mortier's protection. They were in rags. These ladies' situation gives some idea of the state of those women who hadn't had the same advantage.'

And in a carriage with Grimblant (the gendarme who'd dissuaded him from returning to Moscow after Winkovo) Mailly-Nesle again sees some ladies who've come all this way in their white silk slippers. 'Almost unrecognisable, swathed in chiffons scorched by campfires, wholly smoke-blackened', they dine with him and give him

'some pink taffeta used for making cravats and handkerchiefs. Mlle Eléonore's elegant turnout existed only in memory. Clad in hitched up strips of clothing, they had the air of gypsies fallen on evil times.'

Many of the Berezina survivors, perhaps most, are mourning some friend. But only now does Fezensac hear of the death of Alfred de Noailles, his personal friend and former colleague on Berthier's staff:

'Up to that moment I hadn't lost any of my friends, and a sharp pang of grief went through me. But all the consolation Marshal Ney gave me when I spoke to him of it was to say: "Obviously it was his turn, and when all's said and done it's better we're mourning him than for him to be mourning us."'

In such circumstances, Fezensac adds, Ney

'always showed the same lack of feeling. Another time I heard him reply to a poor wounded man who asked him to have him carried: "What d'you expect me to do about it? You're a victim of war." Certainly it wasn't because he was ill-natured or cruel; but he'd become so habituated to the evils of warfare that they'd bitten into his heart. Obsessed with the notion that all military men ought to die on the battlefield, he found nothing simpler than that they should fulfil their destiny. He made no greater case of his own life than he did of others, as we've seen.'

All in sharp contrast to Berthier, whose self-pity when verbally flagellated by his endlessly exacting taskmaster also extends to his fellows, whatever their rank. Dumonceau's just seen him

'giving a bit of sugar to a poor dismounted cuirassier who, dying of hunger, was begging for charity as he dragged himself painfully along the road'.

Here at Zembin Jomini's sharing 'his last 20 peas' with Prince Eugène's chief-of-staff Guilleminot. Always someone's in luck. Tonight it's Gourgaud, whose sole but obsessive extra-military ambition is to get married. Although he has cast his somewhat protruding eyes on the 'neither young nor beautiful' daughter of Senator Roederer, the father, so far hasn't accepted him, he being merely the son of a violinist at the *ci-devant* Versailles court. But who's this, if not Roederer's eldest son? The poor fellow's in an utterly lamentable state. A musket ball has 'passed through his lips, removing his teeth down to the very gums'. Gourgaud takes him to Dr Yvan, who attends to his mouth. And thereafter the *premier officier d'ordonnance* doesn't let this prospective brother-in-law out of his sight.[3]

But Lieutenant Tascher, happy to have come across his wounded brother again, is noticing an odd fact. Coffins, at Zembin, are nothing but 'a bit of wood between two stones'.

The Treasure too has crossed the Berezina and its 'eight or nine vehicles, containing four millions in gold' are lumbering and slithering along the 'sheet of ice' which is the Kamen road. In the evening Berthier writes to tell Davout it's got there; but since IV Corps, now the army's advance guard, is having to keep the road clear of Cossacks, it's Davout who's to 'take the Treasure under your protection. Send one of your staff officers to the Viceroy to reconnoitre or park the Treasure.'

Far from lucky are the 2,000 or so Russian prisoners. No one's maltreating them. But no one has anything to give them either. During this cruelly cold night of 29/30 November Sergeant Bertrand and the 7th Light, around their fires which, 'lit on the snow, sink into the sand and are as it were at the bottom of a well', have to guard some:

'At about midnight the cold increases. Our prisoners either die or escape, we're too few to look after them.[4] The sky, sombre until now, clears, and the icy north wind begins whining. At the bottom of our holes it whips up particles of burning sand which fly at our eyes like silver spangles. By morning many of us had gone blind. Those who'd been spared by the burning sand lead those comrades who couldn't see. For my part, being only slightly affected, I was leading an adjutant-major, M. Rougeaut.'[5]

Kamen, 'four to five leagues further on', where Napoleon had first heard the sound of the guns en route for Witebsk in July, is 'a village of 50 timber houses in a continuous forest'. After passing through 'defiles, conifer forests, very narrow country roads', IHQ after doing 'altogether seven leagues in one day' has reached it at 5 p.m. on 29 November. Lodged 'in a baron's château', Castellane notes in his diary,

'we've found some potatoes; it's an event. You should see us in the Emperor's courtyard, all with potatoes on the tips of our sabres. We've eaten our fill. I'm to sleep in a sort of room on good straw. It's not a beautiful spot, but to be under a roof means a great deal; one night, at least, not spent under the bare sky!'

There, around their campfires in the courtyard, the staff officers are hearing the details of how Partonneaux's division, '4,000 infantry and a light cavalry brigade strong', had gone astray:

'The 29th Light Infantry, a handsome regiment made up of officers and veterans recently returned from English prisons, was part of it. These unfortunates, it must be admitted, are toying with misfortune. A fair number of them had been in the San Domingo expedition. Only one battalion of the 55th, the last left at Borissow, arrived,'
an item of information doubtless contributed by Gourgaud, who'd run into the 55th on the Borissow road. Is he too roasting a potato on the tip of his sabre?

Oudinot had left the battlefield early on the morning of the 29th, well ahead of IHQ 'so as to avoid the scrum'. Despite his pains from the unextractable musket ball in the small of his back 'which had grown worse with the inflammation and fever', he'd been placed in his carriage and, escorted by his ADCs, some military police and a troop of Horse Chasseurs commanded by his son Victor, had gone on ahead. 'Toward 1 p.m. we'd reached Pleschenkowiczi', a village of 30 timber houses. 'His officers suggested he lodge in a château we could see a musket shot off to our left', where, as it happens, the insouciant Mailly-Nesle, after admiring the timber manor house's charming French-style garden, has just passed a pleasant evening listening to one of Gourgaud's subordinates 'singing very well and very gaily'. Evidently the imperial household, too, has come on from Kamen, for

'the bread they were baking *chez l'Empereur* was of rye, hardly ground up at all and very poorly leavened. It tasted of mildew. Although I was almost dying of hunger I could hardly bring myself to eat it. It was also said to cause dysentery.'

But Oudinot's unwilling to leave the road, and one of his aides, M. de la Chaise, goes into the village where he chooses a Jew's house instead. The wounded Marshal's anxiety turns out to be justified.

For things have been happening at Pleschenkowiczi.

Only yesterday the Russian General Lanskoi had fallen on it and captured the Polish General Kaminski. He'd also attacked its château and captured some of the *fourriers* [quartermaster sous-lieutenants] who'd come on ahead to prepare 'the Palace'. No sooner has Oudinot been installed in the Jew's house and his wound attended to by Dr Capiomont and he's trying to get some rest, than his son Victor rushes in. '"My dear father," he cries. "We must accept it! We're all prisoners!" "What!" Oudinot replies, in a terrible voice, forgetting the state he's in. "Get the hell out of here and fight!"' At 10 a.m., so Lejeune'll hear afterwards,

'a Cossack officer had come with 200 men to surround the house where Oudinot and Pino were with 25 or 30 officers or soldiers of their suite and addressing them in good French had summoned them to surrender.'

Pils, of course, is there:

'Through the windows we saw some Cossack lances. The Duke of Reggio, who was only wearing a simple pelisse, sat up and said to me: "Hand me my great ribbon [of the *Légion d'honneur*]. At least if they take me alive they'll see who it is they have to do with."'

After putting his pistols and a hunting gun beside him, Pils, like everyone else, rushes out to the horses. 'Hastily I bridle one, grab up a sabre and bring it to him, leaving its sheath behind. Meanwhile M. Jacqueminot [still clad no doubt in his 'magnificent uniform'] has run out into the square, shouting in a loud voice: "Everyone rally around me!"'

'Quickly a troop was formed up and fell on the Cossacks with its sabres, who fled away down all the streets that abutted on the square, charging and pursuing them until they were out of the village. The greater part of their regiment took refuge in the château we'd seen on the left of the road, where they captured several of the Emperor's carriages which, commanded by an officer of the Horse Grenadiers, were just then arriving.'

Other Cossacks are still glimpsed roving about. And after placing scouts around Pleschenkowiczi in case they should come back, M. Le Tellier and Colonel Jacqueminot come and fetch Oudinot, lift him into the saddle, and take him

'to a house at the end of the village, already occupied by the Italian General Pino and able to sustain a siege. All the mounted men surrounded this fortress and those who were on foot went inside. A big fire was lit in the courtyard to pass the night while awaiting an attack.'

According to Cesare de Laugier, who'll soon be somewhere in the vicinity, the house has a gate barred by a timber grill and is 'guarded by some carabiniers of the 3rd Italian Regiment, commanded by a Lieutenant Catilini.' Besides Pino, Oudinot's companions include General Anthouard (IV Corps' former artillery commander whom Griois had replaced after he'd been wounded just before the Wop crossing), General Fontana and various other Italian officers who've just installed themselves in the house. – 'But the Russians,' Pils goes on faithfully in his *Journal de Marche,*

'probably thought we were far more numerous than we really were, and began attacking us with their cannon. A roundshot, passing through the roof, broke a truss, a splinter of which hit *M. le Maréchal* and knocked him over backwards. Surgeon Capiomont, who was at his side, was immediately able to dress this new wound, which had no serious consequences. Two Russian guns were firing grape at the six horses harnessed to the Marshal's carriage. The two shaft horses were killed by the same fragment.'

Afterwards Lejeune will hear how,

'between salvoes the Marshal himself, though suffering greatly and lying on his mattress, fired his pistols at the Cossacks through two or three little openings, and didn't miss. Already four roundshot had made holes but not wounded anyone. In the Spaniards' fashion our officers immediately used these holes to aim at the enemy. A fifth roundshot came and smashed the pallet where the Marshal was lying and at the same time shattered the wall of an oven where five or six little children of the Russian peasant whose dwelling it was had hidden themselves. Terrified to death, these little mites scattered through the room amidst all the smoke and the combatants, who were greatly surprised to see them there.'

After a considerable affray, during which Cossack 'hurrahs' are repeatedly repulsed by volleys of well-aimed musketry, the assailants,

'charged by our mounted men, are driven back on their units. In one of these pursuits a Chasseur of the Guard even managed to capture a Cossack he'd just wounded with a pistol shot and brought him back to us.'

But help is at hand:

'Finally, at about 4 p.m., we saw on the horizon a line which seemed to grow as it came closer. Accompanied by a trumpeter, Captain Delamarre galloped off in that direction.'

It's some of General Hammerstein's Westphalian cavalry, from VIII Corps.[6] 'Soon the Duke of Abrantès arrived and the Marshal embraced him as his liberator.' It's the only useful thing Junot has done throughout the campaign. The two corps commanders go back to the Jew's house, where they spend 'almost the whole night talking together'. Interrogated by an officer of the 7th Polish Lancers who's serving as Oudinot's interpreter, the captured Cossack tells them how after Lanskoi had ordered his regiment to capture 'a wounded general', they'd been expecting some Russian infantry to come up in support and seize Pleschenkowiczi during the night.

Now other units are beginning to arrive at Pleschenkowiczi, and several circumstantial accounts of Oudinot's private battle immediately begin to circulate. 'Having hastened our steps at the sound of the gunfire' Lejeune gets there with I Corps: 'The Cossacks, with some 50 wounded and a few dead, not daring to continue, fled at our approach. What a good thing we'd turned up.'[7] Also reaching Pleschenkowiczi in the evening, von Muraldt's little group of Bavarian chevauléger officers spend the night in the very same cabin where Oudinot had fought his private battle. 'An infantryman showed us the wretched bed from which the Marshal had led its defence and where he'd been wounded' by the splintering roof truss.

As Delaborde's group approaches the village, Paul de Bourgoing sees coming towards him – in the wrong direction – 'an officer on a handsome horse, followed by a trooper leading another.' Who can it be, if not his own brother, an officer in the no longer extant 4th Chasseurs! Hearing of Oudinot's plight, he'd decided to retrace his steps, bought a horse off Jacqueminot and is going to offer him his services. Not half an hour ago he's met Napoleon, 'accompanied by Berthier, Sébastiani, Grouchy and several other generals', complaining bitterly about Partonneaux's surrender and

'reflecting how easy it would have been, but for this, to have made the crossing of the Berezina one of the finest and most glorious military operations ever undertaken – rumours were current that Partonneaux hadn't been with his troops, but had been marching by himself.'[8]

Napoleon had called him over and asked him:

'Where are you off to like this?'

Asked for details of Oudinot's condition, he'd told the Emperor all about the Marshal's fight. And Napoleon had exclaimed 'with emotion':

'"Brave Oudinot! Brave Oudinot! Always the same!"'
And to his informant:
'"At least you aren't losing courage."'
Then the Bourgoing brothers part, each in his own direction.
But here's a surprise. When IHQ stays in the 'rather pretty château Oudinot hadn't dared to occupy, someone comes across 'Baraguay d'Hilliers' portfolio and uniforms' in one of its attics. Sick and disgraced and en route for France after his court-martial at Smolensk, he has felt he'll never again be needing either.[9]

That Sunday evening Le Roy gets there too and lodges together with several other of the 85th's officers

'in a house occupied by its proprietor, a German national, who received us in Austrian fashion, with plenty of bowings and scrapings. That was all we could get out of Baron de Rudorf, a big talker and in supreme degree a braggart. We'd have been only too happy to listen to him if a starving stomach hadn't had first call on our ears. All these fine promises turned into some potatoes and a half-firkin of fermenting red beetroot juice, of the kind used for colouring vodka.'

One officer gets the crimson liquid all over his nose and moustaches. The juice is also a powerful laxative, and will act as such for several days. 'Eight days later Captain Mabou, our newsmonger [*fureteur*], died of it, victim of his own greed.' Kergorre, for his part, spends the night in just such a house as Oudinot's 'fortress':

'We were very snug. However the great numbers of mice which kept scurrying over our faces all night were a nuisance, though I'd taken the precaution of covering mine with a handkerchief.'

At 2 a.m. Berthier again writes to Davout. The halt for the Treasure and the prisoners on 1 December is to be at Stagenki 'if you find nothing inconvenient about doing so and the day's march isn't excessive'. He asks for an officer to be sent to him to say where in fact Davout will be stopping. At 6 p.m. he writes again, from Staïki, exhorting Davout to leave next morning 'at 6 a.m. precisely with your army corps and your prisoners' and to follow Junot, who's following Eugène. There's to be about a league's interval between the corps. The order to 'march closed up and in good order' is again reiterated. 'His Majesty will try to go and spend the night at Selitchi, which is about half-way between Iliya and Molodeczno.'

The morrow is an icy sunny day. In a temperature of -25° Réaumur [-15.6° C] Marbot's gallantry in a violent clash with Don Cossacks almost costs him his life.[10] Dumonceau, less impressed by the heroic qualities of Oudinot's fight than by what it implies, is finding it

'most unpleasant, proving as it did that the Cossacks, whom we'd been hoping we'd seen the last of, weren't yet counting on leaving us in peace'.

Which they certainly aren't. Pion des Loches sees they've

'dressed themselves up in gold-braided hats and coats they'd found in the many artillery vehicles, wagons and generals' carriages that had been left behind, and were pursuing us in this grotesque getup'.

But for most of the thousands in that sad cortege the time for heroics is over. 'Yesterday evening,' an unhappy Franz Roeder notes in his diary,

'Vogel and I pilfered a loaf of bread and, this morning, a copper saucepan. Overmastering need! We've had to do as everyone else is doing!'

After seven or eight hours on the road, leaning on his sergeant-major 'who's endured everything for me', Roeder 'without knowing it' again catches up with the relics of his Young Guard division, bivouacked in a village to the left of the road. And at 4 a.m. 'after another sleepless night' is heartily glad to get going again, naturally in pitch darkness. – Tascher, 1 December:

'Heavy snowfall. Thick flakes all day. Road hardly discernible, no longer flanked either by trees or ditches. The countryside is savage, deserted and covered in forests.'

Castellane too is finding the Lithuanian countryside 'vile. All we have to cheer us up are conifers by the wayside.' All that first December day the snow falls heavily. Nevertheless as Brandt sets off for the next little town the temperature is still going down. The road, marked by corpses around campfires, goes through a forest. Under a sky of glittering stars from time to time Brandt and his companions halt

'at bivouac fires. But we seemed to be among the dead. No one stirred. Sometimes an unfortunate fellow would raise his head, throw us a glassy look and lie back again, doubtless never more to get up. What above all made this night's march disagreeable was the glacial wind that was lashing our faces. At about 8 a.m. we saw a church tower: "It's Molodeczno!" we all exclaimed with one voice. Imagine our amazement when we learnt on reaching it that it was only Iliya, and that we still hadn't gone more than half way to Molodeczno.'

Although the loss of so much baggage has 'considerably lightened the army's march' and it's less encumbered now by stragglers, it has, by the same token, very few horses left to eat. Le Roy's carefully organised pocket larder has long been empty – and neither he nor anyone else has any hope of getting a mouthful for days to come, 'the whole countryside having been ravaged by both armies for 20 miles around'. Yet amazingly, all along the narrow icy-surfaced road with its endless forests, many *fricoteurs* are still plodding on with 'their immense booty'. Now and then Mailly-Nesle – still in his carriage of course – sees

'a man leading three heavily laden unnourished horses which can hardly stand up. To have less trouble leading them, he tied them to one another's tail, only concerning himself with the first. Now someone would cut the rope holding the horses together, and some robber profit by it. Now a movement of impatience caused one of these innocent animals to be killed, and sometimes even the driver would be felled to the ground.'

Suddenly whole rows of demoralised soldiers, clinging to one another, fall like packs of cards, or 'turn and flee if the tip of a lance appeared or the word 'Cossack' was repeated two or three times'. 'Bands of marauders' are still being formed, Caulaincourt notices, 'in full view of everyone, so as to recruit fresh stragglers'. Marc-Bussy's little band of Swiss runs into just such a small private army

'from all the corps: the Imperial Guard, light infantry, troopers, marching like demons. The colonel of the 123rd Line, who knows what such marauders go for, shouts to us: "Soldiers of the 3rd Brigade, distribution time!" We leave our ranks, the colonel among us, and fling ourselves on them as if they were an advancing enemy column. All had food and effects they'd pillaged.'

Bussy, for his part, fills his pocket handkerchief with valuables, and gets

'a Russian woman's overcoat of thick white cloth which one of these marauders had let fall from his shoulders. The colonel, seeing one of them, fine as if on parade, with the cross of the *Légion d'honneur* on his coat, rips it off him, calling him a straggler, a marauder. The other doesn't answer a word. This body is twice as numerous as our brigade. The grenadiers of the 123rd furnished themselves with fur bonnets of the Guard in exchange for their own, which were worthless.'

But now even the staunch Swiss are beginning to melt away:

'Often we hear someone say: "*Ma foi!* it's all up! We can't do any more. We're always getting fewer. I'm going to do as the others." Of all the brigade we're only fifteen in the ranks, all Swiss! The colonel of the 123rd tells our Major Graffenried: "Major, I put you in command of the brigade. I'm pushing off too." The major replies: "I shan't be commanding it for long, shall I? You see what's left!" Whereupon Graffenried makes us all present arms, and says: "Good-bye, my friends. You must march as far as you can." I think they left together. The night was so dark we couldn't see them leave, and on the snow you can't hear horses' footfalls. Each of us is trying to get on as best he can, without losing his comrades for fear of the Cossacks. At 8 a.m. there are still a few of us together.'

But later that day (2 December), lingering too long in a village but – unlike many others – still clinging to his musket, the little voltigeur from the Vaud suddenly finds he's all alone.

Throughout the retreat the white-haired 57-year-old Narbonne's behaviour at IHQ has been impeccable. Although 'used to enjoying all the ease and pleasures of life' he's been showing 'all the activity and ardour of a young man'. 'In the midst of our disasters,' attests his ADC Castellane admiringly – and Gourgaud and Ségur confirm it –

'his courage, his gaiety were remarkable. He wore the "royal bird" hairstyle, had himself powdered in the mornings at the bivouacs, often seated on a roof-beam, the steps of some house or a bench, even in the nastiest weather, as if he'd been in the most agreeable boudoir. During this operation he amused the bystanders with his jokes.'

If it weren't for Napoleon's marble features (every morning he shaves himself while Constant holds the mirror), Narbonne's clean-shaven face would be almost unique. Castellane hasn't shaved for two weeks and Kergorre for six. But Daru is no less imperturbable than Narbonne. According to his valet, 'he made almost the whole route from Moscow to Posen on foot and shaved himself every morning with as carefree an air as if we'd been at the Tuileries.'

Not that IHQ is immune to alarms. One at least, turns out to be a comic mistake. Someone starts shouting for an officer whose name is Ozanne. The cry is taken up by others, and immediately turns into '*Aux armes!*' which brings the whole Guard to arms! Even Napoleon comes out to ask what's going on. At IHQ things are happening that have never happened before. 'Two mules from the Emperor's transport wagons which had fallen behind,' it's reported to Caulaincourt, have been stolen

'while their driver was a little way off. No one knew who'd taken them. I mention this insignificant event because it's the only one of its kind to have happened throughout the campaign.'

Roustam says the thieves, starving soldiers, had taken the canteen, carried on the backs of the three mules which, under Ségur's command, always followed with wine, bread or biscuit and provisions in baskets on their saddles, and was always conducted by three gendarmes and two of the kitchen and table staff:

'The soldiers could see, written on it, who it was for; but stole it even so. The Emperor excused these men. Yet he wanted to know which regiment they belonged to. "A day will come when they'll have plenty of food and I'll review them on parade. But no, the reproach would be too cruel: On such or such a day you stole your Emperor's bread!"'

'On the last of these mules', Roustam explains, 'was the little iron bed which we erected everywhere and which was folded up with a mattress.'

Now even the Old Guard's beginning to disintegrate. The Master of the Horse keeps on coming across its veterans

'who'd succumbed to frost-bite and fallen to the ground. Should one help them along, which meant laboriously carrying them? They begged you to let them be. Should one take them to one of the bivouac fires which lined the route? Once these poor wretches fell asleep they were dead. If they resisted the craving for sleep, some other passer-by would help them on a bit further, thus prolonging their agony a little while, yet not saving them. In this state the drowsiness brought on by the cold is irresistible. Sleep comes inevitably; and to sleep is to die. In vain I tried to help several of these unfortunate men. The only words they uttered were to beg me, for pity sake, to leave them to sleep a little. Alas! It was the poor wretch's last wish; but at least his sufferings were over, without pain or death-throes. Gratitude, a smile even, was imprinted on his discoloured lips.'

For Pierre Auvray the first two days of December are

'days the like of which has never been seen. The cold had become so bad that the hoar frost, attaching itself to one's face, formed on it a 2-inch icicle. We marched through forests amidst the most terrible sufferings.'

And all the time the snow falls steadily. Dumonceau's lancers are finding it 'hardly possible to make out the road. Its whereabouts is no longer marked either by rows of trees or ditches.' Of all the survivors of the Berezina crossing, only the Polish Guard Lancers, who are taking 'the wars of Batory, Zamoyski and Chodkiewicz for our models', are feeling quite at home. Indeed more and more so:

'From day to day our march was getting easier. Order, morale, the language, all were facilitating everything for us in this fraternal country. For us the winter, though harsh, was in no way extraordinary. Above all when marching in the evening or in extreme cold we were in the habit of dismounting and, holding our horses by the bridle, singing march tunes or "Cracow songs", as much to relieve the horses as to keep our men warm and prevent them from falling asleep on horseback. It's an officer's duty to keep up a spirit of gaiety and confidence in his subordinates. Supported by the example of the French veterans we persevered in supporting our own.'

Griois too is noticing that

'virtually all our army's Poles were using such means that their knowledge of the country and the language facilitated for them, and they felt little of our terrible distress.'

By and by orders come to V Corps for all Poles to branch off left toward Olita, where it has its depots. All dismounted cavalry, on the other hand, are to make for the big remount depot at Merecz.

And still no one has anything to give the Russian prisoners, most of them bleeding from Doumerc's cuirassiers' long sword-thrusts and slashes. All day Lejeune and his party are

'passing through an immense forest with difficult defiles at every step. In these woods we lost almost all our prisoners. The two to three thousand we were taking with us were a great source of embarrassment to us. We hadn't a scrap of food to give them, and I was happy to shut my eyes when they took their chance and escaped while we were passing through some forest. Because I couldn't be so cruel as to let them be maltreated into going on with us.'

Le Roy too sees the futility of keeping a 25-year-old Russian who's been allotted to him. As evening begins to fall he makes a sign to his prisoner, seated beside him on some pine branches; and together they get up and walk a few paces away from the fireside:

'I showed him where the rearguard was: *"Franzozi, Rusqui!"* Then I showed him the forest, crooking my arm, my hand pointing toward the Russian army that was behind us, saying: *"Nein franzozi."* Then, putting my hand to my mouth: *"Nein cleba, niema mieuza"*[neither bread nor meat]. I put a little bit of biscuit into his hand, saying: *"Pachol"* [March!] – a word I'd remembered from the time I was myself a prisoner [in 1807]. This poor young man understood me perfectly. He threw himself on my hand, which he kissed several times.'

Jacquet praises Le Roy for his action. At least one person's happy! Only the men of Morand's division evidently have greater resources. Captain

François, too, is in charge of some prisoners. 'We shared everything with them. Afterwards they were very useful to us in procuring us some food.'

The row between Ney and Victor is inspiring little confidence in IX Corps' support. And Ney 'wants to set the remainder of III Corps, i.e., a few officers and the regiments' Eagles, at a distance'. Ney's personal escort against the Cossacks, 'a little sacred squadron, scarcely 100 men still under arms, and all the eagles', is provided by one of Fezensac's subordinates, a Captain Delachau:

'A drummer of the 24th Line marched at our head. He was all that was left of III Corps' regimental drummers and musicians.'

The rest of the corps tries to catch up with IHQ, which isn't easy, since it's already a whole day's march ahead.

'For two days and three nights we marched almost without halting; and when excessive fatigue forced us to take a moment's rest we all gathered in a barn with the regiments' Eagles and some soldiers still under arms, who watched over their defence.'

But when an order comes to break all the Eagles and bury them Fezensac simply can't bring himself to obey. 'I had the pole broken and the Eagle put into the pack of one of the Eagle-bearers who was always marching at my side.'

The second manor house to provide overnight quarters for IHQ is at Staïki (fifteen houses, plunged in the depths of an endless forest). Although

'the barns attached to it are full of forage, so far we haven't had so miserable a lodging. The Emperor and staff officers each had a little corner measuring 7 or 8 feet square. All the rest were packed together in another room. It was freezing so hard that everyone took shelter in this little hole of a place. When we lay down we had to lie on top of one another to save space. A pin couldn't have been dropped between us.'

Least of all is Napoleon's plump major-domo ever likely ever to forget his night here:

'All the way from Moscow M. de Bausset, suffering from gout, had been in a carriage. Someone, moving about in the dark, trod on his foot. The wretched cripple began screaming "Monstrous! I'm being murdered!" Those of us who were awake shouted with laughter, which woke up those who were asleep. And everyone – including the unfortunate invalid himself – paid tribute to this momentary foolishness with roars of laughter. We nicknamed Staïki "Miserowo".'

When morning comes, Larrey's scientific eye notes how the night's freshly fallen snow is

'crystallising in six-pointed stars, of various sizes. In the little stars the same distribution as in the big ones, and the same symmetry of the crystals was to be seen.'

CHAPTER 21

THE EMPEROR QUITS

'They danced while others froze' – a bulletin that doesn't lie – 'Sire, I'm old. Take me with you' – 'One must always trust one's luck – 'Kill me rather than let me be taken' – a hermetically sealed carriage and its escort – 'they'd been dancing while others froze' – 'the Emperor was shivering as with the ague'

Now IHQ's making for Molodeczno, near the junction with the Minsk–Vilna highway. This day, 2 December, is a double anniversary – of Napoleon's self-coronation, and of Austerlitz, that great victory only eight years ago which had 'rolled up the map of Europe'. But this freezing day no one feels like celebrating either. Left behind at Sedlichë to communicate with Victor, Castellane places himself under a tree, where

'all day, near a campfire on the highway, I've had the spectacle of the stragglers of all nations, all arms, most of whom have thrown away their muskets, the men of the Old Guard excepted. They're keeping theirs. All this forms a close column of twelve to fifteen men abreast.'

From a disgruntled Marshal Victor, when he turns up, he hears how IX and II Corps had taken up position to protect the stragglers as they'd passed through the narrow passage across the swamps near Ilya, and how the same disorder had reigned as at the Berezina. His colleague d'Aremberg has been sent on the same mission; but somehow they've missed each other. At 7 p.m., after passing the Vilna–Minsk junction on foot, Castellane gets to Molodeczno 'and the Emperor's headquarters, set up in a house which almost has the air of a proper château.' Molodeczno is quite a large town, but most of its timber houses, 'following our men's praiseworthy habit', are already in flames.' As for the château,

'standing by itself to the left on some high ground at the entrance to the bridges, it's a fine timber manor house, the property of Count Oginski. The King of Naples had his campfire a few paces away from us.'

The sheet ice has prevented no fewer than twenty couriers from coming further. Fourteen of the leather dispatch-cases all, Fain notes (sent between 1 and 19 November, Caulaincourt sees), are from Paris; the rest 'from all along the line'. They don't only contain official correspondence. Castellane, who hasn't had any letters from home for a long time and has 'been deprived of news from Paris since Krasnoië', now gets nine. Several others, he gathers from their contents, must have been captured by Cossacks.

The most important dispatches are from Maret, at Vilna. Some report on Schwarzenberg's now useless advance. More relevantly they tell Napoleon that twelve battalions of Loison's [34th] division[1] had reached Vilna on 21 November and been ordered forward to Ochmiana, the last town before it, to cover the last stage of the army's retreat. Loison himself is still at Königsberg, organising the rest of his scattered division.[1] To send forward Loison's untried Neapolitan and Bavarian conscripts from the Confederation of the Rhine has been Hogendorp's idea. And Napoleon immediately tries to inhibit it. Writes to Maret:

'"The 34th Division's movement must be stopped. If it has left, how shall we feed it? It will become disbanded, like the rest of the army."'

Some of his ministers he declares himself pleased with. Others not. Particularly not – indeed very far from pleased – with his ambassador-extraordinary at Warsaw, Abbé *D.-G.-F. de Pradt* who – he's been telling Caulaincourt over and over again – has ruined all his plans.[2] Where, for instance, are the 'Polish Cossacks'? There quite simply aren't any. And it's all Pradt's fault! The fact is, however, as Maret writes, the Grand Duchy's finances are exhausted. So is Lithuania. And Caulaincourt, listening no doubt to Napoleon's comments as he rips open the leather dispatch-cases and glances at their dates of dispatch, realises that from now on

'we'd have to make do without all the other supports the Emperor had been counting on. Obviously neither Vilna, nor even the Niemen, would be the end of the army's retreat, and therefore of our troubles either. The Emperor busied himself reading his dispatches from France, and everyone was glad to have news from home. In Paris there'd been some worry about news from the army being interrupted, but no notion of the extent of our disasters.'

Also shivering at Molodeczno is a M. de Forget, Councillor of State, with the ministerial portfolio. Napoleon questions him on the state of the roads, etc. Is anything known of the army's catastrophe? Nothing? Well, that's just as well. The main thing now is that the Austrian, Prussian and American ambassadors who've been at Vilna all this time are on no account to be allowed to witness the débâcle.[3] And an urgent message is sent off to Maret to clear the diplomatic corps out of Vilna post-haste.

Ever since the Berezina, Caulaincourt's been aware that Napoleon's preparing a bulletin. And this evening at Molodeczno he dictates its text. For an Imperial Bulletin the 29th is quite exceptionally candid.[4] It dates the catastrophe from 6 November (*'until which time the weather was perfect ... the army's movement had been carried out with greatest success'*), and goes on to describe how *'30,000 horses perished in a few days, those of the cavalry, artillery and the Train were perishing every night, not by hundreds but by thousands'*, how much of the artillery and 'munitions of war and mouth' had had to be abandoned for lack of teams; and how, as the result of the sudden cold of 7 November, *'this army, so handsome on the 6th, was already very different by the 14th'*, and had been unable to risk a battle for lack of artillery:

'"*The men seemed stunned, lost their gaiety, their good humour, and dreamed only of misfortunes and catastrophes. The enemy, seeing on the roads the traces of this terrible calamity that was striking the French army, tried to profit from it. He enveloped all the columns with his Cossacks who, like the Arabs of the desert, carried off the trains and vehicles that were following on.*"'

In sum, the largest army ever raised in Europe no longer exists. What a shock it's going to be for the Parisians! For France!

Already, yesterday evening, Castellane's friend Quartermaster Anatole de Montesquiou has been sent on his way to Paris with eight captured Russian flags and orders to everywhere spread news of the victory won on the banks of the Berezina and insert it instantly in the Vilna and Mainz newspapers. Above all he's to tell Marie-Louise all this verbally, before the terrible news becomes public:

'The Emperor's idea was to prepare public opinion. He was determined to hide none of his disasters.'

Boulart's among those who profit from the courier's departure to send a letter to his wife.

But Napoleon has reached an even more important decision – to leave the army. He tells Caulaincourt:

'"With things as they are, it's only from the Tuileries I can keep my grip on Europe." He was counting on being able to set out within 48 hours. He was eager to start, so as to forestall the news of our disasters.'

As soon as contact's been made with Loison's fresh division, based at Vilna – where 'as he saw it the army would no longer be at risk' – he'll be off. Caulaincourt is dubious. Obviously Napoleon still has no real idea of the completeness of the catastrophe. But when he says he doubts that the army'll be able to make a stand at Vilna, Napoleon merely replies: "You're laughing at me!"

On another important point, however, he affects to listen to Caulaincourt's advice. To whom should he hand over supreme command – Murat or Eugène? Caulaincourt, in his blunt frank way that so often gives offence, repeats what he's already said several times before. The army has more confidence in Eugène. Murat, though a hero on the battlefield, isn't generally thought to have either the force of character, the sense of order or the foresight that'll be needed to save or re-organise what's left of the army. People are even accusing him of

'having instigated His Majesty to undertake the Moscow expedition and of having lost the magnificent cavalry force there'd been at the start of the campaign.'[5]

Well, that's true, Napoleon agrees. But a king can't serve under a viceroy; so for reasons of rank it's not possible for him to hand over to Eugène. As Berthier, Caulaincourt adds, agrees.[6]

'Certain other remarks he'd made earlier, and which I recalled because they recurred during this conversation, gave me the idea that he'd prefer to leave to his brother-in-law the honour of rallying the army, and that he was loth to let his stepson have the credit for this further achievement,'

a typical instance, Caulaincourt thinks to himself, of Napoleon's distrust of anyone who enjoys a well-deserved personal reputation. His impending departure, Napoleon goes on, is to be kept secret for the time being. Caulaincourt's preliminary preparations likewise:

'Under pretext of making arrangements for officers to be sent with dispatches, I gave orders to the post-stages. But our troops soon disorganised these relays and I had to make other arrangements by sending several transport detachments on ahead whose horses would serve our purpose.'

Then there's the question – which is the Master of the Horse's business – of transporting Napoleon himself. *Quâ* organiser of all headquarters transports Caulaincourt's to accompany him to Paris:

'Our situation was such that if steps weren't taken well in advance the least trifles were liable to place obstacles in our way, even insurmountable ones. We wouldn't be able to use our relays to get along the highway, for instance – it was like a sheet of glass – if I hadn't kept a sack of coal under lock and key, to forge shoes for the horses. We'd only been able to do our forging at night, the transport wagons being on the move for 12–15 hours every day. The cold was so severe, even beside the forge fire, that the farriers could only work in gloves and even then had to rub their hands together at every moment so they shouldn't freeze.'

Who else is to come? Not Berthier, anyway. Roustam is eavesdropping 'in the next room. I heard loud words being spoken. It was the Emperor reprimanding Berthier at the top of his voice for wanting to go with him.

'"I'm going to France because my presence is indispensable."

'"Sire, Your Majesty has known for a long time I want to leave the service. I'm old. Take me with you."

'"You'll stay, together with Eugène and Murat. You're ungrateful. You're a coward! I'll have you shot in front of the whole army!"'

Berthier, Roustam hears, was weeping and sobbing. It seems he isn't the only one listening through the half-open door – or else it's thanks to him that a Major Dariale, Commandant of the Palace, knows how Berthier has pleaded in tears to be allowed to come too, pointing out that he'd never yet abandoned him: 'That's not possible,' Napoleon had replied, so Dariale tells Castellane.

'"It's necessary you remain with the King of Naples. I know very well, I do, that you're good for nothing.[7] But no one believes it, and your name'll have some effect on the army."'

So long as Berthier remains with the army it'll at least *seem* to have a headquarters. Murat is least of all an administrator. And Berthier's routines will be necessary to re-organise the army when it gets to Vilna.

This scene, Roustam declares, 'took place on 3 December. Next day Berthier had become resigned.'

Tascher. 4 December:

'Rigorous cold. Silent road. Thoughts worth remembering. Anniversary of my birth. Memory of my mother ... tears, agony. Did six leagues, lodged in a village, half a league ahead of headquarters. Fever and diarrhoea. Eugène's sufferings.'

But miracles do happen, if only petty ones. By now Sorbier's taken a complete loathing to the miserly sycophantic Drouot (who incidentally is also shaving every day), even forbidden him to appear in his presence unless summoned – but the thick-skinned Drouot appears even so. Again and again he's been sending him back to make sure his guns (which he, Sorbier, anyway doesn't think he'll be able to save) are following on. But today is St Barbara's day – a day for gifts. And Drouot astounds everyone by making 'a generous gesture. From his ammunition cart he took out his wine keg and a few bottles of wine', and distributes them to his fellow-officers. Peering into his wagon, Pion and Boulart both see in it a whole ham; and consider pinching it. But desist. Which is a pity, because in a few days it'll go the way of all the other wagons. The wine, however, will be enough to sustain their little group for more four days. That day the Guard artillery, following on, is attacked by Cossacks, who among other booty relieve it of Boulart's wagon:

'A real catastrophe for me. The cold increases to -20° [-25° C]. Fire breaks out in the next house to mine. Had to flee hastily, portmanteau under my arm.'

En route Castellane, too, bumps into his 'dragoon', who tells him his servant boy and horses have fallen to the Cossacks. 'The only fur I've got left is a woman's fox pelisse. I've been marching all day with holes in my boots.' But I Corps' little party is lucky. It runs into

'some vehicles of a convoy coming from Germany which had got as far as Markowo, a little village, just as we were about to enter it. They'd brought an abundance of fresh and varied foods, and our brave soldiers were able to eat bread, butter, cheese and drink a glass of wine. What a repast, after 40 days on short rations!'

For once something has been rationally arranged:

'General Guilleminot and his division [sic], who'd got there first, had taken measures to see to it that these vehicles' contents shouldn't be wasted. He invited the men to dine at the village's little château. On fine tables of chestnut there was an enormous soup tureen, all the china of a tea service, many white loaves and several baskets of Breton butter. At this sight, so novel for people who for two months had been living under the most frightful privations, our eyes, our nostrils, opened like those of an Arab horse that hears the trumpet. Each of us ate enough – not for two, but for ten. Afterwards it was painful to leave this comfortable place with its warmth and food to go on and lie out in the open at a bivouac near Smorgoni in 25 degrees of frost.'

Leaving Molodeczno at 9 a.m., IHQ reaches the village of Bienitze, halfway to Smorgoni. Here it's met, as protocol requires (but also in response to an order sent off to him at 1.30 a.m., 2 December), by General Dirk van Hogendorp, governor of Vilna province. A bluff, square-minded 51-year-old Dutchman who'd once had been governor of Java then Dutch ambassador at St Petersburg, Hogendorp enjoys the enviable status of ADC to the Emperor.[8] Now, leaving Loison's lightly clad division behind him at Ochmiana, he has come to report on the state of affairs in the rear. He finds IHQ lodged in Count Zoçal's manor house, whose barns are yielding any amount of 'oats, flour, peas, potatoes and oatmeal'– all of which are being distributed to the Staff and the Guard. After being cross-examined by

Napoleon, Hogendorp sets off back again, to prepare the unsuspecting Vilna to receive the wreckage of what had been the Grand Army.

Another major worry is the Treasure. Ever since the Berezina, order after order, inquiry after inquiry, has been sent back to Davout and Eugène, whose officers and NCOs are escorting it. While IHQ had been at Molodeczno, the convoy – which also comprises Pajol's convoy of carriages containing wounded generals – has been attacked by Lanskoi's troops, together with 600 Cossacks. In the affray Generals Pino and Fontana are gallantly defended by three Italian carabiniers. So far Pajol's convoy has managed to survive by always keeping ahead of the column,

'ignoring such habitations as the route offered. From time to time we ran into magazine guards, employees of the Administration, who'd remained behind during the campaign. To them, they who'd lacked for nothing, the tale of our sufferings seemed a fable!'

Tascher. 5 December:

'Reached Smorgoni, little town; lodged there. Resources here which we have the misery of seeing pillaged without being able to profit from it. Found a detachment of the regiment. Amazement at seeing clean well-turned out men.'

Also getting to this major 'country town [*bourg*] of 200 timber houses with a number of villages within reach' where Charles XII's army had gone into winter quarters for the last time in 1708–9, Boulart finds

'some horses come from France, which are being distributed among the various batteries of the Guard. My battery still being the best mounted, I'm not given any.'

Noting that the thermometer on this upland has fallen to -20° Réaumur [-25° C], Cesare de Laugier, as he trudges on along the 'good road' that leads to Smorgoni, is struck by 'some birds falling from frozen trees' a phenomenon which had even impressed Charles XII's Swedish soldiers a century ago:

'The ground no longer presents anything but an enormous crystallised and impracticable surface. No one who still has a horse can any longer make use of it. In the air a great silence. Not a breath of wind. Anything that lives or stirs, even the wind, seems to be pierced through, frozen, stricken dead. Those of our men who've so far been able to preserve the greatest constancy are at the end of their tether.'

Many men remember Smorgoni very well, having been there in early July. It's 'a long village strung out along the road and situated in a region of immense forests. Its inhabitants hunted bears, sold their furs, and trained the young bears to do gymnastics in Europe as a spectacle. Not waiting for us they've fled with their merchandise and their pupils.'

Continuous suffering can be relieved by weird, almost surrealistic outbursts. A good comrade of Griois', a Colonel Cottin, still has his servant. The party have just reached Smorgoni and are having to defend the house they've occupied, and Cottin's 'threatening to run our assailants through with his sword and lunging out with great thrusts through the crack of the door and windows.' He's just giving orders to his servant when, for the first time, he notices the man's face is as smoke-blackened as everyone else's. 'What shocked him most was the dirtiness of the man's ears.' His arms flailing 'like two telegraphs' Cottin shouts at him:

"How dare you present yourself in front of superior officers, colonels, with your face and ears smothered in filth! Have you forgotten the respect due to them? Since we left Moscow I've lost part of my belongings and my horses by your fault, and I've never reproached you. *But to present yourself with a dirty face like yours, that's the limit!* Get out, go and wash, and for God's sake *wash your ears!*

Everyone, not least the servant, who's 'stupefied', thinks Cottin must be joking. But he isn't. 'Probably it was the last straw.' The party doesn't think poor Cottin who, for all his firmness of character, is coughing 'mouthfuls of blood' where he lies on the ground at nights, will even get as far as the next bivouac. But he does. And one day distributes to them all he has left: 'For my part I got a shirt and four blocks of chocolate.' Cottin himself will live to laugh at his own strange outburst.

This isn't an army where secrets can be kept; and by now almost everyone, at least on the staff, knows what's in the wind – that the Emperor's leaving. At 2 p.m. on 5 December IHQ reaches Smorgoni. 'One hour after his arrival,' Napoleon says to Roustam:

"Roustam, fix everything in my carriage. We're leaving."

They're to take all the cash they can – Roustam's to ask First Secretary Méneval to supply it. Upon Méneval's applying to Paymaster *Guillaume Peyrusse* – who, unlike himself, is still in the best of health – Peyrusse gives him 60,000 francs in gold. Of this Méneval passes on 14,000 francs to *Constant Wairy*, the chief valet. As for the remainder, Roustam divides it up into three parts: 'one-third in a compartment of the carriage, one-third in a silver-gilt chocolate pot, and the last third, in rolls, in the double-bottomed case'. Everyone's asking him what's afoot. Castellane, in the *salon de service,*[9] is 'greatly astonished to hear that the Emperor's leaving'. But not, among others, his valet:

'About half an hour later the Emperor sent for me in his room and said to me:

"Constant, I'm leaving. I thought I'd been able to take you with me; but on reflection I see that several carriages would draw attention. It's essential I'm not held up. I've given orders for you to be able to leave as soon as my horses get back. So you'll be following me at a short distance."

'I was feeling very ill,'

which, Constant thinks, is 'why the Emperor didn't want me to leave on the box, as I asked to, to give him all the care he was accustomed to.'[10]

All the army corps commanders – Murat, Eugène, Ney, Mortier, Bessières, Lefèbvre and Davout – have been summoned to a meeting at 7 p.m. Only the wounded Oudinot, who's gone on ahead, and Victor, some miles behind with the rearguard, are absent. For form's sake Napoleon pretends to seek the marshals' advice. Of course everyone knows it's a foregone conclusion. But Bessières has been ordered to take it upon himself to broach the matter. Should not His Majesty leave for Paris?

'No sooner had the first words been said than he flew into a violent rage, saying that "only my most mortal enemy could propose I should abandon the army in its present situation." He even went further, for he made a movement to draw his sword and throw himself at the Marshal.' Whereupon Bessières (so at least he'll tell Baudus afterwards) replies 'with studied coldness':

'"Even when you've killed me, it'll be no less true that you no longer have an army, that you can't stay here because we can no longer protect you."'

Pure amateur theatricals, says Baudus, 'because we have proofs that his project to leave had already been decided on'. However, the ritual has to be gone through. And Napoleon, who's not above such amateur theatricals, pretends to let himself be convinced. Only his choice of Murat to take over as commander-in-chief causes universal dismay. Least of all does 'King Murat' want it. Ever since the Winkovo camp only his wife's urgent warnings have dissuaded him from emulating Jérôme Bonaparte,[11] quitting the army, and going home. Now his presence of mind deserts him completely. In vain he invokes his ignorance of army administration. As for matters of protocol, he protests, he'll be only too glad to waive them and step aside in favour of Eugène (whom he openly detests). Napoleon tells his 'Neapolitan *pantalone*' sharply do as he's told. Meeting over. To Rapp he says:

'"Well, Rapp, I'm leaving tonight for Paris. France's welfare and that of this unfortunate army necessitate my presence there. I'm leaving the King of Naples in command."'

When Rapp objects that his departure will depress the army, he replies:

'"I must keep an eye on Austria and keep Prussia under control."'

Rapp, aware of the intensity of Prussian hatred from his time as governor of Danzig, says he's sceptical about the latter possibility. For a while, hands clasped behind his back, Napoleon paces to and fro. Says nothing. Then:

'"When I'm at the head of the 120,000 men I'm going to organise, the Prussians will think twice before declaring war on me."'

To Rapp it's obvious that Napoleon's still labouring under a delusion that the army only has to go into winter quarters at Vilna to be able to put up a firm resistance. Finally Napoleon orders him to second Ney.

Soon the rumour has reached everyone. Told by his servant Louis that things are being prepared for the Emperor's departure ('which at first I didn't believe') Mailly-Nesle – 'for the first time during the retreat' – is stricken by anxiety. What if he can't get his promised certificate to allow him to take the waters in France?

'But a few moments later a page told us the Emperor's carriage was ready, and that he was leaving for Vilna to prepare victuals *for fear of wastage*'
– the explanation, so Dariale's told Castellane, that's to be put about, 'I know very well he's going further than that.' This is the moment, Mailly-Nesle feels, to turn to one of his fellow-aristocrats. Slipping in among the top brass, he gets Narbonne to promise him he'll have his certificate. Narbonne also sends for his ADC Castellane and tells him he's to be sent on mission to Berlin. The suave, well-liked diplomat of the *ancien régime* is to do what he can to play down the news of the Grand Army's destruction – which will certainly throw King Frederick William's subjects into transports of joy – and keep him faithful to the French alliance. Not that Narbonne's leaving right now. He and his aides still have many icy days marching ahead of them.

General Delaborde still has his carriage, but his supply of candles has run out. Dryly humorous as usual he, told he'll soon be receiving an official proclamation, merely tells Paul de Bourgoing to keep their 'spluttering light of a splinter of resinous wood' burning, to read it by:
'"You see, my friend, it's a vestal's job I'm entrusting you with. Bear in mind it's to read the Emperor's order that you're going to keep the sacred fire burning. It's said he wants to talk to some of his generals this evening. Perhaps he'll summon me. I must be able to read his orders on the spot. Under such circumstances I shouldn't like to be a moment late.'"
Whereupon Delaborde quietly takes a nap.

Evidently Caulaincourt has prepared everything for immediate departure and the meeting with the marshals can't have taken long. Under its commanding officer, Szeptycki, Zalusky's squadron of Polish Guard Lancers, 'bivouacked along an enclosure', is on duty. 'A brazier was burning in front of us.' A relative of the same name, Lieutenant Adam Zalusky, is standing at the head of 'a column of dismounted cavalrymen'. The two officers are enjoying
'a honeycomb for dessert and it was getting rather late, when suddenly we were told to order the squadron to mount.'
Some Cossacks in the offing? Zalusky, not regarding his cousin or another officer as fit for such a foray, leaves them in charge of others of the same ilk, and
'the squadron assembled. We were ordered to go into the courtyard of the château, a vast antique timber building. We found the courtyard's right wing already occupied by the Horse Chasseurs. Extremely curious to know what was afoot, we drew up to their left.'
It's between 8 and 9 p.m. Suddenly Zalusky sees
'two coaches with lanterns lit come forward. The Emperor, with a numerous suite, appeared on the steps of the house.'
Henckens, in the Sacred Squadron, standing there beside his superb steed Cerberus and unfamiliar with these personages' appearance, asks his aristocratic young Colonel Talhouët – who until Moscow had been one of Napoleon's adjutants – to identify them for him.

'The Emperor came out of the house where the conference had taken place. His air altogether pensive and with his characteristic cowlick hanging down on his forehead, he sat down on a milestone.[12] As we made to mount, he gave Grouchy the order to leave the officers standing by their horses. After quite a long wait General Caulaincourt turned up with four sleighs, very well harnessed up.'

After which everything goes at its usual breakneck speed:

'The Emperor took his seat with Caulaincourt in the first carriage. Lobau, Duroc and Lefèvre-Desnouëttes in the second. And in the third two other persons of his suite.'

So quickly is it all happening that Castellane sees how Count Lobau,

'hasn't even time to speak to his nephew. The carriage had already been brought out when he was told to get into it.'

Captain Count Wonsowicz, 'a Polish officer who'd been through the whole campaign, a man of proven courage and devotion', is to ride at one side of the first carriage, as guide and interpreter. Roustam on the other. Fagalde and Amodru are to be outriders. A footman and a workman are to follow in a barouche on runners. The second carriage is to leave a few minutes later. The 'personages' in the third, Fain, Bacler d'Albe,[13] Doctor Yvan, and Baron Mounier (Third Secretary), are to follow on. Paul de Bourgoing sees the first carriage get under way,[14] escorted by *Chasseurs à Cheval.* 'The Chasseurs set off,' Zalusky goes on. 'Our squadron followed the carriages at a gallop.' Outside Smorgoni, Colonel Szymanowski, meeting the first carriage with another squadron of the Polish Guard Lancers, notices on its doors the letters 'SA':

'The French, not losing their sense of sardonic humour even now, said they stood for '*Sans adieu'* ['without so much as a good-bye'].'

And as it flits by, Roman Soltyk's friend Grabowski, also of the Polish Guard lancers, thinks he hears some of the 'old grumblers' muttering: 'Ah yes, it's *Colin-qui-court* ('Colin who's running away'), a sarcastic pun on Caulaincourt's name:[15] About one mile outside Smorgoni', Brandt, with the few survivors of the Vistula Legion,[16] is overtaken by

'a big vehicle, a sort of coach, on which a front seat had been improvised, arriving at a considerable speed through the mass of fugitives. It was preceded by a horseman [Amodru] wearing a green riding-coat and who'd taken no other precaution against the unspeakable cold than to wrap his ears in a small shawl. I don't know what happened; but suddenly I saw him draw his sword and strike out at a man who was on the road and who tottered and fell over backwards. The carriage instantly passed on. Later it was said that it was the Emperor's carriage, that the man was an orderly officer, and that the soldier who'd been corrected in this way had probably said some unsuitable word.'[17]

In a long village beyond the town Dumonceau, too, has been ordered to be ready to leave at 9 p.m. in command of an imperial escort. To go where? No one tells him. But since it's not his turn for duty, he, 'pleased to escape a nocturnal ride which looked like being most painful', lets his friend Captain

Post command it instead. ('Though I afterwards regretted having been excused when I became aware of the mission's importance.') And at 10 p.m. Napoleon's carriage turns up[18] and Post's escort replaces the Chasseur detachment. That Colbert's men – by now most of them are Poles – are to escort the carriage is explicable. Already some 500 Chasseurs have died en route. But the Poles, as we've seen, are in good trim. And they've just been joined by their '5th squadron, newly formed at Danzig'. But, says Zalusky, 'it was fitted out in its parade uniforms and made up of young, still inexperienced men. So it was suffering greatly from the sharpest cold (-22°) of the whole campaign.'[19]

By midnight Napoleon, 'sound asleep' in his carriage, reaches Ochmiana; but by now the night's so cold that one-third of its escort has fallen behind. Getting down 'to heed a call of nature' Roustam sees

'a light, quite close to me, in a hut. I go inside to light my pipe, I see some people lying on straw. I recognise an officer of the Gendarmes of the Guard, who seemed astounded to see me, and said. "What chance brings you here?" I told him the Emperor was there. "How lucky he didn't get here earlier!" he said. "An hour ago the Cossacks were here. They made a *hurrah* on the village.'

Roustam realises the party isn't yet out of trouble. Far from it. For only a quarter of an hour ago two light infantry regiments and a detachment of Loison's Neapolitan cavalry have been attacked by 600 Cossacks under the Russian Colonel Seslavine, together with regular cavalry and light artillery on sledges. The Russians are only a few hundred yards outside Ochmiana. So cold is the night that Loison's men (so Kergorre will hear next day) 'hadn't been able to fire their muskets'. Even so, they've driven off their assailants by sheer weight of numbers. Hogendorp's idea of sending them forward to Ochmiana may prove fatal to Loison's men. But it has saved Napoleon – so far – from falling into Russian hands! When Caulaincourt sees them he notices that

'these troops, believing the main army was covering them, were so full of confidence that, the cold being so extreme, they hadn't even posted proper outposts'.

The night is extremely cold and pitch dark. The carriage has drawn up – an hour will pass before the second will arrive – in the main square, where two fresh detachments of Polish cavalry, 'one of Guard Lancers, the other of the 7th Regiment of Lancers of the Vistula', are 'drawn up in line of battle'. Among the officers who place 'themselves in a semicircle around the carriage door' is General Gratien, commanding Loison's division in Loison's continued absence. Another is a Saxon surgeon named *Geissler*, who notices that the carriage, 'drawn by six little Lithuanian horses, is draped in furs'. Utterly impressed by this man whose word has made and unmade most of Europe's states and monarchs, Geissler studies his features:

'His face hadn't changed at all since 1807, 1808 and 1809. We closely considered this powerful mortal from distance of a few paces. He wore a serious air and seemed to be in very good health.'

The troops' acclaim has to be suppressed – the local situation, everyone's aware, is utterly precarious. What are His Majesty's chances of getting through? One in three? One in ten?

'Such a secret couldn't be kept for long, and already the Russians might well have sent troops to intercept him. Going into the house of the local military governor, he studied his map of Lithuania, examining it very closely. His generals tried to dissuade him from going on. But he rejected their advice. To set off in broad daylight, indeed, seemed the most dangerous of all expedients.'

Wonsowicz is amazed at his determination to press on. And when he asks Wonsowicz whether he has any escort for him, Wonsowicz says there are 266 lancers. That'll do, says, Napoleon. He'll take them:

'"We're leaving at once. The night's dark enough for the Russians not to see us. Besides, one must always trust to one's luck. Without that one gets nowhere."'

So the fresh lancers are ordered to mount:

'But before leaving again he summoned his orderly officer, took a pair of pistols into his *coupé* and gave them to him, recommending that he place himself on the seat with General Lefèvre-Desnouëttes. The mameluke Roustam got into a sledge immediately following the Emperor's carriage; and Colonel Stoïkowski, commanding the escort, was given orders to keep close to the carriage door. Here are the ever-memorable words the Emperor, after all these preparations, addressed to those around him:

'"I'm counting on you all. Let's go! Keep a sharp lookout to right and left of the road."'

Then, turning to these devoted and fearless men, to whom he'd given his pistols, he added:

'"In the event of certain danger, kill me rather than let me be taken."

'Count Wonsowicz, deeply moved at an order no one would have obeyed except in the barbarous ages of paganism, said:

'"Does Your Majesty permit me to translate what I've just heard to our Poles?"'

'"Yes, let them know what I've said."'

'Those words were repeated in the Polish language, and the lancers shouted with one voice: "We'll rather let ourselves be cut in pieces than allow anyone come near you." All this happened at 2 a.m. on 6 December, at a time of year and in a latitude where the nights last seventeen hours. And Napoleon was prepared to confront such dangers! The Russians had only withdrawn a short distance.'

Roustam returns to the carriage. A crack of the whip, and off it goes again 'at top speed' into the black icy night. Outside the town the Cossacks are only a few hundred yards from the road:

'Where the mist was thinner their lights could be seen on the skyline just outside Ochmiana, especially to the left of the road. The silent procession could even hear the voices of the enemy sentries.'

But nothing happens. The Cossacks don't spot the carriage. Are left behind.

It's one of those fiercely cold nights one gets in the north. No snow is falling. So extreme is the cold that after a few miles 50 at most of the Poles are still with the carriage: 'The horses kept falling, and as a result, the riders having no remounts, at the second relay we'd none left.' Only a small advance guard's been sent ahead to the next post- house, at Rownopol, reached at dawn. Two others have been placed out in echelon along the road:

'By the time they reached Rownopol there were only 36! These were divided, half going before and half after us. Of all the detachments there weren't fifteen men still with us when we reached the relay.'

There, in a temperature that's fallen to -28° C, new horses are waiting, and the remaining Poles are replaced by a detachment of Neapolitan Horse Guards, under the Duke of Rocca Romana, who'd got there with Hogendorp. 'Some of these Neapolitan troopers, dressed in [sky-blue and yellow] parade uniforms, froze during the transit and littered the route with their corpses' – tomorrow Labaume will see them lying by the roadside 'showing that Napoleon had passed that way'.

The third relay post is at Miednicky. Here the Duke of Bassano himself, alias Foreign Minister Maret, has been waiting for it. Getting into Napoleon's carriage he gives Caulaincourt his own in exchange – and the Master of the Horse goes on ahead to Vilna which he reaches almost simultaneously with the returning Hogendorp. Going straight to his headquarters, he finds the Dutchman

'having to rouse to action people who were just leaving M. de Bassano's ball. They'd been dancing while others froze.'

Caulaincourt asks Hogendorp urgently to obtain some post-horses for the next stage of the imperial transit.

At 10.15 a.m. Napoleon's carriage reaches Vilna. But doesn't enter it. Circumventing the town wall, it halts at 'a country house half-destroyed by fire' in the Kovno suburb. Now there are

'barely eight of the escort left, including General Lefèbvre-Desnouëttes. Such of the Neapolitans as were still acting as escort had frost-bitten hands and feet.'

Just then or a moment later Caulaincourt comes out from the town, where he has bought fur-lined boots for the whole party. To his alarm he sees the Duke of Rocca Romana

'pressing both his hands against the stove. I'd great difficulty in making him realise he was risking losing them, and in making him go out and rub them in the snow – a treatment which so increased his pains that it was more than he could do to persevere in it',

so that Rocca Romana loses several fingers and toes. Meanwhile Hogendorp, in response to Caulaincourt's urgent request, has ordered the governor of Vilna city, General Roch-Godart to provide 27 relay horses, 'which I was so very fortunate, albeit only with great difficulty, as to find in the midst of a mob of troopers who were in the main square. I also managed to assemble some 60 mounted men to escort the carriages, so great was the disorder beginning to be.'

Having furnished the escort and the relays with six of Maret's horses and his own postilion, Hogendorp, *quâ* ADC to the Emperor, wants to go to him. But now it's nearly midday. And Napoleon has gone – at 11.30 a.m. 'Such had been his haste, he'd already left. Just as we were leaving' the second carriage, with Duroc and Lobau in it, had caught up.

An hour and a quarter has sufficed for Vilna. In no time Napoleon is speeding westwards toward the Niemen – which no doubt he's privately regretting ever having crossed.

Throughout that day and the following night, the carriage flies on over the snowy plains. Never will Caulaincourt

'remember suffering so much as on that journey between Vilna and Kovno. The Emperor was wearing thick wool and was covered with a good rug, with his legs in fur boots, thrust into a bearskin bag. Yet he complained so of the cold that I had to cover him with my own bearskin rug. Our breaths froze on our lips, forming small icicles under the nose and eyebrows and around the eyelids. All the carriage's upholstery, particularly its hood, was frozen hard and white from our rising breath. When we reached Kovno, two hours before dawn, the Emperor was shivering as with the ague.'

That's at 5 a.m. on 7 December. They halt at 'a kind of tavern kept by an Italian scullion who'd set up in business since the army had passed that way' where Amodru, riding on ahead, has had a fire lit. 'The meal seemed superb, simply because it was hot. Good bread and a fowl, a table and chairs, a tablecloth – to us all these were novelties.'

But dare they pass through Prussia? Napoleon insists it's Caulaincourt's sole responsibility to decide which route to take to Warsaw – 'which, I confess, seemed to me a heavy responsibility, and worried me a lot'. He decides to chance it, and they set off. Crossing the Niemen bridge they turn left for Mariempol and Gumbinnen. Climbing the

'the almost perpendicular slope which one must surmount en route for Mariempol, we were forced to get down. At every moment the horses kept falling or losing their foothold and the carriage was on the verge of slipping backwards and tumbling over the precipice. We heaved at the wheels; and at last reached Mariempol.'

And all the time Napoleon is talking and talking – an endless monologue which Caulaincourt scribbles down at their overnight halts while he snatches a few moment's sleep...

CHAPTER 22

'THE VERY AIR SEEMED FROZEN'

Reactions to Napoleon's departure – a splendid dawn – 'we were completely iced up' – 'I've seen soldiers carrying officers on their shoulders' – 'only a very few were still themselves' – 'they couldn't even assemble the Old Guard's service battalion ... a sentry had frozen solid on his feet' – 'but Ney was there!' – not a very cruel death? – Le Roy's prayer – 'We've done everything humanly possible' – 'they told us it was Vilna'

The army, Paul de Bourgoing thinks, reacts to the Emperor's departure 'differently as between the regiments and the staffs, according to the character of each'. Emerging from the last Imperial Headquarters at Smorgoni just as it's being dissolved, Philippe de Ségur, Assistant Prefect of the Palace, runs into

'Colonel Fezensac with his regiment's eagle, escorted by some officers and NCOs, the sole remains of his unit. In a voice full of emotion I told him: "the Emperor's leaving us." After a moment this colonel, at first silent and pensive, replied: "He's doing the right thing!" Fezensac's position and mine were different; but this firm word, said in passing, restored my firmness of will. Such sangfroid gave me back my own. I tacitly accepted this noble example, to which it today pleases me to bear witness.'

But to Roman Soltyk, that ardent Polish patriot and Bonapartist in the Topographical Department, Napoleon's departure seems to be the signal for the army's complete dissolution. 'Everyone', says Fezensac, 'did whatever came into his head.' 'A great man cannot be replaced,' Ségur thinks. 'The Guard's veterans fell into disorder. It was a general *sauve-qui-peut*'. 'As long as he'd stuck with us,' Dumonceau confesses,

'our total confidence in him had helped to reassure and support us in our resignation. Now he was abandoning us, and all hope of any happy outcome vanished with him.'

Even the Old Guard seems smitten. 'No one was expecting Napoleon to leave us,' least of all Dr Réné Bourgeois:

'He'd left the army about a quarter of an hour and I'd gone up to one of the Guard's bivouacs where there were some senior officers, when a major of the Grenadiers came up to me and addressing one of them, said in a loud voice:

'"Well, there you are then. So the brigand's gone, has he?"

'"He's just gone by," the other replied, "same as in Egypt."

'Astonished at this expression – "brigand" – and not knowing whom it referred to, I paid close attention, and as a result of this conversation learnt that it was Napoleon who was being spoken of.'

Captain François, who'd himself been in the army General Bonaparte had abandoned in Egypt in 1799, is categorical:

'This news destroyed what was left of the army's courage. The men were sombre, and lost all hope of ever seeing their own country again.'

But others, perhaps most, are already too stunned for it to have much effect one way or the other. On Griois' party for instance it makes 'little impression'[1] Many, like Griois, Dupuy and Vionnet, realise on reflection that it's the only thing Napoleon could have done: 'He had to think as much about his empire as his army.' Others again are philosophical. When the remains of I Corps reach Smorgoni next day (6 December) and hear that the Emperor's gone, Le Roy, Guillaume and Jacquet take it for granted 'he'd be collecting fresh troops to come to our aid while we were at Vilna or on the Niemen. Soon we didn't bother our heads any more about it. We had other things than politics to attend to!'

They're only kept going by thinking how nice it'll be to get home. It's the only thought that's keeping up their courage. To von Muraldt, too, it seems that though the Emperor's departure 'soon became known, it made no particular impression on the great majority. Each was too preoccupied with himself and his own misery.' But Castellane has a private grief. He'd spent 'part of the night copying out the 29th Bulletin from the draft corrected by His Majesty's hand. It had been passed to me by the amiable and witty secretary Baron Mounier. The words *"gèle difficilement"* [incorrect French for 'it's freezing badly'] were written in His Majesty's handwriting.'

From Narbonne he's heard that, like the Emperor's other ADC's, he's been given 30,000 francs and been promoted. But while Gourgaud and the other *officiers d'ordonnance* have been given 6,000 francs a head, the adjutants 'have been overlooked' though 'they've done quite as much service'. The oversight festers.

Dumonceau, 6 December:
'Even before dawn we were on the march again in a beautiful winter twilight under a splendid starry sky. The atmosphere was calm and limpid but the cold more rigorous than ever. It was said to be touching -30° Réaumur [-37.5° C]. Even the very air seemed frozen into light flakes of transparent ice which were flitting about in space. Then we saw the horizon gradually lighting up with a burning red, the sun appear radiant through a light misty radiation its fires set fire to. The whole snowy plain became splendid with purple, and scintillated as if sown with rubies. It was magnificent to behold. The road wasn't encumbered with its usual crowd. We marched at our ease, though always tiringly because of the ice.'

Some debris of a convoy of biscuit intended for the army's rearguard, scattered over its surface, looks repulsive, but is avidly consumed by all who're passing by. Tascher:

'Excessive cold. Great number of men dropping dead on the road, sometimes stripped before expiring and left there naked on the snow, still alive. Bivouacked with the Army of Italy, 2½ leagues behind headquarters.'

In the breathtaking cold Lejeune, like everyone else, sees
'the road littered with dead men. The carriage wheels, turning with difficulty, caught up these ice-covered corpses and dragged them along, sliding. Haxo and I were marching arm in arm to support each other on

the ice. A soldier and an officer were marching beside us. The soldier took a bit of Russian black bread somewhat bigger than a man's fist out of his pocket and greedily bit into it. The officer, surprised to see this bread, offered the grenadier a 5-franc piece for it.

'"No," replied the soldier, biting furiously into his bit of hard bread, like a lion jealous of its prey.

'"I beg of you, sell me your bread. Here's 10 francs."

'"No, no, no!" And the bread dwindled by half.

'"I'm dying. Save my life. Here are 20 francs."

'At this, with a savage air, the grenadier's teeth took away another enormous mouthful. He took the 20 francs. and gave away what was left, regretting the deal.'

'We were completely iced up,' Lejeune goes on:

'The breath coming from one's mouth was thick as smoke, and attached itself in icicles on our hair, our eyebrows, our beard and our moustache. These icicles became so thick they intercepted our vision and respiration. Breaking the ones which were getting in my way, General Haxo, seeing my face and nose were discoloured and waxen, told me they were frost-bitten. In fact I felt nothing at all. I had to make haste to rub them with snow. A minute or two's rubbing got the blood circulating again. But the reaction of the heat after the cold on the hand I'd used to do it with caused me horrible pain, and I needed all my willpower to stand it. A moment later Engineer-Colonel Emi had the same pains for the same reasons. He threw himself down and rolled on the ground in despair. Not wishing to abandon him, we had to hit him violently to make him get up.'

Constant, the Emperor's abandoned valet, sees 'gunners putting their hands under their horses' nostrils, to try to get a little warmth from those animals' forceful breathing'. Dysentery, too, – or anyway diarrhoea[2] – is ravaging the column:

'Its victims were promenading their frightful skeletons, covered with a dry and livid skin. The nakedness of these unfortunates, who had to halt at every step, was the most terrifying picture death could show us. Others, almost all of them cavalrymen, having lost or burnt their shoes, were marching with bare legs and feet. The frozen skin and muscles were exfoliating themselves like successive layers of wax statues. The bones were exposed, and their temporary insensitivity to any pain in them sustained them in the vain hope of again seeing their own homes.'

Le Roy, getting to Smorgoni, sees

'several soldiers and officers unable to do their trousers up. I myself helped one of these unfortunates to put his *** back and button himself up. He was crying like a child. With my own eyes I saw a major make a hole in the seat of his trousers so as not to have to undress to relieve himself. For the rest, he wasn't the only one to take this disgusting precaution.'

Franz Roeder, too, is heeding a call of nature in the bushes when some Cossacks ride up. They immediately strip him of his fur coat – the one that had belonged to the voltigeur officer killed at Krasnoïe – torn and bloodstained though it is. But then, to Roeder's amazement – and also Sergeant-Major Vogel's, who's staring helplessly from another bush – the raiders suddenly desist and gallop away. What's happened? Luckily they've mistaken Roeder's Hessian Order of Merit for the Order of Vladimir, which has the same ribbon! 'Now, Vogel,' declares Roeder, 'I'm really beginning to believe it's God's will we shall get to Vilna!'

But the equally faithful Guillaume has caught cold – last night he seemed to have a slight temperature. How's he feeling? Get up, let's go, says Le Roy when morning comes and all the others in their group have already left Smorgoni. Guillaume takes the reins of horse and pony, but 'the poor devil couldn't stay on his legs, kept falling down'. Le Roy suggests he get on the horse he'd provided them with, and ride on ahead to the next overnight halt. He and Jacquet will follow on, leading the pony: "Get on with it, then! There's the rearguard firing!" But the end has come for poor ever-faithful, ever-resourceful Guillaume. Both his feet are frost-bitten. He has a splitting headache. The fever's strangling him. If he goes on it'll only be for them helplessly to see him die en route. They're just passing Smorgoni's last houses when they see an open door:

'"Carry me inside," says Guillaume, "and get going."'

But at least they can leave him the pony, the bearskin rug and the food bag? 'If you can't catch up today, try to make it tomorrow!' Guillaume's just protesting he's still got the money Le Roy had entrusted to him at the Berezina, when one of Ney's ADCs comes by and – though Le Roy protests he can't leave his brave servant – drags him out into the street:

'It was then, seeing the road deserted, I got going. And I did well to, for I hadn't done one league before I saw Cossacks behind me trying to carry off the rearguard. But Ney was there!'

One man sorry to leave Smorgoni is Brandt:

'It was the first place where we could get something for money. We'd also found some troops there who were in quite good order. We bought some bread at not too excessive a price, as well as some rice and a little coffee, from an old Jewess. It seemed to break her heart to separate herself from her victuals. It was the first coffee I'd drunk for several months [Brandt had only briefly halted in the Moscow suburbs] and though there was neither sugar nor milk it was a great comfort to me.'

Then Smorgoni too is left behind.

From there to Ochmiana, as Napoleon's escort had found out, is 24 versts (fifteen miles). An 8-hour march for what until yesterday was IHQ. To have been overlooked while Gourgaud and the other wearers of sky-blue and silver uniforms have each been accorded 6,000 francs, is evidently causing resentment. Ever since Moscow, where the egocentric Gourgaud was made a baron of the Empire, Castellane, who's merely been promoted, has been finding the arrogance of this 'bad bedfellow hard to live with' insufferable. Now, this night at Ochmiana ('nasty little timber town') the staff officers are 'piled up on top of one another in a wretched barn' and Gourgaud's 'leaning against a barrel, violently complaining of there being no room for him on the floor. His stupid monologue irritated me. Since his Moscow nomination his pride knows no limits, I reproached him for it. One word led to another, I got up, grabbed my sabre, he his; we went outside to fight.'

Their comrades protest that this is neither the time nor the place for a duel. But it's the cold that

'did more to send us back inside. We couldn't hold our sabres. To risk one's life for a place on the ground after escaping so many dangers proves the extent of our recklessness and indifference.'

Also no doubt the dissolution of headquarters morale. Now

'we're often being refused any water. Because of the cold the Grenadiers of the Guard, [though] well paid [to do so], often prefer not to go and look for any. Then we have snow melted in our pannikins.'

That night Prince Eugène and his remaining 500–600 men bivouac in a church. Hitherto the wives of Colonel Dubois of the 2nd Line and of the intendant-commissary of Pino's division, who'd joined their husbands in Moscow, have been travelling, well wrapped up in furs and straw, in a sleigh. That morning they'd left Smorgoni and, as usual, gone on ahead. But now the Réaumur mercury falling to -24° has been too much for them. Both are dead when their husbands catch up with the sleigh at Zapray. But hard-frozen corpses are part of the landscape. Le Roy's just about to lie down supperless to get some sleep on the earthen floor of a cottage where there's at least a stove burning, when he sees two corpses underneath it. They smell so nasty he goes out and sleeps in some hay beside a bivouac fire instead:

'Anyone who wanted to profit from it had to keep it going. They did this so well that all the horse cloths and timbers went into it.'

At Ochmiana Dumonceau and the rest of the Lancer Brigade come upon Loison's division – some 10,000 men, he thinks, in summer uniforms. Also some squadrons of no less lightly clad Neapolitan cavalry. And hears about the previous evening's clash with the Cossacks just before Napoleon had got there, during which part of the town's large supplies of provisions had gone up in flames. Even so, the lancers get a more than welcome ration of meat, flour and brandy. As for Loison's men, when Fezensac gets there he's shocked to see how

'after only two days of bivouacking, the cold had reduced them to almost the same state as ourselves. Finally the other regiments' bad example had discouraged them. They were being swept away in the general rout.'

To Kergorre the division seems to have been

'wiped out by the cold during the night. These troops were totally use-less and even harmful, since they swelled the number of the famished and the disbanded. The men could no longer hold their muskets with their frozen hands, even though they'd taken the precaution of wrap-ping them up in linen.'

For General Count *Wilhelm Hochberg*, future Margrave of Baden, com-manding a unit in what had been IX Corps, 7 December is 'the most terrible day in my life. There were 30 degrees of frost. I could only assemble 50 of my men; the others, 200 to 300 of them, lay on the ground, frozen. The last remains of IX Corps were annihilated. Doumerc's cavalry, which had made up the extreme rearguard, was destroyed, it too, during that unhappy night of 6/7 December.'

On the other hand the wind, when morning comes, isn't quite so strong and Colbert's men are entertained to another brilliant dawn. But soon they're shocked to come across more detritus of Loison's ill-fated division, left behind while advancing along the Ochmiana road:
'We found the sides of the road littered with dead soldiers whose regular turnout and fine clothing contrasted with the rags we were used to seeing. Coming as they had out of good cantonments and consequently less acclimatised than ourselves, they'd seen themselves instantly decimated.'
All along the roadside Cesare de Laugier keeps seeing
'the corpses of the Neapolitan vélites. Recognisable by their rich brand-new clothes, they showed the Emperor had gone this way.'
Kergorre, sharing some potatoes with his three companions and General Grandeau, notes that the thermometer has fallen from -16° to -28° Réaumur (-20° to -35° C):
'That morning the snow had a sharper sound than usual. The sun was so red you could look straight into it, as you do the moon, though the sky was cloudless. An icy mist swathed us, we could only breathe by putting some cloth over mouth and nose.'

That day Berthier sends off a dispatch to the Emperor that won't reach its addressee – so fast is his transit – until he's in Paris. Line by line, wasting no words, he details the catastrophe:
'Almost all the men of the Train have disappeared ['disparu' also means 'dead']. Only the gunners, out of a sense of honour, are leading horses, but many are succumbing, not even being able to hold a bridle. The Young Guard is completely disbanded. The Old presents scarcely 600 men together. The cavalry is almost completely disbanded. I've had all the vehicles carrying the trophies burnt, except one that carries everything that's most precious. The whole of Rapp's face is frost-bitten. Three of your muleteers have just been found dead. Last night 20 of the horses pulling the Treasure died. We've taken horses belonging to individuals in hopes it will reach Vilna.'
Catching up with the 85th toward evening at Polé, Le Roy bivouacs almost alone with Jacquet in a barn full of grain, straw and hay. For 10 francs they buy a chicken, mix it with some beef that's been left over and make soup:
'Ah, what a soup! Poor Guillaume, I said at each spoonful. If you could only have such a beef-tea you'd soon be well again!'
All night he can't sleep for thinking of him:
'Poor lad, he was so attached to me! Took such care of my interests! He's certainly the only servant I've had who never deceived me.'

Every evening Paul de Bourgoing's teenaged servant Victor, also so gallant, so cheerful, so devoted, has always been turning up – even if half an hour late – at Delaborde's bivouac. But now an evening comes when the lad doesn't show up at all. 'I inquired after him in vain. And I've never seen him since.' So ends the epic of the heroic little Parisian street-urchin who'd so desperately wanted to be a drummer-boy but who'd been turned down because of his puny physique.[3]

Berthier has got over his fit of despair and is riding with 'King Murat in the Emperor's berline, surrounded by 200 grenadiers of the Guard'. The adjutants, among them Castellane and Flahaut (promoted general of brigade at Napoleon's departure), are 'taking turns to sit on the box behind':

'I did one league like this, then I went ahead on foot. No better proof of our misery, as Flahaut caused me to observe, than to see a general and a superior officer count themselves happy to be able to sit up behind a carriage! For the rest, the greatest personages were regarding it as a stroke of luck. M. de Narbonne and others of the Emperor's ADCs took turns to sit up behind his Majesty's carriage.'

Murat has immediately shown his strategic, logistic and administrative ineptitude by wanting to send the feeble wreckage of III Corps, now marching with the Guard, back to support Victor. An order impossible to implement. And therefore quite simply ignored. 'General Ledru, who commanded us, just continued his march.'

Now no one's riding a horse. Hardly anyone has one, even at headquarters. And those who have one can't use it. All those belonging to Murat's chief-of-staff Belliard have long since died and been eaten. For three days now Belliard himself – still suffering from his Borodino wound – has had to be 'carried on the backs of a 27-year-old ADC, Colonel Robert, his intendant Pierre Aumann, and his foster-brother'. Cesare de Laugier admires other instances of such devotion. Though himself feverish with 'dysentery', Surgeon-Major Filippi of the Royal Italian Guard has flown to the assistance of several officers and

'without a thought to the musketballs flying about his ears, given first-aid to the wounded, put them in a carriage, and with great difficulty didn't rejoin his regiment for a long while, without anyone giving a thought to him in the meantime. At last he rejoined us, and his comrades, who'd thought he was lost, welcomed him with delirious shouts of joy.'

Then there's Major Maffei, who, like several other officers, is being carried by his men (but will die at Kovno). In this most desperate of straits Larrey's still being accorded special treatment by one and all:

'In the midst of the army and above all of the Imperial Guard I could not perish. And in fact I owe my existence to the soldiers. Some ran to help me when, surrounded by Cossacks, I was about to be killed or taken prisoner. Others made haste to pick me up and lead me on when, my physical strength having abandoned me, I fell down in the snow. Others again, seeing me tormented by hunger, gave me such food as

they possessed. And if I presented myself at their bivouac each made room for me and I was immediately wrapped in some straw or their clothes. How many generals or superior officers were repulsed or pitilessly sent packing by their own men! But at the name of Larrey everyone got up and acclaimed it with friendly respect,'
he'll write proudly to his wife in January. Not that officers and generals, as Labaume sees with more jaundiced eye, aren't for the most part being avoided, 'so as not to have to serve them'. Generals, officers, NCOs, rankers, are all one. Bonnet comes across a grenadier sergeant named Logeat commanding

> 'ten or twelve men of the regiment, guarding a cart at the roadside, in full dispute with General Ledru, commanding a division of our corps. This general had taken a great fancy to what was on this cart, and Logeat was defending himself with very disrespectful words. I took his side and the general had to make do with treating us as pillagers. That evening, to console him, I sent him half a turkey and some bread the little detachment had been bringing back.'

But the adjutant-major of what once was the resplendent, the privileged Guardia d'Onore[4] sees even more shocking sights:

> 'I saw soldiers of the Imperial Guard stripping Intendant Joubert, who they thought was dead, while he was crying out to them: "At least let me die before you strip me of my clothes!"'

But, Cesare de Laugier consoles himself in his diary (can it be he's keeping it, like Labaume, with 'crows' feathers dipped in gunpowder'?) 'I've also seen soldiers carrying their officers on their shoulders.' The Swiss regimental doctor Heumann is such a hero. When others – among them, regrettably, Thomas Legler (but he's promised his fiancée first and foremost to look after himself) – abandon his acting-colonel Zingg, he refuses to leave him. And then there's Berthier, always charitable to beggars along the route.

Such devotion from men for their officers has been hard-earned by years of campaigning. 'All honour to the nation that could produce such men,' writes Caulaincourt in an unusual outburst of emotion, 'and to the army that can boast such soldiers!' Perhaps it's Labaume, among others, Caulaincourt is thinking of when he adds:

> 'And shame on the scoundrels and disloyal Frenchmen who've in any way tarnished a glory so valiantly acquired!'

Tascher. 8 December:

> 'Extreme fatigue forces us to make an early halt by the wayside. Did four leagues; bivouacked in a hamlet on the road, sixteen miles from Vilna. Alacrity in all eyes. Hopes of Vilna!'

The cold, it seems to Boulart,

> 'has become more intense. I sleep in a church, on a pew and close to a nice fire which brings on the most acute pains in my feet. The nave is packed, lots of men are dying there. Terrifying cries of "Run away! Get out! Everyone here's dying!" awaken me. I'm in a maddening state of exhaustion.'

Jomini's suffering from pleurisy. Before reaching Ochmiana the intense cold had forced him to get down from Eblé's travelling coupé and bivouac, together with the Duke of Piacenza, inside the hard-frozen cadaver of a horse, where he'd paid 3 ducats for as many spoonfuls of honey. Even so they'd had to drive away marauders armed with axes. Buying a sledge off a soldier, together with the little pony that's drawing it, he'd stipulated as condition that the soldier should take him as far as Vilna. Dozed off in the sledge. But been woken up abruptly – in a ditch. The soldier had simply tossed him into it! Now a gigantic Swiss drum-major is shaking him by the shoulders and a familiar voice is asking in a Vaudois accent: Does he really intend to end his brilliant military-literary career in a Lithuanian ditch? Helped on to Ochmiana by the drum-major, he finds a fine house intact at the entrance to the town which is in flames. The drum-major hammers on the locked door. And who should come and open if not General Barbanègre, he who five months ago had been governor of Vilna town and welcomed him as his successor? 'Along a road marked only by rigid frozen corpses' Vilna's two ex-governors pursue their way in the latter's carriage.

There are occasional Cossack incursions. Already Caulaincourt has noticed that, glutted with booty, they're neither bothering to kill men nor even take prisoners. At one point Paul de Bourgoing sees some and some Russian hussars lying dead by the roadside. But is too cold to pay much attention. And in fact the Russians are finding the going almost as hard:

'The Russian general headquarters wasn't able to follow the French as swiftly as we were, the route being so pillaged, burnt and devastated that there was no means of engaging any other troops.'

All along the road Rochechouart and Wilson have been seeing

'both sides littered with dead bodies in all postures, or with men expiring from cold, hunger and fatigue. Each of us could individually take an incredible number of prisoners. Most, stripped of their clothes by the Cossacks, were wandering about half-naked, begging us, for mercy sake, to take them prisoner. Some said they knew very well how to cook, others that they were clever hairdressers, valets, etc. We were deafened by those cries: "*Monsieur le Baron*, take me with you. I can do this, I can do that. For the love of God a bit of bread, of anything at all.'

As for the body of the Russian army, it has

'spread itself out to left and right, where it at least could subsist, even though submitting to the effects of the lethal cold which was falling equally on us all'.

In a tavern at Ochmiana the French *émigré* sees something which

'put the finishing touch to the picture of the horrible sufferings the most beautiful, the most valiant army in the world was having to endure. Two big thin faces, with no flesh on them.'

They're two Portuguese officers, stripped of their uniforms by Cossacks. One of them is

'dressed in the most bizarre fashion, long underpants, torn stockings, shoeless, a wretched waistcoat, a shirt in shreds, and for head-dress only a black silk stocking whose foot dangled negligently behind his head.' To their astonishment Rochechouart, who'd spent some time in Portugal in 1801–2, addresses them in Portuguese. The man so oddly dressed turns out to be 'the Viscount d'Asseca, from the house of Souza', from d'Alorna's Portuguese Legion. Only by threats can he prevail on the Jewish innkeeper to provide them with sheepskins; and provides them with 'a pair of boots taken at the Berezina and destined for myself'. They'll serve for both of them until they get to Vilna with him. Just as they're about to leave Ochmiana

'a skeleton of a woman presented herself to our shocked eyes, asking for something to eat, and adding after having devoured what we'd given her: "Messieurs, take me with you. I'm young and beautiful, I'll do anything you want." Poor woman, we left her there.'

And all they can do while passing through 'the miserable town of Ochmiana' is to get the town's *starotz* (elder), against payment, to light a fire in the town gaol, where

'a hundred or so prisoner officers were behind bars, in their shirtsleeves, having been stripped of their coats, trousers, etc., by Cossacks and Jews'.

From the barred unglazed windows they call out to Rochechouart and his three companions that they're dying of cold and hunger,

'adding to their screams signs that were well understood by my comrades, who hastened to given them what was left of our provisions, adding some clothing'.

His companion Wlodeck explains that they're Freemasons, 'and that being Freemasons like them and being able to do so they had to come to their brothers' help'.

Miedniki, 'a village of 40 houses, with a brick manor house, 28 versts (17½ miles) from Vilna', is the Lancer Brigade's goal for the day. There Dumonceau catches up with his fellow-captain Post and the remains of his detachment that had escorted Napoleon. The road is hilly. Castellane's following on:

'The King's headquarters goes on to Miednicky (thirteen miles). Leaving at 9 a.m., we get there at 3 p.m. Horrible day. We've seen lots of corpses of the Neapolitan division. First it had come to meet us, then fallen back toward Vilna. Its soldiers fall. A little blood comes out of their mouths, then it's over. Seeing this sign of imminent death on their lips, their comrades are often giving them a blow on the shoulders, throwing them to the ground and stripping them before they're quite dead. Any number of frost-bitten feet, hands, ears.'

During that terrible night, Larrey's little Réaumur thermometer, still hanging from his coat lapel, falls to -26°, -27° and -28° (-32.5° to -35° C). Afterwards he'll realise that 8/9 December had been the coldest days of the entire retreat.[5]

Griois' misery is at its height. His clothing 'suitable at best for a mild southern autumn, is wholly inadequate in a Russian winter'. Ever since the Winkovo camp back in October it' has consisted of 'a gold-laced red kerseymere waistcoat, a tailcoat of light cloth, over it a one-piece riding-coat, a pair of cloth trousers buttoning up on the side, no underpants, very tight Suvarov-style boots and woollen socks. How-ever, it had been impossible to change it, and the bearskin I'd got hold of was no substitute for the mantle-style overcoat I'd been robbed of when crossing the Berezina.'

Excellent to sleep in at nights, his bearskin is far too heavy for the road, and he has to drape it over his horse. Cutting some strips from it he's made himself

'a kind of sheath, 7 or 8 inches long, attached at the ends by a string I passed round my neck. When on the march I thrust my hands into it, for lack of gloves, and made a kind of sleeve. But when on horseback I put it in my stirrups, and it was then my feet, more sensitive to the cold than my hands, that profited from it. From another strip of bearskin I'd made myself a chin-band which covered the lower part of my face and which I attached behind my head.'

It's in this 'singular getup, my head sheltered by a tattered hat, my skin chapped by the cold and smoke-blackened, my hair powdered by hoarfrost and my moustaches bristling with icicles', he's struggling on toward Vilna. Yet he's one of the few

'whose costume still kept something of a uniform about it. Most of our wretched companions seemed to be phantoms dressed up for a carnival [*en chienlits*]. One day I saw Colonel Fiéreck wrapped in a soldier's old greatcoat, wearing on his head over his forage cap a pair of trousers but-toned up under his chin. All these grotesque accoutrements were pass-ing unnoticed. Or if anyone did notice them, it was only to profit from such inventions as seemed most appropriate to keep out the cold.'

The future Margrave of Baden, with IX Corps, sees

'a cavalry general on a *konya*, his legs wrapped in tatters, enveloped up to the ears in a fur. A cuirassier officer in a fur-bordered satin mantle on a similar horse, trailing his feet along the ground. A civilian employee with a gold-embroidered collar, wearing a woman's hat and toddling along in yellow pantaloons, etc.'

Surgeon-General Larrey, just as exposed to the cold and to hunger as everyone else, is keeping himself alive by noting, scientifically, the exact effects of extreme cold on starving men:

'The deaths of these unfortunates was preceded by a facial pallor, by a sort of idiocy, by difficulty in speaking, feeble-sightedness or even the total loss of this sense. And in this state some went on marching for a while, longer or shorter, led by their comrades or friends. The muscular action became noticeably weaker. Individuals staggered like drunken men. Their weak-ness grew progressively until the subject fell – a sure sign that life was totally extinct. The swift and uninterrupted march of men *en masse*,'

he goes on remorselessly,

'obliged those who couldn't keep up with it to leave the centre of the column to get to the roadside and flank it. Separated from the closed column, abandoned to themselves, they soon lost their balance and fell into snow-filled ditches, which they found it hard to get up out of again. Instantly they were stricken by a painful stupor, from which they went into a state of lethargic stupor, and in a few moments they'd ended their painful existence. Often, before death, there was an involuntary emission of urine. In some, nasal haemorrhages, something we'd noticed more particularly on the heights of Miednicky, one of the points in Russia which seemed to me to have the greatest altitude. I have reason to believe the barometer, in this high region, had fallen considerably.'

Such a death doesn't seem to Larrey to be a cruel one:

'The vital forces being gradually extinguished, they drew with them the overall sensitivity, and with it disappeared any awareness of the sensitive faculties. It seems probable that at the last moment the heart became paralysed, and at the same time the vital organs ceased to function. The fluids, already reduced in volume by privations and the lack of calories, promptly coagulated. We found almost all the individuals who'd perished like this prone on their stomachs. Their bodies were stiff, their limbs inflexible. The skin remained discoloured and apparently without any gangrenal blemishes. In general, death was more or less prompt, according to whether the subject had suffered from a longer or shorter abstinence.'

All this he's noting with scientific eye though

'we ourselves were all in such a state of prostration and torpor that we could scarcely recognise one another. We marched in a depressed silence. The organ of life and of the muscular forces was enfeebled to a point where it was very hard to keep a sense of direction and maintain one's equilibrium. Death was heralded by the pallor of the face, by a sort of idiocy, by difficulty in speaking, by weakness of vision.'

Lejeune, like Bourgogne before him, like thousands of others, has an irresistible desire to sit down. And does so. He's just letting the blissful torpor of death overcome him when his comrades at Davout's headquarters force him to get up and keep going. At every step Kergorre's seeing men drop:

'The habit of seeing them grow weaker enabled us to predict the moment when an individual would fall down and die. As soon as a man began to totter you could be sure he was lost. Still he went on a little way, as if drunk, his body still leaning forward. Then he fell on his face. A few drops of blood oozed from his nose. And he expired. In the same instant his limbs became like bars of iron.'

Von Muraldt's companions are

'giving vent to our pain in various ways. Some wept and whimpered. Others, totally stupefied, didn't utter a sound. Many behaved like lunatics, especially at the sight of a rousing fire or when, after starving for several days, they got something to eat. Only very few indeed were still themselves.'

That day Castellane, for the first time but for a very good – or rather, painful – reason, ceases to make entries in his journal. His swollen right hand isn't merely useless. It's agonising. At the evening meal he can't even raise it to 'dispute the morsels' of food. But one of Berthier's ADCs, d'Hautpoul[6] 'an excellent comrade, took my plate and had the *maître d'hôtel* put everything into it.' That night of 7/8 December d'Hautpoul is his bedfellow. 'Some thirty of us were heaped up in that barn: generals, ADCs to the Emperor, officers.'

Now despondency has even hit a member of the marshalate. At 8 a.m. on 8 December the *générale* was being beaten in the King's courtyard. Castellane, helped to attach his last portmanteau ('my servants, chilled, frost-bitten, demoralised, were telling me it was impossible') by Augustin, the only one of Narbonne's domestics who's still 'quite healthy', hears why:

'It's due to the arrival of the Duke of Bellune, who's abandoned his two army corps. He only had 50 men under arms, and therefore has chosen to return in person to general headquarters. The Prince of Neuchâtel, who'd lost his head, came into the room where we were having our breakfast, shouting at us that we were dishonouring ourselves by finishing it and pointing out that the stand-to was being beaten. We didn't pay him much attention. They weren't even being able to assemble the Old Guard's service battalion. It was leaving its dead at its bivouac and a sentry frozen to death on his feet. The cold didn't permit the men to hold their muskets.'

Berthier's been unnerved by Victor's attitude. 'Having asked him where his corps was,' he'll write in his next report to Napoleon,

'he replied that it was several leagues away. I told him that when one has the honour of commanding the Grand Army's rearguard one should be with those of its men who are closest to the enemy. To this he countered that he only had 300 men left.'

Murat and Berthier tell Victor he's 'a miserable wretch' [*le traitaient en misérable*]. All he replies is

'"Don't attack me. I'm quite unhappy enough as it is."'

How are things with the Treasure? That morning Davout writes to Berthier:

'*Monseigneur.* I have the honour to inform Your Highness that the Treasure is having the greatest difficulty in keeping up. The wagons are too heavily loaded and won't move at all. At every moment it's being cut off without any human strength being able to prevent it. It seems to me necessary to replace the wagons by sledges which we would use our authority to seize in the columns or obtain in some other way. If this measure isn't taken the Treasure will never be able to keep up and be lost at the first slightly steep hill.'

'One Treasury wagon was looted by stragglers,' Berthier will write, passing on Davout's report to Napoleon, now far away:

'Only 12,000 francs were saved. We've done everything humanly possible to save the other wagons. But each hill is an obstacle. On the downward slopes, despite putting the brakes on, the cannon carry away the horses. Yesterday six out of a post of eight men of the *Chasseurs à Cheval* died.'

Only yesterday their Captain Dieudonné (ever-famous from Géricault's heroic masterpiece, just now being exhibited at the Paris Salon) was seriously wounded, evidently in some affray with a Cossack.

But in spite of everything, Captain Duverger, I Corps' paymaster, has managed to keep his Treasury wagon on the move. Now he's only got three more hours to go to reach Vilna. Alas, just then another wagon, containing 2 million francs, gets stuck in a deep snowdrift. Least of all does Duverger want to spend another horrible night under the open sky. His comrade who's in charge of it implores his help. Only when the Paymaster-General himself implores him to give a hand does he do so. And he and his fellow-treasurers have to pass the night in a little shed. There, sharing some provisions filched from the Paymaster-General's cook, whose wagon's been looted by Cossacks, they find 'an old sapper'.[7] He could symbolise the whole vanished army:

> 'His long red beard, sprinkled with icicles, flashed like diamonds. A bear's skin, fixed by a rope on his right shoulder, draped part of his bust. Aslant his head he was wearing his regulation bearskin, but it been shaved bare on one side by being habitually rubbed against the ground as a pillow, and on the other preserved only a few short hairs. The old sapper was pale and shattered. A deep bleeding wound furrowed his brow. His grey sombre eyes wandered mournfully around him.'

And when they try to wake him in the morning he too is dead.

That last night, only six miles from Vilna but in a temperature of -28° Réaumur (-35° C), Boulart too, whose feet are hurting so much that he's travelling 'in the cart of a *vivandière* of my artillery – though deep in its straw, I'm suffering cruelly from the cold' – has to sleep 'in a wretched forge, without a door or windows, open to all the winds'. Le Roy too, after the house where he and Jacquet have spent that icy sleepless night has nearly burnt down, spends its last hours going over his experiences in detail. Only the reflection that very likely his sergeant son would have succumbed during this – at last he gets the word out – 'rout' if the Cossacks hadn't captured him outside Moscow[8] consoles him for his probable death. As for Vilna, which is now so near, he's fearing it may be 'Smolensk all over again'. At this thought the convinced deist and hater of all priests and theologians is reduced to again praying to that God he believes in, but who, he assumes, takes but scant interest in the sufferings of mortal men. "My God," I said fervently,

> "'I who find such happiness in living and admiring your beautiful sun, accord me the mercy of once again being warmed by him [*sic*] and not leaving my wretched remains in this barbarous icy country! Let me see my family again for one hour! only one hour! I'll die content. I've never asked anything of you, God, as you know! I've only thanked you in all circumstances, happy or unhappy, as they've befallen me. But this one's beyond my strength, and if you don't come to my aid I'm going to succumb under its weight."

'Jacquet, who'd heard me, said: "*Mon major,* your prayer goes for both of us. I ask half of it. I've been listening and, *ma foi,* if these gentlemen aren't asleep they must have heard you too, as I've done. But believe me, with such courage as ours I've got it into my head we're going to get out of Russia safe and sound."'

Now it's morning. And they've only gone a few yards along the road when they come across someone who's evidently had neither their faith nor their strength. 'Where the road leaves Rokow it makes a little right-angle bend, after which it makes straight for Vilna.' Inside the elbow of this bend they see

'a Negro, a musician of the 21st Light Infantry. Probably he'd sat down on the edge of the ditch; then, trying to get up again, had used both hands to do so. But lacked the strength. The cold had gripped him. His arms were stiff. His legs stretched out. His knees weren't even touching the ground, only his stomach seemed supported by the road. His neck and head were arched up, as if he'd tried to sit down. His face was turned toward the town. I touched his face. It was frozen, frozen in this position! A child of a burning climate, it was as if he'd been struck by lightning, killed by 26 degrees of frost [-32.5° C]. I heard several passers by laughing at this unfortunate's eccentric posture.'

Victor Dupuy and his Major Lacroix, walking together along the highway, count up to 900 rank and file, almost all Bavarians or Württembergers, who 'within a very short space of time had fallen dead on the road'. Out of sheer curiosity Le Roy and Jacquet too, walking on down the middle of the road, start counting the dead bodies to right and left. Near a little village just outside Vilna they see nine men seated around a dead fire. Six have just died. Three others are already covered with snow. This depressing sight puts an end to their counting. 'In a little under a league and a half [4½ miles] 58 corpses.'

As Lejeune, Davout, Haxo and Gérard reach the hills outside Vilna they see that only 300 men of the once resplendent I Corps, mostly officers, are still with them, 'and the colonels and generals were reduced to carrying the Eagles'. A single drummer, the only one they have left, marches at their head.

'At 2.30 p.m.,' Jean-Marc Bussy notes, his feet soaked and frost-bitten, 'we enter a big town full of unfortunates like ourselves. We're told it's Vilna.'

The extreme limit of human endurance has been reached – and passed.

CHAPTER 23

PANIC AND CHAOS AT VILNA

A city of hospitals – another governor with a gammy leg – 'from time to time one changes hand, step and lady' – 'all vanished in the twinkling of an eye, as if by enchantment' – a general sauve-qui-peut *– a long narrow gate – restaurants and cafés – 'confusion had reached its peak' – 'I'd only enough strength left to eat' – Murat loses his head – 'Napoleon's cipher seemed covered by a veil' – 'He asked as a last favour to be allowed to embrace the Eagle' – those who could go no further*

Although otherwise intact and stuffed with stores of every kind, Vilna is already one huge hospital. Only at Ghjat, on 3 September, had Napoleon at last yielded to Larrey's appeals and ordered the War Office to send the extra surgeons and medical supplies the Grand Army had needed all along. Whereupon, says Caulaincourt, 'a certain number of surgeons had been sent, but the hospital supplies we lacked so grievously hadn't arrived; nor could they do so quickly, as the road beyond the Niemen offered no means of transporting them'. A man who'd got back to Vilna from Smolensk in September to help supply the acute want of doctors had been Surgeon *Déchy*. He and his 13-year-old son,[1] too, had found Vilna
'nothing but a vast hospital, with men arriving sick with typhus and dysentery. The former convent known as the Hospital of the Cadets, a big three-storey building, had fallen to my father's lot, with five or six hundred men confided to his care. No one could stay in these halls without fumigating them, so fetid was the air. The floors, on all three storeys, were covered with the intestinal evacuations of our unhappy compatriots, dying there in great numbers. There was no bedding, as one can imagine.'
But Déchy had been a man of action. To provide bedding
'my father had a lot of pinewood planks brought, and by having them planed down reduced them to shavings that could replace maize leaves. He had them spread out five or six inches thick, thus forming beds on which each man rested his head on his pack.'
No less devoted a doctor than a father, Surgeon Déchy had himself caught the typhus and died.
But though Vilna's fifteen hospitals and five depots crammed with sick and wounded lack for everything, any amount of other stores have been arriving from the rear. On 2 November a Polish officer named *Bangowski* had got to Vilna with a convoy of 60 wagons loaded with clothes, weapons and harness, plus 500 troopers from various regiments.[2] Hearing that the Moscow army was retreating, and some 'intuition' warning him to go no further, he'd decided to deposit his stores – actually destined for Minsk – in a Vilna church. After which he'd managed to find himself asylum in a damp and unbearably cold cellar room owned by a Jew and already occupied by 'four officers, sick or amputees'. Next day his intuition had been confirmed when the 120 survivors of the newly formed 3rd (Lithuanian)

Guard Lancers had come struggling back into town after two Russian light cavalry regiments had wiped out all the rest 'within the hour'. 'Vilna presents the most lamentable appearance,' Bangowski had written in his diary: 'Streets encumbered with wounded, dead and dying, ravaged by the plague [*sic*]. No room in the churches, in the hospitals. No means even of removing horses' carcasses. And ever more convoys of wounded turning up all the while from Moscow! Everyone's doing what he can to get by, without compassion for anyone else.'

Though the very first refugees' arrival on 22 October had caused a certain consternation, as yet no one had had an inkling of what was afoot. Only after the fall, first of Polotsk then of Minsk, and more especially after the annihilation of the Lithuanian Lancers, had Hogendorp and Roch-Godart, the two governors, begun to worry about its vulnerability. Vilna has a town wall, but no fortifications to speak of. So Roch-Godart had proposed to Hogendorp (who of course will claim the idea as his own) that all avenues and suburbs should be barricaded, and cavalry and infantry pickets placed out on all the approach roads. These and other dispositions,[3] Roch-Godart had thought, had done something to restore confidence. But since 1 December everyone's been getting extremely jittery. Each day Roch-Godart's been anxiously consulted by

'the chief families of Lithuania, who'd all sided with the French and were holding posts under the government. No more than they could I guess that the Grand Army had ceased to exist.'

By sending out Polish detachments he's managed to 'hasten in supplies of grain and build up stores to feed an army of 120,000 men for 36 days'. But his staff haven't had a free moment, and everything's been becoming utterly complicated. In poor health anyway, he's been finding 'the government of Vilna an intolerable burden to bear'. A man with a 'loud harsh voice' who's risen from the ranks and has a rough way with inferiors and superiors alike,[4] Roch-Godart has been wounded nine times 'with a particular attention [five times] to my left leg' – which is making it more and more difficult to mount his horse. And since the turn of the month he's been ill. His duties are crushing him:

'No hospital had any basic supplies. Men were dying in great numbers without receiving any help. Abuses were spreading rapidly in all branches of the administration. The town was filling up with people from all quarters. Vilna had become a real labyrinth, you simply didn't know where you were. But I didn't let anyone lose heart and forced myself to mount my horse and myself saw to everything.'

The anniversary of the Coronation, of course, had had to be duly celebrated. Lieutenant *Porphyre Jacquemot* of the 5th Company of the 5th Artillery Regiment had been ordered to fire a 21-gun salute at 8 a.m.; as many shots again while the *Te Deum* was being sung in the cathedral; and again the same salute at 4 p.m. By that time the whole town had been lit up. And in the evening there'd been a great ball at Hogendorp's palace, which Jacquemot had attended with a colleague:

'As usual, it opened with a *polonaise*, which is nothing but a promenade. Each cavalier chooses a lady and the most respectable person at the ball takes the lead, all the couples following after. From time to time one changes hand, step and lady. In this way one promenades for half an hour accompanied by a march, in such a way that, when it comes to an end, the last lady has become the first. It's the custom for all officers to go to the ball booted and spurred and wearing stable trousers. The women present spoke French, as they all generally do at Vilna.'

Next morning, a Thursday, Jacquemot and his gunners still had no suspicion of the disaster. But since Loison's artillery still hadn't arrived at Vilna, a battery of 6-pounders had been sent off, half of it manned by foot and half by horse gunners:

'It's being said in Vilna that this division has been sent out to prevent any Cossacks who may be marching ahead of the retreating army from seizing the Emperor, who's intending to leave it.'

On the other hand some 'very unpleasant rumours' had been spread by a courier who'd passed through the town.' On the banks of the Berezina we're said to have lost more than 20,000 men, 200 guns and a lot of baggage. The troops are in the greatest disorder.' What's happening? Rumours are rife.

Some days earlier Abramovitch had reached Vilna with Napoleon's dispatch from the Berezina and closeted himself with Maret; and Oudinot's young wife, noticing how reserved her friend's husband had become, had had her own grave suspicions that all was far from well. But then Oudinot himself had arrived. After spending two nights in Davout's bivouacs he'd slept 'a second time (1 December, 'one of the dreariest days' Pils will afterwards remember, 'the men lacked everything'),

'at Ilya. But how times had changed! The first time he'd passed through here his staff had attended a fête in the home of the *seigneurs* living in the château. Everyone had danced all night. This time the château was deserted and no one in this countryside was welcoming us.'

Determined to reach Smorgoni and, despite the loss of his coachman Chalon, who'd been so shaken by the Cossacks' roundshot hitting the coach at Pleschenkowiczi that he'd gone out of his mind, wandered off into the snow and had to be replaced on the box by Oudinot's *maître d'hôtel*, the party had pushed on. That evening Oudinot had asked his staff to get hold of some post-horses and had set off again early next morning to reach Vilna the same day. By about 11 a.m. they'd been at Ochmiana:

'Three miles further on we met a detachment of Loison's division which was marching out to meet the Grand Army. These young men, mostly fresh levies, had an air of great alacrity. They were singing to shorten their road, which was a foot deep in snow, and forget its difficulties.'

This had cheered him up. His faithful and resourceful ADC Le Tellier had gone on ahead, reached Vilna, and come back and a few versts outside the town met the party with Oudinot's great carriage:

'We were amazed to see horses in such good shape and rough-shod for ice. A few moments later we met a regiment of horse chasseurs of the

Neapolitan Guard, it too on its way to join the Grand Army. These horsemen were well mounted and magnificently turned out.'
Shortly before nightfall the wounded Marshal's carriage had rolled up and
stopped in the great square in front of the archbishop's palace. To his
young wife it seems his attendants are 'frozen stiff on the box. *Mme la
Duchesse,*' Pils goes on,

'at the foot of the staircase, took him into her arms. Doubled up with
pain, frozen, the Marshal, unrecognisable from head to foot, reached
the waiting fireside,'

and at the sight of the dinner table, laid with silver, etc., exclaims:

'"It's a dream, gentlemen, is it not, to be back at a properly laid table?"'

Then, suddenly, on 5 December, all illusions had vanished. The astounding news spreads. The Emperor has circumvented the town and left for
France, leaving behind him the frozen relics of his escort. Only five of
them, Jacquemot notes in his diary, formed

'from the debris of three cavalry regiments, will ever see Italy again!
They'd marched in 22 degrees of frost [-27.5° C]. Hunger and cold have
totally annihilated them.'

This, even Caulaincourt had noticed during his brief visit to Hogendorp, had
'quickly became known, and been the signal for almost universal departure. The Duke of Bassano with his *bureaux*, all the foreign ministers, the
members of the provisional government, all the provincial authorities, the
mayor, most members of the municipality – all vanished in the twinkling
of an eye, as if by enchantment. I've never seen such a panic terror like
the one which struck all minds at once.'

One of the first refugees to get here in advance is Dedem van der Gelder.
And Maret, before quitting the archiepiscopal palace where for four
months he's been the Emperor's plenipotentiary, provides him with transport to Warsaw. Not that he expects the Dutch ex-diplomat to get that far.
Dedem seems so desperately ill that Maret privily tells the courier who's to
accompany him that, if he doesn't survive, he's to obtain a burial certificate
for Dedem's family in Holland. Naturally he also goes to tell the Oudinots
what's happened:

'The Emperor has passed by tonight on his way back to France.'

Everyone's leaving, he tells them. They should do the same. The 'Bayard
of the French Army' is shattered. 'Catastrophe,' his young duchess realises,
'was a word he didn't understand'. Two francophile Lithuanian ladies she's
made friends with immediately beg to be allowed to leave Vilna with them.
Few indeed are the fugitives who do so as snugly as her severely wounded
husband, 'lying down and carefully wrapped up'. Her 'good coach, with its
mattresses, a *dormeuse* [sleeper]', has been hastily stocked with food and is
almost comically full. Also in it are four members of Oudinot's entourage,
all suffering from dysentery. A fifth, his *maître d'hôtel*, M. Roget,

'to whom notably belonged the glory of having grilled the mutton chops
the Emperor had partaken of shortly before crossing the Berezina, was

now on his knees, now lying partly stretched out on top of the others and twisting himself into every shape, and exciting their acute compassion.'

Escorted by 20 of Hogendorp's perfectly equipped cuirassiers, wrapped in their big white mantles, the *dormeuse* rolls through Vilna's paved but snow-laden streets:

'Not a soul was to be seen, except some pale shivering Jews, on their way to their speculations, which nothing ever abates.'

Such is the state of affairs in this town that's about to be invaded – as Maret has informed Roch-Godart – by 'a troop of 20,000 fugitives who, frozen and starving, are about arrive and are intending to pillage the magazines'.

Until this moment Roch-Godart's had no inkling of the extent of the disaster. The news horrifies him. Sick and ailing as he is, he summons the mayor and chief of police and impresses on them the dangers of the situation. All householders are at once to begin baking bread and give it to any soldiers needing it. But orders are one thing. Actions another. Within 24 hours

'no one was any longer bothering about anything except their own safety. All the Polish families were leaving for Warsaw or Königsberg. The mayor of the city, the police commissary and the principal civil authorities were abandoning their functions and fleeing the country.'

So are the ambassadors of the foreign powers. General Trechkoff (Austria), General Baron Krusemarck (Prussia), the Danish envoy, and Mr Barlow, Minister of the United States (he'll freeze to death en route for Warsaw) – all are leaving head over heels.

There's no doubt about it. The greatest military force in Europe's history, the incomparable, invincible Grand Army, no longer exists.

The Napoleonic tide has turned. At last.

Vilna's 'many monasteries', Roch-Godart goes on, 'belonged to various orders' and he has 'persuaded all the monks to retire into only one of them, to avoid all danger when the army arrived in disorder' – hardly well-advised (all the monasteries and convents, after all, have been turned into typhus-ridden hospitals) the order seems to be the only feasible one. Dirk van Hogendorp, too, is taking his measures. That day, 7 December, in a temperature of -27° to -30° Réaumur (-34° to -37.5° C), he has big placards put up,

'showing in large letters which monastery the men of each army corps were to report to, and where they'd find soup ready made, meat, bread and warm apartments'.

And three hours after dark, at 7 p.m. on Tuesday, 8 December, the first refugees begin to arrive. The approach to the town gate, Mailly-Nesle notices, goes

'by a road through a gully in the hillside. Palisades had been erected in front of the gates and soldiers were prohibiting anyone from entering. But we passed though in spite of their jabbing bayonets.'

Soon the road's 'encumbered for a mile and a half with carts and carriages entangled in each other and unable to move'. Even while still 25 miles away Pion des Loches' usual prescience has foreseen that 'we'd have to get there in good time if we were to find lodgings and food'. Telling his servant to stick with Drouot, 'whose *matériel* had been reduced to one gun and an ammunition cart' – himself he only has three caissons left – he promises to

'come back to the town gate and wait for them. Three miles from Vilna a line of French and Bavarian soldiers had been detailed off to protect our entry; and even at that point the crush was already beginning to be noticeable.'

Reaching the gate Pion des Loches finds it blocked by

'a broken vehicle. The men on foot were going in one by one, without bothering to get rid of what was left of it to clear a path for men on horseback. These, having their feet split open by the cold and wrapped up and unable to dismount, were patiently waiting their turn. It was one of the saddest sights I'd seen in the retreat.'

Inside the town walls Lieutenant Jacquemot has been ordered to station himself at what he calls 'the Minsk Gate' with eight gunners and a corporal, to prevent artillery vehicles from coming into town and make them take a side road to go and park on the Kovno highway. But though he stays there until 5 p.m., it's no good: 'because no one listened to me'. All he gets for his pains is a frost-bitten hand.

Morning comes, and Hogendorp, as protocol requires, rides out to meet the army's new commander-in-chief. By and by, coming toward him on the road, he sees

'the King of Naples and the Prince of Neuchâtel on foot because of the intense cold. Murat was all wrapped up in huge and superb furs. A very tall fur hat added to his already great stature, making him resemble a walking colossus. Beside him Berthier, his small frame weighed down by heavy clothing, contrasted oddly.'

The town gate is 'narrow, deep and vaulted'. And outside it there's already a growing mass of freezing men. To get through it takes Griois more than an hour; afterwards he'll remember how, even though the gate's only 200 yards away, 'seeing its long vaulting packed with men and horses being pushed over and suffocated by the mob I'd have given everything in the world to still be far away from it'. Victor Dupuy – he who five months ago had galloped into Vilna to the ecstatic applause of Polish ladies watching from their open windows – has to wait for the gate to open. 'Overcome with lassitude and drowsiness, gripped by the frost', he longs to sit down. But his fellow-officers of the 7th Hussars, knowing it'll be the death of him if he does so, hold him up and walk him to and fro to get his circulation going again:

'The King of Naples was about to come by. At the head of the officers I had with me I placed myself in his path. I saluted him. He recognised me, signed to me to follow him. For him the town gates opened up. We entered at his heels.'

At last Griois tumbles into the town: 'But I was alone. I'd lost the gunner who'd been with me. There I got my breath back, for my strength had almost wholly abandoned me.'

Once inside, an amazing sight greets his eyes. A perfectly normal town, going about its everyday business! 'The houses were still intact, the inhabitants busy with their normal occupations.' Entranced, Mailly-Nesle too enters the town

'with a feeling of prodigious happiness. We saw glittering shop windows, chimneys smoking, well-dressed people. And, above all, the restaurant keepers' signs.'

Sent on ahead by Colonel Dubois of the 2nd Cuirassiers – only three have survived – Sergeant-Major Thirion is also among the first to enter. And finds the town

'very calm and well provisioned. I went into the first cafe I came to; and there, seated near a rousing fire, I had myself served *café au lait!* How many cups of it didn't I consume, and little cakes besides!'

After which he takes rooms for Colonel Dubois.

By now it's between 9 and 10 a.m. Roch-Godart, aghast, sees 'all the army's debris arriving'. Even if Hogendorp, after what he's already seen at Ochmiana, isn't quite so surprised as Roch-Godart, he's no less stupefied – some will say paralysed:

'The head of the unfortunate column began entering Vilna. In vain, efforts were made to draw their attention to the placards I'd put up to direct them to the convents. Everyone, generals and soldiers, forced their way into the first house that seemed suitable, looked for its warmest apartment, lay down, and had themselves brought something to eat. The strongest drove out the weakest. Generals and officers, if they could assert a vestige of their authority, made the soldiers give up a place to them, even if it was only a room or a bed. The town would indubitably have burnt down if all its houses hadn't been built of stone.'

Yet there's an abundance of victuals. And, so Hogendorp will protest afterwards, they're being distributed 'without any formality to the first-comer who presented himself'. This, however, isn't how von Muraldt will remember it. According to an 'order of the day as cruel as it was half-witted' – and which he ascribes, precisely, to Hogendorp – 'only men who're still with their colours' are to get any food from the stores:

'Only those with the colours! No army corps, no divisions, no brigades, no regiments existed any longer. Not even any individual troops.'

Few, it seems, see Hogendorp's placards anyway; or if they do, ignore them. Muraldt may scorn what he's heard is Hogendorp's order that rations are only to be distributed to men with the colours. But Le Roy sees in it the paradoxical reason for the catastrophe that's building up at the long narrow vaulted gate:

'Perhaps you'll ask why these unfortunates didn't try to shelter for the night, like we did. To this I'll reply that most of the men who were marching on their own had left their regiments, thrown away their arms and, for that reason alone, found themselves repulsed by their comrades, who'd often had to do service in their place. These men were driven away and banished from the distributions. That's the reason why they had to march with their unit, but nevertheless without communicating with it.'

Now, having to rejoin the mass to get into the town, they're

'afraid the superior officers detailed off to supervise the entrance would have them arrested as fugitives if they entered on their own'.

This, as Le Roy sees it, is why the *fricoteurs* and 'the army' are

'pressing one another to suffocation point, while they could have entered by a side-gate, which was free. Where one went, another followed, like Dindoneau's sheep.'

Everyone who survives the crush is making a bee-line for the nearest restaurant or cafe, above one of which Mailly-Nesle sees

'written for example in good French: "*Au Veau qui Tette*" [The Sign of the Suckling Calf] – "*A la Renommé des Pieds de Mouton*" ['Famous for Sheeps' Trotters']. First we entered a German hostelry where everything had already been demolished and where, despite our resources and pecuniary offers, it was impossible for us to get anything. So we dragged ourselves off to the "*Veau qui Tette*", which, like all the town's other inns, was packed to the roof.'

There he and his companions, 'grabbing *en passant* some boiled potatoes destined for someone else', have to make do with a chimney corner and a bottle of brandy. The Marquis de Bonneval – 'a bizarre fact' – has

'one fixed idea: to eat some *crêpes* in company with some comrade! Someone pointed out a Jew who had this as his speciality. But alas I couldn't eat in moderation.'

Dupuy and his party of 7th Hussars, for their part, dive into

'a liquor shop a short distance from the gate. There were only a few bottles, about half a litre each, at the price of a gold *Frédéric* apiece [21.50 francs]. Everyone went through his pockets, his belt. The needful sum being put together, we each took one and, drinking to a better future, we quickly drained it off straight out of the bottle. It was cinnamon liqueur, so weak it didn't go to our heads at all; yet was of such comfort to us, even so, that I felt no ill effects afterwards.'

Lieutenant Vossler's group of Prussian hussars make for the big Café Lichtenstein, as do also von Suckow and his good friend Captain von Klapp – but not before they've already eaten the largest omelette a Jew can make them. They'd been putting a glass of stout to their lips when they'd noticed, under the table, a scarlet-faced corpse, dead from an overdose of brandy. 'From his coquettish uniform I saw it was a gunner of the horse artillery.' Not that this has damped their appetite. Throwing the corpse out into the street, they've gobbled up their omelette, refused to pay the Jew more than 4 francs for it[5] – he'd wanted 7 silver roubles or 28 francs – and gone on to the Lichtenstein, where they've found the Württemberg war commissary Schoenlin, who gives von Suckow his arrears of pay: 14 ducats (about 175 francs). With this he goes out and buys himself some clothes, muffs and a fur cap. Coming back to the Café Lichtenstein he sees some of his fellow Württemberg officers throwing an insolent French hussar officer out into the street for insulting their young Prince Eugène. Then they all have a game of billiards. And von Suckow falls asleep under the billiard table. Emerging from the vintner's, meanwhile, Victor Dupuy has again fallen in with some his officers:

'I established myself in a wretched gin shop, also run by a Jew. None of us had any money. I had a few payments of arrears of pay due to me as captain. I gave part of them to Lieutenant Korte, who went and got the cash from the army's paymaster, a man named Bresson. Korte brought me back about 1,000 francs. I took 150 of them and said to my companions:

'"Share the rest out among yourselves. Here's my notebook and my pencil. Each of you can write his name and how much he takes."

'And so they did.'[6]

Some high-ups such as Lariboisière are finding a room prepared for them and their staffs, with a nice fire and a dinner

'on a little table covered with a white tablecloth. Such a sudden change seemed like a fairy tale. We thought we were dreaming. It was a delightful dream. But it had a fateful effect on several of us,'

notably on Captain Lebreton de Vanoise, one of Planat's six artillery captains,[7] who 'went out of his mind'. Like everyone else, the first thing Major Boulart has done has been to

'try to provide for myself, the lack of food having completely exhausted my strength. In this my comrade Cottin and I were rather successful, though the crowd of starving men was making it difficult. But this meal so stupefied me and gave me such an urgent longing for sleep that, forgetting to rally either my servants or my horses, I only thought of going to take possession of the billet I'd been given.'

The house, Boulart finds, belongs to a cordwainer and is already occupied by an old acquaintance – none other than Captain Lignières of the 1st Guard Chasseurs. For 20 francs Lignières has bought bread and some potatoes off some Line soldiers; and off his host, for a further 20 francs, a small pig. Boulart, 'dying of cold', is admitted.[8] Likewise a gunner captain 'whose face had been burnt by a powder explosion'. His sleep is only protected by a dragoon and one of Lignières' chasseurs, who point a loaded musket 'though a hole made expressly for the purpose' to keep out intruders. But unwonted warmth, too, if excessive, can be fatal:

'Woe to the man who, stunned by the cold and whose animal functions had almost been annihilated and in whom all exterior sensibility was extinct, if he suddenly came into too hot a room! The exposed or frozen parts [of his body], far from the centres of circulation, were stricken by gangrene, which instantly manifested itself, and developed with such rapidity that its progress was noticeable to the eye. Or else to the individual who was suddenly suffocated by a sort of swollenness which seemed to seize on the pulmonary and cerebral system. He perished as if asphyxiated.'

Larrey sees Chief Pharmacist Sureau, of the Guard – he who during the night before Borodino had been sent to the rear to fetch a plasma to help Napoleon's cough and migraine – die like this:

'He'd got to Vilna without mishap. Only his vitality was enfeebled by cold and abstinence. Offered asylum in a very hot room in the hospital's pharmacy, he'd hardly spent a few hours in this novel atmosphere than his members swelled up, became bloated; and soon afterwards, without being able to utter a single word, he expired in the arms of his son and another of his colleagues.'

But outside the city gate the scrum's becoming utterly awesome. With evident satisfaction Lieutenant Jean-Roch Coignet sees the colonel who'd looted icons from Moscow churches drop dead – and his possessions being plundered by his servants. Any number of wagons and carriages are getting stuck and having to be abandoned. Seven of the thirteen horses of I Corps' paymaster Duverger have died in the night. Now, says his colleague Kergorre, his Treasury Wagon No. 48, containing 2 millions in gold and 'what remained of the trophies which Commissary Duverger with infinite pains had brought so far' gets stuck in the jam outside the gate and is snatched by Cossacks. So, immediately behind young Peyrusse's wagon, is the section of the Treasury convoy commanded by a certain Paymaster Roulet, 'a good fellow'. Peyrusse himself, 'dead with cold and hunger', gets through – though his convoy has been scattered, Luckily Kergorre (who witnesses Duverger's disaster) has got through with his horse and even a little box full of silver

'at the heels of General Grandeau, who cut a path for himself with his cane, shouting: "Make way, make way for the General!" – even at risk of being knocked down by those he was jostling. We were all dressed in such a way no one could be distinguished from anyone else. I don't mean merely the soldier from the general, but even a man from a woman.'

Then Kergorre, with his 'six weeks' growth of beard and a face black as coal and icicles hanging from my nostrils', goes and finds his *ordonnateur* – who doesn't even recognise him:

'I had to whisper my name in his ear – for a fortnight now I'd lost my voice terribly. One hour after I'd got there they served us up some hams. I ate one almost whole. So little did I feel my stomach, the more I devoured, the hungrier I became! Joly, my comrade from Mojaisk, objected vainly. Seeing how I went on, he wrested the ham away from me almost by force.'

But the Bordeaux does him good:

'I don't understand how it was that I didn't get drunk. In a normal state a quarter as much would have turned my head.'

But in the night Kergorre vomits it all up, undigested; and two of his colleagues die.

Delaborde's carriage too has to be abandoned outside the gate. And so does that of Pion des Loches, with its superb Chinese porcelain dinner set. As he fights his way through, Fezensac, who's been given General Ledru's permission to come on ahead to find out what arrangements have been made, is reminded of the crush at the Berezina:

'No precaution had been taken to establish any order there. Yet while everyone was stifling everyone else at the gate there were other side passages open we didn't know of and to which no one was showing the way.'

Planat and several other officers have to wait nearly two hours to get in. 'We were so stunned, everyone regarded himself as lost if he separated himself even a few paces from the column.' Reaching the gate at last with Sergeant-Major Vogel, Franz Roeder too is

'threatened with a horrible death. Swept off my feet, I was flung down between two fallen horses, on top of which a rider then stumbled with a third. I gave myself up for lost. Then dozens of people began to pile up on top of us, screaming horribly as their arms and legs were broken or they were being crushed. Suddenly one of the horses' heavings flung me into an empty space, where I could pick myself up and stagger in through the gate.'

Ill though he is, Roeder isn't so shattered by his experience that he can't lament the 'loss of a splendid English lorgnette made by Ramsden'. When the Red Lancers get there, at about midday, Dumonceau is horrified to see dead, dying and struggling men and horses

'heaped up on top of one another in a little hill more than two metres high. It was a veritable moving mountain.'

Slowly, ever so slowly, his Dutchmen clamber over it,

'pushing, shoving, hemmed in on all sides, horrified at having to get over it and at each step risking being overthrown by the quiverings, the convulsive spasms of the victims we were trampling underfoot'.

Yes, it's the Berezina all over again. Or even worse. There it had been a river to get across. Now only a long deep narrow gate to squeeze through. And yet the town has other – wide open – side gates! Taking one look at the horrific scene, Davout, Haxo, Gérard and Lejeune decide they'll never be able to get through:

'I couldn't get into the town except by some gardens, where I found a ladder which fitted into another ladder, and by means of it easily climbed over the wall.'

Inside the town the first sight to meet Lejeune's eyes is

'a cart belonging to the army's Paymaster-General. Its barrels had been smashed in and partly pillaged. But this icy metal had become so painful to the touch that the passers-by, utterly exhausted and hardly having enough strength left to drag themselves along, hadn't the courage to bend down and pick up the crowns, which were too heavy for them to carry.'

Happily he comes across his sister, who's been nursing General Vasserot, who'd saved her life at the Berezina. Marshal Lefèbvre's carriage, too, has got through the crush immediately in Murat's wake; and with it Louise Fusil, who's nursing his wounded son:

'Pressing forward, the crowd seemed to fancy they'd reached the Promised Land. It was there almost all the French from Moscow perished. Fighting cold and hunger, they couldn't get into the town.'

Once through, she drives to a house where Lefèbvre 'had lodged when passing through the first time'. It belongs to the wife of a Polish francophile, Countess Kasakoska:

'But the house was all at sixes and sevens. The Count was preparing to leave. We couldn't find a servant to give us something to eat or even make us a fire. The cold was at -28 degrees and we spent a horrible night. From the agitation reigning in people's faces I could see we shouldn't be staying long.'

Neither has Fezensac, once inside the town, seen any of Hogendorp's placards:

'Arrived in the middle of the town, it was impossible to find out where III Corps was to be put up. Everything was in confusion at the governor's palace and the municipality.'

In the end, utterly exhausted and unable to find out where III Corps is supposed to go, he pushes his way into Berthier's lodgings, where he finds 'his servants scattered. Having supped on a pot of jam without any bread, I fell asleep on a plank.' Yet the notices are certainly there. For when Le Roy and Jacquet at last get through the gate they see them written up on the first houses:

'Some orderly officers guided us, each to the place allocated to him. "Such or such a unit to the Benedictines, such another the Dominicans." The whole of I Corps was lodged in a large monastery.'

When Griois sees such a notice it's in the hall of the municipal offices, where one of his group has put it up to tell them where to go. But the instruction is vague, the house hard to find, and 'most of the inhabitants had shut themselves up inside their homes, and those I met with didn't speak French'. Luckily he falls in with one of his gunners, who shows him the way to their billet,

'the ground floor of a house, truly a very small one. But there were two rooms anyway, one for us [officers] and one for the gunners and servants. There was good stove in each, wood to heat it up and a narrow courtyard for the horses.'

A bottle of Spanish wine – 'whose taste one had almost forgotten' – brings him back to life. 'You'll laugh at me and pity me when I tell you that this moment, preceded and followed by such dangers, was one of the moments in my life when I felt the most real and complete happiness.' He shaves off a month's growth of beard and throws his reserve shirt, which he's had with him in his portmanteau but is aswarm with lice, into the fire,

'refusing pitilessly to give it to the servant girl who was helping me clean myself up. Then I took off my boots which hadn't left me for six weeks. Lying down on a mattress with some other comrades I had the delicious sensation of an unfortunate prisoner from whom the irons he's long been wearing are taken off.'

The 85th Line, Le Roy goes on, 'occupied two rooms on the first floor' of the monastery assigned to it:

'There I was charged with the Eagle and policing the unit. The staff officers and the colonel had gone out to have dinner in a hotel. They were to have sent me something to eat. But either by oversight or neglect, I only got the food portion due to my rank. This meant I had to share a room with some exhausted officers, who kept me company for the last time. Most of them had made up their minds not to leave Vilna until they'd recovered.'

He counts 50 officers,

'half of whom, unable to go any further, were determined to stay in Vilna, and a little more than 200 NCOs and men, only half of them armed. I'm sure that including its isolated men, the regiment, 4,000 strong when it had entered the campaign, couldn't have assembled 300 at Vilna. And we weren't at the end of our troubles.'

Someone tells him there's a magazine full of clothing, both for officers and men:

'Someone came and advised us to go and get some of these effects. But few soldiers, I saw, loath to be disturbed, were in a hurry to do so. I'd a trunk at the depot. I had it brought up to the room where I was. I found some new effects and took what seemed needful, notably a pair of brand new riding-boots.'

After which he distributes his few remaining possessions among his comrades.

Is Vilna defensible? Napoleon has certainly thought so. Surely this is the end of the endless retreat? Certainly the Poles are assuming it is.

But what's going on at headquarters, now not even imperial? Everyone except the Poles, Chlapowski thinks, is losing his head. In the troops of the Confederation of the Rhine he sees,

'the utmost demoralisation reigned. And the best proof of it is my meeting with General de Wrede and some Bavarians.'

Little is left of them either. Withdrawing parallel with the main army from Polotsk via Veleika and Nemenczini, VI Corps too has been almost destroyed. Approaching Vilna, Wrede had been ordered to liaise with Ney, but acted insubordinately. Now Labaume sees his 'half-routed' Bavarians turn up with a few guns, whose horses can no longer pull them, after – according to Lejeune – 'all day with the few troops left him he valiantly fought the enemy, who didn't cease to cannonade us'. 'In the morning', Chlapowski goes on,

'I went to King Murat's headquarters at the château. I met a man wearing a civilian cloak, a kind of turban on his head, with a sword in his hand, gloveless, and running, followed by some fifteen men armed with muskets, with bayonets levelled as if to charge. Catching sight of me and recognising my *czapka* and my uniform, he shouted excitedly: "Where's the headquarters? The Cossacks are in town!'"

Examining him closely, Chlapowski recognises his interlocutor as Wrede, whom he'd often seen in the 1809 campaign. And answers calmly:

'"I'm just on my way there and if you permit, General, I'll show you the way there. There's no need for us to panic. The town gates are being guarded by infantry, the military police are everywhere, and I assure you there still aren't any Cossacks in the town. But General, sheath your sword, or you'll frighten King Murat."'⁹

If only the Emperor were here! Then, Chlapowski's sure, order would soon be re-established. As it is, though Hogendorp has

'had a circular order printed and taken round to every house and posted up at each street corner, inviting the Marshals and generals to assemble there',

Berthier's being depressingly unsuccessful in assembling the generals of brigade, and even of division, at his headquarters.

'There were at least 100 generals in Vilna – but hardly ten came. Generals refused to listen to the orderly officers and the ADCs sent them by the Major-General.'

But in Berthier's house on the main square, next door to the palace – the one that was by rights the Archbishop's but by turns had been the Tsar's, then Napoleon's, then Maret's, and now, if only fleetingly, is Murat's – the Belgian Sergeant *Scheltens* and the 30 survivors of the 2nd Guard Grenadiers have broken into the Imperial Staff's food stores and are treating themselves to

'some fine flour, lard, fine oil, rice and good wine, even champagne, and some excellent cognac, baked some bread and pancakes and roasted a ham in the oven'.

If chaos reigns at Murat's headquarters, Hogendorp says his own house

'resembled a hospital. I owe it to myself to say that the enormous expense contributed greatly to the ruin of my fortune.'

Hogendorp had 'so little believed what I'd told him,' says Dedem, 'that he didn't even save his own carriages.'¹⁰ And when Ney comes to his headquarters to reprimand him for having sent the newly raised Lithuanian regiments behind the Niemen, he finds him 'with his ADCs, eating hastily, without any crockery – he too had lost everything'. Pion des Loches, too, turns up. While Hogendorp writes out an order allocating billets for what remains of the Guard Artillery,

'I read, furtively, a pile of printed orders of the day, dated I don't know which day, announcing that the Emperor had post-haste taken the road to his capital, having handed over command to the King of Naples. So, the deserter of Egypt was deserting Russia, abandoning us to our wretched lot and to all the follies and caprices of an adventurer who'd have been the world's biggest lunatic if he hadn't been its emperor.'

Asked to explain what's going on, Hogendorp can't. But tells Pion des Loches he's welcome to take some copies of his proclamation. 'I rolled some up, put them in my pocket, and left.' His three remaining caissons will remain in Vilna.

All that Wednesday the ghastly struggle to get through the town gate goes on and on. And by now, inside the town
'the houses were full. Unfortunates who'd managed to drag themselves as far as this in hope of finding succour, fell down from fatigue in the streets and squares and soon died of cold. All the town's doorways were so packed you could no longer get in or out. In a word, it was a real débâcle. Already the Cossacks had seized several suburbs and so to speak were all jumbled up with our men.'
Lieutenant Jacquemot sees
'troops are still arriving *en masse*. I believe a small effort has been made to assemble them, but it's not been possible. They haven't been given a single loaf of bread, though all the magazines were overflowing with flour and grain. Since 6 December they've even ceased making any distributions to the garrison.'
Jacquemot himself takes a lot of artillery officers to his lodgings, but has nothing to give them, 'and they were badly off, even if warmly so'. Von Muraldt has pneumonia. All his limbs are aching, 'but otherwise I'm all right'. Once inside the town Dumonceau has found
'the streets comparatively deserted; calm reigned, the dwellings were shut up from top to bottom, as in a town taken by assault'.
Behind closed shutters the Belgian lancer captain glimpses the pale faces of invalids. Even while proud of the good order prevailing in what's left of his own regiment, he imagines how it must feel for the French who'd stayed at Vilna to see what a state the army's in. Planat too notices that the 'men who'd been at Vilna or were on their way to join the army' are almost more terrified than the locals. At the sight of
'a kind of mob, more like a legion of convicts or hideous hobgoblins than troops, they became much more demoralised than we were. When he saw the demoralised columns [*sic*] passing through the town, Roche, chief veterinary artist of the artillery parks, who'd remained at Vilna throughout the campaign – a very fine fellow, kind and obliging beyond comparison [he'd lent Planat money to equip himself when he'd first been commissioned] – had a stroke and died.'
After the tiny relics of III Corps have elbowed their way through the mob Captain Bonnet goes to an inn and buys a pound of sugar for a gold napoleon. By now stragglers from the 85th who're still rejoining at I Corps' convent are reporting that the Cossacks are already at the town gates, trying to force their way through the rearguard; and already Le Roy doesn't 'believe the army will be staying very long'. Especially as there's no sign of any fresh troops. Everywhere Fezensac sees
'our ragged and starving soldiers straying about. Some were paying for the most wretched food with its weight in gold. Others were begging a bit of bread from the inhabitants and imploring their pity. Terrified, the

latter contemplated the remains of this formerly so formidable army which five months ago had stirred their imagination. The Poles were sorry because of the miseries that were ruining their hopes. The partisans of Russia were triumphant. The Jews only saw an opportunity to make us pay through the nose for everything we needed. Already on the first day the shops, the inns and cafes, not being able to cope with the numbers of clients, had closed, and the inhabitants, fearing our greed would soon bring on a famine, were hiding their provisions.'

A few distributions are being made to the Guard, but all the other army corps are so chaotic it's impossible to help them. Sent on ahead, the Guard Lancer Brigade's farriers, however, have

'obtained for us regulation billets, distributed to us immediately on our arrival. It was the first time such a favour had fallen to our lot since we'd set out from here last July'.[11]

Although given proper billets in the main street leading to the Kovno Gate and issued with food and forage, Dumonceau and Post go to a restaurant which they find 'packed with starving hungry men like ourselves, loquacious and noisy with joy as a synagogue'. Squeezed in at a corner table, they have to content themselves with 'a simple morsel of grilled meat and a bottle of mediocre wine, paid for heavily'.

Unable to get any sense out of the civil authorities, Pion des Loches and his friend Bitche push their way into a cafe where they manage to get themselves served two cups of bad coffee. Also, after insisting, a bottle of mediocre Bordeaux and 2-pound loaf which, though piping hot, isn't fully baked. Then pushing open a street door at random they enter a huge room,

'rather over-decorated, heated by a big stove whose warmth however couldn't melt an inch of ice on the floor tiles. Two ladies were there. We saluted them and took our place on a big sofa, loudly telling each other that we weren't going to be put out again at any price.'

The ladies, horrified at their appearance, give a servant some silver to get some food, regretting they can't offer the two Guards artillery officers beds. 'Beds, *Mesdames*! Since leaving Moscow we've slept on snow.' Greedy above all for eggs and meat, they're told good food is already in short supply.

'The ladies, doubtless afraid they'd be eaten up alive, brought us some wretched lukewarm soup, which we threw ourselves on avidly.'

It's now between 4 and 5 p.m. As darkness falls Dumonceau and Post are on their way back from their meagre and expensive meal and are hoping for a comfortable night in billets for once – when they hear a cannonade starting up outside the city. Good-bye to all hopes of a comfortable night!

'Fate didn't have one in store for us. Already the guns were beginning to rumble outside the town, mingled not far away with musketry. On all sides the drums were beating the fall-in. The men, grumbling, were running to arms. Others were staying where they were to get food from the magazines, which were said to have been given over to pillage. Still others were lying on the snow, against the walls of houses, not knowing whom to turn to to obtain a bed or help. By contrast, some unfortunate wounded or sick men were fleeing from homes where they'd previously been received, so as not to expose themselves to the vindictiveness of their hosts, become inhospitable at the enemy's approach.'

Orders come for Colbert's men to be ready to leave at 11 o'clock. Not daring to relax in his billet in the meantime for fear of being left behind, Dumonceau takes refuge among his stable horses.

No one at headquarters, least of all the King of Naples, is giving a thought to defending Vilna – not even for twenty-four hours – 'even though some remaining units of Loison's division are still staving off the Russians' advance guard on the heights outside'. Rapp, in obedience to his orders, has reported to Ney:

'We had a long talk. Ney too, urged the necessity of continuing the retreat. He regarded it as indispensable. "We can't stay here a day longer." Hardly were the words out of his mouth than the cannon were heard. The Russians were approaching in some strength. Fighting was going on to fend them off from the town. Immediately we saw the Bavarians. They were retiring in disarray, mingling with our stragglers. Confusion had reached its peak.'

At first, according to Rapp, Murat had hoped to make a stand. But now the reports coming in from the heights around the town 'remove all hope of doing so. He gave orders to retreat.' Telling Rapp he's to return to Danzig and resume his governorship of that city,[12] he utters the memorable words: "'I'm not going to be taken here in this piss-pot.'"

The first thing Zalusky had done had been to

'take a bath; and having got rid of the dust of our marches I dressed myself from head to foot in a brand-new uniform, made in Paris, and which I'd only put on once, in Moscow, since we'd crossed the Niemen'.

For him and all his colleagues in the Polish Guard Lancers it had been obvious this was the end of the great retreat. Resplendent in his dark-blue uniform with its scarlet facings and trimmings, its tall Polish-style *czapka* with its massive silver plaque and its silver aiguillette dangling from his shoulder, he'd gone out into the town to look for acquaintances. What a disappointment!

'I met with many friends who avoided me, partly out of shame, partly because of the jealousy Napoleon's Guard inspired. It was thought that we owed our having stood up to the privations better than others had to imperial favour, not to our own efforts.'

While he's studying the mobs swirling about the streets he's summoned to the regimental paymaster, 'who pressed me to draw my arrears, and wanted to pay me in Dutch thalers known as albertus. He explained to me that we were going to evacuate Vilna.' What a shock! Zalusky's pained and astounded:

'Our youthful Polish imaginations couldn't imagine we shouldn't be staying here. If the French leaders had done their duty as well as the Polish ones had there'd have been no question but that the army would have gone into winter quarters at Vilna. After a lot of trouble I prevailed on him not to burden me down with silver, so as not to spoil my horse. And in fact the trumpet was sounding the 'To horse!' I take off my fresh uniform, put on the one I've been marching in, with my sheepskin waist-coat and my mantle. I reach the square of alarms. I learn that King Murat wants to retreat further and that he's taking us with him. So that's how it's to be, our last hopes vanish and we must continue our peregri-nation beyond the Niemen!'

Orders come to the Lancer Brigade to be ready to leave at 11 p.m. 'At 5 p.m.', Rossetti notes in his diary, 'the King, the Viceroy and Marshal Berthier left the town and went on foot to establish themselves in a house on the outside fringe of the Niemen suburb.'

'In the midst of the tumult Prince Murat rushed out of his palace, pushed his way through the mob without his guards, and went and estab-lished himself in the suburb on the Kovno road, where, Your Majesty' (Berthier will explain to Napoleon afterwards) 'parked the artillery on our arrival in June.'

As he leaves the Archbishop's palace, Murat orders Rossetti 'to stay in town until the moment when Marshal Lefèbvre, with the remains of the Imper-ial Guard, should be forced to evacuate it'. Cesare de Laugier, that stickler for military honour, is utterly shocked:

'Who'd ever have thought that Murat, that soldier without peer for intrepidity, for courage, despising danger, accustomed to throw himself sabre in hand on the enemy – that this same Murat, no sooner than invested with high command, should be weighed down to the ground by so heavy a responsibility and become timid and irresolute?'[13]

To an indignant Cesare de Laugier it seems as if Murat's only concern is 'to save himself and abandon us all to our fate. Happily, it's only a ques-tion of moving his headquarters to a café on the Kovno road, a musket shot from the town.'

Murat's courage may have abandoned him, but not his customary gallantry toward the ladies. Through his secretary he has assured the Countess de Choiseul-Gouffier she has nothing to fear. Since Vilna isn't going to be defended, neither is she in danger of being taken by storm! The scene in the main square that night reminds the art-loving countess of a Teniers genre-painting:

'The men were lighting fires in the streets to keep themselves warm. A thousand men were to be seen spread out among the flames and leap-ing sparks. The Town Hall still bore some festive decorations. Looked at through the clouds of smoke rising to the sky, Napoleon's cipher seemed to be covered by a veil.'

Yes, the scene even reminds her of a yet greater artist: 'The night effects had something Rembrandt-like about them.'

Only this morning of 9 December have the imperial carriages 'escorted by the Dragoons of the Guard and which should have got to Vilna on 6 or

7 December, arrived in the greatest disorder' – Berthier writes that evening in a dispatch to Napoleon (now nearing Warsaw). They'd had immense trouble negotiating a frozen gradient:

'"Your Majesty knows the slope down into the town. It was nothing but a sheet of ice. Despite the lock-chains most of the carriages carried away and turned over on top of one another. The cold had stunned almost all the men. Most had frost-bitten hands or feet."'

Ordered to get under way again at midday

'"the élite gendarmes abandoned them. The coachmen and postilions refused to march. There was even a moment of insurrection against the stable-master.[14] They all wanted to stay in Vilna. At 5 p.m. we still hadn't got your carriages to leave. We have decided to burn some of them.'

It's from the burning carriages that some of the smoke veiling Napoleon's cipher is coming. Also (his doctor Desgenettes will tell Wilson) from 'his state tent lined with shawls, etc., all his table-linen, his state bed, etc. Here were buried or destroyed all the trophies that he took from Moscow' and of which 'he'd previously ordered drawings to be made' so that he could 'remake them in Paris'. Included among them, Bacler d'Albe had seen, 'the flags taken from the Turks during the last hundred years, old weapons, and a Madonna'. Doubtless also the cross of solid gold, 'about 10 inches high' which had been found inside the great silver-plated Cross of Ivan when it had been pulled down from the cathedral in the Kremlin. All night the countess watches

'the Emperor's carriages being burnt in the university courtyards opposite the palace, as well as a heap of other things – tents, camp beds, etc., etc. One young academician wanted to buy a magnificent gold mathematical case, bearing the imperial arms, off a sentry. But the soldier just poked the case into the flames with the tip of his bayonet.'

In the end, Berthier goes on, enough men have been scraped together to get the remaining carriages on the move:

'"But, Sire, I owe you the whole truth. The army is totally disbanded. The staff officers, our ADCs, can march no further. We're all tired out, can only walk."'

As for Murat's carriages, which had 'come from Naples under the orders of Fontanier, his stable-master' Rossetti doesn't say. But he's found 'three of my horses and two grooms who'd been in the King's convoy also waiting for me'.

Vilna's much despised Jews – a very large segment of the population – may be driving hard bargains and showing little or no compassion for the French who all these months have been behaving so arrogantly toward them. But now they're being

'very useful. When no one could supply any more bread or sugar, or coffee, or tea, etc., they brought us spiced bread. Better still, they could even un-nest – God knows where from – means of transport, horses, sledges, when there were none to be had anywhere. Thanks to them some hundreds of officers managed to escape from Russia's frozen plains. But "*le monsieur* had to have money", even a lot of money, because they were robbers beyond all expression.'

Sledges and sleighs, above all, are in maximum demand. The otherwise unprejudiced von Suckow has to pay 20 roubles for a sledge which, he assumes, 'hadn't cost our noble intermediary more than a tenth part of that sum'.

Hearing the drums sounding the 'Fall-in!', Griois and his comrades assume

'these warlike sounds only applied to the Vilna garrison, charged with driving away the enemy from the town. They troubled us very little. Nor had I paid much attention, on getting here, to Marshal Ney, whom I'd seen on the square forming up such soldiers as he'd been able to reunite into platoons.'

Fezensac says the 'officers of III Corps, like the rest of the army, had spent the day quietly enough in the houses, and troubled themselves very little when they heard the *générale* go, or about the approach of the enemy'. And Hochberg, Margrave of Baden – loth even to pause at Vilna and wanting to make a bee-line for the German frontier – sees '74 officers and doctors of the Baden troops refusing to leave'. Griois and his friends are calmly having supper when the orderly officer they've sent to Eugène's headquarters returns:

'Never in my life shall I forget how we felt when he told us the Prince, like the rest of the army, was about to get going and that Vilna was going to be entirely evacuated during the night. I was stunned. The most utter discouragement seized hold of me. Death seemed preferable to the fatigues and sufferings we were again going to have to endure.'

He longs to get a fever, as an excuse to stay. But his temperature remains obstinately normal. His feet, however, have swollen so he can't get his boots on again. 'So I was going to have to stay at Vilna or else leave in the icy cold, legs bare and with no other shoes except a pair of old slippers I'd had great difficulty in finding in the house.' 'So in this terrible cold,' von Muraldt hears to his despair,

'now at -28° (-35° C), this unexampled retreat was to go on! My strength didn't suffice for me to continue the journey on horseback, still less so on foot.'

At the same time he can't bear the thought of being taken prisoner. Fortunately a Captain von Hagens 'of the Bavarian Lifeguards' [*sic*] who's just joined his group, overhears him discussing with his friend Knecht what to do now, and his own horse having just died, but who has a little cart and a servant to drive it, suggests they harness up Muraldt's horse to it, so that the feverishly coughing Muraldt can ride in it. Well, for lack of a sleigh, a cart will do. Said and done. The benevolent Hagens arranges everything. Since Knecht is to proceed on horseback with the rest of the group, they bid each other a fond farewell 'hoping to meet again in better times'. And Muraldt takes his seat in the cart. But Hagens feels he must go off and get some bread and food for the journey; and suggests they drive to the market place and wait for him there. Which they do:

'From all the town's streets and alleyways crowds of people were already crossing the square en route for Kovno. Already we could hear cannon-fire and even some musketry from the surrounding hills. Each moment the disorder and noise were growing worse. I waited impatiently for my fellow-traveller to come back. In vain I looked to right and left. A long while we waited; but still he didn't come. Meanwhile the cannonade was growing and coming closer to the town. From the men hurrying past us we caught the words: "We're cut off. The Cossacks have occupied the Kovno road", and so forth.'

Muraldt and the servant discuss what to do, decide to wait a little while longer. But when, after two hours, von Hagens still doesn't put in an appearance, they decide to leave without him. Bonneval for his part is still obsessively guzzling *crêpes* when 'fortunately the sound of the Russian guns wrenched us away from our feast, and we got going again'. Now it's 11 p.m. In I Corps' monastery Le Roy hears

'a shout of "To arms!" The drums beat the "Fall-in!" Half asleep, still not believing my ears, I'm just sitting up, when the colonel tells me to bring the regiment downstairs, says he's waiting to take us to new lodgings.'

Pushing the regiment's Eagle-bearer in front of him and lit by several fine candles, Le Roy tries to encourage his exhausted comrades of the 85th by telling them they've better lodgings waiting for them in the suburbs, where they'll be better able to defend themselves if attacked. But several officers, he sees in the candlelight, are in no mood to obey:

'Come along, captains! Come along, lieutenants! You who've got this far, surely you aren't going to let me leave all on my own? Are you going to abandon your Eagle just when you're getting back to a friendly country? Come, lads, just a little more courage! I'm in the same wretched state you are, and yet here you are, wanting to add to my sufferings the chagrin of seeing brave men abandon themselves to the tender mercies of a enemy who's furiously determined to ruin us. Oh, believe me, you can hope for no pity. Stay here, and you're giving yourselves over to death.'

(At least that's what he, as a grandfather, will say he said.) One of the older captains, who's been with the 85th since Egypt and fought in innumerable battles, can't resist Le Roy's stirring harangue and gets up with difficulty:

'"Help me up, even if I'm going to die at the foot of the stairs. Help me up," he said to his comrades, "so I can die a bit further on." We set him on his legs. He couldn't take even one step. His legs, so long stiff and swollen, could no longer support him. Collapsing again into a sitting position, he asked as a last favour to be allowed to embrace the Eagle. Three of his friends and several soldiers tried in vain to come with us. Like him they embraced the Eagle and shed tears at this symbol of a distant fatherland. We left them with two sappers to look after them until the enemy got there.'[15]

The cold beer offered to Pion des Loches and his friend Bitche by the ladies has immediately given him diarrhoea. Even so, they're still at table when, at 11 p.m., they too hear the *générale* being beaten. Realising what's going to happen and afraid of waking up too late tomorrow morning, des Loches convinces the others to come with him to Murat's headquarters at the café in the suburbs, where they spend the small hours with other artillerymen and officers, most of whom have severe colds and whose coughing makes a hellish din all night:

'I was bent double on a bale of hay and unable to stretch my legs. My diarrhoea was getting worse and worse. Unable to get out, I was reduced to shoving aside the bales of hay I was lying on.'

All that's left of Pion's wagonful of provisions, wines, liqueurs, etc., so carefully stocked in Moscow, is 'a few sugar loaves'.

Rapp, his nose, one ear and two fingers frost-bitten, has meanwhile dismounted at Hogendorp's headquarters, where he inquires after Ney, to whom Napoleon had ordered him to give his support. And Ney tells him:

'I've just had the *générale* beaten, and have hardly been able to assemble 500 men. They're all frost-bitten, exhausted and despondent. No one wants to hear another word about fighting. You look as if you're in a bad way?'

That night Roch-Godart's feeling so ill he could die:

'But my worst affliction, much though I was suffering physically, was not to be able to mount a horse in these critical moments and support the fatigues and cold I was going to be exposed to.'

Many, perhaps most, of the 20,000 or so of those who can go no further are wounded men. After a few hours rest to recover from his own utter exhaustion, Larrey has made

'a quick visit to the hospitals, to make sure they were being served in those respects which concerned me. At the Hospice of Charity I gathered together the sick surgeons and principal wounded officers, whom I confided to the especial care of the good Grey Sisters. In all the hospitals, beside all such medical officers, I left a sufficient number of surgeons of all grades to treat the wounded. I left them letters of recommendation to the senior medical officers of the Russian army; and got ready to join the Guard and the staff.'

Neither is Lefèbvre's son – known to the whole army as 'Coco' – in a state to be transported any further. So at their host's house, where comfortable lodgings and a good dinner had been prepared in advance, the terrible decision is taken to leave him too behind. And Louise Fusil – remembering how the old Marshal had saved her life between Krasnoïe and the Berezina – nobly volunteers to stay on as his son's nurse:

'Late that evening the Marshal came back and told us everyone was leaving; and he wrote to the Russian general commanding the outposts that, forced to leave his son in the town, he trusted in his loyalty to treat him generously as an enemy.'

One of Lefèbvre's ADCs is sent off with the message.

Obviously Sergeant Scheltens and his 29 comrades of the 2nd Grenadiers have strong digestions; for they, at least, have survived their sudden banquet. They're just coming out of Berthier's house when Scheltens sees

'a soldier killed in a manner in which no one, perhaps, can ever before have left for the next world. Our Lieutenant Seraris was just coming out. He was carrying a ham under each arm. Appears a soldier, barring his way and demanding one of his hams. By way of reply our man instantly got a blow on the head with the ham, applied with such force it felled him to the ground. He was so weak, it's only fair to add, little was needed to slay him.'

Out there on the main square Lefèbvre has 'drawn up the 600 Grenadiers of the Guard that still remained to him in battle formation'. But Captain Lignières sees how the agonising prospect of having to abandon his sick son is causing the poor old man utterly to lose his head:

'Standing in front of us, the 1st Regiment of Chasseurs of the Old Guard – to be more correct, of the remains of the Old Guard – he said: "Look, here's this Old Guard which was the terror of Europe, of the world. Look what a state it's in! You think you'll see France again? Not one of you will ever see it again." And pointing:

'"D'you hear the guns here, d'you hear them over there?"

'A voice shouted: "Silly old fool, shut up! If we've got to die, we'll die."

'One of the King of Naples' ADCs who'd retained all his vigour and activity [Rossetti perhaps?] came to tell him to report to the king. [Afterwards] we were informed that the king had sharply reprimanded him. We never saw him again.'[16]

Although 'furiously tempted to remain behind' with his faithful servant-cum-foster-brother Louis, Mailly-Nesle too has decided he'll have to leave him behind to the tender mercies of the enemy. Reluctantly he entrusts him to the care of a Jew who at first refuses 'to take in someone who was so ill'. He leaves him all his money; 'and we parted, tears in our eyes'. Once again blue blood has recourse to its peers. Going to the palace just after Murat has evacuated it, he finds everything there in turmoil. Flouting the efforts of some officers who fail to recognise him, swear at him and try to turn him away, the young aristocrat gets hold of Narbonne[17] who at once offers Mailly-Nesle 200 gold napoleons – 'but I only accepted half'. Thanks to Caulaincourt's wise measures no fewer than 80 of the 715 IHQ horses have reached Vilna safe and sound. And once again Mailly-Nesle's given one of them.

Bumping into his brigade commander General Jacqueminot and his chief-of-staff Tavernier, Victor Dupuy hears that Sébastiani, as captain of the Sacred Squadron's 2nd Company, has occupied the palace courtyard. All its members are to assemble there at midnight with their horses. So he and his remaining officers of the 7th Hussars do so. Invited upstairs, they're officially informed of the Emperor's departure for France. 'We were told not to become disunited and that in a few moments we'd be marching for Kovno.' News which causes Dupuy – as he himself admits – to lapse from virtue:

'Coming closer to the fire in General Sébastiani's drawing-room, I saw in a corner of the mantelpiece a bottle with its cork half out. I picked it up. It was full. Stuffing it hurriedly under my cloak, I went out, signing to one of my comrades to follow me. As soon as we were in an antechamber I sampled the bottle's contents. It was excellent wine. We drained it quickly. I went back into the drawing-room, put the bottle back in its place, and left, laughing at its owner's disappointment when he found it empty.'

Boulart, meanwhile, is

'just giving myself up to the delight of being able to sleep in a good bed, when someone came and told me Vilna was being evacuated and that we'd better get going.'

A long time he lies there, trying to make up his mind whether he can't afford to sleep on until morning:

'But at length, at midnight, I pulled myself together and went to General Sorbier, where I got into Colonel Lallemand's[18] carriage, together with Captain Evain who, having been burnt at Krasnoïe by the explosion of an ammunition box, had been travelling in it for several days.'

Neither has Griois, with his swollen feet still in slippers, been able to face up to the prospect of having to resume the march. Come what may, he has decided he's going to stay where he is. But then, suddenly, a fellow-officer, 'a M. Guyot, who'd left from Verona with a detachment of remounts and conscripts and been kept at Vilna by the governor' and who'd been lingering in Vilna for the past month, turns up. Both he and his men and horses, Guyot says, are in tiptop condition,

'and were at my disposal. With a zeal and an urgency I'll never forget as long as I live, he undertook to find a sledge, harness two of his best horses to it, and come and fetch me in an hour or two.'

Which Guyot does. What's more he brings with him a pair of his own boots, large enough for Griois' swollen feet. This gives Griois back his courage 'which, I admit, had entirely abandoned me that evening'. Some time after 1 a.m. Guyot comes back and fetches him. Others of his party have already gone on ahead;

'Only two of those who'd shared our billet, utterly worn out by fatigue and with frost-bitten feet, preferred to wait for the enemy.'

Giving up all hope of ever again seeing his adjutant-major 'M. Lenoble,[19] who'd never left my side throughout the campaign' and whom he hasn't seen since their last bivouac, Griois climbs into a sledge filled with hay. And off they go, Guyot riding and then walking beside it, followed by some gunners, one them leading Griois' horse. Rossetti's servant, too, has swapped his wagon for a sleigh, 'loading it with my effects and the new provisions of food he'd got hold of in Vilna'. Now at 2 a.m., 'an adjutant of the Guard came to warn me that Marshal Lefèbvre was getting ready to leave the town, and that Marshal Ney, who'd resumed command of the rearguard, would be following him at one hour's distance. I went to the King and spent the rest of the night at his headquarters.'

After buying himself 'a fur hat, fur gloves and fur boots', Lieutenant Vossler together with some Prussian cavalry officers who've have placed themselves under the command of General Count Norman have decided to follow side roads to the Niemen and then each make his own way home. Unfortunately no one's been giving any orders to von Suckow. At the Café Lichtenstein he's awakened by a violent kick in the ribs

'from M. Lichtenstein in person. With a ferocious air this café-keeper who'd earned so much money from us and who'd always received us in the most flattering manner and with the humblest and deepest bows, now shouted at me: "Get up, you dog of a German! And get the hell out of here! Your comrades have already run away and are getting the treatment from the Cossacks they deserve." Yes, the Cossacks were in the streets. On all sides one heard shouts, oaths, whiplashes being applied, and groans in I don't know how many languages.'

Franz Roeder, in the home of a drunken English vet named Mr Drew who'd been his host in July, is feeling too dreadfully ill to go on. With the best will in the world neither he nor his Sergeant-Major Vogel can go a step further. Roeder, that sharply intellectual, humane if at times arrogant man, that stickler for justice who could never resist the temptation of another campaign, has undergone a religious conversion more heartfelt and decisive and certainly less rhetorical than Le Roy's: '10 December: I'm sitting here in Vilna! It's morning and I've slept in a bed, completely undressed!' Roeder thanks God from the bottom of his heart; prays he, even so, may reach the frontier: 'God, what appalling misery! And all this has been survived by a man in failing health, with swollen feet and hands, thin as lath! But God be praised, the pain in my chest has abated.' With this pious but heartfelt reflection he falls into a kind of delirium, in which he dreams he's

'still on the icy road, where the dead, as if on a battlefield, lie in frozen ranks along the roadside, and an infinite number of horses.'

Sometimes he thinks he's going mad ...[20]

'More than 20,000 men, almost all sick,' Fezensac sums up, 'several generals, many officers, almost all sick, fell into the power of the enemy, as well as stocks of victuals, armaments and clothing.' Among them are 3,000 to 4,000 officers. Also numerous women. One, after being tragically separated from her two children en route, is Mme Marie-Rose Chalmé – she who'd been interviewed by Napoleon in the Petrovskoï Palace outside Moscow.[21] Like so many others – like Franz Roeder, almost – she'll die in Vilna – probably from typhus.

CHAPTER 24

PONARI'S FATAL HILL

Why the arsenal wasn't blown up – Ney's new rearguard – Mouton the poodle's last fight – 'he was like one of the heroes of olden time' – gold millions in the snow – 'the sharpest cry I'd ever heard him utter' – a poor Polish maidservant – Ambassador Pradt is dismissed

At 4 a.m., in a sudden brief but heavy snowfall, III Corps, a mere couple of hundred men, leaves at Murat's heels. Of the 4th Line all that's left is a sergeant and ten men. The temperature, Larrey notices as he leaves, has 'risen a few degrees. A great deal of snow fell in those few moments.' Marching out through the Kovno suburb with the Old Guard in pitch darkness and the heavily falling snow, III Corps is followed by the debris of all the others. And when at 6 a.m. IV Corps – also only a mere hundred or so men still under arms – leaves the St-Raphael monastery, Labaume and Cesare de Laugier everywhere see

'the courtyards, galleries, stairs of buildings full of soldiers. We left in silence, leaving the streets littered with soldiers drunk, dead or asleep. Neither shouts nor orders could get anyone to obey.'

Those of the 85th who'd responded to Le Roy's exhortations had made up their bivouac fires 'from newly constructed but dismantled houses in the Kovno suburb' just opposite Murat's headquarters. Leaving them, they too follow on.

But before leaving his café Murat – or is it Berthier? – has suddenly remembered something. A hundred or so miles way to the north-west Macdonald's X Corps, which has been besieging Riga but done little fighting, is still virtually intact. For some time now he's been without orders. 'Macdonald', says Hogendorp, 'had been forgotten about.' Now Berthier hurriedly entrusts a dispatch to a Prussian staff-major who's been waiting for them in Vilna. X Corps, of which two-thirds consist of General Yorck's 'superbly equipped' Prussians, is to withdraw immediately to the Niemen at Kovno. The Prussian major having been sent off with his dispatch, 'an hour before daybreak the King, the Viceroy and the Prince of Neuchâtel left the Vilna suburb and took the Kovno road.'

As a parting administrative gift to the Lithuanian capital Hogendorp has ordered Eblé to blow up its arsenal. The task devolves on Lieutenant Jacquemot, whose company of the 5th Artillery Regiment has left prematurely. This snowy or, as it soon turns out to be, icy clear morning Jacquemot's kicking his heels in the town square, longing for something to eat, when his major comes by. Why's he idling there? Why isn't he getting busy? The captain who's been charged with the job, Jacquemot replies, has gone to get orders from the Marshal. At that moment his own superior turns up and

'has the fuzes cut and placed, ready for lighting, on some planks pierced expressly for the purpose'.

By now it's 8.30 a.m., and already the Cossacks are infiltrating the town from all quarters. Some, Jacquemot's gunners see,

'together with some infantrymen, had climbed the hill beside the arsenal and would soon be reaching it in spite of us'.

And though some of his men have already been detailed off to cope with them, the others decide to light the fuzes forthwith:

'One man lights the one leading to the powder magazine, and a corporal and some gunners in my company those that led to the ammunition wagons. With my own hand I placed two on a little bag.'

But then everything goes wrong. 'Suddenly I see all the gunners who're with me in the arsenal running off as fast as their legs can carry them.' Jacquemot runs after them, shouting to them to come back. There's no danger, he shouts, the fuzes will take five minutes to burn off. Reaching the square in front of the cathedral he finds another squad posted there under a fellow lieutenant:

'He shouted to me: "Did you see them?" "No! who?" "The Cossacks, behind you, removing the fuzes you'd placed!" It was their arrival that put my gunners to flight.'

And who save the Vilna arsenal.

Now it's the Traka Gate, leading to Novo-Troki and Kovno, that's jammed with fugitives. Outside it Hogendorp, with the help of a fellow-Dutchman, a Major During, has managed to assemble a variegated battalion of 400–500 men – including Jacquemot's fugitive gunners. 'He ordered me to form up my platoon and follow on after two companies of the Imperial Guard, to protect the retreat against Cossacks who'd already circumvented Vilna to our left.' On reaching Vilna yesterday, Séruzier, too, had divided his battery into two sections and sent each by the side road that circumvents the town walls. Jacquemot remains at his new post, to let the column pass on. 'The night was magnificent,' Griois will recall,

'and the moon was shining with a brilliance reflected on the carpet of snow covering the countryside. The cold was more rigorous than ever. The ice crackled under the feet of men and horses. Everyone was pressing on, even more so as to stand up to the cold by marching quickly than to flee from the Cossacks.'

There in the moonlight the road is flanked by extraordinary and terrible sights. Bonnet and his little party of the 18th Line had only got into the town

'towards 2 or 3 o'clock – such was the encumbrance at the gate I'd lost touch with my companions but got in by dint of my elbowings, gone to a tavern, been given some food for silver, bought a pound of sugar for gold.'

But immediately leaving again yesterday evening, he had passed

'between lines of stacked muskets abandoned by men who neither would nor could stay out there in the open fields. They were fresh troops of Grandjean's or Lorge's division¹ who'd seen our rout and been stricken by our example.'

But, more terribly, Captain François sees there
'thousands of corpses, completely naked, many of them bearing marks
of dagger blows. But it certainly wasn't the Poles who'd committed these
crimes; they showed us great attachment. It was Platov's Cossacks who'd
assassinated the sick and wounded whom the inhabitants, terrified of
these brigands, had driven out of their houses.'

Now Murat and Berthier are riding in one of the few imperial carriages to
have survived the night's *auto-da-fé*, followed by the men of the 85th, 'in
support of the cavalry [i.e., the Sacred Squadron],
'marching just ahead of him. Murat was between the two bodies, accompanied by his staff and a feeble escort.'
With them, besides Eugène, either on foot or horseback, are Lefèbvre,
shattered at having to leave his dying son, Mortier and Bessières, all accompanied by what remains of their staffs. Davout, Labaume notices, has a high
fever and is travelling by sleigh. The remaining mounted cavalry are commanded by Sébastiani,[2] who 'at this moment of distress, when egoism was
the order of the day' has 'generously offered the hospitality of his headquarters to Narbonne. He and his little group, too, are travelling in three
sledges: Narbonne and Castellane's fellow-ADC Chabot in the first; 'I
myself with Ayherts, the servant, in the second; the valet and cook in the
third.' But soon the moon sets and 'in the darkness of the night' the three
sledges become separated.

If Le Roy's finding the going difficult it's because of his new boots. Slithering about in the deep freshly fallen snow, he's beginning to fall behind,
even by the time the men of the 85th reach the suburb's last houses.

Vilna's outskirts have already been left behind when someone on Murat's
staff suddenly remembers something. What about that picket of 40 men
(François says 30), half from the 29th Line and half from the 113th, who'd
been guarding the long bridge over the Vilia? General Gratien sends a Captain Paolo Lapi back to bring it in. Although attacked by numerous Russian
cavalry, Lapi shows a coolness and self-possession worthy of Ney himself. Withdrawing the picket from the bridge, he closes the ranks and beats the charge:
'Attacked by Cossacks and a furious mob, the men, obeying their officer,
formed a ring and fired by ranks. Then, levelling their bayonets, they
marched off, cleared themselves a path,'
and so rejoin the rearguard 'without the loss of a single man'.

Meanwhile Ney himself, 'destined up to the last moment to save what
was left of the army', has appeared with yet another rearguard. This one is
made up of 'some of Wrede's Bavarians and the remains of Loison's division', in all some 2,300 infantry and 200 cavalry. As Hogendorp moves on
with his own scratch battalion, he can't help seeing how Ney
'by his extreme ability in the profession of war seemed to augment its
strength. He made it manoeuvre in such fashion as to occupy the Cossacks, halt them, and attract them on to itself, and thus cover the general retreat – or rather, rout.'

Not that Hogendorp likes Ney personally: 'he thought he was the only man who was doing his duty, or even knew how to'. Nor has Wrede, 'who couldn't disguise his hatred of the French', have a good word to say for him:

'Marching with his staff and the debris of his cavalry under this little rearguard's protection, he kept grumbling with a morose and discontented air at what the Marshal was doing. The Marshal, he was telling his ADCs in German, was giving himself and his men a ridiculous lot of trouble and only making the retreat more difficult.'

Which certainly isn't true. Co-ordinating his rearguard's Bavarians with Séruzier's horse artillery, Ney is protecting the remaining transports. Notably the Treasure, whose wagons had been supposed to leave Vilna at midday yesterday, but in fact have only got going at 7 a.m.

Not far away in the chaotic column Sergeant Bourgogne and his fellow-sergeant Daubenton are fighting for their lives. Not against Cossacks but – a rare mention of regular Russian troops at this stage – with a Russian cuirassier. Daubenton himself, though 'half dead from cold and hunger, his face thin, pale and blackened by the bivouac fires' is 'still seemingly full of energy'. But his movements are being hampered by the regimental dog, 'a handsome poodle' named Mouton – whose name of course means 'sheep'. Sheep by name, but certainly not by nature, Mouton has been with the Fusiliers-Grenadiers ever since 1808, when they'd found him in Spain. He'd been at the battles of Essling and Wagram; gone back with the regiment to Spain; but in Saxony, en route for Russia, had gone missing, perhaps stolen. Yet in Moscow there he was: 'A 15-man detachment had left Paris some days after ourselves, and as they passed through the place where he'd disappeared the dog had recognised the regimental uniform and followed the detachment.' Out of pity for Mouton's frost-bitten paws Daubenton has attached him to his knapsack, where he's 'barking like a good dog'. Which is just the trouble:

'The cuirassier gave Daubenton a second blow on his shoulder, which struck Mouton on the head. The poor dog howled enough to break one's heart. Although wounded and with frozen paws, he leapt off his master's back to run after the man; but being fastened to the straps of the knapsack he pulled Daubenton down. I thought it was all over with him.'

Bourgogne takes aim, but the priming of his musket doesn't burn; and 'the man, shouting savagely, threw himself on me'. He just has time to scramble in under an abandoned wagon

'and present my bayonet at him. Seeing he couldn't do anything to me, he went back to Daubenton, who because of Mouton hadn't had time to get up. All the time that devil of a dog was barking and dragging him sideways.'

But Daubenton's musket goes off and the Russian cuirassier

'uttered a savage cry, made a convulsive movement, and at the same moment his sword fell, also the arm that held it. Then a stream of blood came from his mouth, his body fell forward over the horse's head, and in this position he remained as if dead.'

Freeing himself, Daubenton grabs the cuirassier's horse. At that moment they hear behind them a lot of noise, followed by cries of "Forward! Fix bayonets!":

'I came out from under my wagon and saw Marshal Ney, musket in hand, running up at the head of a party of the rearguard. At the mere sight of him the Russians fled in all directions. The rearguard seized several horses, and made their riders march among themselves.'

But they're soon left behind. 'What else could we do? Never shall I forget the Marshal's commanding air at that moment,' Bourgogne concludes admiringly,

'his splendid stance in face of the enemy and the confidence he inspired in the unhappy sick and wounded around him. At that moment he was like one of the heroes of olden time. In the last days of this disastrous retreat he was the saviour of what was left of the army.'

But it's been poor Mouton's last fight. 'I never saw him again.'

Each of the remaining Treasury wagons – these caissons which Kergorre, Peyrusse and others have been conducted at such immense pains all the long way to Moscow and back – contains 12 million francs in gold; and – as Davout had already pointed out on 8 December on the eve of reaching Vilna – 'is much too heavily laden'. Together with others which have been picked up in Vilna, they too are now to meet their Nemesis.

Three miles outside Vilna, just beyond a bend in the river Vilia, there's a short steep slope. Ponari Hill.[3]

Three days ago, on 7 December, the Oudinots' carriage, drawn by its rough-shod horses, had had no difficulty in 'vigorously mounting this straight steep slope', though even then the Duchess of Reggio, peering out into the murk through its window, had

'made out some motionless soldiers scattered all over the slope they'd vainly tried to climb. Overcome by the cold, they'd collapsed; and no one who'd fallen there had got up again. A few dribbles of blood had escaped from their lungs and nostrils and reddened the snow.'

Neither do the Polish Lancers of the Guard, who're forming the advance guard, 'have the least difficulty' in climbing it. 'The first-comers,' Griois goes on,

'had been able to reach the top. The hill wasn't very high; but it was steep, and covered in ice. The greater part had halted on the road.'

But then, as the surface has become more and more slippery – 'like marble' – under successive sleighs, sledges and other vehicles, more and more have failed to make the gradient, slithered backwards, and ended up all at a criss-cross at the bottom. 'Since they were blocking it,' Griois sees,

'those coming on behind had decided not to go any further tonight. Grouped around fires fed by the debris of broken or abandoned vehicles, their drivers made a picturesque tableau as they waited for daybreak.'

Approaching in their three sleighs along the road in the darkness, Narbonne's scattered party, too, see 'the mountain covered by the campfires of drivers who'd realised it was impossible to get on.' And at once all the Grand Army's remaining artillery and its few surviving headquarters vehicles – they'd had left Vilna at 8 a.m. – get hopelessly stuck. So that by the time IV Corps headquarters arrives on the chaotic scene it finds that 'no vehicle had been able to pass for the last 24 hours':

'After marching for about an hour, the column came to a sudden halt and we saw in front of us a veritable sea of men. Several of us went to find out what the matter was and we reported back that the first carriage hadn't been able to climb the hill.'

Are they even on the Kovno road, Labaume wonders. 'The Poles were making for Novo-Troki.'[4] Should IV Corps have taken that smaller road which, a mile or so to the rear, had borne off to the right? But no. It simply isn't possible, Le Roy and Jacquet realise, 'to go off to right or left, the roadsides being steep and wooded'.

After two hours painful marching during which they've diverted themselves by swapping memories from Spain, Jean-Marc Bussy and his sergeant, who've long ago lost touch with any of their Swiss comrades, are also brought to a standstill by this 'mass of cannon, ammunition wagons, carts, halted pell-mell at the foot of a hill'. Obviously neither guns nor Treasury wagons are going to get up it, nor indeed anything else much that moves by horsepower. For all that moves on wheels this icy slope's the end of the road.

But sledges? All the rest of the long icy night Castellane tries to 'move my sledge on, through the guns, the wagons'. Soon the jam has become inextricable; and by the time von Muraldt gets there the gunners are already detaching their horses and spiking their guns. Clothes, uniforms, effects of every sort lie scattered on the snow. Although Paymaster Guillaume Peyrusse, who'd left Vilna at 7 a.m., no longer has his own calèche, he still has his Treasury wagon. At 10 a.m., together with the others, it reaches the foot of Ponari Hill:

'I spent the hours of darkness looking for roads, trying out ways through. Neither my horses nor I could keep our feet. Since it's impossible to get on, I hoped it'd clear tomorrow,'

he'll afterwards write to his friend André in Paris:

'That fatal day 25 degrees of frost were killing me. The reflux of men running away from the Cossacks, who'd been masters of the town since 9 a.m., was causing an appalling disorder. The blockage grew; finally nothing could get by. Already the Cossacks were reaching the summit, bringing cannon with them.'

What to do? Someone's sent to consult Murat. Who tells the emissary from the Treasury:

'"There isn't a moment to lose to save as much as we can for His Majesty." I was ordered to take everything I could out of my wagon, load it on to my horses and reach the top of the hill, where we were to rally.

I don't know how I found the strength to do so. From all sides I took whatever sacks I could find on the vehicles. I broke open my cases of gold and put all of it, my roubles,[5] my jewels, into the sacks. Taking any men of the Household I could find, I gave each a horse to take by the bridle, took some effects, and set fire to all the rest; and there I go, walking on foot with my convoy.'

Truly Peyrusse is earning the position of the Emperor's travelling cashier, the object of his burning ambition! 'We busied ourselves thrusting aside the overturned vehicles,' Berthier will write to Napoleon,[6]

'setting fire to everything that got in the way, so as to get the rest of the Treasure through. Almost all the vehicles had only got there after we'd put 20 horses to each. Of Your Majesty's carriages only three got to the top. Your Majesty's table silver and that of the paymaster of your household was put into bags and carried on horses. None of it was lost.'

But at the foot of the hill someone breaks open one of the ordinary Treasury wagons:

'It was like a signal. Everyone flung himself on these vehicles, smashed them open, dragged out the most precious things. The men of the rearguard, passing in front of this disorder, threw away their weapons to load themselves with booty. So furiously did they fling themselves into it, they didn't even hear the whistling of musket balls or the Cossacks' howlings. One even saw Russians and Frenchmen, forgetting all about the war, jointly pillaging the same wagon. Ten millions of gold and silver vanished.'

Already the lids of several caissons – among them perhaps the two which Coignet had brought from Paris in June?[7] – have been smashed open with musket butts and are being plundered of their little casks of gold napoleons:

'Even so, we saw many men hurry by, indifferent, only being interested in saving their lives and paying not the least heed to the bags of cash being flung about on the ground. A struggle had broken out among the plunderers. Several bags full of gold and silver had fallen from hands frozen too stiff to hold them, and now the coins were rolling about on the ice.'

Among the Treasury vehicles that have to be abandoned, Kergorre sees, is the new one designated by Berthier before reaching Vilna 'for the most precious items' and into which Paymaster Duverger, at Vilna, has put the precious jewel-encrusted Madonna, worth so many millions, taken from Moscow.

Is there really no way round? Planat de la Faye recalls having carefully studied the map on his way to Vilna in June, and that there's another road 'not a mile to our rear' that leads to Novo-Troki and which mounts the hill at a gentler gradient. 'We'd be able to regain the Kovno road cross-country.' Lariboisière's carriage, Planat sees, as he stands there watching not only soldiers but officers fighting for the gold lying in the snow, hasn't a ghost of a chance of getting through this chaos, let alone up the hill. No more than Roch-Godart's or Delaborde's. 'The General hesitated,' Planat goes on:

'Honoré thought we ought to unharness the horses, load on to them all we could save of the baggage, set his father on one of the pack-horses, and try to pass through the woods flanking the road on either side.'

But Planat's sure that Lariboisière, weak and depressed as he is, isn't up to sitting a horse:

'At this moment General Pernetty, whose calèche was just behind us, having heard our discussion, dismounted and agreed with me. Without wasting more time on discussion, I took the lead-horse's bridle and turned our calèche around. Since the vehicles coming behind us had passed to right and left of us in hopes of finding a way through, we went back without meeting any obstacle; and by the end of a quarter of an hour we were on the Novo-Troki road, where we soon heard musketry and hurrahs. Vehicles, admittedly in no sort of order, were moving on along this road, which wasn't encumbered. So General Pernetty and I galloped ahead to organise two regular files of vehicles and to halt every-thing which wasn't an ammunition or baggage wagon.'

Many other individuals besides the Poles – who've taken this route as a mat-ter of course – are doing the same. Lejeune for instance.

But at the foot of Ponari Hill the jam's only getting worse, and all the time the sound of Séruzier's cannon fire and Ney's fusillades is coming closer. Likewise the noise from the ever-growing mass of men pouring out from Kovno.

How to get up this mountain of ice? Certainly not up the road, even on foot. Many individuals, among them Le Roy, still gravely handicapped by his new boots, are therefore struggling to get up through the brushwood on each side.[8] Taking off from the road, he's cut himself a stick in the woods, heavy as they are with the night's fresh-fallen snow, and crawls slowly upwards. But Muraldt's feverish legs won't even carry him. 'Thereto my dri-ver was showing clear signs of wishing to mingle with the other plunderers around the bags of gold and leave me in the lurch.' But somehow or other he dissuades him; and they too keep to one side of the road:

'Thanking God and after inexpressible difficulties and at almost every moment, often having had to halt to let our poor horse get its breath back',

Muraldt gets his light vehicle up to the summit. Cursed and sworn at by the crowd all round them, Griois and Guyot, too, take off to the left and put their backs into heaving their sleigh upwards over the virgin snow:

'We were half-way up when some terrifying shouts were heard from above us and spread swiftly down to the bottom. It was a cannon which, held up at the summit and disturbed from its place by some shock, was hurtling downwards with a terrible noise, smashing and dragging with it everything it met with.'

All tangled up no doubt with its team of six or eight horses, it rushes down past them. And at long last Griois and Guyot reach the summit with their sleigh. So, at dawn, does Castellane; but without his. 'Three-quarters of the way up', fed up with his slow progress, he'd decided to abandon it and walk, leaving it with Ayherts the servant.

Still at the rear of the column – or rather the inchoate mass – Sergeant Daubenton has had the Russian cuirassier's horse snatched from him and disappeared into the crowd to assert his rights, leaving Bourgogne to suffer acutely from colic and wonder whether that Jew's wine he'd drunk yesterday at Vilna wasn't poisoned? Trudging on 'in the midst of men, women, and even some children', he looks about him in vain for some glimpse of his friend. Some Hessians – he assumes they're from Victor's IX Corps – have just tried to make a stand on a little hillock, but been wiped out by Russian cavalry:

'Behind, only Marshal Ney and his rearguard were to be seen, taking up position on a little eminence.'

And ahead of him Bourgogne too surveys Ponari Hill

'from the foot to the summit. The road about three-fourths up the slope to our left could be traced by the number of wagons, carrying more than seven [sic] millions in gold and silver, as well as other baggage and carriages drawn by horses whose strength was so exhausted they'd had to be left on the road.'

Now he reaches the abandoned bivouacs where some men are still warming themselves at the still smouldering fires. Lieutenant Jacquemot, whose horses have been roughshod ever since late November and who has therefore managed to get up the hill with his gunners, even sees

'two companies of the Guard thrown into disorder, never to reassemble. The carriages abandoned at the foot of the hill were being burnt and all sorts of things were being pillaged. The standards taken from the enemy, even the enormous cross of St Ivan, taken from the Kremlin[9] were lying abandoned on the ground.'

For Fezensac it's

'a singular sight to see men covered in gold and dying of hunger, and to find spread out on the snows of Russia [sic] all the objects invented by Parisian luxury'.

Bourgogne, all on his own now, rounds

'the hill to the right. Here several carts had tried to pass, but they'd all been overturned into the ditch at the roadside. One wagon still had many trunks in it. I should have liked to carry one off, but in my feeble state didn't dare risk it, afraid, having once got down, I'd not be able to climb out of the ditch again.'

But someone from the Vilna hospital corps 'seeing my dilemma, was kind enough to go down and threw me a box' containing four fine linen shirts and some cotton trousers. Which are almost more welcome than gold – especially as he has 800 francs on him anyway, and hasn't changed his shirt since 5 November, and his 'shreds and tatters' like everyone else's are 'filled with vermin. A little farther on I picked up a band-box containing two superb hats.' And here's his old friend and fellow-countryman

Sergeant Picard, who helps himself to a pair of Marshal's epaulettes! A little further on, through some brushwood, the path 'beaten out by the first men who'd crossed the hill at daybreak' turns left; and he rejoins the highway. Shortly afterwards little Jean-Marc Bussy – for his part he has contented himself with filling his empty cartridge pouch with cartridges – sees two men in gold-braided hats by the roadside, whom he at first takes for Russians; but then recognises as two Swiss colonels. Has he seen their carriages, they ask. He says he hasn't and, after some words of mutual encouragement, passes on. Half an hour after reaching the summit, Bourgogne hears

'a heavy fusillade, accompanied by loud cries from the direction of the wagons. Marshal Ney, seeing the booty couldn't be saved, was having it distributed among the men, and at the same time was keeping the Cossacks off by steady volleys.'

A moment later, just as he sees some Cossacks advancing towards him, he sinks 'more than five feet, up to my eyes' into the snow. Almost suffocates.

But at the foot of Ponari's fatal slope the remains of the Guard artillery, the rest of Napoleon's carriages and most of the Imperial Treasure have all been lost. Roch-Godart, too, has lost his carriage and sledges, just as Jomini, still very sick, has lost the brand-new sledge he'd just got hold of at Vilna, together with its coachman. For all his sapience Pion des Loches, too, has to abandon his last three vehicles. 'They didn't leave again. We clambered up the slope through trees and rocks.' All that's left of II Corps' artillery also gets stuck and is left behind:[10]

'It was there the remains of the army's carriages disappeared. Thus of 1,100 guns that had gone into Russia, not one would recross the Niemen.[11] As for the carriages of the Emperor and his suite, the only ones I saw after Vilna were the calèches of Generals Sorbier and Lallemand; and I guarantee each of them had cost at least 100 artillery horses. Drouot lost the two carriages left to him,'

concludes Pion des Loches with a certain smug satisfaction.

'"It was 12 millions my troops looted at Vilna,"' Napoleon will tell his minister Molé in February. Just now, however, he has other things to think about. At the Gragow post-house he and Caulaincourt have abandoned the 'hermetically sealed' imperial berline for what they've been told is

'a very comfortable one mounted on runners which the local squire had had made for his daughter, recently married. At first this Polish gentleman had refused to sell it, no matter what price was offered him;'

but on hearing who it's for has insisted on giving him it for nothing. Napoleon tells Caulaincourt:

"Hours flit by, and in my position if I lose a moment I may have lost everything," and he won't 'accept the gift, for which (according to Bourgoing/Wonsowicz) he paid 1,000 ducats (10,000 francs)'; but according to Caulaincourt:

'a few gold pieces. In view of the Emperor's impatience to reach his destination it was a piece of good luck. We left the carriage in the charge of the footman. The Emperor hardly gave us time to transfer our rugs and weapons. For lack of space in the sleigh he was even forced to abandon his *nécessaire* he found so useful,'
– a gold item of equipment which, according to Constant, contained 'everything that was agreeable or useful in a bedroom, together with a breakfast service for several persons'. – 'Uncomfortably seated and hemmed in still worse,' Caulaincourt continues, 'he was sacrificing everything that makes a long journey endurable'. At Mariempol they'd been caught up by the second carriage, with Duroc, Lobau and Lefèvre-Desnouëttes in it, but soon left it behind. And that's the last they'll see 'either of a carriage or a man of those who'd left Smorgoni'. Their new vehicle, alas, turns out to be less than cosy:

'The aged box, which had been once been red, had been set on a sled and had four large windows, or rather panes of glass set in worm-eaten frames, which didn't close properly. The joints of this hulk, three-quarters rotten, gaped open on all sides, freely letting in the wind and snow, which I had to be sweeping out all the time so that we shouldn't get soaked through by letting it melt on the seats.'

Caulaincourt has again had to sacrifice half his cloak to keep his imperial fellow-traveller even moderately warm. So far from being cast down, however, Napoleon seems to be more than a little euphoric. When Caulaincourt expresses doubts as to whether the army will be able to rally at Vilna he dismisses them out of hand: "Vilna's well-stocked with food," he tells him, "and that'll set everything to rights again. I've anticipated everything in the orders I've left with M. de Bassano."[12] And all the time he's making brilliant analyses – seen from his point of view – of the power situation in Europe: "Everyone should see the Russians as a scourge. The war against Russia is a war wholly in the interests – if rightly judged – of the older Europe and of civilisation. Europe should envisage only one enemy – the Russian colossus."

To this, Caulaincourt ventures, with his usual frankness: 'It's Your Majesty who's the cause of everyone's anxiety, which is preventing them from seeing other dangers.'

The crazy old vehicle flies on over the snow. As Napoleon blithely talks on and on, good-naturedly replying to the more pertinent of Caulaincourt's criticisms, he

'felt up for my ear to tweak it; and as he couldn't find it under my bonnet, it was my neck or my cheek that received the pinch – a kindly rather than an irritable one. He was in such a good mood that he admitted the truth of some of the points I'd brought forward. Others he refused. One would have thought he had no immediate concern in them. So far was the Emperor from checking my frankness that he listened and replied not only without ill-humour but with real cordiality.'

Only one thing – or rather, person – infuriates him. His ambassador at Warsaw, Abbé Pradt. Why hadn't he appointed Talleyrand instead? Well, it

had been Maret's wife, terrified at the idea of having her husband's predecessor, that arch-intriguer, in Warsaw, who'd intrigued him out of the
job. And then, Duroc and others had spoken so well of Pradt:
'"He has ruined all my plans with his indolence. He's a chatterbox, nothing more,"' declares Napoleon angrily.

By now Caulaincourt has 'dispensed with the services of our worthy
[Mariempol] post-master, whom the Emperor rewarded suitably'. Some 32
miles north of Warsaw lies Pultusk, scene of the battle of 26 December
1806, reached two hours before dawn:

'A Polish servant-girl, half-dressed, poked and puffed at the fire for all
she was worth and nearly burnt her eyes over the most miserable one
that ever was lit. The Emperor inquired what this poor girl earned. It was
so little that he remarked that the sum would hardly suffice to keep his
heavy clothing in order. He bade me give her a few crowns and tell her
they were for her dowry. The poor girl couldn't believe her eyes. The
Emperor remarked that it was possible to make many people of that
class happy with very little money. "I'm impatient, Caulaincourt," he
added, "for the day of a general peace, so as to get some rest and be able
to play the part of the good man. We shall spend four months in every
year travelling within our own frontiers. I shall go by short stages with my
own horses. I shall see the cottage firesides of our fair France."'

He goes on to dilate on all he'll do, when that day comes, for France and
Europe:

'The soup and the coffee were taking time to come, and the Emperor,
numb from the cold and the fire's increasing heat, fell asleep. I seized
the opportunity to make some notes. When he woke up his sorry meal
was soon gulped down and we clambered back into our sledges.'

Half-way between Pultusk and Warsaw

'although the snow was knee-deep, the Emperor visited the defences of
Sierock and Praga. We shook the snow off as best we could before getting back into our cage – for such, exactly, was the shape of the antique
box which housed us.'

But here at last is the Vistula:

'The Emperor's vanity didn't reassert itself until we got to the gates of
Warsaw. On reaching the [Praga] bridge we couldn't repress a humble
reflection on the modest carriage of the King of Kings. He seemed
delighted to find himself in Warsaw, and was very curious to see whether
he'd be recognised. I think he wouldn't have been sorry if someone had
guessed his identity.'

But, even though it's 'the hour when that part of the city is at its most
crowded' no one does:

'The Emperor's magnificent green velvet cloak with gold braid only
drew the attention of a few humble passers-by. They turned to look, but
didn't stop, being in a hurry to get back to their own firesides. Anyway
it would have been difficult to recognise the Emperor, for he wore a
hood, also of green velvet, and his fur cap covered half his face.'[13]

Amodru the outrider has 'only got there a few moments before', having been ordered to arrange accommodation not at the French Embassy but at the Hôtel d'Angleterre: "I refuse to stay with a man I'm going to dismiss," says Napoleon, and asks 'to be taken to the hotel by way of the Cracow Boulevard, which at that time was Warsaw's main thoroughfare.'

"'I'd like to find myself in that street again," Wonsowicz hears him say, "because I once held a great review in it."' At 11 a.m. after walking up it – 'we didn't take our seats in the sleigh until we'd crossed the main square' – they alight at the Hôtel d'Angleterre. (Pradt says it was at 1.30.) And Napoleon tells Caulaincourt to go and fetch the wretched ambassador.

It's to be a confrontation neither Caulaincourt nor Pradt will ever forget.

'The doors of my room,' Pradt begins his account of his last interview with the Emperor Napoleon,

> 'were flung open and admitted a tall man, who stalked in, supported by one of my embassy secretaries. "Let's go. Come, follow me!" said this phantom. His head was wrapped in a silk shawl. His face was lost to view in the depths of the fur, in which he seemed to be buried. His gait was hampered by fur-lined top boots. It was a kind of ghost-scene.'

'Dressed as I was,' Caulaincourt concedes, 'the Ambassador was no little amazed to see me. But he was even more astounded, couldn't believe his ears or his eyes, when I said the Emperor was there[14] and was asking for him.'

'"The Emperor?"' he repeats again and again, in astonishment, as Caulaincourt gives the lie to Maret's inflated reports, e.g., of 6,000 prisoners taken at the Berezina. '"Why, in such grave circumstances, write to an Ambassador as if he were the editor of *Le Moniteur*, when it's vital he should know the truth? The number of prisoners is of little import, seeing we can't keep them." Pradt flatters Caulaincourt for having been against the war from the outset: "Your Grace will have justice done you now, for it's well-known you did your best to prevent it."

No comment. Caulaincourt declines some breakfast but asks Pradt to send Napoleon a bottle of Bordeaux; and leaving the flurried ambassador to change his clothes, goes back to the hotel. While waiting for Pradt, Napoleon has been opening his other mail. One item informs him that the playboy Count Montholon – his minister plenipotentiary at Würzburg – has married the divorcée Albine Vassel (both of whom will accompany him to St Helena). Since such marriages are forbidden – except in his own case, for reasons of state – Montholon too is instantly dismissed. By and by Pradt arrives and is admitted to

> 'a low-ceilinged little room, freezing cold, with its shutters half-closed to prevent his being recognised and where a wretched Polish maidservant was on her knees puffing at a fire of green wood which rebelled at her efforts, sputtering out more damp into the chimney than heat into the room.'

Unadvisedly – but, Caulaincourt thinks, spontaneously – Pradt declares his concern for the health of this phenomenal man who seems to have dropped out of the sky:

'But this seemed to be even less in his favour. The Emperor would rather have been blamed, even criticised by any other man, and wasn't disposed to tolerate this man-to-man air of concern from a man with whom he was deeply angry.'

Caulaincourt tactfully tries to leave the room. But Napoleon, evidently 'to increase M. de Pradt's discomfiture by the presence of a third party', tells him to stay. Upon Caulaincourt pointing out that he must fetch His Majesty a cloak and make other arrangements for the onward journey, he's told, in that case, to summon the Polish Prime Minister, Count Stephan Potocki, and the Minister of Finance. Returning, Caulaincourt, 'as the door between the rooms didn't shut properly', can't help eavesdropping. He hears Napoleon berate the wretched Pradt 'for committing nothing but blunders' – and Pradt trying to justify himself, promising betterment, and reiterating the disastrous state the Polish economy:

'The more M. de Pradt justified himself, the angrier the Emperor became. His presence seemed to be infuriating him. His gestures, the way he shrugged his shoulders, so clearly showed the temper he was in that I really shared the embarrassment of his victim, who was in an agony of mortification. It seemed to me his remarks on some grounds weren't unreasonable.[15] Seeing a card on the mantelpiece, the Emperor stopped suddenly in mid-sentence, snatched it up, wrote a few words on it and handed it to me. It said: *"Tell Maret that fear of the Russians has made the Archbishop of Malines lose his head. He's to be sent back and someone else entrusted with his duties."'*

But by and by Napoleon's fury abates and he asks Pradt:

'"What do the Poles really want?"'

'"They want to be Prussian."'

'"Why not Russian?" Napoleon rejoins.

'Indignantly turning his back on M. de Pradt, he told him to return in half an hour with the ministers who'd been summoned.' When he's gone, Caulaincourt points out that it's hardly the right juncture to dismiss his ambassador publicly, it'll produce a bad effect. Very well, says Napoleon, Caulaincourt can write to Maret from Posen: "Now let's have dinner, so I can see the ministers, and we'll be off." His point evidently conceded, Caulaincourt drops the card in the fire.

All this time dinner's been getting cold.

Attended by Pradt, Count Potocki and the Minister of Finance arrive. Say how worried they've been at the personal risks His Majesty's been running and their relief at seeing him safe and sound.

'"Risks? Fatigue nourishes me. Peace and rest are only for lazy monarchs."'

Outside the door as he attends to their travel arrangements, Caulaincourt hears him telling the two Poles:

'"I've committed two errors. One, to go to Moscow; the other to have stayed there too long. Perhaps I'll be blamed, but it was a great and bold measure. But it's true: from the sublime to the ridiculous is but a step. Neither French nor German soldiers are made for this climate. Below 7 degrees they're worth nothing. Up to 6 November I was master of Europe. I am not so any longer.'"

Blatantly exaggerating the army's surviving effectives to 150,000 men, he says that before three months are out he'll have as strong an army as when he'd opened the campaign:

'"I carry more weight when I'm on my throne in the Tuileries than at the head of my army."'

Well yes, at Pradt's suggestion he'll lend the Grand Duchy "the 2 or 3 million francs in copper from the pawnshops that have already been lying in Warsaw for three months; and 3 or 4 million in paper, drawn on the Courland contributions" to raise the country against the Russians. For his part, he assures the two ministers, he'll never abandon them. Is His Majesty going to cross Prussia, they ask with obvious anxiety, as he, in the most cordial manner, dismisses them. Yes, he is. Potocki goes home, and his daughter-in-law notes how

'the fascination this extraordinary man exercised over all who heard him was so powerful that my father-in-law, who'd been in the deepest gloom when he'd left us, returned full of hopes'.

Meanwhile Caulaincourt, outside fixing the horses 'while the Emperor attended to his toilet', jots down

'particulars of what he'd said to the Ambassador. As far as I'd been able to pay attention to what was being said, I'd heard the Emperor ascribing his setbacks solely to the climate. The burning of Moscow, he admitted, had upset his plans.'

But as he climbs back into the sleigh Napoleon the Inexhaustible goes on grumbling about Pradt:

'"He complains of everyone, criticises everything. What's *he* ever done to entitle him to blame others? He's losing this campaign for me."'

Fagalde cracks his whip. And away goes the strange old conveyance, rattling down Warsaw's streets, en route for the Prussian frontier, Posen and Dresden.[16] It'll take Napoleon and Caulaincourt precisely eight days to reach Paris – the fastest transit yet recorded.

CHAPTER 25

NEY'S LAST STAND

Lithuania's icy plateau – What's become of Narbonne? – a diary saved, a diary lost – 'the roar of the distant artillery and the howling of the wind' – 'Ney's absence seem to be the end; his presence set everything to rights' – 'I begged every man to show zeal, man by man' – 'The King of Naples must be replaced' – I'm the rearguard of the Grand Army'

When at last they get to the top of Ponari Hill both Fezensac and Le Roy are surprised to find themselves alone. But then some of Fezensac's men catch up with him; and Le Roy, coming out of a hut he's gone into to scratch the soles of his new boots with his knife, finds himself among a dozen of the rearguard's skirmishers whose 'packs, though not full, seemed to be laden down with something very heavy'. Bourgogne, who's also on his own,[1] 'seeing some people were in it', enters the hut. Inside are

> 'a score of men belonging to the Guard, all with bags containing 5-franc pieces. When they saw me several began calling out: "Who'd like 100 francs for a 20-franc gold piece?"'

But Bourgogne already has '800 francs in gold and more than 100 francs in 5-franc pieces' and at this moment is 'caring more for life than for money'. Outside in the darkness Castellane, he too alone and on foot, having left his sledge to Narbonne's servant Ayherts,[2] is being approached by Ney's men,

> 'Frenchmen and allies who offered to let me buy looted objects, basins, sets of table silver, etc. Our men were only to happy to give 100, even 300 francs in silver for a gold napoleon [20 francs].'

Getting no offers they try to give away their loot. Some musicians, 'terribly weak and their fingers frozen', are too heavily laden to get far:

> 'Shaking the 5-franc pieces out of their bags, they say it'd have been better to have left them in the wagons, especially as there'd been plenty of gold for the taking. But many had sacks of double napoleons.'

Others, 'always the weakest', go on clinging to their loot, only to have it torn from them by those who've omitted to take any. Castellane decides he must get going; and Bourgogne, also trudging along on his own, is surprised to see someone he knows coming toward him. It's a comrade named Pinier 'commissioned eight months ago'. Bourgogne asks him where he's bound for. Instead of replying his friend asks him who he is:

> 'At this unexpected question from someone who'd been my comrade in the same regiment for five years, I couldn't refrain from tears.'

Recognising him, Pinier gives him some wine:

> 'I only had one free hand, so the good fellow supported me with his left hand and with the other poured the wine into my mouth. Only yesterday, and then very vaguely, had he heard of our disasters.'

Bourgogne tells him there's no army left:

'"What's that firing?"

'"That's the rearguard, commanded by Marshal Ney."

'"I shall join the rearguard,"'

says Pinier. And goes to join Loison's men, not one of whose squares (Loison will claim when he finally catches up) have been broken by Russian cavalry, 'only by grape and roundshot', they being pursued by '14 cannon, without a single one to reply with' and are making haste to join up with Ney. '"You're suffering,"' says Ney dryly, when Loison reaches him. '"You'll be better off at Königsberg. I authorise you to go there."' And Loison hands over his remaining 500 men to General Marchand.[3]

At last day dawns. Once again

'the monstrous cold was accompanied by a brilliant sun that gave only light, but no warmth. The air seemed to be filled with innumerable little icy atoms. If for a moment one closed one's eyes to protect them against the snow's blinding whiteness one had all the difficulty in the world to reopen them.'

Von Muraldt, covered though he is from top to toe in warm furs, feels frozen to the bone. 'The cold hurt dreadfully and every breath I drew made a painful hole inside my chest.' Paymaster Peyrusse's morale is only being kept up by the reflection that he hasn't lost a single one of the coins that were entrusted to him. He needs it. For the Cossacks are at his heels – 'those furious devils weren't content with their fine haul' at Ponari. Not until they've marched four leagues do the Treasury officials rally. Their immediate goal, like everyone else's who remembers the district, is Evë,[4] 44 kilometres from Vilna. In a sleigh that's taken him on board at the summit of Ponari Hill and whose two well-nourished horses are being briskly driven by 'one of the regiment's soldiers whom I'd rudely chastised at Moscow', Brandt gets there at 11 p.m. And orders him to drive straight through the town (sleighs just now being more valuable than gold) and only halts at its last house, where he finds the rest of the Vistula Legion bivouacked:

'You can imagine our comrades' joy! I gave eight napoleons to our saviour for handing over the two horses and the sleigh, but on condition that he stay with me.'

Everyone wants to buy the sleigh; but now, if ever, possession is nine points of the law. At Evë, too, Le Roy catches up with the column. But when Griois gets there it's only to realise he's lost something very precious indeed. His diary,

'which I'd been keeping meticulously ever since I'd left Naples. I'd have given all the gold I still had in my belt to get my notes back.'[5]

The gunner who's been leading his horse – a 'novice' from Vilna – has let someone cut its reins en route. The loss of his last horse – the campaign has cost him no fewer than 27 – and his few remaining effects, 'a shirt, some chocolate, my portfolio, some letters' – is nothing compared with such a loss. And he flies into a rage – a rage that goes on for several days and which he'll afterwards regret – with the gunner, who sheds tears of remorse:

'I could even have hit him. Each time I caught sight of that gunner it began again. What I myself, though carried in a sleigh and well covered up, had suffered along that same road should have made me more indulgent, or anyway more just.'

At 5 p.m., Castellane too, 'on foot, exhausted by the fever due to my frost-bitten hand and dying of hunger', has reached Evë, having fallen in en route with Chabot, Narbonne's other ADC, who tells him he'd seen Narbonne on the road some time before dawn, and that 'General Curial assured us he'd seen him in the rear, on foot'. They fear the worst. At 11 p.m. the groom, 'his nose and feet frozen' turns up with his sledge – but still no Narbonne. Nor is there any sign of the servant Ayherts or of Castellane's sledge. Rejoining a headquarters no longer imperial, and after a supper consisting only of 'a bit of black bread, a hunk of meat without even any water', Castellane passes another horrible night 'holding my hand in the air as I shared a bale of hay with Chabot and two of my other comrades'. But, unlike Griois, he consoles himself that when abandoning his sledge at Ponari he'd slipped *his* diary into his pocket 'together with my parents' portraits'. Next day, Friday, he lingers at Evë until 10 a.m.

'in hopes of seeing my general. During all that time the mob of stragglers kept passing by. The Old Guard, reduced to 1,400 men at the moment of the Emperor's departure, now counted no more than 800 under arms.'

Murat, it seems, has recovered from his panic, and is intending to make a stand at Kovno, or at very least evacuate it in an orderly fashion. So at 5 a.m. on 11 December, Berthier sends back a staff officer to Ney, asking him to 'make short day's marches to enable us to establish ourselves at Kovno'. Short marches! When Ney, pressed by some Cossacks with fourteen cannon, hasn't a single gun with which to reply! Just as Murat's leaving Evë for Kovno, Loison's division, now only 600 strong, turns up. Some of them belong to the 113th Line, of whom some are Florentines, whose uniform had struck Castellane 'in that town, by its beauty and good quality'. Now the Italian regiment has only some 120 men left, and when Castellane asks one of its sergeants how so fine a unit can have melted away so quickly, the sergeant replies:

'"We're dying of hunger and cold. The enemy fires a few roundshot at us, we can't send any back."'

So they've melted away, like the rest of the army. Getting into Narbonne's sleigh with their cook – 'the only one of our lot who wasn't at all frost-bitten' – Castellane and Chabot make for Kovno: 'All day our anxiety for M. de Narbonne only grew.' Although his gangrenous hand aches monstrously, he consoles himself by thinking: 'We've seen a spectacle of great horrors. Nothing like it will ever be seen again.'

Now everyone's making for Zismory. Leaving their miserable bivouac at 4 a.m., Lieutenant Jacquemot's gunners, passing through Evë, see on all sides villages in flames and by the roadside, abandoned for lack of teams to draw them, unused guns and ammunition wagons that have belonged to their colleagues of the 18th Company of the 4th Artillery Regiment. This morning, travelling on in his sleigh, he fancies there are even more corpses than yesterday. At one slope he has to get out and – like Napoleon at Liady – 'despite the cold felt by the parts in contact' slide down on his backside. The Fusiliers-Grenadiers (Bourgogne has caught up with them) do the same:

'General Roguet, some officers and several sappers who were marching in front, had fallen over. Some picked themselves up, and those who were strong enough went down it in a sitting position, guiding them- selves with their hands. Others, weaker, trusted to Providence – i.e., they rolled over and over, like barrels.'

In this fashion Bourgogne, bruised all over, reaches the foot of the hill. But he's cheered to note something not seen for a long time:

'The general had ordered a halt to make sure everyone was there. I remember that when a man fell, cries were heard: "Halt! A man's fallen!" A sergeant-major of our battalion shouted: "Halt there! I swear not one of you shall go on until the two left behind have been picked up and brought on." It was by his firmness they were saved.'

Altogether it seems to Bourgogne that

'On this march there was much more readiness to help one another than before. Probably it was the hope of reaching our journey's end. Meanwhile the roar of the distant artillery and the howling of the wind were mingled with the moans and cries of men dying in the snow.'

As for himself, however, he feels he's nearing the end of his tether. Strag- gles repeatedly. Sometimes, though hardly able to drag himself along, he manages to keep up with his comrades. Sometimes, when he doesn't, he falls in with other isolated comrades, most of them too at their last gasp, and they do what they can to help one another along. Again and again he's rescued by his friend Grangier, who refuses to let him make his will and give up in despair.

Somewhere between Evë and Kovno Murat sees Loison's much-delayed artillery coming towards him. To save its sixteen guns he orders it to turn back. So only the Cossacks have any cannon. And when Jacquemot at about 5 p.m. hears the sound of their approaching gunfire,

'our misery didn't leave us enough energy to be afraid of death or try to avoid it. The sound of the hurrahs didn't hasten our march.'

Seeing a village close to the left of the road, they hope to spend the night there. But then, seeing a party of Cossacks forcing some Guard cavalry troopers to evacuate it, are obliged to push on to Zismory. Getting there at 10 p.m., they, like Planat's group, find the village 'packed' and 'entirely dev- astated'. Ruthlessly, Lariboisière's servants turn out two young Dutchmen 'from the latest levy.[6] They'd formed part of one of the route columns that hadn't been through any of the fatigues of the campaign and were vanishing like smoke as soon as they came in touch with our terrifying column. One of them, who wasn't even twenty, burst into tears and begged to be allowed to stay. In vain. Anyway he was very warmly dressed.'

Jacquemot's gunners, too, have to sleep outside in the snow, with not a bite to eat except a little biscuit pillaged from the Vilna stores. And through part of the night Planat and his comrades hear the Dutch youngster's groans. 'Next morning he was dead.' So are many others who – unlike Muraldt who, though he has some brandy in his cart, wisely decides to stick to tea – have drunk themselves silly on it. 'Certainly two-thirds never saw the sun rise.' But here at Zismory, to his two ADCs' infinite relief, is the white-haired Narbonne. After Ponari he too 'had found himself quite alone, on foot, believing he'd lost everything'. Fortunately he'd confided his money, including the sums Napoleon had given him at Smorgoni for his diplomatic mission in Berlin, to a general of the Neapolitan Guard, who has looked after it for him. He and his party take refuge with 'Sébastiani's very well-composed headquarters'.[7] A Warsaw banker, a M. Bignon, 'is there with his carriage'. Even when a Dutch surgeon has treated his hand, Castellane is unable to hold the reins and has to turn down Sébastiani's offer of his own horse.

Now it's the morning of 12 December, and the first-comers are arriving at Kovno – that 'very well-built little town set in an amphitheatre of pine woods' at the junction of the Rivers Vilia and Niemen, which at midsummer had put Vossler in mind of an Italian city. Immense jagged blocks of ice that seem to Thomas Legler taller than Swiss chalets, stick up from the Niemen's surface 'everywhere frozen to a depth of 6–8 feet'. Yet yesterday evening, almost without realising it, Muraldt's group have crossed over and been received in a village whose lights they'd seen on the Polish shore. Now, recrossing the frozen river in the morning, they again make for Kovno by the Vilna road, and notice how

'since we'd left in June, this town had been provided all round with regular fortifications, with bastions and countersinks, palisaded and furnished with numerous artillery,'

all according to Napoleon's order of early July. Although 'its entrance is narrow' there is as yet no crowd, so Muraldt and his companions have no difficulty in getting in and bivouacking in the main square 'in the centre of town and near the Niemen'.

Here too are immense stores.

The garrison consists of Neapolitans, whose prime duty it is to guard them – notably the huge stocks of rum. Presenting himself at such a store, Muraldt, though confronted with a Neapolitan bayonet and volubly shouted at in an incomprehensible Italian dialect, manages to elude the guard and get himself some biscuit, fresh from the oven – only to find that in the dark he has paid not 2 francs but 2 napoleon*s* (40 francs) for it, almost all the cash he has left.

At that moment – some time around midnight of 11/12 December – Murat and Eugène arrive. And though Murat immediately gives orders that the stores be distributed 'without formalities' the pillage continues. Soon the rum is

> 'virtually flowing in the streets. Only with difficulty were the men prevented from drinking it all up, so as to keep something for the rearguard which, under Marshal Ney, was to join us tomorrow. The smell of it spreading and upsetting me, I lay down on the floor in the corner of another room to sleep'.

It's Muraldt's first night in a warm room since leaving Moscow. Here he's luckier than Fezensac. Dead with fatigue, unable to find himself a lodging of any kind, Fezensac has to sleep on the doorstep of a house already occupied by IV Corps – for soon the crowd has begun to arrive, with the usual battles to get in and keep others out. The Treasury personnel become scattered in the crush: 'Some get inside, others aren't strong enough to push through the mob.' By the time Jacquemot's gunners had got to the town gate there'd already been such a crush that it had been 2 p.m. before they could get through. And nightfall before Griois and his 'guardian angel' Guyot get here, even though they'd left their bivouac in the early hours. By now 'an immense crowd was obstructing the avenues to the gate'. Warmly wrapped up though he is in Guyot's sleigh, Griois' teeth are chattering 'so my jaw could break'. Just then, sitting there shivering in the mob, he catches sight of

> 'a man with a cadaverous face, astride a flankless horse, with a half-burnt forage cap on his head and wrapped in shreds of some bed covering. It was Major Petit, of the artillery, my adjutant in the Calabrian campaign and a comrade of mine for many years past. Only when he told me his name did I recognise him and me he'd probably only recognised from what was left of my uniform and Lieutenant Guyot's.'

Remembering how ill Petit had been when he'd left Smolensk, he's not particularly pleased to see him; 'abandoned by his men, stripped of his effects, he was reduced to the most pitiable state'. Although still accompanied by an NCO as ill as himself, neither has been able to help the other. Seeing Griois sitting there, apparently snug in his sledge,

> 'he came up to me and told me of his misfortunes and how utterly alone he was. Doubtless he expected me to offer to let him join me. And indeed that ought to have been my first impulse. I blush as I confess I didn't; and I was even afraid he'd make the request, which a shred of shame would have prevented me from refusing. But a comrade, a friend, would be only one more mouth to feed.'

Guyot, who has gone off to reconnoitre, comes back and tells Griois it's easier to turn off to the left, go to the river bank, and get into Kovno over its ice:

> 'After a cold "good-evening" I hardly expected a reply to, I decided to take this option and it was without regret, or rather with pleasure, I left M. Petit'

– an act so hard-hearted he'll never forgive himself for having committed it. 'The sufferings of six weeks had effaced all human feeling from me, a monstrous egoism had my heart in its grip.'[8] Griois finds the streets full of military men of every rank, all looking for food and shelter for the night:

'Yells, curses echoed on all sides. Barrels of biscuit and rum from the pillaged magazines were being bashed-in in the middle of the streets and each man was watching jealously over this precious loot. The uproar, the disorder was terrible.'

Peyrusse searches about in the mob for his missing colleagues – resorts no doubt to the same means as Griois, 'usual since everyone had been marching on his own: despite the din, to shout out the names of one's companions'. Luckily, an NCO recognises Griois and takes him to a house outside the town wall where IV Corps' artillery staff are being put up, quite lavishly, by a Jewish family:

'Stimulated by our generosity, they were providing us with any amount of sugar, coffee, dairy goods, potatoes, meat and above all some bread of a brilliant whiteness and an exquisite savour.'

The beer's bad but the wine good. A single largish room contains both the party of officers and their hosts,

'who, without getting in our way too much, were hardly less numerous: i.e., a dozen people, among them a swarm of children who, according to the custom of the country, spent the night above the stove.'

The Jewish family sells them sheepskins, shoes (furred and otherwise), sugar, butter and flour. Their hostess has

'a beautiful Jewish face with an aquiline nose, large black eyes surmounted by eyebrows of the same tint and whose hue stood out against a perfectly white complexion,'

which reminds Griois, that lover of Italian art and music, of 'the Rebeccas and Judiths of the Italian school'. What's more to the point, she spends the night baking for them.

At midday the Guard has been followed into town by I and IV Corps, 'represented by the Eagles, the officers, and a hundred or so men. All the rest had been disbanded.'[9] Those of its men who, unlike Bourgogne, haven't been able to cram themselves into a room, have bivouacked in the main square. Many are hopelessly drunk on rum, 'the more dangerous' says Fezensac,

'because the men weren't aware of its effects. Only being accustomed to the country's bad brandy, they thought they could drink the same quantities of rum with impunity.'

Dumonceau's men, who've got here in advance, are billeted in a large inn with a yard; but the crush to get inside is so great that, like Fezensac, Dumonceau prefers to camp outside on the pavement. In one corner of the square a fire breaks out and two houses are burnt down.

How many people even realise they've reached the Niemen? Few, so it seems to von Muraldt, if any. Nor are they expecting any imminent improvement in their conditions. Many disbanded men, he sees, are obsessed by only one thought – to get out of Russia, that 'accursed country'. Fezensac too sees masses of fugitives passing straight through the town without even halting:

'Accustomed to mechanically following those walking in front of them, we saw them risking suffocation as they forced their way over the bridge, without realising they could easily cross the Niemen on the ice.'

'The Niemen had vanished,' Berthier will write to Napoleon:

'Everywhere it was frozen to a depth of 6 feet, and so covered in snow that vehicles were passing over it, as if across a plain. It can bear the weight of the heaviest guns. Only the map showed a river existed there.'

As for the fortified bridgehead, in which optimists at headquarters have been placing their hopes, Berthier explains why one glance at this chaotic scene is enough for the King of Naples to realise there can be no question of halting at Kovno either: 'It's only a big useless redoubt, open at the throat,' i.e., on the river side.

Lejeune's longer route along the Vilia's winding bank has taken more time, of course, than the direct one. And when he gets to Kovno it's

'snowing heavily. You could hardly see ten paces ahead of you. Part of Kovno was on fire. Carefully crossing the bridge in my sledge, I couldn't restrain my tears at the thought of what I'd seen at this same spot on 24 June and the comparison with what was happening here now.'

Already Berthier has notified Ney: 'II and IV Corps have at most 60 men apiece, the Vistula Legion is only a feeble detachment' (of 60 men, says Brandt). And now Ney's reply comes in. It's been impossible for him, he writes, with Loison's division reduced to a mere 500 youngsters, to hold the Cossacks at Evé, and when he gets to Kovno he's very much afraid it'll be with enemy at his heels. So he'll be needing the entire Kovno garrison to defend the town's evacuation. At midday Berthier writes to say he can have it, and that Murat is sending him six of Loison's guns. With this force he must try to hold up the Cossacks at the defile at Rumchiki, at least until tomorrow morning:

'"We have here a kind of bridgehead or sort of entrenched camp, armed with twelve guns, a work where we can make a stand until enemy infantry appears in superior force. Here Loison's division will find everything it lacks. Thus you'll form a respectable body of infantry. The King has ordered the dismounted cavalry, the whole Imperial Guard, both infantry and cavalry, and I and IV Corps to draw food rations for eight days and move over to the left bank this evening. The twelve pieces of artillery that were here have been placed on the high ground over there. In this position the King thinks we can teach the Cossacks a lesson.'"

All of which looks fine on paper. But once again has little to do with reality. And anyway Murat has already decided to clear out – 'you've seen with your own eyes that almost nothing's left of the Imperial Guard'. A second officer is sent off to Macdonald, with new orders. He's not to retire on Kovno, but on Tilsit, 20 leagues further down the Niemen.

All day the indefatigable Daru and his colleagues are busy writing their last orders on Russian soil – for that's what Lithuania must again become. These men, at least, Berthier will certify, have lost nothing of their energy. Once again, everything useful that can't be taken away is to be destroyed. Eblé must blow up the arsenal. The chief medical officer is to evacuate the hospital. As the early night again begins to fall, as much of the Treasure as had been saved at Ponari, plus some more that's been lying in Kovno, is loaded on to new wagons 'harnessed up to artillery horses' and makes its way 'with greatest difficulty' through the crowds down to the bridgehead. There the congestion is immense ('because of the large numbers of sleighs and sledges both officers and men had taken in the villages').* Not that many of the fugitives aren't making their way across the ice above and below the town. 'On the bridge one of the Treasury wagons overturned. A guard was placed over it.'*

Murat's headquarters have already crossed over to the high ground on the left bank, together with twelve guns to command the frozen river. Likewise his Royal Neapolitan Guard which – surprisingly – according to Berthier still amounts to some 700–1,000 men. A meeting of the Marshals is called for 7 p.m. And Bessières informs his colleagues that the Imperial Guard still has 500 cavalry.

Beyond the bridge the road forks – right to Tilsit, left to Gumbinnen. Its for the latter town, the first in Prussia, that Murat intends to march at daylight, leaving Kovno to Ney, in whom 'he has every confidence'.*

Morning comes. Ney, who's had a good night's sleep at lodgings inside the town, insists that IV Corps' staff shall help him defend it:

'An earthwork, hastily [sic] thrown up in front of the Vilna Gate, seemed to him a sufficient defence to hold up the enemy all day. In the forenoon the rearguard again entered the town. Two guns, serviced by some infantry platoons, were placed on the rampart, and this little number of troops made ready to sustain the attack that was already preparing.'

Although his party has woken up at the usual early hour, ready to depart, Griois has to wait for a a pair of fur-lined shoes from a Jewish shoemaker who's been paid in advance for them. He and Guyot can't leave until he does, even though 'a sound of men and horses and some musket shots not far away announced a hurrah'. Cossacks, presenting themselves at the town's exits, are driving in their guards, 'very few in number anyway and stunned by the cold'. They too, being few in number, aren't daring to force their way in, but are

'galloping through the streets of the suburb, firing off pistol shots and pursuing any Frenchmen they caught sight of with their shouts'.

The shoemaker's fur-lined shoes 'whether from inefficiency or by design' turn out to be too small and narrow, and the Jew, 'in atrocious German', wants to discuss how they can be improved,

'certainly intending to keep me there up to the moment when the Cossacks entered the house. It was only by shoving my foot into his chest I got rid of him, and left him the shoes and the silver he'd received.'

At the sound of the very first shots Guyot has harnessed up their sleigh: 'We made haste to put the victuals we'd bought on to it. But our hosts, profiting from the danger the least delay could expose us to, were unloading our sleigh as fast as we were loading it. Father, mother, children, flung themselves at our provisions without taking any other precautions than to elude our kicks; and I still laugh when I recall our anger and oaths at seeing our sugar loaves, our hams and even our bread being whipped from under our noses.'

Now some Cossacks are coming down the street. And the two artillery officers dash off in their sleigh into the town, where all that's left of the Imperial Guard has assembled at dawn in the market place. There General Roguet has had all the trouble in the world to winkle his men out of the houses. For more than an hour a Piedmontese comrade of Bourgogne's, named Faloppa, has

'done nothing but prowl about on all fours, howling like a bear. I realised he fancied he was in his own country amidst the mountains, playing with the friends of his childhood. In short, poor Faloppa had gone mad.'

Just as he's confiding his dying comrade's money to two women who've taken pity on him, Bourgogne hears

'the noise in the street increasing. It was already daylight, but in spite of that we couldn't see much, for the little squares of glass were dimmed with ice, and the sky, covered with thick clouds, foretold a lot of snow still to come. We were making ready to go outside when, all at once and quite close to us, we heard the sound of cannon from the direction of Vilna, mingled with volleys of musketry, shouts and oaths. I thought I could make out the voice of General Roguet. Indeed it was he who was swearing and indiscriminately dealing out blows at officers and NCOs as well as rankers to make them get going. He was entering the houses and making the officers search them to be sure no men were left inside. He did right, and it's perhaps the first good service I ever saw him render the rank and file.'

"Don't you see it's that brute of a General Roguet striking at everybody with his stick?" says another of Bourgogne's comrades – one who means to stay and await his fate, as so many others have done. And fixes his bayonet: 'Just let him come here; I'm waiting for him!' Adjutant-Major Roustan, however, turns them all out. Falling in, the Fusiliers-Grenadiers march slowly through the mob; but have to wait a long time at the Niemen bridge: 'Colonel Bodelin, who commanded our regiment, ordered the officers to prevent anyone from crossing it alone. We were now about 60 men, the remnant of 2,000, all grouped round the colonel. He looked sadly on the remains of his fine regiment, probably drawing a contrast in his own mind. To encourage us he made us a speech. I'm afraid very few listened.'

In the thick morning mist the Lancer Brigade brings up the rear. Only some 600 infantry and 600–800 cavalry of the once 50,000-strong Imperial

Guard – that élite of the élite which at midsummer 'headed by its bands playing fanfares' had crossed Eblé's pontoon bridges – stumble across the narrow Niemen bridge, 'established on very tall piles that resembled stilts'.[10] In the crush someone steals Zalusky's portmanteau containing his fine new uniform 'thanks to which I'd cut such a brilliant figure at Vilna. The saddest part of it was I couldn't impute this theft to the Cossacks, who were doing their best to avoid us.' Dumonceau too notices what a host of carriages and other troops are crossing directly over the ice.

All in all the Guard column totals some 2,500 men under arms. Castellane, who's there, makes a slightly different count. He sees some 2,000 of the 10,000 of the Old Guard who'd left Moscow cross the bridge; and some 300 only, of the 8,000 of the Young Guard. After them come the tiny remnants of I, II, III and IX Corps. 'They hadn't one bayonet between them', Daru says with pardonable poetic licence, meaning a few officers only. IV Corps has 30 men. Wrede's 20th (Bavarian) Division (VI Corps) has 50. Oudinot and Victor's corps, Castellane thinks, are still in reasonably good order. 'Of those who'd reached this point,' Bourgogne notices,

'not half had seen Moscow. They were the garrisons of Smolensk, of Orsha, of Vilna, as well as the remnant of the army of Victor and Oudinot.'

There are individuals who nearly reach the bridge only to drop dead. One such is Colonel Widman of the Italian Guardia d'Onore, who, Labaume writes

'had supported our fatigues until then. Unable to go further, he fell just as he was leaving Kovno to go to the bridge and expired without the satisfaction of dying outside Russia.'

Griois is appalled by the chaos and destruction in the streets:

'The rearguard was still there, and the Cossacks were no longer to be feared. But what horrible spectacle didn't this unhappy town present! All the houses which the soldiers had just left seemed to have been pillaged. Stove-in casks, broken or half-burnt furniture, filled the streets. Numerous corpses added to the horror of this picture. They covered the main square. Almost all of them were Grenadiers of the Guard who, having got there first, had taken possession of the stores of rum and brandy to make good their long privations. Stunned by inebriation and gripped by the cold in the bivouacs they'd established on this square, they didn't wake up again. It looked like a battlefield, or rather a halt where harassed soldiers were lying in closed ranks.'

Bourgogne hears that 1,500 men have perished there during the night. Making for 'the gate on to the Niemen', Griois and Guyot force their way through the crowd. 'I could easily have avoided this dangerous passage by crossing the river over the ice.' But that's very dangerous too. One officer who does so in his sleigh and almost fails to reach the Polish shore is Dessaix's ADC Captain *Girod de l'Ain*. His sleigh gets stuck between two of the immense blocks of ice. Only after he has given up all hope does a passerby come to his aid. Otherwise most people are doing the same as Griois:

'Sufferings and misery had so weakened my intelligence and enervated my will that everyone was mechanically following the path traced by those ahead of him.'

Le Roy, too, is here, with his 'bosom friend' Lieutenant Jacquet:

'As early as 2 a.m. on 13 December I heard the 85th being called. I woke up the gentlemen. "Come on, my dear Jacquet, for the last time on Russian soil, let's go and see what's wanted of us."'

But it's 5 a.m. before they can cross the river.

Outside the town, meanwhile, Séruzier and his horse-gunners are helping Ney to fend off huge swarms of Cossacks – afterwards he'll remember their numbers, perhaps exaggeratedly, as about 15,000. To Grabowski their appearance seems

'very funny. They were so weighed down by loot that their horses could hardly advance. We saw many of them wearing a French general's richly embroidered coat under their cape. Their pockets were stuffed with rings and watches. Hung at their saddle they carried bags of silver and gold.'

Seeing them busy pillaging (or, as the saying goes, 'Cossacking') stragglers, Séruzier's men capture '300 good horses which I hastened to distribute to my dismounted troopers'. With Colonel Pelleport of the 18th Line, Fezensac has spent the night trying, mostly in vain, to stop their few remaining men from drinking too much liquor. Now they're at their posts on the town's defences:

'The Russians' first cannon shot dismounted one of our guns. The infantrymen fled, the gunners were about to follow suit. Any moment now and the Cossacks would be able to enter the town. But just then the Marshal appeared on the rampart. His absence had seemed to be the end of us. His presence was enough to set everything to rights. He himself took a musket. The troops returned to their post.'

'Hardly had the rearguard re-entered Kovno,' Ney will report indignantly two days later to Berthier,

'than the artillery officer ordered his guns to be spiked, thus destroying all possibility of keeping the enemy at a distance from the town'

– an act of 'ineptitude' confirmed, in his own report, by Ney's immediate subordinate General Gérard:[11]

'Towards midday the enemy cavalry approached with some artillery pieces and began firing at the works which are to right and left of the Vilna Gate. Those works were armed with four guns, which, having replied with a few shots, were spiked by the ineptitude of the officer commanding them.'

The rearguard, Gérard goes on,

'consisted of 300 of the 29th Line [Loison's division] and 80 men of a battalion from Lippe. It had been impossible for me to assemble two men from the division's other units. As soon as the Lippe infantry had received some roundshot into its ranks, it broke up, threw away its arms,

and fled, without either *M. le Maréchal* or myself being able to halt even one of them'
– 'except one sergeant,' Ney conscientiously corrects him, 'whose name, I'm sorry to say, I don't know.' – 'There was a moment of terror,' Gérard goes on: 'Everyone was abandoning us, and we ourselves were obliged to fire muskets to hold up the Cossacks who were coming closer and closer.' On the high ground beyond the river, so the 'inept' commandant has told Ney, there should be the twelve guns Murat last night stationed there – or anyway eight of them; Murat, already retreating along the Gumbinnen road, has taken four of them with him. But already 'several hundred' Cossacks are appearing there, 'almost surrounding us by this manoeuvre'. Commanding as they do the Gumbinnen road, the town, the bridgehead and the bridge – on which they're already firing grape – Ney sends General Marchand with the pitiful remains of III Corps and anyone else he can get hold of to support them:

'Although we lost some men there, and only succeeded in gaining a foothold in some barns at the edge of the plateau, this movement was well executed. At the same time the enemy was cannonading the bridgehead on the right of the Vilia River[12] and threatening to carry by force the works at the Vilna Gate whose guns, as I've already said, I'd been deprived of by the artillery officer's incredible blunder. My position then became most alarming, and it was only after the greatest efforts that I managed to place some of the 34th Division's guns and make some detachments of the 29th Regiment protect them. This semblance of resistance began to contain the enemy, and by redoubling my activity, by begging each and every man, man by man, to show some zeal, I managed to last out until night began to fall, without the town being carried by main force [a threat] it had been exposed to for three hours. At 9 p.m. I began my retreat.'

By this time, Gérard adds, only 150 men of Loison's division are left – Ney says 200. Both the Niemen and the Vilia bridges have been set fire to, at both ends. All Kovno's magazines and arsenals have been blown up.

That evening of 13 December the pitiful relics of III Corps pass through Kovno amidst the drunk, the dead drunk, the dead and the dying. 'By the light of the bivouac fires still burning in the streets' Fezensac's companions 'make out some soldiers who look at us indifferently. They said nothing when we told them they'd fall into the power of the enemy, just lowered their heads and huddled together round the fire. The inhabitants, lined up to watch us pass, were regarding us with insolent looks. One of them had already armed himself with a musket. I wrenched it from him. Several soldiers who'd dragged themselves as far as the Niemen fell dead on the bridge. We in our turn crossed the river and, turning our glances toward the terrible country we were leaving, felicitated ourselves on being so fortunate as to get out of it; and above all at being the last to do so.'

But fate has something much crueller in store for the intrepid Séruzier, he who'd been in the army's advance guard all the way to Moscow and then in its rearguard all the long way back. Reaching the bridgehead, he finds there 'more than 15,000 Cossacks, who attacked us'. Seeing he hasn't a chance against such numbers and

'wishing to obtain, if possible, an honourable capitulation, I placed my infantry in a little wood and disposed myself to charge with my cavalry'.

He's hoping the Cossacks, seeing his resolute attitude, will only pillage his vehicles and let his men slip across the Niemen:

'As I was giving the order to sound the charge I saw a Russian horseman coming forward for a parley. He proposed that I lay down my arms and let myself be taken prisoner with my infantry and squadrons.'

Séruzier agrees, on condition that his men and their effects are taken to Russian headquarters. The Russian emissary returns to his commander for orders, and Séruzier goes back to the wood,

'expecting to find my infantrymen there. But found no one. While I'd been doing my best to arrange an honourable capitulation these unworthy soldiers, terrified at the swarms of Cossacks they saw on all sides on the plain, had disbanded themselves and were trying to reach the bridge and escape. You can imagine my anger! I leave the wood, gallop flat out back to my cavalry, only to find ... no one's left! My troopers had done the same as the infantry. I found myself without any troops. Only one man had stuck by me. He deserves to have his name mentioned. He was an Alsatian named Klein.'

All the fugitives are overtaken by the Cossacks, run down and stripped. In the wood Séruzier and Klein, heroically defending themselves to the last, are also attacked by Cossack lances

'which I parried as best I could with my sabre. Then their commander ordered them to fire at me. Six Cossacks fired at a range of fifteen paces, and I was hit by four of their carbines. My horse fell dead, my right leg was caught beneath him. Then these brigands fell on me, gave me 27 lance jabs, tore my clothes off me, seized my decorations, my weapons, my money, and stripped me completely.'

Only the extreme cold, by freezing the blood, saves him from bleeding to death:

'Though I'd been wounded in the cruellest fashion, the Cossack chief, seeing I'd got up and judging from the riches I'd been stripped of that I was an officer of note in the French army, was so barbarous as to force me to march, naked, for nine miles in a cold of -27 to -28 degrees (-34° to -35° C), to Hetman Platov's headquarters. It was about 4 p.m.'

Rejoined by many of his men, all as stark naked as himself, Séruzier reproaches them bitterly for their cowardice. Platov examines him, wants to know who he is and what possessions he's had taken from him: 'Everything. Silver. Jewellery. Effects. Six horses, two from Limousin, two Normands and two Hanoverians.'

But Platov – he who since his son was killed near Moscow has even offered his only daughter in marriage to any Cossack who kills or captures Napoleon and whose hatred for the French knows no bounds – ignores the

code of generous behaviour normal between superior officers. Taking Séruzier's horses for himself, he gives him back nothing:
'I was in front of an immense bonfire, and the warmth unfroze my wounds. My blood began flowing from all parts of my body.'
And he passes out.[13]

Ségur isn't on the spot; but in his moving but far from always accurate epic, he'll write afterwards that Ney
'passed through Kovno and crossed the Niemen, still fighting, falling back and not fleeing, marching behind all the others, sustaining the honour of our arms up to the very last'.

Most of the refugees who have recrossed the Niemen bridge have been taking the left-hand road, following the Guard towards Wilkowiski. But immediately in front of them is another hill at least as steep and frozen as Ponari and no more surmountable. At its foot, where the roads divide, Jacquemot's men see 'calèches, carriages, baggage wagons, an entire artillery park' which had been brought up from Königsberg 'completely abandoned'. Even one of the new Treasury wagons has come to grief. Hochberg can hardly believe his eyes:
'The men were throwing themselves into the wagons but, pushed by those who came after, they fell in headfirst, their feet in the air. Others were succumbing under the weight of sacks they'd filled with silver and the passers-by were maltreating them in the most shameful fashion.'
Jacquemot sees a large amount of the treasure being taken away by a German officer. Getting to the top of the hill Bourgogne realises that nothing's left of the Fusiliers-Grenadiers. And for Dumonceau, whose *konya* had been stolen in Kovno while he and his servant Jean had been snatching some much-needed sleep, there's a small but poignant tragedy in store. After waiting for Jean to catch up, following on no doubt with their last lead-horse, he's riding his favourite 5-year-old mare Liesje,[14] and tries to overtake a Neapolitan unit when Liesje's hindlegs slip as she tries to jump the ditch – and they both tumble into it. One leg trapped beneath her, Dumonceau, after calling out in vain to passers-by, is finally extricated by a fellow-lieutenant of the Red Lancers. But Liesje – she on whose back he'd trotted about so blithely and curiously not far from here on Midsummer Eve – she's done for:
'I tugged at her bridle, shook her impatiently to force her to make an effort. She did all she could to please me, and in the end managed to drag herself up out of the ditch; but that was all I could get out of her, and it was becoming obvious her back was broken. So her state was hopeless. The poor beast seemed to be suffering greatly, was groaning sadly and when she saw I'd made up my mind to go off without her several times dolorously raised her head to follow me with a sad look, her eyes inflamed with tears, expressive of her anxiety, her regrets and as if begging me not to abandon her. I was profoundly moved. I ran off as if

pursued by remorse, carrying my portmanteau under my arm. She was the best horse I ever had in my life.'

It's the only time the Belgian captain, in his lucid but mechanical handwriting, expresses any grief.

Since all too many men seem to be turning right at the bridge, Griois and Guyot too, without knowing where it leads to, have taken the Wilkowiski–Gumbinnen road. Reaching the hilltop they hear behind them 'gunfire and a fusillade' from the other side of the river:

'It was our rearguard, commanded by the brave Marshal Ney, disputing the enemy's entry into Kovno. Despite too unequal a fight he maintained himself there until evening. These were the last cannon shots I heard.'

But to Ney, who's 'hoping to be able to retire to Gumbinnen via Skrauce under cover of the night that hid the feebleness of my means', this new icy slope proves insurmountable. No sooner have Ney's men begun climbing the slope than 'roundshot from the enemy drawn up across the road' begin falling among it. 'This last attack', Fezensac realises,

'was the most unforeseen of all and the one which most vividly struck the men's imagination. Marchand and Ledru managed to form a kind of battalion by uniting all isolated men present to III Corps. In vain we tried to force our way through. Since the men's muskets didn't carry that far, they didn't dare advance. They stubbornly refused to open the passage by force. I ordered some tirailleurs to advance. Two-thirds of the muskets didn't go off.'[15] To advance or retreat was equally impossible, it would be to expose themselves 'to a charge. Our loss would have been certain.'

Deaf to his appeals to them to stay and if necessary die with him, some of Fezensac's officers,

'just embraced me, weeping, and went back to Kovno. Two others suffered the same fate. One had got drunk on rum and couldn't keep up. The other, whom I was particularly fond of, disappeared shortly afterwards.'

This breaks Fezensac's heart. Heroism can do no more. It's the end:

'But then Marshal Ney appeared. In so desperate a situation he evinced not the least disquietude. He decided to follow the Niemen downstream and take the Tilsit road in hopes of reaching Königsberg by cross-country roads,'

even if it means depriving Murat of any rearguard. Nor can Ney even notify Murat where he's gone to. But there's nothing for it. Under cover of night Ney's party march back downstream, and though many don't realise what's happened and wander on downstream towards Tilsit, about six miles from the Kovno bridge they turn off left into a lane. Major Bonnet is one of them: 'At 10 p.m., having got back some of our martial air thanks to the 29th Regiment which the Marshal had recruited I don't know where, we halted at a fine village.'

By now Headquarters is at Skrauce, and as Murat leaves again, wondering of course what's become of his rearguard, he sends an officer back to find out:

'Getting to the first houses, he finds a post of twelve Cossacks, who arrest him, take his money, his watch, his Cross, his epaulettes, and then let him go, together with the sledge he'd come in. They gave him back one napoleon.'

Ashamed of such humiliation, it'll be a day and more before he rejoins to tell the tale. Meanwhile Murat, still hearing nothing, has sent back a second officer, an *officier d'ordonnance* named Atthalin, who, after hearing guns firing in the direction of Kovno, returns without any news.

Deep in the night Ney's little party, struggling on through Poland's snow-laden forests, are sharing a single 'white horse, which we mounted one after the other'.

On 15 December Headquarters reaches Wilkowiski, that village where on 22 June Napoleon 'in a terrible voice' had declared war on Russia. Now Berthier writes to him: 'There were not 300 men of the Old Guard [on parade]; of the Young Guard fewer still, most of them unserviceable.' And next day, at Wirballen in a ciphered PS:

'The King of Naples is the first of men on the battlefield ... the King of Naples is the man least capable of commanding in chief. He should be[16] replaced at once.'

Himself, he possesses only what he stands up in. Even the carriage with the campaign's maps and documents has been lost. Fortunately, thanks to the energy and intelligence of its driver, it turns up next day at Gumbinnen. There 'for the first time since leaving Moscow' Larrey eats

'a complete meal, slept in a warm room and in a good bed. Lariboisière was so ill, so shattered, he could no longer speak. That evening he went to bed, never to get up again.'

Not very far away, across the Baltic, the former Marshal Bernadotte, now Crown Prince Elect of Sweden,[17] has just heard about Napoleon's disaster at the Berezina. He too adds a hasty PS, to his letter to the Tsar:

'I had expected, Your Majesty, that on being informed of your state's evacuation I should be able to congratulate you on having seized his person near Borissow. The opportunity was excellent, but it would have been to hope for too much at once.'

After unsuccessfully trying next day (18 December) to convince the Prussian provincial governor Schön at Gumbinnen (where Griois finds the heroic Eblé 'in a state of utter weakness and dejection ... no more than a shadow of himself')[18] that Murat has a whole French army at his heels, *Intendant-Général* Dumas and some friends are just

'drinking some excellent coffee when a man in a brown greatcoat entered. He had a long beard. His face was blackened. And he looked as if he'd been burnt. His eyes were red and gleaming.

'"At last I'm here," he said. "Why, General Dumas, don't you know me?"

'"Why no. Who are you?"

'"I'm the rearguard of the Grand Army. I'm Marshal Ney."'

A few hours later, 'just as the clock was striking the last quarter before midnight', a shaky old post-chaise, 'one of those cumbersome vehicles mounted on two enormous wheels and with old-style shafts', gallops into Paris. Its two occupants are Napoleon and Caulaincourt. It dashes through the still unfinished Arc de Triomphe[19] – 'only Amodru had stuck with us' – so rapidly the sentries have no time to halt it, and into the courtyard of the Carousel at the Tuileries. When they knock at the door of the Empress's apartments the Swiss porter, not even recognising them, refuses at first to admit them.

'Never in my life have I had such a sense of satisfaction,' writes Caulaincourt, who has hardly enjoyed a wink of sleep for the three weeks it's taken them to dash across Europe. At his levée next morning Napoleon tells his amazed ministers:

"Well, gentlemen, fortune has dazzled me. I've let it lead me astray. Instead of following the plan I'd in mind I went to Moscow. I thought I'd sign peace there. I stayed there too long. I've made a grave mistake, but I'll have the means to repair it."

And gets down to work, raising fresh armies to defend his crumbling empire.[20]

TWO EPILOGUES

In the spring of 1813, Heinrich von Roos, after spending the winter at Borissow practising his medical arts, would visit Studianka. From a Russian engineer officer who was 'cleaning out the river and extracting from it anything that had fallen in during the crossing' he would hear how 'in the nearby forests an ample harvest of watches, silver, decorations, weapons, epaulettes, etc., had been gathered from hard-frozen corpses found seated against trees'. The officer, who'd built himself some shacks out of the wreckage of the bridge which had once been the wreckage of Studianka, would make Roos

'a present of a sword, a sabre and an English saddle. We explored the houses [i.e., the three which had been left standing and evidently not demolished by Victor, as per Napoleon's order]. Many weapons, shreds of clothing, helmets, peaked caps, papers, books, plans were still left there. I found officers' commissions, death certificates that concerned the units I'd belonged to and which I handed in two years later to the Petersburg embassy.'

The Russian major's special business is to collect all letters, documents, maps and other papers being found there in such vast numbers, and sort them out by language. Roos helps him with the German ones, and a French sergeant with the French, which include

'the correspondence of Marshals, their notebooks, even some letters from Napoleon, some addressed to his wife and others to his ministers. The first proved the Emperor could be tender, and the other that despite the difficulties of this unhappy retreat he was busying himself paying close attention to everything that was going on in France.'

The sergeant weeps every time anything crops up that wounds his patriotic feelings. Roos also hears how

'after the army had left, the village's inhabitants had wanted to rebuild it, but were forbidden to do so by a decree of the Emperor Alexander, according to which the village of Studianka was to be utterly razed and not exist for the future. At the limits of what had been the village we saw two big sepulchres. One stood not far from where I'd spent the night of 26/27 November. It was as tall as a peasant's cottage and completely surrounded by conifers. According to the professor this tomb dated from a hundred years ago and the sharply disputed passage of the Swedes under Charles XII,'

en route for their last victory at Toloczin and final defeat at Poltava.

'One only had to scratch the surface to find bones. The Eastern sepulchre, which encloses our warlike companions dead of hunger, cold and exhaustion, is even loftier and takes up a larger surface area. The number of corpses buried there is estimated to be several thousands.'

In his study at Staroï-Borissow Prince Radziwil's *intendant*, a Baron de Korsak, whom Roos had helped back to health, was making a collection of relics:

'Here I saw successfully used for the first time the iron hand-mills Napoleon had had sent from France for his army. Also an incredible collection of decorations of almost all the nations that had taken part in the war. Some had been compulsorily handed over by the peasantry, some had been bought off them.'

In 1822 a Prussian engineer officer, Major J. L. U. Blesson, would visit the scene. Emerging from the dark forests between Borissow and Studianka, he'd begin to notice:

'just think of it, ten years after the catastrophe – a mass of leatherware, strips of felt, scraps of cloth, shako covers, etc., strewn on the ground and fields. As one approached the river, these melancholy relics lay thicker and even in heaps, mingled with the bones of human beings and animals, skulls, tin fittings, bandoliers, bridles and suchlike. Scraps of the Guard's bearskins had survived.'

Close to the bank where the main (artillery) bridge had been he'd be surprised to find:

'an island divides the river into two arms. It owes its origin to the vehicles and bodies which had fallen off the bridge and to the corpses which had been carried down to this point and then covered with mud and sand. We made our way with difficulty along the bank amid relics of all kinds, and soon reached the second [foot] bridge.'

Here are no more mounds of skeletons, only piles of fittings and mountings. The bodies had been swept downstream. 'Below the island three muddy mounds had formed, and these, we found, were covered with forget-me-nots.'

Revisiting Russia on business in 1828, Paul de Bourgoing, one-time lieutenant of the 5th Tirailleurs,[1] would keep halting for deep and sad reflections:

'I recognised these feeble undulations of Russia's verdant terrain, these long avenues of immense silver birches, that graceful tree of the North with its pale and lightsome foliage. I remembered very distinctly the sight of our two battalions of the Young Guard as it had windingly mounted this succession of hills, deserted now. It seemed to me these narrow valleys should have retained some faint echo of the singing of so many joyous voices,[2] of the song of that regiment which could have no inkling of the fate awaiting it. But no sound, no whisper was heard in the distance among these solitudes. The greatest number of these voices, so full of life and hope, had been frozen by the cruel onslaught of these countries' climate, so smiling and so flower-bedecked in the fine season, so deserted, so cold, so desolate in the depths of winter.'

To this day mounds can be seen along the Moscow road where the Grand Army lies buried.

NOTES

Chapter 1. 'A Word Unknown in the French Army'

1. For Albrecht Adam, see *1812 – The March on Moscow*, hereinafter referred to as *The March*, index.

2. See *1812 – Napoleon in Moscow*, hereinafter referred to as *Moscow*, pp. 218 et seq.

3. Following the fatal route a year later, when the Grand Army's 1,100 abandoned guns were on display outside the Kremlin, the English travel writer J. T. James would be told how it had been 'curious to trace, in the course of their flight, the successive diminution in size of the different pieces of ordnance which were taken; first the 12-pounders, then the eights, and then the sixes, their means of transport constantly decreasing as they advanced further on their march'.

4. See *Moscow*, Chapter 8.

5. Virtually every one of our eye-witnesses reiterates the same thing. 'Hurrah' is in fact a Cossack word, meaning 'death'.

6. See *The March*, p. 179.

7. See *Moscow*, p. 197.

8. Since the Revolution tents had not been regulation issue in the French armies.

9. For the load the ranker had to carry in and on his pack, see *The March*, p. 32.

10. This according to General *Guillaume de Vaudoncourt* who would himself be taken prisoner. 'The massacre at Moscow seems to have been very terrible,' Wilson was noting in his *Journal*: 'The captives pay dear for their master's crimes. Those are the happiest, indeed, who quit their chains and their lives together. But the Russians have great wrongs to avenge. Buonaparte was very cruel in the capital, executing many without proof of guilt, for offences which he had no right to punish with death.'

11. See *Moscow*, pp. 171 *et seq*.

12. See Moscow, pp. 202 *et seq*.

13. Marshal A.-J. Mailly had been wounded in the head and captured at Rossbach. Created a Marshal of France in 1783, he tried in vain to defend the Tuileries but resigned when Louis XVI had tried to flee the country. Arrested at the age of 86, he was guillotined on 25 March 1794 at Arras, presumably under the very eyes of the detestable terrorist-Jacobin Lebon, who enjoyed dining on a balcony opposite, watching the executions. 'Despite his 86 years he mounted the scaffold unaided and died crying "*Vive le Roi!* I die faithful to my king, as my ancestors have always been!" Doubtless it was this that in 1815 would cause Mailly-Nesle to be raised to the peerage.

14. 'A white's always a white, a blue always a blue,' Napoleon would say on St Helena.

15. See *Moscow*, p. 228.

16. See *Moscow*, illustration facing p.141.

17. See *The March*, p. 42.

18. See *The March*, index; also *Moscow*, with Le Roy's portrait.

19. Bonnet wouldn't write anything more in his diary until Smolensk.

20. See *Moscow*, index.

21. As I pointed out in *The March*, the term 'dysentery' denoted any kind of diarrhoea.

22. See *The March*, p. 324.

23. The Portuguese Chasseurs attached to the Young Guard wore brown jackets, sky-blue trousers and Bavarian-type helmets with a heavy crest hanging down over the brow. He'd see them still in good shape at the Berezina.

24. For the 5th Tirailleurs and their redoubtable Colonel Hennequin, see *The March*, p.113.

25. Winzingerode had been an inveterate supporter of the successive coalitions and in 1806 been active in getting Prussia to declare war on France, with disastrous consequences.

26. Among them perhaps General Count *Philippe de Ségur*, Assistant Prefect of the Palace (who, Roman Soltyk says, was in charge of the headquarters mules during the retreat 'and made a very good job of

it') and – clearly – Marshal Bessières' ADC Lieutenant-Colonel Baudus, whose account of the incident is in Bertin: *Etudes sur Napoléon*, p. 163. My account fuses that of Baudus with Caulaincourt's more extensive one, and with those of Ségur, Fain, Denniée, Rapp, and A. F. de Beauchamp's *Histoire de la Déstruction de Moscoue en 1812*. All essentially agree.

27. Ségur may very well have been present and thus is exempt on this occasion from Gourgaud's scornful charge of reporting mere gossip.

28. See *Moscow*, p.198.

29. See *Moscow*, pp. 115–18. Despite Mme Anthony's tears, both actresses would get back to France.

30. Marbot, however, calls Friederichs an 'excellent, very brave officer, the handsomest man in the French armies'. He would die the following year, two days after being wounded at the Battle of Leipzig.

31. See *The March*, p. 334.

32. See *The March*, pp. 205, 207, 208.

33. Dedem saw 'the dead unburied after our first passage' and next day Captain Charles François would see several of his former companions' putrefying corpses. One of the 30th Line's captains 'still had his mouth on his own arm, eaten to the bone'.

34. See *The March*, pp. 325–6.

Chapter 2: Borodino Revisited

1. See *Moscow*, p. 235.

2. See *Moscow*, index.

3. The Napoleonic soldier measured distances in leagues. A league was about an hour's march or rather more than three miles.

4. See *The March*, p.132.

5. See *The March*, and illustration.

6. Crossing it a week or so earlier in a convoy escorted by 300 Poles of his own regiment, the wounded Polish Captain Heinrich von Brandt had sat up in his wagon and thought that 'seen in perspective from the hilltops these heaps of corpses, stripped of everything, looked like immense flocks of sheep'.

7. Von Suckow's rendering seems less faithful than Vossler's. See *The March*, p. 318 and J. T. James's illustration, p.193. By the time James sketched it, already leaning to its fall, in 1813, all the corpses had apparently been burned or buried.

8. See *The March*, pp. 299 *et seq*.

9. 'Some Baden grenadiers, who escorted Napoleon's baggage, treasure and kitchen as far as the Berezina. Later on, at Borissow, two NCOs of that regiment who, prisoners like myself, were serving me as orderlies, assured me it was Napoleon himself who'd given this order. Some officers of his staff had been of his opinion; others, like Berthier, had stood up against him. The latter had even hinted to some of the grenadiers to let their prisoners gradually escape under cover of night.' Captain Count M.-H. Lignières, of the 1st Foot Chasseurs of the Guard, says it was Spaniards and Portuguese, not Frenchmen, who'd committed the atrocity. Zalusky: 'In his critique of Ségur's *History*, p. 200, General Gourgaud exonerates us completely from the reproach made us by M. de Ségur in saying that there were some Poles among the Spanish and Portuguese escort. Never has a Pole struck his disarmed enemy!'

10. Presumably one of the five temporary bridges thrown over the Kolotchka on 6 September, not the one leading into Borodino village.

11. It's not clear to me whether François means the Kolotskoïe abbey or the village of Kolotskaya, which had been burnt down during the battle and could hardly have been rebuilt. Nor, presumably, would he have 'approached' it because his unit must have followed the main road through the ruins of Borodino village and its church.

12. Not that discipline in the French armies was always what it could have been. In 1807 the starving Guard infantry refused to share what food it had even with Murat.

13. 'This heroic carabinier', Sergeant Bertrand concludes, 'got himself another musket when we left Smolensk and was killed by a roundshot on 17 November at the battle of Krasnoïe.'

14. But a few days later the 'secretary' would be carried off by Cossacks while

foraging in a village; 'the other, ill and almost blind, got lost on the road before reaching Vilna'.

15. 'Thanks to the brave Captain Berchet, paymaster of the 18th, and to the honesty of my brave comrades, *the 120,000 francs were put back in the chest after the campaign* [Pelleport's italics]. I don't know whether many regiments were as fortunate as the 18th Line. Anyway, I'll always regard it as an honour to have commanded men capable of accomplishing such acts of heroism.'

Chapter 3: Getting Through at Viazma

1. See *The March*, index.

2. See *The March*, pp. 240 et seq.

3. See *The March*, pp. 90, 91, where Everts is wrongly ranked as sergeant.

4. See *The March*, pp. 174–5.

5. See *The March*, p. 112.

6. Rossetti says 'we', i.e., presumably Murat's staff, had got to Viazma 'towards midday', and that Napoleon had sent the Guard 'which had marched for part of the night' on ahead to seize the town, and that it had got there at 9 a.m. But Rossetti (see *The March*, pp. 110–11) isn't always too reliable about times.

7. A repeat performance, that is, of what had been done on the way out. See *The March*, p. 238.

8. Brandenburgs were tassel-ended loops, usually of black but in Napoleon's case gold lace.

9. The master of HMS *Northumberland* too would record Napoleon as having a 'loud harsh voice'.

10. John R. Elting's *Military History & Atlas of the Napoleonic Wars* summarises the movements of II, VI and X corps as follows: 'In the north, Macdonald moved on Riga, ignoring Steingell, who marched south to join Wittgenstein. The two Russian commanders tried to trap Saint-Cyr between them. Administering a bloody repulse to Wittgenstein's assault on Polotsk, Saint-Cyr successfully withdrew from that town after dark on the 19th, burning his bridges behind him, and sending Wrede against Steingell on 20 October, the Russians retreating to Disna

in disorder. (Lacking a bridging train, Wittgenstein could not interfere.) Thereafter, Saint-Cyr sent Wrede to Glubokoië with the remains of the VI Corps to cover the direct road to Vilna. He himself retired towards Lepel to be on the flank of any advance against Wrede, but had to relinquish his command because of a painful wound. Learning of Saint-Cyr's plight, Victor marched to his aid on 20 October, reaching the crippled II Corps near Tchasniki on the 29th. Here he clashed indecisively with Wittgenstein, and retired on Sienno. Wittgenstein did not pursue.'

11. In July Jérôme, initially in command of three army corps, had gone off back to Cassel in a huff. See *The March*, index.

12. There seems to be some confusion here. The Guard had surely left on 2 November? In view of what followed and the Russians' approach, it seems strange that Napoleon did not wait for IV and I Corps to arrive. But doubtless he was anxious to secure the Dnieper bridge at Doroghobouï. In general, Caulaincourt criticises his lack of foresight during this part of the retreat.

13. Afterwards Planat would find that he had few memories of this first part of the retreat after Ghjat, because of being exposed to sudden sharp cold. 'Later I'd stand up to much more rigorous cold without my faculties being noticeably affected.'

14. See *The March*, p.128 and illustration.

15. Young Moncey 'who'd just come from the imperial pages'. See *The March*, pp. 193, 214, 374.

16. See Guesse's painting of the Russians thrusting the French rearguard at bayonet point down Viazma's main street.

17. See *The March*, p. 241.

18. Wilson even went so far as to send off his ADC to Petersburg to complain to the Tsar. A little more energy, Wilson thinks, and Kutusov might have got to Viazma still earlier – but in that case he'd have had to confront Napoleon and the Imperial Guard, an eventuality which, to judge by later developments beyond Smolensk, Kutusov was rightly scared of. My pen-friend Colonel John Elting, however, has little use for Wilson's *Geschäft*: 'Wilson was

easily taken in – in fact he probably became a catspaw in the Bennigsen (a former Hanoverian and so *almost* an Englishman) v. Kutusov feud.' Certainly he was very full of himself and a considerable knowall.

19. The Russians of course celebrated Viazma as a victory.

20. See *The March*, index, and *Moscow*, p.195.

Chapter 4: Handmills at Doroghoboui

1. Thus Ney himself, in his so-called *Mémoires*: 'A retreat *en échiquier* upon two lines may be effected according to the principles laid down in the [1791] regulations. This movement may be made alternately in the two lines, and by even and uneven battalions, during the whole time the retrograde movement lasts.'

2. My eye-witnesses' texts all describe the same developments, in very similar words. The above is from a Russian account.

3. See *Moscow*, Chapter 8.

4. For Grouchy and the semi-imbecilic Lahoussaye, see *The March*, p. 331 and *Moscow*, index.

5. Chlapowski had started the retreat with nine horses, of which seven would survive 'all in good condition'. He himself had been wounded nine times, always in the same arm. Having a very large income, he had been married off by Napoleon, but not happily.

6. 'While on campaign,' Jean-Michel Chevalier, an officer of the Guard's *Chasseurs à Cheval*, tells us, 'Napoleon ate very little. He breakfasted at 9 or 10 a.m. and had nothing more to eat until 8 or 9 p.m., and very little then. He always wore our regiment's green jacket or dress coat, with very small, general's epaulettes, without any aiguillettes, a single star, that of the [Grand] Eagle and the decoration of a simple knight of the Legion of Honour, a white cashmere waistcoat and similar short breeches, riding boots (indoors, silk stockings and slippers with gold buckles), the great red sash [of the Legion of Honour] between coat and waistcoat, his historic little hat, and a sword. When it was cold he put on the grey overcoat everyone knows over his coat. When he was riding along

the route on horseback, in our midst, he had the air of being our colonel. Then nothing – rain, hail, snow, storm – nothing prevented him from pursuing his way; he paid it no attention. Prince Berthier always rode at his side, then [came] the generals, the ADCs, the *officiers d'ordonnance* and his Mameluke Roustam. If it was cold and he dismounted, the chasseurs of the escort hastened to make up a small fire. Then he would amuse himself by pushing the firewood with his feet, or turn his back to the fire, his hands behind his back. If he needed to pay a minor call of nature en route, he dismounted in our midst and did his business without ceremony. Sometimes I saw him change his linen. One can say that Napoleon, in our midst, was at the centre of his family and seemed to be quite at home [*chez lui*].'

7. See *The March*, pp. 232, 233.

8. See *Moscow*, pp. 70, 71.

9. See *Moscow*, p. 161.

10. 'That', he adds, 'is just about all I had on me when I recrossed the Niemen.'

11. A napoleon, sometimes also referred to as a *louis*, was worth 24 livres, or 20 francs, say £500/$1000 in modern money. But such calculations are notoriously problematic.

Chapter 5: Snow

1. Joubert commanded Razout's (11th) Division's 1st Brigade (4th and 18th Line).

2. Together with a few fellow-conspirators Malet, a former Jacobin who'd taken up with the Catholic reaction, had 'arrested' Pasquier, head of the Paris police and Police Minister Savary in the name of an imaginary provisional government, announcing that Napoleon was dead in Russia. Desmarest, another police officer he'd conned and arrested, had instantly imagined 'Bernadotte at the Russian headquarters, coming after the fatal blow to offer himself to our bewildered generals as a mediator, arranging with them a new government under Alexander's auspices and then, in concert with them, having sent orders and agents to Paris'. A veteran of the Paris Municipal Guard witnessed Malet's and his fellow conspirators' execution:

'The conspirators had been condemned to death. They were to be shot on the Grenelle plain. The battalion of veterans in barracks at the Rue du Foin were ordered to attend the execution, maintain order, form line ... Naturally, I went with the battalion. The condemned men arrived in cabs at Grenelle [beyond the *Champ de Mars*], where they were made to stand in a single row. I believe there were twelve of them. The platoons which were to shoot them were some tirailleurs of the Young Guard, taken from the depots. I was struck again by the spectacled man, as at the council. They fired. I hardly saw the unfortunate men fall: the smoke prevented it. I heard heart-rending cries, then a succession of musket shots to finish them off. The veterans I was with, who were at a great distance from the place of execution, said the condemned men had been massacred, the tirailleurs not knowing how to fire a shot. The troops' movements, the noise of the crowd which *we* veterans were holding at a distance, the drums, together all that suppressed emotion ... I only saw the spectacled man who'd been condemned, the smoke of the gunpowder prevented me from seeing him fall. But when I got home I was very pale, extremely agitated, and people tumbled to it that I'd gone with our veterans at Grenelle: I was reprimanded. I seem to remember that Parisian Guard, white coats, green turn backs, were present, unarmed, at the execution. It was dissolved, I believe, and its men absorbed into other regiments. The conspirators' punishment had no more effect on the lower part of the population, that of my quarter, than the conspiracy had. Everyone kept his mouth shut. As long as the Great Empire lasted I always heard people speak in very low voices, even in the family, about political events. Any individual who spoke aloud, fearlessly, was counted as a police spy.'

3. See *The March*, p. 62.

4. The troops invariably referred to the regimental eagles as '*les coucous*'. It is curious to think that the first symbol of empire to be proposed to Napoleon had been the cock – which he'd dismissed as 'ridiculous'.

5. The so-called *halte des pipes*, made normally every two hours. See *The March*, p. 28.

6. Did he? According to John R. Elting 'it was an old army yarn'.

7. Some men would afterwards forgive themselves – and one another – for such sins against the code of *camaraderie* and military honour. Others not. Bourgogne's immortal *Memoirs*, written to exorcise his horrible memories, are as much a military man's confession of human weakness as of its powers of survival.

8. Larrey himself, to judge from his portrait, was a typical Celt. His observation is correct, but not of course his explanation. As we now know, it wasn't the southerners' blood or intelligence that saved them, but their smaller heat losses, due to having less skin area in proportion to bulk. Small individuals tend to feel cold less than big ones.

9. But many would fall in battle at Krasnoïe. See Chapter 10.

10. Like many other letters, Compans' to his wife from Smolensk owes its survival to its being captured by Cossacks.

11. Jean Victor Moreau, Napoleon's rival for power during the last years of the Republic, had gone over to his enemies after being exiled for plotting to overthrow the Bonapartist regime.

12. Even this incident is only mentioned in a footnote. Whether or not one agrees with the victim's assessment of Napoleon, it must be remembered that Bourgeois' book, like Labaume's, came out in 1814, under the first Bourbon restoration. Not that Bourgeois seems to have had any strong Bonapartist feelings.

13. An attitude that seems to have been spreading even as early as at Smolensk in August. Dedem is even more crushing. After the first serious snowfalls, he says, 'not a single French general was at his post' – certainly an exaggeration. And Caulaincourt adds that the 'most public-spirited' of them, seeing that Napoleon, marching along with everyone else, was all too well aware of the extent of the disaster, 'exempted themselves from talking about or indeed from taking any notice of it'.

14. This is a question I must leave hanging in the air. If I could re-read many of the memoirs I first made excerpts from before reading all the others but to which I no longer have access, I should certainly be

able to provide many a missing piece in this jigsaw puzzle.

15. Labaume, a cavalry captain on Eugène's staff, published his embittered and critical book in 1814 during the first Bourbon restoration. He sees Napoleon above all as a man who, despite all his imperial and rationalistic rhetoric, was in love with war and adventure, no matter at what cost. Labaume wrote 'to the end and the moral of rendering odious this fatal expedition which forced civilised peoples to make war on barbarians'. His history would afterwards come out in numerous editions, in French, English and other languages.

Chapter 6: Disaster at the Wop

1. During the '16-hour long night' before leaving Doroghoboui's smouldering ruins, one of Cesare de Laugier's fellow-officers, a Lieutenant Bandai, dying in a roofless stone building in thickly falling snow, foretold the moment of his death: 'At the end of 50 minutes [Raffaglia, as he'd ordered, had his watch in his hand] he asked what time it was. "11.50", came the reply. "Then I've ten more minutes, and my pains are finished. Bring me a bit closer to the fire." We saw him die at the exact moment he'd predicted.'

2. See *Moscow*, pp. 76 *et seq.*

3. See *Moscow*, p. 201 for their kindness to him.

4. Apparently he'd tried them out. His text contradicts itself.

5. Marshal Berthier's son, Anthouard, wrote his own account. See Bibliography.

6. In his *Mémoires* Ney specifies the duties of an adjutant-commandant. He was the equivalent of a 20th-century colonel assigned to staff duty.

7. See *The March*, p. 232.

8. It was Del Fante who'd led the storming of the Great Redoubt at Borodino, captured the Russian general Litchacheff and taken him to Napoleon. See *The March*, pp. 303, 305.

9. Even so it was only a dress-rehearsal for what would happen to the entire army three weeks later.

10. Ségur, with IHQ and just then entering Smolensk, would hear the details afterwards.

Chapter 7: How Witebsk was Lost

1. Elting points out that Napoleon would now and again go through the army lists looking for deserving but no longer active officers. But our memoirists' pages frequently echo the belief that absence meant imperial oblivion.

2. See *The March*, pp. 103, 104.

3. For Jomini and Hogendorp's embittered squabbles and Napoleon's order, see *The March*, p. 243.

4. For Napoleon's insoluble Polish problem, see *The March*, p. 101, etc.

5. The small country town where the campaign's first major action had been fought on 25/26 July. See *The March*, pp. 131 *et seq.*

6. For Charpentier at Witebsk, see *The March*, pp. 174, 178. See also pp. 153 *et seq.*

7. On the other hand it was partly because considerable forces had to be left in the rear that the army had lacked decisive superiority at Borodino.

8. See *The March*, pp. 174, 175.

9. 'If poor Amédée de Pastoret were one day to write his memoirs he would have a lot to tell!' – Stendhal.

10. On the eve of the campaign Oudinot had married Mlle de Coussy (who had now come out to Vilna to nurse his shattered shoulder) in a double wedding where Lorencez, his chief-of-staff, had espoused one of Oudinot's daughters. Lorencez had remained with II Corps when Saint-Cyr had taken over.

11. For Beschenkowiczi, see *The March*, index.

12. Castex's light cavalry brigade, consisting of the 23rd and 24th Chasseurs, was actually part of II Corps. After evacuating Polotsk, a badly wounded Saint-Cyr had met Victor, resigned and gone back to France. This had placed II Corps temporarily under Victor's command.

13. Taken to St Petersburg and released after the wars, Pouget, like Balzac's Colonel Chabert, would be a victim of his Bonapartist sympathies and apply in vain

to the Bourbon government for any recompense for his services at Witebsk, or even for his 'costs for espionage, which amounted to about 1,200 francs'. Napoleon's only comment when he heard of Pouget's last fight and his refusal to abandon his wretched Berg soldiers was: 'Eh bien, he should have run off and left them stuck there.' An opinion which Pouget, writing his memoirs, would be inclined to share.

Chapter 8: Smolensk Again

1. 'The main street, the great square, all had suffered the same destruction, even the very house pointed out as having been the lodging of Buonaparte. The walls were breached in several parts, and the towers, on which batteries of howitzers had been planted, were in a very shattered state' – but that would be after they'd been partially blown up by Ney's Illyrians on 17 November. *J. T. James*, visiting Smolensk in 1813.

2. An immeasurably popular *opéra comique* by C. S. Favart (1710– 92).

3. Mainly because Murat had given orders to deceive Napoleon as to his losses by burying the French dead first. See *The March*, p. 213.

4. An old comrade in arms from Italy, the elderly and tight-fisted Baraguay d'Hilliers, Colonel-General of Dragoons, was a man on a level with Junot. Reaching Berlin, he'd die of chagrin and/or whatever illness it was he was suffering from.

5. All according to Ségur, but other eyewitnesses in the rear at Smolensk, e.g., Honoré Beulay, confirm it.

6. These were men of Platov's corps. Kutusov's main army had circumvented Smolensk to the south and gone on to try and cut off the French retreat at Krasnoië.

7. See *The March*, p. 217.

8. During the advance the invaders had found the population as far as Smolensk able to speak Polish or Lithuanian and therefore anti-Russian.

9. 'Banding themselves together, they'd been going on ahead of the army and been the first to get to any houses they found, or camped separately in villages. When the army had got there, these

thieves had come out of their hiding, prowled around the bivouacs, stolen their horses as quietly as possible and the officers' portmanteaux, and set out again very early before the army started out. Such was their daily plan.'

10. 'By prodigious economies' these would be made to last as far as Bobr. Le Roy's chicken would keep him going as far as the Berezina.

11. On 6 November, in addition to his own duties as responsible for the entire Administration, such as it was, Daru had also officially replaced Mathieu Dumas, who'd been ill ever since leaving Moscow.

12. This, no more than Kergorre's statement to the same effect, isn't quite true. Getting there in September from Minsk with Partonneaux's division (IX) Honoré de Beulay had found all the hospitals full of sick men from the Moscow army 'shivering in infected and stinking barns, lying on rotten straw and devoured by fleas and lice ... dying like flies'. The former inhabitants, 'finding time go slowly in the depths of inhospitable forests, were beginning to return to their homes. We'd been described to them as bloodthirsty barbarians. They were very much surprised to find us civilised people, who liked to laugh when we weren't ill and showed ourselves amiable to women and children and paid for what we bought.' But very few had come back. When Everts had got there on 31 October he'd found the garrison 'in a kind of barracks' and the officers in some uninhabited houses abandoned by their occupants.'

13. Roustam's statement, reiterated by Denniée in his *Itinéraire*, that Napoleon, contrary to all his habits, shut himself up in the governor's palace 'and didn't come out until the 14th at 5 a.m. to continue his retreat', cannot stand up to Caulaincourt's.

14. See *The March*, p. 42.

15. It was by this road that Barclay de Tolly's army had retrograded after the battle of 14 August. See *The March*, p. 375.

16. For the Neuchâtel battalion, see *Moscow*, p. 113.

17. Paul de Bourgoing, who was certainly present, assures us that this happened at Smolensk, not during the ensuing battle

of Krasnoïe, as popular historians would afterwards make out: 'How could the wretched men, even if they'd been standing to the right of the regiment, have blown down their instruments, or used their poor frost-bitten fingers? This on the other hand was quite possible at Smolensk, as there were fires where they could warm themselves.' Bourgogne agrees.

Chapter 9: The Icy Road to Krasnoïe

1. 'Of these four ADCs,' Mailly-Nesle writes, 'M. Giroux died of wounds received while rejoining us, and M. de Bugueville received three musket balls in his body.'

2. Domergue was one of the French civilian hostages taken from Moscow by Rostopchin.

3. See *Moscow*, pp. 116, 117, 118.

4. See *The March*, pp. 187 *et seq.*

5. See *Moscow* pp. 149, 150.

6. See *Moscow*, p. 242.

7. The Krasnoïe ravine had already played an important part at the First Battle of Krasnoïe in August, when Griois' guns had got stuck in it. See *The March*, p. 172.

8. The one Napoleon had ordered to be burnt on the eve of Borodino, but which Narbonne had saved from the flames. See *The March*, pp. 251, 252.

9. J. T. James, following the route a year later, would be astonished to see how all the trees in the forests lining the road were half-burnt.

10. See *The March*, pp. 172–3.

Chapter 10: The Guard Strikes Back

1. This is Chambray's estimate in his attempt at a dispassionate and objective account of the campaign (published in 1825). He errs in assuming the Russian army had 'suffered few privations' – it too was suffering dreadfully from cold and starvation. 'Having received some reinforcements [it] was almost as numerous as when it had left Malojaroslavetz. The French army, including the debris of Baraguay-d'Hillier's division and the Smolensk garrison, added up to no more

than about 49,100 combatants, of whom 5,500 cavalry were in the worst possible state. More than 30,000 stragglers were marching with the columns, embarrassing their movements.'

2. See *The March*, Chapter 21.

3. On leaving Moscow on 19 October, according to the returns assembled afterwards by Chambray, the Imperial Guard had still consisted of 22,480 officers and men, including gunners and Train, and 112 guns. Since then it had lost horses and wagons, and certainly several hundred men.

4. Including those regiments which were sometimes classed as Middle Guard, among them the Fusiliers-Grenadiers.

5. For its latest recruits see Bourgoing and Fezensac's accounts in *The March*, pp. 22, 23, 113.

6. A *toise* was more or less a fathom.

7. Roguet says 1 a.m., Bourgogne with his column says 2 a.m.

8. But François' men had at Borodino: See *The March*, p. 282.

9. 'For almost two months', Griois adds, 'this hope of something better that never materialises prevented me from succumbing to fatigue.'

10. For Ornano's ineptitude, see *The March*, p. 293–4, and *Moscow*, pp. 195, 196.

11. Oddly enough Griois makes no mention of this famous episode. Ségur tells the same story, at second or perhaps third hand, in virtually the same words as Laugier, but puts the reply into the mouth of General Guyon, whom he makes claim to have 24,000 men against the Russians' 20,000. Laugier, too, is certainly writing at second hand and, for once, *ex post facto*, and therefore may have got it from Ségur, whose history there is other evidence of his having read. That day, as we've seen, he was in no state to report anything.

12. The Joseph-Napoleon Regiment, whose would-be deserters had caused Coignet such trouble in July (see *The March*, pp. 107, 108), was made up of fragments of Romana's corps who had failed to get themselves evacuated by the British Navy from Denmark, and of Spanish prisoners of war. Its 1st and 4th Battalions formed part of IV Corps; the 2nd and 4th

Battalions had fought at Borodino under their Swiss Colonel Tschudi as part of what had been Dedem's 2nd Infantry Brigade of Friant's 1st Division, which had now been detached to reinforce III Corps, still at Smolensk.

13. Cesare de Laugier adds in a note that Eugène honoured Del Fante's family with a pension and that a street in Leghorn (Livorno) is called Cosimo del Fante. Is it still? The francophile Laugier spells the gallant auditor's name 'Ville-Blanche'.

14. It's a curious trait of human nature that though we have no compunction in shooting or stabbing down an enemy, nothing will induce us to put a friend out of even the worst extremes of agony. We shall see this again in the case of the hated and sadistically minded Delaître. After the Second Battle of Polotsk, Honoré Beulay, too, would hear an officer of the Train 'who'd had a sword thrust through his stomach and whose guts were dragging after him in the snow, calling out to me to finish him off, to put an end to his unspeakable sufferings. I shrank back in horror from the thought of it, and while grieving for this unfortunate man with all my heart, I ran off, abandoning him to his sad fate.'

15. Grabowski assures us that if Klicki – Ségur spells it Kliski – colonel of the 1st Regiment of Lancers of the Vistula, hadn't chanced to be there, IV Corps would have had to surrender.

16. For Napoleon's dream of invading India and the rumour that he intended to, see *The March*, p. 31, and *Moscow*, pp. 146, 240. Taken to St Petersburg, Davout's *bâton* would be put on display at the 'victory' celebrations. Although supposedly out of reach, it vanished! A rumour that it had been taken by some member of the French theatre troupe led to a riot and the troupe was forthwith embarked for Stockholm.

17. The last we saw of Sauvage and Houdart of VIII Corps' artillery park was during the advance through Lithuania in July. See *The March*, pp. 68, 75.

18. In a letter to Napoleon from Königsberg, the 20-year-old Prince Emil of Hesse would receive the highest praise from Berthier for 'constantly marching with his

250 men whom he has known how to preserve, as also five guns'. Bourgoing lauds his 'heroic valour' and Vionnet admired him for 'never quitting his officers, sharing their difficulties, their privations and their dangers as if he were the least of them'.

19. See *The March*, pp. 155, 157.

20. Not to be confused of course with von Suckow of the Württembergers.

21. Paul de Bourgoing confirms Ségur's account on this striking detail.

22. The few survivors of the 33rd Line would be repatriated to the Netherlands after the 1813 campaign, without any representations either from the French or Dutch Ministry of War.

Chapter 11. 'Marching, marching, marching ...'

1. Actually Kutusov, under the impact of the Guard's attack at Kontkovo on 17 November, had assumed that it was acting as rearguard to the rest of the army; cancelled his projected assault on Krasnoïe; and even sent orders to Tormassov to halt his march to the Dnieper.

2. What a scene to delight Gillray and the patriotic hearts of his fellow London caricaturists: 'Buonaparte, Emperor of the Frenchies, whizzing downhill out of Russia on his a**e, like a shot off a shovel!' Naturally neither Caulaincourt nor anyone else at IHQ seems to have seen the funny side of 'the grave situation'.

3. See *The March*, p. 171.

4. 'He joined our march,' Pastoret adds. 'This son of the princes of Lisbon came to die at Königsberg for a foreign prince.' On 27 January 1812 Alorna, wishing to 'prove to himself and his friends that he still wasn't decrepit' and to avenge insults from the British, had written to Napoleon, asking to be allowed to shed his blood for him 'the greatest man in the world' by making war in the North. Altogether it's interesting to note how well the Portuguese performed in Russia, as they were simultaneously doing – against the French – under the victorious Wellington in Spain. – See also Theotonio Banha: *Apontamentos para a historia du Legiao portugueza*, Lisbon, 1865.

5. Brandt, too, thought Jomini was governor at Orsha, and Labaume lists him as such. Elting points out that 'whatever army Jomini accompanied it was noted that he always meddled and interfered'.

6. Future Marshal of France. See *The March*, p. 62.

7. At Vilna on 7 July Napoleon had written to Lariboisière, telling him that Eblé had just been ordered to 'instantly organise a bridging train of 32 boats, with two companies of pontoneers and one of sailors, and place them under the orders of a senior officer'. It was to be at Murat's orders. Faber du Faur had seen part of it parked in the Kremlin. Evidently another part had been left at Orsha, or else subsequently brought up.

8. Doubtless on the broad sandy foreshore Dumonceau had noticed in August, now fringed with ice. See *The March*, p. 139.

9. The one concerning the route from Krasnoïe to Orsha had been sent off the previous day.

10. For the contretemps which could arise when dealing with French arrogance, see *The March*, p.115.

Chapter 12: Ney's Amazing Exploit

1. For these Spaniards, see *The March*, index.

2. See *The March*, p. 178.

3. I.e., ex-Friant, ex-Dufour, now being commanded by General J.-B.-L.-A. de Ricard. A returned *émigré*, Ricard was a relation by marriage to the Marseilles family of Clary, thus to the Bonapartes.

4. A division, in this sense, consisted of two companies, marching in line together.

5. His narrative is to be found in *Les Espagnols de la Grande Armée.*

6. One of them being the Provençal Major Doreille, sole support of his indigent mother at Tarascon, she who had already lost her other six sons in the wars.

7. François confirms that the 2nd Division was almost totally annihilated.

8. François himself, of course, wasn't in Ney's rearguard; he was limping on beyond Krasnoïe, after rescuing the 30th's Eagle. But to judge from the detailed

intensity of his account he seems afterwards to have heard all about it, Unfortunately he doesn't identify his informant for us.

9. François gives the name of the forest as Netinki.

10. Evidently François is identifying with his informant or repeating his words.

Chapter 13: The Terrible News at Toloczin

1. At St Helena he would declare him to have been 'incomparable for the artillery', mentioning him in the same breath as 'Murat for the cavalry'. Promoted General of Brigade, in 1813 and 1814 Drouot would provide notable services in action, accompany Napoleon to Elba and command the Guard artillery at Waterloo.

2. It was near Toloczin that Charles XII's Swedish army had won its last victory before being annihilated at Poltava on 30 June 1709.

3. For Napoleon's Turkish problem, see *The March*, index.

4. These and other town statistics are taken from a report sent in by an anonymous Polish officer, sent on ahead. It is to be found in Chuquet.

Chapter 14: Struggles for the Borissow Bridge

1. Pils too says the 23rd – see *The March*, p. 43. Marbot's tale that he rescued Oudinot in the nick of time after he'd 'barricaded himself in a stone house, adding to his ADCs a dozen French soldiers who were rejoining the army' is obviously purloined from what would happen much later on at Pleschenkowiczi. As we shall see, much of what Marbot, *raconteur par excellence*, writes does not withstand close scrutiny.

2. As I've explained in the introduction to *The March*, there has been no possibility, even within this book's fairly vast framework, to follow the doings of II and VI and then IX Corps around Polotsk; not for lack of memoirs – there are many, a whole account could be sewn together from those of Saint-Chamans, Marbot, Saint-Cyr, Legler, Pils, Lorencez, etc. – but of space. Saint-Cyr's own account of his

operations and the second Battle of Polotsk is lucidity itself, and required reading for war-gamers.

3. Antoine F. de Brack, author of the famous *Avant-postes de Cavalerie légère.*

4. See *Moscow,* Chapter 10.

5. See *The March,* p. 32.

6. See the fascinating texts of this and other 'treaties' imposed by Napoleon on his 'allies' in Nafziger's invaluable book.

7. See *The March,* p. 23.

8. See James R. Arnold's biographical study in Chandler: *Napoleon's Marshals.*

9. On 24 November Victor would write to Berthier: 'My generals of division are complaining a great deal about their troops. Generally speaking they are serving badly. It's difficult to keep them within bounds. They ascribe this to their state of indigence, but I believe it's due to their being so badly composed. The Dutch regiments, above all, are absolute nullities. The only unit which holds up and has always marched in good order is the Baden Brigade.' He had only 800 cavalry left.

10. The non co-ordination of II and IX Corps and its putative effect on the Berezina battle would provide an endless topic of debate among military men for decades afterwards. Lorencez produces documents to defend Oudinot and show that he was all the time trying to edge towards the Moscow army and was fully aware of the Borissow bridge's importance.

11. Second son of a former governor of St Petersburg, Pahlen would one day be the Russian Ambassador in Paris.

12. Having been Jérôme's chief-of-staff during the campaign's opening stages, he'd been given command, after that popinjay king's petulant departure, of II Corps' 8th Division.

13. At the campaign's outset Marbot, too, had been received with polite scepticism and a patronising clap on the shoulder when he'd come rushing with news that Wittgenstein was in presence.

14. For a brief description of Glubokoië, see *The March,* p. 109.

15. Corbineau's other two regiments may not have been so fortunate, for Fain will hear afterwards that '70–80 troopers less well mounted than the others' were lost.'

16. And certainly not Jomini's, who claims it was. At most his general knowledge of the vicinity may have contributed to the decision. Nor was Lorencez right in thinking that the 6th Lancers had crossed by the Studianka ford; in fact they used another, just north of Borissow.

17. After the Swedes had lost Finland to Russia in 1808 it had become a Russian archduchy. This explains the presence of Finnish soldiers at the Berezina.

18. Later that day Oudinot would write to Berthier: 'This contretemps has prevented us from saving the big bridge over the Berezina, which had been set fire to at three points simultaneously.' But added (as if it in any way palliated the disaster): 'We have taken several artillery ammunition wagons and are looking for six cannon we're assured the enemy have abandoned. We've already taken about 800 or 900 prisoners, among them several superior officers and we're still picking up many in the town.'

19. Napoleon would leave him a substantial sum in his will 'to go on defending the honour of French arms'.

20. Oudinot attributes the capture of Pahlen's '300 or 400 vehicles to our voltigeurs who'd crossed the stream to the left' of the small bridge at the town's entrance. 'We'd have entered it', he'll report to Berthier, 'if the enemy hadn't set fire to it.'

21. Actually 'three short leagues, i.e., about eight miles, according to General Bourdesolle, whose light cavalry had reconnoitred it and found 'narrow cross-country roads through the woods and marshes. Log bridges have had to be hastily constructed. The infantry and cavalry would only be able to make this march very slowly and with extreme fatigues and preceded by sappers. The artillery wouldn't get through.' Another officer thought the 'road through the forest is at present practicable for artillery except for certain spots which aren't properly frozen but can be turned. The approach to the village of Oukholoda is marshy.' The river's width was about the same as at Studianka. 'But the inhabitants say it isn't fordable even in summer.' On the right

bank, lined by trees, there were houses for the Russians to fortify, and the ground became marshy. A Polish ADC, the 32-year-old Colonel Falkowski, too, had been to Beresino.

22. 'Saving the Bridge at Borissow', it seems to me, would make a perfect wargame. Starting from the loss of Minsk and Oudinot's and Victor's strategical disputes, it would hinge around an analysis of he accounts given by Vaudoncourt, Victor, Pils, Lorencez, Marbot, Langeron, Rochechouart, Tchitchakov, Calosso and Curély.

Chapter 15: 'How Ever Shall We Get Through?'

1. *'Comment passerons-nous? Comment passerons-nous?'* All this according to Paul de Bourgoing, who however makes the error of thinking Napoleon got the news at Orsha.

2. It was particularly unfair to Davout, who was methodically commanding the rearguard against dwindling forces of Cossacks, 'accompanied as always by an infinite number of all the army corps' stragglers who, halting close to our troops when we take up a position, at the least alert rush to the rear, sweeping the combatants away with them.' Nor has Eugène, a few miles ahead of Davout, lost his head. On the contrary, bivouacked 'three leagues from Toloczin, near Jablonka', he's proving an admirable commander in adversity. Ney, who certainly isn't losing his, is in advance of him. Analysing IX and II Corps' movements, Lorencez writes: 'If Wittgenstein had marched on Bobr or some other place on the major line of communication between Smolensk and the Berezina, Napoleon would have found his Poltava long before reaching Borissow.' But Kutusov, still at Krasnoïe and 'preyed upon by theoretical as well as practical doubts concerning the Russian strategy' (Chandler) as he struggled through hardly less terrible difficulties than the French, had his most advanced units at least 40 miles to the rear. Tchitchakov, as we shall see, would be thrown into confusion by his recommendations.

3. Jomini says his words were: 'Sire, we aren't in Lombardy, nor in Swabia; but in Lithuania, 600 leagues from France, in a desert where winter has already overtaken

us. What matter now the beautiful manoeuvres offered us by a divided enemy on our flanks? Any day that puts distance between the army and its line of retreat will risk the loss of such of it as is still in a state to carry arms.' In reality one doesn't exactly see even 'the insufferably conceited' (Hogendorp) Jomini lecturing Napoleon in such terms!

4. Oddly enough, it had also been at Toloczin that Charles XII had burnt all his State papers. Was there an element of suggestion involved? We know from Bausset that throughout his stay in the Kremlin Napoleon had had the *History of Charles XII* (presumably Adlerbeth's, not Voltaire's, which he had had no use for) open on the roll-top desk in the Tsar's bedroom and 'even on his bedside table'.

5. Three days later Junot would write in the most fulsomely obsequious terms: 'I haven't a single infantryman left, not a gun, and my cavalry has hardly 100 horses. Who could do it more devotedly? What general officer can date the honour of guarding Your Majesty as far back as I can? Etc.' Junot having so disastrously blotted his copy book at Valutina in August, his letter was ignored.

6. For this intelligent young aristocrat's dependence on the experienced Henckens, see *Moscow*, p. 145.

7. At Vilna Oudinot's young wife, living under Maret's direct protection in the governor's palace, had struck up a 'strong and fascinated friendship' with Abramovitch's wife, a Polish woman who'd been divorced by no fewer than 'three husbands, still living'. One of them, Eugénie de Cousset alleges, had been Montholon 'who afterwards went with Napoleon to St Helena' and, according to Sten Forshuvud's researches, finally murdered him. But as far as we know Albine Montholon was his first wife.

8. Bourgogne's unforgettable epic of his survival amidst the icy wastes should be read in his own classic pages.

9. As we have seen, opinions would differ widely about how much of the Sacred Squadron survived intact, and for how long.

10. Lieutenant J. M. Chevalier, a long-serving officer of the Chasseurs à Cheval who'd been with him in Egypt, describes

in minute detail Napoleon's and Murat's costumes at this stage of the retreat: 'The Emperor had had a cap of green velvet made, in the shape of a toque with a tassel, and a little gold tuft, the band and ear pads in black martin skin, a kind of dressing-gown in grass-green velvet like the cap, the collar in black otter, the whole lined with fur, fringed with gold brandenburgs, a white belt around it to support his sword, fur boots, big gloves and a big stick – that's how the Emperor was dressed just then. An accoutrement, for the rest, which didn't seem much to his liking, for he only wore it a few days. The King of Naples wore a huge, opulent, semi-Polish costume: a Polish-style cap with a white ostrich feather, a fur-lined Polish-style mantle, violet like the cap, baggy red trousers, boots over them, a black bear's skin (I believe) in the form of a half-mantle thrown over his left shoulder, which gave his way of walking and his physiognomy a martial and imposing air. Prince Berthier, too, in a blue overcoat and a peasant cap, was marching at the Emperor's side.' As for other members of IHQ, Chevalier adds tersely: 'general carnival'. Chevalier's own clothing at this time may be of interest: 'Here's how I was clad, a complete portmanteau on my person: 1. A flannel waistcoat; 2. a shirt; 3. a knitted woollen waistcoat; 4. a sheepskin waistcoat; 5. a coloured waistcoat; 6. a braided waistcoat; 7. a dolman; 8. a belt; 9. a riding-coat; 10. a cloak over the whole. On my thighs: 1. a pair of underpants; 2. a pair of buckskin breeches; 3. a pair of Hungarian breeches; 4. a pair of cloth trousers; 5. a pair of trousers for riding, and, on my head, a bearskin cap.' We offer these exact descriptions to any tin figurine enthusiast to try to render!

11. No eye-witness authenticates this legendary scene, depicted in the well-known painting and a thousand tin-soldier dioramas; this is the only reference to it I've been able to find.

12. But not, as we shall see, before some residue had got across the Berezina.

13. Caulaincourt (p.105) thinks Napoleon would have done better to have made for Weselovo direct from Kroupki, taking the same road as Corbineau had arrived by. 'The fact is, that if we'd taken it, we'd have gained two marches; and that by making

our manoeuvres seem to be directed toward Borissow, we could have avoided the Admiral altogether, and that all our losses might have been saved.' But, thinks Caulaincourt, 'Pahlen's defeat and other considerations' had made Napoleon opt for Borissow. 'On the whole, though, the probability is that he knew nothing of Corbineau's suggestions, since he never spoke of them at the time they were made, and even deplored the inconvenience to the artillery and transport of having to make so big a detour to reach Weselovo. He spoke to me about the matter, as well as to the Prince of Neuchâtel, grumbling that he was never told about things in time.' There is some obscurity here which it seems impossible to clear up.

14. There is a time-scale problem here. As we have seen, Oudinot, according to Lorencez, had already sent II Corps' 'whole cuirassier division' (Doumerc's) to make a demonstration downstream on 24 November. Yet both Curély and Dumonceau see the movement undertaken 24 hours later? The matter seems to me to bear on the question of whether Oudinot or Napoleon ordered the feint.

Chapter 16: Two Fragile Bridges

1. A native of Crissier, in the Vaud, Jean-Marc Bussy had been a prisoner of war in England and even joined the British army, but feigned sickness so as not to be sent to India. Returning to France, he'd tried to get himself demobbed, but been arrested and sent off to Spain ... and Russia.

2. In his book *Vers la Bérésina*, Paris 1908, B. R. F. van Vlijmen says there were 300 of them; 'those from II Corps, about 200, were mostly Dutchmen'. This is partly confirmed by Dumonceau, below.

3. In his *Campaigns of Napoleon* David Chandler suggests 'some approximations' as to the Grand Army's fighting strength at the Berezina: Guard 8,500; I Corps 3,000; II Corps 11,000; III Corps (after reinforcement) 3,000; IV Corps 2,000; V + VI Corps 1,500; IX Corps 13,500; IHQ 2,500; mounted cavalry 5,500, and some 250–300 guns. Total 49,000 under arms plus some 40,000 stragglers.

4. Castellane, at least, wasn't underestimating the efforts of IHQ's cooks and

maîtres d'hôtel. 'Since Smolensk,' he writes in his diary, 'our meals consist of a very small slice of black bread, in the morning, with a bit of cow or horsemeat. In the evening we also get some soup. Sometimes we've been given mutton.'

5. Marbot (who says Napoleon got to Studianka at midday) says he 'put an end to the dispute by ordering one of the bridges to be built by the artillery, the other by the engineers. Instantly the beams and scantling battens of the village's huts were torn off and the sappers, like the gunners, got down to work.'

6. Oddly, Napoleon always found certain French words unpronounceable, or else didn't bother to try and pronounce them properly. E.g., he always called the infantry '*l'enfanterie*'.

7. Rapp's memories tend to be sporadic, and by no means always accurate. He'd remember the battery as having only twenty guns.

8. Although Berthier, always at hand, must have noted it down in his 'little green notebook' Curély's promotion wouldn't be confirmed until 9 August 1813.

9. Albitte had been famous at Mainz for his melancholy air 'which people took for a sign of remorse' for his revolutionary zeal; obviously mistakenly. – A. Chuquet: *Feuilles d'Histoire du XVII au XX Siècle,* Paris, 1911.

10. Chandler: 'If any one Russian mistake can be singled out for special comment, it is their failure to hold or destroy the crucial causeway leading away from the Berezina toward Zembin.'

11. Next year Tchitchakov, in virtual exile in Paris, would publish a defence of his bungling at the Berezina: *Rélation du passage de la Bérésina,* Paris, 1814; and *Mémoires,* Berlin, 1855. See also Emile Charles: *Documents sur la vie de l'Amiral de Tchitchageff,* Paris, 1854.

12. No one in the army, except Berthier, was allowed to wear a Swiss civilian-style hat like Napoleon's.

13. Duverger saw him in much the same light.

14. The decoration would never reach him. 'Only too soon', sighs Brandt, 'it would enter the category of things one doesn't even dare boast of having had. But he, the brave and chivalrous king, he'd have more unhappiness than I [for lack of] my decoration!' In 1815 Murat, like Ney, would be shot by firing-squad.

15. 'His uniforms, his plume, his boots made after an antique fashion, all appeared to him to be invaluable accessories in the art of seducing the fair sex. With this paraphernalia he really thought himself the most irresistible of men, though in point of fact he was so handsome no one needed such trappings less than he did.' Caulaincourt, of Murat.

16. It will be seen that Dupuy's account contradicts Tascher's. Perhaps Tascher himself and some others 'drifted away', while others remained?

17. He means a 'rag-and-bone man'. See *The March,* p. 111.

18. Unlike Mère Dubois' infant, this one would survive. In 1818 Bertrand would 'next meet with him as a child in the Legion of the Aube'.

Chapter 17: Partonneaux Surrenders

1. Actually Kutusov was four days' march behind but had sent on Platow and Miloradovitch to catch up with and harass French as they approached the Berezina. Clausewitz, serving at Russian headquarters, ascribes Kutusov's dilatoriness and caution to his over-estimating the numbers of French effectives. It was also due to poor reconnaissance on the part of his Cossacks who failed to report that half the Grand Army now consisted of stragglers. Napoleon, Clausewitz says, was 'living on a capital amassed over long years'. His mere name scared all the Russian commanders.

2. Rossetti writes 'this defection', but it seems unlikely that Napoleon should already have used this word, though he'd call it that afterwards. Besides, it still wasn't certain Partonneaux's division was lost. But we have already caught Rossetti out using 'terminological inexactitudes'.

3. Partonneaux's little-known letter is in Chuquet: *op. cit.,* Series 3.

4. At Hamburg Planat had impressed on him 'the dangers and hardships of a campaign. But at that time he'd been full of health and ardour, and told me he'd all

his life wanted to go campaigning with the brave Frenchmen. The poor devil had already had enough when we'd crossed the Niemen and I'd have sent him back as soon as we'd got to Kovno, if I could have replaced him.'

5. For their fate, see Chapter 19, below.

6. Caulaincourt would specifically set the number of individuals finally lost at about 10,000. Fain says 200–300 combatants (after Davout and Victor's withdrawal) and 10 to 12,000 stragglers.

7. Pils' expressive water-colour of the lurid and dramatic scene – here reproduced, unfortunately, only in black and white – in which he perfectly captures the moonlight effect, must have been made the previous night. It is reproduced – in colour – in Gaston Stiegler's book.

Chapter 18: Holocaust at the Berezina

1. In 1816 Kundert, then a corporal drummer in the 31st Swiss Regiment in Dutch service at Duisburg, would remind Legler of the incident. 'He still had the musket ball in his jawbone.'

2. Bourmann lived until he was 89, 'the last Fribourg survivor of the Napoleonic armies. Always upright and walking lightly he seemed to defy time. Each year on 28 November' (also commemorated in '*The Berezina Song*', apparently composed soon afterwards, and still sung in Switzerland) he would make 'a distribution to charity while taking the sacrament. That service was followed by a second in memory of his comrades who'd died on that sanguinary day.' He died in 1877, having seen Napoleon III's defeated army take refuge in his canton.

3. 'As for the poor 22nd [Russian] Chasseurs, old comrades of my first campaigns, they'd been crushed by the cuirassiers on the one hand and on the other by a well-nourished fire of artillery which had taken them in flank.' That evening their colonel, all in tears, would tell Rochechouart: 'Of the 2,000 men I had with me this morning, I've only brought back 150, three officers and my flag.' 'A great part of them had been taken prisoner, and the rest were out of action, dead or wounded.' But many would return to the colours next day.

4. This isn't the only occasion where an attentive reader catches Marbot out arrogating to himself a role which certainly belonged to his superior general. He does the same thing at the campaign's outset, at the Battle of Wilkomir on 28 June, which in his own account he claims to have won almost single-handed but where Calosso and Pils' more sober evidence reduces events to their proper proportions.

5. No doubt the very one Lejeune had designed for Berthier's 'ladykillers' in Spain, or some variant of it. For details of the uniform worn by Berthier's ADCs see *The March*, pp. 44–5.

6. Certainly there's something in Marbot's version, too; for Fain also hears how Cossacks had been 'seen dragging this officer away, striking him as they did so', and that 'the 23rd Chasseurs had done what they could to rescue him. But he was never heard of again.' Bonneval's statement that he'd seen Alfred de Noailles the previous day lying dead at the bridgehead, 'shot though the head by one of our own men' is obviously aprocryphal. Even more so Mailly-Nesle's tale of de Noailles being killed at Zembin next day. What is certain is that he wasn't listed by the Russians as a prisoner. In July 1813 Flahaut would translate an official Russian letter to that effect, but that 'on the other hand, his effects and letters have been found near the Berezina'. Young Noailles' health had been severely impaired as a prisoner in Spain, where Berthier had evidently got him exchanged. See Chuquet, vol. III, pp. 370–7.

7. But a few days later they became separated and 'I never saw him again.'

8. Fezensac says the little girl got back safely out of Russia 'without even catching cold'.

9. Several of our writers mention this gap, so difficult to surmount, between the bridge and the river bank. One wonders how the carriages and artillery had got over it? Doubtless thanks to their own ramps they had with them.

10. Hardly one of our 'cameramen' but has left an equally dramatic and circumstantial account of how he got across the Berezina. These four, Suckow, Le Roy, Kergorre and Griois, must stand for dozens and for the experience of thousands.

11. 'But I heard next day he'd found his brother a little way away, but in a dying condition. Thus perished these two poor brothers, and also a third in the 2nd Lancers.' Bourgogne adds that when he got back to Paris he saw their parents 'who begged me for news of their children. I left them a ray of hope by saying that their sons had been taken prisoners, but I felt certain they'd died.'

12. It's curious to reflect that the shells were being fired at the orders of one of Jomini's most ardent readers and disciples, Wittgenstein's chief-of-staff General Diebitsch.

13. 'A few unfortunates,' Louise will hear, but not being there herself cannot vouch for it, 'nevertheless managed to walk over the ice and get across the river. Those who rejoined us at Vilna', she adds, 'told us of scenes which made us shudder.'

14. The Bashkirs had impressed themselves on the invaders' imagination – and skin – by being armed with bows and arrows.

Chapter 19: Two Prisoners

1. On 9 December, after stumbling on through a devastated countryside, what was left of the column would get to Witebsk. The monstrous sufferings of the Russians' prisoners are related *in extenso* by Roos, Beulay and Faure, *op. cit.*

Chapter 20: Cortege Through the Snows

1. Jomini, it will be remembered, had been appointed official campaign historian after Napoleon had scotched his secret plans for serving under the Tsar, where he'd hoped for more rapid promotion. See *The March*, p. 104.

2. She would survive the retreat.

3. For some reason Roederer didn't accept him even so. For Gourgaud's personality and ambitions, see *The March*, p. 360. For his growing arrogance, see below.

4. 'Almost all would perish from hunger en route for Vilna.' – As for the ones from Rochechouart's 20th Russian Chasseurs, 'the French being unable to guard these prisoners, they were able to rejoin their flags three or four days afterwards'.

5. Luckily the evil was transient. 'Two days later everyone would have got his sight back.'

6. For its virtual annihilation at Valutina, see *The March*, p. 210.

7. Accounts of Oudinot's famous private battle at Pleschenkoviczi differ. Naturally I trust Pils, who was on the spot. Marbot's version, as usual, is wildly inaccurate; he has neither the date nor the place right. Cesare de Laugier, always concerned to defend the honour of Italian arms, is annoyed with Labaume, Ségur, Cambray and Vaudoncourt for their accounts – particularly with Labaume, who, being on Eugène's staff, must have heard Captain Migliorini ('who'd distinguished himself throughout the campaign' and together with the captured Cossack been sent to Eugène on his arrival at Pleschenkoviczi to report on the affair) for not mentioning Pino's gallantry in commanding the defence.

8. Which was untrue. Partonneaux and his headquarters had been at the head of the division, and going on along the straight road toward Staroï-Borissow instead of turning off to the left he had marched with the brigade closest to the Russians. Napoleon would do him less than justice in the celebrated 29th Bulletin, issued a few days later. It was felt that if it hadn't been for the loss of his division all the stragglers and baggage might have been got across the river, and with them such stores as might have enabled much more of the army to reach Vilna. But Napoleon could also be magnanimous. On 19 July 1813 he would give Partonneaux's three sons – their father still being a prisoner in Russia – free places in the Turin Lycée; and on his return from Elba, hearing they'd been deprived during the First Restoration because of Partonneaux's political affiliations, he gave them new ones at the Marseilles Lycée, even though Partonneaux had refused to serve under him any more. Partonneaux himself would afterwards deny that he'd lost his way, claiming instead that he'd heard the bridge over the Berezina was already cut, whereupon he'd tried to find a way northwards and so rejoin the Vilna road.

9. Baraguay d'Hilliers would in fact die in Berlin.

10. It can be read *in extenso* in his *Memoirs.*

Chapter 21: The Emperor Quits

1. Loison's ill-fated division, part of Augereau's XI (reserve) Corps stationed in Germany but at Vilna since 21 November, consisted of three infantry brigades, the first nominally eight battalions strong, but in reality only some 3,000 (Castellane would estimate it at 6,000; but Berthier's figure is to be preferred) of its original 10,000. In March-April 1813 there would be an enquiry into Loison's behaviour, but though subjected to Napoleon's criticism he would be reinstated.

2. For Pradt's point of view, see *Moscow*, pp.109–11, 237–8.

3. It must not be imagined the Tsar had not hastened to inform Europe, or at all events those powers which, openly or secretly, sympathised with his cause, of his great enemy's catastrophe. In Stockholm, for instance, various letters and strangers dispatched from Petersburg and arriving in the Swedish capital had 'caused a certain amount of worry on account of Napoleon's entrance into Moscow and it was assumed St Petersburg would have to be evacuated if, as was being said, he marched against that capital with a large part of his army.' This news, Bernadotte, Sweden's freely elected Crown Prince, had written to Alexander on 25 November, had put heart into the francophile anti-Russian party. In his high-flown rhetoric Bernadotte had reassured the Tsar – and told the Russian Ambassador in Stockholm – that no matter what the war's outcome might be 'Sweden would sooner bury itself among its boulders than change sides.' Why, he'd even signed a treaty of friendship with the ex-King Ferdinand III of Spain (currently held prisoner with his obstreperous family in Berthier's château on the Loire)! On 28 October the Tsar had replied at length, recounting Russian successes from 6 October on: 'Knowing the friendship Your Highness feels for me, I hope Your Highness will be somewhat interested in this good news.' Having failed to detach the Danes from their French alliance and already planning a Swedish-Russian offensive in Germany for 1813, in the event of a catastrophe for the Grand Army in Russia, Bernadotte certainly was.

4. Madame de Staël, herself no mean exaggerator and just then hobnobbing with the Tsar at Petersburg en route for Stockholm, where she'd soon be doing the same with her old friend Bernadotte, would say of her arch-enemy that he was 'a man who so loves to cause strong emotions and who when he can't hide his setbacks exaggerates them, so as always to outdo anyone else.' *Considérations.* Here there was no possibility of exaggeration!

5. The second accusation was of course true (see *The March*, p.123), the first the opposite of the truth. Murat had never wanted any part in the campaign, and at Smolensk, in August, had even begged Napoleon to halt his march on Moscow. See *The March*, pp. 185, 201.

6. Afterwards, when Murat's lack of character and total unreliability had become evident, Berthier, 'overwhelmed by despair, reproached himself with having contributed to the selection of such a leader'. (Caulaincourt)

7. Roustam's memoirs are not perhaps the most reliable of sources. For Berthier's declining efficiency in 1812 and Napoleon's occasionally brutal way of speaking to him, see *The March*, p. 66. But at the Tuileries, hearing of the loss of Vilna, Napoleon would regret not having handed over to Eugène.

8. After Waterloo, Hogendorp would found an agricultural colony in Brazil. Napoleon would rather unaccountably leave him 100,000 francs in his will. In defiance of Napoleon's strict order that no woman should cross the Niemen, his young wife, the Princess Hohenlohe, her mother and their little girl had joined him at Vilna. On his being ordered to send them back at once (see *The March*, p. 243) he did so; but the young Duchess of Reggio (also flouting imperial orders) on her way to join her wounded husband at Vilna in early October, encountered them at their first wretched overnight stop after Kovno on their way back. The daughter seemed sickly, and indeed died six months later; and soon thereafter also her mother.

9. The outermost of the three rooms that invariably constituted Napoleon's personal headquarters. For its routines see *The March*, pp. 93–4.

10. On 16 December Castellane would see Constant and Collin, the major-domo, at Heilsberg, on their way back to France.

11. See *The March*, p. 109

12. *Une borne*. Probably one of the official milestones; but the word also means a stone sticking out from a house to keep carriages from knocking against the wall. Perhaps it was the latter.

13. For d'Albe's function as Chief Cartographer, see *The March*, p. 94. Amodru and his brother would accompany Napoleon to St Helena in the capacity of coachmen.

14. Bourgoing says at 8 p.m. Fain, also on the spot but perhaps having other things to think about just then, says 9 p.m. Roustam says between 8 and 9. Bourgoing's circumstantial account of Napoleon's departure and journey, published in 1869, has high source value, having been based on an unpublished account in Polish by Wonsowicz.

15. The jibe, if it really were made, had been revived in the Paris theatres on the eve of the war when it had become known that Caulaincourt, a friend of the Tsar's and just back from his 4-year Petersburg embassy, was a 'dove' and completely against it. Actually it had originally been invented and stuck at the time of the judicial assassination of the Duc d'Enghien. For Caulaincourt's painful position, see *The March*, p. 16.

16. At Molodeczno its wounded had rejoined its other survivors. It had been virtually wiped out in the Brill Wood, and even been sabred by mistake by Doumerc's cuirassiers, 'notably Colonel Kosinowski who'd been wearing a green pelisse'.

17. Somehow, though Brandt's word isn't to be doubted, there's something unclear about this incident. He describes it as occurring *before* reaching Smorgoni, in which case it can hardly have been after Napoleon had left.

18. Dumonceau, who is usually to be relied on in matters of detail, writes 'in a sledge'. But Caulaincourt, who after all had arranged all the details, says specifically it was a carriage on wheels. A sledge was following, with a workman in it to make any necessary repairs en route. Most historians describe the carriage as being escorted by Polish lancers, but don't mention the Dutch ones who, as we see, were also involved. Dumonceau's account was

only published in 1963. And perhaps by this stage of things, in December 1812, the original writers didn't distinguish too clearly between Colbert's two regiments, both no doubt tightly wrapped up in their cloaks. Is Zalusky's memory, too, failing him when he says that it was at the 'Ochmiana post-house the Dutch Guard Lancers relieved us'?

19. Zalusky, who notes the lowest temperature recorded as -22°, accuses the historian Thiers of exaggerating it to -30°. 'I don't know what our regiment's friend Dr Larrey, who carried a thermometer, noted. But what I know is that in our Polish countries it never falls below -24° or -25°. Around Danzig and Eylau it had frozen at least as low as this during the wars of 1806–7.'

Chapter 22: The Very Air Seemed Frozen

1. Ségur and Labaume, he says, are definitely wrong in saying the army was indignant and that Napoleon's departure put the finishing touch to its discouragement and disorganisation.

2. As I explained in *The March*, the term 'dysentery' was used in those days to cover both conditions.

3. See *The March*, p. 48.

4. See *The March*, p. 46.

5. Thereafter his thermometer would rise slightly to between -24° and -18° R (-15° – 11.25° C).

6. See *The March*, pp. 165, 319, 390.

7. 'Sappers', or as perhaps the word should be translated 'pioneers', regularly had beards, wore bearskins, white leather aprons, and in addition to their muskets carried axes.

8. See *Moscow*, p. 150. Perhaps we even owe something of the vividness of his memoirs to Le Roy's sleeplessness that night, the coldest of the entire retreat?

Chapter 23. Panic and Chaos at Vilna

1. See *The March*, pp. 36, 52; *Moscow*, p. 162. Berthier's letter, dated the Kremlin, 13 October, had arrived shortly afterwards. Sent for by a commissary, the boy had been told the Emperor had given him

all the privileges of a commissioned officer and was sending him back to France to finish his schooling at the imperial expense.

2. He'd embarked them in the yacht *Charlotte de Königsberg* at the Frische-Haf on 20 June, switched them on 30 September to seven barges on the Niemen and had all the trouble in the world reaching Kovno before the rivers froze.

3. 'All I had at Vilna were four Polish regiments made up of recruits who, though they'd officially existed since July, were still neither dressed nor armed. I had to take whatever I could find in the hospitals and stores, and within 24 hours all these men were more or less armed and clothed.' By mid-November, in a cold which had fallen from -20° to -25° Réaumur, the two governors had 'managed to assemble about 12,000 infantry and 2,000 cavalry and had sent them off in two brigades – one towards Smorgoni on the main Minsk road, the other toward Dolhinov, to support II Corps and facilitate the Berezina crossing.' Meanwhile several provisional regiments had arrived from Prussia. Also, more spectacularly, 1,200 Neapolitans, 'two regiments of Murat's Royal Guard and Guards of Honour', all volunteers. Oudinot's young duchess had seen them on parade, no doubt magnificently turned out in their yellow or pale blue and crimson uniforms: 'I couldn't refuse the Duke of Bassano's invitation to be present at a review of the Neapolitan Guard, which was passing through Vilna to go and rejoin Murat. Bright and brilliant, it manoeuvred for an hour or two under our eyes. It was its adieu to the world; a few days later, the cold having got worse, men and horses gradually melted like snow in sunshine.'

All these troops had had to camp around the town. 'From this moment the "fortress of Vilna" presented an imposing aspect.' And when, toward the month's end, Loison's division, twelve German and Italian infantry battalions, had arrived from Germany, Hogendorp had fanned them out strategically 'to support the retiring army and prevent it being surprised by the Russians. Those at Lida were to keep open communications with Reynier. Those at Voronov and Roudzicvhi with Grodno. The units at Sventsiany with Dunaborg. A big cavalry depot was established

at Merecz and the debris of the shattered 3rd Guard Lancers was at Novo-Troki. At Vilna itself 1,500 cuirassiers and carabiniers were stationed to maintain order.'

4. Roch-Godart had first met Bonaparte in 1797. The circumstance of his battalion having been the one that had been active during the *coup d'état* of 18th Brumaire, together with his distinguished service record, doubtless explains his knighthood of the Legion of Honour. By 1812 he'd become disgusted with the decline in public morals among the Napoleonic hierarchy. It was his chronically gammy leg he had to thank for his governorship. Passing through Grodno en route to join Delzons' division of IV Corps at Moscow, he'd found his leg 'was in a frightful state' and applied to be employed in the rear. And a fortnight later he'd received Berthier's orders. It had taken him 10 to 12 days to create order where evidently Jomini, that eminent theorist, had left chaos. Everything had been inadequate. (For Napoleon's orders to Jomini in July, see *The March*, p. 104.) For instance there'd been a grave lack of carts so that even as late as early October Saint-Cyr had begun complaining of II Corps not getting any supplies. – Roch-Godart would write his memoirs as a prisoner of war in Hungary in 1814, so they have a high level of memory-value. Since Hogendorp and Roch-Godart would be made scapegoats for the ensuing débâcle, both men's memoirs try to show they'd done everything they could to avert it.

5. Monetary values are notoriously difficult to render in modern terms. But 28 francs was perhaps worth some £100 or $200, a considerable price for an omelette!

6. Dupuy adds: 'And when the regiment was re-united I got back all my advances.'

7. See *The March*, p. 95.

8. Lignières says Boulart told him to visit him one day and remind him of what he'd looked like at Vilna, 'because he'd saved his life'. But when in fact, years afterwards, Lignières, during the Restoration, sent him a letter at Strasburg, Colonel Boulart never replied. Boulart himself makes no mention of this incident.

9. There are several accounts of this, but Chlapowski's is the most drastic. After-

wards there would be general tendency to accuse Wrede of radical insubordination, even of treason to the French cause, the more so as he'd go over to the Allies in 1813.

10. In Paris Hogendorp lived in Mailly-Nesle's town house. Afterwards he would be made a scapegoat for the chaos at Vilna – which he certainly couldn't have prevented.

11. When they'd had to spend the night in a downpour being soaked to the bone and up to their knees in mud in a monastery courtyard. See *The March*, pp. 74–5

12. Rapp would conduct an epic defence of Danzig throughout 1813, finally have to surrender and himself be sent as prisoner of war to the Ukraine.

13. Hearing at the Tuileries about the headlong evacuation of Vilna, he would say to Caulaincourt: 'There's no example of such a rout, such stupidity. What a hundred men of courage would have saved has been lost under the nose of several thousand brave men by Murat's fault. A captain of voltigeurs would have commanded the army better than he.' But why had he ignored his own assessment of Murat's character? (See *The March*, p. 64). 'When the King of Naples hears bullets whistle,' he'd tell his minister Molé on 13 February 1813, 'when he can see the danger physically in front of him [*matérielle-ment*], he's 12 feet tall. But when he doesn't, when he imagines it, he becomes more timid than a pregnant woman. Sees phantoms. He lacks moral courage; it comes from his lack of intelligence [*esprit*]. I've no one to put in my place and I'd been only too happy if I could make war through my generals. But they aren't used to it and there's none of them can command the others.' To Molé Napoleon would describe Eugène, who'd perhaps have done somewhat better, as 'less brilliant than the King of Naples; less eminent in one respect; even in every way a mediocre man. But there's more proportion and harmony in him. The King of Naples has lost me my army, because I still had one when I left, but haven't one now. As long as I was there people murmured, but they obeyed.'

14. Napoleon's stable-master was a M. de Saluces, formerly squadron-commander

in the Sardinian service. Next year he would be made major in one of the new Guards of Honour regiments.

15. Afterwards Le Roy would hear that 'for several days all these unfortunates had stayed there without any food, having been stripped of their belongings and maltreated. Probably all succumbed to their sufferings. Not one reappeared in the regiment.'

16. Lefèbvre's son would die a couple of days later, and after the old man had reached Königsberg Napoleon would grant him permission to return to France. For his biography, see Gunther E. Rothenberg's article in David Chandler's *Napoleon's Marshals*.

17. 'Although the traces of his fatigues and privations were strongly marked on his face,' Oudinot's duchess would think when she saw him again, 'this courageous old man had survived all the miseries of the retreat without losing, at least to all appearances, his infectious and gracious gaiety.'

18. Lallemand, though not one of those chosen by Napoleon to go with him to St Helena, would be one of the group of officers who went aboard HMS *Bellerophon* in 1815.

19. Lenoble would die, worn out, in the hospital at Königsberg.

20. All students of this or any period owe a debt of gratitude to Miss Helen Roeder for translating and so vividly presenting excerpts from her ancestor's diary, *op. cit.* The account of what happened to him and Vogel at Vilna, and their journey in May through Poland and Pomerania, where they'd be imprisoned by the Swedish authorities, but finally get home to Darmstadt, is particularly fascinating. It gives a vivid impression of the state of affairs in the region after the débâcle.

21. See *Moscow*, pp. 30, 55.

Chapter 24: Ponari's Fatal Hill

1. Grandjean and Lorge's divisions of XI Corps had also been ordered up. Caulaincourt and Napoleon had seen them at Rumchiki, a village just outside Kovno.

2. See *The March* and *Moscow*, indices.

3. See *The March*, p. 70. Strangely enough, various eye-witnesses would afterwards remember Ponari Hill as lying at quite different distances outside Vilna. Professor Algvidas Jakubcionis of Vilnius University, who has so kindly provided me with many details about and pictures of the town in those days, writes that 'the distance in the early 19th century was 6–7 kilometres'. He explains that the hill's exact gradient in those days is hard to determine, 'as the road now follows a gentler one'.

4. See *The March*, index.

5. Characteristically, Caulaincourt says, when Napoleon heard about the loss of the Treasure at Ponari he was less indignant at the loss of so much gold, as that the millions in false rouble notes he'd secretly had printed in Paris before the campaign might fall into the Russians' hands. He, the bourgeois, was worried about the scandal that might follow! Caulaincourt himself had known nothing about these mass forgeries; but doubtless they explain the care with which a Jewish banker in Vilna had scrutinised some roubles that Sergeant Bourgogne, at a heavy discount, had sold him for gold.

6. The several long letters that Berthier would write to Napoleon on 16, 17 and 18 December are in themselves a continuous and lucid account of the retreat's last days, punctuated here and there by *cris de coeur* in which Berthier's likeable personality shines tragically through. I shall acknowledge such material by an asterisk.

7. See *The March*, p. 361, note 12.

8. As at the Berezina, all our survivors either to got up Ponari Hill or had to circumvent it to find themselves, nearly 200 years later, in our book. Once again I've had to content myself with a few samples.

9. Evidently not the one lost to the Cossacks after being tipped into a lake outside Krasnoïe.

10. 'One of the sharpest cries of pain I ever heard him utter,' Oudinot's young wife would write afterwards, 'was when General Maison told him all this *matériel* had been lost.'

11. This isn't true. Poniatowski's Poles arrived in Warsaw on Christmas Day with all their 36 guns intact; and the Hesse-Darmstadt artillery brought out all theirs.

12. But afterwards he'll tell Molé he'd 'foreseen it all', i.e., the catastrophe at Vilna.

13. For brevity's and completeness sake I am here fusing Bourgoing's, Caulaincourt's and the Countess Potocki's accounts. She must have heard these details at second hand later that day.

14. Caulaincourt says repeatedly 'at the Hôtel de Saxe'. But Bourgoing/ Wonsowicz, the Countess Potocki and Pradt himself all say it was the Hôtel d'Angleterre. For Pradt's views of Napoleon and Maret see *Moscow*, pp. 110-11, 238.

15. No doubt Pradt again stressed the state of utter ruin the Grand Army's passage in June had spelt for the Poles. 1812 was a famine year, and the Continental System had made it impossible for them to export their surplus grain, the country's sole export, from the preceding six good years. And in June it had anyway all been commandeered for the Grand Army's horses. See *The March*, p. 35. Neither cash nor credit was to be had. 'Neither functionary nor priest was being paid. The Duchy's revenues amounted to 40 million francs; its expenses exceeded 100 million, etc.' Even the wealthiest Poles had been ruined. The Potockis had been the only Warsaw household able to afford to return Pradt's invitations to dinner, he says. In his book (1814) where he convincingly describes the *de facto* situation in Poland, Pradt accuses Napoleon of being *supérieurement ignorant* of everything he didn't want to know. But Napoleon, as he's just been explaining to Caulaincourt, sees everything 'from a superior viewpoint'.

16. It would take Napoleon and Caulaincourt eight more days to reach Paris – the fastest transit so far on record. And all the time Napoleon would take and talk and talk. Caulaincourt's 150-page record of his immense monologue, jotted down while he dozed for an hour or two at some staging post, is certainly the most vivid close-up of that extraordinary mind we possess. Caulaincourt's percipient, critical but also sympathetic account should be read *in toto*. No résumé can do it the least justice. Among much else he told Caulaincourt, who'd been against the war from the outset: 'Everything has turned out badly because I stayed too long in Moscow. If I'd left four days after occupying it, as I

thought of doing when I saw the town in flames, the Russians would have been lost. All our disasters hinge on that fortnight [*sic*]. Kutusov's retreat [*sic*] has been utterly inept. It's the winter that's been our undoing. We're victims of the climate. The fine weather tricked me." The Emperor talked of his disasters and of the mistake he'd made in staying at Moscow in the same tone as might have been used by a stranger.'

Chapter 25: Ney's Last Stand

1. For a picture of the survivors' individual sufferings in extreme close-up, see Bourgogne's detailed account of his march from Vilna to Kovno. But his dates after Ponari are manifestly wrong.

2. Ayherts, his hands and feet frost-bitten, would be captured by Cossacks and herded back to Witebsk – 'where he turned wigmaker; he came back to France from Russian prisons in 1814, with 3 francs in his pocket'. He'd die at a ripe old age in the bosom of the Castellane family 'for whom he was always more than a servant'.

3. Loison had had extraordinary difficulties in sending forward his division from Königsberg. Only after a court-martial would he be exonerated for having joined them so belatedly at the front.

4. Today's Vievis. See *The March*, p. 63.

5. Griois' account is one of those which deserve to be translated *in toto*, together with Dumonceau's three volumes, Paul de Bourgoing's, Victor Dupuy's, Le Roy's, Louise Fusil's, Roman Soltyk's, Heinrich von Brandt's and Cesare de Laugier's.

6. Some of the 1812 Dutch conscripts were only 15 years old. See *The March*, p. 22.

7. Beyond the Niemen, Bignon would take Castellane up into his carriage 'despite the odour of suppuration' from his gangrenous hand. 'He was a man of a lively intelligence. We chatted gaily about people in Paris.' For Sébastiani's character see *The March*, p. 106.

8. Later Petit, ignored by the passers-by where he'd collapsed in the snow by the wayside, would be picked up by a compassionate colonel 'who, however, had only come from Vilna and hadn't been to Moscow'. 'When my thoughts take me

back to that epoch of my life,' Griois ends the episode, 'I tremble at the moral degradation misery can bring us to.'

9. For the rest of the chapter I shall mark extracts from Berthier's letters to Napoleon with an asterisk.

10. This would be the original Russian bridge, broken by Wittgenstein when withdrawing in June and immediately re-established by the French engineers. So Bourgogne is certainly guilty of an inexactitude when he says he marched back over 'this same bridge as we'd passed over five months before with the great and brilliant army, now almost annihilated!'

11. Readers of *The March* will recall that it was Gérard, one day to be a Marshal of France, who'd replaced Gudin, killed at Valutina in August.

12. This would be a second bridgehead, at the point where the original bridge had been destroyed in June. See *The March*, p. 56.

13. At Vilna Séruzier, in utter indigence, would appeal for help to the Tsar's brother, the Grand Duke Constantine. Before offering him any, that absurd and nugatory personage whom Séruzier had met at Erfurt in 1810 – but who in 1812 had fallen into a panic at the threat of war and begged his brother at all costs to avoid it (during the retreat Wilson had seen him actually decapitate a dying French officer with his sword) – heedless of his applicant's appalling condition would first amuse himself for an hour or so by resuming a conversation on artillery techniques they'd had at Erfurt. Only then would Constantine forward the shivering colonel's letter to Ney, who would promptly sent him some money. Both Wilson and the German patriotic writer Ernst Moritz Arndt give appalling pictures of the horrifying state of affairs in and around Vilna. Arriving in what he describes as that 'Tartar hell' on 11 January, Arndt, whose writings would play a part in the revolt first of Prussia then of all Germany against the Napoleonic regime, would see 'French cockades lying in the streets, dirty plumes, torn hats and shakos that reminded one of how the French had strutted with them through the streets five months earlier but now were humbled in the dust and trodden underfoot.'

14. For Liesje's history and equine qualities, see *The March*, p. 42.

15. '... *ne partirent pas*'. The expression is ambiguous; it could equally well mean that the men refused to attack the hill – presumably the same one from which Faber du Faur had first seen the main body of the Grand Army assembled at the bridgeheads in midsummer. See illustration in *The March*.

16. Less peremptorily, the French word *doit*, used by Berthier, can also mean 'should be'. But Murat himself had had enough: 'It's no longer possible to serve under a lunatic,' he'd rage to Berthier. 'No prince in Europe any longer believes in his word, nor in his treaties ... Oh, if I'd only listened to the proposals made me by the British! I'd still be a great king, like the Emperor of Austria and the King of Prussia!' An indignant Berthier interrupts: 'The King of Prussia and the Emperor of Austria are princes by the grace of God, time and custom. But you're only a king by the grace of Napoleon and French blood. It's black ingratitude that's blinding you, and I'll let him know your words.' At 4 p.m on 17 January at Elbing, Murat, despite Berthier's supplications, would leave for Naples and 'without orders from the Emperor but certain his decision would have his approval' be succeeded by Eugène. Eugène cancelled Murat's orders for a precipitate retreat. 'From then on everything changed aspect.' In a menacing letter Napoleon would take his *pantaleone* of a brother-in-law to task for his 'weakness of character. I imagine you're not one of those people who suppose the lion is dead. If you're counting on that, you're wrong. The title of King has turned your head.' Berthier himself would fall so ill with the lethal fever sweeping through the army that Daru had to sign his dispatches for him.

17. Of Bernadotte the ex-emperor would say at St Helena: 'I can accuse him of ingratitude, but not of treachery. In a manner of speaking he became a Swede.' And in fact he had accepted the Swedish invitation on condition that Napoleon strike out his stipulation that he wouldn't bear arms against France. In 1813 Bernadotte would play a crucial role in planning the Allies' successful strategies.

18. On 26 December at Königsberg, where Lariboisière had already died, Planat de la Faye would ask Eblé 'for his orders for me in Paris. He had none to give. He was completely demoralised. All he did during my visit was to show me his trouser belt, which had become half again too large for him.' That day Planat left for Berlin with Ferdinand Lariboisière's heart preserved in spirits of wine and his father's body 'in a kind of box in such a way that the head reposed on the cushion at my side'. Eblé would die at Königsberg on 30 December.

19. Or rather, according to *Hortense Beauharnais*, ex-queen of Holland, it had been hastily finished off in wood on the occasion of Napoleon's marriage to Marie-Louise.

20. On 11 January 1813 he'd call up 250,000 conscripts. On 13 February he'd tell his minister Molé: 'I'd have been amazed by such a spectacle if I hadn't long ago learnt to control myself. The day before [5 November] I was conqueror of the world, I'd been commanding the finest army of modern times. Next day, nothing of all that was left. I think I showed a calmness, I'd even say preserved an unalterable cheerfulness, and I don't think anyone among those who saw me could give me the lie. But don't believe I, like other men, haven't a soft heart. I'm even quite a good fellow; but since my earliest youth I've applied myself to silencing that string, and in me it doesn't give out a sound.' He admitted that he was not quite so active as formerly in his work, when he'd now and again only asked de Bausset for 'a glass of water'. Now he finds he needs a cup of coffee. The great chemist Chaptal, another eye-witness, scientifically observing Napoleon after the Russian disaster, found his ideas no longer so clear and logical and his conversation fitful and full of outbursts. 'Somnolence and the pleasures of the table gained on him.' Riding fatigued him and he now tended to drop off to sleep and waste a lot of time talking. Though he no longer worked so hard, his passion for power remained unassuaged. On 3 April 1813 he'd call up 180,000 more conscripts, In August 30,000 more. On 9 October 280,000 more. On 15 November 300,000 more. Of France's total population of 25 millions, and his Empire's 50 millions, Napoleon, in the vast struggle between the *ancien* and the post-Revolutionary regimes, would use up

an estimated 2,114,000 lives. His enemies certainly no fewer.

Two Epilogues

1. See *The March*, p. 112

2. When Napoleon reviewed the 5th Tirailleurs at the Trianon in March, only their redoubtable Colonel Hennequin, a few officers and NCOs and one drummer boy remained. Of Lignières' company of the 1st Foot Chasseurs, 245 strong at Moscow, only 52, 'and this was the strongest of all the Old Guard's companies'. Total losses of officers in Russia had been 9,380, whereof 2,965 killed or dead from wounds, and 6,415 wounded, including seven divisional generals killed and 39 wounded, and 22 generals of brigade killed and 85 wounded. Five Marshals had been wounded. Somewhere between 130,000 and 175,000 horses had perished, excluding the innumerable *konyas*. Of 826 surgeons only 175 are registered as being still alive in February: 'the paymasters have had the same fate', Peyrusse would write to his Parisian friend. Of the '600–700 handsome, powerful men' of the 4th Bavarian Chevaulegers, 'the officers admirably mounted and in brilliant uniforms, filled with vitality and courage' who'd left for Russia, a mere 40 to 50 officers, NCOs and troopers got home. Refused sick-leave, the officers were immediately ordered to form cadres of new recruits. According to the complete breakdown of killed and wounded officers, regiment by regiment, drawn up by the statistician Aristide Martinien (to be found at the end of vol. 2 of Chuquet's *Guerre de Russie*, an invaluable anthology of documents), only the 1st and 2nd Grenadiers and Chasseurs of the Old Guard hadn't lost an officer and only one in each regiment had been wounded – all in cruel contrast to the Line regiments, where an average of seventeen officers had been killed. For the expendable rankers no figures are given.

The patient reader will doubtless be wondering what happened in the end to at least some of our principal protagonists. According to Oudinot's young duchess, Narbonne, in whose company we started our tragic tale,

'had survived all the miseries of the retreat without losing, at least to all appearances, his infectious and gracious gaiety. Yet the traces of his fatigues and privations were strongly marked on the face of this courageous old man.'

But a couple of years later, when the Bourbons returned, he'd die suddenly – another victim, thinks the Swedish researcher Sten Forshuvud, of the arsenical arts of Napoleon's arch-enemy the comte d'Artois, who nursed an undying hatred of all persons of standing who'd supported the imperial regime.

The debonaire but frequently self-pitying Murat, after stupidly emulating Napoleon's come-back during the Hundred Days, would be shot by a firing-squad in Calabria. His last words are said to have been: 'Soldiers, spare the face! Fire!'

After acting as Napoleon's last emissary *vis-à-vis* an implacably united Europe in 1814 and as his Foreign Minister during the Hundred Days, Caulaincourt, Duke of Vicenza, would pay the price of his stubborn loyalty to a man whose policies he had disapproved. Implacably cold-shouldered by the Bourbons as the Duke of Enghien's alleged assassin but still befriended by the Tsar, he'd die of cancer in 1827. The publication of his incomparably initiated memoirs in 1935 would be one of the great events of Napoleonic historiography.

Berthier would desert Napoleon's cause, or rather, remain faithful to the Bourbons in 1815. He died at Bamberg by falling out of a third-storey window while standing on a chair to get a better view of Russian troops marching down the street.

Oudinot, who at Königsberg had 'put his head under his pillow so as not to be kept awake by 20 or 30 Prussians drinking to our disasters' (Pils), lived to be the Grand Old Man of the Napoleonic epoch; he became head of the Invalides in Paris, and despite his many wounds died at a ripe old age.

After promising Louis XVIII to 'bring Bonaparte back in an iron cage' on his return from Elba, Ney, whose nerves and presence of mind seem to have been over-strained in Russia, would make a mess of the conduct of Quatre Bras and Waterloo. Arrested by the Bourbons on a charge of high treason, he'd be shot by firing-squad.

Larrey, captured by the Prussians at Waterloo and already facing a firing-squad, would be recognised and saved by a British officer.

Quite a few of our officer-eyewitnesses, the all-observant Dumonceau for example, would end up as generals, and three, Lyautey, Castellane and Gérard, as Marshals of France.

While in Moscow, if Ali's memoirs are to be believed, Napoleon had one day fallen to 'discussing with Duroc the best sort of death. The best, according to Napoleon, was to "die on the field of battle, stricken by a bullet". For his part he feared he wouldn't be so happy. "I'll die", he said, "in my bed, *comè un' coglione*".' His words were prophetic. Deported to St Helena, he would finally – if the Swedish researcher Sten Forshuvud's closely argued and evidenced theory holds water (and Professor David Chandler has said that it's 'an accusation which must stand in any court of law until someone no less painstakingly and convincingly refutes it') – be poisoned by Count Montholon. Summed up by Ben Weider and David Hapgood in *The Murder of Napoleon*, NY, 1982, it is perhaps the 20th century's most brilliant piece of historical-scientific detection.

INDEX